*Calculus: An Intuitive and Physical Approach*

*By the same author*

Morris Kline and Irvin W. Kay, *Electromagnetic Theory and Geometrical Optics* (Interscience Monograph in Pure and Applied Mathematics), Wiley, New York, 1965.

Morris Kline, *Mathematics, a Cultural Approach*, Addison-Wesley, Reading, Mass., 1962.

Morris Kline, *Mathematics and the Physical World*, T. Y. Crowell Co., New York, 1959.

Morris Kline, *Mathematics in Western Culture*, Oxford University Press, New York, 1953.

Morris Kline, *Mathematical Thought from Ancient to Modern Times*, Oxford University Press, 1972.

Morris Kline, *Why Johnny Can't Add: The Failure of the New Math*, St. Martin's Press, 1973.

# CALCULUS:
## An Intuitive and Physical Approach
### SECOND EDITION

## MORRIS KLINE

PROFESSOR EMERITUS
COURANT INSTITUTE OF MATHEMATICAL SCIENCES
NEW YORK UNIVERSITY

VISITING DISTINGUISHED PROFESSOR
BROOKLYN COLLEGE
THE CITY UNIVERSITY OF NEW YORK

*John Wiley and Sons*     New York • Chichester • Brisbane • Toronto

*Library of Congress Cataloging in Publication Data:*

Kline, Morris, 1908–
  Calculus.

  Includes index.
  1. Calculus.  I. Title.
QA303.K68   1977        515        76-22760


Printed in the United States of America

10 9 8 7 6 5 4 3 2

# PREFACE TO
# THE SECOND EDITION

The basic features of the first edition have been retained, such as the intuitive approach and real applications. As to the approach, the last chapter introduces a rigorous treatment. Though this chapter could be used in conjunction with the opening chapters of the book, I do not recommend doing so; the rigorous presentation is difficult to grasp and obscures the understanding. Rigor undoubtedly refines the intuition but does not supplant it. The rigorous approach should be reserved for a course in advanced calculus for mathematicians.

Most of the applications still belong with the physical sciences; however, no knowledge of physics is presupposed. Several sections on physical applications have been dropped and applications to the social and biological sciences have been added instead. These applications are vital. The theory and technique of the calculus are, in themselves, meaningless. Moreover, since most students who take calculus will be scientists or engineers, they will be highly motivated by the applications. Many calculus texts dispose of applications by asking students to calculate centers of gravity and moments of inertia. But since students have no idea of how these quantities are used, the only consequence is that the gravity of the problems produces inertia in the students.

In addition to extending the scope of the applications, I have made a number of other improvements. More drill exercises have been added, the exercises have been carefully graded as to difficulty, and there are more illustrative examples. Students doing homework exercises acquire the habit of searching for an illustrative example which they can imitate and thereby do the exercises without thinking. To counter this many illustrative examples are incorporated into the text instead of being set apart formally. Hopefully the students will read the text instead of mechanically following the technique of the usual illustrative example.

A chapter on differential equations and a section on such numerical methods as Simpson's rule and the trapezoidal rule have also been added. More use has been made of vector analysis, particularly in treating velocity and acceleration.

Chapter 9, "The Definite Integral," has been moved forward so that students using the mathematics in another course taken simultaneously can utilize the concept sooner.

Some changes in notation are unquestionably an improvement. The $\dot{y}$ notation has been restricted to the customary situation where time is the independent variable; in other situations $y'$, $dy/dx$ and $f'(x)$ are used. The notation $\int y\, dx$ has been introduced early to denote antidifferentiation. The use of $dy/dx$ from the outset is the result of numerous requests. Admittedly, a useful notation in showing the variables involved, it also suggests that the derivative is a quotient, whereas we must take great pains to convince the student that it is not.

The pace of the first few chapters has been speeded up somewhat. However, it does seem desirable, because students are weak in algebra, to keep the algebra simple at the outset while students are acquiring the concepts of the calculus.

Two other changes may be helpful. Since not all classes go at the same pace or have the same objectives the two volumes of the first edition have been replaced by the present single volume. Thereby instructors are freer to choose the topics they deem most appropriate. Second, since time may not permit the inclusion of all the applications, those sections that can be omitted without disrupting the continuity have been starred.

Some figures have been improved; where the precise shape is significant the computer has been employed to achieve accuracy.

An instructor's manual which contains full solutions of all the exercises, suggestions for teaching, and additional material for advanced students is available to instructors on request to the publisher.

*Morris Kline*

*New York, N. Y.*
*August, 1976*

# PREFACE TO
# THE FIRST EDITION

Anyone who adds to the plethora of introductory calculus texts owes an explanation, if not an apology, to the mathematical community. I believe that an introductory course in the calculus should present the subject intuitively and should relate it as closely as possible to science. A text for such an approach is not available.

In this book the justification of the theorems and techniques is consistently intuitive; that is, geometrical, physical, and heuristic arguments and generalizations from concrete cases are employed to convince. The approach is especially suitable for the calculus because the subject grew out of physical and geometrical problems. These problems tell us what functions we should take up, what concepts we want to formulate, and what techniques we should develop. In view of the fact that the human mind learns intuitively and that time does not permit both an intuitive and a rigorous presentation in elementary calculus, it seems to me that the approach adopted is the correct one.

The intuitive approach is explained to the student so that he will know what kind of evidence is being used to support arguments. Thus he is told that a graph of a typical function may not represent all functions. On the other hand, he is also told that the elementary functions are well behaved except at isolated points and that he can usually trust his intuition. As he works with the ideas of the calculus, he will sharpen his intuition. If he continues with mathematics, he will learn the analytical foundations and proofs that guard against the failings of intuition.

The use of an intuitive approach in the first treatment of a subject is not an innovation. Arithmetic is learned intuitively in elementary school and then the logic of it is learned gradually through the work in algebra. Geometry is learned intuitively in junior high school and then the formal deductive approach is presented in senior high school. A difficult subject such as the calculus, therefore, should certainly be introduced by an intuitive approach.

This approach has many merits beyond that of being the only feasible one. Every pedagogue today champions discovery, but few teach it. How does one discover in mathematics? By thinking in physical and geometrical terms, by conjecturing or guessing, by formulating hypotheses and testing them, and by generalizing on specific cases. Physical problems that call for the creation of mathematics set the stage for discovery. That the intuitive approach may lead to errors is granted, but "truth emerges more readily from error than from confusion." The student must be allowed to make mistakes, for if he makes no mistakes, he will not progress.

After the basic material has been covered, the need for rigor is motivated, and the last two chapters of Part 2 of this book do offer an introduction to precise language and proof. These chapters are intended as a transition to advanced calculus.

One alternative to an intuitive approach is a rigorous treatment. In my opinion, a rigorous first course in the calculus is ill advised for numerous reasons. First, it is too difficult for the students. Beginners are asked to learn a mass of concepts so subtle that they defied the best mathematicians for two hundred years. Even Cauchy, the founder of rigor, gave formulations that are crude compared to what the current rigorous presentations ask students to absorb. And Cauchy, despite his concern for rigor, missed the distinctions between continuity and differentiability and between convergence and uniform convergence. Before one can appreciate a precise formulation of a concept or theorem, he must know what idea is being formulated and what exceptions or pitfalls the wording is trying to avoid. Hence he must be able to call upon a wealth of experience acquired before tackling the rigorous formulation. Furthermore, having students master a polished deductive organization does not teach them how to think and how to do mathematics, for thinking and doing are not deductive processes. How can discovery take place when students are asked to work with ideas that are already overladen with sophistication and refinement? Finally, the rigorous approach is misleading. Because the introductory calculus course is the student's first contact with higher mathematics, he obtains the impression that real mathematics is deductive and that good mathematicians think deductively.

Rigor has its place in mathematics education. It is a check on the creations and it permits an aesthetic (as well as an anaesthetic) presentation. But it is also to some extent gilt on the lily and an interdiction against the inclusion of functions which rarely occur in practice and which must even be invented with Weierstrassian ingenuity. A rigorous first course in calculus reminds one of the words of Samuel Johnson; "I have found you an argument but I am not obliged to find you an understanding." Even if the rigorous material is understood, its value is limited. As Henri Lebesgue pointed out: "Logic makes us reject certain arguments but it cannot make us believe any argument."

The reasons often given for a rigorous presentation—that students must learn what a real proof is or that students should not be asked to unlearn later what they have already been taught—are hollow. One cannot give the whole truth at once in any subject. Even we, as teachers, do not face the whole truth for, in fact, the whole question of what is rigorous in mathematics was never so much up in the air as it is now. At any rate, what may seem ideally right and efficient is pedagogically intolerable.

There is also the alternative of compromising on rigor by offering precise definitions and proofs in some portions of the text and intuitive or pseudorigorous arguments in others. This alternative seems to me to have almost all of the disadvantages of a rigorous presentation and the additional one of confusing the student about what proof really is.

The second essential respect in which this book differs from current ones is that the relationship of mathematics to science is taken seriously. The present trend to separate mathematics from science is tragic. There are chapters of mathematics that have value in and for themselves. However, the calculus divorced from applications is meaningless. We should also keep in mind that most of the students taking calculus will be scientists and engineers, and these students must learn how to use mathematics. But the step from mathematics to its applications is not simple and straightforward and it creates difficulties for the student from the time he is called upon to solve verbal problems in algebra. The mathematics courses fail to teach students how to formulate physical problems mathematically. The science and engineering courses, on the other hand, assume that students know how to translate physical problems into mathematical language and how to make satisfactory idealizations. The gap between mathematics and science instruction must be filled, and we can do so to our own advantage because thereby we give meaning and motivation to the calculus.

In this book real problems are used to motivate the mathematics, and the latter, once developed, is applied to genuine physical problems—the magnificent, impressive, and even beautiful problems tendered by nature. I have selected those that do *not* require a background in physics. However, if the student is to think properly even about familiar concepts, such as weight, force, velocity, acceleration, light, and work, the book must say a little about them and about the physical laws that are involved. It does. To relegate physical problems only to the exercises is, in my opinion, ineffective in teaching students how to apply mathematics. If the student is not informed about the physics of a problem, all he can do in tackling an exercise is to apply a formula mechanically or guess what technical process is called for, do it, and check his answer. If the book does not supply an answer and if the student's result is off by a factor of 1000, he will not realize it because he has no judgment about what to expect.

I have tried to incorporate several other features that may contribute to the pedagogy. In many instances I have deliberately made false starts so as to have the student realize that correct methods and correct proofs are almost always preceded by groping and to have students appreciate why we finally take one course rather than another. I wish to dispel the impression that good mathematicians are able to proceed directly to the right conclusion because strict logic or a God-given insight guides them. I have given full details on the mathematical steps in the hope that the book will be readable. The style is informal.

The pace of the first few chapters of Part 1 has been deliberately made slow. It is well known that calculus students are still struggling with elementary algebra. By keeping the opening algebra simple, I trust that the calculus ideas will stand forth. In later chapters the algebra becomes more difficult.

The order of the mathematical concepts and topics was chosen so that applications could be introduced almost from the beginning. However, no artificial or complicated arrangement was necessary. Differentiation and antidifferentiation are the key concepts in the first thirteen chapters and then summation is introduced. The early introduction of applications should permit good correlation with physics courses if these are taken concurrently. The concept of differentials was deliberately delayed until Chapter 12 of Part 1. Most books do stress that the derivative is a limit of a quotient, but often present differentials early. No matter how much the student is cautioned that the derivative is not a quotient, if he is allowed to work almost at once with the quotient of the differentials, he tends to forget the true meaning of the derivative.

Beyond the matter of the proper approach, there are a few other points that may warrant comment. Despite my own preference for a course in analytic geometry which precedes the calculus, I have included the former. This is a concession to the current fad. Some work with vectors is included, but I have not done much with the differentiation and integration of vector functions. I believe that this topic requires a new way of thinking and that we should not try to teach two major classes of techniques at the same time. The calculus of scalar functions is the basic one, and this should be mastered first. Apropos of the inclusion of vector analysis, the present trend to include this topic, linear algebra, probability, and differential equations in a three- or four-semester analytic geometry and calculus course, seems to me to be attempting the impossible.

Any book should be adjustable to the needs of a particular course. Most of the applications are in separate sections, and therefore the number of those that need to be included is optional. Even whole chapters, such as Chapter 13 of Part 1 on further techniques of integration, Chapter 16 of Part 1 on further physical applications of the definite integral, and Chapter 19 of Part 2 on polar parametric equations, can be omitted. The last two chapters of Part 2 (Chapters 24 and 25), the introduction to rigor, can be omitted or, on the other hand, they can be read before the chapters on solid analytic geometry and functions of two or more variables.

I wish to express my thanks to the publishers for their generous support of this approach to the calculus and for their efficient handling of the production.

*New York*                                                              *Morris Kline*
*November 1966*

# CONTENTS

# CHAPTER ONE
# WHY CALCULUS?

***1. The Historical Motivations for the Calculus.*** Each branch of mathematics has been developed to attack a class of problems that could not be solved at all or yielded to a solution only after great efforts. Thus elementary algebra was created to find answers to simple physical problems which in mathematical form called for solving first, second, and higher degree equations with one or two unknowns. Plane and solid geometry originated in the need to find perimeters, areas, and volumes of common figures and to state conditions under which two figures, say two triangles, are congruent or have the same shape—that is, are similar. Trigonometry, introduced by astronomers, enabled man to determine the sizes and distances of heavenly bodies.

In high school algebra and trigonometry we usually learn the fundamentals of another branch of mathematics, called coordinate or analytic geometry. Thus we learn to graph linear equations such as $x + 2y = 5$, to represent a circle of radius $R$ by an equation of the form $x^2 + y^2 = R^2$, and to determine which curves correspond to such equations as $y = \sin x$ and $y = \cos x$. The primary purpose of relating equations and curves is to enable us to use the equations in the study of such important curves as the paths of projectiles, planets, and light rays. Of course, each of the above-mentioned branches of mathematics has also helped to treat problems of the physical and social sciences which arose long after the motivating questions had been disposed of.

During the seventeenth century, when modern science was founded and began to expand apace, a number of new problems were brought to the fore. Because the mathematicians of that century, like those of most great periods, were the very physicists and astronomers who raised the questions, they responded at once to the problems. Let us see what some of these problems were.

Seventeenth-century scientists were very much concerned with problems of motion. The heliocentric theory created by Nicolaus Copernicus

(1473–1543) and Johannes Kepler (1571–1630) introduced the concepts of the earth rotating on its axis and revolving around the sun. The earlier theory of planetary motion, dating back to Ptolemy (c. A.D. 150), which presupposed an earth absolutely fixed in space and, indeed, in the center of the universe, was discarded. The adoption of the theory involving an earth in motion invalidated the laws and explanations of motion that had been accepted since Greek times. New insights were needed into such phenomena as the motion of a projectile shot from a cannon and an answer to the question of why objects stay with the moving earth seemed called for. Furthermore, Kepler had shown on the basis of observations that the path of each planet around the sun is an ellipse, although no theoretical explanation of why the planets move on such paths had been offered. However, the notion that all bodies in the universe attract one another in accordance with the force of gravitation became prominent, and scientists decided to investigate whether the motions of planets around the sun and of moons around planets could be deduced from the proper laws of motion and gravitation. The motion of celestial bodies became the dominant scientific study.

All of these motions—those of objects near the surface of the earth and those of the heavenly bodies—take place with variable velocity, and many involve variable acceleration. Although the difficulties in handling variable velocities and accelerations may not be apparent at the moment, the branches of mathematics that existed before the calculus was created were not adequate to treat them. We shall see later precisely what the difficulties are and how they are surmounted. In pre-calculus courses students often work on problems involving variable velocity—for example, the motion of a body falling to earth—but the intricacy is circumvented there by one dodge or another.

The second major problem of the seventeenth century was the determination of tangents to various curves (Fig. 1-1). This question is of some interest as a matter of pure geometry, but its deeper significance is that the tangent to a curve at a point represents the *direction* of the curve at the point. Thus, if a projectile moves along a curve, the direction in which the projectile is headed at any point on its path is the direction of the tangent at that point. To determine whether the projectile will strike its target head on or merely at a glancing angle, we must know in which direction the projectile is moving at that point on its path at which it strikes

Figure 1-1                          Figure 1-2

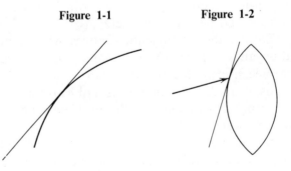

the target. The invention of the telescope and microscope in the seventeenth century stimulated great interest in the action of lenses. To determine the course of a light ray after it strikes the surface of a lens, we must know the angle that the light ray makes with the lens, that is, the angle (Fig. 1-2) between the light ray and the tangent to the lens. Incidentally, the study of the behavior of light was, next to the study of motion, the most active scientific field in that century. It may now be apparent why the question of finding the tangent to a curve was a major one.

A third class of problems besetting the seventeenth-century scientists may be described as maxima and minima problems. The motion of cannon balls was studied intensively from the sixteenth century onward. In fact, the mathematicians Nicolò Tartaglia (1500–1557) and Galileo Galilei (1564–1642) made significant progress in this investigation even before the calculus was applied to it. One of the important questions about the motion of cannon balls and other kinds of projectiles was the determination of the maximum range. As the angle of elevation of a cannon (angle $A$ in Fig. 1-3) is varied, the range—that is, the horizontal distance from the cannon to the point at which the projectile again reaches the ground—also varies. The question is, at what angle of elevation is the range a maximum? Another maximum and minimum problem of considerable importance arises in planetary motion. As a planet moves about the sun, its distance from the sun varies. A basic question in this area is, what are the maximum and minimum distances of the planet from the sun? Some simple maxima and minima problems can be solved by the methods of elementary algebra and elementary geometry, but the most important problems are beyond the power of these branches and require the calculus.

Still another class of problems in the seventeenth century concerned the lengths of curves and the areas and volumes of figures bounded by curves and surfaces. Elementary mathematics suffices to determine the areas and volumes of simple figures, principally figures bounded by line segments and by portions of planes. However, when curves or curved surfaces are involved, elementary geometry is almost helpless. For example, the shape of the earth is an oblate spheroid, that is, a sphere somewhat flattened on the top and bottom (Fig. 1-4). The calculation of the volume of this figure cannot be performed with elementary geometry; it can be done with the calculus. Euclidean geometry does have a method, called the method of exhaustion, for treating a very limited number of area and volume problems involving curves and surfaces, respectively. This method

**Figure 1-3**

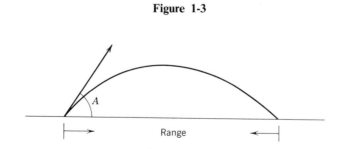

Range

**Figure 1-4**

is difficult to apply and, moreover, involves concepts that can with considerable justification be regarded as belonging to the calculus, although the
Greeks did not formulate them in modern terms. In any case, the method of
exhaustion could not cope with the variety and difficulty of the area and
volume problems that appeared in the seventeenth century. Closely related
to these problems were those of finding the center of gravity of a body and
the gravitational attraction exerted by, say, the earth on the moon. The
relation may not be evident at the moment, but we shall see that the same
method solves both types of problem.

The efforts to treat the four classes of problem that we have thus far
briefly described led mathematicians to methods which we now embrace
under the term calculus. Of course, similar problems continue to be
important in our time; otherwise the calculus would have only historical
value. In fact, once a mathematical method or branch of any significance is
created, many new uses are found for it that were not envisioned by its
creators. For the calculus this has proved to be far more the case than for
any other mathematical creation; we shall examine later a number of
modern applications. Moreover, the most weighty developments in
mathematics since the seventeenth century employ the calculus. Indeed, it is
the basis of a number of branches of mathematics which now comprise its
most extensive portion. The calculus has proved to be the richest lode that
the mathematicians have ever struck.

**2. The Creators of the Calculus.** Like almost all branches of mathematics,
the calculus is the product of many men. In the seventeenth century Pierre
de Fermat (1601–1665), René Descartes (1596–1650), Blaise Pascal (1623–
1662), Gilles Persone de Roberval (1602–1675), Bonaventura Cavalieri
(1598–1647), Isaac Barrow (1630–1677), James Gregory (1638–1675), Christian Huygens (1629–1695), John Wallis (1616–1703), and, of course, Isaac
Newton (1642–1727) and Gottfried Wilhelm Leibniz (1646–1716) all contributed to it. Newton and Leibniz are most often mentioned as the creators
of the calculus. This is a half-truth. Without deprecating their contributions,
it is fair to say, as Newton himself put it, that they stood on the shoulders
of giants. They saw more clearly than their predecessors the generality of
the methods that were gradually being developed and, in addition, added
many theorems and processes to the stock built up by their predecessors.

Even Newton and Leibniz did not complete the calculus. In fact, it may be a comfort to students just beginning to work in the calculus to know that Newton and Leibniz, two of the greatest mathematicians, did not fully understand what they themselves had produced. Throughout the eighteenth century new results were obtained by, for example, James Bernoulli (1654–1705), his brother John Bernoulli (1667–1748), Michel Rolle (1652–1719), Brook Taylor (1685–1731), Colin Maclaurin (1698–1746), Leonhard Euler (1707–1783), Jean Le Rond d'Alembert (1717–1783), and Joseph-Louis Lagrange (1736–1813). However, the final clarification of the concepts of the calculus was achieved only in the nineteenth century by, among others, Bernhard Bolzano (1781–1848), Augustin-Louis Cauchy (1789–1857), and Karl Weierstrass (1815–1897). We shall find many of these great names attached to theorems that we shall be studying.*

**3. The Nature of the Calculus.** The word *calculus* comes from the Latin word for pebble, which became associated with mathematics because the early Greek mathematicians of about 600 B.C. did arithmetic with the aid of pebbles. Today a calculus can mean a procedure or set of procedures such as division in arithmetic or solving a quadratic equation in algebra. However, most often the word means the theory and procedures we are about to study in the differential and integral calculus. Usually we say *the calculus* to denote the differential and integral calculus as opposed to other calculi.

The calculus utilizes algebra, geometry, trigonometry, and some coordinate geometry (which we shall study in this book). However, it also introduces some new concepts, notably the derivative and the integral. Fundamental to both is the limit concept. We shall not attempt to describe the notion of limit and how it is used to formulate the derivative and integral, because a brief explanation may be more confusing than helpful. Nevertheless, we do wish to point out that the calculus in its introduction and utilization of the limit concept marks a new stage in the development of mathematics.

The proper study of the calculus calls for attention to several features. The first is the theory, which leads to numerous theorems about the derivative and the integral. The second feature is the technique; to use the calculus, one must learn a fair amount of technique in differentiation and integration. The third feature is application. The calculus was created in response to scientific needs, and we should study many of the applications to gain appreciation of what can be accomplished with the subject; these applications also give insight into the mathematical ideas.

The theory of the calculus, which depends primarily on the limit concept, is rather sophisticated. Complete proofs of all the theorems are difficult to grasp when one is beginning the study of the subject. Our approach to the theory attempts to surmount this hurdle. Many of our proofs are complete. However, other proofs are made by appealing to geometric evidence; that is, we use curves or other geometric figures to substantiate our assertions. The geometric evidence does not necessarily

---

*The history of the calculus is presented very well in Carl B. Boyer, *The Concepts of the Calculus*, Dover Publications, New York, 1959.

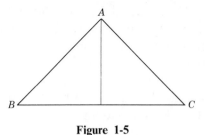

**Figure 1-5**

consist of complete geometric proofs, so that we cannot say that we are *proving* geometrically. Nevertheless, the arguments are quite convincing. For example, we can be certain even without geometric proof that the bisector of angle *A* (Fig. 1-5) divides the isosceles triangle *ABC* into two congruent triangles.

This approach, which will become clearer when we begin considering specific cases, is called the intuitive approach. It is recommended for several reasons. The first, as already suggested, is pedagogical. A thoroughly sound, deductive approach to the calculus, one which the modern mathematician would regard as logically rigorous, is meaningless before one understands the ideas and the purposes to which they are put. One should always try to understand new concepts and theorems in an intuitive manner before studying a formal and rigorous presentation of them. The logical version may dispose of any lingering doubts and may be aesthetically more satisfying to some minds, but it is not the road to understanding.

The rigorous approach, in fact, did not become available until about 150 years after the creation of the calculus. During these years mathematicians built up not only the calculus but also differential equations, differential geometry, the calculus of variations, and many other major branches of mathematics that depend on the calculus. In achieving these results the greatest mathematicians thought in intuitive and physical terms.

The second reason for adopting the intuitive approach is that we wish to have time for some techniques and for applications. Were we to study the rigorous formulations of limit, derivative, integral, and allied concepts, we would not have time for anything else. These concepts can be carefully and most profitably studied in more advanced courses in the calculus after one has some appreciation of what they mean in geometrical and physical terms and of what one wishes to do with them. As for the applications, the calculus more than any other branch of mathematics was created to solve major physical problems, and one should certainly learn what the calculus accomplishes in this connection.

After we have become reasonably familiar with the ideas, techniques, and uses of the calculus, we shall consider in the last chapter how the intuitive approach may be strengthened by a more rigorous one.

# CHAPTER
# TWO
# **THE**
# **DERIVATIVE**

**1. The Concept of Function.** Before considering any ideas of the calculus itself, we shall review a concept that is, no doubt, largely familiar—the concept of a function.

If an object moves in a straight line—for example, a ball rolling along a floor—the time during which it moves, measured from the instant it starts its motion, is a variable. In the case of the ball, the time continually increases. The distance the object moves, measured from the point at which it starts to move, is also a variable. The two variables are related. The distance the ball travels depends on the time the ball has been in motion. By the end of 1 second it may have moved 50 feet, by the end of 2 seconds, 100 feet, and so on. The relation between distance and time is a function. Loosely stated for the moment, a function is a relation between variables.

There are, of course, thousands of functions. If the ball were started on its journey with a different speed, the relation between distance traveled and time in motion would be different. All kinds of motions take place around us, and for each of them there is a function or relation between distance traveled and time in motion. The idea of a relation between variables is not confined to motion. The national debt of this country varies as time varies, and the relation between these variables is also a function. If money is allowed to accumulate interest in a bank, the amount in the account increases with time. Here, too, we have a function. Obviously, many other examples could be cited.

The notion of a function as used in the calculus is more restricted than we have thus far indicated. The statement that a person's obligation to society increases with his age expresses a function, the variables of which are obligation and age. However, it is not possible to measure the extent of this obligation in numbers. The calculus is concerned only with variables whose values can be expressed numerically. Thus time, distance, and money accumulating in a bank are variables whose various values can be measured and therefore can be expressed as numbers.

The most effective mathematical representation of a function is what we shall call a *formula*. Suppose that an object is dropped and falls straight down. The time during which it falls continually increases as does the distance that it falls. The formula

**(1)**                                                                    $$s = 16t^2,$$

whose correctness we shall establish later, expresses the relation between the two variables if the resistance of air is neglected. In this formula $t$ is the number of seconds the object falls measured from the instant it starts to fall and $s$ is the number of feet it falls measured from the point at which it is dropped. (The letter $s$ is used to denote distance because the Latin word for it is *spatium*.) The formula thus says that when $t = 2$, then $s = 16 \cdot 2^2$ or 64. For each value that we may substitute for $t$ there is a corresponding value of $s$. This example not only illustrates a formula but also possesses a property which is important for the functions that the calculus treats. For each value we may choose for $t$ there is no more than one value of $s$. We say that $s$ is a *single-valued* function of $t$.

When written in the form (1), that is, when solved for $s$, formula (1) shows how $s$ depends on $t$ or expresses $s$ as a function of $t$. Then $t$ is called the *independent* variable and $s$, the *dependent* variable.

Formula (1) also tells us something about how $t$ depends on $s$, for example, when $s = 64$, we find that $t$ can be $+2$ or $-2$. To express more clearly the dependence of $t$ on $s$, we can solve (1) algebraically for $t$ and obtain

**(2)**                                                                    $$t = \pm\sqrt{\frac{s}{16}} \cdot$$

Formula (2) expresses $t$ as a function of $s$, so that $s$ is the independent variable and $t$ is the dependent variable. Here we can say that $t$ is a double-valued function of $s$ or we can say that there are two functions,

**(3)**                                          $$t = \sqrt{\frac{s}{16}} \quad \text{and} \quad t = -\sqrt{\frac{s}{16}},$$

each of which is single-valued. Because the techniques of the calculus apply to single-valued functions, we use either one or the other of these two functions, depending on the physical problem.

## EXERCISES

**1.** The amount $A$ of money that accumulates in $n$ years if one dollar is invested and if the interest is compounded annually at the fixed rate of $i$ per cent per year is $A = (1 + i)^n$. As the formula is written, which is the independent variable? Which is the dependent variable?

**2.** Solve $v = 32t$ for $t$. Is the resulting function single-valued?

**3.** Solve $y = 5.3x^2$ for $x$. Is the resulting function single-valued?

**4.** Write the formula for:
   (a) the area $A$ of a circle in terms of the radius;
   (b) the area $A$ of a circle in terms of the diameter.

**5.** Write the formula for the radius of a circle in terms of the area. Is the function single-valued? If not, which of the single-valued functions do you think would be more useful and why?

**6.** One arm of a right triangle is 3 units and the hypotenuse is $x$ units. Write a formula for the length of the other arm.
   *Suggestion:* Use the Pythagorean theorem.

**7.** An automobile travels at 30 miles per hour. Write a formula which expresses the distance $d$ traveled in feet as a function of the time $t$ which represents the number of seconds of travel.

**8.** A rectangle is required to have an area of 4 square feet but its dimensions may vary. If one side has length $x$, express the perimeter $p$ of the rectangle as a function of $x$.

We shall be working with functions constantly. Thus we may have to deal with

**(4)**
$$s = t^2$$

**(5)**
$$y = x^3 + 3x^2 + 5$$

and a great variety of other functions. If we wish to refer to any of these specific functions repeatedly it is cumbersome to have to repeat the entire function each time, and yet some device is needed to avoid confusion with other functions. Moreover, there will be times when we shall want to speak about properties of all functions or all functions of some class. How should we handle these tasks without a lot of extensive repetition or verbiage?

There is a notation which solves our problems and even has additional advantages. Suppose we wish to refer to the function in (4) repeatedly. We use the notation $f(t)$ and $f(t)$ then stands for the entire expression on the right side of (4). [The notation $f(t)$ is read "$f$ of $t$"; moreover the notation does *not* mean $f$ times $t$. The symbol $f(t)$ must be taken as a whole.] Similarly, to denote the function in (5) one writes $f(x)$. To speak of a class of functions one can say, let $f(x)$ be any function of such and such a class.

The notation $f(x)$ has many advantages. First of all, as opposed to $s$ or $y$, it tells us what the independent variable is. Second, suppose one wished to speak of the value of the function $f(x) = x^2 - 9$ when $x = 3$. We could, of course, calculate the value of the function. But, often knowing the value is not as important as is speaking about it. The notation $f(3)$ does it. That is, $f(3)$ means the value of $f(x)$ when $x = 3$. In the case of $f(x) = x^2 - 9$, $f(3) = 0$. Similarly, $f(-2) = -5$.

The function notation has another advantage. Suppose that in some discussion we wish to talk about two different functions, say $y = x^2 - 9$ and $y = (x - 1)/2$. To refer to both as $f(x)$ would be confusing. What we can do is refer to $x^2 - 9$ as $f(x)$ and refer to $(x - 1)/2$ as $g(x)$. In this situation $f(5)$ is 16 and $g(5)$ is 2.

The function notation also lends itself to a distinction that is most often honored in the breach. Strictly speaking, a function is a relation between two variables, $x$ and $y$ say. The relation might be that $y$ is the square of $x$. Then the relation is neither $x$ nor $y$ but something connecting the two. Thus when one says that John is the father of William, the relationship is fatherhood, and this relation is neither John nor William but a connection between them. Yet in speaking about these people one might use the word father to mean John, whereas the word strictly refers to the relationship. Likewise in dealing with functions we should distinguish between the relation and the value $y$ of the function. We could use $f$ to denote the relation between $y$ and $x$ and use $f(x)$ to mean $y$. However, we often use $y$ or $f(x)$ to mean the relation. Fortunately, this use of $y$ or $f(x)$ in the double sense causes no confusion and avoids a lot of unnecessary words.

**Example 1.** If $f(x) = x^2 - 7x + 5$, $f(2) = 2^2 - 7 \cdot 2 + 5 = -5$; $f(-2) = (-2)^2 - 7(-2) + 5 = 23$; $f(2a) = (2a)^2 - 7(2a) + 5 = 4a^2 - 14a + 5$; $f(x + 3) = (x + 3)^2 - 7(x + 3) + 5 = x^2 - x - 7$.

**Example 2.** If $f(x) = x^3 + 5$, $f(-2) = (-2)^3 + 5 = -8 + 5 = -3$; $f(t) = t^3 + 5$; $f(2t) = (2t)^3 + 5 = 8t^3 + 5$.

**Example 3.** If $f(x) = x^2 + 9x$ and $g(x) = x^3 - 7$, $f(x) \cdot g(x) = (x^2 + 9x)(x^3 - 7) = x^5 + 9x^4 - 7x^2 - 63x$.

## EXERCISES

1. If $f(x) = x^2 - 9x$, calculate $f(0)$, $f(2)$, $f(-1)$, and $f(9)$.     *Ans.* $0, -14, 10, 0$.
2. If $f(x) = -x^2 - 9x$, calculate $f(0)$, $f(2)$, $f(-2)$, $f(9)$, and $f(-9)$.
3. For the functions in Exercises 1 and 2, calculate $f(a)$ and $f(x_0)$.
     *Ans.* $a^2 - 9a$; $-a^2 - 9a$.
4. If $f(x) = x - \dfrac{1}{x}$ show that (a) $f(-x) = -f(x)$, (b) $f\left(\dfrac{1}{x}\right) = -f(x)$.
5. If $f(x) = \dfrac{x^2 - 9}{-x^2 + 7}$, find $f(0)$, $f(2)$, $f(-2)$, and $f(\sqrt{7})$.
6. If $f(x) = x^2 - 7x$, what is $f(2x)$? What is $f(x + h)$?
7. If $f(x) = \tan x$, find $f(0)$, $f(\pi/4)$, and $f(-\pi/4)$.     *Ans.* $0, 1, -1$.
8. If $f(x) = x^2 + 5$ and $g(x) = x^3 - 7$, how much is $f(-2) \cdot g(-2)$.
9. If $f(x) = \dfrac{3}{x} - x^3$, find $f(3)$, $f(-1)$, $f\left(\dfrac{1}{x}\right)$.
10. If $f(x) = \dfrac{x^2 + 32}{x + 4}$ find $f(0)$, $f(4)$, $f(g^2)$.
11. Let $g(x) = x^3$. Show that $g(-x) = -g(x)$.
12. Let $g(x) = x^4 + 2x^2 + 1$. Show that $g(x) = g(-x)$.
13. We learn in trigonometry that $\sin x \equiv \sin(\pi - x)$. Hence $f(\sin x) = f(\sin[\pi - x])$. Now let $f(x) = x \sin x$. Then $x \sin x = (\pi - x) \sin(\pi - x)$, or $x = \pi - x$. Hence $\pi = 2x$ and since $x$ is any value we choose, so is $\pi$. What is wrong?

**2. The Graph or Curve of a Function.** We learn in algebra that formulas may be pictured as curves. The powerful method of interpreting formulas geometrically is known as coordinate or analytic geometry. This subject was created in the early part of the seventeenth century by René Descartes (1596–1650) and Pierre de Fermat (1601–1665) to expedite the study of functions, which were just beginning to be used, and to study geometric problems by algebraic means.

The main idea of coordinate geometry is that a function relating two variables, such as $y = x^2$ or $y = x^2 + 6x$, can be represented geometrically by a curve and, conversely, that a curve can be represented by a function, although the function may not be single-valued. It is customary to speak of the function as the equation of the curve.

The basic device of coordinate geometry is a coordinate system, that is, a scheme that locates points in a plane by means of a pair of numbers. The most important coordinate system is the one that utilizes two mutually perpendicular lines (Fig. 2-1), called the $x$- and $y$-axes. These lines intersect at some point $O$, called the origin. Along the $x$-axis, which is usually taken to be a horizontal line, we assign to each point its distance from the origin $O$. This distance is taken to be positive if the point lies to the right of $O$ and negative if it lies to the left. Thus point $T$, which is 3 units to the right of $O$, has the number 3 or $+3$ assigned to it, whereas point $U$, which is 3 units to the left of $O$, has the number $-3$ assigned to it. Likewise numbers that represent their distances from $O$ are assigned to points on the $y$-axis, but in this case points above $O$ are assigned positive numbers and points below $O$, negative numbers. It is customary and usually convenient to use the same unit of distance in assigning numbers to points on both axes.

We are now able to locate or describe the positions of all points in the plane in relation to the axes. Consider point $P$ in Fig. 2-1. To reach it from $O$ we can travel 2 units to the right along the $x$-axis and 3 units up in the direction of or parallel to the $y$-axis. Point $P$ is located by the numbers 2 and 3, which are usually written as (2, 3), the first number indicating the

**Figure 2-1**

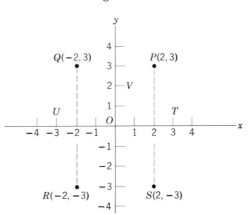

distance along the $x$-axis and the second, the distance parallel to the $y$-axis. The two numbers are called the coordinates of $P$; the first is called the *abscissa* and the second, the *ordinate*.

The coordinates of point $Q$ in Fig. 2-1 are $(-2, 3)$; the minus sign enters because we must travel 2 units to the left to reach $Q$. Similarly, the coordinates of $R$ are $(-2, -3)$ and the coordinates of $S$ are $(2, -3)$.

Our method of attaching coordinates to points assigns two coordinates to each point. Accordingly, point $T$ on the $x$-axis in Fig. 2-1 has the coordinates $(3, 0)$ and point $V$ on the $y$-axis has the coordinates $(0, 2)$.

The coordinate system we have examined is called the rectangular Cartesian system. The word Cartesian honors Descartes who introduced it, although in cruder form, and the word rectangular refers to the fact that the axes meet at right angles.

With the help of the rectangular Cartesian coordinate system we can obtain curves that represent or picture formulas. To obtain the curve corresponding to $s = 16t^2$ we first introduce the usual horizontal and vertical axes of a rectangular coordinate system. We may as well label these axes $t$ and $s$ instead of $x$ and $y$ to remind us of the letters we are actually using for the variables in our formula. We can now graph the formula $s = 16t^2$ by making a table of values. Thus when $t = 0$, $s = 0$; when $t = 1$, $s = 16$; and so forth. The table then reads:

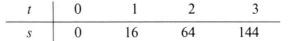

| $t$ | 0 | 1 | 2 | 3 |
|---|---|---|---|---|
| $s$ | 0 | 16 | 64 | 144 |

Because the $s$-values are large, we use a smaller unit of length on the $s$-axis than on the $t$-axis. We now plot the points $(0, 0)$, $(1, 16)$, $(2, 64)$, . . . , and join them by a smooth curve (Fig. 2-2). In the present case there is no need to include negative values of $t$ in the table because we see that for each negative value of $t$, say $-2$, the $s$-value is the same as that for the corresponding positive value of $t$. Geometrically this means that the curve

**Figure 2-2**

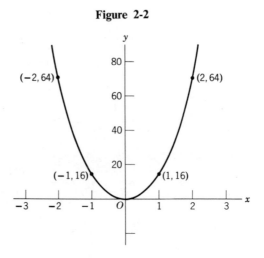

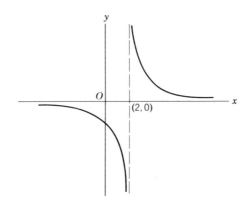

**Figure 2-3**

rises to the left in precisely the same way as to the right. The full curve in Fig. 2-2 is called a *parabola*.

The graph of a formula, that is, the curve corresponding to a formula, is a useful picture of how the variables in the formula behave. Thus we see in Fig. 2-2 that $s$ not only increases as $t$ increases from 0 onward through positive values but does so much more rapidly than $t$. We must, however, be careful to distinguish the curve from the *physical* situation. The motion described by $s = 16t^2$ is that of an object that falls straight down. There is a correspondence between the physical happening and the curve, but the latter is usually not a picture of the physical motion. It is also important to note that both the formula and the curve differ in another essential respect from the physical motion. An object that is dropped from a point near the surface of the earth may fall for, say, 5 seconds and then hit the earth. The physical motion, then, is represented by the formula and the curve only for the values of $t$ from 0 to 5. However, the mathematical formula and mathematical curve have meaning for every positive and negative value of $t$.

The function $s = 16t^2$ is especially simple in that to *each* value of $t$ that we may select there is a corresponding value of $s$. The concept of a function does not require this. Consider, for example, the function

**(6)**
$$y = \frac{1}{x - 2} .$$

For each value of $x$ other than 2, there is a definite value of $y$. For $x = 2$ the expression on the right side becomes $1/0$, which is meaningless because division by 0 is not defined.* Hence this function is defined or, as the mathematician says, this function exists for each value of $x$ other than 2. The graph of the function is shown in Fig. 2-3. There is no point on the graph corresponding to $x = 2$.

---

*Let us recall why a quantity such as $a/0$ is not defined. Suppose first that $a$ is not 0. Were there a number $b$ such that $a/0 = b$, then by multiplying both sides of this equation by 0 we would have $a = 0 \cdot b$. However, $0 \cdot b$ cannot equal $a$, for $a$ is not 0. If $a$ is 0, by the same steps we obtain $0 = 0 \cdot b$; now the trouble is that $b$ can be any number. Because there is no unique answer to $0/0$, the expression is meaningless.

As another example, let us consider the function

(7)                                    $f(x) = \sqrt{1 - x}$ ,

wherein the radical sign denotes the positive square root. When $x$ is greater than 1, the radicand is negative, and the square root of a negative number is a complex number. In elementary calculus we prefer not to deal with complex numbers. Hence we restrict the values of $x$ to 1 and numbers algebraically less than 1; that is, the permissible values of $x$ are the positive numbers less than or equal to 1, 0, and all negative numbers. The graph of the permissible $x$- and $y$- values is shown in Fig. 2-4. Whether we label the vertical axis $y$ or $f(x)$ is immaterial here.

Thus the concept of a function does not require that there be a $y$-value for each value of $x$, but it does require a $y$-value for each value of $x$ in some collection or set of $x$-values. The technical word for the collection of $x$-values for which the $y$-values exist is *domain*; the collection of corresponding $y$-values is called the *range* of the function.

Let us consider as an example the function

(8)                                    $y = \dfrac{x^2 - 4}{x - 2}$ .

The temptation in studying this function is to use algebra at once and write

$$y = \frac{x^2 - 4}{x - 2} = \frac{(x + 2)(x - 2)}{x - 2} ,$$

and now one almost naturally cancels the factor $x - 2$ in numerator and denominator and obtains

(9)                                    $y = x + 2.$

There seems to be nothing wrong about yielding to temptation and, in fact, one seems to gain a lot by doing so, contrary to all the moralists: the function (9) is much simpler than (8).

Figure 2-4

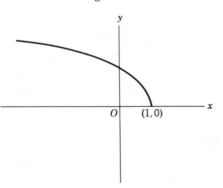

Nevertheless, there is a vital distinction between (8) and (9). To arrive at (9) we canceled the factor $x - 2$ in numerator and denominator. What this operation really amounts to is dividing numerator and denominator by $x - 2$. However, division by $x - 2$ is legitimate except when $x = 2$. Hence the steps from (8) to (9) are correct except when $x = 2$. Let us look at (8) when $x = 2$. The numerator and denominator are each 0, and what we obtain for $y$ is $0/0$. Now, division by 0 is meaningless, and therefore $y$ in (8) has no value at $x = 2$. On the other hand the function in (9) has a very definite value when $x = 2$, namely $y = 4$. Thus the two functions (8) and (9) differ in their behavior at $x = 2$.

Let us look at the graphs of the two functions. To graph (8) we must calculate the $y$-values for various $x$-values. For this purpose we can use the simpler function (9), which is the same as (8) except at $x = 2$. We find that the graph of (9), which is a first degree equation in $x$ and $y$, is a straight line; this is shown in Fig. 2-5$b$. Then the graph of (8) must also be the same straight line *except* at $x = 2$. At $x = 2$ the function (8) has no value, and therefore there is no point on the graph corresponding to $x = 2$. The graph of (8) then consists of two half lines or rays emanating from point $P$ of Fig. 2-5$a$, but point $P$ itself is *not* part of the graph.

The distinction we have drawn between the functions (8) and (9) may seem to be much ado about nothing, but let us withhold judgment and undertake a further study of (8). What can we say about the behavior of that function as $x$ takes on values closer and closer to 2? For values of $x$ close to 2, other than 2 itself, the function (9) has the same values as (8), and we see from (9) that as $x$ takes on values closer and closer to 2, the $y$-values come closer and closer to 4. Hence the same must be true of the function (8). We say that the number 4 is the *limit* of the $y$-values in (8) as $x$ approaches 2. We shall explain the notion of limit and its implications more fully later, as we probe more deeply into the calculus. We should note at this point, however, that although a function is not defined, that is, it has no value, at a given value of $x$, the value $x = 2$ in (8), the values of the function may approach a given number more and more closely as the values of $x$ approach that given value of $x$. In other words, a function may approach a limit at a given value of the independent variable even when the function has no value.

**Figure 2-5**

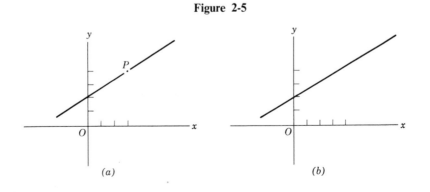

(a)            (b)

## EXERCISES

**1.** Sketch the graphs of the following functions by the method of plotting points:

(a) $y = 3x^2$.

(b) $y = \sqrt{1 - x^2}$.

(c) $y = -\sqrt{1 - x^2}$.

(d) $y = \dfrac{1}{x - 3}$.

(e) $f(x) = x^3$.

(f) $y = \dfrac{1}{x^2}$.

(g) $y = \dfrac{x^2 - 9}{x - 3}$.

(h) $y = \dfrac{x^3 - 1}{x - 1}$.

(i) $f(x) = x^2 - 7x$.

(j) $y = -x^2$.

(k) $y = -x^2 + 7x$.

(l) $y = -x^2 - 7x$.

(m) $f(x) = \sqrt{x^2}$.

**2.** There is of course no obligation to use $y$ and $x$ as the symbols for the dependent and independent variables, respectively. We may use $k$ and $h$. Sketch the following functions:

(a) $k = \dfrac{16h + h^2}{h}$.

(b) $k = \dfrac{h^3}{h}$.

(c) $k = \dfrac{9h + h^3}{h}$.

(d) $k = \dfrac{9h^2 + h^3}{h}$.

(e) $k = \dfrac{(h - 1)^2}{h - 1}$.

**3.** Since the function $y = \dfrac{x^3 - 1}{x - 1}$ is the same as the function $y = x^2 + x + 1$ except at $x = 1$ what is the limit of $\dfrac{(x^3 - 1)}{x - 1}$ as $x$ approaches 1?

### 3. Average and Instantaneous Speed.

The primary concept of the calculus deals with the rate of change of one variable with respect to another. Let us approach an understanding of this concept by discussing the notion of speed, the very concept with which Newton started. By speed we usually understand the rate of change of distance with respect to time. Thus, if a person travels 90 miles in 3 hours, his speed, he says, is 30 mi/hr (miles per hour). He has, of course, divided the distance traveled by the time during which he has traveled that distance to obtain the speed. This speed is more properly called the *average* speed or the *average* rate of change of distance with respect to time.

Of course, the person who travels at the average speed of 30 mi/hr does not necessarily travel at that fixed speed throughout the 3 hours. He may slow down or speed up at various times during the 3 hours. For many purposes, however, it suffices for people to know the average speed at which they have traveled or can expect to travel on some journey.

However, the average speed is not the significant quantity in many daily happenings and scientific phenomena. If a person traveling in an automobile strikes a tree, it is not his average speed during the time he has traveled from the starting point to the tree but his speed at the *instant of collision* that determines whether he will survive the accident. Likewise, when a bullet strikes a target it is the speed of the bullet at the *instant it strikes* rather than its average speed over the time it has been traveling that determines what damage the bullet will do. Many other more agreeable examples of where speed at an instant matter will be encountered later.

In contrasting average speed with instantaneous speed we have implicitly utilized a distinction between interval and instant, which is vital for what follows. An average speed is one that concerns what happens over an *interval* of time—3 hours, 5 seconds, one half second, and so forth. The interval may be small or large, but it does represent the passage of a definite amount of time. We use the word instant, however, to state the fact that something happens so fast that no time elapses. The event is momentary. When we say, for example, that it is 3 o'clock, we refer to an instant, a precise moment. If the lapse of time is pictured by length along a line, then an interval is represented by a line segment, whereas an instant corresponds to a point. The notion of an instant, although it is also used in everyday life, is strictly a mathematical idealization.

Our ways of thinking about real events do cause us to speak in terms of instants and of speed at an instant, but closer examination shows that the concept of speed at an instant presents difficulties. Average speed, which is simply the distance traveled during some *interval* of time divided by that amount of time, is easily calculated. Suppose, however, that we try to carry over this process to instantaneous speed. The distance an automobile travels in one instant is 0 and the time that elapses during one instant is also 0. Hence the distance divided by the time is $0/0$, which is meaningless. Thus, although instantaneous speed is a physical reality, there seems to be a difficulty in calculating it, and unless we can calculate it, we cannot work with it mathematically.

Let us see if we can devise some method of calculating instantaneous speed. If an object travels at a constant speed, say 30 mi/hr or 44 ft/sec (feet per second), there is no problem. We can take its speed at each instant to be 44 ft/sec. Suppose, however, that an object moves with variable speed and we wish to determine its instantaneous speed, say, exactly 3 seconds after it has been in motion. A practical beginning might be to calculate the average speed during the fourth second of the motion. Of course, during the fourth second the object would have changed its speed, because it is moving with variable speed, and the average for the fourth second might not be the speed we seek. This average would be an approximation.

We can improve this approximation if we calculate the average speed for the half second from 3 to $3\frac{1}{2}$ seconds. This average should be a better approximation because even though the object is moving with a variable speed the average is not so likely to differ in a half second as in a full second from the speed which the object possesses at the end of the third second. Nevertheless, even the average speed during the half second is only an approximation to the speed at the end of the three seconds.

The way to obtain better approximations is now clear. We could calculate the average speed over a quarter second from 3 to $3\frac{1}{4}$. This average should be better than the average over a half second because there is less time in which the object's speed can depart from the speed at the end of the third second. Still better approximations would be obtained by calculating the average speed for one eighth of a second from 3 to $3\frac{1}{8}$, then for one sixteenth of a second from 3 to $3\frac{1}{16}$, and so on.

Let us suppose that our calculations of average speeds yielded the following table:

| Time interval after 3 seconds | 1 | $\frac{1}{2}$ | $\frac{1}{4}$ | $\frac{1}{8}$ | $\frac{1}{16}$ | $\frac{1}{32}$ | $\cdots$ |
|---|---|---|---|---|---|---|---|
| Average speed | 100 | 96.5 | 96.3 | 96.1 | 96.05 | 96.01 | $\cdots$ |

This table suggests that, as the time intervals over which the average speeds are computed become smaller and smaller, the average speeds get closer and closer to 96. Moreover, the average speeds represent the speed of the moving object for a time interval closer and closer to the end of the third second. Would it not then be reasonable to take the number approached by these average speeds, namely 96, to be the speed precisely at the end of the third second? Physically this seems most advisable. After all, as the intervals of time measured from the end of the third second become very small, the average speeds in those intervals cannot differ much from what the object possessed at the end of the third second, for the object does not have much time to change its speed.

This indication of how the speed at an instant might be determined is the kernel of the mathematical method of obtaining instantaneous rates. Before we attempt to make the method more precise and more efficient, let us repeat a very important point. The average speeds over the various time *intervals* are easy to compute. An average speed is simply the distance traveled over an interval of time divided by the interval of time. However, the instantaneous speed, the speed at the end of the third second, is *not* obtained by dividing a distance by a time interval. It is obtained *by observing the number that the average speeds approach*—the number 96 in our illustration. In mathematical language we say that the number 96 is the *limit* of the average speeds as the time intervals over which the average speeds are computed approach 0. Hence the instantaneous speed is obtained by a totally new process, namely, by finding the limit of average speeds. By this process we avoid the meaningless expression 0/0 which we would have to face if we tried to compute the instantaneous speed as distance traveled divided by time of travel. Also, as we have already seen, it makes excellent sense from the physical standpoint to choose this limit to be the speed at the end of the third second.

## EXERCISES

1. Suppose that in order to obtain the speed of an object at the end of the third second of its motion you calculated the average speed during the third second, then during the time interval from $2\frac{1}{2}$ to 3, then during the time interval $2\frac{3}{4}$ to 3, and so on. Would you expect the average speeds to come closer and closer to the speed at the end of the third second? Why?                    *Ans.* Yes.

2. Suppose that the average speeds of a moving object for smaller and smaller intervals of time after the third second prove to be 129, 128.5, 128.2, 128. 05, . . . . What would you expect the speed at the end of the third second to be?
                                                                    *Ans.* 128 ft/sec.

The indication above of how instantaneous speed might be calculated was, of course, sketchy. We presumed that we knew the average speeds for smaller and smaller intervals of time, and from them we determined the instantaneous speed. Given a real problem, how do we know these average speeds? We could calculate them if we knew the distance the objects travels as a function of the time it travels. In other words, we must know the formula that relates distance and time traveled.

Let us see how the formula can be used to calculate average speeds and then instantaneous speed. We shall take the case of a ball that is dropped near the surface of the earth. The relevant formula is $s = 16t^2$. The formula presupposes that the time $t$ is measured in seconds from the instant the ball starts to fall and the distance $s$ in feet is measured from the point at which the ball is dropped. (Just how such formulas are obtained will be a later concern.)

We shall seek the speed at the end of the fourth second of fall, that is, the speed at the instant $t = 4$. We have already pointed out that we cannot obtain this speed in the same manner in which we calculate the average speed over some interval of time because it is meaningless to divide the zero distance traveled at $t = 4$ by the zero time elapsed. We therefore start with the calculation of the average speed *during the fifth second*. At the beginning of the fifth second, that is, when $t = 4$, the distance covered by the falling body is obtained by substituting 4 for $t$ in the formula $s = 16t^2$. This distance is then $16 \cdot 4^2$ or 256. The distance covered by the end of the fifth second, that is, when $t = 5$, is $16 \cdot 5^2$ or 400. Hence the distance covered during the fifth second is $400 - 256$ or 144, and the average speed during the fifth second is

$$\frac{144}{1} \quad \text{or} \quad 144 \text{ ft/sec.}$$

Of course, the quantity 144 is no more than an approximation of the instantaneous speed. We may, however, improve the approximation by calculating the average speed in the interval of time from 4 to 4.1 seconds, for during this interval the average speed can, on physical grounds, be expected to approximate more closely the speed actually possessed by the body at $t = 4$. We therefore repeat the procedure of the preceding paragraph, this time using the values 4.1 and 4 for $t$. Thus for $t = 4.1$, $s = 16(4.1)^2 = 16(16.81) = 268.96$. For $t = 4$ we know that $s = 256$. Hence the distance traveled during the 0.1 second from $t = 4$ to $t = 4.1$ is $268.96 - 256$ or 12.96, and the average speed during the interval $t = 4$ to $t = 4.1$ seconds is then

$$\frac{12.96}{0.1} = 129.6.$$

We note that the average speed during this tenth of a second is quite different from the value 144 for the fifth second.

Of course, the average speed during the interval $t = 4$ to $t = 4.1$ is not the speed at $t = 4$, because even during one tenth of a second the speed of the falling body changes and the average is not the value at $t = 4$. We can obtain a still better approximation to the speed at $t = 4$ if we calculate the average speed during the one one-hundredth of a second from $t = 4$ to $t = 4.01$, because the speed during this short interval of time near $t = 4$ ought to be almost equal to that at $t = 4$. Hence we again apply our previous procedure. For $t = 4.01$, $s = 16(4.01)^2 = 16(16.0801) = 257.2816$. For $t = 4$ we know that $s = 256$. Thus the distance traveled during the 0.01 of a second from $t = 4$ to $t = 4.01$ is $257.2816 - 256$ or $1.2816$. Then the average speed during the interval $t = 4$ to $t = 4.01$ is

$$\frac{1.2816}{0.01} = 128.16.$$

We could continue this process. The speed during the interval $t = 4$ to $t = 4.01$ is not the exact speed at $t = 4$, because the speed of the falling body changes even in one one-hundredth of a second. We could therefore calculate the average speed in the interval $t = 4$ to $t = 4.001$ and expect this average to be even closer to the speed at $t = 4$ than the preceding ones. (The result is 128.016 ft/sec.) Of course, no matter how small the interval over which the average speed is calculated, the result is *not* the speed at the instant $t = 4$. However, we now see that the average speeds for the intervals of time 1, 0.1, 0.01, and 0.001 are 144, 129.6, 128.16, and 128.016, respectively. These numbers seem to be approaching, or getting closer to, the fixed number 128. Hence we take 128 to be the speed of the falling body at $t = 4$. This number is the *limit* of the set of average speeds. We should note again that the instantaneous speed is *not* defined as the quotient of distance and time. Rather it is the limit approached by average speeds as the intervals of time over which they are computed approach zero.

Instead of computing average speeds during smaller and smaller intervals of time after the fourth second we could have computed average speeds for smaller and smaller intervals of time just preceding the fourth second, that is, from 3 seconds to 4 seconds, from 3.5 to 4 seconds, from 3.9 to 4 seconds, etc. Again we would expect that the limit approached by these average speeds would be the instantaneous speed at $t = 4$. (See Exercise 6.)

Two objections to what we have done may occur. First, what right have we to take the number approached by the average speeds to be the speed at $t = 4$? The answer, as we have already implied, is that mathematicians have adopted a definition that makes good physical sense. They argue that the smaller the interval of time starting at $t = 4$ for which the average speeds are computed, the closer the behavior of the falling body must be to that at $t = 4$. Hence the number approached by average speeds over the smaller and smaller intervals of time starting at $t = 4$ should be the speed at $t = 4$. Because mathematics seeks to represent physical phenomena, it naturally adopts definitions that seem to be in accord with physical facts. It can then expect the results obtained by mathematical reasoning and calculations to fit the physical world.

The second possible objection to our definition of instantaneous speed is a more practical one. Apparently, we must calculate average speeds over many intervals of time and attempt to discern what number these average speeds seem to be approaching. However, there appears to be no guarantee that the fixed number chosen is the correct one. Thus, if in our above calculations we had obtained only the average speeds 144, 129.6, and 128.16, we might have decided that these speeds were approaching the number 128.15; this result would be in error by 0.15 ft/sec. The answer to this objection is that we can generalize the entire process of obtaining the instantaneous speed so that it can be carried out more quickly and with certainty. We shall describe this new method in the next section.

## EXERCISES

1. Distinguish between the change in distance that results when an object moves for some interval of time and the rate of change of distance compared to time in that interval.

2. Suppose that an object falls a distance $s$ given by $s = 16t^2$. What is the change in distance, or distance traveled, from $t = 3$ to $t = 5$? What is the average rate of change of distance compared to time in that time interval? What is the average speed in that time interval?          *Ans.* 256 ft; 128 ft/sec; 128 ft/sec.

3. Distinguish between average speed and instantaneous speed.

4. What mathematical concept is used to obtain instantaneous speed from average speed?

5. If the distance $s$, in feet, that a body falls in $t$ seconds is given by the formula $s = 16t^2$, calculate the following:
   (a) The average speed of the body during the first 5 seconds of fall.
                                                               *Ans.* 80 ft/sec.
   (b) The average speed during the fifth second of fall.
   (c) The instantaneous speed at the end of the fifth second of fall.
                                                               *Ans.* 160 ft/sec

6. In the text we calculated the instantaneous speed at $t = 4$ of an object falling according to the formula $s = 16t^2$ by first calculating average speed over intervals of time following $t = 4$; that is, we calculated average speeds over the intervals 4 to 5, 4 to 4.1, 4 to 4.01, and so on. Calculate the instantaneous speed at $t = 4$ by working with average speeds over the time intervals 3 to 4, 3.9 to 4, 3.99 to 4, and so on.

7. If at some instant during its motion an object has the speed of 30 mi/h, will the object travel 30 miles in the next hour?          *Ans.* Not necessarily.

**4. The Method of Increments.** We have already stated that we can formulate the process of calculating instantaneous speed in such a way as to avoid tedious calculation and at the same time be certain of the limit that the average speeds approach. To examine this method, let us again calculate the instantaneous speed of a dropped body at the end of the fourth second of fall, that is, at the instant $t = 4$. The formula that relates distance fallen and time of travel is, of course,

**(10)** $$s = 16t^2.$$

Again we can calculate at once the distance fallen by the end of the fourth second. This distance, which we denote by $s_4$, is $16 \cdot 4^2$ or

**(11)** $$s_4 = 256.$$

The generality of our new process consists in calculating the average speed not over a specific interval of time, such as 0.1 of a second, but over an arbitrary interval of time. We introduce a quantity $h$ that is to represent any interval of time beginning at $t = 4$ and extending before or after $t = 4$. The quantity $h$ is called an *increment* in $t$ because it is some additional interval of time. If $h$ is positive, it represents an interval after $t = 4$; if it is negative, it denotes an interval before $t = 4$.

To calculate the average speed in the interval 4 to $4 + h$ seconds, we must first find the distance traveled in this interval of time. We therefore substitute $4 + h$ for $t$ in (10) and obtain the distance fallen by the body in $4 + h$ seconds. This distance is denoted by $s_4 + k$, where $s_4$ is the distance the body falls in four seconds and $k$ is the additional distance fallen, or the *increment* in distance, in the interval of $h$ seconds. Thus

$$s_4 + k = 16(4 + h)^2.$$

We multiply $4 + h$ by itself and obtain

**(12)**         $s_4 + k = 16\,(16 + 8h + h^2) = 256 + 128h + 16h^2.$

To obtain $k$, the distance traveled in the interval of $h$ seconds, we have but to subtract (11) from (12). The result is

**(13)**                          $k = 128h + 16h^2.$

The average speed in the interval of $h$ seconds is the distance traveled in that time divided by the time, that is $k/h$. Let us therefore divide both sides of (13) by $h$. Then

**(14)**                          $\dfrac{k}{h} = \dfrac{128h + 16h^2}{h}.$

When $h$ is *not* zero, it is correct to divide the numerator and denominator on the right-hand side of (14) by $h$. The result is

**(15)**                          $\dfrac{k}{h} = 128 + 16h.$

Hence (15) is also a correct expression for the average speed when $h$ is not zero.

To obtain the instantaneous speed at $t = 4$, we must determine the number approached by the average speeds as the interval $h$ of time over which these speeds are computed becomes smaller and smaller. We can readily obtain it from (15). If $h$ decreases, $16h$ must also decrease; when $h$ is close to zero, $16h$ is also close to zero. In view of (15), then, the fixed number that the average speed approaches is 128. This number is taken to be the instantaneous speed at $t = 4$.

The process we have just examined, called the *method of increments*, is basic to the calculus. It is subtler than it appears at first sight. We should not expect to appreciate its finer points on first contact, any more than one gets to know another person well on the basis of one meeting. As a step in the right direction, however, we shall make one or two observations.

First, we wish to determine the speed at $t = 4$. Because $h$ is the increment in time beyond $t = 4$ and $k/h$ is the average speed in this interval, we may think that to determine the speed at $t = 4$ we should let $h$ be 0 in (14). However, when $h = 0$, we see from the right side that the numerator and denominator are 0, so that we obtain $0/0$. This result should no longer surprise us. We have already recognized that we cannot get instantaneous speed by dividing the 0 distance traveled at an instant by the 0 time that an instant amounts to. However, if we agree to consider average speeds, then $h$ is not 0 and the right side of (14) is a meaningful expression. Moreover, when $h$ is not 0, it is correct to divide numerator and denominator by $h$ and to obtain the simpler expression in (15) for the average speeds. This latter expression happens to be especially simple, and therefore we can determine from it the limit approached by the average speeds as $h$ approaches 0, namely, the number 128. The difference between (14) and (15) is precisely the difference between the function

$$y = \frac{x^2 - 4}{x - 2}$$

and the function

$$y = x + 2,$$

which we discussed in Section 2.

For the rather elementary function $s = 16t^2$, instead of finding the limit of $k/h$ in (15) by letting $h$ approach 0, we may let $h$ be 0 in (15); the result then is also 128. This agreement between the value of the right side of (15), namely $128 + 16h$, when $h$ is 0 and the number approached by $128 + 16h$ as $h$ gets closer to 0 will appear in a number of fairly simple functions.* However, let us not lose sight of the fact that we seek the limit of $128 + 16h$ as $h$ approaches 0 rather than the value when $h$ is 0.

The main point that emerges from this section is the possibility of finding instantaneous speed by a general process—the method of increments. No tedious arithmetical calculations are necessary, nor is there any doubt about the limit approached by the average speeds.

**Example.** Find the instantaneous speed or instantaneous rate of change of distance with respect to time at $t = 5$ of an object which falls according to the formula $s = 16t^2 + 96t$.

**Solution.** We first calculate the distance fallen at the end of $5 + h$ seconds. This distance is

**(16)** $\qquad s_5 + k = 16(5 + h)^2 + 96(5 + h) = 880 + 256h + 16h^2.$

*We could pursue the point further and learn just when the limit approached by $k/h$ as $h$ approaches 0 must agree with the "value" of $k/h$ when $h$ is 0. But to do so would involve a long digression into theory which at the moment is of secondary importance. We shall return to this point in Chapter 25.

The distance fallen at the end of 5 seconds is

**(17)**                                   $s_5 = 16 \cdot 5^2 + 96 \cdot 5 = 880.$

The distance fallen in the $h$ seconds is obtained by subtracting (17) from (16). Then

$$k = 256h + 16h^2.$$

The average speed during the $h$ seconds is

$$\frac{k}{h} = \frac{256h + 16h^2}{h}.$$

Fortunately we can simplify this expression to

$$\frac{k}{h} = 256 + 16h.$$

We now evaluate the limit of $k/h$ as $h$ approaches 0. This limit is clearly 256 and this number is the instantaneous speed at the end of 5 seconds of fall.

## EXERCISES

1. For each of the following functions find the number or limit approached by the numerator, by the denominator, and by the entire function as $h$ approaches 0:

   (a)  $\dfrac{3h^2}{h^2}$.             *Ans.* 0, 0, 3.    (d)  $\dfrac{3h^3 + 3h^2 + h}{h}$.

   (b)  $\dfrac{h^2}{2h^2}$.                                (e)  $\dfrac{h^2}{h}$.              *Ans.* 0, 0, 0.

   (c)  $\dfrac{3h^2 + h}{h}$.           *Ans.* 0, 0, 1.    (f)  $\dfrac{3h^2}{h}$.

2. Describe in your own words the essence of the method of increments.
3. Suppose that the fall of an object is described by the formula $s = 16t^2$. Use the method of increments to calculate the following:
   (a)  The instantaneous speed at the end of the third second of fall.
   
   *Ans.* 96 ft/sec.
   (b)  The instantaneous speed at the end of the fifth second of fall.
   (c)  The instantaneous speed when $t = 6$.                   *Ans.* 192 ft/sec.
4. Suppose that the formula that relates the height above the ground and the time of travel of a ball thrown up into the air is $s = 128t - 16t^2$.
   (a)  How high is the ball when $t = 3$?                      *Ans.* 240 ft.
   (b)  What is the average speed during the fourth second of flight?
   (c)  Calculate the instantaneous speed when $t = 3$.        *Ans.* 32 ft/sec.
5. Find the limit as $h$ approaches 0 of $h/(\sqrt{h + 4} - 2)$.

   *Suggestion:* Multiply the numerator and denominator by $\sqrt{h + 4} + 2$.
   
   *Ans.* 4.
6. (a)  Is the function $(3h^2 + h)/h$ identical with the function $3h + 1$?

(b) Can we use the latter function in place of the former to determine the number approached by the former as $h$ approaches 0? Justify your answer.

**5. A Matter of Notation.** The method of increments, which we examined in Section 4, begins by giving an increment $h$ to the value of the independent variable. An increment $h$ in this variable causes an increment $k$ to occur in the dependent variable. We then calculate $k/h$—the average rate of change of one variable with respect to the other—and finally obtain the limit approached by $k/h$ as $h$ approaches 0.

We have used $h$ and $k$ to denote the increments in $t$ and $s$, respectively, and we could very well continue to use these symbols to denote increments throughout the calculus. However, history has something else to say on this matter. It has been customary since the days of Euler to use $\Delta t$ (pronounced delta $t$) for the increment in $t$ and $\Delta s$ for the increment in $s$. These symbols are both bad and good. The notation $\Delta t$ is *not* a product of $\Delta$ and $t$, but must be taken as a whole. It means a change in the value of $t$, that is, some numerical change. Thus if $t$ is increased from 3 to 4, then $\Delta t = 1$. If $t$ increases from 3 to $3\frac{1}{2}$, $\Delta t = \frac{1}{2}$. If $t$ decreases from 3 to $2\frac{1}{2}$, $\Delta t = -\frac{1}{2}$. Thus $\Delta t$ has the same meaning as $h$. Likewise, $\Delta s$ has the same meaning as $k$.

It is, of course, more awkward to write $\Delta t$ instead of $h$ and $\Delta s$ instead of $k$. There is, however, a slight advantage in that $\Delta t$ denotes explicitly an increment in $t$ and $\Delta s$, an increment in $s$; that is, we do not have to remember the variable to which the increment refers. Like better men before us, we shall bow to history and use $\Delta t$ and $\Delta s$.

Let us repeat the calculation of the preceding section in this new notation; that is, we shall calculate the speed at the end of the fourth second of an object that falls according to the formula $s = 16t^2$. The method of increments calls for first calculating the average speed in an interval of time $\Delta t$ bordering on the fourth second. When $t = 4$, the value of $s$, which we denote by $s_4$, is 256; that is,

**(18)**                                            $$s_4 = 256.$$

If we change the value of $t$ by some amount $\Delta t$, the new value is $4 + \Delta t$. The new value of $s$ is denoted by $s_4 + \Delta s$. Then

**(19)**          $$s_4 + \Delta s = 16(4 + \Delta t)^2 = 256 + 128\Delta t + 16(\Delta t)^2.$$

By subtracting (18) from (19) we obtain

**(20)**                               $$\Delta s = 128\Delta t + 16(\Delta t)^2.$$

The quantity $\Delta s$ is, of course, the distance traveled in the time $\Delta t$. To obtain the average speed in the interval of time $\Delta t$, we must calculate $\Delta s/\Delta t$. Division of both sides of (20) by $\Delta t$ yields

**(21)**                                      $$\frac{\Delta s}{\Delta t} = 128 + 16\Delta t.$$

To obtain the instantaneous speed at $t = 4$, we seek the limit of $\Delta s/\Delta t$ as the values of $\Delta t$ become smaller and indeed approach 0 in value. However, as $\Delta t$ approaches 0, $16\Delta t$ also approaches 0, so that the right-hand side of (21) approaches 128. Hence the instantaneous speed at $t = 4$, which is the limit of the average speed as the increment $\Delta t$ approaches 0, is 128.

It is desirable to have some short notation for the statement that we have evaluated the limit of $\Delta s/\Delta t$ as the values of $\Delta t$ approach 0. We can express it in the abbreviated form

$$\lim_{\Delta t \to 0} \frac{\Delta s}{\Delta t} .$$

Here lim is an abbreviation for limit, the arrow symbolizes approach, and the whole expression means the limit of $\Delta s/\Delta t$ as $\Delta t$ approaches 0. In this notation what we showed in the calculation above is that

**(22)** $$\lim_{\Delta t \to 0} \frac{\Delta s}{\Delta t} = 128.$$

Even this notation in (22) is somewhat lengthy. Hence mathematicians replace it by a still briefer one. Newton used $\dot{s}$. Leibniz used $ds/dt$. Still another notation $s'$ was introduced by Lagrange and if Euler's notation $f(t)$ is used then the limit (22) is denoted by $f'(t)$. Thus

$$\lim_{\Delta t \to 0} \frac{\Delta s}{\Delta t} = \dot{s} = \frac{ds}{dt} = s' = f'(t).$$

The four notations, $\dot{s}$, $ds/dt$, $s'$, and $f'(t)$, are identical in meaning but all fall short of perfection. Newton's symbolism is concise but poor because the dot above the $s$ is often overlooked; moreover it fails to show what the independent variable is. Leibniz's notation suggests that the limit is a quotient whereas the limit of average speeds definitely is *not* a quotient. In fact, the very idea of using the limit of average speeds for the instantaneous speed is to avoid the meaningless quotient $0/0$. Leibniz's symbol $ds/dt$ must be taken in its entirety. Nevertheless, Leibniz's notation, properly understood, does remind us that the limit, although not itself a quotient, is obtained from a quotient, that is, average speed. Moreover, it does show the independent and dependent variables. Lagrange's notation, $s'$, like Newton's, fails to show what the independent variable is. The notation $f'(t)$ is informative but clumsier than $\dot{s}$ or $s'$. Since all four notations are in use we shall employ all of them just to become accustomed to them. However, we shall usually use the dot notation as in $\dot{s}$ only when the independent variable is the time.

## EXERCISES

**1.** Give the argument that convinces you that, as the values of $\Delta t$ approach 0, $16\Delta t$ also approaches 0.

**2.** If $s = 16t^2$, how much is $\Delta s$ when $t = 3$ and $\Delta t = 1$? When $t = 4$ and $\Delta t = 1$? When $t = 4$ and $\Delta t = \frac{1}{2}$?                                    *Ans.* 112; 144; 68.

**3.** Use the delta notation to calculate the instantaneous speed at the end of the fifth second of an object that falls according to the formula $s = 16t^2$.

**4.** Use the delta notation to calculate the instantaneous speed at the instant $t = t_1$ of an object that falls according to the formula $s = 16t^2$.                *Ans.* $32t_1$.

**5.** An object dropped near the surface of the moon falls to the surface in accordance with the formula $s = 2.6t^2$. Use the delta notation to calculate the speed of the object at the end of the fourth second.

**6.** An object dropped near the surface of the sun falls to the surface in accordance with the formula $s = 432t^2$. Use the delta notation to calculate the speed of the object at the end of the fifth second.                   *Ans.* 4320 ft/sec.

**7.** Consider the function $s = t^2$. At $t = 2$ and for $\Delta t = 0.1$, $\Delta s/\Delta t$ is a good approximation to $\dot{s}$. How could you improve this approximation to $\dot{s}$?

**8.** Calculate the instantaneous speed of the following relations between distance and time at the instant indicated:

(a) $s = 4t^2$ at $t = 3$.          *Ans.* 24.     (c) $s = 3t^2$ at $t = 0$.          *Ans.* 0.
(b) $s = \frac{1}{4}t^2$ at $t = 3$.                    (d) $s = \frac{5}{2}t^2$ at $t = 2$.

**9.** Is a limit a variable or a constant?

**10.** Is a limit an exact value or an approximate value?

### 6. The Method of Increments Applied to $y = ax^2$.
It is characteristic of mathematics to seek to generalize a process which has proved useful in a number of particular situations and so make it applicable to a whole class of problems. Science is concerned with thousands of rates of change; the rate of change of air pressure with respect to altitude, the rate of change of the altitude of an airplane with respect to velocity, and the rate of change of temperature with respect to time or to altitude are a few familiar examples. Let us investigate then a generalization of what we have been doing in finding instantaneous speed. In stead of the symbols $t$ and $s$ for our variables, we shall use $x$ and $y$, without specifying what $x$ and $y$ may stand for physically. Furthermore instead of, the particular function $s = 16t^2$, let us work with

**(23)**                                    $$y = ax^2,$$

where $a$ is some constant whose value is not specified but plays the role that 16 does in $s = 16t^2$. Finally, instead of calculating the instantaneous speed, which is the instantaneous rate of change of $s$ with respect to $t$, we shall calculate the instantaneous rate of change of $y$ with respect to $x$.

To calculate the instantaneous rate of change of $y$ with respect to $x$ means, of course, to calculate the rate of change at a value of $x$ as opposed to an average rate of change over some interval of $x$-values. The word instantaneous really does not apply, because $x$ need not represent time. However, the word is used because in the original and in many current applications of the calculus the independent variable represents values of time.

To compute the instantaneous rate of change of $y$ with respect to $x$ we use the method of increments and the customary $\Delta x$ and $\Delta y$ for the increments of $x$ and $y$. Also, the rate of change is always computed at a value of $x$, and to be general we let this be $x_1$. We compute first the value of $y$ when $x$ has the value $x_1$. This value of $y$, which we shall call $y_1$, is obtained by substituting $x_1$ for $x$ in (23). Then

(24) $$y_1 = ax_1^2.$$

We now consider a change or increment $\Delta x$ in the value of $x$, so that the new value of $x$ is $x_1 + \Delta x$. To compute the new value of $y$, which we denote by $y_1 + \Delta y$, we must substitute the new value of $x$ in (23). Then

$$y_1 + \Delta y = a(x_1 + \Delta x)^2.$$

Because

$$(x_1 + \Delta x)^2 = x_1^2 + 2x_1 \, \Delta x + (\Delta x)^2,$$

it follows that

(25) $$y_1 + \Delta y = ax_1^2 + 2ax_1 \, \Delta x + a(\Delta x)^2.$$

Our next step is to determine the change $\Delta y$ in $y$ which results from the change $\Delta x$ in $x$ by subtracting (24) from (25). Thus

(26) $$\Delta y = 2ax_1 \, \Delta x + a(\Delta x)^2.$$

To arrive at the average rate of change of $y$ in the interval $\Delta x$, we must find $\Delta y / \Delta x$. Accordingly, we divide both sides of (26) by $\Delta x$ and obtain

(27) $$\frac{\Delta y}{\Delta x} = \frac{2ax_1 \, \Delta x + a(\Delta x)^2}{\Delta x}.$$

To secure the rate of change of $y$ compared to $x$ at the value $x_1$ of $x$ we must determine the limit of the right side of (27) as $\Delta x$ approaches 0. We are fortunate in that we can divide the numerator and denominator of (27) by $\Delta x$ and obtain

(28) $$\frac{\Delta y}{\Delta x} = 2ax_1 + a \, \Delta x.$$

As $\Delta x$ becomes smaller and approaches 0, the quantity $a \, \Delta x$, which is merely a constant times $\Delta x$, also approaches 0, and the quantity $\Delta y / \Delta x$ approaches the value $2ax_1$. This last quantity is the limit approached by the average rates of change, $\Delta y / \Delta x$, and so is the rate of change of $y$ with respect to $x$ at the value $x_1$ of $x$. Just to check our result, we note that when $a = 16$ and $x_1 = 4$, the quantity $2ax_1$ is 128, which is the limit that we obtained in the special case of (22).

Thus the instantaneous rate of change of $y$ with respect to $x$ at the value $x_1$ of $x$ is $2ax_1$. We have already indicated the notation for the instantaneous speed. Now we merely change the notation for the variables.

The following

**(29)** $$\lim_{\Delta x \to 0} \frac{\Delta y}{\Delta x} = 2ax_1,$$

**(30)** $$y' = 2ax_1,$$

**(31)** $$\frac{dy}{dx} = 2ax_1$$

**(32)** $$f'(x_1) = 2ax_1$$

are then equivalent statements.

To speak of the instantaneous rate of change of $y$ with respect to $x$ at the value $x_1$ of $x$ is lengthy. Hence we call this rate the *derivative* of $y$ with respect to $x$ and, when necessary, specify "at $x_1$." The process of applying the method of increments to obtain the derivative is called *differentiation*.

We should note the significance of what we have accomplished so far. We have proved that the derivative of $y = ax^2$ at the value $x_1$ of $x$ is $2ax_1$. Hence, given any function that is a special case of $y = ax^2$, we can write down at once the derivative of this function. We do not have to go through the entire method of increments. Thus, given $s = 16t^2$, the value of the derivative at $t_1$ is $2 \cdot 16 \cdot t_1$. If $t_1$ were 4, the value of the derivative would be $2 \cdot 16 \cdot 4$ or 128.

As another example let us consider the relation of the area of a circle to the radius. The formula that expresses the function is, of course,

$$A = \pi r^2.$$

In relation to $y = ax^2$, here $A$ plays the part of $y$, $r$ plays the part of $x$, and the constant $\pi$ is the value of $a$. If we use the notation $A'$ for the derivative, formula (30) tells us that at $r = r_1$

$$A' = 2\pi r_1.$$

This result has a simple geometrical meaning (Fig. 2-6). It says that the instantaneous rate of change of the area of a circle with respect to the radius at any given value of the radius is the circumference. More loosely stated, the rate at which the area increases when $r$ increases is the size of

**Figure 2-6**

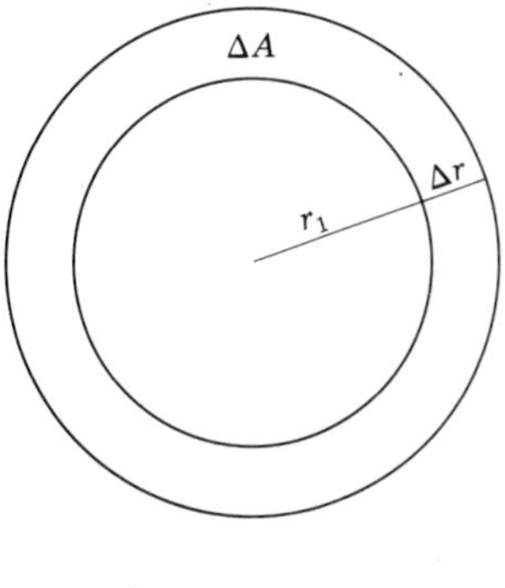

the circumference. This result is very reasonable. When the radius $r_1$ is increased by an amount $\Delta r$, the area $A$ of the circle increases by an amount $\Delta A$. We may think intuitively of $\Delta A$ as a thin band whose area is approximately the circumference $2\pi r_1$ times the width $\Delta r$. The ratio $\Delta A / \Delta r$ is then approximately $2\pi r_1$. This average rate of change of area with respect to the radius comes closer to $2\pi r_1$ as $\Delta r$ approaches 0. The circumference $2\pi r_1$ is the instantaneous rate at which the area increases at the given value $r_1$ or $r$.

## *EXERCISES

1. Calculate the derivatives of the following functions at the specified values of the independent variable:

   (a)  $y = 16x^2$ at $x = x_1$   Ans. $32x_1$.    (e)  $A = \pi r^2$ at $r = 5$.    Ans. $10\pi$.

   (b)  $y = 16x^2$ at $x = 4$.                 (f)  $s = 2.6t^2$ at $t = 5$.

   (c)  $y = bx^2$ at $x = 4$.   Ans. $8b$.    (g)  $y = -2x^2$ at $x = 4$. Ans. $-16$.

   (d)  $s = 16t^2$ at $t = 5$.              (h)  $y = \frac{1}{2}x^2$ at $x = x_1$.

2. The functions in the following items relate distance and time. Calculate the instantaneous speed at the specified value of $t$.

   (a)  $s = 16t^2$ at $t = 6$.

                  Ans. 192 ft/sec.   (c)  $s = \dfrac{g}{2} t^2$ at $t = t_1$.

   (b)  $s = 10t^2$ at $t = 3$.                          Ans. $gt_1$ ft/sec.

3. A man lays out a circular area of radius 100 feet. If he increases the radius by 10 feet, how much does he increase the area? When $r_1 = 100$ and $\Delta r = 10$, how much is $\Delta A$?                      Ans. $2100\pi$ ft; $2100\pi$ ft.

4. Determine the derivative of $y = x^2$ at $x = x_1$ by the method of increments or any other legitimate method. Compare the results with that for $y = ax^2$. Does the comparison suggest any general statement about the effect on the derivative of the constant factor $a$ in the function?

5. Find the rate of change of the area $A$ of a square with respect to a side $s$ at a given value $s_1$ of the side. Is the result intuitively reasonable?   Ans. $A' = 2s_1$.

6. The area of a rectangle is given by the formula $A = lw$, where $l$ and $w$ are the length and width, respectively. Suppose that $l$ is kept fixed. Find the rate of change of $A$ with respect to $w$ at a given value of $w$. Interpret the result geometrically.

7. If $y = f(x)$, what does $f(x) - f(x_0)$ denote in the delta notation?

8. If $y = f(x)$, what does $\dfrac{f(x) - f(x_0)}{x - x_0}$ denote in the delta notation?

9. If $y = f(x)$ what does $\lim\limits_{x \to x_0} \dfrac{f(x) - f(x_0)}{x - x_0}$ denote?

10. If $y = f(x)$, what does $f'(x_0)$ denote?

11. In using the method of increments we encounter the function $\Delta y / \Delta x$. What are the independent and dependent variables in this function?

**7. The Derived Function.** We have found that the derivative of $y = ax^2$ at the value $x_1$ of $x$ is $2ax_1$; in symbols

(33) $$\frac{dy}{dx} = y' = f'(x_1) = 2ax_1$$

The derivative is, of course, the rate of change of $y$ with respect to $x$ at a value of $x$. However, by using the letter $x_1$ for the value of $x$ at which we calculated (33), we actually accomplished more than we intended. The value $x_1$ of $x$ is *any* value of $x$. Its value is not limited. Hence we can say that at any value of $x$ the derivative $y'$ of $y = ax^2$ is $2ax$; that is,

**(34)**                    $$y' = 2ax.$$

By writing (34) instead of (33) we merely emphasize that $x_1$ is really any value of $x$. Because for each value of $x$ there is a corresponding value of the derivative $y'$, we have in (34) a new function. The independent variable is $x$, and the dependent variable is $y'$. We might prefer to use a more conventional symbol for the dependent variable. We cannot use $y$ because it already denotes $ax^2$ in the present context. We could use $z$ or some other letter. However, there is really no objection to using $y'$ (or $dy/dx$ or $f'(x)$) if we remember that, in addition to denoting the derivative of $y$ with respect to $x$, it also denotes the dependent variable in the function $y' = 2ax$. Sometimes, however, we do use a special symbol for the dependent variable $y'$. Thus for the function $s = 16t^2$ the derived function is $\dot{s} = 32t$. The symbol often used for $\dot{s}$ is $v$, the first letter of the word velocity, because $\dot{s}$ does give physically the instantaneous speed or instantaneous velocity. (We shall distinguish between speed and velocity later.)

To distinguish the derivative at a value of $x$ from the function that arises when we consider the various values of the derivative as $x$ changes, we call the function the *derived function*. Thus $y' = 2ax$ is the derived function of $y = ax^2$. Sometimes the word derivative is used to denote the function, and this is permissible if no confusion results.

When we discussed the concept of a function, we pointed out that it does not require that there be a $y$-value for each value of $x$. There need be a $y$-value only for the values of $x$ in some domain. The same remark applies to derived function. In the case of $y' = 2ax$ there is a value of $y'$ for each value of $x$. Let us, however, consider the function $y = 1/(x - 2)$. As we pointed out, this function has no value or does not exist for the value 2 of $x$. Therefore, the derived function does not exist at $x = 2$ because the derivative at $x = 2$ depends, by its very definition, on the value of the original function at $x = 2$. Thus a derived function, like any function, has a domain and a range, and the domain need not include all values of $x$.

# ✳ EXERCISES

1. Suppose that an object falls in accordance with the formula $s = 5t^2$. Find the formula for the speed at any time $t$.                    *Ans. $ds/dt = v = 10t$.*

2. State in words what the following represent symbolically:
   (a) $\dot{s} = 32t$.
   (b) $\dot{s} = 5t$.
   (c) $\dot{v} = -32$.
   (d) $y' = 4x$.
   (e) $\dfrac{dy}{dx} = 8x$.
   (f) $f'(x) = -3x$.

3. State at once what the derived functions are for the following functions:
   (a) $s = 3t^2$.                    *Ans. $\dot{s} = 6t$.*

(b)   $s = -3t^2$.                                    (h)   $y = 27x^2$.
(c)   $s = \frac{7}{2}t^2$.          *Ans.* $\dot{s} = 7t$.    (i)   $y = \frac{4}{3}x^2$.     *Ans.* $dy/dx = \frac{8}{3}x$.
(d)   $y = 8x^2$.                                     (j)   $y = -\frac{15}{2}x^2$.
(e)   $y = x^2$.           *Ans.* $y' = 2x$.    (k)   $y = 0.03x^2$.   *Ans.* $f'(x) = 0.06x$.
(f)   $y = -x^2$.                                    (l)   $y = \sqrt{2}\,x^2$.
(g)   $y = -3x^2$.        *Ans.* $y' = -6x$.

**8. The Differentiation of Simple Monomials.** We have seen that by considering the general function $y = ax^2$ we could determine the derivative at
once; therefore we can now find the derivative of all functions of that form
without going through the method of increments each time. To be able to
utilize other particular functions as readily in applications we may as well
treat general forms. Because we shall find later that our applications will
involve functions such as $y = 3x$ and $y = 5x$, let us determine the derivative of functions of the form $y = bx$.

   This function is so simple that we may be able to see on an intuitive
basis what the derivative should be. Let us consider a special case. If an
automobile travels at the constant speed of 30 mi/hr, the formula that
relates distance traveled (in miles) and time of travel (in hours) is $s = 30t$.
However, if the automobile travels at a constant speed, its speed at each
instant is the same. In other words, its instantaneous rate of change of
distance with respect to time is 30. Then the derivative of $s = 30t$ should be
30. What then should we expect the derivative of $y = bx$ to be? The answer
should be $b$. We can readily confirm this inference by using the method of
increments and we shall leave the confirmation to an exercise. Let us note
the result.

**Theorem:**   If

**(35)**                                  $$y = bx$$

then

**(36)**                                  $$\frac{dy}{dx} = b.$$

   Now let us consider the function $y = c$, where $c$ is a constant. What is
$dy/dx$? If $y$ is a constant for all values of $x$ then $y$ does not change when $x$
changes and so the instanteous rate of change of $y$ with respect to $x$ must
be 0. Our result then is:

**Theorem:**   If

**(37)**                                  $$y = c$$

then

**(38)**                                  $$\frac{dy}{dx} = 0.$$

This result, too, can readily be confirmed by the method of increments.

## EXERCISES

1. Use the method of increments to show that if $y = bx$, then $y' = b$.
2. Use the method of increments to show that if $y = c$, then $y' = 0$.
3. Find the derived functions of the following functions:
   (a)  $f(x) = 2x^2$.     *Ans.* $f'(x) = 4x$.     (d)  $d = -9t$
   (b)  $y = -2x^2$.                               (e)  $y = 7$.     *Ans.* $dy/dx = 0$.
   (c)  $y = 3x$.          *Ans.* $y' = 3$.         (f)  $s = 6$.
4. Apply the method of increments to find the derived function of the function $y = ax^3$.     *Ans.* $y' = 3ax^2$.
5. We found that the instantaneous rate of change of the area of a circle with respect to the radius at a given value of the radius is the circumference of the circle. What is your guess as to the instantaneous rate of change of the volume of a sphere with respect to the radius at a given value of the radius? Apply the result of Exercise 4 to the formula for the volume of a sphere, $V = \frac{4}{3}\pi r^3$ and see if your guess was correct.
6. When $y = ax^2$, $y' = 2ax$; when $y = ax^3$, then you should have found in Exercise 4 that $y' = 3ax^2$. Now suppose that $y = ax^4$. What would you expect $y'$ to be? Verify your conjecture by applying the method of increments to $y = ax^4$.     *Ans.* $y' = 4ax^3$.
7. Suppose that an object moves along the arc of a circle of radius 5 and that arc length and central angle are as shown in Fig. 2-7. How much is $ds/d\theta$ if $\theta$ is measured in radians?

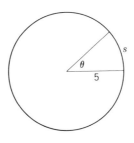

**Figure 2-7**

8. The speed of an object that is dropped and falls toward the earth from some point near the surface is given by the formula $v = 32t$. By definition the instantaneous acceleration is the instantaneous rate of change of speed with respect to time at any given value of $t$. Find the acceleration in the present case.     *Ans.* $\dot{v} = 32$.
9. Express the following statements in symbols:
   (a)  The instantaneous rate of change of $y$ with respect to $x$ is $n$ times $y$.
   (b)  The rate of change of $y$ with respect to $x$ at a value of $x$ is a constant times $x$.     *Ans.* $y' = kx$.
   (c)  The rate of change of $y$ with respect to $x$ at a value of $x$ is proportional to $x$.
   (d)  The rate of change of the area of a circle with respect to the radius is proportional to the radius.     *Ans.* $dA/dr = kr$.
10. Criticize the following argument. The derivative of any function is defined at a

value of $x$. The function is constant at that value of $x$. Hence the derivative is 0 because the derivative of a constant is 0.

**9. The Differentiation of Simple Polynomials.** The functions which occur in actual scientific work do not usually consist of single terms such as $3x^2$ or $5t$, that is, monomials. For example, the formula that represents the height above the ground of a ball that is thrown up with an initial speed of 100 ft/sec is $s = 100t - 16t^2$. To find the derivative, that is, the instantaneous rate of change, of such functions at various values of $t$, or to find the derived function, we must treat polynomials, that is, functions that are a sum or difference of two or more monomials. We are now able to differentiate such polynomials.

We have learned that if $y = ax^2$ then $dy/dx = 2ax$; if $y = bx$, then $dy/dx = b$; and if $y = c$, then $dy/dx = 0$. Suppose that we are required to differentiate the function

(39) $$y = ax^2 + bx + c.$$

Were we to go through the method of increments we would obtain a contribution to the derived function from the term $ax^2$ and this contribution would be $2ax$. Similarly, the term $bx$ in (39) would contribute $b$, and the term $c$ in (39) would contribute 0. These contributions to the derivative would be added because $y$ in (39) is a sum of terms. Hence we have a general result which we shall state as a theorem, though it will be superseded later by a more general theorem.

**Theorem:**    If

(40) $$y = ax^2 + bx + c$$

then

(41) $$\frac{dy}{dx} = 2ax + b.$$

**Example.**    We may use the preceding theorem to save a lot of work. Suppose that the height of a ball above the ground is given by the function $s = 100t - 16t^2$. What is the speed of the ball at any time $t$?

We can write our function as

(42) $$s = -16t^2 + 100t.$$

It is then a special case of the function in the theorem in that $a = -16$, $b = 100$, and $c = 0$. Hence

(43) $$\frac{ds}{dt} = -32t + 100$$

and since the derivation of distance with respect to time is the speed, $ds/dt$ gives the speed.

## EXERCISES

1. Find by any method the derived functions of the following functions:

   (a) $s = 10t^2 - 32t$.

          *Ans.* $\dot{s} = 20t - 32$.

   (b) $s = 10t^2 + 7$.

   (c) $s = 4t^2 + 16t + 8$.

          *Ans.* $\dot{s} = 8t + 16$.

   (d) $s = 16t - 4t^2 + 8$.

   (e) $y = x^2 - 7x + 12$.

   (f) $y = -x^2 + 14x - 12$.

   (g) $y = -7x + 2$.

   (h) $y = 3\sqrt{2}\, x^2 + \sqrt{3}\, x$.

2. Prove by the method of increments that if $y = ax^2 + bx + c$ then $dy/dx = 2ax + b$.

3. If $f(x) = x^2 - 9$, what is $f'(2)$, $f'(-2)$?

4. Show that $y = x^2 + 5$ and $y = x^2$ have the same derived function. Can you give any plausible argument for this result?      *Ans.* $dy/dx = 2x$.

5. If an object is thrown downward with an initial speed of 100 ft/sec, the distance that it falls in $t$ seconds is given by the formula $s = 100t + 16t^2$. Determine the formula for the speed at any time $t$. Calculate the speed of the object at the end of the fourth second of fall.

6. The temperature $T$ in degrees at a point $x$ feet above sea level is $T = 55 - 0.004x$. What is the rate of change of temperature with respect to altitude at (a) sea level, (b) 100 feet above sea level, and (c) 1000 feet above? What physical significance do you attach to the fact that the rate of change is negative?
        *Ans.* (a) $-0.004$; (b) $-0.004$; (c) $-0.004$.

7. In one kind of chemical reaction two separate substances combine to form a third substance, much as hydrogen gas and oxygen gas combine to form water vapor. Suppose that the third substance amounts to $x$ grams after $t$ minutes and that $x = 18t - 3t^2$. What is the rate in g/min (grams per minute) at which the third substance is produced after the following time intervals?

   (a) 2 minutes.      *Ans.* 6 g/min.      ∶NOTE∶ UNITS ◦F $\frac{dx}{dt} = 18 - 6t$

   (b) 3 minutes.

   (c) 4 minutes.      *Ans.* $-6$ g/min.      GRAMS/MIN

   (d) Is there any question about the physical significance of the answer to part (c)?

8. The total cost $C$ of producing $x$ units of some item is a function of $x$. (Of course physically $x$ takes on only positive integral values but it is convenient to think of it as taking on all real values in some domain.) Economists use the term *marginal cost* for the rate of change of $C$ with respect to $x$. Suppose that $C = 5x^2 + 15x + 200$, what is the marginal cost when $x = 15$? Would this marginal cost be the cost of the 16th unit?

9. Using the definition of marginal cost in the preceding exercise, suppose that the cost $C$ of producing $x$ units of a toy is $C = 3x^2 - 4x + 5$. What is the marginal cost for any value of $x$? Would the marginal cost necessarily increase with $x$ in any realistic situation?

10. Suppose that the revenue $R$ from selling $x$ units of a commodity is $R = 2x^2 + 4x$ and the cost $C$ of producing the $x$ units is $C = 10x$. The profit $P$ in selling the $x$ units is the revenue minus the cost or $P(x) = 2x^2 + 4x - 10x = 2x^2 - 6x$. The marginal profit is defined to be $dP/dx$. Calculate it. Suppose the marginal profit is negative for some value of $x$. Does this mean that the businessman is losing money?

11. The total cost $C$ in dollars of producing $x$ units of a commodity is $C = 8500 + 6x - 0.002x^2$. Find the marginal cost $dC/dx$ when $x = 1200$. Is a low or high marginal cost desirable?

**10. *The Second Derivative.*** We have seen so far that, given the formula that relates the distance and time traveled by an object, we can calculate the speed or the instantaneous rate of change of distance with respect to time. Thus, when

**(44)** $$s = 16t^2,$$

then at any time $t$

**(45)** $$\dot{s} = 32t.$$

We have already pointed out that the derivative calculated at an arbitrary time $t$ is itself a function of $t$ which is called the derived function. Then (45) is the derived function in which $t$ is the independent variable and $\dot{s}$ is the dependent variable. Here $\dot{s}$ represents speed, and, as already noted, it is customary to use the letter $v$ (the first letter of velocity) in place of $\dot{s}$. Then

$$v = 32t.$$

Now the speed $v$ is a function of $t$, and we can ask for the instantaneous rate of change of $v$ with respect to $t$. This rate has important physical meaning. It is the instantaneous acceleration. Let us first be clear about the notion of acceleration.

Loosely speaking, acceleration is a change in speed which takes place during some interval of time. To go anywhere acceleration is as important as speed. If an object is at rest it has zero speed. To move it must acquire some speed, say 30 miles per hour, which is 44 feet per second. But to go from 0 speed to a speed of 44 feet per second there must be some acceleration. If the change in speed from 0 to 44 takes place in 4 seconds, say, then the average acceleration is 11 feet per second per second and this is abbreviated as 11 ft/sec$^2$.

Suppose now that the object, perhaps a person in an automobile, has acquired the speed of 44 ft/sec. If there were no acceleration he would be doomed to spend the rest of his life moving at that speed. If he wished to stop he would have to lose speed and this means there must be a negative acceleration or a deceleration. Thus if the person applies the brakes he may reduce his speed from 44 to 0 in, say 2 seconds. Then the average negative acceleration is 22 ft/sec$^2$.

The acceleration, positive and negative, that we have been describing is the average acceleration per second. As in the case of speed, it is often the instantaneous acceleration rather than the average acceleration that matters. Thus, if the brakes of an automobile are applied suddenly, the automobile suffers an instantaneous deceleration or a negative acceleration. Unfortunately, the passengers do not receive the same deceleration and they continue to move forward, often through the windshield of the automobile.

If the speed of an object is given as a function of time, we can find the instantaneous acceleration because it is the instantaneous rate of change of speed with respect to time. Thus, if

**(46)** $$v = 32t,$$

then in view of what we learned about the derivatives of functions of the form $y = bx$, we know that

**(47)** $$\dot{v} = 32.$$

There is nothing really new mathematically in obtaining the derivative or the derived function of formulas such as (46). However, we may wish to call attention to the fact that the acceleration is the derived function of a function which is itself the derived function of still another function; that is, the acceleration is the derived function of the speed function which is the derived function of the distance function. To indicate this, we use the notation

$$\ddot{s} \qquad \text{or} \qquad \frac{d^2s}{dt^2}$$

for the acceleration. The function denoted by either symbol is called the *second derived function* of $s = 16t^2$ or, if we should be calculating $\ddot{s}$ or $d^2s/dt^2$ at a particular value of $t$, we speak of these values of $\ddot{s}$ or of $d^2s/dt^2$ as the *second derivative* of $s = 16t^2$ at the value of $t$ in question. Thus in place of (47) we can write

$$\ddot{s} = 32 \qquad \text{or} \qquad \frac{d^2s}{dt^2} = 32.$$

Here the second derived function happens to be a constant; hence its value at any given value of $t$ is always 32.

The notation just introduced for the second derivative applies, of course, regardless of what letters we use for the variables. If we use $x$ and $y$, the second derived function of $y$ with respect to $x$ is denoted by

$$\frac{d^2y}{dx^2} \qquad \text{or} \qquad y'' \qquad \text{or} \qquad f''(x).$$

## EXERCISES

**1.** Suppose that an object falls according to the formula $s = 16t^2 + 100t$.
   (a)  Calculate the second derived function $\ddot{s}$.          *Ans.* $\ddot{s} = 32$.
   (b)  Calculate $d^2s/dt^2$.
   (c)  Calculate the function that gives the acceleration at any time $t$.
                                                                    *Ans.* $\dot{v} = 32$.
   (d)  Calculate the acceleration at the instant $t = 3$.
   (e)  Calculate the derived function of the velocity as a function of time.
                                                                    *Ans.* $\dot{v} = 32$.

2. Suppose that the height of an object above the ground at time $t$ is given by $s = 100t - 16t^2$. Answer the same questions raised in Exercise 1.

$$Ans.\ \ddot{s} = d^2s/dt^2 = \dot{v} = -32.$$

3. Write in symbols: the acceleration of an object is proportional to its speed.

4. What is the second derived function of $y = bx$?      *Ans.* $y'' = 0$.

5. Calculate the second derived functions of the following functions:

  (a)   $s = -16t^2$.     *Ans.* $\ddot{s} = -32$.   (f)   $y = -4x^2 - 8x + 20$.

  (b)   $s = -16t^2 + 100t$.                *Ans.* $d^2y/dx^2 = -8$.

  (c)   $y = -t^2 + 100t$.         (g)   $y = 8x - 10$.

          *Ans.* $d^2y/dt^2 = -2$.   (h)   $y = \sqrt{5}\,x^2 - 7x$.

  (d)   $y = -3t^2 + 100t + 50$.      (i)   $y = 3\sqrt{5}\,x^2 - 7x$.

  (e)   $y = 4x^2 + 8x$.                  *Ans.* $y'' = 6\sqrt{5}$.

                                 (j)   $s = 16t^2 - 100t + 3$.

# CHAPTER THREE
# THE ANTIDERIVED FUNCTION OR THE INTEGRAL

**1. The Integral.** Suppose that we are given the derived function

**(1)** $$\dot{s} = 32t$$

and are obliged to find the original function, that is, the function which relates $s$ and $t$. How can we do so? Of course, in the case of (1) we happen to know that the original function is $s = 16t^2$, but, generally, given a derived function we might not know beforehand what the original function is. For example, we might be given that

$$\dot{s} = 7t^2 - 3t$$

or

$$y' = \tfrac{1}{3}x^3 - 7x,$$

and in these cases it is not clear how to find the respective original functions.

Before we bother to look into the problem of finding the original function, we may well ask why we should entertain such a task. The answer is that when we formulate physical problems mathematically the given physical information usually leads to derived functions, and the primary objective in solving the physical problems is to find the original functions. We shall see later that this is the basic use of the calculus.

Let us start with the problem of finding the original function corresponding to (1) and let us suppose for the moment that we do not know the answer. We do know that there is some formula relating $s$ and $t$ such that $\dot{s} = 32t$. We can ask ourselves, what do we do in going from a formula to its derived function? Having answered this question, perhaps we can reverse the process. In Chapter 2 we learned that when $y = ax^2$ then $y' = 2ax$. Evidently, $y'$ can be obtained from $y$ by taking the quantity 2, which appears as the exponent in the original function, multiplying it into the coefficient $a$, and then reducing the exponent by 1. Hence, if we start with $2ax$ and wish to obtain the original function, we should increase the exponent of $x$ by 1, thus obtaining $2ax^2$, and then divide the whole term by the new exponent 2. We then obtain $ax^2$.

Let us apply this method to $\dot{s} = 32t$, which is a special case of $y' = 2ax$. We increase the exponent by 1, obtain $32t^2$, and then divide the latter quantity by the new exponent 2 to obtain $16t^2$. Then $s = 16t^2$ is a function whose derived function is $\dot{s} = 32t$. Thus for derived functions of the form $y' = 2ax$ we can obtain the original function.

We have overlooked one point. It is true that if $y = ax^2$ then $y' = 2ax$. However, it is also true that if $y = ax^2 + C$, where $C$ is any constant, then $y'$ is still $2ax$. In other words, a constant term that may be present in the original function does not contribute to or show up in the derived function. Hence, given $y' = 2ax$, we do know that the term $ax^2$ belongs in the original function but we do not know whether this function should also contain a constant term and, if it should, we have no information as to the value of this constant term. All we can say is that if

$$\text{(2)} \qquad\qquad\qquad y' = 2ax$$

then

$$\text{(3)} \qquad\qquad\qquad y = ax^2 + C,$$

and, unless we know more about the original function, we cannot say how much $C$ is. For the moment let us recognize the necessity of including this $C$ in the original function and not pursue the question of what we might do about determining it.* What appears to be an unfortunate circumstance will soon be seen to be a considerable advantage.

As an example of the use of our result, let us find the original function for which

$$y' = 8x.$$

If we increase the exponent by 1, we obtain $8x^2$, and, if we then divide by 2, we obtain $4x^2$. Thus

$$y = 4x^2 + C.$$

The process of going from the derived function to the original function is called *antidifferentiation* or *integration*. The original function is called the *primitive function*, the *antiderived function*, or the *indefinite integral* of the given derived function. We most often use the third term and even shorten it to *integral*.

Before we can make use of antidifferentiation or integration, we must be able to carry it out for at least a few types of functions. Suppose we are

---

* We have not shown that there may not be functions even more complicated than (3) whose derived function is $2ax$. It is certainly conceivable that other functions may exist. We shall return to this point later and prove that if two functions have the same derived function over an interval of $x$-values then these two functions can differ at most by a constant.

given that the instantaneous acceleration, that is, the instantaneous rate of change of speed with respect to time, of some moving object is

**(4)** $$\dot{v} = 32.$$

What formula relates $v$ and $t$? (We know that the independent variable is $t$ because $\dot{v}$ is acceleration.) Formula (4) should remind us of the formula

**(5)** $$y' = b,$$

which, as we found earlier, is the derived function of $y = bx$. Hence the integral of $\dot{v} = 32$ should be $v = 32t$. Furthermore, in view of the possibility that there may be a constant term in the original function, we must say that

**(6)** $$v = 32t + C.$$

Hence we can find the integrals of derived functions such as (4).

Let us note that we can use the same process to go from (4) to (6) as in going from $32t$ to $16t^2$. The quantity 32 in (4) can be thought of as $32t^0$. If we now increase the exponent by 1 and divide $32t$ by the new exponent, which is 1, we obtain $32t$.

We may summarize what we have been discussing by noting the

**Theorem 1:** If

$$\frac{dy}{dx} = ax$$

then

$$y = \frac{ax^2}{2} + C$$

and if

$$\frac{dy}{dx} = b$$

then

$$y = bx + C.$$

Moreover, since the derived function of the sum of two functions is the sum of the derived functions, the integral of a sum of two derived functions is the sum of the two separate integrals. Thus

**Theorem 2:** If

$$\frac{dy}{dx} = ax + b$$

then

$$y = \frac{a}{2} x^2 + bx + C.$$

**Example.**   Find the integral if

$$\frac{dy}{dx} = 3x + 7.$$

To reverse differentiation we increase each exponent of $x$ by one and divide by the new exponent. Moreover, since the integral is a sum of two functions, it is the sum of the separate integrals. We may think of 7 as $7x^0$ and we obtain $y = \frac{3}{2}x^2 + 7x + C$.

## EXERCISES

1. Find the primitive function or integral of the following derived functions:

(a) $\dot{s} = 2t$.          Ans. $s = t^2 + C$.

(b) $y' = 5$.

(c) $\dot{s} = -32t$.

          Ans. $s = -16t^2 + C$.

(d) $\dot{v} = -32$.

(e) $\dfrac{dy}{dx} = x$.          Ans. $y = \dfrac{x^2}{2} + C$.

(f) $\dfrac{dy}{dx} = 3x$.

(g) $\dot{v} = 32t$.          Ans. $v = 16t^2 + C$.

2. Remembering that the derived function of the sum (or difference) of functions is the sum (or difference) of the derived functions (Chapter 2, Section 9) find the integrals of the following derived functions:

(a) $\dot{s} = 32t + 100$.

          Ans. $s = 16t^2 + 100t + C$.

(b) $\dot{s} = 32t - 100$.

          Ans. $s = 16t^2 - 100t + C$.

(c) $\dfrac{ds}{dt} = -16t + 50$.

(d) $y' = 3x + 7$.

(e) $\dfrac{dy}{dx} = \sqrt{2}\,x - 7$.

          Ans. $y = \dfrac{\sqrt{2}}{2}x^2 - 7x + C$.

(f) $\dfrac{dy}{dx} = -\sqrt{2}\,x + 8$.

(g) $y' = 50 - 3x$.

(h) $y' = 50x - 3$.

(i) $\dfrac{dy}{dx} = 100 - 32x$.

          Ans. $y = 100x - 16x^2 + C$.

(j) $\dot{s} = 96 - 6t$.

          Ans. $\dot{s} = 96t - 3t^2 + C$.

(k) $\dot{s} = 50 - \sqrt{2}\,t$.

(l) $\dot{s} = \sqrt{2}\,t + 50$.

(m) $\dot{s} = \frac{1}{3}t - \frac{1}{4}$.

          Ans. $s = \frac{1}{6}t^2 - \frac{1}{4}t + C$.

(n) $\dot{s} = -2.5t + 3.2$.

(o) $y' = \sqrt{12}\,t + 5$.

(p) $y' = \sqrt{24}\,x - 5\sqrt{3}$.

**2. Straight Line Motion in One Direction.** The simplest problem in which the calculus and antidifferentiation in particular prove to be effective is vertical motion near the surface of the earth. Before we investigate this problem, it is important to understand how mathematics is employed in physical problems. Mathematics proper can give us facts about numbers and geometrical figures. However, the concepts of speed, acceleration, mass, force, light, sound, molecular structure, and kinetic energy are not part of mathematics but of physics, chemistry, or some other science. Hence the axioms and theorems of mathematics can tell us nothing about these concepts. To deduce conclusions about them, we must have physical facts or what the physicist calls laws or principles. To these physical facts, which generally are quantitative statements, we can apply the processes of mathematics. Thus it is the combination of physical principles and mathematics that makes possible the fruitful application of mathematics to physical problems. The accomplishments of the collaboration of mathematics and physics will become clearer as we advance further into the subject of the calculus.

For vertical motion near the earth's surface, Galileo obtained a basic physical principle: if one *neglects air resistance*, all objects fall to earth with the same acceleration, which is a constant. Specifically, all objects near the surface of the earth are subject to a downward acceleration of 32 ft/sec². (In the metric system the acceleration is 980 centimeters per second per second.) In symbols

**(7)**
$$a = 32.$$

This acceleration is caused by the gravitational attraction of the earth.

Let us consider our first physical problem and try to find out how long it takes an object dropped from a point 400 feet above the earth's surface to reach the surface. To solve this problem it seems reasonable that we must find the function that relates the distance and the time traveled by the object.

Before we tackle any physical problem, it is well to be certain that the signs of the quantities involved are correctly chosen. We know in the present case that the object has a downward acceleration of 32 ft/sec². Should we take this acceleration to be positive or negative? The answer depends on what direction we choose as positive for the distance traveled. Suppose that we choose the downward direction to be the positive one for distance. Now let us see what happens if we take the acceleration to be positive. If an object is dropped, it starts out with 0 speed. Because the acceleration is positive—and acceleration means a change in speed—the object acquires more and more positive speed as it falls. A positive speed causes the distance to increase with time and, if the distance is 0 at the start, the distance traveled is positive. To sum up, if we wish the downward direction for distance to be the positive one, then a downward acceleration should be taken as positive.

Let us choose the downward direction to be the positive one for distance and accordingly write

**(8)**
$$a = 32.$$

We know that by antidifferentiation we can proceed from the acceleration to the speed and from the speed to the distance traveled. Hence let us carry out these antidifferentiations or integrations. To remind ourselves that instantaneous acceleration is the instantaneous rate of change of speed with respect to time let us rewrite (8) as

**(9)**
$$\dot{v} = 32.$$

In Section 1 we learned that by antidifferentiation we can write

**(10)**
$$v = 32t + C.$$

The presence of the unknown quantity $C$ seems to be an obstacle but actually is not. If an object is dropped, it leaves the hand with zero speed. This means that if time is measured from the instant the object leaves the hand, then, when $t = 0$, $v = 0$. Let us use this information in (10). Substitution of 0 for $t$ and 0 for $v$ gives

$$0 = 32 \cdot 0 + C$$

or

$$C = 0.$$

Hence the correct formula for speed is

**(11)** $$v = 32t.$$

Instantaneous speed is, of course, the instantaneous rate of change of distance with respect to time. To state this explicitly, we rewrite (11) as

**(12)** $$\dot{s} = 32t.$$

By using antidifferentiation we can state that

**(13)** $$s = 16t^2 + C.$$

We must use some physical information to determine the constant of integration. If we agree to measure distance from the point at which the object is dropped and if, as we have already agreed, we measure time from the instant the object is dropped, then $s = 0$ when $t = 0$. Substitution of these values in (13) gives

$$0 = 16 \cdot 0^2 + C$$

or

$$C = 0.$$

Then

**(14)** $$s = 16t^2$$

is the formula that gives the distance (in feet) the body falls in $t$ seconds.

To answer the original question of how long it takes the object to fall 400 feet, we have but to substitute 400 for $s$ in (14) and calculate the corresponding value of $t$. It so happens that there are two answers; $t = 5$ and $t = -5$. Of course, both are correct mathematical answers, but only the positive one answers the *physical* problem.

The preceding example shows how the constants $C$ that arise in integration can be determined in a given physical problem. The information we used to determine both constants concerned values of $v$ and $s$ at $t = 0$. These values of $v$ and $s$ at $t = 0$ are called *initial* values or initial conditions for the obvious reason.

Before considering other applications, let us note that we could have proceeded differently in the problem above. We could have insisted that the upward direction be the positive direction for $s$. However, the acceleration is downward. As we have already pointed out, a downward acceleration means a downward speed and a downward distance covered with increasing time. If the positive direction for distance is to be upward, the downward distance that the object falls is in the negative direction. We can take care of the signs if we agree to start with the fact that $a$ or $\dot{v}$ is $-32$; that is

$$\dot{v} = -32.$$

Then by antidifferentiation

$$v = -32t + C.$$

Now it is still true that $v = 0$ when $t = 0$, because at $t = 0$ a dropped object has 0 speed. Then $C = 0$ and

$$v = \dot{s} = -32t.$$

By antidifferentiation

**(15)** $$s = -16t^2 + C.$$

To determine this $C$, we must first establish the origin for $s$. Suppose that we agree to measure $s$ from the ground. Moreover, the upward direction has been chosen as positive. Then, since the object is dropped from a point 400 feet above the ground, at $t = 0$, $s = 400$. If we substitute these values in (15), we have

$$400 = -16 \cdot 0^2 + C$$

or

$$C = 400.$$

The final formula is

**(16)** $$s = -16t^2 + 400.$$

We must, however, be careful about how we describe this result. The variable $s$ is *not* the distance traveled by the object. This distance is $16t^2$. The quantity $400 - 16t^2$ is the original height of the object measured from the ground upward minus the distance fallen by the object in time $t$ (Fig. 3-1). Thus $s$ is the *height above the ground* at time $t$. To call attention to this meaning of $s$, we can write (16) as

**(17)** $$h = -16t^2 + 400,$$

where $h$ denotes height above the ground.

To answer the original question of how long it takes the object to fall 400 feet, we must now say that when the object hits the ground $h = 0$. If we

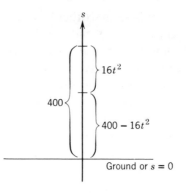

**Figure 3-1**

substitute 0 for $h$ in (17), we see that the equation for $t$ becomes precisely the same as the one obtained from (14), namely, $16t^2 = 400$. The positive value of $t$, $t = 5$, is still the correct answer to the physical problem because $t$ is measured from the instant the object begins to fall.

In this second method we introduced a negative acceleration and consequently a negative speed. It is customary when the sign of the speed enters significantly into a problem to use the word *velocity* in place of speed. A velocity can be positive or negative. The word speed is then used to denote the numerical value of the velocity without regard to sign. In the second method the velocity is always negative for $t$ greater than 0. The word acceleration, however, is used to cover positive and negative rates of change of velocity.

We see from the examples already considered that the occurrence of the constant of integration is not a disadvantage but may even be an advantage. It permits us to adjust the formulas for velocity and distance to the specific situation we wish to describe.

With the same mathematical theory we can also tackle a class of problems in which an object is not just dropped but is thrown downward and then continues to fall under the acceleration of gravity. To throw an object downward as opposed to dropping it means that when the object leaves the hand it already has some velocity. Suppose, for example, that an object is thrown downward with a velocity of 100 ft/sec from a height of 1000 feet. Let us find the formula for the distance traveled in time $t$. Suppose that we choose the downward direction of distance as positive. We know that as soon as the object is released by the hand it possesses a downward acceleration due to gravity of 32 ft/sec$^2$. This downward acceleration generates a downward velocity, and the downward velocity causes the object to move downward. Because we have chosen the downward direction of distance as positive, we must start with

**(18)** $$a = \dot{v} = 32.$$

Then by antidifferentiation

**(19)** $$v = 32t + C.$$

The essential change in treating objects that are thrown downward as opposed to objects that are dropped comes in the next step. Suppose that we agree to measure time from the instant the object leaves the hand. Then at $t = 0$, $v = 100$. We substitute these values in (19) and obtain

$$100 = 32 \cdot 0 + C$$

or

$$C = 100.$$

Then from (19) we have

**(20)**                                $v = 32t + 100.$

We should compare this result with (11).
     To obtain the distance traveled we note that $v = \dot{s}$, so that

$$\dot{s} = 32t + 100.$$

Then by antidifferentiation

**(21)**                                $s = 16t^2 + 100t + C.$

To determine the constant of integration we must decide what our origin for distance is to be. Let us agree that distance is to be measured from the point at which the object is released. Then, at $t = 0$, $s = 0$. If we substitute these values in (21), we see that $C = 0$, and the formula for the distance traveled downward is

**(22)**                                $s = 16t^2 + 100t.$

We can now answer such questions as how long it takes the object to fall a given distance or how far it falls in a given time.
     The rather simple problems discussed in this section show how the process of antidifferentiation or integration enables us to start with physical information about derived functions and produce useful formulas. We shall consider weightier examples subsequently.


# EXERCISES

1. An object is dropped from the top of the Empire State Building, which is 1000 feet high. Derive the formula for the distance the object falls in time $t$. Then calculate the time it takes the object to reach the ground and the velocity with which it hits the ground.          *Ans.* $s = 16t^2$; $5\sqrt{10}/2$ sec; $80\sqrt{10}$ ft/sec.

2. Suppose that an object is dropped from the tenth floor of a building whose roof is 50 feet above the point of release. Derive the formula for the position of the object $t$ seconds after its release if distance is measured from the *roof*, the positive direction of distance is downward and time is measured from the instant the object is dropped. What is the distance fallen by the object in $t$ seconds?

3. An object is dropped from a stationary balloon which is 1000 feet above the ground. Derive the formula for the position of the object after $t$ seconds if the distance is measured from the ground, the positive direction is upward, and time is measured from the instant the object is dropped.

   *Ans.* $s = -16t^2 + 1000$.

4. Suppose that an object is dropped from a height of 1000 feet at 10 seconds after 12 o'clock. Derive the formula for the position of the object in $t$ seconds if distance is measured from the starting point, the positive direction is downward, and time is measured from 12 o'clock.

5. Suppose that an object is thrown downward so that as it leaves the hand it has a speed of 100 ft/sec. Derive the formula for the distance fallen in $t$ seconds after it is thrown if the distance is measured from the starting point and the downward direction is chosen positive. *Ans.* $s = 16t^2 + 100t$.

6. Suppose that an object is set into straight line motion along the ground by giving it an initial speed of 100 ft/sec. If we suppose that the ground is smooth and flat, there is no horizontal acceleration. Derive the formula for the distance traveled in $t$ seconds.

7. An object that is dropped from a point 500 feet above the surface of the moon falls to the surface with a constant acceleration of 5.3 ft/sec². If the distance is measured from the surface and the upward direction is positive, derive the formula for the position of the object (i.e., its height above the surface) after $t$ seconds. Incidentally, the moon has no atmosphere and therefore air resistance does not enter into motions near the surface. *Ans.* $s = -(5.3/2)t^2 + 500$.

8. Suppose that an object is thrown downward from the roof of a building that is 200 feet high and that the initial speed is 50 ft/sec. Derive the formula for the height above the ground if the distance is taken positive in the upward direction.

9. An object is dropped from a height of 1000 feet. What is its velocity when it hits the ground? *Ans.* $80\sqrt{10}$ ft/sec.

10. An object dropped near the surface of the earth acquires the velocity $v = 32t$ in $t$ seconds. Suppose that it falls for $T$ seconds. Is it correct to take the arithmetic mean of the initial and final velocities as the equivalent constant velocity in order to calculate the distance traveled?

11. A train runs at a velocity of 45 mi/hr along a straight track. When the brakes are applied, the deceleration (negative acceleration) is $1\frac{1}{3}$ ft/sec². For how long and how far from the station should the brakes be applied so that the train stops at the station? *Ans.* 49.5 sec; 1633.5 ft.

12. Water drops flow out from a small opening at the rate of one drop per second and fall vertically with an acceleration of 32 ft/sec². Determine the distance between two successive drops exactly 1 second after the second one has left the opening.

13. The landing velocity of an airplane (i.e., the velocity at which it touches the ground) is 100 mi/hr. It decelerates at a constant rate and comes to a stop after traveling $\frac{1}{4}$ mile along a straight landing strip. Find the deceleration or the negative acceleration. *Ans.* 20,000 mi/hr².

14. A body is dropped. At the instant when it has fallen 100 feet a second body is to be projected downward with an initial velocity which will enable it to catch up with the first body in 10 seconds after the second body is released. What is the requisite initial velocity?

15. If an object moves along a circle of radius $R$, its position can be described by specifying the angle $\theta$ through which it has rotated (Fig. 3-2). The derivative of

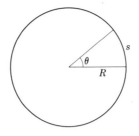

**Figure 3-2**

$\theta$ with respect to $t$ is called the angular velocity and is usually denoted by $\omega$; that is, $\dot{\theta} = \omega$. The derivative of the angular velocity with respect to $t$ is called the angular acceleration and is usually denoted by $\alpha$; that is, $\ddot{\theta} = \dot{\omega} = \alpha$. The linear distance covered by the object is $s = R\theta$ if $\theta$ is measured in radians. Answer the following questions concerning circular motion:

(a)  What is the linear velocity?                                    *Ans. $R\dot{\theta}$.*

(b)  What is the linear acceleration?

(c)  Find the constant angular acceleration of an object moving along a circle if starting from rest it makes 3600 revolutions during the first 2 minutes.

*Ans. $\pi$ rad/sec².*

(d)  The end of a shaft rotates about the other end with a constant acceleration. It starts from rest and makes 12.5 revolutions in the first 5 seconds. What is its angular velocity at the end of the fifth second?

(e)  The initial angular velocity of a wheel turning about a fixed axle is $2\pi$ rad/sec. After 10 revolutions the wheel is brought to rest by friction in the bearings. Find angular deceleration on the assumption that it is constant.

*Ans. $0.1\pi$ rad/sec².*

(f)  A wheel of radius 1 foot starts from rest and rotates with a constant acceleration. After 10 minutes any point on the rim of the wheel has a linear velocity of $v = 100$ ft/sec. Find the linear velocity of the point and angular velocity of the wheel after 15 seconds.

*Ans. $\frac{5}{2}$ ft/sec; $\frac{5}{2}$ rad/sec*

**3. Up and Down Motion.** Among straight line motions, that of an object projected upward is very important physically and of considerable interest mathematically. Let us seek the formulas that govern such motions. We shall continue to restrict ourselves to motions near the surface of the earth and to neglect air resistance, so that we may use the fact that the acceleration of gravity is constant and equal to 32 ft/sec². It is convenient to measure distance from the surface of the earth and to take the upward direction as positive. However, the acceleration is downward, which gives the object a downward speed and, in turn, causes the object to fall downward. To ensure that the distance traveled *by reason of this acceleration* is recorded as downward, we must regard the acceleration as negative. We start then with the basic fact that

**(23)**                                   $a = \dot{v} = -32.$

Then by antidifferentiation

**(24)**                                   $v = -32t + C.$

If an object is projected upward, it must have an initial velocity upward; that is, if we measure time from the instant it is projected upward, at the instant $t = 0$ the object must be given an upward or positive velocity. Let us suppose that this velocity is 128 ft/sec. Then, at $t = 0$, $v = 128$. If we substitute these values in (24), we find that

$$128 = -32 \cdot 0 + C$$

or

$$C = 128,$$

so that

**(25)**                               $v = -32t + 128.$

We have in (25) the formula for the velocity of the moving object at any time $t$. To find the height reached by the object, that is, the distance traveled upward, at any time $t$, we use the fact that the velocity is the instantaneous rate of change of distance with respect to time. Hence $v$ is $\dot{s}$, and by antidifferentiation applied to (25) we obtain

**(26)**                               $s = -16t^2 + 128t + C.$

To establish the value of $C$ we may use the physical fact that, when $t = 0$, the object is on the ground. Because we have agreed to measure distance from this surface, $s = 0$ at $t = 0$. Thus from (26)

$$0 = -16 \cdot 0^2 + 128 \cdot 0 + C.$$

Then $C = 0$ and

**(27)**                               $s = -16t^2 + 128t.$

We have derived formula (27) by considering what happens when the object travels upward. However, we know from experience that the object reaches some highest point and then falls downward. Does formula (27) apply to the falling motion? We started with the fact that the acceleration is $-32$ ft/sec$^2$. This acceleration applies at every instant that the object is in the air because gravity acts constantly on an object in motion, to produce a downward acceleration of 32 ft/sec$^2$. Hence this fact applies to the upward and downward motion. We also used the fact that the object is projected upward with an initial velocity of 128 ft/sec. Surprisingly, this velocity also applies throughout the motion. If we ignore for the moment the effect of gravity, only the velocity of 128 ft/sec operates. Now Newton's first law of motion, an axiom of physics thoroughly grounded in experience, states that if an object is at rest and no force acts it remains at rest and if it is in motion and no force acts it continues to move indefinitely in a straight line at a constant speed. If an object is set into upward motion at 128 ft/sec and gravity does not act, the object continues to move upward *indefinitely* at 128 ft/sec. The correctness of Newton's first law of motion can be appreciated if we think of what happens when an object is projected horizontally along a smooth surface such as ice. Gravity does not affect the horizontal motion, and therefore the object keeps skimming along the ice. If there were no air resistance and if the ice were ideally smooth, the object would move indefinitely at the velocity with which it was projected.

In vertical motion, however, gravity does act to produce the acceleration of $-32$ ft/sec$^2$ and, accordingly, the velocity of $-32t$ ft/sec. Hence the object moves upward at 128 ft/sec while gravity produces a downward velocity of $32t$ ft/sec; that is, at any instant of time during the upward *and* downward motion the object is impelled upward with a speed of 128 ft/sec and downward at $32t$ ft/sec. The *net* velocity then is $-32t + 128$. Hence formula (25) holds at each instant of the motion.

What about (27)? Because (25) is the correct expression for the velocity during the downward as well as the upward motion and because the velocity is the rate of change of distance with respect to time, the integral of the velocity function should give the distance traveled downward as well as upward. The function in (27) thus represents the upward and downward motion. What, however, does $s$ represent? For some interval of $t$-values starting at $t = 0$, the object rises and the corresponding $s$-values represent distance traveled upward or height above the ground. At some value of $t$ (which happens to be 4 here) the object reaches a maximum height and then, because the net velocity becomes negative, the object moves downward. The distance traveled during the downward motion is a negative distance, which, added to the positive distance already covered by the object, gives the *net height* of the object above the ground. Then $s$ represents the *height of the object above the ground*.

To be certain that we understand the meaning of $s$ in (27), let us look at Fig. 3-3. We see from (25) that $v$ is positive from $t = 0$ to $t = 4$. Hence in this interval the object moves upward, and during this motion the value of $s$ is both the distance traveled and the height above the ground. At $t = 4$, $v$ is 0. At this instant the object begins its downward motion. From $t = 4$ to $t = 5$, for example, the object falls some distance, and this negative distance, when added to the positive distance already covered, gives the net height of the object above the ground.

**Figure 3-3**

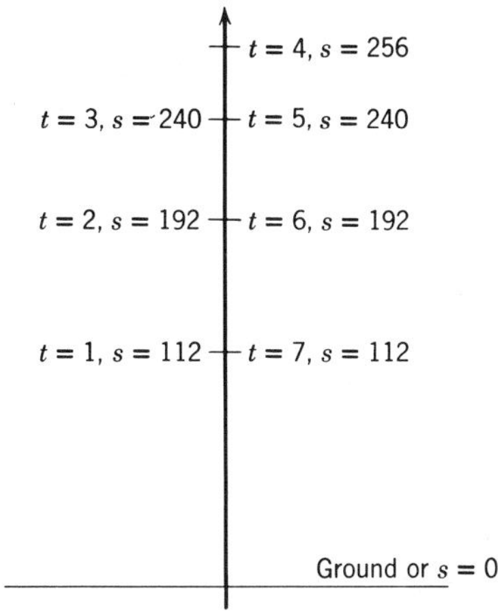

$s$

$t = 4, s = 256$

$t = 3, s = 240$  $t = 5, s = 240$

$t = 2, s = 192$  $t = 6, s = 192$

$t = 1, s = 112$  $t = 7, s = 112$

Ground or $s = 0$

Thus (27) does hold for the upward and downward motion, provided we remember that $s$ is not distance traveled throughout the motion but the height above the ground. With formula (27) available, we can answer all kinds of questions about the motion.

One question of interest is the maximum height attained by an object that is thrown or shot up into the air. This question is easily answered. Let us consider the motion represented by formula (27), namely,

**(28)** $$s = 16t^2 + 128t.$$

We happen to know the maximum height in this case; it is shown in Fig. 3-3. Let us suppose, however, that we do not know it and therefore seek a method of finding it. The problem of finding the maximum height could be answered if we knew at what instant of time, that is, at what value of $t$, the object attains maximum height because we could then substitute this value of $t$ in (28). But we seem to lack this information. However, we do know but have not yet utilized the formula for velocity, namely,

**(29)** $$v = -32t + 128.$$

A distinctive fact about the velocity of the object at the instant it attains maximum height is that the velocity is 0; for the object rises until its velocity is 0 and then falls. Hence we substitute 0 for $v$ in (29) and solve

**(30)** $$0 = -32t + 128$$

for $t$. We see then that, when the object is at maximum height, $t = 4$. We now substitute this value of $t$ in (30) and obtain

**(31)** $$s = -16 \cdot 4^2 + 128 \cdot 4 = 256.$$

Thus the maximum height attained by the object is 256 feet.

We should note that to solve the problem of maximum height we used a physical argument, namely, that the velocity of the object is 0 at the maximum point. We may indeed be convinced that this physical fact is correct. Nevertheless, we must go outside of mathematics to obtain it. Although some physical information must enter into all applications of mathematics to physical science, it is desirable to prove by mathematical means as much as we can because we are then more certain of our facts. We shall see later, when studying maxima and minima, that we can prove by *mathematical means* that the velocity is 0 at the highest point of the object's path.

## EXERCISES

1. For the motion represented by formula (27), what is the height above the ground at $t = 5$? What is the distance traveled by the object from $t = 0$ to $t = 5$? *Ans.* 240 ft; 272 ft.

2. Suppose that an object is projected upward from the ground with a velocity of 160 ft/sec. Choose the upward direction to be the positive one for the height above the ground and derive the formulas for the velocity at any time $t$ and for the height above the ground at any time $t$.

3. The height of a ball which is thrown up from the ground with a velocity of 192 ft/sec is given by the formula $s = +192t - 16t^2$. Find $t$ when $s = 512$. What physical significance do the two answers have?          *Ans.* $t = 4, 8$.

4. The height of a ball which is thrown upward from the ground with a velocity of 144 ft/sec is given by the formula $s = 144t - 16t^2$. Find the velocity when $t = 9$ and interpret the result physically.

5. If a gun is capable of firing a bullet at the speed of 1000 ft/sec and if the gun is fired straight up, how high will the bullet go?          *Ans.* 15,625 ft.

6. Because man is preparing for activities on the moon, it may be worthwhile to consider this question: Suppose that a ball is thrown up from the surface of the moon with a velocity of 96 ft/sec. How high will it go and how long will it take to reach that maximum height? The acceleration due to gravity near the surface of the moon is 5.3 ft/sec².

7. A stone is thrown upward from the ground with an initial velocity of 96 ft/sec. (a) How long does it take to reach the ground again? (b) What velocity does it have at the instant it returns to the ground?          *Ans.* 6 sec; $-96$ ft/sec.

8. A stone is thrown upward from the surface of a planet where the acceleration due to gravity (the attraction of that planet) is $g$ ft/sec². The initial velocity is $v_0$ and distance upward is taken to be positive. Find the formulas for the velocity and the height above the ground.          *Ans.* $v = v_0 - gt$; $s = v_0 t - \dfrac{gt^2}{2}$.

9. A bullet is shot straight up and returns to earth in 20 seconds. What is its initial velocity?

10. Suppose that an object is thrown upward with an initial velocity of 200 ft/sec and that the upward direction is taken to be positive for height above the ground. However, time is measured from the instant 5 seconds before the object is thrown up. Derive the formula for the height above the ground at any time $t$.

11. Suppose that an object is thrown upward with an initial velocity of 200 ft/sec and that another one is thrown upward 5 seconds later with an initial velocity of 300 ft/sec. When and where do they meet?          *Ans.* 2.3 sec after second object is thrown.

12. Calculate the velocity with which an object must be shot straight up in order to just reach a height of 1000 feet. By just reaching the specified height we mean that the velocity of the object should be 0 at that height.

13. Calculate the minimum ejection velocity with which a shell must be fired to strike a target 1000 feet high and directly overhead.          *Ans.* $80\sqrt{10}$ ft/sec.

14. Show that an object thrown up into the air near the surface of the earth with a velocity $V$ will rise to a maximum height of $V^2/64$.

15. A subway train travels 400 feet between two stations. It starts from rest and accelerates at the rate of 8 ft/sec² until its velocity reaches 20 ft/sec. It then moves at this constant velocity for a while and then decelerates to rest at the rate of 12 ft/sec². Find the total time between the stations.

16. A rocket is shot straight up into the air to a height of 10 miles at which point its velocity is 120 mi/hr (176 ft/sec). Its fuel is now exhausted, and therefore the

rocket receives no further acceleration from the fuel. Assuming that the acceleration due to gravity is still 32 ft/sec², write a formula for the subsequent velocity of the rocket and for its height above the ground.

*Suggestion:* Choose the instant at which the rocket reaches the 10-mile height as the zero point for time.

*Ans.* $v = -32t + 176$; $s = -16t^2 + 176t + 52,800$.

17. (a) A ball is thrown straight up into the air from the roof of a building with a velocity of 96 ft/sec. Write a formula for its subsequent height above the roof as a function of time. *Ans.* $s = -16t^2 + 96t$.

(b) If the roof is 112 feet above the ground, how long after it is thrown up does the ball reach the ground?

18. (a) A ball is thrown straight up into the air from the roof of a building with a velocity of 96 ft/sec. If the roof is 112 feet above the ground, write a formula for the height of the ball above the ground.

*Ans.* $s = 96t - 16t^2 + 112$.

(b) How long after it is thrown up does the ball reach the ground?

*Ans.* 7 sec.

19. Suppose that an object which travels along a horizontal straight road at a velocity of 88 ft/sec starts to lose velocity, that is, decelerates at the rate of 11 ft/sec². What distance does it travel by the time it comes to rest? The answer, incidentally, is the minimum distance in which one can stop a car that is traveling at 60 mi/hr. Actually, it takes about 1 second before a person who decides to apply the brakes actually does so. Hence the car travels another 88 feet between the instant the decision is made and the instant at which the car comes to rest.

20. Suppose that a ball is thrown up with a velocity of 128 ft/sec. Decide on the basis of experience or intuition whether it takes as much, more, or less time for the ball to travel from the starting point to the maximum height as it does to travel from that position to the ground. Now obtain the answer mathematically.

21. A motorist is traveling at a constant speed $v_0$ and is approaching a traffic light. He wishes to stop the car at the light. However, his reaction time, that is, the time it takes him to put his foot on the brakes, is $\tau$ and the maximum deceleration of the braked car is $a$. What is the minimum distance from the light in which he can bring his car to a stop? *Ans.* $\frac{1}{2}(v_0^2/a) + v_0\tau$.

22. The traffic department of a town wishes to put a warning sign reading "Slow Down, Stoplight Ahead" sufficiently in advance of the stoplight for oncoming motorists to have time to slow down and stop at the light. If automobiles can decelerate at the rate of 5 ft/sec² and if the maximum speed allowed on the road is 30 mi/hr (44 ft/sec), how far in advance of the light should the warning sign be placed to permit motorists to stop in time?

23. A subway train travels over a distance $s$ in $t$ seconds. It starts from rest (zero velocity) and ends at rest. In the first part of its journey it moves with constant acceleration $f$ and in the second part with constant deceleration (negative acceleration) $r$. Show that $s = [fr/(f + r)]t^2/2$.

24. A bomber releases a bomb while flying vertically *upward* at a velocity of 1500 ft/sec at a height of 10,000 feet. (The bomb when released also has an upward velocity of 1500 ft/sec.)

(a) How long after it is released will it take the bomb to reach the ground?

*Ans.* 100 sec.

(b) Immediately after releasing the bomb the bomber flies away horizontally at the rate of 1200 ft/sec. How far away from the point at which the bomb strikes the ground is the plane when the bomb strikes?

25. In a chemical reaction two substances are combining to form a third one. The rate $\dot{x}$ at which the third substance is being formed in grams/min is given by the function $\dot{x} = 9 - \frac{1}{2}t^2$ when the reaction has been underway for $t$ minutes. How much substance is formed in 4 minutes?          *Ans.* $25\frac{1}{3}$ g.

26. A body is dropped from a height of 100 yards. After falling for 2 seconds a second body is projected vertically upward from a point on the earth directly below and with a velocity of 40 yd/sec (yards per second). Find the time and height at which the two bodies meet.

     *Ans.* Approx. 3.3 sec after first body is dropped; approx. 42 yd.

27. A balloon is ascending with a velocity of 20 ft/sec when a stone is dropped from it. The stone reaches the ground in 6 seconds. Find the height of the balloon when the stone was dropped. (When dropped from the balloon, the stone has the upward velocity of the balloon.)

28. Show that a body thrown upward has the same speed when passing a given point on the upward and the downward motions.

29. A body is thrown into the air with an initial velocity of $v_0$ ft/sec. What initial velocity is required to double the maximum height previously attained?

     *Ans.* $\sqrt{2}\ v_0$ ft/sec.

**4. *Motion Along an Inclined Plane.**** Motion along a straight line is not confined to vertical or horizontal paths. Trains and automobiles move up and down hills, and airplanes rising or descending from a field follow essentially straight line paths. Such paths are studied under the concept of motion along an inclined plane. We shall consider how the calculus helps to study the motion of objects down or up inclined planes.

   If an object $M$ is placed on a smooth (frictionless) inclined plane (Fig. 3-4), we know that it will slide down. To obtain quantitative information about the motion, we must know something about the acceleration, velocity and distance it travels. The force that causes the motion, as in the case of objects that fall straight down, is gravity. Gravity pulls straight down, whereas the object slides down the plane. Hence we are obliged to look into the question of how a force which acts in one direction can be effective in another direction.

   Forces are peculiar animals. Suppose an object rests on a horizontal smooth table at $P$ (Fig. 3-5). If a force of magnitude or numerical value $F_1$

**Figure 3-4**

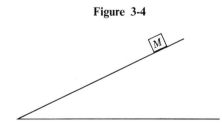

---

* This section can be omitted without disrupting the continuity.

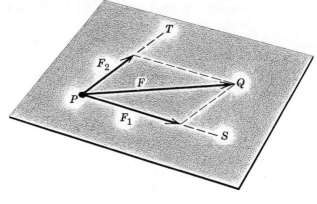

**Figure 3-5**

pulls it toward $S$ and another force of magnitude $F_2$ pulls it toward $T$, the object actually moves along the diagonal $PQ$ of the parallelogram determined by the two forces. That is, the two sides of the parallelogram which determine it are the side of length $F_1$ in the direction of $F_1$ and the side of length $F_2$ in the direction of $F_2$, both starting at $P$, which is the point of application of the two forces. The magnitude $F$ of the total or resultant force is the length of the diagonal $PQ$. Why do the combined forces behave in this way? The only answer is that this is what we find to be the case in experimenting with forces. We cannot quarrel with nature, but we can be grateful that we can describe the action of forces by a simple mathematical law.

Forces are a prime example of what are known as vectors, that is, entities that have magnitude and direction. When we obtain the effect of two forces by using the parallelogram law, we say that we *add* the forces. This meaning of the word "add" differs from that used to describe the addition of two numbers. In fact, as the parallelogram law implies, a force of 3 poundals and a force of 4 poundals (a poundal is one unit of force) do not generally add up to 7 poundals. The mathematicians have reasons for using the word "add" in combining forces, but the reasons are irrelevant here. It is important to note, however, that the statement that forces are being added means that they are being combined under the parallelogram law.

The most important case of the addition of two forces is that in which they are at right angles to each other (Fig. 3-6). Here the parallelogram

**Figure 3-6**

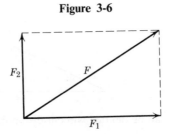

becomes a rectangle, and the resultant of magnitude $F$ is the diagonal of the rectangle.

Let us return to our object at $P$ on the inclined plane (Fig. 3-7). Gravity acts on this object and pulls straight down. We can think of this force of gravity of magnitude $F$ as the resultant of two forces—one of magnitude $F_1$ which is directed down the plane and the other of magnitude $F_2$ which is directed perpendicular to the plane. These summands or components of the gravitational force are determined by dropping perpendiculars from the endpoint $Q$ of $F$ onto the plane and onto the line perpendicular to the plane, so that $F$ is the diagonal of the rectangle determined by $F_1$ and $F_2$. Thus we can think of the force whose magnitude is $F$ as having been replaced by the forces with magnitudes $F_1$ and $F_2$. Now $F_2$ is the magnitude of the force with which gravity presses the object against the inclined plane. The plane resists this force; that is, the plane, because it is rigid, does not permit the object to move into or perpendicular to the plane. This reaction of the plane, denoted by $N$ in Fig. 3-7, offsets or exactly counteracts $F_2$. Hence the force which causes the object to slide down the plane is the other component or summand of the gravitational force, the one with magnitude $F_1$.

How large is $F_1$? Suppose that the plane is inclined at angle $A$ to the horizontal (Fig. 3-7). Then the angle at $Q$ is also $A$, because both are complementary to the angle between $F_1$ and $F$ at $P$ and therefore

**(32)**                                   $$F_1 = F \sin A.$$

To obtain the numerical value of $F_1$, we must make use of one more physical fact. The force that the earth's gravity exerts on an object is called the *weight* of the object. Each of us is constantly being pulled toward the earth by the earth's gravitational force, and the magnitude of this force is the person's weight. Thus $F$ in (32) is the weight of the object on the inclined plane.

We know as a physical fact that when an object is allowed to fall straight down, the force of gravity or the weight of the object gives it an acceleration of 32 ft/sec². Because the force acting on the object along the inclined plane is $F \sin A$, it would seem reasonable that the acceleration given to the object should be 32 sin $A$. We are assuming, in other words, that the force is proportional to the acceleration. Let us make this physical

**Figure 3-7**

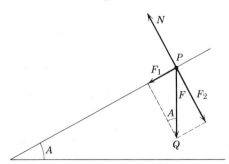

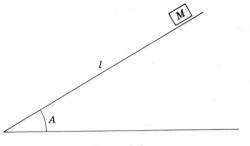

**Figure 3-8**

assumption; later, when we have had occasion to look further into the relation between force and acceleration, we shall see that it is correct.* What we have decided then is that the acceleration $a$ of an object sliding down a plane inclined at an angle $A$ to the horizontal is

(33) $$a = 32 \sin A.$$

We are now in a position to answer some questions about motion down an inclined plane. Suppose that an object is placed on a plane inclined at an angle $A$ to the horizontal (Fig. 3-8). What velocity does it acquire after sliding for 10 seconds? We know that $a = \dot{v}$. Hence

$$\dot{v} = 32 \sin A.$$

Now $32 \sin A$ is a constant for a given inclined plane. Hence

$$v = (32 \sin A)t + C = 32t \sin A + C.$$

Because the object starts with 0 velocity, $v = 0$ when $t = 0$. Hence $C = 0$ and

(34) $$v = 32t \sin A.$$

Thus after 10 seconds the object acquires a velocity of $320 \sin A$ ft/sec. Given the value of $A$, we can of course find $\sin A$.

We can also find how far the object travels in 10 seconds. If we let $s$ be the distance traveled down the plane in $t$ seconds, $v = \dot{s}$. By (34)

$$\dot{s} = 32t \sin A.$$

Again we must remember that $32 \sin A$ is a constant, and integration yields

$$s = 16t^2 \sin A + C.$$

If $s$ is measured from the point at which the object begins to slide, $s = 0$ when $t = 0$ and therefore $C = 0$. Thus

(35) $$s = 16t^2 \sin A$$

is the formula for the distance traveled in $t$ seconds. We can now calculate $s$ for any value of $t$.

* The reader who already knows Newton's second law of motion, $F = ma$, where $m$ is the mass of the object and $a$ the acceleration, will see at once the correctness of the assumption.

## EXERCISES

1. Suppose that an object starts from rest and slides 200 feet down a hill whose inclination is 30°. How long does it take to slide this distance and what velocity does the object acquire?  *Ans.* 5 sec; 80 ft/sec.

2. Suppose that an object starts from rest and slides down a hill whose inclination is 30°. The object slides from a height of 100 feet above the horizontal ground to the ground. How long does it take to slide down the hill and what velocity does the object acquire?

3. Answer the questions of Exercise 2 if the conditions are the same except for the fact that the inclination of the hill is 15°.  *Ans.* 10 sec approx.; 80 ft/sec.

4. If a plane is inclined at an angle of 90° to the horizontal, that is, if $A = 90°$, the motion down the plane of a body which starts from rest should be the same as that of a body which is dropped and falls vertically. Do formulas (33), (34), and (35) reduce to the formulas for the latter kind of motion when $A = 90°$?

5. (a)  Suppose than an object is allowed to slide down an inclined plane from a point which is $h$ feet above the horizontal ground, and that the object slides $l$ feet along the plane to the ground (Fig. 3-8). How long does it take to slide this distance?  *Ans.* $l/4\sqrt{h}$ .

   (b)  Under the conditions of part (a), what velocity does the object acquire?

   *Ans.* $8\sqrt{h}$ .

   (c)  Is there anything remarkable about the answer to part (b)?

6. (a)  Suppose that an object slides down two different inclined planes from a height of $h$ feet above a horizontal plane to the horizontal plane itself. One inclined plane slopes gradually and is $l_1$ feet long; the other is steep and $l_2$ feet long. Show that the respective times of descent $t_1$ and $t_2$ satisfy the equation $t_1/t_2 = l_1/l_2$.

   (b)  Under the conditions of part (a), compare the velocities acquired at the bottoms of the two paths.  *Ans.* Equal.

7. An object slides down an inclined plane $OP'$ (Fig. 3-9) starting from rest at 0. Show that the point $Q$ reached in the time $t_1$ required to fall straight down to $P$ lies on a circle with $OP$ as diameter.

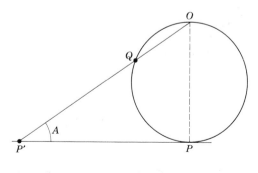

**Figure 3-9**

8. In Fig. 3-10, $OQ$, $OQ'$, $OP$, ... are pieces of straight wire all emanating from $O$ and lying in one vertical plane. A bead is slipped on each wire at $O$, and all

are released simultaneously to slide down their respective wires. Show that at any instant of time the beads lie on a circle.

*Suggestion:* Use the result of Exercise 7.

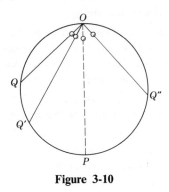

**Figure 3-10**

9. Find the straight line path for which the time required for an object to slide from $O$ to some point of the curve $C$ is least (Fig. 3-11).

*Suggestion:* Use the result of Exercise 8.

*Ans.* The path $OQ$ for which the circle on $OQ$ has $O$ as its highest point and is tangent to $C$.

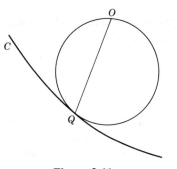

**Figure 3-11**

10. Suppose that an object slides down a hill whose inclination is $A$ and that at the instant it starts to slide it has a velocity of $v_0$ ft/sec. Derive the formula for the distance the object slides in time $t$.

# APPENDIX*
# THE COORDINATE GEOMETRY
# OF STRAIGHT LINES

**A1. *The Need for Geometrical Interpretation.*** Thus far in our work on the calculus we have dealt with formulas. It is a wise procedure in all mathematical work to try to think in geometrical as well as algebraic (or

* This appendix may be omitted by readers familiar with the elements of coordinate geometry.

analytical) terms. The geometrical mode of thinking not only helps us to understand what we are doing algebraically but may also suggest new results.

The way to associate geometrical figures with formulas has already been indicated in Chapter 2. We use the technique of coordinate geometry to associate a curve with a formula. Our method of doing this so far has been to make a table of $x$- and $y$-values which satisfy the formula, plot a point on a rectangular Cartesian coordinate system for each pair of $x$- and $y$-values, and join these points by a smooth curve. This method is crude and laborious; it can be replaced by more effective ones. In this Appendix we begin a deeper and more systematic study of the relation between formulas and the curves representing them or, as one also says in coordinate geometry, between equations and curves.

**A2. The Distance Formula.** Before we can take up the main task of coordinate geometry—the interpretation of given formulas as curves and the attachment of the proper formula to a given curve—we must acquire a few subsidiary ideas. The first is a formula or algebraic expression for the distance between two points in terms of the coordinates of these points.

To denote two specific points and at the same time to indicate that they can be any two points, we use the notation $(x_1, y_1)$ for one point and $(x_2, y_2)$ for the other. The subscripts 1 and 2 distinguish the points. Suppose, then, that $P_1$ with coordinates $(x_1, y_1)$ and $P_2$ with coordinates $(x_2, y_2)$ are the two points (Fig. 3A-1). If we draw the horizontal line through $P_1$ and the vertical line through $P_2$, they intersect at a point $Q$. We see at once that $P_1P_2$ is the hypotenuse of the right triangle $P_1QP_2$. Moreover, we see from the figure that

$$QP_2 = SP_2 - SQ = SP_2 - RP_1 = y_2 - y_1.$$

Also,

$$P_1Q = TQ - TP_1 = x_2 - x_1.$$

**Figure 3A-1**

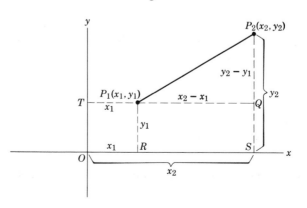

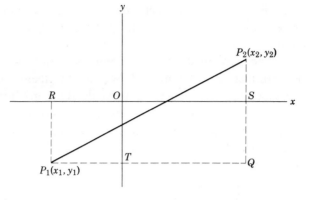

**Figure 3A-2**

Hence by the Pythagorean theorem

$$(P_1P_2)^2 = (x_2 - x_1)^2 + (y_2 - y_1)^2,$$

and therefore

(1)                    $$P_1P_2 = \sqrt{(x_2 - x_1)^2 + (y_2 - y_1)^2} \, .$$

We take the positive square root because the distance is usually taken to be positive. Formula (1) gives the distance between two points in terms of their coordinates.

Our proof of the distance formula begged a question. Suppose that one or both of the points has negative coordinates. Would formula (1) still be correct in such cases? Let us take $P_1$ to be the third quadrant (Fig. 3A-2) and see if (1) is still correct.

Previously we found that $QP_2$ is $y_2 - y_1$. We see in Fig. 3A-2 that now $QP_2$ is $QS + SP_2$ and we want $QP_2$ to be the actual sum of the positive lengths $SP_2$ and $QS$. Now $SP_2$ is $y_2$. However, the actual length of $QS$ is the length of $P_1R$. If we took $y_1$ to be the length of $P_1R$, we would have a negative quantity, because $y_1$ here represents a negative number. Hence we take the positive length of $QS$ to be $-y_1$. Then

$$QP_2 = SP_2 + QS = y_2 - y_1.$$

Likewise the length $P_1Q$ is the sum of the positive lengths $P_1T$ and $TQ$. Because $x_1$ is negative, we take $-x_1$ to represent the positive length $P_1T$. Then

$$P_1Q = TQ + P_1T = x_2 - x_1.$$

We see then that our results for $QP_2$ and $P_1Q$ are the same as the previous ones, and formula (1) holds.

**Example.**  Find the distance between two points whose coordinates are (3, 5) and (−2, 1).

**Solution.**     We may let either point be $(x_1, y_1)$ and the other $(x_2, y_2)$ and we use formula (1). Thus let $(3, 5)$ be $(x_1, y_1)$ and $(-2, 1)$ be $(x_2, y_2)$. Then

$$\sqrt{(x_2 - x_1)^2 + (y_2 - y_1)^2} = \sqrt{(-2 - 3)^2 + (1 - 5)^2} = \sqrt{25 + 16} = \sqrt{41} .$$

## EXERCISES

1. Find the distance between the points whose coordinates are the following:
   (a)  $(3, 2)$ and $(5, 7)$.        *Ans.* $\sqrt{29}$ .   (d)  $(-7, -5)$ and $(-1, -3)$.
   (b)  $(-3, 2)$ and $(5, 7)$.                     (e)  $(1, 2)$ and $(1, -2)$.        *Ans.* 4.
   (c)  $(-3, -1)$ and $(-4, 2)$.

                                *Ans.* $\sqrt{10}$ .

2. Show that in finding the distance between two points it does not matter which point we denote by $P_1$ and which by $P_2$.
3. Show that $(-1, -4)$, $(5, 4)$, and $(-6, 6)$ are the vertices $A$, $B$, and $C$ respectively of an isosceles triangle.
4. Show that the triangle whose vertices are $(0, 5)$, $(-3, 0)$, and $(3, 0)$ is or is not equilateral.
5. Show that the coordinates of the midpoint of the line segment joining $(x_1, y_1)$ and $(x_2, y_2)$ are $\left( \dfrac{x_1 + x_2}{2} , \dfrac{y_1 + y_2}{2} \right)$.

**A3.  *The Slope of a Straight Line.*** In our everyday experience we use the notion of the slope of a hill. What we mean by the slope is the number of feet we travel up, which is called the rise, divided by the number of feet of horizontal travel, which is called the run. Thus if we walk from $P$ to $Q$ (Fig. 3A-3) and rise 2 feet while moving horizontally 6 feet, we say that the slope is 2/6 or 1/3. This notion of slope is utilized to specify the slope of any line with respect to the horizontal or x-axis.

Consider the line through $P_1$ and $P_2$ of Fig. 3A-4 and, in particular, the segment $P_1P_2$. The rise is $QP_2$ and the run is $P_1Q$. Then the slope is $QP_2/P_1Q$. We found in deriving formula (1) that $QP_2 = y_2 - y_1$ and $P_1Q = x_2 - x_1$. Then the slope of the segment $P_1P_2$, which is usually denoted by $m$, is

(2)                                $$m = \frac{y_2 - y_1}{x_2 - x_1} .$$

**Figure 3A-3**

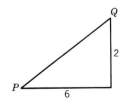

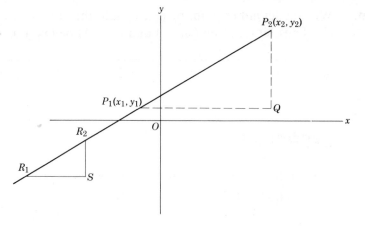

**Figure 3A-4**

Suppose that we take any other two points, say $R_1$ and $R_2$ on the line $P_1P_2$. Would the slope of the segment $R_1R_2$ be the same as the slope of $P_1P_2$? Triangles $R_1SR_2$ and $P_1QP_2$ are similar because the corresponding sides are parallel. Hence $QP_2/P_1Q = SR_2/R_1S$. Thus the slope of $R_1R_2$ is the same as that of $P_1P_2$. This means that any two segments of a line have the same slope, and therefore we can speak of the slope of a line and mean by it the slope of any segment of that line. Then formula (2) gives the slope of the line.

Let us note that it does not matter which of the two points determining the segment is called $P_1$ and which $P_2$. For, if we interchange $(x_1, y_1)$ and $(x_2, y_2)$ in (2), we change the signs of numerator and denominator but not the sign of the fraction.

To distinguish lines which "fall" as $x$ increases from lines which rise as $x$ increases we make a slight extension of the usual notion of slope. We continue to use formula (2) for the value of the slope. However, as we can see from Fig. 3A-5, although $y_2 - y_1$ is positive, the quantity $x_2 - x_1$ is negative. Hence formula (2) gives a negative slope for a line which falls to the right or as $x$ increases. Let us note that here too it does not matter which point we call $(x_1, y_1)$ and which $(x_2, y_2)$. If $P_1$ and $P_2$ are interchanged, $x_2 - x_1$ becomes positive, but $y_2 - y_1$ becomes negative and therefore the ratio remains the same.

**Figure 3A-5**

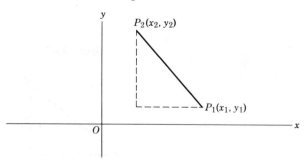

There are two exceptional cases of slope. If a line is parallel to the $y$-axis, $x_2 - x_1 = 0$ and the slope of the line is not defined. If the line is parallel to the $x$-axis, formula (2) yields the slope 0.

## EXERCISES

**1.** Draw the line joining the two given points and calculate its slope:
  (a)  (3, 4) and (5, 7).        *Ans.* $\frac{3}{2}$.  (e)  $(-3, 7)$ and $(-5, -2)$.
  (b)  $(-1, 2)$ and (5, 7).                                                *Ans.* $\frac{9}{2}$.
  (c)  (3, 7) and (5, 2).        *Ans.* $-\frac{5}{2}$.  (f)  (3, 7) and (3, 10).
  (d)  $(-3, 7)$ and (5, 2).

**A4. The Inclination of a Line.** An alternative method of describing the slope of a line with respect to the horizontal or $x$-axis utilizes the angle which the line makes with the axis. This angle of inclination is the counterclockwise angle whose initial side is the $x$-axis taken in the positive direction and whose terminal side lies on the line itself taken in the upward direction. Figure 3A-6 shows 4 lines in different positions with respect to the $x$-axis, and the angle of inclination $A$ of each of these lines is indicated. We note that angle $A$ can vary from 0 to 180°. These extreme values are assigned as the inclination of a line which is parallel to the $x$-axis.

The slope of a line and the angle of inclination both give the direction of the line. The slope of a line, according to (2), is

$$m = \frac{y_2 - y_1}{x_2 - x_1} .$$

If the line rises to the right as in ($a$) of Fig. 3A-7, the slope is positive and is the ratio $QP_2/P_1Q$. However, this ratio is also tan $A$. Hence*

**(3)**                               $m = \tan A.$

If the line falls to the right as in ($b$) of Fig. 3A-7, the slope is still $QP_2/P_1Q$ but the ratio is negative. The ratio of the positive lengths $QP_2$ and $QP_1$ is

**Figure 3A-6**

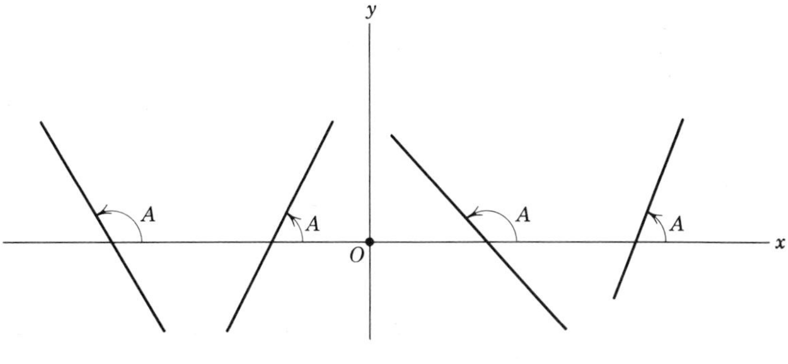

---

* Strictly speaking, formula (3) is correct only if we use the same unit of distance on the $x$ and $y$ axes.

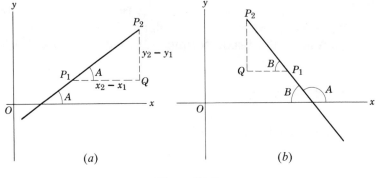

**Figure 3A-7**

tan $B$. However, because $A = (180 - B)$,

**(4)**    $$\tan A = \tan(180 - B) = -\tan B.$$

Then tan $A$ is negative and still gives the slope. Thus formula (3) still holds.

If the angle of inclination $A$ of a line is given, we can always find the slope by finding the tangent of the angle. If $A$ is acute, we merely look up its tangent in a table of trigonometric ratios. If $A$ is obtuse, we look up the tangent of the supplementary angle $B$, and, as (4) shows, tan $A = -\tan B$.

Conversely, if the slope is specified, we know tan $A$. We can now use trigonometric tables to find the angle $A$. If the tangent value is positive, angle $A$ is the acute angle found directly in the table. If the tangent value is negative, say $-3$, then, because we have the identity (4), we find the angle $B$ whose tangent value is $+3$, and the identity (4) tells us that $180 - B$ is the angle whose tangent value is $-3$. Hence $180 - B$ is the angle of inclination $A$ of the line whose slope is $-3$.

## EXERCISES

**1.** Find the slope of the line whose angle of inclination is the following:

(a)  30°.                    *Ans.* $\sqrt{3}/3$.    (g)  0°.                    *Ans.* 0.
(b)  45°.                                             (h)  $\pi/4$.
(c)  70°.                    *Ans.* 2.7.             (i)  $\pi/3$.                *Ans.* $\sqrt{3}$.
(d)  110°.                                            (j)  $\pi/2$.         *Ans.* Undefined.
(e)  120°.                   *Ans.* $-\sqrt{3}$.     (k)  $\pi$.
(f)  170°.

**2.** Find the angle of inclination of the line whose slope is the following:

(a)  1.                      *Ans.* $\pi/4$.    (e)  $-\frac{1}{2}$.              *Ans.* 153° 26'.
                                                (f)  $-0.7270$.
(b)  $\dfrac{\sqrt{3}}{3}$.                      (g)  2.748.                      *Ans.* 70°.
(c)  $\sqrt{3}$.             *Ans.* $\pi/3$.    (h)  0.
(d)  $\frac{1}{2}$.                              (i)  $-2.748$.                   *Ans.* 110°.

**3.** Find the angle of inclination of the line through the following points:

(a)  (1, 1) and (4, 4).      *Ans.* $\pi/4$.    (d)  $(-5, -7)$ and (1, 1).
(b)  $(-4, 4)$ and $(-1, 1)$.                   (e)  (3, 2) and (3, 7).          *Ans.* $\pi/2$.
(c)  (1, 1) and (5, 7).      *Ans.* 56°19'.

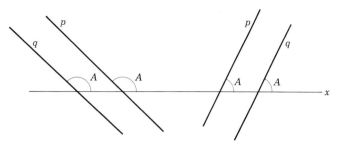

**Figure 3A-8**

**A5. Slopes of Parallel and Perpendicular Lines.** If two lines are parallel, as are the lines $p$ and $q$ in each pair of Fig. 3A-8, their angles of inclination are equal because they are what in plane geometry are called corresponding angles of parallel lines. If two angles are equal, their tangent values are the same. Hence if two lines are parallel, their slopes are equal.

Conversely, if two lines, say $p$ and $q$, have the same slope, then by (3) the tangents of their respective angles of inclination are equal. Moreover, given the tangent of an angle, there is just one angle between 0 and 180° which has this tangent value. Then the angles of inclination of the two lines are equal; but if the corresponding angles of two lines are equal the lines are parallel; hence the lines $p$ and $q$ must be parallel. Thus we have proved the following theorem:

**Theorem:**  If two lines are parallel, their slopes are equal, and conversely if two lines have equal slopes, then the lines are parallel.

Now let us consider two lines $p$ and $q$ which are perpendicular (Fig. 3A-9). Since an exterior angle of a triangle is equal to the sum of the two remote interior angles, we have that

$$A_2 = A_1 + 90°.$$

Then

$$\tan A_2 = \tan(A_1 + 90°) = -\cot A_1 = -\frac{1}{\tan A_1}.$$

Thus the slope $m_2$ of $q$ is the negative reciprocal of the slope $m_1$ of $p$, that is, $m_2 = -1/m_1$.

**Figure 3A-9**

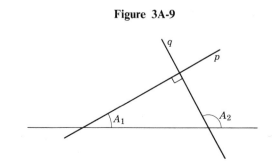

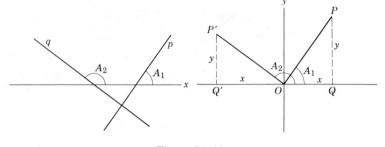

**Figure 3A-10**

Conversely, if we start with two lines $p$ and $q$ (Fig. 3A-10) whose slopes are the negative reciprocals of each other and if we let $A_2$ and $A_1$ be the angles of inclination of these lines, we know that

**(5)** $$\tan A_2 = -\frac{1}{\tan A_1} = -\cot A_1.$$

We now ask what, in view of (5), is the relation between $A_2$ and $A_1$? Because angles of inclination cannot be larger than 180°, one of the angles must be acute and the other obtuse. Suppose that $A_2$ is the larger angle. Let us take $OP$ parallel to $p$ and $OP'$ parallel to $q$. Then, if we suppose that $A_1$ is $A_2 - 90°$, Fig. 3A-10, in which $OP = OP'$, shows that (5) holds for this $A_1$. Moreover, there is no other acute angle with the same cotangent value as $A_1$. Hence the only $A_1$ which satisfies (5) is $A_2 - 90°$. Geometrically this means that, because $A_1$ and $A_2$ are angles of inclination, the lines $p$ and $q$ are perpendicular to each other. Thus we have proved the following theorem:

**Theorem:** If two lines are perpendicular to each other, their slopes are negative reciprocals of each other and conversely.

## EXERCISES

**1.** Show that the line through $(1, 2)$ and $(7, 3)$ is parallel to the line through $(-4, -3)$ and $(8, -1)$.      *Ans.* $m = \frac{1}{6}$ for both.

**2.** Show that the line joining $(1, 4)$ and $(3, 7)$ is perpendicular to the line through $(1, -4)$ and $(4, -6)$.

**3.** What is the inclination of a line which is perpendicular to the line through the points $(2, 1)$ and $(5, 4)$?      *Ans.* 135°.

**4.** What is the inclination of a line which is perpendicular to a line whose slope is 2?

**5.** What is the inclination of any line perpendicular to the line through the points $(2, 1)$ and $(-5, 7)$?

**6.** A triangle is determined by each of the following sets of three points. Which sets represent a right triangle?
(a) $(0, 7)$, $(-4, -2)$, $(5, 2)$.      (c) $(8, 6)$, $(4, 4)$, $(-1, 10)$.
(b) $(4, 5)$, $(-4, -1)$, $(2, -9)$.      (d) $(5, 5)$, $(5\sqrt{3}, -5\sqrt{3})$, $(-5, -5)$.

**7.** Draw a line through $(0, 3)$ with slope $\frac{2}{3}$.

**8.** Draw a line through $(0, 3)$ with slope $-\frac{2}{3}$.

**9.** Show that the points $(-1, 3)$, $(6, 6)$, $(8, 2)$, and $(1, -1)$ are the vertices of a parallelogram.

**A6. *The Angle Between Two Lines.*** If two lines are not parallel, they intersect at some angle, say $\theta$. As Fig. 3A-11 shows, there are really two different angles formed at the intersection, one of which is the supplement of the other. To be specific about which angle we mean, we take the upward direction of each line as the positive direction on the line and take the angle between the positive directions as the angle between the two lines.

Now let $A_2$ and $A_1$ be the inclinations of the two lines, with $A_2$ the greater inclination. We see from Fig. 3A-11 that

$$A_2 = \theta + A_1$$

or

$$\theta = A_2 - A_1.$$

Then

$$\tan \theta = \tan(A_2 - A_1).$$

We learn in trigonometry an identity for the tangent of the difference of two angles. According to this identity

**(6)**
$$\tan \theta = \frac{\tan A_2 - \tan A_1}{1 + \tan A_2 \tan A_1}.$$

If we now let $m_2$ be $\tan A_2$ and $m_1$ be $\tan A_1$, we have the following theorem:

**Theorem:** If $m_2$ and $m_1$ are the slopes of two lines, the tangent of the angle $\theta$ between the two lines is given by the formula

**(7)**
$$\tan \theta = \frac{m_2 - m_1}{1 + m_1 m_2}.$$

The quantity $m_2$ must be taken to be the slope of the line with the larger inclination.

**Figure 3A-11**

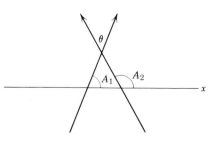

**Example.**   Find the angle between the two lines whose slopes are $-2$ and 4.

**Solution.**   We use (7). Since $m_2$ must be the slope of the line with the larger inclination, and $-2$ must be the slope of the line whose angle of inclination lies between 90° and 180°, we let $m_2$ be $-2$ and $m_1 = 4$. Then, by (7),

$$\tan \theta = \frac{-2-4}{1+(-2)(4)} = \frac{-6}{-7} = \frac{6}{7}.$$

We now use our trigonometry table to find the angle whose tangent is $\frac{6}{7}$ or .8571. To the nearest 10′ of angle the answer is 40° 40′.

## EXERCISES

1. Find the angle between two lines:
   (a)  Whose slopes are 3 and 4.         (c)  Whose slopes are 3 and $-2$.
                   *Ans.* 4° 24′.                                     *Ans.* 45°.
   (b)  Whose inclinations are 30° and 135°.
2. Find the angle between the line through (1, 3) and (5, 7) and the line through (1, 3) and $(-2, 7)$.

***A7. The Equation of a Straight Line.*** We come now to the main concern of coordinate geometry, namely, relating equations and curves. We begin with the straight line, which is also spoken of as a curve in coordinate geometry.

    To know a line implies that one knows some facts which determine that line. Thus if we know a point $(x_1, y_1)$ on a line and the slope $m$ of the line, the line is fixed or unique (Fig. 3A-12). We shall find its equation. Let $(x, y)$ be the coordinates of *any* other point on the line. Then by (2) we have that

$$m = \frac{y - y_1}{x - x_1}$$

or

(8)                         $$y - y_1 = m(x - x_1).$$

**Figure 3A-12**

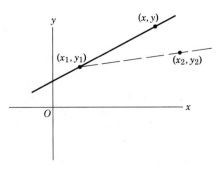

Equation (8) is the equation of the line because the coordinates $(x, y)$ of *any* point on the line satisfy the equation. Moreover, any point not on the line does not satisfy the equation because such a point, say $(x_2, y_2)$ in Fig. 3A-12, and $(x_1, y_1)$ determine a line with a different slope. Equation (8) is known as the *point-slope equation* of a straight line.

Our discussion of equation (8) illustrates the general definition.

**Definition:** The equation of a curve is an equation involving $x$ and $y$ which is satisfied by the coordinates of any point on the curve but is not satisfied by the coordinates of any point not on the curve.

Equation (8) gives the equation of a straight line, if we know one point on the line and its slope. There is a special case of (8) which is often used. Suppose that the known is a point on the $y$-axis (Fig. 3A-13) and its coordinates are $(0, b)$. The quantity $b$ is called the $y$-intercept of the line. Then equation (8) becomes

**(9)** $$y = mx + b.$$

Equation (9) is known as the *slope-intercept equation* of a straight line.

A straight line is also determined if two points on the line are fixed. Suppose that the two points are $(x_1, y_1)$ and $(x_2, y_2)$. Then by (2) we know that

$$m = \frac{y_2 - y_1}{x_2 - x_1}.$$

We now know a point on the line and its slope. Then by equation (8) the equation of the line is

$$y - y_1 = \frac{y_2 - y_1}{x_2 - x_1}(x - x_1)$$

or, in the more symmetrical form obtained by dividing both sides by $(x - x_1)$,

**(10)** $$\frac{y - y_1}{x - x_1} = \frac{y_2 - y_1}{x_2 - x_1}$$

Equation (10) is known as the *two-point form of the equation* of the straight line. For the moment we exclude the possibility that $x_2 = x_1$.

**Figure 3A-13**

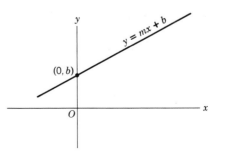

**Example 1.** Find the equation of the line that goes through the point (3, 2) and has a slope of 4. Do the points (6, 5) and (5, 10) lie on that line?

**Solution.** We use (8) to find the equation of the line. Thus (3, 2) are $(x_1, y_1)$ and $m = 4$. Hence

$$y - 2 = 4(x - 3).$$

To test whether (6, 5) lies on this line we use the fact that the coordinates of any point on the line satisfy the equation. Hence is $5 - 2 = 4(6 - 3)$? The equality does not hold and so (6, 5) does not lie on the line. On the other hand, for the point (5, 10), is $10 - 2 = 4(5 - 3)$? The latter equality does hold and the point (5, 10) lies on the line.

**Example 2.** Find the equation of the line determined by the points $(-2, 4)$ and (5, 6).

**Solution.** We may use (10) and let $(x_1, y_1)$ be $(-2, 4)$ and $(x_2, y_2)$ be (5, 6). Then

$$\frac{y - 4}{x - (-2)} = \frac{6 - 4}{5 - (-2)}$$

or

$$\frac{y - 4}{x + 2} = \frac{2}{7}$$

or

$$2x - 7y = -32.$$

## EXERCISES

1. (a) Find the equation of the line which passes through the point (1, 2) and has a slope of 5.      *Ans.* $y - 2 = 5(x - 1)$.
   (b) Does the point with coordinates (2, 3) lie on the line?
2. Find the equation of the line:
   (a) Passing through (2, 3) and (7, $-5$).      *Ans.* $y - 3 = -\frac{8}{5}(x - 2)$.
   (b) Passing through (0, 5) and having the slope $-2$.
   (c) Passing through (3, 0) and having the slope 2.      *Ans.* $y = 2(x - 3)$.
   (d) Whose $y$-intercept is 5 and has the slope $-4$.
3. Show that the three points whose coordinates are (3, 6), (4, 7), and (5, 8) lie on one straight line.      *Ans.* $y = x + 3$.
4. Find the equation of the line:
   (a) Passing through (3, 4) and parallel to the line whose slope is 2.
        *Ans.* $y - 4 = 2(x - 3)$.
   (b) Passing through (4, 2) and perpendicular to the line whose slope is 2.
5. Find the tangent of the angle between $y = 3x + 7$ and $y = -2x + 5$.      *Ans.* 1.

Let us now note that the equation of any straight line can be written in the form

**(11)** $$Ax + By + C = 0.$$

Thus equation (8) when written in this form is

$$mx - y - mx_1 + y_1 = 0.$$

Here $A = m$, $B = -1$, and $C = -mx_1 + y_1$. We see then that the equation of any line is of the form (11) and we note that (11) is an equation of the first degree in $x$ and $y$.

The converse is also true, that is, an equation of the first degree in $x$ and $y$ represents a straight line. To prove this, suppose that we start with $B \neq 0$. Then (11) can be written in the form

$$y = -\frac{A}{B} x - \frac{C}{B}.$$

If we compare this equation with (9), we see that it represents a straight line with slope $m = -A/B$ and $y$-intercept $b = -C/B$.

If $B = 0$ and $A \neq 0$ in (11), it reads

$$Ax + 0y + C = 0$$

or

$$x = -\frac{C}{A}.$$

Where are all the points for which $x = -C/A$? Because all the points have the same $x$-coordinate, they must lie on the line parallel to the $y$-axis and at a distance $-C/A$ to the right or to the left depending on whether $-C/A$ is positive or negative.

Thus we have proved the following theorem:

**Theorem:** The equation of any straight line can be written in the form

**(12)** $$Ax + By + C = 0$$

and every equation of the form (12) in which $A \neq 0$ or $B \neq 0$ represents a straight line.

The first degree equation in $x$ and $y$ is also called a linear equation because it represents the straight line.

## EXERCISES

1. Find the slope and the $y$-intercept of the straight line whose equation is the following:

(a) $2x + 3y + 5 = 0$.  
                                       *Ans.* $-\frac{2}{3}$; $-\frac{5}{3}$.

(b) $3x - 4y = 7$.

(c) $3x + 4y = 0$.      *Ans.* $-\frac{3}{4}$; $0$.

2. Describe the line whose equation is $y = 3$.

3. Find the equation of the line passing through $(1, 2)$ and parallel to the line $3x + y + 7 = 0$.                        *Ans.* $3x + y - 5 = 0$.

4. Find the equation of the line passing through $(5, -1)$ and perpendicular to the line $3x + y + 7 = 0$.

5. Show that if the line $Ax + By + C = 0$ passes through the origin, then $C = 0$.

6. Find the condition that the lines $Ax + By + C = 0$ and $ax + by + c = 0$ be parallel.                        *Ans.* $Ab = aB$.

7. Show that the lines $3x + 2y = 7$ and $2x - 3y = 7$ are perpendicular.

8. What is the inclination of the line $3x + 2y = 7$?

9. Find the tangent of the angle between $3x + 2y = 5$ and $x - 7y = 6$.
                                                         *Ans.* 2.09.

10. Determine which of the following sets of three points lie on one line.

    *Suggestion:* One method is to find the equation of the line joining two of the points and then see if the coordinates of the third point satisfy the equation of the line.

(a)   $(-7, -2), (5, 3), (-\frac{11}{5}, 0)$.          (c)   $(-6, 3), (-4, -3), (-2, -10)$.

(b)   $(-1, -3), (2, -1), (14, 6)$.

11. What does each statement below imply about $A$, $B$, and $C$ in the line whose equation is $Ax + By + C = 0$?

(a)   The slope is $\frac{3}{2}$.

(b)   The $x$ and $y$ intercepts are 4 and 3, respectively.

(c)   The line goes through $(0, 0)$.

(d)   The line is parallel to the $x$-axis.

(e)   The line is perpendicular to the $x$-axis.

12. If we take any point $(x, y)$ on any straight line, then by the distance formula $x^2 + y^2 = r^2$ where $r$ is the distance from $(x, y)$ to the origin. Accordingly, the equation of the straight line should be $x^2 + y^2 = r^2$ because the coordinates of any point on the line satisfy the equation. What is wrong with this argument?

**A8. The Distance from a Point to a Line.** A formula that is occasionally useful is the one which shows us how to obtain the distance from a known point $(x_1, y_1)$ to a known line $Ax + By + C = 0$. What we wish to calculate, then, is the distance $PR$ of Fig. 3A-14. There seems to be no direct method of finding $PR$ but, if we introduce the point $S$ which has the same $x$-value as $P$ and lies on the line $Ax + By + C = 0$, we can find the distance $PS$. The $x$-value of $S$ is $x_1$, and because $S$ lies on the line, the $y$-value of $S$, namely $y_2$, must satisfy the equation

$$Ax_1 + By_2 + C = 0.$$

Then

$$y_2 = -\frac{A}{B}x_1 - \frac{C}{B}.$$

Now $PS = y_1 - y_2$ so that

$$PS = y_1 - \left(-\frac{A}{B}x_1 - \frac{C}{B}\right) = y_1 + \frac{A}{B}x_1 + \frac{C}{B}.$$

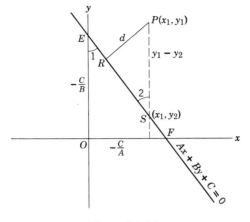

**Figure 3A-14**

If we could obtain some additional fact about triangle $PRS$, we might be able to use it and the value of $PS$ to obtain what we want, that is, $PR$. We note that the given line cuts the $x$- and $y$-axes at $F$ and $E$, respectively, and so forms the triangle $FOE$. Moreover, because $PS$ is parallel to $EO$, $\angle 1 = \angle 2$, and both triangles $FOE$ and $PRS$ are right triangles. Hence the two triangles are similar. Then

**(13)**
$$\frac{PR}{PS} = \frac{OF}{EF}.$$

We can, however, find $OF$ and $EF$. $OF$ is the $x$-intercept of our line, and because $y = 0$ at $F$, we have only to set $y = 0$ in $Ax + By + C = 0$ to find that the abscissa of $F$, $OF = -C/A$. Likewise $OE = -C/B$. Then $EF = \sqrt{(C/A)^2 + (C/B)^2}$. We now know $PS$, $OF$, and $EF$ in (13). If we substitute their values, we have

$$PR = \frac{OF \cdot PS}{EF} = \frac{-\dfrac{C}{A}\left(y_1 + \dfrac{A}{B}x_1 + \dfrac{C}{B}\right)}{\sqrt{\dfrac{C^2}{A^2} + \dfrac{C^2}{B^2}}}.$$

A little algebra simplifies the result. We factor out the $C^2$ from the radical and cancel it and the $C$ above. Then we add the fractions in the radical and take out $AB$. The result thus far is

$$PR = \frac{-\dfrac{1}{A}\left(y_1 + \dfrac{A}{B}x_1 + \dfrac{C}{B}\right)}{\dfrac{1}{AB}\sqrt{A^2 + B^2}}.$$

Inversion of $1/AB$ and multiplication yields

**(14)**
$$PR = \frac{Ax_1 + By_1 + C}{\sqrt{A^2 + B^2}}.$$

We have neglected the minus sign, which usually is not of interest.

Let us note that (14) is easy to remember. The numerator is the result of substituting the coordinates $(x_1, y_1)$ of the given point into $Ax + By + C$. The denominator is the square root of the sum of the squares of the coefficients of $x$ and $y$.

The above proof fails when the line goes through the origin, but formula (14) is still correct. We shall not bother with a proof for this special case.

## EXERCISES

**1.** Find the distance in the following cases:
- (a)  From the point $(2, 1)$ to the line $4x - 3y + 15 = 0$.          *Ans.* 4.
- (b)  From the point $(3, 2)$ to the line $4x - y + 2 = 0$.
- (c)  From the point $(-1, 3)$ to the line $4x + 2y = 0$.          *Ans.* $\sqrt{5}/5$.
- (d)  From the point $(2, 7)$ to the line $3x + 4y - 2 = 0$.

**A9. Equation and Curve.** We have already pointed out that the main concern of coordinate geometry is to associate curves with equations and equations with curves. Thus far we have carried out this task for straight lines. We shall study the relation of curve and equation for more complicated cases throughout the book. For the present, however, we shall resort when necessary to the method introduced in Chapter 2 for finding the curve of a function, namely, making a table of values of $x$ and $y$ and plotting the corresponding points.

# CHAPTER FOUR
# THE GEOMETRICAL SIGNIFICANCE OF THE DERIVATIVE

***1. The Derivative as Slope.*** We have mentioned the desirability of thinking geometrically as well as algebraically in order to help us understand what we are doing. Let us, therefore, attempt to find a geometrical meaning for the derivative.

To pursue this objective, let us review the process of finding the derivative of

**(1)** $$y = x^2$$

at the value $x_0$ of $x$ and let us interpret each step geometrically. We introduce a rectangular Cartesian coordinate system (Fig. 4-1) in which, as usual, the positive $x$-axis is directed to the right and the positive $y$-axis is directed upward. The function $y = x^2$ is then pictured geometrically by the parabola shown in the figure. The first step in obtaining the derivative at $x_0$ is to calculate the $y$-value at $x_0$. This value is given by

**(2)** $$y_0 = x_0^2.$$

The choice of $x_0$ and the corresponding $y_0$ places us at some point, say $P$, on the curve. We now let the value of $x$ change to $x_0 + \Delta x$ and denote the corresponding value of $y$ by $y_0 + \Delta y$. Then by substituting $x_0 + \Delta x$ in (1) we have

**(3)** $$y_0 + \Delta y = (x_0 + \Delta x)^2 = x_0^2 + 2x_0 \Delta x + (\Delta x)^2.$$

Because $y_0 + \Delta y$ is the value of $y$ corresponding to the value $x_0 + \Delta x$ of $x$, the point whose coordinates are $(x_0 + \Delta x, y_0 + \Delta y)$ is some new point, say

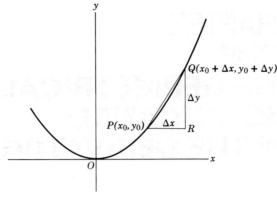

**Figure 4-1**

$Q$, on the curve. In accordance with the method of increments, we now subtract (2) from (3). Then

**(4)** $$\Delta y = 2x_0 \, \Delta x + (\Delta x)^2.$$

The quantity $\Delta y$ is the difference in the ordinates of $P$ and $Q$; geometrically it is the length $RQ$. The quantity $\Delta x$ is the length $PR$.

We now obtain the average rate of change of $y$ with respect to $x$ in the interval $\Delta x$ by dividing both sides of (4) by $\Delta x$. Then

**(5)** $$\frac{\Delta y}{\Delta x} = 2x_0 + \Delta x.$$

The quantity $\Delta y / \Delta x$ has an important geometrical interpretation. The slope of a line is given by (see formula (2) of the Appendix to Chapter 3)

$$m = \frac{y_2 - y_1}{x_2 - x_1}.$$

**Figure 4-2**

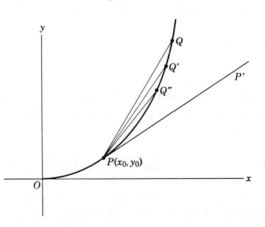

In this formula $(x_1, y_1)$ and $(x_2, y_2)$ are the coordinates of any two points on the line. Now $\Delta y$ is the difference in the $y$-values of $P$ and $Q$ in Fig. 4-1. Likewise $\Delta x$ is the difference in the $x$-values of $P$ and $Q$. Hence

$$\frac{\Delta y}{\Delta x} = \text{slope of secant } PQ.$$

To obtain the derivative $dy/dx$ at $x_0$, we must now let $\Delta x$ approach 0 and then determine the limit of $\Delta y/\Delta x$. That $\Delta x$ becomes smaller means geometrically that $Q$ moves along the curve toward $P$. Thus, for some smaller value of $\Delta x$ than shown in Fig. 4-1, $Q$ might move to $Q'$ (Fig. 4-2). Of course, when $\Delta x$ becomes smaller, $\Delta y$ also becomes smaller, as we can see geometrically or from (4). For the $\Delta x$ and $\Delta y$ that correspond to $Q'$, $\Delta y/\Delta x$ is the slope of the secant line $PQ'$.

Algebraically the limit of $\Delta y/\Delta x$ is $2x_0$; that is,

**(6)**
$$\frac{dy}{dx} = 2x_0.$$

As $\Delta x$ approaches 0, the points $Q, Q', Q'', \ldots$ approach $P$. Geometrically, the lines $PQ, PQ', PQ'', \ldots$ seem to approach a fixed line, namely, the line through $P$ which just touches the curve at $P$, the line $PP'$ in the figure. That is, the line $PP'$ seems to be the limit of the lines $PQ, PQ', \cdots$. Because for each choice of $\Delta x$, $\Delta y/\Delta x$ is the slope of one of the secants through $P$ and $dy/dx$ is the limit of $\Delta y/\Delta x$, then $dy/dx$ should be the slope of the limit approached by the secants, that is, the slope of $PP'$. To be specific, when $x_0$ is 1, then $dy/dx$ is 2 and the slope of the line $PP'$ is 2.

**2. The Concept of Tangent to a Curve.** We propose to pursue more carefully the nature of the line $PP'$ which is the limit of the secants $PQ, PQ', PQ'', \cdots$. The line $PP'$ just touches the curve $y = x^2$ at $(x_0, y_0)$; that is, it has only point $P$ in common with the curve. For if it cut the curve in some point, say $\overline{Q}$, near $P$, $P\overline{Q}$ would be one of the secant lines. The fact that $PP'$ is the limit of secant lines $PQ$ as $Q$ approaches $P$ and that $PP'$ has only point $P$ in common with the curve near $P$, suggests that we take $PP'$ to be the tangent to the curve at $P$. Moreover, we learn from the argument in Section 1 that *the slope of the tangent at $(x_0, y_0)$ is the derivative of the function $y = f(x)$ evaluated at $x_0$.*

We have, then, not only obtained a geometric meaning for the derivative, but have introduced a new definition of tangent, namely that it is the

**Figure 4-3**

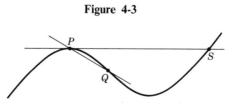

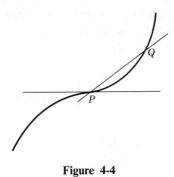

**Figure 4-4**

limit of secants through the point $P$ of tangency. One might ask, how does this notion of tangent square with the notion used in Euclidean geometry in which the tangent to a curve is a line which has only one point in common with a curve and does not cross the curve? The answer is that the present notion generalizes the older Euclidean notion. This generalization is needed to treat the variety of curves with which the calculus deals. Consider, for example, the line $PS$ of Fig. 4-3. It has two points in common with the curve, namely, $P$ and $S$. Yet intuitively we feel that it is a tangent at $P$. It would not be a tangent in the Euclidean sense because it has two points in common with the curve. It is a tangent in our more general sense because it is the limiting line of the secants $PQ$ as $Q$ approaches $P$.

Again, the horizontal line through $P$ of Fig. 4-4 is not a tangent in the Euclidean sense because it crosses the curve at $P$. It is a tangent under the more general definition because it is the limiting line of the secants $PQ$ as $Q$ approaches $P$.

Let us see if our geometrical interpretation of the derivative holds up. The derivative of $y = x^2$ at $x_0 = -2$, in view of (6), is $-4$. According to Fig. 4-5, the line through $(-2, 4)$ on the curve with slope of $-4$ does seem to be the tangent to the curve at the point $(-2, 4)$.

**3. *Application of the Derivative as the Slope.*** From the standpoint of application the fact that the derivative at any value $x_0$ of $x$ is the slope of

**Figure 4-5**

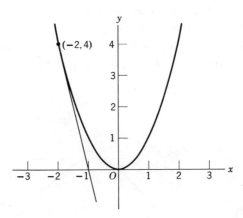

**Figure 4-6**

the tangent at the point $(x_0, y_0)$ of the curve is very significant. First, the derivative solves the purely geometrical problem of finding the tangent to a curve at any point on that curve. Because the derivative gives the slope of the tangent line and because we have a point on that line, we know the line precisely.

Second, we often have to consider the physical situation of an automobile or a train climbing a hill. It is important to know the slope of the hill or curve at any point. We define the slope of the *curve* at a point to be the slope of the tangent to the curve at that point. This definition is quite reasonable. The slope of the curve at $P$ in Fig. 4-6 is approximated, although poorly, by the slope of $PQ$. However, as $Q$ approaches $P$, the slope of the line $PQ$ approximates the slope of the curve better and better. Hence the slope of the curve at $P$ should be the slope of the tangent at $P$.

To understand how useful this definition of the slope of a curve can be, let us consider the roadway of a bridge which is shown as the arc $AOB$ in Fig. 4-7. For the purpose of our illustration we can assume that this arc is part of the parabola $y = -x^2$. The slope of the curve at $x = -2$ is given by the derivative. Because the derived function of $y = -x^2$ at an arbitrary value of $x$ is $-2x$, the derivative at $x = -2$ is $+4$. This then is the slope of the roadway at $x = -2$; that is, at $x = -2$ the roadway rises at the rate of 4 feet for every foot of horizontal distance. This rate of climb is totally impractical, because no automobile or truck has the power to climb at such a rate. Our example thus makes the general point that the derivative enables us to calculate the slope of an inclined roadway and to determine whether the slope is or is not too steep for the vehicles that are to use that road.

**Figure 4-7**

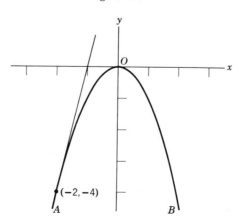

There is another use for the tangent to a curve and hence for the derivative. Suppose that an object moves along a curve. Then the direction in which the object is moving, when at any point on the curve, is taken to be the direction of the tangent to the curve at that point. The reasonableness of this definition of direction of motion is readily seen from Fig. 4-2. If the object at $P$ were to move directly to $Q$, we would surely take $PQ$ to be its direction of motion. If, instead, the object were to move from $P$ directly to $Q'$, we would take $PQ'$ to be its direction of motion. The more the object tends to follow the curve, the closer its direction of motion approaches the direction of the tangent at $P$. Hence for an object which moves along the curve, the direction of its motion when at $P$ is the direction of the tangent at $P$.

There is another use for the interpretation of the derivative as the slope of the curve of the formula. In Chapter 3 we found, for example, that the formula which represents the height above the ground of an object that is thrown up with an initial velocity of 128 ft/sec is given by

(7)
$$h = -16t^2 + 128t.$$

The graph of this formula, obtained by point-for-point plotting, is shown in Fig. 4-8. We know now that the slope of this curve at any point $P$ is the value of the derivative of formula (7) at the abscissa of $P$. However, the derivative of (7) is the velocity of the object at the point $P$. Hence the velocity can be interpreted geometrically as the slope of the curve representing the relation between height above the ground and time.

We should note that the curve in Fig. 4-8 is not a picture of the physical motion, which would be straight up and down. Nevertheless, the curve does show how the height varies with time, and its slope shows how the velocity changes. It is often convenient, as in Fig. 4-8, to use a different unit for length on the $y$-axis from that on the $x$-axis. In such cases the slope of the *graph* will not agree with the value of the derivative. Nevertheless, the knowledge that the slope is the velocity is still helpful.

To solve some problems involving the tangent to a curve at a point, it

**Figure 4-8**

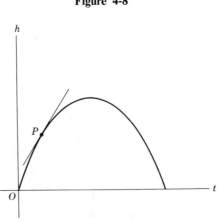

is desirable to employ the equation of the tangent. Let us consider the tangent to $y = 2x^2$ at $x = 3$ and $y = 18$. We know that the slope of this tangent is the value of the derivative $y'$ at $x = 3$. The slope at any value of $x$ is

$$y' = 4x$$

and the slope at $x = 3$ is 12. Because at $x = 3$, $y = 18$, the tangent passes through the point (3, 18). We have then the slope of the tangent line and the coordinates of one point on that line. To find the equation of the tangent, we can use the point-slope form of the equation of a straight line, namely,

$$y - y_1 = m(x - x_1).$$

In the present case we obtain

$$y - 18 = 12(x - 3)$$

or

$$y = 12x - 18.$$

## EXERCISES

1. Draw carefully the graph of $y = x^2$ and from it find the slope of the tangent at the point (3, 9). Does your measurement of the slope agree with the value of $y'$ at $x = 3$?

*Ans.* $m = 6$.

2. Calculate the slope of the tangent to the curve of the following formulas:
   (a)  $s = 4t^2$ at $t = 2$.       *Ans.* 16.   (c)  $y = -x^2 + 6x$ at $x = 2$.
   (b)  $y = 2x^2$ at $x = 1$.

   *Ans.* 2.

   (d)  $y = -x^2 + 6x$ at $x = 3$.
   Draw the graph in each case and see if the calculation agrees with the visual estimate of the slope of the tangent.

3. Find the angle of inclination of the tangent to the curve of the following:
   (a)  $y = x^2$ at $x = 3$.                 (d)  $y = -x^2$ at $x = 0$.
   
   *Ans.* 80° 32'.          (e)  $y = -x^2 + 6x$ at $x = 3$.
   
   (b)  $y = 16x^2$ at $x = 2$.                                    *Ans.* 0°.
   (c)  $y = x^2$ at $x = -2$.
   
   *Ans.* 104° 2'.

4. Suppose that an object is moving along a curve whose equation is $y = -4x^2 + 16x$ and is at the point whose abscissa is 3. Specify the direction of motion of the object in terms of the slope and the angle of inclination of the tangent.

   *Ans.* $-8$; 97° 7'.

5. Suppose that an object moving along the curve whose equation is $y = -4x^2 + 16x$ strikes a (vertical) wall whose equation is $x = +2$. Would you describe the direction of impact as head-on or glancing?

6. Find the equation of the tangent to the curve whose equation is the following:
   (a)  $y = x^2$ at $x = -3$.                 (b)  $y = x^2 - 6x$ at $x = 2$.
   
   *Ans.* $y = -6x - 9$.

7. Suppose that a path up a hill can be represented by the function $y = \frac{1}{100} x^2$ for $x$ in the interval 0 to 6.
   (a)  What is the slope of the hill at $x = 3$?                 *Ans.* $\frac{3}{50}$.
   (b)  Is the slope steeper at $x = 3$ or at $x = 5$?

8. Prove that no two tangents of the curve $y = x^2$ are parallel.

9. Find the slope of the tangent to the curve $y = x^3$ at $x = 0$, $x = 1$, and $x = -1$. (We found in Chapter 2, Section 8, Exercise 4 that the derived function of $y = x^3$ is $3x^2$.) Draw the curve and the tangents. Note that the tangent crosses the curve at $x = 0$.        *Ans.* 0, 3, 3.

10. Find a point on the curve $y = x^3$ at which the tangent is parallel to the tangent at $x = 4$.

11. Given a function whose graph for the domain from $a$ to $b$ is shown in Fig. 4-9, describe the variation in the value of the derivative as the values of $x$ vary from $a$ to $b$.

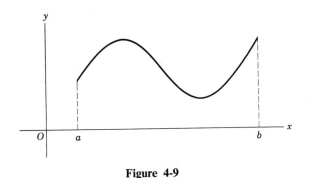

Figure 4-9

12. Suppose that the height above the surface of the earth of some object which moves along a vertical path varies during the time interval from 0 to $b$ as shown in Fig. 4-10. When was the velocity greatest? Least? Zero?
                               *Ans.* At 0; at $t = b$; at maximum point.

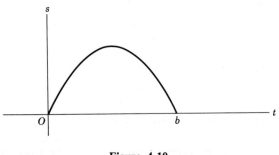

Figure 4-10

13. Show geometrically that the functions $y = x^2$ and $y = x^2 + 5$ must have the same derived function.

14. Express the following statements in symbols:
   (a)  The slope of a curve at any point equals the abscissa of that point.
                                        *Ans.* $y' = x$.

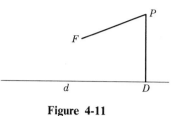

**Figure 4-11**

    (b)   The ordinate of a curve at any point is a constant times the square of the slope at that point.

    (c)   At any point $P$ of a curve the slope is equal to one half of the slope of the line joining $P$ to the origin.                        *Ans.* $y' = y/2x$.

**4. The Equation of the Parabola.** Because we intend to make intensive use of the parabola in a variety of applications, let us establish a few facts about that curve. Geometrically a parabola is defined as follows:

**Definition:** The set of all points each of which is equidistant from a fixed point and a fixed line is a curve called the parabola. The fixed point is called the focus of the parabola and the fixed line is called the directrix.

    Thus, in Fig. 4-11, $F$ is a given fixed point, the focus, and $d$ is a given fixed line, the directrix. Then $P$ is a point on the parabola determined by $F$ and $d$, if and only if $PF = PD$.

    To apply the methods of the calculus to the parabola we need the equation of the parabola, that is, the functional relation between the coordinates $x$ and $y$ of all points on the parabola. We can make the equation as simple as possible if we make the following choice of axes. We choose the perpendicular line from the focus to the directrix as the $y$-axis (Fig. 4-12) and we choose the $x$-axis as the line which passes halfway between the focus and the directrix. With this choice of axes and if $2p$ is the (fixed) distance between the focus and the directrix, the coordinates of the focus become $(0, p)$ and the equation of the directrix is $y = -p$.

**Figure 4-12**

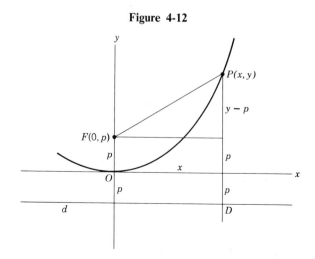

Now let the coordinates of any point $P$ on the parabola be $(x, y)$. According to the definition of the parabola

(8) $$PF = PD.$$

The length $PF$ is the hypotenuse of a right triangle whose sides have length $y - p$ and $x$. Then

$$PF = \sqrt{x^2 + (y - p)^2} \ .$$

The length $PD$ is seen from the figure to be $y + p$. Then, in view of (8),

$$\sqrt{x^2 + (y - p)^2} = y + p.$$

We could stop at this point and rightly maintain that we have the equation of the parabola, but a little algebra simplifies the result. If we square both sides, we obtain

$$x^2 + (y - p)^2 = (y + p)^2$$

or

$$x^2 + y^2 - 2py + p^2 = y^2 + 2py + p^2.$$

We subtract equal quantities from both sides and obtain

(9) $$y = \frac{1}{4p} x^2.$$

Equation (9) is the equation of the parabola. We should note that there is not one parabola but an indefinite number of them. Each choice of a value of $p$, which means each choice of a distance from focus to directrix, determines a different parabola.

If we did not happen to know what a parabola looks like, we could choose a value of $p$ and sketch the curve. Figure 4-12 shows the general appearance of a parabola. Each such curve is symmetric about a line which is called the *axis* of the parabola. This axis happens to be the $y$-axis when the coordinate system is chosen as in Fig. 4-12. The point at which the axis cuts the parabola, the point $O$ in Fig. 4-12, is called the *vertex* of the parabola.

Thus we have the following result.

**Theorem:** The equation of the parabola whose focus is $(0, p)$ and whose directrix is $y = -p$ is $y = \frac{1}{4p} x^2$.

**Example.** Find the equation of the parabola whose focus is at $(0, 6)$ and whose directrix is the line $y = -6$.

**Solution.** The given focus and directrix meet the conditions in the theorem if we take $p$ to be 6. Then the equation of the parabola is $y = \frac{1}{24} x^2$.

## EXERCISES

1. Find the equation of the parabola:
   (a)  whose focus is at $(0, \frac{5}{2})$ and whose directrix is $y = -\frac{5}{2}$.
   (b)  whose focus is at $(0, 1.5)$ and whose directrix is $y = -1.5$.

2. Suppose that the equation of a parabola is $y = \frac{1}{12} x^2$. What are the coordinates of the focus and what is the equation of the directrix?

3. Suppose that the equation of a parabola is $y = \frac{1}{12} x^2$. What is the width of the parabola at the height of the focus? This width is called the *latus rectum*. Can you generalize the result for any parabola whose equation is $y = (1/4p)x^2$?

   *Ans.* $4p$.

4. Suppose that the focus and directrix lie as shown in Fig. 4-13 and that the axes are chosen as shown. Guess what the equation of the parabola is and then derive it in the manner indicated in the text.           *Ans.* $x = (1/4p)y^2$.

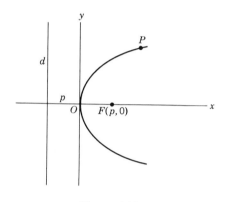

**Figure 4-13**

5. Suppose that the focus and the directrix lie as shown in Fig. 4-14 and that the axes are chosen as shown. Guess what the equation of the parabola is and then derive it in the manner indicated in the text.

   *Suggestion:* Remember that $p$ is positive and that the $y$-values of the points $P$ are negative. Hence, for example, the distance $PD$ is $-y + p$.

   *Ans.* $y = -(1/4p)x^2$.

**Figure 4-14**

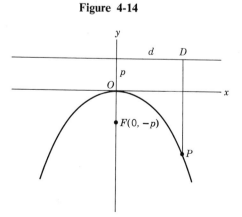

6. For each of the parabolas in exercises (a) to (d) find the coordinates of the focus, the equation of the directrix and the length of the latus rectum. (Cf. Exercises 3, 4 and 5.) Draw a sketch of the curve.
   (a) $x^2 = 16y$   (b) $y^2 = -8x$   (c) $2y^2 - 9x = 0$   (d) $3x^2 + 4y = 0$

7. Find the equation of the parabola having the given properties:
   (a) focus $(5, 0)$; directrix $x = -5$;   (b) focus $(0, -2)$; directrix $y - 2 = 0$;
   (c) focus $(\frac{1}{2}, 0)$; directrix $2x + 1 = 0$.

8. Given the focus and the directrix of a parabola and the axes as shown in Fig. 4-15, derive the equation of the parabola. Now that you have the answer, compare the position of the parabola with that in Fig. 4-12 and see if you can derive the answer from the equation $y = (1/4p)x^2$.   *Ans.* $y = [(1/4p)x^2] - p$.

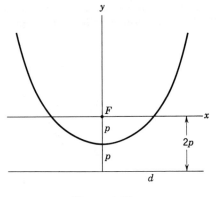

**Figure 4-15**

9. Suppose that the coordinate axes are chosen so that the focus of a parabola has the coordinates $(4, 0)$ and the directrix has the equation $y = -8$ (Fig. 4-16). Find the equation of the parabola.        *Ans.* $y = \frac{1}{16}x^2 - \frac{1}{2}x - 3$.

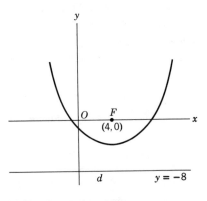

**Figure 4-16**

10. Describe in words how:
    (a)   $y = x^2 + 6$ differs from $y = x^2$.
    (b)   $y = 3x^2$ differs from $y = x^2$.
    (c)   $y = (x + 6)^2$ differs from
          $y = x^2$.

**11.** (a) Prove that the tangent at any point of the parabola $y = x^2/4p$ cuts the $x$-axis halfway between the origin and the abscissa of the point of tangency.

  (b) Using this result give a construction for the tangent to a parabola at a given point.

**12.** A high voltage cable is supported by two towers 2800 feet apart and 348 feet high. The cable hangs in approximately the shape of a parabola, and the lowest point on the cable is 200 feet above the ground. Find the equation of the parabola.                    *Ans.* $y = 37x^2/490,000$.

**13.** A parabolic arch supports a bridge over a roadway. The width of the roadway is 50 feet and the center of the arch is 25 feet above the center of the roadway. A truck 10 feet high wishes to pass under the arch and plans to keep its right-hand wheels 2 feet from the right-hand edge of the roadway. Is there enough overhead clearance for the truck?

**14.** A ship wishes to sail along a path which will keep it equidistant from a battery of guns located at $F$ (Fig. 4-17) and along the shore 30 miles away. Write an equation for the path that the ship should take.

$Ans.$ $y = x^2/60$ if origin is midway and $x$-axis is parallel to shore.

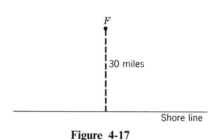

**Figure 4-17**

**15.** Prove that the foot of the perpendicular from the focus to any tangent of a parabola lies on the tangent to the vertex.

  *Suggestion:* If two lines are perpendicular to each other, the slope of one is the negative reciprocal of the slope of the other.

**16.** Prove that the point of intersection of two tangents to a parabola which are perpendicular to each other lies on the directrix.

**17.** In Fig. 4-18 the length $QT$, which is described as the projection of $PT$ on the axis of the parabola, is called the subtangent. The line $PR$, which is perpendic-

**Figure 4-18**

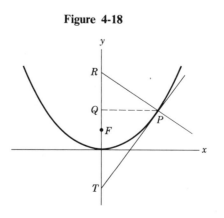

ular to the tangent at $P$, is called the normal to the parabola at $P$ and the length $QR$, which is the projection of $PR$ on the axis, is called the subnormal. (a) Prove that the vertex bisects the subtangent of any tangent to the parabola. Hence describe a method of constructing the tangent at $P$. (b) Prove that the length of the subnormal is $2p$.

**5. Physical Applications of the Derivative as Slope.** One of the most important uses of the parabola is to concentrate light, sound, and radio waves in a particular direction. Let us see first what this means. Suppose that a source of light, say a flashlight bulb with nothing surrounding it, is placed at some point in space and that by somehow feeding electric current to it the bulb is lit. Then light rays emanate from the bulb and spread out into space uniformly in all directions. This light is not concentrated at all. We know, however, that by using a suitable reflector which partially surrounds this bulb we obtain a strong beam in one direction. Such reflectors are used, for example, in powerful searchlights and in automobile headlights. What shape should the reflector have in order to reflect in one direction all the rays that strike it?

It seems evident on physical grounds that a surface of revolution should be sought. For suppose that the source of light is placed at $F$ (Fig. 4-19) and the reflector is placed below and about $F$ so as to reflect the light in the upward direction $FF'$. Now suppose that a ray making some angle $A$ with the upwardly directed line $FF'$ leaves $F$ and strikes the point $P$ on the surface and that at $P$ the surface is so shaped that the reflected ray takes the upward course $PD$. Consider next another ray leaving $F$ and making the same angle $A$ with $FF'$. If the surface of revolution has the axis $FF'$, this ray strikes the surface at some point $P'$ at the same level as $P$. Moreover, because the shape of the surface at $P'$ is the same as at $P$, this ray is also reflected directly upward. What we want then is a surface of revolution generated by revolving the curve $OPQ$ of Fig. 4-19 about the line $OFF'$. If $OPQ$ is correctly designed, the whole surface will direct the reflected light upward.

Our problem reduces then to choosing the shape of the curve $OPQ$, so that light rays from $F$ striking various points on this curve are all reflected upward. To design $OPQ$ correctly, we must know how light rays behave

**Figure 4-19**

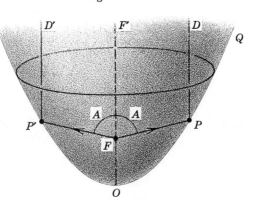

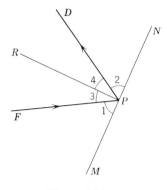

**Figure 4-20**

when they strike a reflecting surface. The relevant behavior of light rays is embodied in the *law of reflection*. Suppose for the moment that *MN* is a *flat* reflecting mirror (Fig. 4-20) and that a light ray emanating from *F* strikes the mirror at *P*. Then the reflected ray takes the path *PD* for which ∢1 = ∢2. Alternatively stated, if we introduce the perpendicular or normal *PR* to the mirror at *P*, the reflected ray takes the path for which ∢3 = ∢4. Of course, the equality of angles 1 and 2 is equivalent to the equality of angles 3 and 4. In physics ∢3 is called the angle of incidence and ∢4 is the angle of reflection, so that the law of reflection states that the angle of incidence equals the angle of reflection. Where convenient, we can also call ∢1 the angle of incidence and ∢2 the angle of reflection.

Now suppose that we reintroduce the curve *OPQ* (Fig. 4-21) and the light ray *FP* that strikes the curve at *P*. At *P* the curve behaves as though it were replaced by the tangent at *P*. This behavior is to be expected, for only a very little bit of the curve at *P* has anything to do with the reflection of the ray *FP*. What does count about the curve at *P* is the direction in which it is going, so to speak, or the angle that it makes with *FP*. However, at *P* the direction of the curve is the direction of the tangent. In other words, for the purpose of studying the reflection of light, at each point a curve may be replaced by its tangent.

What do we want now? We know that at *P* the reflected light ray takes the path which makes ∢2 = ∢1. We want to fix the curve so that the

**Figure 4-21**

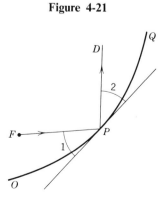

reflected ray takes the upward path *PD*. Hence we must choose a curve *such that the line FP makes the same angle with the tangent at P as the upward direction PD makes with the tangent at P*. If the curve is so chosen, the light ray *FP* is automatically reflected in the upward direction.

To find the proper curve we could set up in mathematical terms the condition we have just described and then try to determine the curve. This problem can be solved, but it is also wise to see if some known curve possesses this property. Actually, the Greeks discovered that the parabola reflects light rays issuing from the focus, so that the reflected rays all travel out parallel to the axis of the parabola. We shall prove that the parabola does this, that is, we shall prove that for the parabola *OPQ* (Fig. 4-22) the lines *FP* and *PD*, when *PD* is parallel to the axis *OF*, make equal angles with the tangent at *P* or that $\angle 1 = \angle 2$.

The proof is straightforward. We choose the *x*- and *y*-axes as shown in Fig. 4-22. We see, first, that $\angle 3 = \angle 2$ because *PD* is parallel to the *y*-axis. Hence we should prove that $\angle 1 = \angle 3$. We can prove this if we can prove that *FP = FT*. Let us try to do this.

If we designate $(x_1, y_1)$ to be the coordinates of *P* and if the coordinates of the focus are, as usual, $(0, p)$, we see that *FP* is the hypotenuse of a right triangle whose arms are $y_1 - p$ and $x_1$. Then

**(10)** $$FP = \sqrt{x_1^2 + (y_1 - p)^2} = \sqrt{x_1^2 + y_1^2 - 2y_1 p + p^2}.$$

However, because $(x_1, y_1)$ is a point on the parabola, by (9)

**(11)** $$x_1^2 = 4py_1.$$

If we substitute this value of $x_1^2$ in (10), we obtain

**(12)** $$FP = y_1 + p.$$

Now let us obtain an expression for *FT*. We see from Fig. 4-22 that

**(13)** $$FT = FO + OT = p + OT.$$

**Figure 4-22**

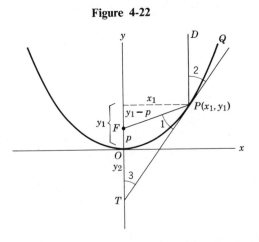

However, $OT$ is the $y$-value of the point at which the tangent at $P$ cuts the $y$-axis; that is, $OT$ is the $y$-intercept of the tangent. Let us therefore find the equation of the tangent at $P$ and find its $y$-intercept. To find the equation of the tangent, we use the point-slope form of the equation of a line; this calls for the slope of the tangent. The slope of the tangent is the derivative of the curve at $(x_1, y_1)$. The equation of the curve is

$$y = \frac{1}{4p} x^2.$$

Because the derived function of $y = ax^2$ is $y' = 2ax$, in our case

$$y' = \frac{1}{2p} x,$$

and at $(x_1, y_1)$

$$y' = \frac{1}{2p} x_1.$$

Then by using the point-slope form of the equation of the straight line [Chap. 3, Appendix, (8)] the equation of the tangent becomes

$$y - y_1 = \frac{x_1}{2p} (x - x_1),$$

where $x$ and $y$ refer to *coordinates of points on the tangent*. The $y$-intercept of the tangent is the point at which $x = 0$. Hence the $y$-value of $T$, say $y_2$, is

$$y_2 - y_1 = \frac{x_1}{2p} (0 - x_1) = - \frac{x_1^2}{2p}$$

or

$$y_2 = y_1 - \frac{x_1^2}{2p} .$$

However, in view of (11)

$$y_2 = y_1 - 2y_1 = -y_1.$$

Now $y_1$ is a positive quantity and therefore $y_2$ is negative as indeed it should be. We are, however, interested in the *geometric* length $OT$ and therefore we may say that

$$OT = y_1.$$

Then by (13)

**(14)** $$FT = p + y_1.$$

If we now compare (12) and (14), we see that we have proved that $FP = FT$. Then $\angle 3 = \angle 1$ and therefore $\angle 1 = \angle 2$. Thus we have proved an important geometrical property of the parabola: The line from the focus to any point $P$ on the parabola and the line through $P$ and parallel to the axis make equal angles with the tangent. Because light rays obey the physical law that the angle of incidence must equal the angle of reflection, a light ray issuing from $F$ and striking the parabola at $P$ takes the direction $PD$. The point $P$ is any point on the parabola. Hence *all* rays from $F$ travel after reflection in the direction of the axis of the parabola.

If a surface is formed by rotating the arc $OPQ$ of the parabola about its axis, we obtain what is called a paraboloid of revolution, and all rays issuing from $P$ and striking any point on the paraboloid travel out parallel to the axis of the paraboloid. The paraboloid is such a powerful concentrator of light, sound, and radio waves that its use has become very widespread. It is used not only in the reflectors of flashlights and searchlights but in hundreds of different types of radio antennas.

## EXERCISES

1. Where does the calculus enter into the proof of the reflection property of the parabola?
2. Review the proof of the reflecting property of the parabola and determine whether it also establishes that the parabola is the only curve which reflects rays from a point source into a parallel beam of rays.
3. Prove that if the chord (Fig. 4-23) joining the points of tangency of two tangents to a parabola goes through the focus, the tangents are perpendicular to each other.

    *Suggestion:* Use the reflection property of the parabola.

**Figure 4-23**

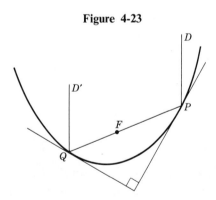

4. Prove the reflection property of the parabola by the following method. Use the formula for the tangent of the angle between two lines [Chap. 3, Appendix, (7)].

Our knowledge of the calculus enables us to solve another physical problem of considerable significance*—the problem of determining the shape of the cable of a bridge when the total weight of the load, the cable

* This application can be omitted without disrupting the continuity.

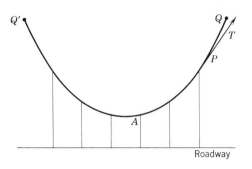

Figure 4-24

and the roadway per horizontal foot is constant. The cable is assumed to be perfectly flexible (that is, it offers no resistance to bending) and inelastic (that is, it does not stretch or contract). Both properties are possessed, for example, by a piece of ordinary rope.

Consider the cable $Q'APQ$ shown in Fig. 4-24. Because the cable supports the roadway, there is tension in the cable. Let us first satisfy ourselves that at any point on the cable the tension that any part of the cable exerts on an adjoining part is along the cable. Specifically we should see that the tension exerted by the arc $QP$ on the rest of the cable has the direction of the tangent at $P$. Intuitively this fact is rather obvious, for if the pull at $P$ were not along the tangent the cable would bend (because it is perfectly flexible) inward or outward. Nevertheless, we may consider a supporting argument.

Suppose that the cable were made up of short rods (Fig. 4-25) which were linked at the joints and that the rods were free to move at the joints. At any point within any rod the tension is merely along the rod, because one part of a rod can pull another part of the same rod only along the rod. At a joint such as $P$ the pull of the rod $PR$ on the rod $PQ$ is along $PR$, whereas the pull of the rod $PQ$ on the rod $PR$ is along $PQ$. The two rods make an angle with each other at $P$, and the two pulls are in different directions. We now imagine that the rods are made smaller and smaller and that of course more joints are introduced to connect adjacent rods. As the rods become smaller, the shape of the whole chain of rods approaches that of the original, completely flexible cable and the directions of the pulls or tensions within a rod or at a joint of two rods approaches that of the tangent to the flexible cable at the corresponding point.

Now let us consider any section of the flexible cable, say the section from $A$ to $P$ in Fig. 4-26. Because the pull at $A$ by the section to the left of $A$ is tangential to the cable, at $A$ the pull or tension is horizontal and to the

Figure 4-25

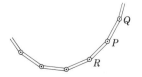

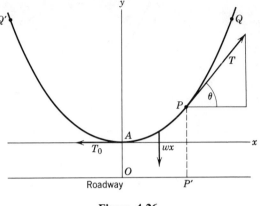

**Figure 4-26**

left. This tension is some constant which we shall denote by $T_0$. The tension on $AP$ at $P$ exerted by the section $PQ$ of the cable is along the tangent at $P$. Let us call the magnitude of this tension $T$. Because this tension also has a direction, namely, the direction of the tangent at $P$, it is represented geometrically by a directed line segment or a vector. We shall let $\theta$ be the angle which the direction of the tension (or the tangent) at $P$ makes with the horizontal.

There is one more force acting on the section $AP$ of the cable, namely, the pull of that portion of the cable, load and the roadway which extends from $O$ to $P'$ (Fig. 4-26). Because the total pull or weight is assumed to be the same per horizontal foot, then, if $w$ is the weight per horizontal foot, the load supported by the arc $AP$ is $wx$, where $x$ is the abscissa of $P$. (We are here using the fact that the $y$-axis passes through $A$.) The pull of this load is actually distributed along $AP$, but all the pulls are downward, and we need to know only that there is a total downward pull on $AP$ amounting to $wx$.

Thus there are three forces acting on $AP$: the horizontal pull $T_0$ to the left, the downward pull $wx$ of the total load, and the tension or pull $T$ tangential at $P$. Because the arc $AP$ is at rest or in equilibrium, the three forces must somehow offset one another, for if there were some net force the cable would move or bend under the action of that force. Alternatively, we may say that the horizontal forces must offset one another and that the vertical forces must do likewise. The tension $T$ is equivalent to a horizontal and a vertical tension acting simultaneously, for a tension is a force and, as we saw, in Section 4 of Chapter 3, any force may be replaced by the proper horizontal and vertical components. Specifically, the tension of magnitude

**Figure 4-27**

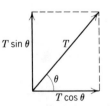

$T$ (Fig. 4-27) is equivalent to the combined action of the horizontal component $T \cos \theta$ and the vertical component $T \sin \theta$.

The horizontal component $T \cos \theta$ must offset the only other horizontal force that is acting, namely, $T_0$. Hence

**(15)**
$$T \cos \theta = T_0.$$

The vertical component $T \sin \theta$ of the tension must offset the only other vertical force that is acting, namely, $wx$. Hence

**(16)**
$$T \sin \theta = wx.$$

If we divide (16) by (15), we obtain

**(17)**
$$\tan \theta = \frac{w}{T_0} x.$$

Now $\tan \theta$ is the slope of the tangent line at $P$, and this slope is $y'$ where $y'$ is the derived function of whatever function represents the shape of the cable. Thus

$$y' = \frac{w}{T_0} x.$$

By antidifferentiation we obtain

$$y = \frac{w}{2T_0} x^2 + C.$$

To fix the constant $C$ we can choose the $x$-axis so as to pass through the point $A$ of Fig. 4-26. Then $y = 0$ when $x = 0$, so that $C = 0$. Thus

**(18)**
$$y = \frac{w}{2T_0} x^2.$$

We note the important result that the shape of the cable must be parabolic. We have of course used the fact that the total load must be the same for each horizontal foot. Later we shall study the shape of a cable when the load is differently distributed.

Let us note one or two implications of the result (18). Although the equation seems to involve two unknown quantities $w$ and $T_0$, only their ratio is involved. We can in fact write the equation as $y = kx^2$ where $k = w/2T_0$. To determine the equation of the parabola, we need to know only the value of $k$, which we can find if we know the coordinates of one point through which the parabola must go.

Suppose that we do specify the coordinates of one point (Fig. 4-28), say the point $(2, 3)$. Because the curve is symmetric with respect to the $y$-axis, the point $(-2, 3)$ must also be on the curve. Moreover, the lowest point of the cable must be the origin if (18) is presupposed. Hence to specify the coordinates of one point means really that the width from $(-2, 3)$ to $(2, 3)$ and the depth, 3, are specified. We know, however, that the

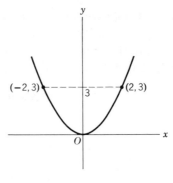

**Figure 4-28**

cable must have an equation of the form $y = kx^2$, and there is only one parabola of this form through a given point. Hence it would seem that if we fix one point, that is, fix the width and depth, there is no freedom to choose the load that the cable will support. However, this is not true. The quantity $k = w/2T_0$. Fixing $k$ fixes only the ratio of $w$ to $T_0$. If we increase $w$, the load per horizontal foot, then $T_0$ must increase in the same ratio. To sum up, if the width of a cable and the depth at that width are specified, there is only one shape for the cable regardless of the load, provided only that the load is constant over each horizontal foot.

## EXERCISES

1. With reference to the derivation of the equation of the cable, (a) Does the horizontal component of the tension $T$ vary from point to point on the cable? (b) Does the vertical component of the tension $T$ vary from point to point on the cable?                                                      *Ans.* (a) No; (b) Yes.

2. Assuming that $w$, the load per horizontal foot, is given, calculate the tension $T$ at any point on the parabola $y = (w/2T_0)x^2$.

   *Suggestion:* Square (15), square (16), and add. Then use the equation of the parabola to eliminate $T_0$ from the expression for $T$.

   $$Ans.\ \ T = (wx/2y)\sqrt{x^2 + 4y^2}\ .$$

3. Find the tension at the points at which the cable of a suspension bridge is attached to the towers, if the width of the cable between the two points of attachment is 120 feet (Fig. 4-29), the depth of the cable is 15 feet and the cable supports a roadway whose weight of 150 tons is uniformly distributed horizontally.

   *Suggestion:* Use the result in Exercise 2.                         *Ans.* $75\sqrt{5}$ tons.

**Figure 4-29**

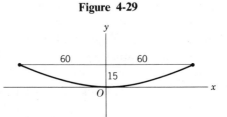

4. Consider the cable described in Exercise 3. Because it passes through the point (60, 15), the equation of the cable is $y = x^2/240$. Using the result of Exercise 2, study the variation of the tension $T$ along the cable. At what point or points is the tension greatest and at what point is the tension least?

*Ans.* Greatest at ($\pm 60$, 15); least at (0, 0).

5. We have required in our derivation of the equation of the cable that the weight of the roadway per horizontal foot be constant. Can the roadway itself be curved?

6. Suppose that the load on the cable treated in the text were not the constant weight $w$ per horizontal foot but that the load varied with the horizontal distance from the midpoint of the bridge in accordance with the formula $w = 5x^2$. What would the shape of the cable be?

### 6. *Further Discussion of the Derivative as the Slope.*

We may recall that in our original discussion of speed at an instant we pointed out that we could calculate the speed at the instant $t = 3$, say, by taking average speeds over intervals following $t = 3$ and shrinking to 0 or over intervals preceding $t = 3$ and shrinking to 0. That is, we arrive at the same limit for $\Delta s/\Delta t$, whether the quantity $\Delta t$ is positive or negative. The same argument applies to any $\Delta y/\Delta x$. Let us examine geometrically what a negative $\Delta x$ implies.

Suppose that the function is again $y = x^2$ and that the value of $x$ at which we consider the derivative is $x = 3$. Let the point $P$ of Fig. 4-30 be the point (3, 9). If now we take $\Delta x$ to be some negative quantity, the point $(3 + \Delta x, 9 + \Delta y)$ might be the point $Q$ which lies *below* $P$. It is still true that $\Delta y/\Delta x$ represents the slope of $PQ$. As $\Delta x$ becomes numerically smaller (although algebraically larger), the point $Q$ moves toward $P$, and of course $\Delta y/\Delta x$ continues to represent the slope of $PQ$. Our concept of the derivative requires that $\Delta y/\Delta x$ should approach the same limit at $x = 3$ when $\Delta x$ goes through negative values as when it goes through positive values. Then geometrically our concept of the derivative requires that the secants $QP$ approach the same line as $Q$ approaches $P$ from below as from above, because we took the tangent at $P$ to be the line whose slope at $P$ is the derivative.

Let us consider, however, the curve shown in Fig. 4-31. As $Q$ approaches $P$, the secants $QP$ approach a limiting line at $P$, namely $PR$. As $Q'$ approaches $P$, the secants $Q'P$ approach another limiting line at $P$, namely $PS$. The lines $PR$ and $PS$ are not the same, and therefore we do *not* speak of a tangent at $P$. Put otherwise, a point traveling toward $P$ from $Q$

**Figure 4-30**

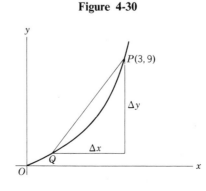

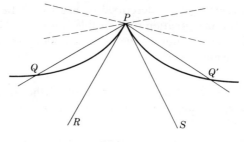

**Figure 4-31**

has one direction of motion as it reaches $P$, namely $RP$, whereas a point traveling toward $P$ from $Q'$ has another direction of motion as it reaches $P$, namely $SP$. Let us note also that if we had been content to take as our definition of tangent a line which has one point in common with the curve (cf. Section 2), any of the broken lines shown in the figure would have had to be accepted as a tangent.

The fact that the secants through $P$ approach different limiting lines means in algebraic terms that if we calculated the limit of $\Delta y/\Delta x$ at the $x$-value or abscissa of $P$, we would obtain a different limit for $\Delta y/\Delta x$ when $\Delta x$ approaches 0 through negative values than when $\Delta x$ approaches 0 through positive values. Just as we say that there is no tangent at $P$, so we must say that the function which represents the curve has no derivative at $P$.

## EXERCISES

1. By $|x|$ we mean the positive value of $x$, whether the value of $x$ in question be negative or positive. Thus $|-3| = 3$ and $|3| = 3$. Graph $y = |x|$ for negative and positive $x$. What can you say about the existence of a tangent at negative values of $x$? At positive values of $x$? At $x = 0$?

    *Ans.* Tangent exists everywhere except at (0, 0).

2. Does $y = |x|$ have a derivative at $x = 0$?

3. Graph the function $y = \frac{1}{2}(x + |x|)$. At what values of $x$ does the derivative exist and what is the value of the derivative when it does exist?

    *Ans.* For $x < 0, y' = 0$; for $x > 0, y' = 1$.

4. Interpret geometrically $\dfrac{f(x_0 + \Delta x) - f(x_0 - \Delta x)}{2\,\Delta x}$.

5. Prove that

$$\lim_{\Delta x \to 0} \frac{f(x_0 + \Delta x) - f(x_0 - \Delta x)}{2\,\Delta x} = f'(x_0).$$

*Suggestion:* Add and subtract $f(x_0)$ in the numerator.

# CHAPTER FIVE
# THE DIFFERENTIATION AND INTEGRATION OF POWERS OF $x$

**1. Introduction.** So far our work in the calculus has involved only simple functions of the form $y = ax^2 + bx + c$. The calculus would be rather limited and uninteresting if it were confined to these functions. To increase its applicability we must consider more complicated functions. In this chapter we shall study the differentiation and integration of functions of the form $y = x^n$.

**2. The Functions $x^n$ for Positive Integral $n$.** We start with the function $y = x^n$. For the present we consider only the case when $n$ is a positive integer, and our purpose is to find $dy/dx$. Before we attempt this task, let us consider what we already know about special cases. When $n = 1$, we have

$$y = x \qquad \text{and} \qquad \frac{dy}{dx} = 1.$$

When $n = 2$, we have

$$y = x^2 \qquad \text{and} \qquad \frac{dy}{dx} = 2x.$$

When $n = 3$ (see Chapter 2, Section 8, Exercise 4),

$$y = x^3 \qquad \text{and} \qquad \frac{dy}{dx} = 3x^2.$$

If we study these special cases, we find that the exponent in the function becomes a coefficient in the derived function and the exponent of the derived function is one less than it is in the original function. We would guess that when

$$y = x^n \qquad \text{then} \qquad \frac{dy}{dx} = nx^{n-1}.$$

Let us see if we can prove that this is correct.

To find the derived function we must first find the derivative at some fixed value of $x$. When we wish to find the derivative of a function which we do not know how to differentiate, we usually resort to the method of increments.

Let $x_0$ be the value of $x$ at which we seek the derivative. Then

(1) $$y_0 = x_0^n.$$

We change $x_0$ by some amount $\Delta x$ to the value $x_0 + \Delta x$. The corresponding value of $y$ is denoted by $y_0 + \Delta y$. Then

(2) $$y_0 + \Delta y = (x_0 + \Delta x)^n.$$

We seek next the increase in $y$, that is $\Delta y$. This results from subtracting (1) from (2). Then

(3) $$\Delta y = (x_0 + \Delta x)^n - x_0^n.$$

The method of increments now calls for finding the average rate of change of $y$ with respect to $x$ in the interval $\Delta x$. We therefore divide both sides of (3) by $\Delta x$ to obtain

(4) $$\frac{\Delta y}{\Delta x} = \frac{(x_0 + \Delta x)^n - x_0^n}{\Delta x}.$$

We must now find the limit of $\Delta y/\Delta x$ as $\Delta x$ approaches 0.

The natural thing to try is to expand $(x_0 + \Delta x)^n$ by means of the binomial theorem. Let us recall that

$$(a + b)^n = a^n + na^{n-1}b + \frac{n(n-1)}{2} a^{n-2}b^2 + \cdots + c_{n-1}ab^{n-1} + c_n b^n.$$

(5)

We have used $c_{n-1}$ and $c_n$ as coefficients in the last two terms instead of writing them out explicitly because, as we shall see in a moment, their precise values do not matter.

If we now apply (5) to $(x_0 + \Delta x)^n$ and substitute the expansion in (4), the terms $x_0^n$ cancel and we are left with

$$\frac{\Delta y}{\Delta x} =$$

$$\frac{nx_0^{n-1}\,\Delta x + \dfrac{n(n-1)}{2}\, x_0^{n-2}(\Delta x)^2 + \cdots + c_{n-1}x_0(\Delta x)^{n-1} + c_n(\Delta x)^n}{\Delta x}.$$

(6)

Now $\Delta x$ is not 0, and so we may divide the numerator and the denominator by $\Delta x$. Then

$$\frac{\Delta y}{\Delta x} = nx_0^{n-1} + \frac{n(n-1)}{2} x_0^{n-2}(\Delta x) + \cdots + c_{n-1}x_0(\Delta x)^{n-2} + c_n(\Delta x)^{n-1}.$$

**(7)**

To determine the limit of $\Delta y/\Delta x$ as $\Delta x$ approaches 0 we rewrite (7) as

$$\frac{\Delta y}{\Delta x} = nx_0^{n-1} + \Delta x \left[ \frac{n(n-1)}{2} x_0^{n-2} + \cdots + c_{n-1}x_0(\Delta x)^{n-3} + c_n(\Delta x)^{n-2} \right].$$

**(8)**

There are $n-1$ terms in the bracket. Suppose that for a given value of $\Delta x$, the value of the largest term is $A$. Then the value of all the terms is at most $(n-1)|A|$. As $\Delta x$ approaches 0 in value, the absolute value of each term in the bracket cannot increase because $\Delta x$ is the only variable quantity. In fact, for values of $\Delta x$ less than 1, the quantities $(\Delta x)^2$, $(\Delta x)^3$, and so on are smaller than $\Delta x$, and these powers of $\Delta x$ decrease in value even more than $\Delta x$. The bracket is itself multiplied by $\Delta x$, and therefore the value of the product is at most $\Delta x(n-1)|A|$. As $\Delta x$ approaches 0, this product must also approach 0. Then the limit of the right side of (8) is $nx_0^{n-1}$. That is,

**(9)**
$$\frac{dy}{dx} = \lim_{\Delta x \to 0} \frac{\Delta y}{\Delta x} = nx_0^{n-1}.$$

The proof of (9) holds for every value $x_0$ of $x$. Hence we have proved a general result which is sufficiently significant to be recognized as a theorem. Before stating the theorem let us note that if the original function had been $y = ax^n$, where $a$ is a number, the factor $a$ would have been present in steps (2) to (9). Hence the theorem we have established reads thus:

**Theorem:** If

$$y = ax^n$$

then the derived function is

**(10)**
$$\frac{dy}{dx} = anx^{n-1}$$

when $n$ is a positive integer.

We shall call the result (10) the power rule.

## EXERCISES

**1.** For each of the following function find the derived function:

(a)  $y = x^6$        Ans.  $\dfrac{dy}{dx} = 6x^5$    (e)  $y = x^{10}$

(f)  $y = 7$        Ans. $y' = 0$

(b)  $y = x$

(c)  $y = x^5$

(g)  $y = x^8$

(d)  $y = 4x^5$

(h)  $y = (1/2)x^7$

**2.** The proof of the power rule is valid for positive integral values of $n$. Why is it necessary to impose this limitation?

**3.** Is it true for $n = 0$ that if $y = x^n$ then $y' = nx^{n-1}$?        Ans. Yes.

**4.** Show that  $\lim\limits_{\Delta x \to 0} \dfrac{(x + \Delta x)^3 - x^3}{\Delta x} = 3x^2$.

**5.** Show that the rate of change of the volume of a cube with respect to the edge is three times the area of any face.

**6.** What is  $\lim\limits_{b \to 0} \dfrac{(a + b)^3 - a^3}{b}$ ?

**7.** What is  $\lim\limits_{q \to 0} \dfrac{f(p + q) - f(p)}{q}$ ?        Ans. $f'(p)$.

**8.** What is  $\lim\limits_{\Delta x \to 0} \dfrac{f(x + 2\Delta x) - f(x)}{\Delta x}$ ?

*Suggestion:* Let $2\,\Delta x = t$.

Let us now consider the inverse process to differentation. What is the function for which

**(11)**                          $\dfrac{dy}{dx} = x^n$?

We know that to differentiate a function of the form $x^n$ we must make the exponent a multiplier of the derivative and reduce the exponent by 1. Hence to antidifferentiate or integrate we should reverse the process. That is, we should increase the exponent in (11) by 1 and divide by the new exponent. Hence we form $x^{n+1}$ and divide by $n + 1$. However, we should recall what was discussed in Chapter 3. The original function or integral might contain a constant which would leave no trace in the derivative. Then, given (11),

**(12)**                          $y = \dfrac{x^{n+1}}{n + 1} + C.$

Because we shall have many occasions to integrate functions we should have a notation which indicates that this is what we wish to do. To indicate that we wish to find the function whose derived function is $x^n$, we indicate this fact by the notation

$$y = \int x^n \, dx.$$

The symbol just to the right of the equal sign is an elongated $S$ and is called the integral. The function to be integrated is $x^n$ and the $dx$ following $x^n$ denotes that we are integrating with respect to $x$. The origin of this notation will be noted later.

Before stating the theorem which embodies the result (12) let us note that if we had been given

$$\frac{dy}{dx} = ax^n$$

the antiderived function or integral would have to be

$$y = a\frac{x^{n+1}}{n+1} + C.$$

The reason is simply that when we differentiate this result the factor $a$ must appear in the derivative in accordance with (10). Hence we have the

**Theorem:** If

$$\frac{dy}{dx} = ax^n$$

then

(13) $$y = \int ax^n\, dx = a\frac{x^{n+1}}{n+1} + C.$$

**Example.** Given $dy/dx = 3x^7$, find $y$.

**Solution.** The constant 3 can be ignored for the moment and we integrate $x^7$. According to (13) the integral of $x^7$ is $x^8/8$. We now multiply this result by the constant 3 so that

$$y = \int 3x^7\, dx = 3\frac{x^8}{8} + C.$$

## EXERCISES

**1.** For each of the following derived functions find the integral:

(a) $y' = x^3$.    *Ans.* $y = \dfrac{x^4}{4} + C.$    (e) $y' = x^5$.

(b) $\dfrac{dy}{dx} = x^3$.    (f) $y' = 7x^{10}$.

(c) $y' = 3x$.    (g) $f'(x) = 4x^5$.

(h) $f'(x) = 2x$.

(d) $\dfrac{dy}{dx} = 5$.    *Ans.* $y = 5x + C.$    (i) $f'(x) = 4x^2$.

2. Evaluate:

(a)   $y = \int x^2 \, dx.$ 

*Ans.* $y = \dfrac{x^3}{3} + C.$

(b)   $y = \int x^3 \, dx.$

(c)   $y = \int 3x^7 \, dx.$

*Ans.* $y = \dfrac{3x^8}{8} + C.$

(d)   $y = \int x \, dx.$

(e)   $y = \int 1 \, dx.$

### 3. A Calculus Method of Finding Roots.

The ability to differentiate and integrate $y = x^n$ will serve us in many applications. Here we discuss how Newton used the derivative to devise a method of obtaining the $n$th root of a number. Let us suppose that we wish to obtain $\sqrt[3]{5}$. The number that we seek will be denoted by $x_0 = \sqrt[3]{5}$. Then $x_0^3 = 5$ or $x_0^3 - 5 = 0$. We shall consider how to approximate $x_0$. This means that we shall consider values of $x^3 - 5$ such that $x^3 - 5$ may not exactly equal 0 but may come close to 0. In other words, let us study the function $y = x^3 - 5$ and see what we can learn about values of $x$ that come close to making $y$ zero.

We graph the function $y = x^3 - 5$ (Fig. 5-1). The point $(\sqrt[3]{5}, 0)$ is, of course, the point at which the graph cuts the $x$-axis. We note that if we take a point $P$ on the curve and near $(\sqrt[3]{5}, 0)$, the tangent to the curve at $P$ cuts the $x$-axis at a point $Q$ whose abscissa should be close to $(\sqrt[3]{5}, 0)$. Hence let us find the equation of the tangent at $P$ and then determine its $x$-intercept.

Suppose that the coordinates of $P$ are $(x_1, y_1)$. Then the slope of the tangent at $P$ is the derivative of $y = x^3 - 5$ at $x_1$. This slope is $y' = 3x_1^2$. Because the tangent goes through $(x_1, y_1)$, the equation of the tangent is

$$y - y_1 = 3x_1^2(x - x_1).$$

We agreed earlier that we would find the $x$-intercept of the tangent. Hence

**Figure 5-1**

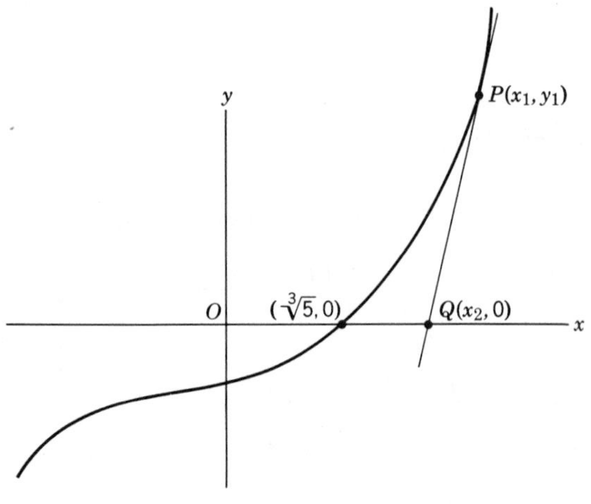

we set $y = 0$ and solve for the $x$-intercept, which we shall denote by $x_2$. Then

$$-y_1 = 3x_1^2(x_2 - x_1)$$

or

**(14)**
$$x_2 = \frac{-y_1}{3x_1^2} + x_1.$$

This number $x_2$ is then an approximation to $\sqrt[3]{5}$. In view of the fact that $y_1$ is a $y$-value on the curve, we know that $y_1 = x_1^3 - 5$, and we can rewrite (14) as

$$x_2 = -\frac{x_1}{3} + \frac{5}{3x_1^2} + x_1$$

or

**(15)**
$$x_2 = \frac{1}{3}\left(2x_1 + \frac{5}{x_1^2}\right).$$

If we examine Fig. 5-2, we see that had we taken the point $P'$ whose coordinates are $(x_2, y_2)$ in place of $P$, the approximation would have been a better one because the tangent at $P'$ cuts the $x$-axis at $R$ which is closer to $\sqrt[3]{5}$ than $Q$ is. There is, however, no need to redo the whole derivation with $(x_2, y_2)$ in place of $(x_1, y_1)$. Because the point $(x_1, y_1)$ was any point on the curve, the result (15) is quite general. If in (15) we substitute $x_2$ for $x_1$ and write $x_3$ for the $x$-value of $R$, we obtain

**(16)**
$$x_3 = \frac{1}{3}\left(2x_2 + \frac{5}{x_2^2}\right).$$

This value $x_3$, which is the abscissa of the point $R$, is a better approximation to $\sqrt[3]{5}$ than $x_2$.

Now we can repeat the argument of the preceding paragraph. If we substitute $x_3$ for $x_2$ in (16), we obtain a still better approximation $x_4$. The process can be continued as long as necessary to secure the approximation

**Figure 5-2**

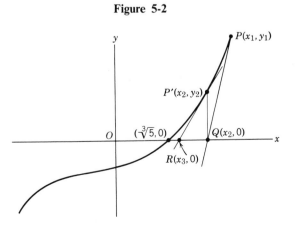

that is desired. Thus if we want an approximation to 3 decimal places and find that the next approximation after a given one no longer affects the third decimal place, we know that we have the right approximation.

The method that we employ to obtain better and better approximations to $\sqrt[3]{5}$ in effect solves approximately the equation $x^3 - 5 = 0$. The method can be used to solve more complicated equations approximately.

The essence of the method of finding $\sqrt[3]{5}$, then, is to guess an approximate value. Let us choose 1. This is our choice of $x_1$. Then according to (15)

$$x_2 = \frac{1}{3}\left(2 \cdot 1 + \frac{5}{1^2}\right) = \frac{7}{3}$$

is another approximation (though in this instance not necessarily better). We now let $x_2$ be $\frac{7}{3}$ and use (16), or what amounts to the same thing, use (15) with $x_1$ and $x_2$ replaced by $x_2$ and $x_3$. Then

$$x_3 = \frac{1}{3}\left(2 \cdot \frac{7}{3} + \frac{5}{\left(\frac{7}{3}\right)^2}\right) = 1.8 \text{ approximately}.$$

This value, $x_3$, is a better approximation to $\sqrt[3]{5}$ than $\frac{7}{3}$. We can now continue the process and obtain $x_4$, $x_5$, and so on, until we achieve the desired accuracy.

## EXERCISES

1. Using formula (15), calculate an approximate value of $\sqrt[3]{5}$ correct to 3 decimal places.                                                          *Ans.* 1.710.

2. Suppose that instead of $\sqrt[3]{5}$ we seek $\sqrt[3]{a}$. How is formula (15) altered to generalize from 5 to $a$?

3. Derive a formula, analogous to (15), which would furnish an approximate value of $\sqrt{5}$.
$$\text{Ans. } x_2 = \frac{1}{2}\left(x_1 + \frac{5}{x_1}\right).$$

4. Generalize the result of Exercise 3 to obtain an approximate formula for $\sqrt{a}$. Note that the answer gives a very useful method for finding square roots.
$$\text{Ans. } x_2 = \frac{1}{2}\left(x_1 + \frac{a}{x_1}\right).$$

5. Use Newton's method to obtain a general formula analogous to (15) for $\sqrt[n]{a}$.
$$\text{Ans. } x_2 = \frac{1}{n}\left\{(n-1)x_1 + \frac{a}{x_1^{n-1}}\right\}.$$

6. Suppose that you had to find one or more solutions of $x^3 - 7x + 5 = 0$. Do you think Newton's method applies to this equation? If so, describe the method.

7. Suppose that you apply Newton's method to find an approximation to the abscissa $r$ where the function graphed in Fig. 5-3 cuts the $x$-axis and suppose that you start at the point $P$ or $(x_1, y_1)$. Is the approximate value $x_2$ necessarily a better approximation to $r$ than $x_1$? Although criteria for the success of Newton's

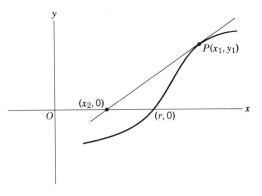

**Figure 5-3**

method can be given, it is just as well at this stage to draw the graph of the function and to rely upon geometric evidence as to whether the successive approximations $x_2$, $x_3$, . . . approach the root.

**8.** Leaving aside some theoretical considerations show that to find a root $r$ of $f(x) = 0$ one can choose an approximate value $a_1$ and obtain a better approximation $a_2$ which is given by $a_2 = a_1 - f(a_1)/f'(a_1)$.

**4. *Differentiation and Integration of* $x^n$ *for Fractional Values of n*.** We have so far restricted the value of $n$ in $y = x^n$ to positive integral values of $n$. However, functions such as $y = x^{1/2}$, $y = x^{2/3}$, and other fractional powers of $x$ are also useful, and therefore it is desirable to know how to find their derivatives. Before we consider this question let us note a few facts about the meaning of such functions.

The (multiple-valued) function $y^2 = x$ has real values only for positive values of $x$ and for $x = 0$. For positive values of $x$ there are two values of the function, a positive and a negative value. We take the symbols $x^{1/2}$ or $\sqrt{x}$ to stand for the positive value. For each value of $x$, positive or negative, the function $x^{1/3}$ or $\sqrt[3]{x}$ has 3 values if we include complex numbers. Another way of saying this is that if $y = x^{1/3}$, then $y^3 = x$, and that to each value of $x$ there are 3 values of $y$. However, whether $x$ is positive or negative there is just one value of $x^{1/3}$ which is real. If $x$ is positive, the real value of $x^{1/3}$ is positive; thus $\sqrt[3]{8} = 2$. If $x$ is negative, the real value of $x^{1/3}$ is negative; thus $\sqrt[3]{-8} = -2$.

Generally, by $\sqrt[q]{x}$ or $x^{1/q}$, where $q$ is a positive integer, we mean one real number. If $x$ is positive or zero, $q$ may be odd or even, and $\sqrt[q]{x}$ is the positive root. If $x$ is negative, $q$ must be odd, and $\sqrt[q]{x}$ is the negative real root. Further, $x^{p/q}$ means $(\sqrt[q]{x})^p$, with the understanding that if $x$ is negative $q$ must be odd.*

Before tackling the problem of the derivative of $y = x^{p/q}$, let us consider the simpler case of $y = x^{1/2} = \sqrt{x}$. To find the derivative at the

*It is also true, by a theorem on exponents, that

$$(\sqrt[q]{x})^p = \sqrt[q]{x^p}.$$

value $x_0$, we proceed by the method of increments. We start with the values of $x$ and $y$ at $x_0$. That is,

$$y_0 = \sqrt{x_0} \ .$$

We now let $x$ change to the value $x_0 + \Delta x$. Then

$$y_0 + \Delta y = \sqrt{x_0 + \Delta x} \ .$$

The change in $y$ is

$$\Delta y = \sqrt{x_0 + \Delta x} - \sqrt{x_0} \ .$$

Then the average rate of change of $y$ with respect to $x$ in the interval $\Delta x$ is

$$\text{(17)} \qquad \frac{\Delta y}{\Delta x} = \frac{\sqrt{x_0 + \Delta x} - \sqrt{x_0}}{\Delta x} \ .$$

We seek the limit approached by $\Delta y / \Delta x$ as $\Delta x$ approaches 0. However, the value of this limit is not evident from an examination of the right-hand side of (17). Nor can we divide numerator and denominator by $\Delta x$ to obtain a simpler function from which the limit might be evident.

The way out of the dilemma is a trick. We multiply the numerator and denominator on the right side of (17) by $\sqrt{x_0 + \Delta x} + \sqrt{x_0}$. This does not change the value of $\Delta y / \Delta x$. Then

$$\frac{\Delta y}{\Delta x} = \frac{\sqrt{x_0 + \Delta x} - \sqrt{x_0}}{\Delta x} \times \frac{\sqrt{x_0 + \Delta x} + \sqrt{x_0}}{\sqrt{x_0 + \Delta x} + \sqrt{x_0}} \ .$$

By multiplying the two numerators and then the two denominators we obtain

$$\frac{\Delta y}{\Delta x} = \frac{x_0 + \Delta x - x_0}{\Delta x \left\{ \sqrt{x_0 + \Delta x} + \sqrt{x_0} \right\}} \ .$$

The numerator reduces to $\Delta x$, and we may then cancel the $\Delta x$ in the numerator and denominator. This leaves us with

$$\text{(18)} \qquad \frac{\Delta y}{\Delta x} = \frac{1}{\sqrt{x_0 + \Delta x} + \sqrt{x_0}} \ .$$

The right-hand side of (18) yields exactly the same values as the right side of (17). From (18), however, we can see what the desired limit should be. When $\Delta x$ approaches 0, $\sqrt{x_0 + \Delta x}$ approaches $\sqrt{x_0}$, because the square root of a number changes gradually as the number changes. Hence we see from (18) that

(19)
$$\frac{dy}{dx} = \lim_{x \to 0} \frac{\Delta y}{\Delta x} = \frac{1}{2\sqrt{x_0}}.$$

This result can be written in terms of negative exponents. Thus

(20)
$$\frac{dy}{dx} = \frac{1}{2\sqrt{x_0}} = \frac{1}{2x_0^{1/2}} = \tfrac{1}{2} x_0^{-1/2}.$$

The interesting point about the result in this form is that, because the original function is $y = x^{1/2}$, the derivative is obtained by the same rule as is used for the derivative of $y = x^n$, that is, by the power rule. In the present case $n = \tfrac{1}{2}$, and the derivative is indeed of the form $nx^{n-1}$ in accordance with (10).

Let us note next what the derived function of $y = \sqrt{x}$ is. The derived function exists wherever the derivative of $y = \sqrt{x}$ exists. The derivative at $x_0$ is $1/2\sqrt{x_0}$. This derivative is meaningful for any $x_0$ except $x_0 = 0$ and negative values of $x$. Hence the derived function

(21)
$$\frac{dy}{dx} = \frac{1}{2\sqrt{x}}$$

exists or has a value only for positive values of $x$ although the original function exists also at $x = 0$.

What does the nonexistence of the derived function at $x = 0$ mean geometrically? The derivative at any value of $x$ is the slope of the tangent to the curve at that value of $x$. If we examine Fig. 5-4, we see that for $x$ closer and closer to 0 the slope of the tangent increases more and more. Moreover, this slope can be one million, ten million, and in fact a number as large as one pleases if $x$ is close enough to 0. We describe this unbounded increase in the slope by saying that the slope becomes infinite as $x$ approaches 0. We do *not* say that there is a number infinity which is the value of the slope at $x = 0$. In fact, although there is a tangent to $y = \sqrt{x}$ at $x = 0$, this tangent, which is a vertical line, does not have a slope, that is, there is no number to represent its slope.

What we have said about slope applies to the derived function $1/2\sqrt{x}$. As $x$ approaches 0, the derived function becomes larger and,

**Figure 5-4**

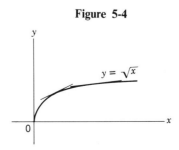

indeed, by taking $x$ close enough to 0, the derived function can be as large a number as one pleases. However, there is no value of the derived function for $x = 0$.

The statement that *as $x$ approaches* 0 *the values of* $1/2\sqrt{x}$ *become larger and larger and, in fact, as large as any number one can name*, is of course very lengthy. Hence a symbolic shorthand is used, namely,

$$\lim_{x \to 0} \frac{1}{2\sqrt{x}} = \infty.$$

This shorthand is somewhat unfortunate because it suggests that $\infty$ is a number and that the function is approaching that number. In fact, we have often said that a limit is a number. However, the symbol $\infty$ here does *not* represent a number, and the entire equation must be understood in the sense of the italicized statement above.

We have just considered the differentiation of $y = x^{1/2}$ and we should now like to differentiate $y = x^{p/q}$, wherein $p$ and $q$ are positive. We might guess that since the derivation of $y = x^{1/2}$ can be obtained by the power rule, the same should apply to $y = x^{p/q}$. However, the evidence supplied by the special case is not a proof for the general case. We cannot conclude that all Indians walk single file through the woods because one does. We could give a direct proof of the general case here but with the technique presently at our disposal the proof would be cumbersome. We shall give a simple proof later (Chap. 7, Sect. 4). For the present we shall use the result on the basis of the evidence that the power rule works for positive integral $n$ and $n = 1/2$.

Before stating the result let us note that, just as in the case of $x^n$ when $n$ is a positive integer, when the factor $a$ is present, that is, if the function is $ax^{p/q}$, the constant $a$ appears as a factor in the derivative. This is also evident in the case of $ax^{1/2}$ or $a\sqrt{x}$ if one reviews the steps leading to (21).

We may embody these results in the following theorem:

**Theorem:**   Suppose that

**(22)** $$y = ax^{p/q}$$

where $p$ and $q$ are positive integers. The function is defined for positive $x$ and zero when $q$ is even and for positive and negative $x$ when $q$ is odd. Then the derived function is

**(23)** $$\frac{dy}{dx} = a\,\frac{p}{q}\,x^{(p/q)-1}$$

with the understanding that the derived function is subject to the same limitations on the values of $x$ as is the original function and the additional limitation that the derived function does not exist at $x = 0$ if $(p/q) - 1$ is less than 0.

Now that we know that the derived function of (22) is (23), we may also consider the integral of (23). Because finding the integral means finding the function that has the given derived function, the integral is $y = ax^{p/q} + C$. However, as in the case of $y = x^n$, we are not usually given the derived function in the form (23) but in the form

**(24)** $$\frac{dy}{dx} = ax^{p/q}.$$

We seek therefore

$$y = \int ax^{p/q}\, dx.$$

We know that in finding the derived function one multiplies the function by the exponent and then reduces the exponent by 1; to find the integral we increase the exponent by 1 and divide by the new exponent. Thus we have the following theorem:

**Theorem:**   If

$$\frac{dy}{dx} = ax^{p/q}$$

then

**(25)** $$y = \int ax^{p/q}\, dx = a\,\frac{x^{(p/q)+1}}{(p/q) + 1} + C.$$

Because we restricted $p/q$ in (22) to be positive, the quantity $(p/q) + 1$ must be greater than 0.*

We can remember (23) and (25) separately or we can remember that the combination of the results obtained here and in Section 2 amounts to the following. If $y = ax^n$, where $n$ is a positive integer or positive fraction, $dy/dx = anx^{n-1}$; if $dy/dx = ax^n$, where $n$ is a positive integer or fraction greater than $-1$, then

$$y = a\,\frac{x^{n+1}}{n+1} + C.$$

**Example 1.** Differentiate $y = 3x^{7/2}$.

**Solution.**   We ignore the constant factor 3 for the moment and differentiate $x^{7/2}$. By the power rule (23) the derived function is

$$\tfrac{7}{2}x^{7/2-1}.$$

We now multiply the result by 3, so that $dy/dx = (21/2)x^{5/2}$.

*This limitation will be removed later.

**Example 2.** Find the integral if $dy/dx = \sqrt{8x}$ .

**Solution.**  We write first that $dy/dx = \sqrt{8}\ \sqrt{x} = \sqrt{8}\ x^{1/2}$. Then $\sqrt{8}$ can be treated as a constant factor and ignored for the moment. The integral or antiderived function of $x^{1/2}$ is $x^{3/2}/(3/2)$ or $(2/3)x^{3/2}$. Then $y = \sqrt{8}\ (2/3)x^{3/2} + C = (4\sqrt{2}\ /3)x^{3/2} + C$.

## EXERCISES

1. Find the derived function for the following functions:
   (a)  $y = x^7$.           Ans. $y' = 7x^6$.
   (b)  $y = 3x^{7/2}$.       Ans. $y' = \frac{21}{2}x^{5/2}$
   (c)  $y = 2x^{1/3}$.
                             Ans. $dy/dx = \frac{2}{3}x^{-2/3}$.
   (d)  $y = 5\sqrt[3]{x}$ .
   (e)  $y = \sqrt[3]{x^2}$ .
                             Ans. $dy/dx = \frac{2}{3}x^{-1/3}$.
   (f)  $y = \sqrt[4]{x}$ .
   (g)  $y = x^{p/3}$.

   (h)  $y = x^{5/q}$.
                             Ans. $dy/dx = \frac{5}{q}x^{(5/q)-1}$
   (i)  $y = t^{5/3}$.
   (j)  $s = 3t^{1/2}$.
   (k)  $s = \sqrt{t^3}$ .       Ans. $\dot{s} = \frac{3}{2}t^{1/2}$.
   (l)  $s = \sqrt[3]{t}$ .
   (m)  $f(x) = x^{5/3}$.
   (n)  $f(x) = x^{5/3} + 3x + 7$.

2. Find the antiderived function or integral for the following:
   (a)  $dy/dx = x^{4/3}$.
                             Ans. $y = \frac{3}{7}x^{7/3} + C$.
   (b)  $dy/dx = x^{3/2}$.
                             Ans. $y = \frac{2}{5}x^{5/2} + C$.
   (c)  $y' = 5\sqrt[3]{x}$ .
   (d)  $y' = \sqrt[3]{x^2}$ .
   (e)  $\dot{s} = 3t^{2/3}$.
   (f)  $\dot{s} = t^{-1/3}$
   (g)  $dy/dx = x^{-1/2}$.
                             Ans. $y = 2x^{1/2} + C$.

   (h)  $y' = (\sqrt[5]{x}\ )^7$.
                             Ans. $y = \frac{5}{12}x^{12/5} + C$.
   (i)  $\dot{s} = t^{3/5}$.
   (j)  $\dot{s} = \sqrt[4]{t^3}$ .   Ans. $s = \frac{4}{7}t^{7/4} + C$.
   (k)  $\dot{s} = 4t^{1/2}$.
   (l)  $\dot{s} = t^{-2/3}$.
   (m)  $f'(x) = x^{5/3} + x^{3/2}$.
   (n)  $f'(x) = 2x^{1/2} + x^{-1/2}$.

3. Evaluate the following:
   (a)  $y = \int x^{1/3}\, dx$.
                             Ans. $y = \frac{3}{4}x^{4/3} + C$.
   (b)  $y = \int x^{-1/2}\, dx$.
   (c)  $y = \int \sqrt[4]{x}\, dx$.
                             Ans. $y = \frac{4}{5}x^{5/4} + C$.

   (d)  $s = \int t^{-1/2}\, dt$.
   (e)  $s = \int \sqrt{t}\, dt$.
                             Ans. $s = \frac{2}{3}t^{3/2} + C$.
   (f)  $s = \int t^{3/5}\, dt$.

4. Suppose that a variable (independent or dependent) takes on larger and larger values. Does it follow that the variable is becoming infinite? Can you give an example to support your answer?

5. What does the statement $\lim\limits_{x\to 0} 1/x^2 = \infty$ mean?

6. Use the method of increments to find the derived function of $y = 1/x$.

7. Discuss the variation of the slope of $y = x^{1/2}$ as $x$ increases from 0 to $\infty$. Base your discussion on the derived function and verify your conclusions by using the curve of the function.

**8.** The equation of a parabola which opens to the right (see Fig. 4-13) is $y^2 = 8x$. Find the slope at the point $(2, 4)$ and at the point $(2, -4)$.

**9.** Find the equation of the tangent to the parabola $y^2 = 16x$ at the point $(4, 8)$ and at the point $(4, -8)$.

**10.** Describe the behavior of the slope of the upper half of the parabola $y^2 = 4px$ both analytically and verbally as $x$ varies from 0 to $\infty$.

**11.** If an object falls straight down from rest and if the air resistance is negligible then the velocity (in ft/sec) is related to the distance it falls (in ft) by the formula $v = 8\sqrt{s}$. Does the velocity increase more rapidly as the object falls a greater and greater distance?

**12.** The period of a pendulum, that is, the time it takes in seconds to make one complete swing, is given by the formula $T = 2\pi\sqrt{l/32}$. (We shall derive this formula later.) In the formula $l$ is the length of the string in feet and 32 is the acceleration of gravity. Find $dT/dl$. Does the period change more rapidly as $l$ becomes smaller and smaller?

# CHAPTER SIX
# SOME THEOREMS ON DIFFERENTIATION AND ANTIDIFFERENTIATION

**1. *Introduction.*** Thus far we have learned how to differentiate and antidifferentiate only the simplest functions. Fortunately, or unfortunately, the uses of the calculus call for a great variety of functions. To encompass them we must extend our knowledge of the basis processes of differentiation and antidifferentiation. For example, suppose that we have to differentiate

**(1)** $$y = x^7 + x^5.$$

We might guess that the derivative, $y'$, is the sum of the derivatives of $x^7$ and $x^5$. Indeed, in some very simple cases treated earlier we saw that the derivative of a sum of two functions is the sum of the derivatives. We certainly do not wish to go through the lengthy method of increments each time, if we can establish a general result for all sums. We know that the derived function of $x^7$ is $7x^6$ and that of $x^5$ is $5x^4$. If we knew generally that the derivative of a sum of two functions is the sum of the derivatives, we could write down the derivative of the function in (1) immediately. Similarly, if we had general rules for finding the derivative of the difference, product and quotient of two functions the process of differentiation would be easier to perform. The results in each case may seem obvious, but there are some surprises in store for us.

**2. *Some Remarks About Functions.*** While working with a specific function, we can examine the function itself to see if it possesses some requisite property. For example, if we are interested in the derivative of $y = x^2$, we can go through the method of increments to see if the limit of $\Delta y / \Delta x$ exists as $\Delta x$ approaches 0 and to find the limit if it does exist. However, we now wish to prove theorems about functions in general and therefore cannot examine individual functions to see, for example, that $\Delta y / \Delta x$ approaches a limit. We can, however, specify that we shall restrict the functions studied to those that have the requisite properties. One of these properties is that $\Delta y$

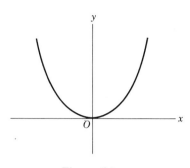

Figure 6-1

must approach 0 as $\Delta x$ does. This is known as the property of continuity. The property is so important that we shall consider it at some length.

We can best understand what continuity means if we consider the graphs of functions. In graphical terms a function is continuous if the curve can be drawn with one uninterrupted motion of a pencil. Thus $y = x^2$ is continuous because the curve (Fig. 6-1) can be so drawn. We can start as far to the left and go as far to the right as we wish without lifting the pencil from the paper.

The function $y = x^2$ is especially simple. To pursue the notion of continuity a little further, let us consider the function

**(2)** $$y = \frac{1}{x - 2}.$$

The graph of this function (Fig. 6-2) consists of two parts. We can draw the first part but cannot without lifting the pencil from the paper proceed to draw the second part. The trouble, of course, arises from the fact that the function has no value at $x = 2$. Moreover, as $x$ approaches 2 through values larger than 2, the corresponding $y$-values become larger and larger without bound, and as $x$ approaches 2 through values smaller than 2, the $y$-values become smaller and smaller without bound. Hence no matter how much we draw of the curve for values of $x$ less than 2, we must skip from these values of $x$ to values of $x$ greater than 2 to draw the right-hand portion of the curve. We can say that the function (2) is continuous for

Figure 6-2

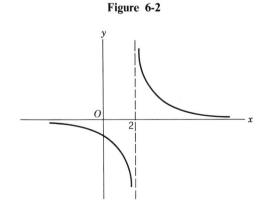

$x < 2$ and continuous for $x > 2$ but is discontinuous for $x = 2$. The fact that the function is discontinuous at $x = 2$ does not detract from its usefulness. We may be interested in using the function to describe some physical phenomenon in which $x$ represents values greater than 2. For such an application we do not care how the function behaves when $x = 2$ or when $x$ is less than 2.

Let us consider the matter of continuity in connection with another function. In trigonometry we study the function

**(3)**                            $y = \tan x.$

The graph of this function is shown in Fig. 6-3. We see from the graph that from values of $x$ arbitrarily close to $-90°$ or $-\pi/2$ radians to values arbitrarily close to $x = 90°$ or $\pi/2$ radians the graph is one uninterrupted curve and is therefore continuous in this interval of $x$-values. However, at $x = 90°$ the function has about the same behavior as the function in (2) at $x = 2$. That is, the function values jump from larger and larger positive values as $x$ approaches $90°$ from the left to values that become smaller and smaller as $x$ approaches $90°$ from the right. At $x = 90°$ the function has no value. We can draw the portion of the curve that belongs to $x$-values less than but as close as we wish to $90°$, but to draw the portion that corresponds to $x$-values larger than $90°$ we must lift the pencil from the paper and then start afresh. This function is then discontinuous at $x = 90°$, and for that matter it is discontinuous at $x = 270°$, $450°$, and at every value of $x$ that results from adding a multiple of $180°$ to $90°$; the function is also discontinuous at $x = -90°$ and at every value of $x$ that results from subtracting a multiple of $180°$ from $-90°$.

The discontinuities in (2) and (3) are examples of a common type. The function is not defined at one or more specific values of $x$, and in addition the function values become larger and larger without bound or smaller and smaller without bound as the values of $x$ approach these specific values.

**Figure 6-3**

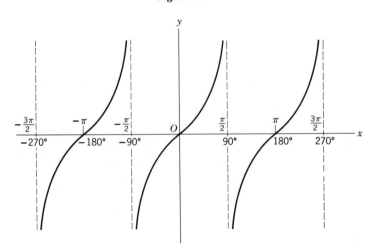

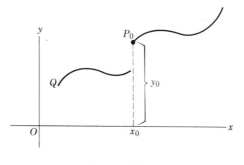

**Figure 6-4**

A function can fail to be continuous, that is, it can be discontinuous, for another reason. Suppose that the graph of a function is that shown in Fig. 6-4. It is understood there that the value of the function at $x_0$ is the $y_0$ indicated. If we attempt to draw this curve by starting at $Q$, we can carry out an uninterrupted motion until the vertical line at $x_0$ is reached. But then to draw the portion at $x_0$ and to the right of $x_0$, we must move up suddenly at $x_0$ to the level of $P_0$. We say that the function values jump at $x_0$ and the function is discontinuous at $x = x_0$. The behavior of this function might seem outlandish and we might think that no self-respecting function would behave in this way. We may stand fast in this moral judgment for the present because we intend to ignore such functions; all we are trying to do here is to learn what to avoid.

The derivative is calculated at a value of $x$, say $x_0$. When differentiating a function, we expect $\Delta y$ to approach 0 as $\Delta x$ approaches 0, because if $\Delta y$ should approach some non-zero number or become infinite, the quotient $\Delta y / \Delta x$ would not approach a definite number. For the derivatives to exist what we really presuppose is that the function is continuous. Suppose that the curve in Fig. 6-5 is the graph of some function and that we are considering the derivative at $P_0$ which has the coordinates $(x_0, y_0)$. If we consider any point $P$ to the right of $P_0$ or any point $Q$ to the left, then $\Delta x$ is the difference in the $x$-values of $P_0$ and $P$ or $P_0$ and $Q$, while $\Delta y$ is the difference in the $y$-values of $P_0$ and $P$ or $Q_0$ and $Q$. If $\Delta y$ is to approach 0 as $\Delta x$ does then the $x$ and $y$ of $P$ and the $x$ and $y$ of $Q$ must approach the $(x_0, y_0)$ of $P_0$. Thus we see that $P$ and $Q$ must approach $P_0$. This is what we mean when we say that the curve can be drawn with uninterrupted motion

**Figure 6-5**

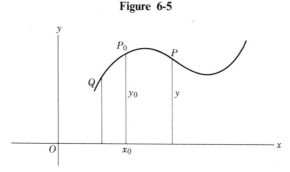

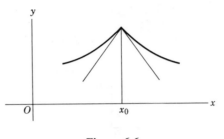

**Figure 6-6**

of the pencil; that is, we can go from $Q$ to $P$ through $P_0$ without taking the pencil from the paper. In other words, the function must be continuous at $P_0$.

We can of course require our mathematical functions to be continuous at those values of $x$ at which the derivative is to be calculated, but are such functions useful? Fortunately, physical phenomena are usually continuous. As a ball falls, the distance it travels changes continuously with the time of travel. The distance does not jump abruptly from one value to another or become infinite at a finite value of the time. We shall see as we take up many other physical applications that the functions representing them are continuous at least in the intervals of $x$-values that matter for the applications. Hence requiring continuity of our mathematical functions does not detract from their usefulness.

In calculating the derivative of a function at a value $x_0$ of $x$, more is involved than continuity. The continuity of a function at $x_0$, for example, guarantees that $\Delta y$ approaches 0 as $\Delta x$ does. We are, however, interested in

$$\text{(4)} \qquad\qquad \lim_{\Delta x \to 0} \frac{\Delta y}{\Delta x} \, .$$

Despite the fact that $\Delta y$ and $\Delta x$ both approach zero, it is conceivable that the ratio $\Delta y / \Delta x$ may not approach a definite number. For example, the function whose graph is shown in Fig. 6-6 is continuous at all values of $x$ but it does not have a derivative at $x_0$ because there is no unique tangent at $x_0$ (review the discussion in Chap. 4, Sect. 6). The curve shown in Fig. 6-6 changes direction abruptly at $x_0$ and is said to have a corner or cusp there. Because we wish to consider functions that do have derivatives at least in the domain of $x$-values in which we shall be interested we shall limit ourselves to those for which the limit (4) does exist at each $x$-value in the domain. Such functions are said to be differentiable at the $x$-values in question. If a function is continuous and differentiable in a domain or an interval of $x$-values, its graph is smooth, that is, without corners, and the function is often described as smooth.*

Thus we impose two restrictions on the general functions that we shall treat. *The first is that they must be continuous, at least in the intervals in which we shall use them, and the second is that they must be differentiable.*

---

* Some authors use the word smooth to include the additional condition that the derived function be continuous in the interval.

We shall not bother to state these hypotheses in our theorems because to do so would mean enormous repetition. Where we depart from these conditions, we shall discuss the situation.

## EXERCISES

1. Sketch the following functions and determine from the graphs the values of $x$ for which they are continuous and those for which they are discontinuous:
   (a) $y = 3x$.
   (b) $y = \sin x$.
   (c) $y = \sqrt{1 - x}$.
   (d) $y = \dfrac{1}{x^2}$.

   (e) $y = \dfrac{x^2 - 9}{x - 3}$.

   *Suggestion:* See Chapter 2, Section 2.

   (f) $y = \dfrac{x^3 - 1}{x - 1}$.

2. Associated with each point $P$ of a curve (Fig. 6-7) is its abscissa $x$ and the angle of inclination $A$ of the tangent at $P$. Corresponding to each value of $x$ in the interval $OC$ there is a unique value of $A$. Hence $A$ is a function of $x$. Determine whether $A$ is a continuous function of $x$ in the interval $OC$.  *Ans.* No.

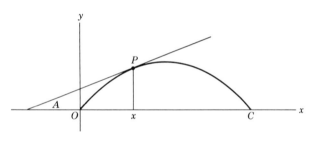

**Figure 6-7**

3. The slope of the curve in Fig. 6-7 at any point $P$ is, by definition, the slope of the tangent at $P$. The slope is $\tan A$, which we now denote by $z$. This $z$ also varies with $x$. Determine whether $z$ is a continuous function of $x$ in the interval $OC$.  *Ans.* Yes.

4. The statement that $y$ approaches $\infty$ describes $(a)$ the number that $y$ approaches, $(b)$ a state of mind, $(c)$ the fact that the values of $y$ surpass any number however large, and $(d)$ the fact that $y$ takes on the value $10^{12}$. Which alternative is most appropriate?  *Ans.* $(c)$.

**3. The Differentiation of Sums and Differences of Functions.** Let us now turn to the problem mentioned in Section 1, and let us start with the case of a function that is a constant times another function. When we differentiated $y = 16x^2$, we found the result to be $y' = 32x$. We can obtain the same result by keeping the constant separate, differentiate $x^2$ to obtain $2x$, and then multiply 16 by $2x$. What we are really saying then is that the derivative of a constant times a function, that is $16 \cdot x^2$, is the constant times the derivative, that is $16 \cdot 2x$. Hence we have reason to believe that the derivative of a constant times a function is the constant times the derivative of the function. Let us express this statement symbolically. Suppose that $u$ is a function of $x$ and

(5) $$y = cu.$$

Then what we believe is that

(6) $$y' = cu'.$$

Let us see if we can prove (6). To prove basic facts about differentiation we go back to the method of increments. Suppose that $x_0$ is the value of $x$ at which we wish to calculate $y'$. At $x_0$, the value of $u$ is, say, $u_0$ and the value of $y$ is $y_0$. Then

(7) $$y_0 = cu_0.$$

We change $x$ to the value $x_0 + \Delta x$. Consequently, $y$ and $u$ both change, and we denote the changes by $\Delta y$ and $\Delta u$, respectively. Then

(8) $$y_0 + \Delta y = c(u_0 + \Delta u) = cu_0 + c\Delta u.$$

We subtract (7) from (8), so that

(9) $$\Delta y = c\Delta u.$$

In accordance with the method of increments we divide both sides of (9) by $\Delta x$. To divide the product $c\Delta u$ by $\Delta x$, it is correct to divide only one of the factors. Then

(10) $$\frac{\Delta y}{\Delta x} = c\,\frac{\Delta u}{\Delta x}\;.$$

We now wish to determine the limit of $\Delta y/\Delta x$ as $\Delta x$ approaches 0. On the right side we have a product. Because $u$ is a function of $x$, the quantity $\Delta u/\Delta x$ approaches the limit $u'$. As $\Delta u/\Delta x$ gets closer and closer to its limit $u'$, the product should get closer and closer to $cu'$. Thus, as $x$ approaches 2, $x^2$ approaches 4, and therefore $3x^2$ approaches 12. Of course, this argument by example is not a mathematical proof. What we need to know is that if any function, which in our case is $\Delta u/\Delta x$ as a function of $\Delta x$, approaches a certain limit, a constant times that function approaches the constant times the limit. At the present time we shall rely on what intuitively seems to be a very reasonable fact and conclude that $y' = cu'$. Although our proof is incomplete, we affirm our result as a theorem.*

**Theorem 1:** If $y$ and $u$ are functions of $x$ and $y = cu$, then

(11) $$y' = cu'.$$

That is, the derivative (and derived function) of a constant times a function is the constant times the derivative (derived function) of that function.

* The reader who wishes to delve further into the proofs of this and the next few theorems at this time should consult Chapter 25.

Let us consider next the problem of how to differentiate the sum of two functions. Suppose that $u$ and $v$ are functions of $x$ and $y = u + v$. Thus $u$ could be $x^2$ and $v$, $7x^3$; then $y$ would be $x^2 + 7x^3$. Is it true that $y' = u' + v'$? We shall resort to the method of increments. Let $x_0$ be the value of $x$ at which we calculate the derivatives. Then, with the usual meanings,

$$(12) \qquad\qquad y_0 = u_0 + v_0.$$

We change $x$ to $x_0 + \Delta x$. Let $\Delta y$, $\Delta u$, and $\Delta v$ denote the changes in the respective functions. Then

$$(13) \qquad\qquad y_0 + \Delta y = u_0 + \Delta u + v_0 + \Delta v.$$

Subtraction of (12) from (13) yields

$$\Delta y = \Delta u + \Delta v.$$

The average rate of change of $y$ with respect to $x$ in the interval $\Delta x$ is

$$(14) \qquad\qquad \frac{\Delta y}{\Delta x} = \frac{\Delta u}{\Delta x} + \frac{\Delta v}{\Delta x} .$$

We now wish to determine the limit of $\Delta y / \Delta x$ as $\Delta x$ approaches 0, and we face a problem analogous to that encountered above. We want the limit of the entire right-hand side of (14), that is,

$$\lim_{\Delta x \to 0} \left( \frac{\Delta u}{\Delta x} + \frac{\Delta v}{\Delta x} \right).$$

May we conclude that this limit is the same as

$$(15) \qquad\qquad \lim_{\Delta x \to 0} \frac{\Delta u}{\Delta x} + \lim_{\Delta x \to 0} \frac{\Delta v}{\Delta x} \, ?$$

That is, may we conclude that the limit of a sum of two functions is the sum of the limits of the summands? The answer would seem to be affirmative. For example, we know that as $x$ approaches 1, $5x^2$ approaches 5 and $3x$ approaches 3. Then as $x$ approaches 1, $5x^2 + 3x$ certainly approaches 8. Again we must point out that this example does not constitute a proof of the theorem on limits, but we rest on this limited evidence for the present and assert the following theorem:

**Theorem 2:** If $u$ and $v$ are functions of $x$ and $y = u + v$, then

$$(16) \qquad\qquad y' = u' + v'.$$

That is, the derivative (derived function) of a sum of two functions is the sum of the derivatives (derived functions).

What holds for a sum of *two* functions, holds for a sum of three and more functions. Thus suppose that $y = u + v + w$, where $u$, $v$, and $w$ are functions of $x$. We may regard $y$ as

**(17)**
$$y = (u + v) + w.$$

Certainly, $u + v$ can be regarded as a single function of $x$ because to each value of $x$ in some domain, $u + v$ has a value, namely, the sum of the values of $u$ and $v$. Then, as expressed in (17), $y$ is the sum of two functions, $u + v$ and $w$. Hence by Theorem 2

$$y' = (u + v)' + w'.$$

Here $(u + v)'$ means the derivative of the entire function $u + v$. However, by Theorem 2 again, $(u + v)' = u' + v'$. Hence

**(18)**
$$y' = u' + v' + w'.$$

This argument can be extended to a sum of four or more functions by repeated application of Theorem 2. Hence we have the following theorem:

**Theorem 3:** If $y$ is the sum of any fixed finite number of functions, that is, if $y = u_1 + u_2 + \cdots + u_n$, then

**(19)**
$$y' = u_1' + u_2' + \cdots + u_n'.$$

That is, the derivative (derived function) of a sum of a finite number of functions is the sum of the derivatives (derived functions).

Finding the derivative of a difference of two functions, that is, the derivative of $y = u - v$ where $u$ and $v$ are functions of $x$, could be considered as a separate problem. However, we can write $y = u + (-v)$ and regard $y$ as the sum of $u$ and $-v$. Then, by Theorem 2, the derivative of $y$ is the sum of the derivatives of $u$ and $-v$. The derivative of $-v$ is the derivative of $-1 \cdot v$ and, by Theorem 1, this derivative is $-v'$. Hence $y' = u' - v'$. Thus we have the following theorem:

**Theorem 4:** If $u$ and $v$ are functions of $x$ and if $y = u - v$, then

**(20)**
$$y' = u' - v'.$$

That is, the derivative (derived function) of a difference of two functions is the difference of the derivatives (derived functions) of the separate functions.

Before considering additional theorems on differentiation, let us see how those already given are used in actual problems of differentiation. Suppose that we must find $y'$ when

$$y = 10x^7 + 6x^3.$$

We see, first, that $y$ is the sum of two functions. Hence, by Theorem 2, we may differentiate each separately. We consider then the function $10x^7$. According to Theorem 1, the derived function of this function is the constant 10 times the derived function of $x^7$. In Chapter 5 we learned that the derived function of $x^7$ is $7x^6$. Hence the derived function of $10x^7$ is $70x^6$. Likewise the derived function of $6x^3$ is $6 \cdot 3x^2$ or $18x^2$. Hence

$$y' = 70x^6 + 18x^2.$$

## EXERCISES

1. Find the derived functions of the following functions:
   (a) $y = 10x^6$.      *Ans.* $y' = 60x^5$.
   (b) $y = 10x^{2/3}$.
   (c) $y = x^3 + 7x^5$.
          *Ans.* $y' = 3x^2 + 35x^4$.
   (d) $y = 5x^4 + 7x^{1/3}$.
   (e) $y = x^3 - 7x^2$.
          *Ans.* $y' = 3x^2 - 14x$.
   (f) $y = (x^2 + x)7x$.
   (g) $y = x^{5/2}(x^2 + 3x)$.
          *Ans.* $y' = \frac{9}{2}x^{7/2} + \frac{21}{2}x^{5/2}$.
   (h) $y = (x^2 + x)(x - 3)$.
   (i) $y = 8\sqrt{x}$.
          *Ans.* $dy/dx = 4x^{-1/2}$.
   (j) $y = 4\sqrt{x} + 6\sqrt[3]{x}$.
   (k) $y = \sqrt{8x}$.
          *Ans.* $dy/dx = \sqrt{\dfrac{2}{x}}$.
   (l) $y = \sqrt{4x} + \sqrt[3]{6x}$.

2. If $y = f(x) + g(x)$, what is $y'$?        *Ans.* $y' = f'(x) + g'(x)$.

3. If $y = f(x) - g(x)$, what is $y'$?

4. If $y = cf(x)$, what is $y'$?        *Ans.* $y' = cf'(x)$.

5. An airplane reaches an altitude of $15x^2 - x^3$ feet after having traveled $x$ miles (horizontally).
   (a) Find the rate of increase of altitude with respect to horizontal distance traveled when the airplane has traveled 2 miles.        *Ans.* 48 ft/mi.
   (b) Graph the function $y = 15x^2 - x^3$ from $x = 0$ to $x = 10$.
   (c) Find the slope of the graph at $x = 2$, $x = 5$, $x = 7$, and $x = 10$.
          *Ans.* 48, 75, 63, 0.
   (d) Taking into account any change of scale you may have used for the $y$-axis, would you say that the graph could be an actual picture of the airplane's flight path?

6. The rate of change of the area of a circle with respect to the radius is geometrically the circumference of the circle. [See Chap. 2, Sect. 6.] Generalize this result for circles to spheres and prove that your generalization is correct.

7. The total cost of producing $x$ units of a commodity is $C = x^3/3 + 2x + 4$. Economists call the rate of change of $C$ with respect to $x$ the marginal cost. Calculate the marginal cost.

8. The demand for a commodity is a function of the price. Suppose that the demand for a commodity, that is, the number $x$ of units of the commodity which people will buy at the price $p$ is given by $x = 10p + 80$ where $p$ is the price per unit. The revenue $R$ from the sale of $x$ units is $xp$. What is the marginal revenue, that is, the rate of change of $R$ with respect to $x$?
          *Suggestion:* To find $R$ in terms of $x$, use the demand function to express $p$ as a function of $x$.

9. Suppose that the revenue $R$ from the sale of $x$ units of a commodity is $R = 4x^3 - 3x^2 + 2x$. What is the marginal revenue? (See Exercise 8.)

10. Suppose that the cost $C$ of producing $x$ units of a commodity is $x^3/3 + 2x + 4$ and that the revenue $R$ from the sale of $x$ units is $R = x^2 + 4x$. The profit $P$ is $R - C$. What is the marginal profit, that is, the rate of change of $P$ with respect to $x$?

11. If the cost $C$ of producing $x$ units of an article is $50 + 3x + 2x^2$, what is the marginal cost (see Exercise 7) when $x = 50$? What is the cost of producing the 51st unit?

**4. The Differentiation of Products and Quotients of Functions.** Let us consider now the problem of how to differentiate the product of two functions. For example, we might have to differentiate the function

(21) $$y = (x^2 + 3)x^3.$$

It is true in this case, although it will not be true of problems we shall encounter later, that we can avoid the product form by multiplying $x^3$ into each term in the parentheses. However, just to be perverse let us insist on trying to differentiate this product.

To obtain $y'$ we might apply the reasonable conjecture that the derived function of a product of two functions is the product of the derived functions. Accordingly,

(22) $$y' = 2x \cdot 3x^2 = 6x^3.$$

To check our conjecture let us multiply out, that is, let us apply the distributive axiom in (21). Then

$$y = x^5 + 3x^3.$$

If we differentiate this function, we obtain

(23) $$y' = 5x^4 + 9x^2$$

Now (22) and (23) do not agree. Hence our conjecture must be wrong. Let us not be too dejected, however, because Leibniz made the same conjecture and it took him quite a while to see what was wrong with it.

Let us resort to the method of increments. Suppose that

(24) $$y = uv$$

where $u$ and $v$ are functions of $x$. At $x = x_0$, $u$, $v$, and $y$ have values that we denote by $u_0$, $v_0$, and $y_0$. Then

(25) $$y_0 = u_0 v_0.$$

We let $x$ change to the value $x_0 + \Delta x$. Then

$$y_0 + \Delta y = (u_0 + \Delta u)(v_0 + \Delta v)$$

or

(26) $$y_0 + \Delta y = u_0 v_0 + u_0 \Delta v + v_0 \Delta u + \Delta u \Delta v.$$

We subtract (25) from (26) to obtain

$$\Delta y = u_0 \Delta v + v_0 \Delta u + \Delta u \Delta v.$$

The average rate of change of $y$ with respect to $x$ in the interval $\Delta x$ is obtained by dividing by $\Delta x$. Of course, to divide a product by $\Delta x$ it is correct to divide either factor by $\Delta x$. Hence

**(27)**
$$\frac{\Delta y}{\Delta x} = u_0 \frac{\Delta v}{\Delta x} + v_0 \frac{\Delta u}{\Delta x} + \Delta u \frac{\Delta v}{\Delta x}.$$

To obtain the limit of $\Delta y / \Delta x$ as $\Delta x$ approaches 0, we note first of all that the right-hand side of (27) consists of three terms, whereas we want the limit of the entire sum. However, we have already had occasion to point out in connection with Theorem 2 that intuitively it is reasonable that the limit of a sum of functions should be the sum of the limits of the summands. Hence we take the limit of each term separately. The first two terms are alike in that each contains a constant, $u_0$ in the first term and $v_0$ in the second, multiplied into a function of $\Delta x$. To find

$$\lim_{\Delta x \to 0} u_0 \frac{\Delta u}{\Delta x}$$

we recall the proof of Theorem 1. We found it reasonable to conclude there that the limit of a constant times a function is the constant times the limit of the function. Hence

**(28)**
$$\lim_{\Delta x \to 0} u_0 \frac{\Delta v}{\Delta x} = u_0 v.'$$

Likewise

**(29)**
$$\lim_{\Delta x \to 0} v_0 \frac{\Delta u}{\Delta x} = v_0 u'.$$

The third term on the right side of (27) presents a new problem. Here we have a product of two functions of $\Delta x$, namely, $\Delta u$ and $\Delta v / \Delta x$. Both functions vary as $\Delta x$ approaches 0. The function $\Delta u$ approaches 0 as $\Delta x$ approaches 0 because the smaller the increment in $x$, the smaller is the increment in the function $u$. The function $\Delta v / \Delta x$ approaches some number $v'$ as $\Delta x$ approaches 0. What does the product of $\Delta u$ and $\Delta v / \Delta x$ approach?

Let us consider the two functions $2x^2$ and $3x$. As $x$ approaches 1, $2x^2$ approaches 2 and $3x$ approaches 3. What does the product $6x^3$ approach? Certainly, as $x$ approaches 1, $6x^3$ approaches 6. Judging from this example, then, the limit of a product of two functions is the product of the limits. This example is not a proof, but it gives some ground for believing that the conclusion is correct.

We shall rest on this crude argument for the present and assert that the limit of the product

$$\Delta u \cdot \frac{\Delta v}{\Delta x}$$

is the product of the limits. We have already noted that the separate limits are 0 and $v'$. Hence

**(30)**
$$\lim_{\Delta x \to 0} \Delta u \cdot \frac{\Delta v}{\Delta x} = 0.$$

If we now use (28), (29), and (30), we see from (27) that

$$\lim_{\Delta x \to 0} \frac{\Delta y}{\Delta x} = u_0 v' + v_0 u' + 0$$

or that the derived function $y'$ is given by

$$y' = uv' + vu'.$$

Hence we have proved the following theorem:

**Theorem 5:** If $y = uv$ where $u$ and $v$ are functions of $x$, then

**(31)**
$$y' = uv' + vu'.$$

That is, the derivative (and derived function) of a product of two functions is the first factor times the derivative (derived function) of the second plus the second times the derivative (derived function) of the first.

We see from Theorem 5 that the procedure for differentiating the product of two functions is not what we guessed at the outset but is slightly more complicated.

The type of argument that we used to derive Theorem 3 from Theorem 2 can now be applied to derive the following theorem:

**Theorem 6:** If $y = uvw$, where $u$, $v$, and $w$ are functions of $x$,

**(32)**
$$y' = uvw' + uwv' + vwu'.$$

We consider next the procedure for differentiating the quotient of two functions. Thus

$$y = \frac{x^2 + 1}{x + 7}$$

is a quotient of the functions in the numerator and denominator. We might conjecture that $y'$ is the quotient of the derivative of the numerator and the derivative of the denominator. However, our experience with obtaining the derivative of a product of two functions might forewarn us that this conjecture may be erroneous, and in fact it is. To see that it is we can differentiate $y = x^3/x^2$ by forming the quotient of the derivative of the numerator and the derivative of the denominator and comparing with the derivative of $y = x$. To obtain the correct procedure we use the method of increments.

Let $u$ and $v$ each be a function of $x$ and let

**(33)**
$$y = \frac{u}{v} .$$

To obtain $y'$ at the value of $x_0$ of $x$, we first substitute $x_0$ for $x$ in the functions $u$, $v$, and $y$. If, as usual, we denote the function values by $u_0$, $v_0$, and $y_0$, then

**(34)**
$$y_0 = \frac{u_0}{v_0} .$$

We now replace $x$ by $x_0 + \Delta x$ in (33) and denote the new values of $u$, $v$, and $y$ by $u_0 + \Delta u$, $v_0 + \Delta v$, and $y_0 + \Delta y$. Then

**(35)**
$$y_0 + \Delta y = \frac{u_0 + \Delta u}{v_0 + \Delta v} .$$

In accordance with the method of increments we subtract (34) from (35) and obtain

**(36)**
$$\Delta y = \frac{u_0 + \Delta u}{v_0 + \Delta v} - \frac{u_0}{v_0} .$$

Let us simplify this expression by carrying out the subtraction. The lowest common denominator is $(v_0 + \Delta v)v_0$, and therefore we obtain

$$\Delta y = \frac{v_0(u_0 + \Delta u) - u_0(v_0 + \Delta v)}{(v_0 + \Delta v)v_0} .$$

The numerator can be simplified to yield

**(37)**
$$\Delta y = \frac{v_0 \Delta u - u_0 \Delta v}{(v_0 + \Delta v)v_0} .$$

Now we divide both sides by $\Delta x$. To divide the right side by $\Delta x$, it is correct algebra to divide the numerator by $\Delta x$. Moreover, in dividing each of the products in the numerator, we must divide one factor only. Hence

**(38)**
$$\frac{\Delta y}{\Delta x} = \frac{v_0 \dfrac{\Delta u}{\Delta x} - u_0 \dfrac{\Delta v}{\Delta x}}{(v_0 + \Delta v)v_0} .$$

To determine the limit of $\Delta y / \Delta x$ we face a new difficulty. The right-hand side of (38) is a quotient, and both the numerator and the denominator vary as $\Delta x$ approaches 0. May we determine the limit of the quotient by determining the limits of the numerator and denominator separately? Suppose, for example, that we are faced with the quotient

$$\frac{x^2 + 3x + 2}{x + 1}$$

and that we must find the limit approached by the quotient as $x$ approaches 0. The numerator certainly approaches 2 as $x$ approaches 0, because $x^2$ and $3x$ become smaller and smaller and approach 0. The denominator approaches 1. Hence the quotient of the limits is $2/1$ or 2. It so happens that the numerator can be factored into $(x + 2)(x + 1)$ and the value of the fraction is $x + 2$; thus we see that this fraction approaches 2 as $x$ approaches 0. Hence it does seem as though the limit of a quotient can be obtained by taking the quotient of the limit of the numerator and the limit of the denominator (provided that the limit of the denominator is not zero).

For the present we shall accept the evidence of this example and proceed to evaluate the limit in (38) by calculating the limit of the numerator and the limit of the denominator. The limit of the numerator is evaluated by practically the same argument that enabled us to proceed from (27) to (31). The limit of the difference of the two terms in the numerator is the difference of the limits. The limit of $v_0 \Delta u / \Delta x$, as in (28), is $v_0 u'$ and the limit of $u_0 \Delta v / \Delta x$, as in (29), is $u_0 v'$. Hence the limit of the numerator is

$$v_0 u' - u_0 v'.$$

The limit of the denominator in (38) is readily determined. As $\Delta x$ approaches 0, $\Delta v$ approaches 0. Hence $v_0 + \Delta v$ approaches $v_0$. The other factor $v_0$ is constant as $\Delta x$ varies. Because the limit of a constant times a function is the constant times the limit of the function, the limit of the product $(v_0 + \Delta v)v_0$ is $v_0^2$.

Then the derivative of $y$ with respect to $x$ at $x = x_0$ is

$$(39) \qquad y' = \lim_{\Delta x \to 0} \frac{\Delta y}{\Delta x} = \frac{v_0 u' - u_0 v'}{v_0^2}.$$

The derived function exists for all $x_0$ for which the derivative $y'$ exists. We see from (39) that the derivative exists for all $x_0$ for which $v_0$ does not equal zero. Of course, if $v_0$ is 0, the original function also has no meaning at $x_0$. We then have the following theorem:

**Theorem 7:** If $y = u/v$, where $u$ and $v$ are functions of $x$, then

$$(40) \qquad y' = \frac{vu' - uv'}{v^2}.$$

That is, the derivative (and derived function) of a quotient of two functions is the denominator multiplied into the derivative (derived function) of the numerator minus the numerator multiplied into the derivative (derived function) of the denominator, all divided by the square of the denominator. The derivative (derived function) exists where $v$ does not equal 0.

The use of the theorems on the derivative of a product and quotient of functions is somewhat novel, and we might therefore consider one or two examples. Suppose that we must find the derived function of

$$y = (x^2 - 1)(x^2 + 6x + 5).$$

We could, of course, multiply the two polynomials and obtain a single polynomial. We could then apply the theorem on the derived function of a sum of functions and obtain the required result. However, it is easier to apply Theorem 5 on the derived function of a product of two functions. We think of $x^2 - 1$ as a function $u$ of $x$ and of $x^2 + 6x + 5$ as a function $v$ of $x$. Then

$$y' = uv' + vu' = (x^2 - 1)(2x + 6) + (x^2 + 6x + 5)(2x).$$

We can, of course, simplify the result by purely algebraic processes. Whether or not we should do so depends on what we plan to do with the derived function.

Let us consider next an example of the use of the theorem on the derived function of a quotient. Suppose that

$$y = \frac{x^2 + 3}{2x - 1}.$$

Such a function, that is, a quotient of two polynomials, is called a *rational function*. To obtain the derived function we apply the theorem on quotients. We think of $x^2 + 3$ as a function $u$ of $x$ and of $2x - 1$ as a function $v$ of $x$. Then

**(41)** $$y' = \frac{vu' - uv'}{v^2} = \frac{(2x - 1)(2x) - (x^2 + 3)(2)}{(2x - 1)^2}.$$

Again, we can simplify the result if the use to be made of it warrants doing so.

## EXERCISES

1. Find the derived function of each of the following functions:

(a) $y = (x^2 - 1)(x + 2)$.
   Ans. $y' = 3x^2 + 4x - 1$.

(b) $y = x(x^2 - 1)(x + 2)$.

(c) $y = \dfrac{x}{x - 1}$.
   Ans. $y' = \dfrac{-1}{(x - 1)^2}$.

(d) $y = \dfrac{x^2 - 1}{x + 3}$.

(e) $y = \dfrac{x^2 - 1}{x^2 + 3}$.
   Ans. $y' = \dfrac{8x}{(x^2 + 3)^2}$.

(f) $y = \dfrac{x(x^2 - 1)}{x + 3}$.

(g) $y = \dfrac{x^3 + 3x^2 + 7}{x - 1}$.
   Ans. $dy/dx = \dfrac{2x^3 - 6x - 7}{(x - 1)^2}$.

(h) $y = 7x^2 + \dfrac{3}{x - 1}$.

2. If $y = f(x)g(x)$, what is $y'$?
   Ans. $f(x)g'(x) + f'(x)g(x)$.

3. If $y = f(x)/g(x)$, what is $y'$?

4. If $f(x) = x^4$, $g(x) = x^2 + 7$ and $y = f(x)g(x)$, calculate $y'$.

5. If $f(x) = \sqrt{x}$, $g(x) = x^2 + 1$, and $y = f(x)/g(x)$, calculate $y'$.

6. If $f(x) = \dfrac{x+1}{x-1}$, $g(x) = \dfrac{1}{x}$, and $y = f(x) + g(x)$, calculate $y'$.

7. If $f(x) = \sqrt{x}$, $g(x) = \dfrac{1}{x}$, and $y = f(x)g(x)$, calculate $y'$.

8. The numbers in the following problem have been chosen to simplify the arithmetic. Suppose that the population $P$ of a country increases according to the formula $P = 100 + 2.5x^2$ in $x$ years from 1970. The gross national income $I$ increases according to the formula $I = 2500 + 3x + 7x^2$. The per capita income $C$ is then $I/P$. Calculate the rate of change of per capita income per year.

9. If in step (27) of the proof of Theorem 5 we had written $(\Delta u/\Delta x)\Delta v$. would it have been correct and would the proof still go through?　　　　　*Ans.* Yes.

10. Had we established earlier in the logical development of the calculus the theorem on the derived function of a product of two functions, we could have given another proof on the power rule for positive integral $n$; that is, if $y = x^n$, then $y' = nx^{n-1}$. The alternative proof uses mathematical induction, the idea of which is the following. We know by application of the method of increments that when $n = 1$, $y' = 1x^0$. Now assume, in accordance with the method of mathematical induction, that for $n = k - 1$, $y' = (k-1)x^{k-2}$, and let us prove that for $n = k$, $y' = kx^{k-1}$. Hence consider $y = x^k = x \cdot x^{k-1}$. Complete the proof.

11. If $p$ is the price per unit at which $x$ units of a commodity can be sold then $R = xp$ is called the total revenue and $dR/dx$ is called the marginal revenue. Show that the marginal revenue is $p + x\,dp/dx$.

12. A firm produces $x$ cans per week at a total cost of $C$ dollars. The average cost per unit is $A = C/x$ and $dC/dx$ is the marginal cost $M$. Show that $dA/dx$ is $(xM - C)/x^2$.

13. A car depreciates according to the law that the value $V$ in $t$ years is given by the formula $V = 2500/(1 + t)$. When is the rate of depreciation greatest?

14. A firm can sell $x$ chairs at $p$ dollars per chair when $p = [640/(x+9)] - 40$. Its revenue $R$ is $xp$. Calculate the marginal revenue $dR/dx$ and determine the largest number it can sell and still keep the marginal revenue positive.


**5. The Integration of Combinations of Functions.** Whenever a theorem on differentiation is established it is helpful to think immediately of the inverse process of antidifferentiation, because the inverse process is equally important. Theorem 1 tells us that if $y = cu$, then $y' = cu'$. It tells us that the constant factor $c$ can, so to speak, be ignored for the moment while we differentiate the function $u$ and that we then multiply the result of the differentiation by $c$. The very meaning of antidifferentiation, that is, finding the function that has a given derived function, enables us to state the following theorem:

**Theorem 8:** If $y' = cu'$ then

(42) $$ y = \int cu' \, dx = c \int u' \, dx = cu + C. $$

In practice this means that in antidifferentiation or integration we may ignore the constant factor for a moment, integrate the function, and then multiply the antiderivative or integral by the constant. Of course, the constant of integration $C$ must be added on.

Just as Theorem 8 follows from Theorem 1, so a consequence of Theorem 2 on the differentiation of a sum of functions is the following theorem:

**Theorem 9:** If $y' = u' + v'$ then

**(43)** $$y = \int (u' + v')dx = \int u'\, dx + \int v'\, dx = u + v + C.$$

That is, the integral of a sum of functions is the sum of the integrals plus the constant of integration.

In view of Theorem 3, we could of course extend Theorem 9 to a sum of $n$ functions. There is no need to state a separate theorem.

Suppose $y' = 3x^3 - 5x^{1/2}$, that is, $y'$ is a difference of two functions. We noted in Theorem 4 that a difference $u - v$ of two functions $u$ and $v$ can always be regarded as the sum $u + (-v)$ or $u + (-1)v$. In view of Theorem 8 the $(-1)$ can be handled. Thus

**Theorem 10:** If $y' = u' - v'$, then

**(44)** $$y = \int (u' - v')dx = \int u'\, dx - \int v'\, dx = u - v + C.$$

We might ask next, what theorems on antidifferentiation correspond to Theorems 5 and 7 on the differentiation of products and quotients? There is a very useful inverse to Theorem 5, called *integration by parts*. However, we shall delay studying it until we can make significant use of it. (See Chapter 14, Section 2.) As for Theorem 7, we can indeed state that if

**(45)** $$y' = \frac{vu' - uv'}{v^2}$$

then

$$y = \int \left( \frac{vu' - uv'}{v^2} \right)dx + C = \frac{u}{v} + C.$$

However, this result is rarely useful. The reason is that a derived function is seldom presented to us in the explicit form (45). A derived function may indeed have resulted from the application of the theorem on quotients, as was the case in (41), but when the result is simplified algebraically, it is no longer possible to recognize what the original $u$ and $v$ were. Hence the antidifferentiation must be performed in accordance with some other theorem.

**Example.**   If $y' = 3x^3 - 5x^{1/2}$, what is $y$?

**Solution.**   To integrate we may, by reason of Theorem 10, integrate $3x^3$ and $5x^{1/2}$ separately and subtract the second result from the first. In integrating $3x^3$ we may for the moment ignore the 3, integrate $x^3$, and then multiply the result by 3. The final antiderivative is $3x^4/4$. Likewise to integrate $5x^{1/2}$ we integrate $x^{1/2}$, obtain $x^{3/2}/\frac{3}{2}$ or $\frac{2}{3}x^{3/2}$ and multiply this result by 5. Then $y = 3x^4/4 - 10x^{3/2}/3 + C$.

## EXERCISES

1. Find the integrals of the following derived functions:

(a)  $y' = 8x^2$.     Ans. $y = \frac{8}{3}x^3 + C$.

(b)  $y' = 7x^{2/3}$.

(c)  $y' = \sqrt{8x}$ .

Ans. $y = \dfrac{4\sqrt{2}}{3}x^{3/2} + C$.

(d)  $y' = 7x^{2/3} + \sqrt{8x}$ .

Ans. $y = \frac{21}{5}x^{5/3} + \dfrac{4\sqrt{2}}{3}x^{3/2} + C$.

(e)  $y' = 7x^2 + 6x - 3$.

Ans. $y = \frac{7}{3}x^3 + 3x^2 - 3x + C$.

(f)  $y' = \sqrt{4x}$ .

(g)  $y' = -7x^2 - 6x + 3$.

(h)  $dy/dx = \dfrac{x^4 + 3x^2}{x^2}$ .

Ans. $y = \dfrac{x^3}{3} + 3x + C$.

(i)  $dy/dx = \dfrac{x^4 + 3x^2}{\sqrt{x}}$ .

(j)  $dy/dx = ax^2 + bx + c$.

Ans. $y = \dfrac{a}{3}x^3 + \dfrac{b}{2}x^2 + cx + C$.

(k)  $dy/dx = 3x^4 - 7x^2 + 5x - 6$.

2. Evaluate:

(a)  $\displaystyle\int 8x^2\, dx$.     Ans. $y = \frac{8}{3}x^3 + C$.

(b)  $\displaystyle\int 7x^{-1/2}\, dx$.

(c)  $\displaystyle\int (7x + 8x^2)dx$.

(d)  $\displaystyle\int (9x^2 + 6x - 3)dx$.

Ans. $3x^3 + 3x^2 - 3x + C$.

(e)  $\displaystyle\int (x^2 - 7x^{2/3})dx$.

(f)  $\displaystyle\int (x^{1/2} + 3x^{2/3})dx$.

(g)  $\displaystyle\int (s^{1/2} + 3s^{2/3})ds$.

Ans. $\frac{2}{3}s^{3/2} + \frac{9}{5}s^{5/3} + C$.

(h)  $\displaystyle\int (3t^2 - 4t)dt$.

**6.  All Integrals Differ by a Constant.** The theorems on the differentiation of combinations of functions, in conjunction with what we have already learned about the geometrical interpretation of the derived function as the slope of a curve, permit us to give a rather convincing geometrical argument in support of a fact that we have been using right along. We have said, for example, that if

**(46)** $$y' = 4x$$

then

**(47)** $$y = 2x^2 + C;$$

that is, *all* integrals of (46) are comprised in (47). In other words, all integrals of a given derived function are obtained by finding one integral and adding a constant. Let us prove this geometrically.

It is more convenient here to use the function notation. Suppose that

**(48)** $$y' = f'(x).$$

Then certainly

$$y = f(x)$$

is one integral of (48). Now let $g(x)$ be any other integral of (48); that is, $g'(x) = f'(x)$. We should like to show that $g(x)$ can differ from $f(x)$ by at most a constant. Then let

**(49)** $$w = f(x) - g(x).$$

By the theorem on the differentiation of the difference of two functions,

$$w' = f'(x) - g'(x) = 0.$$

We now ask, what function has the derived function that is 0 over some interval of $x$-values? Geometrically it seems clear that if the slope of some curve is always 0, this curve must be a straight line parallel to the $x$-axis. Then the equation of $w$ as a function of $x$ must be $w = $ constant. Hence we see from (49) that $g(x) = f(x) + $ constant. Because $g(x)$ is *any* integral of (48) other than $f(x)$, we see that all integrals of (48) are given by

$$y = f(x) + C.$$

**7. The Power Rule for Negative Exponents.** The general theorems on differentiation that we proved in Section 4 enable us to extend at once the range of the power rule. We have already proved that when $n$ is a positive integer or a positive fraction,* the derived function of $y = x^n$ is $y' = nx^{n-1}$. We now prove that the power rule holds when $n$ is a negative integer or negative fraction. The proof is simple. We start with

**(50)** $$y = x^n$$

where $n$ is a negative integer or a negative fraction. By the very meaning of a negative exponent we have

$$y = \frac{1}{x^{-n}}$$

where, of course, $-n$ is positive. We can regard this function as a quotient of two functions, namely, 1 and $x^{-n}$. We know how to differentiate a quotient and we know how to differentiate $x^{-n}$ because the exponent is

---

* Strictly we have not proved the power rule for positive fractional exponents but we shall (Chap. 7, Sect. 4).

positive. We apply (40). Then

$$\frac{dy}{dx} = \frac{x^{-n}(0) - 1(-nx^{-n-1})}{(x^{-n})^2}.$$

or

$$\frac{dy}{dx} = \frac{nx^{-n-1}}{x^{-2n}} = nx^{-n-1-(-2n)}$$

or

**(51)**
$$\frac{dy}{dx} = nx^{n-1}.$$

If we compare (50) and (51), we see that $y'$ is obtained from $y$ by a straightforward application of the power rule, even though $n$ is a negative whole number or a negative fraction. Hence the power rule holds when $n$ is a positive or negative whole number or fraction. We should note that for negative $n$, for example $x^{-3}$, the function is not defined at $x = 0$, and therefore neither the derivative nor the derived function has any meaning at $x = 0$.

If we combine what we proved in Chapter 5, Section 4, with what we just proved, we have the following theorem:

**Theorem 11:** If $y = x^n$, where $n$ is a positive or a negative whole number or fraction or zero, then

**(52)**
$$y' = nx^{n-1}.$$

Of course in view of (11) a constant multiplier of $x^n$ will also appear in the derivative.

Corresponding to the theorem on differentiation is a theorem on antidifferentiation. We could state the new theorem thus: If $y' = nx^{n-1}$, where $n$ is a positive or negative fraction or zero, then $y = x^n + C$. However, in practice we generally encounter $y'$ in the form $y' = x^n$, and we seek $y = \int x^n \, dx$. To obtain the integral we reverse what is done when differentiating a power of $x$; that is, we increase the exponent by 1 and divide by the new exponent. Hence

$$y = \int x^n \, dx = \frac{x^{n+1}}{n+1} + C.$$

We notice now that the result is meaningless when $n = -1$. In other words, the derived function $y' = 1/x$ cannot be integrated, at least not by the power rule. Our result then is the power rule for integration:

**Theorem 12:** If $y' = x^n$ where $n$ is any positive or negative whole number or fraction or zero except $-1$, then

**(53)**
$$y = \int x^n \, dx = \frac{x^{n+1}}{n+1} + C.$$

Since a constant multiplier $a$ as in $y = ax^n$ appears as a constant multiplier in the derivative, it follows that in integration a constant multiplier in $y'$ must appear in the integral. That is,

$$y = \int ax^n \, dx = a \frac{x^{n+1}}{n+1} + C.$$

## EXERCISES

1. Find the derived functions of the following functions:
    (a) $y = x^{-7}$.    Ans. $y' = -7x^{-8}$.
    (b) $y = x^{-3/2}$.
    (c) $y = \dfrac{2}{x}$.    Ans. $y' = -2x^{-2}$.
    (d) $y = \dfrac{1}{\sqrt{x}}$.
    (e) $y = \dfrac{1}{\sqrt{3x}}$.
      Ans. $dy/dx = -\dfrac{1}{2\sqrt{3}} x^{-3/2}$.
    (f) $y = \dfrac{x^2 + 7x}{x^3}$.

2. Find the integrals of the following derived functions:
    (a) $y' = x^{-7}$.
      Ans. $y = -\dfrac{x^{-6}}{6} + C$.
    (b) $dy/dx = x^{-1/2}$.
    (c) $y' = \dfrac{1}{\sqrt{x}}$.
      Ans. $y = 2x^{1/2} + C$.
    (d) $y' = \dfrac{1}{8x^2}$.
    (e) $dy/dx = \dfrac{1}{\sqrt{8x}}$.
      Ans. $y = \dfrac{1}{\sqrt{2}} x^{1/2} + C$.

3. Evaluate:
    (a) $\int x^{-5} \, dx$.
      Ans. $y = -\frac{1}{4} x^{-4} + C$.
    (b) $\int (x^{-5} + x^{-3/2}) \, dx$.
    (c) $\int x^{-3/4} \, dx$.
    (d) $\int x^{-7/2} \, dx$.
    (e) $\int (x^3 + x^{-5/2}) \, dx$.
      Ans. $y = \frac{1}{4} x^4 - \frac{2}{3} x^{-3/2} + C$.
    (f) $\int (3x^{-3} + 2x^{-2}) \, dx$.

4. Show that the segment of the tangent at any point (Fig. 6-8) of the curve $y = 1/x$ (the curve is called a hyperbola) that is cut off by the axes is bisected at the point of contact.

**Figure 6-8**

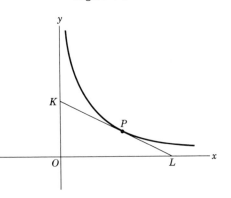

5. Show that the tangent at any point of the curve $y = 1/x$ (Fig. 6-8) cuts off from the axes a triangle which always has the same area.

6. When light is given off by a source, which is often idealized as a point, it spreads out in all directions. At some subsequent time it illuminates a spherical area of radius $r$ feet or an area of $4\pi r^2$ square feet. If the intensity given off by the source is $A$ units (lumens is the technical name for the unit), the intensity per square unit of area illuminated is $I = A/4\pi r^2$. Find the rate of change of the intensity with distance when $r = 20$ feet and when $r = 200$ feet. How would you explain physically that the numerical value or absolute value of the rate of change is much less when $r = 200$ feet than when $r = 20$ feet?

   *Ans.* At $r = 20$, $dI/dr = -A/16000\pi$; at $r = 200$, $dI/dr = -A/16,000,000\pi$.

7. The total cost of producing $x$ glasses is given in dollars by the function $C = 500 + \sqrt{x} + \dfrac{1}{\sqrt{x}}$. Find the rate of change of cost per unit, that is, the marginal cost, for the hundredth glass. Would the marginal cost generally for all products be positive?

## 8. The Concept of Work and an Application.* An important concept for scientific and engineering purposes is work. As used in these fields the word has a technical meaning, but for the moment let us rely upon our intuitive understanding and consider why one should be interested in it. A train or an airplane which pulls a load over some distance, a crane which lifts a steel girder from the ground to some height, and a rocket which shoots up into the air all do work. Of course, the work that these mechanisms do is powered by engines and fuel. To design the engines and to choose the suitable kind and amount of fuel one must know how much work is to be done. Thus a quantitative measure of the work is called for.

The performance of work involves the application of a force. Pushing or pulling an object along the ground is a force which is needed to overcome the force or friction between the object and the ground. Raising an object calls for the exertion of a force by a person or an engine to overcome the force of gravity. In the technical use of the concept of work the force applied must cause motion. If one pushes against a heavy object but fails to move it, even though great effort may be expended, there is, technically speaking, no work done. Loosely speaking, work is force multiplied by the distance through which the force acts.

The unit of force in the British system is the poundal or the pound which is 32 poundals. In the centimeter-gram-second (c.g.s.) metric system it is the dyne. Because work is force times distance and distance is measured in feet, the unit of work is the foot-poundal. In the metric system the unit of work is the erg or the dyne-centimeter. Thus if a force of 50 poundals pushes an object for 10 feet, the work done is 500 foot-poundals (ft-pdl) or 500/32 foot-pounds (ft-lb).

The examples of work that we shall consider here involve the action of gravity, that is, the gravitational attraction which the earth exerts on objects. When gravity acts on an object and, for example, causes it to fall, we say that gravity does work on the object. If we raise an object, we say

---

* This section can be omitted without disrupting the continuity.

that we have done work against gravity. The same amount of force is involved in both cases and, if the object moves the same distance, the work done is the same.

Let us consider the force of gravity. The force which the earth's gravity exerts on an object is called the *weight* of the object. This concept of weight involves the notion of *mass*. Every piece of matter has mass, which is a property quite different from weight. Technically the mass of an object is the resistance it offers to any change in its velocity. However, for our purposes it is adequate to think of the mass of an object as the quantity of matter in it. It is intuitively clear that a cubic foot of lead has more mass than a cubic foot of wood, which in turn has more mass than a cubic foot of sponge.

Near the surface of the earth the *weight* of an object is always 32 times the amount of *mass*; in symbols,

**(54)** $$w = 32m.$$

This fact is established by direct measurement of mass and weight. The unit of mass is pounds and the unit of weight, because it is a force, is poundals. Unfortunately, the use of the pound for 32 poundals of force causes some confusion, but is also convenient because 1 pound of mass weighs 1 pound.

If an object moves near the surface of the earth, its weight does not change appreciably. Hence if gravity pulls an object weighing 100 poundals down a distance of 25 feet, the work which gravity does is 2500 ft-pdl. Certainly, we do not need the calculus to calculate this work.

If an object is at a great distance from the surface of the earth, its weight or the gravitational force exerted on it by the earth is no longer the weight near the surface and, in fact, the weight varies with the distance from the earth. The force which the earth exerts on any object at any distance from the earth's center is given by the famous axiom of physics known as Newton's law of gravitation. This law states that *any* two objects in the universe attract each other, and the force with which each attracts the other is given quantitatively by the formula

**(55)** $$F = \frac{GmM}{r^2}.$$

In this formula $G$ is a constant; it is the same number no matter what the masses involved and no matter what the distance between them. The quantities $m$ and $M$ are the *masses* of the two objects measured in pounds. As to the quantity $r$, Newton's law applies to particles, that is, to objects which, in the situation being studied, can be idealized as concentrated at one point and in such cases $r$ is the distance between the point–particles. An object which is treated as a particle is not necessarily small. Thus in treating some aspects of the motion of the earth around the sun it may be adequate to regard the earth and sun as particles or point-masses. It is likewise often possible to treat an object which falls to earth as a particle. However, the earth is vast compared to the object, and the various portions of the earth pull the object in different directions and with different strengths because their distances from the falling object vary considerably. Hence it does not seem possible to treat the earth as a particle. There is, nevertheless, a remarkable theorem, which we shall prove much later and which states that the earth, if regarded as a sphere, attracts particles *as though* the earth's mass were concentrated at its center. Hence we can take the distance between the earth and the object, the quantity $r$ in (55), to be the distance from the *center* of the earth to the object. The quantity $r$ is measured in feet (centimeters in the metric system).

Because the quantity $G$ is constant, we can take two known masses, measure the distance between them, measure the force with which they attract each other, and then calculate $G$, the only unknown in (55). This has been done many times, and the value of $G$ turns out to be, in the foot-poundal-second system, $1.07 \cdot 10^{-9}$ (in the metric system $G$ is $6.67 \cdot 10^{-8}$).

If, now, $M$ stands for the mass of the earth and $m$ is the mass of an object above the earth, then $F$ in (55) is the force with which the earth attracts the object or the weight of the object. We see that the weight of an object does vary with its distance from the center of the earth; in fact, the weight decreases as the distance increases.

How does this formula for weight compare with formula (54), namely, $w = 32m$? When the value of $G$ is substituted in (55), when $M$ is replaced by the mass of the earth, and when $r$ is taken to be $4000 \cdot 5280$, that is, when the object is at or practically at the surface of the earth, the quantity $GM/r^2$ reduces to 32, so that $GMm/r^2$ becomes $32m$ and $w$ is then only a special designation of $F$. In other words, for the values of $G$, $M$, and $r$ just mentioned

**(56)**
$$\frac{GM}{(4000 \cdot 5280)^2} = 32.$$

In practice we often use this equation to find the product $GM$.

To calculate the work done by gravity in pulling an object some distance straight down, we cannot multiply the force by the distance because the force varies from point to point along the path. We must use the calculus. Let us actually compute the work done by gravity in pulling an object some distance downward.

Let us choose the direction from the center of the earth upward as the positive direction for $r$ (Fig. 6-9). Because the force of gravitation acts toward the center, we write

**(57)**
$$F = -\frac{GmM}{r^2}$$

where $M$ is the mass of the earth and $m$ is the mass of the object. Suppose that the object is at some distance $r$ from the center of the earth and gravity pulls the object downward a small distance $\Delta r$. Even over this small distance $\Delta r$ the force of gravity is not constant, and therefore strictly we cannot say that the force is given by (57). However, it is reasonable to

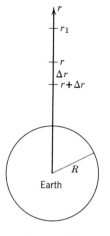

**Figure 6-9**

suppose that there is some value $\bar{r}$ in the interval $\Delta r$ at which the force

$$\bar{F} = -\frac{GMm}{\bar{r}^2} .$$

Let us denote the work done by gravity in moving the object over the interval $\Delta r$ by $\Delta W$. Then

$$\Delta W = \bar{F}\Delta r.$$

By division

$$\frac{\Delta W}{\Delta r} = \bar{F}.$$

We now determine the limit of $\Delta W / \Delta r$ as $\Delta r$ approaches 0. As $\Delta r$ approaches 0, $\bar{r}$ must come closer and closer to $r$ because $\bar{r}$ is between $r$ and $r + \Delta r$. Then $\bar{F}$ must come closer and closer to the value of $F$ at $r$. That is,

$$\frac{dW}{dr} = \lim_{\Delta r \to 0} \frac{\Delta W}{\Delta r} = F$$

or, in view of (55),

$$\frac{dW}{dr} = -\frac{GmM}{r^2} .$$

We may now apply formula (53), the inverse of the power law, to assert that

**(58)** $$W = \frac{GmM}{r} + C.$$

To determine the constant of integration we suppose that the object starts at the distance $r_1$ from the center of the earth and that no work has been done as yet by gravity. This means that when $r = r_1$, $W = 0$. Then

$C = -GmM/r_1$ and

(59) $$W = \frac{GmM}{r} - \frac{GmM}{r_1} .$$

This is the formula for the work done by gravity in pulling an object of mass $m$ down from a point $r_1$ feet from the center of the earth to a point $r$ feet from the center.

To use formula (59) we must know the value of the product $GM$. It is given by (56) which shows that

(60) $$GM = 32(4000 \cdot 5280)^2.$$

If we should happen to need the values of $G$ and $M$ separately, we could use the measured value of $G$, which is

$$G = 1.07 \cdot 10^{-9},$$

and calculate $M$, which proves to be

$$M = 13.1 \cdot 10^{24} \text{ pounds.}$$

We also note that for the purpose of simple algebraic transformations it is convenient to let $R$ denote the radius of the earth, that is,

$$R = 4000 \cdot 5280;$$

then (60) reads

(61) $$GM = 32R^2.$$


## EXERCISES

1. Show that the work done by gravity in pulling an object of mass $m$ straight down from a distance $r_1$ from the center of the earth to the surface of the earth is $W = 32mR[1 - (R/r_1)]$.

2. Calculate the work that gravity does in pulling a mass of 100 pounds from a height of 500 miles above the earth to the surface of the earth.

    *Ans.* $\dfrac{22{,}528 \cdot 10^6}{3}$ ft-pdl.

3. Suppose that we use $32m$ as the constant force of gravity and calculate the work done by gravity in pulling an object over the same path as in Exercise 2. Before calculating, determine whether the answer will be greater or smaller than the answer in Exercise 2 and then carry out the calculation.

    *Ans.* $8{,}448 \cdot 10^6$ ft-pdl.

4. How much work is done in raising a satellite with a mass of 1000 pounds from the surface of the earth to a height of 1500 miles?

5. Formula (59) gives the work done by gravity in pulling an object down when the work is 0 at the height $r_1$. Suppose that we want to measure work so that it

is 0 when the object is at the surface of the earth, that is, when $r = R$. Obtain the appropriate formula for the work done in moving the object from the distance $r$ to the surface.

$$Ans. \quad W = 32mR\left(\frac{R}{r} - 1\right).$$

6. A cable weighing 2 pounds per foot of length (and so having a mass of 2 pounds per foot) is suspended from the top of a well 200 feet deep and extends to the bottom. Find the work done in raising the cable to the surface. Over the distance of 200 feet you may use $32m$ as the constant weight of a mass $m$.

7. Suppose that the cable described in Exercise 6 has a tool weighing 300 pounds attached to the lower end. Calculate the work done in raising the tool to the surface. *Ans.* 3,200,000 ft-pdl.

8. The law of gravitation applies of course also to the moon and to any object which the moon attracts. The mass of an object is the same everywhere, so that an object with mass $m$ on the earth has mass $m$ on or near the moon. However, the weight of an object of mass $m$ is $5.3m$ on the surface of the moon. The moon's radius is about 1100 miles so that [cf. (56)] if $M$ is the mass of the moon

$$\frac{GM}{(5280 \cdot 1100)^2} = 5.3.$$

(a) Determine first whether formula (59) applies to work done by the moon's gravity. *Ans.* Yes.

(b) Derive the formula analogous to that given in Exercise 1, that is, the formula for the work done by the moon's gravity in moving an object of mass $m$ from a distance of $r_1$ from the center to the surface of the moon.
*Ans.* $W = 5.3mR[1 - (R/r_1)]$; $R$ is the radius of the moon.

9. Using the data of Exercise 8, calculate the work which the moon's gravity does in pulling a mass of 100 pounds from a height of 500 miles above the surface to the surface (cf. Exercise 2).

10. How much work must be done to raise a satellite with a mass of 1000 pounds from the surface of the moon to a height of 1500 miles (cf. Exercise 4).

$$Ans. \quad \frac{230,868 \cdot 10^6}{13} \text{ ft-pdl.}$$

11. (a) To push an object up a smooth inclined plane, one must overcome the force of gravity which causes the object to slide down the plane. Hence according to formula (32) of Chapter 3 the force which must be applied is $w \sin A$ where $w$ is the weight of the object and $A$ is the angle of inclination of the plane. Suppose that you push the object from the ground level to a point $h$ feet above the ground. How much work is done?
*Ans.* $wh$.

(b) Is the result remarkable in any respect?

# CHAPTER SEVEN
# THE CHAIN RULE

**1. Introduction.** The functions we have been able to differentiate and integrate thus far have been rather simple ones. Essentially they have been polynomials, terms of the form $x^{p/q}$, and simple combinations of such functions formed by the four operations of addition, subtraction, multiplication, and division. However, physical problems lead to more complicated algebraic functions, for example, $y = \sqrt{x + 1}$. This function arises when one wishes to work with the upper half of the parabola $y^2 = x + 1$. Thus far we have no method of differentiating

$$(1) \qquad y = \sqrt{x + 1} .$$

We can regard this function as a combination or composite of two functions

$$(2) \qquad y = \sqrt{u} , \quad u = x + 1.$$

What we have done in (2) is to express $y$ as a function of $u$, which is a function of $x$, and $y$ is said to be a function of a function. Now we can find $dy/du$ and $du/dx$ by methods of differentiation we have already learned. What is $dy/dx$?

**2. The Chain Rule.** The Leibnizian notation for the derivative suggests that

$$(3) \qquad \frac{dy}{dx} = \frac{dy}{du} \cdot \frac{du}{dx} .$$

We might conclude in looking at (3) that all we must do to prove the equality is to cancel the $du$'s. We recall, however, that the symbolism $dy/du$, for example, does not mean a quotient. The entire symbol stands for

**144**

a limit, which is not a quotient but a number approached by the entire fraction $\Delta y/\Delta u$ as $\Delta u$ approaches 0.

However, (3) is correct, and the method of increments yields the desired proof. Before using it, let us note that (3) is a meaningful statement, first of all, at a point. That is, if $x_0$ is some value of $x$, $u_0$ the corresponding value of $u$, and $y_0$ the corresponding value of $y$, then $dy/dx$ at $x = x_0$ is the product of $dy/du$ at $u_0$ and $du/dx$ at $x_0$, if $du/dx$ exists at $x_0$ and if $dy/du$ exists at $u_0$. Second, (3) is also a statement about the derived *functions* $dy/dx$, $dy/du$, and $du/dx$ for those $x_0$'s and $u_0$'s for which the equality holds among the derivatives.

To prove (3) we now apply the method of increments. We note that if we change $x$ from $x_0$, the value of $x$ at which we seek the derivative, by an amount $\Delta x$, then $u$ changes by some amount $\Delta u$ because $u$ is a function of $x$. However, if $u$ changes by an amount $\Delta u$, then $y$ changes by an amount $\Delta y$. We can write the purely algebraic relation

**(4)**
$$\frac{\Delta y}{\Delta x} = \frac{\Delta y}{\Delta u} \cdot \frac{\Delta u}{\Delta x} .$$

Each of these fractions is a true quotient, and therefore this equation is justified merely because we can cancel $\Delta u$'s on the right side. We intend to apply a limit process, but before doing so we note that when $\Delta x$ approaches 0, $\Delta u$ approaches 0. This is true when $du/dx$ exists, for if $\Delta u$ did not approach 0 when $\Delta x$ does, the limit $du/dx$ could not exist—it would be infinite. Hence, to require that $\Delta x$ approach 0 is to require that $\Delta u$ approach 0. Likewise when $\Delta u$ approaches 0, $\Delta y$ approaches 0. If we take the limit as $\Delta x$ approaches 0 in (4), the limit on the right side, which is a product, can be calculated as the product of the limits. The limit of $\Delta u/\Delta x$ is of course $du/dx$; the limit of $\Delta y/\Delta u$ is $dy/du$. Then*

**(5)**
$$\frac{dy}{dx} = \frac{dy}{du} \cdot \frac{du}{dx} .$$

Thus we have proved the following theorem:

**Theorem 1:** If $y$ is a function of $u$ and $u$ is a function of $x$, then

**(6)**
$$\frac{dy}{dx} = \frac{dy}{du} \cdot \frac{du}{dx} .$$

This theorem is called the chain rule because it deals with a "chain" of functions or a function of a function.

Because the function notation is often useful let us express the chain

---

*This proof of (5) is not quite complete. It is possible for $\Delta u$ to be 0 when $\Delta x$ is not 0. Then the algebraic equation (4) is not justified. Actually if $\Delta u$ is not 0 for any small interval about $u_0$, the proof is right, for we need to consider only small $\Delta x$ to obtain the limit as $\Delta x$ approaches 0. However, $\Delta u$ may be 0 at values of $x$ arbitrarily close to $x_0$. Nevertheless, (5) can be shown to be true in this case also.

rule in this notation also. Suppose, then, that we have

$$y = f(u) \quad \text{and} \quad u = g(x).$$

Then the chain rule states that

$$\frac{dy}{dx} = f'(u)\,g'(x)$$

where, of course, $f'(u)$ denotes the derivative of $f(u)$ with respect to $u$ and $g'(x)$ denotes the derivative of $g(x)$ with respect to $x$. To indicate that $y$ is a composite function of $x$ the notation

$$y = f(g(x))$$

is also used.

**3. Application of the Chain Rule to Differentiation.** We shall make extensive use of the chain rule. The first advantage we derive from it is to enlarge considerably the class of functions we can differentiate and integrate. At present we consider differentiation.

   Let us consider the function

(7)                                  $$y = \sqrt{x^2 + 1}\ .$$

and let us find $dy/dx$. With the chain rule at hand we can proceed as follows. We let

$$u = x^2 + 1.$$

Then in place of (7) we have

(8)                          $$y = \sqrt{u} \quad \text{and} \quad u = x^2 + 1.$$

Now we see that

$$\frac{dy}{du} = \tfrac{1}{2}u^{-1/2} \quad \text{and} \quad \frac{du}{dx} = 2x.$$

Then by the chain rule

$$\frac{dy}{dx} = \frac{dy}{du} \cdot \frac{du}{dx} = \tfrac{1}{2}u^{-1/2} \cdot 2x.$$

In view of the value of $u$ in (8),

(9)                                  $$\frac{dy}{dx} = \frac{x}{\sqrt{x^2 + 1}}\ .$$

   The chain rule can also be used to expedite differentiations that could be performed without it but are more readily done with it. Thus suppose that

**(10)**
$$y = (x^2 + 1)^5.$$

We could, of course, expand the binomial and obtain a polynomial and then differentiate the polynomial by using earlier theorems. However, it is easier to proceed as follows. Let

$$u = x^2 + 1.$$

Then

$$y = u^5 \quad \text{and} \quad u = x^2 + 1.$$

Furthermore,

$$\frac{dy}{du} = 5u^4 \quad \text{and} \quad \frac{du}{dx} = 2x.$$

Then by the chain rule

$$\frac{dy}{dx} = \frac{dy}{du} \cdot \frac{du}{dx} = 5u^4 \cdot 2x = 5(x^2 + 1)^4 \cdot 2x.$$

Thus by the application of the chain rule we have obtained $dy/dx$ rapidly, and we have the answer in a compact form. Let us pay particular attention to the appearance of the factor $2x$ in the answer. It enters the answer because of the factor $du/dx$ in the chain rule.

This example suggests that we can profitably generalize Theorem 11 of Chapter 6. There we learned that if

$$y = x^n$$

where $n$ is a positive or negative integer or fraction or zero, then

**(11)**
$$\frac{dy}{dx} = nx^{n-1}.$$

Now suppose that we have $y = u^n$ where $u$ is a function of $x$. Then the chain rule tells us that

$$\frac{dy}{dx} = \frac{dy}{du} \cdot \frac{du}{dx}.$$

To find $dy/du$ we can apply (11) because $u$ is as much a variable as $x$ is. Then

$$\frac{dy}{dx} = nu^{n-1} \frac{du}{dx}.$$

This result, which is basic in differentiation, is worthy of being stated as a theorem:

**Theorem 2:** If $y = u^n$ where $u$ is a function of $x$ and $n$ is a positive or negative integer or fraction or zero, then

**(12)**
$$\frac{dy}{dx} = nu^{n-1} \frac{du}{dx}.$$

We call this result the generalized power rule for differentiation.

**Example 1.** Find $dy/dx$ when $y = \sqrt{x^2 + 6x + 4}$ .

**Solution.**   We can apply the chain rule in the form (12). We let $u = x^2 + 6x + 4$. Then our function is

$$y = u^{1/2}.$$

Then by (12)

$$\frac{dy}{dx} = 1/2u^{-1/2}(2x + 6) = \frac{2x + 6}{\sqrt{x^2 + 6x + 4}} .$$

**Example 2.** Find $dy/dx$ when $y = x^3/(x^2 + 3)^2$.

**Solution.**   We must treat the given function as a quotient of two functions. Hence first

$$\frac{dy}{dx} = \frac{(x^2 + 3)^2 \dfrac{d(x^3)}{dx} - x^3 \dfrac{d(x^2 + 3)^2}{dx}}{(x^2 + 3)^4} .$$

Now the only remaining difficulty is to differentiate $(x^2 + 3)^2$. We let $u = x^2 + 3$. Then

$$\frac{dy}{dx} = \frac{(x^2 + 3)^2(3x^2) - x^3 \cdot 2(x^2 + 3)(2x)}{(x^2 + 3)^4} .$$

We can, of course, simplify the answer and would do so if we had to do further work with it.

## EXERCISES

1. Differentiate the following functions:

(a)   $y = (x^3 + 1)^4$.

        Ans.  $\dfrac{dy}{dx} = 12(x^3 + 1)^3x^2$.

(b)   $y = (x^2 - 7x + 6)^4$.

(c)   $s = (t^2 - 5)^4$.

(d)   $y = \dfrac{1}{(a^2 - x^2)^2}$ .

(e)   $y = \dfrac{5 + 2x}{5 - 2x}$ .

(f)   $y = \sqrt[3]{x^2 + 1}$

        Ans.  $\dfrac{dy}{dx} = \dfrac{2}{3}(x^2 + 1)^{-2/3}x$.

(g)   $y = \left(\dfrac{x}{x + 1}\right)^4$.

(h)   $y = \sqrt{x^2 - x}$ .

        Ans.  $\dfrac{dy}{dx} = \dfrac{1}{2}(x^2 - x)^{-1/2}(2x - 1)$.

(i)   $y = \sqrt{x^2 - x}\,(x^2 + 1)$.

(j)   $y = \sqrt{\dfrac{x}{1 + x}}$ .

        Ans.  $\dfrac{dy}{dx} = \dfrac{1}{2\sqrt{x}\,(1 + x)^{3/2}}$ .

(k)   $y = \sqrt{1 + x}\,\sqrt{1 - x}$ .

(l)   $y = (y')^2$.    Ans. $y' = 2y'y''$.

2. As an object increases its height $x$ above the surface of the earth, its weight $w$ decreases because the pull of gravity on the object decreases. Suppose that a rocket weighs $80/(x + 4000)^2$ million pounds at an altitude of $x$ miles and is rising at the constant rate of 100 mi/min. Find the rate of change of weight with respect to time at any instant.      *Ans.* $dw/dt = -16{,}000/(x + 4000)^3$.

3. If $p$ is the price at which $x$ units of a certain product can be sold then $xp$ is called the revenue $R$. The rate of change of $R$ with respect to $x$ is called the marginal revenue. Calculate the marginal revenue if $p = \sqrt{250 - 9x}$ .

4. Differentiate the following functions:
   (a)   $y = (x^2 + 2)^3(x - 3)$.
      *Ans.* $y' = (x^2 + 2)^2(7x^2 - 18x + 2)$.    (b)   $y = \sqrt{\dfrac{x - 1}{x + 1}}$ .
      (c)   $y = (5x^2 - 1)^{-2/3}$.

## 4. The Differentiation of Implicit Functions.

A function is a relation between two variables such that given a value of one in some domain a unique value of the second is determined. Thus $y = x^3 - 7x^2$ is a typical function. Functions often occur in less convenient form. Thus the relation between abscissa and ordinate of a circle (Fig. 7-1) of radius 5 is, by the Pythagorean theorem,

**(13)** $$x^2 + y^2 = 25.$$

Here $y$ is not expressed in terms of $x$. We can, of course, solve for $y$ and obtain

$$y = \pm \sqrt{25 - x^2} .$$

We should note that (13) gives rise to two functions:

**(14)** $$y = \sqrt{25 - x^2} \quad \text{and} \quad y = -\sqrt{25 - x^2} .$$

The first function represents the positive $y$-values as $x$ ranges from —5 to 5 and the second the negative $y$-values for the same domain of $x$-values. Thus in our sense of the term two (single-valued) functions are needed to represent the circle. We say that (13) represents each of these functions *implicitly*, whereas (14) gives each one explicitly.

We might be interested in either of these functions. Let us suppose

**Figure 7-1**

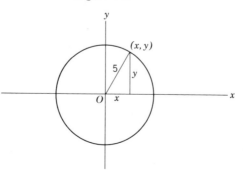

that we are interested in

**(15)**
$$y = \sqrt{25 - x^2}\,,$$

and that we wish to calculate the derived function, $dy/dx$, but are given (13) instead of (15). How then do we find $dy/dx$? One procedure that can often be followed is to solve (13) for $y$, as in (15), and then differentiate by using the chain rule. However, even if we can solve for $y$ for many purposes it would be easier to work with the implicit function (13) if we could find some method of differentiating it as it stands.

There is at least one other reason for trying to work with implicit functions. Consider the equation

**(16)**
$$y^3 + xy^2 + x^2 = 0.$$

As far as $y$ is concerned, this is a cubic equation and can be solved for $y$ in terms of $x$ and the constants. In fact, there are (usually) three distinct solutions; that is, the equation (16) represents implicitly three distinct functions. If we wanted to work with any one of these functions, we could solve for $y$, but the expression that results is quite complicated. It would be simpler to work with (16) as it stands. Furthermore, suppose that we have the equation

**(17)**
$$y^5 + 4y^3 - 3xy^2 + xy + 7 = 0.$$

Here we have a fifth degree equation in $y$, and only exceptional fifth degree equations can be solved algebraically. Hence even if we were willing to work with a complicated expression of $y$, we could not obtain it. If we have to work with any one of the five functions represented implicitly by (17), we must learn how to work with the implicit representation.

Let us consider the problem of differentiating a function which is given implicitly and let us start with the simple case of (13). We know that $y$ in (13) represents some function of $x$, but we do not care to know or utilize the precise form of this function. If we recognize that the left side of (13) is then only a set of terms in $x$, we may be able to differentiate it. The derivative of $x^2$ is $2x$. The real problem is, what is the derivative of $y^2$ with respect to $x$? Here we have a function of $y$, namely $y^2$, and $y$ itself is a function of $x$. Finding the derivative of $y^2$ with respect to $x$ should remind us of the chain rule. This rule tells us ($y$ plays the role of $u$ in the chain rule) that we must differentiate with respect to $y$ and then multiply by $dy/dx$; that is,

$$\frac{d(y^2)}{dx} = 2y\,\frac{dy}{dx}\,.$$

We have then the derivative of the left side of (13). The right side is a constant and its derivative is 0. Hence we obtain

**(18)**
$$2x + 2y\,\frac{dy}{dx} = 0.$$

From this we have

(19)
$$\frac{dy}{dx} = -\frac{x}{y}.$$

It is true that the derivative involves $y$ as well as $x$. Sometimes the derivative can be used in exactly this form. For example, to calculate the slope of the circle at $(3, 4)$, we can substitute directly in (19). Alternatively, if we can find $y$ explicitly, and we can in this case, we can substitute the value of $y$ in (19) and obtain $dy/dx$ as a function of $x$. We must be careful, however, to keep in mind which function is involved. If we are interested in the upper half of the circle, we must use $y = \sqrt{25 - x^2}$, and if in the lower half of the circle, then $y = -\sqrt{25 - x^2}$.

The differentiation of an equation such as (16) involves another, minor consideration. We have

(20)
$$y^3 + xy^2 + x^2 = 0.$$

Again we argue that because this equation defines $y$ as a function of $x$, the left side is a function of $x$. To differentiate $y^3$ we again use the chain rule and obtain

$$\frac{d(y^3)}{dx} = 3y^2 \frac{dy}{dx}.$$

To differentiate the term $xy^2$ we must first take into account the fact that we have a product of two functions of $x$. Then

$$\frac{d}{dx}(xy^2) = \frac{d(x)}{dx} y^2 + x \frac{d(y^2)}{dx} = y^2 + x \cdot 2y \frac{dy}{dx}.$$

The derivative of the third term in (20), namely $x^2$, is of course $2x$. Because the right side of (20) is 0, its derivative is 0. We now put together the result of differentiating the several terms in (20) and obtain

$$3y^2 \frac{dy}{dx} + y^2 + 2xy \frac{dy}{dx} + 2x = 0.$$

To obtain $dy/dx$ we must solve this equation for $dy/dx$. This process gives

$$\frac{dy}{dx} = \frac{-y^2 - 2x}{3y^2 + 2xy}.$$

In this case it is almost necessary to leave the result in terms of $x$ and $y$ because the explicit expression for any of the functions $y$ would be cumbersome.

Now that we know how to differentiate functions defined implicitly we can obtain a proof of the power law for positive fractional $n$ which we promised in Section 4 of Chapter 5. The problem is to obtain the derivative of

(21)
$$y = x^{p/q},$$

where $p$ and $q$ are positive integers and $x$ may be positive, zero, or negative if $q$ is odd but only 0 or positive if $q$ is even. By raising both sides of this equation to the $q$th power, we have

(22)
$$y^q = x^p.$$

Now let us differentiate this equation. By the chain rule

$$\frac{d(y^q)}{dx} = qy^{q-1}\frac{dy}{dx}.$$

The derivative of $x^p$ is $px^{p-1}$. Then

$$qy^{q-1}\frac{dy}{dx} = px^{p-1}.$$

By solving for $dy/dx$ we obtain

$$\frac{dy}{dx} = \frac{p}{q}\frac{x^{p-1}}{y^{q-1}} = \frac{p}{q}\frac{x^{p-1}y}{y^q}.$$

We have the values of $y$ and $y^q$ in (21) and (22). If we use these, we obtain

$$\frac{dy}{dx} = \frac{p}{q}\frac{x^{p-1}x^{p/q}}{x^p} = \frac{p}{q}x^{-1}x^{p/q} = \frac{p}{q}x^{(p/q)-1}.$$

Thus we see again that the power rule is correct for positive fractional exponents. The extension to negative fractional and negative integral exponents can now be made as in Chapter 6, Section 7.

## EXERCISES

1. Find $dy/dx$ for the functions defined implicitly by the following equations:

(a) $xy = 1$.　　Ans. $\dfrac{dy}{dx} = -\dfrac{y}{x}$.

(b) $x^2 + y^2 - 5 = 0$.

(c) $3x^2 + 2y^2 - 5 = 0$.

　　Ans. $\dfrac{dy}{dx} = -\dfrac{3x}{2y}$.

(d) $x^2 + xy + y^2 + 7 = 0$.

(e) $y^3 + xy^2 + y + 2x = 0$.

　　Ans. $\dfrac{dy}{dx} = -\dfrac{y^2 + 2}{3y^2 + 2xy + 1}$.

(f) $y^2 = 4x$.

2. Find the expression for the slope at points on the lower half of the circle $x^2 + y^2 = 25$.　　　　　Ans. $dy/dx = x(25 - x^2)^{-1/2}$.

3. Find the slope at the point $P$ (Fig. 7-2) whose abscissa is 2 of the parabola $y^2 = 8x$.

4. Given that $dy/dx = -x/y$, find $d^2y/dx^2$ in terms of $x$ and $y$.　　　　Ans. $d^2y/dx^2 = -(y^2 + x^2)/y^3$.

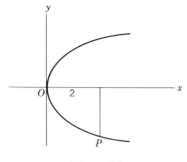

**Figure 7-2**

5. Show that the equation of the tangent to the parabola $y^2 = 4px$ at the point $(x_0, y_0)$ is $y - y_0 = \dfrac{2p}{y_0}(x - x_0)$.

6. Show that the $x$-intercept of the tangent to the parabola $y^2 = 4px$ at the point $(x_0, y_0)$ is $-x_0$.

7. Show that the $x$-intercept of the normal (the line perpendicular to the tangent) to the parabola $y^2 = 4px$ at the point $(x_0, y_0)$ is $x_0 + 2p$.

**5. Equations of the Ellipse and Hyperbola.**\* The method of differentiating implicit functions is especially useful when applied to the functions representing the conic sections, that is, the parabola, circle, ellipse, and hyperbola. Let us consider first the equations of the ellipse and hyperbola.

The ellipse is usually defined in the following way. We start with two points, $F$ and $F'$ of Fig. 7-3, which are called the foci. The two points are a given fixed distance apart, denoted by $2c$. (We could say $c$ but the ensuing algebra is simpler if we use $2c$.) We choose a number $2a > 2c$ and consider all points (in one plane) whose distances from $F$ and $F'$ add up to $2a$. This set of points constitutes an ellipse. Thus if $P$ is a point on the ellipse, then

**(23)** $$PF + PF' = 2a.$$

We note, incidentally, that $2a$ must be greater than $2c$ because the sum of two sides of a triangle is greater than the third side.

To find the equation of the ellipse, we locate the coordinate axes in a way that, experience shows, gives the simplest equation (Fig. 7-4). That is,

**Figure 7-3**

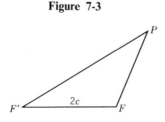

\*This section can be omitted by those students who are familiar with the analytic geometry of the ellipse and hyperbola.

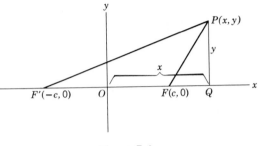

**Figure 7-4**

we let the $x$-axis be the line joining the two foci and we let the $y$-axis be the line perpendicular to the $x$-axis and halfway between $F'$ and $F$. Then the coordinates of $F$ are $(c, 0)$ and the coordinates of $F'$ are $(-c, 0)$. Let the coordinates of any point $P$ on the ellipse be $(x, y)$. Because $PFQ$ is a right triangle, we see that

$$PF = \sqrt{(x - c)^2 + y^2} \, ,$$

and because $PF'Q$ is a right triangle and the (geometric) distance $F'Q$ is $x + c$, we see that

$$PF' = \sqrt{(x + c)^2 + y^2} \, .$$

Then the algebraic equivalent of (23) is

**(24)**              $$\sqrt{(x - c)^2 + y^2} + \sqrt{(x + c)^2 + y^2} = 2a.$$

We could maintain that this result is the algebraic equation of the ellipse because it expresses the condition which the coordinates $(x, y)$ of any point on the ellipse must satisfy. However, we can simplify this equation.

The easiest way to simplify it is to first rewrite (24) as

$$\sqrt{(x - c)^2 + y^2} = 2a - \sqrt{(x + c)^2 + y^2} \, .$$

Now let us square both sides. This step gives

$$(x - c)^2 + y^2 = 4a^2 - 4a\sqrt{(x + c)^2 + y^2} + (x + c)^2 + y^2.$$

If we expand $(x - c)^2$ on the left side and $(x + c)^2$ on the right, subtract equal terms from both sides, and put all terms except the radical on one side, we obtain

$$- 4cx - 4a^2 = -4a\sqrt{(x + c)^2 + y^2} \, .$$

Dividing both sides by $-4$ yields

$$+ cx + a^2 = a\sqrt{(x + c)^2 + y^2} \, .$$

We square both sides again and obtain

$$c^2x^2 + 2a^2cx + a^4 = a^2\left[(x + c)^2 + y^2\right].$$

Expanding $(x + c)^2$ and multiplying the terms in the brackets by $a^2$ gives

$$c^2x^2 + 2a^2cx + a^4 = a^2x^2 + 2a^2cx + a^2c^2 + a^2y^2.$$

If we subtract $2a^2cx$ from both sides and rearrange terms, we obtain

$$a^2x^2 - c^2x^2 + a^2y^2 = a^4 - a^2c^2$$

or

$$x^2(a^2 - c^2) + a^2y^2 = a^2(a^2 - c^2).$$

The combination $a^2 - c^2$ occurs twice. Because $a > c$, $a^2 - c^2$ is a positive quantity and we can let

**(25)**
$$a^2 - c^2 = b^2.$$

Then

**(26)**
$$b^2x^2 + a^2y^2 = a^2b^2.$$

This form of the equation of the ellipse is simple. We can also divide the equation by $a^2b^2$ and write*

**(27)**
$$\frac{x^2}{a^2} + \frac{y^2}{b^2} = 1.$$

It is helpful to know the shape and size of the ellipse in terms of the quantities $a$, $b$, and $c$. We see from (26) that when $y = 0$, $x = \pm a$. The two points $(a, 0)$ and $(-a, 0)$ are the points at which the ellipse cuts the $x$-axis (Fig. 7-5). Likewise when $x = 0$, we see from (26) that $y = \pm b$. These two points $(0, b)$ and $(0, -b)$ are the points at which the ellipse cuts the $y$-axis.

*Because we squared an equation twice to derive (27) from (24), there is the possibility that we introduced values of $x$ and $y$ which satisfy (27) but not (24). That squaring can introduce new solutions is obvious from the example $x = y$. Squaring produces $x^2 = y^2$, and there are many $x$ and $y$ satisfying the latter equation which do not satisfy the former. To show that (27) has exactly the same solutions $(x, y)$ as (24), let us suppose that $(x_1, y_1)$ satisfies (27) but not (24). $(x_1, y_1)$ are the coordinates of some point. The sum of the distances of this point from the foci is then not $2a$ but, say, $2k$. Moreover $2k > 2c$ because if we take any point $Q$ [other than those on the segment $FF'$ which points can be ruled out at once as not satisfying (27)], $QF + QF' > 2c$. By starting with an equation which is (24) except that $2a$ is replaced by $2k$ and by going through steps (24) to (27) we obtain the result

$$\frac{x_1^2}{k^2} + \frac{y_1^2}{k^2 - c^2} = 1.$$

Suppose that $k < a$. Then $x_1^2/k^2 > x_1^2/a^2$ and because $k^2 - c^2 < a^2 - c^2$, $y_1^2/(k^2 - c^2) > y_1^2/b^2$. Then $(x_1, y_1)$ cannot satisfy (27). If we suppose that $k > a$, we can obtain a similar contradiction.

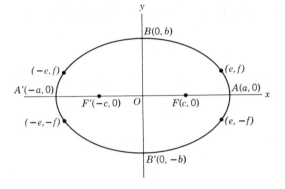

**Figure 7-5**

To obtain some idea of how the curve behaves, we note first that if $(e, f)$ are the coordinates of a point that satisfy equation (26) or (27), then $(-e, f)$ also satisfy the equation. This means geometrically that the curve is symmetric with respect to the $y$-axis, because $(-e, f)$ is, so to speak, the mirror image of $(e, f)$ in the $y$-axis. We also observe from (26) or (27) that if $(e, f)$ are the coordinates of a point on the curve, then $(e, -f)$ are the coordinates of another point on the curve because if $(e, f)$ satisfy (26) then so do $(e, -f)$. Geometrically this means that the curve is symmetric with respect to the $x$-axis because $(e, -f)$ is the mirror image of $(e, f)$ in the $x$-axis.

The significance of knowing that a curve is symmetric with respect to the $x$-axis, or the $y$-axis, or both is that if we know what the curve looks like in the first quadrant, that is, where $x$ and $y$ are both positive, we also know how it looks in one or more of the other quadrants. In the case of the ellipse, if we could find out what the curve looks like in the first quadrant, then, because it is symmetric with respect to the $x$-axis, we also know how it looks in the fourth quadrant. Also, because the curve is symmetric with respect to the $y$-axis, we know how it looks in the second and third quadrants. Hence, as far as the ellipse is concerned, determining the shape of the curve reduces to determining what the curve looks like in the first quadrant.

We could use the geometrical definition of the ellipse to determine the shape in the first quadrant. Thus, to be concrete, choose a number for $2c$, say 8, and a number for $2a$, say 12. We could then place two points 8 units apart, which would be the foci. A point on the ellipse must have the sum of its distances from these two points equal to 12. We pick any two numbers whose sum is 12, say 9 and 3. Then we draw a circle with $F'$ as center and radius 9 and another circle with $F$ as center and radius 3 (Fig. 7-6). Where these two circles intersect, we have a point on the ellipse. In this way we can locate a number of points and then join them by a smooth curve.

We can also use the equation of the ellipse to determine the shape in the first quadrant. We see from (26) that

$$a^2y^2 = a^2b^2 - b^2x^2$$

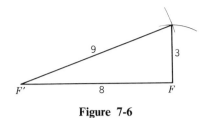

**Figure 7-6**

or that

**(28)**
$$y = \pm \frac{b}{a} \sqrt{a^2 - x^2} \, .$$

If we wish to locate points in the first quadrant, we use the function

$$y = \frac{b}{a} \sqrt{a^2 - x^2} \, .$$

For a given ellipse, that is, for a definite choice of $2a$ and $2c$, say 12 and 8 again, we can calculate $b$ by (25). In this case $b = \sqrt{20}$ and $a$ of course equals 6. Then our function becomes

$$y = \frac{\sqrt{20}}{6} \sqrt{36 - x^2} \, .$$

Next we can choose a few values of $x$, calculate the corresponding values of $y$, and plot the points corresponding to each pair of $x$-and $y$-values. The shape of the curve in the first quadrant and consequently in all four quadrants is shown in Fig. 7-5. We shall see in the next section how we can learn more about the curve.

The shape of the ellipse is, of course, the same no matter where we choose the axes. Hence we see that an ellipse is symmetrical about two lines which are mutually perpendicular. The intersection of these two lines, the point $O$ in Fig. 7-5, is called the *center* of the ellipse. (This center is also the midpoint of $FF'$.) The longest chord through $O$, the segment $AA'$ in Fig. 7-5, is called the *major axis* and its length is $2a$. The shortest chord through $O$ is the segment $BB'$ and it is called the *minor axis*. Its length is $2b$.

For each choice of $a$ and $c$ with $a > c$ there is an ellipse. Hence there is not one ellipse but an infinity of ellipses. How do they differ from each other? If $a$ and $c$ are altered but the ratio is kept the same, we obtain an ellipse of the same shape but of different size. We can prove this readily. Because

$$b^2 = a^2 - c^2,$$

if we replace $a$ by $ra$ and $c$ by $rc$, the new $b$ value is $r$ times the old $b$ value. Furthermore, if we denote by primes the coordinates of the ellipse determined by $ra$ and $rc$, we have from (27)

**(29)**
$$\frac{x'^2}{r^2 a^2} + \frac{y'^2}{r^2 b^2} = 1.$$

If we set

$$x' = rx, \qquad y' = ry,$$

(29) reduces to (27). That is, to each $x$ and $y$ of the ellipse determined by $a$ and $c$, there are an $x'$ and $y'$ of the ellipse determined by $ra$ and $rc$ which are $r$ times $x$ and $y$, respectively. This new ellipse has the same shape as the original one.

To distinguish ellipses by shapes we must change the ratio of $a$ to $c$. We define a new quantity called the *eccentricity*, which is denoted by $e$, namely,

$$e = \frac{c}{a}.$$

When the eccentricity changes, the shape of the ellipse changes. Since only the ratio $e$ counts as far as shape is concerned, we may keep $a$ fixed and vary $c$. Because $2c$ is the distance between the foci, $c$ can be 0 or positive. When $c$ is 0, the two foci coincide and, since $b^2 = a^2 - c^2$, $a = b$. We see then from (26) that when $e = 0$, the ellipse becomes a circle. As $c$ increases, while $a$ remains fixed, (25) tells us that the ellipse becomes flatter. Because $c$ must be less than $a$, $e$ is always less than 1.

The equation of the hyperbola is in many respects similar to that of the ellipse. Geometrically the curve is defined as follows. We start with two fixed points, $F$ and $F'$ in Fig. 7-7, which are called the foci. The two points are a given fixed distance apart denoted by $2c$. Now we consider all points (in one plane) whose distances from $F$ and $F'$ *differ* by the same constant which we denote by $2a$. The set of all points which satisfy this condition is called a hyperbola. That is, the hyperbola consists of all points $P$ for which

$$PF - PF' = 2a \qquad \text{or} \qquad PF' - PF = 2a.$$

We note that the $2a$ must be less than $2c$ because if $P$ is a point on the hyperbola, then $|PF' - PF|$ must be less than $F'F$, for the difference of any two sides of a triangle must be less than the third side.

Let us find the equation of the hyperbola. The geometrical definition requires that for any point $P$ on the hyperbola either

$$PF - PF' = 2a \qquad \text{or} \qquad PF' - PF = 2a.$$

**Figure 7-7**

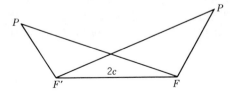

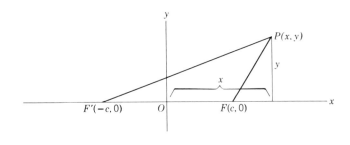

**Figure 7-8**

We locate the coordinate axes in a way that, experience shows, gives the simplest equation. That is, we let the $x$-axis (Fig. 7-8) be the line through $F$ and $F'$ and we let the $y$-axis be the line perpendicular to the $x$-axis and halfway between $F$ and $F'$. Because the distance $FF'$ is $2c$, the coordinates of $F$ are $(c, 0)$ and the coordinates of $F'$ are $(-c, 0)$. If we denote the coordinates of any point $P$ by $(x, y)$, then as in the case of the ellipse

$$PF = \sqrt{(x - c)^2 + y^2} \, ,$$

$$PF' = \sqrt{(x + c)^2 + y^2} \, .$$

The definition of the hyperbola then states that the curve consists of all $(x, y)$ for which

**(30)** 
$$\sqrt{(x - c)^2 + y^2} - \sqrt{(x + c)^2 + y^2} = 2a$$

or

**(31)** 
$$\sqrt{(x + c)^2 + y^2} - \sqrt{(x - c)^2 + y^2} = 2a.$$

Let us consider the first of these equations and simplify it. The easiest way to begin the simplification is to rewrite (30) as

**(32)** 
$$\sqrt{(x - c)^2 + y^2} = 2a + \sqrt{(x + c)^2 + y^2} \, .$$

We now repeat the processes we used to simplify the analogous case—equation (24) for the ellipse; that is, we square both sides of (32), eliminate equal terms on both sides, and rearrange the terms. We obtain

**(33)** 
$$- cx - a^2 = a\sqrt{(x + c)^2 + y^2} \, .$$

We again square both sides, subtract equal terms, and simplify precisely as in the corresponding steps for the ellipse to obtain

**(34)** 
$$x^2(a^2 - c^2) + a^2 y^2 = a^2(a^2 - c^2).$$

Before we proceed, we might go back and look at (31). We know that (30) leads to (34), but presumably the points $(x, y)$ satisfying (31) would satisfy some other equation than (34). However, if we write (31) as

$$-\sqrt{(x - c)^2 + y^2} = 2a - \sqrt{(x + c)^2 + y^2}$$

and perform the steps leading to (33), the only difference is that we obtain

**(35)** $$- cx - a^2 = - a\sqrt{(x + c)^2 + y^2} .$$

If we now square again, as we did in going from (33) to (34), we obtain (34). In other words, the second squaring operation, which we performed to obtain (34), introduces automatically the points satisfying the condition (31), and (34) represents *both* (30) and (31).

We may then confine ourselves to (34) and because, in the case of a hyperbola $2a < 2c$, we set

$$c^2 - a^2 = b^2,$$

and (34) becomes

**(36)** $$b^2x^2 - a^2y^2 = a^2b^2$$

or, by dividing each term by $a^2b^2$,

**(37)** $$\frac{x^2}{a^2} - \frac{y^2}{b^2} = 1.$$

Either equation, (36) or (37), represents all points on the hyperbola.

To use either equation effectively, it is desirable to know not only the shape of the hyperbola but what the quantities $a$, $b$, and $c$ mean geometrically. We can use either equation to obtain this information. We note from equation (36) that when $y = 0$, $x = \pm a$. The points $(a, 0)$ and $(-a, 0)$ are then the $x$-intercepts, that is, the points at which the curve cuts the $x$-axis (Fig. 7-9). However, when we set $x = 0$, we see that there are no real values for $y$. This means that the curve does not cut the $y$-axis.

**Figure 7-9**

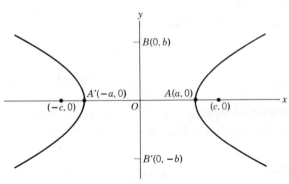

The argument we gave for the ellipse showing that curve is symmetric with repect to the $x$- and $y$-axes, applies equally well to the hyperbola. Hence, as in the case of the ellipse, the problem of determining the shape of the curve reduces to determining the shape in the first quadrant. However, we see from (36) that

$$a^2y^2 = b^2x^2 - a^2b^2$$

or that

$$y = \pm \frac{b}{a} \sqrt{x^2 - a^2} \; .$$

To discuss the curve in the first quadrant, we need to consider only

$$y = \frac{b}{a} \sqrt{x^2 - a^2} \; .$$

We see first of all that if $x < a$, then $y$ is complex. Hence there are no points on the curve with abscissas less than $a$. We see also that as $x$ increases, $y$ increases; moreover $x$ can become infinite and, as it does so, $y$ also becomes infinite. Of course, so far we do not know the precise shape of the curve in the first quadrant. We can choose specific values of $a$ and $c$, and therefore of $b$, and calculate the $y$-values for a few $x$-values. The shape is shown in Fig. 7-9. Now by using the symmetry of the curve we obtain the entire figure. We see that the full curve consists of two separate or disjoined branches. The two branches make up the hyperbola.

The hyperbola is symmetric with respect to two lines which are perpendicular to each other. With the choice of coordinate axes that we made, the two lines are of course the $x$- and $y$-axes. The intersection of the two lines, the origin in the case of Fig. 7-9, is called the *center*. The segment $AA'$ is called the *major* or *transverse* axis. Its length, as we know, is $2a$. Although the curve does not cut the $y$-axis, it is helpful to mark off the segment $BB'$ (Fig. 7-9) of length $2b$, which is called the *minor* or *conjugate* axis. The usefulness of this length will be apparent shortly.

We have seen that the equation of a hyperbola is

$$b^2x^2 - a^2y^2 = a^2b^2.$$

Associated with the hyperbola is a pair of lines, called the *asymptotes*, whose equation is

$$b^2x^2 - a^2y^2 = 0.$$

To see that this equation represents a pair of lines, we have but to factor it and write it as

**(38)** $$(bx - ay)(bx + ay) = 0.$$

The curve corresponding to (38) consists of all points which satisfy

**(39)** $$bx - ay = 0 \quad \text{or} \quad bx + ay = 0.$$

The reason is that if the coordinates of some point $(x_1, y_1)$ satisfy $bx - ay = 0$, the left factor in (38) is 0 whether or not the right factor is. Likewise if $(x_1, y_1)$ are coordinates which satisfy $bx + ay = 0$, the right factor in (38) is 0 whether or not the left factor is. Then the curve belonging to (38) is the curve of the first equation in (39) *and* the curve of the second equation in (39).

Now the equations in (39) can be written as

$$(40) \qquad\qquad y = \frac{b}{a} x \qquad \text{and} \qquad y = -\frac{b}{a} x.$$

We see, then, that each is a straight line (Fig. 7-10), the first having the slope $\frac{b}{a}$ and the second, the slope $-\frac{b}{a}$

The importance of these lines, the asymptotes, is that the branches of the hyperbola lie between them as shown in Fig. 7-10, As the figure suggests, the points farther and farther out along the curve in the first quadrant come closer and closer to the asymptote, but the curve does not ever touch or cut the asymptote. The same is true in each of the other quadrants. We shall not prove this assertion. (See Exercise 19.)

For each value of $a$ and $c$, with $c > a$, a hyperbola is determined. Hence there is not one hyperbola but an infinite number of them. We can distinguish them by specifying the values of $a$ and $c$. However, as in the case of the ellipse, the shape of the hyperbola is determined not by the individual values of $a$ and $c$ but by the ratio $c/a$. We call this ratio the *eccentricity* and denote it by $e$; that is,

$$e = \frac{c}{a} .$$

Since $c > a$, $e$ is always greater than 1. To see how $e$ determines the shape, let us note that

$$b^2 = c^2 - a^2 = a^2 \left( \frac{c^2}{a^2} - 1 \right) = a^2 (e^2 - 1).$$

**Figure 7-10**

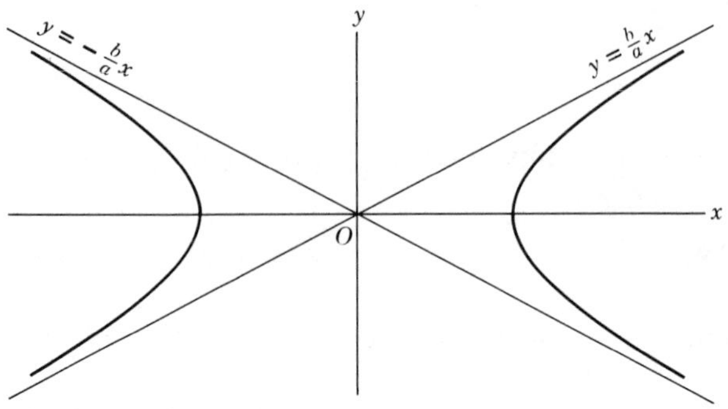

If $a$ is kept fixed and $e$ varies, we see that $b$ varies. We now recall that the equations of the asymptotes are $y = bx/a$ and $y = -bx/a$. Hence the asymptotes lie close to the $x$-axis when $b$ is small and farther away when $b$ is large. Because the hyperbola always lies between the asymptotes, as shown in Fig. 7-10, the curve is narrower or wider depending on the value of $b$ or the related value of $e$.

## EXERCISES

1. Show that $x^2 + y^2 = r^2$ is the equation of a circle with radius $r$.
2. Triangle $ABC$ is inscribed in a semicircle of radius 1 (Fig. 7-11). Prove that $\angle ACB$ is a right angle by computing the slopes of $AC$ and $BC$.

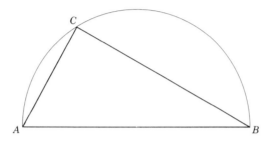

**Figure 7-11**

3. Given the equation $(x^2/16) + (y^2/9) = 1$ for an ellipse, how much are $a$, $b$, $c$, and $e$? *Ans.* $a = 4$, $b = 3$, $c = \sqrt{7}$, $e = \sqrt{7}/4$.
4. Given the equation $8x^2 + 10y^2 = 80$ for an ellipse, how much are $a$, $b$, $c$, and $e$?
5. How long are the major and minor axes of the ellipse $(x^2/36) + (y^2/10) = 1$? *Ans.* $12$, $2\sqrt{10}$.

6. Write the equation of the ellipse for the following cases:
   (a) $a = 8$, $b = 2$. *Ans.* $(x^2/64) + (y^2/4) = 1$.
   (b) $a = 8$ and the distance between the foci is 4.
   (c) $a = 5b$ and passing through the point $(7, 2)$.
   (d) The major axis is 12 and the minor axis is 8.
   *Ans.* $(x^2/36) + (y^2/16) = 1$.

7. The width of an ellipse is often specified by giving the length of the chord passing through a focus and perpendicular to the $x$-axis. Show that this length, which is called the *latus rectum*, is $2b^2/a$.
8. Suppose that the foci of an ellipse which are $2c$ units apart lie on the $y$-axis (Fig. 7-12) and the $x$-axis is halfway between them and, of course, perpendicular to the $y$-axis. If we continue to use $2a$ for the sum of the distances of any point on the ellipse from the two foci, show that the equation of the ellipse is $(x^2/b^2) + (y^2/a^2) = 1$.

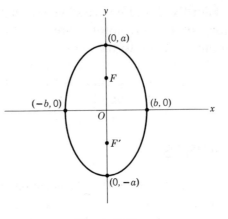

**Figure 7-12**

9. An arch in the shape of the upper half of an ellipse is to support a bridge over a roadway 50 feet wide. The center of the arch is to be 25 feet above the center of the roadway. Write the equation of the ellipse.

*Ans.* $(x^2/625) + (y^2/625) = 1$.

10. The orbit of the earth about the sun is practically an ellipse with the sun at one focus. The ratio of the earth's least distance from the sun (which occurs when the earth is at one end of the major axis) to the greatest distance (which occurs at the other end of the major axis) is $29/30$. Find the eccentricity of the ellipse.

*Ans.* $1/59$.

11. Given the equation $(x^2/16) - (y^2/9) = 1$ for a hyperbola, how much are $a$, $b$, $c$, and $e$?   *Ans.* $a = 4$, $b = 3$, $c = 5$, $e = \frac{5}{4}$.

12. Given the equation $8x^2 - 10y^2 = 80$ for a hyperbola, how much are $a$, $b$, $c$, and $e$?

13. How long are the transverse and conjugate axes of the hyperbola $(x^2/36) - (y^2/9) = 1$?   *Ans.* $12$, $6$.

14. Write the equation of the hyperbola for the following cases:
    (a) $a = 8$, $b = 2$.   *Ans.* $(x^2/64) - (y^2/4) = 1$.
    (b) $a = 8$ and the distance between the foci is 20.
    (c) $a = 8$ and $b = 10$.   *Ans.* $(x^2/64) - (y^2/100) = 1$.
    (d) The transverse axis is 12 and the conjugate axis is 8.

15. In the case of an ellipse $a$ is always greater than (or at least equal to) $b$. What is the corresponding relation of $a$ to $b$ for the hyperbola?

16. The width of a hyperbola is often specified by giving the length of the chord passing through a focus and perpendicular to the $x$-axis. Show that this length, which is called the latus rectum, is $2b^2/a$.

17. Suppose that the foci, which are $2c$ units apart, of a hyperbola lie on the $y$-axis (Fig. 7-13) and the $x$-axis lies halfway between them and perpendicular to the $y$-axis. If we continue to use $2a$ for the difference of the distances of any point on the hyperbola from the foci, show that the equation of the hyperbola is $(x^2/b^2) - (y^2/a^2) = -1$.

18. If we multiply the equations of the two lines $5x + 2y = 25$ and $5x - 2y = 16$, we obtain $25x^2 - 4y^2 = 400$. According to the argument given in connection with (38), the equation of the product should still represent the two lines. However, the points $(4, 0)$ and $(-4, 0)$ satisfy the product but do not satisfy either of the linear equations. What is amiss?

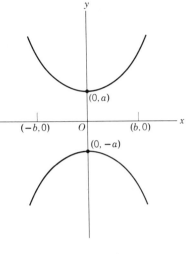

**Figure 7-13**

**19.** Given the hyperbola $(x^2/a^2) - (y^2/b^2) = 1$, so that $y = \pm(b/a)\sqrt{x^2 - a^2}$, let $y_1 = (b/a)\sqrt{x^2 - a^2}$ and let $Y_1 = bx/a$. Show that $Y_1 - y_1$ approaches 0 as $x$ becomes arbitrarily large (approaches infinity).

*Suggestion:* $Y_1 - y_1 = (b/a)(x - \sqrt{x^2 - a^2})$. Now multiply by $(x + \sqrt{x^2 - a^2})/(x + \sqrt{x^2 - a^2})$.

**6. Differentiation of the Equations of Ellipse and Hyperbola.** Our chief concern in this chapter has been the chain rule, and we have seen so far that it enables us to differentiate many functions that we could not handle previously, including implicit functions. Let us apply the chain rule to the particular implicit functions which represent the equations of the ellipse and hyperbola.

We found that the equation of the ellipse is of the form

**(41)** $$b^2x^2 + a^2y^2 = a^2b^2$$

when the coordinate axes are chosen as in Fig. 7-4. In trying to determine the curve which belongs to this equation, we found that, by reason of symmetry with respect to the $x$- and $y$-axes, all we had to do was to determine the shape in the first quadrant. At that point the best suggestion we could make was to solve (41) for $y$, obtaining for the first quadrant

**(42)** $$y = \frac{b}{a}\sqrt{a^2 - x^2},$$

and then calculate a few pairs of $x$- and $y$-values. With the calculus we can do a little more to determine the shape of the curve.

The derivative of a function representing a curve tells us the slope of the curve. Let us find the slope at any point of the ellipse. We could differentiate the function in (42), but it is easier to work with the implicit equation (41). If we differentiate it with respect to $x$, we obtain

$$2b^2x + 2a^2y \frac{dy}{dx} = 0$$

or

**(43)**
$$\frac{dy}{dx} = -\frac{b^2x}{a^2y}.$$

We see at once that, because $x$ and $y$ are positive in the first quadrant, $dy/dx$ is always negative (except at $y = 0$). Moreover, as $x$ increases from 0 to $a$, we see from (42) that $y$ decreases from $b$ to 0. Hence as $x$ increases from 0 to $a$, the slope becomes more and more negative, starting at $x = 0$ with 0 slope. We know then that the slopes of the tangents to the curve must behave as shown in Fig. 7-14. Then the curve itself must have the shape shown in that figure. Thus we obtain a somewhat better picture of the graph than if we had plotted a few points and had connected them with a smooth curve.

We can also find the equation of the tangent to the ellipse at any point. Let $(x_1, y_1)$ be a point on the curve. By (43) we know that the slope of the curve which is the slope of the tangent, must be

$$\frac{dy}{dx} = -\frac{b^2x_1}{a^2y_1}.$$

We now use the fact (Chap. 3, Sec. A7) that the equation of a line passing through the point $(x_1, y_1)$ and having slope $m$ is given by

$$y - y_1 = m(x - x_1).$$

In our case we have

**(44)**
$$y - y_1 = -\frac{b^2x_1}{a^2y_1}(x - x_1).$$

**Figure 7-14**

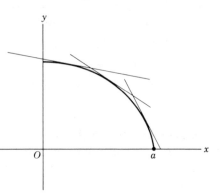

We must, of course, be careful about what value we use for $y_1$. If we are dealing with a point that lies on the upper half of the ellipse, then for a given $x_1$, $y_1$ is given by

$$y_1 = \frac{b}{a} \sqrt{a^2 - x_1^2}.$$

If we are dealing with a point that lies on the lower half of the ellipse, then for a given $x_1$, $y_1$ is given by

$$y_1 = -\frac{b}{a} \sqrt{a^2 - x_1^2}.$$

Let us note that we can do the same for the hyperbola. The equation of the hyperbola is

**(45)** $$b^2x^2 - a^2y^2 = a^2b^2.$$

Then the slope of the hyperbola is given by $dy/dx$, which we calculate from (45) by differentiating the implicit equation. We find first that

$$2b^2x - 2a^2y \frac{dy}{dx} = 0$$

and therefore

**(46)** $$\frac{dy}{dx} = \frac{b^2x}{a^2y}.$$

Thus in the first quadrant the slope is always positive.

## EXERCISES

1. Determine the shape of the hyperbola in the first quadrant by analyzing the formula for the slope.
2. Find the equation of the tangent to the ellipse $4x^2 + 5y^2 = 40$ at $x = 1$. There are two points on the ellipse at which $x = 1$; hence there should be two answers.
$$Ans. \ y \pm \frac{6}{\sqrt{5}} = (x - 1)\left(\pm \frac{2\sqrt{5}}{15}\right).$$
3. Find the equation of the tangent to the ellipse in Exercise 2 at $x = -1$. Again there should be two answers.
4. Find the equation of the tangent to the ellipse $(x^2/16) + (y^2/9) = 1$ at $x = \sqrt{7}$. There are two answers.
$$Ans. \ y \pm \tfrac{9}{4} = (x - \sqrt{7})\left(\pm \frac{\sqrt{7}}{4}\right).$$
5. Find the equation of the tangent to the hyperbola $4x^2 - 5y^2 = 40$ at $x = 5$. There are two answers.
6. Find the equation of the tangent to the hyperbola $(x^2/9) - (y^2/16) = 1$ at $x = -5$. There are two answers. $\quad Ans. \ y \pm \tfrac{16}{3} = (x + 5)(\pm \tfrac{5}{3}).$

**7.** (a)   Show that the lines $FP$ and $F'P$ from the foci to any point $P$ on the ellipse (Fig. 7-15) make equal angles with the tangent at $P$.

    (b)   Suppose that a light ray issues from $F'$ and strikes an elliptical mirror at $P$. What direction does the reflected ray take?                     *Ans.* Toward $F$.

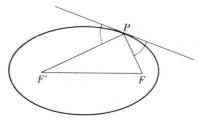

**Figure 7-15**

**8.** Consider the equation $\dfrac{x^2}{a^2 - k} + \dfrac{y^2}{b^2 - k} = 1$, with $a^2 > b^2$.

    (a)   Discuss the loci represented by this equation for fixed $a$ and $b$ but as $k$ varies.

           *Suggestion:* First let $k$ vary from 0 to $b^2$; then let $k$ vary from $b^2$ to $a^2$; and finally let $k$ vary from $a^2$ upward. *Ans.* Ellipse for $0 \le k < b^2$; hyperbola for $b^2 < k < a^2$; no locus for $k > a^2$.

    (b)   Calculate the foci of the various conics represented by the equation.

**9.** Show that an ellipse and any confocal hyperbola, that is, any hyperbola which has the same foci as the ellipse, intersect at right angles.

    *Suggestion:* Use the representation given in Exercise 8.

**10.** Show that the product of the distances from the foci to any point of any tangent to an ellipse is $b^2$ where $b$ is the semi-minor axis.

**11.** Show that the tangent at any point $P$ of a hyperbola (Fig. 7-16) bisects the angle $F'PF$, where $F$ and $F'$ are the foci.

**Figure 7-16**

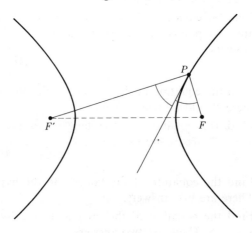

**12.** Show that the segment of a tangent to a hyperbola which lies between the asymptotes is bisected at the point of tangency.

**13.** Show that the tangent at any point $P$ of the parabola $y^2 = 4px$ cuts the $x$-axis at a point $T$ (Fig. 7-17) whose abscissa is the negative of the abscissa of $P$.

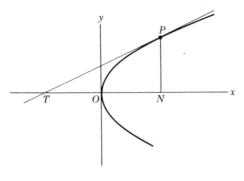

Figure 7-17

**14.** Show that if $PG$ is the normal (Fig. 7-18) to the ellipse $(x^2/a^2) + (y^2/b^2) = 1$ at the point $P$ then $OG = e^2 \cdot ON$ where $e$ is the eccentricity of the ellipse. $ON$ is the abscissa of $P$.

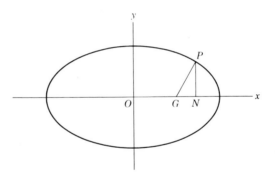

Figure 7-18

**15.** Show that if $TPt$ (Fig. 7-19) is the tangent to the ellipse $(x^2/a^2) + (y^2/b^2) = 1$ at the point $P$, then $ON \cdot OT = a^2$ and $OM \cdot Ot = b^2$. $ON$ is the abscissa of $P$ and $OM$ is the ordinate.

Figure 7-19

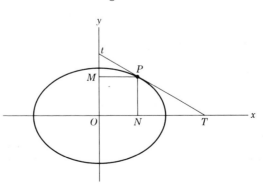

**7. Integration Employing the Chain Rule.** The increased power to differentiate functions means, of course, increased power to integrate because the
latter process is merely the inverse of the former. In Theorem 2 of this
chapter we learned that if $y = u^n$, where $u$ is a function of $x$, then
$dy/dx = nu^{n-1} du/dx$. Given $dy/dx$ in this form, we can state at once that
$y = u^n + C$. However, as in the case of the simpler formula $dy/dx = nx^{n-1}$, the derived function is generally not given us in precisely the form
$nu^{n-1} du/dx$. Rather, we are given

$$\frac{dy}{dx} = u^n \frac{du}{dx}$$

and are required to find $y$. However, we know that in differentiating $y = u^n$
the exponent becomes a coefficient and the new exponent is one less.
Hence we must reverse this process. To indicate that we wish to find $y$ we
use the usual integral sign and to indicate that we are integrating with
respect to $x$ we use the usual $dx$ and write

$$y = \int u^n \frac{du}{dx} \, dx.$$

If we now reverse what happens in differentiation we obtain

$$y = \frac{u^{n+1}}{n+1} + C.$$

The result is the single most important formula for integration:

**Theorem 3:** If

**(47)**
$$\frac{dy}{dx} = u^n \frac{du}{dx}$$

where $u$ is a function of $x$ and $n \neq -1$, then

**(48)**
$$y = \int u^n \frac{du}{dx} \, dx = \frac{u^{n+1}}{n+1} + C.$$

This theorem generalizes Theorem 12 of Chapter 6, and therefore we refer
to it as the generalized power rule for integration or the inverse of the
generalized power rule.

Let us see how useful Theorem 3 can be. Suppose that we are given

**(49)**
$$\frac{dy}{dx} = 5(x^2 + 1)^4 \cdot 2x$$

and are obliged to find $y$ as a function of $x$. Knowing Theorem 3, we try to
think of the right side of (49) as a function of $u$ times $du/dx$. The obvious
candidate for $u$ is $x^2 + 1$ because then the $2x$ is $du/dx$. Hence we let

$$u = x^2 + 1$$

and write (49) as

**(50)**
$$\frac{dy}{dx} = 5u^4 \frac{du}{dx} \, .$$

We now compare (50) with (47). Apart from the factor 5, (50) is in the form (47). However, a constant factor can be ignored during integration and then multiplied into the integral. By (48) we obtain

$$y = 5 \frac{u^5}{5} + C = u^5 + C.$$

In view of the value of $u$

**(51)**
$$y = (x^2 + 1)^5 + C.$$

The result in (51) appears peculiar at first sight. Corresponding to the factor $5(x^2 + 1)^4$ in (49), we do have $(x^2 + 1)^5$ in (51), but nothing in (51) corresponds to the factor $2x$ in (49). This is as it should be. In differentiating (51) by the chain rule, we would let $u = x^2 + 1$. Then the chain rule calls for

$$\frac{dy}{dx} = \frac{dy}{du} \cdot \frac{du}{dx} \, .$$

The factor $du/dx$ is, in the present example, $2x$ and this appears in the derivative in addition to whatever $dy/du$ calls for. We must expect then that in reversing the chain rule the quantity $du/dx$ will "disappear."

Let us consider another example. Given

$$\frac{dy}{dx} = \frac{x}{\sqrt{x^2 + 1}} \, ,$$

we shall try to find $y$ as a function of $x$. We can, of course, write this derived function as the product

**(52)**
$$\frac{dy}{dx} = \frac{1}{\sqrt{x^2 + 1}} \cdot x.$$

A likely candidate for the function $u$ is $x^2 + 1$, but then $du/dx$ is $2x$, whereas we have only the factor $x$ in (52). However, it is algebraically correct to write (52) as

$$\frac{dy}{dx} = \frac{1}{2} \frac{1}{\sqrt{x^2 + 1}} \cdot 2x.$$

If we now let $u$ be $x^2 + 1$, we have

$$\frac{dy}{dx} = \frac{1}{2} \frac{1}{\sqrt{u}} \frac{du}{dx} = \tfrac{1}{2} u^{-1/2} \frac{du}{dx} \, .$$

Apart from the constant factor $\frac{1}{2}$, this derivative is in the form (47). Then by (48)

**(53)** $$y = \frac{1}{2}\frac{u^{1/2}}{\frac{1}{2}} + C = u^{1/2} + C = \sqrt{x^2 + 1} + C.$$

In using (48) in the examples, we replaced a function of $x$ in the integrand by $u$. This device, which will be employed often later, is called *integration by substitution* of a new variable.

## EXERCISES

1. Integrate the following functions:
   (a)  $dy/dx = 4(x^2 + 1)^3 2x$.
   $\quad\quad$ *Ans.* $y = (x^2 + 1)^4 + C$.
   (b)  $dy/dx = (x^2 + 1)^3 \cdot 2x$.
   (c)  $dy/dx = (x^2 + 1)^3 \cdot x$.
   $\quad\quad$ *Ans.* $y = \dfrac{(x^2 + 1)^4}{8} + C$.
   (d)  $dy/dx = 4(x^2 + 7x)^3(2x + 7)$.
   (e)  $dy/dx = (x^2 + 7x)^3(2x + 7)$.
   $\quad\quad$ *Ans.* $y = \dfrac{(x^2 + 7x)^4}{4} + C$.
   (f)  $dy/dx = (x^2 + 6x)^4(x + 3)$.
   (g)  $dy/dx = \dfrac{2x}{(x^2 + 6)^5}$.
   $\quad\quad$ *Ans.* $y = -\dfrac{1}{4(x^2 + 6)^4} + C$.
   (h)  $dy/dx = (1 + 5x)^5$.

   (i)  $f'(x) = \sqrt{1 + 5x}$.
   $\quad\quad$ *Ans.* $f(x) = \dfrac{2(1 + 5x)^{3/2}}{15} + C$.
   (j)  $f'(x) = \dfrac{1}{\sqrt{2 - 3x}}$.
   (k)  $dy/dx = \dfrac{x}{(x^2 + 4)^{3/2}}$.
   $\quad\quad$ *Ans.* $y = -(x^2 + 4)^{-1/2} + C$.
   (l)  $f'(x) = \left(1 + \dfrac{x}{2}\right)^3$.
   (m)  $dy/dx = x\sqrt{4 + 5x}$.
   $\quad\quad$ *Suggestion:* Let $u = 4 + 5x$ and replace $x$ by its value in terms of $u$.
   $\quad\quad$ *Ans.* $y = \dfrac{2(4 + 5x)^{5/2}}{125}$
   $\quad\quad\quad\quad - \dfrac{8(4 + 5x)^{3/2}}{75} + C$.

2. Evaluate:
   (a)  $\int (x^2 + 5)2x\, dx$.
   $\quad\quad$ *Ans.* $y = (x^2 + 5)^2/2 + C$.
   (b)  $\int (x^2 + 5)^2 x\, dx$.
   (c)  $\int \dfrac{x}{(x^2 + 5)^2}\, dx$.
   (d)  $\int \dfrac{3x}{(x^2 + 5)^2}\, dx$.

   (e)  $\int (x^3 + x^2)^2(3x^2 + 2x)dx$.
   $\quad\quad$ *Ans.* $y = (x^3 + x^2)^3/3 + C$.
   (f)  $\int \dfrac{2x + 7}{\sqrt{x^2 + 7x}}\, dx$.
   (g)  $\int (x^2 + 2x)^{-2}(x + 1)dx$.
   (h)  $\int 3(x^2 + 2x)^{-2}(x + 1)dx$.

3. A particle moving along $AM$ (Fig. 7-20) is attracted to a fixed point $O$ with a force which varies inversely as the square of the distance from $O$. Find the work done on the particle as it moves the distance $l$ from $A$ to $B$.

   *Suggestion:* Let $x$ be the distance from $A$ to any point $P$ on $AB$ and let $r$ be the variable distance from $P$ to $O$. The force $F$ attracting $P$ to $O$ is $k/r^2$. But only the component of this force along $AB$ serves to move the particle

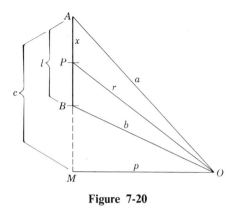

**Figure 7-20**

along $AB$. This component is $(k/r^2)$ cos $OPM = (k/r^2)(c - x)/r$. Then $dW/dx = k(c - x)/r^3$ and $r = \sqrt{p^2 + (c - x)^2}$.

*Ans.* $\dfrac{k}{b} - \dfrac{k}{a}$.

**4.** The integral of $(2x - 1)^3$ obtained by replacing $2x - 1$ by $u$ and applying the chain rule is $(2x - 1)^4/8 + C$. On the other hand, we can expand $(2x - 1)^3$ by the binomial theorem and integrate without using the chain rule. The result is $2x^4 - 4x^3 + 3x^2 - x + C$. Do these two integrals agree?

**5.** If $y' = f(x)g(x)$ and if $g'(x) = f(x)$, find $y$.      *Ans.* $y = \dfrac{[g(x)]^2}{2} + C$.

**8. The Problem of Escape Velocity.**\* The problem of calculating the velocity with which an object must be shot straight up into the air in order to have it reach a given altitude is important for scientific and practical purposes. For example, an antiaircraft gun that seeks to hit an airplane flying directly overhead must be able to fire the shells with sufficient initial velocity to have them reach the plane. The launching of satellites requires sending them up to a given height before they are directed around the earth, and the launching of rockets and spaceships involves similar problems.

    The velocity with which an object is to be shot up to reach a given height must be such that though the object loses velocity as it rises, it will have enough velocity to keep going until it reaches the desired height. To send an object to a point not too high above the surface of the earth, we can apply the fact that gravity causes a downward acceleration of 32 ft/sec². Then the problem of calculating the initial velocity is rather easy (see Chap. 3, Sect. 3, Exercise 12). However, if an object is to be sent to a great height, the acceleration of 32 ft/sec² is no longer a reliable figure. What then is the proper acceleration?

    The acceleration toward the earth that any object experiences is due to the earth's gravitational attraction. This force, as we already know, is given by the formula

**(54)** $$F = G\,\frac{mM}{r^2}\,,$$

\*This section can be omitted without disrupting the continuity.

where $M$ is the mass of the earth, $m$ is the mass of the object, and $r$ is the distance of the object from the center of the earth. Thus we know the force that the earth exerts on the object but not the acceleration.

To determine the acceleration we must have recourse to a basic law of physics. Newton's first law of motion states that if no force acts on an object and the object is at rest, the object remains at rest, and if the object is in motion, it continues to move at a constant speed in a straight line. However, suppose that a force does act. What does the force do? Newton's second law of motion states that the force changes the speed or the direction of motion or both This second law of motion is a physical principle established on the basis of observations and measurements. The quantitative statement of Newton's second law that suffices for present purposes is

**(55)** $$F = ma;$$

here $F$ is the force acting on the mass $m$ and producing the acceleration $a$. As in our earlier treatments of forces and accelerations acting to produce straight line motion both $F$ and $a$ can be positive or negative.*

We entered into the discussion of Newton's second law because, given the force of gravitation (54) acting on a mass $m$, we wished to know the acceleration that this force imparts to $m$. Formula (54) answers this question. If we write (54) as

**(56)** $$F = m\,\frac{GM}{r^2}$$

and compare it with (55) which holds for *any* force, we see that the acceleration that the force of gravity gives to the object of mass $m$ is

**(57)** $$a = \frac{GM}{r^2}\ .$$

We pointed out in Chapter 6, Section 8 [see formula (56) there] that when $r$ is the radius $R$ of the earth, that is, $4000 \cdot 5280$ feet, then

**(58)** $$32 = \frac{GM}{(4000 \cdot 5280)^2} = \frac{GM}{R^2}\ .$$

If we compare (57) and (58), we see that the acceleration due to gravity of an object at or practically at the surface of the earth is 32 ft/sec², a fact we already know but which we now see is a special case of the general formula for the acceleration of gravity.†

Let us now undertake to calculate the velocity with which an object must be shot up to reach a given height. We seek, of course, the minimum

---

*Actually Newton's second law of motion is a vector law. When we have occasion to use this more general formulation of Newton's second law we shall state it.
†We have been using 32 ft/sec² as the acceleration due to gravity at the surface of the earth. Actually, the acceleration is not exactly the same at all points on the surface even at sea level. It is common practice to use $g$ in place of 32 as the value of $GM/R^2$, and then one can take $g$ to be the correct value for any given location. We shall, however, use the value 32 most of the time.

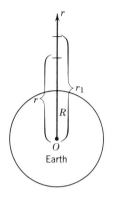

**Figure 7-21**

velocity needed to do the job. If the velocity is greater than this minimum, the object will go even higher. Let us suppose then that the object is shot up with the proper initial velocity and is $r$ feet from the center of the earth.*

We have the acceleration to which an object $r$ feet from the center of the earth (and above the earth) is subject. If we take $r$ to be positive in the upward direction (Fig. 7-21), then, because the acceleration causes a downward motion and therefore a downward velocity and so a decrease in $r$, we must write

$$a = - \frac{GM}{r^2} .$$

Moreover, $a$ is the second derivative of $r$ with respect to $t$. To remind ourselves of the variables involved, we use the Leibnizian notation and write

**(59)**
$$\frac{d^2r}{dt^2} = - \frac{GM}{r^2} .$$

We know that the acceleration is the derivative of the velocity. Hence by integrating (59) with respect to $t$ we should obtain the velocity of an object that moves under the attraction of gravity. However, here we face a difficulty. If the right side of (59) were a function of $t$, we could integrate that function and state that it is the velocity, that is, $dr/dt$. However, the right side is a function of $r$.

The chain rule resolves our difficulty. Let us denote the velocity by $v$. Then

**(60)**
$$\frac{d^2r}{dt^2} = \frac{dv}{dt} .$$

Now $v$ is a function of $r$ because the velocity varies with distance from the center of the earth, and $r$ is a function of $t$ because the distance from the center of the earth varies with the time. Hence the chain rule says that

**(61)**
$$\frac{dv}{dt} = \frac{dv}{dr} \cdot \frac{dr}{dt} = \frac{dv}{dr} \cdot v.$$

*Recall the discussion in Chap. 6, Sect. 8 on the meaning of $r$.

Thus we may write (59) as

**(62)**
$$v \frac{dv}{dr} = -\frac{GM}{r^2}.$$

The new equation (62) does not seem to be more tractable than (59) because the factor $v$ on the left side seems to bar what would otherwise be a straightforword integration. However, the chain rule helps us again. If the left side of (62) were merely $dv/dr$, we would say that the integral is $v$. What we do have on the left side is $v$ multiplied by $dv/dr$. This is precisely the situation that can be handled by reversing the chain rule. According to theorem 3 of Section 7, if we have $dy/dr = v\,dv/dr$, the integral is $v^2/2$. This is the integral of the left side of (62).

As for the right side of (62), the integral with respect to $r$, by the inverse of the power rule, is $GM/r$. Hence

**(63)**
$$\frac{v^2}{2} = \frac{GM}{r} + C.$$

To see more clearly what we have done in the integration process we should now differentiate (63) by regarding it as defining $v$ implicitly as a function of $r$.

To fit the formula for velocity to the problem in hand, we must determine $C$. Because we wish to treat the situation in which the velocity is to be 0 at some distance $r_1$ from the center of the earth, we can require that $v$ be 0 at $r = r_1$. Then

$$0 = \frac{GM}{r_1} + C$$

or

$$C = -\frac{GM}{r_1}.$$

Then from (63)

**(64)**
$$\frac{v^2}{2} = \frac{GM}{r} - \frac{GM}{r_1}.$$

This formula, as it stands, does not yet answer the question of what velocity must be given to an object at the surface of the earth to reach a height $r_1$. The formula gives the velocity acquired under the action of gravity by an object that starts with 0 velocity at the distance $r_1$ from the center of the earth and falls to a distance $r$ from the center of the earth but external to the earth. If we wish to find the velocity $v_0$ acquired at the surface of the earth, we have but to let $r = 4000 \cdot 5280$. As before, we denote the radius of the earth by $R$. Hence the velocity acquired at the surface of the earth is given by

**(65)**
$$\frac{v_0^2}{2} = \frac{GM}{R} - \frac{GM}{r_1}.$$

To answer the original question of what velocity must be imparted to an object at the surface of the earth so that the object reaches $r_1$ with zero velocity we can reason as follows. Because an object rising from the earth with an initial velocity $v_0$ loses velocity in exactly the reverse order of that in which it gains velocity in falling, we can say that (65) gives the initial velocity that must be imparted to an object at the surface of the earth in order that it reach a height $r_1$ and have velocity 0 there. In applying (65) we can use the fact that $GM = 32(4000 \cdot 5280)^2 = 32R^2$.

A very interesting deduction from (65) is the quantity known as the escape velocity. This is the least velocity that one must give to an object so that it never falls back to earth, that is, so that it escapes. By contrast, (65) gives the initial velocity that enables the object to reach the distance $r_1$ but when it reaches this point, its velocity is 0 and gravity pulls it back to the earth. For the object to escape it must be able to travel up indefinitely. That is, no matter how far up it goes, it must continue to have some velocity to enable it to keep going. The mathematical formulation of this physical requirement is that as $r_1$ becomes infinite, the velocity should approach 0. The phrase, $r_1$ becomes infinite, does not mean that the distance $r_1$ is approaching a definite value but merely that $r_1$ is getting larger and larger and its values exceed any number, no matter how large, that anyone may name.

Now (65) does give the (least) initial velocity $v_0$ required to send an object to a height $r_1$. Hence we have but to see what happens to (65) as $r_1$ becomes infinite. In mathematical notation we seek

**(66)**
$$\lim_{r_1 \to \infty} \frac{GM}{r_1} .$$

We should note that we do not substitute $\infty$ for $r_1$. As we have previously noted, $\infty$ is not a number.

As $r_1$ becomes larger and larger, the fraction in (66) must become smaller because the numerator is a constant. Moreover, because $r_1$ takes on values such as $10^6$, $10^{12}$, . . . , the fraction becomes as small and smaller than any small quantity one may name. That is, the fraction must come closer and closer to 0 in value as $r_1$ becomes infinite. Then

$$\lim_{r_1 \to \infty} \frac{GM}{r_1} = 0.$$

Now we see from (65) that the escape velocity $v_0$ is given by

**(67)**
$$v_0 = \sqrt{\frac{2GM}{R}} .$$

To simplify calculation, we can use the fact that $GM = 32R^2$ and therefore

**(68)**
$$v_0 = \sqrt{64R} = 8\sqrt{R} .$$

Because $R$ is $4000 \cdot 5280$,

$$v_0 = 36{,}800 \text{ ft/sec} = 7 \text{ mi/sec approximately} .$$

If we use 3960 miles for $R$, we find that $v_0$ is 6.93 mi/sec.

Before leaving the subject of escape velocity, let us note that in our method of integrating (59) we used a special transformation, namely (61). This transformation is important, but there is another device that is also very useful. We start again with (59), namely,

$$\textbf{(69)} \qquad\qquad \frac{d^2r}{dt^2} = -\frac{GM}{r^2}.$$

Now we multiply both sides of (69) by $dr/dt$. This gives

$$\textbf{(70)} \qquad\qquad \frac{dr}{dt} \cdot \frac{d^2r}{dt^2} = -\frac{GM}{r^2} \cdot \frac{dr}{dt}.$$

On the left side of (69) we can regard $dr/dt$ as some function $u$. Then $d^2r/dt^2$ is the derivative of $u$. Thus the form of the left side is

$$u\frac{du}{dt}.$$

This form is precisely the one that permits us to integrate by reversing the chain rule. Then the integral with respect to $t$ of the left side is $u^2/2$. Because our $u$ is $dr/dt$ or the velocity $v$, the integral of the left side of (70) is $v^2/2$. The right side of (70) is also in the form that permits reversing the chain rule. It contains a function of $r$ multiplied by $dr/dt$. Hence the integral with respect to $t$ is $GM/r$. Thus we obtain from (70)

$$\frac{v^2}{2} = \frac{GM}{r} + C.$$

This is exactly what we obtained in (63); therefore from here on the work is the same.

## EXERCISES

1. Calculate the velocity that an object acquires in falling from a height of 1000 miles to the surface of the earth.               *Ans.* $640\sqrt{660}$ ft/sec.

2. Calculate the least velocity required to send an object up to a height of 4000 miles.

3. Assume that the acceleration of gravity is 32 ft/sec$^2$ at any height and calculate the least velocity required to send an object up to a height of 4000 miles. Would you expect this velocity to be greater or less than that called for in Exercise 2? Give the physical justification for your expectation.
                                                              *Ans.* $6400\sqrt{33}$ ft/sec.

4. A particle falls from rest at a point $A$ whose height above the surface of the earth equals the radius of the earth. Show that the velocity on reaching the surface of the earth is equal to that acquired by a particle falling from rest through half the distance under the constant acceleration of 32 ft/sec$^2$.

5. Show that the velocity of escape from the earth is equal to the velocity required to send up an object to the height equal to the radius of the earth if the acceleration due to gravity were 32 ft/sec$^2$ at all heights.

6. Obtain a formula for the velocity attained by a body falling under the force of gravity if the initial velocity at height $r_1$ is not 0 but $V$. What velocity does the body acquire when it reaches the earth's surface?

$$Ans.\ -\sqrt{V^2 + 2GM/R - 2GM/r_1}\ .$$

7. Find the velocity with which an object should be sent straight up so that it has a velocity of 1000 ft/sec when it reaches a height of 4000 miles above the earth's surface.

8. If an object falls from rest and reaches the earth's surface with a velocity of 10,000 ft/sec, from what height did it fall?

9. An object is projected upward with a velocity of 1 mi/sec. Find the maximum height it will reach.                                    *Ans.* 84 mi approx.

10. What can you say about the motion of an object that is shot up from the earth with a velocity greater than the escape velocity?

11. How would you modify the theory of escape velocity if the object were shot up from the moon instead of the earth?

12. If the radius of the moon is 4/15 of the earth's radius and the mass of the moon is 1/81 of the earth's mass, find the least velocity with which an object must be projected upward from the moon to escape from the moon.

*Ans.* 1.50 mi/sec.

13. With what velocity must an object be projected upward from the earth's surface to reach the moon 240,000 miles away. The moon's gravitational attraction is not to be considered.                        *Ans.* 6.88 mi/sec.

14. With what velocity must a body be projected from the moon to reach the earth? Neglect the attraction of the earth. Use the data of Exercises 12 and 13.

*Ans.* 1.49 mi/sec.

15. Suppose that we determine the constant of integration in (63) so that $v = v_0$ when the object is at the surface of the earth. What is the formula for the velocity at the distance $r$ from the center of the earth?

$$Ans.\ \frac{v^2}{2} = \frac{v_0^2}{2} + \frac{GM}{r} - \frac{GM}{R}\ .$$

16. (a) Calculate the velocity with which an object must be shot up from the earth (away from the sun) to just reach a given height $r_1$ from the center of the earth, but this time take into account the sun's gravitational attraction as well as the earth's. Suppose that the sun and earth are at rest (Fig. 7-22) and the object is shot out in the direction of the line joining the sun to the earth (which means perpendicularly to the earth's path around the sun).

**Figure 7-22**

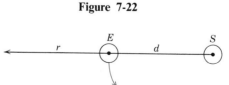

*Suggestion:* Let $d$ be the distance from the center of the sun to the center of the earth. Let $S$ be the mass of the sun. Then the *differential equation* is

$$\frac{d^2r}{dt^2} = -\frac{GM}{r^2} - \frac{GS}{(r + d)^2} .$$

(b)  Using the result of part (*a*) calculate the escape velocity. Use the following data. The mass $S$ of the sun is 330,000 times the mass of the earth; the distance $d$ between the earth and sun is 93,000,000 miles. To save calculation use the result from the text that $\sqrt{2GM/R} = 7$ mi/sec approximately.                                    *Ans.* 27 mi/sec approx.

17.  In exercise 13 we calculated the velocity required to send an object from the earth to the moon on the assumption that the moon's attraction was to be neglected. Because the moon attracts the object, this attraction should help the object to reach it. To obtain some estimate of the help that the moon's attraction furnishes, let us reason as follows. We assume that the earth and the moon are at rest. At some point on the line joining the earth to the moon (Fig. 7-23) the moon's gravitational attraction just offsets the earth's attraction for the object, and from that point on, which we call the stagnation point, the moon's attraction pulls the object to the surface of the moon. Hence it is necessary only to shoot the object up to reach the stagnation point. To calculate the location of the stagnation point let us use the fact that the moon's mass is $1/81$ of the earth's mass. Also, the distance between the centers of the earth and moon is $60R$, where $R$ is the earth's radius. Then if $m$ is the mass of the object sent up and $r_s$ denotes the distance out from the earth's center to the stagnation point,

$$\frac{GMm}{r_s^2} = \frac{GMm}{81(60R - r_s)^2} .$$

If we solve this equation for $r_s$, we find that $r_s = 54R$. Now calculate the velocity required to send an object up from the earth's surface to just reach the stagnation point, assuming that during this motion the moon exerts no attraction. We also neglect the sun's attraction.                         *Ans.* 6.86 mi/sec.

Figure 7-23

18.  Using the approach discussed in the preceding exercise, calculate the velocity required to send an object *from the surface of the moon* to the surface of the earth by projecting the object upward with just enough velocity to reach the stagnation point. The moon's radius is $4/15$ of the earth's radius.
                                                        *Ans.* 1.40 mi/sec.

19.  (a)  The calculation of the velocity required to send an object up from the surface of the earth to the moon by sending it to the stagnation point (Fig. 7-23) is only an approximate answer, because it neglects the fact that the moon attracts the object while it is traveling to the stagnation point and then gives it an acceleration so that it reaches the surface of the moon

with more than 0 velocity. Moreover the earth's attraction continues to be effective even after the object passes the stagnation point. To take into account the continuing action of the earth's and the moon's gravitational attraction, show that the correct differential equation is

$$\frac{d^2r}{dt^2} = -\frac{GM}{r^2} + \frac{(GM/81)}{(60R - r)^2}.$$

(b)  We should like to have the object hit the moon with the least possible velocity. If we send the object up so that it has more than zero velocity at the stagnation point, then since from there on the moon's attraction is stronger than the earth's the object will hit the moon with greater than zero velocity. Hence the best one can do is to send the object up so that the velocity at the stagnation point is zero. Using this condition, solve the differential equation and find the velocity with which an object must be sent up from the earth to hit the moon with the least possible velocity.

**9. Related Rates.** The chain rule permits us to answer a number of questions concerning the rate at which some variable is changing with respect to time. Suppose that a box-shaped tank with square base (Fig. 7-24) of dimensions 5 by 5 ft is being filled with water at the constant rate of 50 cu ft of water per minute. We might be interested in the rate at which the height $x$ of the water is rising at any instant of time. In the present example, because water is being poured in at the constant rate of 50 cu ft/min and the area of the base is 25 sq ft, the height of the water rises 2 ft/min. Moreover, because the water is being poured in at a constant rate and the cross section of the tank is uniform, the height $x$ of the water increases at the same rate at any instant of time, the rate of 2 ft/min. In calculus symbols, $dx/dt = 2$.

However, suppose that the water is poured at the same rate of 50 cu ft/min into a conical tank (Fig. 7-25). At what rate is the water level $x$ rising? In this situation it is not possible to state at once what $dx/dt$ is, because a fixed volume of water per minute does not increase the height of the water as much when $x$ is large as when $x$ is small. Let us see what we can do about calculating $dx/dt$.

**Figure 7-24**                                    **Figure 7-25**

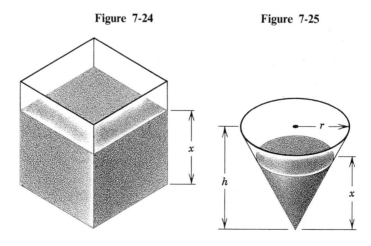

We know that the volume of a cone of height $h$ and radius $r$ is

$$V = \tfrac{1}{3}\pi r^2 h.$$

To be concrete, suppose that $r = h/2$ in our case, so that

$$V = \tfrac{1}{12}\pi h^3.$$

When the height $h$ is the variable amount $x$,

**(71)**                                                   $$V = \tfrac{1}{12}\pi x^3.$$

Now we know $dV/dt$; this is 50 cu ft/min at any time $t$, and we would like to know $dx/dt$. This statement suggests the chain rule, because

$$\frac{dV}{dt} = \frac{dV}{dx} \cdot \frac{dx}{dt}.$$

Application of the chain rule to (71) yields

$$\frac{dV}{dt} = \tfrac{1}{4}\pi x^2 \frac{dx}{dt}.$$

By solving for $dx/dt$, we obtain

**(72)**                                              $$\frac{dx}{dt} = \frac{4(dV/dt)}{\pi x^2}.$$

We see that the rate at which the water level is rising depends not only on $dV/dt$ but, as we expected, on the value of $x$ itself. If this value is specified, we can compute $dx/dt$.

A very important rate that occurs in physical problems is power. Power is defined as the rate of change of work with respect to time. To put the matter loosely for the moment, if we intend to do a certain amount of work, say raise an object from a height $R$ to a height $r$ from the center of the earth, we can do it either slowly or rapidly. To do it rapidly requires more power during the time it is applied. An engine pulling a load uphill does work to pull the load from one place to another. The power the engine delivers determines the rate at which it pulls the load or does the work. This concept of power is the same as that used in electricity. An electric light operates at a certain power (measured in watts), which determines the brightness of the light.

The rate at which work is to be done is not always a matter of choice. A generator supplying electricity to a community must be prepared to supply power at the rate called for by the demand on the electricity. Hence the operating company must know whether its generators are adequate.

If the work done in any given operation is $W$, the definition of the power is $dW/dt$. Thus if an object of mass $m$ is lifted straight up and if we assume that the distance is small so that we may use $32m$ for the weight, the work done is

$$W = 32mh$$

where $h$ is the height to which the object is lifted, measured, say, from the surface of the earth. Then the power

$$\frac{dW}{dt} = 32m\,\frac{dh}{dt}\,.$$

We see then that the power varies with $dh/dt$ or with the velocity with which the object is raised.

The unit of power, because it is the product of force ($32m$ in the example) and velocity, is foot-poundals per second or, because it is also possible to use pounds of force, foot-pounds per second. In engineering practice the unit of horsepower is used, 1 horsepower being 550 ft-lb/sec; that is, 1 horsepower means that 550 pounds of force are applied at the rate of 1 ft/sec or 275 pounds of force are applied at the rate of 2 ft/sec and so on. (In the centimeter-gram-second system, 1 horsepower equals $7.457 \times 10^9$ watts.)

If an object is raised to a great height so that we must take into account the varying force of gravity, we know from Section 8, formula (59), of Chapter 6 that the work done by gravity in pulling an object down from a distance $r_1$ from the center of the earth to a distance $r$ is

$$W = \frac{GmM}{r} - \frac{GmM}{r_1}\,.$$

By the chain rule we have

$$\frac{dW}{dt} = -\frac{GmM}{r^2}\,\frac{dr}{dt}\,.$$

Again we see that the power is the force applied, namely, $GmM/r^2$ times the velocity $dr/dt$ with which the power is applied.

## EXERCISES

1. The edge $e$ of a metal cube is expanding at the rate of 0.05 in./hr. At what rate is the volume $V$ increasing?                      *Ans.* $dV/dt = 3e^2/20$ cu in./hr.

2. Suppose that fluid flows out of the bottom of a cone-shaped vessel at the rate of 3 cu ft/min. If the height of the cone is three times the radius (Fig. 7-26), how fast is the height of the fluid decreasing when the fluid is 6 inches deep in the middle?

**Figure 7-26**

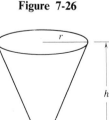

3. A mothball of radius $\frac{1}{2}$ inch evaporates to leave a mothball of radius $\frac{1}{4}$ inch at the end of 6 months. Express the radius of the ball as a function of time.

   *Suggestion:* Make the physical assumption that the rate of change of volume with respect to time is proportional to the surface area.

   $$Ans. \ r = \frac{1}{2} - \frac{t}{24}.$$

4. If a mass of 10 pounds is raised from the surface of the earth to a height of several hundred miles at the rate of 25,000 ft/sec, what power must be applied at the surface of the earth and at a height of 100 miles?

   *Ans.* $8 \cdot 10^6$ ft-pdl/sec; $8 \cdot 10^6 (40/41)^2$ ft-pdl/sec.

5. (a) Find the rate at which the area of a circle changes with respect to time in terms of the time rate of change of the radius. *Ans.* $dA/dt = 2\pi r \, dr/dt.$

   (b) If, when the radius of a circle is 5 feet, it is increasing at the rate of $\frac{1}{2}$ ft/sec, at what rate is the area changing? *Ans.* $5\pi$ sq ft/sec.

   (c) Since when the radius is 5, it is changing at the rate of $\frac{1}{2}$ ft/sec, and the area is then changing at the rate of $5\pi$ sq ft/sec, does the area increase by $5\pi$ sq ft in the next second?

   (d) Suppose that the radius' rate of increase of $\frac{1}{2}$ ft/sec is *constant*, that is, the same at all values of $r$. Does the area increase by $5\pi$ sq ft in the next second after the radius is 5 ft? *Ans.* No.

6. Find the rate of change of the area of a square when the sides are increasing at the rate of 1 ft/min and are 5 feet long.

7. Two ships start at the same point, but the first ship leaves at noon and sails east at the rate of 20 mi/hr and the second leaves at 1 P.M. and sails south at 25 mi/hr. How fast is the distance between them changing at 2 P.M.?

8. A conical tank is 14 ft across the top and 12 ft deep. Water is flowing in at the rate of 30 cu ft/min and flowing out at the rate of 20 cu ft/min. How fast is the surface of the water rising when it is 6 ft high?

9. If $y^2 = 2x$ and $x$ is increasing at the rate of $\frac{1}{2}$ unit per minute, how fast is the slope of the graph changing when $x = 32$?

   *Ans.* Decreasing at the rate of $1/1024$ units per minute.

10. (a) A train leaves a station which we take to be the origin of our coordinate system and travels along the upper half of the parabola $y^2 = 4x$. At what rate is the distance of the train from the station changing when the train is at the point $(9, 6)$ on the curve and $x$-value of the train's position is increasing at the rate of 2 units per minute.

    *Ans.* $22/\sqrt{117}$ units per min.

    (b) The answer in part (a) is just a little more than 2 units per minute. Show by geometrical evidence that this answer is reasonable.


# APPENDIX
# TRANSFORMATION
# OF COORDINATES


***A1. Introduction.*** When we derived the equations of the ellipse and the hyperbola in Chapter 7, we stated that experience indicates how to locate the axes in reference to the foci so that the resulting equation would be as simple as possible. However, more than a mere desire to satisfy curiosity recommends looking into the question of a change in the location of the axes.

**A2. Rotation of Axes.** Because we know the full story of the general first degree equation

$$Ax + By + C = 0,$$

let us look into second degree equations in $x$ and $y$. We know that for special positions of the axes the equations of parabola, ellipse and hyperbola are of the second degree. The most general equation of the second degree in $x$ and $y$ has the form

**(1)**                $$Ax^2 + Bxy + Cy^2 + Dx + Ey + F = 0.$$

This equation looks formidable, and there seems to be no obvious way of determining what curve or curves it may represent for various values of the coefficients. One might pick particular values of $A$, $B$, $C$, and the other coefficients, solve for $y$ as a function of $x$, make a table of values, and plot the corresponding points. However, such an approach is not likely to be fruitful not only because there is an infinite number of possible values for each of the coefficients, but because we know in fact that this equation includes parabolas, ellipses, and hyperbolas as special cases and we would only be confused by the variety of results. However, the thought that the equation of a curve depends on the location of the axes suggests approaching the problem of analyzing (1) by considering what happens when we change axes.

Suppose that we consider what happens when the axes are rotated through some angle $\theta$. That is, suppose that we have already the set of $x$- and $y$-axes and that we introduce a new pair (Fig. 7A-1), the $(x', y')$-axes such that the $x'$-axis makes an angle $\theta$ with the $x$-axis. Moreover, to start with let us suppose that the origin is the same for both pairs. If we take any point $P$ in the plane, its location with respect to the $x$- and $y$-axes is specified by the coordinates $x$ and $y$ of $P$, $x$ being $OM$ and $y$ being $PM$. With respect to the $(x', y')$-axes, the *same* geometric point $P$ has different

**Figure 7A-1**

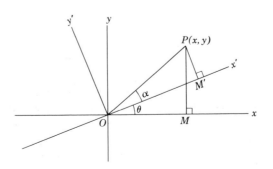

coordinates, say $(x', y')$, $x'$ being $OM'$ and $y'$, $PM'$. How are the coordinates $(x, y)$ of $P$ related to the coordinates $(x', y')$ of $P$?

Let us start with the $x$-value of $P$. If we introduce the angle $\alpha$ shown in the figure, we can say that

$$\text{(2)} \qquad\qquad x = OP \cos(\theta + \alpha).$$

We can use the trigonometric identity

$$\cos(A + B) = \cos A \cos B - \sin A \sin B$$

to rewrite (2) as

$$x = OP \cos \theta \cos \alpha - OP \sin \theta \sin \alpha.$$

However, $OP \cos \alpha$ is $OM'$ or $x'$ and $OP \sin \alpha$ is $PM'$ or $y'$. Hence

$$\text{(3)} \qquad\qquad x = x' \cos \theta - y' \sin \theta.$$

Thus we see so far how $x$ is related to $x'$ and $y'$.

If in place of (2) we consider

$$\text{(4)} \qquad\qquad y = OP \sin(\theta + \alpha)$$

and apply the trigonometric identity

$$\sin(A + B) = \sin A \cos B + \cos A \sin B,$$

we obtain from (4) that

$$y = OP \sin \theta \cos \alpha + OP \cos \theta \sin \alpha.$$

Because $OP \cos \alpha$ is $x'$ and $OP \sin \alpha$ is $y'$,

$$\text{(5)} \qquad\qquad y = x' \sin \theta + y' \cos \theta.$$

Thus we have the following theorem:

**Theorem:** If $(x, y)$ are the coordinates of a point relative to the $(x, y)$-axes and $(x', y')$ the coordinates of the same point relative to $(x', y')$-axes which have the same origin but are rotated an angle $\theta$ with respect to the first pair of axes, then

$$x = x' \cos \theta - y' \sin \theta$$
$$\text{(6)} \qquad\qquad y = x' \sin \theta + y' \cos \theta.*$$

We see from (6) how the coordinates of a single point are related to the new coordinates under rotation. How does this help to analyze equation

---

*If $\theta$ is a counterclockwise angle then $\theta$ is taken to be a positive angle. If $\theta$ is a clockwise angle then it must be taken to be negative to insure the correctness of formulas (6).

(1)? The equation represents a particular collection of points, those whose coordinates satisfy the equation. Suppose that we consider what happens to the coordinates of all these points. Because the equations (6) hold for any $(x, y)$, we certainly can substitute them for the $x$ and $y$ of points belonging to (1). The algebra involved in simplifying the resulting equation is lengthy. However, only multiplication is utilized. If we substitute the values of $x$ and $y$ given by (6) into (1), carry out the indicated multiplications and rearrange the terms we obtain

$$[A \cos^2 \theta + B \sin \theta \cos \theta + C \sin^2 \theta] x'^2$$
$$+ [-2A \sin \theta \cos \theta + B(\cos^2 \theta - \sin^2 \theta) + 2C \sin \theta \cos \theta] x'y'$$
$$+ [A \sin^2 \theta - B \sin \theta \cos \theta + C \cos^2 \theta] y'^2$$

**(7)** $$+ [D \cos \theta + E \sin \theta] x' + [-D \sin \theta + E \cos \theta] y' + F = 0.$$

Equation (7) is certainly no improvement over (1). However, there is the chance that by picking $\theta$ properly we may obtain a simplification of (7). If we examine the equations of the parabola, ellipse, and hyperbola, which we have already encountered, we observe that they do not contain an $xy$-term. Perhaps we should choose $\theta$ so as to eliminate the $x'y'$-term in (7); we might then see more clearly what the equation represents. To eliminate the $x'y'$-term, we must have a $\theta$ for which

**(8)** $$-2A \sin \theta \cos \theta + B(\cos^2 \theta - \sin^2 \theta) + 2C \sin \theta \cos \theta = 0.$$

As an aid in determining the value of $\theta$, we use the trigonometric identities

$$\sin 2\theta = 2 \sin \theta \cos \theta$$
$$\cos 2\theta = \cos^2 \theta - \sin^2 \theta.$$

Then (8) becomes

**(9)** $$(C - A) \sin 2\theta + B \cos 2\theta = 0.$$

Division by $\cos 2\theta$ gives

**(10)** $$\tan 2\theta = \frac{B}{A - C}.$$

Because $A$, $B$, and $C$ are known from (1), we see that we can pick a $\theta$ which eliminates the $x'y'$-term in (7). Of course, there are many values of $\theta$ satisfying (10), but no matter what value $B/(A - C)$ might have we can find a value of $2\theta$ lying between $0°$ and $180°$ and therefore a value of $\theta$ lying between $0°$ and $90°$. There is the special case in which $A - C = 0$, but in this case (9) tells us that $\cos 2\theta = 0$ and therefore $2\theta = 90°$.

For the value of $\theta$ which satisfies (10) the coefficients in (7) have definite values. We cannot make any significant statements as yet about these coefficients, but let us note for the moment that because the $x'y'$

-term is eliminated (7) has the form

**(11)** $$A'x'^2 + C'y'^2 + D'x' + E'y' + F = 0.$$

To practice what we have learned so far, let us eliminate the $xy$-term from the equation

**(12)** $$3x^2 - 10xy + 3y^2 = 0.$$

We first use (10) to determine $\theta$. Because our $A = 3$, $B = -10$, and $C = 3$, we see that

$$\tan 2\theta = \frac{-10}{3-3}.$$

Of course, division by 0 is meaningless, but what this equation tells us, in view of a previous remark, is that $2\theta = 90°$. We can see this in another way; by (10)

$$\cot 2\theta = \frac{A - C}{B}$$

and because $\cot 2\theta = 0$, $2\theta = 90°$. Hence $\theta = 45°$. Now $\sin 45° = \sqrt{2}/2$ and $\cos 45° = \sqrt{2}/2$. Then equations (6) become

$$x = x'\frac{\sqrt{2}}{2} - y'\frac{\sqrt{2}}{2}$$

$$y = x'\frac{\sqrt{2}}{2} + y'\frac{\sqrt{2}}{2}.$$

We substitute these values of $x$ and $y$ in (12). Thus

$$3\left(x'\frac{\sqrt{2}}{2} - y'\frac{\sqrt{2}}{2}\right)^2 - 10\left(x'\frac{\sqrt{2}}{2} - y'\frac{\sqrt{2}}{2}\right)\left(x'\frac{\sqrt{2}}{2} + y'\frac{\sqrt{2}}{2}\right)$$

$$+ 3\left(x'\frac{\sqrt{2}}{2} + y'\frac{\sqrt{2}}{2}\right)^2 = 0.$$

We carry out the indicated multiplications and obtain

**(13)** $$x'^2 - 4y'^2 = 0.$$

Of course, the $x'y'$-term should not appear in the result, and the fact that it does not is a partial check on the correctness of the algebra.

The curve corresponding to (13) consists of the two straight lines

$$x' - 2y' = 0 \quad \text{and} \quad x' + 2y' = 0.$$

In fact, we encountered an equation such as (13) in our discussion of the

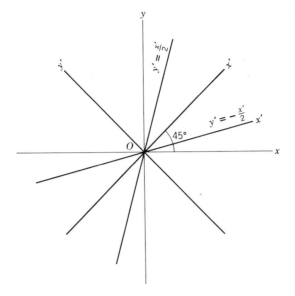

**Figure 7A-2**

asymptotes of the hyperbola [see (38) of Chap. 7], and the argument given there applies here. Figure 7A-2 shows the curve of Equation (13). We should note that the curve—the two straight lines in this case—must be graphed with respect to the $(x', y')$-axes, which are turned 45° from the $(x, y)$-axes. Moreover, the graph of the original Equation (12) consists of the same two straight lines. In fact, having obtained the graph we could now forget about the $(x', y')$-axes and regard the two straight lines as the graph of (12) with respect to the $(x, y)$-axes.

In this example we found that $\theta = 45°$, and therefore we knew at once that $\sin \theta = \sqrt{2}\,/2$ and $\cos \theta = \sqrt{2}\,/2$. In other cases we may find $\tan 2\theta$ by using (10) and we may not be able to state at once what $\sin \theta$ and $\cos \theta$ are. We could of course go to the trigonometric tables to find $2\theta$; then $\theta$, $\sin \theta$, and $\cos \theta$ can also be determined. However, there is no need to resort to trigonometric tables and to decimal expressions if one does not wish to. We know that $1 + \tan^2 A = \sec^2 A$ and $\cos A = 1/\sec A$. Hence

$$\cos 2\theta = \pm \frac{1}{\sqrt{1 + \tan^2 2\theta}} \,.$$

The signs of $\cos 2\theta$ and $\tan 2\theta$ must be the same. Next we may resort to the half-angle trigonometric identities to state that

$$\sin \theta = \sqrt{\frac{1 - \cos 2\theta}{2}} \quad , \quad \cos \theta = \sqrt{\frac{1 + \cos 2\theta}{2}}$$

to find the $\sin \theta$ and $\cos \theta$ we need to use formulas (6).

## EXERCISES

1. Transform the following equations by rotating the axes through the indicated angle. Graph the curve and show both sets of axes:

   (a)   $x^2 + 4xy + y^2 = 16$;  45°.              (c)   $3x^2 - 3xy - y^2 = 5$; $\tan\theta = 3$.
             Ans. $3x'^2 - y'^2 = 16$.        (d)   $x^2 + 4xy + 4y^2 = 0$; $\tan\theta = 2$.

   (b)   $3x^2 - 4xy + 10 = 0$; $\tan\theta = 2$.

2. Would you expect the equation $x^2 + y^2 = r^2$ to remain the same under a rotation of axes? If so, why?

3. Remove the $xy$-term from the following equations by rotating the axes. Graph the curve and show both sets of axes:

   (a)   $x^2 + 2\sqrt{3}\,xy - y^2 = 4$.              (e) $x^2 - 2xy + y^2 = 12$.
             Ans. $x'^2 - y'^2 = 2$.                      Ans. $y'^2 = 6$.

   (b)   $17x^2 - 16xy + 17y^2 = 225$.              (f)   $xy = 12$.

   (c)   $3x^2 - 4\sqrt{3}\,xy - y^2 = 9$.               (g)   $25x^2 + 14xy + 25y^2 = 288$.
             Ans. $-3x'^2 + 5y'^2 = 9$.                  Ans. $16x'^2 + 9y'^2 = 144$.

   (d)   $x^2 + 4xy + y^2 = 16$.

4. Could rotation of axes be used to simplify the general equation $Ax + By + C = 0$ of the straight line?

**A3.  Translation of Axes.** Now let us consider whether we can carry further our analysis of the general second degree equation (1). We have found so far that we can, by rotation of axes, transform it to (11), namely,

**(14)**                    $$A'x'^2 + C'y'^2 + D'x' + E'y' + F = 0.$$

There is the possibility that by a further change in the location of the axes we can simplify (14). This suggestion arises from the following example.
    Consider the equation

**(15)**                    $$(x - 3)^2 + (y - 2)^2 = 25.$$

The left-hand side is the square of the distance from $(x, y)$ to (3, 2), and this distance, according to the right side, is always 5. Hence the curve corresponding to (15) is a circle with center at (3, 2) and radius 5. If we square the terms in (15), we obtain

**(16)**                    $$x^2 - 6x + y^2 - 4y - 12 = 0.$$

On the one hand we see that (16) is of the form (14). On the other, we know that the equation of a circle with center at the origin and radius 5 is

**(17)**                    $$x^2 + y^2 = 25.$$

If we chose axes in Fig. 7A-3 with origin at (3, 2) and parallel to the existing $x$- and $y$-axes, the equation of the circle would be (17) with respect to the new axes, whereas it is (16) or (15) with respect to the original axes.
    The suggestion that we derive from this example is that we may be able to simplify (14) by introducing new axes parallel to the original ones

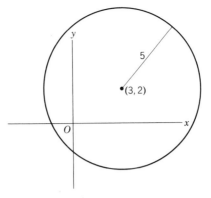

**Figure 7A-3**

but at some new origin $(h, k)$, that is, by *translating* the axes. Let us try this. If we introduce new axes, the $x''$- and $y''$-axes of Fig. 7A-4, then for any point $P$ with coordinates $(x', y')$

$$x' = x'' + h$$

**(18)**
$$y' = y'' + k.$$

Let us substitute these values of $x'$ and $y'$ in (14) and see if we can determine $h$ and $k$ so as to simplify the equation materially.

Substitution of (18) in (14) gives

**(19)**    $A'(x'' + h)^2 + C'(y'' + k)^2 + D'(x'' + h) + E'(y'' + k) + F = 0.$

Multiplication yields

$$A'x''^2 + 2A'x''h + A'h^2 + C'y''^2 + 2C'y''k + C'k^2$$

**(20)**
$$+ D'x'' + D'h + E'y'' + E'k + F = 0.$$

We hope to eliminate the $x''$- and $y''$-terms. The coefficients of $x''$ and $y''$ are

$$2A'h + D' \quad \text{and} \quad 2C'k + E'.$$

**Figure 7A-4**

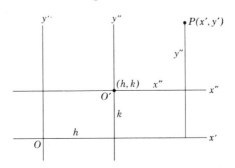

Let us set them equal to 0. Thus

$$2A'h + D' = 0, \qquad 2C'k + E' = 0.$$

If $A'$ and $C'$ are not 0, we have

(21) $$h = -\frac{D'}{2A'}, \qquad k = -\frac{E'}{2C'}.$$

Thus we can determine $h$ and $k$ to eliminate the $x''$- and $y''$-terms in (20), and (20) reduces to

(22) $$A'x''^2 + C'y''^2 + G = 0,$$

where $G$ is the sum of all the constant terms in (20).

Now we are on familiar ground. If $A' = C'$ and if $G$ is opposite in sign to $A'$ and $C'$, Equation (22) represents a circle. If $A' \neq C'$ but are alike in sign and $G$ is of opposite sign, Equation (22) represents an ellipse. If $A'$ and $C'$ are of opposite signs, whether numerically equal or not, Equation (22) represents a hyperbola.

The derivation of (21) presupposed that $A'$ and $C'$ are not 0. Now, both cannot be 0 because these $A'$ and $C'$ are the $A'$ and $C'$ of (14), and if they were both 0, (14) would be a straight line; because (14) represents the same curve as (1), the latter would represent a straight line and therefore would not be of the second degree. However, $A'$ or $C'$ of (20) may be 0. Let us suppose that $C' = 0$. Then we cannot determine $k$ in (21), but we can determine $h$ to eliminate the $x'$-term in (20). Then (20) reduces to

(23) $$A'x''^2 + E'y'' + H = 0,$$

where

(24) $$H = A'h^2 + D'h + E'k + F.$$

Because $h$ is already fixed we can use (24) to determine $k$ so that $H = 0$. Then (23) reduces to

(25) $$A'x''^2 + E'y'' = 0,$$

which is a parabola.

Likewise, if $A'$ should be 0 but $C'$ not 0 in (20), we could reduce (20) to

(26) $$C'y''^2 + D'x'' = 0,$$

which is again a parabola.

We note, incidentally, that instead of remembering (21) or the special cases such as (24), it is just as well, given (14), to make the substitution (18) and determine $h$ and $k$ directly.

Thus we have learned much about (1). Rotation of axes eliminates the $xy$-term. Then translation of axes reduces it to one of the standard forms that we have already encountered for the ellipse, parabola, or hyperbola.

Our proofs did omit a couple of degenerate cases. For example, if $E'$ were 0 in (23), we could not use (24) to determine $k$. But then if $A'$ and $H$ are of opposite signs, for example, if (23) degenerates to $3x''^2 - 7 = 0$, the graph consists of two coincident straight lines.

The grand conclusion that results from our analysis of (1) is that every equation of the second degree represents a parabola, ellipse (including the circle), or hyperbola, apart from a few degenerate cases. Moreover, by a rotation and translation of axes we can write the equation of the curve in one of the simplified forms that we learned earlier.

## EXERCISES

1. Simplify each of the following equations by translating the axes. Graph the curves and show both sets of axes:

   (a) $x^2 - y^2 + 32x + 4y + 40 = 0$.
   
                 *Ans.* $x'^2 - y'^2 - 212 = 0$.

   (b) $3x^2 + 4y^2 - 12x - 6y + 7 = 0$.

   (c) $x^2 + 4y^2 + 10x - 12y + 14 = 0$.

   (d) $x^2 + 6x + 4y + 8 = 0$.
   
                 *Ans.* $x'^2 + 4y' = 0$.

   (e) $4x^2 - 32x - 4y - 13 = 0$.
   
                 *Ans.* $4x'^2 - 4y' = 0$.

   (f) $y^2 - 6x - 10y + 19 = 0$.

   (g) $x^2 - y^2 + 8x - 14y - 35 = 0$.
   
                 *Ans.* $x'^2 - y'^2 - 2 = 0$.

   (h) $x^2 + y^2 - 6x + 4y - 12 = 0$.

   (i) $y^2 - 4x + 8 = 0$.
   
                 *Ans.* $y'^2 = 4x'$.

   (j) $y^2 - 8x - 6y + 17 = 0$.

2. Could translation of axes be applied to the equation $Ax + By + C = 0$ to simplify this equation?

3. Show that by translation of axes the equation

$$\frac{(x-3)^2}{9} + \frac{(y+2)^2}{4} = 1$$

   can be reduced to the standard form of the ellipse, that is, $(x^2/a^2) + (y^2/b^2) = 1$.

4. (a) Show that the equation $y = ax^2 + bx + c$ can be reduced by translation of axes to the standard form $y = x^2/4p$ of the parabola.

   (b) Find the coordinates of the focus and vertex of the original parabola.
   
      *Ans.* Focus$\left( \dfrac{-b}{2a}, \dfrac{4ac - b^2 + 1}{4a} \right)$; vertex$\left( -\dfrac{b}{2a}, \dfrac{4ac - b^2}{4a} \right)$.

   (c) Find the equation of the directrix of the original parabola.
   
      *Ans.* $y = \dfrac{4ac - b^2 - 1}{4a}$.

5. Determine the major and minor (transverse and conjugate) axes and the coordinates of the center of the following hyperbolas:

   (a) $16x^2 - 25y^2 - 128x - 150y = 369$.      *Ans.* $a = 5, b = 4, (4, -3)$.

   (b) $36x^2 - 36y^2 - 288x - 360y + 972 = 0$.

   (c) $9x^2 - 4y^2 + 54x + 16y = 79$.      *Ans.* $a = 4, b = 6, (-3, 2)$.

   (d) $16x^2 - 9y^2 + 192x + 72y = 288$.

   (e) $25x^2 - 16y^2 + 200x + 160y = -400$.      *Ans.* $a = 5, b = 4, (-4, 5)$.

6. Determine the major and minor axes and the coordinates of the center of the following ellipses:
   (a) $36x^2 + 25y^2 - 216x + 300y = -324$      *Ans. $a = 6, b = 5, (3, -6)$*
   (b) $16x^2 + 25y^2 - 96x - 100y - 156 = 0$.
   (c) $9x^2 + 25y^2 + 36x + 150y + 36 = 0$.      *Ans. $a = 5, b = 3, (-2, -3)$.*
   (d) $9x^2 + 36y^2 + 54x - 216y + 81 = 0$.
   (e) $49x^2 + 16y^2 - 196x - 96y - 444 = 0$.      *Ans. $a = 7, b = 4, (2, 3)$.*

7. Reduce to standard form and graph the curve whose equation is
   (a) $x^2 + 4xy + 4y^2 + 12x - 6y = 0$.      *Ans. $y'' = \sqrt{5}\, x''^2/6$.*
   (b) $5x^2 + 6xy + 5y^2 + 22x - 6y + 21 = 0$.      *Ans. $4x''^2 + y''^2 = 16$.*
   (c) $x^2 - 2xy + 4y^2 - 4 = 0$.
   (d) $5x^2 + 4xy - y^2 + 24x - 6y - 5 = 0$.
   (e) $x^2 - 2xy + y^2 - 5y = 0$.      *Ans. $4y''^2 - 5\sqrt{2}\, x'' = 0$.*
   (f) $x^2 + 2xy + y^2 + 4x - 4y = 0$.
   (g) $x^2 + 6x - 3y + 6 = 0$.      *Ans. $x'^2 - 3y' = 0$.*
   (h) $13x^2 + 10xy + 13y^2 - 42x + 6y - 27 = 0$.

**A4. Invariants.** Coordinate geometry, useful as it is in furnishing equations for curves, also embarrasses us with its abundance of equations for the same curve. We have seen that rotation of axes and then translation of axes give us two more equations for the very same curve with whose equation we begin. If we wished to determine some facts about the curve without having to go through rotation and translation of axes, it would certainly be desirable to do so by working with the original equation. Some of these facts can be so determined.

For example, given any second degree equation in $x$ and $y$, we know now that it must represent a parabola, ellipse, hyperbola, or some degenerate case. Which curve it does represent can be determined without going through the processes of rotation and translation. We were able to show that the general equation (1), namely,

(26) $$Ax^2 + Bxy + Cy^2 + Dx + Ey + F = 0$$

can be transformed by rotation and translation into (22), that is,

(27) $$A'x''^2 + C'y''^2 + G = 0,$$

or into (25), that is,

(28) $$A'x''^2 + E'y'' = 0,$$

or into (26), which is

(29) $$C'y''^2 + D'x'' = 0,$$

or possibly into some degenerate case. By examining $A'$ and $C'$ we were able to state what curve we had. If we could relate $A'$ and $C'$ to $A$ and $C$, we might be able to state, merely by examining the original Equation (1), what the curve is. How are $A'$ and $C'$ related to $A$ and $C$?

We know from (7) and (11) that

**(30)**                 $A' = A \cos^2 \theta + B \sin \theta \cos \theta + C \sin^2 \theta$

**(31)**                 $C' = A \sin^2 \theta - B \sin \theta \cos \theta + C \cos^2 \theta.$

We see at once, by adding (30) and (31), that

**(32)**                              $A' + C' = A + C.$

This relation is useful but not sufficient. A review of the discussion following Equation (22) shows that we had to know whether $A' = C'$ or $A' \neq C'$ and, if the latter, whether $A'$ and $C'$ agreed or disagreed in sign. This information cannot be secured from (32). Hence we shall look for additional relations between the original and transformed coefficients. Since we do not know what relations beyond (32) may hold, let us explore a little bit.

We see from (30) and (31) that

$$A' - C' = A \cos 2\theta + B \sin 2\theta - C \cos 2\theta$$

or

**(33)**                 $A' - C' = (A - C)\cos 2\theta + B \sin 2\theta.$

This relation is not very useful because it involves $\theta$. However, we know something essential about $\theta$. We chose it to satisfy equation (9), namely,

**(34)**                 $0 = (C - A)\sin 2\theta + B \cos 2\theta.$

Now, if we square (33), we obtain

$$(A' - C')^2 = (A - C)^2 \cos^2 2\theta + 2B(A - C)\sin 2\theta \cos 2\theta + B^2 \sin^2 2\theta.$$

**(35)**

If we square (34), we obtain

**(36)**        $0 = (C - A)^2 \sin^2 2\theta + 2B(C - A)\sin 2\theta \cos 2\theta + B^2 \cos^2 2\theta.$

By adding (35) and (36), we obtain

**(37)**                         $(A' - C')^2 = (A - C)^2 + B^2.$

Equations (32) and (37) give two equations in the two unknowns $A'$ and $C'$ in terms of the known quantities $A$, $B$, and $C$, and therefore we could stop right here. However, we may be able to avoid the necessity of solving these two simultaneous equations every time we wish to know what $A'$ and $C'$ are. If we square (32), we obtain

**(38)**                         $(A' + C')^2 = (A + C)^2.$

And if we subtract (38) from (37), we obtain

**(39)**                          $-4A'C' = B^2 - 4AC.$

   This single relation tells us all we need to know. Thus in the discussion following (22) we found that if $A'$ and $C'$ are alike in sign (whether equal or unequal), the curve is an ellipse (or the special case of a circle). But then $-4A'C'$ is negative. Hence

**(40)**              if $B^2 - 4AC$ is negative, the curve is an ellipse.

If $A'$ and $C'$ are unlike in sign, we know from (22) that the curve is a hyperbola. But then $-4A'C'$ is positive. Hence

**(41)**              if $B^2 - 4AC$ is positive, the curve is a hyperbola.

If $A'$ and $C'$ is 0, then (25) and (26) tell us that the curve is a parabola. In these cases $4A'C' = 0$, and therefore

**(42)**              if $B^2 - 4AC = 0$,   the curve is a parabola.

This listing of possibilities (40), (41), and (42) does not tell us what degenerate cases may arise, but it is rarely necessary to use such tests.
   Thus we see from (40), (41), and (42) that we can tell from the original equation (1) exactly what curve we have. The answer to this question is often important in itself; it also serves as a check on what we obtain by rotation and translation if we have reason to go through these processes. Equation (39) serves still another purpose. The ellipse, hyperbola, and parabola are called conic sections because such curves can be obtained as the intersection of a cone and a plane (Fig. 7A-5) (we shall not examine this geometrical fact). The ellipse and hyperbola are called central conics because they have a center, the point of intersection of the axes of symmetry. If we start with the equation of a central conic, there is a slight reduction in the algebra of rotation and translation of axes if the translation is performed first. Equation (39) tells us which conic we are dealing with.
   The relation (39) is significant for another reason. We know that in rotating the axes by some angle $\theta$ we fix $\theta$ so that $B' = 0$. Then we could write (39) as

**(43)**                          $B'^2 - 4A'C' = B^2 - 4AC.$

This equation says that the quantity $B^2 - 4AC$ remains the same or, one says, is *invariant* under rotation of axes. We found in (32) that the quantity $A + C$ is also invariant under rotation of axes. The entire subject of invariants under change of axes or under transformation of coordinates, is enormously important because such invariants express geometric properties of curves, that is, properties that are independent of the particular set of axes used to describe the equation of the curve.

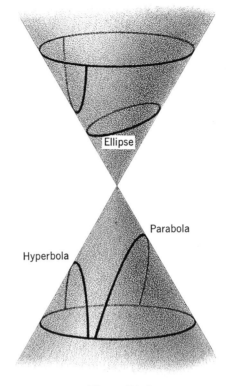

**Figure 7A-5**

Rotation and translation of axes are used to study equations of degrees higher than the second and to study the equations of other types of curves. We shall use these transformations in later work.

## EXERCISES

1. Test the equations in Exercise 7 of Section $A3$ to determine what curves they represent. Check your results against the standard forms given in the answer.

2. If we multiply the equations of the straight lines $3x - 2y = 0$ and $4x - 5y = 0$, we obtain the equation $12x^2 - 23xy + 10y^2 = 0$. According to the argument given in Chapter 7 in connection with (38), the equation of the product should represent the two straight lines. However, by using the $B^2 - 4AC$ test we find that the equation represents a hyperbola. Explain the seeming contradiction.

3. (a)   Would you expect the slope of a line to be invariant under rotation of axes?

   (b)   To test whether the slope of a line is invariant under rotation of axes, we can take any line $y = mx + b$ and consider what happens to it under rotation of axes. Find the transformed equation and determine its slope.

   $$Ans. \quad m' = \frac{m \cos \theta - \sin \theta}{\cos \theta + m \sin \theta}.$$

4. (a)   Would you expect the angle between two lines to be invariant under rotation of axes?

    (b)  Prove your conjecture by considering what happens under rotation of axes to $\tan \theta = (m_2 - m_1)/(1 + m_1 m_2)$.

          *Suggestion:* Use the result of Exercise 3*b*.

5. Would you expect the slope of a curve to be invariant under translation of axes?

6. (a)  Would you expect the slope of a line to be invariant under rotation of axes?
   (b)  Prove your conjecture by considering what happens to the slope of $y = mx + b$ under translation of axes.

7. Would you expect the angle between two lines to be invariant under translation of axes?

8. (a)  Consider the quantity $x^2 + y^2$. Would you expect it to be invariant under rotation of axes?

          *Suggestion:* What is the geometric meaning of the quantity?

   (b)  Prove that the quantity $x^2 + y^2$ is invariant under rotation of axes.

9. (a)  Would you expect the quantity $x^2 + y^2$ to be invariant under translation of axes?

   (b)  Prove your conjecture.

# CHAPTER
# EIGHT
# MAXIMA
# AND MINIMA

**1. Introduction.** We mentioned at the very outset that one of the major problems which troubled mathematicians of the seventeenth century was that of finding greatest or least values of varying quantities. The greatest range that could be obtained by varying the angle of elevation of a cannon and the greatest and least distance of a planet from the sun are examples of real problems of those times. Why should these problems have led to thinking about the calculus, that is, about instantaneous rates of change?

Physically, it was clear to the scientists that a rate of change was involved. Consider a ball thrown straight up into the air. As it rises, its velocity decreases; when it reaches the highest point, the maximum height, its velocity is 0 or else it would continue to rise. It then starts its downward motion. In other words, the velocity is 0 at the maximum height. But the velocity is the instantaneous rate of change of height with respect to time. Hence the instantaneous rate of change or the derivative is involved. We therefore expect that it is also involved in other maxima and minima problems.

Let us consider the problem of maximum range. The range of a shell fired from a cannon located at $O$ (Fig. 8-1) depends on the angle $A$ at which the cannon is inclined. It is intuitively clear that if the shell is fired at a very high angle or a very low angle, the range is small. Presumably, there is some value of $A$ for which the range is a maximum. Let us suppose that we have the precise function which relates range and angle $A$. How should we proceed to find the value of $A$ that yields maximum range? The motion of a ball thrown straight up furnishes a clue. Here the relevant function is the height of the ball as a function of the time, and at the maximum point the derivative of height with respect to time, the velocity, is 0. This suggests that to find the maximum range we must find the derivative of the range with respect to $A$ and set this derivative equal to 0.

More generally, if $y$ is a function of $x$, it seems that to find the maximum value of $y$ we must find $y'$ and set this equal to 0. With this clue

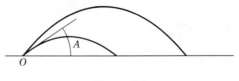

**Figure 8-1**

in mind let us study the behavior of functions and see if we can find a method of determining maximum and minimum values of the dependent variable.

### 2. The Geometrical Approach to Maxima and Minima. Let us take a specific function, which is nevertheless representative of what happens generally, and study its geometrical behavior. Consider the function

$$y = \frac{x^3}{3} - 2x^2 + 3x + 2.$$

To obtain the graph of this function we make a table of $x$- and $y$-values, graph the points whose coordinates are given in the table, and join these points by a smooth curve (Fig. 8-2).

Judging by the graph, the function that we are studying seems to have a maximum value of about 3 near $x = 1$ and a minimum value of about 2 near $x = 3$. Because the behavior of the derivative of the function seems to be important in finding maximum and minimum values of functions, let us observe the behavior of the derivative near the maximum and minimum points. At a point such as $A$, to the left of the maximum point $P$, the derivative of $y$ with respect to $x$, which is the slope of the curve at $A$, is positive. At a point such as $B$, the derivative is negative. At the maximum point $P$, the derivative seems to be 0, for the tangent line seems to be horizontal. Thus on the basis of the geometrical evidence we see that the derivative is 0 at the maximum point; it is positive at points to the left and negative at points to the right.

Now let us consider the behavior of the derivative near the minimum value of the function. At the point $C$ to the left of the minimum point $Q$ the derivative is negative; at $Q$ the tangent is horizontal and therefore the derivative is 0; at $D$ the derivative is positive. Hence at a minimum point, as at a maximum point, the derivative is 0, but in the case of a minimum

**Figure 8-2**

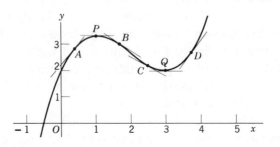

the derived function changes from negative values at points to the left to positive values at points to the right.

The geometrical evidence suggests that we use the following algebraic procedure to determine the maximum and minimum values of a function. We have

**(1)**
$$y = \frac{x^3}{3} - 2x^2 + 3x + 2.$$

Then

**(2)**
$$y' = x^2 - 4x + 3.$$

We now find the values of $x$ where $y' = 0$. Fortunately, we can write $y'$ as

**(3)**
$$y' = (x - 1)(x - 3),$$

and we see that

**(4)**
$$y' = 0 \quad \text{when} \quad x = 1 \quad \text{and when} \quad x = 3.$$

To determine whether $x = 1$ is the abscissa of a maximum point or a minimum point, we test the behavior of $y'$. It is apparent from (3) that when $x$ is a little less than 1, the first factor is negative and the second is negative. Hence $y'$ is positive. However, when $x$ is a little greater than 1, the first factor is positive and the second is negative. Hence $y'$ is negative. Thus $y'$ changes from positive to 0 to negative as $x$ changes from values somewhat less than 1 to 1 and to values somewhat greater than 1. Then $x = 1$ should be the abscissa of the maximum point $P$. To find the $y$-value of $P$, that is, the maximum value of the function, we substitute $x = 1$ in (1) and obtain $y = 3\frac{1}{3}$.

To determine whether $y$ is a maximum or a minimum at $x = 3$, we again observe the behavior of the derived function (3) for values of $x$ near 3. For $x$ somewhat less than 3, $y'$ is the product of a positive and a negative factor and therefore is negative. For $x$ somewhat larger than 3, $y'$ is positive. Hence the derived function $y'$ changes from negative to positive as $x$ passes through the value 3. Then $x = 3$ is the abscissa of a minimum value of the function. To find the value of $y$ at $x = 3$, we substitute 3 for $x$ in (1) and obtain $y = 2$.

We seem to have a procedure for finding the maximum and minimum values of a function. Before discussing the subject any further, it may be well to practice this procedure.

## EXERCISES

**1.** Find the maximum and minimum values of the following functions:

(a) $y = 2x^3 - 9x^2 - 24x - 12$.
    *Ans.* Max., 1; min., $-124$.

(b) $y = -x^3 - 3x^2 + 9x + 15$.

(c) $y = x^4 - 2x^2$.
    *Ans.* Max., 0; min., $-1$.

(d) $y = x^2 + \dfrac{1}{x^2}$.

(e) $y = \dfrac{6x}{x^2 + 1}$.
    *Ans.* Max., 3; min., $-3$

There are a few additional considerations about maxima and minima which are important for the effective handling of the method. First, we did not really find the maximum or minimum values of the functions that we investigated above. Let us examine the function (1) and its graph (Fig. 8-2). For $x$ greater than 3 the function increases continuously and becomes indefinitely large. In particular it becomes larger than the value $3\frac{1}{3}$ which we found to be the maximum value at $x = 1$. If we really want the maximum value of the function, then $3\frac{1}{3}$ is not the answer. In fact, because the function gets larger and larger as $x$ increases to the right, the function has no maximum value. In what sense, then, is $3\frac{1}{3}$ the maximum value of the function? It is a *relative maximum*; that is, the value $3\frac{1}{3}$ is larger than the function values in the *immediate neighborhood* of $x = 1$. What we found, then, by our procedure is a relative maximum.

Likewise the $y$-value of 2 which occurs at $x = 3$ is not the minimum value of the function. In fact, for negative values of $x$ the function values are not only less than 2 but they decrease more and more as $x$ becomes more and more negative. The function in question has no minimum value, for it continues to decrease indefinitely as $x$ becomes smaller. However, $y = 2$ is a *relative minimum*; that is, the $y$-value at $x = 3$ is smaller than $y$-values in the *immediate neighborhood* of $x = 3$.

To summarize, our procedure for finding the maximum and minimum values of a function is really a procedure for finding relative maxima and minima. It may seem then that our procedure is worthless. However, we shall see shortly that for scientific applications relative maxima and minima are very important.

There may, however, be problems in which the true or absolute maximum or minimum of a function is of interest. Let us note, first, that if we consider the function (1) over a definite interval of $x$-values, say from $-2$ to 5, the true or *absolute maximum* value of $y$ in this interval is (Fig. 8-2) the $y$-value at $x = 5$ itself, namely $\frac{26}{3}$. The true or *absolute minimum* value of $y$ in the same interval is $-\frac{20}{3}$, which occurs at $x = -2$. If instead of the interval $-2$ to 5 we consider the interval 0 to 3, we see that the relative maximum of $3\frac{1}{3}$ for $y$ at $x = 1$ is also the absolute maximum for that interval. The absolute minimum is 2, which occurs at two values of $x$ in the interval, namely, at $x = 0$ and at $x = 3$.

We can determine the absolute maxima and minima. Let us consider any finite interval of $x$-values. Such an interval is denoted by $a \leq x \leq b$, which means all $x$-values between $a$ and $b$ and including $a$ and $b$. The absolute maximum must occur either at one or both ends of the interval or it must occur at some value $x_0$ interior to the interval. Thus in the case of the function (1) and the $x$-interval of $-2$ to 5, the absolute maximum occurs at the end value $x = 5$. If the $x$-interval is 0 to 3, the absolute maximum occurs at $x = 1$ which is inside or interior to the interval 0 to 3. If the absolute maximum occurs at an interior value $x_0$, it must also be a relative maximum because the function values on either side of $x_0$ must be smaller than at $x_0$. Hence the derivative $y'$ must be 0 at $x_0$, and we can use our procedure for relative maxima to find the absolute maximum. If the absolute maximum does not occur at an interior value, it must occur at an end value. Hence we have but to find the values of the function at the two end values and compare them with the values of the relative maxima to see which is the greatest value.

A second consideration is involved in the following examples. Let us seek the relative maxima and minima of the function

**(5)**
$$y = x^3.$$

We first obtain

**(6)**
$$y' = 3x^2$$

and set $y'$ equal to 0. We find, then, that $x = 0$ should be the abscissa of a relative maximum or minimum of the function. However (Fig. 8-3), the derivative is positive for $x$ slightly less than 0 *and* for $x$ slightly greater than 0. Thus the derivative does not change sign, and one of the conditions for a maximum or minimum is not fulfilled. This example shows that the vanishing of the first derivative at some value of $x$ does not imply that the function has a maximum or a minimum at that value of $x$.

On the other hand, let us consider the function

**(7)**
$$y = x^{2/3}.$$

Here

**(8)**
$$y' = \tfrac{2}{3} x^{-1/3} = \frac{2}{3 \sqrt[3]{x}} .$$

The derivative of the function is never 0. We might then be led to conclude that the function has no relative maximum or minimum. However, an examination of the function (Fig. 8-4) shows that it does indeed have a relative minimum at $x = 0$. The trouble here is that because the derivative does not exist at $x = 0$, it cannot give us information about the relative maxima and minima of the function.

**Figure 8-3**

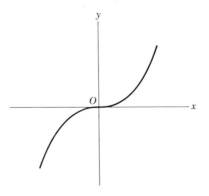

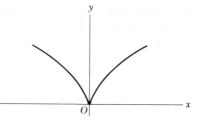

**Figure 8-4**

*3. Analytical Treatment of Maxima and Minima.* So far our arguments have been based on graphs of particular functions; let us now try to be more analytical and more general. First, what do we mean by a relative maximum of a function relating $y$ and $x$? A function has a *relative maximum* $y_0$ at $x = x_0$ if $y < y_0$ for all values of $x$ less than and greater than $x_0$ at least in some small interval about $x_0$. A function has a *relative minimum* $y_0$ at $x = x_0$ if $y > y_0$ for all values of $x$ less than and greater than $x_0$ at least in some small interval about $x_0$.

If a function does not have a relative maximum or relative minimum at $x = x_1$, what is its behavior? It may be increasing as $x$ passes through $x_1$ or it may be decreasing. To be more precise, the function is said to be *increasing* at $x = x_1$ if for all $x$-values in some interval about $x_1$ it is true that when $x < x_1$ then $y < y_1$ and when $x > x_1$ then $y > y_1$ (Fig. 8-5$a$). Correspondingly, a function is said to be *decreasing* at $x_1$ if for all $x$-values in some interval about $x_1$, it is true that when $x < x_1$ then $y > y_1$ and when $x > x_1$ then $y < y_1$ (Fig. 8-5$b$).

We may now prove the following theorem:

**Theorem 1:** If the derivative $y'$ is positive at $x = x_1$, the function is increasing at $x = x_1$. If the derivative $y'$ is negative at $x = x_2$, the function is decreasing at $x = x_2$.

The proof is rather simple. Let $x = x_1$ be a value of $x$ at which $y'$ is positive. Now

$$y' = \lim_{\Delta x \to 0} \frac{\Delta y}{\Delta x} .$$

**Figure 8-5**

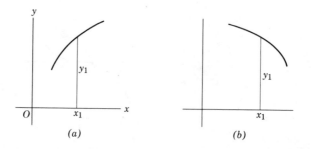

(a)                                    (b)

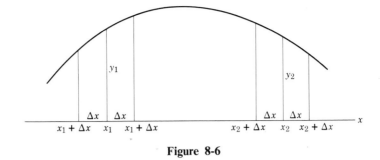

**Figure 8-6**

If $y'$ is positive, $\Delta y / \Delta x$ must be positive for $\Delta x$ sufficiently small because the quotient comes closer and closer to $y'$ as $\Delta x$ approaches 0. Now let us consider $x_1 + \Delta x$ for small $\Delta x$. For negative $\Delta x$, $x_1 + \Delta x$ is to the left (Fig. 8-6) of $x_1$. The quantity $\Delta y$ is, by definition, the value of $y$ at $x_1 + \Delta x$ minus the value of $y$ at $x_1$. If $\Delta x$ is negative and $\Delta y / \Delta x$ is positive, $\Delta y$ must be negative. This means that at $x_1 + \Delta x$, $y$ must be less than at $x_1$. That is, $y$ increases as $x$ changes from $x_1 + \Delta x$ to $x_1$.

Now let us suppose that $\Delta x$ is positive, so that $x_1 + \Delta x$ is to the right of $x_1$. The quantity $\Delta y$, which is the $y$-value at $x_1 + \Delta x$ minus its value at $x_1$, must now be positive because $\Delta y / \Delta x$ is positive. Hence $y$ increases as $x$ changes from $x_1$ to $x_1 + \Delta x$. We conclude then that at a point $x_1$ where $y'$ is positive the function increases as $x$ changes from values less than $x_1$ to values greater than $x_1$.

A similar argument would show that at a point $(x_2, y_2)$ where $y'$ is negative the function decreases as $x$ changes from values less than $x_2$ to values greater than $x_2$.

We may now prove the following theorem:

**Theorem 2:** If $y$ is a function of $x$, and $y$ has a relative maximum or minimum at $x = x_0$ and if $y'$ exists at $x_0$, then $y'$ is 0 at $x = x_0$.

If $y'$ is positive at $x = x_0$, then according to Theorem 1 the function must be increasing at $x_0$, and if $y'$ is negative at $x = x_0$, the function must be decreasing there. However, at a relative maximum or a relative minimum the function is neither increasing nor decreasing. Hence the derivative $y'$ (if it exists) must be 0 at $x_0$.

If a function has a relative maximum at $x_0$, the derivative must vanish there. However, the vanishing of the derivative, as we saw in the case of $y = x^3$, does not guarantee that the function has a relative maximum at $x_0$. What does guarantee it?

**Theorem 3:** If $y'$ is 0 at $x = x_0$ and if $y'$ changes from positive values to negative values as $x$ passes through $x_0$, the function $y$ has a relative maximum at $x_0$.

Because $y'$ is positive for $x < x_0$, then, by Theorem 1, $y$ must be increasing at such values of $x$. Also, because $y'$ is negative for $x > x_0$, $y$

must be decreasing for these values of $x$. This behavior of $y$ is precisely what we mean by $y$ having a relative maximum at $x = x_0$.*

There is, of course, the corresponding theorem about a relative minimum.

**Theorem 4:** If $y'$ is 0 at $x = x_0$ and if $y'$ changes from negative to positive values as $x$ passes through $x_0$, the function $y$ has a relative minimum at $x_0$.

The proof here is practically the same as for Theorem 3 with appropriate changes corresponding to the fact that $y'$ now goes from negative to positive values.

Theorems 3 and 4 give what are called sufficient conditions for a relative maximum or minimum. That is, if the conditions are fulfilled the function has a relative maximum or minimum. If the derivative does not exist at some value of $x$ in an interval under consideration, no information about relative maxima or minima can be deduced readily.

Let us summarize what the above theorems say. A function has a relative maximum (or minimum) at a value $x_0$ of $x$ if the derivative is 0 there and if it changes sign as $x$ changes from values less than $x_0$ to values greater than $x_0$. Also, as we saw in the preceding section, to obtain the absolute maximum (or minimum) of a function in an interval $a \leq x \leq b$, the values of the function at $x = a$ and $x = b$ must also be considered. The absolute maximum (or minimum) may occur at one or both of these end values or it may occur at an interior point. If it does occur at an interior point, it is a relative maximum (or minimum). To determine the absolute maximum (or minimum) in the interval, one must compare the values of the function at the relative maxima (or minima) and the values at the end points $a$ and $b$.

**Example.**   Find the relative maxima and minima of the function $y = 2x^3 + 3x^2 - 72x$.

**Solution.**   The relative maxima and minima occur at $y' = 0$. Hence let us first find $y'$.

$$y' = 6x^2 + 6x - 72.$$

We now set $y' = 0$. Thus

$$6x^2 + 6x - 72 = 0.$$

Dividing through by 6 gives

$$x^2 + x - 12 = 0.$$

We can solve this quadratic equation by factoring. We find that

$$(x + 4)(x - 3) = 0$$

*This proof is not complete because the notion of an increasing or decreasing function is defined at a value of $x$. However, the proof is readily completed when the mean value theorem is available. See Chapter 13, Section 2, and Exercise 1 there.

so that

$$x = -4 \qquad \text{and} \qquad x = 3.$$

Let us consider $x = -4$. Since $y'$ can be written as

$$y' = 6(x + 4)(x - 3)$$

we see that for $x$ slightly less than $-4$, $(x + 4)$ is negative and $(x - 3)$ is negative. Hence $y'$ is positive. Similarly for $x$ slightly greater than $-4$, say $-3\frac{3}{4}$, $(x + 4)$ is positive and $(x - 3)$ is negative so that $y'$ is negative. Thus as $x$ changes from values slightly less than $-4$ to values slightly more than $-4$, $y'$ changes from positive to 0 to negative. Hence the original function has a relative maximum at $x = -4$.

The same method shows that $x = 3$ is a relative minimum of the function.

## EXERCISES

1. Find the relative maxima and minima of the following functions:
   (a) $y = 16 - 3x - 9x^2$.
   (b) $y = -8x + 2$.
   (c) $y = 2x^3 - 6x$.
   (d) $y = 2x^3 + 8x + 3$.
   (e) $y = x^3$.
   (f) $y = x^4 - 2x^2 + 12$.
   (g) $f(x) = x^4$.
   (h) $f(x) = x + \dfrac{1}{x}$.
   (i) $f(x) = x\sqrt{x - 1}$.
   (j) $f(x) = \dfrac{x^2}{x - 1}$.

2. Find the relative maxima and minima and the absolute maxima and minima of
   (a) $y = -x^2 + 6x + 7$ over the interval $0 \le x \le 5$.
   
   $\qquad\qquad\qquad\qquad$ *Ans.* Rel. max. 16; abs. max. 16; abs. min. 7.
   
   (b) $y = x^3 - 3x^2 + 4$ over the interval $-2 \le x \le 4$.

3. Find the relative maxima and minima of $y = (x - 1)^2(x + 1)^2$. Graph the function. $\qquad\qquad\qquad\qquad\qquad\qquad$ *Ans.* Max., 1; min., 0.

4. Find the relative maxima and minima of $y = 3 - (x - 1)^{2/3}$ by any method you find effective.

5. Show by exhibiting curves representing functions that
   (a) if $y = f(x)$ increases at each value of $x$ of some interval $(a, b)$ that $f'(x)$ is not necessarily an increasing function;
   (b) if $y = f(x)$ increases at each value of $x$ of some interval $(a, b)$ that $f'(x)$ can actually decrease;
   (c) if $y = f'(x)$ is increasing at each value of $x$ of some interval $(a, b)$ that $f(x)$ may decrease.

6. We found in Theorem 1 that if $y'$ is positive at a value of $x$, then $y$ is increasing there. Is the converse true? $\qquad\qquad\qquad\qquad\qquad\qquad$ *Ans.* No.

**4. An Alternative Method of Determining Relative Maxima and Minima.** The use of the fact that the first derivative changes sign at a relative maximum or minimum can be replaced by a test which is sometimes more convenient.

Let us suppose that $y'$ is 0 at some value $x_0$ of $x$ and that $y''$ is negative

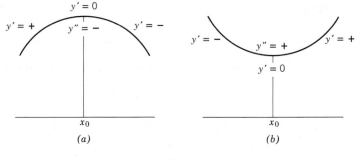

**Figure 8-7**

at this point (Fig. 8-7*a*). Now $y''$ is itself the derived function of $y'$. Hence, by Theorem 1, the *derived function* $y'$ is a decreasing function at $x_0$. Because $y'$ is 0 at $x_0$ and is decreasing there, it must be changing from positive to negative values. However, the conditions of $y' = 0$ at $x_0$ and $y'$ changing from positive to negative are precisely the sufficient conditions of Theorem 3 that $y$ have a relative maximum at $x_0$. Hence we may replace these conditions by the condition that $y''$ is negative.*

Likewise if $y''$ is positive at $x_0$ (Fig. 8-7*b*), then $y'$ is an increasing function, and because it is 0 at $x_0$, it must be changing from negative to positive values as $x$ passes through $x_0$. Then, by Theorem 4, $y$ must have a relative minimum at $x_0$.

Thus our second test for the relative maxima and minima of a function runs as follows:

**Theorem 5:** The function $y$ has a relative maximum at $x = x_0$ if

$$y' = 0 \quad \text{and} \quad y'' < 0 \quad \text{at} \quad x = x_0;$$

the function $y$ has a relative minimum at $x = x_0$ if

$$y' = 0 \quad \text{and} \quad y'' > 0 \quad \text{at} \quad x = x_0.$$

If $y''$ is 0 or does not exist at $x = x_0$, this test is not helpful.

The use of this theorem is illustrated by the following example. Suppose that we wish to determine the relative maxima and minima of the function

**(9)** $$y = x^3 - 3x^2 + 5.$$

We find $y'$, namely,

**(10)** $$y' = 3x^2 - 6x.$$

The function $y'$ is 0 when

$$3x^2 - 6x = 0$$

---

* Let us recall (Chap. 2, Sect. 10) that $y''$ is the second derivative of the function $y$ and that another notation for $y''$ is $d^2y/dx^2$.

or when

$$x = 0 \quad \text{and} \quad x = 2.$$

Thus $x = 0$ and $x = 2$ are possible abscissas of relative maxima and minima. To determine what happens at these values of $x$ we first find $y''$. This is

$$y'' = 6x - 6.$$

Now when $x = 0$, $y''$ is negative. Hence a relative maximum of the function occurs at $x = 0$. At $x = 2$, $y''$ is positive. Hence a relative minimum of the function occurs at $x = 2$. The actual relative maximum and minimum values of the functions are obtained from (9). For $x = 0$, $y = 5$; for $x = 2$, $y = 1$.

## EXERCISES

1. Use the second test to determine the relative maxima and minima of the functions:

(a) $y = x^3 - 3x^2 - 9x + 2$.
    *Ans.* Max., 7; min., $-25$.

(b) $y = x^2 + \dfrac{16}{x}$.    *Ans.* Min., 12.

(c) $y = (x + 1)^2(x - 2)^2$.
    *Ans.* Max., $\frac{81}{16}$; min., 0.

(d) $y = x^4 - 2x^3 - 2x^2 + 1$.

(e) $y = \dfrac{ax}{x^2 + a^2}$, $a$ positive.
    *Ans.* Max., $\frac{1}{2}$; min., $-\frac{1}{2}$.

(f) $y = 3x^4 - 4x^3 - 36x^2 + 60$.
    *Ans.* Max., 60; min., $-4$ and $-149$.

(g) $y = x^4 - 2x^2 + 10$.

(h) $y = x^3 + 3x^2 + 9x + 6$.

2. What is the maximum slope of $y = -x^3 + 3x^2 + 9x - 27$?    *Ans.* 12.

**5. *Some Applications of the Method of Maxima and Minima.*** We have now a method of finding the relative maxima and minima of a function. In practical applications there is the additional step of formulating mathematically the function that expresses the physical quantity whose maximum or minimum value we seek. We shall examine a few applications.

One of the classic applications of the method was made by the mathematician Pierre de Fermat to derive what is called the law of refraction for light. First, let us be clear about the difference between reflection and refraction. When light strikes a mirror, whether the mirror is flat or curved (see Section 5 of Chapter 4), it is reflected in accordance with the principle that the angle of incidence, angle $i$ of Fig. 8-8, equals the angle

**Figure 8-8**

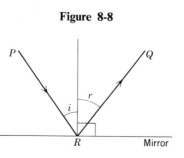

of reflection, angle $r$ of the figure. (In our past work we used the complementary angles of $i$ and $r$, which of course are also equal.) Thus under
reflection the light goes back into the medium from which it came; that is,
in Fig. 8-8 it returns to the region above the mirror. In refraction there are
two media, say air and water, and the light passes from one medium into
the other. Thus (Fig. 8-9) the light ray emanating from $P$ strikes the
boundary between the air and the water at $R$, enters the water, and then
travels through the water. What is remarkable about this process is that the
light ray changes its direction as it enters the water, so that the path $RQ$ is
not a continuation of the straight line $PR$. The problem that baffled
scientists and mathematicians from the time of Euclid until the seventeenth
century was, how is the direction of $RQ$ related to that of $PR$, or how is the
angle of refraction $r$ related to the angle of incidence $i$? There did not seem
to be any simple relation between $i$ and $r$.

In 1621 the Dutch mathematician Willebrord Snell and in 1637 René
Descartes gave crude physical arguments to support their discovery of the
correct law of refraction. Of course, physical arguments are more suspect
than mathematical arguments, and in fact Descartes' argument was wrong
even though his conclusion was correct. Fermat then took up the question
of establishing the correct law of refraction on a sounder basis.

The Alexandrian Greek mathematician and engineer Hero (first
century) had proved in the case of reflection that the path $PR + RQ$ (Fig.
8-8) is the shortest path that light could take in going from $P$ to *any* point of
the mirror and then to $Q$; that is, the path that light actually takes so as to
make angle $i$ equal angle $r$ is shorter than any other path from $P$ to the
mirror to $Q$. In the case of refraction (Fig. 8-9) light does not take the
shortest path from $P$ to $Q$ because the shortest path is the straight-line path.
However, it was known by Fermat's time that light travels with a finite
velocity and that the velocity is a constant in a uniform medium. In the
case of reflection the light goes back into the same medium from which it
came and therefore, assuming that the atmosphere is of uniform character
as it is over short distances, the velocity is constant over the entire path
$PRQ$. Hence the fact that the light takes the shortest path under reflection
also means that it takes the least time. Fermat decided that light in traveling

**Figure 8-9**

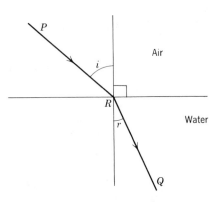

from one point to another always takes the path requiring least time, and he adopted this assertion as a basic physical principle or, one might say, as a physical axiom about light, just as Newton's laws of motion and of gravitation are physical axioms in the field of mechanics.

With the principle of least time as his physical axiom, Fermat established the correct law of refraction. Let us follow Fermat's derivation. Suppose that the light goes from $P$ in the first medium to $Q$ in the second. Because the points $P$ and $Q$ (Fig. 8-10) are given and fixed, the distance $d$ between the feet of perpendiculars from $P$ and $Q$ to the boundary of the medium is also fixed. This distance $d$ is the distance $AB$ in the figure. The light takes a straight-line path to *some* point $R$ on the boundary, because medium 1 is homogeneous or uniform and the straight-line path takes least time. Likewise the light takes a straight-line path from $R$ to $Q$ in the homogeneous medium 2. What we do not know is where the point $R$ lies on the boundary. Let us denote $AR$ by $x$. Then $RB = d - x$. Let $v_1$ be the velocity of light in medium 1. In medium 2, the velocity is different, and therefore we denote it by $v_2$. Then the time light requires to travel from $P$ to $R$ and from $R$ to $Q$ is

$$t = \frac{PR}{v_1} + \frac{RQ}{v_2},$$

or, if $a$ is the length $PA$ and $b$ is the length $QB$,

**(11)**
$$t = \frac{\sqrt{a^2 + x^2}}{v_1} + \frac{\sqrt{b^2 + (d - x)^2}}{v_2}.$$

We can now find the value of $x$ for which $t$ is a minimum. To do this we first find $dt/dx$. To differentiate each radical, we use the chain rule. Thus

$$\frac{dt}{dx} = \frac{1}{v_1}\frac{1}{2}\frac{1}{\sqrt{a^2 + x^2}}\, 2x + \frac{1}{v_2}\frac{1}{2}\frac{1}{\sqrt{b^2 + (d - x)^2}}\,\frac{d}{dx}\left[b^2 + (d - x)^2\right]$$

$$= \frac{x}{v_1\sqrt{a^2 + x^2}} + \frac{1}{v_2}\frac{1}{2}\frac{1}{\sqrt{b^2 + (d - x)^2}}\left[2(d - x)(-1)\right].$$

**Figure 8-10**

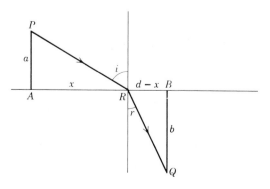

Then

(12)
$$\frac{dt}{dx} = \frac{x}{v_1\sqrt{a^2 + x^2}} - \frac{d - x}{v_2\sqrt{b^2 + (d - x)^2}}.$$

We now must set $dt/dx$ equal to 0. Thus

(13)
$$\frac{x}{v_1\sqrt{a^2 + x^2}} - \frac{d - x}{v_2\sqrt{b^2 + (d - x)^2}} = 0.$$

If there is a relative minimum at some value of $x$, this last equation must be satisfied at that value. We could solve equation (13) for $x$, but fortunately there is a simpler way to obtain the result.

From Fig. 8-10 we see that

(14)     $$\sin i = \frac{x}{\sqrt{a^2 + x^2}} \quad \text{and} \quad \sin r = \frac{d - x}{\sqrt{b^2 + (d - x)^2}}.$$

Hence equation (13) says that

(15)
$$\frac{\sin i}{v_1} - \frac{\sin r}{v_2} = 0$$

or

(16)
$$\frac{\sin i}{\sin r} = \frac{v_1}{v_2}.$$

This is the law of refraction. It tells us that the relation between $i$ and $r$ involves not only the sines of the angles but also the velocities of light in the two media. This law is the basis for the design of all optical lenses.

We have not shown that equation (15) really yields a relative minimum of our original function (11). However, by applying the first test we shall now see that it does. Let us note that in view of equation (14) the value of the derivative in (12) can be written as

(17)
$$\frac{dt}{dx} = \frac{\sin i}{v_1} - \frac{\sin r}{v_2}.$$

If the value of $x$ is slightly less than the value determined by (13), we see from Fig. 8-10 that angle $i$ and therefore $\sin i$ decreases, whereas angle $r$ and therefore $\sin r$ increases. Hence the value of $dt/dx$ in (17) must be less than 0. Likewise if $x$ is slightly greater than the value determined by (13), it is again evident from the figure that $\sin i$ increases and $\sin r$ decreases, and therefore $dt/dx$ is greater than 0. Hence $dt/dx$ changes from a negative value to a positive one as $x$ passes through the value determined by $dt/dx = 0$. Then this value of $x$ must be the value at which the function (11) is a relative minimum.

Let us consider next a problem which is simpler, but which involves another point. Let us prove that of all rectangles with the same perimeter the square has maximum area. As a matter of fact, Fermat, who was one of the first to develop the calculus method of finding relative maxima and minima of functions, used this problem to show that the method works.

Let us denote by $x$ and $y$ the dimensions of any rectangle (Fig. 8-11). Then the area is given by

**(18)** $$A = xy.$$

However, we are interested only in rectangles with the same perimeter. Suppose that we denote this common perimeter by $p$. Then for all rectangles of perimeter $p$

**(19)** $$p = 2x + 2y.$$

We may now state from (19) that

**(20)** $$y = \frac{p - 2x}{2}.$$

Then by substituting in (18) we obtain

$$A = x\left( \frac{p - 2x}{2} \right) = \frac{px}{2} - x^2.$$

We should now like to know, for what value of $x$ is $A$ a maximum? We can apply the standard method. We find $dA/dx$ and set it equal to 0. Thus

$$\frac{p}{2} - 2x = 0$$

or

**(21)** $$x = \frac{p}{4}.$$

Because $d^2A/dx^2$, the second derivative of $A$ with respect to $x$, is $-2$, we see that the value $p/4$ furnishes a relative maximum. The rectangle of maximum area is a square.

Problems in which the function to be maximized or minimized involves two variables related by another equation often exhibit a peculiarity which is illustrated by the following example (Fig. 8-12). Suppose that we

**Figure 8-11**

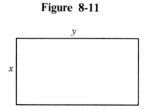

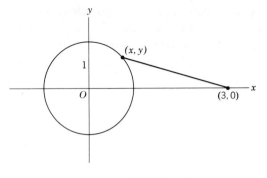

**Figure 8-12**

had to find the shortest distance from the point (3, 0) to the circle $x^2 + y^2 = 1$. The answer happens to be geometrically evident. The point on the circle which is closest to (3, 0) is clearly (1, 0). However, let us apply the method of the calculus.

Let $(x, y)$ be the coordinates of any point on the circle. Then the distance from (3, 0) to the point $(x, y)$ (see the Appendix to Chapter 3) is

**(22)** $$d = \sqrt{(x-3)^2 + y^2} \, .$$

Our goal is to find the $(x, y)$ for which $d$ is a minimum. We note that the $(x, y)$ that makes $d$ a minimum also makes $d^2$ a minimum. Hence let us investigate the minimum of

**(23)** $$s = d^2 = (x-3)^2 + y^2$$

or of

**(24)** $$s = x^2 - 6x + 9 + y^2.$$

As the problem now stands, $s$ is a function of $x$ and $y$. However, $x^2 + y^2 = 1$. Then choosing the positive $x$ gives

$$x = \sqrt{1 - y^2}$$

and therefore

$$s = 1 - y^2 - 6\sqrt{1 - y^2} + 9 + y^2$$

or

**(25)** $$s = -6\sqrt{1 - y^2} + 10.$$

We now apply differentiation and find that

$$\frac{ds}{dy} = \frac{6y}{\sqrt{1 - y^2}} \, .$$

We see that $ds/dy = 0$ when $y = 0$. Moreover, $ds/dy$ is negative for $y < 0$ and positive for $y > 0$. Hence $y = 0$ is the $y$-value of a relative minimum. Of course, when $y = 0$, $x = 1$. (We have already rejected negative values of

$x$.) Thus (1, 0) is the point on the circle that is at a minimum distance from (3, 0), just as we expected.

In eliminating one of the variables from (24), we deliberately eliminated $x$ and obtained (25). We could, however, eliminate $y$ from (24). Using the fact that $y^2 = 1 - x^2$, we obtain instead of (25)

**(26)**
$$s = x^2 - 6x + 9 + 1 - x^2$$

or

**(27)**
$$s = -6x + 10.$$

Now let us differentiate. We find that

$$\frac{ds}{dx} = -6.$$

Because the derivative is never 0, we might be tempted to conclude that there is no value of $x$ that furnishes a minimum $s$. However, let us recall that our calculus method furnishes *relative* maxima or minima. There may very well be an absolute maximum or minimum. The $x$ that we are concerned with can vary from $-1$ to $1$. We see from (27) that when $x = 1$, $s$ is least and is indeed 4. Also, when $x = 1$, $y = 0$. Hence again we find that (1, 0) is the point on the circle which is least distant from (3, 0).

## EXERCISES

1. If the height of a ball above the ground is given by the formula $h = 80t - 16t^2$, find the maximum height the ball attains. *Ans.* 100.
2. Show that of all rectangles with the same area the square has least perimeter.
3. Suppose that a rectangular plot is to be fenced off with one side along a river where no fencing is needed. What are the dimensions of the maximum area that can be fenced in with 100 feet of fencing? *Ans.* 25 by 50.
4. Show that of all triangles with a given base and a given area, the isosceles triangle has the least perimeter.

    *Suggestion:* Let the given base be $AB$ (Fig. 8-13). Choose an $x$-axis along $AB$ and let the $y$-axis bisect $AB$. Because the areas are fixed, the altitude $h$ must

**Figure 8-13**

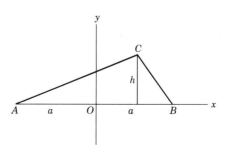

be the same for all triangles considered. Now show that for the triangle of least perimeter $CA = CB$.

5. Show that of all triangles with a given base and a given perimeter, the isoceles triangle has the greatest area.

   *Suggestion:* Use Hero's formula for the area, namely,

$$A = \sqrt{s(s - a)(s - b)(s - c)}$$

   where $a$, $b$, and $c$ are the sides and $s$ is half the perimeter.

6. Find the dimensions of a rectangular plot containing 864 sq ft and requiring least fencing with the condition that a fence parallel to one pair of sides be included so as to divide the plot into two rectangles.       *Ans.* 24 by 36.

7. Find the dimensions of the rectangle of largest area whose diagonal is 10 feet.
   *Ans.* $5\sqrt{2}$ by $5\sqrt{2}$ .

8. Find the dimensions of a cylindrical can containing 1 cu. ft. but with minimum surface area (including top and bottom).    *Ans.* $r = 1/ \sqrt[3]{2\pi}$ , $h = (2\pi)^{2/3}/\pi$.

9. Find the rectangle of given area which has the shortest diagonal.
   *Ans.* Square.

10. Find the rectangle of maximum area inscribed in the circle $x^2 + y^2 = 1$.

11. Given a point $R$ with coordinates $(a, b)$ in the interior of the parabola $y^2 = 4px$, show that the shortest path from $R$ to a point $P$ of the parabola and from $P$ to the focus $(p, 0)$ is the one determined by the point $P$ which lies on the line through $R$ parallel to the axis. (If we recall that light from the focus after reflection at the parabola goes out parallel to the axis, this problem shows that light takes the shortest path and, because it travels in one medium, it takes the least time.)

12. Suppose that two fixed masses $m$ and $M$ attract each other in accordance with the law of gravitation $F = GmM/r^2$. For what value of $r$ is $F$ least? Greatest?
    *Ans.* None.

13. Can the value of the relative maximum of a function be less than a relative minimum of the function?

    *Suggestion:* Consider $y = x + (1/x)$.                          *Ans.* Yes.

14. Prove or disprove the assertion that if a function of $x$ is 0 at $x = a$, the derivative must be 0 at $x = a$.

15. What conditions must any or all of the coefficients $a$, $b$, and $c$ of the function $y = ax^2 + bx + c$ satisfy in order that the function have a relative maximum point?                                                *Ans.* $a < 0$.

16. Given $y = x^3 + bx^2 + 3x + 5$, what condition must be imposed on $b$ in order that the function have no relative maxima or minima?       *Ans.* $|b| < 3$.

17. Find the maximum value of the function $y = x^3$ in the domain $-1 \leq x \leq 4$.
    *Ans.* 64.

18. A 100-feet long straight fence is in place. We wish to add 200 more feet of fencing, so that the 100 feet are fully utilized and so that the 300 feet enclose a rectangle of maximum area. Find the dimensions of the rectangle of maximum area.                                              *Ans.* 50 by 100.

19. Find the point on the parabola $y^2 = 4x$ which is at the shortest distance from $(1, 0)$. Carry out the work by eliminating $y$ from the distance function and then by eliminating $x$.                                *Ans.* (0, 0).

**20.** Find the point $(x, y)$ on the ellipse $b^2x^2 + a^2y^2 = a^2b^2$ such that the distance to the focus $(c, 0)$ is a minimum.

    *Suggestion:* Express the distance as a function of $x$ and work the problem. Then express the distance as a function of $y$ and work the problem.

*Ans.* $(a, 0)$.

**21.** A man is in a boat at $P$ 1 mile from the nearest point $A$ on the shore (Fig. 8-14). He wishes to go to $B$ which is farther along the straight shore 1 mile from $A$. If he can row at 3 mi/hr and walk at 5 mi/hr, toward what point $C$ between $A$ and $B$ should he row in order to reach $B$ in least time?

*Ans.* $AC = \frac{3}{4}$ mi.

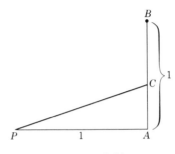

**Figure 8-14**

**22.** The conditions are the same as in Exercise 21, except that the man can row at 4 mi/hr.
*Ans.* $C = B$.

**23.** The conditions are the same as in Exercise 21, except that the man can row at 5 mi/hr.
*Ans.* $C = B$.

**24.** Given the isosceles triangle $ABC$ (Fig. 8-15), in which $AB$ is 12 inches and the altitude $CD$ is 3 inches, find the point $P$ on $CD$ such that the sum of the distances of $P$ from the vertices is a minimum.
*Ans.* The point $C$.

**Figure 8-15**

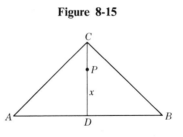

**25.** We shall "prove" that given a point inside a circle of radius $r$, there is no point on the circle which is nearest or farthest from the given point. We choose the origin of our coordinate system (Fig. 8-16) to be the center of the circle and we choose the $x$-axis so that it passes through the given point. Then the given point has coordinates $(a, 0)$. Let $(x, y)$ be any point on the circle. The distance of $(x, y)$ to $(a, 0)$ is given by $D = \sqrt{(x - a)^2 + y^2}$ . Because $D^2$ is a maximum or a minimum when $D$ is, we may as well consider $D^2$. Because $x^2 + y^2 = r^2$,

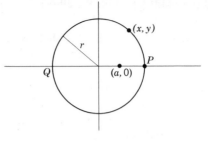

**Figure 8-16**

$D^2 = (x - a)^2 + r^2 - x^2$. Then, if we denote $D^2$ by $s$, $ds/dx = -2a$. This derivative is not 0 for any value of $x$, and therefore there is no maximum or minimum distance.

Intuitively it is evident, however, that $P$ is the point on the circle at the minimum distance from $(a, 0)$ and $Q$ is the point on the circle at the maximum distance from $(a, 0)$. What is wrong with the proof?

**26.** When measurements $m_1, m_2, \ldots, m_n$ of a certain length or other quantity are made, a common practice is to take the arithmetic mean $m = (m_1 + m_2 + \cdots + m_n)/n$ as the true value of the length. We call $m_1 - m, m_2 - m, \ldots, m_n - m$ the errors in the individual measurements. Show that the arithmetic mean makes the sum of the squares of the errors a minimum.

**27.** Use Fermat's principle of least time to deduce the law of reflection of light.

*Suggestion:* Use the method in the text but remember that you are dealing here with reflection rather than refraction. In terms of Fig. 8-17, the answer is $\alpha = \beta$.

**Figure 8-17**

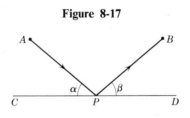

**28.** A pier is to be built at some point $P$ along the shore $CD$ of a river, so that merchandise can be unloaded from a ship on it and then trucked to towns $A$ and $B$ (Fig. 8-17). Where should $P$ be located so that $AP + PB$ is least?

*Suggestion:* In view of the fact that light travels at a constant velocity in a uniform or homogeneous medium, least time means least distance. Hence use the result of Exercise 27.

**29.** In Fig. 8-18 $CD$ and $EF$ are parallel shores of a river and $A$ and $B$ are towns each at some distance from the respective shores. The towns want to build a bridge $PQ$ across the river and perpendicular to the shores so that the total distance from $A$ to $B$ is a minimum. Show that $P$ must be chosen so that $AP$ and $QB$ are parallel.

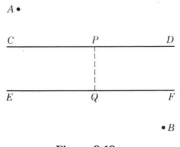

**Figure 8-18**

**30.** The specific weight $s$ of water, that is, the weight of a cubic centimeter of water in the temperature range $0 < t < 100$, wherein water is liquid, is given by the formula $s = 10^{-6}(1 + 53t - 6.53t^2 + 0.014t^3)$ when $t$ is the Centigrade temperature. At what temperature is the specific weight a maximum?

*Ans.* $t = 4.09°C.$

**6. *Some Applications to Economics.*** * If any one group of people is interested in maxima and minima problems it is business people. They wish to maximize profits and, where necessary, to minimize losses. However, economic problems are far more complicated than physical problems because many more substantial factors enter into economic events than in physical ones. Moreover, some of these factors, particularly those which involve human responses, either are not measurable or do not follow the same laws all the time. Nevertheless some progress is being made in mathematical economics.

The problems we can tackle with elementary calculus are oversimplified and therefore unrealistic. The numbers we shall use are also unrealistic; they have been deliberately chosen to minimize the arithmetic. Despite these limitations the problems will give some indication of how the calculus can be useful in the rapidly developing science of economics.

Perhaps the first function of interest to a manufacturer is the cost function, that is, the total cost of producing $x$ units of an article. A typical example might be

**(28)** $$C(x) = 3000 + 10x + 0.1x^2,$$

where $C(x)$ is the cost in dollars for $x$ units. The 3000 would represent the fixed costs of, say, rent and machinery. The variable terms would then represent labor, materials used to manufacture the units, and perhaps depreciation of machinery. Now $x$ takes on only positive integral values but it is convenient mathematically to think of $x$ as varying continuously through all positive real values and to take the nearest integral value as the practical answer if the mathematical answer should be a fraction or an irrational number.

---

*This section can be omitted without disrupting the continuity.

The manufacturer would certainly like to know what happens to this cost as he produces more and more articles. He can, of course, graph the function. However, a very useful aid is what economists call the marginal cost and which is, by definition, the rate of change of cost with respect to the quantity produced, that is, $dC/dx$. In the case of the above example

$$dC/dx = +10 + 0.2x.$$

This marginal cost function shows that the cost of producing additional units increases steadily with $x$. It would, of course, be possible to produce more and more units of a commodity so that the rate of change of cost decreases with $x$; this would mean more efficient production.

Although the cost function and marginal cost are useful to know, an even better measure is the average cost. If $x$ units are produced at a total cost of $C$ dollars, then the average cost, $A(x) = C(x)/x$. The significance of average cost may be seen in the following consideration. If the average cost can be made as small as possible then clearly the manufacturer is producing at greatest efficiency. Given the cost function $C(x)$, when is the average cost least? We shall use our calculus test. Since

**(29)**
$$A(x) = \frac{C(x)}{x}$$

let us find $A'(x)$. We differentiate the right side as a quotient of two functions. Thus

$$A'(x) = \frac{xC'(x) - C(x)}{x^2} = \frac{C'(x)}{x} - \frac{C(x)}{x^2}.$$

Now $A(x)$ is a minimum when $A'(x) = 0$. Hence

$$\frac{C'(x)}{x} - \frac{C(x)}{x^2} = 0$$

or

$$C'(x) = \frac{C(x)}{x}.$$

Now $C'(x)$ or $dC/dx$ is the marginal cost and the right side is the average cost. Hence (granted the second derivative test for the moment) the average cost is the minimum when it equals the marginal cost.

Let us consider an example. Suppose the cost function of some product is

$$C(x) = 200 + 15x + 5x^2.$$

Then by (29)

$$A(x) = \frac{200}{x} + 15 + 5x.$$

The average cost $A(x)$ will be a minimum when $A'(x) = 0$. Now

$$A'(x) = -\frac{200}{x^2} + 5,$$

and

$$A'(x) = 0$$

when

$$-\frac{200}{x^2} + 5 = 0$$

or

$$x = \sqrt{40}.$$

It is also evident that the marginal cost

$$\frac{dC}{dx} = 15 + 10x,$$

has at $x = \sqrt{40}$ the value

$$\frac{dC}{dx} = 15 + 10\sqrt{40}.$$

If we calculate the average cost at $x = \sqrt{40}$ we find that

$$A(\sqrt{40}) = \frac{200}{\sqrt{40}} + 15 + 5\sqrt{40}.$$

Since $200/\sqrt{40} = 5 \cdot 40/\sqrt{40} = 5\sqrt{40}$, $A(\sqrt{40}) = 15 + 10\sqrt{40}$ and this is the value of $dC/dx$.

Knowing all about his cost of producing articles does not suffice for a manufacturer. He wants to make money. Hence he would like to know what price he can get for his product. The price is usually a function of how many units are put up for sale. Thus if $p(x)$ is the price in dollars, say, at which $x$ units can be sold then a typical $p(x)$ is

**(30)**                      $$p(x) = 1000 - 2x.$$

This function says that the more units are placed on the market the lower the price they will command. The price function is often called the *demand* function.

After knowledge of the market price the next quantity of interest to the manufacturer is the revenue, or income. This is

**(31)**                      $$R(x) = x\,p(x).$$

However, revenue is not profit because the cost must be taken into account. The profit function $P(x)$ is

**(32)** $$P(x) = R(x) - C(x).$$

The manufacturer can now determine for what value of $x$, $P(x)$ is a maximum. The value of $x$ for which $P(x)$ is a maximum need not be the one for which average cost is least. If the manufacturer can command a good price for his product then his profit may be a maximum even though he is not producing at the most efficient cost per unit.

Let us consider an example of maximizing profit. Suppose that the cost function $C(x) = 300 + 10x + 0.1x^2$ and that the price function $p(x)$ is $1000 - 2x$. Then the profit $P(x)$ is, by (32),

$$P(x) = x(1000 - 2x) - (300 + 10x + 0.1x^2).$$

We shall find when $P(x)$ is a maximum. First of all

$$P(x) = -300 + 990x - 2.1x^2.$$

Then

$$P'(x) = 990 - 4.2x.$$

When $P'(x) = 0$, $x = 236$, approximately. We see at once that $P''(x)$ is negative so that the profit is a maximum when about 236 units are sold. The value of 236 for $x$ is not necessarily the value at which maximum revenue can be obtained, nor, as already noted, the value at which minimum average cost of manufacture is achieved.

Businessmen do not always seek maximum profit. If a merchant has a large stock of some article and needs cash he will seek maximum revenue.

**Example.** A furniture store can sell 100 sofas per month at $500 each. However, it can sell 20 additional units for each $10 reduction in price. At what price should it sell the sofas to maximize the revenue?

**Solution.** Let $x$ be the price at which the sofas are to be sold. The number of sofas that will be sold depends on the number of multiples of $10 that the reduced price is below $500. The reduction in price is $500 - x$. The number of multiples of $10 in $500 - x$ is $(500 - x)/10$. For each such multiple the store sells 20 additional units. Hence the number of units sold will be $100 + 20[(500 - x)/10]$ or $100 + 1000 - 2x$. Since the price is $x$ dollars per sofa the revenue is

$$R = x(1100 - 2x) = 1100x - 2x^2.$$

To obtain the maximum revenue we apply the usual method,

$$\frac{dR}{dx} = 1100 - 4x.$$

When $dR/dx = 0$,

$$x = 275.$$

Thus maximum revenue will be received when the sofas are sold at $275 apiece.

## EXERCISES

1. Suppose that the (total) cost of producing $x$ units of a product is $C(x) = x^3 - 6x^2 + 15x$. Find the number of units for which the average cost $A(x)$ is a minimum. Verify that for this number of units the minimum average cost equals the marginal cost.

2. Suppose that the (total) cost of producing $x$ units is $C(x) = x^3 - 15x^2 + 76x + 10$ and that the demand function is $p(x) = 55 - 3x$. Find the number of units for which the profit will be a maximum.

3. Prove generally that when the profit is a maximum, the marginal revenue $dR/dx$ equals the marginal cost.

4. Suppose that the demand function of some article is $p(x) = 75 - 2x$ and the cost function is $C(x) = 350 + 12x + x^2/4$. Find the number of units and price at which the total profit is a maximum. What is the maximum profit?

5. A manufacturer sells $x$ units of a product when the price $p(x)$ per unit is $100 - 0.10x$ dollars. The cost of $x$ units is $C(x) = 1000 + 50x$ dollars. How many should he sell to maximize his profit?

6. The manufacturing cost of an article involves a fixed overhead of $100 per day, 50 cents for material, and $x^2/100$ dollars per day for labor and machinery to produce $x$ articles. How many articles should be produced per day to minimize the average cost per article?

7. The total cost of producing $x$ units of an article is $C(x) = a + c\sqrt{x}$. What number of units will minimize average cost?

8. A bank knows that the amount of money people will invest is proportional to the interest rate it will pay on the investment. The bank can earn 7% on the money. What interest rate should it offer to maximize its profit?

9. A store is to be built with a rectangular floor area of 10,000 square feet. The front wall will cost twice as much per linear foot as the side and back walls. The height of the store is to be 10 feet. What should the dimensions be to keep the total cost a minimum?

10. To run a ship costs $125 per hour of fixed costs plus fuel. The cost of fuel per hour is $\frac{1}{10}v^3$, where $v$ is the speed. At what speed should the ship be run to minimize the cost per *mile* of operation?

11. An oil field has 25 wells. Each produces 100 barrels of oil per day. If new wells are drilled the yield of all the wells decreases by 3 barrels per day for each new well. How many wells should be drilled to maximize the number of barrels of oil produced?

12. A printer can print greeting cards at an initial cost of $100 for the plate and at the cost of $0.05x + 0.01x^2$ for $x$ cards to cover wear and tear on his machinery. He can sell the cards he prints at $1 each. How many should he print to maximize his profit?

13. The fixed cost of land for a building is $500,000. If the building is one story high the additional cost is $100,000. However, if additional floors are built, because the foundation must be stronger, each additional floor costs $100,000 more than the next lower one. The space for each floor can be rented at $300,000 per year. (a) How high should the building be to maximize the profit for the first year? (b) How high should the building be to maximize the per cent return on the investment?

14. If a truck travels at $x$ miles per hour the cost per hour of operating the truck is $10 + x^2/50$ dollars. At what speed is the cost a minimum for a 100-mile trip?

15. A store can sell 100 tennis rackets a year at $30 each. For each $2 drop in price it can sell 10 more rackets. What sale price would produce the greatest revenue?

16. A restaurant charges $25 a couple for its meals and attracts 100 couples per evening at that price. For each $2 that it reduces the price it attracts 10 more couples. What price would produce the greatest revenue?

A great number of significant problems in economics concern the effect of taxation imposed by a local or the federal government. Taxes can be of various sorts. The tax may be imposed on the producer or manufacturer. In this situation the producer's cost is increased. If, let us suppose, a tax of $t$ dollars per unit is imposed by a government the cost to the producer of producing $x$ units will not be the old $C(x)$ but $C(x) + tx$. The *demand function* will remain the same. The producer may or may not raise the price at which he offers his product. Of course if he raises the price then the demand $x$ will fall. The producer's problem is, in fact, to decide what price he should charge so as to maximize his profit despite the tax or how many articles he should sell to maximize his profit in view of the increase in cost to him. The profit function will now be

(33) $$P(x) = xp(x) - C(x) - tx.$$

The situation is different if the government imposes a tax on the consumer, say in the form of a sales tax. Now the manufacturer's cost remains the same. But since the price to the consumer is higher, the number $x$ of units demanded will decrease. Thus if the original demand function is $p = 10 - 3x$ and a 25% tax on the sale price is imposed, the new price is $(5/4)p$. When the manufacturer calculates his revenue, which is $xp$, he will have to take into account that the number of units demanded will be determined by the $x$ which corresponds to $(5/4)p$ instead of $p$. Or one can say that the new demand function is $p = (4/5)(10 - 3x)$. Since the manufacturer does not get the sales tax it is this $p$ that enters into his revenue. The profit $P(x)$ is given by

$$P(x) = xp - C(x)$$

wherein $p$ is the *new* demand function.

The interesting questions that arise when a tax of either type is imposed are what effect does this have on the manufacturer's profits and how much does the tax affect the consumer's total cost. The following exercises, while the numbers are not realistic, illustrate what happens.

## EXERCISES

1. Suppose that the cost function of a commodity is $C = 3x$ and the demand function is $p = 10 - 3x$, where $p$ is in dollars. The government imposes a tax of $2 per unit to be paid by the manufacturer. Find the maximum profit for the producer. What price per article produces maximum profit?

2. Find the number of articles sold to yield the maximum profit under the conditions of Exercise 1 but without the tax and find the price at which the articles will be sold.

3. Suppose that the cost function of a commodity is $C = 3x$ and the demand function is $p = 10 - 3x$. The government imposes a sales tax of 25% (to be paid by the purchaser, or course). Find the maximum profit for the producer and the price at which the articles will be sold.

4. Suppose that the cost function is $C = 4x$ and the demand function is $p = 20 - 4x$. A sales tax of 10% is imposed; find the price and quantity sold to produce maximum profits.

*7. Curve Tracing.* We have pointed out several times that the graph or curve of a formula is immensely useful in helping us to understand its behavior. Up to now we have obtained the curves of formulas by relying largely on point-for-point plotting. For simple functions the graphs are readily obtained. However, for more complicated functions even the seemingly simple task of plotting points can be a problem. This process can be time-consuming and can lead to serious errors at that.

Let us consider the very simple function

(34)
$$y = \frac{1}{x}.$$

By calculating values of $y$ for various values of $x$ and by plotting, we might obtain the four points shown as black dots on the right-hand portion of Fig. 8-19 and the four points similarly pictured on the left. Joining the four points on the right by a smooth curve and doing the same on the left gives correct portions of the full graph. However, we still do not know how the two portions should be joined. We might be tempted to join them by the

**Figure 8-19**

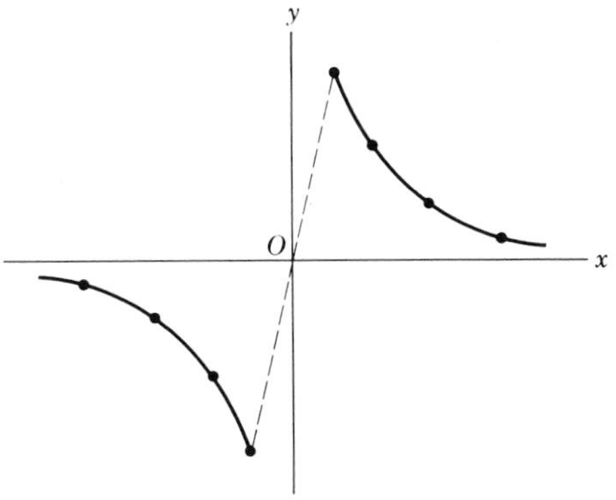

broken line shown in the figure or perhaps, for art's sake, round out the junctions. In the case of this simple function we know the correct curve through previous contact with it. We can also see readily that as $x$ approaches 0 through positive values, $y$ becomes infinite through positive values, and as $x$ approaches 0 through negative values, $y$ becomes negatively infinite.

However, let us consider the relatively simple function

**(35)**                                    $$y = 4x^3 - 15x^2 + 18x.$$

If we make a table of values for this function, we obtain the table shown below. By joining the four plotted points, we obtain the continuous curve shown in Fig. 8-20. Actually the graph dips between $x = 1$ and $x = 2$ and has a relative maximum at $x = 1$ and a relative minimum at $x = \frac{3}{2}$. We can determine these facts by means of our calculus method of determining relative maxima and minima. In other words, the calculus is an aid to graphing.

In this section we shall investigate how the calculus can help in graphing functions when we know the formula for the function. One aid, as the preceding example illustrates, is the determination of the relative maxima and minima of the function. There are others, which we consider next.

A helpful procedure is to find the first derivative and to note where it is positive and where negative. We know from our work on maxima and minima that where $y'$ is positive, the function must be increasing and where it is negative, the function must be decreasing. Thus in the example of (35) $y'$ is $12x^2 - 30x + 18$ and at $x = 2$, $y'$ is 6; therefore, the function must be increasing at $x = 2$.

Another aid in graphing is the determination of what is called the concavity of the graph. Figure 8-21 shows four ways in which a curve can lie in relation to its tangent. In the upper two cases the curve lies above its

**Figure 8-20**

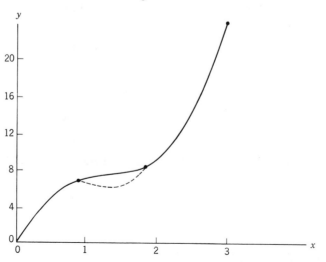

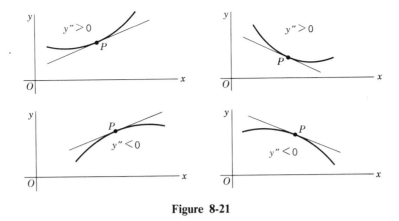

**Figure 8-21**

tangent. This means that near $P$ the $y$-values of points on the curve are larger than the $y$-values of the tangent at $P$ for the same $x$-values. The curve is then said to be *concave upward* at $P$. In the two lower cases shown in Fig. 8-21 the curve lies below its tangent at $P$, and the curve is said to be concave downward at $P$.

To know whether a curve is concave upward or downward at a point is certainly a help in graphing the curve. A useful test is the value of the second derivative at the point. Suppose that $y''$ is positive at a point $P$. We proved earlier that if the derivative of a function is positive at a point, the function is increasing at that point. If $y''$ is positive, the function $y'$ is increasing. However, $y'$ is the slope of the curve, and this is increasing at $P$. Hence the slope of the curve is less to the left of $P$ and more to the right of $P$ than it is at $P$. The curve then must have the shapes of either of the upper two cases in Fig. 8-21. (We must remember in the second case that as the angle of inclination of the tangent approaches $180°$, the slope increases algebraically.)

Similarly, if $y''$ is negative at $P$, $y'$ is a decreasing function. Hence the slope of the curve is greater to the left of $P$ and less to the right of $P$ than it is at $P$. Then the curve must behave as shown in the lower two cases of Fig. 8-21. Thus we can test readily for upward and downward concavity.

In this discussion of concavity we omitted consideration of the case in which $y'' = 0$ at a point on a curve. This case is of considerable interest. If $y''$ is 0, we do not know whether $y'$ is increasing or decreasing, just as when $y'$ is 0, we do not know whether $y$ is increasing or decreasing. In fact, usually when $y'$ is 0, $y$ has a relative maximum or minimum. Hence when $y''$ is 0, we should look into the possibility that $y'$ has a relative maximum or minimum. Figure 8-22 shows the most common situation. At the point $Q$ and at all other points to the left of $P$, $y''$ is positive and the curve is concave upward. At the point $R$ and at all other points to the right of $P$, $y''$ is negative and the curve is concave downward. Alternatively, we may say that at points to the left of $P$, the derived function $y'$ is an increasing function, and at points to the right of $P$, $y'$ is a decreasing function. Then $y'$ has a relative maximum at $P$, and its derivative, namely $y''$, must be 0 at $P$. In other words, at a point at which $y''$ is 0, it does seem as though $y'$ has a

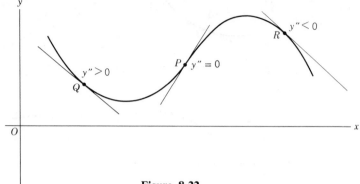

**Figure 8-22**

relative maximum or minimum. We must, however, be careful. The vanishing of the derivative of a function is necessary at a relative maximum or minimum but it is not sufficient. The derivative must, in addition, change sign in passing through the relative maximum or minimum point. In the present case, if $y'' = 0$ and if $y''$ changes from positive to negative as $x$ passes through the value at $P$ or if $y''$ changes from negative to positive, $y'$ has a relative maximum or minimum.

Thus at *a point at which $y'' = 0$ and changes sign, the first derived function has a relative maximum or minimum*. Moreover, the curve changes at that point from concave upward to concave downward or the reverse. At such a point the tangent *crosses* the curve, for at points immediately to the left the curve must be above the tangent and at points immediately to the right, below the tangent, or vice versa. A point at which $y'' = 0$ and changes from positive to negative or negative to positive is called a *point of inflection*. The location of such points is also an aid in graphing a function.

To tie together the various aids that the calculus offers toward graphing functions, let us consider an example. Suppose that we know that the formula representing some function is,

**(36)** $$y = \frac{2(x - 2)}{x^2}.$$

For a function such as (36), which we observe at once to have no value at $x = 0$, it is well to determine exactly what the behavior is near $x = 0$. The numerator approaches $-4$ as $x$ approaches 0, and because the denominator approaches 0, the value of the function becomes infinite as $x$ approaches 0. Moreover, whether $x$ approaches 0 through negative values or through positive values, the function becomes negatively infinite. Hence we know already that the function drops rapidly toward $-\infty$ as $x$ approaches 0 through positive values as well as through negative values. The line $x = 0$ is an asymptote [See Chap. 7, equation (40)].

It is also useful to know where the curve cuts the $x$-axis; that is, the $x$-intercepts. In the present case $y = 0$ when $x = 2$. Hence the curve cuts the $x$-axis on the right of the $y$-axis but not on the left.

We note next that

**(37)** $$y' = \frac{-2x + 8}{x^3}.$$

Let us consider first the behavior of $y'$ for positive values of $x$. When $x$ increases from 0 to 2, $y'$ is always positive. Hence $y$ increases steadily from $x = 0$ to $x = 2$. The curve crosses the $x$-axis at $x = 2$ and, because $y'$ remains positive until $x = 4$, the function still increases. At $x = 4$, $y' = 0$. Here we have a possible relative maximum or relative minimum of the function. Because $y'$ changes from positive to negative as $x$ passes through 4, the value $x = 4$ is the abscissa of a relative maximum. When $x = 4$, $y = \frac{1}{4}$.

For $x > 4$, $y'$ is negative. Hence the function must decrease steadily. Yet we see from (36) that the function remains positive. Moreover, the denominator increases faster than the numerator, and the function values approach 0.

We know now the essential behavior of the function for positive $x$-values, but we may confirm what we have learned by testing for points of inflection. We find that

**(38)**
$$y'' = \frac{4x - 24}{x^4} .$$

Because $y'' = 0$ at $x = 6$, this value of $x$ is a possible location of a point of inflection. We see that $y''$ changes sign as $x$ passes through the value 6, and therefore there is a point of inflection at $x = 6$. At the value 6 of $x$, $y$ is $\frac{2}{9}$.

For negative values of $x$ we note that $y'$ is always negative because the numerator is positive and the denominator is negative. A negative $y'$ means that the function is constantly decreasing *as $x$ increases*. This means that as $x$ increases from $-\infty$, that is, from large negative values, and approaches 0, the $y$-values decrease constantly. From what value do they start to decrease? When $x$ is very large and negative, we see from (36) that $y$ is negative and near 0 in value. Hence as $x$ increases from $-\infty$ to 0, $y$ starts from 0 and steadily decreases.

Figure 8-23 assembles all of the information that we have gathered about the graph. Of course, the graph is not exact. It gives the essential behavior of the function. To make the graph more accurate we would have to calculate the $y$-values for a number of $x$-values.

**Figure 8-23**

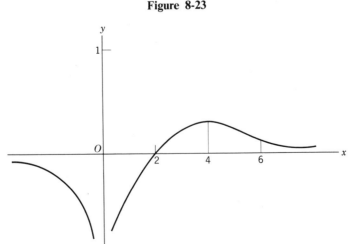

## EXERCISES

1. Sketch the graphs of the following functions. Use all the information that you can obtain from studying the first and second derived functions of the functions.
   (a)  $y = x^3 - 6x^2 + 9x + 1$.
   (b)  $y = x^3 + 3x^2 + 3x + 5$.
   (c)  $y = x^3 + 2x^2 + 3x + 5$.
   (d)  $y = x^{5/3}$.
   (e)  $y = \dfrac{1}{x^2 + 1}$.
   (f)  $y = x^4$.
   (g)  $y = x^4 - 4x^3$.
   (h)  $y = \dfrac{x}{x^2 + 1}$.
   (i)  $y = \dfrac{x(x - 3)}{(x + 3)^2}$.
   (j)  $y = \dfrac{2x}{x + 4}$.

2. Given the function shown in Fig. 8-24, describe how the second derived function varies from $A$ to $B$, $B$ to $C$, ..., $G$ to $H$, $H$ to $I$.

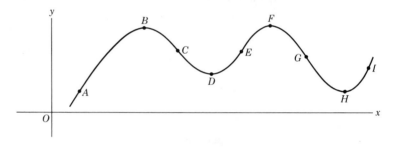

**Figure 8-24**

3. Show that the point of inflection of the general cubic polynomial function $y = ax^3 + bx^2 + cx + d$ is the average of the three zeros of the function (the three values of $x$ at which $y$ is 0).

   *Suggestion:* From algebra we know that $y = a(x - r_1)(x - r_2)(x - r_3)$. Two of the quantities $r_1$, $r_2$, and $r_3$ may be complex, but you may apply the calculus to the function.

4. The function $y = ax^3 + bx^2 + cx + d$ has a point of inflection and a horizontal tangent at the same value of $x$. Show that $b^2 - 3ac = 0$.

5. Find the points of inflection of $y = x^4 - 8x^3 + 64x + 8$.

# CHAPTER
# NINE
# THE
# DEFINITE
# INTEGRAL

**1. Introduction.** Thus far we have learned two of the basic notions of the calculus, the derivative and the antiderivative. The latter we have also called the integral. It should more properly be called the *indefinite integral*. The third basic notion of the calculus, which we shall now investigate, is called the *definite integral*. It may seem at first that the definite integral has nothing to do with differentiation and antidifferentiation. But we shall see that all three are intimately involved with each other though not to the extent of a scandal.

We mentioned at the beginning of this book that one of the major classes of problems that led to the calculus was the determination of areas, volumes, and centers of gravity of a variety of figures. Let us consider the subject of area. The calculation of areas of figures bounded by *straight-line segments* can be performed with the methods of Euclidean geometry. Thus the areas of triangles, rectangles, and parallelograms are readily found. More complicated rectilinear figures, that is, figures bounded by line segments, can at the very worst be broken up into triangles, and the area can then be obtained as the sum of areas of the triangles. It is in this way that, for example, the areas of regular polygons are calculated.

The first really difficult figure is the circular region. The Greeks solved the problem of finding its area by taking a very natural step. First, they approximated the area by inscribing a square (Fig. 9-1). Then they improved the approximation by inscribing the regular octagon, then the regular 16-sided polygon, and so on. Each new polygon is evidently a better approximation to the desired area. The Greeks then noted that the areas of these successive inscribed polygons approached more closely the area of the circle. They also used circumscribed regular polygons which, as the number of sides increased, also approached the area of a circle through larger values.* Euclid (circa 300 B.C.), following Eudoxus (406–355 B.C.), then

---

* The Greeks did not use limits explicitly. They used an indirect method of proof known as the method of exhaustion. For simplicity we speak in this section of the Greeks using limits.

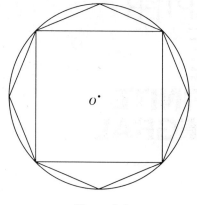

**Figure 9-1**

proved that the areas of any two circles are to each other as the squares of their respective radii. From this it follows that for any circle the area $A = kr^2$ where $k$ is a constant and $r$ is the radius. Archimedes (287–212 B.C.) then calculated the value of $k$, which is denoted by $\pi$, of course, by calculating the perimeters of inscribed and circumscribed regular polygons of more and more sides in a circle of diameter 1, and showed that $\pi$ lies between $3\frac{1}{7}$ and $3\frac{10}{71}$.

The next major result in the determination of areas was Archimedes' calculation of the area between an arc of a parabola and a chord, that is, the area bounded by the arc $BA'AA''C$ and the chord $BC$ in Fig. 9-2. Because regular polygons are not inscribable in this area, Archimedes hit upon the idea of using triangles. His first approximation was the triangle $ABC$, the point $A$ having been chosen as the one at which the tangent to the parabola is parallel to $BC$. His next approximation was obtained by adding to triangle $ABC$ the triangle $AA''C$, which takes in area between the arc $AA''C$ and the chord $AC$, and the triangle $AA'B$, which takes in area between the arc $AA'B$ and the chord $AB$. To obtain his third approximation, he inscribed triangles in each of the four regions still not included—the region between arc $A'B$ and chord $A'B$ is one such region—and so the third approximation was the sum of triangles $ABC$, $AA'B$, $AA''C$, and the

**Figure 9-2**

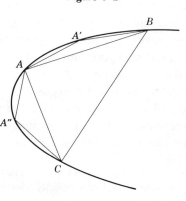

four new triangles. By observing the limit approached by these successive approximations, Archimedes showed that the area of the parabolic segment is $\frac{4}{3}$ of the area of triangle $ABC$.

A few other striking results about area were obtained by Archimedes. However, each problem that he tackled required a specially designed set of approximating figures. Moreover, the determination of the limit was a problem of considerable difficulty for the Greeks because they did not possess our algebra and analytic geometry.

From Greek times until the seventeenth century very little progress was made in finding areas and volumes bounded in whole or in part by curved figures. However, in that century some mathematicians—Pascal, Fermat, and notably Leibniz—introduced a general method of approximating curvilinear areas by rectilinear figures and of coming closer and closer to the desired area by improving the rectilinear approximation. When we understand what these men did we shall be able to outdo Archimedes, who was one of the greatest mathematicians of all times.

**2. Area as the Limit of a Sum.** Consider the area shown in Fig. 9-3, that is, the area bounded by the curve $CD$, by the vertical lines at $x = a$ and $x = b$, and by the $x$-axis. We can obtain an approximation to it by choosing the minimum $y$-value in $(a, b)$ and multiplying it by $b - a$. In anticipation of future steps, we write $b - a$ as $\Delta x$ and we denote the minimum $y$-value by $m_1$. Thus the first approximation is $m_1\Delta x$. Geometrically, this approximation is the area of the rectangle shown in the figure. We write

$$\underline{S_1} = m_1 \, \Delta x.$$

The $S$ refers to the sum that, as we shall see, enters into our process; the subscript reminds us that we have the first approximation; the bar underneath is to indicate that we have used the minimum $y$-value in $\Delta x$.

We can obtain a better approximation to the area in question if we divide the interval $(a, b)$ into two equal parts (Fig. 9-4), each of which we denote by $\Delta x$, if we take the minimum $y$-value in each part, and then form the sum

$$\underline{S_2} = m_1 \, \Delta x + m_2 \, \Delta x.$$

**Figure 9-3**

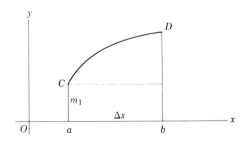

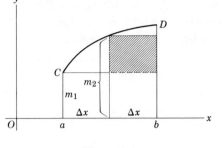

Figure 9-4

Geometrically, $\underline{S_2}$ is the sum of two rectangles, and it is clear that $\underline{S_2}$ is a better approximation to the area under the curve than $\underline{S_1}$, because it includes the shaded area in Fig. 9-4, whereas $\underline{S_1}$ did not include it.

We can now divide $(a, b)$ into three equal parts and form $\underline{S_3}$, then into four equal parts and form $\underline{S_4}$, and so on. Let us try to be general. Suppose that we divide the interval $(a, b)$ into $n$ equal parts (Fig. 9-5) and denote each by $\Delta x$. In each part or subinterval $\Delta x$ we choose the minimum $y$-value, which we denote by $m_1, m_2, \cdots, m_n$, respectively. We now form the sum

(1)                 $$\underline{S_n} = m_1\, \Delta x + m_2\, \Delta x + \cdots + m_n\, \Delta x,$$

where the dots indicate the missing terms. Geometrically, $\underline{S_n}$ is a sum of $n$ rectangles.

The important point to see now is that the larger we make $n$, which means that $\Delta x$ becomes smaller and smaller, the closer does the sum $\underline{S_n}$ approach the area under the curve. Geometrically this statement is evident, because the smaller $\Delta x$ is, the less the minimum $y$-value in any subinterval $\Delta x$ can differ from the other $y$-values in that subinterval.

Now, the quantity $n$ can be made larger and larger without bound. To each $n$ there is a sum $\underline{S_n}$, and therefore the quantity $\underline{S_n}$ varies with $n$. Hence we can speak of

$$\lim_{n \to \infty} \underline{S_n};$$

Figure 9-5

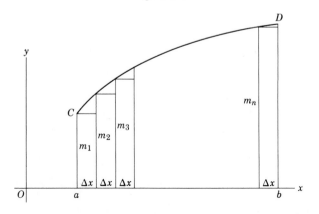

geometrically, this limit seems to be the exact area under the curve $CD$. If we denote this area by $A$, we can say that

**(2)**
$$\lim_{n \to \infty} \underline{S_n} = A.$$

The limit concept involved in (2) is in some respects different from the limit of, say, $x^2$ as $x$ approaches 2 or of $1/x$ as $x$ becomes infinite, but for the moment, let us not pursue the difference.

The approximations to the area $A$ that we obtained in $\underline{S_1}, \underline{S_2}, \ldots, \underline{S_n}$ were all less than $A$ because in each $\Delta x$ we chose the minimum $y$-value. We can obtain another sequence of approximations to $A$ if we use the *maximum* $y$-value in each $\Delta x$. Because the considerations are the same as those we have just considered, let us jump at once to the $n$th approximation. We divide the interval $(a, b)$ into $n$ equal parts (Fig. 9-6) and, as before, denote the width of each part or subinterval by $\Delta x$. In each $\Delta x$ we take the maximum $y$-value and denote them by $M_1, M_2, \ldots, M_n$. We now form the sum

**(3)**
$$\overline{S_n} = M_1 \, \Delta x + M_2 \, \Delta x + \cdots + M_n \, \Delta x.$$

We use the notation $\overline{S_n}$ to remind ourselves that we have used the maximum $y$-value in each $\Delta x$. Each term in this sum is the area of a rectangle, and each rectangle is larger than that portion of the area under the curve which it approximates. Our argument now is that as $n$ is taken larger, and as $\Delta x$ becomes smaller accordingly, the corresponding sum $\overline{S_n}$ is a better approximation to the area under the curve, because in a smaller $\Delta x$ the maximum $y$-value differs less from the other $y$-values in that $\Delta x$. Since $n$ can increase without bound, we can at least speak about

$$\lim_{n \to \infty} \overline{S_n},$$

and on geometric grounds it appears that

**(4)**
$$\lim_{n \to \infty} \overline{S_n} = A.$$

**Figure 9-6**

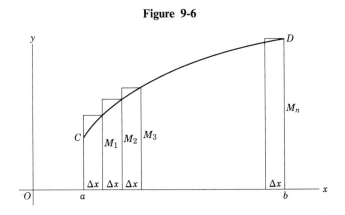

This scheme of approximating a given area by a sum of rectangles is entirely analogous to the Greek scheme of approaching the area of a circle by regular polygons. Each sum of rectangles that approaches the area from below is analogous to an inscribed regular polygon. Each sum of rectangles that approaches the area from above is analogous to a circumscribed regular polygon. Moreover, just as the area of the circle lies between the increasing areas of the set of inscribed regular polygons and the decreasing areas of the circumscribed regular polygons, so the area under the curve lies between the increasing areas of the sums of rectangles that approximate the area from below and the decreasing areas of the sums of the rectangles that approximate the area from above.

Before we develop further our new approach to area, let us see how it works out in a particular case. Let us find the area (Fig. 9-7) under the straight line $y = 2x$ and between $x = 1$, $x = 5$, and the $x$-axis. We want to calculate the limit called for in (2). Hence we must first find $S_n$, which is defined in (1). We break up the interval from $x = 1$ to $x = 5$ into $n$ equal parts, each of width $\Delta x$. In each subinterval we choose the smallest $y$-value. In the first subinterval this is the $y$-value at $x = 1$. Then, because $y = 2x$,

$$m_1 = 2 \cdot 1.$$

In the second subinterval the smallest $y$-value is the left-hand $y$-value. The corresponding $x$-value is $1 + \Delta x$; hence

$$m_2 = 2(1 + \Delta x).$$

In the third subinterval the smallest $y$-value is again the left-hand $y$-value and the corresponding $x$-value is $1 + 2\Delta x$. Hence

$$m_3 = 2(1 + 2\Delta x).$$

We see that the same procedure applies to each subinterval. Let us therefore note only the last one. The smallest $y$-value is the left-hand

**Figure 9-7**

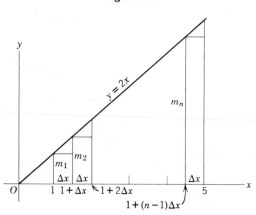

$y$-value and the corresponding $x$-value is $1 + (n - 1)\Delta x$. Then

$$m_n = 2[1 + (n - 1)\Delta x].$$

The sum $S_n$ in this example is

$$S_n = 2\Delta x + 2(1 + \Delta x)\Delta x + 2(1 + 2\Delta x)\Delta x$$

**(5)**
$$+ \cdots + 2[1 + (n - 1)\Delta x]\,\Delta x$$

or

$$S_n = 2\Delta x + 2\Delta x + 2(\Delta x)^2 + 2\Delta x + 2 \cdot 2(\Delta x)^2$$

**(6)**
$$+ \cdots + 2\Delta x + 2(n - 1)(\Delta x)^2.$$

We would like to find the number approached by $S_n$ as $n$ becomes infinite. First, let us rearrange the terms. We see that the quantity $2\Delta x$ occurs in each term. Because there are $n$-terms, these amount to $2n\,\Delta x$. In addition, we have the quantities

$$2(\Delta x)^2 + 2 \cdot 2(\Delta x)^2 + \cdots + 2(n - 1)(\Delta x)^2$$

or

$$2(\Delta x)^2[1 + 2 + \cdots + (n - 1)].$$

The quantity in the brackets is the sum of an arithmetic progression of $n - 1$ terms. The formula for the sum of $n$ terms of such a progression is

$$s = \frac{n}{2}(a + l)$$

where $n$ is the number of terms, $a$ is the first term, and $l$ is the last term. In our case

$$s = \frac{n - 1}{2}(1 + n - 1) = \frac{(n - 1)n}{2}.$$

Hence

**(7)**
$$S_n = 2n\,\Delta x + 2(\Delta x)^2 \frac{(n - 1)n}{2}.$$

If we try to use the facts that $n$ becomes infinite and $\Delta x$ approaches 0 in (7) we do not see clearly what number $S_n$ approaches. However, we know that we divided the interval from $x = 1$ to $x = 5$ into $n$ equal parts each of width $\Delta x$, so that

**(8)**
$$\Delta x = \frac{5 - 1}{n}.$$

Let us substitute the value of $\Delta x$ given by (8) in (7). Then

$$\underline{S_n} = 2n\,\frac{4}{n} + 2\left(\frac{4}{n}\right)^2 \frac{(n-1)n}{2} = 8 + 16\,\frac{(n-1)n}{n^2}$$

or

$$\underline{S_n} = 8 + 16 - \frac{16}{n}\,.$$

It is now clear that as $n$ becomes infinite, $16/n$ approaches 0 and $\underline{S_n}$ approaches 24. That is,

**(9)**                                    $$\lim_{n\to\infty}\underline{S_n} = 24.$$

We have found that the area under $y = 2x$ between $x = 1$ and $x = 5$ is 24. In the present case the figure is a trapezoid whose bases are the ordinates at $x = 1$ and $x = 5$, that is, 2 and 10, and whose altitude is 4. Because the area of a trapezoid is one half the altitude times the sum of the bases, we see that the area as given by plane geometry agrees with the result obtained by the calculus method.

Let us consider next a more difficult example. We shall evaluate the area (Fig. 9-8) under the parabola $y = x^2$ and lying between $x = 0$ and $x = 5$ by using (1) and (2). We divide the interval from 0 to 5 into $n$ equal parts, each of width $\Delta x$. In each subinterval the smallest $y$-value is the left-hand value. The abscissas at the left-hand end points of the subintervals are

$$0,\ \Delta x,\ 2\Delta x,\ 3\Delta x,\ \cdots,\ (n-1)\,\Delta x.$$

Because $y = x^2$, the ordinates at these abscissas are

$$0^2,\ (\Delta x)^2,\ (2\Delta x)^2,\ \cdots,\ \{(n-1)\,\Delta x\}^2.$$

**Figure 9-8**

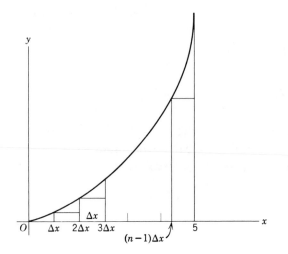

These successive $y$-values are, of course, the $m_1, m_2, m_3, \cdots, m_n$ of (1). Then, in accordance with (1),

$$\underline{S_n} = 0^2 \cdot \Delta x + (\Delta x)^2 \, \Delta x + (2\Delta x)^2 \, \Delta x + \cdots + \{(n-1)\,\Delta x\}^2 \, \Delta x$$

or

**(10)**          $$\underline{S_n} = (\Delta x)^3 \big[\, 1^2 + 2^2 + 3^2 + \cdots + (n-1)^2 \,\big].$$

To simplify this result, let us accept for the moment that the sum of the squares of the first $n$ integers is given by the formula*

**(11)**          $$s = \frac{n^3}{3} + \frac{n^2}{2} + \frac{n}{6}\,.$$

Because our expression (10) calls for the sum of the squares of the first $(n-1)$ integers, we could substitute $n-1$ for $n$ in (11) or we can obtain the result faster by noting that we want $s - n^2$, which is

$$\frac{n^3}{3} - \frac{n^2}{2} + \frac{n}{6}\,.$$

We substitute this value for the quantity in brackets in (10) and obtain

$$\underline{S_n} = (\Delta x)^3 \left( \frac{n^3}{3} - \frac{n^2}{2} + \frac{n}{6} \right).$$

As $\underline{S_n}$ now stands, it is difficult to determine the limit as $n$ becomes infinite because $\Delta x$ approaches 0. However, we divided the interval from $x = 0$ to $x = 5$ into $n$ parts so that

$$\Delta x = \frac{5}{n}\,.$$

Then

$$\underline{S_n} = \left( \frac{5}{n} \right)^3 \left( \frac{n^3}{3} - \frac{n^2}{2} + \frac{n}{6} \right) = 125\left( \frac{1}{3} - \frac{1}{2n} + \frac{1}{6n^2} \right).$$

We now see that

$$\lim_{n \to \infty} \underline{S_n} = \tfrac{125}{3}\,.$$

This number is the area under the parabola $y = x^2$ between $x = 0$ and $x = 5$.

Before we do more with the above method of finding areas, we should become a little more familiar with it through use.

---

* The proof is given in the Appendix to this chapter.

## EXERCISES

1. Find the area under the line $y = 3x$ between $x = 1$ and $x = 5$ by the method employed in the text.                                           *Ans.* 36.

2. Find the area of Exercise 1 but use the largest $y$-value in each subinterval in place of the smallest $y$-value.

3. Find the area under the parabola $y = x^2$ from $x = 0$ to $x = 5$ by using the largest $y$-value in each subinterval.                          *Ans.* $\frac{125}{3}$.

4. Find the area under the curve $y = x^2$ from $x = 1$ to $x = 5$.          *Ans.* $\frac{124}{3}$.

5. Compute approximately the area under $y = x^2$ from $x = 0$ to $x = 5$ by using 10 subintervals $\Delta x$ to fill out the interval $(0, 5)$ and by using the largest $y$-value in each subinterval.

6. Compute approximately the area under the curve $y = 1/(1 + x^2)$ for the interval $0 \leq x \leq 1$. Use $n = 10$ and the smallest $y$-value in each subinterval.
                                                                *Ans.* 0.75.

**3. The Definite Integral.** The method of finding areas that we examined in Section 2 introduces several new concepts into the calculus, and we should obtain a clearer understanding of them before considering whether we can do anything more significant with the method.

There is, first, a new limit concept. Each approximation to the area under a curve is a sum of rectangles. We have denoted these sums, when the minimum $y$-value is used in each $\Delta x$, by

$$\underline{S_1}, \ \underline{S_2}, \ \underline{S_3}, \ \cdots, \ \underline{S_n}, \cdots .$$

This set of successive sums is called an *infinite sequence*. More generally, an infinite sequence is a set of numbers such that there is a first member, a second member, and in fact a member corresponding to each positive integer $n$. Thus the set is unending. What is of interest in sequences is the number which the members of the sequence approach, that is, the *limit* toward which the members tend. We denote the number which the members approach by the notation

$$\lim_{n \to \infty} \underline{S_n} .$$

If we consider any infinite sequence, we need not use the bar underneath, and we can write it as

$$S_1, S_2, S_3, \cdots, S_n, \cdots .$$

Thus if the sequence consists of the numbers

$$1, \ \frac{1}{2}, \ \frac{1}{3}, \cdots, \ \frac{1}{n}, \cdots,$$

then $S_1 = 1$, $S_2 = \frac{1}{2}$, $S_3 = \frac{1}{3}, \cdots, S_n = 1/n$. It is evident in this case that

$$\lim_{n \to \infty} S_n = 0$$

because as $n$ gets larger and larger, the quantity $1/n$ comes closer and closer to 0. Thus if $n = 10^6$, $1/n = 0.000,001$; if $n = 10^9$, $1/n = 0.000,000,001$; and so on.

If the sequence consists of the numbers

$$1, 1\frac{1}{2}, 1\frac{1}{3}, 1\frac{1}{4}, \cdots, 1\frac{1}{n}, \cdots,$$

it is evident that the limit is 1 because the additional quantity $1/n$ in the $n$th term approaches 0.

Not every sequence has a limit. Thus the members of the sequence

$$1, 4, 9, \cdots, n^2, \cdots$$

become larger and larger and increase beyond bound. They do not approach a definite number. We sometimes say that the $n$th term becomes infinite, but this means only that the successive terms increase and become larger than any number that one may name.

A sequence may not have a limit or, one says, may fail to converge even if the terms do not become infinite. For example, consider

$$1, 2, \frac{1}{2}, 1\frac{1}{2}, \frac{1}{4}, 1\frac{1}{4}, \frac{1}{8}, 1\frac{1}{8}, \cdots.$$

Here the odd-numbered terms approach 0 and the even-numbered terms approach 1. Because *all* the terms do not come closer and closer to one fixed number, the sequence does not have a limit.

It is desirable to distinguish between a sequence and a function. The function $y = x^2$ takes on values for *all* values of $x$ in some domain. If, for example, we were interested in this function over the domain $x = 3$ to $x = 5$, the possible values of $x$ would be the whole numbers, fractions, and irrational numbers between 3 and 5. On the other hand, if we have a sequence whose $n$th term is, say, $n^2$, then only the values of $n^2$ for $n = 1$, $n = 2$, $n = 3$, and so on are of interest. One can regard $n$ as a variable and $n^2$ as a function, but only the values of $n^2$ for positive integral values of $n$ matter.

The difference between a function and a sequence insofar as the values that $x$ can take on in the former case and $n$ in the latter is reflected in the corresponding limit concepts. For example,

$$\lim_{x \to 2} x^2$$

is the number that $x^2$ approaches as $x$ takes on *all* values closer and closer to 2. On the other hand, when one considers, for example,

$$\lim_{n \to \infty} \frac{1}{n^2},$$

he is interested in the number that $1/n^2$ approaches as $n$ takes on larger and larger positive integral values.

We shall say more about sequences in connection with the work on infinite series. At the present time some acquaintance with the notions of infinite sequence and limit of a sequence is sufficient, and we may return to the subject of the area under a curve.

## EXERCISES

**1.** Write the first 5 terms of the sequence whose $n$th term is the following:

(a) $\dfrac{n}{3}$.

(b) $n^2$.

(c) $\dfrac{n+1}{n+2}$.

(d) $\dfrac{n+3}{\sqrt{n}}$.

**2.** Write the $n$th term of the following sequences:

(a) $3, 2\frac{1}{2}, 2\frac{1}{3}, 2\frac{1}{4}, \cdots$.    *Ans.* $2 + (1/n)$.

(b) $\frac{1}{2}, \frac{1}{4}, \frac{1}{8}, \frac{1}{16}, \cdots$.    *Ans.* $1/2^n$.

(c) $2\frac{1}{2}, 2\frac{1}{4}, 2\frac{1}{8}, 2\frac{1}{16}, \cdots$.

(d) $1, -\frac{1}{2}, \frac{1}{3}, -\frac{1}{4}, \frac{1}{5}, \cdots$.

(e) $\dfrac{1}{1 \cdot 2}, \dfrac{1}{2 \cdot 3}, \dfrac{1}{3 \cdot 4}, \dfrac{1}{4 \cdot 5}, \cdots$.

(f) $1, \frac{1}{2}, \frac{1}{6}, \frac{1}{24}, \frac{1}{120}, \cdots$.    *Ans.* $1/n!$.

**3.** Determine by inspection the limit, if there is one, of each of the following sequences. The symbol $s_n$ denotes the $n$th term of the sequence.

(a) $s_n = \dfrac{1}{\sqrt{n}}$.    *Ans.* 0.

(b) $s_n = \dfrac{n}{n+1}$.    *Ans.* 1.

(c) $s_n = \dfrac{1/n}{1/(n+1)}$.    *Ans.* 1.

(d) $s_n = (-1)^n \dfrac{n-1}{n+1}$.    *Ans.* None.

(e) $s_n = \sqrt{n}$.

(f) $s_n = (-1)^n \dfrac{1}{n!}$.

(g) $s_n = 1^n$.

(h) $s_n = \dfrac{n^2 + 3n}{n+2}$.    *Ans.* None.

(i) $s_n = \dfrac{2(n-1)}{n^2 - 1}$.

(j) $s_n = 5 + \dfrac{1}{n} + \dfrac{6}{n^2}$.

We can generalize somewhat our method of finding the area under a curve. When we discussed previously approximating the area under a curve by rectangles, we decided that in each subinterval $\Delta x$ we would choose the smallest $y$-value or the largest $y$-value. With either choice the successive sums obtained by utilizing narrower and narrower rectangles approach the area under the curve. If, however, we should select in each subinterval *any* $y$-value (Fig. 9-9), then the sum of the rectangular areas should likewise approach the area under the curve. This fact is rather easy to establish. Suppose that we have subdivided the interval $(a, b)$ into equal subintervals $\Delta x$. As before, we denote by $m_i$ the smallest $y$-value in the $i$th subinterval and by $M_i$, the largest $y$-value. Now let $y_i$ denote any $y$-value in the $i$th subinterval. Thereby we obtain three different sequences of sums whose $n$th terms are

$$\underline{S_n} = m_1 \, \Delta x + m_2 \, \Delta x + \cdots + m_n \, \Delta x,$$

$$S_n^* = y_1 \, \Delta x + y_2 \, \Delta x + \cdots + y_n \, \Delta x,$$

$$\overline{S_n} = M_1 \, \Delta x + M_2 \, \Delta x + \cdots + M_n \, \Delta x.$$

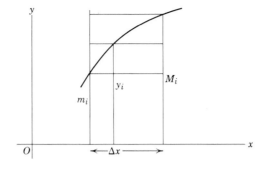

**Figure 9-9**

From the fact that

$$m_i \leq y_1 \leq M_i$$

we have that

$$\underline{S_n} < S_n^* < \overline{S_n} .$$

Now, when $n$ becomes infinite, both $\underline{S_n}$ and $\overline{S_n}$ approach the area under the curve. Because $S_n^*$ lies between the other two, it must approach the same limit. Hence, if we should find it convenient to choose some $y$-value in each subinterval $\Delta x$ other than the minimum or maximum one, we may do so.

We may take another liberty with respect to the construction of the sequence of approximating sums. We introduced this concept by starting with subdivisions of the interval $(a, b)$ into equal parts of width $\Delta x$. However, our main concern is to have the sum of the rectangles that we form come closer, as the number of rectangles increases, to the area under the curve. The way to attain this end is to make each rectangle narrower and narrower, even though in any one subdivision the rectangles are not of equal width. That the essential point is the narrowness of each rectangle is easily seen. Why is each rectangle $y_i \Delta x$ only an approximation to a portion of the area under the curve? An examination of Fig. 9-9 or of any of the foregoing figures in this chapter shows that the $y_i$ we choose in any subinterval $\Delta x$ is not necessarily the right choice because the $y$-values that correspond to the $x$-values in $\Delta x$ vary and the $y_i$ we choose may differ from the others. However, if $\Delta x$ is small, the $y$-values corresponding to the $x$-values in $\Delta x$ cannot differ very much from the $y_i$ we choose, and the smaller $\Delta x$ is, the less these $y$-values can differ from $y_i$. Hence what matters in forming the sequence of sums of rectangles is not that the $\Delta x$'s in each subdivision of $(a, b)$ be equal but that the $\Delta x$'s approach 0 in size as $n$, the number of subintervals, increases. This requirement is usually stated thus: the maximum $\Delta x$ in the $n$th subdivision must approach 0 as $n$ becomes infinite. For if the maximum $\Delta x$ approaches 0, so must each of the others.

If we do choose unequal subintervals to fill out the interval $(a, b)$, we cannot denote the width of each subinterval by $\Delta x$. In place of this we use $\Delta x_1$, $\Delta x_2$, and so on for the successive widths (Fig. 9-10). If we let $y_1$ be the $y$-value corresponding to any $x$-value in $\Delta x_1$, let $y_2$ be the $y$-value corresponding to any $x$-value in $\Delta x_2$, and so on, the $n$th term of the sequence of

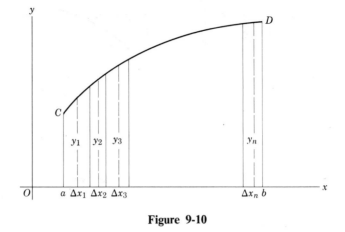

**Figure 9-10**

approximating sums is

$$S_n = y_1 \, \Delta x_1 + y_2 \, \Delta x_2 + \cdots + y_n \, \Delta x_n$$

and the area is given by

**(12)**
$$\lim_{n \to \infty} S_n,$$

provided that the maximum or largest $\Delta x$ in $S_n$ approaches 0 as $n$ becomes infinite.

We see, then, that we can form many different kinds of sequences, each of which approaches the area under a curve, or, we may say, has the area under the curve as its limit. If we are given a particular curve and are to find the area between that curve and the $x$-axis and between two vertical lines at $x = a$ and $x = b$, we could choose any one of the sequences of approximating sums and then seek

$$\lim_{n \to \infty} S_n.$$

There is another notation for this limit which is very helpful in keeping before us the factors that determine the area. If $y = f(x)$ is the equation of the curve under which the area lies, then we write for the limit

**(13)**
$$\int_a^b y \, dx \qquad \text{or} \qquad \int_a^b f(x) \, dx.$$

That is, no matter which of the approximating sequences we may use,

$$\lim_{n \to \infty} S_n = \int_a^b y \, dx \qquad \text{or} \qquad \lim_{n \to \infty} S_n = \int_a^b f(x) \, dx.$$

The notation in (13) must not be taken too literally. The symbol $\int$ is the elongated $S$ which we have already used to denote integration. It was introduced by Leibniz to remind one that he is dealing with the limit of a sequence of sums. The symbols $a$ and $b$ are the left- and right-hand end values of the $x$-domain over which the area is being calculated. The $y\,dx$ or $f(x)\,dx$ is a reminder that we took rectangles of height $y_i$ and width $\Delta x_i$. If one is dealing with the specific function $y = x^2$ and wishes to indicate that function instead of $y$ or $f(x)$, he can write

**(14)** 
$$\int_a^b x^2\,dx.$$

Clearly the notation (13) or (14) is more informative than

$$\lim_{n\to\infty} S_n.$$

The quantity (13) is called the *definite integral*. The use of the word integral is not justified by what we have said so far, for integrals in the past have arisen through antidifferentiation. The connection between definite integrals and antidifferentiation remains to be discussed. The word "definite," however, is intended to convey the fact that the symbol (13) stands for a number, whereas ordinary integrals, or indefinite integrals as they are often called, are functions.


## EXERCISES

1. Describe the area represented by the following:

   (a)  $\int_1^3 x^2\,dx.$

   (b)  $\int_0^5 x^3\,dx.$

   (c)  $\int_2^5 (x + 3)\,dx.$

   (d)  $\int_{-1}^4 x^2\,dx.$

   (e)  $\int_1^3 (9 - x^2)\,dx.$

   (f)  $\int_3^8 (x - 3)\,dx.$

   (g)  $\int_0^5 \sqrt{x}\,dx.$

2. The definite integral is (a) a sum, (b) a sequence of sums, (c) a limit of a sequence of sums, or (d) a limit of many sequences of sums. Which of the alternative answers is most appropriate?

3. Given that $S_n = x_1{}^3\,\Delta x_1 + x_2{}^3\,\Delta x_2 + \cdots + x_n{}^3\,\Delta x_n$, where $\Delta x_1, \Delta x_2, \cdots, \Delta x_n$ fill out the $x$-interval $(0, 1)$ and $x_i$ is any value of $x$ in $\Delta x_i$, express $\lim_{n\to\infty} S_n$ as a definite integral.  *Ans.* $\int_0^1 x^3\,dx.$

4. Let $S_n = y_1\,\Delta x_1 + y_2\,\Delta x_2 + \cdots + y_n\,\Delta x_n$, where the $\Delta x_i$ fill out the $x$-interval from $x = 1$ to $x = 5$ and $y_i$ is a value of $3x^2$ in $\Delta x_i$. Express $\lim_{n\to\infty} S_n$ as a definite integral.

5. Let $S_n = 3x_1{}^2\,\Delta x + 3x_2{}^2\,\Delta x + \cdots + 3x_n{}^2\,\Delta x$, where the $\Delta x$ are equal subintervals which fill out the $x$-interval from $x = -2$ to $x = 6$ and $x_i$ is any value of $x$ in each $\Delta x$. Express $\lim_{n\to\infty} S_n$ as a definite integral.

6. Let $S_n = x_1\sqrt{x_1{}^2 - 2}\,\Delta x_1 + x_2\sqrt{x_2{}^2 - 2}\,\Delta x_2 + \cdots + x_n\sqrt{x_n{}^2 - 2}\,\Delta x_n$, where the $\Delta x_i$ fill out the $x$-interval from $x = 2$ to $x = 10$ and $x_i$ is any value of $x$ in $\Sigma x_i$. Express $\lim_{n\to\infty} S_n$ as a definite integral.

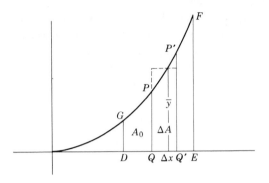

**Figure 9-11**

**4. The Evaluation of Definite Integrals.** Thus far in this chapter we have improved on the Greek method of finding areas bounded in whole or in part by curves by using sums of rectangles as the approximating figures and by using the equation of the curve and algebra to calculate the limit approached by the sequence of sums of rectangles. There is some question, however, as to whether we have gained very much. The few examples we have studied which show how to find an area by finding the limit of a sequence of sums also show that the process is cumbersome. Indeed, if the equation of the curve should be complicated, the summation technique might not be practical at all for the actual calculation. Is there an easy way of evaluating definite integrals?

Consider the area $DEFG$ (Fig. 9-11). We can regard this area as swept out by the line segment $QP$ that starts at $DG$ and moves to the right. Suppose that $QP$ has reached the position shown. The position of $QP$ is specified by the $x$-value of $Q$, say $x_0$, and the area generated for this position of $QP$, namely $DQPG$, can be denoted by $A_0$. Suppose that $QP$ moves to $Q'P'$. Let the distance $QQ'$ be denoted by $\Delta x$. When $QP$ moves to $Q'P'$, the area increases by the amount $QQ'P'P$, which we denote by $\Delta A$. This increment in area is larger than $QP \times \Delta x$ and smaller than $Q'P' \times \Delta x$. Because the ordinates between $QP$ and $Q'P'$ increase continuously, there must be some ordinate between them, say $\bar{y}$, such that

$$\Delta A = \bar{y} \times \Delta x.$$

Then

$$\frac{\Delta A}{\Delta x} = \bar{y}.$$

To obtain the instantaneous rate of change of area, that is, the rate of change of $A$ with respect to $x$ at the value $x_0$ of $x$, we must find the limit of $\Delta A / \Delta x$ as $\Delta x$ approaches 0. As $\Delta x$ approaches 0, $Q'$ moves to $Q$ and $Q'P'$ moves to $QP$. For any value of $\Delta x$ the ordinate $\bar{y}$ is always between $QP$ and $Q'P'$. Hence $\bar{y}$ must also approach $QP$. The value of $QP$ is the ordinate or $y$-value corresponding to $x_0$; that is, $QP$ is $y_0$. Hence

$$\frac{dA}{dx} = y_0$$

or, if the equation of the curve is $y = x^2$,

$$\frac{dA}{dx} = x_0^2.$$

Because this result is true for any value of $x$ in the interval $DE$, we may as well write the derived function, namely,

$$\frac{dA}{dx} = x^2.$$

To find the area $A(x)$ itself we apply antidifferentiation. Then

**(15)** $$A(x) = \int x^2 \, dx = \frac{x^3}{3} + C.$$

The problem of determining $C$ arises. Here when $QP$ is at $DG$, the value of $A$ is 0. To be more specific, suppose that the $x$-value of $D$ is 3. Then we know that when $x = 3$, $A = 0$. If we substitute these values in (15), we obtain

$$0 = \frac{3^3}{3} + C$$

or

$$C = -9.$$

Then

$$A(x) = \frac{x^3}{3} - 9$$

is the function which expresses the area from $DG$ to any position of $QP$, the abscissa of $Q$ being $x$.

To find the area $DEFG$, which we originally set out to do, we have but to note that this area is attained when $QP$ reaches $EF$. Suppose that the abscissa of $E$ is 6. Then we merely substitute 6 for $x$ in the expression for $A$ and obtain

$$A = \frac{6^3}{3} - 9 = 72 - 9 = 63.$$

Thus we have found the area bounded at least in part by a curve through the process of antidifferentiation or integration. To apply this process, we must of course know the equation of the curve.

We can obtain the same result if we take the expression (15) for the area, namely $(x^3/3) + C$, substitute 6 for $x$, then substitute 3 for $x$, and subtract the second result from the first. Thus

$$\frac{6^3}{3} + C - \left( \frac{3^3}{3} + C \right) = 63.$$

The constant of integration is eliminated in the process.

This area, which we obtained by antidifferentiation, is precisely the area we have already indicated by the symbol

(16)
$$\int_3^6 x^2 \, dx.$$

Thus the definite integral (16) can be evaluated by antidifferentiation and the substitution of the end values 6 and 3 as indicated just above.

The result—that the definite integral, which is a limit of sequences of sums of rectangles, is evaluated essentially by antidifferentiation—is fundamental. It is, in fact, called the *fundamental theorem of the calculus*. We signalize it by stating it separately as a theorem:

**Theorem:**  The definite integral $\int_a^b y \, dx$ or $\int_a^b f(x)dx$, which is a limit of sequences of sums of rectangles, is evaluated by finding the indefinite integral of the function $y$ or $f(x)$ and by subtracting the result of substituting $a$ in this integral from the result of substituting $b$ in this integral.

In symbols we may state the fundamental theorem thus:

(17)
$$\int_a^b f(x)dx = F(x)|_a^b = F(b) - F(a).$$

In this symbolism $F(x)$ is any antiderivative of $f(x)$; the symbol $F(x)|_a^b$ denotes that we intend to substitute $b$ in $F(x)$, substitute $a$ in $F(x)$ and subtract the second result from the first; the symbols $F(b) - F(a)$ indicate just what we get by carrying out what $F(x)|_a^b$ calls for.

We have stated a theorem but what have we done about its proof? We gave an argument based on the geometry of Fig. 9-11. However, the function represented geometrically there does not have the behavior of all functions. Hence the argument is incomplete. However, let us use this evidence as our "proof." It is intuitively sound. We shall examine a rigorous proof at a later time.

The definite integral, or the integral as the limit of sequences of sums, is a concept independent of the derivative, and it has been customary in the literature to think of the calculus as consisting of two parts: the differential calculus, concerned with differentiation and antidifferentiation, and the integral calculus, concerned with the definite integral and its ramifications. However, the fundamental theorem shows us that there is only one calculus. Nevertheless the definite integral is indeed something new and will prove to be a more important concept for tackling problems.

Let us consider an example of how the fundamental theorem is used.

**Example.**  Find the area (Fig. 9-12) between the curve $y = x^2 + x + 1$, the $x$-axis, and the ordinates at $x = 2$ and $x = 4$.

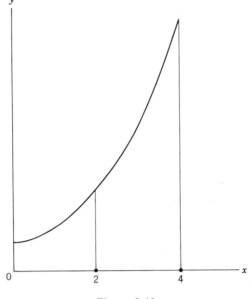

**Figure 9-12**

**Solution.** This area is represented by the definite integral

$$A = \int_2^4 (x^2 + x + 1)\,dx.$$

According to the fundamental theorem, we may evaluate the area by first finding an indefinite integral of

$$y = x^2 + x + 1.$$

One indefinite integral is

$$F(x) = \frac{x^3}{3} + \frac{x^2}{2} + x.$$

We ignore the constant of integration because this will drop out in the next step. The fundamental theorem tells us next that

$$A = F(x)\Big|_a^b = \frac{x^3}{3} + \frac{x^2}{2} + x \Big|_2^4$$

$$= \frac{4^3}{3} + \frac{4^2}{2} + 4 - \left( \frac{2^3}{3} + \frac{2^2}{2} + 2 \right)$$

$$= \frac{80}{3}$$

## EXERCISES

**1.** Compute the following by using the fundamental theorem.

(a) $\int_1^3 x^2\,dx.$  *Ans.* $\frac{26}{3}$. (b) $\int_0^1 y\,dx$ where $y = x^3$. *Ans.* $\frac{1}{4}$.

(c) $\displaystyle\int_1^2 \frac{1}{x^2}\, dx.$                          (g) $\displaystyle\int_1^5 (3x^2 - 2x + 5)dx.$

(d) $\displaystyle\int_{-3}^2 x^2\, dx.$                          (h) $\displaystyle\int_1^5 \sqrt{4x + 1}\ dx.$

(e) $\displaystyle\int_0^5 3x^3\, dx.$                          (i) $\displaystyle\int_1^4 (5x - x^2)dx.$

(f) $\displaystyle\int_0^{10} \sqrt{5x}\ dx.$

2. Find the area bounded by the curve $y = x^2$, the $x$-axis, and the following:
   (a) The ordinates at $x = 2$ and    (b) The ordinates at $x = 4$ and
   $x = 6$.                          *Ans.* $69\frac{1}{3}$.    $x = 8$.

3. By the method of the calculus find the area bounded by the straight line $y = x$, the $x$-axis, and the ordinates at $x = 4$ and $x = 6$. Check your result by using plane geometry.                          *Ans.* 10.

4. Find the area bounded by the curve $y = 9x$, the $x$-axis, and the ordinates at $x = 3$ and $x = 6$.

5. Find the area bounded by the curve $y = x^{1/3}$, the $x$-axis, and the ordinates at $x = 2$ and $x = 8$.                          *Ans.* $12 - \frac{3}{2}\sqrt[3]{2}$.

6. Find the area bounded by the curve $y = x^2$, the $x$-axis, and the ordinate at $x = 5$.

7. Find the area between the curve $y = \sqrt{x + 1}$ , the $x$-axis, and the ordinates at $x = 1$ and $x = 5$.                          *Ans.* $\frac{2}{3}(6^{3/2} - 2^{3/2})$.

8. Given that $S_n = x_1{}^3\, \Delta x_1 + x_2{}^3\, \Delta x_2 + \cdots + x_n{}^3\, \Delta x_n$, where $\Delta x_1, \Delta x_2, \ldots, \Delta x_n$ fill out the interval $(0, 1)$ and $x_i$ is a value of $x$ in $\Delta x_i$, show that, provided the maximum $\Delta x_i$ of any subdivision of $(0, 1)$ approaches 0 as $n$ becomes infinite, $\displaystyle\lim_{n\to\infty} S_n = \frac{1}{4}$.

   *Suggestion:* Express the limit of $S_n$ as a definite integral and then use the fundamental theorem.

9. Let $S_n = y_1\, \Delta x_1 + y_2\, \Delta x_2 + \cdots + y_n\, \Delta x_n$, where the $\Delta x_i$ fill out the $x$-interval from $x = 1$ to $x = 5$ and $y_i$ is a value of $y = 3x^2$ in $\Delta x_i$. If the maximum $\Delta x_i$ approaches 0 as $n$ becomes infinite, evaluate $\displaystyle\lim_{n\to\infty} S_n$.

   *Ans.* 124.

10. Let $S_n = 3x_1{}^2\, \Delta x_1 + 3x_2{}^2\, \Delta x_2 + \cdots + 3x_n{}^2\, \Delta x_n$, where the $\Delta x_i$ fill out the $x$-interval from $x = -2$ to $x = 6$ and $x_i$ is any value of $x$ in $\Delta x_i$. Evaluate $\displaystyle\lim_{n\to\infty} S_n$ with the understanding that the maximum $\Delta x_i$ approaches 0 as $n$ becomes infinite.

11. Let $S_n = 2x_1{}^2\, \Delta x + 2x_2{}^2\, \Delta x + \cdots + 2x_n{}^2\, \Delta x$, where the $\Delta x$ are equal subintervals that fill out the $x$-interval from $x = 3$ to $x = 6$ and $x_i$ is a value of $x$ in the $i$th subinterval $\Delta x$. If $\Delta x = (6 - 3)/n$, evaluate $\displaystyle\lim_{n\to\infty} S_n$.                          *Ans.* 126.

12. Let $S_n = x_1\sqrt{x_1{}^2 - 2}\ \Delta x_1 + x_2\sqrt{x_2{}^2 - 2}\ \Delta x_2 + \cdots + x_n\sqrt{x_n{}^2 - 2}\ \Delta x_n$, where the $\Delta x_i$ fill out the $x$-interval from $x = 2$ to $x = 10$ and $x_i$ is any value of $x$ in $\Delta x_i$. Assuming that the maximum $\Delta x_i$ approaches 0 as $n$ becomes infinite, evaluate $\displaystyle\lim_{n\to\infty} S_n$.

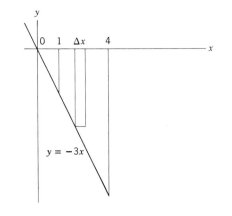

**Figure 9-13**

**5. Areas Below the *x*-Axis.** The areas we have considered so far were situated above the *x*-axis. Let us now consider the area illustrated in Figure 9-13, that is, the area between the *x*-axis, $y = -3x$, $x = 1$, and $x = 4$. Were we to approach this area by considering first a sequence of sums of rectangles, the *n*th term of which is

$$S_n = y_1 \, \Delta x + y_2 \, \Delta x + \cdots + y_n \, \Delta x,$$

everything we said previously about such sequences would hold except that the $y_i$ would be negative. Hence $\lim_{n \to \infty} S_n$ would be a negative number.

As for the fundamental theorem, the argument we gave above as to the justification of the theorem applies here too. The fact that the *y*-values are negative does not in any way affect the argument because negative numbers are as respectable and as legitimate as positive numbers. In the present example

$$\lim_{n \to \infty} S_n = \int_1^4 -3x \, dx.$$

According to the fundamental theorem

$$\int_1^4 -3x \, dx = -\tfrac{3}{2} x^2 \big|_1^4 = -\tfrac{3}{2} \cdot 4^2 - \left( -\tfrac{3}{2} \cdot 1^2 \right) = -22\tfrac{1}{2}.$$

What significance should we attach to the fact that the area is negative? The area itself as a purely geometrical quantity or physical quantity is positive. The fact that our method of representing curves by equations in which *y* or *x* or both can take on negative values leads, in the case where the area lies below the *x*-axis, to a negative area may be unfortunate but if we recognize this fact and take it into account where relevant, it does not cause any difficulty.

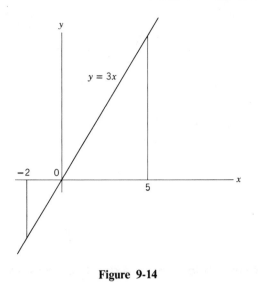

**Figure 9-14**

To see how we can handle this peculiar fact that areas lying below the x-axis turn out to be negative let us consider another example. Suppose we now seek the area (Fig. 9-14) bounded by the line $y = 3x$, the x-axis, and the ordinates at $x = -2$ and $x = 5$. If we evaluate

**(18)**
$$\int_{-2}^{5} 3x \, dx$$

the result will not be the correct area because the integral is negative in part of the domain from $-2$ to 5 and positive in the other part. However, since the integral is a limit of a sequence of sums of rectangles we can consider the rectangles that "fill out" the area from $-2$ to 0 and the rectangles that fill out the area from 0 to 5 and consider the integral (18) as the sum of two integrals thus:

**(19)**
$$\int_{-2}^{5} 3x \, dx = \int_{-2}^{0} 3x \, dx + \int_{0}^{5} 3x \, dx.$$

If we now apply the fundamental theorem to all of these integrals we obtain

$$\tfrac{3}{2} x^2 \big|_{-2}^{5} = \tfrac{3}{2} x^2 \big|_{-2}^{0} + \tfrac{3}{2} x^2 \big|_{0}^{5}$$

or

$$\tfrac{63}{2} = -6 + \tfrac{75}{2}.$$

The value of the definite integral on the left side of (19) is $\tfrac{63}{2}$. However, if we are interested in the *geometrical* area between $y = 3x$, the x-axis, $x = -2$, and $x = 5$ then, knowing that the integral gives a negative area when the area lies below the x-axis, we ignore the minus sign in the $-6$ and take the entire geometrical area to be $6 + \tfrac{75}{2}$ or $\tfrac{87}{2}$.

## EXERCISES

1. Find the geometrical area between $y = -3x$, the $x$-axis, $x = 0$, and $x = 5$.

2. (a) Evaluate $\displaystyle\int_{-3}^{4} 3x\ dx$.

   (b) Find the geometrical area between $y = 3x$, the $x$-axis, $x = -3$, and $x = 4$.

3. (a) Evaluate $\displaystyle\int_{-3}^{3} -x^2\ dx$.

   (b) Find the geometrical area between $y = -x^2$, the $x$-axis, $x = -3$, and $x = 3$.

4. Find the geometrical area between $y = -\sqrt{2x + 1}$, the $x$-axis, $x = 1$, and $x = 5$.

5. Find the geometrical area between the curve of $y = (x - 3)(x - 2)(x + 1)$, the $x$-axis, $x = 0$, and $x = 4$.  *Ans.* $\frac{71}{6}$.

**6. *Areas Between Curves.*** Our use of the definite integral and the fundamental theorem to find areas has been confined thus far to areas lying between a curve and the $x$-axis. Actually our new tools enable us to solve more complicated area problems.

Suppose that we wished to find the area between the curves $y = 5x$, $y = x^2$ and the ordinates at $x = 1$ and $x = 4$ (Fig. 9-15). Clearly this area is the difference of two areas, the area under $y = 5x$ and the area under $y = x^2$ both taken between $x = 1$ and $x = 4$. Then since each area is given by a definite integral the area we seek is given by

(20)
$$\int_{1}^{4} 5x\ dx - \int_{1}^{4} x^2\ dx.$$

We can now use the fundamental theorem to evaluate each integral. Thus (20) yields

(21)
$$\tfrac{5}{2}x^2\Big|_{1}^{4} - \frac{x^3}{3}\Big|_{1}^{4} = \tfrac{75}{2} - 21 = \tfrac{33}{2}.$$

**Figure 9-15**

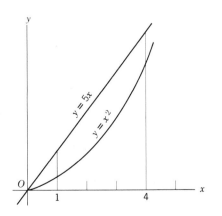

However, in using the fundamental theorem we first find the indefinite integrals of $5x$ and of $x^2$, that is, we first find

$$\int 5x \, dx \qquad \text{and} \qquad \int x^2 \, dx.$$

Since (20) calls for the subtraction of the two definite integrals we can use the fact (Chap. 6, Sect. 5) that the difference of the two indefinite integrals is the indefinite integral of the difference of the two functions, that is,

(22)
$$\int 5x \, dx - \int x^2 \, dx = \int (5x - x^2) dx$$

and since we then substitute the end values 1 and 4 in each of the separate integrals as in (21) we may as well substitute the end values 1 and 4 in the single integral on the right side of (22). Thus the area we seek is given by

$$\int_1^4 (5x - x^2) dx = \frac{5x^2}{2} - \frac{x^3}{3} \Big|_1^4 = \tfrac{5}{2} \cdot 4^2 - \tfrac{64}{3} - \left( \tfrac{5}{2} \cdot 1^2 - \tfrac{1}{3} \right) = \tfrac{33}{2} .$$

The point we have just made, stated in general terms, is that if $u$ and $v$ are functions of $x$ then

(23)
$$\int_a^b u \, dx \pm \int_a^b v \, dx = \int_a^b (u \pm v) dx.$$

Sometimes the calculation of the right-hand integral in (23) is simpler because terms in $u$ and $v$ may combine or offset each other. Whether or not one uses (23) the main point of this section is that we can find the area between curves by means of the definite integral.

Let us consider another example.

**Example.**   Find the area between the curves $y = 3x - x^2$ and $x - 3$.

**Solution.**   Our first task is to recognize the area we wish to find. This is shown in Fig. 9-16. We must first find the abscissas of points $A$ and $B$. This is done by

**Figure 9-16**

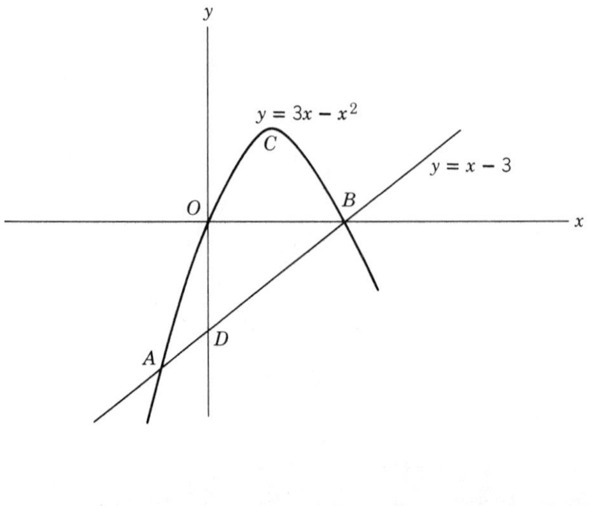

solving simultaneously

$$y = 3x - x^2$$
$$y = x - 3.$$

Then

$$3x - x^2 = x - 3$$

or

$$x^2 - 2x - 3 = 0.$$

Then $x = -1$ and $x = 3$. The value $-1$ is the abscissa of $A$ and the value 3 is the abscissa of $B$. The respective ordinates are $-4$ and 0.

Now let us consider the area between $O$ and $B$. Part of this area lies below the $x$-axis. We could find the area $OBC$ and the area $ODB$ and add the numerical values. However, if we form

$$\int_0^3 \left[ (3x - x^2) - (x - 3) \right] dx$$

then because we have *subtracted* $x - 3$ we have changed the sign of the area $ODB$ and the entire integral will give the correct geometrical area $OCBD$. In the region $AOD$, the $y$-values of $y = 3x - x^2$ are negative but the $y$-values of $y = x - 3$ are still more negative. Then

$$3x - x^2 - (x - 3)$$

will give precisely the vertical lengths between $AO$ and $AD$ and with the proper sign. Hence

$$\text{Area } AOD = \int_{-1}^0 \left[ (3x - x^2) - (x - 3) \right] dx.$$

Then as in (19) the entire area $AOCBD$ is given by

$$\int_{-1}^3 \left[ (3x - x^2) - (x - 3) \right] dx = \int_{-1}^3 (3 + 2x - x^2) dx$$

$$= 3x + x^2 - \frac{x^3}{3} \Big|_{-1}^3 = 10\tfrac{2}{3}.$$

# EXERCISES

1. Evaluate $\int_1^4 (x^2 + x^3) dx$.  *Ans.* $84\tfrac{3}{4}$.

2. Express the area under the curve of $y = 9 - x^2$ between $x = 0$ and $x = 1$ as a definite integral and then calculate it.  *Ans.* $8\tfrac{2}{3}$.

3. Express the area between $y = x^3 + 9$, $y = x^2$, $x = 1$, and $x = 5$ as a definite integral and then evaluate it.                                    *Ans.* $150\frac{2}{3}$.

4. Find the area between the curves $y = 3x^2$ and $y = 5x^2$ and between the ordinates at $x = 2$ and $x = 4$.                                    *Ans.* $37\frac{1}{3}$.

5. Find the area between the curve $y = 1/x^2$ and the x-axis and between $x = 1$ and $x = 3$.

6. Find the area between the curve $y = x^2$ and the line $y = 2x$.                *Ans.* $\frac{4}{3}$.

7. Find the area between the curves $y = x^2$ and $y = \sqrt{5x}$ .

8. Find the area between the curves $y = 9 - x^2$ and $y = x^2$.                *Ans.* $18\sqrt{2}$ .

9. Find the area between the curve $y = x^2$ and the straight line $y = 8x - 4$.

10. Find the area between the parabolas $y = 2x^2 + 1$ and $y = x^2 + 5$.
                                                                        *Ans.* $10\frac{2}{3}$.

11. Find the area between $y^2 = 16x$ and $y^2 = x^3$.                *Ans.* $8\frac{8}{15}$.

12. Calculate the physical area in the region bounded by the curve $y = x^3 - 8$, the x-axis, and the vertical lines $x = 1$ and $x = 3$.                *Ans.* $12\frac{1}{2}$.

13. Prove with the aid of the fundamental theorem that

$$\int_a^b cy\ dx = c \int_a^b y\ dx.$$

14. Show by using a counterexample that $\int_a^b u\ dx - \int_a^b v\ dx \neq \int_a^b uv\ dx$ where $u$ and $v$ are functions of $x$.

15. By appealing to geometric evidence show that $\int_0^8 x^n\ dx + \int_0^1 x^{1/n}\ dx = 1$ for $n$ a positive integer.

16. Show that the area under $y = x^a$, $a \neq -1$, and between $x = c$ and $x = d$ equals $1/a$ times the area bounded by $y = x^a$, the y-axis, $y = c^a$, and $y = d^a$.

**7. Some Additional Properties of the Definite Integral.** There are a few simple properties of the definite integral that are frequently used. The definition of the definite integral

**(24)**                                    $$\int_a^b y\ dx$$

assumes that the upper end value $b$ is larger than the lower end value $a$. There is, however, no objection to considering the definite integral

**(25)**                                    $$\int_b^a y\ dx$$

where, with $a < b$, the upper end value is smaller than the lower one. We can, in fact, take over everything that applied to (24) with one exception. Previously, when we used equal subintervals in the interval $(a, b)$, we took $\Delta x$ to be $(b - a)/n$. For the sake of consistency we agree in the case of (25) that

$$\Delta x = \frac{a - b}{n} .$$

When $a < b$—the case that we are now discussing—$\Delta x$ is negative. Moreover, even if we choose unequal subintervals in the interval $(a, b)$, we take them to be negative. The choice of $y$-values in each subinterval can be the same for both (24) and (25). Hence the effect of our choice of sign for $\Delta x$ is to make each $S_n$ that we form for (25) the negative of the corresponding $S_n$ for (24). However, if the sequence

$$\frac{1}{2}, \frac{3}{4}, \frac{7}{8}, \ldots, \frac{n-1}{n}, \ldots$$

approaches 1, the sequence

$$-\frac{1}{2}, -\frac{3}{4}, -\frac{7}{8}, \ldots, -\frac{n-1}{n}, \ldots$$

approaches $-1$. Hence

**(26)**
$$\int_b^a y \, dx = -\int_a^b y \, dx.$$

We can consider the same fact from the standpoint of antidifferentiation. The left-hand integral calls for finding the indefinite integral of the function represented by $y$ and then subtracting the result of substituting $b$ in this indefinite integral from the result of substituting $a$. The right-hand integral calls for the same indefinite integral and then subtracting the result of substituting $a$ from the result of substituting $b$. Then the final numbers will be the negatives of each other.

There is one more fact about the definite integral which is occasionally useful. Instead of considering the definite integral $\int_a^b f(x)dx$ we could consider

$$\int_a^x f(x)dx$$

wherein the upper end value $x$ is variable; this is still called the definite integral. Of course now the value of the definite integral depends on the value of $x$; that is, it is a function of $x$. One can therefore ask, what is

**(27)**
$$\frac{d}{dx}\int_a^x f(x)dx?$$

The notation just used, although perhaps understandable, is not quite satisfactory. The symbol $x$ is used in two different senses. In $f(x)$, $x$ stands for a variable which runs through some interval of values from $a$ on. The symbol $x$ at the upper end of the integral sign stands for the end of the interval of integration. To remove the ambiguity it is better to write

**(28)**
$$\frac{d}{dx}\int_a^x f(u)du$$

wherein $u$ runs through the values from $a$ to $x$. Thus if $f(x)$ is $x^2$, $f(u)$ is $u^2$ and the integral in (28) is taken over the interval from $a$ to $x$. Our question now is, what is the value of (28)?

The answer is readily obtained. By the fundamental theorem

$$\int_a^x f(u)du = F(x) - F(a)$$

where $F(x)$ is an antiderivative of $f(x)$.* Then

$$\frac{d}{dx} \int_a^x f(u)du = f(x)$$

because the derivative of $F(x)$ is $f(x)$ and $F(a)$ is a constant. This result is often labeled the *corollary to the fundamental theorem*. Given the definite integral $\int_a^x f(u)du$, wherein the upper end value $x$ is variable, then

**(29)** $$\frac{d}{dx} \int_a^x f(u)\,du = f(x).$$

This corollary is occasionally useful.

Our treatment of the definite integral has been motivated by the problem of finding areas bounded by curves. We shall see later that the definite integral has many applications.

## EXERCISES

1. Evaluate $\dfrac{d}{dx} \displaystyle\int_a^b x^3\,dx$ when $a$ and $b$ are constants.

2. Evaluate $\dfrac{d}{dx} \displaystyle\int_a^x u^3\,du$ by using the corollary to the fundamental theorem and by actually evaluating the integral.

3. If $g(x) = \displaystyle\int_0^x \sqrt{u^2 + 2}\,du$, what is $d^2g/dx^2$?

4. If $g(x) = \displaystyle\int_0^{x^2} f(u)du$, what is $dg/dx$?

   *Suggestion:* Let $x^2 = v$ and use the chain rule.

5. Criticize the following argument which "proves" that every triangle is isosceles. Consider triangle $ABC$ (Fig. 9-17) and let $AD$ be the altitude from $A$ to $BC$. Now let $PQ$ be any parallel to $BC$ and $PR$ and $QS$ parallel to $AD$. Then $PR = QS$. By drawing parallels such as $PQ$ we can cover triangle $BAD$ by lines such as $PR$. Similarly, we can cover triangle $CAD$ by lines such as $QS$. Hence triangle $BAD$ equals $CAD$ and triangle $ABC$ is isosceles.

* One could also say, where $F(u)$ is an antiderivative of $f(u)$.

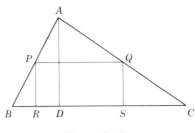

**Figure 9-17**

**8. Numerical Methods for Evaluating Definite Integrals.** By virtue of the fundamental theorem of the calculus we know that we can evaluate the definite integral

**(30)** $$\int_a^b f(x)\,dx$$

by finding an antiderivative of $f(x)$, say $F(x)$, and then calculating $F(b) - F(a)$. For the functions we have studied thus far the problem of finding an antiderivative of $f(x)$ is readily solved and we can calculate the definite integral. However, we intend to apply the concept of the definite integral to many more complicated functions and even though we shall find that there are many more techniques of finding antiderivatives (Chap. 14), it is a sad fact that we cannot find antiderivatives for all of the $f(x)$ that occur in mathematical and physical problems even when $f(x)$ is an elementary function. For example, one cannot evaluate

$$\int_0^{\pi} \sqrt{1 + \cos^2 x}\ dx,$$

which gives the length of one arch of the sine curve (Fig. 10-1) by finding an antiderivative of the integrand. Moreover, in practical work some functions are known only as graphs or as statistical tables and even though it may be possible to find a formula to represent such functions the formula will surely be an approximate one and therefore, even if one can antidifferentiate the formula, the answer will still be approximate.

In both situations, that is, where one cannot find an antiderivative or where the antiderivative is an approximation, it is useful to be able to evaluate the definite integral numerically using only numerical values of $f(x)$.

One method of numerical evaluation is called the trapezoidal rule and this is readily derived. We know from our work on the definite integral (Sect. 3) that an approximate value of $\int_a^b f(x)\,dx$ is given by

$$S_n = y_0\,\Delta x_1 + y_1\,\Delta x_2 + \cdots + y_{n-1}\,\Delta x_n$$

where the subintervals $\Delta x_1, \Delta x_2, \ldots, \Delta x_n$ fill out the interval $(a, b)$ and $y_i$ is any value of $y = f(x)$ in $\Delta x_i$. Let us use equal subintervals and call each $h$.

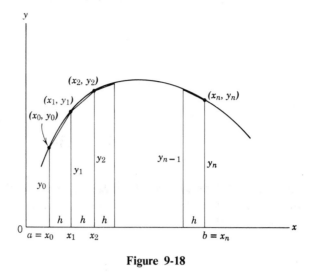

**Figure 9-18**

Then if we choose the $y_i$ to be the left-hand $y$-values in each subinterval $h$ (Fig. 9-18),

$$\underline{S}_n = y_0 h + y_1 h + \cdots + y_{n-1} h$$

is an approximation to the definite integral (30). It is also true that

$$\overline{S}_n = y_1 h + y_2 h + \cdots + y_n h,$$

where the $y_i$ are the right-hand $y$-values in each subinterval $h$, is an approximation to the definite integral (30). Hence the average of the two should be a better approximation. This average is

**(31)** $\quad S_n = \frac{1}{2}(y_0 + y_1)h + \frac{1}{2}(y_1 + y_2)h + \cdots + \frac{1}{2}(y_{n-1} + y_n)h.$

Each of these terms is the area of a trapezoid formed by, for example, $y_0$, $y_1$, $h$ and the chord joining $(x_0, y_0)$ and $(x_1, y_1)$, because the area of a trapezoid is one-half the altitude times the sum of the bases. Hence the approximation (31) is called the trapezoidal rule. We can rewrite (31) in the more convenient form

**(32)** $\quad \displaystyle\int_a^b f(x)\,dx \approx h\left[\frac{1}{2}y_0 + y_1 + y_2 + \cdots + y_{n-1} + \frac{1}{2}y_n\right]$

wherein the symbol $\approx$ means approximately. Generally, the larger $n$ is, the better the approximation.

**Example.**  Approximate the area under the curve $y = 1/(1 + x^4)$ from $x = 0$ to $x = 2$ (Fig. 9-19).

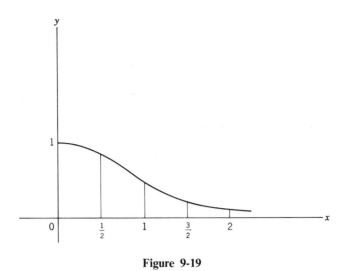

**Figure 9-19**

**Solution.**     Let us divide up the interval from $x = 0$ to $x = 2$ into 4 subintervals. Then $x_0 = 0$, $x_1 = \frac{1}{2}$, $x_2 = 1$, $x_3 = \frac{3}{2}$, and $x_4 = 2$, while $h = \frac{1}{2}$.

By actual substitution in the function $y = 1/(1 + x^4)$ we find that

$$y_0 = f(x_0) = f(0) = 1; \quad y_1 = f(x_1) = f(\tfrac{1}{2}) = .94;$$

$$y_2 = f(x_2) = f(1) = .5; \quad y_3 = f(x_3) = f(\tfrac{3}{2}) = .165;$$

$$y_4 = f(x_4) = f(2) = .059.$$

Substitution in (32) yields

$$\tfrac{1}{2}\left[\tfrac{1}{2}(1) + .94 + .5 + .165 + \tfrac{1}{2}(.059)\right] = 1.067.$$

## EXERCISES

1. Evaluate $\int_1^5 x^2 \, dx$ approximately by using the trapezoidal rule and 4 subintervals. Then determine the accuracy of the approximation by using the fundamental theorem.

2. Approximate $\int_0^{\frac{1}{2}} \dfrac{dx}{1 + x^2}$ by using five subintervals.                    *Ans.* 0.463.

3. Approximate $\int_0^3 \sqrt{1 + x^3} \, dx$ using six subintervals.                    *Ans.* 7.39.

4. Suppose a function $y = f(x)$ is known to us only through the following table:

| $x$ | 0 | 1 | 2 | 3 | 4 | 5 | 6 | 7 | 8 | 9 | 10 |
|---|---|---|---|---|---|---|---|---|---|---|---|
| $y$ | 1.72 | 1.60 | 1.44 | 1.24 | 1.06 | 0.92 | 0.80 | 0.70 | 0.63 | 0.56 | 0.50 |

Approximate $\int_0^{10} f(x) \, dx$.

The trapezoidal rule approximates a curve by a set of line segments or chords and in effect uses the formula for the area of a trapezoid. One would expect to do better by approximating the given curve by another curve which is readily integrated or whose values are readily computed. The simplest approximating curve which usually improves on the trapezoidal rule and which is easy to handle is a parabola of the form $y = ax^2 + bx + c$. Such a parabola is determined by three points. Hence we divide up the interval $(a, b)$ of the definite integral $\int_a^b f(x)dx$ into $n$ equal subintervals. Corresponding to the endpoints $x_0, x_1, x_2, \ldots, x_n$ of these subintervals there are the points $P_0, P_1, \ldots, P_n$ of the given curve (Fig. 9-20). We approximate the curve through $P_0$, $P_1$, and $P_2$ by an arc of a parabola; then do the same for $P_2$, $P_3$, and $P_4$, for $P_4$, $P_5$, and $P_6$, and so on. Since each parabolic arc covers two subintervals, we see that the number of these must be even.

Now let us investigate what the area under a typical parabolic arc is. The equation of the parabola is $y = ax^2 + bx + c$ and it is to be determined by three points on the curve, say $(x_{i-1}, y_{i-1})$, $(x_i, y_i)$, and $(x_{i+1}, y_{i+1})$. We can come closer to our ultimate goal if we write the equation of the parabola as

(33) $$y = a(x - x_i)^2 + b(x - x_i) + y_i.$$

This form insures that the parabola goes through $(x_i, y_i)$. Now since we choose equal subintervals of the width $h$, say, then the area we want is

$$\int_{x_i-h}^{x_i+h} \left[ a(x - x_i)^2 + b(x - x_i) + y_i \right] dx$$

$$= \left. \frac{a(x - x_i)^3}{3} + \frac{b(x - x_i)^2}{2} + y_i x \right|_{x_i-h}^{x_i+h}$$

$$= 2y_i h + \frac{2ah^3}{3}$$

(34) $$= h\left( 2y_i + \frac{2ah^2}{3} \right).$$

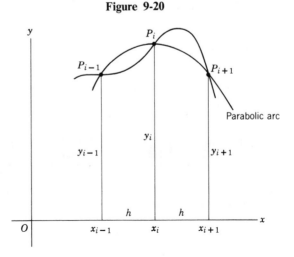

**Figure 9-20**

To make the parabola pass through $(x_{i-1}, y_{i-1})$ we must have from (33), since $x - x_i$ must be $-h$,

$$y_{i-1} = ah^2 - bh + y_i;$$

and to make the parabola pass through $(x_{i+1}, y_{i+1})$ we must have

$$y_{i+1} = ah^2 + bh + y_i.$$

If we now add these last two equations and rearrange terms we get

$$2ah^2 = y_{i-1} - 2y_i + y_{i+1}.$$

Hence by (34) the area under the parabola through $(x_{i-1}, y_{i-1})$, $(x_i, y_i)$ and $(x_{i+1}, y_{i+1})$ is

**(35)**
$$\frac{h}{3}(y_{i-1} + 4y_i + y_{i+1}).$$

We planned to divide the interval $(a, b)$ into $n$ subintervals, with $n$ even, and to approximate each arc of the curve through $P_0$, $P_1$ and $P_2$, $P_2$, $P_3$ and $P_4$, and so on by an arc of a parabola. The areas under these parabolic arcs are given by (35) by letting $i = 1, 3, 5, \ldots, n - 1$. Then the approximation to the desired integral is given by adding these successive areas so that

**(36)**
$$\int_a^b f(x)\,dx = \frac{h}{3}\left[y_0 + y_n + 2(y_2 + y_4 + \cdots + y_{n-2})\right.$$
$$\left. + 4(y_1 + y_3 + \cdots + y_{n-1})\right].$$

This result is known as Simpson's rule.

**Example.** Let us calculate $\int_1^2 \frac{dx}{x}$ and let us choose 10 subintervals. Then $h = 0.1$ and $y_0 = \frac{1}{1}$, $y_1 = 1/1.1$, $y_2 = 1/1.2, \ldots, y_{10} = \frac{1}{2}$. If we substitute these values in (36) we find that the definite integral is approximately 0.693150. We shall find later that the value of this integral is the logarithm of 2 to a base $e$ which we have yet to discuss. A more accurate value of the integral computed by other means is 0.693147.

## EXERCISES

**1.** Approximate $\int_0^1 \frac{dx}{1+x}$ using 4 subintervals.      *Ans.* 0.693.

**2.** Evaluate $\int_1^5 x^2\,dx$ by using Simpson's rule and 4 subintervals. Compare the result with the exact value obtained by using the fundamental theorem. Would you expect the two values to agree?

**3.** Approximate $\int_0^3 \sqrt{1 + x^3}\ dx$ by using Simpson's rule and 6 subintervals.

**4.** Given the following data on a function $y = f(x)$

| $x$ | 0 | 1 | 2 | 3 | 4 | 5 | 6 |
|-----|----|----|----|----|----|----|----|
| $y$ | 32 | 38 | 29 | 33 | 42 | 44 | 38 |

calculate approximately $\int_0^6 f(x)dx$.                                    *Ans.* 37.33.

**5.** Evaluate $\int_0^{\frac{1}{2}} \dfrac{dx}{1 + x^2}$ approximately by using Simpson's rule and 4 subintervals.

# APPENDIX
# THE SUM OF THE SQUARES
# OF THE FIRST $n$ INTEGERS

We wish to prove that

$$S = 1^2 + 2^2 + 3^2 + \cdots + n^2 = \frac{n^3}{3} + \frac{n^2}{2} + \frac{n}{6}.$$

**Proof:**      One method of proof depends on a trick. We have the identity

$$n^3 - (n - 1)^3 = 3n^2 - 3n + 1.$$

By replacing $n$ by $n - 1$, we have

$$(n - 1)^3 - (n - 2)^3 = 3(n - 1)^2 - 3(n - 1) + 1.$$

Similarly,

$$(n - 2)^3 - (n - 3)^3 = 3(n - 2)^2 - 3(n - 2) + 1.$$
$$\cdots \cdots \cdots \cdots \cdots \cdots \cdots \cdots$$
$$3^3 - 2^3 = 3 \cdot 3^2 - 3 \cdot 3 + 1.$$
$$2^3 - 1^3 = 3 \cdot 2^2 - 3 \cdot 2 + 1.$$
$$1^3 - 0^3 = 3 \cdot 1^2 - 3 \cdot 1 + 1.$$

If we now add the left sides and then the right sides, we have

$$n^3 = 3(1^2 + 2^2 + \cdots + n^2) - 3(1 + 2 + \cdots n) + n$$

$$= 3S - 3\frac{n}{2}(n + 1) + n.$$

If we solve this equation for $S$, we obtain the result above.

The proof can also be made by mathematical induction.

# CHAPTER TEN
# THE TRIGONOMETRIC FUNCTIONS

**1. Introduction.** We have learned the basic concepts of the calculus, differentiation, antidifferentiation, and the definite integral. We have also seen that these three concepts are intimately related. However, we have applied these concepts only to simple functions, that is, polynomials such as $x^2 - x + 5$, rational functions, which are quotients of polynomials, and to simple expressions involving fractional powers of $x$ or algebraic functions of $x$ as, for example, $\sqrt{(x + 5)/(x^2 + x)}$. Because we have been limited to just these few types of functions we have been limited in the applications we could make. To extend the power of the calculus we must learn how to handle new types of functions.

Our next concern will be the class known as trigonometric functions. These are important because they represent periodic phenomena. The motion of a bob on a spring and the motion of a pendulum are obvious periodic phenomena, but many others, such as sound waves, alternating electric current, and radio waves, are also periodic, although this fact is not at once apparent. However, even if one recognizes that a phenomenon is periodic and that trigonometric functions should be involved, he must still answer the question of precisely which function represents that phenomenon and how one can extract physical information from the function. After presenting a few technical facts about the trigonometric functions we shall consider a few of these applications.

**2. The Sinusoidal Functions.** The basic periodic function is $y = \sin x$. To refresh our minds about this function, let us look at the graph in Fig. 10-1. As the function arises in trigonometry, $x$ stands for the size of an angle, which is measured in degrees or in radians. Both units are shown in the figure. In the calculus the radian measure is preferred for a reason that will be evident shortly.

There is a common misconception about the function $y = \sin x$ which stems from the fact the $x$-values originate as a measure of angles. The

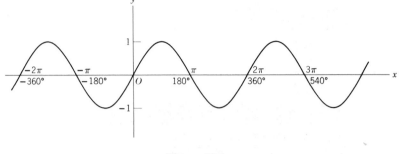

**Figure 10-1**

function $v = 32t$ originally represented and still represents the velocity of a body which is dropped and falls (in a vacuum) under the pull of the earth's gravity. The values of $t$ in this application are time values and the $v$-values are, of course, velocity values. However, as a mathematical function the values of $v$ and $t$ are pure numbers and not time and velocity values. All one can say mathematically is that when $t = 1$, $v = 32$. Indeed, the same mathematical function might be used in a totally different physical context where $t$ might represent any number of oxen and $v$ the combined lengths of their tails. The same point applies to $y = \sin x$. As a mathematical function $x$ and $y$ represent pure numbers, and the fact that $x$ originally represented the sizes of angles is irrelevant. If we choose to let the values of $x$ represent, for example, values of time and the values of $y$ to represent distance, we are entirely free to do so, and we shall do so when this interpretation fits the physical phenomenon under study. In other words, once we have some way of determining the $y$-value which belongs to a given $x$-value, we have a mathematical function that can be applied to any physical situation in which the function may be useful.

To obtain the value of $y$ for a given value of $x$ we do interpret $x$ as the number of radians in an angle and then look up our trigonometric tables for the sine of the angle of that many radians or, if necessary, first convert the radians to degrees. This reversion to angles and sines of angles is utilized *only because the values of y happen to be recorded in trigonometric tables.*

The function $y = \sin x$ is periodic, that is, the $y$-values repeat in successive intervals the values that $y$ takes on in the interval 0 to $2\pi$. The interval $2\pi$ is called the *period*, a term which, incidentally, comes from the physical situation in which $x$ represents time. (In applications in which $x$ represents distance, the interval $2\pi$ is called the *wavelength.*) As Fig. 10-1 shows, the maximum $y$-value is 1, and this number is called the *amplitude* of the function.

The great usefulness of the trigonometric functions derives from the fact that for each of the six fundamental functions, $y = \sin x, y = \cos x, y = \tan x, y = \cot x, y = \sec x,$ and $y = \csc x$, there is an infinitude of variations. We shall discuss these in connection with the function $y = \sin x$, but the same remarks apply to the other five functions.

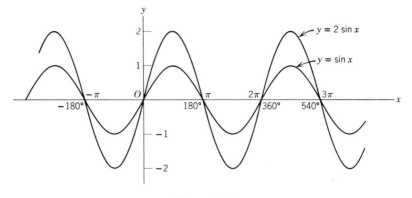

**Figure 10-2**

A common variation of $y = \sin x$ is

**(1)** $$y = 2 \sin x.$$

It is easy to see in this case how the second function differs from the first.
For each value of $x$, $2 \sin x$ is twice $\sin x$. Figure 10-2 shows the effect of
the factor 2. The period of $y = 2 \sin x$ is still $2\pi$, but the amplitude is 2. Of
course, any number can occur in place of the 2, and so we already have the
infinite number of functions $y = a \sin x$.

Another equally common variation of $y = \sin x$ is exemplified by

**(2)** $$y = \sin 2x.$$

The effect of the 2 in this function is different from that in $y = 2 \sin x$. In
the case of (2), given any value of $x$, say $\pi/4$, we first multiply by 2,
obtaining $\pi/2$, and then find $\sin \pi/2$, which is of course 1. That is, for
$y = \sin 2x$ when $x = \pi/4$, $y = 1$. We can readily see that as $x$ takes on the
values from 0 to $\pi$, $2x$ takes on the values from 0 to $2\pi$ and $\sin 2x$ runs
through the complete set of $y$-values that occur in the interval from 0 to $2\pi$
of $y = \sin x$. That is, $y$ increases from 0 to 1, then decreases to 0, decreases
still further to $-1$, and then increases to 0. This range of $y$-values is called a
cycle. The behavior of $y = \sin 2x$ is represented in Fig. 10-3. We see that
the amplitude is 1 but the period is $\pi$. It is worth remembering that the

**Figure 10-3**

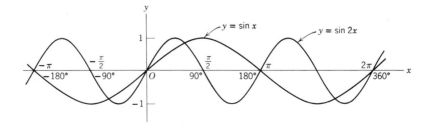

period can be obtained by dividing the normal period $2\pi$ by the coefficient of $x$. It is perhaps unnecessary to add that in place of the 2 in $y = \sin 2x$, any number can occur, so that there is another infinity of sinusoidal functions of the form $y = \sin bx$.

Another kind of variation on $y = \sin x$ is that which combines the two types we have discussed. It is generally represented by the formula $y = a \sin bx$. A few other variations are suggested in the exercises.

## EXERCISES

1. Sketch on the same axes $y = \sin x$ and
   (a) $y = \sin 3x$.
   (b) $y = 3 \sin x$.
   (c) $y = 3 \sin 2x$.
   (d) $y = 2 \sin 4x$.
   (e) $y = \sin\left(x + \dfrac{\pi}{2}\right)$.
   (f) $y = \sin x + \dfrac{\pi}{2}$.
   (g) $y = \sin(x - 1)$.
   (h) $y = -2 \sin 3x$.

2. Sketch $y = x + \sin x$.

   *Suggestion:* Sketch $y = x$ and $y = \sin x$ on the same axes. Then at a number of values of $x$ add the ordinates of the two curves. If one ordinate is positive and the other negative, you must of course add the signed values.

3. Sketch $y = x \sin x$.

4. Sketch $y = 3 \sin 2(x - 1) + 4$.

   *Suggestion:* Sketch in order $y = \sin x$, $y = \sin 2x$, $y = \sin 2(x - 1)$, $y = 3 \sin 2(x - 1)$, and $y = 3 \sin 2(x - 1) + 4$.

5. Sketch $y = x^2 + \sin x$.

**3. Some Preliminaries on Limits.** In the calculus we are interested in what we can do with the derived functions and integrals of the trigonometric functions. To find the derivative of $y = \sin x$, we use the method of increments. In the course of this work we must determine certain limits and so we shall dispose of these now. The first is

$$(3) \qquad\qquad \lim_{x \to 0} \frac{\sin x}{x}.$$

The determination of this limit is more difficult than that of, say,

$$(4) \qquad\qquad \lim_{x \to 2} \frac{x^2 - 4}{x - 2}.$$

Here we can divide numerator and denominator by $x - 2$, which is certainly correct when $x \neq 2$; having obtained $x + 2$, we can see that the function approaches 4 as $x$ approaches 2. For (3), however, where the same difficulty arises as in (4), namely, both numerator and denominator approach 0, it is not possible to divide numerator and denominator by some quantity in order to determine the limit readily. Moreover, substituting 0 for $x$ in (3), which sometimes gives the same result as finding the limit as $x$ approaches 0, does not help because in the present case it gives $0/0$.

Before trying to determine the limit of a function, it is wise to convince oneself that it does indeed have one. To obtain some indication of whether there may be a limit and what number to expect, we choose values of $x$ and calculate the values of the fraction (3). Thereby we obtain the following table:

| $x$ | 0.5 | 0.3 | 0.2 | 0.1 | 0.05 | 0.01 |
|---|---|---|---|---|---|---|
| $\sin x$ | 0.479 | 0.2955 | 0.1987 | 0.0998 | 0.049979 | 0.00999998 |
| $\dfrac{\sin x}{x}$ | 0.959 | 0.985 | 0.9933 | 0.9983 | 0.99958 | 0.999998 |

It seems quite clear that the limit in question is 1.

We shall prove that this is so. We may regard $x$ as the size of a positive central angle in a circle (Fig. 10-4) of radius 1 and center $O$. Let $AD$ be the arc of the circle intercepted by the angle. At $A$ we drop the perpendicular $AB$ to the side $OD$ of the angle and at $D$ we erect the perpendicular to the side $OD$. This perpendicular meets $OA$ in some point which we denote by $E$.

We see from the figure that

**(5)** $$\text{area } OBA < \text{area of sector } ODA < \text{area } ODE.$$

But

$$\text{area } OBA = \tfrac{1}{2} OB \cdot BA = \tfrac{1}{2} \cos x \sin x.$$

Further, the area $ODA$ of the sector of the circle is that part of the entire area of the circle which the central angle $x$ is of $2\pi$. That is,

$$\text{area } ODA = \frac{x}{2\pi} \cdot \pi(1)^2 = \frac{x}{2}.$$

Finally,

$$\text{area } ODE = \tfrac{1}{2} ED \cdot OD = \tfrac{1}{2} \tan x = \frac{1}{2}\frac{\sin x}{\cos x}.$$

**Figure 10-4**

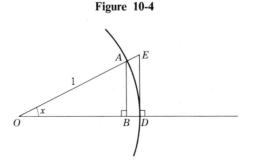

With these values of the individual areas the inequality (5) reads

$$\tfrac{1}{2}\cos x \sin x < \frac{x}{2} < \frac{1}{2}\frac{\sin x}{\cos x}.$$

If we divide the inequality by the positive quantity $(\sin x)/2$ we obtain

**(6)**
$$\cos x < \frac{x}{\sin x} < \frac{1}{\cos x}.$$

We recall from the study of trigonometry (see Fig. 10-5) that as $x$ approaches 0, $\cos x$ approaches 1. However, we see from (6) that as $x$ approaches 0, $x/\sin x$ always lies between two quantities, $\cos x$ which approaches 1 and $1/\cos x$ which must also approach 1 because $\cos x$ does. Hence

$$\lim_{x \to 0} \frac{x}{\sin x} = 1.$$

Because this limit is 1, it is also true that the reciprocal approaches 1, that is,

**(7)**
$$\lim_{x \to 0} \frac{\sin x}{x} = 1.$$

We have considered the limit of $(\sin x)/x$ as $x$ approaches 0 through positive values. However, when $x$ is negative, we may use the fact that

**(8)**
$$\frac{\sin x}{x} = \frac{\sin(-x)}{-x},$$

because $\sin(-x) = -\sin x$. Moreover, if $x$ is negative, $-x$ is positive. Because the right side of (8) deals with a positive variable and the fraction approaches 1 as $x$ approaches 0, the left side of (8) also approaches 1.

We should note that the convenience of radian measure is utilized in the proof of (7). Had we used $x$-values which are associated with the degree measure of angles, our statement about the area of sector $ODA$ would have had to be modified to read

$$\text{area } ODA = \frac{x}{360} \cdot \pi(1)^2,$$

and as a consequence the final result would have been

$$\lim_{x \to 0} \frac{180}{\pi}\frac{\sin x}{x} = 1.$$

When the values of $x$ are associated with the radian measure of angles, we dispense with the factor $180/\pi$. Of course, nothing important in the calculus would really be affected if we did have to carry this factor.

There is one more limit that we shall utilize shortly, namely,

**(9)**
$$\lim_{x \to 0} \frac{1 - \cos x}{x}.$$

The difficulty in evaluating this limit is the usual one—both numerator and denominator approach 0. However, the limit is readily evaluated. We utilize the trigonometric identity

$$\textbf{(10)} \qquad \sin\frac{x}{2} = \sqrt{\frac{1 - \cos x}{2}}$$

so that

$$1 - \cos x = 2\sin^2\frac{x}{2}.$$

If we substitute this value in (9), we obtain

$$\lim_{x\to 0}\frac{2\sin^2\frac{x}{2}}{x}.$$

It is correct algebraically to write this last expression as

$$\lim_{x\to 0}\sin\frac{x}{2}\;\frac{\sin\frac{x}{2}}{\frac{x}{2}}.$$

If, for convenience, we regard $x/2$ as $y$, we see that we must determine the limit as $y$ approaches 0 of a product one factor of which is $\sin y$ and the other $(\sin y)/y$. We know that the limit of a product of two functions is the product of the limits. However, as $y$ approaches 0, $(\sin y)/y$ approaches 1 and $\sin y$ approaches 0. Hence the product of the limits is 0. Thus

$$\textbf{(11)} \qquad \lim_{x\to 0}\frac{1 - \cos x}{x} = 0.$$

## EXERCISES

1. Show that $\displaystyle\lim_{x\to 0}\frac{1 - \cos x}{x} = 0$ by multiplying numerator and denominator by $1 + \cos x$ and then making any appropriate steps.

2. Evaluate the following limits:

   (a) $\displaystyle\lim_{x\to 0}\frac{\sin 2x}{x}$.       *Ans.* 2.      (d) $\displaystyle\lim_{x\to 0}\frac{1 - \cos x}{x^2}$.

   (b) $\displaystyle\lim_{x\to 0}\frac{\sin ax}{x}$.      (e) $\displaystyle\lim_{x\to 0}\frac{\tan x}{x}$.      *Ans.* 1.

   (c) $\displaystyle\lim_{\Delta x\to 0}\frac{\sin \Delta x}{\Delta x}$.      *Ans.* 1.

**4. Differentiation of the Trigonometric Functions.** To differentiate $y = \sin x$ we apply the method of increments. Let $x_0$ be the value of $x$ at which we desire the derivative. Then

$$y_0 = \sin x_0.$$

If $x$ changes to the value $x_0 + \Delta x$, then

$$y_0 + \Delta y = \sin(x_0 + \Delta x)$$

and

$$\frac{\Delta y}{\Delta x} = \frac{\sin(x_0 + \Delta x) - \sin x_0}{\Delta x}.$$

We cannot obtain the limit of the right side as $\Delta x$ approaches 0 by merely inspecting the expression; hence we shall try to transform it on the chance that some other form may be more perspicuous. The presence of $\sin(x_0 + \Delta x)$ suggests that we try to use the identity

$$\sin(A + B) = \sin A \cos B + \cos A \sin B.$$

Then

$$\frac{\Delta y}{\Delta x} = \frac{\sin x_0 \cos \Delta x + \cos x_0 \sin \Delta x - \sin x_0}{\Delta x}.$$

Again, a direct evaluation of the limit of the fraction does not seem possible, and therefore we try collecting the terms in $\sin x_0$ and breaking up the fraction into two fractions. Thus

**(12)** $$\frac{\Delta y}{\Delta x} = \sin x_0 \cdot \frac{\cos \Delta_x - 1}{\Delta x} + \cos x_0 \frac{\sin \Delta x}{\Delta x}.$$

To obtain $dy/dx$ we must determine the limit of $\Delta y/\Delta x$ as $\Delta x$ approaches 0. The right side is a sum of two terms, and according to the theorem that the limit of a sum is the sum of the limits we may consider each term separately. As for the term

**(13)** $$\sin x_0 \cdot \frac{\cos \Delta x - 1}{\Delta x},$$

the quantity $\sin x_0$ is a constant. A theorem on limits tells us that the limit of the product is the constant times the limit of the second factor. This limit is precisely the one we considered in (11), except for a factor of $-1$ and the fact that the $x$ in (11) is the $\Delta x$ in (13). Hence the limit of (13) is 0.

The term

**(14)** $$\cos x_0 \frac{\sin \Delta x}{\Delta x}$$

in (12) is again a constant times a function of $\Delta x$, and the limit of this term is the constant times the limit of $(\sin \Delta x)/\Delta x$. By (7) we see that the limit of (14) is $\cos x_0$.

We have, then, from the consideration of (13) and (14) that

$$\frac{dy}{dx} = \lim_{\Delta x \to 0} \frac{\Delta y}{\Delta x} = \cos x_0.$$

This result holds at every value of $x_0$, and therefore we have that if $y = \sin x$ the derived function is

**(15)**
$$\frac{dy}{dx} = \cos x.$$

Now that we have the derived function in (15), the chain rule enables us to handle more complicated sine functions. Suppose that $y = \sin 3x$. To obtain $dy/dx$ we regard $3x$ as $u$; we then have

**(16)**
$$y = \sin u, \qquad u = 3x.$$

The chain rule states that

$$\frac{dy}{dx} = \frac{dy}{du} \cdot \frac{du}{dx}.$$

Hence from (15) we have

$$\frac{dy}{dx} = \cos u \cdot 3 = 3 \cos 3x.$$

In fact, no matter how complicated the function of $x$ whose sine is being considered, we may always call it $u$ and write $y = \sin u$ with $u$ representing that function of $x$. Then

**(17)**
$$\frac{dy}{dx} = \cos u \frac{du}{dx}.$$

The derivatives of the other five trigonometric functions are readily obtained. Let us remind ourselves first of the behavior of the function $y = \cos x$. This is shown in Fig. 10-5.

To obtain the derivative of $y = \cos x$, we can go through the method of increments, but it is easier to obtain it from (17). We know that we can relate $\cos x$ to $\sin x$ through the trigonometric identity

$$\cos x \equiv \sin\left(x + \frac{\pi}{2}\right).$$

**Figure 10-5**

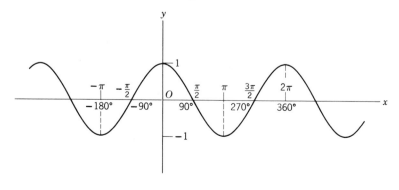

This identity holds for every value of $x$. Hence to differentiate $y = \cos x$, we may differentiate $y = \sin(x + \pi/2)$. With the chain rule the result is immediate. We regard $x + \pi/2$ as $u$, so that

$$y = \sin u, \qquad u = x + \frac{\pi}{2}.$$

Then by (17)

$$\frac{dy}{dx} = \cos u \cdot 1 = \cos\left(x + \frac{\pi}{2}\right).$$

But we have the identity

$$\cos\left(x + \frac{\pi}{2}\right) \equiv -\sin x.$$

Hence, if $y = \cos x$,

**(18)**
$$\frac{dy}{dx} = -\sin x.$$

As in the case of $y = \sin x$, if we have $y = \cos u$, where $u$ is some function of $x$, we may apply the chain rule to write

**(19)**
$$\frac{dy}{dx} = -\sin u \frac{du}{dx}.$$

For the function $y = \tan x$, whose behavior is shown in Fig. 10-6, the derived function is readily obtained. We have only to note that

$$y = \tan x = \frac{\sin x}{\cos x},$$

and we may now apply the theorem on the derivative of the quotient of two functions. We leave the details for an exercise and merely note the result. If

**Figure 10-6**

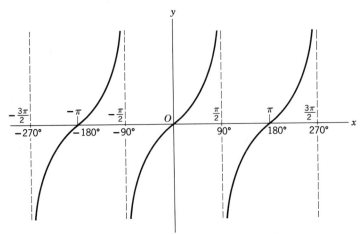

$y = \tan x$, then

**(20)**
$$\frac{dy}{dx} = \sec^2 x.$$

Here we should note that the derived function exists at all values of $x$, except when $x$ is an odd multiple of $\pi/2$ (see Fig. 10-8). As in the case of $y = \sin x$, if we have $y = \tan u$, where $u$ is a function of $x$, then

**(21)**
$$\frac{dy}{dx} = \sec^2 u \, \frac{du}{dx} \, .$$

The case of $y = \cot x$ is practically the same as $y = \tan x$. The graph of the function is shown in Fig. 10-7. To obtain the derived function of $y = \cot x$, we have only to note that

**(22)**
$$y = \cot x = \frac{\cos x}{\sin x}$$

and apply the theorem on the derivative of a quotient of two functions. Again we leave the details for an exercise and note the result. If $y = \cot x$, then

**(23)**
$$\frac{dy}{dx} = -\csc^2 x,$$

and if $y = \cot u$, where $u$ is a function of $x$, then

**(24)**
$$\frac{dy}{dx} = -\csc^2 u \, \frac{du}{dx} \, .$$

The derived function in (23) fails to exist when $x$ is any multiple of $\pi$ (see Fig. 10-9).

**Figure 10-7**

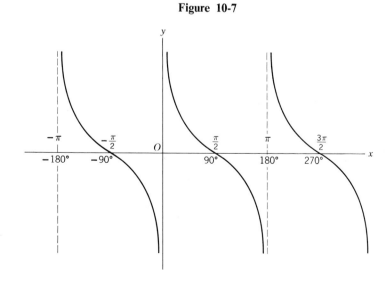

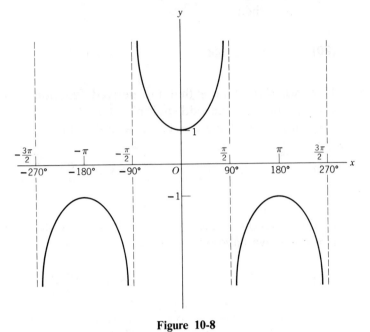

**Figure 10-8**

  The derived function of $y = \sec x$, whose behavior is shown in Fig. 10-8, is also obtainable at once. Because

**(25)**        $$y = \sec x = \frac{1}{\cos x} ,$$

the theorem on the derived function of a quotient of two functions can be applied and yields

**(26)**        $$\frac{dy}{dx} = \sec x \tan x.$$

Also, if $y = \sec u$, where $u$ is a function of $x$, then

**(27)**        $$\frac{dy}{dx} = \sec u \tan u \frac{du}{dx} .$$

The derived function in (26) does not exist when $x$ is an odd multiple of $\pi/2$.

  Finally, we consider the sixth trigonometric function $y = \csc x$, whose behavior is shown in Fig. 10-9. The derived function is obtainable from the fact that

**(28)**        $$y = \csc x = \frac{1}{\sin x} .$$

The result is

**(29)**        $$\frac{dy}{dx} = -\csc x \cot x.$$

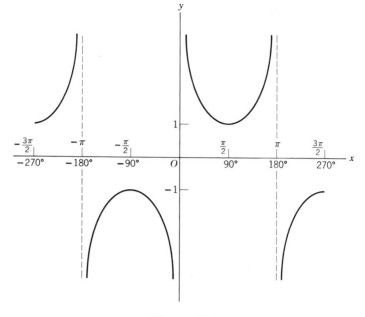

**Figure 10-9**

If $y = \csc u$, where $u$ is a function of $x$, then

**(30)**
$$\frac{dy}{dx} = -\csc u \cot u \frac{du}{dx} .$$

The derived function in (29) fails to exist when $x$ is any multiple of $\pi$.

Let us put together our results on the six functions. In all cases to be stated $u$ is a function of $x$.

**Theorem:**

**(31)**    If $y = \sin u$, then $\dfrac{dy}{dx} = \cos u \dfrac{du}{dx}$ .

**(32)**    If $y = \cos u$, then $\dfrac{dy}{dx} = -\sin u \dfrac{du}{dx}$ .

**(33)**    If $y = \tan u$, then $\dfrac{dy}{dx} = \sec^2 u \dfrac{du}{dx}$ .

**(34)**    If $y = \cot u$, then $\dfrac{dy}{dx} = -\csc^2 u \dfrac{du}{dx}$ .

**(35)**    If $y = \sec u$, then $\dfrac{dy}{dx} = \sec u \tan u \dfrac{du}{dx}$ .

**(36)**    If $y = \csc u$, then $\dfrac{dy}{dx} = -\csc u \cot u \dfrac{du}{dx}$ .

## EXERCISES

1. Find the derived functions of each of the following functions:

   (a)  $y = \sin 2x$.

           *Ans.*  $dy/dx = 2 \cos 2x$.

   (b)  $y = \cos 5x$.

   (c)  $y = 3 \cos 2x$.

           *Ans.*  $dy/dx = -6 \sin 2x$.

   (d)  $y = 6 \tan 5x$.

   (e)  $y = \sec 4x$.

           *Ans.*  $dy/dx = 4 \sec 4x \tan 4x$.

   (f)  $y = \sin x \cos x$.

   (g)  $y = \dfrac{1}{\cos 2x}$.

           *Ans.*  $dy/dx = \dfrac{-2 \sin 2x}{\cos^2 2x}$.

   (h)  $f(x) = \sin x \cot x$.

   (i)  $f(x) = \cos x \tan x$.

           *Ans.*  $f'(x) = \cos x$.

   (j)  $y = \sqrt{1 - \cos^2 x}$

   (k)  $y = \sqrt{1 + \tan^2 x}$ .

           *Ans.*  $dy/dx = \sec x \tan x$.

   (l)  $y = \sqrt{2 - \cos^2 x}$ .

           *Ans.*  $dy/dx = \dfrac{\sin x \cos x}{\sqrt{1 + \sin^2 x}}$.

2. Find the derived functions of each of the following functions:

   (a)  $y = \sin^3 x$.

           *Ans.*  $dy/dx = 3 \sin^2 x \cos x$.

   (b)  $y = \sin^3 x \cos x$.

   (c)  $y = \sin^3 2x$.

           *Ans.*  $dy/dx = 6 \sin^2 2x \cos 2x$.

   (d)  $y = \sqrt[3]{\sin x}$ .

   (e)  $y = \cos^2 2x$.

           *Ans.*  $dy/dx = -4 \sin 2x \cos 2x$.

   (f)  $y = \sin x^3$.

   (g)  $y = \tan 2x \cot 2x$.

           *Ans.*  $y' = 0$.

   (h)  $y = \sin \dfrac{1}{x}$ .

   (i)  $f(x) = x \cos \dfrac{1}{x}$ .

           *Ans.*  $f'(x) = \cos \dfrac{1}{x} + \dfrac{1}{x} \sin \dfrac{1}{x}$.

   (j)  $f(x) = \sqrt{\sin x^3}$ .

   (k)  $y = \cos(\sin x)$.

           *Ans.*  $dy/dx = -\sin(\sin x)\cos x$.

   (l)  $y = \sin^2 x + \cos^2 x$.

   (m)  $f(x) = \dfrac{\sin 2x}{\tan x}$ .

           *Ans.*  $f'(x) = -4 \sin x \cos x$.

3. Given that  $\dfrac{\Delta y}{\Delta x} = \dfrac{\sin(x_0 + \Delta x) - \sin x_0}{\Delta x}$  use the identity

$$\sin A - \sin B = 2 \cos \frac{A + B}{2} \sin \frac{A - B}{2}$$

   to find  $dy/dx$.

4. To differentiate  $y = \cos x$, we might use a trigonometric identity and write  $y = \sin\left(\dfrac{\pi}{2} - x\right)$. Obtain  $dy/dx$  from this form of  $\cos x$.

5. Using the fact that  $\tan x = \sin x/\cos x$, find  $y'$  when  $y = \tan x$.

6. Using the fact that  $\cot x = \cos x/\sin x$, find  $y'$  when  $y = \cot x$.

7. Using the fact that  $\sec x = 1/\cos x$, find  $y'$  when  $y = \sec x$.

8. Using the fact that  $\csc x = 1/\sin x$, find  $y'$  when  $y = \csc x$.

9. Given  $y = \sin x$, find  $d^2y/dx^2$.     *Ans.*  $d^2y/dx^2 = -\sin x$.

10. Given  $y = \cos x$, find  $d^2y/dx^2$.

11. Let us accept for the present the fact that the range of a projectile fired from a gun which is inclined at an angle  $A$  to the ground is given by the formula  $R = (V^2/16) \sin A \cos A$, where  $V$, the initial velocity of the projectile, is fixed. Find the value of  $A$  for which the range is maximum.     *Ans.*  $\pi/4$.

**12.** Find the value of $\displaystyle\lim_{\Delta x \to 0} \frac{\sin(2x + 2\Delta x) - \sin 2x}{\Delta x}$ .

**13.** Find the value of $\displaystyle\lim_{x \to \pi/2} \frac{\sin x - 1}{x - \pi/2}$ .  *Ans.* 0.

**14.** A mass $M$ is drawn up a straight incline of given height $h$ by a mass $m$ which is attached to the first mass by a string passing from it over a pulley at the top of the incline (Fig. 10-10) and which hangs vertically. Find the angle of the incline in order that the time of ascent be a minimum.

  *Suggestion:* The net force acting on $M$ is $32m - 32M \sin A$.

                   *Ans.* $\sin A = m/2M$.

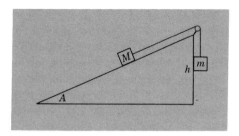

**Figure 10-10**

**15.** Given a point and a vertical line distant $d$ from it, find the inclination of the straight line which would guide a particle acted on only by gravity from the point to the vertical line in the shortest time.      *Ans.* $\pi/4$.

**16.** A swinging pendulum is 4 feet long and is rotating at the rate of $18°/\sec$ when it makes an angle of $30°$ with the vertical. How fast is the end of the pendulum rising or falling at that moment?        *Ans.* $\pi/5$ ft/sec.

**17.** An airplane, flying at an altitude of 2 miles, passes directly over an observer on the ground. A few moments later the observer notes that the airplane's angle of elevation is $30°$ and is decreasing at the rate of $15°/\min$. How fast is the plane traveling?              *Ans.* $2\pi/3$ mi/min.

**18.** A revolving beacon 3600 feet off a straight shore makes 2 revolutions per minute. How fast does its beam sweep along the shore (a) at the point on the shore nearest the beacon? (b) at the point on the shore 4800 feet away from the beacon?      *Ans.* (a) $14,400\pi$ ft/min.; (b) $25,600\pi$ ft/min.

**19.** A ferris wheel 50 feet in diameter makes 1 revolution every 2 minutes. If the center of the wheel is 30 feet above the ground, how fast is a passenger in the cab rising when he reaches a height of 40 feet?

  *Suggestion:* Let $A$ be the angle between the line from the center of the wheel to the cab and the line from the center of the wheel to the ground. Then the height of the cab above the ground is $h = 30 - 25 \cos A$.

                *Ans.* $5\sqrt{21}\ \pi$ ft/min.

**20.** A destroyer at $A$ sights a battleship at $B$, 2 miles away (Fig. 10-11). The latter is sailing due east at 10 mi/hr and the former is capable of sailing at 8 mi/hr. In what direction should the destroyer sail to come as close as possible to the battleship?

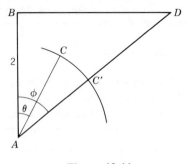

**Figure 10-11**

*Suggestion:* Suppose that the destroyer takes the direction $\theta$ and sails for some time $t$ until it is closest to the battleship. The destroyer may then be at $C$ and the battleship at $D$. The destroyer can do better by sailing in the direction $\phi$, the angle determined by the straight line from $A$ to $D$, for in that same time $t$ it can travel the distance $AC'$ equal to $AC$, and $DC'$ is then less than $DC$. Hence it is necessary to consider only the situations in which the destroyer heads directly for the position of the battleship. However, this still leaves open a domain of possible values for $\phi$, and the problem then becomes, which value of $\phi$ is best?                               *Ans.* $\sin \phi = 0.8$.

21. A steel girder 27 feet long is moved on rollers along a passageway and into a corridor 8 feet wide and at right angles to the passageway. How wide must the passageway be for the girder to go around the corner?

    *Suggestion:* Idealize the girder as the line segment $AB$ of Fig. 10-12. As the girder is moved around the corner it is best to keep it touching the inner vertex at 0 and touching the outer wall of the corridor. Then $\theta$ varies as the girder is moved into the corridor. The largest value of $x$ as $\theta$ varies from $90°$ to $0°$ is the required width of the passageway.                               *Ans.* $5\sqrt{5}$.

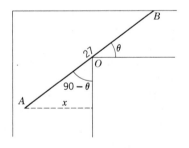

**Figure 10-12**

**5. Integration of the Trigonometric Functions.** Every new formula of differentiation gives us a new formula for integration. Thus from formulas (31) to (36) we have the following

**Theorem:**   If $\dfrac{dy}{dx} = \sin u \, \dfrac{du}{dx}$, then

**(37)**                    $y = \displaystyle\int \sin u \, \dfrac{du}{dx} \, dx = -\cos u + C.$

If $\dfrac{dy}{dx} = \cos u \dfrac{du}{dx}$, then

**(38)** $$y = \int \cos u \frac{du}{dx}\, dx = \sin u + C.$$

If $\dfrac{dy}{dx} = \sec^2 u \dfrac{du}{dx}$, then

**(39)** $$y = \int \sec^2 u \frac{du}{dx}\, dx = \tan u + C.$$

If $\dfrac{dy}{dx} = \csc^2 u \dfrac{du}{dx}$, then

**(40)** $$y = \int \csc^2 u \frac{du}{dx}\, dx = -\cot u + C.$$

If $\dfrac{dy}{dx} = \sec u \tan \dfrac{du}{dx}$, then

**(41)** $$y = \int \sec u \tan u \frac{du}{dx}\, dx = \sec u + C.$$

If $\dfrac{dy}{dx} = \csc u \cot u \dfrac{du}{dx}$, then

**(42)** $$y = \int \csc u \cot u \frac{du}{dx} = -\csc u + C.$$

As in the case of the algebraic functions, integration is more difficult than differentiation. Let us consider a few examples involving the trigonometric functions.

Given

$$\frac{dy}{dx} = \cos 2x,$$

let us find $y$. If we think of $2x$ as $u$, we have $dy/dx = \cos u$. If we had in addition the factor $du/dx$, we could integrate by applying (38). In the present case, because $du/dx$ is 2, we write

$$\frac{dy}{dx} = \tfrac{1}{2} \cos u \cdot 2.$$

Now, apart from the factor $\tfrac{1}{2}$, our derivative is in the form called for by (38). However, a constant factor can be kept separate and merely multiplied into the integral. Hence

$$y = \tfrac{1}{2} \sin u + C = \tfrac{1}{2} \sin 2x + C.$$

We may recall that the factor $du/dx$, which is 2 in this example, does not itself give rise to any term in the integral.

Let us consider next

$$\frac{dy}{dx} = \cos^2 x \sin x.$$

If we regard $\cos x$ as $u$, we have

$$\frac{dy}{dx} = u^2 \cdot \sin x.$$

To have the proper $du/dx$, in view of the fact that $u = \cos x$, we need $-\sin x$. However, this is easily introduced, because it involves only multiplying and dividing by a constant factor, namely $-1$.
Thus

$$\frac{dy}{dx} = -u^2(-\sin x) = -u^2 \frac{du}{dx}.$$

Now apart from the constant factor $-1$ we are in a position to apply the generalized power rule of Chapter 7, Section 7. Then

$$y = -\frac{u^3}{3} + C = -\frac{\cos^3 x}{3} + C.$$

As a third example let us consider

**(43)**                    $$\frac{dy}{dx} = \tan 2x \sec^2 2x.$$

The fact that the derived function of $\tan x$ is $\sec^2 x$ suggests setting

$$u = \tan 2x.$$

Then by (33)

**(44)**                    $$\frac{du}{dx} = \sec^2 2x \cdot 2.$$

With this choice of $u$ as $\tan 2x$, we see from (43) and (44) that

$$\frac{dy}{dx} = \frac{1}{2} u \frac{du}{dx}.$$

Again, apart from the factor $\frac{1}{2}$, we are in a position to apply the generalized power rule. From this we have

**(45)**                    $$y = \frac{1}{4} u^2 + C = \frac{1}{4} \tan^2 2x + C.$$

There is another way of doing the integration. Let us write (43) as

**(46)**                    $$\frac{dy}{dx} = \sec 2x \sec 2x \tan 2x.$$

Now we try letting

$$u = \sec 2x.$$

Then by (35)

$$\frac{du}{dx} = \sec 2x \tan 2x \cdot 2.$$

We see then that we can write (46) as

$$\frac{dy}{dx} = \frac{1}{2} u \frac{du}{dx},$$

from which

**(47)**          $$y = \frac{1}{4} u^2 + C = \frac{1}{4} \sec^2 2x + C.$$

If we compare (45) and (47), we see that we presumably have two different answers. However, there is the trigonometric identity

$$\sec^2 2x = 1 + \tan^2 2x.$$

Then

$$\frac{1}{4} \sec^2 2x = \frac{1}{4} + \frac{1}{4} \tan^2 2x.$$

Hence (47) becomes

$$y = \frac{1}{4} + \frac{1}{4} \tan^2 2x + C = \frac{1}{4} \tan^2 2x + C',$$

where $C'$ is some new constant of integration. If we now compare with (45), we see that we have the same result.

In integrating trigonometric functions we should keep in mind that the numerous identities of trigonometry often aid in transforming a given function into one which is identical in its values to the given one but more amenable to integration.

## EXERCISES

1. Given the following information, find $y$:

(a)  $y' = \cos 3x.$

  Ans. $y = \dfrac{\sin 3x}{3} + C.$

(b)  $y' = \sin 4x.$

(c)  $y = \int \sin^2 x \, dx.$

  Ans. $y = \dfrac{x}{2} - \dfrac{\sin x \cos x}{2} + C.$

(d)  $dy/dx = \cos^2 x.$

(e)  $y = \int \sin^2 x \cos x \, dx.$

  Ans. $y = \dfrac{\sin^3 x}{3} + C.$

(f)  $y' = \sin^2 3x \cos 3x.$

(g)  $y' = \sec^3 x \tan x.$

  Ans. $y = \dfrac{\sec^3 x}{3} + C.$

(h)  $dy/dx = \cot^4 x \csc^2 x.$

(i)  $dy/dx = \tan^3 2x \sec^2 2x.$

  Ans. $y = \dfrac{\tan^4 2x}{8} + C.$

(j)  $y' = \dfrac{\csc^2 2x}{\cot^3 2x}.$

(k)  $f'(x) = \sqrt{\cot^3 x} \, \csc^2 x.$

  Ans. $f(x) = \dfrac{-2 \cot^{5/2} x}{5} + C.$

(l)  $f'(x) = \csc^4 ax \cot ax.$

(m)  $y = \int \sec^5 x \tan x \, dx.$

  Ans. $y = \dfrac{\sec^5 x}{5} + C.$

(n)  $y' = \dfrac{\sec^2 x}{\sqrt{\tan x + 3}}.$

(o)  $f'(x) = x \cos x^2.$

2. If $y' = \sin x \cos x$, then by letting $u = \sin x$ we see that $y = (\sin^2 x)/2$. By letting $u = \cos x$, we see that $y = -(\cos^2 x)/2$. Then $\sin^2 x/2 = -\cos^2 x/2$. What is wrong?

3. If $y = f(x)$ is a periodic function, is $y' = f'(x)$ necessarily periodic? Defend your answer.                          *Ans. Yes.*

4. Show by an example that if $y' = f'(x)$ is periodic, then $y = f(x)$ need not be.

5. Find the area between the curve $y = \sin x$ and the $x$-axis from $x = 0$ to $x = \pi$.                                            *Ans.* 2.

6. Find the geometrical area between the curve $y = \cos x$, the $x$-axis, the line $x = 0$, and the ordinate at $x = 2\pi$.

7. Find the area between $y = \cos x + 1$, $y = 3/2$, $x = 0$, and $x = \pi$.                                     *Ans.* $\sqrt{3} + \pi/6$.

8. Evaluate $\int_0^{\frac{\pi}{2}} \sin^2 x \, dx$.

9. Find the area bounded by the $y$-axis, $y = 8 \cos x$ and $y = \sec^2 x$.                                  *Ans.* $3\sqrt{3}$.

10. $\int_0^{4\pi} \sqrt{\dfrac{1 - \cos x}{2}} \, dx = \int_0^{4\pi} \sin \dfrac{x}{2} \, dx = -\dfrac{1}{2} \cos \dfrac{x}{2} \Big|_0^{4\pi} = 0$. But the original integrand is positive in $(0, 4\pi)$ (except at isolated points) and so the area cannot be 0. What is wrong?

## 6. Applications of the Trigonometric Functions to Periodic Phenomena.*

We have already stated that the trigonometric functions are immensely important in the study of periodic phenomena, and we are now in a position to look at a few of them. We consider first the motion of a bob on a spring—an investigation launched by Robert Hooke as part of the seventeenth-century efforts to design simple, portable clocks.

Suppose that the upper end (Fig. 10-13) of the spring is fixed and a bob is attached to the lower end. The weight of the bob extends the spring. Because the spring is extended, it exerts a tension or pull upward, and this tension increases as the spring becomes more and more extended. The spring stretches to the point at which the upward tension in the spring just offsets the weight of the bob. The position of the bob at which the two forces, the upward pull of the spring and the downward pull of the weight, offset each other is called the equilibrium position. If no new forces are introduced, the bob stays in this equilibrium position indefinitely.

If the bob is pulled down still more and then released, it oscillates about the equilibrium position and, if air resistance (and strictly, internal losses in the spring) are ignored, the bob continues to oscillate endlessly. We propose to study the motion of the bob mathematically. Our program is to obtain a function that describes its motion and then to try to learn some facts from the function which are not apparent from mere observation of the bob's motion.

We introduce a vertical coordinate line, the $y$-axis of Fig. 10-13, and choose the origin $O$ to be the equilibrium position of the bob. Let us denote by $d$, which we take to be positive, the length by which the spring is

*This section can be omitted without disrupting the continuity.*

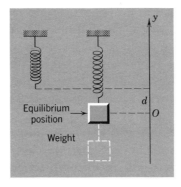

**Figure 10-13**

extended when the bob is attached to it. After the bob is set in motion by pulling it down from the equilibrium position and then releasing it, its position, of course, varies continuously with time. The $y$-value of this varying position that the bob may have at any time $t$ is called the displacement. When the bob is below the equilibrium position, the $y$-values are negative numbers; when above, they are positive.

   We seek the relation between displacement and time, that is, between $y$ and $t$. To obtain the motion of the bob, we must have some physical principle or principles. In the present case we apply Hooke's law which says that the tension in the spring or force exerted by the spring is proportional to the extension or contraction of the spring beyond its normal length. To be specific, suppose that the bob is pulled down a distance $y$ below the equilibrium position. Because this $y$-value is itself negative, the spring is extended to an amount $d - y$. Hooke's law states that the force exerted by the spring on the bob is

**(48)**
$$k(d - y)$$

where $k$ is the proportionality constant and is positive. This constant has a direct physical meaning. Some springs are very "tight", that is, it is hard to extend them. Hence when extended they exert a strong force to contract. For such springs $k$ is large. Alternatively, there are springs that are easily extended, and these exert a small restoring force. For such springs $k$ is a small number. Thus $k$ represents the "stiffness" of the spring and is called the spring constant.

   One force acting on the bob is the pull of the spring. Also acting on the bob is the weight of the bob, $32m$, where $m$ is the mass of the bob. In representing these forces mathematically, we must be careful about the signs. The significance of a force insofar as motion is concerned is that it causes acceleration. We know this through Newton's second law of motion which states that a force acting upon a mass gives it an acceleration. We have already pointed out that an acceleration in a given direction produces a velocity in that direction and the velocity produces a distance moved in that same direction. Then the positive direction of a force must be that which causes the distance traveled to be in the positive direction.*

Let us now look at the forces acting on the bob with a view to assigning the proper signs to them and let us keep in mind that we have chosen the upward direction to be the positive one for $y$. The spring force, by (48), is $k(d - y)$. When $y$ is positive but less than $d$, and when $y$ is negative, the quantity $k(d - y)$ is positive. However, for the values of $y$ in question, the spring is extended and therefore pulls the bob upward. The force then is in the positive direction, and because $k(d - y)$ is positive, it has the correct sign. To check the sign let us consider the situation when $y$ is positive and greater than $d$. Then $k(d - y)$ is negative. However, when $y > d$, the spring is contracted beyond its normal length; it therefore seeks to expand and so presses downward on the bob. It causes the bob to travel downward and because the downward direction is negative, the sign of $k(d - y)$ is correct in this case too.

The only other force acting on the bob is the weight $32m$. This force always acts downward and, because it causes the bob to move downward, it should be negative. We represent this force then by $-32m$.

Thus the algebraic sum of the forces acting on the bob is

**(49)**  $$k(d - y) - 32m.$$

When the bob is in the equilibrium position, the upward pull of the spring just offsets the downward pull of the weight. Consequently,

**(50)**  $$kd = 32m.$$

Hence the *net force* acting on the bob is

$$- ky.$$

We note incidentally that equation (50) enables us to measure the spring constant $k$. If we attach a known weight to the spring, we can measure $d$ and solve for $k$.

Now that we know the net force acting on the bob we may use Newton's second law of motion which states that $F = ma$, where $F$ is the force in poundals, $m$ is the mass in pounds, and $a$ is the acceleration in feet per second per second. In the present case of straight-line motion, $a$ is $d^2y/dt^2$ or $\ddot{y}$ and $F$ is $-ky$.[†] Hence

**(51)**  $$m\ddot{y} = -ky.$$

---

*Likewise a negative force causes a negative acceleration, which causes the distance traveled to be in the negative direction. Nevertheless, even when a negative force and therefore a negative acceleration is acting, the actual motion may be upward. This can happen because some other velocities or accelerations may also be acting and may dominate. Thus when a ball is thrown up into the air and the upward direction is taken positive, there is a negative acceleration, due to gravity, always acting on the ball which causes the distance traveled to be downward. However, the initial velocity given to the ball by the hand is positive, and this dominates the motion during the upward motion of the ball.

† We are using the dot notation for the derivative because the independent variable is time.

Thus the implication of Hooke's law and Newton's second law of motion in calculus terms is a statement about the second derivative of $y$ as a function of $t$.

This equation is of the same form as that encountered in dealing with escape velocity. We could solve the present one by the same trick, that is, by replacing $d^2y/dt^2$ by $v\,dv/dy$, where $v$ is the velocity, but here we can do something simpler. If we examine (51), we see that it calls essentially for a function whose second derivative equals the function. This suggests sine or cosine. By mere trial we find that

$$y = \sin\sqrt{\frac{k}{m}}\ t \quad \text{and} \quad y = \cos\sqrt{\frac{k}{m}}\ t$$

will serve, for if

$$y = \sin\sqrt{\frac{k}{m}}\ t,$$

then

$$\dot{y} = \sqrt{\frac{k}{m}}\ \cos\sqrt{\frac{k}{m}}\ t$$

and

$$\ddot{y} = -\sqrt{\frac{k}{m}}\ \sqrt{\frac{k}{m}}\ \sin\sqrt{\frac{k}{m}}\ t = -\frac{k}{m}\ \sin\sqrt{\frac{k}{m}}\ t = -\frac{k}{m}\ y.$$

Likewise, $y = \cos\sqrt{k/m}\ t$ satisfies (51). Moreover, if we introduce a constant multiplier in either choice of $y$, we also obtain a function that satisfies (51). Finally, we can state that

**(52)** $$y = A\sin\sqrt{\frac{k}{m}}\ t + B\cos\sqrt{\frac{k}{m}}\ t,$$

where $A$ and $B$ are any constants we choose, is also a solution of (51) because when we substitute this value of $y$ in that equation, we see that the left side equals the right side.

Thus by trial we have obtained a function that satisfies (51). We do not know that this is the only function that can satisfy it, but at the moment we should be thankful that we have at least one; let us see if it tells us anything about the bob's motion. We shall return later (Chap. 11, Sect. 4) to the question of whether (52) is the unique solution, that is, the one and only one.

Formula (52) is the sum of a sine function and a cosine function of the same period. Such a sum is sinusoidal; we can see this in the following way. We multiply and divide through the right-hand side of (52) by $\sqrt{A^2 + B^2}$.

Thus

**(53)**

$$y = \sqrt{A^2 + B^2} \left[ \frac{A}{\sqrt{A^2 + B^2}} \sin\sqrt{\frac{k}{m}} \, t + \frac{B}{\sqrt{A^2 + B^2}} \cos\sqrt{\frac{k}{m}} \, t \right].$$

We now introduce an angle $\phi$, which is defined as shown in Fig. 10-14; that is, $\phi$ is the angle for which

**(54)**         $$\cos \phi = \frac{A}{\sqrt{A^2 + B^2}} \, , \qquad \sin \phi = \frac{B}{\sqrt{A^2 + B^2}} \, .$$

Such an angle can be defined for any value of $A$ and $B$; of course, if $A$ or $B$ or both prove to be negative, $\phi$ is not an acute angle. Also, because $A$ and $B$ are constants, so is $\sqrt{A^2 + B^2}$, and we may as well replace it by the constant $C$. Then (53) becomes

$$y = C \left( \sin\sqrt{\frac{k}{m}} \, t \cos \phi + \cos\sqrt{\frac{k}{m}} \, t \sin \phi \right)$$

or by a trigonometric identity

**(55)**                    $$y = C \sin\left( \sqrt{\frac{k}{m}} \, t + \phi \right).$$

Equation (55) is fully equivalent to (52). The constants $A$ and $B$ in (52), as yet undetermined, are replaced in (55) by the constants $C$ and $\phi$. Moreover, if we determine $A$ and $B$ from some physical facts, we can calculate $C$ and $\phi$. Conversely, if we know $C$ and $\phi$, we know $\sqrt{A^2 + B^2}$ and $\cos \phi$ and $\sin \phi$. Hence we can find $A$ and $B$ from (54).

The advantage of (55) as opposed to (52) is that we see at once that $y$ is a sinusoidal function of $t$; that is, the curve is a sine curve of some period and amplitude. The amplitude is clearly $C$. The quantity $\phi$ is usually called a phase constant; that is, $y$ is not 0 when $t$ is 0, as in the simple sine function $y = \sin t$, but $y$ is 0 in (55) when $t$ is $-\phi/\sqrt{k/m}$ and of course whenever the argument $\sqrt{k/m} \, t + \phi$ is a multiple of $\pi$. The period $T$ of

**Figure 10-14**

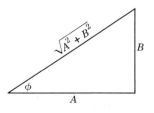

(55) is, as in all sine curves, $2\pi$ divided by the coefficient of $t$; that is,

**(56)**
$$T = \frac{2\pi}{\sqrt{\frac{k}{m}}} \quad \text{or} \quad T = 2\pi\sqrt{\frac{m}{k}} \; .$$

This means that for each increase in $t$ of $2\pi\sqrt{m/k}$, the $y$-values go through one cycle of values. Or, in terms of time, it takes $2\pi\sqrt{m/k}$ seconds for the curve to go through one full cycle of sine values. If it takes this many seconds to go through one cycle, the number of cycles per second, or the frequency per second, is

**(57)**
$$f = \frac{1}{2\pi\sqrt{\frac{m}{k}}} = \frac{1}{2\pi}\sqrt{\frac{k}{m}} \; .$$

Thus we have learned that the motion of the bob is sinusoidal. Moreover, we see from (56) that it takes $2\pi\sqrt{m/k}$ seconds to go through one cycle; that is, it takes this much time for the bob to make one complete oscillation, or one complete up and down motion.

This last fact is rather remarkable, for it says that the period is *independent of the amplitude.* Thus regardless of whether the bob moves far up and down from its equilibrium position or just oscillates slightly above and below its equilibrium position the period is the same. This fact is very important in the use of springs in watches or clocks, because though air resistance and friction cause the motion to die down, that is, cause the amplitude to decrease, the period is not affected. Moreover, if we restore the amplitude by giving the bob an occasional push or pull, the period is still not affected. Hence the period can be used as a constant measure of time.

We learn also from (57) that we can fix the period or frequency as we wish. The frequency depends on $k$ and $m$. This means that if we choose $k$ and $m$ properly, we can make $f$, say, 1 per second. If we pick a particular spring, $k$ is fixed and, as we pointed out in connection with (50), can be measured. Then we select $m$, the mass of the bob, so that

$$\frac{1}{2\pi}\sqrt{\frac{k}{m}} = 1.$$

It is of interest to find out how the constants $A$ and $B$ of (52) or the $C$ and $\phi$ of (55), which are in effect the constants of integration, are determined in a particular situation. Suppose that we work with $A$ and $B$. When we considered the motion of a ball thrown up into the air, we found that the initial velocity and the position from which we measured height determined the constants of integration. The situation is similar here. We start the bob off by pulling it down some distance, say $D$, and then let it go. If we agree to measure time from the instant it is released, we have that at

$t = 0, y = -D$. If we substitute these values in (52), we obtain

**(58)**         $$-D = A \sin\left(\sqrt{\frac{k}{m}} \cdot 0\right) + B \cos\left(\sqrt{\frac{k}{m}} \cdot 0\right).$$

This tells us that $B = -D$.

If the bob is merely released after it is pulled down, the velocity $\dot{y} = 0$ when $t = 0$. This second condition is met by first obtaining $\dot{y}$ from (52). Thus

**(59)**         $$\dot{y} = A\sqrt{\frac{k}{m}} \cos\sqrt{\frac{k}{m}} \, t - B\sqrt{\frac{k}{m}} \sin\sqrt{\frac{k}{m}} \, t.$$

Because $\dot{y} = 0$ when $t = 0$,

$$0 = A\sqrt{\frac{k}{m}} \cos\left(\sqrt{\frac{k}{m}} \cdot 0\right) - B\sqrt{\frac{k}{m}} \sin\left(\sqrt{\frac{k}{m}} \cdot 0\right).$$

Then

$$A = 0.$$

Thus the final description of the motion for the initial conditions specified above is

**(60)**         $$y = -D \cos\sqrt{\frac{k}{m}} \, t.$$

The amplitude of the motion is precisely the distance down to which the bob is pulled before being released. Figure 10-15 shows the graph of the motion called for by (60). Of course, the bob's motion is up and down.

We can start the bob's motion differently. We can pull it down to a distance $-D$ below the equilibrium position and then give it an upward velocity of, say, $v_0$. Time can still be measured from the instant the bob is pushed upward at $y = -D$. The first condition still requires that (58) hold,

**Figure 10-15**

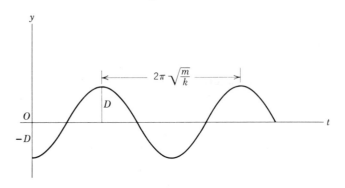

so that $B = -D$. However, to meet the condition on the initial velocity we now use (59) and require that $\dot{y} = v_0$ when $t = 0$. Hence

$$v_0 = A\sqrt{\frac{k}{m}}\ \cos\left(\sqrt{\frac{k}{m}} \cdot 0\right) - B\sqrt{\frac{k}{m}}\ \sin\left(\sqrt{\frac{k}{m}} \cdot 0\right).$$

From this equation we see that

$$A = v_0\sqrt{\frac{m}{k}}\ .$$

Now our description of the motion is

(61) $$\qquad y = v_0\sqrt{\frac{m}{k}}\ \sin\sqrt{\frac{k}{m}}\ t - D\cos\sqrt{\frac{k}{m}}\ t.$$

## EXERCISES

1. Suppose that we use the representation (55), namely,

$$y = C\sin\left(\sqrt{\frac{k}{m}}\ t + \phi\right),$$

to represent the motion of the bob. Use the initial conditions that $y$ is $-D$ and $\dot{y}$ is 0 at $t = 0$ to determine $C$ and $\phi$. $\qquad$ *Ans.* $C = -D$, $\phi = \pi/2$.

2. Use the representation (52) of the bob's motion and determine $A$ and $B$ under the initial conditions that the bob is at the equilibrium position when $t = 0$ but is given an initial velocity of 5 ft/sec. What is the amplitude of the motion?

3. What is the amplitude of the motion represented by (61)?
    *Suggestion:* Utilize the form (55).

4. Consider the motion of the bob given by (60). When is the velocity of the bob greatest? When is the acceleration of the bob greatest?

5. Suppose that the effect of gravity is ignored in the motion of a bob on a spring. How is (51) affected? What can you say about the solution of the equation in this case? $\qquad$ *Ans.* $d = 0$;
    (51) remains same but $y$ is measured from end of unextended spring.

6. A mass weighing $\frac{1}{4}$ pound and attached to one end of a spring is in equilibrium when the extension of the spring is 4 inches. The mass is raised 2 inches from its equilibrium position and then released. Find the displacement of the mass $t$ seconds after the start of the motion.

7. An elastic string stretches $\frac{1}{2}$ inch for every pound of mass attached to one end. If the upper end is fixed and a mass of 3 pounds is attached to the lower end and suddenly released, how far will the mass fall before reversing its motion and what is the period of oscillation of the mass? $\qquad$ *Ans.* 3 in.; 0.393 sec.

8. A spring, one end of which is fixed, stretches $\frac{1}{2}$ inch for every pound of mass attached to the free end. A 4-pound mass is attached to the free end and allowed to reach the equilibrium position. The mass is then struck so as to give

it instantaneously an upward velocity of 1 ft/sec. Find the function relating displacement and time of motion of the mass.

9.  A particle is attached to the middle of a uniform elastic string which is stretched between two points $A$ and $B$ on a smooth horizontal table (Fig. 10-16). If the particle is pulled to some point in the line $AB$ and then released, determine its subsequent motion. Assume that the displacement of the particle is small enought to keep the two parts of the string taut.

    *Suggestion:* If the length $AB$ is $2a$, if the unstretched length of the string is $2l$, $l < a$, and if the displacement of the particle at any instant is $x$, the two forces acting on the particle are $k(a - l - x)$ and $k(a - l + x)$. These forces oppose each other.

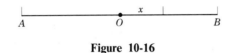

**Figure 10-16**

10. The balance wheel of a watch oscillates sinusoidally; that is, the angular displacement of any point on the rim is a sinusoidal function of the time. The maximum angular displacement of any point is $\pi/2$ and the period is $\frac{1}{2}$ second. Find the angular velocity and angular acceleration of any point (and therefore of the wheel) 2 seconds after it passes through the equilibrium position.                                    *Ans.*  $2\pi^2$ rad/sec; 0.

Our second application of the trigonometric function is to the study of the motion of a simple pendulum. This device, like that of a bob on a spring, was investigated during the seventeenth century as a possible standard of time, and the principal men in this work were Galileo and Huygens. The device is still important today, although its use in clocks is out of date. The simple pendulum consists of a string suspended from a fixed point $T$ (Fig. 10-17) and a bob attached to the other end. The equilibrium position of the pendulum is, of course, that in which the string is vertical. When the bob is pulled to one side and released, it continues to swing forward and back and, were there no air resistance, would continue this motion indefinitely.

When the bob is in any position to the right or left of its equilibrium position, it is said to be displaced; this displacement can be represented mathematically by the arc length $s$, which is measured positive to the right of $O$ and  negative to the left. Alternatively, the displacement of the bob can be represented by the angle $\theta$ which the string in any position makes with the vertical. The angle $\theta$ is taken to be positive when the bob is to the right of $O$ and negative when the bob is to the left of $O$. Because $s = l\theta$, where $l$ is the constant length of the string, we can readily convert from one variable to the other. Our first objective is to find the function that relates displacement and time.

What force keeps the bob moving? The answer is that the force of gravity, which in this case is the weight of the bob, gives the bob an acceleration. The weight, if $m$ is the mass of the bob, is $32m$. Let us see how

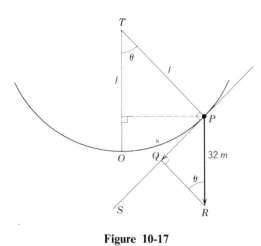

**Figure 10-17**

this force acts on the bob. Suppose that it is in a typical position, $P$ in Fig. 10-17. The force of gravity pulls straight down, whereas the bob moves along a circular arc. Hence we must determine what component of the force of gravity is effective in causing motion along the circle. The direction of the motion when the bob is at $P$ is tangential to the circle, and so we must ask for the component of gravity along the tangent $PS$. Let $PR$ be a vector that represents the force of gravity. The component of $PR$ along $PS$ is obtained by dropping a perpendicular from $R$ onto $PS$ thus obtaining $PQ$. The angle at $R$ is readily seen to be equal to $\theta$, and therefore the component is

$$PQ = 32m \sin \theta.$$

This component is directed toward the left when $s$ or $\theta$ is positive. However, a force that causes $s$ or $\theta$ to decrease must be negative. Hence we must write

$$PQ = -32m \sin \theta.$$

This force is the only one acting along the circle.

As in the case of the motion of the bob on the spring, we now utilize Newton's second law of motion, $F = ma$, to state that

**(62)** $$ma = -32m \sin \theta.$$

The acceleration is the second derivative of the distance traveled by the bob; that is, $a = d^2s/dt^2$ or $\ddot{s}$. Hence (62) becomes

**(63)** $$m\ddot{s} = -32m \sin \theta.$$

To obtain an equation in two variables, we use the fact that

$$s = l\theta.$$

Because $\theta$ is also a function of $t$, $ds/dt = (ds/d\theta)d\theta/dt$. Since $l$ is a constant,

$$\dot{s} = l\dot{\theta};$$

by differentiating once more, we obtain

$$\ddot{s} = l\ddot{\theta}.$$

Then (63) becomes, after dividing through by $m$ and by $l$,

**(64)** $$\ddot{\theta} = \frac{-32}{l} \sin \theta.$$

We would, of course, like to know the functional relation btween $\theta$ and $t$ which satisfies (64). Actually, the integration of (64) to find $d\theta/dt$ as a function of $t$ could be performed, but the step from $d\theta/dt$ as a function of $t$ to $\theta$ as a function of $t$ involves a difficulty that cannot be overcome at this time. (See Chap. 20, Sect. 12). Our alternative move at present is one which is commonly employed in the application of mathematics to physical problems, namely, to make a reasonable approximation. For the pendulum motion that occurs in a clock the angle $\theta$ does not become very large. We proved earlier that

$$\lim_{\theta \to 0} \frac{\sin \theta}{\theta} = 1.$$

This means that for $\theta$-values near 0, $\sin \theta$ and $\theta$ must be nearly equal in value. In fact, our table in Section 3 shows that for $\theta$ equal to 0.3 radians or less, $\sin \theta$ and $\theta$ differ at most in the third decimal place. Now 0.3 radians is more than 17°. Hence it would appear that the error committed in replacing $\sin \theta$ by $\theta$ when $\theta$ is small could not be very much. Therefore, we replace $\sin \theta$ by $\theta$ in (64) and consider the equation

**(65)** $$\ddot{\theta} = - \frac{32}{l} \theta.$$

We now compare (65) with (51) which reads

$$\ddot{y} = - \frac{k}{m} y.$$

These two equations are precisely the same except for the symbols. There is therefore no need to repeat the steps by which we determined the solution of (51). We have but to change the symbols in (52) and write

**(66)** $$\theta = A \sin \sqrt{\frac{32}{l}} \, t + B \cos \sqrt{\frac{32}{l}} \, t.$$

Moreover, we may take over at once from (56) the conclusion that the period $T$ of a pendulum is given by

**(67)** $$T = 2\pi \sqrt{\frac{l}{32}}$$

and that the number of oscillations per second or the frequency per second of the pendulum is, in view of (57),

**(68)**
$$f = \frac{1}{2\pi} \sqrt{\frac{32}{l}} \ .$$

The conclusions we drew about the motion of the bob on the spring also apply to the pendulum, except that an approximation is made in deriving the results for the pendulum. We see, in particular, that the period and frequency are independent of the amplitude of the motion.* Hence in the case of the pendulum, too, the decrease in amplitude caused by air resistance does not affect the period, and if the amplitude is maintained, as it is in pendulum clocks, by periodically giving the pendulum a little "push," the period is not affected. We see also that the period can be adjusted by varying the length $l$ of the string.

There is an additional point about the pendulum that does not apply to the bob on the spring. The period of the pendulum depends on the quantity 32, which is the acceleration due to gravity. If a pendulum clock has been set so that its period is 1 second and it is then taken to another location where the acceleration due to gravity is no longer 32—the top of a mountain, for example—the period no longer is 1 second. This dependence of the period on the acceleration of gravity is a defect in pendulum clocks. However, it is an ill wind that blows no good. If we carried through the mathematical work on the pendulum using $g$ for the acceleration of gravity in place of 32, the formula for the period would be

**(69)**
$$T = 2\pi \sqrt{\frac{l}{g}} \ .$$

Now suppose that the period of a pendulum is measured at some location by another timepiece; then (69) can be used to determine the acceleration of gravity at that location. The pendulum is, in fact, one of the most sensitive devices for measuring the acceleration of gravity.

We still must see how (66) can be adjusted to the initial data of any particular problem. Suppose that the bob of a pendulum is pulled aside, so that $\theta$ is 0.1 radian, and then released and suppose that time is measured from the instant the pendulum is released. These physical conditions mean in mathematical terms that $\theta = 0.1$ when $t = 0$ and that $\dot{\theta}$, which is the instantaneous rate of change of $\theta$ with respect to $t$ or what is called the *angular velocity*, is 0 when $t = 0$. If we substitute $\theta = 0.1$ and $t = 0$ in (66), we obtain

$$0.1 = A \sin 0 + B \cos 0$$

or

$$B = 0.1.$$

*This is not true for the solution of the *exact* pendulum equation (64).

To use the initial conditions on the angular velocity, we first find $\dot{\theta}$. This is

$$\dot{\theta} = A\sqrt{\frac{32}{l}} \cos\sqrt{\frac{32}{l}}\, t - B\sqrt{\frac{32}{l}} \sin\sqrt{\frac{32}{l}}\, t.$$

Because $\dot{\theta} = 0$ when $t = 0$,

$$0 = A\sqrt{\frac{32}{l}} \cos 0 - B\sqrt{\frac{32}{l}} \sin 0.$$

Then

$$A = 0.$$

Thus the function which represents the motion in this case is

(70)
$$\theta = 0.1 \cos\sqrt{\frac{32}{l}}\, t.$$

## EXERCISES

1. Given the equation $\ddot{y} = -ky$, write out at once the functional relation between $y$ and $t$.    Ans. $y = A \sin \sqrt{k}\, t + B \cos \sqrt{k}\, t$.

2. Suppose that the bob of a pendulum is pulled to the right so that $\theta = 0.1$ and is then given an initial angular velocity of $-0.05$ rad/sec. Find the function relating $\theta$ and $t$.

3. Suppose that a pendulum is in the equilibrium position and is given an initial velocity of 0.1 rad/sec to the right. Find the function relating $\theta$ and $t$.

$$\text{Ans. } \theta = 0.1\sqrt{\frac{l}{32}} \sin\sqrt{\frac{32}{l}}\, t.$$

4. What function relates the displacement $s$ of the pendulum and time $t$?

5. Discuss the variation in the angular velocity of the pendulum motion whose equation is given in (70).

6. Suppose that the period of a pendulum is half of what you would like it to be. How would you change $l$ to obtain the desired period?

7. How does the period of a pendulum depend on the mass of the bob?

8. Suppose that you wish to hit a target which moves like the bob of a pendulum. At what point in its path would you seek to hit it and why?
      Ans. When $\dot{\theta} = 0$.

9. A pendulum oscillates in a vertical plane about a fixed horizontal axis $O$. From the equilibrium position to the position of maximum deflection of $\theta = \pi/16$ radians, it takes $\frac{2}{3}$ seconds.

   (a)  What is the equation of motion of the pendulum?    Ans. $\theta = \dfrac{\pi}{16} \sin \dfrac{3}{4} \pi t$.

   (b)  Where will the pendulum have its maximum angular velocity and what is it?
      Ans. $\dot{\theta}_{max} = \dfrac{3}{64} \pi^2/\text{sec}$.

10. What is the linear velocity, that is, the velocity along the circular path, of the bob of the pendulum whose motion is described by (70)?

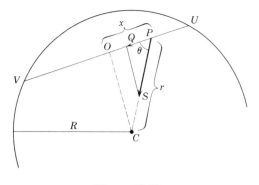

**Figure 10-18**

We consider next a third "application" of the trigonometric functions. Suppose that a straight tunnel is dug through the earth from point $U$ to point $V$ (Fig. 10-18). An object is placed just inside the tunnel at $U$ and then released. What is its subsequent motion?

Of course, if the object is to move from $U$, some force must act on it to provide acceleration and thus permit it to gain velocity. This force is the force of gravity. The force of gravity of the entire earth acts differently on objects *inside* the earth than on objects outside. We recall that the usual formula for the force with which an object of mass $M$ attracts another of mass $m$ external to the first one is

$$(71) \qquad\qquad F = \frac{GMm}{r^2}.$$

When the mass $m$ is inside the earth, the earth's gravitational force is given by

$$(72) \qquad\qquad F = \frac{GM}{R^3}\, mr$$

where $G$ is the usual gravitational constant, $M$ is the mass of the earth, $R$ is the radius of the earth, $m$ is the mass being attracted, and $r$ is the distance of the mass $m$ from the center of the earth. This force, too, acts to pull objects toward the center of the earth. As we shall see later (Chap. 16, Sect. 7), formula (72) is a consequence of (71). Since $G$, $M$, and $R$ are constants, let us write for convenience

$$(73) \qquad\qquad F = kmr$$

where $k$ is $GM/R^3$.

The object is free to move along the tunnel $UV$. Hence we should first determine how effective the force of gravity is along the tunnel. Suppose that the object of mass $m$ is at $P$. The force of gravitation pulls it in the direction $PC$, where $C$ is the center of the earth. Let $PS$ represent the direction and magnitude of the force $F$ given by (73). The effectiveness of this force in causing the object at $P$ to move along the tunnel is the component of $PS$ in the direction $UV$. As usual, to obtain this component we drop a perpendicular from $S$ onto $UV$; this determines the point $Q$. The length $PQ$ is the component of $PS$ along $UV$, and $PQ$ equals $|PS|\cos\theta$ where $|PS|$ is the magnitude of the vector $PS$ and $\theta$ is the angle shown in Fig. 10-18.

To study the motion of the mass $m$ along the tunnel, it is desirable to introduce coordinates that indicate its position. The most convenient way to do this is to choose the midpoint $O$ of $UV$ as the origin and let distances from $O$ along $UV$ be denoted by $x$, $x$ taken positive in the direction $OU$ and negative in the direction $OV$.

When the object is at $P$, the distance $PC$ is $r$ and $OP$ is $x$. From Fig. 10-18 it is at once evident that

$$\cos\theta = \frac{x}{r}.$$

Because $PQ$ is $|PS|\cos\theta$ and, by (73), $|PS|$ is $kmr$, then $PQ = kmx$. However, $PQ$ acts to decrease $x$. Hence we must write

$$PQ = -kmx.$$

Newton's second law of motion is, of course, $F = ma$. In the present case the acceleration is $d^2x/dt^2$ or $\ddot{x}$. Hence

$$m\ddot{x} = -kmx$$

or

**(74)**                                $$\ddot{x} = -kx.$$

What function relates $x$ and $t$? We need but compare (74) with (51). The two are identical if $k$ here replaces the $k/m$ there. We know then from (52) that

**(75)**                          $$x = A\sin\sqrt{k}\,t + B\cos\sqrt{k}\,t.$$

We now fix $A$ and $B$ to meet the initial conditions of our present problem. At time $t = 0$ the object is at $U$. Suppose that the distance $OU$ is $x_0$. Then at time $t = 0$, $x = x_0$. Because the object is just placed at $U$, it has no initial velocity; that is, at $t = 0$, $\dot{x}$ is 0. The first initial condition yields from (75)

$$x_0 = A\sin 0 + B\cos 0.$$

Hence

$$B = x_0.$$

From (75) we obtain by differentiation

$$\dot{x} = A\sqrt{k}\,\cos\sqrt{k}\,t - B\sqrt{k}\,\sin\sqrt{k}\,t.$$

The initial condition that $\dot{x} = 0$ when $t = 0$ yields

$$0 = A\sqrt{k}\,\cos 0 - B\sqrt{k}\,\sin 0,$$

so that

$$A = 0.$$

The resulting function is then

**(76)** $$x = x_0 \cos \sqrt{k}\, t.$$

The motion of the object placed at $U$ is now clear. The object oscillates back and forth from $U$ to $V$ to $U$. We can even calculate the period of the motion. Formula (56) applied to the present case, where $k$ replaces the $k/m$ in (56), becomes

$$T = \frac{2\pi}{\sqrt{k}}.$$

However, $k = GM/R^3$ and, as we may recall from formula (61) of Chapter 6, $GM = 32R^2$. Hence $k = 32/R$. Then

**(77)** $$T = 2\pi\sqrt{\frac{R}{32}}.$$

If we use $4000 \cdot 5280$ for $R$, then $T = 5100$ seconds or 85 minutes.

Formulas (76) and (77) are interesting not only because of what they do say but also because of what they do not say. Neither involves a particular location for the tunnel $UV$. If we choose any two points on the earth's surface and connect them by a tunnel, the resulting motion is still described by (76) and the resulting period by (77). Formula (76) involves the length of the tunnel, because $x_0$ is half the length, but the period of the motion is the same no matter where the tunnel is located.

The subject of motion in a tunnel through the earth has an interesting variation. Instead of building a straight tunnel from $U$ to $V$, we might fashion a curved tunnel (Fig. 10-19). Then the acceleration at the outset, being directed more toward the center of the earth, is greater and an object sliding along the tunnel acquires more velocity sooner than in a straight tunnel. Of course, the path is longer for a curved tunnel, and therefore the gain in velocity can be offset by the increased length of the path. What path requires least time? This question cannot be answered by the methods of

**Figure 10-19**

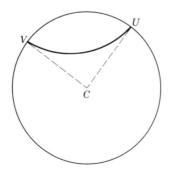

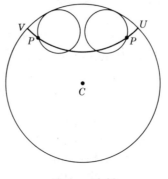

**Figure 10-20**

the ordinary calculus—it is a problem belonging to the subject of the calculus of variations—but the answer, which was supplied by Newton, is worth noting.

Newton showed that the best path is an arc of a hypocycloid joining $U$ and $V$. A hypocycloid is the path traced by a definite point $P$ of a small circle rolling on the inside of a larger circle (Fig. 10-20). In the case of a tunnel through the earth, the larger circle is the circumference of the earth and the size of the smaller circle depends on the location of $U$ and $V$. The hypocycloid starts out with a vertical drop (that is, the tangent at $U$ goes through the center of the earth), and so an object sliding along it has the maximum possible acceleration at the outset.

The following data give some idea of what can be gained by using a hypocycloidal path. Suppose that a straight tunnel is dug between New York and San Francisco. Along the surface of the earth the two cities are about 2,575 miles apart, but the tunnel would be 2,530 miles long (Fig. 10-21). At the midpoint the tunnel would be 206 miles below the surface; the maximum velocity acquired by the object, which would be at the midpoint, would be 1.57 mi/sec; and a one-way journey, according to (77), would take about $42\frac{1}{2}$ minutes. The hypocycloidal path would be 2940

**Figure 10-21**

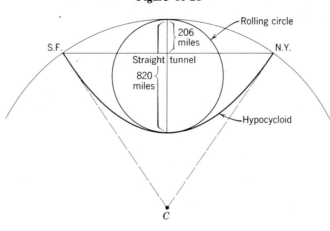

miles long. At the midpoint the tunnel would be 820 miles below the surface; the velocity of the object at that point would be 3 mi/sec; and the one-way journey would take 26 minutes.*

## EXERCISES

1. How do you account physically for the fact that the period of the motion is the same whether the tunnel $UV$ (Fig. 10-18) is a short one or even as long as the one through the center of the earth?

2. Suppose that a straight tunnel is bored from London to Paris, a distance of 200 miles, and an object is placed inside the tunnel at London. What is the maximum velocity that the object acquires during its journey?     *Ans.* $100\sqrt{k}$ .

3. Suppose that an object is placed in the tunnel $UV$ (Fig. 10-18) at a point two-thirds of the way from $U$ to $O$ and then released. What function describes its motion and what is the period of the motion?

$$\textit{Ans. If } OU = x_0, \text{ then } x = \frac{x_0}{3} \cos \sqrt{kt} \; ; 2\pi/\sqrt{k} \; .$$

4. Suppose that an object is placed at the center of the tunnel $UV$ (Fig. 10-18) and then released. What is its subsequent motion?                    *Ans.* No motion.

5. Suppose that an object is placed at any distance $\bar{x}$ from the center of the tunnel $UV$ (Fig. 10-18) and then released. Graph the period of the motion as a function of $\bar{x}$. Of course, $\bar{x}$ can vary from $-x_0$ to $x_0$, where $x_0$, as in the text, is one half of $UV$. The results of Exercises 3 and 4 would come in handy here.

6. A circularly cylindrical block of wood 1 foot in diameter and weighing 100 pounds floats in water with its axis vertical (Fig. 10-22). The cylinder is depressed 2 feet and then released. What function describes its subsequent motion?

   *Suggestion:* This problem involves Archimedes' principle which states that an object immersed (partly or entirely) in water is buoyed up by a force that is equal to the weight of the displaced water. Suppose that, when the cylinder just floats in the water, $d$ feet of it are immersed (this is the equilibrium position). The volume of displaced water is then $\pi(\frac{1}{2})^2 d$ and, because water weighs 62.5 lb/cu ft, the weight of the displaced water is $\pi(\frac{1}{2})^2 d(62.5)$ pounds. The cylinder weighs 100 pounds (in air) and because it floats, the weight of the cylinder must just equal the weight of the displaced water. Then
   (a)   $100 = (\frac{1}{2})^2(62.5)\pi d = 15.6\pi d$.
   Introduce a vertical coordinate axis and let the origin $O$ be at the water's surface. Let the cylinder now be depressed, so that the point $P$ which in the equilibrium position is at the surface is now $y$ feet below. Then $d - y$ feet of its length are in water ($y$ is positive upward). Gravity still exerts a force of 100 pounds downward, but the upward (buoyant) force of the displaced water is now $15.6\pi(d - y)$. The net force on the cylinder is now
   (b)   $15.6\pi(d - y) - 100$.

*Newton considered the motion of an object in a tunnel just as an interesting phenomenon. But this phenomenon is being taken seriously by present-day railroad engineers. See L. K. Edwards: "High Speed Tube Transportation," *Scientific American*, August 1965. For further details on curved tubes see the *American Mathematical Monthly*, June-July, 1969, pp. 708-709.

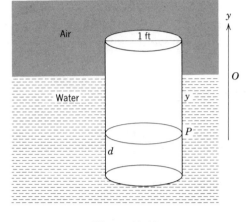

**Figure 10-22**

In view of ($a$), the net force is
(c)    $- 15.6\pi y$.
This net force causes acceleration and therefore an up and down motion of the bob. Now use Newton's second law of motion. Note that the mass of the cylinder is also 100 pounds and the net force of the water, which should be in poundals, is 32 times the quantity in (c).

> *Ans.* The diff. equation is $100\ddot{y} = -32 \cdot 15.6\pi y$.

7. Suppose that a tunnel similar to that discussed in the text is dug through the moon. Given that the mass of the moon is $\frac{1}{81}$ of that of the earth, the radius of the moon is $\frac{3}{11}$ of that of the earth and the acceleration of gravity on the surface of the moon is $\frac{1}{6}$ that on the surface of the earth, if an object is placed at one end of the tunnel and released, what is the period of the motion in the tunnel?

> *Ans.* $T = 54\sqrt{3}\,\pi/11\sqrt{11k}$ .

The applications that we have considered—the motion of a bob on a spring, the motion of a simple pendulum, and motion along a tunnel in the earth—illustrate some important applications of the calculus of trigonometric functions. But they also show something more. The same mathematical technique applies to a variety of different physical situations, so that if one masters the technique, he can immediately obtain insight into a variety of situations. In all of the above applications the fundamental physical fact, when expressed in mathematical terms, is that some function $y$ of the independent variable $x$ satisfies the equation

**(78)**
$$\frac{d^2y}{dx^2} = -Ky$$

and, as we have seen, the function turns out to be of the form

**(79)**
$$y = A \sin\sqrt{K}\,x + B \cos\sqrt{K}\,x$$

or

**(80)**
$$y = C \sin(\sqrt{K}\,x + \phi).$$

We then fix the constants $A$ and $B$ or the constants $C$ and $\phi$ to suit particular conditions of the physical situation. Motions obeying the differential equation (78) or its consequence (79) are called *simple harmonic motions*.

## EXERCISES

1. The amplitude of a body undergoing simple harmonic motion is $a$ and its period is $\tau$. Find its maximum velocity. *Ans.* $2\pi a/\tau$.

2. The maximum velocity of a body undergoing simple harmonic motion is 2 ft/sec and its period is $\frac{1}{5}$ second. What is its amplitude? *Ans.* $1/5\pi$ ft.

# CHAPTER ELEVEN
# THE INVERSE TRIGONOMETRIC FUNCTIONS

**1. The Notion of an Inverse Function.** Functions are, of course, used to express relationships between variables, and it is helpful both from the standpoint of physical meaning and mathematical technique to designate one variable as the independent variable and the other as the dependent variable. Thus in studying the relation between the velocity of a body which is dropped near the surface of the earth and the time of fall, that is, the function $v = 32t$, it is usually desirable to regard the time as the independent variable and the velocity as the dependent variable. Certainly, to answer the question of what velocity is acquired in a given number of seconds of fall, the choice of $t$ as the independent variable is helpful.

However, one may be interested in determining how many seconds are required for the velocity to reach 100 ft/sec, 200 ft/sec, etc. To answer this question it is more convenient to write the formula as $t = v/32$, substitute the given values of $v$, and then calculate $t$. That is, it is more convenient to regard $v$ as the independent variable and $t$ as the dependent variable. One says that $t = v/32$ is the *inverse function* of $v = 32t$.

Let us look at the concept of inverse function graphically. If we graph the independent variable along the horizontal axis and the dependent variable along the vertical axis, the graph of $v = 32t$ looks as shown in Fig. 11-1, and the graph of $t = v/32$ appears as in Fig. 11-2. Actually, either graph represents both the original function and its inverse. Just as we can choose a value of $t$, find the point on either graph that has this $t$-value, and then find the corresponding value of $v$, so we can choose a value of $v$, go over to the point on the graph having this $v$-value, and find the corresponding value of $t$.

As far as the basic relation between $t$ and $v$ is concerned, both functions $v = 32t$ and $t = v/32$ say the same thing and both graphs illustrate the same relation. The choice of one function and graph rather than the other is merely a matter of convenience in answering particular questions.

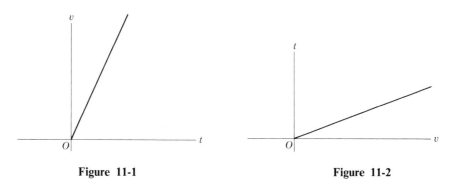

Figure 11-1                          Figure 11-2

A slight difficulty arises when we consider such functions as

**(1)**
$$d = \frac{v^2}{64}.$$

This function tells us the distance $d$ that a dropped body has fallen when it has acquired a given velocity $v$; thus, by the time the body has acquired a velocity of, say 10 ft/sec, it has fallen $\frac{25}{16}$ feet. We may be interested in how much velocity a body acquires in falling a given number of feet. In this case it is more convenient to express $v$ as a function of $d$. If, however, we proceed to solve for $v$, we find, first, that

**(2)**
$$v^2 = 64d.$$

This function is called multiple-valued, because to each value of $d$ there are two values of $v$, namely,

**(3)**
$$v = +8\sqrt{d} \quad \text{and} \quad v = -8\sqrt{d}.$$

We pointed out in Chapter 2 that the calculus cannot work effectively with multiple-valued functions. Given a value of $d$, we must know which value of $v$ is to be taken or, if we want the instantaneous rate of change of $v$ with respect to $d$, we must know which of the two single-valued functions in (3) we should differentiate. In simple falling-body problems, we would most likely use $v = 8\sqrt{d}$, because we usually take distance and velocity to be positive.

Which function is the inverse function to $d = v^2/64$? Let us look at the situation graphically. The original function is shown in Fig. 11-3 and

Figure 11-3

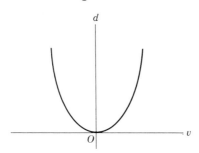

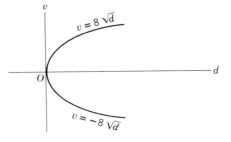

**Figure 11-4**

the multiple-valued function $v^2 = 64d$ is graphed in Fig. 11-4. In the domain 0 to $-\infty$ for $v$, the original function $d$ increases from 0 to $\infty$. This behavior of $v$ and $d$ is also shown in the lower half of Fig. 11-4, although there $d$ is the independent variable. As $v$ varies from 0 to $\infty$ in the original function, $d$ increases from 0 to $\infty$. This relation is shown in the upper half of Fig. 11-4 where, again, $d$ is shown as the independent variable.

The graphs suggest the following. We can and do define the inverse function of $d = v^2/64$ to be the multiple-valued function $v^2 = 64d$ or $v = \pm 8\sqrt{d}$. This function is said to have two branches: $v = 8\sqrt{d}$ and $v = -8\sqrt{d}$. The first branch serves as the inverse function to $d = v^2/64$ when $v$ runs from 0 to $\infty$, and the second branch serves as the inverse function to $d = v^2/64$ when $v$ varies from $-\infty$ to 0.

In other words, when the original function rises and falls or falls and rises, we must break up the entire domain of the independent variable into separate domains, in each of which the function is continually increasing or continually decreasing. In each separate domain the original function has a distinct inverse function. The collection of separate inverse functions belongs to one multiple-valued function, just as $v = 8\sqrt{d}$ and $v = -8\sqrt{d}$ belong to $v^2 = 64d$. The multiple-valued function is the inverse function to the *entire* original function. Each separate single-valued inverse function is also called a branch of the entire multiple-valued inverse function.

**2. The Inverse Trigonometric Functions.** As in the case of the algebraic functions, it is often convenient to utilize the inverse functions of the trigonometric functions. Let us first acquire a little information about the inverse trigonometric functions.

We start with the original function $y = \sin x$. Its graph is repeated here (Fig. 11-5) for convenience. We now wish to define the inverse function of $y = \sin x$. By definition, this inverse function assigns to each value of $y$ the value or values of $x$ which correspond to $y$ in $y = \sin x$. We cannot solve $y = \sin x$ for $x$, at least not so as to express the solution in terms of available notation, and therefore we introduce a new one. We write

**(4)**                     $x = \sin^{-1} y.$

This is read "$x$ is the inverse sine function of $y$." This inverse function is multiple-valued, because to each value of $y$ in the interval $-1 \leq y \leq 1$ there is an infinite number of values of $x$. However, in view of what we

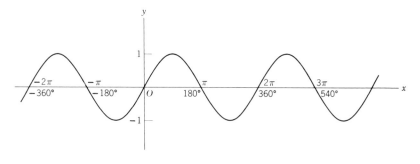

**Figure 11-5**

pointed out about inverse functions for functions that increase and decrease, we may be able to break up the domain of $x$ into a number of separate domains, so that in each domain there is just one $x$ for a given $y$. Thus consider the domain $-\pi/2$ to $\pi/2$ for $x$; here $y = \sin x$ always increases, and we can now say that as $y$ varies from $-1$ to $1$, $x$ varies from $-\pi/2$ to $\pi/2$. In other words, if we restrict $x$ to the range $-\pi/2$ to $\pi/2$, there is only one branch of the inverse function. We can also limit $x$ to the domain $\pi/2$ to $3\pi/2$; then we can say that as $y$ varies from $-1$ to $1$, $x$ varies from $3\pi/2$ to $\pi/2$. This range of $x$-values furnishes another branch of the inverse function $x = \sin^{-1} y$.

Because we must work with single-valued functions, it is necessary to restrict the domain of $x$-values. When the $x$-range is $-\pi/2$ to $\pi/2$, the corresponding branch of (4) is called the principal branch and the values of $x$ are called the principal values. When the function $x = \sin^{-1} y$ is used without mention of the range of $x$-values, it is understood that the principal branch is meant. Then for the principal branch of

$$x = \sin^{-1} y$$

as $y$ varies from $-1$ to $1$, $x$ varies from $-\pi/2$ to $\pi/2$.

The notation $\sin^{-1}$ is both good and bad. It is suggested by the fact that the inverse of the number 2, say, is $2^{-1}$. On the other hand, we do *not* mean $1/\sin y$ by $\sin^{-1} y$. Rather, we mean to denote the inverse function to $y = \sin x$ in the sense of inverse function already discussed. An alternative notation, $x = \text{arc} \sin y$, which is an abbreviation for $x$ is the arc (or angle) whose sine is $y$, is really preferable to avoid ambiguity but takes more time and space to write. We use the notation in (4) because it is standard. If we really wish to denote $1/\sin y$ in terms of negative exponents, we write $(\sin y)^{-1}$ or $\csc y$.

The function (4) is the inverse function to $y = \sin x$. However, mathematicians like to use $x$ for the independent variable and $y$ for the dependent variable, so that we write

**(5)**                                    $$y = \sin^{-1} x$$

for the inverse function. For the principal branch the domain of $x$ is $-1$ to $1$ and the range of $y$ is $-\pi/2$ to $\pi/2$. Figure 11-6 shows the graph of $y = \sin^{-1} x$.

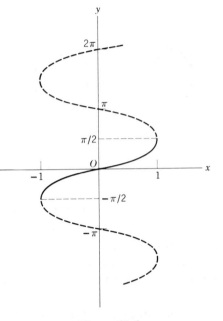

**Figure 11-6**

To each trigonometric function there is an inverse function, which is multiple-valued. The problem of choosing the principal branch is the same as for $y = \sin x$; that is, we must choose a domain of $x$ in which the original function is either continually increasing or continually decreasing and define the principal branch for that domain of $x$. Let us dispose of the details.

For the function $y = \cos x$, which is illustrated in Figure 10-5, we can introduce the inverse function

$$x = \cos^{-1} y,$$

or, letting $x$ denote the independent variable and $y$ the dependent variable,

**(6)**                                   $y = \cos^{-1} x.$

Figure 11-7 illustrates this function. To choose a principal branch, we note that for $y = \cos x$, $y$ decreases from 1 to $-1$ as $x$ increases from 0 to $\pi$. In this domain of $x$-values there is only one value of $x$ for each value of $y$. Hence the principal branch of $y = \cos^{-1} x$ is chosen to be from $-1$ to 1 for $x$ and, as $x$ varies from $-1$ to 1, $y$ varies from $\pi$ to 0. As in the case of (5), when no range of $y$ is mentioned, the principal values are understood to be the ones to be used.

For the function $y = \tan x$, whose behavior is shown in Fig. 10-6, the inverse function is

$$x = \tan^{-1} y$$

or, to use the more customary convention regarding independent and dependent variable,

**(7)**                                   $y = \tan^{-1} x.$

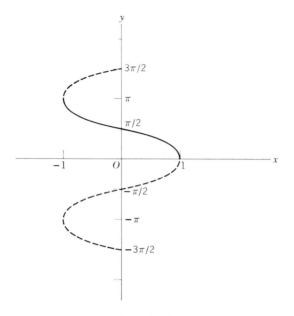

**Figure 11-7**

The graph of this function is shown in Fig. 11-8. The principal branch is the one for which, as $x$ varies from $-\infty$ to $\infty$, $y$ varies from $-\pi/2$ to $\pi/2$.

The function $y = \cot x$, which is graphed in Fig. 10-7, has as its inverse function

**(8)**                         $$y = \cot^{-1} x$$

whose graph is shown in Fig. 11-9. The principal branch is that for which, as $x$ varies from $-\infty$ to $\infty$, $y$ varies from $\pi$ to 0.

The definition of the inverse function of $y = \sec x$ presents a bit of a

**Figure 11-8**

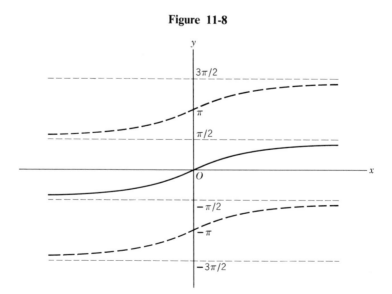

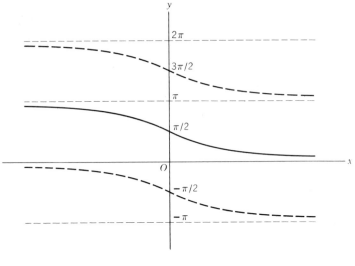

**Figure 11-9**

problem. The inverse function

**(9)** $$y = \sec^{-1} x$$

is illustrated in Fig. 11-10. There is no way of selecting a principal branch so that, as $x$ increases continuously from $-\infty$ to $\infty$, $y$ will continually increase or continually decrease. We therefore choose to be guided by the desirable relation that

$$\sec^{-1} x = \cos^{-1}\left(\frac{1}{x}\right),$$

that is, that the angle whose secant is $x$ equals the angle whose cosine is $1/x$. We define the principal branch of (9) to be the one for which, as $x$

**Figure 11-10**

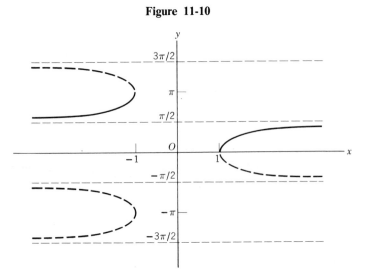

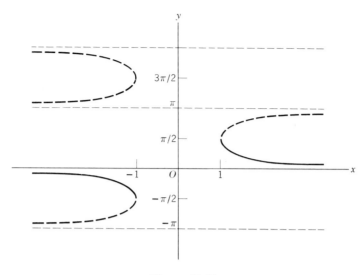

**Figure 11-11**

varies from $-\infty$ to $-1$, $y$ varies from $\pi/2$ to $\pi$, and as $x$ varies from 1 to $\infty$, $y$ varies from 0 to $\pi/2$. Thus if, for example, $x = 2$, then $\sec^{-1} 2 = \cos^{-1} \frac{1}{2}$. Now $\cos^{-1} \frac{1}{2} = \pi/3$. As we can see from Fig. 11-10, our choice of the principal branch permits $\sec^{-1} 2$ to be $\pi/3$. The same applies, for example, to $x = -2$.

The problem of choosing the principal branch presents itself also in defining the inverse function of $y = \csc x$. The graph of

**(10)** $$y = \csc^{-1} x$$

is shown in Fig. 11-11. There is no way of choosing a principal branch so that, as $x$ varies from $-\infty$ to $\infty$, $y$ will continually increase or continually decrease. Because it is desirable that

$$\csc^{-1} x = \sin^{-1}(1/x),$$

we define the principal branch to be the one for which, as $x$ varies from $-\infty$ to $-1$, $y$ varies from 0 to $-\pi/2$, and as $x$ varies from 1 to $\infty$, $y$ varies from $\pi/2$ to 0.

## EXERCISES

**1.** What is the inverse function of the function $y = (x - 1)(x - 2)$?
$$\text{Ans. } x = \frac{3 + \sqrt{1 + 4y}}{2} \text{ and } x = \frac{3 - \sqrt{1 + 4y}}{2}.$$

**2.** Find the principal values of:
   (a)  $\sin^{-1} 0.5$.                *Ans.* $\pi/6$.  (e)  $\tan^{-1}(-1)$.         *Ans.* $-\pi/4$.
   (b)  $\sin^{-1}(-0.5)$.                         (f)  $\sin^{-1}(-0.3)$.
   (c)  $\cos^{-1}(0.5)$.             *Ans.* $\pi/3$.  (g)  $\cos^{-1}(0.7)$.         *Ans.* 45° 34′.
   (d)  $\cos^{-1}(-0.5)$.                         (h)  $\cos^{-1}(-1)$.

3. What is
   (a) $\lim\limits_{x\to\infty} \tan^{-1}x$?    *Ans.* $\pi/2$.   (b) $\lim\limits_{x\to-\infty} \tan^{-1}x$?

4. Evaluate:
   (a) $\sin(\sin^{-1}0.5)$.    *Ans.* 0.5.   (e) $\sin(\sec^{-1}(-2))$.   *Ans.* 0.8660.
   (b) $\cos(\sin^{-1}0.5)$.        (f) $\cos(\sec^{-1}2)$.
   (c) $\sec(\sin^{-1}0.5)$.    *Ans.* 1.15.   (g) $\sin(2\sin^{-1}0.5)$.   *Ans.* $\sqrt{3}/2$.
   (d) $\sin(\sec^{-1}2)$.        (h) $\cos(2\sin^{-1}1)$.

**3. The Differentiation of the Inverse Trigonometric Functions.** The calculus is concerned with the use of derivatives and integrals of functions. Let us then consider the question, what is the derivative of $y = \sin^{-1}x$? Because this is a new type of function, it would be natural to try to find its derivative by applying the method of increments. This approach proves to be difficult. However, an inverse function is intimately related to its original function, and perhaps we can learn something about the derivative of the inverse function from that of the original function.

Let us consider

(11) $$y = \sin x$$

and its inverse function

(12) $$x = \sin^{-1}y.$$

In the present discussion of the inverse function we use $y$ for the independent variable and $x$ for the dependent variable to help keep in mind how these variables relate to the original function.

What we seek in terms of the notation in (12) is

$$\lim_{\Delta y\to 0} \frac{\Delta x}{\Delta y}$$

where $\Delta y$ is the increment in $y$ at some value $y_0$ and $\Delta x$ is the corresponding increment in $x$ at the value $x_0 = \sin^{-1}y_0$. Because $\Delta x$ and $\Delta y$ are numbers and not 0,

(13) $$\frac{\Delta x}{\Delta y} = \frac{1}{\dfrac{\Delta y}{\Delta x}}.$$

Moreover, as $\Delta y$ approaches 0, $\Delta x$ approaches 0 because they are related by the function (12) and, as in the case for any continuous function (see Chap. 6, Sect. 2), when the value $y_0 + \Delta y$ of the independent variable approaches $y_0$, the corresponding values $x_0 + \Delta x$ of the dependent variable approach $x_0$. However, the $y$ and $x$ in (12) are the same as the $y$ and $x$ in (11), and for (11) we know that as $\Delta x$ approaches 0, $\Delta y$ approaches 0. Hence to speak of $\Delta y$ approaching 0 for the difference quotient $\Delta x/\Delta y$ is equivalent to speaking of $\Delta x$ approaching 0 for the difference quotient $\Delta y/\Delta x$. Because the left and right sides of (13) are equal for all $\Delta x$ and $\Delta y$

as both of these approach 0 simultaneously,

**(14)**
$$\lim_{\Delta y \to 0} \frac{\Delta x}{\Delta y} = \lim_{\Delta x \to 0} \frac{1}{\dfrac{\Delta y}{\Delta x}} .$$

Finding the limit of the right side of (14) calls for finding the limit of the quotient of two functions, namely, 1 and $\Delta y / \Delta x$. However, the limit of a quotient is the quotient of the limits provided that the limit of the denominator is not 0.* Hence

**(15)**
$$\frac{dx}{dy} = \frac{1}{\dfrac{dy}{dx}} .$$

Of course, (15) also holds for the derived functions wherever both exist.

This result is of general use in the calculus and we state it more formally for future reference.

**Theorem:** If $y$ is a function of $x$ and $x$ as a function of $y$ is the inverse function corresponding to some domain of $x$-values of the original function, then

**(16)**
$$\frac{dx}{dy} = \frac{1}{\dfrac{dy}{dx}}$$

provided that $dy/dx$ is not 0.

The statement of the result (16) in the Leibnizian notation can be misleading. It appears that all we are saying, for example, is that

$$\frac{7}{3} = \frac{1}{\dfrac{3}{7}} .$$

However, (16) is not that simple because neither $dx/dy$ nor $dy/dx$ is a quotient, and we must go through a proof involving limits, as we did, in order to establish (16). The Leibnizian notation may help us to remember the result, as it does in the case of the chain rule, but it is deceptive as to the thought behind the symbols.

Let us see how this theorem can be used to find the derived functions of the inverse trigonometric functions. We return to (11) and (12), namely, $y = \sin x$ and its inverse function $x = \sin^{-1} y$. According to (16),

$$\frac{dx}{dy} = \frac{1}{\dfrac{dy}{dx}} .$$

* See the discussion preceding Theorem 7, Chapter 6.

The $dy/dx$ refers to the derived function of the original function. Because this is $y = \sin x$, we have

$$\frac{dx}{dy} = \frac{1}{\cos x} .$$

The independent variable in the inverse function is $y$, and we want to express the derived function of the inverse function in terms of its independent variable, as we did for all other functions that we have studied. We know that

$$\frac{1}{\cos x} = \frac{1}{\pm\sqrt{1 - \sin^2 x}} = \frac{1}{\pm\sqrt{1 - y^2}} .$$

Thus we have the result in terms of $y$, but there is still the question of which sign to take for the radical. We must recall here that we chose as the principal branch of $x = \sin^{-1} y$ the range $-\pi/2$ to $\pi/2$ for $x$. In this interval $\cos x$ is always positive. We must then choose the positive radical. Our result is

$$\frac{dx}{dy} = \frac{1}{\sqrt{1 - y^2}} .$$

If we represent the independent variable in the inverse function by $x$ and the dependent variable by $y$, our result can be formulated thus:

**Theorem:**   If $y = \sin^{-1} x$, then in the interval $-\pi/2$ to $\pi/2$ for $y$

(17) $$\frac{dy}{dx} = \frac{1}{\sqrt{1 - x^2}} .$$

Let us determine next the derived function of the inverse cosine function. The original function is $y = \cos x$, and we write the inverse function as $x = \cos^{-1} y$, again to keep the identities of the $x$'s and $y$'s clear. In view of (16),

$$\frac{dx}{dy} = \frac{1}{\dfrac{dy}{dx}} = -\frac{1}{\sin x} .$$

To express $dx/dy$ in terms of the independent variable of the inverse function, we do much the same as we did in the case of the inverse sine function. Thus

$$-\frac{1}{\sin x} = -\frac{1}{\pm\sqrt{1 - \cos^2 x}} = -\frac{1}{\pm\sqrt{1 - y^2}} .$$

To determine which sign to use we note that the $x$-values of $y = \cos x$ are restricted to the interval $0$ to $\pi$ for the purpose of defining the principal branch of the inverse function. In this interval sin $x$ is positive. Hence we must use the positive sign for the *radical*. Our result then is

$$\frac{dx}{dy} = -\frac{1}{\sqrt{1-y^2}} .$$

If we represent the independent variable in the inverse function by $x$ and the dependent variable by $y$, our result is the following:

**Theorem:**  If $y = \cos^{-1} x$, then in the interval 0 to $\pi$ for $y$

(18) $$\frac{dy}{dx} = -\frac{1}{\sqrt{1-x^2}} .$$

We determine next the derived function of the inverse tangent function. The original function is $y = \tan x$ and the inverse function is $x = \tan^{-1} y$. By (16)

$$\frac{dx}{dy} = \frac{1}{\dfrac{dy}{dx}} = \frac{1}{\sec^2 x} .$$

To write the result in terms of the independent variable $y$ of the inverse function, we note that

$$\frac{1}{\sec^2 x} = \frac{1}{1+\tan^2 x} = \frac{1}{1+y^2} .$$

Then

$$\frac{dx}{dy} = \frac{1}{1+y^2} .$$

If we represent the independent variable in the inverse function by $x$ and the dependent variable by $y$, we have the following theorem:

**Theorem:**  If $y = \tan^{-1} x$, then

(19) $$\frac{dy}{dx} = \frac{1}{1+x^2} .$$

This result holds for every branch of $y = \tan^{-1} x$.

We should, of course, remember in connection with each differentiation formula that *the chain rule extends the scope of these formulas* immeasurably. Thus suppose that we wish to find the derived function of

(20) $$y = \cos^{-1} \frac{1}{x} .$$

Before we differentiate, let us note the domain of values for $x$. Because the cosines of angles can vary only from $-1$ to $+1$, that is, $1/x$ can vary from

$-1$ to $+1$, $x$ in (20) can vary from $-\infty$ to $-1$ and from 1 to $\infty$. To use the chain rule, we let

$$u = \frac{1}{x}.$$

Then (20) becomes

$$y = \cos^{-1} u, \qquad u = \frac{1}{x}.$$

By the chain rule and by (18),

$$\frac{dy}{dx} = \frac{dy}{du} \cdot \frac{du}{dx} = - \frac{1}{\sqrt{1 - u^2}} \cdot \frac{-1}{x^2} = \frac{1}{\sqrt{1 - \left(\frac{1}{x}\right)^2}} \frac{1}{x^2}.$$

To simplify the result we can write first

$$\frac{dy}{dx} = \frac{1}{\sqrt{\frac{(x^2 - 1)}{x^2}}} \frac{1}{x^2}.$$

Now we must be careful. The radical must yield a positive quantity because this is what we have agreed to mean by it. When both roots are possible, we have written $\pm\sqrt{\phantom{x}}$ and when the negative root is called for, we have written $-\sqrt{\phantom{x}}$. Hence in taking the $x^2$ out of the radical we *cannot* write

$$\frac{dy}{dx} = \frac{1}{\frac{1}{x}\sqrt{x^2 - 1}} \frac{1}{x^2}$$

because when $x$ is negative, as it can be, the value of the left factor is negative. Rather, we must write

$$\frac{dy}{dx} = \frac{1}{\frac{1}{|x|}\sqrt{x^2 - 1}} \frac{1}{x^2}.$$

To simplify further, we note that $1/x^2$ is always positive. $|x|$ is also always positive. Hence the division of $|x|$ into $x^2$ must yield $|x|$. Thus the final result is

(21)
$$\frac{dy}{dx} = \frac{1}{|x|\sqrt{x^2 - 1}}.$$

For convenient reference we list our results on the differentiation of the inverse trigonometric functions. Although we did not derive the last three of these, the method of deriving them is exactly the same as that employed for the first three.

**Theorem:** It is understood in the following formulas that $u$ is a function of $x$, and that $y$ is restricted to the principal branch.

(22) $\qquad$ If $y = \sin^{-1} u$, then $\dfrac{dy}{dx} = \dfrac{1}{\sqrt{1 - u^2}} \dfrac{du}{dx}$ .

(23) $\qquad$ If $y = \cos^{-1} u$, then $\dfrac{dy}{dx} = -\dfrac{1}{\sqrt{1 - u^2}} \dfrac{du}{dx}$ .

(24) $\qquad$ If $y = \tan^{-1} u$, then $\dfrac{dy}{dx} = \dfrac{1}{1 + u^2} \dfrac{du}{dx}$ .

(25) $\qquad$ If $y = \cot^{-1} u$, then $\dfrac{dy}{dx} = -\dfrac{1}{1 + u^2} \dfrac{du}{dx}$ .

(26) $\qquad$ If $y = \sec^{-1} u$, then $\dfrac{dy}{dx} = \pm\dfrac{1}{u\sqrt{u^2 - 1}} \dfrac{du}{dx}$ .

The plus sign holds if $u > 1$ and the minus sign for $u < -1$. The formula presupposes that for $1 < u < \infty$, $y$ runs from 0 to $\pi/2$ and for $-\infty < u < -1$, $y$ runs from $\pi/2$ to $\pi$.

(27) $\qquad$ If $y = \csc^{-1} u$, then $\dfrac{dy}{dx} = \mp\dfrac{1}{u\sqrt{u^2 - 1}} \dfrac{du}{dx}$ .

In this formula we use the upper sign if $u > 1$ and the lower sign if $u < -1$. The formula presupposes that for $-\infty < u < -1$, $y$ runs from 0 to $-\pi/2$ and for $1 < u < \infty$, $y$ runs from $\pi/2$ to 0.

## EXERCISES

**1.** Deduce the derived function for $y = \cot^{-1} x$.

**2.** Differentiate each of the following functions:

(a) $y = \sin^{-1} \dfrac{x}{3}$ .

$\qquad$ *Ans.* $y' = \dfrac{1}{\sqrt{9 - x^2}}$ .

(b) $y = \cos^{-1} x^2$.

(c) $y = \tan^{-1} \dfrac{1}{x}$ .

$\qquad$ *Ans.* $y' = -\dfrac{1}{x^2 + 1}$ .

(d) $y = \sin^{-1} \dfrac{x - 1}{x}$ .

(e) $f(x) = (\sin^{-1} x)^2$.

$\qquad$ *Ans.* $f'(x) = 2(\sin^{-1} x)/\sqrt{1 - x^2}$ .

(f) $f(x) = \tan^{-1} \sqrt{x^2 + 1}$ .

(g) $y = \sin^{-1} (\cos x)$.

(h) $f(x) = \tan^{-1} \sqrt{x - 1}$ .

(i) $y = \sec^{-1} 3x$.

(j) $y = \sec^{-1} (2x - 3)$.

(k) $f(x) = \operatorname{arc cot} 3x^2$.

**3.** Draw the graph of $y = \cos^{-1} (1/x)$ and check whether (21) has the right sign.

**4.** Draw the graph of $y = \cos^{-1}(\sin x)$ as $x$ varies from 0 to $2\pi$.

**5.** Determine the point of inflection of

(a)   $y = \sin^{-1} x$.      *Ans.* $x = 0$.   (c)   $y = \tan^{-1} 2x$.      *Ans.* $x = 0$.

(b)   $y = \sin^{-1} 2x$.

**6.** If $x = g(y)$ is the inverse function of $y = f(x)$, determine whether $d^2y/dx^2 = 1/d^2x/dy^2$.

     *Suggestion:* Because $y'$ is a function of $x$ and $x$ is a function of $y$, differentiate $y' = 1/x'$ with respect to $x$, but use the chain rule on the right side.

                                                 *Ans.* $y'' = -x''/x'^3$.

**7.** Evaluate

(a)   $\displaystyle\lim_{x \to 0} \frac{\tan^{-1} x}{x}$.      *Ans.* 1.   (b)   $\displaystyle\lim_{x \to 1} \frac{\tan^{-1} x - \dfrac{\pi}{4}}{x - 1}$.      *Ans.* $\frac{1}{2}$.

**8.** A particle $P$ moves (Fig. 11-12) along the line $x = a$ with constant speed $v$. If the line $OP$ joining the particle to the origin makes an angle $\theta$ with the $x$-axis, find the angular velocity and angular acceleration of the line $OP$ in terms of $v$, $a$, and $\theta$.

     *Suggestion:* The problem calls for $\dot{\theta}$ and $\ddot{\theta}$. Introduce the quantity $y$ shown in the figure and find an expression for $\theta$.

$$\textit{Ans. } \dot{\theta} = \frac{v}{a}\cos^2\theta, \quad \ddot{\theta} = -\frac{2v^2}{a^2}\sin\theta\cos^3\theta.$$

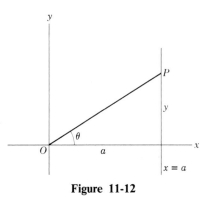

**Figure 11-12**

**9.** A particle $P$ falls down (Fig. 11-13) the straight line $x = a$ starting from the axis of $x$. If its distance from the $x$-axis is $\frac{1}{2}gt^2$ when it has been moving $t$ seconds, find the angular velocity and angular acceleration of the line $OP$.

     *Suggestion:* The problem calls for $\dot{\theta}$ and $\ddot{\theta}$. Find an expression for $\theta$.

$$\textit{Ans. } \dot{\theta} = \frac{4agt}{4a^2 + g^2t^4}, \quad \ddot{\theta} = \frac{4ag(4a^2 - 3g^2t^4)}{(4a^2 + g^2t^4)^2}.$$

**Figure 11-13**

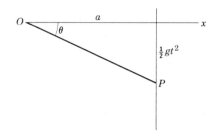

**4. Integration Involving the Inverse Trigonometric Functions.** Because new techniques of differentiation generally yield new techniques of integration, we should see to what extent our power to integrate is increased by formulas (22) to (27) for the inverse trigonometric functions. The surprising fact about the derived functions of the inverse trigonometric functions is that they do not involve trigonometric functions or their inverses but algebraic functions. We are enabled thereby to integrate new types of algebraic functions, and we shall examine one or two in a moment. The integration of functions that are themselves inverse trigonometric functions can be carried out but requires a technique that we shall study later, namely, integration by parts.

Let us note first the integration formulas that result from inverting the differentiation formulas (22) to (27). With the understanding that $u$ is a function of $x$ and that $y$ is in the principal branch, we have the

**Theorem:**

If $\dfrac{dy}{dx} = \dfrac{1}{\sqrt{1-u^2}} \dfrac{du}{dx}$, then

$$(28) \qquad y = \int \frac{1}{\sqrt{1-u^2}} \frac{du}{dx}\, dx = \sin^{-1} u + C.$$

If $\dfrac{dy}{dx} = -\dfrac{1}{\sqrt{1-u^2}} \dfrac{du}{dx}$, then

$$(29) \qquad y = \int -\frac{1}{\sqrt{1-u^2}} \frac{du}{dx}\, dx = \cos^{-1} u + C.$$

If $\dfrac{dy}{dx} = \dfrac{1}{1+u^2} \dfrac{du}{dx}$, then

$$(30) \qquad y = \int \frac{1}{1+u^2} \frac{du}{dx}\, dx = \tan^{-1} u + C.$$

If $\dfrac{dy}{dx} = -\dfrac{1}{1+u^2} \dfrac{du}{dx}$, then

$$(31) \qquad y = \int -\frac{1}{1+u^2} \frac{du}{dx}\, dx = \cot^{-1} u + C.$$

If $\dfrac{dy}{dx} = \pm\dfrac{1}{u\sqrt{u^2-1}} \dfrac{du}{dx}$, then

$$(32) \qquad y = \int \pm\frac{1}{u\sqrt{u^2-1}} \frac{du}{dx}\, dx = \sec^{-1} u + C.$$

If $\dfrac{dy}{dx} = \mp\dfrac{1}{u\sqrt{u^2-1}} \dfrac{du}{dx}$, then

$$(33) \qquad y = \int \mp\frac{1}{u\sqrt{u^2-1}} \frac{du}{dx}\, dx = \csc^{-1} u + C.$$

In the last two formulas the upper sign holds if $u > 1$ and the lower sign holds if $u < -1$.

As a simple application of these formulas, let us consider the problem of integrating

$$\frac{dy}{dx} = \frac{2x}{\sqrt{1 - x^4}}.$$

As we know from past work on differentiation, a given derived function may not seem to fall directly under one of the known integration formulas, but by the proper choice of $u$ as a function of $x$ it can be so handled. In the present case the $2x$ in the numerator suggests that it may play the role of $du/dx$, and therefore we choose $u = x^2$. Then

$$\frac{dy}{dx} = \frac{1}{\sqrt{1 - u^2}} \frac{du}{dx}.$$

We may now state by virtue of (28) that

$$y = \sin^{-1} u + C = \sin^{-1} x^2 + C.$$

Let us consider another example of integration, namely, to find $y$ as a function of $x$ when

(34)
$$\frac{dy}{dx} = \frac{1}{\sqrt{a^2 - b^2 x^2}}.$$

We assume that $a$ and $b$ are positive. The troublesome quantity in this derived function is the $a^2$, for if it were just 1, we could let $u = bx$ and then manage to apply (28). However, a slight algebraic step removes the difficulty. We write

(35)
$$\frac{dy}{dx} = \frac{1}{a\sqrt{1 - \dfrac{b^2}{a^2} x^2}}.$$

We would now like to let $u = bx/a$, but to use (28) we need the proper $du/dx$. This is $b/a$. Hence we write (35) as

$$\frac{dy}{dx} = \frac{1}{b} \frac{1}{\sqrt{1 - \dfrac{b^2}{a^2} x^2}} \frac{b}{a}.$$

With the understanding that $u = bx/a$,

$$\frac{dy}{dx} = \frac{1}{b} \frac{1}{\sqrt{1 - u^2}} \frac{du}{dx}.$$

The factor $1/b$ can be ignored for the moment because it is a constant factor. We may then apply (28) and state that

**(36)** $$y = \frac{1}{b} \sin^{-1} u + C = \frac{1}{b} \sin^{-1} \frac{bx}{a} + C.$$

## EXERCISES

**1.** Integrate the following derived functions:

(a) $y' = \dfrac{x}{\sqrt{1 - x^4}}.$

*Ans.* $y = \frac{1}{2} \sin^{-1} x^2 + C.$

(b) $y' = \dfrac{x^2}{\sqrt{1 - x^6}}.$

*Ans.* $y = \frac{1}{3} \sin^{-1} x^3 + C.$

(c) $dy/dx = \dfrac{1}{a^2 + x^2}.$

*Ans.* $y = \dfrac{1}{a} \tan^{-1} \dfrac{x}{a} + C.$

(d) $dy/dx = \dfrac{1}{a^2 + b^2 x^2}.$

(e) $y' = \dfrac{1}{2x\sqrt{x^2 - 1}}.$

(f) $y' = \dfrac{1}{\sqrt{5 - 4x^2}}.$

*Ans.* $y = \frac{1}{2} \sin^{-1} \dfrac{2x}{\sqrt{5}} + C.$

(g) $dy/dx = \dfrac{1}{16 + 9x^2}.$

*Ans.* $y = \frac{3}{4} \tan^{-1} \dfrac{3x}{4} + C.$

(h) $dy/dx = \dfrac{1}{\sqrt{16 - 9x^2}}.$

*Ans.* $y = \frac{1}{3} \sin^{-1} \dfrac{3x}{4} + C.$

(i) $dy/dx = \dfrac{1}{2x\sqrt{4x^2 - 1}}.$

(j) $f(x) = \displaystyle\int \dfrac{x^2}{\sqrt{1 - x^6}} \, dx.$

(k) $f'(x) = \dfrac{x}{x^4 + 3}.$

(l) $y = \displaystyle\int \dfrac{\sec x \tan x}{9 + 4 \sec^2 x} \, dx.$

(m) $y = \displaystyle\int \dfrac{x + 3}{\sqrt{1 - x^2}} \, dx.$

(n) $y = \displaystyle\int \dfrac{dx}{x^2 + 10x + 30}.$

**2.** Find the area between the curve $y = 1/(9 + x^2)$, the $x$-axis, and the lines $x = \pm\sqrt{3}$.

*Ans.* $\pi/9.$

Our ability to integrate the types of algebraic expressions in formulas (28) to (33) empowers us to dispose of some unfinished business. In Chapter 10 we had occasion to integrate an equation of the form

**(37)** $$\ddot{y} = -Ky,$$

where $\ddot{y}$ is the second derivative of $y$ with respect to $t$ and $K$ is positive. This equation arose in the motion of the bob on the spring, the motion of the pendulum, and the motion of an object along a tunnel through the earth. We found by mere trial that there is an integral of the form [see (52) of Chapter 10]

**(38)** $$y = A \sin \sqrt{K} \, t + B \cos \sqrt{K} \, t.$$

Of course, the $K$ here is the quantity $k/m$ in the reference just cited. The point we did not settle in the preceding chapter is that (38) is the *only* solution of (37). We shall find (38) by a systematic process and determine that (38) is indeed the only solution of (37).

Our first step is one we have made in other applications [see Chapter 7, step (70)]. We multiply both sides of (37) by $2\dot{y}$. Then

$$\textbf{(39)} \qquad\qquad 2\dot{y}\ddot{y} = -2Ky\dot{y}.$$

Now $y$ is some function of $t$ (although we do not know the precise form of this function). For this function, no matter what it turns out to be, the left side of (39) and the right side are identical functions of $t$. Hence the integrals of these two functions can differ at most by a constant. Let us then integrate each side separately and equate the results.

On the left side we regard $\dot{y}$ as $u$. Then $\ddot{y} = du/dt$. We have then

$$2u\,\frac{du}{dt}\;.$$

To integrate with respect to $t$, we have precisely the form required for the chain rule, namely, a function of $u$, multiplied by $du/dt$. According to the procedure for reversing the chain rule, we integrate the function of $u$ with respect to $u$. The integral then is $u^2$ or $\dot{y}^2$.

On the right side we have a similar situation. If we think of $y$ as $u$, again we have, apart from the constant factor $-2K$, a function of $u$ multiplied by $du/dt$. Thus the chain rule can be applied. We integrate the function of $u$, which is $u$ itself, with respect to $u$ and obtain $u^2/2$, and in view of the factor $-2K$ we get $-Ku^2$ or $-Ky^2$.

We may therefore state that

$$\textbf{(40)} \qquad\qquad \dot{y}^2 = -Ky^2 + C.$$

We wish, however, to find $y$ as a function of $t$. We have that

$$\textbf{(41)} \qquad\qquad \dot{y} = \pm\sqrt{C - Ky^2}\;.$$

Unfortunately, the right side is a function of $y$ rather than of the independent variable $t$. Hence ordinary integration seems to be impossible. However, here we can use another device that is very much worth noting. The quantity $\dot{y}$ is, of course, $dy/dt$, and it refers to $y$ as a function of $t$. We can, however, think of the *inverse* function where $t$ is a function of $y$. Moreover, we know from (16) that

$$\frac{dt}{dy} = \frac{1}{\dfrac{dy}{dt}}\;.$$

Then we have from (41) that

$$\textbf{(42)} \qquad\qquad \frac{dt}{dy} = \pm\,\frac{1}{\sqrt{C - Ky^2}}\;.$$

Now that we have the derived function expressed as a function of the independent variable, there is some hope of carrying out the integration.

The right side of (42) is in the form of (34) if we think of $a$ in (34) as $\sqrt{C}$ and $b$ in (34) as $\sqrt{K}$. Hence in view of (36)

**(43)**
$$t = \pm \frac{1}{\sqrt{K}} \sin^{-1} \frac{\sqrt{K}}{\sqrt{C}} y + D,$$

where $D$ is another constant of integration. Because we want to obtain $y$ as a function of $t$, we solve for $y$ as follows. From (43)

$$\pm \sqrt{K}\, (t - D) = \sin^{-1} \frac{\sqrt{K}}{\sqrt{C}} y$$

or

$$\frac{\sqrt{K}}{\sqrt{C}}\, y = \sin \left\{ \pm \sqrt{K}\, (t - D) \right\}$$

or

**(44)**
$$y = \frac{\sqrt{C}}{\sqrt{K}}\, \sin \left\{ \pm \sqrt{K}\, (t - D) \right\}.$$

This result can be written in a simpler form. The quantity $K$ is given to start with. But $C$ is a constant of integration and therefore is fixed by the initial conditions. We can replace $\sqrt{C}/\sqrt{K}$ by a new constant, say $E$, and fix it when the initial conditions are applied. The same argument applies to $\sqrt{K}\, D$, which we therefore replace by $F$. Then

$$y = \pm E \sin (\sqrt{K}\, t - F).$$

By agreeing that $E$ can take on positive or negative values we eliminate the need to write the $+$ and $-$ signs in front, so that

**(45)**
$$y = E \sin (\sqrt{K}\, t - F).$$

We have but to compare (45) with the result (55) of Chapter 10 to see that the result is the same. Of course, the quantity $F$ here is the quantity $-\phi$ there. Because both are arbitrary and are fixed by initial conditions, it does not matter which way we write this constant.

Thus what we should see is that equation (37), which we integrated by trial and error in the preceding chapter, can be integrated by two successive antidifferentiation processes, and the two constants of integration, which we previously introduced on the trial-and-error basis, arise through the two successive antidifferentiations. Moreover, because two integrals of a given derived function can differ at most by a constant and we used this fact in integrating (37), the result (45) is unique.

**5. Change of Variable in Integration.** When we integrated the derived function

$$\frac{dy}{dx} = \frac{2x}{\sqrt{1 - x^4}} \tag{46}$$

in the preceding section we let $u = x^2$. Then $du/dx = 2x$. Thus

$$y = \int \frac{1}{\sqrt{1 - u^2}} \; \frac{du}{dx} \; dx$$

and by (28)

$$y = \sin^{-1} u + C = \sin^{-1} x^2 + C. \tag{47}$$

We may characterize this process of introducing $u$ by saying that we *substitute a new variable u for a function of x.*

In the integration of roots of algebraic expressions, of which (46) is typical, another process is often employed which is actually only a minor modification of the use of substitution but is sufficiently different to warrant attention and even to justify the introduction of a new name. We could illustrate this new process by working with the derived function in (46), but for the sake of variety let us integrate

$$\frac{dy}{dx} = \sqrt{a^2 - x^2} \; .$$

That is, we seek

$$y = \int \sqrt{a^2 - x^2} \; dx. \tag{48}$$

We note first that this integral form does not appear among any of those we have encountered so far.

The troublesome element in (48) is, of course, the presence of the square root, and therefore it seems wise to see what we can do about eliminating it. Toward this end the trigonometric functions seem to be helpful. Thus, suppose that we let

$$x = a \sin \theta \tag{49}$$

and substitute this value of $x$ in (48). Then

$$y = \int \sqrt{a^2 - a^2 \sin^2 \theta} \; dx = a \int \cos \theta \; dx. \tag{50}$$

Now we cannot integrate a function of $\theta$ with respect to $x$. However, we can use the chain rule. This states that

$$\frac{dy}{d\theta} = \frac{dy}{dx} \frac{dx}{d\theta} \; .$$

That is, we can convert $dy/dx$ to $dy/d\theta$ by multiplying by $dx/d\theta$. Then

**(51)**
$$y = \int \frac{dy}{dx} \frac{dx}{d\theta} \, d\theta.$$

The quantity $\cos\theta$ in (50) is really $dy/dx$ expressed in terms of $\theta$, as we can see from the given $dy/dx$. If we multiply by $dx/d\theta$ then (51) tells us that we may indeed integrate with respect to $\theta$. Since $dx/d\theta$ in our case is $a\cos\theta$, we may write

$$y = a\int \cos\theta \, dx = a\int (\cos\theta)a\cos\theta \, d\theta = a^2\int \cos^2\theta \, d\theta.$$

To integrate $\cos^2\theta$ we use the trigonometric identity

$$\cos\theta = \pm\sqrt{\frac{1 + \cos 2\theta}{2}} \ .$$

Then

$$y = a^2\int \cos^2\theta \, d\theta = a^2\int \left( \frac{1}{2} + \frac{\cos 2\theta}{2} \right) d\theta$$

$$= \frac{a^2}{2} \int d\theta + \frac{a^2}{2} \int \cos 2\theta \, d\theta$$

or

**(52)**
$$y = \frac{a^2\theta}{2} + \frac{a^2}{4} \sin 2\theta + C.$$

We have the integral as a function of $\theta$, whereas we were concerned with $y$ as a function of $x$. However, from (49) we obtain

$$\theta = \sin^{-1} \frac{x}{a} \ .$$

To replace $\theta$ by $x$ in (52), we need also the value of $\sin 2\theta$. Because

$$\sin\theta = \frac{x}{a}$$

and

$$\sin 2\theta = 2\sin\theta\cos\theta$$

or

$$\sin 2\theta = 2 \frac{x}{a} \sqrt{1 - \frac{x^2}{a^2}} = 2 \frac{x}{a^2} \sqrt{a^2 - x^2} \ ,$$

we have from (52) that

**(53)**
$$y = \frac{a^2}{2} \sin^{-1} \frac{x}{a} + \frac{x}{2} \sqrt{a^2 - x^2} + C.$$

Thus we have integrated (48).

The key idea in the integration is to let

**(54)**
$$x = a \sin \theta,$$

and then to replace $x$ by this new function of $\theta$. The $dx$ in the integrand (50) reminds us that we must replace $dx$ by $(dx/d\theta)\, d\theta$ and then the integrand becomes a function of $\theta$ to be integrated with respect to $\theta$.

For the sake of identification let us say that when we replace $x$ by a function of $\theta$, we make a *change of variable* and when we introduce $u$ as a function of $x$, we use *substitution of a new variable*. These two methods, substitution and change of variable, are and are not essentially different. From the standpoint of what we do to carry out the integration, there is a difference. In substitution, after introducing $u$ as a function $x$, we do *not* change the given derived function (except for algebraic steps that leave its value unchanged) and merely single out the $f(u)\, du/dx$ as in treating (46). In change of variable, where $x$ is replaced by a function of $\theta$, we must also replace the $dx$ by $(dx/d\theta)\, d\theta$. From the standpoint of the underlying theory, the methods of substitution and change of variable are essentially the same. Both are applications of the chain rule.

We may see the relation between the two methods by observing that if $x = g(\theta)$ then

$$\int f(x)\, dx = \int f(g(\theta))\, g'(\theta)\, d\theta.$$

In change of variable we go from left to right. We replace $x$ by $g(\theta)$ and $dx$ by $g'(\theta)\, d\theta$. In the method of substitution we go from right to left. We face a function of $\theta$, namely, $f(g(\theta))$. If we can replace $g(\theta)$ by $x$ and still find $g'(\theta)$ within the existing integrand (except for a constant multiplier), we may make the substitution and replace the integral on the right by the one on the left.

There is one more point to note about the use of change of variable. We first obtained $y$ in (52) as a function of $\theta$ and then because $\theta$ is a function of $x$ we obtained $y$ as a function of $x$ in (53). For some purposes it may be sufficient to use $y$ as a function of $\theta$ and not bother to reexpress it as a function of $x$. Thus if we wished to fix the constant of integration so that $y = 0$ when $x = 0$ in (53) we would obtain $C = 0$. We can argue as well that because $x = a \sin \theta$, when $x = 0$, $\theta = 0$ and require that $y = 0$ when $\theta = 0$ in (52). Again we find that $C = 0$. Moreover if we wished to know the value of $y$ at say $x = a$ we could calculate this from (53) in which $C$ is now 0 or we could argue that because $x = a \sin \theta$, at $x = a$, $\theta = \pi/2$ and calculate $y$ for $\theta = \pi/2$ in (52), with $C = 0$. In other words, after a change of variable, say from $x$ to $\theta$, we can often work with $y$ as a function of $\theta$ instead of reexpressing $y$ as a function of $x$.

## EXERCISES

**1.** Integrate $dy/dx = \sqrt{a^2 - x^2}$ by using the change of variable $x = a \cos \theta$.

$$\textit{Ans. } y = -\frac{a^2}{2}\left[\cos^{-1}\frac{x}{a} - \frac{x\sqrt{1 - (x^2/a^2)}}{a}\right] + C.$$

**2.** Find the area in the first quadrant of the ellipse $(x^2/a^2) + (y^2/b^2) = 1$.

Ans. $\pi ab/4$.

**3.** Integrate by making a change of variable for $x$ in terms of some appropriate function of $\theta$:

(a) $y' = \dfrac{1}{\sqrt{9 - x^2}}$.

Ans. $y = -\cos^{-1}\dfrac{x}{3} + C.$

(b) $dy/dx = \dfrac{1}{\sqrt{16 - 9x^2}}$.

(c) $dy/dx = \dfrac{1}{16 + 9x^2}$.

Ans. $y = \dfrac{1}{12} \tan^{-1}\dfrac{3x}{4} + C.$

(d) $y' = \sqrt{9 - x^2}$.

(e) $f'(x) = \dfrac{1}{(a^2 + x^2)^{3/2}}$.

Suggestion: Let $x = a \tan \theta$.

Ans. $f(x) = \dfrac{x}{a^2\sqrt{a^2 + x^2}} + C.$

(f) $dy/dx = \dfrac{1}{(a^2 - x^2)^{3/2}}$.

(g) $y' = \dfrac{x^2}{\sqrt{16 - x^2}}$.

Ans. $y = 8 \sin^{-1}\dfrac{x}{4}$

$- \dfrac{x}{2}\sqrt{16 - x^2} + C.$

(h) $y = \displaystyle\int \dfrac{x^2}{(25 - x^2)^{3/2}}\, dx.$

Ans. $\dfrac{x}{\sqrt{25 - x^2}} - \sin^{-1}\dfrac{x}{5} + C.$

(i) $y = \displaystyle\int \dfrac{\sqrt{25 - x^2}}{x^2}\, dx.$

**4.** Calculate the area of the portion of the ellipse $9x^2 + 16y^2 = 144$ between the $y$-axis and $x = 2$.

Ans. $\pi + 3\sqrt{3}/2$.

There is one caution about integrating a function of $x$ by introducing a new variable, whether by substitution or by change of variable. Suppose that we denote the new variable by $t$. Then $x$ *must be a (continuous) single-valued function of $t$ and $dx/dt$ must also be continuous in the domain of $t$-values that corresponds to the domain of $x$-values over which one wishes to consider the integral.* Let us see why this must be so by using a simple example. Suppose that we wish to calculate the integral of (Fig. 11-14)

**(55)**
$$\frac{dy}{dx} = x^2 + 1$$

and evaluate it over the interval from $x = -1$ to $x = 4$. By integration

$$y = \frac{x^3}{3} + x + C.$$

**Figure 11-14**

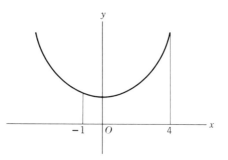

We must now substitute 4 for $x$, then substitute $-1$ for $x$, and subtract the second result from the first. Thus

**(56)**                    $y = \frac{64}{3} + 4 - \left(-\frac{1}{3} - 1\right) = \frac{80}{3}$ .

The constant of integration, we note, is canceled out.

Suppose that we decide to perform the integration by the change of variable $x = \sqrt{t}$ . We have from (55) that

$$y = \int (x^2 + 1) \, dx = \int (t + 1)\tfrac{1}{2} t^{-1/2} \, dt.$$

If we now integrate with respect to $t$ we obtain

**(57)**                    $y = \tfrac{1}{3} t^{3/2} + t^{1/2} + C.$

To evaluate this integral over the interval $x = -1$ to $x = 4$ we can argue that when $x = -1$, $t = 1$ and when $x = 4$, $t = 16$. If we substitute $t = 16$ in (57), substitute $t = 1$, and then subtract the second result from the first one we will obtain

**(58)**         $y = \tfrac{1}{3} \cdot 16^{3/2} + 16^{1/2} - \left(\tfrac{1}{3} \cdot 1^{3/2} + 1^{1/2}\right) = 24.$

The result in (58) does not agree with that in (56), because the domain for the new variable $t$, namely from 1 to 16, does not correspond to the domain $-1$ to 4 for $x$. In fact, if we substitute 1 for $t$ in $x = \sqrt{t}$ , we obtain $+1$ for $x$ and not $-1$.

Figures 11-15 and 11-16 tell the story. In the domain $-1$ to 0 for $x$, it is true that $t = x^2$, but the inverse function is $x = -\sqrt{t}$ ; in the domain 0 to 4 for $x$, the inverse function is $x = \sqrt{t}$ . This point is precisely the one we made earlier in this chapter, namely, that if the original function falls and rises (is not monotonic), we must break it up into intervals in which it is monotonic and define a separate branch of the inverse function for each domain in which this original function is monotonic. In the range of $-1$ to 4 for $x$, $x$ is not a single-valued function of $t$, as Fig. 11-16 shows.

Let us redo the problem by change of variable, but this time let us be careful about the inverse functions. We can calculate the desired integral by calculating it from $-1$ to 0 for $x$ and then from 0 to 4 for $x$ (see Fig. 11-14).

**Figure 11-15**

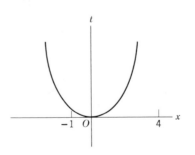

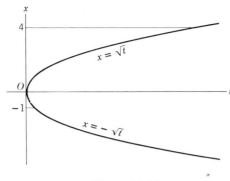

**Figure 11-16**

Now in any case

$$\frac{dy}{dx} = x^2 + 1.$$

Then

**(59)**
$$y = \int (x^2 + 1)\, dx.$$

In the interval from $x = -1$ to $x = 0$ we use the change of variable $x = -\sqrt{t}$. Then

**(60)**
$$y = \int (t + 1)\left(-\tfrac{1}{2}t^{-1/2}\right) dt$$

or

**(61)**
$$y = -\tfrac{1}{3}t^{3/2} - t^{1/2} + C.$$

When $x = -1$, $t = 1$ and when $x = 0$, $t = 0$. If we substitute 0 for $t$ in (61), then 1 for $t$, and, finally, subtract the second result from the first we obtain $\tfrac{4}{3}$. To calculate the integral of (55) from $x = 0$ to $x = 4$ we use the change of variable $x = \sqrt{t}$ [see (57)] and this yields $\tfrac{76}{3}$. The sum of $\tfrac{4}{3}$ and $\tfrac{76}{3}$ yields the correct result of $\tfrac{80}{3}$.

**6. Time of Motion Under Gravitational Attraction.*** The inverse trigonometric functions are helpful in carrying further the study of motion in a straight line caused by gravitational attraction. In Chapter 7, Section 8, we found the velocity which an object acquires when it starts from rest at a distance $r_1$ from the center of the earth (Fig. 11-17) and falls to a distance $r$. To produce this motion, gravity introduces an acceleration

$$a = -\frac{GM}{r^2},$$

*The section can be omitted without disrupting the continuity.

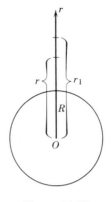

**Figure 11-17**

where $G$ is the gravitational constant, $M$ is the mass of the earth, and $r$ is the variable distance of the falling object from the center of the earth. The velocity $v$ acquired by the object is given by

**(62)**
$$\frac{v^2}{2} = \frac{GM}{r} - \frac{GM}{r_1} .$$

We can now ask the question, how long does it take the object to fall from the distance $r_1$ to the distance $r$? There is a possibility of answering this question because $v$ in (62) is $dr/dt$, and if we could find $r$ as a function of $t$ or $t$ as a function of $r$ we could calculate the time in question.

Equation (62) tells us that

$$v = \pm \sqrt{2GM} \sqrt{\frac{1}{r} - \frac{1}{r_1}} .$$

We shall use the minus sign because the acceleration downward was taken to be negative (in Chapter 7) and the velocity acquired then must also be negative. Also, because $v = dr/dt$, we have

$$\frac{dr}{dt} = -\sqrt{2GM} \sqrt{\frac{1}{r} - \frac{1}{r_1}} .$$

We face the fact that the right side is a function of the dependent variable rather than of the independent variable, and therefore we work with $t$ as a function of $r$. By using (16) we have

**(63)**
$$\frac{dt}{dr} = -\frac{1}{\sqrt{2GM}} \frac{1}{\sqrt{\dfrac{1}{r} - \dfrac{1}{r_1}}} .$$

The problem now is how to integrate the function of $r$ on the right side. As it stands, there is no apparent antidifferentiation theorem that seems to be applicable. Let us try rewriting by combining the fractions in the radical.

Then

$$\frac{dt}{dr} = -\frac{1}{\sqrt{2GM}} \sqrt{\frac{rr_1}{r_1 - r}} \quad.$$

We must calculate, then,

**(64)**
$$t = \int -\frac{1}{\sqrt{2GM}} \sqrt{\frac{rr_1}{r_1 - r}} \; dr.$$

There is still no clearly applicable integration process, but the presence of the square root and the knowledge that some root expressions can be handled by a trigonometric change of variable suggest trying

**(65)**
$$r = r_1 \cos^2 \theta.$$

We use $\cos^2 \theta$ to have $r$ decrease as $\theta$ increases from 0. If we make this change of variable in (64) we obtain

$$t = \int \frac{\sqrt{2}}{\sqrt{GM}} \; r_1^{3/2} \cos^2 \theta \; d\theta.$$

Now the use of the trigonometric identity

$$\cos^2 \theta = \frac{1 + \cos 2\theta}{2}$$

permits us to integrate. We have

$$t = \frac{\sqrt{2} \; r_1^{3/2}}{\sqrt{GM}} \int \frac{1 + \cos 2\theta}{2} \; d\theta$$

or

**(66)**
$$t = \frac{\sqrt{2} \; r_1^{3/2}}{\sqrt{GM}} \left( \frac{\theta}{2} + \frac{\sin 2\theta}{4} \right) + C.$$

We can now replace $\theta$ by its value in terms of $r$ by means of (65). We have that

**(67)**
$$\cos \theta = \sqrt{\frac{r}{r_1}}$$

wherein we use the plus sign for the radical because $r$ can vary from $r_1$ to some lower positive value and so $\cos \theta$ can be taken to be positive in that range of $r$. Also

$$\sin 2\theta = 2 \sin \theta \cos \theta$$

so that

**(68)**
$$\sin 2\theta = 2\sqrt{1 - \frac{r}{r_1}}\,\sqrt{\frac{r}{r_1}}\,.$$

If we use (67) and (68) in (66) we obtain

$$t = \frac{\sqrt{2}\,r_1^{3/2}}{\sqrt{GM}}\left[\frac{1}{2}\cos^{-1}\sqrt{\frac{r}{r_1}} + \frac{1}{2}\sqrt{1 - \frac{r}{r_1}}\,\sqrt{\frac{r}{r_1}}\right] + C.$$

Now let us agree to fix $C$ so that $t = 0$ when $r = r_1$. Then $C = 0$ and our final formula is

**(69)**
$$t = \frac{r_1^{3/2}}{\sqrt{2GM}}\left(\cos^{-1}\sqrt{\frac{r}{r_1}} + \sqrt{1 - \frac{r}{r_1}}\,\sqrt{\frac{r}{r_1}}\right).$$

This formula also presupposes that $v = 0$ when $r = r_1$ because this condition was used in Chapter 7, Section 8, to derive (62).

The result (69) is useful if we are interested in the functional relation between $t$ and $r$. However, if we wish only to calculate the value of $t$ for a specific motion from $r = r_1$ to $r = r_2$, say, we can work with $t$ as a function of $\theta$ as given by (66). We would usually fix the constant of integration in (66) so that $t = 0$ when $r = r_1$, that is, when the object is at the point from which it starts to fall. However, when $r = r_1$, we see from (65) that $\cos^2\theta = 1$ and $\theta = 0$. We substitute 0 for $t$ and 0 for $\theta$ in (66) and obtain $C = 0$. Then (66) becomes

**(70)**
$$t = \frac{\sqrt{2}\,r_1^{3/2}}{\sqrt{GM}}\left(\frac{\theta}{2} + \frac{\sin 2\theta}{4}\right).$$

If we wish to calculate the time of fall to some point $r_2$, we must use (65) to calculate the corresponding value of $\theta$ and then substitute this value of $\theta$ in (70). Furthermore, if we wish to calculate the time of fall from a distance $r_2$ to a distance $r_3$, we can find the corresponding values of $\theta$ in (65) and substitute them in (70).

## EXERCISES

For convenient reference we list the following values: $G = 1.07 \cdot 10^{-9}$, $M = 13.1 \cdot 10^{24}$ pounds, $GM = 14 \cdot 10^{15}$, $R = 21 \cdot 10^6$ feet, $GM/R^2 = 32$ ft/sec².

1. Calculate the time required to reach the earth's surface by an object which is dropped from a height of 2000 miles above the earth's surface.

                                           *Ans.*   1250 sec approx.

2. Suppose that we use the acceleration of 32 ft/sec² in place of the true gravitational acceleration and that an object falls from a height of 2000 miles above the

earth's surface. Will the object take more or less time to fall to the surface than if accelerated by the true acceleration? Calculate the time of fall and compare with the answer to Exercise 1.

3. Suppose that an object is shot up from the earth's surface to just reach a height of 100,000 feet, that is, so that its velocity is 0 when it reaches that height. Calculate the time of flight. *Ans.* 98 sec approx.

4. Find the time required for an object to reach the moon 240,000 miles away if the object is shot up with just enough velocity to reach the moon. The moon's gravitational attraction is not to be considered. *Ans.* 4 days, 20 hours.

5. Suppose that an object is shot up with the escape velocity. How long does it take to reach a height $r$?

   *Suggestion:* Neither formula (69) nor (70) is useful because if we let $r_1$ become infinite we cannot evaluate $t$. It is best to rederive the formula for velocity (in place of (62) with the velocity specified at the surface of the earth). This was done in Exercise 15 of Chapter 7, Section 8. Now let the initial velocity at the surface of the earth become the escape velocity and derive an expression for the time of flight to height $r$. Fix the constant of integration so that $t = 0$ at the surface of the earth.
   $$\text{Ans. } t = \frac{\sqrt{2}}{3\sqrt{GM}}\, r^{3/2} - \frac{\sqrt{2}}{3\sqrt{GM}}\, R^{3/2}.$$

6. Two identical spheres each of mass 2000 pounds and radius 1 foot are located with their centers 6 feet apart. Each sphere attracts the other as though its mass were concentrated at a point. If they are attracted to each other by their mutual force of gravitation, how long will it take for them to come into contact?

   *Suggestion:* Because the same force acts on each sphere, they will meet halfway between the two points at which they started. Choose an origin there; let $x$ be the variable distance from this origin to the center of either sphere, and let $m$ be the mass of either sphere. Then the motion of each sphere is given by $m\ddot{x} = -Gm^2/4x^2$. When they come into contact, $x = 1$. You can use the theory of the text, except that $Gm/4$ replaces $GM$ there.
   *Ans.* $t = 2$ hrs approx.

7. A body of unit mass is attracted to a center by the gravitational force of a mass $M$ located at the center. Suppose that the unit mass is released at infinity with 0 velocity. (This means that as the distance from the center becomes infinite, the velocity approaches 0.) Let us agree to measure time from the instant the body reaches the center.
   (a) Find the formula for the distance from the center as a function of time.
   $$\text{Ans. } r = (-\tfrac{3}{2})^{2/3}(2GM)^{1/3}t^{2/3}.$$
   (b) How long does it take the body to travel the infinite distance from infinity to the center? *Ans.* ∞.
   (c) What is the velocity of the body when it reaches the center? *Ans.* ∞.
   (d) Does the solution to (a) have mathematical meaning for positive $t$?
   (e) What physical meaning does the solution to (a) have for positive $t$?

# CHAPTER TWELVE
# LOGARITHMIC AND EXPONENTIAL FUNCTIONS

**1. Introduction.** Suppose that there are 100 bacteria in a culture and that each bacterium doubles on the average once every hour; then at the end of one hour there are 200 bacteria, at the end of two hours, 400, and so on. The number $N$ of bacteria present after $t$ hours might then be represented by the formula:

**(1)** $$N = 100 \cdot 2^t.$$

Of course, this formula is at best a mathematical idealization of the actual physical situation. For many values of $t$, $N$ turns out to be a whole number plus a decimal. This decimal part has no physical significance. Apart from this fact, however, the formula appears to be a realistic description of the increase in the number of bacteria. It represents, as it should, a steady increase in the number $N$ as $t$ increases. Moreover, the formula gives the correct number at positive integral values of $t$.

Formula (1) is an example of an exponential function. What characterizes exponential functions is that the independent variable, $t$ in formula (1), occurs as an exponent, whereas, for example, in $y = x^n$ the independent variable is the base and the exponent $n$ is constant. This example also shows that to represent some physical phenomena we seem to need a greater variety of functions than we have studied so far. The diversity of natural phenomena is almost endless, and mathematics must supply a multiplicity of types of functions to represent and deduce knowledge about these happenings. In this chapter we shall study exponential functions and the closely related logarithmic functions; we shall also see how useful they can be. We begin with logarithmic functions because it is more convenient to do so.

**2. A Review of Logarithms.** The concept of logarithms is probably not new, for the reader has undoubtedly met them in connection with arithmetic calculation. Nevertheless, let us review the essential facts. The ordinary or common logarithm of a number is the exponent to which 10 must be raised to obtain the number. Thus the logarithm of 100 is 2 because $100 = 10^2$ and the logarithm of 0.1 is $-1$ because $0.1 = 10^{-1}$. The logarithms of most numbers are irrational and we represent them as decimals usually only to four places. Thus the logarithm of 5 (which for the present we take from a table) is 0.6990 because $5 = 10^{0.6990}$.

Logarithms exist for all positive numbers.* For convenience in determining and calculating with logarithms, we first consider the logarithms of numbers between 1 and 10. These logarithms are always between 0 and 1. Then the whole-numbered part of the logarithm, called the characteristic, is 0 and the rest of it, called the mantissa, is some decimal. Thus for 5 the logarithm is 0.6990; here 0 is the characteristic and .6990 is the mantissa. Now let us consider a number greater than 10. Since

$$50 = 5 \cdot 10 = 10^{0.6990} \, 10^1 = 10^{1.6990},$$

the logarithm of 50 has the characteristic 1 and the mantissa .6990. Any number greater than 10 is some positive integral power of ten times a number between 1 and 10, and so the logarithm of that number has a positive integral part and a decimal, which is also the mantissa of the corresponding number between 1 and 10. As another example, because

$$325 = 3.25 \cdot 10^2$$

and because (again resorting to a table)

$$3.25 = 10^{0.5119},$$
$$325 = 10^{0.5119} \cdot 10^2 = 10^{2.5119}.$$

Thus the mantissa of 325 and 3.25 is the same, but the characteristic of 325 is 2, whereas that of 3.25 is 0.

For numbers between 0 and 1 it is still true that each is some power of 10 multiplied by a number between 1 and 10. Thus

$$0.325 = 3.25 \cdot 10^{-1}$$

and because

$$3.25 = 10^{0.5119},$$

it follows that

$$0.325 = 10^{0.5119} \cdot 10^{-1}.$$

But now we must be careful. The logarithm 0.5119 is a positive number, whereas the logarithm $-1$ is negative. For purposes of *arithmetic* it is better not to add these numbers and to write

$$0.325 = 10^{\bar{1}.5119}.$$

---

* There are logarithms for negative and even complex numbers, but they are not considered in elementary calculus.

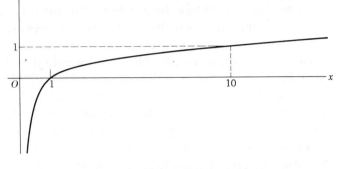

**Figure 12-1**

By putting the minus sign over the 1 we indicate that only the 1 is negative. If we are not interested in using logarithms to do arithmetic, we can just as well calculate $-1 + 0.5119$, which is $-0.4881$, and write

$$0.325 = 10^{-0.4881}.$$

Then the logarithm of 0.325 is $-0.4881$, a negative number. Moreover, the closer a number is to 0, the more negative is its logarithm. For example, because

$$0.000001 = 10^{-6},$$

the logarithm of 0.000001 is $-6$.

   We repeat that the numbers between 0 and 1 have negative logarithms and the closer the number is to 0 the more negative its logarithm. As the numbers increase from 1 onward, their logarithms are positive and increase. A graph (Fig. 12-1) shows how the logarithms of numbers increase with the numbers. The numbers from 0 on are plotted along the $x$-axis, and the $y$-value corresponding to each $x$-value is the logarithm of that $x$-value.

   The graph thrusts to the fore what has been implicit in the subject of logarithms from the outset—there is a functional relation between numbers and their logarithms. We can, in fact, let $x$ stand for any positive number and $y$ for any logarithm. Then the formula

**(2)**                                $y = \log x$

represents the relation between numbers and their logarithms.


## REVIEW EXERCISES
## ON LOGARITHMS

**1.** Given $\log 7 = 0.8451$, find the following:
   (a)  $\log 70$.                    *Ans.* 1.8451.   (d)  $\log 0.07$.
   (b)  $\log 700$.                                     (e)  $\log 0.007$.    *Ans.* $-3 + 0.8451$.
   (c)  $\log 0.7$.        *Ans.* $-1 + 0.8451$.

**2.** Given $\log 7 = 0.8451$ and $\log 9 = 0.9542$, find the following:

(a) $\log 63$.              *Ans.* 1.7993.    (d) $\log 9^2 \cdot 7$.

(b) $\log 7^3$.                         (e) $\log 21$.

(c) $\log(90/7)$.        *Ans.* 1.1091.

### 3. The Derived Functions of Logarithmic Functions.

In the calculus we are naturally interested in what we can do with the derivative and integral of the logarithmic function. Let us look first into the derivative. When we have no prior theorems to tell us how to differentiate a given function, we fall back on the definition of the derivative, which means applying the method of increments. At a value $x_0$ of $x$ we have

$$(3) \qquad y_0 = \log x_0.$$

If $x$ changes to the value $x_0 + \Delta x$, $y$ changes to $y_0 + \Delta y$, and

$$(4) \qquad y_0 + \Delta y = \log(x_0 + \Delta x).$$

Then subtraction of (3) from (4) gives

$$\Delta y = \log(x_0 + \Delta x) - \log x_0,$$

and therefore

$$(5) \qquad \frac{\Delta y}{\Delta x} = \frac{\log(x_0 + \Delta x) - \log x_0}{\Delta x}.$$

We wish, of course, to find the limit of $\Delta y/\Delta x$ as $\Delta x$ approaches 0. However, the limit of the quotient on the right side of (5) is not evident, and so we shall try to change the form of it in the hope that the limit may be more apparent. We shall use the fact that the logarithm of the quotient of two numbers is the logarithm of the numerator minus the logarithm of the denominator. If we first put the factor $1/\Delta x$ in (5) in front of the expression and then use the fact just cited, we obtain

$$(6) \qquad \frac{\Delta y}{\Delta x} = \frac{1}{\Delta x} \log\left( \frac{x_0 + \Delta x}{x_0} \right) = \frac{1}{\Delta x} \log\left( 1 + \frac{\Delta x}{x_0} \right).$$

This form is not an improvement because as $\Delta x$ approaches 0, the quantity in parentheses approaches 1, its logarithm approaches 0, and the entire right side approaches $0/0$. Let us try another transformation. Because the logarithm of a power is the exponent times the logarithm of the base (for example, $\log 9^3 = 3 \log 9$), we may write (6) as

$$(7) \qquad \frac{\Delta y}{\Delta x} = \log\left( 1 + \frac{\Delta x}{x_0} \right)^{1/\Delta x}.$$

This form seems equally useless, for as $\Delta x$ approaches 0, the quantity in parentheses approaches 1 and the exponent becomes infinite; thus it is not at all clear what the entire power approaches.

We shall investigate the right side of (7). It is easier to do so after making the following change: we raise the number

$$\left(1 + \frac{\Delta x}{x_0}\right)^{1/\Delta x}$$

to the power $x_0$ and compensate by dividing the logarithm by $x_0$; that is,

$$(8) \qquad \frac{\Delta y}{\Delta x} = \frac{1}{x_0} \log\left(1 + \frac{\Delta x}{x_0}\right)^{x_0/\Delta x}.$$

The point in making this change is that if we now let $\Delta x / x_0$ be $t$, we can consider the simpler expression

$$(9) \qquad (1 + t)^{1/t}$$

and see what happens as $t$ approaches 0. To get some idea of how this quantity varies with $t$, we do a little arithmetic. The results, which are obtained by using logarithms, are

| $t$ | 1 | 0.5 | 0.25 | 0.1 | 0.03 | 0.01 | 0.001 | 0.0001 |
|---|---|---|---|---|---|---|---|---|
| $(1 + t)^{1/t}$ | 2 | 2.250 | 2.441 | 2.594 | 2.6786 | 2.7048 | 2.7169 | 2.7181 |

Because $\Delta x$ may be negative as well as positive, we consider also some negative values of $t$. The results are

| $t$ | $-0.01$ | $-0.001$ | $-0.0001$ |
|---|---|---|---|
| $(1 + t)^{1/t}$ | 2.7320 | 2.7196 | 2.7184 |

It seems from these tables that, as $t$ approaches 0,

$$(1 + t)^{1/t}$$

approaches a definite number whose value to three decimal places is 2.718. Further calculations would show that there is an unending number of digits in the decimal part of the number, but that it does not become so large as 2.719 or less than 2.718. These calculations do not really prove that the expression (9) has a limit as $t$ approaches 0, for there is a chance that for very small $t$ the expression may, for example, suddenly start to increase rapidly and even become infinite. There is, however, a geometric argument that does convince us that (9) approaches a limit. The limit, if it exists, of $\Delta y / \Delta x$ in (8) is the derivative of $y = \log x$ and therefore is the slope of the curve in Fig. 12-1 at $(x_0, y_0)$. However, the curve clearly has a definite slope at each point. Hence $\lim \Delta y / \Delta x$ as $\Delta x$ approaches 0 exists, and because (9) is another form of (8) and $1/x_0$ is merely a constant factor,

$$(10) \qquad \lim_{t \to 0}(1 + t)^{1/t}$$

does exist. For the present we shall rely on this geometric argument (which is not a rigorous proof) to establish the fact that the limit in (10) does exist.

This limit has an unending number of digits in the decimal part, as, for example, $\sqrt{2}$ and $\pi$ have. Because it is not possible to write out the exact number, it is designated by $e$ in honor of the mathematician Leonhard Euler, who made fundamental contributions to the calculus and, for that matter, to all other branches of the mathematics and physics of the eighteenth century.

We may now return to (8). In view of the value of $t$, we can say that

**(11)** $$\left(1 + \frac{\Delta x}{x_0}\right)^{x_0/\Delta x}$$

approaches $e$ as $\Delta x$ approaches 0. Then the logarithm of (11) should approach $\log e$ because, judging at least by the graph in Fig. 12-1, when $x$ approaches a definite number, $\log x$ approaches the logarithm of that number.* Then we have from (8)

**(12)** $$\frac{dy}{dx} = \lim_{\Delta x \to 0} \frac{\Delta y}{\Delta x} = \frac{1}{x_0} \log e.$$

We could use this result for the derivative of the logarithmic function. However, the quantity $\log e$, which means, of course, the logarithm of the number $2.718\ldots$, then always occurs as a multiplier of the essential quantity $1/x_0$. To avoid carrying this constant, $\log e$, it is customary in the calculus and in higher mathematics to introduce another system of logarithms. The usual or common system employs 10 as the base, and, as we know, the logarithm of any number is the exponent to which we must raise 10 so that the resulting power equals the number. Although 10 is indeed the best base for calculations with logarithms, it is possible to use other bases. In particular, it is possible to choose $e$ itself as the base. In this natural or Naperian system the logarithm of a number is the exponent to which $e$ must be raised so that the power equals the number. For example, it happens to be arithmetically correct that

$$10 = e^{2.3026}$$

(we give only four decimal places in the exponent). Then the logarithm of 10 to the base $e$ is 2.3026, whereas the logarithm of 10 to the base 10 is 1. All of the theorems that we learn about logarithms to base 10 apply to logarithms to base $e$, because these theorems are really a translation of theorems on exponents. Thus the theorem that if $a$ and $b$ are positive numbers,

$$\log(ab) = \log a + \log b$$

holds for base $e$ because, if we suppose that $l_1$ is the logarithm of $a$ to the base $e$,

$$a = e^{l_1}.$$

*That is, $\log x$ is a continuous function of $x$.

Likewise, if $l_2$ is the logarithm of $b$ to the base $e$,

$$b = e^{l_2}.$$

Then

$$ab = e^{l_1} \cdot e^{l_2} = e^{l_1 + l_2},$$

and therefore the logarithm of $ab$ is the sum of the logarithms of $a$ and $b$. Of course, the rules for finding the characteristic and mantissa of a logarithm are different for base $e$ than for base 10.

How do we obtain the logarithms of numbers to base $e$? There is a very simple relation between the logarithms of numbers to base $e$ and the logarithms of numbers to base 10. Suppose that $N$ is any (positive) number and $l$ is its logarithm to base $e$. This means that $N = e^l$. Suppose that $m$ is the logarithm of $N$ to the base 10. This means that $N = 10^m$. Then

$$e^l = 10^m.$$

Now let us take the logarithm to base $e$ of both sides of this equality. Then

$$\log_e e^l = \log_e 10^m.$$

Because the logarithm of a power is the exponent times the logarithm of the base, we have

$$l \log_e e = m \log_e 10.$$

Now $\log_e e$ is 1 because $e^1 = e$. In view of the meanings of $l$ and $m$, this equation says that

**(13)** $$\log_e N = \log_{10} N \cdot \log_e 10.$$

Equation (13) tells us that to obtain the logarithm of a number $N$ to the base $e$ we should take the logarithm of that number to base 10 and multiply it by the logarithm of 10 to base $e$. All we need, then, to obtain logarithms of numbers to base $e$ is the constant factor $\log_e 10$ and an ordinary logarithm table.

How can we obtain $\log_e 10$? Suppose that we let $N$ be $e$ in (13). Then

$$1 = \log_{10} e \cdot \log_e 10.$$

Thus $\log_e 10$ is $1/\log_{10} e$, and the latter can be found by using the ordinary logarithm tables. It turns out that

$$\log_e 10 = 2.3026.$$

Despite the fact that logarithms to base $e$ can be calculated by using (13), tables of logarithms to base $e$ have been made up and a brief one is appended to this book. Actually, logarithms to the base $e$ are more readily calculated than common logarithms, and in modern times the latter are computed from the former. (See Chap. 20.)

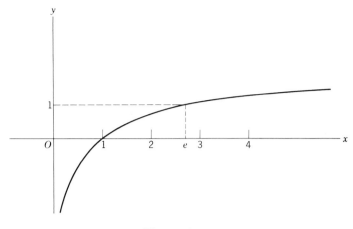

**Figure 12-2**

If we agree hereafter that by logarithms we mean logarithms to base $e$, our logarithm function is

**(14)** $$y = \log x,$$

with base $e$ understood (Fig. 12-2). Then (12) says, because $\log_e e = 1$, that

**(15)** $$\frac{dy}{dx} = \frac{1}{x_0}.$$

The derived function is, of course,

**(16)** $$\frac{dy}{dx} = \frac{1}{x}.$$

We note for the logarithmic function, as for the inverse trigonometric functions, that the derived function is an algebraic function.

Formula (16) also provides a new integral. Previously (Chap. 6, Sect. 7) we proved that if

$$\frac{dy}{dx} = x^n,$$

then

**(17)** $$y = \frac{x^{n+1}}{n+1} + C$$

for all positive and negative integral and fractional values of $n$, except $n = -1$. When $n = -1$, we have formula (16), and we now see that when

**(18)** $$\frac{dy}{dx} = \frac{1}{x},$$

then

**(19)** $$y = \int \frac{1}{x} \, dx = \log x + C, \quad x > 0.$$

Let us not forget the ubiquitous chain rule. If

$$y = \log u,$$

where $u$ is a positive function of $x$, that is, a function whose values are positive, then

(20) $$\frac{dy}{dx} = \frac{1}{u}\frac{du}{dx}.$$

Conversely, if (20) holds, then

(21) $$y = \int \frac{1}{u}\frac{du}{dx}\,dx = \log u + C, \quad u > 0.$$

There is one point about the passage from (18) to (19) that is worthy of note. The function $\log x$ is defined or has meaning only for positive values of $x$. However, the derivative $dy/dx = 1/x$ is defined for positive and negative values of $x$. If we were given $dy/dx = 1/x$ and were interested in some application with negative values of $x$, could we still integrate this $dy/dx$? The answer is yes, because if $x$ stands for negative numbers, then $-x$ is positive. We can write

(22) $$\frac{dy}{dx} = \frac{1}{x} = \frac{1}{-x}(-1).$$

We may now think of $-x$ as $u$, which meets the condition in (20) that $u$ be positive, and the following factor, $(-1)$ in (22), is $du/dx$. Hence by (21)

$$y = \log u + C$$

or

(23) $$y = \log(-x) + C \quad \text{for } x < 0.$$

We may also generalize the inverse of the chain rule. If

$$\frac{dy}{dx} = \frac{1}{u}\frac{du}{dx}$$

when $u$ is a negative function of $x$, then we may set

$$u = -v,$$

where $v$ is a positive function of $x$. We have that

$$\frac{du}{dx} = -\frac{dv}{dx}.$$

Now

(24) $$\frac{dy}{dx} = \frac{1}{u}\frac{du}{dx} = \frac{1}{-u}\left(-\frac{du}{dx}\right) = \frac{1}{v}\frac{dv}{dx}.$$

Because $v$ is a positive function, we may use (21) and write

(25)      $$y = \log v + C = \log(-u) + C \quad \text{for } u < 0.$$

Let us put these various results together for convenient reference.

**Theorem:**    If $y = \log x,\ x > 0$, then

(26)      $$\frac{dy}{dx} = \frac{1}{x} .$$

If $dy/dx = 1/x$, then

(27)    $y = \log x + C$ when $x > 0$ and $y = \log(-x) + C$ when $x < 0$.

We may express (27) in the form:

(28)  If $dy/dx = 1/x$, $y = \log |x| + C$, whether $x$ is positive or negative.

Next, in view of the chain rule, if $y = \log u$ where $u$ is a positive function of $x$, then

(29)      $$\frac{dy}{dx} = \frac{1}{u} \frac{du}{dx} .$$

If

$$\frac{dy}{dx} = \frac{1}{u} \frac{du}{dx} ,$$

then

(30)    $y = \log u + C$ for $u > 0$   and   $y = \log(-u) + C$ for $u < 0$.

We may express (30) in the form: if for positive or negative $u$

$$\frac{dy}{dx} = \frac{1}{u} \frac{du}{dx} ,$$

then

(31)      $$y = \log |u| + C.$$

**Example 1.** Find $dy/dx$ when $y = \log(x^2 + 7)^2$.

**Solution.**    First of all we can write $y = 2 \log(x^2 + 7)$. Now let $u = x^2 + 7$. Then by (29)

$$dy/dx = \frac{2}{x^2 + 7} (2x) = \frac{4x}{x^2 + 7} .$$

**Example 2.** Find $dy/dx$ when $y = \log[(x^2 + 5)(x^3 - 7)]$.

**Solution.**   The simplest way to perform the differentiation is to rewrite $y$ as

$$y = \log(x^2 + 5) + \log(x^3 - 7).$$

We now apply (29) to each term, letting $u$ be $x^2 + 5$ in the first one and $u$ be $x^3 - 7$ in the second one. Then

$$dy/dx = \frac{2x}{x^2 + 5} + \frac{3x^2}{x^3 - 7}.$$

**Example 3.** Evaluate

$$\int \frac{x}{x^2 + 1}\, dx.$$

**Solution.**   There is the possibility that if we let $u = x^2 + 1$ then the integrand can be put into the form $(1/u)du/dx$. However, if $u = x^2 + 1$ then $du/dx = 2x$. We may multiply the integrand by 2 provided we compensate by multiplying the entire integral by $\frac{1}{2}$. Thus

$$\int \frac{x}{x^2 + 1}\, dx = \frac{1}{2} \int \frac{2x}{x^2 + 1}\, dx = \frac{1}{2} \int \frac{1}{u}\frac{du}{dx}\, dx$$

$$= \frac{1}{2} \log u + C = \frac{1}{2} \log(x^2 + 1) + C.$$

## EXERCISES

1. Estimate the integral part of the following:
   (a)  $\log_e 3$.                    *Ans.* 1.    (c)  $\log_e 100$.                    *Ans.* 4.
   (b)  $\log_e 9$.                                 (d)  $\log_e 1$.
2. Suppose that 2 is used as the base of a system of logarithms. What then are the following:
   (a)  $\log 8$.                     *Ans.* 3.    (c)  $\log 1$.
   (b)  $\log 16$.                                 (d)  $\log \frac{1}{2}$.                     *Ans.* $-1$.
3. Look up in the table of natural logarithms the following quantities:
   (a)  $\log 3$.            *Ans.* 1.0986.    (d)  $\log 0.1$.
   (b)  $\log 5$.                               (e)  $\log 0.5$.            *Ans.* $-0.6931$.
   (c)  $\log 10$.           *Ans.* 2.3026.
4. Find the numbers whose natural logarithms are the following:
   (a)  $-0.5108$.                             (c)  $3.4012$.
   (b)  $0.7885$.            *Ans.* 2.2.    (d)  $4.3820$.            *Ans.* 80.
5. On the same set of axes sketch $y = \log_{10} x$ and $y = \log_e x$.
6. On the same set of axes sketch the following pairs of curves. Base $e$ is understood.
   (a)  $y = \log x$ and $y = 3 \log x$.
   (b)  $y = \log x$ and $y = \log x + 2$.
   (c)  $y = \log x$ and $y = \log(x + 3)$.

(d)   $y = \log x$ and $y = 3 \log(x + 2)$.

(e)   $y = \log x$ and $y = \log(5 - x)$ for $x < 5$.

**7.** Given the function $y = \log_a x$, where the notation indicates the logarithm to base $a$, find $y'$.

   *Suggestion:* Rewrite $y = \log_a x$ in terms of $\log_e x$.

$$\text{Ans. } y' = 1/x \log_e a.$$

**8.** Find the derived functions of the following functions:

(a)   $y = \log x^2$.

$$\text{Ans. } \frac{dy}{dx} = \frac{1}{2x}.$$

(b)   $y = (\log x)^2$.

(c)   $y = \log \dfrac{x}{1 + x}$.

$$\text{Ans. } \frac{dy}{dx} = \frac{1}{(x + x^2)}.$$

(d)   $y = \log \sin x$.

(e)   $y = \log(x^2 + 3x)$.

$$\text{Ans. } \frac{dy}{dx} = \frac{2x + 3}{x^2 + 3x}.$$

(f)   $f(x) = x \log x$.

(g)   $y = x \log x - x$.

$$\text{Ans. } \frac{dy}{dx} = \log x.$$

(h)   $f(x) = \dfrac{\log x}{x}$.

(i)   $y = \log(\log x)$.

$$\text{Ans. } \frac{dy}{dx} = \frac{1}{x \log x}.$$

**9.** Is there something especially worth noting in the result of Exercise 8(g)?

**10.** Find the integrals of the following derived functions:

(a)   $\dfrac{dy}{dx} = \dfrac{1}{3x}$.

$$\text{Ans. } y = \tfrac{1}{3} \log x + C.$$

(b)   $\dfrac{dy}{dx} = \dfrac{1}{x + 2}$.

(c)   $\dfrac{dy}{dx} = \dfrac{2x}{x^2 + 1}$.

$$\text{Ans. } y = \log(x^2 + 1) + C.$$

(d)   $\dfrac{dy}{dx} = \dfrac{x}{x^2 + 1}$.

(e)   $\dfrac{dy}{dx} = \dfrac{x - 3}{x^2 - 6x + 10}$.

$$\text{Ans. } y = \tfrac{1}{2} \log(x^2 - 6x + 10) + C.$$

(f)   $\dfrac{dy}{dx} = \dfrac{\cos x}{\sin x}$.

$$\text{Ans. } y = \log|\sin x| + C.$$

(g)   $f'(x) = \dfrac{\sin x}{\cos x}$.

$$\text{Ans. } f(x) = -\log|\cos x| + C.$$

(h)   $f'(x) = \tan x$.

(i)   $\dfrac{dy}{dx} = \cot x$.

$$\text{Ans. } y = \log|\sin x| + C.$$

(j)   $f'(x) = \dfrac{\sin x}{1 - \cos x}$.

(k)   $f'(x) = \dfrac{\sec^2 x}{\tan x}$.

$$\text{Ans. } y = \log|\tan x| + C.$$

(l)   $\dfrac{dy}{dx} = \dfrac{1}{x \log x}$.

**11.** Evaluate:

(a)   $\displaystyle\int \dfrac{3x}{x^2 + 2} \, dx$.

$$\text{Ans. } \tfrac{3}{2} \log(x^2 + 2) + C.$$

(b)   $\displaystyle\int \dfrac{x^2}{1 - x^3} \, dx$.

(c)   $\displaystyle\int \dfrac{x + 1}{x^2 + 2x + 5} \, dx$.

(d)   $\displaystyle\int \left( \dfrac{1}{2x - 5} - \dfrac{1}{2x + 3} \right) dx$.

(e)   $\displaystyle\int \tan \dfrac{x}{2} \, dx$.

**12.** Find the area between the curve $y = 1/x$, the $x$-axis and the ordinates at $x = 1$ and $x = 10$.

$$\text{Ans. } 2.3026.$$

**13.** The response of a human sense organ is not directly proportional to the stimulus; that is, $R$ is not $kS$. For example, the human hand will detect a difference between a 2-pound weight and a 1-pound weight far more readily than the difference between a 21-pound weight and a 20-pound weight. The general law of response versus stimulus was first enunciated by Ernst Heinrich Weber in 1834 and developed by G. H. Fechner in 1860. Roughly, in calculus terms it says that $\Delta R = k \, \Delta S / S$ where $\Delta R$ is the difference in response, $\Delta S$ is the difference in the stimulus, and $S$ is a measure of the stimulus. Find the precise relation between $R$ and $S$.

**14.** Show by mathematical induction that for positive integral $n$

$$\frac{d^n}{dx^n} \log x = (-1)^{n-1} \frac{(n-1)!}{x^n}.$$

The left-hand side means the $n$th derivative of $\log x$ and $(n-1)!$ means $1 \cdot 2 \cdot 3 \cdots (n-1)$.

**15.** Evaluate $\lim\limits_{x \to 1} \dfrac{\log x}{x-1}$.          *Ans.* 1.

**4. Exponential Functions and Their Derived Functions.** We have often converted statements about logarithms to statements about exponents. It is apparent therefore that exponential functions are closely related to logarithmic functions. In fact, the statement

**(32)**                               $y = \log x$

means

**(33)**                               $x = e^y.$

Because the same $x$ and $y$ are involved in (32) and (33) but (33) expresses the relation with $y$ as the independent variable, (33) is the inverse function of (32). A glance at Fig. 12-2 shows that there is a unique $x$ for each $y$, so that we do not have the problem of multiple values. If we write $x$ for the independent and $y$ for the dependent variable, the exponential function is

**(34)**                               $y = e^x;$

its graph is shown in Fig. 12-3. This graph, of course, is only Fig. 12-2 with the $x$- and $y$-axes interchanged.

**Figure 12-3**

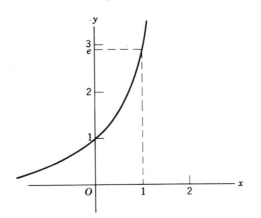

To find the value of $y$ in (34) for various values of $x$ we could work backwards in the table of natural logarithms; that is, because (34) says that $x$ is the natural logarithm of $y$, we could look up the $x$-value in the logarithm table and find the number, the $y$-value, which has that logarithm. However, because the exponential function is widely used, a separate table of $e^x$ and even $e^{-x}$ values has been prepared and a brief one is included in the Appendix to this book.

## EXERCISES

1. On the same set of axes sketch each of the following pairs of curves:
   (a)  $y = e^x$ and $y = 3e^x$.
   (b)  $y = e^x$ and $y = e^{-x}$.
   (c)  $y = e^x$ and $y = e^{(x+2)}$.
   (d)  $y = e^x$ and $y = e^x + 2$.
   (e)  $y = e^x$ and $y = x + e^x$.
   (f)  $y = e^x$ and $y = e^{3x}$.
   (g)  $y = e^x$ and $y = e^{-3x}$.

The calculus is, of course, concerned with differentiation and integration. Let us see what these processes amount to for exponential functions. Because the basic exponential function is the inverse of the basic logarithmic function and because we have a theorem on the derivative of inverse functions, let us approach the derivative of the basic exponential function in this way. To keep the relation between $x$ and $y$ clear we write the original function as

**(35)** $$y = \log x$$

and the inverse function as

**(36)** $$x = e^y.$$

We know from the theorem on the derived function of an inverse function that

$$\frac{dx}{dy} = \frac{1}{\dfrac{dy}{dx}}.$$

Since the derived function of (35) is $1/x$,

$$\frac{dx}{dy} = \frac{1}{1/x} = x = e^y.$$

If now we write the inverse function with $y$ as the dependent variable and $x$ as the independent one, we have the following result. If

$$y = e^x,$$

then

**(37)** $$\frac{dy}{dx} = e^x.$$

Peculiarly, the derivative of $e^x$ is $e^x$.

Of course, the chain rule helps us to extend the utility of the result (37).

**Theorem:**   If $y = e^u$, where $u$ is any function of $x$, then

(38) $$\frac{dy}{dx} = e^u \frac{du}{dx}.$$

Thus we can now differentiate a variety of exponential functions. We also have at once the integration formulas:

**Theorem:**   If $dy/dx = e^x$, then

(39) $$y = \int e^x \, dx = e^x + C,$$

and if $dy/dx = e^u(du/dx)$, then

(40) $$y = \int e^u \frac{du}{dx} \, dx = e^u + C.$$

To apply (40) we can proceed as follows. Suppose that

(41) $$\frac{dy}{dx} = xe^{-x^2}.$$

If we let $u = -x^2$, then $du/dx = -2x$. We rewrite (41) as

$$\frac{dy}{dx} = -\frac{1}{2} e^{-x^2}(-2x).$$

With our choice of $u$

$$\frac{dy}{dx} = -\frac{1}{2} e^u \frac{du}{dx}.$$

Then

$$y = \int -\frac{1}{2} e^u \frac{du}{dx} \, dx = -\frac{1}{2} e^u + C = -\frac{1}{2} e^{-x^2} + C.$$

## EXERCISES

1. Find the derived functions of the following functions:
   (a)   $y = e^{x^2}$.   *Ans.* $dy/dx = 2xe^{x^2}$.
   (b)   $y = e^{-2x}$.
   (c)   $y = e^{-1/x}$.
           *Ans.* $dy/dx = (1/x^2)e^{-1/x}$.
   (d)   $y = e^{\sin x}$.
   (e)   $y = e^x \log x$.
   (f)   $f(x) = x^2 e^{-x}$.
           *Ans.* $f'(x) = (2x - x^2)e^{-x}$.
   (g)   $f(x) = e^{-x} \cos 2x$.
   (h)   $y = (e^x)^2$.   *Ans.* $dy/dx = 2e^{2x}$.
   (i)   $y = \dfrac{e^x - e^{-x}}{e^x + e^{-x}}$.
   (j)   $y = \dfrac{e^x}{1 + e^x}$.
           *Ans.* $y' = 1/(1 + e^x)$.

**2.** Find the slope of $y = e^x$ at $x = 0$.

**3.** Graph the function $y = e^{-x^2}$.

**4.** Find the integral when the derived function has the following values:

(a)  $dy/dx = e^{-x}$.

             *Ans.* $y = -e^{-x} + C$.

(b)  $dy/dx = xe^{x^2}$.

(c)  $dy/dx = e^{\sin x} \cos x$.

             *Ans.* $y = e^{\sin x} + C$.

(d)  $dy/dx = \dfrac{e^{-1/x}}{x^2}$.

(e)  $f'(x) = e^{-x/2}$.

**5.** Find $y$ when $y'$ has the following values:

(a)  $y' = \dfrac{e^x - e^{-x}}{e^x + e^{-x}}$.

             *Ans.* $y = \log(e^x + e^{-x}) + C$.

(b)  $y' = \dfrac{e^{2x} - 1}{e^{2x} + 1}$.

(c)  $y' = \dfrac{e^{2x}}{1 + e^{2x}}$.

             *Ans.* $y = \tfrac{1}{2}\log(1 + e^{2x}) + C$.

**6.** Evaluate:

(a)  $\displaystyle\int e^{4x}\, dx$.      *Ans.* $\tfrac{1}{4}e^{4x} + C$.

(b)  $\displaystyle\int \dfrac{e^{1/x^2}}{x^3}\, dx$.

(c)  $\displaystyle\int e^{-x^2+3}x\, dx$.

(d)  $\displaystyle\int (e^x + 2)^2\, dx$.

(e)  $\displaystyle\int (e^x + 1)^4 e^x\, dx$.

(f)  $\displaystyle\int \dfrac{e^{2x}}{e^{2x} + 5}\, dx$.

**7.** Find the area under the curve $y = xe^{x^2}$ from $x = 0$ to $x = 1$.

**8.** The function $y = e^{-x^2}$ is immensely useful in the theory of probability; its graph is shown in Fig. 12-4. If we consider the area under the curve from $x = 0$ to $x = t$, the area is a function of $t$, say $F(t)$, and $F(t) = \displaystyle\int_0^t e^{-x^2}\, dx$. Using geometric evidence, show that the following hold:

(a)  $F(2)$ is positive.

(b)  $F(-2) = -F(2)$.

(c)  $F(3) > F(2)$.

(d)  $F(t)$ is an increasing function for positive $t$.

        *Suggestion:* Note the corollary to the fundamental theorem in Chapter 10.

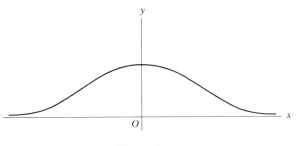

**Figure 12-4**

**9.** Graph the function $y = e^{-x}$.

**10.** Graph the function $y = e^{-x} \sin x$.

**11.** Show that if a phenomenon obeys the law $y = e^{kx}$, then for successive values of $x$ that are in arithmetic progression the corresponding values of $y$ are in geometric progression.

   *Suggestion:* Suppose that the successive values of $x$ are $0, h, 2h, \ldots$, and calculate the corresponding values of $y$.

12. Evaluate $\lim\limits_{h \to 0} \dfrac{e^h - 1}{h}$ .                                                    *Ans.* 1.

13. Show that $y = De^{kx}$ satisfies the equation $dy/dx = ky$.

14. The total cost $C$ of producing $x$ units of a commodity is $C = 5e^{x/8}$. Find the minimum average cost.

**5. Problems of Growth and Decay.** One class of applications employing the exponential and logarithmic functions deals with quantities that increase or decrease continuously at a rate that is some constant times the amount present at any time. Thus the temperature in a steel bar may decrease at any instant at a rate of 0.1 per minute times the actual temperature at that instant. We are already accustomed to the notion of an instantaneous rate of change and this idea may no longer disturb us, but the notion of an instantaneous rate that is some constant times the amount already present calls for an understanding of the significance of the constant that may not be intuitively apparent.

   Let us therefore begin with a more familiar situation. Suppose that we deposit 1 dollar in a bank that pays 4 per cent interest per year and compounds the interest annually. This means that the bank adds 4 cents to the account at the end of the first year. Then the total amount to the credit of the depositor at that time is $1.04. At the end of the second year the bank pays 4 percent interest on $1.04. Hence the amount at the end of the second year is

$$1.04 + (1.04)(0.04) = 1.04(1 + 0.04) = (1.04)^2.$$

At the end of the third year the bank pays 4 per cent on the amount present, namely $(1.04)^2$. Hence the amount at the end of the third year is

$$(1.04)^2 + (1.04)^2(0.04) = (1.04)^3.$$

At the end of $n$ years the amount $A$ accumulated is

**(42)**                            $A = (1.04)^n.$

We should note that under annual compound interest the bank pays interest on the *amount present*, but it pays this interest once a year; the rate of 0.04 is *not* applied continuously to the amount present. Moreover, if formula (42) is to fit the actual situation, the values of $n$ must be positive integers.

   Now suppose that the bank pays 4 per cent per year compounded quarterly. This means that the annual rate is divided by 4 and the interest of 1 per cent is paid at the end of each quarter year on the amount present at that time. The amount accumulated at the end of $n$ years is readily calculated by the same argument that led to (42), except that now the interest rate is $0.04/4$ and the number of times interest is compounded is $4n$. Hence the amount accumulated at the end of $n$ years is

**(43)**
$$A = \left(1 + \frac{0.04}{4}\right)^{4n}.$$

If, instead of quarterly, the interest is compounded $r$ times a year at the rate of 4 per cent per year, the amount accumulated at the end of $n$ years is

**(44)**
$$A = \left(1 + \frac{0.04}{r}\right)^{rn}.$$

We now ask the seemingly pointless question: suppose that $r$ becomes infinite, that is, suppose that the interest is compounded *continuously* at the rate of 4 per cent per year; how much money is accumulated at the end of $n$ years?* What we want is the value of $A$ in (44) as $r$ becomes infinite. We can write (44) in the form

$$A = \left[\left(1 + \frac{0.04}{r}\right)^{r/0.04}\right]^{0.04n}.$$

If we let $0.04/r$ be $t$, then the quantity in the brackets looks familiar; in fact, it is what we encountered in (9), where $t = 0.04/r$. Because $r$ becoming infinite is equivalent to $t$ approaching 0, we have that

$$\lim_{r \to \infty} \left[\left(1 + \frac{0.04}{r}\right)^{r/0.04}\right]^{0.04n} = \lim_{t \to 0} \left[(1 + t)^{1/t}\right]^{0.04n} = e^{0.04n}.$$

Then

**(45)**
$$A = e^{0.04n}.$$

There are several features of this result that warrant attention. First, in formula (42), $n$ is a number of years but limited to a positive integer (or zero). In (43) $n$ is still a number of years but, because the formula represents quarterly compounding, it is logical to ask how much money is accumulated at the end of 6 quarters for example. In this case $n$ is one and one half years or $\frac{3}{2}$. In other words, $n$ can take on values such as $\frac{1}{4}$, $\frac{2}{4}$, and $\frac{3}{4}$. For the case of compounding $r$ times a year, when (44) obtains, it is logical to ask how much money is accumulated in any number of intervals. Thus if $r$ were 13, and we wanted to know how much money accumulated after 16 intervals, we would let $n$ be $16/13$. The permissible values of $n$, in other words, are $m/13$ where $m$ is any positive interger. In the case of (45), where the money is compounded continuously, it is logical to ask how much money is accumulated at any time. Hence $n$ can be any positive real number. To emphasize the fact that $n$ can now stand for any interval of time, we write (45) as

**(46)**
$$A = e^{0.04t}.$$

*Actually many banks do compound interest continuously.

The next point to note about (46) is the rather surprising result that 1 dollar bearing interest at the rate of 4 per cent per year but compounded *continuously* throughout the year amounts to $e^{0.04}$ at the end of 1 year. The table of the exponential function shows that $e^{0.04} = 1.0408$. Hence 1 dollar invested at the rate of 4 per cent per year compounded continuously produces 1.0408. This amount is not much more than 1.04 but, of course, if 1 million dollars is so invested, the return is \$1,040,800 in 1 year instead of \$1,040,000, and the difference between 4 per cent per year compounded only at the end of the year and 4 per cent per year compounded continuously is \$800. Moreover, if the million dollars is left to accumulate interest for 10 years at the rate of 4 per cent per year compounded continuously, it amounts to

$$1 \cdot 10^6 \, e^{0.04(10)},$$

and because $e^{0.4}$ is 1.4918, the amount accumulated is \$1,491,800, whereas if the interest were 4 per cent per year compounded annually for 10 years the amount accumulated, according to (42), would be

$$1 \cdot 10^6 (1.04)^{10}$$

or \$1,480,244.

Let us return to reality. The most important point about the above discussion is that continuous compounding of interest at the rate of 0.04 per year is an example of the phenomenon in which a quantity changes continuously at a rate that is applied constantly to the amount present at any instant. Moreover, a rate of 0.04 *per year applied continuously* to the amount present is equivalent to the rate of 0.0408 applied at the end of each year.

Let us now look at the problem of continuous compounding of interest in another way. To say that interest is continuously compounded means that at any instant of time the interest is being applied to the amount present. If $A$ is the amount present at any instant, the amount that is added in time $\Delta t$, if the annual rate is 0.04 and if $\Delta t$ is measured in years, is $A(0.04) \, \Delta t$. Then $\Delta A = A(0.04) \, \Delta t$ and $\Delta A / \Delta t = 0.04A$. The instantaneous rate of increase of $A$ is, by definition, $dA/dt$. Hence

**(47)** 
$$\frac{dA}{dt} = 0.04A.$$

Let us see what this equation implies about the relation between $A$ and $t$.

We can integrate this equation readily. By the theorem on inverse functions it can be written as

$$\frac{dt}{dA} = \frac{1}{0.04} \frac{1}{A}.$$

Then by (27)

$$t = \frac{1}{0.04} \log A + C.$$

We could evaluate the constant of integration at once, but we save time later if we first rewrite the equation as

$$\log A = 0.04t - 0.04C.$$

By the definition of logarithms to base $e$,

$$A = e^{0.04t - 0.04C} = e^{0.04t} \cdot e^{-0.04C}.$$

For the moment $C$ is some unknown constant that is still to be determined. Then so is $e^{-0.04C}$. Let us call the latter $D$. Hence

**(48)**                          $$A = De^{0.04t}.$$

Suppose that 1 dollar was invested to start with. Then when $t = 0$, $A = 1$. Hence $D = 1$ and

**(49)**                          $$A = e^{0.04t}.$$

This is the same result as (46).

We see, then, that continuous compounding at the rate of 0.04 per year means, in view of (47), that the instantaneous rate of change of $A$ is some constant times $A$, and this constant is the annual rate. There is another point to be noted about the statement of the rate of change. We stated that the money is compounded *continuously at the rate of 4 per cent per year* of the amount present. The phrase "per year" is essential. It is because the 0.04 is a rate per year that we must interpret the $t$ in (49) as standing for a quantity in terms of years.

Let us now return to the problem of what happens to a steel bar which is initially at 100° and which loses temperature continuously at the rate of 0.1 per minute of the amount present. If the bar lost 0.1 of its existing temperature *at the end of* each minute, it would have a temperature of 90° at the end of 1 minute, a temperature of 81° at the end of the second minute, and so on. However, the condition is that the loss of 0.1 of the existing temperature be continuous. A continuous loss of temperature at the rate of 0.1 per minute times the temperature prevailing at that instant means that the instantaneous rate of change of temperature equals 0.1 times the temperature. In symbols, if $T$ is the temperature,

$$\frac{dT}{dt} = 0.1T.$$

This statement is not quite correct. Because the temperature is decreasing, its derivative must be negative. Then we must state that

$$\frac{dT}{dt} = -0.1T.$$

In this equation $t$ stands for the time in minutes. Our problem now is to find the functional relation between $T$ and $t$.

This equation is of exactly the same form as (47). The $-0.1$ here corresponds to 0.04 there and, of course, $T$ here corresponds to $A$ there. In view of (48) we can state at once that

$$\textbf{(50)} \qquad\qquad T = De^{-0.1t}.$$

To fit this formula to the specific situation in which the temperature is 100° at the outset, we can agree that if time is measured from the instant when the temperature is 100°, then when $t = 0$, $T = 100°$. If we substitute these values in (50), we have

$$100 = De^{-0.1(0)}.$$

Then $D = 100$ and

$$\textbf{(51)} \qquad\qquad T = 100e^{-0.1t}.$$

This formula tells us how the temperature of the body decreases with time. The unit of $t$ must be minutes because the rate of 0.1 is 0.1 per minute.

To calculate $T$ at various values of $t$, we could utilize common logarithms. Thus at $t = 3$, say,

$$\textbf{(52)} \qquad\qquad T = 100e^{-0.3}.$$

Now

$$\log_{10} T = \log_{10} 100 - 0.3 \log_{10} e.$$

Because $e$ is about 2.718, we could complete the calculation by using the table of common logarithms. However, with a table of the exponential function available we only need to look up $e^{-0.3}$. The rest of the arithmetic is obvious. In the present case, the value of $T$ in (52) is about 74.1°. When $t = 10$, since $e^{-1} = 0.368$, $T = 36.8°$ approximately.

Phenomena such as the continuous compounding of money and the loss of heat in an object are examples of exponential growth and decay, respectively. In these examples we knew the rate at which the continuous change is taking place. However, there are situations in which we know that a quantity is changing continuously at a rate that is some constant times the amount present but do not know the constant. Such a situation is sometimes stated in the language of proportion; that is, one is told that some quantity $y$ is changing continuously at a rate with respect to time which is proportional to the amount present. In symbols, this statement is written as

$$\frac{dy}{dt} = ky,$$

where $k$ is unknown. However, enough information may be given to determine $k$ and also $y$ as a function of $t$. Let us consider some examples.

Let us examine first a problem in the growth of a population. If the physical conditions in an area are stable, we might expect that the birth and death rates would remain constant and that there would be some net rate, say a rate of growth, if the birthrate exceeds the death rate. It may be sufficient in some population studies to know that if there are 3 births per one hundred of population per year and 1 death per hundred per year, the net rate of increase is 2 people per hundred *per year*. We can then write a formula for the population in $t$ years. In fact, if the population is 500 at $t = 0$, then

$$P = 500 + 500(0.02)t.$$

However, in other such studies it may be necessary to take into account that the population increases *continuously* at some annual rate applied to the existing population. This fact is certainly pertinent in a large population because births and deaths are continually taking place. Let us see what can be done with the assumption of a continuous change whose rate is proportional to the number present at any time.

The statement that the population changes continuously at some annual rate applied to the existing population or that the instantaneous rate of change of population is proportional to the existing population can be expressed in mathematical language as

**(53)**                                       $$\frac{dP}{dt} = kP$$

where $P$ is the population, $t$ is the time in years, and $k$ is the proportionality constant whose value we do not know. Now (53) leads, in the same way as (47) led to (48), to

**(54)**                                       $$P = De^{kt}.$$

Suppose that we know that the population was 10,000 twenty years ago and is 20,000 today. Let us agree to measure time from the instant when the population was 10,000. Then at $t = 0$, $P = 10,000$. This implies that $D$ in (54) is 10,000. So far then

**(55)**                                       $$P = 10,000e^{kt}.$$

Because our unit of time is years, we can say that at $t = 20$, $P = 20,000$. From (55) we have

$$20,000 = 10,000e^{k \cdot 20}.$$

Then

**(56)**                                       $$2 = e^{20k},$$

and by taking the logarithms of both sides

**(57)**                                       $$20k \log e = \log 2.$$

This statement is correct in base 10 or base $e$. If we choose base $e$, then, because $\log_e e = 1$,

**(58)** $$k = \frac{\log_e 2}{20} = \frac{0.693}{20} = 0.0347.$$

If we choose base 10, then, by (56),

**(59)** $$k = \frac{1}{20} \frac{\log_{10} 2}{\log_{10} e} = \frac{1}{20} \frac{0.3010}{0.4343} = 0.0347.$$

This value of $k$ is the rate per year which operates continuously. By substituting this value in (55) we obtain the precise law of population growth. We can then use this law to calculate the population to be expected at some time in the future. Of course, the law is an idealization. Strictly the population does not change continuously because the values of $P$ must be integral.

## EXERCISES

1. The more general statement of how an object loses heat, known as Newton's law of cooling, is that the rate of decrease of temperature of an object is continuous and proportional to the difference between the temperature of the object and that of the surrounding medium. Suppose that the surrounding medium is so vast that the heat it absorbs from the object does not appreciably change the medium's temperature so that it remains constant. Suppose that the object is initially at a temperature of 100° and loses temperature continuously at the rate of 1/100 per minute of the difference between its temperature at time $t$ and the constant temperature $T_0$ of the surrounding medium. Derive the formula that relates the temperature of the object and time.
   *Ans.* $T - T_0 = (100 - T_0)e^{-0.01t}$.

2. Suppose that an object loses temperature at the rate of 0.01 of the existing temperature not continuously but at the end of each minute. If the temperature is initially 100°, derive the formula that relates the temperature of the object and the time. *Ans.* $T = 100(0.99)^t$. To fit the physical situation $t$ can take on only the values 0, 1, 2, . . . , where the numbers refer to minutes.

3. Suppose that an object, initially at a temperature of 100°, loses temperature continuously at the rate of 0.01° per minute. Derive the formula that relates the temperature and the time. *Ans.* $T = 100 - 0.01t$.

4. Suppose that the population of a town increases at the net rate *per year* of 0.03466 of its population *at the beginning* of the year. Find the formula that relates the population and time. *Ans.* $P = P_0(1.03466)^t$.

5. Suppose that the population of a town was 5000 twenty years ago and that it increased continuously at a rate proportional to the existing population. Suppose that the population reached 15,000 at the end of the twenty years. What formula relates the population and the time? *Ans.* $P = 5000e^{0.06t}$.

6. A steel ball heated to a temperature of 100° is placed in a medium which is held at a constant temperature of 40°. At the end of 2 minutes the temperature of the ball is 80°. At what time will the temperature be 43°? *Ans.* 14.6 min.
   *Suggestion:* See Exercise 1.

7. Sugar in water dissolves continuously at a rate proportional to the undissolved amount. If the amount of sugar is initially 200 grams and 100 grams are dissolved in 2 minutes, how long does it take to dissolve 150 grams? How long does it take to dissolve all 200 grams? $\qquad$ *Ans.* 4.1 min; ∞.

8. Suppose that the population of a town increases at an annual rate of *r* people per hundred per year. Find the equivalent rate if the same population is assumed to increase continuously and at a rate proportional to the existing population. $\qquad$ *Ans.* $k = \log_e (1 + r)$.

9. Bacteria in a culture increase continuously at a rate proportional to the number already attained. If the proportionality constant is 0.2 per minute, find the number of bacteria in *t* minutes if there are 100 to start with.

$$\text{\textit{Ans.} } N = 100e^{0.2t}.$$

10. A beam of light passing through water loses intensity continuously at a rate that is proportional to the intensity present at a given depth. If the proportionality constant is denoted by *k*, that is, if *k* is the percentage of loss per foot of depth, and if the intensity is reduced by $\frac{1}{2}$ after the light passes through 10 feet of water, how much is *k*? $\qquad$ *Ans.* $k = 0.07$.

11. A radioactive substance such as uranium emits particles from the nucleus of each atom. After emitting this particle the atom is no longer uranium (it becomes thorium). We say then that the uranium atom has decayed or disintegrated. There are billions of atoms even in a small amount of uranium, and in any small interval of time some of the atoms disintegrate. Because some disintegration is continually taking place, it is reasonable to speak of the instantaneous rate of change with respect to time of the number of atoms of uranium. Moreover, even though two different atoms may emit particles at quite different instants, the number of atoms is so large that we can assume that the rate at which the atoms emit is proportional to the number of atoms present. Then if *N* is the number of uranium atoms present at time *t*, the rate of decrease of *N* per unit of time (in years) is

$$\dot{N} = -kN$$

where *k* is the proportionality constant. If there are $10^{12}$ uranium atoms present at $t = 0$, and if half of these are present after 4,500,000,000 years, find the value of *k*. $\qquad$ *Ans.* $k = 1.6 \cdot 10^{-10}$.

12. In a certain chain of nuclear reactions that take place in a nuclear reactor plutonium decays to uranium 235 and the uranium decays to thorium. The amount of uranium derived from plutonium at any time *t* is given by $u = P(1 - e^{-\lambda t})$ where *P* is the original amount of plutonium. The amount of uranium that has decayed at any time *t* is given by $U = u(1 - e^{-\lambda t})$. Let us assume that $P = 3400$ grams and that $\lambda = \frac{1}{10} \log 2$. If the amount of uranium present at any time exceeds what is called the critical mass, namely 800 grams, the reactor will explode. Is the reactor safe? $\qquad$ *Ans.* Disaster.

13. A tank contains 100 gallons of salt water in which 150 pounds of salt is dissolved. Salt water containing one pound of salt per gallon enters continuously at the rate of 2 gal/min. If the mixture in the tank is kept uniform by stirring and the mixed salt water flows out continuously at the rate of 2 gal/min, what is the amount of salt in the tank at the end of 1 hour?

$\quad$ *Suggestion:* Let *Q* be the number of pounds of salt in the tank at the end of *t* minutes. Show that $\dot{Q} = 2 - 2Q/100$. Find *Q* as a function of *t*. $\qquad$ *Ans.* 115 lb.

**14.** A fishtank, which holds 10 gallons, contains impure water, that is, a mixture of impurities and water. A filter is placed in the tank which draws out the impure water continuously at the constant rate of 10 gal/hr and replaces it at the same rate by pure water. How long does it take to replace half of the impurity by pure water? This problem is a somewhat idealized version of a typical problem in biology. If a drug (or dye) is injected in an organ of the body and thereafter the drug is thinned out by the influx of blood not containing the drug, the dilution of the drug follows the law involved in this problem.

*Suggestion:* Let $y =$ the number of gallons of impurity present.

*Ans.* 0.7 hr.

**15.** The half-life of a radioactive mass of atoms $N(t)$, which disintegrate according to the law $N(t) = N(0)e^{-kt}$ where $t$ is time in years, is the time required for $N(t)$ to equal $N(0)/2$. Find the half-life in terms of $k$.     *Ans.* $0.693/k$.

**16.** (a)   A quantity of radium atoms disintegrates according to the law $N(t) = N(0)e^{-0.000433t}$, the number 0.000433 meaning the per cent of atoms per year. How many of the original number $N(0)$ are left after 100 years?

*Ans.* $0.958N(0)$.

(b)   What is the half-life (see Exercise 15) of radium?   *Ans.* About 1600 years.

**17.** The sales of a product are decreasing at a rate which is $s$ times the number selling at any time $t$. In how many years will the sales decrease to half of those sold at time $t = 0$?

**18.** The population of the earth was about 3 billion in 1970. It is estimated that the world's population is increasing continuously at a rate of 2% per year of the existing population. When will the population of 20 billion be reached?

**19.** Suppose that the earth cannot support a population greater than 20 billion and that the rate of population growth is proportional to the difference between 20 billion and the existing population at any time. Find the law of population growth.     *Ans.* $P = 20 - De^{-kt}$.

**20.** Carbon 14, denoted by $C^{14}$, is a radioactive isotope of carbon. The amount of $C^{14}$ present in any unit volume of the atmosphere remains constant and living organisms manage to maintain the same amount per unit volume of their bodies. However, if the organism dies it loses $C^{14}$ at a rate proportional to the amount present. The amount present can be used to date the death. If the half-life (see Exercise 15) of $C^{14}$ is 5570 years how old is a dead organism which has $\frac{1}{10}$ of the $C^{14}$ present when the organism was alive?     *Ans.* 18,500 years.

**21.** Under reasonable conditions the blood pressure in the aorta (the main artery from the heart) during what is known as the diastolic phase (when the heart relaxes) is subject to the law $P'(t) = (-c/w)P(t)$. Find $P(t)$.

**22.** A drug is injected into the blood and is gradually absorbed and then eliminated. The concentration $y$ of the drug at any time $t$ is given by the formula $y = [A/(C_2 - C_1)](e^{-C_1 t} - e^{-C_2 t})$, wherein $A$, $C_1$, and $C_2$ are positive constants. Find the time $t$ at which the concentration is a maximum.

*Ans.* $t = [1/(C_1 - C_2)] \log(C_1/C_2)$.

**6. *Motion in one Direction in a Resisting Medium.*** \* When Galileo investigated the laws of falling bodies in the early part of the seventeenth century, he neglected air resistance because it is a secondary effect compared to the action of gravity. Had he undertaken to consider this effect, he

---

\*This section can be omitted without disrupting the continuity.

might have been frustrated in any case, because the mathematics required to handle it was not available. One hundred years later, by which time the calculus had been founded, the mathematicians were empowered and proceeded to tackle problems of motion in resisting media. Such problems, which include the motion of raindrops, meteorites, ships, trains, and automobiles, have always been important, and today are even more important in view of the greater variety of motions that modern man utilizes.

To consider motions in media that offer resistance, say, air or water, we must know something about the kind of resistance that takes place. This information is not derived from mathematics but from physical investigations. Perhaps the first point to note is that the resistance of the medium is a force, which acts in conjunction with other forces such as the force of gravity. Second, the resistance that an object experiences in falling through air or in being propelled through water depends on many factors, for example, the density of the medium, the shape and size of the object, the smoothness of the surface of the object, and its velocity. If it is necessary to obtain a precise expression for the resistance of the medium, all of these factors must be taken into account, as is done, for example, in the design of airplanes. However, of all these factors the *velocity* of the object as it moves through the medium is usually the most important in determining what resistance the object will encounter. In our introduction to the problem of motion in resisting media we consider the dependence of the resistance only on the velocity of the moving object. The other factors will be contained in a proportionality constant. This simplification or idealization is a very realistic one, as we shall soon see.

How, then, does the resistance depend on the velocity? For comparatively small speeds, say up to about a few hundred feet per second, it is found by experiment that the resistance offered by the medium is proportional to the velocity of the moving object; for higher speeds the resistance is proportional to the square of the velocity. These are the physical facts; however, for the purpose of getting to know how to treat motions in resisting media we shall not worry much about the proper range of the actual speeds.

Let us consider first a rather simple situation. Suppose that an object is projected along smooth ground and that the resistance of the air is *proportional to the velocity* of the object. The action of gravity can be neglected because the surface opposes downward motion. What formula relates the velocity of the object and time and what formula relates the distance traveled and time?

When we say that the object is projected along smooth ground we mean that the object is launched with some initial velocity and thereafter is subject to the resistance that slows down its motion. Suppose that the body is projected to the right, which we take to be the positive direction. Then the air resistance acts to the left and slows down the object. We can obtain the mathematical representation of this motion in either of two ways. We can argue that at any instant the object loses velocity at a rate that is proportional to the velocity. The instantaneous loss in velocity is $dv/dt$ or $\dot{v}$. Because this is proportional to the velocity, we have so far that $\dot{v} = kv$. If the object is moving to the right, $v$ is positive; however, the resistance acts to the left, so that

**(60)** $$\dot{v} = -kv,$$

where $k$ is a positive constant. To see that the minus sign is necessary we can also argue that $v$ is positive but is decreasing. Hence $dv/dt$ must be negative, and therefore we must interpose the minus sign if the right side is to equal the left side.

The second method of deriving (60), which is worth noting because it is more useful in other problems, argues that there is a resistive force acting to the left which is proportional to the velocity. This force is $-Kv$. According to Newton's second law of motion, this force must equal the mass of the object times its acceleration, and therefore

$$m\dot{v} = -Kv.$$

If we divide both sides by $m$ and replace $K/m$ by $k$, we again obtain (60).

The form of equation (60) is quite familiar, and by now we know that the integral is

**(61)** $$v = De^{-kt}.$$

To determine $D$ we must know some physical facts. If, for example, we know that the object was launched with an initial velocity of 100 ft/sec and if we measure time from the instant the object is launched, then at $t = 0$, $v = 100$. These values substituted in (61) yield $D = 100$, and therefore the final formula for the velocity as a function of the time is

**(62)** $$v = 100e^{-kt}.$$

Of course, to calculate $v$ for various values of $t$ we must know $k$. This quantity can be obtained from measurements of actual resistance experienced by objects in the medium in question; alternatively, by measuring $v$ at a definite value of $t$ one can calculate $k$. Figure 12-5 shows how $v$ varies with $t$.

From (62) we can derive the formula for distance traveled in time $t$. If $x$ is the distance traveled in time $t$, then $v = dx/dt = \dot{x}$, so that

**(63)** $$\dot{x} = 100e^{-kt}.$$

**Figure 12-5**

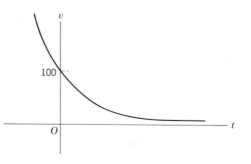

The exponential factor on the right is of the form $e^u$ where $u = -kt$. To apply the inverse of the chain rule we need $du/dt$, which is $-k$. Hence we write (63) as

$$\frac{dx}{dt} = -\frac{100}{k} e^{-kt}(-k).$$

Now we can apply (40) wherein we let $u = -kt$. Then

**(64)** $$x = -\frac{100}{k} e^u + C = -\frac{100}{k} e^{-kt} + C.$$

Again we need some physical information to determine $C$. If, for example, we measure distance traveled from the position of the object at time $t = 0$, then $x = 0$ when $t = 0$. If we substitute these values in (64), we have that

$$0 = -\frac{100}{k} + C.$$

Then

$$x = -\frac{100}{k} e^{-kt} + \frac{100}{k}$$

or

**(65)** $$x = \frac{100}{k} (1 - e^{-kt}).$$

It is helpful to see what this result means geometrically. The graph of this function is best obtained by first determining the graph of $x = -e^{-kt}$, which is shown in Fig. 12-6a. By adding 1 to each $x$-value in this graph we obtain Fig. 12-6b. If we now "stretch" each ordinate by the factor $100/k$, we obtain the graph of (65) shown in Fig. 12-6c. We note that as $t$ becomes infinite, that is, as $t$ takes on larger and larger values without bound, $x$ approaches $100/k$. This fact is also apparent in (65) because $e^{-kt} = 1/e^{kt}$. In other words, the object approaches a fixed point $100/k$ feet away from the starting point more and more closely as $t$ becomes infinite, but never quite reaches this point.

**Figure 12-6**

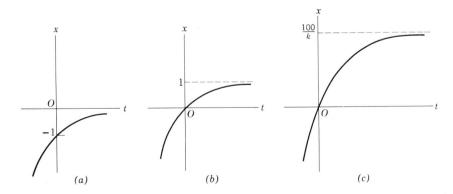

(a)          (b)          (c)

## EXERCISES

1. Suppose that an object is launched horizontally over some smooth surface with an initial velocity of 100 ft/sec and that the air resistance varies as the square of the velocity. We may neglect gravity for the reason given in the text. Find the formula that relates velocity and time. Compare the result with (62).

   *Ans.* $v = 100/(1 + 100kt)$.

2. Under the conditions of Exercise 1 and using the result obtained there, find the formula that relates distance traveled and time of travel. Compare the result with (65).             *Ans.* $x = (1/k) \log(1 + 100kt)$.

3. According to the result of Exercise 2 when an object travels subject to a resistance that varies as the square of the velocity, the distance traveled becomes infinite with increasing time. The text showed that when the resistance of the medium is proportional to the velocity, the distance traveled approaches a finite limit with increasing time. Because the resistance of the medium seems to be greater in Exercise 2, we would expect the distance traveled to be less than in the text example. How would you explain this paradox?

   *Suggestion:* Consider what happens when $v$ becomes less than 1.

4. A particle starts from the origin with velocity $V$ and moves along a horizontal smooth surface in a medium whose resistance is proportional to $\sqrt{v}$ , where $v$ is the variable velocity. Find the following:
   (a)   The relation between velocity and time.        *Ans.* $v = \left(\sqrt{V} - kt/2\right)^2$.
   (b)   The relation between distance and time.
   (c)   The relation between velocity and distance.   *Ans.* $x = 2(V^{3/2} - v^{3/2})/3k$.
   (d)   How far the particle moves.                                  *Ans.* $2V^{3/2}/3k$.

5. A man rowing at $v_0$ ft/sec in still water rests his oars. Thereafter the resistance of the water, which we may assume to be proportional to the velocity, slows down his speed. Find the formulas for the velocity and distance traveled $t$ seconds later.             *Ans.* $v = v_0 e^{-kt}$; $x = (v_0/k)(1 - e^{-kt})$.

6. Using the relation $dv/dt = v\, dv/dx$ and the conditions of Exercise 5, find the formula for the velocity $v$ in terms of the distance $x$ traveled after the oars are rested.             *Ans.* $v = v_0 - kx$.

7. A torpedo is ejected under water with an initial velocity $V$. It is known experimentally that the resistance of the water is $0.0068v^2$, that is, $k = 0.0068$. If the torpedo must strike with a velocity of at least $V/2$ to cause damage, what is the maximum effective striking distance?

   *Suggestion:* See Exercises 1 and 2.             *Ans.* 101.9 ft.

8. Exercise 7 can be done by following the procedures of Exercises 1 and 2 and then calculating the time at which $v$ becomes $V/2$. However, because we are interested in the relation between distance traveled and velocity, we can use an old device, namely, $dv/dt = (dv/dx)(dx/dt) = v\, dv/dx$. Redo Exercise 7 by this method.

As another example of motion in a resisting medium let us consider the motion of an object of mass $m$ falling downward in air. If the motion takes place near the surface of the earth, we can take the acceleration of gravity to be 32 ft/sec$^2$. We assume that the resistance of the air is *proportional to the velocity*. The force of gravity acts on the object, and the amount of this force is the weight of the object or $32m$. To keep the signs straight, we must take the positive direction of force to be the positive direction of the distance. Let us take the downward direction as positive. Hence the force of gravity is $+32m$. The magnitude of the air resistance is $Kv$, where we take $K$ to be positive, and because this force acts to resist the motion, its direction is upward. Since $v$ is positive downward the force of the air resistance is $-Kv$. The net force acting on the object is

$$32m - Kv.$$

By Newton's second law of motion this force is the mass of the object times the acceleration; hence

$$m\dot{v} = 32m - Kv.$$

If we divide both sides of this equation by $m$ and replace $K/m$ by another constant $k$, our equation becomes

**(66)**
$$\dot{v} = 32 - kv.$$

The integration of this equation seems to pose a problem. Since the right side is a function of the *dependent* variable, let us write it as

**(67)**
$$\frac{dt}{dv} = \frac{1}{32 - kv} \,.$$

It seems likely that we can apply formula (30) if we can choose a suitable $u$. We let

$$u = 32 - kv.$$

Then

$$\frac{du}{dv} = -k.$$

We therefore write (67) in the form $dt/dv = (dt/du)(du/dv)$, that is,

$$\frac{dt}{dv} = -\frac{1}{k}\frac{1}{u}(-k).$$

The constant $-1/k$ can be ignored for the moment while we apply (30). Then

$$t = -\frac{1}{k}\log u + C = -\frac{1}{k}\log(32 - kv) + C.$$

Because we want $v$ as a function of $t$, we solve for $v$. First,

$$\log(32 - kv) = -kt + kC$$

or

$$32 - kv = e^{-kt+kC} = e^{-kt}e^{kC} = De^{-kt},$$

where $D = e^{kC}$. Thus we obtain

**(68)** $$v = \frac{32}{k} - \frac{D}{k} e^{-kt}.$$

To determine $D$ we need some physical information. Suppose that the object is just dropped from some point above the surface of the earth. This means in mathematical terms that $v = 0$ when $t = 0$ if time is measured from the instant the object is dropped. If we substitute these values in (68), we find that $D = 32$. Then

**(69)** $$v = \frac{32}{k}(1 - e^{-kt}).$$

Again, it is instructive to picture the relation between $v$ and $t$. Let us recall that positive $v$ is directed downward. We first graph $v = -e^{-kt}$ as shown in Fig. 12-7$a$. We then add 1 to each $v$-value and obtain Fig. 12-7$b$. Finally, we multiply each $v$-value by $32/k$ and obtain Fig. 12-7$c$.

The surprising fact which the last figure reveals but which can also be deduced from (69) is that the velocity of the falling object does not increase indefinitely; it approaches a limiting value of $32/k$ as $t$ becomes infinite. This limiting value is called the *terminal velocity*.

The fact that there is a finite terminal velocity is very important in some situations. Suppose that a man drops out of an airplane and opens his parachute immediately. Then the air resistance is considerable. Let us suppose that the value of $k$ in this case is 2. The man's downward velocity is 0 at the outset and increases thereafter, but it never becomes larger than $\frac{32}{2}$ or 16 ft/sec. He may then land without injuring himself.

Having obtained (69), we may as well see if we can find the formula that relates distance fallen and time of fall. We let $y$ represent the variable distance; the downward direction has already been chosen to be the positive one. Let us rewrite (69) as

**(70)** $$\dot{y} = \frac{32}{k} - \frac{32}{k} e^{-kt}.$$

**Figure 12-7**

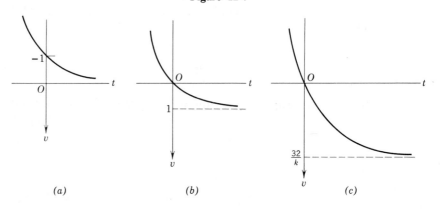

(a)             (b)             (c)

The integration here is practically straightforward. The first term on the right is a constant and the second can be handled in the same way as (63). Then

$$y = \frac{32}{k} t + \frac{32}{k^2} e^{-kt} + C.$$

If we measure distance from the position of the object at $t = 0$, then at this instant $y = 0$. If follows that $C = -32/k^2$, and

**(71)**
$$y = \frac{32}{k} t + \frac{32}{k^2} e^{-kt} - \frac{32}{k^2}.$$

To obtain a sketch of the graph of (71), we first sketch (Fig. 12-8) $y = (32/k^2)e^{-kt}$. We then subtract from this sketch the constant value $-32/k^2$. This *raises* the first sketch by a constant amount. We then graph independently but on the same set of axes the function $y = 32t/k$. This is a straight line whose slope depends, of course, on the value of $k$. Now, according to (71), the $y$ we seek is the sum of the $y$-values on the second sketch and the $y$-values on the straight line. Hence, as $t$ increases from 0 onward, we estimate what the sum of these $y$-values is and thus obtain the final graph which is the final curve in Fig. 12-8.

We note from the graph that the object does not fall quite as far during the first few seconds as it does later in the same period of time. This is, of course, understandable because the object starts with 0 velocity and takes time to gain appreciable velocity. However, it soon acquires a velocity close to the terminal velocity of $32/k$ and thereafter falls at almost this velocity.

**Figure 12-8**

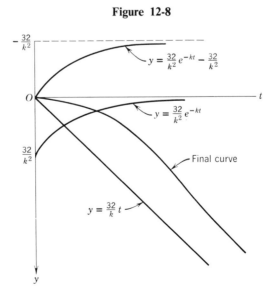

## EXERCISES

1. Suppose that we redo the problem considered in the text of an object falling from some height in a medium whose resistance is proportional to the velocity, but that this time we take the upward direction as positive. Derive the formula that relates velocity and time.

   *Suggestion:* Since $v$ is negative the resistance is $-Kv$ where $K$ is positive.

2. Compare the result (69) with the corresponding formula for an object that falls straight down under the action of gravity in a vacuum.

3. Suppose that an object is thrown downward with an initial velocity of 1000 ft/sec in a medium whose resistance is proportional to the velocity. Find the expression for the velocity as a function of time.

   *Ans.* $v = (32/k) - [(32/k) - 1000]e^{-kt}$.

4. Suppose that an object is thrown downward with an initial velocity $V$ in a medium whose resistance is proportional to the velocity.
   (a) Find the expression for the velocity as a function of time and discuss the motion for the cases $V > 32/k$, $V = 32/k$, and $V < 32/k$.

   *Ans.* $v = \dfrac{32}{k} - \left(\dfrac{32}{k} - V\right)e^{-kt}$.

   (b) What is the terminal velocity in each case? Explain physically why the answers are correct. *Ans.* $32/k$.

5. Using the result of Exercise 3, find the expression for the distance fallen as a function of time $t$. *Ans.* $y = (32/k)t + (1/k)[(32/k) - 1000](e^{-kt} - 1)$.

6. A body falls from rest in a medium whose resistance is proportional to the velocity. If the terminal velocity is 12 ft/sec, find the velocity and distance fallen after 2 seconds. *Ans.* $v = 12(1 - e^{-16/3})$; $y = 12(2 + \tfrac{3}{8}e^{-16/3}) - \tfrac{9}{2}$.

7. An aviator drops out of an airplane and falls freely for 10 seconds (during which time we may suppose the air resistance to be negligible). He then opens his parachute and the air resistance becomes proportional to his velocity. Find the formula that expresses his velocity as a function of time from the instant he opens his parachute.

   *Ans.* $v = \dfrac{32}{k} - \left(\dfrac{32}{k} - 320\right)e^{-kt}$.

8. Suppose that a body has acquired a downward velocity $v_0$ and that thereafter it gains velocity proportional to the distance traveled. Find the formulas for distance traveled, velocity, and acceleration as functions of time. Distance and time are measured from the instant and place where the object already has the velocity $v_0$. *Ans.* $y = (1/k)v_0(e^{kt} - 1)$.

9. Suppose that an object is dropped and falls freely in a vacuum and suppose that we consider, as Galileo seriously did for a while, that the velocity acquired by the object is proportional to the distance fallen. Show that this assumption leads to an absurdity.

10. Suppose that a body has acquired a downward velocity $v_0$ and that thereafter the acceleration is proportional to the distance traveled. Measure time and distance from the instant and place where the object has acquired the velocity $v_0$ and find the formula for the distance traveled as a function of time.

    *Suggestion:* Use at once the fact that $dv/dt = v\,dv/dy$.

    *Ans.* $y = \left(v_0/2\sqrt{k}\right)\left(e^{\sqrt{k}\,t} - e^{-\sqrt{k}\,t}\right)$.

**7. Up and Down Motion in Resisting Media.**\* The motions in resisting media that we have considered so far are motions in one direction, that is, either horizontal or downward. Let us consider next an object of mass $m$ that is projected upward with some initial velocity, say 1000 ft/sec. We suppose that the air resistance is *proportional to the velocity*. The object, of course, rises and then falls. What function relates velocity and time and what function relates height above the ground and time?

Let us choose the upward direction as positive. The force of gravity acts continuously in the downward direction and therefore is represented by $-32m$. The resistance of the medium acts downward when the object is rising and upward when it is falling. This reversal of the direction in which the air resistance acts raises the question of its sign. When the object rises, its velocity $v$ is positive, and therefore the air resistance is $-Kv$ if we take $K$ to be positive. When the object falls, $v$ itself is negative, so that $-Kv$ is positive and represents an upward force. Thus $-Kv$ is the correct representation of the air resistance for both the upward and the downward motion. The net force acting on the object at any instant is

$$-32m - Kv,$$

and by Newton's second law of motion we have that at any instant

$$m\dot{v} = -32m - Kv.$$

If we divide both sides by $m$ and replace $K/m$ by $k$, we obtain

**(72)** $$\dot{v} = -32 - kv.$$

To integrate we may use the method already applied to (66). That is, we can write (72) in the form

$$\frac{dt}{dv} = -\frac{1}{32 + kv}$$

and, if we again introduce

$$u = 32 + kv,$$

we can write

$$\frac{dt}{dv} = -\frac{1}{k}\frac{1}{u}\frac{du}{dv}.$$

Then by (30)

$$t = -\frac{1}{k}\log u + C$$

\*This section can be omitted without disrupting the continuity.

or

**(73)** $$-kt + C' = \log u$$

where $C' = kC$. In view of the value of $u$,

$$\log(32 + kv) = -kt + C'.$$

Then by the meaning of the logarithm

**(74)** $$32 + kv = e^{-kt+C'} = De^{-kt},$$

where $D = e^{C'}$.

To determine the constant of integration we use the physical fact that at $t = 0$, the instant at which the object is thrown up, $v = 1000$. Then

$$32 + k \cdot 1000 = D.$$

With this value of $D$ substituted in (74), we have that

**(75)** $$v = -\frac{32}{k} + \frac{32 + 1000k}{k} e^{-kt}.$$

Thus we have obtained the formula for the velocity as a function of the time.

A graph of (75) is instructive. The graph of the second term on the right is an exponentially decaying function which, at the value $t = 0$, is $(32 + 1000k)/k$. We subtract the constant value $32/k$ from this graph and obtain the result shown in Fig. 12-9.

Having obtained the formula for the velocity as a function of the time, we can now reasonably ask for the relation between height above the ground and time. If we denote height above the ground by $y$, we have from (75) that

$$\dot{y} = -\frac{32}{k} + \frac{32 + 1000k}{k} e^{-kt}.$$

To find $y$ we have but to integrate in a straightforward manner. Then

**(76)** $$y = -\frac{32}{k} t - \frac{32 + 1000k}{k^2} e^{-kt} + C.$$

**Figure 12-9**

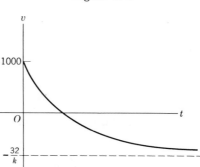

At $t = 0$ the object is at the ground so that $y = 0$; by substituting these values in (76), we find that

$$C = \frac{32 + 1000k}{k^2}.$$

With this value of $C$, (76) becomes

**(77)** $$y = -\frac{32}{k}t + \frac{32 + 1000k}{k^2}(1 - e^{-kt}).$$

A graph of (77) is helpful in interpreting its significance. To obtain a sketch we might pick a possible value of $k$, say $k = 0.5$. We start by sketching $y = -e^{-kt}$; we then add 1 to each $y$-value of this graph to obtain the graph of $y = 1 - e^{-kt}$; next we "stretch" each $y$-value of the latter graph by the factor $(32 + 1000k)/k^2$. Then we graph separately but on the same set of axes $y = (-32/k)t$ and by adding ordinates of these last two graphs at a number of values of $t$ we obtain the result shown in Fig. 12-10.

Because motion in a resisting medium is more realistic than motion in a vacuum, we should explore the implications of the major results (75) and (77). Some pertinent questions are considered in the exercises.

Our entire discussion of motion in resisting media illustrates a very important feature of applied mathematics. As we noted at the beginning of Section 6, when Galileo decided to study motion he consciously neglected air resistance. When he was challenged about this neglect, he answered that

**Figure  12-10**

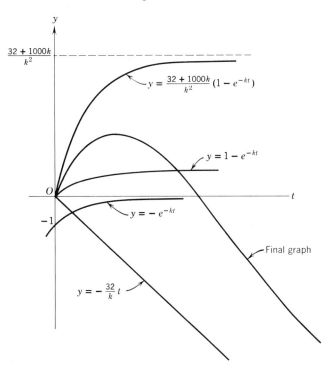

we must first consider the primary phenomenon and then, if necessary,, consider any additional factors. Galileo initiated what is still today regarded as the sound approach to the problems of applied mathematics and mathematical physics. One always idealizes a physical problem, which means neglecting any effects or subsidiary phenomena that may not matter for the usefulness of the desired results. If, however, the results are not accurate enough for the application, one must seek a better idealization, that is, one which hews closer to reality. Thus including resistance of the medium gives a better idealization than the assumption of no resistance for motions in the atmosphere and in water. A better idealization may also mean the need to employ more advanced mathematical techniques, as we can see by comparing what we did in Chapter 3 with the work in this section. Practical application may require even a third or fourth improvement in the idealization. For example, we ignored the shape of the moving object; in fact, we lumped such factors as shape, size, and frictional effects due to the surface of the object together in the value of the constant $K$ and took into account only the effect of velocity on resistance. Such an idealization would not suffice if one were designing the wings of an airplane.

## EXERCISES

1. What is the physical significance of the value of $t$ where the curve cuts the $t$-axis in Fig. 12-9?

2. Suppose that an object is thrown straight up with an initial velocity of 1000 ft/sec and that air resistance is neglected. What formula relates velocity and time? How does the graph of this formula compare with that in Fig. 12-9?
   *Ans.* $v = 1000 - 32t$.

3. Suppose that an object is projected upward with an initial velocity of 1000 ft/sec and that air resistance is proportional to the velocity. Find the time $t_1$ at which it reaches maximum height.    *Ans.* $t_1 = (1/k) \log[1 + (1000/32)k]$.

4. Under the conditions of Exercise 3 find the maximum height $y_1$ reached by the object.    *Ans.* $y_1 = (1000/k) - (32/k^2) \log[1 + (1000k/32)]$.

5. Suppose that an object is projected upward with an initial velocity of 1000 ft/sec and air resistance is neglected. Find the time to reach maximum height and the maximum height.    *Ans.* 125/4 sec; 15,625 ft.

6. Compare the results of Exercise 5 with those of Exercises 3 and 4. For the purposes of comparison, use the value of 0.5 for $k$.

7. The point of Exercises 5 and 6 is that it takes less time for an object to each its maximum height when air resistance is taken into account than when it is not. Because air resistance slows up the object, how do you account for the seeming contradiction?

8. It is not possible with the present means at our disposal to find the time of flight of an object that is projected upward under the conditions in Exercise 3, that is, the time elapsed from the instant the object starts upward to the instant it returns to the ground.* However, if we call $T$ the time of flight, we can show

---

*In our work on infinite series (Chap. 20) we shall learn additional techniques.

readily that the velocity with which the object returns to the ground is $1000 - 32T$. Use (75) and (77) to show that this result is correct. Also, how does this result compare with the analogous one in the case of no air resistance?

9. (a)  Suppose that a body is projected upward in a medium whose resistance is proportional to the square of the velocity. Write the differential equation that represents the motion.

(b)  Does your differential equation represent the upward and downward motion?

10. (a)  Given that the differential equation $\dot{v} = -32 - kv^2$ represents the motion of an object which is shot up in a medium whose resistance is proportional to the square of the velocity use the method in the text to find $v$ as a function of $t$.

$Ans.$ $v = \sqrt{32/k} \ \tan(-\sqrt{32k} \ t + C)$.

(b)  To determine the constant of integration in the answer to (a) suppose the initial velocity is 1000 ft/sec,

$Ans.$ $v = \sqrt{32/k} \ \tan(\alpha - \sqrt{32k} \ t)$ where $\alpha = \tan^{-1} \sqrt{k/32} \ 1000$.

(c)  Let $k = 0.005$ in the answer to (b) and find the value of $t$ when $v = 0$.

$Ans.$ 3.7 sec approx.

11. (a)  Using the answer to exercise 10(b) find the function which relates height $y$ above the ground and time $t$.

*Suggestion:* To integrate $\tan x$ regard it as $\sin x / \cos x$.

$Ans.$ $y = (1/k) \log \cos(\alpha - \sqrt{32k} \ t) + C$.

(b)  Determine the constant of integration in the answer to (a) by using the fact that $y = 0$ when $t = 0$. $Ans.$ $(-1/k) \log \cos \alpha$.

(c)  Using the value $k = 0.005$ and the answer to exercise 10(c) calculate the maximum height reached by the object. Compare the result with that of Exercise 5.

12. Suppose that an object is projected upward with an initial velocity of 1000 ft/sec in a medium whose resistance is proportional to the square of the velocity. Calculate the time $t_1$ to reach maximum height. See Exercise 10(b).

$$Ans. \ t_1 = \frac{1}{\sqrt{32k}} \ \tan^{-1}\left(\sqrt{\frac{k}{32}} \ 1000\right) = \frac{1}{\sqrt{32k}} \ \tan^{-1} \alpha.$$

13. Under the conditions of Exercise 12 calculate the maximum height $y_1$ attained by the object. See Exercises 11 and 12.

$$Ans. \ y_1 = \frac{1}{2k} \ \log\left[1 + (1000)^2 \frac{k}{32}\right].$$

## 8. Hyperbolic Functions.

In working with exponential functions we often encounter, as we shall shortly see, expressions of the form

$$\frac{e^x + e^{-x}}{2}.$$

Mathematicians have therefore introduced a name for this and similar functions. Specifically we introduce a new function called hyperbolic cosine of $x$ and abbreviated to $\cosh x$ (pronounced as spelled). By definition

(78) $$y = \cosh x = \frac{e^x + e^{-x}}{2}.$$

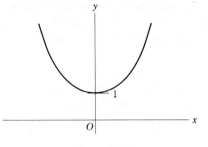

**Figure 12-11**

The graph of $y = \cosh x$ is shown in Fig. 12-11. The derivative of this function also occurs frequently; it is called the hyperbolic sine of $x$ and is abbreviated to sinh $x$ (pronounced like "cinch"). Then

**(79)**                     $$y = \sinh x = \frac{e^x - e^{-x}}{2} .$$

The graph of $y = \sinh x$ is shown in Fig. 12-12.

These two functions are analogous to the ordinary sine and cosine functions, although there are differences. Thus, whereas

$$\frac{d}{dx} \cos x = -\sin x.$$

we have, as we can see by differentiating in (78),

**(80)**                     $$\frac{d}{dx} \cosh x = \sinh x.$$

Just as it is convenient in ordinary trigonometry to introduce four additional functions that can be defined in terms of $\sin x$ and $\cos x$, so for

**Figure 12-12**

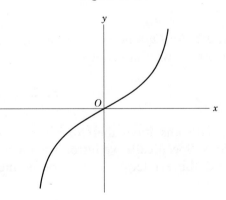

the hyperbolic functions we introduce four additional functions, namely,*

**(81)**

$$\tanh x = \frac{\sinh x}{\cosh x}, \qquad\qquad \coth x = \frac{1}{\tanh x},$$

$$\text{sech } x = \frac{1}{\cosh x}, \qquad\qquad \text{csch } x = \frac{1}{\sinh x}.$$

The graph of $y = \tanh x$ is shown in Fig. 12-13 and for handy reference we include the graphs of $y = \coth x$, $y = \text{sech } x$, and $y = \text{csch } x$ (Figs. 12-14 through 12-16).

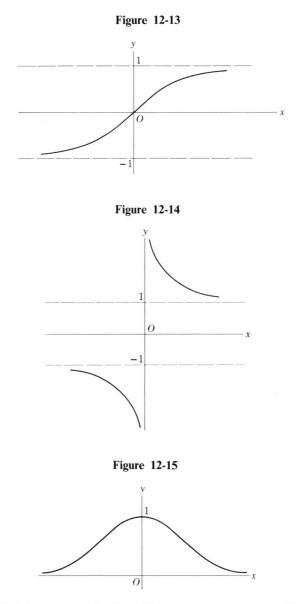

**Figure 12-13**

**Figure 12-14**

**Figure 12-15**

*There are no verbal abbreviations for these. We refer to them as hyperbolic tangent, and so on.

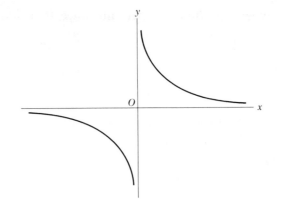

**Figure 12-16**

For these six hyperbolic functions, as for the ordinary trigonometric functions, many identities hold. For example, we see immediately from the definitions of the hyperbolic functions that

**(82)**

$$\sinh x = -\sinh (-x),$$

$$\cosh x = \cosh (-x),$$

$$\cosh^2 x - \sinh^2 x = 1.$$

As these examples show, some of the identities are entirely analogous to those for the ordinary trigonometric functions, whereas others differ somewhat. We leave for the exercises the establishment of a few other identities for the hyperbolic functions.

The term hyperbolic functions suggests that somehow the hyperbola is involved. Let us recall that the familiar trigonometric functions are defined in terms of ordinate, abscissa, and distance of any point $P$ in the coordinate plane that lies on the terminal side of the angle when the initial side (Fig. 12-17) is the positive $x$-axis. As the angle $A$ varies, point $P$ on the terminal side can always be taken to have the same distance from the origin. Hence these points lie on a circle and the ordinary functions are often called the circular functions to distinguish them from the hyperbolic functions. The latter can be defined in terms of properties of the hyperbola but because the definitions are not often used we shall not look into them.

In view of the fact that $\sinh x$ and $\cosh x$ are defined in terms of the exponential function, it is easy to obtain the derivatives of the hyperbolic

**Figure  12-17**

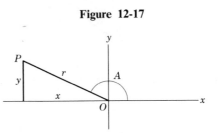

functions. Moreover by using the chain rule we may state the results in the following form:

**Theorem:** Let $u$ be a differentiable function of $x$. Then

(83)
$$\frac{d(\sinh u)}{dx} = \cosh u \ \frac{du}{dx} \ .$$

(84)
$$\frac{d(\cosh u)}{dx} = \sinh u \ \frac{du}{dx} \ .$$

(85)
$$\frac{d(\tanh u)}{dx} = \operatorname{sech}^2 u \ \frac{du}{dx} \ .$$

(86)
$$\frac{d(\coth u)}{dx} = -\operatorname{csch}^2 u \ \frac{du}{dx} \ .$$

(87)
$$\frac{d(\operatorname{sech} u)}{dx} = -\operatorname{sech} u \tanh u \ \frac{du}{dx} \ .$$

(88)
$$\frac{d(\operatorname{csch} u)}{dx} = -\operatorname{csch} u \coth u \ \frac{du}{dx} \ .$$

As usual, to each differentiation formula there is an integration formula. For convenience we state them.

**Theorem:** If $u$ is a differentiable function of $x$ then

(89)
$$\int \sinh u \ \frac{du}{dx} \ dx = \cosh u + C.$$

(90)
$$\int \cosh u \ \frac{du}{dx} \ dx = \sinh u + C.$$

(91)
$$\int \operatorname{sech}^2 u \ \frac{du}{dx} \ dx = \tanh u + C.$$

(92)
$$\int \operatorname{csch}^2 u \ \frac{du}{dx} \ dx = -\coth u + C.$$

(93)
$$\int \operatorname{sech} u \tanh u \ \frac{du}{dx} \ dx = -\operatorname{sech} u + C.$$

(94)
$$\int \operatorname{csch} u \coth u \ \frac{du}{dx} \ dx = -\operatorname{csch} u + C.$$

Just as the ordinary or circular trigonometric functions give rise to inverse functions, so do the hyperbolic functions. Thus to the function

$$y = \sinh x$$

there corresponds the inverse hyperbolic function

(95)                                      $x = \sinh^{-1} y.$

To write down the inverse function is not enough. We must also ascertain that there is a unique $x$ for each $y$ or at least a unique $x$ for each $y$ in some domain. However, Fig. 12-12 shows that this is the case for every value of $y$.

Because $y = \sinh x$ has a meaning in terms of the exponential functions, let us see if we can obtain some corresponding meaning for $x = \sinh^{-1} y$. We know that

$$y = \sinh x = \frac{e^x - e^{-x}}{2} .$$

Let us see if we can solve for $x$ in terms of $y$. We let

$$e^x = z.$$

Then

$$e^{-x} = \frac{1}{z}$$

and

$$y = \frac{z - \dfrac{1}{z}}{2} .$$

This equation is easily solved for $z$ and yields

$$z = y \pm \sqrt{y^2 + 1} .$$

We seem to have a choice here, but if we wish to stick to real values of our variables then because $z$ or $e^x$ is necessarily positive,

$$z = y + \sqrt{y^2 + 1} .$$

In view of the value of $z$

$$x = \log\left(y + \sqrt{y^2 + 1}\right).$$

This function is defined for every real value of $y$.

Because it is customary to use $x$ for the independent variable and $y$ for the dependent variable, we now write

(96)                  $y = \sinh^{-1} x = \log(x + \sqrt{x^2 + 1})$

and this function is defined for every real $x$ (Fig. 12-18).

We may define an inverse hyperbolic function for each of the original

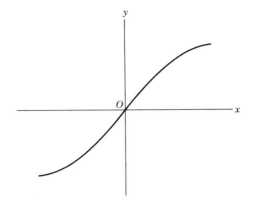

**Figure 12-18**

hyperbolic functions. Thus to $y = \cosh x$ there corresponds

$$x = \cosh^{-1} y.$$

As in the case of $x = \sinh^{-1} y$, we can find an expression for $x = \cosh^{-1} y$ in terms of the logarithmic function. Here we find by the above method that

$$x = \log\left(y \pm \sqrt{y^2 - 1}\,\right).$$

In this case we must be careful as to which of the two functions we choose. The graph of $y = \cosh x$ (Fig. 12-11) shows that there are two values of $x$ for each value of $y$ greater than 1. The two choices for $x$ show up in the above equation by the presence of $\pm\sqrt{y^2 - 1}$. We use for the principal branch

$$x = \log\left(y + \sqrt{y^2 - 1}\,\right) \qquad \text{for} \quad y \geq 1.$$

If we now revert to the use of $x$ and $y$ as independent and dependent variables, respectively, we have for the principal branch

**(97)** $\qquad y = \cosh^{-1} x = \log(x + \sqrt{x^2 - 1}\,) \qquad \text{for} \quad x \geq 1.$

Figure 12-19 shows the graph of the double-valued function. The principal branch is the upper half and the logarithmic expression in (97) represents only this half.

Corresponding to the function $y = \tanh x$, there is the inverse function

$$x = \tanh^{-1} y.$$

To obtain an expression for $x$ in terms of ordinary functions, we go back to

$$y = \tanh x = \frac{\sinh x}{\cosh x} = \frac{e^x - e^{-x}}{e^x + e^{-x}}\,.$$

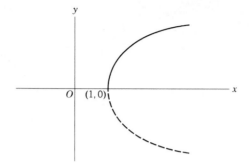

**Figure 12-19**

If we use our earlier device of letting $e^x = z$ and solve for $z$, we find that

$$z^2 = \frac{1 + y}{1 - y}.$$

and because $z^2 = e^{2x}$,

$$x = \tfrac{1}{2} \log \frac{1 + y}{1 - y}.$$

This function is defined for all $y$ between $-1$ and $+1$. With the usual use of $x$ and $y$, we write

**(98)**     $y = \tanh^{-1} x = \tfrac{1}{2} \log \dfrac{1 + x}{1 - x}$     for   $-1 < x < 1.$

Figure 12-20 shows the graph of this function.

We see from the manner in which we have treated the first three inverse hyperbolic functions that we can make the analogous definitions for

**Figure 12-20**

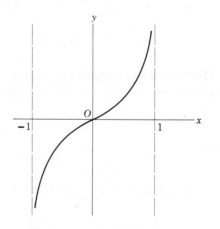

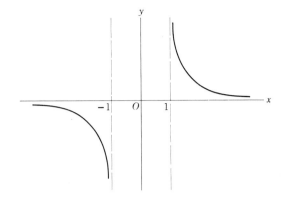

**Figure 12-21**

the last three. For reference we note that

**(99)** $\quad y = \coth^{-1} x = \frac{1}{2} \log \frac{x + 1}{x - 1} \qquad$ for $\quad x < -1 \quad$ and $\quad x > 1.$

Figure 12-21 shows the graph of this function.

Furthermore, we have

**(100)** $\qquad y = \operatorname{sech}^{-1} x = \log \frac{1 + \sqrt{1 - x^2}}{x} \qquad$ for $\quad 0 < x \leq 1.$

The graph of this function is shown in Fig. 12-22; the principal branch is the upper half of the graph and the logarithmic expression in (100) represents only this half.

Finally, we have the function

**(101)** $\qquad y = \operatorname{csch}^{-1} x = \log\left( \frac{1}{x} + \frac{\sqrt{1 + x^2}}{|x|} \right) \qquad$ for $\quad x \neq 0.$

**Figure 12-22**

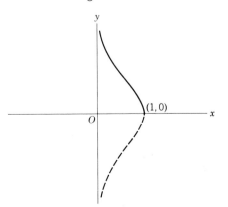

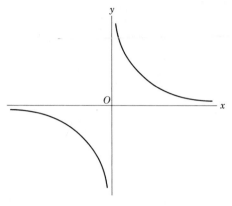

**Figure 12-23**

The graph of this function is given by Fig. 12-23.

We can obtain the formulas for the derivatives of the inverse hyperbolic functions in several ways. The easiest way would be to use the logarithmic expressions in formulas (96) to (101). For reference we note the results:

**Theorem:**

$$(102) \quad \frac{d(\sinh^{-1} x)}{dx} = \frac{1}{\sqrt{1 + x^2}} .$$

$$(103) \quad \frac{d(\cosh^{-1} x)}{dx} = \frac{1}{\sqrt{x^2 - 1}}$$

for $x \geq 1$ and for the principal branch.

$$(104) \quad \frac{d(\tanh^{-1} x)}{dx} = \frac{1}{1 - x^2} \qquad \text{for} \quad |x| < 1.$$

$$(105) \quad \frac{d(\coth^{-1} x)}{dx} = \frac{1}{1 - x^2} \qquad \text{for} \quad |x| > 1.$$

$$(106) \quad \frac{d(\operatorname{sech}^{-1} x)}{dx} = - \frac{1}{x\sqrt{1 - x^2}}$$

for $0 < x < 1$ and for the principal branch.

$$(107) \quad \frac{d(\operatorname{csch}^{-1} x)}{dx} = - \frac{1}{|x|\sqrt{1 + x^2}} .$$

Of course, the chain rule extends the usefulness of these formulas in the usual way. Let us also keep in mind that to each differentiation formula (102) to (107) there is a corresponding integration formula.

We see from the discussion of the hyperbolic functions and their inverse functions that they are no more than special combinations of exponential functions and logarithmic functions. Nevertheless, it is easier to work with the hyperbolic and inverse hyperbolic functions as such.

## EXERCISES

1. Establish the following identities:

   (a) $\tanh x = -\tanh(-x)$.

   (b) $\sinh x = \dfrac{2 \tanh \dfrac{x}{2}}{1 - \tanh^2 \dfrac{x}{2}}$.

   (c) $\sinh x = \dfrac{\tanh x}{\sqrt{1 - \tanh^2 x}}$.

   (d) $\sinh 2x = 2 \sinh x \cosh x$.

   (e) $\cosh 2x = \cosh^2 x + \sinh^2 x$.

   (f) $\cosh 2x = 2 \cosh^2 x - 1$.

   (g) $\cosh 2x = 1 + 2 \sinh^2 x$.

   (h) $\tanh 2x = \dfrac{2 \tanh x}{1 + \tanh^2 x}$.

   (i) $\sinh(x \pm y) = \sinh x \cosh y \pm \cosh x \sinh y$.

   (j) $\cosh(x \pm y) = \cosh x \cosh y \pm \sinh x \sinh y$.

2. Show that the following relations hold:

   (a) $\dfrac{d}{dx}(\sinh x) = \cosh x$.

   (b) $\dfrac{d}{dx}(\tanh x) = \operatorname{sech}^2 x \, dx$.

   (c) $\dfrac{d}{dx}(\coth x) = -\operatorname{csch}^2 x$.

3. Show that the following relations hold:

   (a) $\dfrac{d}{dx}(\sinh^{-1} x) = 1/\sqrt{1 + x^2}$.

   (b) $\dfrac{d}{dx}(\cosh^{-1} x) = 1/\sqrt{x^2 - 1}$.

   (c) $\dfrac{d}{dx}(\tanh^{-1} x) = 1/(1 - x^2)$.

We shall look into one use of the hyperbolic functions at this point. In the exercises of Section 7 we considered the motion of an object which is projected upward in a medium whose resistance is proportional to the square of the velocity.* The differential equation (cf. (72))

$$m\dot{v} = -32m - Kv^2$$

does not represent the downward motion because during this motion the resistance is upward, whereas the term $-Kv^2$, with $K$ positive, represents a downward force. The correct differential equation for the downward motion, if the *downward direction* is taken as positive, is

$$m\dot{v} = 32m - Kv^2.$$

The $-Kv^2$ now represents an upward force. After dividing through by $m$ we have

$$\frac{dv}{dt} = 32 - kv^2$$

where $k = K/m$.

To integrate this differential equation we note first that the right side is a function of the dependent variable. Hence we use the theorem on inverse functions to write

**(108)** $$\frac{dt}{dv} = \frac{1}{32 - kv^2}.$$

*It is not necessary to go through the exercises of Section 7 to understand what follows here. This application of the hyperbolic functions can be omitted.

How to integrate (108) is not immediately obvious. However, it has some resemblance to (104), which reexpressed with the aid of the chain rule, reads

**(109)**
$$\frac{d\,(\tanh^{-1}u)}{dx} = \frac{1}{1-u^2}\,\frac{du}{dx}\,.$$

Let us see if we can put the right side of (108) in the form of the right side of (109).

We can certainly write (108) as

$$\frac{dt}{dv} = \frac{1}{32} \cdot \frac{1}{1 - \dfrac{k}{32}\,v^2}\,.$$

Now let

$$u = \sqrt{\frac{k}{32}}\ v.$$

Then

$$\frac{dt}{dv} = \frac{1}{32}\,\frac{1}{1-u^2}\,.$$

If we multiply and divide by $du/dv$, which is $\sqrt{k/32}$ , then

**(110)**
$$\frac{dt}{dv} = \frac{u}{\sqrt{32k}}\,\frac{1}{1-u^2}\,\sqrt{\frac{k}{32}}\,.$$

Now (110) is in precisely the form (109) so that we may integrate and say

$$t = \frac{1}{\sqrt{32k}}\ \tanh^{-1}u + C$$

or since $u = \sqrt{\dfrac{k}{32}}\ v$

$$t = \frac{1}{\sqrt{32k}}\ \tanh^{-1}\sqrt{\frac{k}{32}}\ v + C.$$

If we now solve for $v$ we obtain

$$v = \sqrt{\frac{32}{k}}\ \tanh(\sqrt{32k}\ t + C')$$

where $C'$ is a new constant.

We can determine this constant. Since the object starts its downward motion at $t = 0$ with velocity $v = 0$, and since $\tanh 0 = 0$, we see that $C' = 0$. Hence the downward velocity is given by

**(111)**
$$v = \sqrt{\frac{32}{k}}\ \tanh\sqrt{32k}\ t.$$

We can also find the distance $y$ fallen in time $t$ where $y$ is positive in the downward direction. From (111) we have

$$\frac{dy}{dt} = \sqrt{\frac{32}{k}} \ \tanh \sqrt{32k} \ t.$$

To integrate we use a device we have previously used for $\tan x$. We write

**(112)**
$$\frac{dy}{dt} = \sqrt{\frac{32}{k}} \ \frac{\sinh \sqrt{32k} \ t}{\cosh \sqrt{32k} \ t}.$$

Now let us keep in mind that $d(\cosh x)/dx = \sinh x$ [see (80)]. To take care of the factor $\sqrt{32k}$ in (112) we shall write it as

**(113)**
$$\frac{dy}{dt} = \frac{1}{k} \ \frac{\sinh \sqrt{32k} \ t}{\cosh \sqrt{32k} \ t} \ \sqrt{32k}.$$

If we let $u = \cosh \sqrt{32k} \ t$, then

$$\frac{du}{dt} = \sinh \sqrt{32k} \ t \sqrt{32k}.$$

Hence apart from a constant factor (113) is in the form

$$\frac{dy}{dt} = \frac{1}{u} \ \frac{du}{dt},$$

and

**(114)**
$$y = \frac{1}{k} \ \log \cosh \sqrt{32k} \ t + C.$$

To determine $C$ we use the fact that $y = 0$ when $t = 0$. Since $\cosh 0 = 1$ and $\log 1 = 0$, $C = 0$ and

**(115)**
$$y = \frac{1}{k} \ \log \cosh \sqrt{32k} \ t.$$

To use formula (111) for the downward velocity and formula (115) for the distance fallen one could go to tables for the respective hyperbolic functions. These do exist. But it is almost as fast to use the definitions of the hyperbolic functions and use the $e$ tables. In terms of $e$ formula (111) is

**(116)**
$$v = \sqrt{\frac{32}{k}} \ \frac{e^{\sqrt{32k} \ t} - e^{-\sqrt{32k} \ t}}{e^{\sqrt{32k} \ t} + e^{-\sqrt{32k} \ t}}$$

or if we multiply numerator and denominator by $e^{\sqrt{32k} \ t}$

**(117)**
$$v = \sqrt{\frac{32}{k}} \ \frac{e^{2\sqrt{32k} \ t} - 1}{e^{2\sqrt{32k} \ t} + 1}.$$

Similarly formula (115) becomes

**(118)**
$$y = \frac{1}{k} \log\left( \frac{e^{\sqrt{32k}\, t} + e^{-\sqrt{32k}\, t}}{2} \right).$$

# EXERCISES

1. Use the value of 0.005 for $k$ and calculate the velocity and distance fallen by an object that starts from rest and falls for 3.7 seconds in a medium whose resistance is $0.005v^2$. We may recall from Exercise 10 of Section 7 that 3.7 seconds is the time it takes the object to reach the maximum height of 219.5 feet, if it is projected upward with an initial velocity of 1000 ft/sec. Hence the purpose of this exercise is to see how much velocity the object acquires by falling downward for the same amount of time as it took to reach the maximum height and to see how the distance it falls during the 3.7 seconds compares with the distance it rose during that time.    *Ans.* 72 ft/sec; 170.9 ft.

2. Suppose that an object starting from rest falls 219.5 feet in a medium whose resistance is 0.005 $v^2$. How long does it take to fall that distance?

    *Suggestion:* We are given $k$ and $y$ in (118), and our goal is to find $t$. Let $a = e^{\sqrt{32k}\, t}$. Then note that $e^{-\sqrt{32k}\, t} = 1/a$. Find $a$ and then $t$. Do you expect the result for $t$ to be more or less than 3.7 seconds, which is the time it takes to *rise* 219.5 feet, and what physical argument can you give to support your expectation?    *Ans.* 4.38 sec.

3. Having found the time required to fall 219.5 feet under the conditions of Exercise 2 use that result to find the velocity that the object acquires in falling that distance. This velocity should be compared with the velocity of 1000 ft/sec with which the object was projected upward so as to reach the maximum height of 219.5 feet.    *Ans.* 75.2 ft/sec.

4. If we were interested in finding the formula that relates velocity and distance fallen by an object which starts from rest and falls in a medium whose resistance is $kv^2$, we could take the value of $t$ given by (117), substitute this in (118), and then simplify the resulting relation between $y$ and $v$. We can, however, proceed as follows. We may use the fact that $dv/dt = (dv/dy)(dy/dt) = v(dv/dy)$. Then our differential equation becomes

$$v\frac{dv}{dy} = 32 - kv^2.$$

Find $y$ as a function of $v$.    *Ans.* $y = \dfrac{1}{2k} \log \dfrac{32}{32 - kv^2}$.

5. Suppose that a raindrop falls from a cloud with an initial velocity $v_0$ in a medium whose resistance is $kv^2$. Find the distance fallen as a function of $v$.

$$\textit{Ans. } y = \frac{1}{2k} \log \frac{32 - kv_0^2}{32 - kv^2}.$$

6. Using the result of Exercise 5, solve for $v$ as a function of $y$ and then find the terminal velocity. Note that the terminal velocity is by definition the velocity approached as $t$ becomes infinite. But by (118) we see that as $t$ becomes infinite, $y$ becomes infinite. Is the terminal velocity independent of the initial velocity $v_0$?

$$\textit{Ans. } v = \sqrt{\frac{32e^{2ky} + kv_0^2 - 32}{ke^{2ky}}}.$$

**7.** An object that falls from rest in a medium whose resistance is proportional to the square of the velocity has a terminal velocity of 16 ft/sec. How long does it take to acquire a velocity of 15.8 ft/sec.? Use Exercise 6.          *Ans.* 1.267 sec.

**8.** A parachute jumper falls in a medium whose resistance is proportional to the square of the velocity. If he does not open his parachute, $k = 0.0015$. If he does open it, $k = 0.142$. Compare the terminal velocities in the two cases. See Exercise 6.                              *Ans.* 170 ft/sec; 15 ft/sec.

**9.** With the data of Exercise 8 determine for both cases how far the parachute jumper falls by the time he reaches a velocity of 95 per cent of the terminal velocity.                              *Ans.* 915.8 ft; 8.7 ft.

**10.** A particle is projected upward with an initial speed $V$ in a medium whose air resistance is $kv^2$ where $v$ is the velocity. Find the velocity of the particle when it falls back to its starting point.

    *Suggestion:* By using the result of Exercise 13 of Section 7 we learn the maximum height the particle will attain. It will then fall from that height to the ground starting with a zero initial velocity.          *Ans.* $v = V/\sqrt{1 + (kV^2/32)}$ .

**9. Logarithmic Differentiation.** We return for a moment to the pure technique of differentiation. We can now dispose of one more case of the power rule that we were unable to treat earlier. We proved that if

**(119)**                                     $$y = x^n$$

and $n$ is a rational number, that is, an integer or quotient of two integers, positive or negative, or zero,

$$\frac{dy}{dx} = nx^{n-1}.$$

Those proofs do not apply to cases such as

$$y = x^{\sqrt{2}}$$

because the exponent here is an irrational number, that is, neither a whole number nor a ratio of two whole numbers. The question then is, what is the derivative of $x^n$ when $n$ is irrational?

    Let us note first that we limit the function to values of $x$ greater than 0. The reason is that if $x$ should be negative, the meaning of a negative number raised to an irrational exponent becomes complicated. The difficulty here is basically of the same kind as that involved in $(-2)^{1/2}$; that is, we run into complex numbers.

    To differentiate the function in (119), we first take the logarithm of both sides. Then

$$\log y = n \log x.$$

To help our thinking we may introduce the variable $u$ such that

$$u = \log y = n \log x.$$

Then $u$ is a function of $x$ for which we may assert

**(120)**
$$\frac{du}{dx} = n\frac{1}{x}.$$

But

$$\frac{du}{dx} = \frac{du}{dy}\frac{dy}{dx} = \frac{1}{y}\frac{dy}{dx}.$$

By equating the two results for $du/dx$ we have

$$\frac{1}{y}\frac{dy}{dx} = n\frac{1}{x}.$$

Multiplication of both sides by $y$ and replacement of $y$ by $x^n$ yields

**(121)**
$$\frac{dy}{dx} = nx^{n-1}.$$

Thus we see that the same power rule applies when $n$ is an irrational number as when it is rational. Of course, the corresponding theorem, namely, if

$$\frac{dy}{dx} = x^n$$

then

**(122)**
$$y = \frac{x^{n+1}}{n+1} + C$$

applies when $n$ is irrational, as does the chain rule in the case of

$$y = u^n$$

where $n$ is irrational and $u$ is a positive function of $x$.

The device of taking the logarithm of $y$ in the function $y = f(x)$ before differentiating is known as logarithmic differentiation. Its utility extends beyond the proof of the power rule for irrational $n$. Let us consider, for example, the function

**(123)**
$$y = x^x, \qquad x > 0.$$

This function is not a power of $x$ in the usual sense, for in $y = x^n$ the exponent is a constant. Nor is (123) an exponential function in the usual sense, for in $e^x$ or $a^x$ the base is constant. Nevertheless, (123) is a function of $x$, and it is meaningful to ask for its derivative. By the technique of logarithmic differentiation we can obtain it immediately. For

$$\log y = x \log x.$$

Then, in the same way,

$$\frac{1}{y}\frac{dy}{dx} = x \cdot \frac{1}{x} + \log x$$

or

$$\frac{dy}{dx} = y(1 + \log x)$$

or

$$\frac{dy}{dx} = x^x(1 + \log x).$$

The device of logarithmic differentiation proves useful especially when we must differentiate functions of the form

$$y = u^v$$

where $u$ and $v$ are functions of $x$.

## EXERCISES

**1.** Find $y'$ when $y$ has the following values:

(a)  $y = (x^2)^x$.                          *Ans.* $y' = (2 + 2 \log x)(x^2)^x$.

(b)  $y = (x^2)^{2x}$.

(c)  $y = \dfrac{\sqrt{2x + 5}}{\sqrt{x^2 + 7}}$.   *Ans.* $y' = \left(\dfrac{1}{2x + 5} - \dfrac{x}{x^2 + 7}\right)\dfrac{\sqrt{2x + 5}}{\sqrt{x^2 + 7}}$.

(d)  $y = (x^2 + 2)^3(1 - x^3)^4$

(e)  $y = (x^2 + 1)^6(3x^3 - 5)^4(x^4 - 2x)^3$.

(f)  $y = \dfrac{x(1 - x^2)^2}{(1 + x^2)^{1/2}}$.

# CHAPTER
# THIRTEEN
# DIFFERENTIALS
# AND THE LAW
# OF THE MEAN

**1. Differentials.** Suppose that we are working with the function $y = x^2$ and wish to calculate $\Delta y$ when $x = 5$ and $\Delta x = 0.2$. The need to do this might arise in experimental or engineering work where the value of $x$ has been measured and found to be 5 with a possible error of as much as 0.2. One might then wish to know how much $y$ could be in error because of the error in $x$. We can, of course, calculate $\Delta y$. For any $x$ it is $(x + \Delta x)^2 - x^2$, so that

**(1)** $$\Delta y = 2x\,\Delta x + (\Delta x)^2.$$

We observe that when $\Delta x$ is small, 0.2 in our case, $(\Delta x)^2$ is much smaller. A good approximation, then, to $\Delta y$ is given by $2x\,\Delta x$; to have a notation for this approximation we shall use $dy$. Then

**(2)** $$dy = 2x\,\Delta x.$$

We can picture (Fig. 13-1) what the approximation amounts to. The function $y = x^2$ can represent the area of a square of side $x$, and $\Delta x$ can represent an increase in $x$. We see then what $2x\,\Delta x$ and $(\Delta x)^2$ are. Certainly, for small $\Delta x$, the latter is much smaller than the former.

The advantage gained in approximating $\Delta y$ by $dy$ is minor for the function $y = x^2$, but only because the function is so simple. For even a slightly more complicated function the advantage can be considerable. Let us take $y = x^4$. Here

**(3)** $$\Delta y = 4x^3\,\Delta x + 6x^2(\Delta x)^2 + 4x(\Delta x)^3 + (\Delta x)^4.$$

For small $\Delta x$, not only is $(\Delta x)^2$ smaller, but $(\Delta x)^3$ and $(\Delta x)^4$ are even smaller. Hence the approximation $dy$, where

**(4)** $$dy = 4x^3\,\Delta x,$$

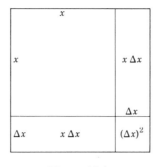

**Figure 13-1**

should be good, and we see here how much simpler it would be to calculate $dy$ as opposed to $\Delta y$. When we consider how much more complicated than even $y = x^4$ are the functions that we deal with in the calculus, we must agree that there is some point to having a useful approximation to $\Delta y$.

Let us try to see what the proper generalization of (2) and (4) might be. We usually introduce $\Delta y$ to calculate the derivative of the function. We then divide $\Delta y$ by $\Delta x$ and take the limit as $\Delta x$ approaches 0. To do this in (1) and in (3), we would find that the derivative is the coefficient of the term containing $\Delta x$ in (1) and (3). For example, (3) can be written as

**(5)**        $\Delta y = y' \, \Delta x + $ terms involving higher powers of $\Delta x$.

Equation (5) suggests that if we start with any function $y = f(x)$ and form $\Delta y$, we obtain

**(6)**                        $\Delta y = f'(x) \, \Delta x + \epsilon \, \Delta x,$

where $\epsilon$ is some quantity that approaches 0 when $\Delta x$ does. (Mathematicians love to use Greek letters, such as epsilon here, because Greek letters seem more mysterious and more impressive to nonmathematicians and suggest that mathematicians are deep thinkers.) As a matter of fact, $\Delta y$ must have the form in (6) because we know that $\Delta y/\Delta x$ is not $f'(x)$ but is $f'(x)$ plus some quantity that approaches 0 as $\Delta x$ does. If the difference

$$\frac{\Delta y}{\Delta x} - f'(x)$$

did not approach 0 as $\Delta x$ does, the quotient would not approach the derivative.

Because (6) is the correct form of $\Delta y$ for any function, then because $\epsilon$ is small when $\Delta x$ is small,

**(7)**                        $dy = f'(x) \, \Delta x$

is a good approximation to $\Delta y$. The quantity $dy$ is called the *differential* of $y$. It is customary when working with differentials to write $dx$ in place of $\Delta x$, although both have the identical meaning, namely, a change in $x$. Thus

(7) is usually written as

**(8)** $$dy = f'(x)\ dx.$$

We note that with the meanings just given to $dy$ and $dx$ the quotient of $dy$ and $dx$ equals the derivative.

   Let us see what $dy$ means geometrically. Suppose that we are at point $P$ on the curve (Fig. 13-2$a$ and $b$) of $y = f(x)$. If we change $x$ by some amount $\Delta x$ or $dx$, then $y$ changes by some amount $\Delta y$, which is shown in the two figures. As for $dy$, in view of (8), the quotient $dy/dx$ must equal the derivative at $P$ and the derivative is the slope of the tangent line at $P$. However, the slope of a line is the tangent of the angle of inclination $A$. Then $dy$ must be the length shown in each of the two figures. We could say that $dy$ is the increment in the function represented by the tangent line at $P$, or that if the function $y = f(x)$ were replaced by its tangent line at $P$, $dy$ would be the increment in the function representing the tangent line corresponding to the increment $dx$ in $x$. We see that for the function $y = f(x)$, $dy$ is not the same as $\Delta y$; however, for small $dx$, $dy$ is a good approximation to $\Delta y$.

   Let us return to an observation made earlier, namely, that the quotient of the differentials $dy$ and $dx$ at a value of $x$ is the derivative of the function at that value of $x$. We have learned that the derivative $y'$ or $f'(x)$ of a function $y = f(x)$ is the *limit of a quotient*, namely, the quotient $\Delta y/\Delta x$, but we have emphasized that the derivative is not itself a quotient. That is, we cannot take the limit of $\Delta y$ and divide it by the limit of $\Delta x$ to obtain the derivative, because this procedure leads to $0/0$. However, once the notion of the derivative of a function is established, it is possible to *define*, as we did in (7), a new quantity, namely, $dy$, so that the quotient $dy/dx$ does equal the derivative. The notation $dy/dx$, then, has two meanings. So far we have used it as an alternative notation for $y'$ and in this sense it is *not* a quotient but the limit of $\Delta y/\Delta x$ as $\Delta x$ approaches 0. From now on it also means the quotient of $dy$ and $dx$, where $dy$ is defined in (8) or (7) and $dx$ is an alternative symbol for $\Delta x$.

   The notation $dy/dx$ is a bit confusing, particularly because when it represents a derivative it is not a quotient. Why have we used it in that sense? The reason is largely historical and not without interest. When Leibniz attempted to define the derivative he realized that $\Delta y/\Delta x$ was not the correct quantity. He thought, however, that when $\Delta x$ was sufficiently small and yet not zero, the quotient $\Delta y/\Delta x$ reached a value that was the derivative, that is, it yielded the slope of the tangent to the curve. When $\Delta x$ and $\Delta y$ were such sufficiently small quantities, Leibniz denoted them by $dy$ and $dx$, and thus the derivative was truly a quotient for him. He called $dy$ and $dx$ infinitesimals. We might wonder how Leibniz could have been so crude because, surely, we see clearly that no matter how small $\Delta x$ is, $\Delta y/\Delta x$ is not exactly the value of the derivative. However, we must remember that the limit concept was not yet fashioned in the early days of the calculus, although Newton, working independently, had the beginnings

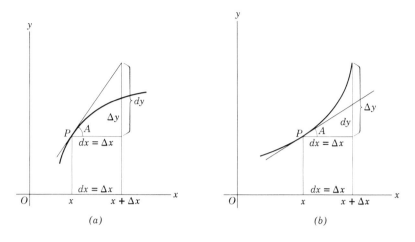

Figure 13-2

of a grip on this idea. Moreover, Leibniz believed that a continuous curve was really a series of very small line segments and that the tangent to the curve and the curve coincided over such a segment, the segment $PQ$ of Fig. 13-3. (Of course, the segment in this figure is much enlarged over what Leibniz took its size to be.) In this view, if $dx$ were no greater than the change in $x$-value between the two ends of the segment, then $\Delta y$, the change in $y$-value of the curve, and $dy$, the change in $y$-value on the tangent line, would be equal.

We might think that the notation $dy/dx$ to stand for the derivative would have been abandoned long ago. But Newton and Leibniz quarreled. The Continental mathematicians, who were far more numerous and more active than the English mathematicians, were partial to Leibniz's ideas and notation and ignored Newton's work. For about 150 years the proper foundation for the derivative and other calculus concepts was not laid, and Leibniz's notation and use of differentials became standard in the calculus.

However, there is some advantage to Leibniz's notation. Aside from the fact that $dy/dx$ indicates what the independent and dependent variables are, now that $dy$ and $dx$ are properly defined as separate quantities, it is often convenient, when $dy$ and $dx$ are being used separately and the quotient does occur, to use the fact that $dy/dx$ is the derivative. Otherwise, to indicate the derivative we would be obliged to replace this quotient by $y'$ or $f'(x)$. The use of $dy$ itself as a separate concept is certainly advantageous, as our opening remarks on approximation indicated.

Figure 13-3

**Example 1.** Find $dy$ if $y = x^5$.

**Solution.**   Since, by definition $dy = f'(x)dx$ and here $f'(x)$ is $x^5$, $dy = 5x^4dx$.

**Example 2.** Find the approximate error in the volume of a cube when the side measures 10 inches with possible error of 0.5 inches.

**Solution.**   The formula for the volume of a cube is $V = x^3$. Then the approximate change in $V$ for a change in $x$ is

$$dV = 3x^2dx.$$

If the change or error in $x = 0.5$ when $x = 10$, then

$$dV = 3.10^2(0.5) = 150 \text{ cu in.}$$

## EXERCISES

1. Find $dy$ for each of the following functions:
   (a)  $y = x^3$.        *Ans. $dy = 3x^2dx$.*
   (b)  $y = \sqrt{x}$ .                      (f)   $y = \log x$.
   (c)  $y = x^{3/2}$.   *Ans. $dy = \frac{3}{2}\sqrt{x}\,dx$.*   (g)   $y = e^x$.
   (d)  $y = \sin x$.                         (h)   $y = e^{2x}$.   *Ans. $dy = 2e^{2x}\,dx$.*
   (e)  $y = \cos x$.                         (i)   $y = (x^2 + 1)^4$.
                      *Ans. $dy = -\sin x dx$.*

2. Compute $\sqrt{101}$ approximately.

      *Suggestion:* Compute $dy$ for the function $y = \sqrt{x}$ when $x = 100$ and $dx = 1$.                                            *Ans.* 10.05.

3. Calculate $\sin 59°$ approximately, knowing that $\sin 60° = \sqrt{3}/2$. Remember that the calculus formulas presuppose radian measure for angles.   *Ans.* 0.8573.

4. What approximate error would arise in the volume of a sphere of radius 3 inches if the radius were in error by 0.2 inch?                     *Ans.* $7.2\pi$.

5. The width of a river is calculated by measuring from a point on one bank the angle of elevation of the top of· a tree 50 feet high and directly across on the opposite bank. The angle is 45° with a possible error of 20′. Find the approximate error in the calculated width of the river.         *Ans.* 0.582 ft.

6. The period of a pendulum is given by the formula $T = 2\pi\sqrt{l/32}$ where $l$ is the length of the pendulum in feet and $T$ is in seconds. Suppose that the pendulum consists of a steel wire and bob and the wire expands by 1 per cent of its length because the temperature of the environment increases.
   (a)   What is the approximate error in the period?         *Ans. $\frac{1}{2}\%$.*
   (b)   What is the approximate error per second?         *Ans.* 0.005 sec.
   (c)   What is the approximate error in the reading of this pendulum clock in one day?                                          *Ans.* 7.2 min.

7. Suppose that you are planning to construct a machine that would calculate $r$ (Fig. 13-4) either by using the values of $s$ and $A$ so that $r = s \cos A$ or by using the values of $h$ and $A$ so that $r = h \cot A$. Let us suppose further that it is

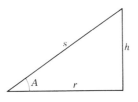

**Figure 13-4**

possible to obtain the values of $s$ and $h$ quite accurately, but that the values of $A$ for small angles cannot be obtained accurately. Which method of calculating $r$ would you use to achieve better accuracy?

> *Suggestion:* Consider $dr$ in each case.                              *Ans.* $r = s \cos A$.

8. With reference to Fig. 13-4, suppose that to calculate $s$ you have the choice of measuring $h$ and $A$ so that $s = h \csc A$ or of measuring $r$ and $A$ so that $s = r \sec A$. As in the preceding exercise, we suppose that lengths can be measured quite accurately, but that the measures of small angles cannot be obtained accurately. Which method of calculating $s$ would you use?

> *Ans.* $s = r \sec A$.

9. A pendulum clock is observed to lose 20 seconds a day when taken to a different locality. If the loss is due to the change in the value of $g$, find the approximate difference in $g$-values between the two localities.

> *Suggestion:* Because the acceleration of gravity is not necessarily 32 ft/sec², you must use the formula $T = 2\pi \sqrt{l/g}$ .          *Ans.* $g/2160$.

10. If the pendulum of a clock is normally 3 feet long and the length increases by $\frac{1}{8}$ inch, how many minutes a day will the clock lose?

11. Using the formula $T = 2\pi \sqrt{l/g}$ for the period of a pendulum, where $g$ has replaced 32, calculate the following:
    (a) Find the percentage change in $T$ if the pendulum is removed to a place where the value of $g$ is 0.2 per cent less.          *Ans.* $\frac{1}{10}$%.
    (b) Suppose that $T$ remains constant but the value of $l$ is in error by about 0.5 per cent. What is the percentage error in the value of $g$?
    (c) Find the percentage error in the value of $g$ if the period is in error by 0.1 per cent.          *Ans.* 0.2%.

12. A given quantity of metal is to be cast in the form of a solid right circular cylinder of radius 5 inches and height 10 inches. If the radius is made $\frac{1}{20}$ of an inch too large, what is the error in the height?

13. Find the approximate difference that 1 minute of angle makes in $\log \tan x$ when $x = 60°$.          *Ans.* 0.0007

14. The range $R$ of a projectile fired at an angle $A$ to the ground and with an initial velocity $V$ is given by $R = (V^2/g) \sin 2A$, $g$ being the acceleration of gravity. Show that for a small change in $g$, the percentage change in $R$ is equal to the percentage change in $g$.

15. Give two interpretations of the notation $dy/dx$.

**2. The Mean Value Theorem of the Differential Calculus.** The differential $dy$ of a function $y = f(x)$ is defined, as we know, by the equation

**(9)**
$$dy = f'(x)dx.$$

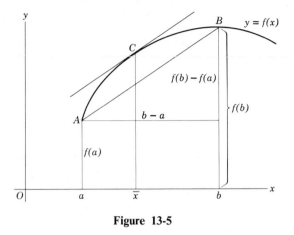

**Figure 13-5**

For small $\Delta x$

**(10)** $\qquad\qquad\qquad \Delta y$ is approximated by $f'(x)dx$.

Can we obtain a better expression for $\Delta y$? The answer to this question is a theorem that is of considerable use in building the calculus.

Suppose that we state the problem a little more broadly. The quantity $\Delta y$ is $f(x + \Delta x) - f(x)$. Instead of considering the values $x$ and $x + \Delta x$, let us consider any two values of $x$, say $a$ and $b$. Then in place of $f(x + \Delta x) - f(x)$ we have $f(b) - f(a)$. In place of $\Delta x$ we have $b - a$. Our question, then, is whether we can find an approximation to $f(b) - f(a)$ which is better than $f'(a)(b - a)$. Suppose that we look at the problem geometrically. Figure 13-5 shows a curve of a typical function, the values $a$ and $b$ of $x$, and $f(a)$ and $f(b)$. We see from the figure that

**(11)** $\qquad\qquad\qquad \dfrac{f(b) - f(a)}{b - a} = $ slope of line $AB$.

However, it is also apparent from the figure that the tangent to the curve at point $C$ is parallel to the chord $AB$. Then the slope of the tangent is the same as the slope of the chord. But the slope of the tangent is algebraically the derivative of the function at $C$. We do not know the abscissa of $C$, but we do know that it lies between $a$ and $b$. Let us denote this abscissa by $\bar{x}$. Then what we have learned is that the right side of (11) is $f'(\bar{x})$ so that

**(12)** $\qquad\qquad f(b) - f(a) = f'(\bar{x})(b - a), \qquad a < \bar{x} < b.$

In other words, we have an exact expression for $f(b) - f(a)$, except that we do not know precisely where $\bar{x}$ lies between $a$ and $b$. Moreover, $b - a$ need not be small.

We should note that there may be more than one value $\bar{x}$ for which (12) is correct. Figure 13-6 shows a curve for which there are two points $C$ and $C'$ between $x = a$ and $x = b$ at which the slope of the tangent equals the slope of the chord $AB$. Hence the abscissa of $C$ or of $C'$ can be used as the $\bar{x}$ for which (12) holds.

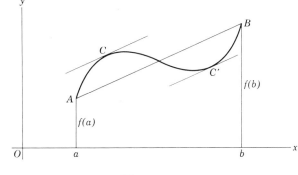

**Figure 13-6**

In relying upon geometric evidence to prove (12) we have made some assumptions. First, the curve joining $A$ and $B$ must be continuous. Figure 13-7 shows a curve that is discontinuous between $A$ and $B$; in this case there is no value of $x$ *between* $A$ and $B$ at which the slope of the tangent equals the slope of the chord $AB$. Secondly, the curve must have a definite slope at each point between $A$ and $B$; that is, $f'(x)$ must exist at each value of $x$ between $A$ and $B$. As Fig. 13-8 shows, nowhere between $a$ and $b$ does the slope of the curve equal the slope of the chord $AB$; the reason is that the slope does not exist at $C$; it changes abruptly from one side of $C$ to the other and therefore fails to take on enough values between $A$ and $B$ to yield a point on the curve at which the slope equals that of the secant $AB$.

These considerations yield a theorem called the *mean value theorem of the differential calculus or the law of the mean of the differential calculus.*

**Theorem:** If $f(x)$ is continuous in the interval $a \leq x \leq b$ and if $f'(x)$ exists at each value of $x$ for which $a < x < b$, then there exists at least one value $\bar{x}$ of $x$ between $a$ and $b$ such that

**(13)** $$f(b) - f(a) = f'(\bar{x})(b - a).$$

There is a special case of (13) that is worth noting. Suppose for the function $y = f(x)$ that $y = 0$ at $x = a$ and at $x = b$; that is, $f(a) = 0$ and $f(b) = 0$. Then we see from (13) that the left side is 0. On the right side we have a product of two factors. One of these, $b - a$, cannot be 0 because $b$

**Figure 13-7**          **Figure 13-8**

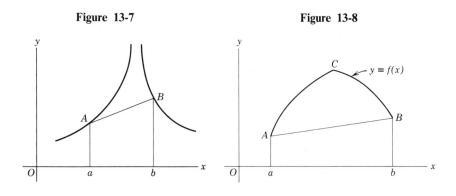

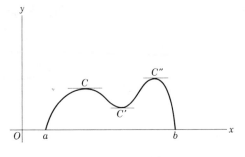

**Figure 13-9**

and $a$ are two different values of $x$. Then the second factor $f'(\bar{x})$ must be 0. Thus the derivative of $y = f(x)$ must vanish at some value of $x$, namely $\bar{x}$, which we know to lie between $a$ and $b$. Figure 13-9 illustrates what we have just proved. We see that the $y$-values are 0 at $x = a$ and $x = b$ and that the slope of the curve is 0 at some values of $x$ between $a$ and $b$; in fact, for the particular function graphed in this figure there are three points on the curve at which the slope is 0 between $a$ and $b$, which means that there are three values of $x$ that can serve as the $\bar{x}$ at which $f'(\bar{x}) = 0$.

The special result we have just obtained is known as *Rolle's theorem*. It is named after Michel Rolle (1652–1719) who first proved it in 1691. The formal statement of Rolle's theorem is as follows:

**Theorem:**    If $y = f(x)$ is continuous throughout the interval $a \leq x \leq b$, if it vanishes at $x = a$ and $x = b$, and if the derivative $f'(x)$ exists at each value of $x$ between $a$ and $b$, then there is at least one value of $x$, say $\bar{x}$, which lies between $a$ and $b$ and at which $f'(\bar{x}) = 0$.

In our order of events we first proved the law of the mean and then derived Rolle's theorem as a special case. It is perhaps worth noting that one can start by proving Rolle's theorem and then prove the more general result, the law of the mean, on the basis of Rolle's theorem. The two results do not differ essentially. If one rotated the axes and curve of Fig. 13-9 so as to obtain Fig. 13-10, part of the former $x$-axis would be a chord and the tangents at $C$, $C'$, and $C''$, which were originally parallel to the $x$-axis, would still be parallel to the chord.*

The mean value theorem will be useful to us in several connections later, but we can also make immediate use of it. Our first application here is to dispose of a question that we have left unanswered for a considerable time. We previously proved by a geometrical argument (Chap. 6, Sect. 6) that given a derived function, any two integrals can differ at most by a constant. That is, given

$$y' = f(x),$$

*Of course, this rough indication of the relation between the two theorems presupposes that the rotation does not convert a single-valued function into a multiple-valued function.

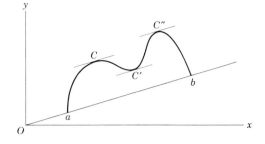

**Figure 13-10**

we showed that all integrals can be obtained by antidifferentiation and then by the addition of some constant. We can and do now prove this fact on the basis of the mean value theorem, although of course the latter was established here only by an intuitive argument.

Suppose that $F(x)$ and $G(x)$ have the same derivative $f(x)$ over some interval $a \le x \le b$. Then consider the function.

$$H(x) = F(x) - G(x).$$

Let $c$ be any value of $x$ in the interval $a \le x \le b$. We apply the mean value theorem to $H(x)$ using the values $x = a$ and $x = c$. Then

$$H(c) - H(a) = H'(\bar{x})(c - a),$$

where $\bar{x}$ lies between $a$ and $c$. Now $H(x) = F(x) - G(x)$, and because $F(x)$ and $G(x)$ have the same derivative everywhere in $(a, b)$, $H'(\bar{x}) = 0$. Then $H(c) - H(a) = 0$ and

$$H(c) = H(a)$$

or, by the definition of $H(x)$,

**(14)** $$F(c) - G(c) = F(a) - G(a).$$

The quantity $a$ is fixed, and therefore $F(a) - G(a)$ is some fixed quantity that we shall denote by $C$. However, $c$ was *any* value of $x$ in $(a, b)$. Hence, by (14), $F(x)$ and $G(x)$ can differ only by the constant $C$. Thus $F(x)$ and $G(x)$, which are any two integrals of $f(x)$, can differ only by a constant $C$.

## EXERCISES

**1.** Show by use of the mean value theorem that if $f'(x) > 0$ for all $x$ in the interval $a < x < b$ then $f(b) > f(a)$.

**2.** Given the function $y = x^2$ and the values $x = 1$ and $x = 4$, find the value $\bar{x}$ at which the mean value theorem holds. Illustrate the result graphically.

*Ans.* $\bar{x} = \frac{5}{2}$.

**3.** Do the same as in Exercise 2 but for the function $y = x^3$.     *Ans.* $\bar{x} = \sqrt{7}$.

4. Show that if we choose $a = -1$ and $b = 1$, the mean value theorem cannot hold for the function $y = 1/x$; that is, there is no $\bar{x}$ satisfying the theorem. Why does the mean value theorem not hold in this case?

5. Show by use of the mean value theorem that for positive $x$, $x > \sin x$. You may use the fact that $|\cos x| \le 1$.

6. Show by use of the mean value theorem that $\log (1 + h) > h/(1 + h)$ and that $h > \log(1 + h)$ for $h > 0$.

7. Show by use of the mean value theorem that $e^x > 1 + x$ for all $x > 0$.

8. Show that for the parabola $y = ax^2 + bx + c$, the value of $\bar{x}$ for which the mean value theorem (13) holds is $\bar{x} = (b + a)/2$.

9. Suppose $f(b) - f(a)$ is the distance traveled in the time $b - a$. What is the meaning of $f'(\bar{x})$?

### 3. Indeterminate Forms.

In Chapter 12 we showed [see formula (65)] that if an object is set into motion along smooth ground with an initial velocity of 100 ft/sec but the air resists the motion with a force proportional to the velocity, the object will travel a distance $x$ in time $t$ given by the formula

$$(15) \qquad\qquad x = \frac{100}{k}(1 - e^{-kt}).$$

The quantity $k$ is the proportionality constant, and the smaller the $k$, the less is the resistance of the air. We would expect on physical grounds that when $k$ is 0, the formula would yield the one which holds when there is no air resistance, in which case the formula for $x$ in terms of $t$ is $x = 100t$. Unfortunately the substitution of 0 for $k$ in (15) yields the meaningless form $0/0$. It is possible, however, that as $k$ approaches 0, the limit of the right side of (15) does exist and may have the value of $100t$. Hence let us see what happens to the formula for $x$ in (15) as $k$ approaches 0. The numerator and the denominator both approach 0 as $k$ does, and in such a case we cannot argue that the limit of the entire expression is the limit of the numerator divided by the limit of the denominator. The problem that we face then is to find the limit of a quotient of two functions when the numerator and the denominator both approach 0 as the independent variable, $k$ in the above example, approaches 0.

The function of $k$ given in (15) is called an indeterminate form, because the function takes the form $0/0$ when $k$ is 0. The words "indeterminate form" are actually misleading because they suggest that the form has a value at $k = 0$ but that the value is indeterminate. This is not the case. If a quotient of two functions has the form $0/0$ for some value, say, $a$ of the independent variable, the quotient has no value at the value $a$ of the independent variable. However, the quotient may very well have a *limiting value* as the independent variable approaches $a$, and we may seek that value because it may supply us with useful information. Thus if we can prove that the limit as $k$ approaches 0 of the right side of (15) is $100t$, we shall know that when the air resistance approaches 0 the motion becomes more and more like the motion with no air resistance.

Actually, we have been working with indeterminate forms right along.

The derivative of a function $y = f(x)$ is, by definition,

**(16)** $$\lim_{\Delta x \to 0} \frac{\Delta y}{\Delta x}$$

where $\Delta y/\Delta x$ is a function of $\Delta x$. We know that if we were to substitute 0 for $\Delta x$ in the expression for $\Delta y/\Delta x$, we would obtain $0/0$ because $\Delta y$ is 0 when $\Delta x$ is 0. However, we were able to evaluate the limit (16) for a great variety of functions. Thus we can say that we have already evaluated many indeterminate forms. Now we can use this knowledge to evaluate rather easily many other indeterminate forms that do not arise as difference quotients.

Let us consider the general problem exemplified by the above problem of motion. Suppose that we have the expression

$$F(x) = \frac{f(x)}{g(x)}$$

and we know that for $x = a$, $f(a) = 0$ and $g(a) = 0$, but that we should like to evaluate

$$\lim_{x \to a} \frac{f(x)}{g(x)}.$$

To do this we shall prove that

**(17)** $$\lim_{x \to a} \frac{f(x)}{g(x)} = \lim_{x \to a} \frac{f'(x)}{g'(x)}.$$

The proof of this assertion is readily made with the help of a slight extension of the mean value theorem known as the *generalized mean value theorem*.

**Theorem:** If $f(x)$ and $g(x)$ are continuous in $a \le x \le b$ and are differentiable in $a < x < b$, if $g(b) \ne g(a)$ and if $g'(x) \ne 0$, then there exists at least one value $\bar{x}$ such that

**(18)** $$\frac{f(b) - f(a)}{g(b) - g(a)} = \frac{f'(\bar{x})}{g'(\bar{x})}$$

and $a < \bar{x} < b$.*

The essence of this theorem is (18) and the assertion that $a < \bar{x} < b$. To prove it we are tempted to apply the mean value theorem to $f(x)$ separately and to $g(x)$ separately and to divide the results. However, this would give $f'(\bar{x}_1)/g'(\bar{x}_2)$, for the right-hand side of (18), whereas (18) asserts

---

*If $g'(x) \ne 0$, then $g(b) \ne g(a)$ by the mean value theorem. However, this implication of the hypotheses is a detail.

that the *same* $\bar{x}$ can be used in numerator and denominator. Nevertheless, it does seem likely that the law of the mean or possibly the special case, Rolle's theorem, could be used to prove (18). To obtain the same $\bar{x}$ in the numerator and denominator we probably should work with a function that involves $f(x)$ and $g(x)$ simultaneously. However, to enable us to apply the law of the mean or Rolle's theorem to the desired function, the function must satisfy the hypotheses of whichever theorem we use. The construction of the desired function is not immediately obvious but fortunately is not difficult. We set up the new function

$$G(x) = [g(b) - g(a)][f(x) - f(a)] - [g(x) - g(a)][f(b) - f(a)].$$

We see by substitution that $G(a) = 0$ and $G(b) = 0$. Then Rolle's theorem applies to $G(x)$ and there exists an $\bar{x}$ for which $G'(\bar{x}) = 0$ and $a < \bar{x} < b$. However,

$$G'(x) = [g(b) - g(a)]f'(x) - g'(x)[f(b) - f(a)],$$

and because $G'(\bar{x}) = 0$, simple algebra yields

$$\text{(19)} \qquad \frac{f(b) - f(a)}{g(b) - g(a)} = \frac{f'(\bar{x})}{g'(\bar{x})}.$$

Of course, to carry out the algebra we need the fact that the denominators in (19) are not 0.

Now we can establish (17). This equation presupposes that $f(a) = 0$ and $g(a) = 0$. Because $b$ in (19) is any value of $x$, provided only that $\bar{x}$ lies between $a$ and $b$, we can replace $b$ by $x$ in (19) and use the facts on $f(a)$ and $g(a)$. Then

$$\text{(20)} \qquad \frac{f(x)}{g(x)} = \frac{f'(\bar{x})}{g'(\bar{x})}.$$

Now $\bar{x}$ depends on $x$ and since the left and right sides of (20) are equal for all $x$ near $a$,

$$\lim_{x \to a} \frac{f(x)}{g(x)} = \lim_{x \to a} \frac{f'(\bar{x})}{g'(\bar{x})}.$$

However if

$$\lim_{x \to a} \frac{f'(x)}{g'(x)}$$

exists, then $f'(\bar{x})/g'(\bar{x})$ must approach the same limit because the $\bar{x}$ are just values of $x$ that approach $a$ as $x$ does. Then

$$\text{(21)} \qquad \lim_{x \to a} \frac{f(x)}{g(x)} = \lim_{x \to a} \frac{f'(x)}{g'(x)}.$$

This is the statement in (17). Let us note this basic result on indeterminate forms as a theorem:

**Theorem:** Suppose that $f(x)$ and $g(x)$ are continuous in some interval $a \leq x \leq b$, the derivatives $f'(x)$ and $g'(x)$ exist in $a < x < b$, and $g'(x)$ does not vanish in $a < x < b$. Then, if $f(a) = 0$ and $g(a) = 0$,

$$(22) \qquad \lim_{x \to a} \frac{f(x)}{g(x)} = \lim_{x \to a} \frac{f'(x)}{g'(x)}$$

when the right-hand limit exists.

The result (22) tells us that we can evaluate the limit called for on the left side by calculating the limit on the right side if it exists. If in addition to the hypotheses on $f(x)$ and $g(x)$ that we have already made in order to establish (22) we add that $f'(x)$ and $g'(x)$ approach $f'(a)$ and $g'(a)$, respectively, and if $g'(a)$ is not 0, we can derive a better result. Because the limit of a quotient is the limit of the numerator divided by the limit of the denominator provided that the limit of the denominator is not 0,

$$(23) \qquad \lim_{x \to a} \frac{f'(x)}{g'(x)} = \frac{\lim\limits_{x \to a} f'(x)}{\lim\limits_{x \to a} g'(x)} .$$

However, as $x$ approaches $a$, $f'(x)$ approaches $f'(a)$. Likewise, as $x$ approaches $a$, $g'(x)$ approaches $g'(a)$. Then from (22) and (23)

$$(24) \qquad \lim_{x \to a} \frac{f(x)}{g(x)} = \frac{f'(a)}{g'(a)} .$$

This form of the result, as opposed to (22), is more often used in practice. It says that to find the limit of $f(x)/g(x)$ as $x$ approaches $a$, when $f(a)$ and $g(a)$ are 0, we should differentiate the numerator $f(x)$, differentiate the denominator $g(x)$, and evaluate $f'(a)/g'(a)$. The results (22) and (24) are usually credited to G. F. A. L'Hospital (1661–1704), a pupil of the superb Swiss mathematician John Bernoulli, and are known as L'Hospital's rule. However, the idea is due to Bernoulli.

Before we apply the result (24) let us see what it means geometrically. We are dealing with two functions $f(x)$ and $g(x)$ that have the value 0 at $x = a$. Hence the curves of $y = f(x)$ and $y = g(x)$ must cross the $x$-axis (Fig. 13-11) at $x = a$. This is point $P$ in the figure. Let $x$ be an arbitrary value near $x = a$ so that $QU = g(x)$ and $QV = f(x)$. The evaluation of the indeterminate form $f(x)/g(x)$ then amounts to asking what the ratio of $QV$ to $QU$ becomes as $Q$ moves toward $P$. Now

$$\frac{QV}{QU} = \frac{QV/PQ}{QU/PQ} .$$

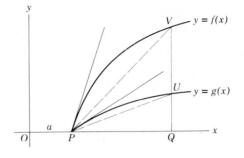

**Figure 13-11**

However, $QV/PQ$ is the slope of the chord $PV$ and $QU/PQ$ is the slope of the chord $PU$. As $Q$ approaches $P$, these chords approach the tangents to the respective curves so that $QV/PQ$ approaches the slope of the tangent to the curve of $y = f(x)$ and $QU/PQ$ approaches the slope of the tangent to $y = g(x)$. Hence what (24) says in geometrical terms is that the ratio of $f(x)$ and $g(x)$, that is, the ratio $QV/QU$, approaches, as $Q$ approaches $P$, the ratio of the slope of the two tangent lines at $P$.

We can now answer the question that we raised in connection with formula (15). What is

$$\lim_{k \to 0} \frac{100(1 - e^{-kt})}{k} \; ?$$

We know already that the numerator and denominator are 0 for $k = 0$. Hence let us apply (24). By differentiating numerator and denominator *with respect to $k$*, we have

$$\frac{100(te^{-kt})}{1}$$

and we evaluate this expression at $k = 0$. The result is $100t$. We are now certain that the motion in the resisting air approaches the motion in a resistanceless medium as $k$ approaches 0.

Let us consider another example. The function

$$\frac{e^x - 1}{\log(1 + x)}$$

has no value when $x = 0$ because both numerator and denominator are 0. However, we might have reason to evaluate

**(25)** $$\lim_{x \to 0} \frac{e^x - 1}{\log(1 + x)} \; .$$

Direct inspection of this quotient does not tell us what the limit is. Hence we apply (24). We differentiate numerator and denominator of (25) and obtain

$$\frac{e^x}{1/(1+x)} \quad \text{or} \quad (1+x)e^x.$$

If we now substitute $x = 0$, we obtain 1, and this is the value of the expression in (25).

From the basic results (22) and (24) we can derive new ones that help us to evaluate other kinds of indeterminate forms. Thus in applying (22) it can happen that in evaluating

$$\lim_{x \to a} \frac{f'(x)}{g'(x)}$$

both $f'(x)$ and $g'(x)$ approach 0 as $x$ approaches $a$ and so the limit of the entire quotient is not discernible. We may then reapply the rule (22) for evaluating a $0/0$ form and determine

$$\lim_{x \to a} \frac{f''(x)}{g''(x)}.$$

In fact, we can continue the process of differentiating the numerator and denominator until we reach a quotient whose limit can be calculated. This limit is the value of the original limit sought.

It may also happen, in evaluating

**(26)**
$$\lim_{x \to a} \frac{f(x)}{g(x)},$$

where $f(a)$ and $g(a)$ are 0 and the limit is not obvious, that the limit

$$\lim_{x \to a} \frac{f'(x)}{g'(x)}$$

is infinite. Then we may consider

**(27)**
$$\lim_{x \to a} \frac{g(x)}{f(x)},$$

and this leads us to considering

$$\lim_{x \to a} \frac{g'(x)}{f'(x)}.$$

This latter limit must be 0. Then the limit in (27) is 0, and because the expression in (26) is the reciprocal of that in (27), the limit in (26) must be infinity, which means that $f(x)/g(x)$ becomes larger and larger without bound.

An example of this case is furnished by the problem of determining

$$\lim_{x \to 0} \frac{\sin x}{1 - \cos x}.$$

The numerator and denominator are 0 for $x$ equal to 0. Hence we apply L'Hospital's rule and seek to determine

$$\lim_{x \to 0} \frac{\cos x}{\sin x}.$$

However, this fraction becomes infinite as $x$ approaches 0. Hence

$$\lim_{x \to 0} \frac{\sin x}{1 - \cos x} = \infty.$$

In the types of indeterminate forms thus far considered, the indeterminacy arose because $f(x)$ and $g(x)$ are 0 for $x$ equal to a finite number $a$. However, we might have the case of $f(x)$ and $g(x)$ becoming 0 as $x$ becomes *infinite* and be interested in the limit of $f(x)/g(x)$ as $x$ becomes infinite. L'Hospital's rule applies in this case, too. We introduce the change of variable $x = 1/z$. Then

$$\lim_{x \to \infty} \frac{f(x)}{g(x)} = \lim_{z \to 0} \frac{f(1/z)}{g(1/z)}.$$

Now we can apply L'Hospital's rule to the right side. We differentiate $f(1/z)$ with respect $z$. To do this we differentiate $f(1/z)$ as though it were $f(u)$ with $u = 1/z$. Thus

$$\frac{df(1/z)}{dz} = f'(u)\frac{du}{dz} = f'(u)\left(-\frac{1}{z^2}\right).$$

The same applies to $g(1/z)$. So far, then, we have

$$\lim_{x \to \infty} \frac{f(x)}{g(x)} = \lim_{z \to 0} \frac{f(1/z)}{g(1/z)} = \lim_{z \to 0} \frac{f'(u)\left[-(1/z^2)\right]}{g'(u)\left[-(1/z^2)\right]} = \lim_{z \to 0} \frac{f'(u)}{g'(u)}.$$

Then

**(28)**
$$\lim_{x \to \infty} \frac{f(x)}{g(x)} = \lim_{z \to 0} \frac{f'(1/z)}{g'(1/z)} = \lim_{x \to \infty} \frac{f'(x)}{g'(x)}.$$

Thus L'Hospital's rule applies in exactly the same way when $x$ approaches $\infty$ as when $x$ approaches 0.

## EXERCISES

1. Evaluate the following indeterminate forms:

(a) $\displaystyle\lim_{x \to 2} \frac{x^2 - 4}{x^2 - 5x + 6}$.    *Ans.* $-4$.   (b) $\displaystyle\lim_{x \to a} \frac{x - a}{x^3 - a^3}$.    *Ans.* $\dfrac{1}{3a^2}$.

(c) $\lim\limits_{x \to n} \dfrac{\log(x/n)}{n - x}$.    *Ans.* $-\dfrac{1}{n}$.

(d) $\lim\limits_{x \to 3} \dfrac{x^2 - 6x + 9}{x^2 - 5x + 6}$.

(e) $\lim\limits_{x \to 0} \dfrac{xe^x - x}{1 - \cos 2x}$.    *Ans.* $\dfrac{1}{2}$.

(f) $\lim\limits_{x \to 0} \dfrac{e^x - e^{-x}}{\sin 2x}$.

(g) $\lim\limits_{x \to 0} \dfrac{\tan x - x}{x - \sin x}$.    *Ans.* 2.

(h) $\lim\limits_{x \to a} \dfrac{\sin x - \sin a}{x - a}$.

(Can you state the answer here at once?)

(i) $\lim\limits_{x \to 5} \dfrac{2 - \sqrt{x - 1}}{x^2 - 25}$.    *Ans.* $-\dfrac{1}{40}$.

(j) $\lim\limits_{x \to 0} \dfrac{\tan x}{\tan 4x}$.    *Ans.* $\dfrac{1}{4}$.

2. To evaluate

$$\lim_{x \to 0} \frac{3x^2 - 1}{x - 1}$$

by L'Hospital's rule we differentiate numerator and denominator and obtain $6x/1$ and now substitute $x = 0$. However, if we look at the original function, we see at once that as $x$ approaches 0 the function approaches 1. Why the discrepancy in the answers?

3. Let us consider

$$\lim_{x \to 0} \frac{x^4 \sin(1/x)}{x^3}$$

with the understanding that $x^4 \sin(1/x)$ is 0 at $x = 0$. We can, of course, divide through by $x^3$ and we then see that the function approaches 0 as $x$ approaches 0. Suppose, however, that we evaluate the limit by L'Hospital's rule. This leads to

$$\lim_{x \to 0} - \frac{x^2 \cos(1/x)}{3x^2} = \lim_{x \to 0} - \frac{\cos(1/x)}{3}.$$

But this limit does not exist. What is wrong?

4. We showed in Chapter 12, formula (69), that if an object falls downward under the action of gravity and with air resistance proportional to the velocity, the velocity at any time $t$ is given by the formula $v = (32/k)(1 - e^{-kt})$ where $k$ is the proportionality constant. Show that as $k$ approaches 0 the formula becomes $v = 32t$,—the formula that obtains when there is no air resistance.

5. In formula (71) of Chapter 12, we obtained the formula for the distance fallen by a dropped object in time $t$ when gravity acts and the air resistance is proportional to the velocity. The distance $y$ is given by $(32/k^2)(kt + e^{-kt} - 1)$, where $k$ is the proportionality constant. Show that as $k$ approaches 0 the formula becomes $y = 16t^2$, which is the distance fallen by an object under the action of gravity but with no air resistance.

6. If an object is launched horizontally over some surface with an initial velocity of 100 ft/sec but the air resistance is proportional to the square of the velocity, then, as we found in Ex. 2, first set of Sect. 6, Chap. 12, the distance traveled in time $t$ is given by $x = (1/k) \log(1 + 100kt)$ where $k$ is the proportionality constant. Show that as $k$ approaches 0 the formula for $x$ approaches the one for the same motion but in a vacuum.

7. If an object is thrown downward with an intial velocity $V$ in a medium whose resistance is proportional to the velocity $v$, the velocity is given by the formula $v = (32/k) - \{(32/k) - V\}e^{-kt}$ where $k$ is the proportionality constant (See Ex. 4, second set in Sect. 6, Chap. 12). Show that as $k$ approaches 0 the formula

approaches $v = 32t + V$—the formula that holds when there is no air resistance.

Another class of indeterminate forms consists of those in which numerator and denominator are both *infinite* when $x$ is some finite number $a$. Thus in

$$\log x / \cot x$$

the numerator and denominator are infinite for $x$ equal to 0. These indeterminate forms are loosely described as $\infty/\infty$ forms. We may however be interested in

$$\lim_{x \to 0} \frac{\log x}{\cot x}$$

and this can be evaluated by L'Hospital's rule.

If $f(x)/g(x)$ is the quantity that approaches $\infty/\infty$ as $x$ approaches $a$, then $1/f(x)$ and $1/g(x)$ approach 0 as $x$ approaches $a$. Now, it is correct algebra to state that

$$(29) \qquad \lim_{x \to a} \frac{f(x)}{g(x)} = \lim_{x \to a} \frac{\dfrac{1}{g(x)}}{\dfrac{1}{f(x)}}.$$

If we apply L'Hospital's rule (22) to the right side of (29), remembering that the numerator and denominator are $1/g(x)$ and $1/f(x)$ respectively, the rule tells us that

$$(30) \qquad \lim_{x \to a} \frac{\dfrac{1}{g(x)}}{\dfrac{1}{f(x)}} = \lim_{x \to a} \frac{\dfrac{-g'(x)}{g^2(x)}}{\dfrac{-f'(x)}{f^2(x)}} = \lim_{x \to a} \left\{ \frac{g'}{f'} \frac{f^2}{g^2} \right\}.$$

We now use the theorem that the limit of a product is the product of the limits to write

$$(31) \qquad \lim_{x \to a} \left( \frac{g'}{f'} \cdot \frac{f^2}{g^2} \right) = \lim_{x \to a} \frac{g'}{f'} \cdot \lim_{x \to a} \frac{f^2}{g^2} = \lim_{x \to a} \frac{g'}{f'} \left\{ \lim_{x \to a} \frac{f}{g} \right\}^2.$$

The steps (29), (30), and (31) provide a series of equalities which show that the first member of (29) equals the last member of (31); that is,

$$(32) \qquad \lim_{x \to a} \frac{f(x)}{g(x)} = \lim_{x \to a} \frac{g'(x)}{f'(x)} \left\{ \lim_{x \to a} \frac{f(x)}{g(x)} \right\}^2.$$

In (32) we see that the entire quantity on the left side is a factor of the right side. We divide through to obtain

$$1 = \lim_{x \to a} \frac{g'(x)}{f'(x)} \cdot \lim_{x \to a} \frac{f(x)}{g(x)} \,.$$

Then

$$\lim_{x \to a} \frac{f(x)}{g(x)} = \frac{1}{\displaystyle\lim_{x \to a} \frac{g'(x)}{f'(x)}} \,.$$

Because the limit of a quotient is the quotient of the limits (provided the limit of the denominator is not 0),

**(33)** $$\lim_{x \to a} \frac{f(x)}{g(x)} = \lim_{x \to a} \frac{1}{\dfrac{g'(x)}{f'(x)}} = \lim_{x \to a} \frac{f'(x)}{g'(x)} \,.$$

Thus we see that L'Hospital's rule also applies in this case where $f(x)$ and $g(x)$ become infinite as $x$ approaches $a$.

We might note the conditions under which this result holds. Because we applied L'Hospital's rule to $1/f(x)$ and $1/g(x)$ to obtain (33), the most direct statement of the conditions is the following: If $f(x)$ and $g(x)$ both become infinite as $x$ approaches $a$, if $1/f(x)$ and $1/g(x)$ are continuous in some interval $a \leq x \leq b$, and if the derivatives of $1/f(x)$ and $1/g(x)$ exist in $a < x < b$, then

**(34)** $$\lim_{x \to a} \frac{f(x)}{g(x)} = \lim_{x \to a} \frac{f'(x)}{g'(x)}$$

when the right-hand limit exists*

As an example of the use of (34) let us evaluate

$$\lim_{x \to 0} \frac{\log x}{\cot x} \,.$$

We see that as $x$ approaches 0 both the numerator and denominator become infinite. Then we may apply (34). Thus

$$\lim_{x \to 0} \frac{\log x}{\cot x} = \lim_{x \to 0} \frac{1/x}{-\csc^2 x} = \lim_{x \to 0} - \frac{\sin^2 x}{x} \,.$$

Unfortunately, as $x$ approaches 0 both $\sin^2 x$ and $x$ approach 0. Hence we

---

*This result is correct also for the case when $x$ becomes infinite. The proof is made in the same way as for (28).

apply L'Hospital's rule for the case of a 0/0 form. We have

$$\lim_{x \to 0} - \frac{\sin^2 x}{x} = \lim_{x \to 0} - \frac{2 \sin x \cos x}{1} = 0.$$

Our final result is

$$\lim_{x \to 0} \frac{\log x}{\cot x} = 0.$$

We may say loosely that $\log x$ becomes infinite more slowly than $\cot x$.


## EXERCISES

**1.** Evaluate the following limits:

(a) $\lim\limits_{x \to 0} \dfrac{\cot x}{\cot 2x}$ .                      *Ans.* 2.

(b) $\lim\limits_{x \to \infty} \dfrac{x^5}{e^x}$ .                      *Ans.* 0.

(c) $\lim\limits_{x \to 0} \dfrac{\tan x}{\tan 3x}$ .

(d) $\lim\limits_{x \to \infty} \dfrac{x^n}{e^x}$ , $n$ a positive integer.                      *Ans.* 0.

(e) $\lim\limits_{x \to \pi/2} \dfrac{\sec x + 1}{\tan x}$ .                      *Ans.* 1.

(f) $\lim\limits_{x \to 0} \dfrac{\log \sin x}{\log \tan x}$ .

(g) $\lim\limits_{x \to \frac{1}{2}} \dfrac{\log(1 - 2x)}{\tan \pi x}$ .                      *Ans.* 0.

(h) $\lim\limits_{x \to \infty} \dfrac{a_0 x^n + a_1 x^{n-1} + \ldots + a_n}{b_0 x^n + b_1 x^{n-1} + \ldots + b_n}$ , $n$ a positive integer.                      *Ans.* $\dfrac{a_0}{b_0}$.

(i) $\lim\limits_{x \to \infty,} \dfrac{a_0 x^m + a_1 x^{m-1} + \ldots + a_m}{b_0 x^n + b_1 x^{n-1} + \ldots + b_n}$ for $m < n$, $m$ and $n$ positive integers.

*Ans.* 0.

**2.** Evaluate

$$\lim_{x \to \infty} \frac{x}{\sqrt{x^2 + 1}}.$$

*Suggestion:* Note that the application of L'Hospital's rule leads to the reciprocal of the given function. Hence the original function and its reciprocal must have the same limit (if any). But if $f(x)$ approaches $l$ and if $l$ is not 0, then $1/f(x)$ should approach $1/l$. What is $l$?                      *Ans.* 1.

Indeterminate expressions may appear in a variety of ways. Thus one might encounter $x \log x$ which for $x = 0$ takes on the "value" $0 \cdot \infty$. Or one might be obliged to treat $\tan x - \sec x$ which for $x = \pi/2$ takes on the value $\infty - \infty$. Indeterminate forms of the class $0 \cdot \infty$ and $\infty - \infty$ can usually be recast by algebraic processes so as to take on the form $0/0$ or

$\infty/\infty$ and we may then seek the appropriate limit. Thus we may treat $x \log x$ as

$$\lim_{x\to 0} x \log x = \lim_{x\to 0} \frac{\log x}{1/x} = \lim_{x\to 0} \frac{1/x}{-1/x^2} = \lim_{x\to 0} (-x) = 0.$$

The passage from the second expression to the third was made in accordance with L'Hospital's rule for the case of $\infty/\infty$.

Still another class of indeterminate forms arises in connection with powers. Thus suppose that we are obliged to determine $\lim_{x\to 0} x^x$. This function $x^x$ takes on the value $0^0$ for $x = 0$ and $0^0$ is meaningless. However, $\lim_{x\to 0} x^x$ may nevertheless exist. To determine this limit we set

$$y = x^x$$

so that

$$\log y = x \log x.$$

We saw above that as $x$ approaches 0, $x \log x$ approaches 0. Hence

**(35)**
$$\lim_{x\to 0} \log y = 0.$$

We think of $y$ as $e^{f(x)}$, where $f(x)$ is some function of $x$, so that $\log y = f(x)$. Equation (35) says that $f(x)$ approaches 0. Then

$$\lim_{x\to 0} y = \lim_{x\to 0} e^{f(x)} = 1.$$

Among indeterminate forms that appear as powers, in addition to the case $0^0$ just described, one encounters $\infty^0$ and $1^\infty$. The method of evaluating the limits the corresponding functions approach is illustrated by the treatment of $x^x$. The method is to take the logarithm of the power and evaluate this logarithm. Then the original limit sought is the antilogarithm of the limit for the logarithm. In fact, all three forms $0^0$, $\infty^0$, and $1^\infty$ derive from the general form

**(36)**
$$[f(x)]^{g(x)}$$

where the expression may take on the values $0^0$, $\infty^0$, or $1^\infty$ at, say, $x = a$. By taking the logarithm of (36) we have

**(37)**
$$\log y = g(x)\log f(x).$$

If $f$ and $g$ take the respective values 0 and 0, then (37) gives the $0 \cdot \infty$ form. If $f$ and $g$ take the respective values $\infty$ and 0, then (37) gives the form $\infty \cdot 0$. And if $f$ and $g$ take the respective values 1 and $\infty$, then (37) gives the form $\infty \cdot 0$. All three cases then usually revert to the indeterminate form

$\infty \cdot 0$, although in special cases $\log y$ may take a simple form (see Exercise 1(w).

## EXERCISES

1. Evaluate the following limits:

(a) $\lim_{x \to 0} (\sqrt{x} \log x)$.       *Ans.* 0.

(b) $\lim_{t \to 0} (t e^{-(1/t)})$.

(c) $\lim_{x \to 0} \left( \csc^2 x - \dfrac{1}{x^2} \right)$.       *Ans.* $\frac{1}{3}$.

(d) $\lim_{x \to \infty} \left( x \tan \dfrac{3}{x} \right)$.

(e) $\lim_{t \to 1} \left( \dfrac{t}{t-1} - \dfrac{1}{\log t} \right)$.       *Ans.* $\frac{1}{2}$.

(f) $\lim_{t \to \infty} (t e^{-(1/t)})$.       *Ans.* $\infty$.

(g) $\lim_{x \to 0} (x \log \tan x)$.

(h) $\lim_{x \to \pi/2} (\tan 3x - \tan x)$.       *Ans.* $\infty$.

(i) $\lim_{x \to 0} (\sin x)^x$.

(j) $\lim_{x \to 0} x^{1/x}$       *Ans.* $\infty$.

(k) $\lim_{x \to 0} (3 \sin x + \cos x)^{\cot x}$.

(l) $\lim_{x \to 0} (e^x + 2x)^{1/x}$.       *Ans.* $e^3$.

(m) $\lim_{x \to \pi/2} (\sec x)^{\cos x}$.

(n) $\lim_{x \to 1} (x^{1/(1-x)})$.       *Ans.* $e^{-1}$.

(o) $\lim_{x \to 2} \left( \dfrac{1}{x-2} \right)^{1/(x-2)}$.

(p) $\lim_{x \to 1} (x-1)^{1/(x-1)}$.

(q) $\lim_{x \to \infty} [\log(1+x) - \log x]$.
       *Ans.* 0.

(r) $\lim_{x \to 0} \sin x \log 2x$.

(s) $\lim_{x \to 0} \left[ \dfrac{1}{\sin x} - \dfrac{1}{x} \right]$.       *Ans.* 0.

(t) $\lim_{x \to \infty} (1+x)^{1/x}$       *Ans.* 1.

(u) $\lim_{x \to 0} x \cot x$.

(v) $\lim_{x \to \pi/2} (\sec x - \tan x)$.       *Ans.* 0.

(w) $\lim_{x \to 0} x^{a/\log x}$.

2. Is an expression that takes the form $\infty^\infty$ at some finite or infinite value of $x$ determinate?       *Ans.* Yes.

3. Answer the same question as in Exercise 2 but for the form $0^\infty$.       *Ans.* Yes.

4. We know from formula (75) of Chapter 12 that the velocity of an object that is thrown up with a velocity of 1000 ft/sec in a medium whose resistance is proportional to the velocity is

$$v = -\frac{32}{k} + \frac{32 + 1000k}{k} e^{-kt}.$$

Show that as $k$ approaches 0, the formula for $v$ approaches that for the vacuum case, namely, $v = 1000 - 32t$.

   *Suggestion:* As the expression for $v$ now stands, when $k = 0$ we have an $\infty - \infty$ type of indeterminate form. Add the fractions.

5. Formula (77) of Chapter 12 states that the height above the ground of an object that is thrown up with an initial velocity of 1000 ft/sec in a medium whose resistance is proportional to the velocity is

$$y = -\frac{32}{k} t + \frac{32 + 1000k}{k^2} (1 - e^{-kt}).$$

Show that as $k$ approaches 0, this formula approaches that for the vacuum case, namely, $y = -16t^2 + 1000t$.

   *Suggestion:* See the preceding exercise.

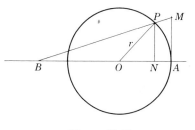

**Figure 13-12**

**6.** In Fig. 13-12, $P$ is a point on a circle with center at $O$ and radius $r$; $AM$ = arc $AP$ and line $MP$ meets $OA$ at $B$. Show that the limiting position of $B$ as $P$ approaches $A$ is given by $OB = 2r$.

   *Suggestion:* Use the similar triangles $BNP$ and $BAM$.

# CHAPTER FOURTEEN
# FURTHER TECHNIQUES OF INTEGRATION

*1. Introduction.* In the foregoing chapters we learned how to integrate a variety of functions by reversing a known differentiation formula. The only exceptions were an occasional use of substitution of a new variable or change of variable. Frequently familiar functions occur in combinations that do not obviously lend themselves to integration; yet there is a considerable number of techniques that enable us to find the integral in such cases. In this chapter we shall study the most important of these techniques.

*2. Integration by Parts.* Among general techniques perhaps the most important is the technique called integration by parts. The procedure stems from a formula for differentiation that we learned much earlier. If $u$ and $v$ are two functions of $x$, we know that

**(1)**
$$\frac{d}{dx}(uv) = u\,\frac{dv}{dx} + v\,\frac{du}{dx}.$$

Then

$$u\,\frac{dv}{dx} = \frac{d}{dx}(uv) - v\,\frac{du}{dx}.$$

If we now indicate integration by using the usual integral sign and the $dx$ notation, then

$$\int u\,\frac{dv}{dx}\,dx = \int \frac{d}{dx}(uv)dx - \int v\,\frac{du}{dx}\,dx + C.$$

Of course, the integral of a derivative gives the function itself, so that

**(2)**
$$\int u\,\frac{dv}{dx}\,dx = uv - \int v\,\frac{du}{dx}\,dx + C,$$

or, since in differential notation,

$$dv = \frac{dv}{dx} \, dx \quad \text{and} \quad du = \frac{du}{dx} \, dx,$$

**(3)**
$$\int u \, dv = uv - \int v \, du + C.$$

Formula (2) or (3) is the formula for integration by parts. At first sight it does not appear to be helpful, for the right-hand side, which presumably gives the answer to the integral on the left, itself contains an integral. However, the right-hand integral is often easier to evaluate than the left one and so the formula is useful. Let us consider some examples.

To evaluate

$$\int x \sin x \, dx$$

let us choose $u = x$ and $dv/dx = \sin x$. It is helpful to arrange the work as follows:

$$u = x \qquad \frac{dv}{dx} = \sin x$$

$$\frac{du}{dx} = 1 \qquad v = -\cos x.$$

Then following (2) we have

$$\int x \sin x \, dx = -x \cos x - \int (-\cos x) \cdot 1 \, dx + C$$

or

**(4)**
$$\int x \sin x \, dx = -x \cos x + \sin x + C.$$

Thus we have obtained the answer readily.

From this example we see that the function chosen for $dv/dx$ must itself be readily integrable. This choice does not guarantee that $\int v(du/dx)dx$ will itself be integrable. That is, the method does not always work. However, by choosing $dv/dx$ to be as complicated as possible and yet integrable we often succeed in making the evaluation of $\int v(du/dx)dx$ possible.

As another example let us consider

$$\int \sec^3 x \, dx.$$

One might try to do integrations involving powers of trigonometric functions by using one or more of the identities, but in the present case integration by parts is the only direct scheme. We regard $\sec^3 x$ as $\sec x \cdot \sec^2 x$ and choose $dv/dx$ to be $\sec^2 x$ because we know how to integrate this function. We first make the preliminary calculations. Thus

$$u = \sec x \qquad\qquad \frac{dv}{dx} = \sec^2 x$$

$$\frac{du}{dx} = \sec x \tan x \qquad v = \tan x.$$

By formula (2)

$$\int \sec x \sec^2 x \, dx = \sec x \tan x - \int \tan x \tan x \sec x \, dx + C$$

The right-hand integral does not seem manageable, and so presumably we did not gain by applying integration by parts. However, let us see what happens if we replace $\tan^2 x$ by $\sec^2 x - 1$. We obtain

$$\int \sec^3 x \, dx = \sec x \tan x - \int (\sec^2 x - 1)\sec x \, dx + C$$

or

$$\int \sec^3 x \, dx = \sec x \tan x - \int \sec^3 x \, dx + \int \sec x \, dx + C.$$

We can transpose the integral involving $\sec^3 x$ from the right side to the left and thus obtain

**(5)** $$2\int \sec^3 x \, dx = \sec x \tan x + \int \sec x \, dx + C.$$

So far we have at least reduced our problem to finding $\int \sec x \, dx$. This is evaluated by a trick that was discovered by someone in the past. The trick is the following:

$$\int \sec x \, dx = \int \sec x \, \frac{\sec x + \tan x}{\sec x + \tan x} \, dx$$

or

**(6)** $$\int \sec x \, dx = \int \frac{\sec^2 x + \sec x \tan x}{\sec x + \tan x} \, dx.$$

Now, if we let

$$u = \sec x + \tan x = \tan x + \sec x,$$

we see that

$$\frac{du}{dx} = \sec^2 x + \sec x \tan x.$$

The integrand on the right side of (6) is of the form

$$\frac{1}{u} \frac{du}{dx} \, dx.$$

Then, by formula (30) of Chapter 12,

$$y = \log u$$

or

**(7)**                     $$\int \sec x \, dx = \log(\sec x + \tan x).$$

We substitute this result in (5) and divide by 2. The final result is

**(8)**          $$\int \sec^3 x \, dx = \frac{\sec x \tan x}{2} + \frac{\log(\sec x + \tan x)}{2} + \frac{C}{2}.$$

Of course, $C/2$ can be replaced by a new constant.

      This example is noteworthy not only for the result but for the peculiar feature that integration by parts leads to the same integral, namely $\int \sec^3 x \, dx$, with which we started; by transposing this term we managed to express the desired integral in terms of something that we could integrate.

## EXERCISES

**1.** Evaluate the following integrals by using integration by parts:

(a)   $\int x \cos x \, dx.$                  *Ans.* $x \sin x + \cos x + C.$

(b)   $\int x \log x \, dx.$

(c)   $\int x e^x \, dx.$                     *Ans.* $x e^x - e^x + C.$

(d)   $\int x^2 e^x \, dx.$

(e)   $\int e^x \sin x \, dx.$         *Ans.* $e^x \dfrac{\sin x}{2} - e^x \dfrac{\cos x}{2} + C.$

(f)   $\int \log x \, dx.$

(g)   $\int x e^{ax} \, dx.$            *Ans.* $\dfrac{x e^{ax}}{a} - \dfrac{e^{ax}}{a^2} + C.$

(h)   $\int e^{ax} \sin nx \, dx.$

(i)   $\int x \sin 2x \, dx.$      *Ans.* $- \dfrac{x \cos 2x}{2} + \dfrac{\sin 2x}{4} + C.$

(j)   $\int x \sec^2 2x \, dx.$

(k)   $\int x \sin^2 \dfrac{x}{2} \, dx.$      *Ans.* $\dfrac{x^2}{4} - \dfrac{x \sin x}{2} - \dfrac{\cos x}{2} + C.$

(l)   $\int \sin x \cos 3x \, dx.$

(m)   $\int \arcsin x \, dx.*$      *Ans.* $x \arcsin x + \sqrt{1 - x^2} + C.$

(n)   $\int \arctan x \, dx.*$

(o)   $\int \dfrac{x e^x}{(1 + x)^2} \, dx.$          *Ans.* $\dfrac{e^x}{1 + x} + C.$

(p)   $\int x \cos^2 \dfrac{x}{2} \, dx.$      *Ans.* $\dfrac{x^2}{4} + \dfrac{x \sin x}{2} + \dfrac{\cos x}{2} + C.$

(q)   $\int x^2 \cos x \, dx.$      *Ans.* $x^2 \sin x + 2x \cos x - 2 \sin x + C.$

*Recall that $\arcsin x = \sin^{-1} x.$

**2.** Let us evaluate $\int(1/x)dx$ by parts. If we let $u = 1/x$ and $dv = 1\ dx$, we obtain $\int dx/x = 1 + \int dx/x$. Then $1 = 0$. What is wrong?

**3.** (a)   Let us try to evaluate $\int dx/(x \log x)$ by integration by parts. Let $u = 1/\log x$ and $dv/dx = 1/x$. Then $du/dx = -(1/(\log x)^2)1/x$ and $v = \log x$.

By the "parts" formula $\int dx/x \log x = 1 + \int dx/x \log x$. It follows that $1 = 0$. What is wrong?

(b)   Evaluate $\int dx/x \log x$ by some other method.          *Ans.* $\log(\log x) + C$.

**4.** Evaluate $\int \sec x\ dx$ by making the substitution $\sec x = \cosh u$, where $x$ is a function of $u$.                    *Ans.* $\cosh^{-1}(\sec x)$ or $\sinh^{-1}(\tan x)$.

**5.** Evaluate $\int \csc x\ dx$ by making the substitution $\csc x = \cosh u$, where $x$ is a function of $u$.                    *Ans.* $-\sinh^{-1}(\cot x)$ or $-\cosh^{-1}(\csc x)$.

**6.** In formula (7) of the text we found that $\int \sec x\ dx = \log(\sec x + \tan x)$. Show that this result is the same as that obtained in Exercise 4.

**3. Reduction Formulas.** There is a technique of integration that is actually an application of integration by parts but whose effectiveness requires a little examination. Let us consider an example.

Suppose that we wish to evaluate

**(9)**                              $$\int \sin^5 x\ \cos^4 x\ dx.$$

This integral can be treated in various ways but let us use integration by parts. We should try to choose our $u$ and $dv/dx$ so that we can integrate $dv/dx$. Let us therefore make the following choice:

$$u = \cos^3 x, \qquad \frac{dv}{dx} = \sin^5 x\ \cos x.$$

Then

$$\frac{du}{dx} = -3 \cos^2 x \sin x, \qquad v = \frac{\sin^6 x}{6}.$$

Formula (2) for integration by parts now gives

**(10)**    $$\int \sin^5 x\ \cos^4 x\ dx = \frac{\sin^6 x}{6} \cos^3 x + 3\int \frac{\sin^7 x}{6} \cos^2 x\ dx.$$

This result may not be very gratifying but if we examine it closely we see that we have accomplished something. We started with $\sin^5 x \cos^4 x$ and we ended, apart from the term already integrated, with $\sin^7 x \cos^2 x$. We have reduced the exponent in the cosine term by 2. One more application of the same procedure will then yield $\cos^0 x$ or 1, so that the cosine term will be eliminated. We shall then have to integrate an expression of the form $\sin^m x$, which, as we shall see, can be done by using trigonometric identities.

In reducing the exponent of the cos $x$ term in (10) we did increase the exponent of the sin $x$ term, and this will lead to more work in integrating the ultimate $\sin^m x$. However, we can improve on (10). We note that

$$\sin^7 x \cos^2 x = \sin^5 x(1 - \cos^2 x)\cos^2 x = \sin^5 x \cos^2 x - \sin^5 x \cos^4 x.$$

**(11)**

If we substitute this result in the last term of (10), we see that we can bring the term involving $\sin^5 x \cos^4 x$ to the left side and combine it with the term already there. The result of this algebra is

**(12)** $$\int \sin^5 x \cos^4 x \, dx = \frac{\sin^6 x \cos^3 x}{9} + \frac{3}{9} \int \sin^5 x \cos^2 x \, dx.$$

This result (12) is better than (10) because we have reduced the integral on the left to that on the right in which the power of sin $x$ *remains the same* and yet the power of cos $x$ is still reduced by 2.

Both formulas (10) and (12) illustrate the major point of this section, namely, that a method of integration, integration by parts in the present case, may not in itself achieve the full result of finding the integral, but it may convert the given integral into one that is simpler. Formulas (10) and (12) are called *reduction formulas* because they reduce the given integral to a form in which some exponent is smaller and thus the resulting integral is easier to handle. Continued application of the formula will often eliminate one of the factors in the original integrand and produce a much simpler integrand. We can see this point more clearly if we first generalize (12). By using the same procedure as we used to obtain (12) we can prove that

$$\int \sin^m x \cos^n x \, dx = \frac{\sin^{m+1}x \cos^{n-1}x}{m + n} + \frac{n - 1}{m + n} \int \sin^m x \cos^{n-2}x \, dx$$

**(13)**

provided that $m + n \neq 0$. We see that continued application of this formula will either eliminate the $\cos^n x$ factor if $n$ is a positive even integer or give only cos $x$ on the right side if $n$ is a positive odd integer. In the latter case we can certainly complete the integration by letting $u = \sin x$. In the former case we can resort to another simpler reduction formula (see Exercise 3) if necessary.

We have used the term reduction formula to mean that the exponent of some power is decreased. However, the term is also used in an extended sense. Suppose that we had started with

**(14)** $$\int \sin^5 x \cos^{-4} x \, dx,$$

wherein $\cos^{-4}x$ means $(\cos x)^{-4}$. If we were to reduce the power of the $\cos^{-4}x$ factor by 2 and end up with

$$\int \sin^5 x \cos^{-6} x \, dx,$$

we would be worse off than when we started. To simplify (14) we would want to increase the exponent of the $\cos^{-4}x$ factor. We can do this. Essentially we have but to use formula (13) in reverse. If we reverse this formula by solving for the last term, we obtain

$$\int \sin^m x \, \cos^{n-2} x \, dx = - \frac{\sin^{m+1} x \, \cos^{n-1} x}{n-1} + \frac{m+n}{n-1} \int \sin^m x \, \cos^n x \, dx$$

**(15)**

or if we replace $n - 2$ by $p$ so that $n = p + 2$, we obtain

$$\int \sin^m x \, \cos^p x \, dx = - \frac{\sin^{m+1} x \, \cos^{p+1} x}{p+1}$$

**(16)**
$$+ \frac{m+p+2}{p+1} \int \sin^m x \, \cos^{p+2} x \, dx,$$

provided that $p + 1 \neq 0$. Thus we see that if $p$ were $-4$, we could convert the left-hand integral to that on the right in which the exponent of the $\cos x$ factor would be $-2$, while the exponent of the $\sin x$ factor would remain the same.

Formula (16) is as much a reduction formula as is (13). The real point, then, about a reduction formula is not that it decreases the exponent of some factor in the original integrand. The formula may increase the exponent or decrease it, but it should change the given integral to another form that may be easier to handle; or continued application of the reduction formula may produce an integral that is easier to handle. There are many reduction formulas, some of which will be given later in a table of integrals. However, all of them are used for the same general purpose that we have just indicated.

## EXERCISES

**1.** Show by generalizing on the example in the text that formula (13) is correct.

**2.** Establish the following reduction formulas:

(a) $\int \cos^n x \, dx = \cos^{n-1} x \sin x + (n-1) \int \cos^{n-2} x \, \sin^2 x \, dx$.
   *Suggestion:* Let $u = \cos^{n-1} x$.

(b)  Convert the result in (a) to

$$\int \cos^n x \, dx = \frac{1}{n} \cos^{n-1} x \sin x + \frac{n-1}{n} \int \cos^{n-2} x \, dx.$$

**3.** Establish the following reduction formula:

$$\int \sin^n x \, dx = - \frac{1}{n} \sin^{n-1} x \cos x + \frac{n-1}{n} \int \sin^{n-2} x \, dx$$

by following the procedure in Exercise 2.

**4.** Evaluate the following:

(a) $\int \sin^6 x \, dx.$

> *Ans.* $-\frac{1}{6}\sin^5 x \cos x - \frac{5}{24}\sin^3 x \cos x - \frac{5}{16}\sin x \cos x + \frac{5}{16}x + C.$

(b) $\int \cos^6 x \, dx.$

(c) $\int \sin^4 x \cos^2 x \, dx.$

> *Ans.* $\frac{1}{6}\sin^5 x \cos x - \frac{1}{24}\sin^3 x \cos x - \frac{1}{16}\sin x \cos x + \frac{1}{16}x + C.$

(d) $\int \sin^4 x \cos^4 x \, dx.$

(e) $\int \sin^4 x \cos^{-2} x \, dx.$*

> *Ans.* $\sin^5 x \cos^{-1} x + \frac{5}{4}\sin^3 x \cos x + \frac{15}{8}\sin x \cos x - \frac{15}{8}x + C.$

(f) $\int \sin^4 x \cos^{-1} x \, dx.$

(g) $\int \sin^{-4} x \, dx.$

> *Suggestion:* Use the result of Exercise 3.

**4. Integration by Partial Fractions.** It is possible to integrate any function that is a quotient of two polynomials. As an example of such a quotient we have

$$\frac{3x^2 - 7x + 2}{x^3 + 5x^2 + 6x + 2}.$$

More generally, a polynomial or rational integral function of $x$ is a function of the form

$$a_0 x^n + a_1 x^{n-1} + \ldots + a_{n-1}x + a_n,$$

wherein $a_0, a_1, \ldots, a_n$ are constants, and a quotient of two polynomials or a rational function of $x$ is of the form

**(17)**
$$\frac{a_0 x^n + a_1 x^{n-1} + \ldots + a_{n-1}x + a_n}{b_0 x^m + b_1 x^{m-1} + \ldots + b_{m-1}x + b_m}.$$

The terms rational integral function and rational function are suggested by the analogy with ordinary numbers; the polynomial is the analogue of the integer and the rational function is the analogue of the quotient of two integers or rational numbers.

To avoid getting lost in a lot of symbols, let us consider concrete examples of (17) instead of working with the general rational function. Suppose, then, that we have the problem of integrating

$$\frac{x^4 + 4x^3 + x^2 + 6}{x^2 + 2x + 1}.$$

* In Exercises (e), (f), and (g) the exponent denotes a power and not the inverse function.

When, as in the present example, the degree of the numerator is equal to or greater than the degree of the denominator, the first useful step is to divide the denominator into the numerator. Let us see what happens when this is done.

The division process, which is entirely analogous to long division of ordinary numbers, is as follows:

$$
\begin{array}{r}
x^2 + 2x - 4 \\
x^2 + 2x + 1 \overline{)\, x^4 + 4x^3 + x^2 + 6} \\
x^4 + 2x^3 + x^2 \\
\hline
2x^3 + 0x^2 + 0x \\
2x^3 + 4x^2 + 2x \\
\hline
-4x^2 - 2x + 6 \\
-4x^2 - 8x - 4 \\
\hline
6x + 10.
\end{array}
$$

The result of the division process then is

(18) $$\frac{x^4 + 4x^3 + x^2 + 6}{x^2 + 2x + 1} = x^2 + 2x - 4 + \frac{6x + 10}{x^2 + 2x + 1}.$$

The advantage of performing the division is that the quotient, $x^2 + 2x - 4$ in the present case, consists of simple powers of $x$ which can be integrated at once, and the remainder, $(6x + 10)/(x^2 + 2x + 1)$ in the present case, in which the degree of the numerator is less than the degree of the denominator, is simpler than the original fraction.

The rational functions that can occur as a remainder are of various types; we shall consider them in turn.

**Case i.** Suppose that the remainder is

(19) $$\frac{x^2 + 2x + 4}{x^3 - 2x^2 - 5x + 6}.$$

The first step is to attempt to express the denominator as a product of linear or first degree factors. To do this we call upon algebra. We learn there that if $a$ is a root of a polynomial equated to 0 then $x - a$ is a factor of the polynomial. To each root there is a factor. This means that we should find the roots of

$$x^3 - 2x^2 - 5x + 6 = 0.$$

The process of finding the roots of a polynomial equation can be a lengthy one. To avoid getting lost in algebra, let us assume that we have found the roots. They are in the present case 1, $-2$, and 3. Then the factors of $x^3 - 2x^2 - 5x + 6$ are $x - 1$, $x + 2$, and $x - 3$; that is,

$$x^3 - 2x^2 - 5x + 6 = (x - 1)(x + 2)(x - 3).$$

We may now write (19) as

$$\frac{x^2 + 2x + 4}{(x - 1)(x + 2)(x - 3)}.$$

At this stage the method of partial fractions enters. We set

**(20)** $$\frac{x^2 + 2x + 4}{(x - 1)(x + 2)(x - 3)} = \frac{A}{x - 1} + \frac{B}{x + 2} + \frac{C}{x - 3}$$

where $A$, $B$, and $C$ are constants that must be determined. The fractions on the right side of (20) are called the partial fractions into which the left side is decomposed. The reasonableness of (20) may be apparent from the fact that when we add the fractions on the right-hand side, the denominator of the sum is the product of the three separate denominators, and in the numerator we have $A$, $B$, and $C$ each multiplied by a quadratic polynomial. Hence for some choice of $A$, $B$, and $C$ the sums of the terms in the numerator might equal the numerator on the left side, namely $x^2 + 2x + 4*$. Our problem then is to find the $A$, $B$, and $C$ for which (20) is a correct statement.

To determine $A$, $B$, and $C$ let us add the fractions on the right. Then

$$\frac{x^2 + 2x + 4}{(x - 1)(x + 2)(x - 3)}$$

$$= \frac{A(x + 2)(x - 3) + B(x - 1)(x - 3) + C(x - 1)(x + 2)}{(x - 1)(x + 2)(x - 3)}$$

**(21)**

We are supposed to choose $A$, $B$, and $C$ in (20) so that the left and right sides are identical, that is, so that they yield the same numbers for all values of $x$. Because we used correct algebra to obtain (21), the same must be true for it. Of course, (20) and (21) have no meaning for $x = 1$, $x = -2$, and $x = 3$. Now, because the denominators in (21) are equal, the numerators must be equal. Moreover, despite the fact that the fractions in (21) have no meaning for the three special values of $x$, the numerators are equal for *all* values of $x$. The reason is a theorem of algebra, namely, if two $n$th degree polynomials are equal for $n + 1$ or more values of $x$, they are equal for all values of $x$. The numerators in (21) are certainly equal for an infinite number of values of $x$ and therefore the theorem applies. Thus the numera-

---

*One can prove that the form assumed in (20) is correct. However, to avoid dependence on theorems of algebra we can, when we have determined $A$, $B$, and $C$, add the partial fractions and see that the sum is the given fraction.

tors in (21) are equal for all values of $x$; that is,

$$x^2 + 2x + 4 \equiv A(x + 2)(x - 3) + B(x - 1)(x - 3) + C(x - 1)(x + 2).$$

If we let $x = 1$, we see that

$$7 = -6A$$

or

$$A = -\frac{7}{6}.$$

If we let $x = -2$, then

$$4 = 15B$$

or

$$B = \frac{4}{15}.$$

If we let $x = 3$, then

$$19 = 10C$$

or

$$C = \frac{19}{10}.$$

With these values of $A$, $B$, and $C$ we return to (20) and we have

$$\frac{x^2 + 2x + 4}{(x - 1)(x + 2)(x - 3)} = -\frac{7}{6(x - 1)} + \frac{4}{15(x + 2)} + \frac{19}{10(x - 3)}.$$

**(22)**

We are now ready to perform integration. That is, given the problem

$$\int \frac{x^2 + 2x + 4}{(x - 1)(x + 2)(x - 3)}\, dx,$$

we may in view of (22) replace this integral by

$$-\frac{7}{6} \int \frac{dx}{x - 1} + \frac{4}{15} \int \frac{dx}{x + 2} + \frac{19}{10} \int \frac{dx}{x - 3}.$$

Each of these integrals is readily evaluated in terms of logarithmic functions.

## EXERCISES

**1.** Evaluate the following integrals:

(a) $\int \dfrac{dx}{(x-3)(x+2)}$.  $\qquad$ *Ans.* $\frac{1}{5} \log \dfrac{x-3}{x+2} + C.$

(b) $\int \dfrac{dx}{x(x-3)(x+2)}$.

(c) $\int \dfrac{dx}{x^2 - 5x + 6}$.  $\qquad$ *Ans.* $\log \dfrac{x-3}{x-2} + C.$

(d) $\int \dfrac{x+2}{(x-3)(x-4)}\, dx.$  $\qquad$ *Ans.* $6 \log(x-4) - 5 \log(x-3) + C.$

(e) $\int \dfrac{x^2 + x + 1}{(x-1)(x+2)(x-3)}\, dx.$

$\qquad$ *Ans.* $-\frac{1}{2} \log(x-1) + \frac{1}{5} \log(x+2) + \frac{13}{10} \log(x-3) + C.$

(f) $\int \dfrac{x^2 + x}{x^3 + 7x^2 + 6x}\, dx.$

(g) $\int \dfrac{dx}{\cos x(1 + \cos x)}$.  $\qquad$ *Ans.* $\log(\sec x + \tan x) - \tan \dfrac{x}{2} + C.$

**2.** In the study of the growth of a population it is often assumed that the rate of growth is proportional to the existing population; then as we saw in Chapter 12, the population increases according to a simple exponential law. However, housing and food supply often set an upper limit to the population that a given region can support. The effect of these limitations is to impede the increase in population long before the upper limit is reached because as people find housing and food more difficult to acquire they either delay having children or decide not to have them. A reasonable assumption about the effect of these limitations is that the rate of increase in population is proportional to the existing population and to the difference between the upper limit, say $L$, and the existing population. This means in mathematical language that if $P$ is the population at any time $t$, then $dP/dt = kP(L - P)$, where $k$ is a constant. Find the formula for $P$ as a function of $t$. The curve corresponding to this formula is called the logistic curve.  $\qquad$ *Ans.* $P = LP_0/[P_0 + (L - P_0)e^{-kLt}].$

**3.** When two substances, say, $A$ and $B$, mix to form a compound substance, the rate of mixing is proportional to the amount (number of atoms) present in the separate or as yet unmixed substances. This law of chemistry is called the law of mass action. Let $a$ and $b$ be the number of atoms of $A$ and $B$ present to start with and suppose that one atom of each combines to form the molecule of the mixed substance $C$. Find the formula giving the number $x$ of molecules of the substance $C$ at time $t$.

$\qquad$ *Suggestion:* If $x$ molecules of $C$ are formed, then $a - x$ is the number of unmixed atoms of $A$. The statement that the rate of mixing is proportional to the number of atoms of the as yet unmixed substances means in mathematical language that $dx/dt = k(a - x)(b - x)$. Assume that $b$ and $a$ are unequal and $b > a$.  $\qquad$ *Ans.* $x = [abe^{(b-a)kt} - ab]/[be^{(b-a)kt} - a].$

**4.** Show that at the inflection point of the logistic curve (Exercise 2) the population is $\frac{1}{2}$ the limiting population $L$.

**5.** To break up $(x^2 + 1)/(x^2 - 1)$ into partial fractions we assume that

$$\frac{x^2 + 1}{x^2 - 1} = \frac{A}{x - 1} + \frac{B}{x + 1} .$$

Then $x^2 + 1 = A(x + 1) + B(x - 1)$. By letting $x = 1$, we obtain $A = 1$ and by letting $x = -1$, we obtain $B = -1$. Then we have that

$$\frac{x^2 + 1}{x^2 - 1} = \frac{1}{x - 1} - \frac{1}{x + 1} .$$

But addition of the partial fractions does not give the left-hand side. What is wrong?

**6.** (a) Consider the motion of an object which is allowed to fall from rest in a medium whose resistance is proportional to the square of the velocity. The differential equation is

$$\frac{dy}{dt} = 32 - kv^2.$$

To solve this we write

$$\frac{dt}{dv} = \frac{1}{32 - kv^2} .$$

Use the method of partial fractions to show that

$$v = \sqrt{\frac{32}{k}} \ \frac{e^{2\sqrt{32k}\ t} - 1}{e^{2\sqrt{32k}\ t} + 1} .$$

(b) Now show that the result in part (a) equals the result in formula (111) of Chapter 12, namely,

$$v = \sqrt{\frac{32}{k}} \ \tanh \sqrt{32k}\ t.$$

**7.** A substance which dissolves in water will usually dissolve at a rate proportional to the undissolved amount and to the difference between a fully saturated solution (the most that can be dissolved in that volume of water) and the concentration at any time $t$. Suppose that a saturated solution of a substance would contain 50 grams in 100 grams of water. If 30 grams of the substance are put into 100 grams of water and ten grams dissolve after 2 hours, how much will be dissolved in another 3 hours?

*Suggestion:* Let $x$ represent the amount of the substance undissolved after $t$ hours.

**8.** (a) The spread of an infectious disease such as the common cold, wherein no deaths occur and no infected people are isolated, is proportional to the number infected and to the number of the total population $M$ who are not yet infected. Let $N(t)$ be the number infected at time $t$ and find the form of $N(t)$.

*Suggestion:* To solve the differential equation you can use the method of partial fractions or for variety let $N = 1/w$.

(b) Find the time $t$ at which the rate of spread of the epidemic is a maximum.

*Suggestion:* You can deduce this result from the solution but you can do it more readily by working with the differential equation.

**9.** If the birth rate in a country is 5 per cent of the population at any time $t$ and the death rate is 2 per cent of the square of the population, what is the law of population growth?

**10.** The rate of change of the spread of a rumor is proportional to those who have heard it and to those who have yet to hear it. Let $x$ be the number of people who have heard the rumor at any time $t$ and let the total population be $N$. Then $dx/dt = kx(N - x)$. Find $x$ as a function of $t$ if $x = x_0$ at $t = 0$ and find the limiting value of $x$ as $t$ becomes infinite.

**Case ii.**    When the rational function to be integrated has a denominator that can be factored into linear factors some of which are repeated the partial fractions procedure we used in Case I still applies but with one modification. Let us suppose that the rational function is

**(23)**
$$\frac{x + 3}{(x - 2)(x - 3)^2} .$$

We might be inclined to try to reexpress this function in the form

**(24)**
$$\frac{A}{x - 2} + \frac{B}{(x - 3)^2}$$

and then determine $A$ and $B$. However, the form (24) is not correct. We can see that this will not do because if we add the fractions the numerator will surely contain a second degree term in $x$ whereas the numerator in (23) does not. The proper way to break up (23) into a sum of partial fractions is to assume that

**(25)**
$$\frac{x + 3}{(x - 2)(x - 3)^2} = \frac{A}{x - 2} + \frac{B}{x - 3} + \frac{C}{(x - 3)^2} .$$

This form takes care of the difficulty that (24) presented because when we add the fractions in (25) the numerator will contain two second degree terms in $x$, and these may offset each other for proper values of $A$ and $B$ and thus yield the first degree numerator on the left side.

The form on the right side of (25) is required for another reason. We are assuming that some sum of fractions will yield the left side of (25). This left side could be a sum of three terms such as we have in (25). If it is, we would be wrong to assume that it necessarily came from the more limited type of sum in (24). In other words, we should assume the most general form from which the sum on the left side of (25) might have come.

Now that we believe that we have the correct partial fractions in (25) the method of determining $A$, $B$, and $C$ is the same as before. From (25), by adding the fractions on the right, we have

(26) $$\frac{x + 3}{(x - 2)(x - 3)^2} = \frac{A(x - 3)^2 + B(x - 2)(x - 3) + C(x - 2)}{(x - 2)(x - 3)^2}.$$

Our argument for determining $A$, $B$, and $C$ is the same as in Case I. The two fractions in (26) are to be identical for all values of $x$ except $x = 2$ and $x = 3$, for which values the fractions are not defined. However, the numerators, which are polynomials, are to be equal for more than two values of $x$. We may regard the left numerator as $0x^2 + x + 3$, so that we have two second degree polynomials equal for more than two values of $x$. Then by the theorem of algebra cited in Case I the numerators must be equal for *all* values of $x$; that is,

(27) $$x + 3 \equiv A(x - 3)^2 + B(x - 2)(x - 3) + C(x - 2).$$

By letting $x = 2$ we see that

$$5 = A.$$

By letting $x = 3$ we see that

$$6 = C.$$

We now choose any other convenient value of $x$. Let us choose $x = 0$. Then

$$3 = 9A + 6B - 2C.$$

Because we know $A$ and $C$, we have from this last equation that

$$B = -5.$$

We substitute the values of $A$, $B$, and $C$ in (25) and obtain

(28) $$\frac{x + 3}{(x - 2)(x - 3)^2} = \frac{5}{x - 2} - \frac{5}{x - 3} + \frac{6}{(x - 3)^2}.$$

Thus, given the problem of evaluating

$$\int \frac{x + 3}{(x - 2)(x - 3)^2},$$

we may in view of (28) replace this integral by

$$5\int \frac{dx}{x - 2} - 5\int \frac{dx}{x - 3} + 6\int \frac{dx}{(x - 3)^2}.$$

Each of these integrals is readily evaluated.

## EXERCISES

**1.** Evaluate the following integrals:

(a) $\int \dfrac{x}{(x-3)(x+1)^2} \, dx.$    *Ans.* $\frac{3}{16} \log \dfrac{x-3}{x+1} - \dfrac{1}{4(x+1)} + C.$

(b) $\int \dfrac{3x+2}{x^2(x+1)} \, dx.$

(c) $\int \dfrac{x+1}{x(x-1)^3} \, dx.$    *Ans.* $\log \dfrac{x-1}{x} + \dfrac{1}{x-1} - \dfrac{1}{(x-1)^2} + C.$

(d) $\int \dfrac{x+1}{(x-2)^2(x-3)^2} \, dx.$

**Case iii.**  Given a rational function such as

**(29)**
$$\frac{4}{x^3 - x^2 + 4x - 4}$$

our first thought would be to factor the denominator. It is at once apparent that 1 is a zero of the polynomial, that is, a root of $x^3 - x^2 + 4x - 4 = 0$, and therefore $x - 1$ is a factor. Then

**(30)**
$$\frac{4}{x^3 - x^2 + 4x - 4} = \frac{4}{(x-1)(x^2+4)}.$$

We can now find the two linear factors of $x^2 + 4$. However, these factors, $x + 2i$ and $x - 2i$, involve complex numbers, and it is desirable in elementary calculus to avoid such numbers because they involve a host of new considerations. Can we then keep the quadratic factor and break up (30) into a sum of two fractions? And if so, can we integrate the separate fractions?

We can reexpress the right side of (30) as a sum of fractions, but because one factor in the denominator is quadratic there is a new element in the picture. We might be tempted to assume that

**(31)**
$$\frac{4}{(x-1)(x^2+4)} = \frac{A}{x-1} + \frac{B}{x^2+4}.$$

However, we can see that if we add the two fractions, the numerator will have an $x^2$-term no matter how we choose $A$ and $B$, but there is no $x^2$-term in the numerator on the left side of (31). The way to eliminate the $x^2$-term in the sum of the two partial fractions is to assume that

**(32)**
$$\frac{4}{(x-1)(x^2+4)} = \frac{A}{x-1} + \frac{Bx+C}{x^2+4}.$$

Let us add the fractions and see if we can determine $A$, $B$, and $C$. Addition of the fractions gives

$$\frac{4}{(x-1)(x^2+4)} = \frac{A(x^2+4) + (Bx+C)(x-1)}{(x-1)(x^2+4)}.$$

Our argument is now the same as in Cases I and II. The numerators on the two sides are polynomials which must be equal for all values of $x$. That is,

$$4 \equiv A(x^2 + 4) + (Bx + C)(x - 1).$$

We choose convenient values of $x$ to determine $A$, $B$, and $C$. When $x = 1$,

$$4 = 5A$$

or

$$A = \frac{4}{5}.$$

When $x = 0$,

$$4 = 4A - C.$$

Then

$$C = -\frac{4}{5}.$$

When $x = -1$,

$$4 = 5A + 2B - 2C.$$

Then

$$B = -\frac{4}{5}.$$

We now have from (32) that

**(33)** $$\frac{4}{(x - 1)(x^2 + 4)} = \frac{4}{5(x - 1)} + \frac{-4x - 4}{5(x^2 + 4)}.$$

To evaluate

$$\int \frac{4}{(x - 1)(x^2 + 4)}\, dx$$

we can instead, in view of (33), evaluate

$$\frac{4}{5} \int \frac{dx}{x - 1} - \frac{4}{5} \int \frac{x + 1}{x^2 + 4}\, dx.$$

The first integral can be handled at once. The second can be expressed as the sum

$$-\frac{4}{5} \int \frac{x}{x^2 + 4}\, dx - \frac{4}{5} \int \frac{1}{x^2 + 4}\, dx.$$

Both of these can be integrated by methods already available.

The evaluation of

$$\int \frac{x+1}{x^2+4} \, dx$$

can be done readily because the $x$-term is missing in the denominator. Let us consider a case in which the full quadratic expression occurs in the denominator. We shall evaluate

**(34)**
$$\int \frac{dx}{x^3+8} \, .$$

We see at once that $-2$ is a zero of $x^3 + 8$ so that

$$x^3 + 8 = (x+2)(x^2 - 2x + 4).$$

However, the quadratic factor $x^2 - 2x + 4$ does not have any real zeros because its discriminant, $b^2 - 4ac$, is $-12$. In accordance with the method we just examined, we set

$$\frac{1}{x^3+8} = \frac{A}{x+2} + \frac{Bx+C}{x^2-2x+4} \, .$$

We need not repeat the process of determining $A$, $B$, and $C$. The results are $A = \frac{1}{12}$, $B = -\frac{1}{12}$, $C = \frac{1}{3}$. Then

$$\frac{1}{x^3+8} = \frac{1}{12}\frac{1}{x+2} + \frac{-\frac{1}{12}x + \frac{1}{3}}{x^2-2x+4} \, .$$

In place of (34) we have

**(35)**
$$\frac{1}{12}\int \frac{dx}{x+2} + \int \frac{-\frac{1}{12}x+\frac{1}{3}}{x^2-2x+4} \, dx.$$

The first integral is readily evaluated. To handle the second integral, we note that we can integrate forms of the type

**(36)**
$$\frac{u}{u^2+a^2} \quad \text{and} \quad \frac{c}{u^2+a^2}$$

where $c$ and $a$ are constants. To put the second integral in (35) into the forms in (36), we complete the square* in the denominator; that is,

$$\int \frac{-\frac{1}{12}x+\frac{1}{3}}{x^2-2x+4} \, dx = \int \frac{-\frac{1}{12}x+\frac{1}{3}}{x^2-2x+1+3} \, dx.$$

*To complete the square in $x^2 + bx + c$ one adds $(b/2)^2$ and then subtracts it, thus $x^2 + bx + c = x^2 + bx + (b/2)^2 + c - (b/2)^2 = (x + b/2)^2 + c - (b/2)^2$.

We now use the method of substitution. That is, let

$$x - 1 = u \quad \text{so that} \quad x = u + 1.$$

Then

**(37)** $$\int \frac{-\frac{1}{12}x + \frac{1}{3}}{(x-1)^2 + 3} \, dx = \int \frac{-\frac{1}{12}u - \frac{1}{12} + \frac{1}{3}}{u^2 + 3} \, dx.$$

To integrate a function of $u$ with respect to $x$, we must also have the $du/dx$ following the function of $u$. However $du/dx$ is 1. Hence we can write in place of the right side of (37)

$$\int \frac{-\frac{1}{12}u + \frac{1}{4}}{u^2 + 3} \, du,$$

and this can be reexpressed as

$$-\frac{1}{2 \cdot 12} \int \frac{2u}{u^2 + 3} \, du + \frac{1}{4} \int \frac{1}{u^2 + 3} \, du.$$

These integrals are known to us. They yield*

$$-\frac{1}{24} \log(u^2 + 3) + \frac{1}{4\sqrt{3}} \arctan \frac{u}{\sqrt{3}}$$

or in terms of $x$,

$$-\frac{1}{24} \log\left[(x-1)^2 + 3\right] + \frac{1}{4\sqrt{3}} \arctan \frac{x-1}{\sqrt{3}} + C.$$

Of course, the full answer to our original problem (34) must include the first integral in (35).

## EXERCISES

**1.** Evaluate the following integrals:

(a) $\displaystyle\int \frac{dx}{x(x^2 + 4)}$          *Ans.* $\frac{1}{4}\log \dfrac{x}{\sqrt{x^2 + 4}} + C.$

(b) $\displaystyle\int \frac{x \, dx}{(x + 1)(x^2 + 1)}.$

(c) $\displaystyle\int \frac{(x + 1)^2}{x^3 + x} \, dx.$          *Ans.* $\log x + 2 \arctan x + C.$

(d) $\displaystyle\int \frac{x^2 \, dx}{x^4 + 5x^2 + 4}.$

*We shall occasionally use arc tan $x$ in place of $\tan^{-1} x$ partly to become familiar with this alternative notation and partly because $\tan^{-1} x$ sometimes occurs in connection with powers of $\tan x$ and there is danger of confusion.

(e) $\int \dfrac{dx}{(x-1)(x^2+4x+5)}$.

  *Ans.* $\frac{1}{10}\log(x-1) - \frac{1}{20}\log(x^2+4x+5) - \frac{3}{10}\arctan(x+2) + C.$

(f) $\int \dfrac{dx}{(x-1)^2(x^2+4x+5)}$.

(g) $\int \dfrac{dx}{x^3+1}$.

  *Ans.* $\frac{1}{3}\log(x+1) - \frac{1}{6}\log(x^2-x+1) + \dfrac{1}{\sqrt{3}}\arctan\dfrac{2x-1}{\sqrt{3}} + C.$

**Case iv.** There is one other situation that can arise in integrating rational functions. The denominator, as we know, is a polynomial of the form

$$b_0 x^m + b_1 x^{m-1} + \ldots + b_{m-1}x + b_m.$$

The linear factors with real coefficients of this polynomial correspond to the real zeros of the polynomial. After determining these linear factors, we may have one or more quadratic factors of which some are repeated. Or the denominator may already be in this form. Thus suppose that we have to integrate the rational function

**(38)** $$\dfrac{5}{(x-1)(x^2+2x+4)^2}.$$

As we might expect from our discussion of the first three cases, the proper partial fractions for this given rational function are

$$\dfrac{A}{x-1} + \dfrac{Bx+C}{x^2+2x+4} + \dfrac{Dx+E}{(x^2+2x+4)^2}.$$

That is, just as in the case in which a linear factor occurs to a higher power than the first, we must allow for all powers of the quadratic factor up to and including the given one, and each partial fraction with this quadratic factor must have a linear numerator. The unknown coefficients $A$, $B$, $C$, and so forth are then determined in the usual way.

From the standpoint of integration the only new problem is how to handle a term such as

$$\dfrac{Dx+E}{(x^2+2x+4)^2}.$$

We must complete the square in the parentheses and introduce $u = x+1$ as in Case III. The expression then reduces to two terms of the form

$$\dfrac{u}{(u^2+a^2)^2} \qquad \text{and} \qquad \dfrac{c}{(u^2+a^2)^2}.$$

The former can be handled at once. The latter must be handled by a reduction formula that reads

$$\int \frac{du}{(u^2 + a^2)^n} = \frac{1}{2a^2(n - 1)} \frac{u}{(u^2 + a^2)^{n-1}}$$

$$+ \frac{2n - 3}{2a^2(n - 1)} \int \frac{du}{(u^2 + a^2)^{n-1}} \, .$$

The correctness of this reduction formula can easily be established by differentiating both sides. We shall not carry out the details of integrating (38) because the procedure is clear.

There is just one more point to be noted in connection with the method of partial fractions. The denominator, we know, is a polynomial

(39)                $b_0 x^m + b_1 x^{m-1} + \ldots + b_{m-1} x + b_m$

where the coefficients are, as usual, real numbers. The question one might raise is, do these four cases take care of all possible factors that may occur in treating polynomials? The answer is yes and results from some theorems of algebra. The zeros of the polynomial (39) are $m$ in number and can be real and complex numbers. To each zero there is a linear factor. The complex zeros occur in conjugate pairs, that is, if $a + bi$ is a zero, then $a - bi$ must also be a zero. Then the corresponding factors are $x - (a + bi)$ and $x - (a - bi)$. The product of two such factors is $x^2 - 2ax + a^2 + b^2$; it is, in other words, a quadratic factor with *real* numbers as coefficients. To each real zero of the polynomial there is a real linear factor. Hence the polynomial must necessarily be factorable into a product of linear and quadratic factors with *real* coefficients.

## EXERCISES

1. Evaluate the following integrals:

(a) $\int \dfrac{dx}{(x^2 + 1)^2}$ .          *Ans.*  $\dfrac{x}{2(x^2 + 1)} + \frac{1}{2} \text{arc tan } x + C.$

(b) $\int \dfrac{2x \, dx}{(1 + x)(1 + x^2)^2}$ .

**5. Integration by Substitution and Change of Variable.** No matter how many formulas for integration are established, it is always necessary to keep in mind that a given integral may have to be reduced to a known formula by a substitution or a change of variable. There are unfortunately no rules to indicate what substitution or change of variable will reduce a given integral to a known formula. We shall, however, consider two classes of integrals that are of sufficient frequency to be worth noting.

The first of these classes deals with integrands involving $\sqrt{x^2 \pm a^2}$ or $\sqrt{a^2 - x^2}$. Let us consider as an example*

**(40)**
$$\int \sqrt{a^2 - x^2} \; dx$$

The radical can be eliminated by a change of variable. Thus let

$$x = a \sin u.$$

To convert the entire integrand to a derivative with respect to $u$ we must replace $dx$ by $(dx / du) \, du$. But

$$\frac{dx}{du} = a \cos u.$$

Then (40) becomes

$$\int \sqrt{a^2 - a^2 \sin^2 u} \; a \cos u \; du$$

or

$$\int a^2 \cos^2 u \; du.$$

In the present case we come down to a simple trigonometric function, and by using the identity

$$\cos u = \sqrt{\frac{1 + \cos 2u}{2}}$$

we can carry out the integration and then replace $u$ by arc sin $(x/a)$ in order to return to a function of $x$.

One may have, to start with, a more complicated function involving $\sqrt{a^2 - x^2}$ or one of the other radicals mentioned earlier, and one of the changes of variable $x = a \sin u$, $x = a \tan u$, or $x = a \sec u$ will at least eliminate the radical. Whether the integration can then be completed depends, of course, on the original function.

The second class of integrands worth noting deals with trigonometric functions and in fact includes many of the trigonometric functions that arise from the change of variable just discussed. The integrands we have in mind are those that involve the trigonometric functions $\sin x$ and $\cos x$ rationally. The integrand

**(41)**
$$\int \frac{dx}{\sin x + \cos x}$$

is an example. The statement that the integrand involves $\sin x$ and $\cos x$ rationally means that if we replace $\sin x$ by $s$, say, and $\cos x$ by $t$, then the

*See also Chapter 11, Section 5.

resulting expression is a rational function of the two variables $s$ and $t$. A rational function in the two variables is a form that involves constants and positive integral powers of $s$ and $t$ joined by the operations of addition, subtraction, multiplication, and division. Thus

$$\frac{3s^3t^2 + 2s^2t^2 - 4st + 5}{3s^2t^2 + 4s + 5t + 7}$$

is a rational function of $s$ and $t$.

If we have a rational function of $\sin x$ and $\cos x$, the change of variable

**(42)**              $x = 2 \text{ arc tan } u$

will convert the rational function into a rational function of $u$. We can see this in the following way. Because

$$\sin \frac{x}{2} = \sqrt{\frac{1 - \cos x}{2}}$$

and

$$\cos \frac{x}{2} = \sqrt{\frac{1 + \cos x}{2}} \ ,$$

then

$$\tan^2 \frac{x}{2} = \frac{1 - \cos x}{1 + \cos x}$$

or, because, by (42), $u = \tan(x/2)$,

$$u^2 = \frac{1 - \cos x}{1 + \cos x} \ .$$

By solving for $\cos x$ we obtain

**(43)**              $\cos x = \dfrac{1 - u^2}{1 + u^2} \ .$

Then, as we can see from Fig. 14-1 or by using the identity

$$\sin x = \sqrt{1 - \cos^2 x} \ ,$$

we have

**(44)**              $\sin x = \dfrac{2u}{1 + u^2} \ .$

Also, because

$$x = 2 \text{ arc tan } u,$$

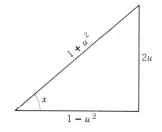

**Figure 14-1**

then

**(45)**
$$\frac{dx}{du} = \frac{2}{1 + u^2} \cdot$$

To see how this change of variable works out in practice let us consider the integral in (41), namely,

$$\int \frac{dx}{\sin x + \cos x} \cdot$$

The process is change of variable as given by (42). We know what $\sin x$, $\cos x$, and $dx$ are by (43), (44), and (45). Then the integral becomes

$$\int \frac{1}{\dfrac{2u}{1 + u^2} + \dfrac{1 - u^2}{1 + u^2}} \frac{2}{1 + u^2} \, du$$

or

$$\int \frac{2}{1 + 2u - u^2} \, du.$$

This integral may be evaluated by completing the square in the denominator.

The class of integrands we have just discussed, namely, those that involve $\sin x$ and $\cos x$ rationally, includes those that involve the other four functions, $\tan x$, $\cot x$, $\sec x$, and $\csc x$, rationally, for each of these functions can be converted to $\sin x$ and $\cos x$ by rational expressions. For example, $\tan x = \sin x / \cos x$. Hence, if the given function involves $\tan x$ rationally, it will involve $\sin x$ and $\cos x$ rationally.

## EXERCISES

**1.** Evaluate the following integrals:

(a) $\displaystyle\int \frac{d\theta}{5 + 4 \cos \theta} \cdot$ 　　　　　　　　*Ans.* $\dfrac{2}{3} \arc \tan\left( \dfrac{1}{3} \tan \dfrac{\theta}{2} \right) + C.$

(b) $\displaystyle\int \frac{dx}{1 + \sin x + \cos x}$ .

(c) $\displaystyle\int \frac{dx}{\sin x + \tan x}$ .        *Ans.* $\dfrac{1}{2}\log\tan\dfrac{x}{2} - \dfrac{1}{4}\tan^2\dfrac{x}{2} + C$.

**6. The Use of Tables.** Let us suppose that we face the problem of integrating a given function and we do not recognize the integral by reversing a familiar differentiation formula. Nor do we find that the techniques of integration by parts, partial fractions, reduction formulas, substitution, and change of variable help us. What can we do? One answer would be to study more techniques or seek to discover a new one. However, the number of techniques and special tricks is quite extensive. It is neither wise nor efficient to spend months or years on what is really an incidental process or means to an end at the expense of the acquisition of more significant knowledge. Fortunately, the results of a large amount of work on integration have been collected in tables, and one utilizes these results. The situation here is entirely analogous to what we do with logarithmic or trigonometric values. We know in principle how these can be calculated* but we do not spend months in calculating these tables ourselves. They were calculated by expert mathematicians, and we are satisfied to use the results. In the case of integral tables we have an additional advantage. We can always differentiate the given integral and check that it gives the derived function that we happen to be facing. The practical procedure, then, when facing an integral which one does not see how to handle immediately, is to look up the tables. Many of the results obtained in the last few sections are given there at once, and one need not use the processes we have been learning. Our purpose in going through many of these processes was to shed light on how so many integrals are obtained.†

A set of tables containing the forms that one is likely to encounter in the ordinary uses of the calculus is appended to this book. From this point on the student may use these tables. There are special collections of tables that contain many more forms than are given here, and one who goes much further in mathematics may want to purchase such a set so as to have it on hand for immediate use.

There are a few points to be noted in the use of tables. First, because there are many forms, they are classified to help the user locate the right one as readily as possible. Thus one finds a class of forms involving $\sqrt{a + bu}$ , another class involving $\sqrt{a^2 + u^2}$ , and still another class involving $\sqrt{2au + u^2}$ . Obviously, one looks among the forms of that class which includes the given integrand.

Secondly, the integrals in the table are deliberately written so as to involve the variable $u$ instead of $x$. Thus instead of

(46) $$\int x^n \, dx = \frac{x^{n+1}}{n + 1} + C$$

*See Chapter 20.
†Now he tells us.

one finds

$$(47) \qquad\qquad \int u^n \, du = \frac{u^{n+1}}{n+1} + C.$$

The use of $u$ instead of $x$ is intended to suggest that $u$ may be any function of $x$. For example,

$$\int (1 + x^2)^{1/2} 2x \, dx$$

comes under (47) if we let $u$ be $(1 + x^2)$. The only point to be careful about is that if $u$ is a function of $x$, the $du$ in (47) is $(du/dx) \, dx$, and this factor *must be present* in the integrand if one is to use (47). This restriction is in accordance with what we learned about integration by substitution. On the other hand, if one has

$$\int x^{1/2} \, dx,$$

the form (47) surely covers it because one has merely to think of $u$ as $x$.

## EXERCISES

**1.** Use the tables to perform the following integrations. Of course, a substitution of a new variable or a change of variable before using the table may be necessary.

(a) $\displaystyle\int \frac{dx}{x^2 \sqrt{x-1}}$.
$\qquad\qquad$ *Ans.* $\dfrac{\sqrt{x-1}}{x} + \arctan\sqrt{x-1} + C.$

(b) $\displaystyle\int \frac{dx}{1 + x + x^2}$.

(c) $\displaystyle\int \frac{\sqrt{1-x}}{x} \, dx$.
$\qquad\qquad$ *Ans.* $2\sqrt{1-x} + \log \dfrac{\sqrt{1-x}-1}{\sqrt{1-x}+1} + C.$

(d) $\displaystyle\int \frac{\sqrt{10-x^2}}{x^4} \, dx$.

(e) $\displaystyle\int \frac{dx}{x^2 \sqrt{1+3x}}$.
$\qquad\qquad$ *Ans.* $-\dfrac{\sqrt{1+3x}}{x} - \tfrac{3}{2}\log \dfrac{\sqrt{1+3x}-1}{\sqrt{1+3x}+1} + C.$

(f) $\displaystyle\int \frac{dx}{x\sqrt{9+x^2}}$.

(g) $\displaystyle\int \frac{\sqrt{3x^2+5}}{x^2} \, dx$.

$$\textit{Ans.} \quad -\frac{\sqrt{3x^2+5}}{x} + \sqrt{3}\,\log(\sqrt{3x^2+5} + x\sqrt{3}\,) + C.$$

# CHAPTER FIFTEEN
# SOME GEOMETRIC USES OF THE DEFINITE INTEGRAL

*1. Introduction.* When we first studied the definite integral (Chap. 9) we introduced it by raising the problem of the area bounded in part or entirely by curves. We shall now extend the use of the definite integral in two respects. First, we have learned how to differentiate and integrate many more types of functions and since the definite integral is evaluated by antidifferentiation we can apply the definite integral to many more area problems. However, if the concept of the definite integral amounted to no more than a way of calculating area, it would not be very significant.

Actually, the definite integral is a very powerful and general concept. We shall see that the definite integral is the tool for casting any number of geometrical and physical problems into mathematical form. The experience of mathematicians with the definite integral is very similar to that with the derivative. The derivative was introduced to represent velocity and acceleration, but proved to be enormously useful in representing any number of instantaneous rates of change. The definite integral likewise proves to be useful in an extraordinary variety of situations, and we shall consider some of them in the next two chapters. Of these a few could still be done by first obtaining a rate of change and then applying antidifferentiation; nevertheless we shall employ the definite integral in order to practice its use.*

*2. Volumes of Solids: The Cylindrical Element.* To know the volumes of solids—such as cans, tanks for oil and water, granaries, and the earth—is obviously useful if somewhat mundane. Some of these problems, such as finding the volume of granaries, are among the oldest to which mathematics was applied. With the calculus that we have thus far developed we cannot find the volumes of all solids. We can, however, find the volumes that are formed by revolving a curve around an axis. For example, the sphere can be generated by revolving a semicircle around a diameter. The solids enclosed by revolving a curve about an axis are called solids of revolution.

---

*The reader should review Chapter 9.

To illustrate the method of finding volumes of figures of revolution by means of the definite integral, let us try to find the volume of the hemisphere (Fig. 15-1) formed by revolving the quarter-circle $ABC$ about the $x$-axis. The problem of finding volumes bounded by curved surfaces presents essentially the same difficulty as that of finding areas bounded by curves. We have no direct method of finding such volumes, and therefore we seek to approximate them by simpler figures whose volume we do know and then improve the approximation. Guided somewhat by success in the area problem, one might introduce the rectangle shown in Fig. 15-1 as an approximation to the area under arc $DE$ and consider rotating the entire rectangle around the $x$-axis. Figure 15-2 shows the figure generated by the rectangle. This figure is a circular cylinder standing on its side. The radius of the cylinder is what we have already denoted by $y_i$ and its height is $\Delta x$. To calculate the volume of this cylinder, we take over from Euclidean geometry the formula for the volume of the circular cylinder. The volume of a cylinder is the area of the base times the altitude, and so in our case it is $\pi y_i^2 \Delta x$.

We now have the basis for an approximation to the desired volume. We divide the interval $OC$ of Fig. 15-1 into $n$ equal subintervals, each of width $\Delta x$. We erect the ordinates at the end points of these subintervals, and in each subinterval we choose the minimum $y$-value of the curve $ABC$. Thus the subinterval $\Delta x$ and the $y_i$ shown in Fig. 15-1 is one of the many subintervals and corresponding $y_i$'s in the interval $OC$. If we now imagine rotating each of these rectangles about $OC$, each generating a cylinder, then the sum of the volumes of these cylinders is an approximation to the volume of the hemisphere. In symbols this sum is

**(1)** $$S_n = \pi y_1{}^2 \, \Delta x + \pi y_2{}^2 \, \Delta x + \cdots + \pi y_n{}^2 \, \Delta x.$$

As $n$ becomes larger, $\Delta x$ becomes smaller, and the sum of the rectangles

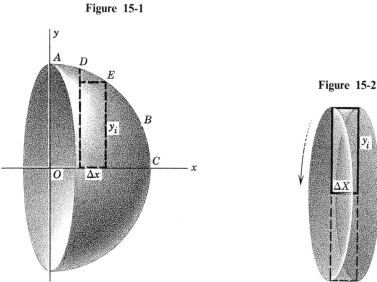

Figure 15-1

Figure 15-2

becomes a better approximation to the area under the curve $ABC$. Then the sum $S_n$ becomes a better approximation to the volume of the hemisphere. The larger $n$ is, the better the approximation. Hence the volume we want is

$$\textbf{(2)} \qquad\qquad \lim_{n\to\infty} S_n.$$

This limit is a definite integral of exactly the same kind as that considered in Chapter 9. There we considered $S_n$ of the form

$$\textbf{(3)} \qquad\qquad S_n = y_1\,\Delta x + y_2\,\Delta x + \cdots + y_n\,\Delta x.$$

If we use $y_i$ to denote any one of the $y$-values in (3), we may say that the $y_i$ in (3) are analogous to the $\pi y_i^2$ in (1). The $y_i$ in (3) are the function values of some function of $x$; but the $\pi y_i^2$ in (1) are also the function values of some function of $x$, namely, the function $\pi y^2$ where $y$ itself represents the ordinates of arc $ABC$ in Fig. 15-1. Hence (2) is the definite integral

$$\textbf{(4)} \qquad\qquad \int_a^b \pi y^2\,dx.$$

The letters $a$ and $b$ in (4) represent, of course, the $x$-values of the end points $O$ and $C$ of the interval filled out by the $\Delta x$. Thus we can evaluate (4) by using the fundamental theorem of the calculus.

Let us evaluate (4) for a specific case. Suppose that the radius of the quarter-circle $ABC$ in Fig. 15-1 is 5. Then $a = 0$ and $b = 5$. Moreover, the equation of the circle with center at the origin and radius 5 is

$$x^2 + y^2 = 25.$$

Hence the equation of the arc $ABC$ is given by

$$y = \sqrt{25 - x^2}\ .$$

Then the volume $V$ that we are seeking, given by (4), is

$$\textbf{(5)} \qquad\qquad V = \int_0^5 \pi(25 - x^2)\,dx.$$

To evaluate the definite integral (5) we use the fundamental theorem. We first find the antiderivative of $\pi(25 - x^2)$, that is, we seek

$$V(x) = \int \pi(25 - x^2)\,dx.$$

We use the notation $V(x)$ to indicate the *function* given by the indefinite integral. In integrating, the constant $\pi$ can be ignored for the moment. The antiderivative of the difference $25 - x^2$ is $25x - x^3/3$. Hence we want

$$V = \pi\left(25x - \frac{x^3}{3}\right)\Bigg|_0^5.$$

The result is $(2\pi/3)125$. Then, the volume of the full sphere is $(4\pi/3)125$; this agrees with the formula, which we usually learn without proof, that the volume of a sphere of radius $r$ is $4\pi r^3/3$.

## EXERCISES

1. If the portion of the line $y = x/3$ lying in the first quadrant is rotated around the $x$-axis, a cone is generated. Find the volume of the cone extending from $x = 0$ to $x = 5$. *Ans.* $125\pi/27$.

2. The upper half of the parabola $y^2 = 16x$ is rotated around the $x$-axis. Find the volume of the solid generated by the arc lying between $x = 3$ and $x = 5$.

3. Find the volume generated by rotating the arc of the parabola $y^2 = 8x$ which lies in the first quadrant between $x = 0$ and $x = 2$ about the $x$-axis.

4. Find the volume generated by rotating the area bounded by $y^2 = 8x$, $x = 2$, and the $x$-axis about the $y$-axis.

5. A segment of a sphere is the volume cut out by two parallel planes. Suppose that the two planes are perpendicular to the $x$-axis of Fig. 15-1 and pass through $x = 2$ and $x = 4$. Find the volume of the segment of the sphere that the planes cut out. *Ans.* $94\pi/3$.

6. The upper half of the ellipse $3x^2 + 6y^2 = 48$ is rotated around the $x$-axis. The surface it generates is a special kind of ellipsoid called a prolate spheroid and has the shape of a football. Find the volume of this spheroid.

7. If the upper half of the ellipse $6x^2 + 3y^2 = 48$ is rotated around the $x$-axis, the surface it generates is another kind of ellipsoid called an oblate spheroid. Find the volume of this spheroid. *Ans.* $128\sqrt{2}\,\pi/3$.

8. The area bounded above by the line $y = 3$, below by the line $y = 0$, on the left by the $y$-axis, and on the right by an arc of the hyperbola $9x^2 - 16y^2 = 144$ is rotated around the $x$-axis. Find the volume of the solid generated.

*Ans.* $24\pi(2\sqrt{2} - 1)$.

**3. Volumes of Solids: The Shell Game.** In Section 2 we found volumes of solids of revolution by approximating the volumes by cylinders and then letting the heights $\Delta x$ of these cylinders approach 0. It is not necessary to restrict the approximating figures to cylinders. We can use any other solid provided that we know the volume of this solid and that, as we increase the number of these solids, the sum of their volumes comes closer and closer to the volume we are seeking. Let us consider an example.

Suppose that we want to find the volume generated by revolving an ellipse around its minor axis; the resulting figure is a special kind of ellipsoid called an oblate spheroid. Let the equation of the ellipse be

**(6)**
$$\frac{x^2}{9} + \frac{y^2}{4} = 1.$$

In Fig. 15-3 we show the part of the ellipse that lies in the first quadrant. The semiminor axis is the length $OB$. If we obtain the volume of the solid enclosed by revolving arc $BCA$ and segment $OA$ around $OB$ and then

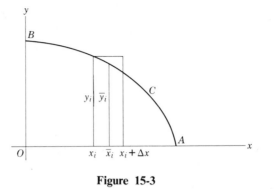

**Figure 15-3**

double the result, we shall have the desired volume. We know that rectangles of width $\Delta x$, such as the one shown, can be used to approximate the area under $BCA$, and therefore if we revolve all these rectangles about the line $OB$, we shall have a set of volumes whose sum approximates the desired volume. We can then let the number of rectangles increase and thus improve our approximation more and more.

Let us see what volume any one rectangle generates when it is revolved around the line $OB$. Figure 15-4 shows the figure generated. It is called a cylindrical shell. We shall find the volume of this shell and then consider summing these volumes to find the volume of the oblate spheroid.

The volume of the shell is the area of its base times its height. The area of the base is the area of the outer circle (Fig. 15-5) of radius $x_i + \Delta x$ minus the area of the inner circle of radius $x_i$. Thus the area of the base is

$$\pi(x_i + \Delta x)^2 - \pi x_i^2.$$

We can obtain a somewhat simpler expression. By factoring we obtain

$$\pi(x_i + \Delta x + x_i)(x_i + \Delta x - x_i).$$

We replace the quantity in the first parentheses by twice the arithmetic

**Figure 15-4**

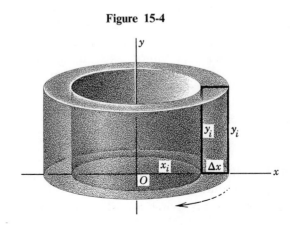

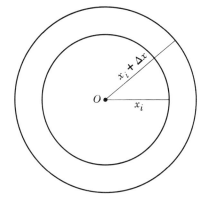

**Figure 15-5**

mean of $x_i + \Delta x$ and $x_i$, namely,

$$2\bar{x}_i = 2\,\frac{x_i + \Delta x + x_i}{2}\,.$$

The area of the base then is

$$2\pi\bar{x}_i\,\Delta x.$$

In other words, the area of the base is the mean circumference $2\pi\bar{x}_i$ times the width of the base. The volume of the shell then is

**(7)** $$2\pi\bar{x}_i y_i\,\Delta x,$$

where $y_i$ is the height of the shell in Fig. 15-4.

 We now sum the volumes of the cylindrical shells, each a result of revolving a rectangle under the curve $BCA$ of Fig. 15-3, about the line $OB$. This sum is

**(8)** $$S_n = 2\pi\bar{x}_1 y_1\,\Delta x + 2\pi\bar{x}_2 y_2\,\Delta x + \cdots + 2\pi\bar{x}_n y_n\,\Delta x.$$

We let the number of rectangles increase, and consequently $\Delta x$ approaches 0. What limit does $S_n$ approach? Compare this $S_n$ with the $S_n$ of the form

**(9)** $$S_n = y_1\,\Delta x + y_2\,\Delta x + \cdots + y_n\,\Delta x$$

considered in Chapter 9. The $y_i$ in (9) are the $y$-values of some function of $x$; in particular, $y_i$ is a $y$-value that belongs to some $x$-value in the typical or $i$th subinterval $\Delta x$. Now (8) is *almost* of the same form. We might say that the typical $2\pi\bar{x}_i y_i$ is the function value of some function of $x$, the function being $2\pi xy$ where $y$ itself represents the equation of arc $BCA$ in Fig. 15-3. This statement is not quite correct. The $\bar{x}_i$ does indeed belong to some $x$-value in the $i$th subinterval $\Delta x$, but the $y_i$ is the $y$-value of *another* $x$-value in the $i$th subinterval $\Delta x$. However, we learned in Chapter 9 that in setting up the $S_n$ which leads to a definite integral we may choose *any* function value in each $\Delta x$. Let us therefore replace $y_i$ in $2\pi \bar{x}_i y_i$ by $\bar{y}_i$ where $\bar{y}_i$ is the $y$-value at $\bar{x}_i$ (see Fig. 15-3). Then $2\pi \bar{x}_i y_i$ is the function value of the function $2\pi xy$ in the $i$th subinterval $\Delta x$, and now

(10) $$S_n = 2\pi \bar{x}_i \bar{y}_1 \, \Delta x + 2\pi \bar{x}_2 \, y_2 \, \Delta x + \cdots + 2\pi \bar{x}_n \bar{y}_n \, \Delta x$$

is exactly like (9), with the $2\pi \bar{x}_i \bar{y}_i$ in (10) corresponding to the $y_i$ in (9). The choice of $\bar{y}_i$ in (10) in place of $y_i$ in (8) means geometrically that instead of the rectangle $y_i \, \Delta x$ in Fig. 15-3 we use the rectangle $\bar{y}_i \, \Delta x$ to generate the cylindrical shell.

What limit, then, does the $S_n$ of (10) approach as $n$ becomes infinite? Because the function whose values are represented in (10) is $2\pi xy$, the limit is the definite integral

(11) $$V = \int_0^3 2\pi xy \, dx.$$

The end values 0 and 3 are the abscissas of $O$ and $A$ in Fig. 15-3.

The evaluation of (11) is straightforward. The process, which we have already used several times, is to find, first, the antiderivative of the function that appears under the integral sign in (11). The function for which $y$ stands is given by (6) and is

$$y = \tfrac{1}{3} \sqrt{36 - 4x^2} \ .$$

Hence

$$2\pi xy = \frac{2\pi}{3} \sqrt{36 - 4x^2} \, x.$$

We must now calculate the indefinite integral, which we denote by $V(x)$, namely,

$$V(x) = \int \frac{2\pi}{3} \sqrt{36 - 4x^2} \, x \, dx.$$

It seems likely in view of the presence of the $x^2$ inside the radical and the $x$ outside that the substitution

$$u = 36 - 4x^2$$

will reduce the integral to a familiar form. With this value of $u$,

$$\frac{du}{dx} = -8x.$$

To have the proper $du/dx$ following the radical, we may write $V(x)$ in the form

(12) $$V(x) = \int - \frac{\pi}{12} \sqrt{36 - 4x^2} \, (-8x) \, dx.$$

The constant $-\pi/12$ can be ignored for the moment. This fact is sometimes indicated by writing

$$V(x) = -\frac{\pi}{12} \int \sqrt{36 - 4x^2} \, (-8x) \, dx,$$

so that our attention can be concentrated on what follows the integral sign or what is called the integrand. In terms of $u$,

$$V(x) = -\frac{\pi}{12} \int u^{1/2} \frac{du}{dx} \, dx.$$

Now by the inverse of the generalized power rule (see (48) of Chapter 7),

$$V(u) = -\frac{\pi}{12} \cdot \frac{2}{3} u^{3/2} = -\frac{\pi}{18} u^{3/2},$$

so that

$$V(x) = -\frac{\pi}{18} (36 - 4x^2)^{3/2}.$$

Then

$$V = -\frac{\pi}{18} (36 - 4x^2)^{3/2} \Big|_0^3.$$

Substitution of 3 for $x$ and then of 0 for $x$ and subtraction of the second result from the first gives

**(13)**
$$V = 0 - \left( -\frac{\pi}{18} \cdot 216 \right) = 12\pi.$$

The volume of the entire oblate spheroid is $24\pi$.

We built up the volume of the oblate spheroid by using cylindrical shells as the fundamental element, that is, as the approximating element. We can use other approximating elements, provided that as the number of elements is increased (while each approaches 0 in size) the sum of these elements approximates more and more closely the desired volume. For example, let us consider the problem of obtaining the volume of a sphere. This time we shall use *spherical* shells.

Figure 15-6 shows a cross section of the sphere of radius $a$. We regard this sphere as consisting of shells such as the one whose cross section is shown in the interior of the figure. The volume of the sphere is exactly the sum of these shells. If we knew the volume of each shell, we could obtain the volume of the sphere merely by adding the sums of the shells. That is, whether we break up the volume of the sphere into five, ten, or fifty shells, the sum of their volumes is the volume of the sphere. However, we do not know the volume of a shell unless we use the formula for the volume of the sphere, and this is what we are trying to find. Instead, let us suppose that the formula for the area of the surface of a sphere is available to us. We

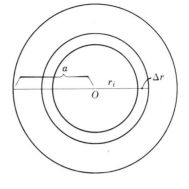

**Figure 15-6**

shall denote by $r_i$ the radius of the inner surface of the typical or $i$th shell. A good approximation to the volume of a shell would be the area of the surface of the inner sphere namely, $4\pi r_i^2$, multiplied by $\Delta r$. This product,

$$4\pi r_i^2 \, \Delta r,$$

is only an approximation because the inner surface is too small.

Now let us break up the interval from $r = 0$ to $r = a$ into $n$ equal subintervals $\Delta r$; each $\Delta r$ fixes the width of a spherical shell just as in Fig. 15-6. Then the sum

**(14)** $$S_n = 4\pi r_1^2 \, \Delta r + 4\pi r_2^2 \, \Delta r + \cdots + 4\pi r_n^2 \, \Delta r$$

is an approximation to the volume of the sphere. As $n$ increases, which implies that $\Delta r$ approaches 0, each term becomes a better approximation to the volume of the corresponding shell because the inner surface $4\pi r_i^2$ is more nearly correct as an average surface for that shell. Thus the larger $n$ is, the more nearly does the sum (14) represent the volume of the sphere. Then the volume $V$ of the sphere should be

$$V = \lim_{n \to \infty} S_n.$$

This limit is expressed in the notation

**(15)** $$V = \int_0^a 4\pi r^2 \, dr.$$

The definite integral (15) is easily evaluated. We consider first

$$V(r) = \int 4\pi r^2 \, dr = 4\pi \int r^2 \, dr = 4\pi \, \frac{r^3}{3}.$$

Then

**(16)** $$V = 4\pi \, \frac{r^3}{3} \Big|_0^a = 4\pi \, \frac{a^3}{3}.$$

The result, of course, is not the important thing here. The main point of this example is that we can employ spherical shells to fill out the volume of a sphere and, by using an approximate expression for the volume of each shell, still obtain the correct volume by a limiting process.

## EXERCISES

1. Consider the curve $y = 9 - x^2$. First, find the volume of the solid of revolution generated by revolving the arc of the curve between $x = 0$ and $x = 3$ around the $x$-axis. Then find the volume of the solid of revolution generated by revolving the same arc about the $y$-axis.                                     *Ans.* $\dfrac{486\pi}{5}$ ; $81\pi/2$.

2. Consider the area lying between an arc of $y = (12 - x^3)/8$, the $y$-axis, and the line $y = 2$. What is the volume of the solid of revolution generated by revolving this area around the $y$-axis?

3. Find the volume of the torus (doughnut) generated by revolving a circle of radius $a$ about a line in the plane of the circle and distant $b > a$ from the center of the circle (Fig. 15-7).                                     *Ans.* $2\pi^2 a^2 b$.

4. Find the volume generated by revolving the area lying under $y = \sin x$ from $x = 0$ to $x = \pi$ about the $y$-axis.

5. A hole 6 inches long (Fig. 15-8) is drilled through the center of a solid sphere of radius $b$ so that the segments of the sphere at the top and bottom of the cylinder are also removed. The resulting figure, incidentally, is that of many napkin rings and wedding bands. What is the volume of the remaining material?
                              *Ans.* $36\pi$ cu in. Is the answer remarkable in any respect?

6. Derive the integral for the mass of the earth on the assumption that the mass per unit volume, that is, the density $\rho$, varies from the center to any point $r$ units from the center in accordance with the formula $\rho = f(r)$.

7. Suppose that in a sphere of radius $R$ the mass per unit volume, that is, the density, at any point is the square of the distance from the center. Find the mass of the sphere.                                     *Ans.* $\frac{4}{5}\pi R^5$.

8. Find the volume of an apple.

    *Suggestion:* Our first task is to represent the apple algebraically. Suppose that we take the circle (Fig. 15-9) with center $(b, 0)$, radius $a$, and $a > b$. The

**Figure 15-7**

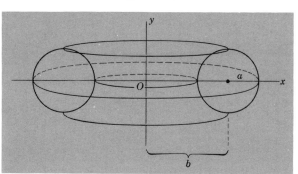

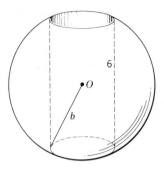

**Figure 15-8**

equation of this circle is $(x - b)^2 + y^2 = a^2$. Consider the arc from $x = 0$ to $x = a + b$ and rotate the area bounded by this arc, the $y$-axis, and the $x$-axis around the $y$-axis. This volume generated is half the volume of the apple.

$$Ans. \quad (4\pi/3)(a^2 - b^2)^{3/2} + 2\pi b[\pi a^2 + b\sqrt{a^2 - b^2} + a^2\sin^{-1}(b/a)].$$

**4. Lengths of Arcs of Curves.** Another major problem that is most readily tackled with the help of the definite integral, that is, as a limit of a sequence of sums, is the calculation of lengths of curves. In practice this problem is very important. If a suspension bridge is to be built and if its main cable is to be a parabolic arc, one would like to know in advance exactly how long this arc is to be.

In Euclidean geometry one commonly works with the lengths of straight lines. This notion of length presents no fundamental conceptual difficulties. When a particular segment of a line has been chosen as the unit of length, the length of any other given segment is the number of times that the unit length can be laid off on the given segment. Of course, this number may not be an integer; it may be a fraction or even an irrational number.

However, the problem of determining the length of a curve cannot be approached in this way. The reason is that curves (except for the circle) change shape from one place to another along the curve, and so it is impossible to find a unit of length whose shape will fit all along the curve. In fact, even if a unit of length could be found to fit all curves, the problem

**Figure 15-9**

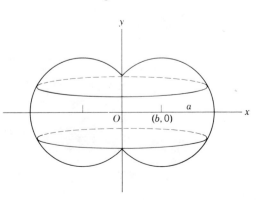

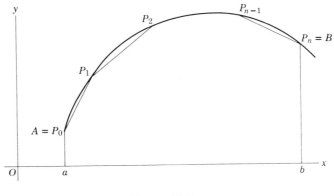

Figure  15-10

of relating that unit to the unit for line segments would still remain, because whatever notion of curve length we might adopt, we should still want to know its relation to the unit for straight-line lengths. For example, if a cable of a bridge is to be built and its length is calculated by some means to be 500 units of "curve length," we would still want to know what these 500 units mean in terms of inches, feet, or yards used for straight line lengths in order to fabricate the proper amount of wire.

The effective approach to curvilinear length, that is, the lengths of an arc, is to build it up on the basis of straight line lengths. The intuitive idea behind what we shall do is that a very small arc should not differ much from a line segment and the smaller the arc the less it will differ. Let $AB$ (Fig. 15-10) be an arc of some curve $C$. We choose points $P_0$, $P_1$, $P_2$, $P_3$, ... with $P_0 = A$ and $P_n = B$, so that the arc is subdivided into subarcs $P_0P_1$, $P_1P_2$, ..., $P_{n-1}P_n$. We now introduce the chords $P_0P_1$, $P_1P_2$, ..., $P_{n-1}P_n$. These chords are approximations to the lengths of the respective arcs in which they are inscribed. Then the sum of the chords

**(17)** $$S_n = P_0P_1 + P_1P_2 + \cdots + P_{n-1}P_n$$

is an approximation to the arc length $AB$.

We can improve this approximation by taking more points of subdivision, which means, of course, that $n$ above will be larger and the various subarcs smaller. Thus, as Fig. 15-11 shows, if $CD$ is a subarc that is approximated by the chord $CD$, then by choosing an additional point $E$, subdividing arc $DC$ into arcs $CE$ and $ED$, and introducing the new chords

Figure  15-11

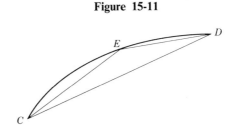

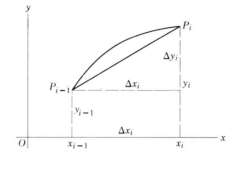

**Figure 15-12**

$CE$ and $ED$, the sum $CE + ED$ thereby obtained is a better approximation to the length of arc $CD$ than chord $CD$ is. Intuitively it seems clear that we can approach the length of arc $AB$ more and more closely as we let $n$, the number of points of subdivision, become larger and larger and, of course, let all chords become smaller and smaller, so that they approximate more closely the subarcs in which they are inscribed. The reasonable conclusion is that $s$, the length of arc $AB$, can be obtained by

**(18)** $$s = \lim_{n\to\infty} S_n = \lim_{n\to\infty} P_0P_1 + P_1P_2 + \cdots + P_{n-1}P_n$$

with the understanding that the maximum chord length must approach 0 as $n$ becomes infinite.

Thus far we have described in geometrical form the way in which we can obtain the arc length $AB$. However, this approach does not help us to calculate the length. The calculation requires the use of analysis. We suppose that the curve is placed in some coordinate system and that we know the equation $y = f(x)$ of the curve. Let us consider (Fig. 15-12) one subarc $P_{i-1}P_i$ and its approximating chord $P_{i-1}P_i$. Corresponding to the chord $P_{i-1}P_i$ there is the subinterval on the $x$-axis determined by the abscissas of $P_{i-1}$ and $P_i$. We call this subinterval $\Delta x_i$. We must say $\Delta x_i$ here rather than $\Delta x$ because our choice of the $P_i$ on the arc does not necessarily result in equal subintervals $\Delta x$. The difference in the ordinates of $P_i$ and $P_{i-1}$ is the actual increment in $y$ that corresponds to the increment $\Delta x_i$ in $x$ and therefore is $\Delta y_i$. By the Pythagorean theorem

$$(P_{i-1}P_i)^2 = (\Delta x_i)^2 + (\Delta y_i)^2 = \left[1 + \frac{(\Delta y_i)^2}{(\Delta x_i)^2}\right](\Delta x_i)^2$$

or*

**(19)** $$P_{i-1}P_i = \sqrt{1 + \left(\frac{\Delta y_i}{\Delta x_i}\right)^2}\;\Delta x_i.$$

*We choose the positive root. However, we shall have occasion to say more about signs later.

When the proper indices are used, such an expression holds for each of the chords. We may now reexpress (18) in the form

$$s = \lim_{n \to \infty} \left\{ \sqrt{1 + \left( \frac{\Delta y_1}{\Delta x_1} \right)^2} \, \Delta x_1 + \sqrt{1 + \left( \frac{\Delta y_2}{\Delta x_2} \right)^2} \, \Delta x_2 + \cdots \right.$$

(20)
$$\left. + \sqrt{1 + \left( \frac{\Delta y_n}{\Delta x_n} \right)^2} \, \Delta x_n \right\}.$$

Unfortunately, the limit called for in (20) apparently is not of the kind that leads to a definite integral. The limit that we have studied is of the form

(21)
$$\lim_{n \to \infty} (y_1 \, \Delta x_1 + y_2 \, \Delta x_2 + \cdots + y_n \, \Delta x_n)$$

where $y_i$ is the $y$-value of some function of $x$ and taken anywhere in the subinterval $\Delta x_i$. However, we can recast (20) so that it takes the form (21). In Section 2 of Chapter 13 we considered the law of the mean which states that if $f(x)$ is any function of $x$ and if $a$ and $b$ are any two values of $x$, then

$$f(b) - f(a) = f'(\bar{x})(b - a)$$

where $\bar{x}$ is some value of $x$ between $a$ and $b$. Now suppose that $a$ is $x_{i-1}$ and $b$ is $x_i$. Then $b - a$ is $\Delta x_i$ and $f(b) - f(a)$ is $\Delta y_i$. We can, therefore, state that

$$\Delta y_i = f'(\bar{x}_i) \, \Delta x_i$$

where $\bar{x}_i$ is some value of $x$ between $x_{i-1}$ and $x_i$. Consequently,

$$\frac{\Delta y_i}{\Delta x_i} = f'(\bar{x}_i).$$

For convenience of notation, we write $y_i'$ for $f'(\bar{x}_i)$ so that

(22)
$$\frac{\Delta y_i}{\Delta x_i} = y_i'.$$

We may apply the law of the mean to each of the quotients in (20), and then this expression becomes

(23) $$s = \lim_{n \to \infty} \left\{ \sqrt{1 + y_1'^2} \, \Delta x_1 + \sqrt{1 + y_2'^2} \, \Delta x_2 + \cdots + \sqrt{1 + y_n'^2} \, \Delta x_n \right\}.$$

Do we now have a limit of the form in (21)? We recall that the derived function of a function is itself a function of $x$ and therefore $\sqrt{1 + y'^2}$ is also a function of $x$. Each term of (23) is a value of the function $\sqrt{1 + y'^2}$ taken at some value of $x$ in the subinterval $\Delta x_i$ and then multiplied by $\Delta x_i$. Hence (23) is of the form (21). Then the limit called for in (23) is representable as

$$(24) \qquad\qquad s = \int_a^b \sqrt{1 + y'^2} \ dx$$

where $a$ and $b$ are the end values of the $x$-interval that the $\Delta x_i$'s fill out (see Fig. 15-10). Thus (24) gives us arc length expressed as a definite integral.

Formula (24) is the basic formula for arc length. There are several points about it to be noted. First, there is the matter of sign. In step (19) we chose the positive square root, and as a consequence formula (24) gives a positive arc length. However, it is often convenient to introduce both a positive and a negative arc length. If in Fig. 15-10 the arc length is taken to be positive in the direction from $A$ to $B$, we should want formula (24) to give us a positive result. If, on the other hand, we choose the direction from $B$ to $A$ as positive, we should want formula (24) to give us a negative result. In this case we should use

$$(25) \qquad\qquad s = \int_a^b -\sqrt{1 + y'^2} \ dx.$$

Secondly, several relations involving arc length prove to be useful in applications. They are readily derived from (24) [or (25)]. To evaluate (24) we would use the fundamental theorem of the calculus, that is, we would first evaluate the indefinite integral

$$s(x) = \int \sqrt{1 + y'^2} \ dx.$$

This statement is equivalent to the statement

$$(26) \qquad\qquad \frac{ds}{dx} = \sqrt{1 + y'^2} \ .$$

Here $s$ is arc length measured from some point on the curve. Which point we choose as the origin for arc length does not matter because if the origin is shifted, the arc length changes by a constant and the derivative is not affected. However, because $ds/dx$ is positive, the arc length must increase with $x$.

Furthermore, if we introduce the tangent to the curve (Fig. 15-13) at point $P$, we can make the following assertions. Let $\alpha$ be the inclination of the tangent line; then

$$y' = \tan \alpha.$$

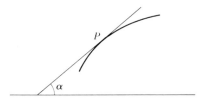

**Figure 15-13**

Consequently, from (26) we have

$$\textbf{(27)} \qquad \frac{ds}{dx} = \sqrt{1 + \tan^2 \alpha} = \begin{cases} \sec \alpha & \text{for} \quad 0 \le \alpha < \pi/2, \\ -\sec \alpha & \text{for} \quad \pi/2 < \alpha \le \pi. \end{cases}$$

By the theorem on inverse functions

$$\textbf{(28)} \qquad \frac{dx}{ds} = \begin{cases} \cos \alpha & \text{for} \quad 0 \le \alpha \le \pi/2, \\ -\cos \alpha & \text{for} \quad \pi/2 \le \alpha \le \pi; \end{cases}$$

this relation is often useful.

Finally, the use of (24) to evaluate arc lengths often leads to difficult integrations. However, we know that a curve can be represented by $x$ as a function of $y$ as well as by $y$ as a function of $x$. Thus the arc $AB$ in Fig. 15-14 might be part of the parabola $y = \sqrt{4x}$ ; then it can also be represented by $x = y^2/4$. By treating $y$ as the independent variable and $x$ as the dependent variable, we can go through a proof very much like the one we used to derive (24) and obtain

$$\textbf{(29)} \qquad s = \pm \int_c^d \sqrt{1 + x'^2} \, dy.$$

Sometimes this integral is more readily evaluated than (24).

**Figure 15-14**

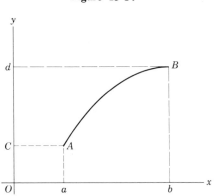

From (29) we have, by the use of the fundamental theorem,

(30) $$\frac{ds}{dy} = \pm \sqrt{1 + x'^2}\ .$$

Also, if we again introduce the angle of inclination $\alpha$ of the tangent line at any point $P$ of the curve, then

$$x' = \frac{1}{y'} = \cot \alpha.$$

From (30)

(31) $$\frac{ds}{dy} = \pm \sqrt{1 + \cot^2 \alpha} = \pm \csc \alpha$$

and

(32) $$\frac{dy}{ds} = \pm \sin \alpha.$$

The proper signs in (29) to (32) must be chosen on the basis of whether $s$ is increasing with $y$ and the value of $\alpha$. Compare (27) and (28).

Equations (27), (28), (31), and (32) are easily remembered by a mnemonic device. We form the triangle shown in Fig. 15-15. Then from this triangle we can read off whatever relation happens to be useful. Thus from the triangle we see that

$$\frac{dx}{ds} = \cos \alpha.$$

The proper signs are not indicated by this triangle but can always be determined in a specific case.

Let us use (24) to find the circumference of the circle $x^2 + y^2 = r^2$. It is, of course, sufficient to find the length of arc in the first quadrant (Fig. 15-16) and multiply by 4.

Because

$$y = \sqrt{r^2 - x^2}\ ,$$

$$y' = \frac{-x}{\sqrt{r^2 - x^2}}\ .$$

**Figure 15-15**

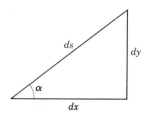

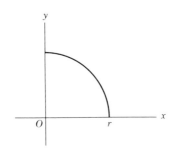

**Figure 15-16**

Then

$$\sqrt{1 + y'^2} = \sqrt{1 + \frac{x^2}{r^2 - x^2}} = \frac{r}{\sqrt{r^2 - x^2}}.$$

By (24)

**(33)**
$$s = \int_0^r \frac{r}{\sqrt{r^2 - x^2}}\, dx.$$

We now call upon the fundamental theorem and first evaluate the indefinite integral

**(34)**
$$s(x) = \int \frac{r}{\sqrt{r^2 - x^2}}\, dx.$$

The integration of this expression is no problem. If we first take a factor $r^2$ out of the radical, we obtain

**(35)**
$$s(x) = \int \frac{1}{\sqrt{1 - \frac{x^2}{r^2}}}\, dx.$$

This form suggests formula (28) of Chapter 11, namely,

**(36)**     if   $\dfrac{dy}{dx} = \dfrac{1}{\sqrt{1 - u^2}} \dfrac{du}{dx}$   then   $y = \sin^{-1} u.$

If we let $u = x/r$ in (35) and then multiply and divide by $r$, we have

$$s(x) = \int \frac{r}{\sqrt{1 - u^2}} \frac{1}{r}\, dx$$

where $1/r$ is $du/dx$. Then by (36)

$$s(u) = r \sin^{-1} u$$

and

$$s(x) = r \sin^{-1} \frac{x}{r}.$$

In view of (33) we want

**(37)**
$$s = r \sin^{-1} \frac{x}{r} \Big|_0^r = \frac{\pi r}{2}.$$

This is the length of one quarter of the circle.

As we have already noted, the calculation of lengths of arcs often presents difficulties because formula (24) involves an awkward integrand. The quantity $\sqrt{1 + y'^2}$, largely because of the square root, is a function for which the antiderivative is not easily found or cannot be found at all. The classic example is that of finding the length of arc of an ellipse. If we start with the equation

**(38)**
$$\frac{x^2}{a^2} + \frac{y^2}{b^2} = 1$$

and follow the procedure used above for the circle, we obtain

**(39)**
$$s = \int_0^a \sqrt{1 + \frac{b^2}{a^2} \frac{x^2}{a^2 - x^2}}\ dx.$$

To obtain a simpler form for the radicand, one might replace $b^2$ by $a^2 - c^2$, then replace $c/a$ by the eccentricity $e$, and simplify. The result is

$$s = \int_0^a \sqrt{\frac{a^2 - e^2 x^2}{a^2 - x^2}}\ dx.$$

One might now try the often helpful change of variable

$$x = s \sin \theta$$

and obtain

**(40)**
$$s = \int_0^{\pi/2} a \sqrt{1 - e^2 \sin^2 \theta}\ d\theta.$$

However, this integral cannot be evaluated in terms of elementary functions, that is, the algebraic, trigonometric, exponential, and logarithmic functions that we have already studied. The integral (40) is called an elliptic integral. The theory of elliptic integrals belongs to a higher branch of analysis than the calculus. We shall say something about the approximate evaluation of (40) in a later chapter.

## EXERCISES

**1.** Find the arc lengths along the following curves:

(a)   $y = x^{3/2}$ from $x = 0$ to $x = 4$.    *Ans.* $\frac{8}{27}(10\sqrt{10} - 1)$.

(b)  $y = \frac{1}{2}(e^x + e^{-x})$ from $x = -1$ to $x = 1$.

(c)  $y^3 = x^2$ from the point $(0, 0)$ to the point $(8, 4)$.                        *Ans.* 9.07.

(d)  $y = \dfrac{x^3}{6} + \dfrac{1}{2x}$ from $x = 1$ to $x = 3$.

(e)  $y = \log \sec x$ from $x = 0$ to $x = \pi/3$.                        *Ans.* $\log(2 + \sqrt{3}\,)$.

(f)  $y = \dfrac{x^4}{4} + \dfrac{1}{8x^2}$ from $x = 1$ to $x = 3$.

(g)  $9\,ay^2 = 4x^3$ from $x = 0$ to $x = x$.

2. A bridge has been designed so that its main cable is to be an arc of a parabola whose equation is $y = x^2/16$. Find the length of the cable from the vertex to $x = 12$.

> *Suggestion:* You may use the integral formula

$$\int \sqrt{x^2 + a^2}\ dx = (x/2)\sqrt{x^2 + a^2} + (a^2/2)\log\left(x + \sqrt{x^2 + a^2}\,\right) + C.$$

*Ans.* $3\sqrt{13} + 4 \log \dfrac{3 + \sqrt{13}}{2}$.

3. Evaluate the integral in (33) of the text by making the change of variable $x = r \sin \theta$.

**5. Curvature.** That a curve curves can be inferred without too much difficulty, but the answer to the question of how much a curve curves is by no means obvious, and this answer is sorely needed in a number of physical phenomena. Let us see why. According to Newton's first law of motion any object in motion will, if no force acts on it, continue to move in the direction in which it is headed. Thus, if some object moves along a curve and is at, say, point $P$ (Fig. 15-17), it will, if no force acts on it, move in the direction in which it is headed, and this means along the tangent to the curve at $P$. For example, an automobile or a train traveling in a curve will shoot off in a straight line if no force is provided to keep it on the curve. In practice this force is provided by sloping or banking the road. Likewise, an object whirled at the end of a string will shoot off along a tangent to its path the instant the hand, which provides the restraining force, lets go of the string. It may be intuitively apparent that the sharper the curve, the more force must be provided to keep the object moving along that curve. To know, then, how much force must be provided, one must know how sharply the curve turns or how sharply it changes direction. In mathematical language we say that one must know the curvature of the curve.

**Figure 15-17**

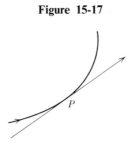

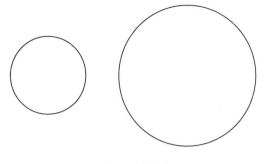

**Figure 15-18**

To calculate the curvature we must first formulate a quantitative definition of what we mean by curvature, and this will be our immediate goal. It is intuitively acceptable that a straight line has no curvature. Hence we shall say that at every point a straight line has zero curvature. A circle does have curvature at each point, and the curvature is certainly the same at all points. What should we take as the measure of curvature? The clue to an answer may come from considering two circles, one large and one small (Fig. 15-18). An object moving along either of the two circles and going once around changes its direction by 360°, but the one moving along the larger circle changes direction less per unit of distance traveled than the one moving along the smaller circle. That is, the curvature of the larger circle is less at any point than that of the smaller one. The larger the circle, the greater is its radius. Hence a possible measure of the curvature would be the reciprocal of the radius, that is, $1/R$, if $R$ denotes the radius. This definition is recommended by the fact that as $R$ increases, $1/R$ decreases. Moreover, the larger $R$ gets, the closer does an arc of a circle approximate a straight line, and the quantity $1/R$ does approach 0 as $R$ becomes larger and larger. We seem, then, to have a satisfactory definition of the curvature of a circle, namely, the curvature of a circle of radius $R$ is $1/R$ at each point.

What should we adopt as a measure of curvature for an arbitrary curve? Our intuitive notion of curvature is how rapidly a curve changes direction. The direction of a curve at a point $P$ is the direction of the tangent (Fig. 15-19), and this direction can be measured by the angle of inclination $\phi$. Then the rapidity of change of direction is really a matter of how much $\phi$ changes from point to point along the curve or rather how

**Figure 15-19**

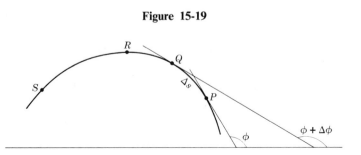

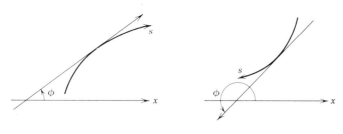

**Figure 15-20**

much $\phi$ changes compared to distance moved along the curve. What this suggests is that the curvature of a curve at any point be taken to be the rate of change of $\phi$ with respect to arc length.

   Before making our definition of curvature precise we must make some conventions for the measure of $\phi$. To make our definition here harmonize with what we shall do later in connection with vectors we shall introduce the following measure. We shall take each tangent to be sensed in the direction of increasing $s$. The inclination $\phi$ of the sensed tangent will be the counterclockwise angle between the positive $x$-axis and the positive sense of the tangent (Fig. 15-20). However, it is not possible to define $\phi$ uniquely so that it varies continuously around a closed curve. According to our conventions thus far, the value of $\phi$ changes abruptly from 0 to 360° at a point such as $P$ in Fig. 15-21. Hence we agree to define $\phi$ to be the value described above plus or minus any multiple of $2\pi$. Thus if the inclination of the tangent at $R$ of Fig. 15-21 should be 330°, for the purpose of discussing curvature at $P$ we shall take $\phi$ to be $-30°$. Then $\phi$ varies continuously over the arc $QPR$. Curvature is a local property of a curve and locally, that is in any small arc, we can define $\phi$ so that it varies continuously.

   Though the inclination angle $\phi$ just defined for the sensed tangent differs from the inclination $A$ which was defined in Chapter 3, Appendix, Section A4, it is still true that the slope of the tangent is given by $dy/dx$. For $dy/dx = \tan A$ and $A$ differs from $\phi$ by a multiple of 180°; since $\tan(180 + A) = \tan A$, we see that $dy/dx$ is still the slope of the sensed tangent.

   Suppose that an object moves from $P$ to $Q$ along a curve (Fig. 15-22). During this motion the change in direction is $\Delta\phi$ and the distance moved is $\Delta s$. Then the average change in direction per unit of distance is $\Delta\phi/\Delta s$. The

**Figure 15-21**

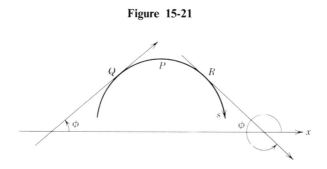

curvature at $P$ should be the limit of this average as $\Delta s$ approaches 0; that is, the curvature at $P$ is $d\phi/ds$. Thus we arrive at the following definition:

**Definition:**   The curvature of a curve at any point is $d\phi/ds$ where $\phi$ is the inclination of the sensed tangent and $s$ is the arc length measured from some fixed point.

We shall now seek a calculable formula for the curvature. Since

$$\phi = \tan^{-1} \frac{dy}{dx}$$

then

$$\frac{d\phi}{ds} = \frac{d}{ds}\left(\tan^{-1}\frac{dy}{dx}\right).$$

Now $dy/dx$ is a function of $x$. Hence it would seem wise to use the chain rule and write

$$\frac{d\phi}{ds} = \frac{d}{dx}\left(\tan^{-1}\frac{dy}{dx}\right)\frac{dx}{ds}.$$

To perform the first differentiation on the right, the chain rule is again needed; let us use $y'$ for $dy/dx$. Then

$$\frac{d\phi}{ds} = \frac{d}{dy'}(\tan^{-1}y')\frac{d^2y}{dx^2}\frac{dx}{ds}.$$

Now we call upon the theorem for differentiating the inverse tangent function to obtain

$$\frac{d\phi}{ds} = \frac{1}{1+y'^2}\frac{d^2y}{dx^2}\frac{dx}{ds}.$$

For $dx/ds$ we may use formula (26) or the negative radical depending upon whether $s$ decreases or increases with $x$. Hence

**(41)**
$$\frac{d\phi}{ds} = \frac{\pm\dfrac{d^2y}{dx^2}}{(1+y'^2)^{3/2}}.$$

**Figure 15-22**

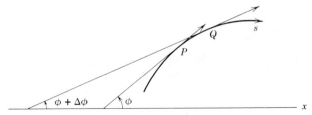

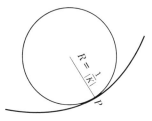

**Figure 15-23**

This expression for the curvature is satisfactory because it calls for $y'$ and $y''$ both of which are readily calculated for a given function $y = f(x)$. The curvature of a curve is often denoted by a single letter $K$ so that

**(42)**
$$K = \frac{d\phi}{ds} = \frac{\pm y''}{(1 + y'^2)^{3/2}}.$$

The sign in (42) is positive if $s$ increases with $x$ and negative if $s$ decreases with $x$.

It is also useful to speak of the radius of curvature of a curve at a given point, and this is defined to be $1/|K|$. Given a curve, we can construct a circle (Fig. 15-23) which passes through point $P$ of the given curve and which has as its center the point along the normal to $P$ at a distance $1/|K|$ from $P$, and on the concave side of the curve. This circle will have the tangent to the curve at $P$ as its tangent because the radius of the circle lies along the normal to the curve at $P$. Because the radius of the circle is $1/|K|$, the curvature of the circle by our definition of curvature for circles is $|K|$. Thus this circle has the same curvature as the curve itself at $P$. For this reason the circle is called the *circle of curvature* of the curve at $P$.

## EXERCISES

1. Show geometrically that the general definition of curvature does yield 0 for the curvature of any straight line.
2. Show geometrically that the general definition of curvature yields $1/R$ for a circle of radius $R$.
3. Show that formula (42) yields 0 for the curvature of a straight line.
4. Show that formula (42) yields $1/R$ for the curvature of a circle of radius $R$.
5. What is the curvature at a point of inflection of a curve?
6. Find the radius of curvature of the following curves at the lowest point:
   (a)  $ay = x^2$.                                              *Ans. $a/2$.*
   (b)  $bay = bx^2 + x$.
   (c)  $y = \sqrt{a^2 + x^2} - a$.                               *Ans. $a$.*
   (d)  $y = b\left(1 - \cos \dfrac{x}{a}\right)$.               *Ans. $a^2/b$.*
   (e)  $\dfrac{x^2}{a^2} + \dfrac{y^2}{b^2} = 1$.

7. Suppose that the ellipse in part (e) of Exercise 6 is a circle, that is, $a = b$. What should the radius of curvature be for this circle and does the answer to part (e) yield this expected value?

8. Prove that the radius of curvature at one end of the major axis of an ellipse is equal to one half of the latus rectum.

### 6. Areas of Surfaces of Revolution.

If an arc of a parabola, an ellipse, or some other curve is revolved around an axis, a surface is generated. Thus a semicircle revolved about its diameter generates the surface of a sphere, and if an arc of a parabola starting from the vertex is rotated around the axis of the parabola, a portion of a paraboloidal surface or of a paraboloid is generated. The areas of such surfaces must often be computed. For example, paraboloidal surfaces are used as antennas for radio systems of various sorts and paraboloidal mirrors are used in searchlights. Before building such devices one usually wants to know the surface area, for this determines the cost and the weight.

To be specific, let us consider (Fig. 15-24) the upper arc of the parabola $y^2 = 8x$ between $x = 0$ and $x = 6$ and let us suppose that this arc is revolved all the way around the $x$-axis and generates a portion of a paraboloid. We seek the area of this paraboloidal surface. As was the case for plane areas, volumes, and lengths of arcs, we have no simple formula for this surface area and we have to obtain it by using the technique of approximating it by rectilinear figures and then improving the approximation.

A possible approximating figure is obtained by first dividing the $x$-interval between $x = 0$ and $x = 6$ into $n$ subintervals $\Delta x_i$ and erecting $y$-values at the points of subdivision. Figure 15-25 shows one subinterval $\Delta x_i$ and the $y$-values erected at its end points. The chord $PQ$ is an approximation to the arc $PQ$. If chord $PQ$ is revolved about the $x$-axis, it generates a surface. This surface is an approximation to the surface generated by the arc $PQ$. We might then sum all the surfaces generated by the chords that approximate the entire arc and then let the number of chords become infinite (while each approaches 0 in length). Because as we know

**Figure 15-24**

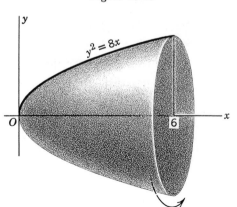

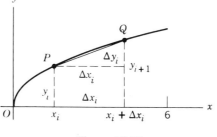

**Figure 15-25**

from our study of arc length, the sum of the chords approaches the arc length, the surface area generated by the sum of the chords should approach the surface area generated by the arc.

We shall calculate first the surface area generated by a chord such as $PQ$. The chord $PQ$ generates the surface of a frustrum of a cone or a truncated cone. Figure 15-26 shows the surface generated by $PQ$ when in the position shown in Fig. 15-25. The area that we seek is the area of the lateral surface of this truncated cone. If we slit the frustrum along $PQ$, say, we can flatten it out and it becomes the area $PP'Q'Q$ in Fig. 15-27. From Fig. 15-26 we see that

$$PP' = 2\pi y_i.$$

But Fig. 15-27 shows that $PP'$ is also an arc of the circle whose radius is $L_1$. If $\alpha$ is the central angle of the circle, the length of this arc is $(\alpha/2\pi)2\pi L_1$ or $\alpha L_1$. Hence

**(43)** $$2\pi y_i = \alpha L_1.$$

Likewise

**(44)** $$2\pi y_{i+1} = \alpha L_2,$$

where $L_2$ is the length $OQ$ of Fig. 15-27. The area $PP'Q'Q$ is the difference in the area of two circular sectors. Because the formula for the area of a

**Figure 15-26**

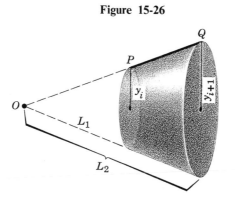

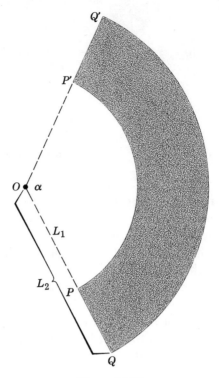

**Figure 15-27**

circular sector is $\alpha r^2/2$ where $r$ is the radius and $\alpha$ is the central angle, the area $PP'Q'Q$ is

$$\frac{\alpha}{2} L_2^2 - \frac{\alpha}{2} L_1^2$$

or

$$\frac{\alpha}{2} (L_2^2 - L_1^2)$$

or

$$\tfrac{1}{2}(\alpha L_2 + \alpha L_1)(L_2 - L_1).$$

We now use (43) and (44) for the values of $\alpha L_2$ and $\alpha L_1$ and we note that $L_2 - L_1$ is $PQ$. Then

$$\text{area } PP'Q'Q = \pi(y_{i+1} + y_2)(PQ) = 2\pi\left(\frac{y_{i+1} + y_i}{2}\right)(PQ).$$

If we replace $(y_{i+1} + y_i)/2$ by the mean $y$-value, $\bar{y}_i$ say, our final result is

**(45)**                     $\text{area } PP'Q'Q = 2\pi\bar{y}_i(PQ).$*

*Had we wished to assume the formula for the lateral surface of a frustrum of a cone, namely, $A = \pi(r_1 + r_2)l$ where $r_1$ and $r_2$ are the radii of the bases and $l$ is the slant height, we could have proceeded at once to this result.

Hence the surface area generated by $PQ$ is

$$2\pi\bar{y}_i(PQ)$$

or (see Fig. 15-25)

$$2\pi\bar{y}_i\sqrt{(\Delta x_i)^2 + (\Delta y_i)^2} \ .$$

This expression can be changed to

$$2\pi\bar{y}_i\sqrt{1 + \left(\frac{\Delta y_i}{\Delta x_i}\right)^2} \ \Delta x_i.$$

We encountered this radical in our derivation of the formula for arc length and we found there that by using the law of the mean we could replace $\Delta y_i/\Delta x_i$ by $y'$ evaluated at some value of $x$ between $x_i$ and $x_{i+1}$. Let us denote the proper value of $y'$ by $y_i'$. Then our expression for the surface area generated by $PQ$ is

$$2\pi\bar{y}_i\sqrt{1 + y_i'^2} \ \Delta x.$$

The surface area generated by the $n$ chords of which $PQ$ is typical is then

$$S_n = 2\pi\bar{y}_1\sqrt{1 + y_1'^2} \ \Delta x_1 + 2\pi\bar{y}_2\sqrt{1 + y_2'^2} \ \Delta x_2 + \cdots + 2\pi\bar{y}_n\sqrt{1 + y_n'^2} \ \Delta x_n.$$

**(46)**

The quantity $\bar{y}_1\sqrt{1 + y_1'^2}$ is the value of a function of $x$, namely, $y\sqrt{1 + y'^2}$ , taken at some value* of $x$ in $\Delta x_1$. Likewise, each of the other terms on the right side of (46) is a value of the same function taken at a value of $x$ within the respective subinterval $\Delta x_i$. Hence we have the typical summation that leads, as the number $n$ of subintervals becomes infinite while the maximum $\Delta x$ approaches 0, to a definite integral. If we denote the desired surface areas by $S$, then

**(47)**
$$S = \int_a^b 2\pi y\sqrt{1 + y'^2} \ dx$$

where $a$ and $b$ are the end values of the $x$-interval that the $\Delta x_i$ fill out.

To apply (47) to the problem of the surface area generated by the arc of

$$y = \sqrt{8} \ x^{1/2}$$

---

*There is strictly an extra point to be considered here. The value $\bar{y}_1$ and the value $y_1'$ are not necessarily taken at the same value of $x$. However, both are taken at values of $x$ within the same $\Delta x_1$. Because we intend to let all the $\Delta x_i$ approach 0, these two different values of $x$ will come closer and closer. We shall consider this point more carefully in Section 7.

that extends from $x = 0$ to $x = 6$, we first calculate $y'$. This is

$$y' = \tfrac{1}{2}\sqrt{8}\; x^{-1/2}.$$

Then by (47)

$$S = \int_0^6 2\pi\sqrt{8}\; x^{1/2}\sqrt{1 + 2x^{-1}}\; dx.$$

In accordance with the fundamental theorem, we first evaluate

$$S(x) = 2\pi\sqrt{8} \int x^{1/2}\sqrt{1 + 2x^{-1}}\; dx.$$

Putting the factor $x^{1/2}$ inside the radical yields

$$S(x) = 2\pi\sqrt{8} \int \sqrt{x + 2}\; dx,$$

and integrating by the inverse of the generalized power rule gives

$$S(x) = 2\pi\sqrt{8}\; \frac{(x + 2)^{3/2}}{\tfrac{3}{2}} = \tfrac{4}{3}\pi\sqrt{8}\,(x + 2)^{3/2}.$$

Then

$$S = \tfrac{4}{3}\pi\sqrt{8}\,(x + 2)^{3/2}\Big|_0^6 = \tfrac{4}{3}\pi 64 - \tfrac{4}{3}\pi\, 8 = \tfrac{4}{3}\pi \cdot 56.$$

What we have done for the parabolic arc applies, of course, to any arc lying in the upper half plane.

We have shown that if an arc of a curve is revolved around the $x$-axis and the arc extends from $x = a$ to $x = b$, the surface area generated is given by

**(48)**
$$S = 2\pi\int_a^b y\sqrt{1 + y'^2}\; dx.$$

This formula is sometimes written in another form. In our work on arc length we showed that

$$\frac{ds}{dx} = \sqrt{1 + y'^2}\;,$$

and this means that in differential form

$$ds = \sqrt{1 + y'^2}\; dx.$$

Hence one can write (48) in the form

**(49)**
$$S = 2\pi\int_a^b y\; ds.$$

Formula (49) has a certain mnemonic value. It suggests that we take little pieces of arc $ds$; then $2\pi y\, ds$ is the surface area generated by revolving the arc $ds$ about the $x$-axis and the integral sign means loosely that we are summing these elements of surface area.

## EXERCISES

**1.** Calculate the surface area of a zone on a sphere of radius $a$.

    *Suggestion:* A zone is generated by revolving an arc $CD$ of the circle of radius $a$ about the $x$-axis (Fig. 15-28).          *Ans.* $2\pi a(d - c)$.

**2.** Find the surface generated by revolving the following arcs about the $x$-axis:

    (a)   The arc of $y = 2\sqrt{x}$ from $x = 0$ to $x = 8$.          *Ans.* $208\pi/3$.

    (b)   The arc of $y = \frac{1}{3}x^3$ from $x = 0$ to $x = 2$.

    (c)   The arc of $y = \frac{1}{2}(e^x + e^{-x})$ from $x = -1$ to $x = 1$.

                              *Ans.* $\pi(e^2 + 4 - e^{-2})/2$.

    (d)   The arc of $y = \sin x$ from $x = 0$ to $x = \pi$.

         *Suggestion:* To integrate, let $u = \cos x$.      *Ans.* $\pi\left(2\sqrt{2} + \log\dfrac{\sqrt{2} + 1}{\sqrt{2} - 1}\right)$.

**3.** Suppose that an arc whose end points have the ordinates $y = c$ and $y = d$ is revolved about the $y$-axis. Write a formula for the area of the surface generated.

**4.** Find the area of the surface generated by revolving each of the following about the $y$-axis:

    (a)   The arc of $x = y^3$ running from $y = 0$ to $y = 3$.   *Ans.* $\pi[(730)^{3/2} - 1]/27$.

    (b)   The arc of $y^2 = x^3$ from $y = 0$ to $y = 8$.          *Ans.* $131.2$.

    (c)   The arc of $y = \frac{1}{4}x^2$ from $y = 0$ to $y = 4$.

**7. *Remarks on Approximating Figures.*** Our procedure for finding areas under curves, the volumes of figures of revolution, arc lengths, and areas of surfaces of revolution has depended on finding the proper simple figures that approximate the desired quantity and then letting the approximating figures decrease in size while the number of them increases. The sum, then, of the areas, lengths, or volumes of the approximating figures approaches the desired quantity. Thus we used rectangles to get at areas under curves, cylinders and cylindrical shells to get at volumes of revolution, chords to

**Figure 15-28**

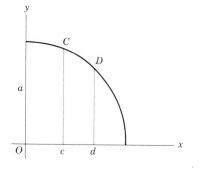

approximate arc lengths, and truncated cones to approximate areas of surfaces of revolution. The choice of the approximating figure was determined entirely by visual evidence, which seemed to assure us that the sum of these approximating figures would approach more and more closely the quantity that we sought. We have, of course, relied on visual and intuitive evidence in many instances and we shall continue to do so. Yet one must be critical and, in the absence of a strict proof, try to check intuitive arguments as much as possible. This is especially true of the choice of approximating elements in obtaining areas, volumes, and similar quantities.

Let us reconsider one or two of the derivations that we have made. When we sought the area under a curve in Chapter 9, we used as an approximating element (Fig. 15-29) the rectangle of width $\Delta x$ and of height $m_i$, where $m_i$ is the minimum $y$-value in $\Delta x$. Our sum $\underline{S_n}$ was

$$(50) \qquad \underline{S_n} = m_1 \, \Delta x + m_2 \, \Delta x + \cdots + m_n \, \Delta x.$$

We then found the limit of $\underline{S_n}$ as $n$ becomes infinite. Although we were, and no doubt still are, reasonably confident that the choice of approximating element was correct, nevertheless some area is, in fact, neglected. Thus the shaded area, $PQR$ in Fig. 15-29, is not included in the $i$th rectangle, and the sum of all these $n$ neglected areas may still approach a nonzero quantity even though the rectangles are made narrower and narrower and their number becomes infinite. We might think that we really disposed of this possible difficulty when we formed the sum

$$(51) \qquad \overline{S_n} = M_1 \, \Delta x + M_2 \, \Delta x + \cdots + M_n \, \Delta x,$$

where $M_i$ is the maximum $y$-value in each $\Delta x$, and concluded that this sum too approaches the area under the curve. But this choice of $M_i \, \Delta x$ as the approximating element includes the area $PSR$ of Fig. 15-29 which is not part of the area that we seek. There is the possibility that the sum of these $n$ additional areas, one in each rectangle $M_i \, \Delta x$, might approach a nonzero quantity even though the rectangles are made narrower and narrower and their number becomes infinite.

We can reassure ourselves that either choice of approximating element, $m_i \, \Delta x$ or $M_i \, \Delta x$, is correct by the following consideration. If we can

**Figure 15-29**

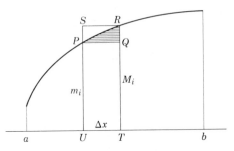

show that the difference between $S_n$ and $\overline{S_n}$ approaches 0 as $n$ becomes infinite, then, because the true area lies between them, either sum must approach the true area. However,

**(52)** $\quad \overline{S_n} - \underline{S_n} = (M_1 - m_1)\Delta x + (M_2 - m_2)\Delta x + \cdots + (M_n - m_n)\Delta x.$

Suppose that we replace the various differences $M_i - m_i$ by the maximum one, say $M_j - m_j$. There are $n$ such differences. Hence

$$\overline{S_n} - \underline{S_n} \leq (M_j - m_j)n\ \Delta x.$$

However, $n\ \Delta x$ is $b - a$ because the $n\ \Delta x$'s fill out the interval $b - a$. Then

**(53)** $\quad\quad\quad\quad\quad\quad\quad \overline{S_n} - \underline{S_n} \leq (M_j - m_j)(b - a).$

Now, as $n$ increases the difference between the maximum and minimum $y$-value in any $\Delta x$ surely approaches 0, because we are dealing with continuous functions that change gradually as $x$ changes and the smaller the change in $x$, that is, the smaller $\Delta x$, the smaller the change in $y$-values (see Section 2 of Chapter 6). Hence the quantity (53) approaches 0 as $n$ becomes infinite.

In other words, not only the sum of the shaded areas (see Fig. 15-29) but also the sum (52) of the rectangles $PQRS$, one for each $\Delta x$, approaches 0 as $n$ becomes infinite; thus the approximating rectangles that we took, namely the $m_i\ \Delta x$, do give the proper approximation to the area under the curve.

What we have just pointed out about the choice of approximating element in connection with area under a curve may seem to elaborate the obvious. Perhaps so, but then there is at least no mental strain involved. Let us reconsider next our method of determining arc length. In this task we choose as our approximating element the chord $PQ$ of Fig. 15-30. Why did we not choose a simpler element, namely, the horizontal segment $PR$? This latter choice would seem as reasonable as the choice of rectangle $PRTS$ in finding area.

**Figure 15-30**

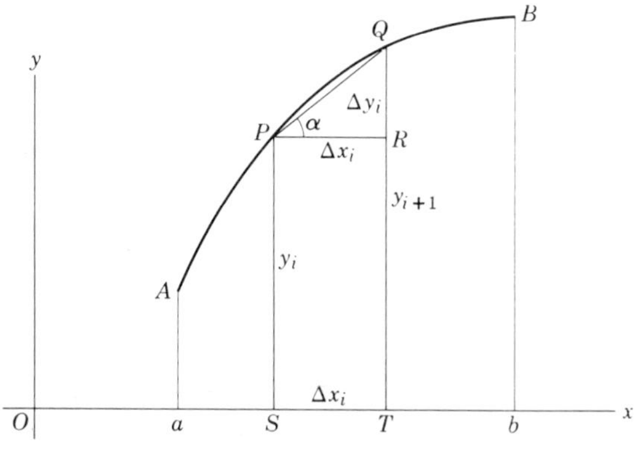

However, we can see almost at once that the choice of $PR$ as the approximating element for arc length will not do. For $PR$ equals $\Delta x_i$ and the sum of the $n$ $\Delta x_i$'s, one for each of the elements into which arc $AB$ is divided, is

$$S_n = \Delta x_1 + \Delta x_2 + \cdots + \Delta x_n = b - a.$$

As $n$ becomes larger and the $\Delta x_i$ become smaller, the sum will still be $b - a$, and so the limit of the sequence of approximations will be $b - a$. This quantity, the horizontal distance from $x = a$ to $x = b$, is not of course, the arc length $AB$.

Let us confirm analytically that the *difference* between the proper approximating element $PQ$ and the improper one $PR$ is significant. We know from our work on arc length [see (23)] that

$$PQ = \sqrt{1 + y_i'^2}\, \Delta x_i$$

where $y_i'$ is the derivative at some value of $x$ in $\Delta x_i$. On the other hand, $PR$ is $\Delta x_i$. Then

$$PQ - PR = \sqrt{1 + y_i'^2}\, \Delta x_i - \Delta x_i$$
$$= \left(\sqrt{1 + y_i'^2} - 1\right)\Delta x_i.$$

Then, because there is one such difference for each approximating element, the sum of the differences is

$$(54) \quad \left(\sqrt{1 + y_1'^2} - 1\right)\Delta x_1 + \left(\sqrt{1 + y_2'^2} - 1\right)\Delta x_2 + \cdots + \left(\sqrt{1 + y_n'^2} - 1\right)\Delta x_n.$$

As $n$ becomes infinite and the maximum $\Delta x$ approaches 0, this sum, which is precisely the kind of sum that we set up as a typical $S_n$, approaches

$$\int_a^b \left(\sqrt{1 + y'^2} - 1\right)dx.$$

This integral is not 0 (except in trivial cases). Hence we see analytically that the difference between the approximating element $PQ$ and the possible element $PR$ is significant.

Now let us compare (52) and (54). Both represent the sum of the differences between two possible choices of approximating elements. In (52) the two choices are the rectangles $M_i\, \Delta x$ and $m_i\, \Delta x$ of Fig. 15-29. In (54) the two choices are $PQ$ and $PR$ of Fig. 15-30. One sum, (52), does approach 0 as $n$ becomes infinite, but the other, (54), does not. How could we characterize them? We note in (52) that the *coefficient* of each $\Delta x$ approaches 0 as $\Delta x$ does. However, in (54) the *coefficient* of each $\Delta x$ does *not* approach 0 as $\Delta x$ does. In fact, because $y_i'$ is the slope of the curve $AB$ at some value of $x$ in $\Delta x_i$ and this slope is generally not 0, $\sqrt{1 + y_i'^2} - 1$ is not 0 no matter how small $\Delta x_i$ is.

Several points can be learned from the foregoing discussion. First, there are correct and incorrect approximating elements. Second, if there is some doubt as to whether we have a correct approximating element, we may be able to settle it by going through a proof similar to the ones we went through to show that $m_i \Delta x$ is a correct approximating element in the case of area and that the element $PR$ or $\Delta x_i$ is not a correct approximating element in the case of arc length. Third, we have a criterion as to whether the difference between two approximating elements is significant: if the difference in the approximating elements, apart from the factor $\Delta x$, does approach 0 as $\Delta x$ does, then the difference is not significant. The formal theorem, which we shall not state precisely, is known as Duhamel's theorem.

Let us make use of this criterion. First, we shall consider a point that we slid over when we determined the appropriate approximating element for the area of surfaces of revolution. We found [see (46)] that the element is

$$\textbf{(55)} \qquad\qquad\qquad 2\pi \bar{y}_i \sqrt{1 + y_i'^2}\ \Delta x_i.$$

We then said that this quantity is the value of a function of $x$, namely, $2\pi y \sqrt{1 + y'^2}$, times $\Delta x_i$ taken at some value of $x$ in the $i$th subinterval $\Delta x_i$. But, as we pointed out in a footnote, this last statement is not strictly correct because $\bar{y}_i$ was determined as an average of $y_i$ and $y_{i+1}$, whereas $y_i'$ was obtained by applying the mean value theorem to $\Delta y_i / \Delta x_i$. Hence $\bar{y}_i$ and $y_i'$ are not values of $y$ and $y'$, respectively, at the *same* value of $x$ in $\Delta x$. Yet to apply the concept of the definite integral we should have chosen $\bar{y}_i$ and $y_i'$ at the same value of $x$. Let us consider the two elements

$$2\pi \bar{y}_i \sqrt{1 + y_i'^2}\ \Delta x_i \qquad \text{and} \qquad 2\pi \bar{y}_i \sqrt{1 + \bar{y}_i'^2}\ \Delta x_i$$

where the latter, apart from $\Delta x_i$, is the value of $2\pi y \sqrt{1 + y'^2}$ taken at the same value of $x$ as $\bar{y}_i$ is taken. The difference of these two elements is

$$2\pi\, \Delta x_i \left( \bar{y}_i \sqrt{1 + y_i'^2} - \bar{y}_i \sqrt{1 + \bar{y}_i'^2}\ \right).$$

As $\Delta x_i$ approaches 0, $y_i'$ will approach $\bar{y}_i'$ because both are values of $y'$ in the same $\Delta x_i$. Hence the quantity in parentheses will approach 0 as $\Delta x_i$ approaches 0. By our criterion the element (55) can be used as a correct approximating element for surface area.

Our criterion also leads to a helpful principle in the choice of approximating element which is very much worth noting. This principle is really a theorem, but we shall not give a strict proof. Suppose that $u$ is any function of $x$. Then $\Delta u$ is the increment in $u$ when $\Delta x$ is the increment in $x$ and $du$ is the differential of $u$ corresponding to this same $\Delta x$. The principle asserts that if $\Delta u$ is the correct approximating element for the limit of a sequence of sums, then so is $du$. For

$$\Delta u - du = \frac{\Delta u}{\Delta x} \Delta x - \frac{du}{dx} \Delta x$$

$$= \left( \frac{\Delta u}{\Delta x} - \frac{du}{dx} \right) \Delta x.$$

As $\Delta x$ approaches 0, the quotient $\Delta u / \Delta x$ approaches $du/dx$. Hence the *coefficient* of $\Delta x$ approaches 0 as $\Delta x$ does. Suppose now that we had to form a sum $S_n$ of approximating elements and the suitable element was $\Delta u$ where $u$ is some function of $x$. What we have just learned is that $du$ would do as well. Moreover, $du$ may be simpler than $\Delta u$ or easier to obtain.

Let us see how we can use this principle. In finding volumes of revolution by the cylindrical shell method (see Fig. 15-4) we had to find the volume of a typical shell. This is the area of the base times the height. Now, the base is a circular disc (Fig. 15-31), and the area of the base is

$$\Delta A = \pi(x_i + \Delta x_i)^2 - \pi x_i^2.$$

We are dealing here with the function

$$A = \pi x^2$$

and $\Delta A$ is the true increment when $x$ has the value $x_i$ and $\Delta x$ is $\Delta x_i$. The differential $dA$ at this value of $x$ is

$$dA = 2\pi x_i \, \Delta x_i.$$

According to our principle, we could use $dA$ in place of $\Delta A$, and had we done so in our work in Section 3, we could have saved a few steps.

We did use the principle without signalizing it when in Section 3 we found the volume of a sphere by using spherical shells. If $r_i$ is the radius of the inner sphere of the shell and $r_i + \Delta r_i$ is the radius of the outer sphere, the true volume of the shell is

$$\Delta V = \frac{4\pi}{3} (r_i + \Delta r_i)^3 - \frac{4\pi}{3} r_i^3.$$

**Figure 15-31**

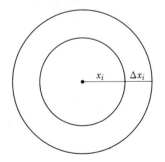

Here we are dealing with the function

$$V = \frac{4\pi}{3} r^3,$$

and the differential $dV$ of this function at $r = r_i$ is

$$dV = 4\pi r_i^2 \, \Delta r_i;$$

this is precisely the approximating element we used in (14).*

We shall use differential elements in place of the actual increments in many of our subsequent applications of the definite integral.

## EXERCISES

**1.** To find the area under a curve (Fig. 15-32) we could use as our approximating element the trapezoid $PQST$ in place of the rectangle $PRST$. Show that the area obtained will be the same in either case.

> *Suggestion:* The difference between the trapezoid and the rectangle is the triangle $PQR$ whose area is $\Delta y_i \, \Delta x/2$.

**Figure 15-32**

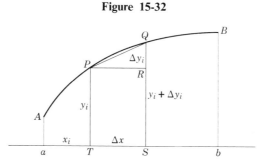

**2.** Suppose that to find the area of the surface of revolution generated by revolving arc $AB$ about the $x$-axis (Fig. 15-32) we used the lateral area of the cylindrical element generated by $PRST$ in place of the area of the truncated cone that is generated by revolving $PQST$ about the $x$-axis. The argument for using the cylinder in place of the truncated cone is that the volume of the cylinder gives the correct result when the cylindrical element is used to find the volume of revolution generated by revolving $AB$ about the $x$-axis, and so its surface area should be a good approximating element in finding the surface area generated by $AB$. Show that the cylinder will not do.

> *Suggestion:* First demonstrate that we can take $2\pi f(x_i)\sqrt{1 + [f'(x_i)]^2} \, \Delta x_i$ to be the element in finding the surface area and compare this with the cylindrical element.

**3.** Consider a right circular cone with radius $r$ and altitude $h$ (Fig. 15-33). To find the lateral surface, let us divide the altitude into $n$ equal segments of length $h/n$.

---

\* Of course, since we were finding the volume of a sphere in that problem, we could not have used the exact $\Delta V$ without reasoning in a circle. However, the principle that we are explaining is still correct.

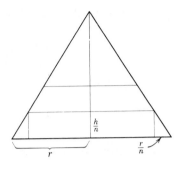

**Figure 15-33**

Now introduce the circular sections made by planes parallel to the base and through the points of subdivision. We now use cylinders as approximating elements. The upper base of each cylinder is one of the sections, and the altitude of each cylinder is $h/n$. In all we have $n - 1$ circular cylinders. The radius of the lowest cylinder is $r(1 - (1/n))$, the radius of the next higher cylinder is $r(1 - (2/n))$, etc. Then

$$S_{n-1} = 2\pi r\left(1 - \frac{1}{n}\right)\frac{h}{n} + 2\pi r\left(1 - \frac{2}{n}\right)\frac{h}{n} + \cdots + 2\pi r\left(1 - \frac{n-1}{n}\right)\frac{h}{n}$$

$$= 2\pi r\frac{h}{n}\left(1 - \frac{1}{n} + 1 - \frac{2}{n} + \cdots + 1 - \frac{n-1}{n}\right)$$

$$= 2\pi r\frac{h}{n}\left[n - 1 - \frac{1}{n}\frac{n(n-1)}{2}\right] = \pi rh\left(1 - \frac{1}{n}\right).$$

Then

$$\lim_{n\to\infty} S_{n-1} = \pi rh.$$

Is the result correct and, if not, what is wrong with the argument?

4. Let $ABC$ be an arbitrary right triangle (Fig. 15-34). To obtain the length of the hypotenuse we might, just to experiment with the method of finding arc length, proceed in the following way. We divide the hypotenuse into $n$ equal parts $CD_1$, $D_1D_2$, $\ldots$ . Through each point of subdivision we draw the perpendiculars such as $D_1C_1$, $D_2C_2$, $\ldots$, and through $C$, $D_1$, $D_2$, $\ldots$ we draw the horizontal

**Figure 15-34**

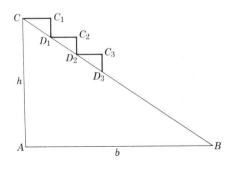

lines $CC_1$, $D_1C_2$, $\ldots$ . The sum of the segments $CC_1$, $C_1D_1$, $D_1C_2$, $C_2D_2$, $\ldots$ is an approximation to the length $CB$. By increasing the number of subintervals on $CB$ and obtaining a new series of "steps," we obtain a new sum that intuitively seems closer to the length of $ACB$. This process can be continued, and the limit of the sequence of sums should be the length $CB$. The merit of this approach is that we apparently do not need to use the Pythagorean theorem, because the sum of the horizontal segments $CC_1$, $C_1C_2$, $\ldots$ is $b$ and the sum of the vertical segments, $C_1D_1$, $C_2D_2$, $\ldots$ is $h$. Hence we know that the first sum obtained as an approximation to the length of $BC$ is $b + h$.

(a) What are the values of the successive approximations and what is $\lim\limits_{n\to\infty} S_n$ where $S_n$ is the $n$th approximation?

(b) Does the method work?

(c) What is wrong with the method?

(d) Do the points of the segments $CC_1$, $C_1D_1$, $D_1C_2$ approach the points of $CB$ as the successive approximations are formed?

**5.** Let $S_n = (2y_1 - \bar{y}_1)\Delta x_1 + (2y_2 - \bar{y}_2)\Delta x_2 + \cdots + (2y_n - \bar{y}_n)\Delta x_n$, where $y_i$ and $\bar{y}_i$ are values of $y = 3x^2$ corresponding to different values of $x$ in $\Delta x_i$. The $\Delta x_i$ fill out the interval from $x = 1$ to $x = 4$. Find $\lim\limits_{n\to\infty} S_n$ with the understanding, of course, that as $n$ becomes infinite the maximum $\Delta x$ approaches 0.

**6.** (a) In view of (26), we can define the differential of arc $ds$ to be $ds = \sqrt{1 + y'^2}\ dx$. Show by a figure what $ds$ is geometrically and distinguish it from $\Delta s$ and from $\sqrt{(\Delta x)^2 + (\Delta y)^2}$ .

(b) Could one use $ds$ in place of $\sqrt{(\Delta x)^2 + (\Delta y)^2}$ in a summation leading to a definite integral?

# CHAPTER
# SIXTEEN
# SOME PHYSICAL APPLICATIONS OF THE DEFINITE INTEGRAL *

**1. Introduction.** The calculation of areas, volumes, lengths of curves, and other geometrical quantities is a very useful task but hardly a very inspiring one. The fact that the volume of a certain figure is 36 cubic inches does not change much, if at all, one's outlook on the world. Indeed, the geometric quantities are often details in significant problems. More exciting and more profound knowledge comes from the study of physical phenomena because this knowledge not only satisfies man's curiosity about the way the physical world functions but has also enabled him to take advantage of nature's behavior. In this chapter we shall consider some physical applications of the definite integral. Of these the calculation of the gravitational force exerted by various bodies is fundamental in physical science, because this force governs basic motions on and near the earth and in the heavens. In particular, we shall establish Newton's famous theorem that every sphere attracts an external object as though the mass of the sphere were concentrated at the center.

The remark made at the beginning of Chapter 15 about the applications treated there applies here also. We could do many of the problems by first calculating the appropriate rate of change and then merely reversing differentiation. However, the summation concept, that is, the definite integral, is often the more natural approach and sometimes the only practical one, and so we shall seek to acquire facility with it.

**2. The Calculation of Work.** In Chapter 6 we had occasion to introduce and utilize the concept of work done by some force on an object. At that time we were able to approach the concept through antidifferentiation; that is, we calculated $dW/dr$, the derivative of work with respect to distance moved, and by antidifferentiation we obtained $W$. Let us now examine similar problems but approached through the notion of summation and the

*This chapter is not essential to the continuity.

476

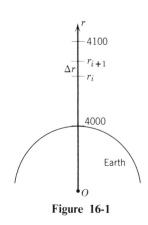

**Figure 16-1**

definite integral. It would be helpful to review Section 8 of Chapter 6 before proceeding.

Let us calculate the work done in raising an object from the surface of the earth to a height of 100 miles above the surface (Fig. 16-1). To do this work, one must exert a force that opposes the force of gravity. The magnitude of this force is

**(1)**
$$F = \frac{GMm}{r^2}$$

where $M$ is the mass of the earth, $m$ is the mass of the object being raised, and $r$ is the distance, positive in the upward direction, from the center of the earth (we are still using without proof the fact that the earth's force acts as though its mass were concentrated at the center). The force of gravity is directed downward, but the force that must be exerted to counteract the gravitational pull must be directed upward, and therefore we shall use (1) with the positive sign to represent the upward force. Because this force varies with distance from the center of the earth, we cannot just multiply the force to be exerted by the distance over which it is exerted to calculate the work done. In accordance with the summation technique, we divide the interval from $r = 4000$ (we shall use miles for the moment) to $r = 4100$ into $n$ equal subintervals $\Delta r$. Thus the $i$th subinterval runs from $r_i$ to $r_{i+1}$. Of course, the force that must be exerted even to move the object over the distance $\Delta r$ is not constant, and so there is some question about how to express even the small elements of work whose sum might yield the total work done.

To see more clearly how we might approach the quantity—total work done—let us look at the graph of the function (1) considered over the interval 4000 to 4100. Let $F_i$ be the value of $F$ at $r_i$. The work done in lifting the object through the typical element $\Delta r$, that is, from $r_i$ to $r_{i+1}$, is less than the rectangle $F_i \, \Delta r$ in Fig. 16-2 because $F$ decreases in $\Delta r$ and more than the rectangle $F_{i+1} \, \Delta r$ because $F_{i+1}$ is too small. In fact, the work done in lifting the object the distance $\Delta r$ is precisely the area under the arc $PQ$ of

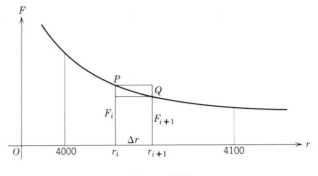

**Figure 16-2**

the curve. We should like to set up a sum

**(2)** $$S_n = F_1 \, \Delta r + F_2 \, \Delta r + \cdots + F_n \, \Delta r$$

that will approximate the work done and then let the number of subintervals $\Delta r$ become infinite. This sum is precisely of the form

**(3)** $$y_1 \, \Delta x + y_2 \, \Delta x + \cdots + y_n \, \Delta x$$

that we considered in our first investigation of the definite integral. We found there that it does not matter which value of $y$ we take in each subinterval $\Delta x$ insofar as the limit of such sums is concerned. Hence to form the sum (2) we can take any value of $F$ in each $\Delta r$. Let us, then, take the value at the left-hand end point of each subinterval $\Delta r$. Thus we take

$$F_i = \frac{GMm}{r_i^2}$$

for the $i$th subinterval $\Delta r$. Then our approximating sum is

**(4)** $$S_n = \frac{GMm}{r_1^2} \, \Delta r + \frac{GMm}{r_2^2} \, \Delta r + \cdots + \frac{GMm}{r_n^2} \, \Delta r.$$

As the number $n$ of subintervals that fill out the interval from $r = 4000$ to $r = 4100$ becomes infinite while, of course, each $\Delta r$ approaches 0, the sum $S_n$ in (4) approaches as its limit the definite integral

**(5)** $$W = \int_{4000}^{4100} \frac{GMm}{r^2} \, dr,$$

where $W$ is the amount of work we are seeking to calculate. To evaluate (5), we calculate the antiderivative

**(6)** $$W(r) = \int \frac{GMm}{r^2} \, dr.$$

Then

**(7)** $$W(r) = -\frac{GMm}{r}$$

and

$$W = - \left. \frac{GMm}{r} \right|_{4000}^{4100}$$

or

**(8)** $$W = - \frac{GMm}{4100} + \frac{GMm}{4000} .$$

To obtain a numerical answer we must, of course, substitute the numerical values of $G$, $M$, and $m$. As for $G$ and $M$, we can use the fact established in formula (61) of Chapter 6, namely,

**(9)** $$GM = 32(4000 \cdot 5280)^2.$$

The value of $m$ is, of course, the mass of the object that is being raised and is therefore some number of pounds. The denominators in (8) must be expressed in feet because the units we are using are in the foot-pound-second system. Then the value of $W$ is in the unit of foot-poundals. As in all calculations of work, the result tells us what work must be supplied by some mechanical, electrical, or chemical agency.

We calculated this same quantity—work—in Section 8 of Chapter 6. Except for the sign, that result is the same as in (6). The difference in sign comes in merely because in Chapter 6 we calculated the work done by gravity in pulling an object downward, whereas here we treated the problem of the work done in raising an object. We see, then, that insofar as this work problem is concerned either approach—that of Chapter 6 using antidifferentiation or the present one using the definite integral—gives the same result.

## EXERCISES

1. Calculate the work done in lifting an object whose mass is 1000 pounds from the surface of the earth to a height of 300 miles.      *Ans.* $4.72 \cdot 10^7$ ft-pdl.

2. Calculate the work done in lifting an object whose mass is 1000 pounds from a height of 300 miles to a height of 600 miles. Before you calculate the work, decide whether the result should be less than that in Exercise 1 or more.

3. Suppose that an object of mass $m$ is pushed up a hill (Fig. 16-3). If the hill is on the surface of the earth, we may take the magnitude $F$ of the force of gravity to be constant and equal to $32m$. However, the force that must be applied along the hill at any point $P$ is the negative of the component of $F$ down the hill. This component is $F \cos \phi = F \sin \theta$. Then the work done is

$$\int_{s_1}^{s_2} - F \sin \theta \, ds$$

where $s_1$ and $s_2$ are the values of the arc length measured from some point $S$ on

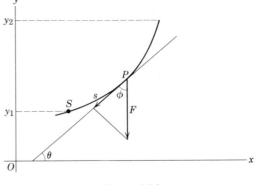

**Figure 16-3**

the hill. However, $\sin \theta = dy/ds$. [See (32) of Chap. 15] Then the work done is

$$-\int_{s_1}^{s_2} F \frac{dy}{ds} \, ds.$$

But by a change of variable $y = g(s)$ this integral equals

$$-\int_{y_1}^{y_2} F \, dy.$$

What conclusion do you draw as to the work done?

4. Suppose that the hill in Exercise 3 were the path that an airplane took in climbing from the surface of the earth to a height of 20 miles. Then it may be desirable to take into account that the magnitude $F$ of the gravitational force is not constant but is $GMm/r^2$ where $m$ is the mass of the airplane and $r$ is, of course, the distance from the center of the earth to any point on the variable path. Would the argument and conclusion of Exercise 3 still apply?

5. Suppose that a rocket is to be lifted from the surface of the earth to a height of 300 miles. Initially the rocket with its fuel may have a mass of 2000 pounds. However, as the rocket goes up, its fuel, which is a considerable part of the mass, burns up gradually. Then the mass of the rocket varies with altitude. Suppose that the variable mass is given by the formula $m = 2000 \, R^3/r^3$ where $R$ is the radius of the earth and $r$ is the distance from the center of the earth. Set up the definite integral which represents the work done in raising the rocket.

6. Express as an integral the work done by gravity in emptying a full cylindrical reservoir 3 feet in radius and 12 feet high by causing the water to flow through a hole in the bottom. Water weighs 62.5 lb/cu ft.

7. A conical reservoir with vertex at the lower end is 12 feet deep. The top of the reservoir is a circle 8 feet in diameter and it is filled to within 4 feet of the top with liquid weighing 80 lb/cu ft. Calculate the work necessary to pump all the liquid over the top of the reservoir. *Ans.* $81,920\pi/9$ ft-lb.

### 3. Applications to Economics.
As in the case of physical problems there are many economics problems that are best formulated as definite integrals. Suppose, for example, that a business has a daily income which, for successive days, is $8, $17, $32, $53, and so on. The proprietor has reason to

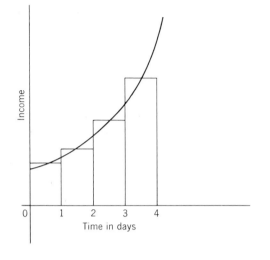

**Figure 16-4**

believe that the income will continue to follow a pattern indicated by the first few days' receipts and would like to know what the total receipts will be for one whole year. By using mathematical techniques* he finds that the income follows the functional law $r(t) = 3t^2 + 5$, where $r$ is income or revenue and $t$ is the time in days. He could now, of course, calculate what $r$ is for $t = 1, 2, 3$, and so on, until $t = 365$ and add the 365 numbers. Instead he idealizes his income and supposes that it comes in continuously according to this law. He now argues that if he breaks up the interval from $t = 0$ to $t = 365$ into small intervals $\Delta t$, then in each $\Delta t$ his income will be $r(t_i)\Delta t$, where $t_i$ is any value of $t$ in $\Delta t$. Then the sum

$$r(t_1)\Delta t + r(t_2)\Delta t + \cdots + r(t_n)\Delta t$$

should be a good approximation to his income for the year. The smaller $\Delta t$ the closer will this sum be to the idealization of continuous income because as is always the case for such approximating sums, the smaller $\Delta t$ the closer $r(t_i)$ is to all the values of $r(t)$ in that subinterval. Then the precise sum of his idealization is given by $R = \int_0^{365} (3t^2 + 5)\,dt$. This quantity can be calculated immediately. Of course the assumption that the income follows the continuous function may cause the final result to be slightly different from the sum of the 365 daily incomes.

The rationale of the method just described may be made more evident if we think in terms of area. The actually discontinuous daily income can be thought of geometrically as the sum of the areas of the rectangles some of which are shown in Fig. 16-4. The height of each rectangle is the income for one day and the base is the time interval of one day. The continuous curve represents the formula fitted to the data and the integral gives the area

*One technique which we shall not take up here is called curve fitting. In the present example another applicable method is finite differences.

under the curve from $t = 0$ to $t = 365$. Clearly the area given by the integral is a good approximation to the sum of the rectangular areas.

## EXERCISES

1. Suppose that the revenue of a business comes in daily but that we idealize the situation, and suppose that the revenue comes in continuously and follows the law $r(t) = 100/(1 + t)^2$ where $t$ is the time in years and $r$ is the revenue in dollars. What will the total revenue be in 5 years?

   *Suggestion:* Since according to the idealization the revenue changes continuously from instant to instant we can approximate the revenue received in the interval $t$ to $t + \Delta t$ by $r(t)\,\Delta t$. The sum of all these products over the interval $t = 0$ to $t = 5$ should be a good approximation to the total revenue in 5 years. What expression would give the exact total revenue?

2. If the income in $t$ days from a business can be idealized by a function such as $r(t) = 3t^2 + 5$, then at each instant of time the income can be calculated. Since there is an infinite number of instants in one day and there is an income at each instant the total income even for one day will be infinite. Thus even in the first day the income at any instant will be at least $5 and in fact will increase to $8 during the day. Even at $5 per instant the sum will be infinite. What is wrong?

3. It is usually the case that when a new product is put into production the time required to build successive units decreases because experience shows how the production process can be improved. Suppose that the time in hours to produce the $x$th unit is given by $T(x) = 80 - 0.05(x - 1)$ wherein 0.05 represents the reduction in time for each successive unit built. The manufacturer wishes to predict the total time $H$ required to build 1000 units.

   *Suggestion:* We idealize the problem and let $x$ vary continuously from 0 to 1000. Then $T(x)\,\Delta x$ is the approximate time required to build the $\Delta x$ part of the unit between the $x$th and the $(x + 1)$st. What expression gives the exact total time $H$ for all 1000 units?

4. Suppose that because of improvements in the production process a firm finds that it can produce the $x$th unit of a product according to the formula $T(x) = 100x^{-1/2}$ where $T(x)$ is the time required to produce the $x$th unit. Find the total time $H$ required to produce 1000 units.

   *Suggestion:* See Exercise 3.

## 4. The Hanging Chain.

**4. The Hanging Chain.** A physical problem of historical and current importance in the design of cables for bridges and of telephone or electric cables hung between two poles is that of determining the shape assumed by a cable suspended from two points $A$ and $B$ (Fig. 16-5). This problem was first solved by John Bernoulli about 1700. The cable is supposed to be made of inelastic material, which means that it will not stretch or contract when suspended, and it is supposed to be perfectly flexible so that it will not resist bending at any point and as a consequence will assume a smooth shape.

   We could approach this problem in practically the same way in which we approached the problem of the cable that supports a uniform horizontal load (Sect. 5 of Chap. 4). However, we shall use this opportunity to learn a

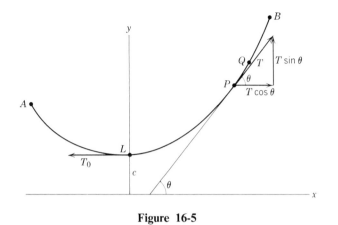

**Figure 16-5**

slightly different method. At point $P$ of the cable the weight of the portion from $A$ to $P$ exerts a pull or tension and the portion $BP$ of the cable exerts an equal and opposing pull. Let us denote the magnitude of the tension by $T$ and consider the direction to be that which $BP$ exerts at $P$. The argument that we gave in Chapter 4 when discussing the parabolic cable to show that the direction of this tension is tangential to the cable at $P$ applies here also.

If $\theta$ is the angle that the tangent at $P$ makes with the horizontal, then the horizontal and vertical components of the tension are $T_x$, which is $T \cos \theta$, and $T_y$, which is $T \sin \theta$, respectively. Let us now consider what the changes in the horizontal and vertical components are if we move from point $P$ to a nearby point $Q$ of the cable.

We may speak of the arc length $s$ of the cable measured from any point on it, say $L$, to $P$. Then the arc length from $L$ to $Q$ is some quantity $s + \Delta s$. We shall consider first the change in $T_x$ as a function of $s$. As we move from $P$ to $Q$, the only new force which is introduced and which might change the value of $T_x$ is the weight of the arc $PQ$ of the cable. If the cable has a weight of $w$ pounds per foot of length, the weight of the arc $PQ$ is $w \, \Delta s$. This weight is directed straight down and thus has no effect on the horizontal force. That is, the horizontal component $T_x$ is not altered in passing from $P$ to $Q$.* Hence

**(10)** $$T_x = C$$

where $C$ is a constant. This result applies in particular at point $L$ of Fig. 16-5, where the entire tension $T$ is horizontal (because the tension is tangential to the curve). Let us denote the tension at $L$ by $T_0$ so that, aside from direction,

**(11)** $$T_x = T_0.$$

Now let us consider the change in the vertical component $T_y$ introduced by passing from $P$ to $Q$. $T_y$ itself is the vertical tension that $BP$

---

*The horizontal force all along the arc $LPQB$ is produced by the pull of the arc $AL$ at $L$, which forces the cable to take a curved form rather than hang straight down.

exerts at $P$. At $Q$ the vertical tension exerted by $BQ$ must offset the additional weight of $PQ$, namely $w \, \Delta s$. Hence, if we regard $T_y$ as a function of $s$, the increase in $T_y$ from $P$ to $Q$ is given by

$$\Delta T_y = w \, \Delta s$$

or

$$\textbf{(12)} \qquad \frac{\Delta T_y}{\Delta s} = w.$$

If we let $\Delta s$ approach 0, we obtain

$$\textbf{(13)} \qquad \frac{dT_y}{ds} = w.$$

We now assume that the cable is uniform; that is, $w$, its weight per unit foot of length, does not change from point to point along the cable. Hence we may integrate (13) at once with respect to $s$ and write

$$\textbf{(14)} \qquad T_y = ws + D,$$

where $D$ is a constant of integration. To evaluate $D$, we note that at $L$, $s = 0$ and $T_y = 0$, the latter because the tension at $L$ is entirely horizontal. Then $D = 0$ and

$$\textbf{(15)} \qquad T_y = ws.$$

If we now divide (15) by (11), we obtain

$$\frac{T_y}{T_x} = \frac{ws}{T_0} .$$

However, $T_y = T \sin \theta$ and $T_x = T \cos \theta$, so that the quotient is $\sin \theta / \cos \theta$. But this is the slope of the curve at $P$. Then

$$\textbf{(16)} \qquad \frac{dy}{dx} = \frac{ws}{T_0} = \frac{s}{c} ,$$

where $c = T_0/w$.

This is what we might call the differential equation of the cable, that is, an equation which the derived function of the equation of the curve satisfies. However, the left side is $dy/dx$ and the right side is a function of $s$. We need, therefore, some relation between $s$ and $x$ or $s$ and $y$ which might help us to obtain an equation involving only two variables. What do we know which relates $s$ and $x$? We know from our work on arc length that

$$\textbf{(17)} \qquad \frac{ds}{dx} = \sqrt{1 + y'^2} .$$

If we now substitute (16) into (17), we see that

$$\frac{ds}{dx} = \sqrt{1 + \frac{s^2}{c^2}}\ .$$

This equation does involve just two variables $s$ and $x$. Because the right side is a function of the dependent variable, we use the theorem on inverse functions to write

$$\frac{dx}{ds} = \frac{1}{\sqrt{1 + \frac{s^2}{c^2}}}\ .$$

Hence

$$x = \int \frac{1}{\sqrt{1 + \frac{s^2}{c^2}}}\ ds.$$

To integrate, we note that the integrand is close to formula 38 in the Table of Integrals.* To make our integrand fit this formula we merely make the substitution $u = s/c$ or the change of variable

$$s = cu.$$

Then

$$x = \int \frac{1}{\sqrt{1 + u^2}} c\ du$$

and

$$x = c \log(u + \sqrt{1 + u^2}) + C.$$

Because we chose to measure arc length from $L$ of Fig. 16-5, $s = 0$ there and so is $u$. If we also choose our $y$-axis to go through $L$, then $x = 0$ when $s = 0$. Hence $C = 0$ and

$$x = c \log(u + \sqrt{1 + u^2})$$

or

(18)
$$x = c \log\left( \frac{s}{c} + \sqrt{1 + \frac{s^2}{c^2}}\ \right).$$

*We can perform the integration by letting $s = cu$ and then letting $u = \tan \theta$. We then have to integrate $\sec \theta$, which we did in (7) of Chapter 14.

We now have a relation between $x$ and $s$ but, to obtain $y$ as a function of $x$ by means of (16), we need $s$ as a function of $x$. Let us therefore solve (18) for $s$ in terms of $x$. First, we have

$$e^{x/c} = \frac{s}{c} + \sqrt{1 + \frac{s^2}{c^2}} \, .$$

If we now write $z$ for $s/c$,

$$e^{x/c} = z + \sqrt{1 + z^2} \, .$$

By subtraction

$$e^{x/c} - z = \sqrt{1 + z^2} \, ,$$

and by squaring both sides and simplifying

$$e^{2x/c} - 2e^{x/c}z = 1.$$

Then

$$z = \frac{e^{2x/c} - 1}{2e^{x/c}} = \frac{e^{x/c} - e^{-x/c}}{2} \, ,$$

and by the meaning of $z$

$$(19) \qquad s = c\,\frac{e^{x/c} - e^{-x/c}}{2} \, .$$

If we now use this relation in (16), we have

$$\frac{dy}{dx} = \frac{e^{x/c} - e^{-x/c}}{2} \, .$$

Each term on the right side is almost immediately integrable, and we obtain

$$(20) \qquad y = c\,\frac{e^{x/c} + e^{-x/c}}{2} + D.$$

If we take $y$ to be $c$ when $x = 0$, then $D = 0$ and

$$(21) \qquad y = c\,\frac{e^{x/c} + e^{-x/c}}{2} \, .$$

This relation between $y$ and $x$ gives the equation of the cable.
We may recall that we introduced the hyperbolic functions $\sinh x$ and $\cosh x$ in Chapter 12. In terms of these functions,

$$(22) \qquad y = c \cosh \frac{x}{c}$$

and

$$(23) \qquad s = c \sinh \frac{x}{c} \, .$$

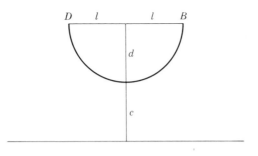

**Figure 16-6**

A curve whose equation is given by (21) or (22) is called a *catenary*. The lowest point, point $L$ in Fig. 16-5, is called the *vertex*, and the line coinciding with the $x$-axis is called the *directrix*.

We have the equation of the catenary, but it contains one constant which is unknown; this is $c$ which equals $T_0/w$. This constant should be determinable from some given conditions. If we fix one point on the curve then by reason of (22), the unknown constant should be determined. Suppose we choose the coordinates of the point $B$ (Fig. 16-6). Let us denote the $x$-value of $B$ by $l$. The $x$-axis has already been chosen so that $y = c$ when $x = 0$. Let us therefore call the $y$-value of $B$, $c + d$. If we substitute these coordinates of $B$ in (21) we have

$$c + d = c \, \frac{e^{l/c} + e^{-l/c}}{2}$$

or

**(24)**
$$c \left( \frac{e^{l/c} + e^{-l/c}}{2} - 1 \right) = d.$$

This equation contains the one unknown $c$. It is not possible to calculate $c$ by any ordinary algebraic method but we could show that there is one and only one positive solution for $c$.*

We note next that the curve of (21) or (22) is symmetric about the $y$-axis (see Fig. 12-11). Hence corresponding to the point $B$ with coordinates

---

*To see that there is one and only one positive solution for $c$, let $x = l/c$ in (24). Then

$$e^x + e^{-x} - 2 - \frac{2d}{l} x = 0.$$

Let

$$f(x) = e^x + e^{-x} - 2 - \frac{2d}{l} x.$$

We see, first, that $f(0) = 0$. Hence the curve of $y = f(x)$ for $x \geq 0$ starts at the origin. As $x$ increases from the value 0, $f'(x)$ or $e^x - e^{-x} - 2d/l$ is negative for small values of $x$. Hence $f(x)$ decreases and the curve is in the fourth quadrant. Next, $f''(x) = e^x + e^{-x}$; this is positive for all $x$. The curve is therefore always concave upward, and therefore if it crosses the positive $x$-axis, it continues upward and does not cross it again. However, for large $x$, $e^x + e^{-x}$ is larger than $-2 - (2d/l)x$, and therefore $f(x)$ is positive. Because $f(x)$ is negative for small $x$, the curve must cross the positive $x$-axis.

$(l, c + d)$, there is the point $D$ (Fig. 16-6) on the curve with coordinates $(-l, c + d)$. The quantity $2l$ is the width of the catenary and the quantity $d$ is called its sag. Thus fixing the width and sag determines the curve completely.

So far we have not specified $w$, the weight per unit length of cable, and yet the catenary is unique. How can this be? The weight $w$ enters into the equation of the catenary through the value of $c$ which is $T_0/w$. Since $c$ is fixed by the width and sag, the ratio $T_0/w$ is fixed. Hence, if $w$ is changed, it must be that $T_0$ also changes. This is physically reasonable because the pull exerted by the arc $AL$ at $L$ in Fig. 16-5 must change if the weight of the cable changes. Since changing $w$ does not change $c$, the shape of the cable is independent of the weight per unit length provided, of course, that it is the same all along the cable. Then if we hang a light rope or a heavy rope from the same two fixed points and if the sag or the length is the same for both ropes their curves will be identical.

## EXERCISES

1. Show that we can determine the value of $c$ in (21) by specifying the width and arc length of the cable. Is the sag then also determined?

2. Calculate the tension $T$ at any point on the catenary (21).

  *Suggestion:* By (11) and (15) $T^2 = T_0^2 + w^2s^2 = w^2c^2 + w^2s^2 = w^2c^2(1 + s^2/c^2)$. Now use (19).

  *Ans.* $T = wy$. Thus the tension at any point is the weight of a length of cable equal to the $y$-value at that point.

3. Suppose that one end of rope is attached to $A$ (Fig. 16-7); the rope hangs between $A$ and $B$; at $B$ it is run over the peg and extends to $C$ on the directrix of the catenary. Show that the rope will not slip in either direction at $B$.

  *Suggestion:* See Exercise 2. You may also use the physical fact that the tension at $B$ due to the weight of $BC$ is offset by the tension at $B$ due to the weight of $LB$.

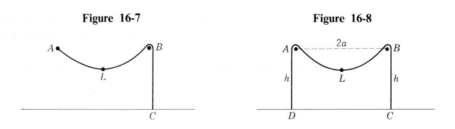

Figure 16-7          Figure 16-8

4. Two smooth pegs are at the same level and $2a$ feet apart (Fig. 16-8). Show that the shortest rope which can be hung over them and which will not slip at $A$ or $B$ is of length $2ea$.

  *Suggestion:* The length of rope is used partly to fill out the arc $ALB$ of the catenary and partly to make the lengths $BC$ and $AD$. We learn from Exercise 3 that the lengths $BC$ and $AD$ must reach to the directrix if the rope is not to slip at $A$ or $B$. Hence we wish to minimize the sum of arc $ALB$ and $2h$ or $2LB + 2h$. The quantity $e$ is the base of the natural logarithms.

**5.** Show that the relation $y^2 - c^2 = s^2$ holds at any point on the catenary. Note that with this result, given the arc length and sag, we can calculate $c$ readily.

**6.** On each catenary $y = c \cosh(x/c)$ there is a point $(x_0, y_0)$ at which the tangent passes through the origin. Show that $x_0$ is determined by the equation $x_0/c = \coth(x_0/c)$.

**7.** Suppose that the mass $\Delta m$ of the element $\Delta s$ of a cable is proportional to the projection $\Delta x$ of $\Delta s$ on the $x$-axis. Show that the curve of the hanging cable is a parabola.

**8.** Calculate the area under the arc of the catenary $y = c(e^{x/c} + e^{-x/c})/2$ from $x = 0$ to $x = d$. Then show that this area is the area of a rectangle whose base has the length of the arc and whose altitude is $c$.          *Ans.* $c^2 \sinh(d/c)$.

**9.** Show that the slope of the catenary at any point is the arc length from the vertex to that point divided by $c$.

**10.** Prove that the radius of curvature at any point of a catenary is $y^2/c$.

**11.** A cable is hung from two points at the same height and 30 feet apart. The length of the cable is 50 feet and the weight per unit foot is 5 pounds. Write an equation for the tension $T_0$ at the lowest point.
                                       *Ans.* $250 = T_0(e^{75/T_0} - e^{-75/T_0})$.

**12.** A cable hangs from two points at the same height and 100 feet apart. The slope of the cable at the right-hand point of support is $\frac{3}{4}$. Find the sag of the cable. It will be necessary to use the $e$-table.          *Ans.* Approx. 18 ft.

**5. *Gravitational Attraction of Rods.*** The calculation of the gravitational attraction exerted by bodies of various shapes is important, because this force causes or enters into an enormous variety of motions including, of course, the motions of the planets about the sun. The problem itself needs some clarification. The usual statement of the law of gravitation is that any two objects attract each other with a force whose magnitude $F$ is given by the formula

**(25)**                              $$F = G\frac{Mm}{r^2},$$

where $G$ is a constant, $M$ and $m$ are the masses of the two objects, and $r$ is the distance between them. As we pointed out in Section 8 of Chapter 6, this statement is somewhat loose. Strictly speaking, the law of gravitation applies to particles, that is, to masses that can be regarded as located each at one point, and then $r$ is the distance between these points. Of course, physically no mass is concentrated at a mathematical point. However, if two masses are very far apart compared to their sizes, as are, for example, the earth and sun, then each mass can be regarded as concentrated at one point. But if we consider the attraction of the earth on a mass which is 10 or 100 miles above the surface of the earth, then, even if the mass is small enough to be regarded as concentrated at one point, the earth cannot be. All that the law of gravitation tells us in this case is that each particle of the earth attracts the small mass according to the law of gravitation but we do not know the force exerted by the whole earth on the small mass. In particular, we would not know what the quantity $r$ should be because each particle of the earth is at a different distance from the small mass.

In other words, to calculate the gravitational force which an extended body such as the earth exerts on a nearby small mass, we must somehow sum up the forces exerted by the separate particles of the earth each at its own distance from the small mass. This summation process requires the calculus.

Our concern in the next few sections will be to calculate the gravitational force exerted by extended bodies of various shapes on other objects. Of course, we are most interested in the attraction exerted by the earth, but to become better acquainted with the calculation of gravitational force we shall start with simple bodies. It is also worth noting that unlike electric charges attract each other in accordance with the same mathematical law as masses do. Hence the mathematical work that we shall undertake is important also for the study of electricity.

Let us begin with a relatively simple problem. Suppose that we have a rod 6 feet long and of mass 18 pounds which is uniformly distributed. The rod is so thin that we think of it as extending in one dimension only. Three feet from one end of the rod (Fig. 16-9) and along the line of the rod is a small object of mass 2 pounds which we shall regard as located at one point. What gravitational force does the rod exert on the 2-pound mass? The difficulty clearly lies in the fact that the rod is an extended body and the various parts of it are at different distances from the 2-pound mass. How should we handle the fact that the mass of the rod is distributed over a 6-foot length?

One might guess that the mass of the rod can be regarded as concentrated at its center, so that the quantity $r$ to be used in (25) is the distance from the center to the 2-pound mass, a distance of 6 feet. This guess is plausible. Each portion of the rod to the left of the center should attract the 2-pound mass with less force than that same mass placed at the center. However, to each such portion to the left there is one equally far to the right which should attract with more force, and therefore the two portions, symmetrically placed with respect to the center, should produce the same total force as when both are concentrated at the center. If we regard the entire mass of the rod as concentrated at the center, the distance between the rod and the 2-pound mass is 6 feet and the force of attraction is

$$(26) \qquad\qquad F = \frac{G \cdot 18 \cdot 2}{6^2} = G \text{ poundals.}$$

The quantity $G$ is, of course, a definite number, but its value is not important at the moment.

Let us now see whether our plausible argument is really sound. Let us introduce an $r$-axis with origin at one end of the rod (Fig. 16-10), so that the rod extends from $r = 0$ to $r = 6$ and the 2-pound mass is located at $r = 9$.

**Figure 16-9**

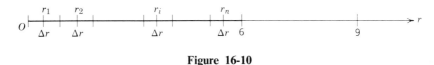

**Figure 16-10**

We next break up the interval from 0 to 6 into $n$ equal subintervals $\Delta r$. Because the rod has a mass of 3 lb/ft, each $\Delta r$ has a mass of $3\Delta r$. We now choose a point $r_1$ in the first subinterval $\Delta r$, $r_2$ in the second subinterval $\Delta r$, and generally $r_i$ in the $i$th subinterval $\Delta r$. This choice of $r_i$ in each subinterval can be the one at which the mass of that subinterval is concentrated for the purpose of determining the gravitational attraction exerted by the mass $3\Delta r$. Actually, we know from our work on the definite integral that it does not matter which $r_i$ we choose.

Then the gravitational attraction of the $i$th subinterval on the 2-pound mass is

$$G\frac{3\,\Delta r \cdot 2}{(9 - r_i)^2}.$$

The sum of the attractions exerted by all the subintervals is

$$S_n = G\frac{3\,\Delta r \cdot 2}{(9 - r_1)^2} + G\frac{3\,\Delta r \cdot 2}{(9 - r_2)^2} + \cdots + G\frac{3\,\Delta r \cdot 2}{(9 - r_n)^2}.$$

We rewrite this as

**(27)** $\quad S_n = G\dfrac{6}{(9 - r_1)^2}\,\Delta r + G\dfrac{6}{(9 - r_2)^2}\,\Delta r + \cdots + G\dfrac{6}{(9 - r_n)^2}\,\Delta r.$

We can now see that we have a function of $r$, namely,

$$G\frac{6}{(9 - r)^2},$$

which is taken at some value $r_1$ in the first $\Delta r$ and multiplied by $\Delta r$, taken at some value $r_2$ in the second $\Delta r_2$ and multiplied by $\Delta r_2$, and so on. As the subintervals $\Delta r$ are made smaller while the number of subintervals is increased so as to always fill out the interval from 0 to 6, the sum $S_n$ approaches the definite integral

**(28)** $$F = \int_0^6 G\frac{6}{(9 - r)^2}\,dr.$$

This integral is readily evaluated. By the fundamental theorem of the calculus, we first evaluate the indefinite integral

**(29)** $$F(r) = 6G\int\frac{1}{(9 - r)^2}\,dr.$$

If we make the substitution

$$u = 9 - r,$$

we see that we need $-1$ in the numerator of the integrand to have the proper $du/dr$. We can of course multiply the integrand by $-1$ and multiply by $-1$ outside the integral sign and not change the value of the integral. By integrating we find that

$$F(r) = -6G \frac{-1}{(9-r)} = \frac{6G}{9-r}.$$

The quantity $F$ is then

$$(30) \qquad F = \frac{6G}{9-r} \Big|_0^6 = 2G - \frac{2}{3}G = \frac{4}{3}G \text{ poundals.}$$

The result in (30) does not agree with (26); if we have not made any mistake in calculating (30), it must be that the plausible argument which led to (26) is wrong. What might be wrong with it? In this argument we supposed that portions of the rod symmetrically placed with respect to the center should exert the same force as if both were placed at the center. Suppose that we consider the two portions, one extending from $r = 1$ to $r = 2$ and the other from $r = 4$ to $r = 5$. According to the argument that the mass of any rod may be regarded, for the sake of calculating its gravitational attraction, as concentrated at its center, the mass of the first portion can be taken at $r = 1\frac{1}{2}$ and the mass of the second at $r = 4\frac{1}{2}$. Then the sum of the attractions of the two masses on the 2-pound mass is

$$G \frac{3 \cdot 2}{\left(9 - 1\frac{1}{2}\right)^2} + G \frac{3 \cdot 2}{\left(9 - 4\frac{1}{2}\right)^2} = \frac{24G}{225} + \frac{24G}{81} = \frac{11}{27}G \text{ approximately.}$$

(31)

If these two portions were placed at the center of the rod, the sum of their attractions would be

$$(32) \qquad 2G \frac{3 \cdot 2}{(9-3)^2} = \frac{12G}{36} = \frac{1}{3}G.$$

If we compare (31) and (32), we see that it is not correct to regard portions of the rod symmetrically located with respect to the center as equivalent to the same two portions located at the center. Functions that vary inversely as the square of $r$, as $F$ does, cannot be treated in this way.

The correct answer, then, to the gravitational attraction exerted by the entire rod is given by (30). We might ask, at what point could the mass of the rod be concentrated so that it would exert the same gravitational force as the extended rod? Let us denote by $\bar{r}$ the point at which the mass might be concentrated. Then the force of attraction of the entire mass of the rod on the 2-pound mass would be

$$G \frac{18 \cdot 2}{(9 - \bar{r})^2}$$

and this, according to (30), must equal $4G/3$. The equation

$$\frac{36G}{(9 - \bar{r})^2} = \frac{4G}{3}$$

leads to

**(33)**                              $\bar{r} = 3.8$ feet.

In other words, the mass could be regarded as concentrated at the point which is 3.8 feet from the left-hand end point. Concentrating it at the center where $r = 3$ would produce too small a force of attraction, as the result (26) shows.

Let us consider another example of the gravitational attraction of rods. We shall calculate the gravitational attraction that a rod of uniformly distributed mass $M$ and of length $2l$ exerts on a particle of mass $m$ situated on the perpendicular bisector of the rod and $h$ units from it. Let us consider the rod $AB$ (Fig. 16-11) as composed of little pieces $\Delta r$ whose sum is $AB$. The mass of the element $\Delta r$ is $(M/2l)\,\Delta r$. This mass attracts the mass $m$ at $P$ in the direction from $P$ to some point $r_i$ in $\Delta r$. The force of attraction $F_i$ has a horizontal component $PQ$ and a vertical component $PR$. Corresponding to each element $\Delta r$ to the right of the center $C$ of the rod there is an element $\Delta r$ symmetrically situated to the left of $C$ and this element attracts the mass $m$ with a force $F_i'$. The horizontal components of $F_i$ and $F_i'$ offset each other. Hence only the vertical components of the forces exerted by the elements $\Delta r$ enter into the gravitational attraction exerted by the elements.

Let us consider then the vertical attraction that the element $\Delta r$ exerts on the mass $m$. The vertical component of $F_i$ (Fig. 16-11) is $F_i \cos \alpha$. But $\cos \alpha = h/\sqrt{h^2 + r_i^2}$ . Hence the vertical component is

$$F_i \frac{h}{\sqrt{h^2 + r_i^2}} \quad .$$

**Figure 16-11**

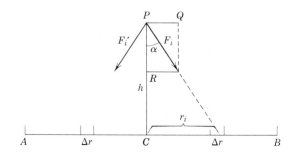

Now $F_i$ itself is, by the law of gravitation,

$$\frac{Gm(M/2l)\,\Delta r}{h^2 + r_i^2}.$$

Thus the vertical component of the force exerted by the typical $\Delta r$ is

(34)
$$\frac{Gm(M/2l)\,\Delta r}{h^2 + r_i^2}\,\frac{h}{\sqrt{h^2 + r_i^2}}.$$

The sum of all such elements of force, one for each $\Delta r$ of the rod $AB$, is an approximation to the total force which the rod exerts. If we let $\Delta r$ approach 0 then the sum approaches the integral

$$F = \int_{-l}^{l} \frac{Gm(M/2l)h}{(h^2 + r^2)^{3/2}}\,dr.$$

By using formula 45 in the Table of Integrals we have that

$$F = \frac{GmMh}{2l}\,\frac{r}{h^2\sqrt{h^2 + r^2}}\,\Big|_{-l}^{l}$$

or

(35)
$$F = \frac{GmM}{h\sqrt{h^2 + l^2}}.$$

This $F$ is the total gravitational attraction exerted by the rod on the mass $m$.


## EXERCISES

1. Find the gravitational force that a rod of uniformly distributed mass $M$ and of length $l$ exerts on a particle of mass $m$ which lies in the line of the rod and $h$ units from one end.                    *Ans.* $GMm/h(h + l)$.

2. Find the gravitational force that a semicircular wire of uniformly distributed mass $M$ and of radius $a$ exerts on a particle of mass $m$ located at the center.
                                                    *Ans.* $2GmM/\pi a^2$.

3. Show that the result in Exercise 2 implies that the wire attracts the particle as if the mass of the wire were located on the radius which bisects the semicircle and at a distance of $a\sqrt{\pi}/2$ from the center.

4. Find the gravitational force that a circular wire of uniformly distributed mass $M$ and of radius $a$ exerts on a particle of mass $m$ located on a line perpendicular to the plane of the wire and passing through its center. The particle is $h$ units from the center.                    *Ans.* $GMmh/(a^2 + h^2)^{3/2}$.

5. (a) Consider a thin rod of uniform mass $M$ per unit foot of length and occupying the length $AB$ (Fig. 16-12). Let a unit mass be placed at a point $P$ which is $p$ units above point $Q$ on the line determined by $AB$. Show that the horizontal and vertical components of the attraction that the rod exerts

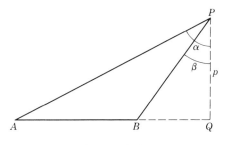

**Figure 16-12**

at $P$ are $(2GM/p) \sin \frac{1}{2}(\alpha + \beta) \sin \frac{1}{2}(\alpha - \beta)$ and $(2GM/p) \sin \frac{1}{2}(\alpha - \beta) \cos \frac{1}{2}(\alpha + \beta)$, respectively, where $\alpha$ is the angle $QPA$ and $\beta$ the angle $QPB$.

(b) Show that the resultant attraction has the magnitude $(2GM/p) \sin \frac{1}{2}(\alpha - \beta)$ or $(2GM/p) \sin \frac{1}{2} APB$ and acts along the bisector of angle $APB$.

**6.** Prove that the attraction of a thin uniform (open-ended) cylindrical shell (Fig. 16-13) of radius $a$ and length $l$ on a unit mass located at a point on the axis of the shell $b$ units from one end and $l - b$ units from the other ($b < l/2$) is

$$\frac{GM}{l} \left[ \frac{1}{\sqrt{a^2 + b^2}} - \frac{1}{\sqrt{a^2 + (l - b)^2}} \right]$$

where $M$ is the mass of the entire shell.

*Suggestion:* Use the result of Exercise 4 and regard the shell as a collection of circular wires, each of rectangular cross section. If $M$ is the mass of the shell $(M/l)\,dh$ is the mass of a wire with thickness $dh$.

**Figure 16-13**

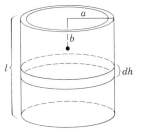

**7.** Having found in Exercise 6 the attraction of a uniform circularly cylindrical shell on a particle of unit mass on the axis of the shell, suppose that the particle is displaced a small distance, say $x$, from the center of the axis along the axis. Show that if $2l$ is the length of the cylindrical shell, $a$ is the radius, and $M$ is its mass, the particle will perform small oscillations about the center with a period of $2\pi(GM)^{-1/2}(l^2 + a^2)^{3/4}$.

*Suggestion:* After changing notation slightly in the result of Exercise 6, assume that $x$ is small and approximate the force on the particle by dropping all terms in $x^2$ and higher powers of $x$. It will be necessary also to expand the radicals by use of the binomial theorem for fractional exponents.

**8.** Find the attraction that a uniform circular wire of mass $M$ and radius $a$ exerts on a thin uniform rod of mass $m$ and length $2l$ lying along the axis of the wire with its middle point at a distance $x < l$ from the center of the wire.

*Suggestion:* Use the result of Exercise 4.

$$Ans. \quad \frac{GMm}{2l} \left\{ \frac{1}{\sqrt{(l-x)^2 + a^2}} - \frac{1}{\sqrt{(l+x)^2 + a^2}} \right\}.$$

**9.** Carrying on from Exercise 8, suppose that the wire is held fixed but the rod is released from rest when its center is at a small distance $x$ from the center of the wire. Show that the rod will oscillate along the axis of the wire with a period of $2\pi(GM)^{-1/2}(a^2 + l^2)^{3/4}$.

*Suggestion:* Use the result of Exercise 8 and approximate it by neglecting all powers of $x$ higher than the first. As in Exercise 7, it will be necessary to use the binomial theorem for fractional exponents.

### 6. Gravitational Attraction of Disks.
Let us consider next a slightly more complicated problem in gravitational attraction. Suppose that a particle of mass $m$ is located at point $P$ which is $h$ feet above the center $O$ of a thin circular disk (Fig. 16-14) of radius $a$. Suppose, too, that the mass of the disk is $M$ pounds per unit volume. What gravitational force does the disk exert on the mass $m$ at $P$?

Before we undertake to solve this problem, let us note one or two facts about handling the mass of the disk. Physically, the disk has some thickness which we denote by $t$. Because the mass *per unit volume* is $M$, the mass of the entire disk is $\pi a^2 t M$. Then the mass of unit area and thickness $t$ of the disk is $Mt$. Some books speak of a very thin disk as infinitely thin or of zero thickness and call it a lamina. They then introduce a mass $\overline{M}$ per unit area. This $\overline{M}$ is our $Mt$.

It is rather apparent from considerations of symmetry that there will be no horizontal force acting on $m$ because, although any one little piece of the disk pulls the mass $m$ both downward and horizontally, to each such

**Figure 16-14**

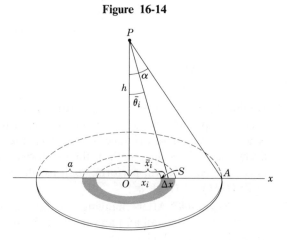

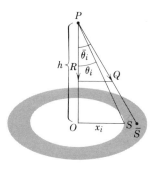

**Figure 16-15**

piece there is another one symmetrically located with respect to the center which will also pull $m$ downward but in the opposite direction horizontally and with the same horizontal force as that exerted by the first piece. Hence the horizontal components offset each other. There is, then, only a downward force acting along $PO$. Thus our problem is, what is the downward force exerted on $m$? Does the entire mass of the disk act as though it were concentrated at $O$? This does not seem reasonable, because the downward component of the force exerted by a piece of the disk far from the center is not as large as if this piece were at the center.

It would be natural to break up the disk into little squares (of thickness $t$), compute the downward attraction of each square, sum these attractions, and then let the squares become smaller while their number increases. However, we do not know how to obtain the limit of a sum whose elements are the areas of little squares.* There is a simpler approach. Suppose that we regard the disk as consisting of a series of successive rings each of width $\Delta x$. Figure 16-14 shows one such ring whose inner boundary has radius $x_i$. Consider this ring as consisting of little pieces of area $\Delta S$ and of mass $Mt\,\Delta S$. Each mass $Mt\,\Delta S$ in this ring pulls the mass $m$ toward it. However, the downward component of the force is the same no matter where the mass $Mt\,\Delta S$ is in the ring, for suppose $PQ$ is the force (Fig. 16-15) exerted by the element of mass in the ring. The direction of $PQ$ is that of $P\overline{S}$ where $\overline{S}$ is some point in the element of mass. The downward component of $PQ$ is $PR$ or $PQ \cos \bar{\theta}_i$, where $\bar{\theta}_i$ is the angle between $P\overline{S}$ and $PO$. Now, $\bar{\theta}_i$ is the same for every element of mass in the ring and the magnitude of $PQ$ is the same for every element of mass in the ring. Hence the entire ring exerts a downward component which is determined by the entire mass in the ring multiplied by $\cos \bar{\theta}_i$.

Let us find the algebraic expression for this downward component. The mass in the ring is

$$Mt\left[\pi(x_i + \Delta x)^2 - \pi x_i^2\right].$$

---

*It is possible to carry out such a plan once we know the theory of double integrals. See Chapter 23, Section 5, Exercise 15.

However, we may replace this by the differential of mass, namely,

$$Mt2\pi x_i \, \Delta x.$$

(See Chap. 15, Sect. 7.)

Then the downward component of the force exerted by this mass is

**(36)** $$F_i = \frac{GMmt2\pi x_i \cos \bar{\theta}_i}{(P\bar{S})^2} \, \Delta x.$$

The quantities $\cos \bar{\theta}_i$ and $P\bar{S}$ in (36) are not strictly functions of $x_i$ but of the $x$-value of some point $\bar{S}$ in $\Delta S$. However, as we pointed out in Section 7 of Chapter 15 in connection with the discussion of surface area, if we replace $\bar{\theta}_i$ by $\theta_i$ and $P\bar{S}$ by $PS$, where $\theta_i$ and $PS$ are determined by $x_i$ (Fig. 16-15), we do not change the value of the limit. For the difference, namely,

$$GMmt2\pi x_i \left| \frac{\cos \bar{\theta}_i}{(P\bar{S})^2} - \frac{\cos \theta_i}{(PS)^2} \right|,$$

approaches 0 as $\Delta x$ does, because $\cos \bar{\theta}_i$ approaches $\cos \theta_i$ and $P\bar{S}$ approaches $PS$ when $\Delta x$ approaches 0. Then the $i$th element of force that we need to consider is

**(37)** $$F_i = GMmt2\pi x_i \frac{\cos \theta_i}{(PS)^2} \, \Delta x.$$

Because, as is evident from Fig. 16-15

$$PS = h \sec \theta_i,$$

**(38)** $$F_i = 2GmMt\pi \frac{x_i \cos \theta_i}{h^2 \sec^2 \theta_i} \, \Delta x.$$

Hence $F_i$ is the value of the function

$$2\pi GMmt \frac{x \cos \theta}{h^2 \sec^2 \theta}$$

taken at some value $x_i$ in the $i$th subinterval $\Delta x$ and multiplied by $\Delta x$. Then the limit of the sequence of the sums of $F_i$ as $\Delta x$ approaches 0 is

**(39)** $$F = \frac{2\pi GMmt}{h^2} \int_0^a \frac{x \cos \theta}{\sec^2 \theta} \, dx.$$

To carry out the integration, we could express $\cos \theta$ and $\sec \theta$ as functions of $h$ and $x$ and then integrate the resulting function of $x$. However, we can work with $\theta$ as the independent variable. We see from

Fig. 16-15 that

$$x = h \tan \theta.$$

Let us make this change of variable in (39). Then we must replace $dx$ by

$$dx = \frac{dx}{d\theta} \, d\theta = h \sec^2 \theta \, d\theta.$$

We must then also change the end values of the interval of integration. When $x = 0$, $\theta = 0$ and when $x = a$, $\theta$ is some value $\alpha$ (see Fig. 16-14) such that $a = h \tan \alpha$. Then (39) becomes

$$F = 2\pi GMmt \int_0^\alpha \sin \theta \, d\theta$$

or

**(40)** $$F = 2\pi GmMt(1 - \cos \alpha).$$

To see how this force of attraction of the entire disk depends on the radius $a$ of the disk and the height $h$ of the mass $m$ above the center of the disk, let us use the fact that

$$\cos \alpha = \frac{h}{\sqrt{a^2 + h^2}}.$$

Then

**(41)** $$F = 2\pi GmMt\left(1 - \frac{h}{\sqrt{a^2 + h^2}}\right).$$

## EXERCISES

1. Suppose that we had assumed that the gravitational attraction exerted by the disk could be computed by regarding the mass of the disk as concentrated at its center. What expression for the gravitational force would we have obtained?

   *Ans.* $\pi GMmt(a^2/h^2)$.

2. Compute the gravitational force exerted on a mass of 2 pounds located 5 feet above the center of a circular disk of radius 10 feet and of mass 3 pounds per unit of area.

   *Suggestion:* $Mt = 3$.                    *Ans.* $12\pi G[1 - (1/5\sqrt{5})]$.

3. Convert the expression (39) for $F$ to a function of $x$ and then integrate.

4. Convert (39) to a function of $PS$ and integrate.

   *Suggestion:* Let $PS = r$ and use the fact that $r^2 = x^2 + h^2$. The answer should be (41).

5. What is the value of $F$ as $a$ approaches infinity? Can you give any physical argument to show why the result is independent of $h$?

6. Obtain a formula for the gravitational attraction exerted by a circular annulus (a circular ring) of thickness $t$, of inner radius 3 feet and outer radius 5 feet, and of mass $M$ per unit volume on a mass $m$ located 10 feet above the center of the annulus.                        *Ans.* $20\pi GMmt[(1/\sqrt{125}) - (1/\sqrt{109})]$.

7. Suppose that the distance $h$ of the mass $m$ of the text becomes larger and larger. On the basis of physical arguments, what would you expect the gravitational attraction of the disk on the mass to become? Establish your conclusion by using (41).

8. A frustum of a right circular cone bounded by planes at right angles to its axis of height $h$, and of mass $M$ per unit volume, may be regarded as a pile of disks each of whose radii subtends the same angle $\alpha$ at the vertex of the cone. Using the result (40) in the text for the disk, calculate the attractive force that the frustum exerts on a mass $m$ at the vertex.

   *Suggestion:* Because $M$ is the mass per unit volume, $M\,dh$ is the mass per unit area of a disk of thickness $dh$.                        *Ans.* $2\pi GMmh(1 - \cos \alpha)$.

9. Calculate the attraction that a solid circular cylinder (Fig. 16-16) of height $l$, radius $a$, and mass $M$ per unit volume exerts on a mass $m$ located at $O$ on the axis of the cylinder $c$ units from the nearer end.

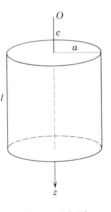

**Figure 16-16**

   *Suggestion:* Regard the cylinder as a sum of disks and use formula (41) of the text for the attraction of each disk.

$$Ans.\ \ 2\pi GMm\left\{l - \sqrt{(l + c)^2 + a^2} + \sqrt{c^2 + a^2}\,\right\}.$$

10. Prove that if the mass per unit volume of a circular disk of radius $a$ at any point $x$ units from the center is $\lambda x$, the attraction at a point on the axis $h$ units above the center is

$$2\pi G\lambda h\left\{\log \frac{\sqrt{a^2 + h^2} + a}{h} - \frac{a}{\sqrt{a^2 + h^2}}\right\}.$$

   *Suggestion:* Use the method of the text to set up the appropriate integral for the attraction.

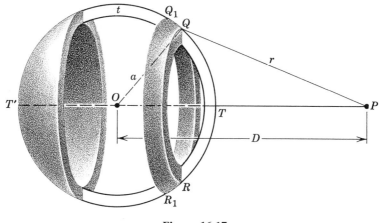

**Figure 16-17**

**7. Gravitational Attraction of Spheres.** The most interesting case of gravitational attraction is, of course, the attraction exerted by the earth. We shall take the earth to be a solid sphere of mass $M$ per unit volume and calculate the force that the sphere exerts on a mass $m$. To start with, we shall suppose that the mass $m$ is external to the sphere and that it is small enough for us to regard its mass as concentrated at one point.

The natural mathematical approach would be to approximate the sphere by a sum of small cubes, to calculate the sum of the gravitational forces exerted by each of the small cubes on the external mass, and then to calculate the limit of this sum as the size of the cubes is decreased while the number of cubes is increased to fill out the sphere. This approach, although a correct one, would lead to a kind of integral that we cannot handle.* We did, however, approach the volume of a sphere as the limit of a sum of thin spherical shells, and so perhaps we can calculate the gravitational attraction exerted by a shell's mass and then sum them to obtain the attraction exerted by the entire sphere.

The calculation of the gravitational attraction that a *thin* spherical shell exerts poses a problem in itself. Suppose that an object of mass $m$ is located at point $P$ (Fig. 16-17) which is $D$ units from the center $O$ of the shell. The shell has a thickness that we shall denote by $t$. The parts of the shell are all at different distances from $P$, and so we cannot apply the law of gravitation at once to the shell and the mass $m$. We can, however, regard the shell as composed of small zones. Thus the circles $QR$ and $Q_1R_1$ bound a zone on the outer sphere of the shell, and if we take this zone to have the thickness $t$ of the shell, we may regard the shell as composed of a number of such zones. If we could calculate the gravitational attraction that the mass of the zone exerts on the mass $m$, we could sum the attractions of all the zones that make up the shell to obtain the attraction exerted by the entire shell.

---

*The integral that results from summing elements involving the small cubes is called a triple integral. See Chapter 23, Section 6.

Let us consider, then, the attraction exerted by any one zone on the mass $m$. We think of the zone (Fig. 16-18) as made up of equal little pieces such as $U_1UTT_1$, each of which pulls the mass $m$. However, we note that the line $OP$ is the axis of symmetry for each zone. In view of this symmetry, the pulls exerted by any two diametrically opposite pieces of the zone, for example, a piece at $QQ_1$ and a piece at $RR_1$, in any direction except $PO$ will offset each other so that the zone pulls the mass $m$ along $PO$. What we should seek, then, is the component along $PO$ that each piece of the zone exerts. These components can all be added to obtain the attraction caused by the zone because they are in the same direction.

The little pieces of any one zone all make about the same angle with $PO$, namely the angle $OPQ$, and each piece is the same distance $r$ from the mass $m$. Hence the component along $PO$ of the force that each piece of the zone exerts is the same. If we let $\Delta V$ be the volume of each piece of the zone, then $M \Delta V$ is the mass of the piece. The force exerted by this piece along $PO$ is

$$\frac{G \Delta V \, Mm}{r^2} \cos \angle OPQ.$$

The sum of all these components is

(42)
$$V \frac{GMm}{r^2} \cos \angle OPQ$$

where $V$ is the volume of the zone. This volume is approximately $t$ times the area of the zone. The area is approximately the circumference of the circle $QR$ multiplied by the arc length $QQ_1$.* This area is

(43)
$$2\pi \cdot QA \cdot a \, d\theta = 2\pi a \sin \theta \cdot a d\theta$$

where $\theta$ is the angle shown in Fig. 16-18. Then the component along $PO$ of the force exerted by the entire zone is, from (42) and (43),

$$t \cdot 2\pi a \sin \theta \cdot a d\theta \frac{GMm}{r^2} \cos \angle OPQ$$

or, if we denote this component by $f$,

(44)
$$f = \frac{GMmt 2\pi a^2 \sin \theta \, d\theta}{r^2} \cos \angle OPQ.$$

Before we reformulate this expression, let us note that we made several approximations. We chose the angle $OPQ$ to represent the angle that the

---

*The area of a zone, according to the formula for the area of a surface of revolution is $S = \int 2\pi y \, ds$. Then $dS = 2\pi y \, ds$. This is an expression for the differential element of surface, which, as we saw in Section 7 of Chapter 15, can be used in place of the actual increment of surface for the purpose of a summation leading to a definite integral. For the present application, $y$ is $QA$ which equals $a \sin \theta$ and $ds = QQ_1 = a \, d\theta$.

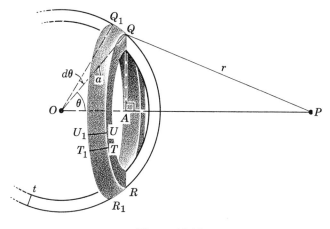

**Figure 16-18**

line from each piece of the zone to $P$ makes with $OP$; to find the surface area of the zone, we used the differential element $2\pi a^2 \sin\theta\, d\theta$; and we chose the length $PQ$ to represent the distance of each piece of the zone from $P$. Will these approximations affect our result? Well, all of these approximations would be eliminated if instead of $Q$ we chose some representative or average point in each piece of the zone. However, we intend to sum the contributions of the various zones that make up the shell and then let the number of zones become infinite; for this purpose any point $Q$ in the zone will do, just as any choice of $y_i$ in $\Delta x_i$ will do for the limit of the sum $y_1\,\Delta x_1 + y_2\,\Delta x_2 + \cdots + y_n\,\Delta x_n$.

Let us now find an expression for $\cos\angle OPQ$ in (44). We have from Fig. 16-18 that

$$\cos\angle OPQ = \frac{AP}{PQ} = \frac{OP - OA}{PQ} = \frac{D - a\cos\theta}{r},$$

where $D$ is the distance from the center of the sphere to the mass $m$ at $P$. Then

**(45)** $$f = \frac{GmMt \cdot 2\pi a^2 \sin\theta\, d\theta}{r^2} \cdot \frac{D - a\cos\theta}{r}.$$

The sum of the forces $f$ exerted by all the zones would be an approximation to that exerted by the whole shell. However, (45) contains two variables $\theta$ and $r$, and we must eliminate one of these to obtain the integrand of our ultimate definite integral. Fortunately, the law of cosines applied to triangle $OPQ$ furnishes

**(46)** $$r^2 = a^2 + D^2 - 2aD\cos\theta.$$

This equation defines $r$ as a function of $\theta$. By differentiating this implicit function with respect to $\theta$, we obtain (in differential form)

$$r\, dr = aD\sin\theta\, d\theta.$$

The use of this relation to replace $a \sin \theta \, d\theta$ in (45) yields

$$\textbf{(47)} \qquad f = \frac{GmMt2\pi ar \, dr}{Dr^2} \cdot \frac{D - a \cos \theta}{r}.$$

To eliminate the remaining term in $\theta$, we again use (46). From it we have that

$$r^2 + D^2 - a^2 = 2D^2 - 2a \, D \cos \theta$$

or

$$\frac{r^2 + D^2 - a^2}{2D} = D - a \cos \theta.$$

If we use this result in (47), we have

$$\textbf{(48)} \qquad f = \frac{GmMt\pi a}{D^2} \cdot \frac{r^2 + D^2 - a^2}{r^2} \, dr.$$

The quantity $f$ is the attractive force along $PO$ which is due to the single zone formed by $QRR_1Q_1$. To obtain the attractive force due to the entire shell, we must first sum all elements of the form (48), one for each zone, and then let the number of zones become infinite while the width $dr$ or $\Delta r$ of each zone approaches 0.* We can see from (48) what the integrand of our definite integral will be. However, we must also know the domain of $r$-values that our summation covers so as to know the end values of the definite integral. If we visualize the various zones that fill out the spherical shell in Fig. 16-17, we see that $r$ will range from the value $PT$ for the nearest zone to $P$ to $PT'$ for the farthest zone from $P$. Then $r$ ranges from $D - a$ to $D + a$.†

Then our definite integral for the attractive force of the entire shell is

$$\textbf{(49)} \qquad F = \int_{D-a}^{D+a} \frac{GmMt\pi a}{D^2} \left( 1 + \frac{D^2 - a^2}{r^2} \right) dr.$$

This integral is readily evaluated. It is, first of all, the sum

$$\frac{GmMt\pi a}{D^2} \int_{D-a}^{D+a} 1 \cdot dr + \frac{GmMt\pi a}{D^2} (D^2 - a^2) \int_{D-a}^{D+a} \frac{1}{r^2} \, dr.$$

---

*$\Delta r$ is geometrically $Q_1P - QP$. $dr$ is the differential of $r$ corresponding to the change $d\theta$ in $\theta$. Hence $dr$ is not exactly the same as $\Delta r$ but can replace $\Delta r$ for purposes of a summation leading to a definite integral.
†Strictly $r$ ranges from $D - a$ to $\sqrt{D^2 + a^2}$ and from $\sqrt{D^2 + a^2}$ to $D + a$. However, the sum of the two integrals with these pairs of end values and the same integrands is given by (49).

The results of the integration are

$$\frac{GmMt\pi a}{D^2}\left[(D+a)-(D-a)\right]$$

$$+\frac{GmMt\pi a}{D^2}(D^2-a^2)\left[\frac{-1}{D+a}+\frac{1}{D-a}\right].$$

By factoring $D^2 - a^2$ and by other simple algebraic steps, we obtain

(50)        $\frac{GmMt\pi a}{D^2}\left[(D+a)-(D-a)-(D-a)+(D+a)\right].$

Then

(51)                              $F = \frac{GmMt4\pi a^2}{D^2}.$

We can interpret this result rather readily. Because the surface area of a sphere of radius $a$ is $4\pi a^2$ and because the mass per unit volume of the sphere is $M$, the quantity $Mt4\pi a^2$ is the mass of the shell. The quantity $m$ is the mass at $P$, and $D$ is the distance from the center of the shell to $P$. Then the quantity (51) is exactly what one would obtain by regarding the mass of the shell as concentrated at the center of the shell and by applying the law of gravitation to the two masses $m$ and $Mt4\pi a^2$ separated by the distance $D$. In other words, *a spherical shell acts, insofar as its gravitational attraction on an external mass is concerned, as though the mass of the shell were concentrated at the center.*

The result that we have just proved must be applied with care. The derivation of (51) is not quite exact, because we used the outer sphere of the shell as the basic one and merely multiplied by the thickness $t$ to take the volume into account. Of course, the volume of the shell is not exactly the area of the outer sphere times the thickness. This means, then, that (51) is not quite justified for a shell of actual thickness, but (51) is a better and better approximation as the thickness approaches 0. Mathematicians idealize the shell by regarding it as a sphere of zero thickness but with mass $M$ per unit *area*. For this idealized shell, the italicized statement is exact. However, we shall soon see that even the gravitational attraction of a thick shell may be computed as if the mass of the entire shell were concentrated at the center.

We are now able to consider the gravitational force that a solid sphere of radius $R$ exerts on an external particle (point mass) of mass $m$. We shall regard the sphere as a sum of $n$ spherical shells (Fig. 16-19). However, in place of the notation $t$ for the thickness of each shell we shall use the quantity $\Delta x$ or $dx$. (They are the same when $x$ is the independent variable.)

The mass of a typical shell whose inner surface has radius $x$ is the volume times the mass $M$ per unit volume, that is

(52)                              $4\pi x^2\,dx\cdot M.$

This expression is not quite correct, because the volume of a shell is not just

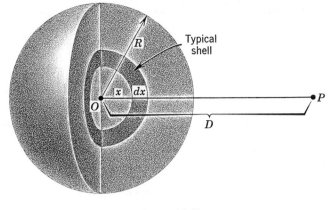

**Figure 16-19**

the area of the inner surface times the thickness. However, the smaller the thickness of the shell, the more accurate (52) will be. In fact, (52) is the differential element of mass and, because we intend to approximate the mass of the sphere by a sum of the masses of a finite number of shells and then let the thickness of each shell approach 0, the use of the differential element of mass is justified in view of what we discussed in Section 7 of Chapter 15.

We did show that the gravitational attraction of a thin shell may be computed by regarding the mass of the shell as concentrated at its center. Hence, by (51), the force that the typical shell exerts on the particle of mass $m$ is

**(53)**
$$\frac{GMm4\pi x^2\, dx}{D^2},$$

where $D$ is the distance $OP$, that is, the distance from the center to the location of the particle.

To obtain the gravitational force exerted by the solid sphere, we sum the forces exerted by the $n$ concentric shells into which the sphere is divided and let the number of shells increase while the width of each shell approaches 0. Such a limit of a sequence of sums is a definite integral. To write down the definite integral, we need only the additional knowledge that $x$ varies from $O$ to $R$. If we let $F$ be the force exerted by the solid sphere, then

$$F = \int_0^R \frac{GMm4\pi x^2\, dx}{D^2}$$

or

**(54)**   $$F = \frac{GMm4\pi}{D^2}\int_0^R x^2\, dx = \frac{GMm4\pi}{D^2}\,\frac{R^3}{3} = \frac{Gm}{D^2}\left(\frac{4\pi R^3 M}{3}\right).$$

This result has a very simple physical interpretation. The quantity $4\pi R^3 M/3$ is the mass of the entire sphere. Because $D$ is the distance from the center of the sphere to the particle at $P$, we see that the whole sphere acts on the external particle as though the sphere's mass were concentrated at the center. The usual law of gravitation applies to the two masses with the distance between them the distance from the center of the sphere to $P$. We have used this fact in earlier chapters.

## EXERCISES

1. Find the attractive force that a thin hemispherical shell of radius $a$ and mass $M$ per unit volume exerts on an external particle $P$ of mass $m$ and $D$ units from the center of the shell. The shell is the right half of the spherical shell in Fig. 16-17.

   *Suggestion:* Use (49) with the proper end values of the integral, namely $D - a$ and $\sqrt{D^2 + a^2}$.

2. Find the attractive force that a thin hemispherical shell of radius $a$ and mass $M$ per unit volume exerts on an internal particle of mass $m$ located at the center of the shell.

   *Suggestion:* Do not apply (55) directly because the integrand is infinite since $D = 0$. Use the method of the text with $P$, of course, at the center $O$. See Fig. 16-20.

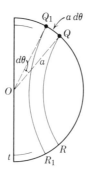

**Figure 16-20**

   *Ans.* $GmMt\pi$. Also, $GmMt\pi = GmMt\pi 2a^2/2a^2$. But $Mt2\pi a^2 =$ mass $\overline{M}$ of shell. Hence the answer can be written also as $Gm\overline{M}/2a^2$.

3. Find the attractive force that a solid hemisphere of mass $M$ per unit volume and radius $R$ exerts on a particle of mass $m$ located at the center.

   *Suggestion:* Use the result of Exercise 2; that is, regard the solid hemisphere as a limit of a sum of shells.

   *Ans.* $\pi GMmR$ or $3Gm\overline{M}/2R^2$ where $\overline{M}$ is the mass of the solid hemisphere.

4. Using the result of Exercise 3, show that the mass of the hemisphere could be regarded as concentrated at the distance $h$ (Fig. 16-21) above the mass $m$, $h$ being $R\sqrt{6}/3$.

**Figure 16-21**

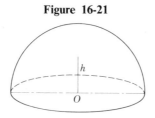

5. What modification would you make in the proof of (54) to obtain the gravitational attraction that a spherical shell of inner radius $b$ and outer radius $a$ exerts on an external point mass which is $D$ units from the center?

6. Prove that a solid sphere of radius $R$, whose mass per unit volume, that is, its density, varies with distance $r$ from the center, attracts an external particle of mass $m$ and $D$ units from the center as if the total mass of the sphere were concentrated at the center.

   *Suggestion:* Let $\rho(r)$ be the density of the earth and use (53).

   $$Ans. \quad \frac{Gm}{D^2} \int_0^R \rho(r)\, 4\pi r^2 \, dr.$$

7. In view of the result of Exercise 6, the attractive force that the earth, whose density varies as $\rho(r)$, exerts on a 1-pound mass at the surface is $G\overline{M}/R^2$ where $\overline{M}$ is the total mass of the earth. Now let $\bar{\rho}$ be the mean density of the earth. Then $\overline{M} = 4\pi R^3 \bar{\rho}/3$. We know that the attractive force of the earth on a 1-pound mass at the surface is 32 poundals. Hence calculate the mean density of the earth. The quantity $G$ in the foot-poundal-second system is $1.07 \cdot 10^{-9}$.

   *Ans.* 340 lb/cu ft.

8. Give a verbal proof of the fact that two spheres attract each other as though both were particles concentrated at their respective centers.

   *Suggestion:* Start by considering the attraction that one sphere exerts on any small element of the second sphere.

The calculation of the attraction exerted by a solid sphere on an external particle is a major result of science and is enormously useful in applications in which the earth is the attracting body. The question also arises, how does the earth act on a particle inside? Suppose, for example, that a deep tunnel were dug in the earth and a particle were placed inside the tunnel. Would the earth attract this particle as though the entire mass of the earth were concentrated at its center and inversely as the square of the distance from the center of the earth to the particle? The answer is surprising.

To consider the attraction of a solid sphere on an external particle, we first had to consider the attraction of a thin shell on an external particle. Apparently, we should now consider the attraction of a thin shell on an internal particle. Let us replace Fig. 16-17 by Fig. 16-22 in which the particle of mass $m$ is located at point $P$ inside the shell. No matter where $P$ is inside the shell, we can take the line $OP$ as an axis and divide the shell into zones that are symmetric about this axis. We now repeat the derivation of (49). There are, however, two essential differences. One is a matter of signs. In the case where $P$ is external to the shell, the angle $OPQ$ is acute for each zone of the shell. However, in the case where $P$ is internal, we can see from Fig. 16-22 and 16-23 that angle $OPQ$ is obtuse for some zones and acute for others. Thus for a zone that lies to the right of $P$, angle $OPQ$ is obtuse, while for a zone that lies to the left of $P$ (Fig. 16-23), angle $OPQ$ is acute. However, (45) is correct for both cases because $\theta$ also changes from acute to obtuse. Thus for a zone that lies to the right of $P$ (Fig. 16-22)

$$\cos OPQ = -\cos QPA = -\frac{PA}{PQ} = -\frac{OA - OP}{r}$$

$$= -\frac{a\cos\theta - D}{r} = \frac{D - a\cos\theta}{r}.$$

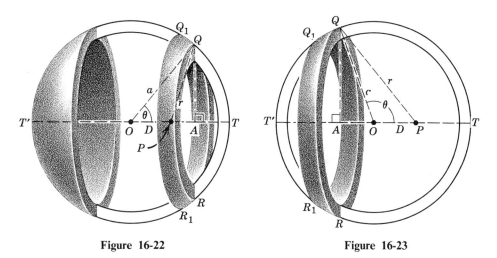

**Figure 16-22**          **Figure 16-23**

For a zone that lies to the left of $P$ (Fig. 16-23)

$$\cos OPQ = \frac{AP}{r} = \frac{OP + OA}{r} = \frac{D - a \cos \theta}{r}.$$

Hence the integrand in (49) is still correct. However, the end values of the interval of integration must be changed. In the present case $r$ varies from $PT$, which is $a - D$, to $PT'$, which is $a + D$. Hence in place of (49) we have

**(55)**
$$F = \int_{a-D}^{a+D} \frac{GMmt\pi a}{D^2} \left( 1 + \frac{D^2 - a^2}{r^2} \right) dr.$$

Then in place of (50) we have

**(56)**   $$F = \frac{GMmt\pi a}{D^2} \left[ (a + D) - (a - D) + (a - D) - (a + D) \right] = 0.$$

Thus we have the surprising result that a thin spherical shell exerts no attractive force on any point mass or particle inside the shell. Of course, the remark we made about (51) also applies here; so far our result is approximate in that we took the volume of the shell to be the surface area of the outer sphere multiplied by the thickness, which is only approximately correct. However, we shall now see that the result is exact even for shells of any thickness.

Consider the shell of thickness $R - h$ (Fig. 16-24). We may regard it as a sum of $n$ shells each of thickness $\Delta x$ where $x$ ranges from $h$ to $R$. Now let us apply (56) to each shell of thickness $\Delta x$. We have but to replace $t$ in (56) by $\Delta x$ to use the result there. However, (56) tells us that the force exerted by a thin shell on a particle $P$ interior to it is 0. This statement, as we have already observed, is not quite correct. The force is approximately 0 for a thin shell, and the approximation becomes better when the shell is thinner. Hence an approximation to the force for each shell of thickness $\Delta x$ (and

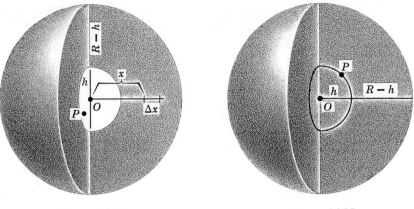

**Figure 16-24**          **Figure 16-25**

mass $M$ per unit volume) is $0 \cdot \Delta x$.* The sum of the forces due to $n$ shells is then $n \cdot 0 \cdot \Delta x$. As $\Delta x$ approaches 0, the approximation to the force exerted by each shell and therefore by the sum of the $n$ shells is better; and the limit as $n$ becomes infinite, which gives the exact force, is 0. Hence we see that even a shell of finite (as opposed to zero) thickness exerts no force on a particle interior to it.

We can now consider the attraction that a solid sphere exerts on a particle of mass $m$ inside the sphere. Figure 16-25 represents a solid sphere of radius $R$ with a particle of mass $m$ at point $P$ which is $h$ units from the center of the sphere. Point $P$ is internal to the spherical shell whose inner radius is $h$ and whose outer radius is $R$, and $P$ is also external to the solid sphere whose radius is $h$. This statement is not quite correct because $P$ is *on* the inner surface of the shell and *on* the surface of the solid sphere of radius $h$. However, let us take the statement as the basis for action at the moment, and we shall see shortly how we correct for the inaccuracy.

Because the particle at $P$ is inside the shell, the shell exerts no force on it. As for the force on the particle at $P$ by the solid sphere of radius $h$, this is, by (54),

**(57)**
$$F = \frac{Gm}{h^2} \left( 4\pi \, \frac{h^3}{3} \, M \right).$$

Hence the action of the entire sphere is equivalent to that of a sphere of radius $h$ and, as (57) shows, the mass of this sphere may be regarded as concentrated at the center.

If one is interested in the variation of $F$ with the distance of the particle from the center, then we have at once from (57) that

**(58)**
$$F = GMm \, \frac{4\pi}{3} \, h.$$

---

*We may state the argument as follows. The exact force exerted by a shell of thickness $\Delta x$ is of the form $f \, \Delta x$, where $f$ replaces the coefficient of $t$ in (56). But $f$ approaches 0 as $\Delta x$ does. Hence $f - 0$ approaches 0 as $\Delta x$ does. By Section 7 of Chapter 15 we may replace $f$ by 0 for the purpose of a summation leading to an integral.

In this form our result states that the attraction of the entire sphere varies with the distance $h$ of the particle from the center. Thus the action of a sphere on a particle inside is quite different from the action on a particle outside. The distance from the center of the sphere to the particle, the quantity $h$, is still the distance to be taken between the two masses, but the dependence of the force $F$ on that distance is no longer inversely as the square of the distance.

The result (58) can be put in a slightly different form. If we multiply numerator and denominator on the right side of (58) by $R^3$, we have

$$F = GmM \frac{4\pi}{3} R^3 \cdot \frac{1}{R^3} h.$$

Because $M$ is the mass per unit volume, the quantity $M 4\pi R^3/3$ is the mass of the *entire* sphere. If we denote this mass by $\overline{M}$, then

**(59)**
$$F = \frac{Gm\overline{M}}{R^3} h.$$

Thus the product $Gm\overline{M}$ enters here as in the law of gravitation for particles. However, the factor $R^3$ in the denominator is new here and, of course, so is the factor $h$.

There is one detail to be taken care of. Point $P$ is not strictly internal to the shell of thickness $R - h$ nor is it strictly external to the solid sphere of radius $h$. Suppose, however, that we introduce the shell of thickness $2e$ and that this shell is devoid of matter (Fig. 16-26). Then the outer shell is of thickness $R - h - e$ and the inner solid sphere has radius $h - e$. Point $P$ is now truly internal to the shell of thickness $R - h - e$, and this shell exerts no attractive force on the particle at $P$. In view of (58) the solid sphere of radius $h - e$ does exert the force

**(60)**
$$GMm \frac{4\pi}{3} (h - e).$$

Now suppose that we let $e$ approach 0. Then the outer shell continues to

**Figure 16-26**

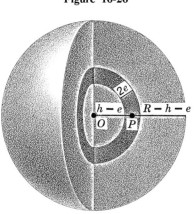

exert no force on the particle at $P$, and the inner solid sphere a force which, in view of (60), approaches (58). The limit as $e$ approaches 0 of the force exerted by the outer shell is 0, and the limit of the force exerted by the inner solid sphere is (58). However, in this limiting situation we have the case of the full sphere of radius $R$ with shell of thickness $R - h$ and inner solid sphere of radius $h$. Thus, considering $P$ in Fig. 16-25 to be internal to the shell and external to the solid sphere of radius $h$ is seen to be justified.

The several results that we have just obtained on the attraction which hollow and solid spheres exert on particles within and without were first demonstrated by Newton in his *Mathematical Principles of Natural Philosophy* (*Philosophiae Naturalis Principia Mathematica*) the first edition of which appeared in 1687. Our results are given in his Propositions 70 to 74 of Book I of the third edition.

The calculation of the gravitational force exerted by the earth is not really disposed of by all of the above theory, for the earth is not a sphere but an oblate spheroid, that is, one type of ellipsoid. For some astronomical calculations the earth may indeed be taken to be spherical but, for example, to calculate the moon's motion the ellipsoidal shape must be taken into account. However, the subject of the gravitational force exerted by ellipsoids extends far beyond the elements of the calculus. This latter problem engaged the best mathematicians of the eighteenth century.

## EXERCISES

1. Calculate the work done by the gravitational force of the earth (of radius $R$) in moving a particle of mass $m$ from the surface *into* the earth to a distance $R_1$ from the center. Assume that the mass of the earth is uniform throughout and is $M$ lb/cu ft.

   *Suggestion:* Use (58).    *Ans.* $W = Gm\frac{4}{3}\pi M\left(\dfrac{R^2}{2} - \dfrac{R_1^2}{2}\right)$.

2. Suppose that $\rho(r)$ is the density of the earth at any point $r$ units from the center. What gravitational force does the earth exert on a unit mass inside the earth $h$ units from the center?    *Ans.* $\dfrac{GM}{h^2}\displaystyle\int_0^h 4\pi\rho(r)r^2\,dr$.

3. Suppose that the earth's density varies directly with the depth below the surface. Show that the attraction of the earth is greatest at a depth equal to $\frac{1}{3}$ of the radius and that the value there is $\frac{4}{3}$ of the value at the surface.

4. The amount of heat in a homogeneous solid mass $m$ at temperature $T$ is given in suitable units by $cmT$ where $c$ is the specific heat of the material.
   (a) Set up an integral for the total heat in a wire of length $a$ and constant cross section $s$ if the density $\rho$ and the temperature $T$ vary with the distance $x$ from one end but $c$ is a constant.
   (b) Do the same as asked in (a) but this time treat $c$ as a function of $T$.
   (c) Under the same general conditions stated at the outset set up an integral for the heat in a solid spherical ball when $\rho$ and $T$ depend only on the distance from the center and $c$ is a constant.

5. The centripetal force at the origin acting on a point mass revolving about the origin at a distance $r$ and with angular velocity $\omega$ is $mr\omega^2$. Suppose that a thin

rod of length $l$, uniform cross section $s$, and variable density $\rho$ rotates at the constant rate of 10 rps around one of its end points. Set up an integral for the total centripetal force acting on the rod.

*Suggestion:* If the notion of centripetal force is not familiar, see Chapter 18, Section 7.

$$Ans. \quad 400\pi^2 s \int_0^l r\rho(r)\, dr.$$

# CHAPTER
# SEVENTEEN
# POLAR
# COORDINATES

***1. The Polar Coordinate System.*** Given a curve, say the circle, we know that we can set up a rectangular coordinate system and express the equation of the curve in the form $x^2 + y^2 = r^2$. If we then wish to study analytically any properties of the curve, we use the relation between $x$ and $y$ given by this equation.

The scheme of locating points by their distances from two mutually perpendicular lines, the $x$- and $y$-axes, is clearly a useful one. However, it is also reasonable when, for example, one is aiming a gun to think in terms of distance from an origin, which would be taken at the location of the gun, and of direction measured from some base line. This scheme for locating points in terms of the distance from an origin and the direction as measured from some base line is known as the *polar coordinate* system. Once one recognizes that there can be alternative coordinate systems, the question arises whether one can represent curves in that system and perhaps use that representation more effectively than the representation in rectangular coordinates.

Let us look into the polar coordinate scheme for representing points and curves and then see what the calculus can do for us in the study of geometrical and physical problems when polar coordinates are utilized.

We start with a point $O$ (Fig. 17-1) called the *pole* and choose the half line or *ray* that starts at $O$ and runs horizontally to the right. This ray is called the *polar axis*. Now let $P$ be a definite point. We imagine a rotation about $O$ of a ray which starts at the polar axis and stops when it passes through point $P$. Suppose that a counterclockwise rotation of 30° or $\pi/6$ radians brings the ray through $P$. Let us suppose also that the length $OP$ is 5 units. The two numbers 5 and 30°, usually written (5, 30°) or (5, $\pi/6$) are the polar coordinates of point $P$. The two coordinates locate the position of $P$ with reference to the pole and the polar axis. Thus, just as in the rectangular coordinate system, two coordinates are required to fix the position of a point in a plane.

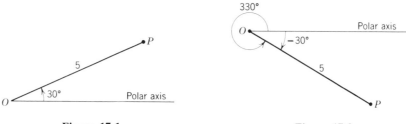

Figure 17-1                    Figure 17-2

A few more conventions are needed to complete the definition of polar coordinates. Suppose that point $P$ lies as shown in Fig. 17-2. If the distance of $P$ from $O$ along the ray $OP$ is 5, this number is still the first of the two polar coordinates of $P$. However, there is some question about what angle the ray $OP$ makes with the polar axis. We can imagine the ray is rotated counterclockwise until it falls on $OP$. Then the angle might be, say, 330°. On the other hand, we can imagine the ray is rotated clockwise until it falls on $OP$. Then the angle is $-30°$ because we regard angles obtained by a clockwise rotation as negative. Hence the polar coordinates of point $P$ can be given in two ways, namely, (5, 330°) or (5, $-30°$). The polar coordinate system thus differs from the rectangular coordinate system in that more than one set of coordinates may describe the same point.

The choices of coordinates to describe one and the same point are even more numerous than we have thus far indicated. Suppose that the ray in Fig. 17-2 rotates counterclockwise through 360° about the point $O$ and then rotates through 330 additional degrees before coinciding with $OP$. Then the angle between the polar axis and $OP$ is 690° and the coordinates of $P$ can be taken to be (5, 690°). Or the ray may rotate clockwise about $O$ through 360° and then through 30 additional degrees before coinciding with $OP$. In this case the angle between the polar axis and $OP$ is $-390°$ and another set of polar coordinates for $P$ is (5, $-390°$). In fact, because the size of an angle between two rays emanating from a point is determined by the amount of rotation that one ray goes through to coincide with the second ray and because any multiple of 360° can be added to the rotation, the size of the angle is not unique, at least to the extent that any multiple of 360° can be included.

There is an additional arbitrariness in the choice of polar coordinates. Let us consider point $P$ of Fig. 17-3. We can imagine a ray is rotated through 150° until it reaches the position $OQ$. Now, instead of proceeding

Figure 17-3

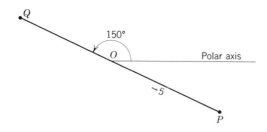

out from $O$ along this ray, we can proceed from $O$ away from $Q$ or, as one says, backward along the ray $OQ$ until we reach point $P$. To denote the fact that point $P$ is reached by proceeding backward along the ray $OQ$, we use negative numbers. If the distance $OP$ is 5, we denote the first coordinate of $P$ by $-5$ and the two coordinates of $P$ are $(-5, 150°)$. Here, too, any other positive or negative angle that locates the ray $OQ$, for example, $-210°$, can be used in place of $150°$. These coordinates $(-5, 150°)$ and the other possible choices described above all denote the same point $P$. The pole $O$ itself has 0 as its first coordinate; its second coordinate can be any angle.

The two coordinates that locate the point in this polar coordinate system are generally denoted by $\rho$ (rho) and $\theta$ (theta), although many books use $r$ and $\theta$. These coordinates are always written in the order $(\rho, \theta)$. We see that $\rho$ can be any number positive, negative, or zero, and that $\theta$, likewise, can be any number, positive, negative, or zero. The line segment $OP$ from $O$, the pole, to a point $P$ is called the *radius vector* to $P$, and the angle $\theta$ that together with $\rho$ locates $P$ is called the *vectorial angle.*

## EXERCISES

**1.** Plot the following points on a polar coordinate system:

(a) $(5, 0)$.         (f) $(3, -390°)$.

(b) $(5, 30°)$.       (g) $(-3, 30°)$.

(c) $(5, \pi/6)$.       (h) $(1, -\pi/4)$.

(d) $(5, -\pi/6)$.     (i) $(-3, -\pi/4)$.

(e) $(3, 390°)$.

**2.** For each point of Exercise 1 give one other set of polar coordinates with positive $\rho$-value and one other set with negative $\rho$-value.

## 2. The Polar Coordinate Equations of Curves.

The reason for using polar coordinates is, as already suggested, that the equations of many curves are more simply represented in polar coordinates. Let us examine the equations of a few common curves.

In the rectangular coordinate system the simplest equations of curves are $x =$ constant, which represents a line parallel to the $y$-axis, and $y =$ constant, which represents a line parallel to the $x$-axis. Let us see first what the analogues of such equations represent in the polar coordinate system. Suppose that we consider the equation

**(1)** $$\theta = 30°.$$

Where are the points for which $\theta = 30°$? If we consider points with positive $\rho$-value, the angle made by the ray from $O$ to any such point must make a $30°$ angle with the polar axis. Hence all such points must lie on the same *ray*, namely $OP$ in Fig. 17-4. However, points on the ray $OQ$, which is the prolongation backward of $OP$, are also described by $\theta = 30°$, although the $\rho$-values of points on $OQ$ are negative. Hence $\theta = 30°$ represents all the

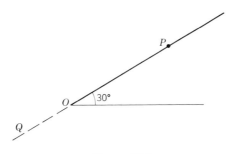

**Figure 17-4**

points on the line $QOP$. Moreover, there are no other points for which $\theta = 30°$ because any such point must have a positive, zero, or negative $\rho$-value, and we have already taken these into account. Thus $\theta = 30°$ represents the entire line that passes through the pole and makes a counter-clockwise angle of $30°$ with the polar axis.

Now let us consider the curve represented by

**(2)**                                       $\rho = 5.$

Where are all the points whose distances from the pole are 5? The answer is the circle of radius 5 (Fig. 17-5). Conversely, if a point lies on the circle of radius 5 with center at the pole $O$, then for this point $\rho = 5$.

The rectangular coordinate equation of a circle of radius 5 and center at the origin is, of course, $x^2 + y^2 = 25$. We see, then, that for the circle, the polar coordinate equation is very much simpler. This fact does not imply, however, that the polar coordinate equation is always preferable when working with the circle.

Let us now start with a curve and ask for its polar coordinate equation. Suppose that we take the straight line which is perpendicular to the polar axis and 5 units from the pole (Fig. 17-6). To obtain the equation of the line, we follow the reasoning used also in working with rectangular coordinates. We ask, what condition must all points on this line satisfy? Let $P$, then, be any point on the line. The polar coordinates of $P$, namely $\rho$ and $\theta$, are indicated in the diagram. We see from the diagram that

**(3)**                                    $\rho \cos \theta = 5.$

**Figure 17-5**

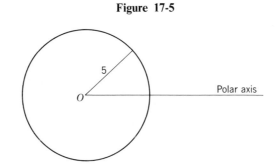

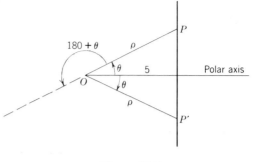

**Figure 17-6**

Because this equation holds for the coordinates of the typical point $P$, this equation presumably is the polar coordinate equation of the line. This answer may be correct, but we must do a little more checking. Let us consider a point such as $P'$. Is it true for the coordinates of $P'$ that $\rho \cos \theta = 5$? Because the $\theta$-coordinate of $P'$ can be the negative angle shown in the figure, and because $\cos \theta$ is positive for $\theta$ between 0 and $-90°$, it is true that the coordinates $(\rho, \theta)$ of $P'$ satisfy this equation.

Strictly speaking, we have not finished showing that the coordinates of any point on the line satisfy the equation $\rho \cos \theta = 5$, because there are many other choices of coordinates for any point on the line. Consider again the point $P$. For a positive $\rho$-value not only $\theta$ but $\theta \pm 2\pi$, $\theta \pm 4\pi$, and so on, all serve as the proper angle for $P$. However, the cosine of all these angles equals $\cos \theta$. Hence for positive $\rho$ any $\theta$-value which belongs to $P$ will, together with $\rho$, satisfy the equation. If a negative $\rho$-value is used to represent $P$, the corresponding angle is $180 + \theta$. However, $\cos(180 + \theta) = -\cos \theta$, and therefore $\rho \cos(180 + \theta) = 5$, because both factors are negative.[*]

We have shown that given any point on the line, its coordinates satisfy the equation $\rho \cos \theta = 5$. We must also show that given a $\rho$ and $\theta$ such that $\rho \cos \theta = 5$, the $\rho$ and $\theta$ belong to a point on the line $PP'$ of Fig. 17-6. We may dispose of this task by noting that if a point is not on the line $PP'$ then for the $\rho$ and $\theta$ of such a point $\rho \cos \theta < 5$ or $\rho \cos \theta > 5$. Hence if $\rho \cos \theta = 5$, the point must lie on the line $PP'$.

To consider another example of finding the polar equation of a curve, let us find the equation of the circle of radius $a$ whose center lies on the polar axis and which passes through the pole (Fig. 17-7). Let $P$ be any point on the upper half of the circle. We know from Euclidean geometry that

---

[*] In the polar coordinate system we do *not* require that every possible choice of coordinates for a point must satisfy the equation. Thus consider the equation $\rho = \sin(\theta/2)$. The coordinates $(-\frac{1}{2}, \pi/3)$ do not satisfy the equation, but the coordinates $(-\frac{1}{2}, 7\pi/3)$, which represent the same point, do satisfy the equation. Hence the point lies on the curve represented by the equation. In other words, a curve and equation correspond if some pair or pairs of coordinates of any point on the curve satisfy the equation and if, whenever at least one pair of coordinates satisfies the equation, the corresponding point lies on the curve.

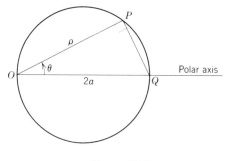

**Figure 17-7**

$OPQ$ is a right angle because it is inscribed in a semicircle. Then we have at once that

**(4)**
$$\rho = 2a \cos \theta.$$

This conclusion holds also when $P$ is on the lower half of the circle because there we can take the coordinate of $P$ to be a positive $\rho$-value and an acute negative value for $\theta$. Because at least one choice of coordinates for each point on the circle satisfies equation (4), this is the equation of the circle. Conversely, if a point $P$ has coordinates $\rho$ and $\theta$ which satisfy (4), $P$ must lie on the circle. For then $\cos \theta = \rho/2a$. If $\rho$ is positive, $\theta$ must be an acute angle (we may ignore any multiple of 360°) and $\rho$ and $2a$ must be the adjacent side and hypotenuse of a right triangle with right angle at $P$. By a theorem of Euclidean geometry, the vertices of all right triangles with hypotenuse $2a$ must be on the circle with diameter $2a$. Then $P$ must lie on the circle. If $\rho$ is negative, for example $-5$, $\theta$ can be between 90° and 270°. Suppose that $\theta$ is obtuse (Fig. 17-8). Then $\phi$, the supplement of $\theta$, is acute and the magnitude of $OP$ is 5. The argument that we gave for $\rho$ positive and $\theta$ acute now applies to $\phi$ and the magnitude of $OP$, and thus $P$ lies on the circle. There are other possibilities for the values of $\rho$ and $\theta$, but they lead in each case to the conclusion that point $P$ whose coordinates $\rho$ and $\theta$ satisfy (4) must lie on the circle.

**Figure 17-8**

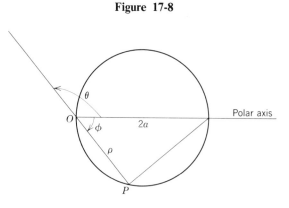

## EXERCISES

**1.** What is the curve corresponding to $\theta = 30°$ and $\rho$ positive?

**2.** What is the equation of a line parallel to the initial ray and 3 units above the pole?                                                    *Ans.* $3 = \rho \sin \theta$.

**3.** What is the equation of a line parallel to the initial ray and 3 units below the pole?

**4.** Give another equation for the line represented by $\theta = 30°$.

**5.** Describe the curve whose equation is the following:

   (a)  $\rho = 10 \cos \theta$.                    (e)  $\rho = 4/\cos \theta$.

   (b)  $\rho = 10 \sin \theta$.                     (f)  $\rho^2 = \sin^2 \theta$.

   (c)  $\rho = -10 \cos \theta$.                  (g)  $\rho \cos \theta = -4$.

   (d)  $\rho = -10 \sin \theta$.                  (h)  $\rho \sin \theta = 1$.

### 3. The Polar Coordinate Equations of the Conic Sections. Next to the straight line and circle the conic sections are the most useful curves. We shall now see what their equations become in polar coordinates.

Most often the conic sections—that is, parabola, ellipse, and hyperbola—are defined by a property peculiar to each one separately (see Chapters 4 and 7). Thus the ellipse is often defined as the set of all points such that the sum of the distances of any one from two fixed points is the same constant. However, all three conic sections can be defined by one common property, called the focus-directrix property. Under this definition, a conic section is the set of all points for which the ratio of the distance from a fixed point and from a fixed line is constant. This means that we start with a fixed line $d$ (Fig. 17-9), called the directrix, and a fixed point $F$, called the focus. Then we consider all points $P$ for which the ratio of the distance $PF$ and the distance $PD$ from $P$ to the line $d$ is a given constant. This set of points is a conic section. If the constant, denoted by $e$ and called the eccentricity, is less than 1, the conic section is called an ellipse; if equal to 1, it is called a parabola; and if greater than 1, it is called a hyperbola.

This definition is somewhat familiar in that it happens to be the one used commonly for the parabola. However, one can show that it applies to

**Figure 17-9**

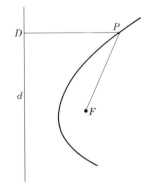

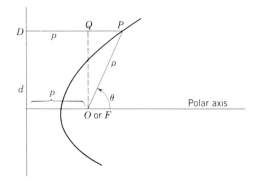

**Figure 17-10**

all the conic sections by using it to find the equation of the curve in rectangular coordinates. This equation proves to be of the second degree in $x$ and $y$, and we have proved (Appendix to Chapter 7) that any equation of the second degree in $x$ and $y$ must represent one of the conic sections. We shall not pursue the application of the focus-directrix definition in rectangular coordinates (see Exercise 15), but we shall apply it in the polar coordinate system.

We do have the possibility of choosing the pole and polar axis so as to make the resulting equation as simple as possible. Suppose that the focus $F$ lies to the right of the directrix $d$. Experience shows that if we choose the point $F$ as the pole and choose the polar axis perpendicular to the directrix $d$ and pointing to the right, so that it points away from the directrix, then the equation is simple. With this choice (Fig. 17-10) let $P$ be any point on a conic section and let $(\rho, \theta)$ be its coordinates. We wish to express in these coordinates the geometric condition

**(5)**
$$\frac{PF}{PD} = e$$

where $e$ is a fixed constant.

The length $PF$ is the $\rho$-value of $P$. The length $PD = PQ + QD$, where $Q$ is the foot of the perpendicular from $F$ to $PD$. Now $PQ = \rho \cos \theta$. The quantity $QD$ is the distance from the focus $F$ to the directrix $d$. This distance is, of course, fixed for any one curve because the focus and directrix are given. Let us denote it by $p$. Then

$$PD = \rho \cos \theta + p.$$

With these values of $PF$ and $PD$ we have from (5)

$$\frac{\rho}{\rho \cos \theta + p} = e.$$

If we solve this equation for $\rho$, we have that

**(6)**
$$\rho = \frac{ep}{1 - e \cos \theta} \cdot *$$

We do not know how the curve of the equation lies in relation to the pole and polar axis, but we can determine this in somewhat the same manner as one does for equations in rectangular coordinates. Suppose, for example, $e = 1$ and $p = 6$. Then (6) becomes

**(7)**
$$\rho = \frac{6}{1 - \cos \theta} \cdot$$

We can now make a table of values for $\theta$ and $\rho$ and thereby locate a few points. Thus

| $\theta$ | 30° | 60° | 90° | 120° | 180° |
|---|---|---|---|---|---|
| $\rho$ | 45 | 12 | 6 | 4 | 3 |

We could continue the table for values of $\theta$ larger than 180°, but we know that we can cover the range from 180° to 360° just as well by covering the range from $-180°$ through $-90°$ to 0°. Since $\cos(-\theta) = \cos \theta$, we should get the same $\rho$-values as $\theta$ ranges from 0° to $-180°$ as when it ranges from 0° to 180°. What this means geometrically is that the curve is symmetric with respect to the polar axis. The curve lies as shown in Fig. 17-10 and is a parabola.

We assumed in the derivation of (6) that the focus lies to the right of the directrix. However, it might equally well lie to the left (Fig. 17-11). If we again choose the pole to be the focus and choose the polar axis perpendicular to the directrix and pointing to the right, so that this time it points from

**Figure 17-11**

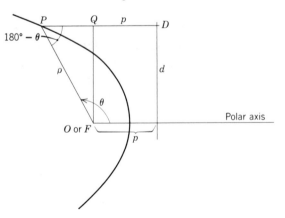

* The circle is a special case in which $e = 0$, $p$ is infinite, and $ep$ is a constant, the radius of the circle.

the focus toward the directrix, the equation of the conic section is slightly altered. We again start with the definition

$$\frac{PF}{PD} = e.$$

$PF$ is again $\rho$. Also $PD = PQ + QD$. But now $PQ = \rho \cos(180 - \theta) = -\rho \cos \theta$. Hence $PD$ is $p - \rho \cos \theta$. Then

$$\frac{\rho}{p - \rho \cos \theta} = e$$

or, by solving for $\rho$,

**(8)**
$$\rho = \frac{ep}{1 + e \cos \theta}.$$

A parabola has just one focus and one directrix. However, the ellipse and hyperbola have two foci (Fig. 17-12) and, as one might guess from the symmetry of these curves, each has a directrix associated with it. We may choose either pair of focus and directrix to write the equation of the curve and our result will be (6) or (8). To be more explicit, if in the case of the ellipse, say, we choose the directrix $d$ and the focus $F$ and the polar axis is, as always, directed from $F$ to the right, then the facts are as in Fig. 17-10 and (6) will result. If we choose $F'$ and $d'$ (for the ellipse) and the polar axis is directed from $F'$ to the right, then the facts are as in Fig. 17-11 and (8) will result. No matter which focus and directrix we pick, the other focus and directrix exist and may play a role. With the choice of $F$ and $d$ for the ellipse, the other focus is to the right of $F$. With the choice of $F'$ and $d'$, the other focus is to the left of $F'$.

We may find it convenient at times to use the polar coordinate equation of a conic section when the focus lies below or above the directrix, the pole is chosen to be the focus, and the polar axis is chosen *parallel* to the directrix and pointing to the right as usual. If the focus lies below the directrix (Fig. 17-13), the equation of the conic section is readily found, by the method above, to be

**(9)**
$$\rho = \frac{ep}{1 + e \sin \theta}$$

**Figure 17-12**

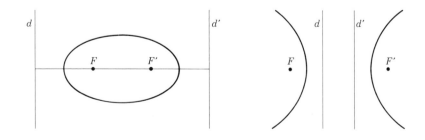

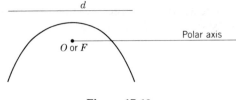

**Figure 17-13**

If the focus lies above the directrix (Fig. 17-14), the equation of the conic section is found to be

**(10)**
$$\rho = \frac{ep}{1 - e \sin \theta} \cdot$$

To plot a curve whose equation falls under one of the forms (6), (8), (9), or (10) we can advance the work considerably if we first determine which form is involved and what $e$ and $p$ are for the curve in question. Thus suppose that we are given the equation

**(11)**
$$\rho = \frac{10}{3 + 4 \sin \theta} \cdot$$

This equation may be reduced to the form (9) if we divide numerator and denominator on the right side of (11) by 3. We obtain

**(12)**
$$\rho = \frac{\frac{10}{3}}{1 + \frac{4}{3} \sin \theta} \cdot$$

If we now compare (12) and (9), we see that $e = \frac{4}{3}$ and $ep = \frac{10}{3}$. Then $p = \frac{5}{2}$. We know now from the fact that $e = \frac{4}{3}$ that the curve is a hyperbola. We also know that the directrix is $\frac{5}{2}$ units above the pole. To obtain a better picture of the curve, we would have to make a table of $(\rho, \theta)$-values belonging to (12) and plot the corresponding points.

## EXERCISES

**1.** What is the equation of the directrix in Fig. 17-10?      *Ans.* $\rho \cos \theta = -p$.

**2.** Sketch the curve whose equation is the following:

(a)   $\rho = \dfrac{10}{5 - \cos \theta} \cdot$        (b)   $\rho = \dfrac{4}{1 + \cos \theta} \cdot$

**Figure 17-14**

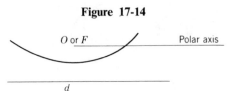

(c) $\rho = \dfrac{5}{3 + 2 \sin \theta}$.

(d) $\rho = \dfrac{4}{1 - 3 \cos \theta}$.

3. Find the equation of the ellipse with the following properties:
   (a) Eccentricity $\frac{2}{3}$ and directrix $\rho \cos \theta = -6$.    *Ans.* $\rho = 12/(3 - 2 \cos \theta)$.
   (b) Eccentricity $\frac{2}{3}$ and directrix $\rho \cos \theta = 6$.

4. Derive (9) under the conditions stated in the text.

5. Sketch the ellipse $\rho = 6/(2 - \cos \theta)$ and by relying on the sketch find the maximum and the minimum values of $\rho$.    *Ans.* Max. = 6, min. = 2.

6. In view of the results of Exercise 5, find the length of the major axis of the ellipse.

7. Sketch the ellipse $\rho = 6/(2 + \cos \theta)$ and answer the same questions as in Exercises 5 and 6.

8. Find the coordinates of the center of the ellipse $\rho = 6/(2 - \cos \theta)$.

9. Find the latus rectum of the ellipse $\rho = ep/(1 - e \cos \theta)$; that is, find the width of the ellipse at the focus.    *Ans.* $2ep$.

10. Find the latus rectum of the parabola $\rho = p/(1 - \cos \theta)$; that is, find the width of the parabola at the focus.    *Ans.* $2p$.

11. Show that the center $C$ of the ellipse $\rho = ep/(1 + e \cos \theta)$ has the coordinates $[e^2 p/(1 - e^2), -\pi]$.

12. Find the semimajor axis of the ellipse $\rho = ep/(1 - e \cos \theta)$. In coordinate geometry this quantity is usually denoted by $a$.    *Ans.* $a = ep/(1 - e^2)$.

13. According to Exercise 9 the latus rectum of the ellipse $\rho = ep/(1 - e \cos \theta)$ is $2ep$. In terms of the semimajor axis $a$ and the semiminor axis $b$, the latus rectum of an ellipse is $2b^2/a$. The value of $a$ was found in Exercise 12. Hence find the value of $b$ in terms of $e$ and $p$.    *Ans.* $b^2 = e^2 p^2/(1 - e^2)$.

14. Suppose that the polar axis is chosen so that it makes the angle $\alpha$ with the line from the focus perpendicular to the directrix (Fig. 17-15). Write the equation of the conic section (here pictured as an ellipse).

*Ans.* $\rho = ep/[1 + e \cos(\theta + \alpha)]$.

**Figure 17-15**

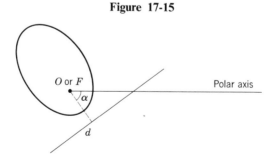

15. Show by use of rectangular coordinates that the focus-directrix definition of the ellipse agrees with the definition usually given in terms of the sum of the distance from two fixed points. That is, show that the focus-directrix definition leads to a second degree equation in $x$ and $y$ and so must be at least one of the conic sections. If you know how to translate axes, you can show that the section is an ellipse.

*Suggestion:* Choose rectangular axes as shown in Fig. 17-16.

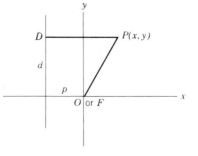

**Figure 17-16**

**16.** Show that if a chord of an ellipse is divided by a focus into two parts of lengths $r_1$ and $r_2$, then $(1/r_1) + (1/r_2) = 2/ep$.

**17.** The following equations do not necessarily represent conic sections. Obtain the curves of the equations by making a table of $(\rho, \theta)$-values and plotting the corresponding points. The names of some of these curves are indicated.
(a)   $\rho = 5 \sin 2\theta$ (four-leaved rose).     (g)   $\rho = a \sec \theta \pm b, b < a$
(b)   $r = \theta$ (Archimedean spiral).                       (conchoid of Nicomedes).
(c)   $\rho = 5(1 + \cos \theta)$ (cardioid).        (h)   $\rho = 5(1 - \cos \theta)$ (cardioid).
(d)   $\rho = 3(1 + \sin \theta)$.                      (i)   $\rho = 5 \cos 3\theta$ (three-leaved rose).
(e)   $\rho = 3(1 - \sin \theta)$ (cardioid).       (j)   $\rho = a \cos 2\theta$.
(f)   $\rho = 5 - 3 \cos \theta$ (limacon).         (k)   $\rho^2 = a^2 \sin 2\theta$ (lemniscate).
                                                      (l)   $\rho^2 = a^2 \cos 2\theta$ (lemniscate).

**4. *The Relation Between Rectangular and Polar Coordinates.*** We could pursue the subject of the polar coordinate equations of various curves and learn how to sketch quickly a variety of curves whose equations are given in polar coordinates. But we shall acquire some of this knowledge as we work with curves. There is, however, one more matter concerning the use of polar coordinates which should be taken up now. Suppose that a curve is given to us through the rectangular coordinate equation and that we wish to see if the polar coordinate equation of the curve is simpler for some purpose we may have in mind. We must know, then, how to obtain the polar coordinate equation from the rectangular one. Conversely, we might have the polar coordinate equation of a curve and might wish to find its rectangular coordinate equation. What we need, then, is a way to transform an equation from one coordinate system to the other.

A relation between rectangular and polar coordinates can be established, if we first agree on how the axes and origin of the rectangular system are to be fixed with respect to the pole and polar axis of the polar system. The most convenient correlation between the two coordinate systems is to have the origin at the pole and the positive half of the $x$-axis coinciding with the polar axis. Figures 17-17$a$ and 17-17$b$ presuppose this arrangement. Point $O$ is the origin of the rectangular system and the pole of the polar system. If we now consider a point $P$ in the first quadrant, it is at once apparent that

**(13)**                            $x = \rho \cos \theta$   and   $y = \rho \sin \theta$.

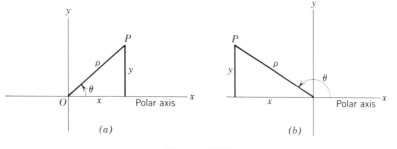

**Figure 17-17**

Fortunately, the relations in (13) hold also when point $P$ is in any of the four quadrants. Figure (17-17$b$) shows that this is so when $P$ is in the second quadrant, because cos $\theta$, by its very definition for second quadrant angles, is $x/\rho$ and sin $\theta$ likewise is $y/\rho$.

Equations (13) are useful in transforming from rectangular coordinates to polar coordinates. To transform from polar to rectangular coordinates, we have from Figs. 17-17$a$ and $b$ that

**(14)** $\qquad \rho = \sqrt{x^2 + y^2}, \qquad \sin \theta = \dfrac{y}{\sqrt{x^2 + y^2}}, \qquad \cos \theta = \dfrac{x}{\sqrt{x^2 + y^2}}.$

These equations also yield unique $\rho$- and $\theta$-values for a given $x$ and $y$ provided that we take $\rho$ to be positive and $0 \le \theta < 360°$. We have seen, however, that negative $\rho$-values may also be used to describe points in polar coordinates; in fact, the same point can be described by a positive $\rho$-value and a $\theta$-value or by a negative $\rho$-value and another $\theta$-value which may differ, for example, by 180° from the first one. If we do use

**(15)** $\qquad\qquad\qquad\qquad \rho = -\sqrt{x^2 + y^2},$

we must also use

**(16)** $\qquad \sin \theta = \dfrac{y}{-\sqrt{x^2 + y^2}} \qquad \text{and} \qquad \cos \theta = \dfrac{x}{-\sqrt{x^2 + y^2}}.$

Most often the use of positive $\rho$-values and therefore equations (14) suffice to transform from polar to rectangular coordinates.

Now let us see how the equations (13) to (16) can be used to transform the equation of a curve from one coordinate system to another. Consider the straight line $\theta = 30°$. To change this to rectangular coordinates, we can state first that tan $\theta = \sqrt{3}/3$ and then, by the latter two equations in (14), $y/x = \sqrt{3}/3$ or $y = \sqrt{3}\,x/3$.*

---

* Strictly speaking, $\theta = 30°$ represents the entire straight line only if we include positive and negative $\rho$-values. If we restrict ourselves to positive $\rho$-values, we must use $\theta = 30°$ and $\theta = 210°$ to describe the entire line. However, in both cases tan $\theta = \sqrt{3}/3$.

As a second illustration let us consider the circle with center at $(a, 0)$ and radius $a$. The rectangular coordinate equation of this circle is

$$(x - a)^2 + y^2 = a^2 \qquad \text{or} \qquad x^2 + y^2 - 2ax = 0.$$

If we use equations (13), we obtain $\rho^2 - 2a\rho \cos \theta = 0$ or $\rho = 2a \cos \theta$, which is the equation (4) obtained earlier in this chapter.

One must be careful, when transforming from polar to rectangular coordinates, to check the resulting equation. It may represent a larger locus than the original polar equation. Thus if we are asked to transform the line $\theta = 60°$ (as noted earlier, this is a line if we include positive and negative $\rho$-values), we might argue

$$\theta = 60°,$$

so that

$$\cos \theta = \frac{1}{2}.$$

Now using (14) we obtain

$$\frac{x}{\sqrt{x^2 + y^2}} = \frac{1}{2}.$$

This equation represents $\theta = 60°$ but for positive $\rho$-values only. If we simplify by squaring both sides we obtain

$$\frac{3}{4} x^2 = \frac{1}{4} y^2$$

or

$$\sqrt{3}\, x = \pm y.$$

This equation represents two full straight lines. The equation $\sqrt{3}\, x = y$ does represent the line $\theta = 60°$ (if we include positive and negative $\rho$ values). However, the equation $\sqrt{3}\, x = -y$ does not correspond to anything in the polar equation $\theta = 60°$ and is called extraneous. The operation of squaring is very likely to introduce extraneous loci.

## EXERCISES

1. Find the rectangular coordinate equations of the following:
   (a)  $\rho = 5 \cos \theta$.                                     *Ans.* $x^2 + y^2 - 5x = 0$.
   (b)  $\rho \cos \theta = 5$.
   (c)  $\rho^2 = a^2 \cos 2\theta$.              *Ans.* $x^4 + y^4 + x^2(y^2 - a^2) + y^2(x^2 + a^2) = 0$.

(d) $\rho = -4 \cos \theta$.

(e) $\rho \sin \theta = -4$. *Ans.* $y = -4$.

(f) $\rho = 5$.

(g) $\rho = 5 \sin 3\theta$.

(h) $\rho = \dfrac{2}{1 - \cos \theta}$. *Ans.* $y^2 = 4(x + 2)$.

(i) $\rho = \dfrac{6}{2 - \cos \theta}$.

(j) $\rho = \dfrac{6}{2 + \cos \theta}$. *Ans.* $\dfrac{(x + 2)^2}{16} + \dfrac{y^2}{12} = 1$.

2. Find the polar coordinate equations of the following:

(a) $x^2 + y^2 = 36$. *Ans.* $\rho = 6$.

(b) $x = 5$.

(c) $x + 2y = 7$.

$\qquad$ *Ans.* $\rho(\cos \theta + 2 \sin \theta) = 7$.

(d) $x^2 + y^2 - 8y = 0$.

(e) $(x - 2)^2 + (y - 3)^2 = 13$.

$\qquad$ *Ans.* $\rho = 4 \cos \theta + 6 \sin \theta$.

(f) $(x^2 + y^2)^2 = a^2(x^2 - y^2)$.

(g) $(x^2 + y^2)^3 = 4a^2x^2y^2$.

$\qquad$ *Ans.* $\rho = a \sin 2\theta$.

(h) $y^2 = 4x + 4$.

3. Change the equation $(x^2/a^2) + (y^2/b^2) = 1$ of the ellipse to polar coordinates. Does the result come under one of the standard forms of section 3? If not, why not?

4. Suppose that a point $P$ has the polar coordinates $(\rho, \theta)$ in a polar coordinate system and a new polar system is introduced whose pole coincides with the pole of the first system but whose polar axis makes the positive angle $\alpha$ with the polar axis of the first system. Let $(\rho', \theta')$ be the coordinates of $P$ with respect to the second system. What equations relate $(\rho', \theta')$ and $(\rho, \theta)$?

$\qquad$ *Ans.* $\rho' = \rho, \theta' = \theta - \alpha$.

## 5. The Derivative of a Polar Coordinate Function.

Let us now see how the calculus serves when functions are expressed in polar coordinates. Given a relation between $\rho$ and $\theta$, say $\rho = 4 \sin \theta$, we can, of course, ask for the instantaneous rate of change of $\rho$ with respect to $\theta$. The values of $\rho$ and $\theta$ are numbers, just as the values of $y$ and $x$ are in any of the functions considered earlier, and therefore the concept of the derivative applies at once. That is,

(17) $$\rho' = \frac{d\rho}{d\theta} = \lim_{\Delta\theta \to 0} \frac{\Delta\rho}{\Delta\theta}.$$

Physically, this meaning of the derivative depends entirely on what $\rho$ and $\theta$ mean physically. If $\theta$ should represent time values and $\rho$ distance along some straight line, then $\rho'$ is instantaneous velocity. In fact, the derivative and its physical meaning are independent of any choice of a coordinate system for plotting $\rho$ and $\theta$ and therefore of the curve representing the function. Even in the case of, say, $s = -16t^2 + 128t$, the physical meaning deals with straight-line motion and the derivative represents velocity; however, the curve, if we choose to plot the function in rectangular coordinates, is a parabola.

The *geometrical* meaning of the derivative is different in the polar coordinate representation from that in the rectangular coordinate system. Let us see why. To obtain the derivative we start with some value $\theta_0$ and the corresponding $\rho$-value, $\rho_0$. The $\theta_0$ and $\rho_0$ are the coordinates of a point, $P$ in Fig. 17-18. We now change the value of $\theta$ to $\theta_0 + \Delta\theta$ and, because $\rho$ is a function of $\theta$, $\rho$ changes to some value $\rho_0 + \Delta\rho$. These values, $(\theta_0 + \Delta\theta, \rho_0 + \Delta\rho)$, are the coordinates of point $Q$ in the figure. Of course, $P$ and $Q$ lie on the curve representing the function. If we draw the circle whose center is the pole $O$ and whose radius is $OP$, the circle cuts $OQ$ in $P'$, say. Then $P'Q = \Delta\rho$. The angle $POQ$ is $\Delta\theta$. To obtain a geometrical meaning for the derivative $\rho'$ we should find one for $\Delta\rho/\Delta\theta$ and then see what the latter becomes as $\Delta\theta$ approaches 0. However *geometrically* $\Delta\rho$ is a length and $\Delta\theta$ is an angle, and there seems to be no significant meaning for the ratio of these two quantities. Certainly, we cannot obtain the geometrical meaning for $\rho'$ that we obtained for $y'$ in rectangular coordinates; that is, $\rho'$ is *not* the slope of the curve at point $P$.

Before we answer the question of what the geometrical meaning of $\rho'$ may be, we would like to point out that some other results that we established when dealing with $y$ as a function of $x$ do hold for functions relating $\rho$ and $\theta$. Thus we gave conditions under which we can find relative maxima and minima of $y$. These conditions involved $y'$ and $y''$. This theory does apply to $\rho$ as a function of $\theta$. To be clear about this point, we must distinguish two approaches that we made to the theory of maxima and minima. In Chapter 8, Section 2, we gave geometrical arguments to show that if $y' = 0$ at some value $a$ of $x$ and if $y'$ changes from positive to negative as $x$ changes from values less than $a$ to values greater than $a$, then $y$ has a relative maximum at $x = a$. The geometrical arguments do *not* carry over to $\rho$ as a function of $\theta$ because we cannot interpret $\rho'$ as a slope. However, in Sections 3 and 4 of that chapter we gave *analytical* arguments for the very same conclusions about relative maxima and minima. These analytical arguments, which do *not* rely upon pictures, do apply to $\rho$ as a function of $\theta$. The arguments should be reviewed at this time.

**Figure 17-18**

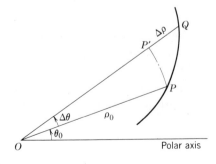

Thus we can conclude that $\rho$ has a relative maximum at $\theta = \theta_0$ if $\rho' = 0$ at $\theta = \theta_0$ and if $\rho'$ is positive for values of $\theta$ near but less than $\theta_0$ and if $\rho'$ is negative for values of $\theta$ near but greater than $\theta_0$. All of the results and tests for relative maxima and minima carry over to $\rho$ as a function of $\theta$.

## EXERCISES

1. Find $\rho'$ for the function $\rho' = ep/(1 - e \cos \theta)$.

          *Ans.* $\rho' = -e^2 p \sin \theta/(1 - e \cos \theta)^2$.

2. (a) For the ellipse $\rho = ep/(1 - e \cos \theta)$ with $e$ between 0 and 1, find the minimum value of $\rho$ and the maximum value of $\rho$.

      *Ans.* Min. $= ep/(1 + e)$, Max. $= ep/(1 - e)$.

  (b) Show geometrically where the minimum and maximum $\rho$-values lie on the ellipse and show the focus from which $\rho$ is measured.

3. For the ellipse in Exercise 2 show that $\rho$ decreases as $\theta$ varies from 0 to $\pi$.

4. In view of the result in Exercise 2, find the length of the major axis of the ellipse in question.        *Ans.* $2ep/(1 - e^2)$.

5. For the parabola $\rho = p/(1 - \cos \theta)$ show that $\rho$ has the minimum value $p/2$ at $\theta = \pi$.

6. For the parabola $\rho = p/(1 - \cos \theta)$ show that $\rho$ decreases as $\theta$ increases from 0 to $\pi$.

7. If $y$ is a function of $x$ and $x$ is the inverse function of $y$, we know that $dy/dx = 1/(dx/dy)$. What is the analogous statement for $\rho$ as a function of $\theta$ and does the analogous statement hold?

Let us return to the question of whether we can find some geometrical meaning for $\rho'$. We shall experiment a bit. We start again with a curve (Fig. 17-19) that represents $\rho$ as a function of $\theta$ and on which lie the points $P$ and $Q$ with coordinates $(\rho_0, \theta_0)$ and $(\rho_0 + \Delta\rho, \theta_0 + \Delta\theta)$, respectively. We draw the circle with center $O$ and radius $OP$ and thus obtain the point $P'$ on $OQ$. The arc $PP'$ has the length $\rho_0 \Delta\theta$ and $QP'$ has the length $\Delta\rho$.

Even though $PP'$ is an arc, let us speak of the triangle $PQP'$. This is a right triangle because the arc of a circle meets a radius at right angles. Then, for the angle $\alpha$, which is the angle between the radius vector to $Q$ and

**Figure 17-19**

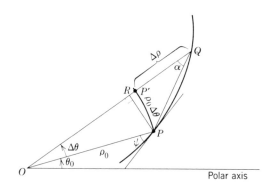

the secant $PQ$, we may say that

**(18)**
$$\cot \alpha = \frac{\Delta\rho}{\rho_0 \, \Delta\theta} = \frac{1}{\rho_0} \frac{\Delta\rho}{\Delta\theta} \, .$$

We now have an expression involving $\Delta\rho/\Delta\theta$ which is approximately correct and may become more accurate as $\Delta\theta$ approaches 0. As $\Delta\theta$ approaches 0, the secant $PQ$ approaches the tangent at $P$ and the radius vector $OQ$ approaches $OP$. Hence $\alpha$ approaches the angle $\psi$, the angle between the radius vector to $P$ and the tangent at $P$. Moreover, as $\Delta\theta$ approaches 0, the right side of (18) approaches $\rho'/\rho_0$, with $\rho'$ denoting the derivative at $(\rho_0, \theta)$. Hence, if the approximation that we made is reasonable in the sense that it yields the same limit as the exact quantity would, we have shown that

**(19)**
$$\cot \psi = \frac{\rho'}{\rho_0} = \frac{d\rho/d\theta}{\rho_0} \, ,$$

where $\psi$ is the angle between the radius vector to $P$ and the tangent at $P$. This result may be valuable because it tells us the angle which the tangent to the curve at $P$ makes with the radius vector to $P$.

The result (19) was obtained by making an approximation; namely, we regarded arc $PP'$ as part of a right triangle. Hence the result may or may not be correct. Let us see if we can establish it by a sounder argument. To obtain a right triangle containing $\alpha$ (Fig. 17-19), let us drop the perpendicular $PR$ from $P$ onto $OQ$. If we use triangle $PRQ$, we can say that

**(20)**
$$\cot \alpha = \frac{RQ}{PR} \, .$$

However,

$$RQ = OQ - OR = \rho_0 + \Delta\rho - \rho_0 \cos \Delta\theta$$

and

$$PR = \rho_0 \sin \Delta\theta.$$

If we substitute these results in (20), we have

$$\cot \alpha = \frac{\rho_0 + \Delta\rho - \rho_0 \cos \Delta\theta}{\rho_0 \sin \Delta\theta}$$

or

$$\cot \alpha = \frac{\rho_0(1 - \cos \Delta\theta) + \Delta\rho}{\rho_0 \sin \Delta\theta} \, .$$

Let us see if we can obtain the limit (19) from this expression for $\cot \alpha$. We divide numerator and denominator by $\Delta\theta$. Then

**(21)**
$$\cot\alpha = \frac{\rho_0 \dfrac{(1-\cos\Delta\theta)}{\Delta\theta} + \dfrac{\Delta\rho}{\Delta\theta}}{\rho_0 \dfrac{\sin\Delta\theta}{\Delta\theta}}.$$

Let us now consider what happens as $\Delta\theta$ approaches 0. We proved in Chapter 10, Section 3 that

$$\lim_{\Delta\theta\to 0}\frac{1-\cos\Delta\theta}{\Delta\theta} = 0 \quad\text{and}\quad \lim_{\Delta\theta\to 0}\frac{\sin\Delta\theta}{\Delta\theta} = 1.$$

Moreover, we do know from our earlier discussion that $\alpha$ approaches $\psi$ as $\Delta\theta$ approaches 0. Hence (21) yields

**(22)**
$$\cot\psi = \frac{\rho'}{\rho_0} = \frac{d\rho/d\theta}{\rho_0}.$$

Because this is true at any point $P$ on the curve, we may drop the subscript and write

$$\cot\psi = \frac{\rho'}{\rho}$$

or

**(23)**
$$\tan\psi = \frac{\rho}{\rho'} = \frac{\rho}{d\rho/d\theta}.$$

Thus we have obtained a geometrical interpretation of the derivative $\rho'$ coupled with $\rho$ as the *tangent of the angle between the radius vector and the tangent line at a point P on the curve.*

A few points should be noted in connection with (23). The first is that there are two angles between the radius vector and the tangent, one being the supplement of the other (Figs. 17-20a and 17-20b). We shall see that the angle that formula (23) gives is the counterclockwise angle from the radius $OP$ to the tangent at $P$. We suppose that we use positive $\rho$-values; moreover, if $\rho$ increases as $\theta$ does, then $\rho'$ is positive (or 0 in exceptional cases). Thus the right side of (23) is positive and $\psi$ must be acute. This is the

**Figure 17-20**

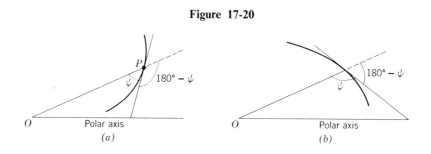

$O$  Polar axis  $(a)$  $O$  Polar axis  $(b)$

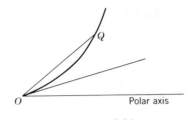

**Figure 17-21**

case in Fig. 17-20$a$. If $\rho$ decreases as $\theta$ increases, then $\rho'$ is negative (or 0 in exceptional cases), and so tan $\psi$ is negative and $\psi$ must be obtuse. Fig. 17-20$b$ shows this case.

The second point to note about (23) is that although the proof does not hold for a point $P$ at which $\rho = 0$, because triangle $OPQ$ of Fig. 17-19 does not exist in this case, the result does hold. For one can regard the radius vector (Fig. 17-21) at point $O$ as the limiting vector of the radius vector $OQ$ as $Q$ approaches $O$. But the tangent at $O$ is also the limiting position of $OQ$ as $Q$ approaches $O$. Hence one can regard the radius vector and the tangent as having the same direction at $O$, and therefore the angle $\psi$ between them is 0. This is what (23) gives when $\rho = 0$.

Our efforts to find a geometrical meaning for $\rho'$ have led to formula (23), which gives the angle between the radius vector and the tangent. However, one may want the slope of the tangent because, as we know from earlier applications, this slope is an important quantity. In Fig. 17-22$a$ we

**Figure 17-22**

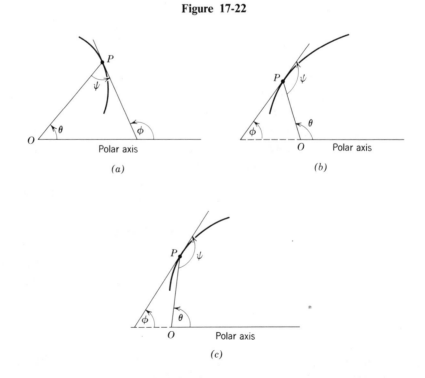

see that $\phi$ is the angle of inclination of the tangent with respect to the polar axis and that $\phi = \theta + \psi$. Then the slope of the tangent line is

**(24)** $$\tan \phi = \tan(\theta + \psi).$$

However, the relation $\phi = \theta + \psi$ does not always hold, as Figs. 17-22b and 17-22c show. In these figures $\theta = \phi + \pi - \psi$, and so $\phi = \theta + \psi - \pi$. But (24) holds in these cases also. Still other geometrical configurations do obtain, because $\theta$ can be arbitrarily large. However, (24) does hold in all cases.

This last statement is true even when the curve passes through the pole. Here $\psi = 0$, as we pointed out in connection with Fig. 17-21, and so $\phi = \theta$. The value of $\theta$ at point $O$ is that value (or values) for which $\rho = 0$, that is, it is the value (or values) of $\theta$ which, when substituted in the polar coordinate equation of the curve, yields $\rho = 0$.

Because (24) holds for the various possible relations among $\phi$, $\theta$, and $\psi$, we now have a method of finding the slope of a curve whose equation is given in polar coordinates. We have from (24), in view of a trigonometric identity, that

**(25)** $$\tan \phi = \frac{\tan \theta + \tan \psi}{1 - \tan \theta \tan \psi}.$$

If, therefore, we wish to find the slope of a curve at a given point whose $\theta$-value is known, we know $\tan \theta$ and by using (23) we have $\tan \psi$. Formula (25) then gives the slope.

**Example 1.** Find the angle between the radius vector and the tangent for the cardioid (Fig. 17-23) $\rho = 2 + \cos \theta$ at $\theta = \pi/4$.

**Figure 17-23**

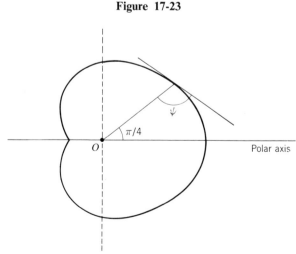

**Solution.**    Since $\psi$ is the angle we want and $\tan\psi = \rho/\rho'$, then

$$\tan\psi = \frac{2 + \cos\theta}{-\sin\theta}.$$

At $\theta = \pi/4$, $\cos\theta = \sqrt{2}/2$ and $\sin\theta = \sqrt{2}/2$. Hence

$$\tan\psi = -(2 + \sqrt{2}/2)/(\sqrt{2}/2) = -(4 + \sqrt{2})/\sqrt{2} = -(\sqrt{2}^{3} + 1).$$

**Example 2.** Find the slope of the curve $\rho = \sin 2\theta$ at $\theta = \pi/6$.

**Solution.**    The portion of the curve which lies in the first quadrant is shown in Fig. 17-24. We use (25). Since $\tan\psi = \rho/\rho' = \sin 2\theta/2\cos 2\theta = (\frac{1}{2})\tan 2\theta$, then at $\pi/6$, $\tan\psi = (\frac{1}{2})\tan\pi/3 = \dfrac{\sqrt{3}}{2}$. Also, $\tan\theta = \tan\pi/6 = 1/\sqrt{3}$. Hence

$$\tan\phi = \frac{\dfrac{1}{\sqrt{3}} + \dfrac{\sqrt{3}}{2}}{1 - \dfrac{1}{\sqrt{3}}\dfrac{\sqrt{3}}{2}} = \frac{2}{\sqrt{3}} + \sqrt{3}.$$

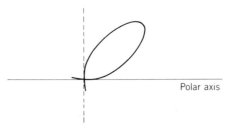

Polar axis

**Figure 17-24**

## EXERCISES

1.  Find the angle between the radius vector and the tangent at the point indicated for each of the following curves:

(a)  $\rho = 10$ at $(10, \pi/2)$.    *Ans.* $\pi/2$.    (c)  $\rho = \dfrac{6}{1 - \cos\theta}$ at $(4, 2\pi/3)$.

(b)  $\rho = a\sin\theta$ at $(a/2, \pi/6)$.

*Ans.* $5\pi/6$.

(d)  $\rho = \dfrac{6}{2 + \sin\theta}$ at $(2, \pi/2)$.

2.  Find the slope of $\rho = 10\cos\theta$ at $\theta = 30°$.    *Ans.* $-\sqrt{3}/3$.

3.  Find the slope of $\rho = 1 + \cos\theta$ at $\theta = \pi/3$.

4.  Find the slope of $\rho = a/\theta$ at $\theta = \pi/3$.

**5.** The curve $\rho = c e^{a\theta}$ is called an equiangular spiral (or logarithmic spiral), because the angle between the radius vector and the tangent is the same at all points on the curve. Prove this fact.

**6.** Prove the converse of the statement in Exercise 5.

**7.** Find the angle between the radius vector and the tangent for the curve $\rho = a(1 - \cos\theta)$ at $(a, \pi/2)$. Also find the angle of inclination of this tangent. Sketch the curve to see the correct relation among $\psi$, $\theta$, and $\phi$.

*Ans.* $\psi = \pi/4$; $\phi = 3\pi/4$.

**8.** Prove the reflection property for the parabola (cf. Chap. 4, Sect. 5); that is, prove that for the curve $\rho = p/(1 - \cos\theta)$ the radius vector $OP$ (or $FP$) and the horizontal line $PD$ make equal angles with the tangent at $P$, $P$ being any point on the curve (Fig. 17-25).

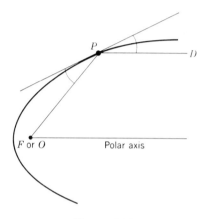

**Figure 17-25**

**9.** Given the ellipse $\rho = ep/(1 - e\cos\theta)$ with $0 < e < 1$, what would you expect $\psi$ to be at the end points of the major axis? Calculate $\psi$.

**10.** Show for any $\rho = f(\theta)$ that $\psi$ is $\pi/2$ at a maximum or minimum value of $\rho$.

**11.** Show that the length $d$ of the perpendicular from the pole to a tangent of $\rho = f(\theta)$ at a point $P$ is given by $\rho^2/\sqrt{\rho^2 + \rho'^2}$, where $\rho$ and $\rho'$ are the values at $P$.

## 6. Areas in Polar Coordinates.

One of the advantages of the polar coordinate representation of curves is that it may be used to find the areas of some regions far more easily than if the same area were described in terms of rectangular coordinates. The shape of areas that are most readily handled in polar coordinates is exemplified by that of $OPQ$ in Fig. 17-26; this region is bounded by the radii vectors $OP$ and $OQ$ and by the arc $PQ$ of some curve.

The procedure for setting up an integral that yields the area $OPQ$ is very much like that used for areas in rectangular coordinates. The independent variable here is $\theta$ and the domain over which it extends is from $\alpha$ to $\beta$; that is, $\theta = \alpha$ is the equation of $OP$ and $\theta = \beta$ is the equation of $OQ$. We divide the domain $\alpha \le \theta \le \beta$ into $n$ subintervals, which we may as well take to be equal. The values of $\theta$ that are selected to subdivide the domain

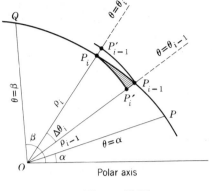

Figure 17-26

are $\theta_0 = \alpha, \theta_1, \theta_2 \cdots \theta_n = \beta$. A typical subinterval $\Delta\theta_i$, which is determined by the end values $\theta = \theta_{i-1}$ and $\theta = \theta_i$, is shown in Fig. 17-26. The equations $\theta = \theta_{i-1}$ and $\theta = \theta_i$ are also the equations of the radii vectors which along with the arc $P_{i-1}P_i$ bound the $i$th subregion $\Delta A_i$ into which the area $OPQ$ is subdivided.

If we could find a suitable expression for the area of these subregions, then by summing them we would have the area of the entire region $OPQ$. Unfortunately, we do not have an exact expression for the area of any one of these subregions. If, however, we draw a circle with $OP_i$ as radius and let $P_i'$ be the point at which the circle cuts $OP_{i-1}$, we have the circular sector $OP_iP_i'$, which is an approximation to $\Delta A_i$. The approximation fails to include the shaded area in $\Delta A_i$. Such circular sectors are analogous to the rectangles that we used to approximate the area under a curve when rectangular coordinates were involved.

The area of a circular sector (Fig. 17-27) of a circle of radius $r$ and central angle $\theta$ (in radians) is given by

**(26)**                                    $\tfrac{1}{2} r^2 \theta,$

for the area of the entire circle is $\pi r^2$ and the area of the sector is to the area of the entire circle as $\theta$ is to $2\pi$, if $\theta$ is expressed in radians. Then the area of the sector is

$$\frac{\theta}{2\pi} \cdot \pi r^2 = \tfrac{1}{2} r^2 \theta.$$

Figure 17-27

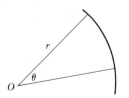

   If we apply (26) to express the area of the circular sector $OP_iP_i'$ we obtain

**(27)** $$\tfrac{1}{2}(OP_i)^2 \, \Delta\theta_i \quad \text{or} \quad \tfrac{1}{2}\rho_i^2 \, \Delta\theta_i$$

where $\rho_i$ is the $\rho$-value of $OP_i$. Then the sum of the $n$ approximating subregions is

**(28)** $$S_n = \tfrac{1}{2}\rho_1^2 \, \Delta\theta_1 + \tfrac{1}{2}\rho_2^2 \, \Delta\theta_2 + \cdots + \tfrac{1}{2}\rho_n^2 \, \Delta\theta_n.$$

It is intuitively clear that as $\Delta\theta$ approaches 0, the area of the circular sector $OP_iP_i'$ approaches the area $\Delta A_i$ of the $i$th subregion. Hence what we want is

$$\lim_{n \to \infty} S_n.$$

   We know from our work on the definite integral that this limit is given by

**(29)** $$A = \int_\alpha^\beta \tfrac{1}{2}\rho^2 \, d\theta$$

where $\rho$ is the function of $\theta$ which describes the curve $PQ$. Thus we have in (29) a formula for the area $OPQ$.

   Before we apply formula (29), we might satisfy ourselves that we were wise to use the circular sector $OP_iP_i'$ as the approximation to the subregion $\Delta A_i$. We did point out in Chapter 15, Section 7, that failure to use a proper approximating element can lead to the wrong result. We can assure ourselves of the correctness of our choice in several ways. Instead of using the sector $OP_iP_i'$ we might use the sector $OP_{i-1}P_{i-1}'$ (Fig. 17-26) determined by the radius vector $OP_{i-1}$. The area of this sector is

**(30)** $$\tfrac{1}{2}\rho_{i-1}^2 \, \Delta\theta_i$$

where $\rho_{i-1}$ is the length of $OP_{i-1}$. This circular sector is larger than the area $\Delta A_i$ because $\rho_{i-1}$ is the largest value of $\rho$ in $\Delta\theta_i$, whereas in (27) $\rho_i$ is the smallest $\rho$-value in $\Delta\theta_i$. In our study of the definite integral we found that

**Figure  17-28**

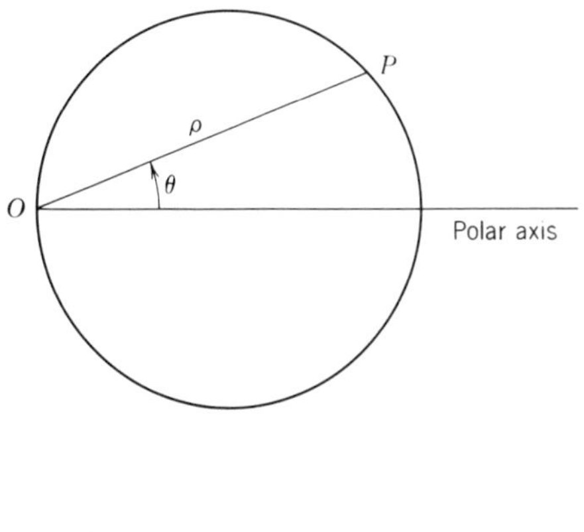

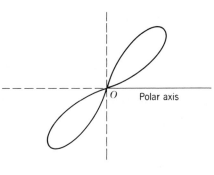

Polar axis

**Figure 17-29**

either choice will lead to the same definite integral. Because the true area lies between what we obtain by using the smallest $\rho$-value in each subinterval and the largest $\rho$-value and because both choices lead to the same definite integral, namely (29), the true area must also be given by this definite integral.

Let us now apply (29) and let us consider, first, finding the area of the circle $\rho = 10 \cos \theta$ shown in Fig. 17-28. To use formula (29), we must know the end values of the domain of $\theta$-values which belong to the area in question. The upper half of this curve is described as $\theta$ varies from 0 to $\pi/2$. The lower half can be obtained by letting $\theta$ run from $\pi/2$ to $\pi$ while $\rho$ takes on negative values. Alternatively, the lower half of the curve is described by letting $\theta$ vary from $-\pi/2$ to 0, while $\rho$ takes on positive values. Hence we can use either of the two integrals,

$$\int_0^{\pi} \tfrac{1}{2}(10 \cos \theta)^2 \, d\theta \quad \text{or} \quad \int_{-\pi/2}^{\pi/2} \tfrac{1}{2}(10 \cos \theta)^2 \, d\theta.$$

To evaluate either of these we, of course, use antidifferentiation. Both lead to the correct result, namely $25\pi$, for the radius of the circle is 5.

As a second example let us consider the curve whose equation is $\rho^2 = 4 \sin 2\theta$. This curve (Fig. 17-29) is called a lemniscate. Our problem is to find the area within the two loops. Actually, the two loops contain the same area; hence we shall find the area within the upper loop. We must determine the range of $\theta$-values which belong to points on this loop. These points are obtained as $\theta$ varies from 0 to $\pi/2$. Hence the area of this loop is

$$\tfrac{1}{2} \int_0^{\pi/2} 4 \sin 2\theta \, d\theta.$$

This area is readily obtained and proves to be 2. Hence the area of both loops is 4.

## EXERCISES

**1.** Find the area enclosed by the cardioid $\rho = a(1 - \sin \theta)$. The curve of this equation is shown in Fig. 17-30.                          *Ans.* $3\pi a^2/2$.

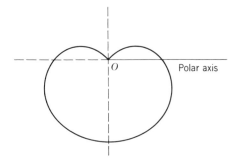

**Figure 17-30**

**2.** Find the area bounded by one loop of the lemniscate $\rho^2 = a \cos 2\theta$.

**3.** Find the area between the parabola $\rho = 8/(1 - \cos \theta)$ and its latus rectum.
*Ans.* 128/3.

**4.** Find the area between the parabola $\rho = 8/(1 + \cos \theta)$ and the vertical line through the pole. *Ans.* 128/3.

**5.** The curve $\rho = a\theta$ is called the spiral of Archimedes. Graph the curve and then find the area swept out by the radius vector in the following number of revolutions:

   (a)  One revolution. *Ans.* $4\pi^3 a^2/3$.

   (b)  Two revolutions.

Archimedes (287–212 B.C.) actually calculated these areas by using the Greek method of exhaustion and the same approximating elements that we used.

**6.** Find the area swept out by the radius vector of the equiangular spiral $\rho = ce^\theta$ in (a) one revolution, (b) two revolutions.

**7.** Find the area between the two circles $\rho = 2a \cos \theta$ and $\rho = a$.

$$Ans.\ (a^2/2)[(5\pi/3) - \sqrt{3}\,].$$

**8.** Criticize the following argument. Suppose that $A$ and $B$ are two concentric circular areas and that the radius of $B$ is twice the radius of $A$. The area of $A$ is the sum of its radii and the same is true of $B$. Because the radii of $B$ are twice as long as the radii of $A$, the area of $B$ is twice the area of $A$.

**7. *Arc Length in Polar Coordinates.*** Just as it may be more convenient to use polar coordinates to find some areas bounded entirely or in part by curves, so it is to find arc lengths of some curves. Our first task is to find the proper expression for arc length in the polar coordinate representation. Suppose that we have the arc $APQB$ of a curve (Fig. 17-31) and that we wish to find the length of this arc.

    Our method of obtaining arc length is to find the sum of inscribed chords and then let the number of these chords become infinite while each approaches zero in size (Chap. 15, Sect. 4). Let $PQ$ in Fig. 17-31 be a typical chord. We should now try to find an expression for it in terms of $\rho$ and $\theta$. Suppose that, as in our treatment of area, we draw a circle with $OP$ as radius. This circle cuts $OQ$ in $P'$. Now the figure $PP'Q$ is almost a right triangle. Certainly, the arc $PP'$ cuts the radius $OP'$ at right angles but, of course, the arc $PP'$ is not a line segment. Nevertheless, let us suppose for a moment that it is; for small $\Delta\theta$, the arc $PP'$ and the chord $PP'$ will not

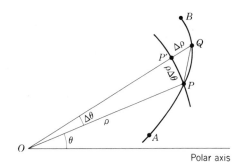

**Figure 17-31**

differ very much. Then we can apply the Pythagorean theorem to triangle $PP'Q$ and assert that

$$PQ^2 = (\rho \, \Delta\theta)^2 + (\Delta\rho)^2$$

or

**(31)**
$$PQ = \sqrt{\rho^2 + \frac{\Delta\rho^2}{\Delta\theta}} \; \Delta\theta.$$

We may now apply the same theorem that we used in the treatment of arc length in rectangular coordinates, namely, the theorem of the mean. According to this theorem

$$\frac{\Delta\rho}{\Delta\theta} = \rho'_i$$

where $\rho'_i$ is the derivative of $\rho$ as a function of $\theta$ taken at some value of $\theta$ in the interval $\Delta\theta$. Then

**(32)**
$$PQ = \sqrt{\rho^2 + \rho'^2_i} \; \Delta\theta.$$

We now have an expression for the chord $PQ$. According to our method of obtaining arc length, we form a sum $S_n$ of such chords and then let $\Delta\theta$ approach 0 so that each chord approaches 0 in length while the number of chords required to fill out the arc from $A$ to $B$ becomes infinite. The arc length from $A$ to $B$ is given by

$$\lim_{n \to \infty} S_n;$$

this limit is expressed by a definite integral, namely,

**(33)**
$$\text{arc length } AB = \int_\alpha^\beta \sqrt{\rho^2 + \rho'^2} \; d\theta$$

where $\alpha$ and $\beta$ are the values of $\theta$ at $A$ and $B$, respectively and $\rho' = d\rho/d\theta$.

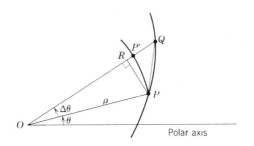

**Figure 17-32**

The derivation of (33) was based on an approximation; we took triangle $QPP'$ in Fig. 17-31 to be a right triangle even though $PP'$ is an arc of a circle. Let us now see if a more accurate approach will yield the same result. Suppose that (Fig. 17-32) we drop a perpendicular from $P$ onto $OQ$ and now actually have a right triangle $PQR$. Then

**(34)** $$\overline{PQ}^2 = \overline{PR}^2 + \overline{QR}^2.$$

We see from the figure that

$$PR = \rho \sin \Delta\theta$$

and

$$QR = QO - RO = \rho + \Delta\rho - \rho \cos \Delta\theta.$$

If we substitute these values in (34), we obtain

$$\overline{PQ}^2 = \rho^2 \sin^2 \Delta\theta + \{(\rho + \Delta\rho) - (\rho \cos \Delta\theta)\}^2.$$

Then, by expanding the binomial in which $\rho + \Delta\rho$ is treated as a single term,

$$\overline{PQ}^2 = \rho^2 \sin^2 \Delta\theta + (\rho + \Delta\rho)^2 - 2\rho(\rho + \Delta\rho)\cos \Delta\theta + \rho^2 \cos^2 \Delta\theta.$$

The first and last terms on the right side amount to just $\rho^2$. Hence, after further squaring and multiplying, we obtain

$$\overline{PQ}^2 = \rho^2 + \rho^2 + 2\rho\,\Delta\rho + (\Delta\rho)^2 - 2\rho^2 \cos \Delta\theta - 2\rho\,\Delta\rho \cos \Delta\theta$$

or

$$\overline{PQ}^2 = 2\rho^2(1 - \cos \Delta\theta) + 2\rho\,\Delta\rho(1 - \cos \Delta\theta) + (\Delta\rho)^2$$

or

**(35)** $$PQ = \left\{ 2\rho^2(1 - \cos \Delta\theta) + 2\rho\,\Delta\rho(1 - \cos \Delta\theta) + (\Delta\rho)^2 \right\}^{1/2}.$$

We would like to put this result for the element of arc in the form of a function of $\theta$ times $\Delta\theta$ so that we could see what the sum of the elements and the limit of this sum should be; that is, we should look for something of the form (32) and, in fact, we hope to show that (32) is correct. Let us multiply the right side of (35) by $\Delta\theta$ and divide inside the square root by $(\Delta\theta)^2$. Then

(36) $\quad PQ = \left\{ 2\rho^2 \frac{(1 - \cos \Delta\theta)}{(\Delta\theta)^2} + 2\rho \frac{\Delta\rho}{\Delta\theta} \frac{(1 - \cos \Delta\theta)}{\Delta\theta} + \left( \frac{\Delta\rho}{\Delta\theta} \right)^2 \right\}^{1/2} \Delta\theta.$

The use of the mean value theorem enables us to replace the third term on the right by $\rho'^2_i$, as we did in obtaining (32). As for the second term on the right, the factor $\Delta\rho/\Delta\theta$ may likewise be replaced by $\rho'_i$. However, the fraction $(1 - \cos \Delta\theta)/\Delta\theta$ approaches 0 as $\Delta\theta$ does, and so the whole term does. We found in Chapter 15, Section 7, that we can neglect in a summation process any term which (apart from $\Delta\theta$) approaches 0. Hence we shall ignore this second term. There remains the term

$$2\rho^2 \frac{(1 - \cos \Delta\theta)}{(\Delta\theta)^2} \, .$$

If the denominator were $\Delta\theta$, this term too would approach 0 when $\Delta\theta$ does and we could ignore it. However, the denominator is $(\Delta\theta)^2$. Let us use the trigonometric identity

$$1 - \cos \theta = 2 \sin^2 \frac{\theta}{2} \, .$$

Then

$$2\rho^2 \frac{(1 - \cos \Delta\theta)}{(\Delta\theta)^2} = \frac{4\rho^2 \sin^2 \frac{\Delta\theta}{2}}{(\Delta\theta)^2} = \rho^2 \frac{\sin^2 \frac{\Delta\theta}{2}}{\left( \frac{\Delta\theta}{2} \right)^2}$$

$$= \rho^2 \frac{\sin \frac{\Delta\theta}{2}}{\frac{\Delta\theta}{2}} \frac{\sin \frac{\Delta\theta}{2}}{\frac{\Delta\theta}{2}} \, .$$

We may replace this term by $\rho^2$ because the difference

$$\rho^2 - \rho^2 \frac{\sin \frac{\Delta\theta}{2}}{\frac{\Delta\theta}{2}} \frac{\sin \frac{\Delta\theta}{2}}{\frac{\Delta\theta}{2}}$$

approaches 0 as $\Delta\theta$ approaches 0, and we found in Chapter 15, Section 7, that if a term of the summation (apart from the factor $\Delta\theta$ itself) approaches 0, it does not contribute to the limit of the sum.

The substance, then, of our consideration of three terms on the right side of (36) is that we may replace this right side by

**(37)** $$PQ = \sqrt{\rho^2 + \rho_i'^2}\, \Delta\theta.$$

We see that we are at the same point as (32), and thus (33) is correct.*

**Example.**   Find the length of one turn of the spiral $\rho = e^\theta$ (Fig. 17-33).

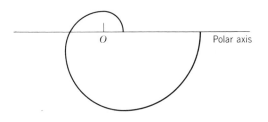

$O$        Polar axis

**Figure  17-33**

**Solution.**   One turn of the spiral means that portion of the curve which is described by $\theta$ running from 0 to $2\pi$. By (33)

$$\text{arc length } s = \int_0^{2\pi} \sqrt{\rho^2 + \left(\frac{d\rho}{d\theta}\right)^2}\, d\theta.$$

Then for $\rho = e^\theta$,

$$s = \int_0^{2\pi} \sqrt{e^{2\theta} + e^{2\theta}}\, d\theta = \int_0^{2\pi} \sqrt{2}\, e^\theta\, d\theta$$

$$= \sqrt{2}\, (e^{2\pi} - 1).$$

# EXERCISES

**1.** Find by use of (33) the following:
   (a)   The circumference of the circle $\rho = a$.
   (b)   The circumference of the circle $\rho = 2a \sin \theta$.                    *Ans.* $2\pi a$.
   (c)   The length of arc of the parabola $\rho = p/(1 - \cos \theta)$ from $\theta = \pi/6$ to $\pi$.
   (d)   The length of arc of $\rho = e^{a\theta}$ from $\theta = 0$ to $\theta = 2\pi$.

                                                   *Ans.* $\sqrt{1 + a^2}\,(e^{2\pi a} - 1)/a$.
   (e)   The length of arc of $\rho = a\theta^2$ from $\theta = 0$ to $\theta = \pi$.
**2.** Find the length of the cardioid $\rho = a(1 - \cos \theta)$. See Fig. 17-34.        *Ans.* $8a$.

*There is still a point to be disposed of. In both (32) and (37) $\rho$ and $\rho_i'$ are not taken at the same value of $\theta$ in the interval $\Delta\theta$. However, we know from the discussion in Chapter 15, Section 7 that this fact does not matter.

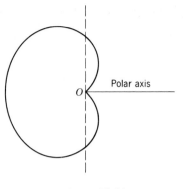

**Figure 17-34**

3. Show that the length of arc of the equiangular spiral $\rho = ce^{a\theta}$ between any two values of $\theta$ is proportional to the increase in the radius vector between those two values of $\theta$.

4. Show that at any point $P$ of a curve whose equation is expressed in polar coordinates, $ds/d\theta = \rho^2/d$ where $d$ is the perpendicular distance from the pole to the tangent at $P$.

5. Find the length of the complete curve $\rho = a \sin^3(\theta/3)$. *Ans.* $3\pi a/2$.

**8. Curvature in Polar Coordinates.** In Section 5 of Chapter 15 we introduced the notion of the curvature of a curve and we found a formula for that curvature when the curve is expressed in a rectangular coordinate equation. Let us now derive the formula for curvature when the curve is represented by a polar coordinate equation.

If $s$ is the arc length measured from some fixed point on a curve (Fig. 17-35) to any point $P$ and if $\phi$ is the angle of inclination of the tangent to the curve at $P$ then, by definition (Chap. 15, Sect. 5), the curvature

**(38)** $$K = \frac{d\phi}{ds}.$$

We should then start with some expression for $\phi$ and calculate $d\phi/ds$. We

**Figure 17-35**

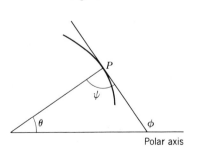

did find in Section 5 that*

$$\phi = \theta + \psi,$$

or where this relation does not hold, that

$$\phi = \theta + \psi - \pi.$$

In either case

**(39)** $$K = \frac{d\phi}{ds} = \frac{d\theta}{ds} + \frac{d\psi}{ds}.$$

To calculate $d\theta/ds$ we need but to recall that the indefinite integral for arc length [see (33)] is

$$s = \int \sqrt{\rho^2 + \rho'^2} \, d\theta$$

so that

$$\frac{ds}{d\theta} = \sqrt{\rho^2 + \rho'^2}$$

and by the theorem on inverse functions

**(40)** $$\frac{d\theta}{ds} = \frac{1}{\sqrt{\rho^2 + \rho'^2}}.$$

We have one of the two quantities that we need in (39). To calculate the second quantity, we first ask ourselves, what formula do we know for $\psi$? We know that

$$\tan \psi = \frac{\rho}{\rho'}$$

or

**(41)** $$\psi = \tan^{-1} \frac{\rho}{\rho'}.$$

This formula really gives us $\psi$ as a function of $\theta$ because $\rho$ and $\rho'$ are functions of $\theta$. However, the chain rule tells us that

**(42)** $$\frac{d\psi}{ds} = \frac{d\psi}{d\theta} \frac{d\theta}{ds}.$$

*The convention adopted in Chapter 15 on the choice of $\phi$-values applies here too.

In view of (40), all we need now is $d\psi/d\theta$. From (41) we have

$$\frac{d\psi}{d\theta} = \frac{1}{1 + \left(\dfrac{\rho}{\rho'}\right)^2} \frac{d}{d\theta}\left(\frac{\rho}{\rho'}\right)$$

$$= \frac{\rho'^2}{\rho'^2 + \rho^2} \frac{\rho'^2 - \rho\rho''}{\rho'^2}$$

so that

(43) $$\frac{d\psi}{d\theta} = \frac{\rho'^2 - \rho\rho''}{\rho'^2 + \rho^2}.$$

Now, by (42) and (40)

(44) $$\frac{d\psi}{ds} = \frac{\rho'^2 - \rho\rho''}{(\rho'^2 + \rho^2)^{3/2}}.$$

We have but to use (40) and (44) in (39). Thus

$$K = \frac{d\phi}{ds} = \frac{1}{(\rho^2 + \rho'^2)^{1/2}} + \frac{\rho'^2 - \rho\rho''}{(\rho'^2 + \rho^2)^{3/2}}$$

or by adding fractions

(45) $$K = \frac{\rho^2 + 2\rho'^2 - \rho\rho''}{(\rho^2 + \rho'^2)^{3/2}}.$$

This quantity can be positive or negative, but we are usually interested in its magnitude, and so we shall not bother with the matter of signs.

## EXERCISES

1. Find the curvature of the following:
   (a) The circle $\rho = a$.
   (b) The circle $\rho = a \sin\theta$.                                    *Ans.* $2/a$.
   (c) The equiangular spiral $\rho = ce^{a\theta}$.          *Ans.* $1/c\sqrt{1 + a^2}\, e^{a\theta}$.
   (d) The parabola $\rho = p/(1 - \cos\theta)$.
   (e) The spiral of Archimedes $\rho = a\theta$.            *Ans.* $(\theta^2 + 2)/a\sqrt{\theta^2 + 1}$.
   (f) The lemniscate $\rho^2 = 4\sin 2\theta$.
2. Use the result of 1(d) to show that the curvature of a parabola is a maximum at its vertex.
3. Use the result of 1(c) to show that the radius of curvature at any point of the equiangular spiral is proportional to $\rho$.
4. Show that the curvature of the cardioid $\rho = a(1 - \cos\theta)$ is $3/4a \sin(\theta/2)$.
5. Show that the curvature of the ellipse $\rho = ep/(1 - e\cos\theta)$ with $0 < e < 1$ is a maximum at either end of the major axis.

# CHAPTER EIGHTEEN
# RECTANGULAR PARAMETRIC EQUATIONS AND CURVILINEAR MOTION

**1. Introduction.** The path of a projectile shot from a cannon, the paths of the planets around the sun, and the path of a ball thrown from one boy to another are examples of curvilinear motion. If, in studying such motions, we were concerned only with the shapes of these paths, we could be content to describe them geometrically or by an equation involving two variables $x$ and $y$. We have, in fact, described such curves—for example, the ellipse—by a geometrical definition and by an algebraic equation. However, the study of motion along curves requires more than either of these representations provides. An equation in $x$ and $y$ that describes the curve itself does not tell us when the moving object is at each point on the curve. Furthermore, we cannot use the equation to calculate such important quantities as the velocity and the acceleration of the moving object at any time. What we seem to need is some relation involving the two coordinates of position, the usual $x$ and $y$, and the time $t$. We shall, therefore, look into a new algebraic scheme for representing curves that will enable us to study motion along these curves.

Some suggestion of how to go about finding the kind of equation or equations involving $x$, $y$, and $t$ may be obtained from our earlier study of rectilinear motion. When an object falls straight down, or is shot straight up and thus moves up and then down, a single function involving $y$ and $t$, that is, height above the ground and time, enables us to describe and study the motion. However, when an object moves along a curve (Fig. 18-1), two coordinates, $x$ and $y$, are needed to describe its position alone, Moreover, both $x$ and $y$ vary with the time $t$. Hence it appears that we need two functions, one relating $y$ and $t$ and the other relating $x$ and $t$, to describe the motion. A clear indication of the kind of functions that we should look for is given by a rather common experience.

Suppose that a person stands on the top of a tall building or cliff and throws a ball straight out horizontally. If there were no gravitational force, the ball would continue to move in the horizontal direction with a constant

**549**

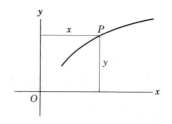

**Figure 18-1**

speed—the speed given to the ball by the hand. This behavior is in accordance with Newton's first law of motion which states that if an object is in motion and if no force acts on it, the object will move at a constant speed in a straight line. Of course, the force of gravity does act on the ball, and this force pulls the ball straight down. What does this fact imply about the horizontal motion? Does it cease when gravity starts to act, that is, as soon as the ball is released from the hand? Apparently not, for if the horizontal motion were abolished by the action of gravity, the ball would travel straight down. What seems to happen is that the ball continues to move horizontally as though there were no gravity and, while doing this, it falls downward under the action of gravity as though there were no horizontal motion. Thus to arrive at the point $A$ of Fig. 18-2 the ball actually travels along the arc $OA$; one can think of it, however, as having moved horizontally the distance $OD$ and, simultaneously, the vertical distance $DA$. Moreover, at any time $t$ after the throw of the ball, the horizontal distance that the ball covers from the starting point is precisely the same as if there had been no gravity and the ball had moved horizontally with the velocity given to it by the hand. And the vertical distance that the ball covers in the same time $t$ is the distance it would have fallen straight down if only gravity had acted from the instant the ball is released at point $O$.

The fact that the curvilinear motion can be regarded as a combination of the horizontal and the vertical motions, each taking place *independently* of the other, can be demonstrated experimentally. If one ball is projected horizontally from a table with some initial speed and another is dropped from the height of the table at the instant the first ball clears the table, the two balls will hit the ground at the same instant. Thus the vertical motions

**Figure 18-2**

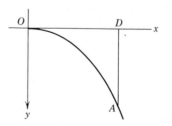

are the same even though the first ball moves out and down. Moreover, if the first ball is projected horizontally with a greater speed, it will travel along a wider arc, that is, it will travel farther horizontally before hitting the ground, but it will still reach the ground in precisely the same time as the ball that falls straight down. The horizontal motion does not detract from the vertical motion, nor does the latter interfere with the horizontal motion. The motion of the ball regarded as a combination of the horizontal and the vertical motions illustrates a principle of motion which is due to Galileo and which is known as the principle of independence of motions.*

**2. The Parametric Equations of a Curve.** Because it is true physically that the horizontal motion and the vertical motion of an object moving along a curved path can be regarded as taking place independently, a possible scheme for involving $x$, $y$, and $t$ in some physically significant equations is to study the horizontal motion separately and the vertical motion separately. Let us consider again a ball thrown out horizontally with a velocity of 20 ft/sec from the top $O$ of a cliff (Fig. 18-3). Since this horizontal motion takes place independently of the vertical motion and since no acceleration or velocity other than the 20 ft/sec enters into the *horizontal* motion, Newton's first law of motion tells us that the ball will travel out indefinitely at the velocity of 20 ft/sec. Then the horizontal distance $x$ that the ball will travel in $t$ seconds is given by

**(1)**                                           $$x = 20t.$$

Now let us consider the vertical motion. If the resistance of the air is ignored the only force causing vertical motion is gravity, and we know that this gives objects (near the earth) a downward acceleration of 32 ft/sec². It is convenient to take the downward direction as positive, and so the acceleration will be positive. We know, then, that the ball will fall downward a distance of $16t^2$ feet in $t$ seconds. Hence

**(2)**                                           $$y = 16t^2$$

describes the downward motion.

The two equations or functions (1) and (2) taken together describe the motion of the ball. They are called the *rectangular parametric equations* of the motion or of the curve along which the motion takes place. The variable $t$ is called the parameter; the word parameter merely expresses the fact that the usual variables $x$ and $y$ in the equation of a curve are expressed in terms of this third, subordinate variable $t$.

Before we attempt to utilize parametric equations in some real problems, let us be clear about how they represent the motion of the ball and the curve along which the ball moves. First, given any value of $t$, that is, the number of seconds the ball is in motion from the instant it was thrown out,

---

*Students familiar with mechanics will recognize that the principle of independence of motions is incorporated in the fact that Newton's second law of motion is a vector law. Each component of the force produces its own acceleration in the direction of that component.

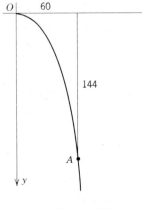

**Figure 18-3**

we can substitute this value in (1) and (2) and calculate the $x$- and $y$-values of the ball's position. Thus, when $t = 3$, $x = 60$ and $y = 144$. Point $A$ on the curve of Fig. 18-3, whose $x$-value is 60 and whose $y$-value is 144, is the position of the ball at $t = 3$. Likewise for any other value of $t$ we can calculate the $x$ and $y$ of the ball's position.

To obtain a good sketch of the curve, we calculate the $x$- and $y$-values corresponding to a number of $t$-values. This can be done systematically by making a table. Although negative values of $t$ have no physical meaning in the situation represented by (1) and (2), the mathematical curve represented by these equations does have points on it corresponding to negative values of $t$. Hence the following table includes such values too.

| $t$ | 0 | 1 | 2 | 3 | 4 | $\cdots$ | $-1$ | $-2$ | $\cdots$ |
|---|---|---|---|---|---|---|---|---|---|
| $x$ | 0 | 20 | 40 | 60 | 80 | $\cdots$ | $-20$ | $-40$ | $\cdots$ |
| $y$ | 0 | 16 | 64 | 144 | 256 | $\cdots$ | 16 | 64 | $\cdots$ |

To plot the curve we take from this table only the $x$- and $y$-values of the various points on the curve. The $t$-values *play no role in plotting the graph.* Thus $x = 20$ and $y = 16$ are the coordinates of one point on the curve, $x = 40$ and $y = 64$ are the coordinates of a second point, and so on. When these points are plotted in the usual way we obtain the curve (Fig. 18-4) represented by the parametric equations (1) and (2).

From the mathematical standpoint we have in the two equations,

**(3)** $$x = 20t, \quad y = 16t^2,$$

a new scheme for representing curves by equations or functions. This scheme does call for two equations rather than one equation involving only $x$ and $y$, and therefore, as far as representing curves algebraically is concerned, the new scheme seems to be more complicated than the old one. However, the parametric equations (3) tell us how $x$ and $y$ vary with time,

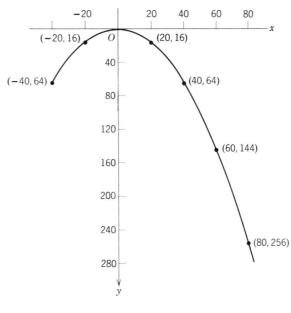

**Figure 18-4**

whereas the old scheme does not, and we shall soon see how important this knowledge is in the study of motion. Moreover, apart from the advantages of the parametric equations in studying motion, we shall find that the study of the purely geometric properties of some curves is best conducted by using parametric equations.

When the parametric equations are simple, it is possible to obtain from them the usual relation between $x$ and $y$ that represents the very same curve. We note in (3) that the $x$ and $y$ that determine any point on the curve correspond to the same $t$-value. Hence, if we take the value of $t$ from one of the equations and substitute it in the other, we obtain the relation between $x$ and $y$. Thus from the first of equations (3) we have

$$t = \frac{x}{20}.$$

If we substitute this value of $t$ in the second equation (2), we obtain

**(4)**
$$y = \frac{x^2}{25}.$$

Equation (4) represents the same curve as do the two parametric equations in (3). We shall call (4) the *direct* relation between $x$ and $y$. Once we have the direct relation, we can, of course, plot the curve by the familiar method of calculating corresponding $x$- and $y$-values and plotting the points. In the case of (4), we recognize from prior work that the curve is a parabola and since the positive $y$-axis is directed downward, the curve opens downward. The ball travels along the right-hand arc of the parabola.

Though it is often possible to obtain the direct equation from the parametric equation one must be careful to check whether the two representations are coextensive. The following example will illustrate the point.

**Example.**   Find the direct equation of the curve represented by

$$x = 3 \cos^2 t, \qquad y = 2 \sin^2 t.$$

**Solution.**   The easiest way to obtain the direct relation is to note that

$$\frac{x}{3} = \cos^2 t \quad \text{and} \quad \frac{y}{2} = \sin^2 t.$$

If we now add the two equations and use the fact that $\sin^2 t + \cos^2 t = 1$, we have

$$\frac{x}{3} + \frac{y}{2} = 1.$$

This is the equation of a straight line. However, the parametric equations represent only positive values of $x$ and $y$. Hence they represent only a segment of the full straight line.

## EXERCISES

1. In the following exercises draw the curve by working with the parametric equations. Then find the direct relation between $x$ and $y$.
   (a)   $x = 2t + 1, y = 1 - t.$                      *Ans.* $y = (3 - x)/2.$
   (b)   $x = t^2, y = 2t.$
   (c)   $x = 2 \sin t, y = 2 \cos t.$                  *Ans.* $x^2 + y^2 = 4.$
   (d)   $x = t^2, y = t^2 - 5t.$
   (e)   $x = e^t, y = e^{-t}.$
         *Suggestion:* Use the $e$-table.                *Ans.* $y = 1/x, x > 0.$
   (f)   $x = \cos t, y = 2 \sin t.$
   (g)   $x = \cos^2 \pi t, y = \sin^2 \pi t.$          *Ans.* $x + y = 1, x > 0, y > 0.$
   (h)   $x = \sin t, y = \sin t.$
   (i)   $x = e^t, y = e^t.$

2. Suppose that an object is thrown out horizontally with a velocity of 50 ft/sec from the top of a cliff 300 feet high. Choose the origin and axes as in Fig. 18-4 and answer the following questions:
   (a)   What are the parametric equations of the motion?
                                                         *Ans.* $x = 50t, y = 16t^2.$
   (b)   Where is the object after three seconds of motion?
   (c)   How long does it take the object to reach the ground?   *Ans.* $\frac{5}{2}\sqrt{3}$ sec.
   (d)   How far out horizontally from the starting point has the object traveled by the time it strikes the ground?

3. Suppose that the conditions of Exercise 2 are changed in just one respect, namely, the horizontal velocity of the object is 100 ft/sec instead of 50 ft/sec. Which of the answers to the four questions raised in Exercise 2 remains the same?                                                        *Ans. (c).*

4. A gun is fired horizontally from point $O$ (Fig. 18-5) with an initial velocity of $V$ ft/sec. At the same instant that the gun is fired an apple is released from point $P$ which is $x_1$ feet from $O$ and on the same level. Show that the bullet must hit the apple.

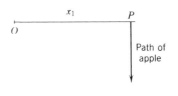

**Figure 18-5**

**5.** Construct the graph of the parametric equations $x = 2 \sin^2 \theta$ and $y = 2 \cos^2 \theta$.

**6.** A ball is thrown out horizontally with a velocity $V$ from the top of a building standing on a horizontal plane. At the same instant another ball is dropped from the top. Show that both reach the ground at the same time.

**7.** The motion of an object released by an airplane is given by the equations $x = Vt, y = h - 16t^2$. These equations presume that the $x$-axis is horizontal and the $y$-axis is directed upward and measured from the ground. Find the following:
 (a) The direct equation of the path.    *Ans.* $y = h - 16(x^2/V^2)$.
 (b) The range, that is, the horizontal distance traveled by the object.
    *Ans.* $(V/4)\sqrt{h}$ .
 (c) In view of the answer to part (b), which factor is more important in increasing the range—the height $h$ from which the object is released or the initial velocity $V$?

**8.** A bomber is flying horizontally at a constant velocity of 240 mi/hr (352 ft/sec), at an elevation of 10,000 feet, and so as to pass over a target on the ground. To hit the target a bomb must be released before the plane is above the target. At what angle of sight, the angle between the vertical and the line of sight to the target, should the bomb be released?    *Ans.* $41° 21'$.

### 3. *Some Additional Examples of Parametric Equations.*

In Section 2 we saw that parametric equations can be used to represent the motion of an object that is thrown out horizontally from the top of a cliff. In later sections we shall again see that we can study various motions effectively by calling upon the parametric representation. However, the value of this representation is not limited to problems of motion. Indeed, we should see that the study of curves generally, whether directed to purely geometrical properties or to physical properties, can be expedited by the use of parametric equations. Let us, therefore, look into a few other examples of parametric equations.

An important curve in applications is the cycloid. This curve is defined as the path traced by any given point on a circle as the circle rolls along a straight line. Thus, if the circle $C$ of Fig. 18-6 rolls along the straight line $L$, point $P$ on the circle which is originally at the bottom of the circle describes a cycloid. The figure shows the curve generated when $P$ has returned to the bottom position of the rolling circle. Actually, the curve extends to the right and left where its shape repeats the portion shown. The arc generated by one complete rotation of $C$ is called a complete arc or an arch of the cycloid. The rolling circle is also called the generating circle.

Let us find the parametric equations of the cycloid. We choose the origin of our coordinate system (Fig. 18-7) to be the location of point $P$

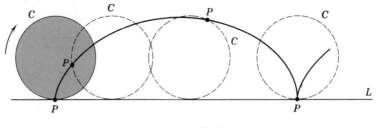

**Figure 18-6**

when it is at the lowest point, that is, when it is on the line $L$, and we choose the $x$-axis along $L$. Suppose that the circle of radius $R$ has rolled to the position shown in the figure. Then the arc $PT$ must equal $OT$, because the circle has rolled along the $x$-axis from the position where $P$ was at $O$ to the position in the figure. We let $\theta$ denote the angle (taken positive) between $CP$ and $CT$, where $C$ is the center of the rolling circle. Then $\widehat{TP} = R\theta$ and because $\widehat{TP} = OT, OT = R\theta$. Also,

$$x = OT - ST = R\theta - PT' = R\theta - R\sin\theta = R(\theta - \sin\theta),$$

and

$$y = CT - CT' = R - R\cos\theta = R(1 - \cos\theta).$$

Then the equations

**(5)** $$x = R(\theta - \sin\theta), \qquad y = R(1 - \cos\theta)$$

are the parametric equations of the cycloid with $\theta$ as the parameter. When the generating circle has completed one rotation, so that $P$ is back on the $x$-axis, $\theta$ has reached the value of $2\pi$; hence one complete arc of the cycloid is generated as $\theta$ varies from 0 to $2\pi$. The parameter $\theta$ in this example is a geometrical quantity, an angle. Thus parametric equations need not always involve time as the parameter.

**Figure 18-7**

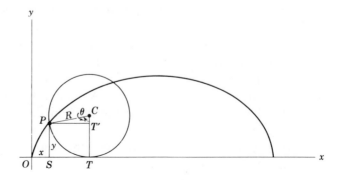

## EXERCISES

**1.** Find parametric equations of the straight line which goes through the origin and makes an angle of 45° with the $x$-axis.

Ans. $x = (\sqrt{2}/2)t, y = (\sqrt{2}/2)t$.

**2.** Find a parametric representation of the straight line through the origin which makes an acute angle $\beta$ with the $x$-axis.

**3.** Could we use the parametric equations $x = 3t, y = 3t$ to represent the straight line through the origin and making an angle of 45° with the $x$-axis? If so, and if $t$ represents time, what would these equations say about motion along this line as compared with the motion represented by the parametric equations of Exercise 1?

**4.** Find the parametric equations of the circle of radius $R$ in terms of the angle $\theta$ shown in Fig. 18-8.

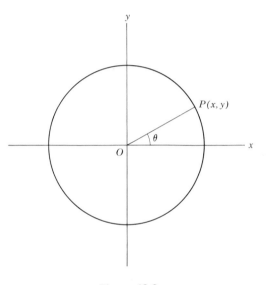

**Figure 18-8**

**5.** Find the parametric equations of the circle of radius $R$ if the angle $\theta$ is measured counterclockwise from the positive $y$-axis.

**6.** Show that the parametric equations (5) of the cycloid hold for points on the cycloid beyond the first complete arc.

**7.** Suppose that the generating circle of the cycloid rolls along the $x$-axis so that it makes one rotation in one second. Then $\theta$ varies with time $t$. Express the parametric equations of the cycloid in terms of $t$.

**8.** The following construction holds for individual points of an ellipse of semi-major axis $a$ and semiminor axis $b$. Draw the circle of radius $OA$; this is called the major circle of the ellipse (Fig. 18-9). Then draw the circle of radius $OB$, which is called the minor circle of the ellipse. Now draw any radius $OCD$. Through $C$ draw a line parallel to the major axis and through $D$ draw a line parallel to the minor axis. These lines meet in a point $P$. Prove that $P$ lies on

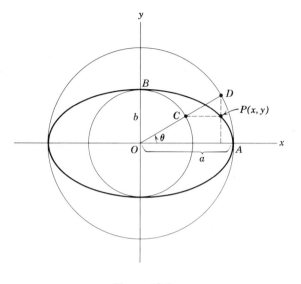

**Figure 18-9**

the ellipse by showing first that the coordinates $(x, y)$ of $P$ satisfy the equations $x = a \cos \theta$, $y = b \sin \theta$, where $\theta$ is the angle shown, and then eliminate $\theta$. What are the parametric equations of the ellipse?

9. Suppose that a string is unwound from a spool of radius $a$ and that the unwound portion is always held taut (Fig. 18-10). The path traced by the end point of the string is called the involute of the circle. Find the parametric equations of the involute.

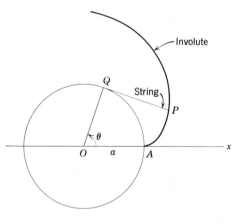

**Figure 18-10**

    *Suggestion:* Let $O$ be the center of the spool and choose the $x$-axis as the line $OA$, where $A$ is the point from which the end point $P$ of the string started its motion. Use the angle $\theta$ as the parameter.

                     *Ans.* $x = a(\cos \theta + \theta \sin \theta), y = a(\sin \theta - \theta \cos \theta)$.

10. (a)   Let $ABP$ be a rigid rod (Fig. 18-11) with the distances of $B$ and $P$ from $A$ fixed. Suppose that as $A$ slides along the $x$-axis, $B$ slides along the $y$-axis. Find the parametric equations of the locus of $P$ in terms of the parameter $\theta$.         *Ans.* If $AP = a$ and $BP = b$, then $x = b \cos \theta, y = a \sin \theta$.

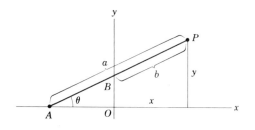

Figure 18-11

Figure 18-11

(b) There is a mechanism for tracing out the locus of $P$. If the $x$- and $y$-axes are slats with a groove along each slat, a nail through $A$ obliges this point on the rod $ABP$ to slide along the groove in the $x$-slot, while a nail through $B$ obliges $B$ to slide along the groove in the $y$-slot. A pencil through a hole at $P$ will then describe the locus of $P$. What is that locus?

**11.** In Fig. 18-12, $ABP$ is a rigid equilateral triangle of side $a$. Suppose that $A$ moves on the $y$-axis while $B$ moves on the $x$-axis. Find the parametric equations of $P$ in terms of the parameter $\theta$.

*Ans.* $x = a \cos \theta + a \cos(120° - \theta), y = a \sin(120° - \theta)$.

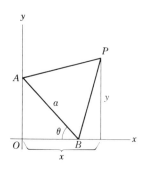

Figure 18-12

**12.** (a) In Fig. 18-13, $AB$ is a fixed line at a fixed distance $a$ above the $x$-axis. Choose any point $Q$ on $AB$ and then choose $P$ on $OQ$ such that $MP = NQ$. Find the parametric equations of $P$ in terms of the angle $\theta$.

*Ans.* $x = a \cot^2 \theta, y = a \cot \theta$.

(b) What is the locus of $P$?

*Ans.* Parabola.

Figure 18-13

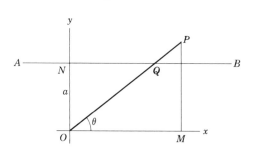

**13.** Show that the parametric equations of the parabola $y^2 = 4px$ in terms of the parameter $\alpha$, where $\alpha$ is the angle of inclination of the normal to the parabola at any point $(x, y)$, are $x = p \tan^2 \alpha$, $y = -2p \tan \alpha$.

   *Suggestion:* The results of Exercises 6 and 7 of Chapter 7, Section 4, will be helpful.

**14.** The parametric equations of the catenary in terms of arc length $s$ are $x = c \log \left[ (s/c) + \sqrt{(s^2/c^2) + 1} \right]$, $y = \sqrt{s^2 + c^2}$. Derive the direct equation and compare your result with that in Chapter 16, Section 3.

**4. *Projectile Motion in a Vacuum.*** We have seen how parametric equations describe curvilinear motion and curves defined purely geometrically. Let us now see how the parametric representation can be used to pursue physical and geometrical investigations. We shall consider the motion of a shell that is shot out from a cannon with an initial velocity whose magnitude is $V$, the cannon being inclined at a fixed angle $A$ to the ground (Fig. 18-14). We shall neglect air resistance. Our first task is to find the parametric equations that represent the motion of the shell. As in the case of a ball thrown out horizontally from the top of a cliff, Galileo's principle that the horizontal and the vertical motions take place independently of each other is applicable. We choose the axes as shown in the figure, the origin $O$ being the point from which the shell is fired.

   Let us denote the horizontal velocity of the shell at any time $t$ by $v_x$. The initial velocity of magnitude $V$ is directed at angle $A$ to the ground. Hence the horizontal velocity of the shell is not $V$ but the component of $V$ along the horizontal. From Figure 18-14 we see that this component is $V \cos A$. Because the only velocity acting in the horizontal direction is $V \cos A$, then according to Newton's first law of motion the shell will continue to travel indefinitely in a horizontal direction with this constant velocity. Thus

**(6)** $$v_x = V \cos A.$$

Then, since $v_x = dx/dt$, the distance traveled in the horizontal direction is

**(7)** $$x = (V \cos A)t = Vt \cos A.$$

**Figure 18-14**

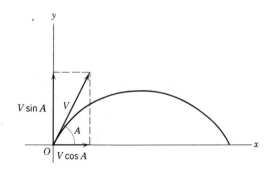

Now let us consider the vertical motion of the shell. Gravity acts to produce a downward acceleration of 32 ft/sec². With the upward direction as the positive one, the acceleration $a_y$ in the $y$-direction is

$$a_y = -32.$$

Now, if we let $v_y$ denote the velocity in the $y$-direction, then $a_y = dv_y/dt$. By antidifferentiation we have

$$v_y = -32t + C.$$

To determine the constant of integration we have the physical fact that at $t = 0$, the shell has an upward velocity of $V \sin A$, for this is the upward component of $V$. Hence

**(8)** $$v_y = -32t + V \sin A.$$

To find the height at any time $t$ we can again integrate, because $v_y = dy/dt$. We obtain

$$y = -16t^2 + Vt \sin A + C,$$

and because $y = 0$ when $t = 0$, then $C = 0$ and

**(9)** $$y = -16t^2 + Vt \sin A.$$

Equations (7) and (9) are the parametric equations of the curve or trajectory along which the shell travels, the parameter being $t$. After fixing particular values for the constants $V$ and $A$ we could plot the curve just as we plotted parametric equations in Section 2. Or, since the parametric equations (7) and (9) are rather simple, we can solve (7) for $t$, obtaining $t = x/V \cos A$, and substitute this in (9). Then

$$y = -16\left( \frac{x^2}{V^2 \cos^2 A} \right) + V \sin A \, \frac{x}{V \cos A}$$

or

**(10)** $$y = -\frac{16}{V^2 \cos^2 A} x^2 + x \tan A.$$

Since $V$ and $A$ are constants, we see that the direct equation of the path is of the form

$$y = ax^2 + bx$$

where $a = -16/V^2 \cos^2 A$ and $b = \tan A$, and therefore (10) represents a parabola (Appendix to Chap. 7, Sect. 3, Exercise 4). Hence the path of the projectile is an arc of a parabola.

There are many questions about the motion of the projectile that we can answer almost immediately by using the parametric equations of the motion. For example, we can find how far out horizontally the projectile travels. This horizontal distance is called the *range*. To obtain it we have but to recognize that when the shell strikes the ground $y$ must be 0. Hence we ask, what is $t$ when $y$ is 0? Let $t_1$ be this value (or values) of $t$. From (9) we have

$$- 16t_1^2 + Vt_1 \sin A = 0,$$

or

$$t_1(-16t_1 + V \sin A) = 0.$$

There are two roots, namely $t_1 = 0$, which physically is the instant when the shell starts out, and

**(11)**
$$t_1 = \frac{V \sin A}{16},$$

which is the time the shell takes to reach the ground again. To find the range we have but to substitute this value of $t$ in (7). Then if $x_1$ is the range,

$$x_1 = V \cos A \cdot \frac{V \sin A}{16} = \frac{V^2}{16} \sin A \cos A$$

or

**(12)**
$$x_1 = \frac{V^2}{32} \sin 2A.$$

In this particular case of projectile motion, in which we happen to have the direct equation (10), we could of course find the range from it. We have but to let $y = 0$ in (10) and solve for $x$. However, it is often the case when parametric equations are used, that the direct equation, even if obtainable, is complicated.

With the general expression for range we can answer another question of interest in the motion of projectiles. Formula (12) is the correct expression for the range for any given $V$ and $A$. Suppose that we keep $V$ fixed but vary $A$, the angle of elevation of the gun. For what value of $A$ is the range a maximum? In this case we do not need the calculus to find a maximum value of a function. We need to note merely that $\sin 2A$ is at most 1 and this occurs when $2A = 90°$ and $A = 45°$. Thus the maximum range is secured when the gun is fired at an angle of 45° and then the range is $V^2/32$.

The parametric equations can be used to find the maximum height to which the shell rises for a given $V$ and $A$. For with a constant $V$ and $A$ the height of the shell at any time $t$ is given by (9), namely,

$$y = - 16t^2 + Vt \sin A.$$

The maximum height attained by the shell is the maximum $y$-value. Hence we find $dy/dt$, which is

$$\frac{dy}{dt} = -32t + V \sin A,$$

and this is 0 at the value $t_2$ given by

**(13)**
$$t_2 = \frac{V \sin A}{32}.$$

The maximum height $y_2$ is then found by substituting this value of $t$ in (9). Thus

$$y_2 = -16 \frac{V^2 \sin^2 A}{(32)^2} + \frac{V^2 \sin^2 A}{32}$$

or

**(14)**
$$y = \frac{V^2 \sin^2 A}{64}.$$

By comparing (11) and (13) we learn something new. We see that $t_1 = 2t_2$; this means physically that the time the shell takes to reach the ground is twice the time it takes to reach maximum height. Or, it takes the shell as long to reach the maximum height as it does to go from that point to the ground again. Moreover, if we substitute the value of $t_2$ into formula (7) for the horizontal distance traveled, we see that the maximum height occurs at the value

**(15)**
$$x_2 = \frac{V^2 \sin 2A}{64},$$

which is one half of the range given by (12). Hence the maximum point occurs midway between the starting point and the point at which the shell hits the ground.

## EXERCISES

1. Use the direct equation (10) to find the range of a projectile and show that your result agrees with (12).
2. A gun can fire a projectile with an initial velocity of 1800 ft/sec. What is the maximum range on a horizontal plane?  *Ans.* 19.1 mi.
3. Apply the calculus method of finding relative maxima and minima to (12) and find the angle $A$ at which a gun should be fired to secure maximum range.
   *Ans.* $A = 45°$.
4. Show that when a shell is fired with a given initial velocity $V$ and at the angle that gives maximum range, the maximum height attained is one fourth of the maximum range.
5. A projectile is fired at some angle so as to attain the range of 450 feet and the time of flight is 5 seconds. Find the initial velocity.  *Ans.* 120.41 ft/sec.
6. If the time of flight of a cannon shot is $T$ seconds and the range is $X$ feet, show that the angle of fire is $\tan^{-1}(16T^2/X)$.
7. For what angle of fire does a shell attain maximum height?  *Ans.* 90°.

8. (a)  Show that for a given range $x_1$ less than the maximum range there are two angles of fire which will give that range and that one angle is the complement of the other.

   (b)  Using the result of part (a), answer the following question: Because there are two angles of fire that permit one to attain a given range, which one requires less time of flight?                    *Ans.* The smaller one.

9. For the parabolic projectile path represented by

$$y = -(16/V^2 \cos^2 A)x^2 + x \tan A$$

   find the following:

   (a)  The equation of the directrix.                 *Ans.* $y = V^2/64.$
   (b)  The coordinates of the vertex.   *Ans.* $(V^2(\sin 2A)/64,\ V^2(\sin^2 A)/64).$
   (c)  The coordinates of the focus.    *Ans.* $(V^2(\sin 2A)/64,\ -V^2(\cos 2A)/64).$

   *Suggestion:* Refer to Chapter 7, Section $A3$, Exercise 4 for material on the equation $y = ax^2 + bx + c.$

10. We know from (14) the maximum $y$-value of the trajectory with angle $A$ and we know from (15) the $x$-value of that maximum. Hence we have the parametric equations of the locus of the maximum points for all trajectories in terms of the parameter $A$. Show that the locus of all these maximum points is

$$\frac{x^2}{\left(V^2/64\right)^2} + \frac{\left[2y - \left(V^2/64\right)\right]^2}{\left(V^2/64\right)^2} = 1.$$

   What curve does this equation represent?                    *Ans.* Ellipse.

11. Suppose that a gun is mounted on a railway car which is moving at the rate of 60 mi/hr (88 ft/sec). The gun is fired at an angle $A$ to the horizontal and with an initial velocity $V$ whose horizontal component is in the direction of motion of the car. Find the formula for the range of the shell (measured from the spot at which the shell is fired).          *Ans.* $(V^2/32)\sin 2A + (88/16)V \sin A.$

12. A shell is fired at an angle $A$ to the ground and with initial velocity $V$. What are the components of the velocity at the instant the shell strikes the ground? Hence, what is the magnitude of the total velocity? How does the direction of the shell's motion on striking compare with the direction in which it was initially fired?

13. (a)  If a shell is fired with initial velocity $V$ and at angle $A$ to the ground, what expression represents the magnitude of the shell's velocity at any time $t$ of its flight?                    *Ans.* $\sqrt{V^2 \cos^2 A + (V \sin A - 32t)^2}.$

   (b)  Show that the result of part (a) can be expressed as $\sqrt{V^2 - 64y}.$

14. Using the result of Exercise 13, find when the magnitude of the velocity is least and interpret the result physically.
                    *Ans.* At $t = V \sin A/32$; the highest point of the path.

15. A projectile is fired at an angle $A$ and after $t$ seconds it appears to have an angle of elevation $B$ as seen from the point of fire. Prove that the initial velocity was $16t \cos B/\sin(A - B).$

16. A ball is hit by a bat at a point $h$ feet above the ground (Fig. 18-15) and the ball is projected with an initial velocity $V$ and at an angle $A$ to the horizontal.

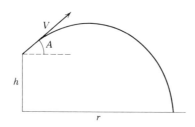

**Figure 18-15**

Find the range $r$, that is, find the horizontal distance from the starting point to the point at which the ball strikes the ground.

$$\text{Ans. } (V^2/64)(\sin 2A + \sqrt{\sin^2 2A + (256h/V^2)\cos^2 A}\ .$$

17. Under the conditions of Exercise 16 and using the result of that exercise, find the angle $A$ for which the maximum range is obtained. Can you give a geometrical argument to show that the value of $A$ should be less than $45°$? Show also that the result reduces to $45°$ when $h = 0$.

$$\text{Ans. } A = \cos^{-1}\sqrt{(K + 4)/(K + 8)} \quad \text{where} \quad K = 256h/V^2.$$

18. Under the conditions of Exercise 16 and using the results of Exercises 16 and 17, show that the maximum range for all possible values of $A$ is $V^2/32 \tan A$, where $A$ is that given in Exercise 17.

19. A projectile is fired at an angle $A$ to the horizontal (Fig. 18-16) and with an initial velocity $V$. However, the ground slopes upward at an angle $B$. Find the range of the projectile; that is, find the distance $OQ$.

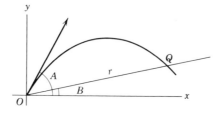

**Figure 18-16**

*Suggestion:* The parametric equations of the line $OQ$ are $x = r \cos B$, $y = r \sin B$. Because $Q$ lies on the path of the projectile, these parametric equations must satisfy the *direct* equation of the projectile's path for the range $r$.                    $\text{Ans. } r = V^2[\sin(2A - B) - \sin B]/32 \cos^2 B.$

20. Under the conditions of Exercise 19, find the maximum range obtainable by varying $A$.                    $\text{Ans. Max. } r = V^2/32(1 + \sin B).$

21. The result of Exercise 20 gives the maximum range or the farthest point that can be reached in the direction $OQ$. If we regard $r$ and $B$ in Fig. 18-16 as the polar coordinates $\rho$ and $\theta$ of this farthest point reached in the direction $\theta$, then the result of Exercise 20 gives the locus of the farthest point reached in any given direction $\theta$. Show that the locus is a parabola. It is called the parabola of surety or parabola of safety because no point outside this locus can be reached by the projectile no matter at what angle it is fired. (See also Chap. 22, Sect. 9.)

22. (a) Suppose that a gun is fired at an angle $A$ to the horizontal to reach a point on the ground which slopes at angle $B$ to the horizontal (Fig. 18-16). Show that the gun will have the same range if fired at the angle $A - B$ to the vertical.

   (b) Show that the statement in (a) is equivalent to the statement that the two directions of fire which give the same range on the sloping ground make equal angles with the bisector of the angle between the vertical and the ground.

23. Using the result of Exercise 20, find the maximum range up a hillside which has a slope of $\frac{1}{20}$ if the gun fires its projectile with a velocity of 600 ft/sec.

   *Ans.* 3550 yd approx.

24. A shrapnel shell strikes the ground and explodes. Its fragments then disperse not only in all horizontal directions around the point of impact but at all angles to the ground and with the same velocity $V$. Calculate the horizontal area endangered by the flying fragments.    *Ans.* $\pi(V^2/32)^2$.

25. Find the greatest distance that a stone can be thrown inside a horizontal tunnel 10 feet high and with an initial velocity of 80 ft/sec. Find also the corresponding time of flight.

26. A projectile is fired at an initial velocity of 160 ft/sec. Find the angle of fire $A$ so that the projectile will strike a wall 480 feet away at the maximum possible height.    *Ans.* $A = 59°$ approx.

27. A golfer seeks to hit a ball across a lake 200 yards wide. He hits the ball at an angle of 30° with the horizontal and gives it an initial velocity of 120 ft/sec. How far from the starting point does the ball hit the water?

28. Equation (10) is the direct equation of the path of a projectile.

   (a) Using the fact that $\sec^2 \theta = 1 + \tan^2 \theta$, find the angle $\theta$ at which the projectile should be launched to reach a given point $(x, y)$. Interpret the answer when the roots are complex, real and distinct, and real and equal.

   $$\text{Ans. } \tan \theta = (V^2/32) \pm \sqrt{(V^2/32)^2 - 2(V^2/32)y - x^2}\ .$$

   (b) What does the discriminant condition that the roots be equal represent geometrically?

29. A coastal gun is located on a cliff at a height of 700 feet above sea level. A projectile is fired from the gun at an angle of 45° to the horizontal and with an initial speed of 1000 ft/sec. Find the horizontal distance (range) traveled by the projectile until it hits the water.    *Ans.* 31,900 ft approx.

30. Suppose that any number of particles are projected simultaneously from the same point, with the same velocity, and in the same vertical plane, but at various angles to the horizontal. Show that at any instant after projection the particles lie on a circle (in the vertical plane).

31. Consider the paths (in one vertical plane) of all projectiles emanating from one point with the same initial velocity (of magnitude) $V$ but with varying angles of fire $A$. The direct equations of these paths are given by formula (10).

   (a) Show that all these parabolas have the same directrix, $y = V^2/64$.

   (b) Show that this common directrix is at the height which the projectile attains when fired directly upward.

   (c) Show that the locus of the foci of all the parabolas is a circle with center at the gun.

   (d) Show that the focus is at the level of the gun when $A = 45°$, below when $A < 45°$, and above when $A > 45°$.

(e)   Show that the locus of the vertices of all the parabolas is an ellipse with center halfway between the gun and the common directrix (cf. Exercise 10).

*Suggestion:* Use the information in Exercise 9.

**32.** (a)   A bomb is dropped and falls straight down from a point $h$ feet above the ground. A gunner on the ground $x_1$ feet away from the point on the ground that the bomb will strike wishes to fire at the bomb so as to explode it in midair. Show that the gunner should aim directly at the point from which the bomb is dropped and should fire the instant the bomb starts to fall.

(b)   What velocity must the shell fired by the gunner have?

**33.** A soldier can throw a hand grenade with an initial velocity $V$, at any angle to the horizontal, and in any direction in the plane on which he stands. Neglect his height and compute the area of the points he can cover with the grenade.

**5. Slope, Area, Arc Length, and Curvature Derived from Parametric Equations.** We have seen that a curve can be represented analytically by two equations–the parametric equations. This parametric representation is the only practical one for some curves such as the cycloid and is certainly more useful than the direct equation in the study of motion along curves. The utility of the parametric equations has already been illustrated and will be equally evident in problems considered in the following sections.

To carry out further work with the parametric representation of curves, we must learn first how to calculate such useful quantities as the slope of a curve, the area bounded in whole or part by a curve, and the length of a curve. We have learned how to find these quantities when we know the direct equation of a curve, whether in rectangular coordinates or polar coordinates. How can we find these quantities when a curve is given to us through its rectangular parameteric equations? The modifications that are necessary to use the parametric equations are rather simple.

Let us agree first on some notation. We are, of course, working with the parametric equations of a curve. These are two functions

**(16)**
$$x = g(t), \qquad y = h(t).$$

We use the letter $t$ here without implying that the parameter represents time. We could as well use some other letter and shall occasionally do so. To indicate derivatives we have often used the Newtonian dot notation. Let us use this now to mean derivatives with respect to $t$. Thus

$$\dot{x} = \frac{dx}{dt} = \dot{g}(t), \qquad \dot{y} = \frac{dy}{dt} = \dot{h}(t).$$

We shall also have occasion to use the direct equation involving $x$ and $y$ that represents the same curve as (16). In dealing with the derivatives of $y$ with respect to $x$, we shall use the Leibnizian notation, $dy/dx$ and $d^2y/dx^2$.

Let us begin with the subject of slope. We know that in terms of the direct equation the slope at any point is $dy/dx$. Now suppose that we have the parametric equations of the curve and let $t_0$ be the value of $t$ at which

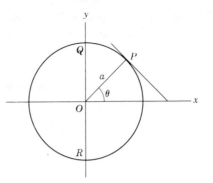

**Figure 18-17**

we wish to calculate the slope. If we let $t$ change from some value $t_0$ to some value $t_0 + \Delta t$, then $x$ will change by some amount $\Delta x$ and $y$ by some amount $\Delta y$. We can then write the purely algebraic equation

**(17)**
$$\frac{\Delta y}{\Delta x} = \frac{\dfrac{\Delta y}{\Delta t}}{\dfrac{\Delta x}{\Delta t}} .$$

If we now let $\Delta t$ approach 0, we may argue that the limit on the left side of (17) is $dy/dx$. The right side is a quotient, and the limit of a quotient is the limit of the numerator divided by the limit of the denominator, provided that the limit of the denominator is not 0. Then we have the result

**(18)**
$$\frac{dy}{dx} = \frac{\dfrac{dy}{dt}}{\dfrac{dx}{dt}} = \frac{\dot{y}}{\dot{x}} , \qquad \dot{x} \neq 0.$$

Thus (18) tells us that we may obtain the slope of a curve from its parametric equations by forming the quotient on the right side.*

As an example let us consider the parametric equations of the circle (Fig. 18-17), namely,

**(19)**
$$x = a \cos \theta, \qquad y = a \sin \theta.$$

To obtain the slope of this curve we shall use (18). However, since the parameter in (19) is $\theta$ we shall replace $t$ by $\theta$. Then

**(20)**
$$\frac{dy}{dx} = \frac{\dfrac{dy}{d\theta}}{\dfrac{dx}{d\theta}} = \frac{a \cos \theta}{- a \sin \theta} = - \cot \theta.$$

---

* Equation (17) might be meaningless if $\Delta x = 0$. However, we suppose that $\dot{x} \neq 0$ and, because $\Delta x / \Delta t$ approaches $\dot{x}$, $\Delta x$ cannot be 0 for small $\Delta t$ because $\Delta t \neq 0$.

It is readily seen that this result makes sense geometrically. The parameter $\theta$ in (19) is the angle shown in the figure. The tangent at $P$ is perpendicular to $OP$ and, because the slope of $OP$ is $\tan \theta$, the slope of the tangent line must be the negative reciprocal of $\tan \theta$ or $-\cot \theta$.

Formula (18) expresses the slope of a curve in terms of the parametric equations. We can also express the second derivative $d^2y/dx^2$ in terms of the parametric equations. We start with the fact that

**(21)**
$$\frac{d^2y}{dx^2} = \frac{d}{dx}\left(\frac{dy}{dx}\right).$$

By the chain rule

**(22)**
$$\frac{d^2y}{dx^2} = \frac{d}{dt}\left(\frac{dy}{dx}\right)\frac{dt}{dx}.$$

Because by the theorem on inverse functions

$$\frac{dt}{dx} = \frac{1}{\dfrac{dx}{dt}},$$

we have from (22) that

**(23)**
$$\frac{d^2y}{dx^2} = \frac{\dfrac{d}{dt}\left(\dfrac{dy}{dx}\right)}{\dfrac{dx}{dt}}.$$

This result is useful if $dy/dx$ is expressed as a function of $t$; otherwise we cannot carry out the differentiation $d(dy/dx)/dt$. However, we can express (23) in another form. In view of the value of $dy/dx$ given by (18), we can write (23) as

$$\frac{d^2y}{dx^2} = \frac{\dfrac{d}{dt}\left(\dfrac{\dot{y}}{\dot{x}}\right)}{\dot{x}}.$$

To carry out the differentiation with respect to $t$, we use the theorem on the derivative of a quotient of two functions. Thus

**(24)**
$$\frac{d^2y}{dx^2} = \frac{\dot{x}\ddot{y} - \dot{y}\ddot{x}}{\dot{x}^3}.$$

As an example of the use of the parametric form of the second derivative, let us find the relative maxima and minima of the curve given by (19). We know from (20) that

**(25)**
$$\frac{dy}{dx} = -\cot \theta.$$

Then to find the possible relative maxima and minima we set

$$\cot \theta = 0.$$

This equation is satisfied when

$$\theta = \frac{\pi}{2} \quad \text{and} \quad \theta = \frac{3\pi}{2} .$$

We now calculate the second derivative. According to (23)

$$\frac{d^2y}{dx^2} = \frac{\dfrac{d}{d\theta}\left(\dfrac{dy}{dx}\right)}{\dfrac{dx}{d\theta}} .$$

In view of (25) and because $x = a \cos \theta$,

$$\frac{d^2y}{dx^2} = \frac{\dfrac{d}{d\theta}(-\cot \theta)}{-a \sin \theta} = -\frac{1}{a}\csc^3 \theta.$$

Of course, the use of (24) in place of (23) would give the same result. At $\theta = \pi/2$, $\csc \theta = 1$, and so $d^2y/dx^2$ is negative. Then at $\theta = \pi/2$, $y$ has a relative maximum. At $\theta = 3\pi/2$, $\csc \theta$ is $-1$, and so $d^2y/dx^2$ is positive. Hence at $\theta = 3\pi/2$, $y$ has a relative mimimum. These two values of $\theta$ correspond to the points $Q$ and $R$ of Fig. 18-17. We should note that if we had worked with the direct equation of the circle, namely $x^2 + y^2 = a^2$, we would have had to deal with the two functions $y = \pm\sqrt{a^2 - x^2}$. The parametric equations represent the entire curve.

## EXERCISES

1. Find $dy/dx$ and $d^2y/dx^2$ for each of the following parametric representations of the functions relating $x$ and $y$:
   (a) $x = 2 - t, y = t^2$.        *Ans.* $dy/dx = -2t, d^2y/dx^2 = 2$.
   (b) $x = 3t^2, y = 4t - 5$.
   (c) $x = te^{-t}, y = e^t$.
          *Ans.* $dy/dx = e^{2t}/(1 - t), d^2y/dx^2 = e^{3t}(3 - 2t)/(1 - t)^3$.

2. Consider the equations of projectile motion in a vacuum, namely, $x = Vt \cos A, y = -16t^2 + Vt \sin A$. We know that at the instant the shell is fired the slope of the curve is $\tan A$. What is the slope at the instant the shell strikes the ground?

3. Find the maximum height of the projectile whose motion is represented by the equations in Exercise 2.        *Ans.* $(V^2 \sin^2 A)/64$.

4. Use the parametric equations of the ellipse, $x = a \cos \theta, y = b \sin \theta$, to find the relative maxima and minima of the ellipse. For the geometrical meaning of $\theta$ see Exercise 4 of Section 3.

5. Use the parametric equations (5) for the cycloid to show that the slope at any point $P$ is $\cot (\theta/2)$.

**6.** Use the parametric equations (5) for the cycloid to find the maximum height of the curve. *Ans. 2R.*

**7.** Prove that the normal to the cycloid at any point $P$ (the perpendicular to the tangent at $P$) passes through the point of contact of the generating circle with the straight line along which the circle rolls. (In terms of Fig. 18-7, the normal at $P$ must pass through point $T$.)

**8.** Show that the tangent to the cycloid at any point $P$ passes through the point of the generating circle diametrically opposite to the point of contact of the circle with the line on which the circle rolls. (In terms of Fig. 18-7, the tangent at $P$ passes through the point on the circle diametrically opposite to $T$.)

**9.** Obtain the direct equation of the cycloid by eliminating $\theta$ between the two equations (5).
$$Ans. \ x = R \cos^{-1} \frac{(R-y)}{R} \pm \sqrt{y(2R-y)}.$$

**10.** Show that for the cycloid $d^2y/dx^2 = -R/y^2$. What does this fact imply about the concavity of the curve?

**11.** Suppose that $y = f(x)$ is the equation of a curve. If we want to obtain a direct expression for its slope in terms of polar coordinates, we can use the fact that the equation is represented parametrically by $x = \rho \cos \theta$ and $y = \rho \sin \theta$ where $\rho$ is some function of $\theta$. Show that

$$\frac{dy}{dx} = \frac{\rho \cos \theta + \sin \theta \, (d\rho/d\theta)}{-\rho \sin \theta + \cos \theta \, (d\rho/d\theta)}.$$

**12.** Obtain the slope of the cycloid at any point $(x, y)$ by using the result of Exercise 9 and compare the ease of doing so with the use of the parametric equations as in Exercise 5.

Another quantity which we often desire to calculate and which can sometimes be obtained more readily by working with parametric equations is the area under a curve. One example is a problem that excited the mathematicians of the seventeenth century when the calculus was in its infancy; it is that of finding the area under one complete arc or an arch of the cycloid. Our formula for area, when the equation of the curve is given in the form of $y = f(x)$ and the area is bounded by the curve, the $x$-axis, $x = a$ and $x = b$, is

**(26)**
$$A = \int_a^b y \, dx = \int_a^b f(x)dx.$$

To apply this to the cycloid (Fig. 18-18), we should have the equation in the form of $y = f(x)$. However, as we can see from the answer to Exercise 9 of the preceding list, it would be difficult to obtain $y$ as a function of $x$.

Let us see if we can use the parametric equations of the cycloid:

**(27)**
$$x = R(\theta - \sin \theta), \qquad y = R(1 - \cos \theta).$$

The presence of $x$ as a function of $\theta$ in (27) suggests that we should try to evaluate (26) by a change of variable; that is, we should replace $x$ by a function of $\theta$ where the relation between $x$ and $\theta$ is given by the first of the parametric equations (27). We should then replace $x$ where it appears in

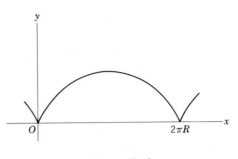

**Figure 18-18**

$f(x)$ by its value in terms of $\theta$. However, we do not know the precise function $f(x)$. But we do know something which is just as good. The function $y = f(x)$ is the equation of the very same curve as is given by the parametric equations (27). Hence, if we were able to replace $x$ in $f(x)$ by the expression for $x$ in terms of $\theta$, we should arrive at $y$ in terms of $\theta$, and this we already have in (27). There is just one other point to be noted. When we do make a change of variable in an integral, we must also replace the $dx$ by

$$dx = \frac{dx}{d\theta}\, d\theta.$$

Hence in terms of $\theta$ our formula (26) for area becomes

$$A = \int y(\theta)\, \frac{dx}{d\theta}\, d\theta.$$

Moreover, when we make a change of variable in a definite integral, there is no need after evaluating the indefinite integral to return to the original independent variable. We merely use the corresponding end values for $\theta$. In the present case one arch of the cycloid is generated when $\theta$ runs from 0 to $2\pi$. Or one can calculate the end values for $\theta$ as follows. Because the change of variable is given by

$$x = R(\theta - \sin \theta),$$

when $x = 0$,

$$\theta - \sin \theta = 0 \quad \text{and so} \quad \theta = 0;$$

when $x = 2\pi R$,

$$R(\theta -\!- \sin \theta) = 2\pi R \quad \text{and so} \quad \theta = 2\pi.$$

Thus the area under one arch of the cycloid is given by

$$A = \int_0^{2\pi} y(\theta)\, \frac{dx}{d\theta}\, d\theta$$

or

**(28)**
$$A \int_0^{2\pi} R(1 - \cos \theta) R(1 - \cos \theta)\, d\theta.$$

More generally, the formula for area under a curve whose parametric equations are

$$x = g(t), \qquad y = h(t)$$

is

**(29)** $$A = \int_{t_1}^{t_2} y(t)\dot{x}(t)\, dt.$$

The values $t_1$ and $t_2$ are the $t$-values of the end points of the arc under which the area lies.

## EXERCISES

1. Evaluate the area given by (28).                           *Ans.* $3\pi R^2$.
2. Given the parametric equations of the ellipse $x = a \cos \theta$ and $y = b \sin \theta$, find the area bounded by the ellipse (see Fig. 18-9).              *Ans.* $\pi ab$.
3. (a)  Show that the equations $x = a \cosh u, y = b \sinh u$, where $a$ and $b$ are positive, represent the right-hand branch of a hyperbola with center at the origin and the $x$-axis as the major axis.
   (b)  Find the area of the region bounded by the $x$-axis, the hyperbola, and the line from the origin to the point on the hyperbola corresponding to the value $u_0$ of $u$.                    *Ans.* $abu_0/2$.
4. The equations $x = 2 \cos^3 \theta, y = 2 \sin^3 \theta$ represent the curve called the four-cusped hypocycloid. Find the area bounded by the curve.        *Ans.* $3\pi/2$.

Length of curve is another quantity that is sometimes more readily obtained from the parametric representation than from the direct equation. Let us see first what formula will yield this. We start with the established result, which, in view of formula (24) of Chapter 15, is

**(30)** $$s = \int_a^b \sqrt{1 + \left( \frac{dy}{dx} \right)^2}\, dx.$$

This formula presumes the direct equation of the curve. If we have the parametric equations

$$x = g(t), \qquad y = h(t),$$

we may make a change of variable from $x$ to $t$ in (30). We must, however, be careful. If we knew $dy/dx$ as a function of $x$, we could replace $x$ by its value in terms of $t$. However, to know $dy/dx$ as a function of $x$ we would have to have the direct equation of the curve, whereas we are seeking a formula that utilizes the parametric equations. We can, however, use (18) and replace $dy/dx$ by

$$\frac{dy}{dx} = \frac{\dot{y}}{\dot{x}}.$$

Also, as in any change of variable, we must replace $dx$ by $(dx/dt)\,dt$. Hence (30) becomes

**(31)**
$$s = \int \sqrt{1 + \left(\frac{\dot{y}}{\dot{x}}\right)^2}\ \dot{x}\ dt$$

or

**(32)**
$$s = \int \sqrt{\dot{x}^2 + \dot{y}^2}\ dt.$$

This integral must be taken between the $t$-values that correspond to the end points of the arc. It is customary to take $s$ to be positive in the direction of increasing $t$.* Thus the final formula for the arc length of the curve

**(33)**
$$x = g(t), \qquad y = h(t)$$

between the points corresponding to $t = t_1$ and $t = t_2$ is

**(34)**
$$s = \int_{t_1}^{t_2} \sqrt{\dot{x}^2 + \dot{y}^2}\ dt.$$

As an example we might consider finding the length of one arch of the cycloid

**(35)**
$$x = R(\theta - \sin\theta), \qquad y = R(1 - \cos\theta).$$

Here the parameter is denoted by $\theta$. Also, we know that one arch of the cycloid is generated when $\theta$ varies from 0 to $2\pi$. The function $x = g(t)$ of (33) becomes the left-hand function in (35), and the function $y = h(t)$ in (33) becomes the right-hand function of (35). To use (34) we need $\dot{x}$ and $\dot{y}$, which are

**(36)**
$$\dot{x} = R(1 - \cos\theta), \qquad \dot{y} = R\sin\theta.$$

Then substitution in (34) gives

**(37)**
$$s = \int_0^{2\pi} \sqrt{2R^2(1 - \cos\theta)}\ d\theta.$$

To integrate, it is helpful to use the trigonometric identity

$$\sin\frac{\theta}{2} = \sqrt{\frac{1 - \cos\theta}{2}}\ .$$

Then (34) becomes

**(38)**
$$s = \int_0^{2\pi} \sqrt{4R^2 \sin^2 \frac{\theta}{2}}\ d\theta = \int_0^{2\pi} 2R \sin\frac{\theta}{2}\ d\theta = 8R.$$

---

* This convention is in agreement with the earlier convention (Chap. 15, Sect. 4) that $s$ be positive with increasing $x$, because we can regard the direct equation of a curve $y = f(x)$ as consisting of the parametric equations $x = t, y = f(t)$.

## EXERCISES

1. Find the circumference of the circle by using the parametric equations $x = a \cos \theta, y = a \sin \theta$.

2. The motion of a particle is described by the parametric equations given below in which $t$ is time. Find the formula for the distance traveled as a function of time starting at $t = 0$.
   (a)  $x = 3t^2, y = 4t^2$. *Ans.* $s = 5t^2$.
   (b)  $x = 3 \sin t, y = 3 \cos t$.
   (c)  $x = a \cos^2 t, y = a \sin^2 t$. *Ans.* $s = a\sqrt{2} \sin^2 t$.
   (d)  $x = 5 \cos 5t^2, y = 5 \sin 5t^2$

3. Find the length of arc of the parabola $x = t^2 - 1, y = 2t$ from $t = 0$ to $t = 5$.
   *Ans.* $5\sqrt{26} + \log(5 + \sqrt{26})$.

4. From a spool of radius 1 inch, 3 turns of thread are unwound, while keeping the thread constantly taut. Find the length of the path described by the end.

   *Suggestion:* In Exercise 9 of Section 3 we derived the parametric equations of the path described by the end of the string. Hence using the parametric equations of that path find its length for the 3 turns of the thread.
   *Ans.* 177.7 in. approx.

5. Suppose that we decided to calculate the length of one arch of the cycloid by calculating the length $ABC$ of Fig. 18-19. Because an arch is symmetric about the line $x = \pi a$ and because the second arch is a repetition of the first one, arc $ABC$ should give the same result as arc $OAB$. We should then use the parametric equations of the cycloid but use as the range of $\theta$, $\pi \le \theta \le 3\pi$. Calculate this length $ABC$.

   *Suggestion:* To have $s$ increase as $\theta$ increases, one must be sure that $ds/d\theta$ is positive.

**Figure  18-19**

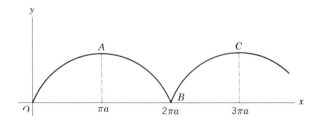

6. (a)  Find the length of the arc of the semicubical parabola $x = t^3, y = t^2$ from $t = 0$ to $t = 2$. *Ans.* $[(40)^{3/2} - 4^{3/2}]/27$.
   (b)  Find the length of the arc of the same curve from $t = -2$ to $t = 2$. Watch out! *Ans.* $2[(40)^{3/2} - 4^{3/2}]/27$.

We shall show how one more useful quantity, the curvature of a curve, can be calculated from the parametric equations of the curve. We know

(Chap. 15, Sect. 5) that, given the direct equation, the curvature $K$ is

**(39)**
$$K = \frac{\dfrac{d^2y}{dx^2}}{\left\{1 + \left(\dfrac{dy}{dx}\right)^2\right\}^{3/2}}.$$

However, if the parametric equations are

$$x = g(t), \qquad y = h(t),$$

we know from (18) that

$$\frac{dy}{dx} = \frac{\dot{y}}{\dot{x}}$$

and from (24) that

$$\frac{d^2y}{dx^2} = \frac{\dot{x}\ddot{y} - \dot{y}\ddot{x}}{\dot{x}^3}.$$

It is just a matter of algebra to substitute these values in (39) and to simplify. The result is

**(40)**
$$K = \frac{\dot{x}\ddot{y} - \dot{y}\ddot{x}}{(\dot{x}^2 + \dot{y}^2)^{3/2}}.$$

Thus the curvature can be readily calculated from the parametric equations. It is worth noting that (40) gives the curvature where (39) fails, namely, where $dy/dx$ is infinite.

There is an alternative expression to (40) for the curvature. In view of (32), we have from (40) that

**(41)**
$$K = \frac{\dot{x}\ddot{y} - \dot{y}\ddot{x}}{\dot{s}^3}$$

where $\dot{s} = ds/dt$.

## EXERCISES

**1.** Show that the curvature of the circle represented by the parametric equations $x = a \cos \theta, y = a \sin \theta$ is $1/a$.

**2.** Find the radius of curvature of the following curves:
(a)   $x = 3t, y = 2t^2 - 1$ at $t = 1$.                                        *Ans.* $\frac{125}{12}$.
(b)   $x = 4t, y = 2/t$ at $t = 1$.
(c)   $x = 4 \sin t, y = 2 \cos t$ at $t = 2$.                               *Ans.* $\frac{15}{8}$.
(d)   $x = 3t^2, y = t^3$ at $t = 1$.
(e)   $x = 20t - \sin 20t, y = 1 - \cos 20t$ at any value of $t$.

3. Find the curvature of the ellipse $x = a \cos \theta$, $y = b \sin \theta$ (see Fig. 18-9) at one end of the major axis (where $\theta = 0$) and at one end of the minor axis (where $\theta = 90°$). *Ans.* $a/b^2$; $b/a^2$.

4. Find the curvature of the cycloid $x = R(\theta - \sin \theta)$, $y = R(1 - \cos \theta)$ at the highest point (where $\theta = 180°$).

5. Find the curvature at the vertex of the right-hand branch of the hyperbola, the branch represented by $x = a \cosh u$, $y = b \sinh u$. *Ans.* $a/b^2$.

6. Find the curvature of the path of a projectile in a vacuum [Equations (7) and (9)] at $t = 0$.

**6. An Application of Arc Length.** * We have seen that we can calculate the arc length of the cycloid by using the parametric equations. This knowledge enables us to solve a problem which plagued the mathematicians of the late seventeenth century and which is still worth considering on several accounts. In their efforts to design a clock they had fastened on the pendulum as a regulating device. However, there is one defect in the pendulum. The period of the pendulum is not strictly independent of the amplitude. A review of the work in Section 6 of Chapter 10 will remind the reader that we made an approximation in order to obtain the fact that the period $T$ of a pendulum is

$$T = 2\pi \sqrt{\frac{l}{32}}$$

where $l$ is the length. Now the bob of a pendulum swings along the arc of a circle. The following question was then formulated by the mathematicians. Suppose that by some suitable mechanical arrangement the bob of the pendulum could be made to swing along some other curve. Could this curve be chosen so that the period of the motion would be absolutely independent of the amplitude? The answer was supplied by Christian Huygens and the curve proved to be the cycloid. Let us see that this is the case.

To have the cycloid serve as the path of the bob the curve must be examined in the position shown in Fig. (18-20) and it is most convenient if the equation of the cycloid can be taken so that $O$, the lowest point on the cycloid, is the origin of the coordinate system. To obtain the parametric equations of the cycloid when the curve is in this position, it is simpler to rederive it. Imagine that the generating circle (Fig. 18-21) is rolling along the line $O'N'$ and below it. To start with, the circle occupies the position shown by the broken-line figure and point $P$ on the circle is at $O$. By the time the circle has rolled so that its point of contact on line $O'N'$ is $N'$, $P$ has moved to the position shown in the figure. The amount of rotation of the generating circle can be specified by angle $\theta$. Then the coordinates of point $P$ as functions of $\theta$ can be obtained by practically the same method as we used in Section 3 of this chapter. Thus

$$x = OM = ON + NM = O'N' + NM = R\theta + R \sin \theta,$$
$$y = PM = CN - CQ = R - R \cos \theta.$$

---

* This section can be omitted without disrupting the continuity.

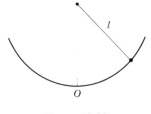

**Figure 18-20**

Then

**(42)** $$x = R\theta + R \sin \theta, \qquad y = R - R \cos \theta$$

are the parametric equations of the cycloid when the curve is in the position of Fig. 18-21.

The bob of the pendulum will move along the curve. To study its motion we can use the distance it moves to the right and to the left of $O$. This distance is the arc length along the cycloid. Let us then calculate the arc length as measured from $O$; this length is to be positive when $P$ is to the right of $O$ and negative when to the left. We need not repeat the steps from (35) to (38) whereby we calculated the arc length of the cycloid. In the present case we use equations (42) and, instead of calculating the length of a complete arc, we merely calculate the length from $O$ to an arbitrary point $P$ whose parameter value is $\theta$. Then [compare (38)]

**(43)** $$s = \int_0^\theta \sqrt{4R^2 \cos^2 \frac{\theta}{2}} = \int_0^\theta 2R \cos \frac{\theta}{2} = 4R \sin \frac{\theta}{2} \Big|_0^\theta = 4R \sin \frac{\theta}{2}.$$

We note that if $\theta$ is taken to be negative when $P$ is to the left of $O$, $s$ will be negative.

We now have an expression for the arc length, and we propose to study the motion of the bob along the cycloid. Suppose that the bob is placed (Fig. 18-22) at some point $P$. What will cause the bob to move? The answer, as in the case of the circular pendulum, is gravity. Let us consider

**Figure 18-21**

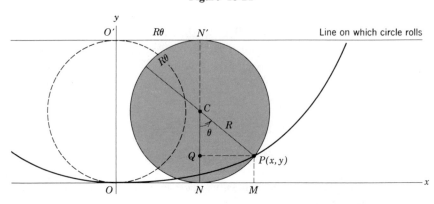

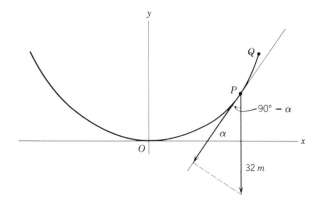

**Figure 18-22**

the force acting at a typical point $P$ on the bob's path. The force of gravity is straight down and is of magnitude $32m$ where $m$ is the mass of the bob. However, again as in the case of the circular pendulum, the force that actually causes the bob to move along the cycloid is the component of gravity tangential to the cycloid. This component is

$$32m \cos (90 - \alpha) = 32m \sin \alpha$$

where $\alpha$ is the inclination of the tangent at $P$. We must remember the matter of signs. We agreed some time ago that the positive direction of the force must agree with the positive direction of the distance. Then in the present case the force acting at $P$ is

$$- 32m \sin \alpha.$$

By Newton's second law of motion,

$$m \frac{d^2 s}{dt^2} = - 32m \sin \alpha$$

or

**(44)** $$\ddot{s} = - 32 \sin \alpha.$$

Unfortunately, (44) is not helpful. The left side involves $s$ and $t$ and the right side involves $\alpha$. If we could replace the right side by some function of $s$ or $t$, we might have a chance of solving the equation by integration. We do have (43) which relates $s$ and $\theta$, namely,

**(45)** $$s = 4R \sin \frac{\theta}{2}.$$

If we could relate $\alpha$ and $\theta$, we might be able to express $s$ in terms of $\alpha$ and then go back to (44) and replace $\alpha$ by some function of $s$. Now, $\alpha$ is the inclination of the tangent to the curve, and so $\tan \alpha$ is the slope. However, we also know how to calculate the slope in terms of $\theta$ by using (18). In fact,

$$\frac{dy}{dx} = \frac{\dfrac{dy}{d\theta}}{\dfrac{dx}{d\theta}} = \frac{R \sin \theta}{R + R \cos \theta} = \frac{\sin \theta}{1 + \cos \theta} = \tan \frac{\theta}{2} .^*$$

Since $dy/dx$ is also $\tan \alpha$, we have

$$\tan \alpha = \tan \frac{\theta}{2}$$

or

**(46)** $$\alpha = \frac{\theta}{2} ;$$

then from (45)

**(47)** $$s = 4R \sin \alpha,$$

and by substituting the value of $\sin \alpha$ in (44) we obtain

**(48)** $$\ddot{s} = \frac{-32}{4R} s.$$

This differential equation we have solved many times (Chap. 10). We know that the motion is sinusoidal or cosinusoidal or a combination of the two depending on the initial conditions. Moreover, and this is the striking point, the period is (cf. (67) of Chap. 10)

**(49)** $$T = 2\pi \sqrt{\frac{4R}{32}} ;$$

this period is independent of the amplitude, as it is in all sinusoidal motions. The result (49) holds no matter how far from the vertex $O$ of Fig. 18-22 we place the bob initially as long as it is on the arch of the cycloid.

We derived (49) by supposing that the bob moves along a track shaped like the arc of a cycloid. We have not shown so far that there is some mechanical arrangement that will cause the bob to follow a cycloidal path and yet swing freely under the action of gravity. Suppose that we suspend the bob from a string (Fig. 18-23) of length $4R$. We then place two rigid cycloids at $A$, as shown in the figure, so that the string wraps itself partly along each of these cycloids in turn as the bob swings from left to right. If these rigid cycloids are generated by rolling circles of radius $R$, the bob will

---

* The last equality follows from the following identities: Because

$$\sin \frac{\theta}{2} = \sqrt{\frac{1 - \cos \theta}{2}} \quad \text{and} \quad \cos \frac{\theta}{2} = \sqrt{\frac{1 + \cos \theta}{2}} ,$$

$$\tan \frac{\theta}{2} = \sqrt{\frac{1 - \cos \theta}{1 + \cos \theta}} = \sqrt{\frac{1 - \cos \theta}{1 + \cos \theta} \cdot \frac{1 + \cos \theta}{1 + \cos \theta}} = \sqrt{\frac{1 - \cos^2 \theta}{(1 + \cos \theta)^2}} = \frac{\sin \theta}{1 + \cos \theta} .$$

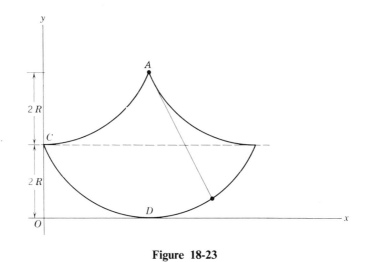

**Figure 18-23**

move along a cycloid of exactly the same size. This last statement requires proof which we shall not supply here. The construction we have just described is due to Huygens.

Because the period of motion of a cycloidal pendulum is independent of the amplitude of its swing, the cycloid is called the tautochrone or the isochronous curve.

## EXERCISES

**1.** Obtain the solution of (48) under the initial conditions that the object is displaced a distance $s_0$ along the cycloidal arc from the lowest point and then released.          *Ans.* $s = s_0 \cos \sqrt{8/R}\ t$.

**2.** Suppose that a cycloidal pendulum of the type illustrated in Fig. 18-23 is constructed. The bob is then pulled back a distance of 1 inch along the arc from the rest position and released. What is the period of oscillation of the bob? Now suppose that the bob is pulled back 2 inches and then released. What is the period?          *Ans.* $T = \pi \sqrt{R/2}$ in both cases.

**3.** Suppose that the cycloid of Fig. 18-22 is a rigid smooth track and that a particle is placed somewhere on it and allowed to slide under the action of gravity. Describe the motion of the particle.

**4.** What is the time required for an object to slide down the cycloid from the point $C$ of Fig. 18-23 to point $D$?          *Ans.* $\pi \sqrt{R/32}$ .

**5.** Suppose that an object slides down a straight line from point $(0, 2R)$ of Fig. 18-23 to point $D$ where $\theta = \pi$. Calculate the time required and compare with the result of Exercise 4.

    *Suggestion:* The acceleration acting on the object is $32 \sin \alpha$ where $\alpha$ is the inclination of the line.

**7. *Velocity and Acceleration in Curvilinear Motion.*** We have already noted that forces, velocities, and accelerations are vectors; that is, they have direction as well as magnitude. However, in our uses of these concepts thus far we were not obliged to do more than obtain the component of a force or

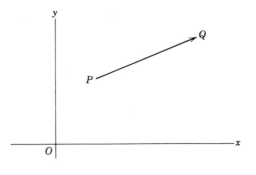

**Figure 18-24**

to recognize that velocities and accelerations have horizontal and vertical components. To obtain further information about the velocities and accelerations of objects that move along curves we must deal more directly with the vector character of velocity and acceleration and we shall therefore introduce vector methods.

A vector, as already noted, has direction and magnitude. It also has a sense. That is, the line $PQ$ of Fig. 18-24 has not only a direction with respect to the $x$- and $y$-axes but it has the sense of $PQ$ as opposed to $QP$. Quantities such as mass and temperature that have magnitude only are called *scalars*.

Vectors are represented geometrically as directed line segments. It is usually immaterial as to where the vector is located so that two parallel line segments having the same direction, sense, and length are considered to be equal. In print vectors are denoted by boldfaced letters, as **v**; in handwritten work an arrow is placed over the symbol as in $\vec{v}$ or a line is placed below as in $\underline{v}$.

If $\mathbf{v}_1$ and $\mathbf{v}_2$ are vectors (Fig. 18-25) then their sum $\mathbf{v}_1 + \mathbf{v}_2$ is defined as follows. One draws $\mathbf{v}_2$ at the terminal point $B$ of $\mathbf{v}_1$. The vector which extends from the initial point $A$ of $\mathbf{v}_1$ to the terminal point $C$ of $\mathbf{v}_2$ is the sum of $\mathbf{v}_1$ and $\mathbf{v}_2$. Alternatively we can draw $\mathbf{v}_2$ as shown in Fig. 18-26, complete the parallelogram determined by $\mathbf{v}_1$ and $\mathbf{v}_2$ and take the sum to be the diagonal $AC$. Since $BC = AD$, the sum just defined is clearly equal to the preceding sum.*

The difference $\mathbf{v}_1 - \mathbf{v}_2$ of two vectors is defined as follows. If both are drawn from a common origin $A$ (Fig. 18-27) then the vector that extends

**Figure 18-25**

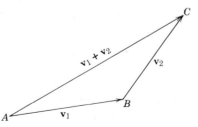

*See also Chapter 3, Section 4.

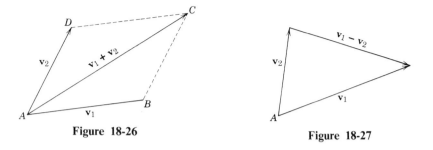

Figure 18-26          Figure 18-27

from the terminal point of $v_2$ to the terminal point of $v_1$ is $v_1 - v_2$. We can see that the sum $v_2 + (v_1 - v_2)$, in accordance with the definition of sum, does indeed yield $v_1$.

To obtain useful results from operations with vectors we must make use of their representation in terms of components. The basic representation uses the rectangular cartesian coordinate system. We introduce (Fig. 18-28) the unit vector **i** which extends along the $x$-axis from the origin to $(1, 0)$. Similarly we introduce the unit vector **j** which extends along the $y$-axis from the origin to the point $(0, 1)$. Then $a\mathbf{i}$, where $a$ is a number, represents a vector parallel to the $x$-axis and having magnitude $|a|$. If $a$ is positive $a\mathbf{i}$ is directed to the right, and if $a$ is negative, $a\mathbf{i}$ is directed to the left. Similarly $b\mathbf{j}$ is a vector parallel to the $y$-axis, of magnitude $|b|$ and directed upward if $b$ is positive and downward if $b$ is negative. The vector **v** which extends from the initial point $A$ of $a\mathbf{i}$ (Fig. 18-28) to the terminal $C$ of $b\mathbf{j}$ is the sum **v** of $a\mathbf{i}$ and $b\mathbf{j}$. That is,

$$\mathbf{v} = a\mathbf{i} + b\mathbf{j}.$$

Moreover $a\mathbf{i}$ and $b\mathbf{j}$ are called the rectangular components of **v**.

It is geometrically obvious that if $v_1 = v_2$ and $v_1 = a_1\mathbf{i} + b_1\mathbf{j}$ and $v_2 = a_2\mathbf{i} + b_2\mathbf{j}$, then $a_1 = a_2$ and $b_1 = b_2$ and conversely.

Figure 18-28

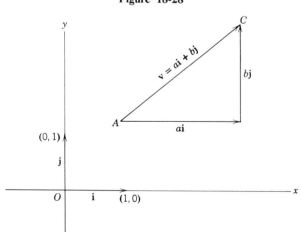

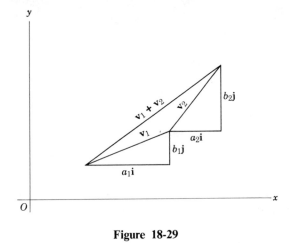

**Figure 18-29**

It is also rather obvious geometrically (Fig. 18-29) that if $v_1 = a_1 i + b_1 j$ and $v_2 = a_2 i + b_2 j$ then

**(50)** $$v = v_1 + v_2 = (a_1 + a_2)i + (b_1 + b_2)j.$$

That is, two vectors may be added by adding the respective components. The analogous result is readily established geometrically for subtraction. That is,

$$v = v_1 - v_2 = (a_1 - a_2)i + (b_1 - b_2)j.$$

In terms of components the magnitude of $v$, denoted by $|v|$, is readily seen (Fig. 18-28) to be

**(51)** $$\sqrt{a^2 + b^2} .$$

A vector $v$ may be multiplied by a scalar. Thus $cv$, where $c$ is a scalar, is a vector having the magnitude $c|v|$ and the direction of $v$. If $c$ is positive the sense of $cv$ is that of $v$; if $c$ is negative the sense is reversed. If $v = ai + bj$ then the similar triangles in Fig. 18-30 show that

**(52)** $$cv = cai + cbj.$$

The zero vector is one whose magnitude is 0. In view of (51), $a$ and $b$ must be 0 so that $v = 0i + 0j$. The vectors $i$ and $j$ already introduced are unit vectors. More generally any unit vector is one whose magnitude is 1.

**Figure 18-30**

**Example.**   Express in component form the vector which extends from (1, 4) to (5, 2).

**Solution.**   Plotting the points shows that the vector can be expressed as the sum of a vector of 4 units in the positive $x$-direction and 2 units in the negative $y$-direction. If we introduce **i** and **j** then the vector is expressible as $\mathbf{v} = 4\mathbf{i} - 2\mathbf{j}$.

In the form just written the initial and terminal points of the vector are not fixed, and as noted in the text, this usually does not matter. If one wishes to specify the position of the vector one must add that the initial point is (1, 4) or that the terminal point is (5, 2).

## EXERCISES

1. Express as vectors in the form $a\mathbf{i} + b\mathbf{j}$:
   (a)   The line segment from the origin to (3, 4).
   (b)   The line segment from (1, 1) to (3, 4).
   (c)   The line segment from (3, 4) to (1, 1).
   (d)   The unit vector making an angle of 45° with the $x$-axis.
   (e)   The unit vector making an angle of 60° with the $y$-axis.
   (f)   The unit vector having the same direction as $\mathbf{i} + 2\mathbf{j}$.
   (g)   The sum of the vectors from (1, 1) to (3, 4) and from (2, 3) to (6, 7).
   (h)   A unit vector tangent to $y = x^2$ at the point (2, 4).

2. Find the magnitude of the following vectors:
   (a)   $2\mathbf{i} + \mathbf{j}$.                          (c)   $-2\mathbf{i} + 4\mathbf{j}$.
   (b)   $3\mathbf{i} - 4\mathbf{j}$.                          (d)   $-2\mathbf{i} - 3\mathbf{j}$.

3. What curve is traced out by the terminal points of the vector $\mathbf{r} = \cos\theta\mathbf{i} + \sin\theta\mathbf{j}$ as $\theta$ varies from 0 to $2\pi$ if the initial point is the origin?

4. Express in the form $a\mathbf{i} + b\mathbf{j}$ the unit vector which has the direction of the tangent to $y = x^2$ at the point (3, 9).

These few facts we have learned about vectors will now enable us to study motion along curves and in particular to study the velocity and acceleration of the moving objects. We know that a curve can be represented by the parametric equations

**(53)**                           $x = g(t), \qquad y = h(t).$

The function $g(t)$ describes the position of the moving object in the horizontal direction while the function $h(t)$ describes the vertical position. The same information is encompassed in the vector expression

$$\mathbf{r}(t) = g(t)\mathbf{i} + h(t)\mathbf{j},$$

where the vector $\mathbf{r}(t)$, (Fig. 18-31), extends from the origin $O$ to the point $P$. The coordinates of $P$ are $(g(t), h(t))$. As $t$ varies the endpoints or terminal points of $\mathbf{r}(t)$ trace out the curve. $\mathbf{r}(t)$ is called a position vector. It can also be written as

$$\mathbf{r}(t) = x\mathbf{i} + y\mathbf{j},$$

where $x$ and $y$ have the values given by (53).

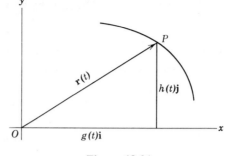

**Figure 18-31**

We shall now see how we can obtain the velocity and acceleration vectors from $\mathbf{r}(t)$. The velocity of a scalar function which represents distance in terms of time has been defined to be the derivative of that function. However, $\mathbf{r}(t)$ is not the vector distance traveled in time $t$ but the position vector of a moving point. Nevertheless let us investigate $d\mathbf{r}/dt$.

Mathematically $d\mathbf{r}/dt$ is defined in the usual manner. That is, we form the difference quotient (Fig. 18-32)

$$\frac{\Delta \mathbf{r}}{\Delta t} = \frac{\mathbf{r}(t + \Delta t) - \mathbf{r}(t)}{\Delta t}$$

and take $d\mathbf{r}/dt$ to be the limit of $\Delta \mathbf{r}/\Delta t$ as $\Delta t$ approaches 0. Thus

$$\frac{d\mathbf{r}}{dt} = \lim_{\Delta t \to 0} \frac{\Delta \mathbf{r}}{\Delta t}.$$

In terms of components, since

$$\mathbf{r}(t) = x(t)\mathbf{i} + y(t)\mathbf{j},$$

$$\mathbf{r}(t + \Delta t) - \mathbf{r}(t) = \Delta x \mathbf{i} + \Delta y \mathbf{j}$$

**Figure 18-32**

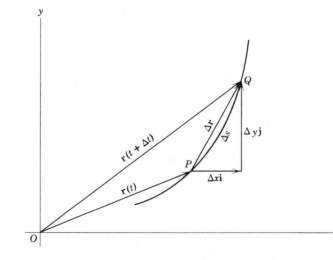

and

$$\frac{\Delta \mathbf{r}}{\Delta t} = \frac{\Delta x}{\Delta t} \mathbf{i} + \frac{\Delta y}{\Delta t} \mathbf{j}.$$

Because **i** and **j** are fixed vectors,

**(54)**
$$\frac{d\mathbf{r}}{dt} = \frac{dx}{dt} \mathbf{i} + \frac{dy}{dt} \mathbf{j} = \dot{x}\mathbf{i} + \dot{y}\mathbf{j}.$$

Hence we can compute $d\mathbf{r}/dt$ by means of its components.

Now let us see whether $d\mathbf{r}/dt$ does indeed give the velocity vector of the moving object. Figure 18-32 shows the geometrical meaning of the various quantities involved in obtaining $d\mathbf{r}/dt$. $\Delta \mathbf{r}$ is the chord joining $P$ and $Q$. As $\Delta t$ approaches 0, $Q$ approaches $P$ and, as we know from earlier work (Chap. 4, Sect. 1), the chord $PQ$ approaches the tangent at $P$. Hence the direction of $d\mathbf{r}/dt$ is that of the tangent to the curve at $P$. Thus $d\mathbf{r}/dt$ has the correct direction for the velocity of the moving object. The slope of $d\mathbf{r}/dt$, since it has the direction of the tangent, is given by $dy/dx$ and, in view of (18),

**(55)**
$$\text{slope of } \frac{d\mathbf{r}}{dt} = \frac{dy}{dx} = \frac{dy/dt}{dx/dt} .$$

The magnitude $|d\mathbf{r}/dt|$ can also be computed by (54) and (51):

$$\left| \frac{d\mathbf{r}}{dt} \right| = \sqrt{ \left( \frac{dx}{dt} \right)^2 + \left( \frac{dy}{dt} \right)^2 } .$$

From (32) we see that

**(56)**
$$\left| \frac{d\mathbf{r}}{dt} \right| = \left| \frac{ds}{dt} \right|$$

where $s$ represents arc length measured from some fixed point on the curve. But $|ds/dt|$ is the speed of the moving object. Hence $d\mathbf{r}/dt$ has the magnitude of speed, which is just what we expect of the velocity vector. The sense of the velocity vector $d\mathbf{r}/dt$ will depend on how **r** varies with $t$.

If we denote the velocity vector by **v**, then

$$\mathbf{v} = \frac{d\mathbf{r}}{dt}$$

and we indicate the components of **v** by

$$\mathbf{v} = v_x \mathbf{i} + v_y \mathbf{j}.$$

In view of (54), $v_x = dx/dt = \dot{x}$ and $v_y = dy/dt = \dot{y}$. When dealing directly with the parametric equations $x = g(t)$, $y = h(t)$ we know that $\dot{x}$ and

$\dot{y}$ represent the horizontal and vertical components of the velocity. This fact is also contained in (54).

The horizontal and vertical components of the acceleration are $\ddot{x}$ or $d^2x/dt^2$ and $\ddot{y}$ or $d^2y/dt^2$. These facts can be expressed vectorially in terms of the derivative of (54). That is, we define the acceleration vector to be

$$\text{(57)} \qquad \mathbf{a} = \frac{d^2\mathbf{r}}{dt^2} = \frac{d^2x}{dt^2}\,\mathbf{i} + \frac{d^2y}{dt^2}\,\mathbf{j} = \ddot{x}\mathbf{i} + \ddot{y}\mathbf{j}.$$

If we denote $d\mathbf{r}/dt$ by $\mathbf{v}$ then

$$\mathbf{a} = \frac{d\mathbf{v}}{dt} = \ddot{x}\mathbf{i} + \ddot{y}\mathbf{j} = a_x\mathbf{i} + a_y\mathbf{j}$$

where $a_x = \ddot{x}$ and $a_y = \ddot{y}$.

The direction (slope) of the acceleration vector is

$$\text{(58)} \qquad \frac{d^2y/dt^2}{d^2x/dt^2}$$

and this vector is therefore generally not tangent to the curve.

We should note that the magnitude of $d^2\mathbf{r}/dt^2$ is given by

$$\text{(59)} \qquad \left| \frac{d^2\mathbf{r}}{dt^2} \right| = \sqrt{\frac{d^2x}{dt^2} + \frac{d^2y}{dt^2}},$$

but this magnitude is not $d^2s/dt^2$. One can readily verify this by computing $d^2s/dt^2$ from

$$\frac{ds}{dt} = \sqrt{\left( \frac{dx}{dt} \right)^2 + \left( \frac{dy}{dt} \right)^2}.$$

What this fact implies is that the *vector* acceleration is not the derivative with respect to time of the speed $ds/dt$. We shall see later that $d^2s/dt^2$ is but one component of the acceleration vector.

We also observe that if an object is moving along a curve other than a straight line, then $\dot{x}$ and $\dot{y}$ cannot both be constant because the slope of the curve is given by $\dot{y}/\dot{x}$ and this changes from point to point. Hence either $\dot{y}$ or $\dot{x}$ or both change with $t$. Then $\ddot{x}$ or $\ddot{y}$ or both cannot be identically zero. Thus, in view of (57), there must be some acceleration in curvilinear motion even if the speed $|ds/dt|$ is constant.

As an example of the direction of the vector acceleration we have the case of a projectile shot out from a cannon inclined at an angle $A$ to the ground (Fig. 18-33). The only acceleration acting is that due to gravity, and this is directed downward at all points of the curve; that is, in this motion $a_x = 0$, $a_y = -32$ and $\mathbf{a} = -32\mathbf{j}$.

Let us consider another example of velocity and acceleration in curvilinear motion. We consider the motion of a particle along a circle—a

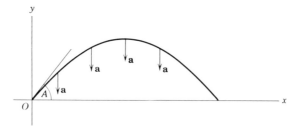

**Figure  18-33**

motion that each of us is constantly undergoing as the earth rotates on its axis. The parametric equations of the circle are (Fig. 18-34)

**(60)**                 $x = R \cos \theta, \qquad y = R \sin \theta.$

However, these equations do not specify the motion until we state how $\theta$ varies with time $t$. It is helpful to introduce the quantity $\omega$, which is the angular velocity of $P$, the position of the particle. By definition $\omega$ is $d\theta / dt$ or $\dot{\theta}$; that is, $\omega$ is the rate of change of $\theta$ with respect to time in radians per second or radians per unit of time for whatever unit of time is used. Then $\theta$ is the number of radians through which $P$ moves in time $t$. If $\omega$ is constant, $\theta = \omega t$. Thus if $\omega$ is, say, 3 and the unit of time is seconds, $\theta = 3t$ and in 2 seconds $\theta$ changes by 6 radians.

Let us suppose that $\omega$ is constant so that $\theta = \omega t$. Then the parametric equations (60) become

$$x = R \cos \omega t, \qquad y = R \sin \omega t.$$

In vector form

**(61)**                 $\mathbf{r}(t) = (R \cos \omega t)\mathbf{i} + (R \sin \omega t)\mathbf{j},$

**Figure  18-34**

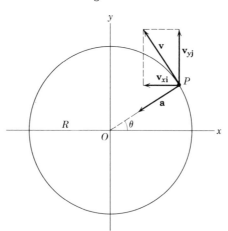

which can also be written as

$$r(t) = iR \cos \omega t + jR \sin \omega t.$$

Then

$$v = \frac{dr}{dt} = (-\omega R \sin \omega t)i + (\omega R \cos \omega t)j.$$

The magnitude $|v|$ of the velocity is

$$\sqrt{(-\omega R \sin \omega t)^2 + (\omega R \cos \omega t)^2} = \omega R.$$

The slope of the velocity vector is

$$\frac{\dot{y}}{\dot{x}} = -\cot \omega t = -\cot \theta$$

and this slope is indeed perpendicular to that of the radius $OP$ (Fig. 18-34) and therefore tangent to the circle at $P$.

Applying (57) to our $dr/dt$ we obtain the acceleration vector

$$a = \frac{d^2r}{dt^2} = (-\omega^2 R \cos \omega t)i + (-\omega^2 R \sin \omega t)j.$$

The magnitude of the acceleration, according to (59), is $\omega^2 R$.

The direction of acceleration is interesting. According to (58) this direction is

$$\frac{-\omega^2 R \sin \omega t}{-\omega^2 R \cos \omega t} = \tan \omega t = \tan \theta.$$

Hence the action of the acceleration is along $OP$ and, because both components are negative when $\omega t < \pi/2$, the sense of the acceleration is

**Figure 18-35**

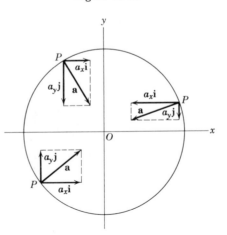

toward $O$ as Fig. 18-35 shows. If account is taken of the signs of the components, one finds that the acceleration is always toward $O$ for all positions of $P$.

The physical meaning of the fact that the acceleration is along $PO$ is that motion in a circle can take place only if there is an acceleration that continually pulls the moving particle toward the center. This physical situation occurs, for example, when one whirls an object at the end of a string. The hand must exert a force, which by Newton's second law of motion implies an acceleration, toward the center to keep the object whirling in a circle. Moreover since the magnitude of the acceleration is $\omega^2 R$ and $\omega$ is the angular velocity, the acceleration must be greater if the angular velocity is increased. This, too, accords with our experience. Acceleration toward a center is called *centripetal* acceleration, centripetal meaning center-seeking. We should note in this example of motion that even though the object moves along the circle at a constant speed there is an acceleration acting. It is this acceleration that continually changes the direction of the motion from what would otherwise be straight-line motion to circular motion.

## EXERCISES

1. Calculate the velocity and acceleration vectors for the motions represented by the following equations:

   (a) $\mathbf{r} = (3t)\mathbf{i} + (4t)\mathbf{j}$.           *Ans.* $\dfrac{d\mathbf{r}}{dt} = 3\mathbf{i} + (8t^2)\mathbf{j}$; $\dfrac{d^2\mathbf{r}}{dt^2} = 16t\mathbf{j}$.

   (b) $\mathbf{r} = (3t^2)\mathbf{i} + (-3t^3)\mathbf{j}$.
   (c) $\mathbf{r} = (\sin 3t)\mathbf{i} + (\cos 3t)\mathbf{j}$.
   (d) $\mathbf{r} = e^t\mathbf{i} + e^{-t}\mathbf{j}$.

2. The vector equation of the cycloid is $\mathbf{r} = R(\theta - \sin\theta)\mathbf{i} + R(1 - \cos\theta)\mathbf{j}$. If $\theta = \omega t$, where $\omega$, the angular velocity, is constant, calculate the magnitudes of the velocity and acceleration of a particle moving along the curve.

   *Ans.* $|\mathbf{v}| = 2R\omega \sin\dfrac{\omega}{2}t$, $|\mathbf{a}| = R\omega^2$.

3. A particle moves on the hyperbola whose parametric equations are $x = r\cosh\omega t$, $y = r\sinh\omega t$, where $\omega$ and $r$ are constants. Calculate the velocity and acceleration vectors.     *Ans.* $\mathbf{v} = (\omega r \sinh\omega t)\mathbf{i} + (\omega r \cosh\omega t)\mathbf{j}$; $\mathbf{a} = \omega^2\mathbf{r}$.

4. Suppose that a particle moves along a cycloid in accordance with $\theta = \omega t$, where $\omega$ is constant:

   (a) When is the magnitude of the velocity 0 and where is the particle at those instants?                                     *Ans.* $t = 0$ or $2\pi/\omega$.

   (b) When is the magnitude of the velocity maximum? Because the generating circle rotates at a constant angular velocity, can you account in physical terms for the fact that $P$ has a maximum magnitude of velocity at the point that you have determined?                     *Ans.* $t = \pi/\omega$.

5. Make a sketch of the cycloid showing the velocity vector and acceleration vector at the four points $t = 0$, $t = \pi/2\omega$, $\pi/\omega$, $3\pi/2\omega$.

6. Use the fact that $ds/dt = |\mathbf{v}|$ to find the distance covered by point $P$ of the cycloid from $t = 0$ to $t = t$.                     *Ans.* $4R[1 - \cos(\omega t/2)]$.

7. Using the result of Exercise 6, obtain the length of one complete arc of the cycloid.                                                                    *Ans.* 8*R*.

8. Show that the direction of the velocity vector at any point on a cycloid for which $\theta$ lies between 0 and 180° is directed toward the highest point on the generating circle. In terms of Fig. 18-36 the velocity at $P$ is directed toward $A$.

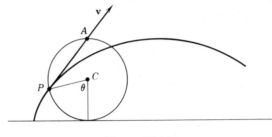

**Figure 18-36**

9. A point on the rim of a train wheel follows a cycloidal path given by the equations $x = 20t - \sin 20t$, $y = 1 - \cos 20t$. Determine the magnitude and direction of the acceleration of the point.
                                              *Ans.* 400; toward the center of the wheel.

10. Show that the direction of the acceleration vector at any point $P$ of the cycloid lies along the line $PC$, where $C$ is the center of the generating circle. (In terms of Fig. 18-36 the acceleration vector is directed along $PC$.)

11. Show that when a particle moving on a cycloid is at the top of its path, its velocity is twice that of the center $C$ of the generating circle.

12. Show that $|d^2s/dt^2|$ is less than the magnitude $\sqrt{\ddot{x}^2 + \ddot{y}^2}$ of acceleration (unless the motion is along a straight line).

13. A wheel 4 feet in diameter rolls along a straight horizontal road at the rate of 20 rpm. Find the magnitude of the velocity and the acceleration of a point on the rim when it is 1 foot below the center of the wheel.

14. Suppose that the gravitational force acting on a particle is proportional to the distance between the particle and a fixed mass. Suppose further that at $t = 0$ the object is on the $x$-axis and moving vertically. Show
   (a)   that the particle travels in an ellipse whose center is at the fixed mass;
   (b)   that the time for one complete orbit is independent of the initial conditions.

   *Suggestion:* Take the fixed mass at $(0, 0)$ and use the fact that $\mathbf{a} = -k\mathbf{d}$, where $\mathbf{d}$ is the variable distance so that $a_x = -kx$ and $a_y = -ky$.

**8. Tangential and Normal Acceleration in Curvilinear Motion.** If a motion takes place along a curve for which we know the parametric equations as functions of the time, we can now calculate the magnitude and direction of the velocity and the magnitude and direction of the acceleration. We obtained these quantities by calculating the components of the velocity and the acceleration in the directions of the $x$- and $y$-axes; that is, we calculated $\dot{x}, \dot{y}, \ddot{x}$, and $\ddot{y}$. In curvilinear motion the direction of the motion is along the tangent to the curve but, as we have already pointed out, there must be some force acting that continually changes the direction of the motion or else the object will move in a straight line. Hence the force that changes the direction of the motion must pull the object away from the tangent direction. To study such motions, it is useful to know what happens in the direction of the tangent and what is acting to cause deviation from that direction. Knowing the acceleration vector as given by (57) does not tell us how much of the acceleration acts along the tangent and how much does not.

We shall first reconsider the tangent vector. The parametric equations we have used thus far to study velocity and acceleration have been functions of a parameter $t$ which represents time. However, as a point $P$ moves along a curve, its position can be specified by the arc length $s$ it has traveled from some fixed point at which $s = 0$. Then the position vector from the origin $O$ to $P$ becomes a function of $s$ and the components of the position vector are likewise functions of $s$. That is,

**(62)** $$\mathbf{r}(s) = x(s)\mathbf{i} + y(s)\mathbf{j}.$$

If the object moves to $Q$, $\mathbf{r}(s)$ changes to $\mathbf{r}(s + \Delta s)$ (Fig. 18-37). Then

$$\frac{\Delta \mathbf{r}}{\Delta s} = \frac{\mathbf{r}(s + \Delta s) - \mathbf{r}(s)}{\Delta s} .$$

We can now define $d\mathbf{r}/ds$ as

**(63)** $$\frac{d\mathbf{r}}{ds} = \lim_{\Delta s \to 0} \frac{\Delta \mathbf{r}}{\Delta s} .$$

However, the ratio of the chord $PQ$ to the arc $PQ$ approaches 1. Hence the magnitude of $d\mathbf{r}/ds$ is 1. The direction of $d\mathbf{r}/ds$ is the limit of the direction of $\Delta \mathbf{r}/\Delta s$. As $\Delta s$ approaches 0, $Q$ approaches $P$. Thus the direction of $d\mathbf{r}/ds$ is that of the tangent at $P$. The sense of the tangent is determined also; $\Delta \mathbf{r}$ is the directed vector $PQ$; $\Delta s$ may be positive, which is the case if $s$ increases from $P$ to $Q$ or negative if $\Delta s$ decreases from $P$ to $Q$ (Fig. 18-38). In the

**Figure 18-37**

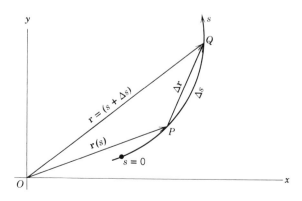

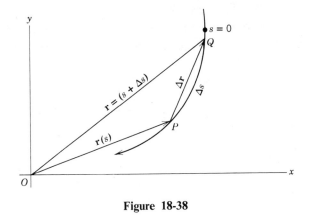

Figure 18-38

first case $\Delta \mathbf{r}/\Delta s$ has the sense of $PQ$ in Fig. 18-37; in the second (Fig. 18-38) $\Delta \mathbf{r}$ has the sense $PQ$ but since $\Delta s$ is negative, the quotient has the sense of $QP$. In both cases the limit $d\mathbf{r}/ds$ has the sense of increasing $s$ on the curve. Thus $d\mathbf{r}/ds$ has the direction of the tangent at $P$ and points in the direction of increasing $s$. The unit vector $d\mathbf{r}/ds$ is generally denoted by **T**.

    The sense of **T** is specified by (Fig. 18-39) the counterclockwise angle $\phi$ between the direction of the positive $x$-axis and the positive sense of **T**. $\phi$ can then vary from 0 to 360°.

    Insofar as the component representation of $d\mathbf{r}/ds$ is concerned, since, by (62),

$$\mathbf{r}(s) = x(s)\mathbf{i} + y(s)\mathbf{j}$$

we have but to repeat the few steps leading to (54) to arrive at

**(64)** $$\mathbf{T} = \frac{d\mathbf{r}(s)}{ds} = \frac{dx}{ds}\mathbf{i} + \frac{dy}{ds}\mathbf{j}.$$

This result (64) may be used to compute $d\mathbf{r}/ds$. If $x$ and $y$ are given in terms of some parameter $t$, say, we must know the relation between $t$ and $s$ in order to use (64). This relation is given by (32).

    The vector **T** has the direction and sense of the velocity vector **v** or $d\mathbf{r}/dt$. To determine the acceleration which causes an object moving on a

Figure 18-39

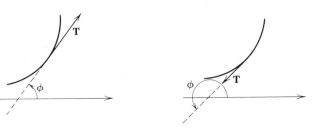

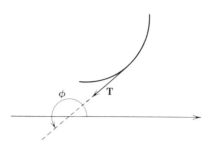

**Figure 18-40**

curve to depart from straight-line motion we shall first study the rate of change of **T**. In terms of the angle $\phi$ which signifies the sense of the unit vector **T**, **T** can always be expressed (Fig. 18-40) as

**(65)** $$\mathbf{T} = (\cos \phi)\mathbf{i} + (\sin \phi)\mathbf{j}.$$

Then

**(66)** $$\frac{d\mathbf{T}}{d\phi} = (-\sin \phi)\mathbf{i} + (\cos \phi)\mathbf{j}.$$

The magnitude of $d\mathbf{T}/d\phi$ is

**(67)** $$\sqrt{\sin^2 \phi + \cos^2 \phi} = 1$$

and the direction of $d\mathbf{T}/d\phi$ is

**(68)** $$\frac{\cos \phi}{-\sin \phi} = -\frac{1}{\tan \phi}.$$

This direction is the negative reciprocal of the direction of **T**; hence $d\mathbf{T}/d\phi$ is perpendicular to **T**. Thus $d\mathbf{T}/d\phi$ is a unit vector perpendicular to **T**, whereas **T** has the direction and sense of the tangent to the curve. We represent the unit vector $d\mathbf{T}/d\phi$ by **N**. It is called the unit normal. Furthermore, we can rewrite (66) as

$$\mathbf{N} = \cos (90° + \phi)\mathbf{i} + \sin (90° + \phi)\mathbf{j}.$$

Thus **N** is the unit normal vector obtained by rotating the unit tangent vector through 90° in the counterclockwise direction (Fig. 18-41).

In terms of **T** and **N** we are now prepared to consider the tangential acceleration and any other acceleration that may be acting on an object moving along a curve. The vectors **T** and **N** that we have just introduced will serve as reference unit vectors much as **i** and **j** do when we study velocity and acceleration in the horizontal and vertical directions.

If the position vector $\mathbf{r}(t)$ is

$$\mathbf{r}(t) = x(t)\mathbf{i} + y(t)\mathbf{j}$$

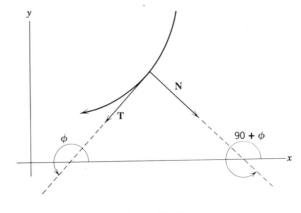

**Figure 18-41**

then we know that the velocity vector is

$$\mathbf{v} = \frac{d\mathbf{r}}{dt}.$$

By the chain rule we may write

**(69)** $$\mathbf{v} = \frac{d\mathbf{r}}{ds}\frac{ds}{dt} = \frac{ds}{dt}\mathbf{T}.$$

Here we see once again that the velocity vector has the direction of the tangent to the curve and has the magnitude $|ds/dt|$.

The acceleration vector is given by $d\mathbf{v}/dt$. We therefore differentiate the right-hand expression in (69). Then

**(70)** $$\mathbf{a} = \frac{d\mathbf{v}}{dt} = \frac{d^2s}{dt^2}\mathbf{T} + \frac{ds}{dt}\frac{d\mathbf{T}}{dt}.$$

But

$$\frac{d\mathbf{T}}{dt} = \frac{d\mathbf{T}}{ds}\frac{ds}{dt}$$

so that

$$\mathbf{a} = \mathbf{T}\frac{d^2s}{dt^2} + \frac{d\mathbf{T}}{ds}\left(\frac{ds}{dt}\right)^2.$$

A somewhat more perspicuous expression for **a** is obtained if we introduce the sensed angle $\phi$ and write

$$\mathbf{a} = \mathbf{T}\frac{d^2s}{dt^2} + \frac{d\mathbf{T}}{d\phi}+\frac{d\phi}{ds}\left(\frac{ds}{dt}\right)^2$$

or since $d\mathbf{T}/d\phi$ is denoted by **N**,

**(71)** $$\mathbf{a} = \mathbf{T}\frac{d^2s}{dt^2} + \mathbf{N}\frac{d\phi}{ds}\left(\frac{ds}{dt}\right)^2.$$

We have now expressed the acceleration vector in terms of two perpendicular components. The first, $\mathbf{T} d^2s/dt^2$, is along the tangent and has the magnitude of the acceleration along the curve. The second component is along $\mathbf{N}$ and has the magnitude

$$\left| \frac{d\phi}{ds} \left( \frac{ds}{dt} \right)^2 \right|.$$

The quantity $(ds/dt)^2$ is simply the square of the instantaneous speed $v$ of the object along the curve. The quantity $d\phi/ds$ is also familiar to us. In Chapter 15, Section 5, [see (42) there] we introduced the curvature of a curve as $d\phi/ds$ and denoted it by $K$. Hence the acceleration can be written as

**(72)**
$$\mathbf{a} = \mathbf{T} \frac{d^2s}{dt^2} + \mathbf{N} K v^2.$$

or in terms of the radius of curvature $R = 1/K$,

**(73)**
$$\mathbf{a} = \mathbf{T} \frac{d^2s}{dt^2} + \mathbf{N} \frac{v^2}{R} = a_T \mathbf{T} + a_N \mathbf{N}.$$

We should also see that the normal component $\mathbf{N} v^2/R$ of the acceleration is directed toward the concave side of the curve. Since $v^2$ is positive, the sense of $\mathbf{N} v^2/R$ or $\mathbf{N} K v^2$ depends on $\mathbf{N} K$. Two illustrations may convince us that the normal component is indeed directed toward the concave side of the curve. In Fig. 18-42$a$, $s$ is positive upward. The unit tangent $\mathbf{T}$ has already been noted to possess the sense of increasing $s$ and $\mathbf{N}$ has been shown to be 90° counterclockwise to $\mathbf{T}$. The curvature $d\phi/ds$ is negative at $P$ because $\phi$ decreases with increasing $s$. Hence $K\mathbf{N}$ has the sense opposite to $\mathbf{N}$ or the sense toward the concave side of the curve.

Let us consider as the second example Fig. 18-42$b$. Here $s$ increases downward. The tangent $\mathbf{T}$ has the sense of increasing $s$ and $\mathbf{N}$ is directed 90° counterclockwise to $\mathbf{T}$. If one moves in the direction of increasing $s$ then $\phi$ increases and so $d\phi/ds$ is positive. Hence $K\mathbf{N}$ is again directed toward the concave side of the curve.

To compute the tangential and normal accelerations one can use (72) or (73). The expression for curvature is available when the curve is given in parametric form [see (40) and (41)]. However, one can sometimes save effort by using the following fact. The acceleration vector at a point $P$ is the same whether it is expressed in components with respect to the cartesian axes or in terms of the tangential and normal components. Thus

$$\mathbf{a} = a_x \mathbf{i} + a_y \mathbf{j} = a_T \mathbf{T} + a_N \mathbf{N}$$

where the various $a$'s have the obvious meanings. Then

$$|\mathbf{a}|^2 = a_x^2 + a_y^2 = a_T^2 + a_N^2.$$

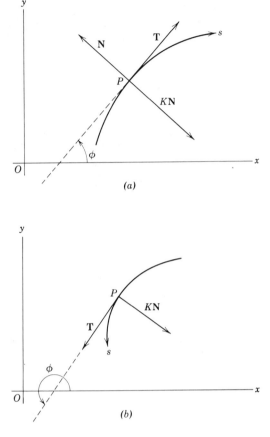

**Figure 18-42**

Hence

**(74)**
$$a_N = \sqrt{|a|^2 - a_T^2} \; .$$

The expressions (72) and (73) for the tangential and normal acceleration show more clearly than the formulas for $a_x$ and $a_y$ a fundamental fact
about curvilinear motion. One tends to think that the time derivative of the
algebraic value $v$ of the velocity, that is $dv/dt$ or $d^2s/dt^2$, is the resultant or
total acceleration. However, the change in the direction of the velocity also
calls for an acceleration. This acceleration is toward the concave side of the
curve and our result for $a_N$ tells us how much this normal acceleration is.
This quantity $a_N$ is also called the *centripetal acceleration*. Because a normal
or centripetal acceleration is present in curvilinear motion, some force must
produce this acceleration. Moreover, in view of (72) or (73), the larger the
curvature of a curve at a point or the larger the velocity along the curve, the
larger $a_N$ must be, and therefore according to Newton's second law of
motion the larger the force must be to produce this acceleration.

Each of us is constantly subject to a normal acceleration, although we
usually do not stop to think about it. The earth is, of course, rotating, and
we say that we "share" in the rotation of the earth; that is, each of us is

constantly moving in a circle. Actually, we would fly off into space if some force did not constantly provide the acceleration that keeps us moving on the circular path. The force that provides the centripetal acceleration is called the centripetal force. What provides the centripetal force? The answer is the earth's gravitational force.

The gravitational force of the earth really exerts two effects on objects. It provides the centripetal force required to keep an object rotating with the earth and it provides the force that we normally call weight—the quantity that we have usually represented as $32m$ for objects near or on the surface of the earth.

The centripetal force required to keep an object on the earth, rotating with the earth, is small compared to the weight of the object. However, if the object should rotate around the earth at a rate of, say, several hours for one rotation, then the centripetal force required to keep it from flying off into space would have to be much greater because $a_N = v^2/R$ and $v$ is large. Specifically if $v$ were 17 times the earth's rotational speed, the centripetal acceleration required to keep an object moving with this velocity along the equator would be equal to the entire gravitational force. Then no force would be available to cause the object to fall to earth, that is, the object would have no weight.

This situation is essentially the one that prevails for satellites and objects in satellites that circle the earth. In fact, suppose the orbit of the satellite is *circular;* the center of its path is the center of the earth; and it orbits at $r$ feet from the center of the earth. The gravitational force exerted by the earth is

$$F_1 = \frac{GMm}{r^2},$$

where $M$ is the mass of the earth and $m$ the mass of the satellite. The centripetal force required to keep the satellite in its circular path is

$$F_2 = \frac{mv^2}{r},$$

because the radius of curvature $R$ is now $r$. If the satellite is to remain in its circular path, that is, if it is not to fall to earth, it must not possess weight. Then the full gravitational force must be used to exert the required centripetal force. That is,

$$\frac{GMm}{r^2} = \frac{mv^2}{r}$$

or

$$\frac{GM}{r} = v^2.$$

This result gives us the velocity at which the satellite must orbit if it is to do

so at the distance $r$ from the center of the earth. Of course, these considerations presuppose a circular path, which is approximately the case for some
of the satellites and balloons that have been set into orbit around the earth.
We shall say more about elliptical paths in Chapter 19.

Let us consider an example of the use of our formulas for tangential
and normal acceleration. Suppose that an object moves along a curve
whose parametric equations are

$$(75) \qquad x = \cos t + t \sin t, \qquad y = \sin t - t \cos t.$$

Find the tangential and normal accelerations. The vectorial form of the
equations of motion is

$$\mathbf{r}(t) = (\cos t + t \sin t)\mathbf{i} + (\sin t - t \cos t)\mathbf{j}.$$

Now the vectorial velocity $\mathbf{v}$ is $d\mathbf{r}/dt$. Hence

$$\mathbf{v} = \frac{d\mathbf{r}}{dt} = (t \cos t)\mathbf{i} + (t \sin t)\mathbf{j}$$

and

$$\mathbf{a} = \frac{d\mathbf{v}}{dt} = (-t \sin t + \cos t)\mathbf{i} + (t \cos t + \sin t)\mathbf{j}.$$

By (72) or (73) the tangential component $a_T$ of the acceleration is $d^2s/dt^2$.
But $|\mathbf{v}| = ds/dt$. Hence

$$\frac{ds}{dt} = \sqrt{(t \cos t)^2 + (t \sin t)^2} = t.$$

Then the tangential component of the acceleration is

$$a_T = \frac{d^2s}{dt^2} = 1.$$

The normal component of the acceleration can be computed directly by
using (72), that is, by computing $Kv^2$ or $K(ds/dt)^2$. However, it is easier to
use (74). Thus

$$a_N = \sqrt{|\mathbf{a}| - a_T^2}$$

$$(76) \qquad = \sqrt{(-t \sin t + \cos t)^2 + (t \cos t + \sin t)^2 - 1} = t.$$

## EXERCISES

1. Suppose that a point moves on the circle of radius $R$ with constant angular
velocity $\omega$. Find the tangential and normal accelerations.

$$\textit{Ans. } a_T = 0, \, a_N = \omega^2 R.$$

**2.** Suppose that a point moves on the circle of radius $R$ with a varying angular velocity and that $\omega$ or $d\theta/dt$ is a function of $t$. Find the tangential and normal accelerations.

**3.** For the cycloid $x = R(\omega t - \sin \omega t)$, $y = R(1 - \cos \omega t)$ calculate the following:
    (a)  The tangential acceleration at an arbitrary point $P$ of the curve.

*Ans.* $R\omega^2 \cos(\omega t/2)$.

    (b)  The normal acceleration of $P$.               *Ans.* $-R\omega^2 \sin(\omega t/2)$.

    (c)  The magnitude of the resultant acceleration.         *Ans.* $R\omega^2$.

**4.** A particle moves along a curve with constant speed. Show that the acceleration is perpendicular to the velocity.

**5.** A bomb is released at point $O$ (Fig. 18-43) from an airplane that is flying horizontally at a velocity of $V$ ft/sec. With the axes chosen as shown in the figure:
    (a)  Write the parametric equations of the motion of the bomb.
    (b)  Calculate the tangential and normal acceleration at any point of the path.

*Ans.* $a_T = (32)^2 t/\sqrt{V^2 + (32t)^2}$ , $a_N = 32V/\sqrt{V^2 + (32t)^2}$ .

    (c)  As a check on the result just obtained consider the magnitude of the total acceleration. Without calculation state what this value is. Now calculate this magnitude by using the components $a_T$ and $a_N$.

    (d)  State on the basis of purely physical facts what $a_T$ and $a_N$ are when $t = 0$. Now use the results of part (b) to see if they yield the proper values at $t = 0$.

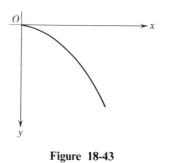

**Figure 18-43**

**6.** Calculate the centripetal acceleration required to keep an object on the equator moving with the earth. What is the tangential acceleration?

*Ans.* 0.11 ft/sec$^2$; 0.

**7.** (a)  What centripetal acceleration is required to keep a satellite moving in a circular path with its center at the center of the earth and at a height of 1000 miles above the surface of the earth?

    (b)  What acceleration does the earth's gravity exert on the satellite?

**8.** Using the equations derived in Section 4 for the motion of a projectile in a vacuum, find the following:
    (a)  The tangential velocity at any point of the path.

*Ans.* $\sqrt{V^2 - 64Vt \sin A + 1024t^2}$ .

    (b)  The velocity in the direction perpendicular to the tangent.

    (c)  The tangential acceleration.      *Ans.* $\dfrac{-32V \sin A + 1024t}{\sqrt{V^2 - 64Vt \sin A + 1024t^2}}$ .

    (d)  The normal acceleration.

(e)  The normal acceleration at the maximum height of the path.    *Ans.* $-32$.

(f)  Could you have answered part (e) without relying on the result of (d)?

**9.** Calculate $a_N$ by using (72) or (73) for the example of the text and show that your result agrees with (76).

We shall consider one more application of the tangential acceleration that will produce some interesting results about motion along curves. Suppose that a particle slides down a smooth curve (Fig. 18-44) under the action of gravity. Let us see what we can find out about the velocity gained during this motion.

The force of gravity which is $32m$, $m$ being the mass of the particle, produces the acceleration. We may, as we know, regard the acceleration as resolved into its tangential and normal components. The particle is free to move only along the curve, and thus only the tangential acceleration is effective. The curve itself, which physically may be of some rigid material, offsets the normal component (and provides the centripetal acceleration). Now the force of gravity acts straight down and its component along the curve is $32m \cos \phi$. Because many of our formulas involve the inclination $\alpha$ of the tangent to the curve, let us use the fact that

$$\alpha = 90 + \phi$$

or

$$\phi = \alpha - 90$$

to write

$$32m \cos \phi = 32m \cos(\alpha - 90) = 32m \sin \alpha.$$

This force is the tangential force and, because $\ddot{s}$ is the tangential acceleration,

$$m\ddot{s} = 32m \sin \alpha.$$

However, we know (Chap. 15, Sect. 4) that

$$\sin \alpha = \pm \frac{dy}{ds}.$$

**Figure 18-44**

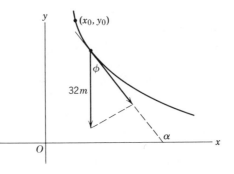

Hence after dividing through by $m$

$$\ddot{s} = \pm 32 \frac{dy}{ds}.$$

The matter of signs must be looked into. If we measure $s$ as increasing from some point $(x_0, y_0)$ on the curve then, because the force is in the direction of increasing $s$, the force should be positive. However, $y$ decreases as $s$ increases. Hence $dy/ds$ itself is negative. Then the proper equation is

**(77)**
$$\ddot{s} = -32 \frac{dy}{ds}.$$

We can derive an interesting result by integrating the present equation. We use an old device of multiplying both sides by $2\dot{s}$. Then

$$2\dot{s}\ddot{s} = -64 \frac{dy}{ds}\dot{s}.$$

We can integrate with respect to $t$. On the left side we have the derivative of $\dot{s}^2$. On the right side, if we again use the chain rule,

$$\frac{dy}{ds}\dot{s} = \frac{dy}{ds}\frac{ds}{dt} = \frac{dy}{dt}.$$

Hence integration yields

$$\dot{s}^2 = -64y + C.$$

Suppose that the particle starts out at $y = y_0$ with 0 velocity. Then $\dot{s} = 0$ at $y = y_0$, and so

$$C = 64y_0.$$

Then

**(78)**
$$\dot{s}^2 = 64(y_0 - y).$$

This result is physically significant. It says that the velocity acquired by the particle is dependent only on the *vertical* distance traveled and is independent of the shape of the curve. In fact, if an object falls straight down the distance $y_0 - y$ and starts with zero velocity, it acquires precisely this velocity of $8\sqrt{y_0 - y}$.

As applied to the motion along the curve of Fig. 18-44 or 18-45, the result (78) tells us the following. If the particle starts at $A$ with 0 velocity, then according to formula (77), because $\ddot{s}$ is positive, the object will gain velocity and from (78) we see that it will gain velocity as long as $y$ decreases. However, after the lowest $y$-value is reached, at $D$ in Fig. 18-45, then, from (77), we see that the acceleration becomes negative because $dy/ds$ is positive. The object will then lose velocity and, in fact, (78) tells us that if the object reaches a height $y_0$, at say $B$, the velocity will be 0.

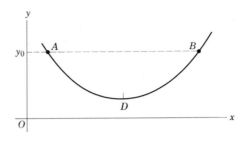

**Figure 18-45**

## EXERCISES

1. Suppose a particle slides down and up the curve $ADB$ of Fig. 18-45 and then back to $A$ and does this repeatedly.
   (a) Will the motion be periodic?
   (b) Must the curve be symmetric about the vertical line through $D$ for the motion to be periodic?
   (c) Will the period be independent of the shape of the curve $ADB$ assuming that $D$ remains at the same $y$-level?

2. Compare the result (78) with the answer to Exercise 5(c) of Chapter 3, Section 4. What relation is there between the two results?

# CHAPTER NINETEEN
# POLAR PARAMETRIC EQUATIONS AND CURVILINEAR MOTION*

**1. Polar Parametric Equations.** We have found that in place of the usual direct representation of a curve by an equation involving the rectangular coordinates $x$ and $y$, we can use rectangular parametric equations where $x$ and $y$ are each expressed in terms of a third variable, say $t$. The same applies to polar coordinates. In place of the direct polar coordinate equation of a curve we can use polar parametric equations, that is, equations that give $\rho$ and $\theta$ each expressed in terms of a third variable $t$. Polar parametric equations are useful in the study of geometric properties of curves when the direct relation between $\rho$ and $\theta$ is complicated and in the study of motion along curves. These values of polar parametric equations are entirely analogous to those of rectangular parametric equations, but, of course, are utilized when the polar coordinate system is more helpful.

Let us consider one or two examples of polar parametric equations. Consider the straight line $PQ$ of Fig. 19-1. Suppose that the perpendicular distance from the pole $O$ to the line is 5 units and that this perpendicular makes an angle of $\pi/6$ with the polar axis. Let $\phi$ be the angle that the radius vector from $O$ to any arbitrary point $P$ on the line makes with the perpendicular. ($\phi$ is positive when taken counterclockwise from $OD$ and

**Figure 19-1**

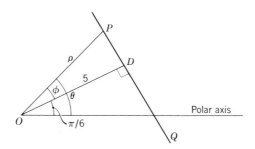

*This chapter is not essential to the continuity.

**605**

negative otherwise.) Then in the right triangle $OPD$ we have

$$\rho = \frac{5}{\cos \phi} \, .$$

Moreover,

$$\theta = \phi + \frac{\pi}{6} \, .$$

These two equations describe the coordinates of point $P$ in terms of parameter $\phi$. The quantities 5 and $\pi/6$ fix the given line. If we eliminate $\phi$ between these two equations by solving the second one for $\phi$ and substituting this result in the first one, we obtain

$$\rho = \frac{5}{\cos\left(\theta - \dfrac{\pi}{6}\right)}$$

as the direct polar equation of the straight line. We might note that in the present case of a line crossing the polar axis obliquely this direct equation between $\rho$ and $\theta$ is obtained more readily through the parametric equations than by other means.

To describe motion with constant speed along the circle $\rho = 5$, polar parametric equations are useful. If the speed along the circle (Fig. 19-2) is constant, the angular velocity $\omega$ is also constant, and the parametric equations are

$$\rho = 5, \qquad \theta = \omega t.$$

Here the first parametric equation does not contain $t$ explicitly, but the two equations are a parametric representation of the $\rho$ and $\theta$ of each point of the circle in Fig. 19-2 in terms of parameter $t$.

Another example is the parametric representation of motion along the line (Fig. 19-3) whose direct equation is $\theta = \pi/6$. If a particle moves out from the pole along this straight line with a constant speed $v$, the parametric equations are

$$\rho = vt, \qquad \theta = \frac{\pi}{6} \, .$$

Again, one of the parametric equations does not contain $t$ explicitly.

**Figure 19-2**

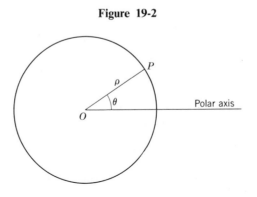

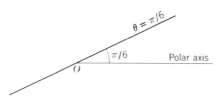

**Figure 19-3**

## EXERCISES

**1.** Given the polar parametric equations $\rho = \rho_0 e^{-kt}$, $\theta = \omega t + \alpha$, find the direct polar equation of the corresponding curve.                    *Ans.* $\rho = \rho_0 e^{-k(\theta - \alpha)/\omega}$.

**2.** Find the direct equation of the curve whose polar parametric equations are $\rho = vt$, $\theta = \omega t$.

**3.** Given a curve whose polar equation is $\rho = a(1 - \cos\theta)$ and the fact that the angular velocity of a particle moving along that curve is a constant, $\omega$, find the parametric equations for $\rho$ and $\theta$ as functions of $t$.

$\quad\quad\quad\quad\quad\quad$ *Ans.* $\theta = \omega(t - t_0)$, $\rho = a[1 - \cos\omega(t - t_0)]$.

**4.** Suppose that the direct polar equation of a curve is $\rho = e^\theta$ and that $d\theta/dt = 2$. If $\theta = 0$ when $t = 0$, write the polar parametric equations that represent the motion along the curve.

**5.** Suppose that a point moves along the curve $\rho = \theta^2$ so that $d\rho/dt = 3$. Find the polar parametric representation of the curve.    *Ans.* $\theta^2 = 3t + \rho_0$, $\rho = 3t + \rho_0$.

### 2. *Velocity and Acceleration in the Polar Parametric Representation.*

Because the primary usefulness of the parametric representation is to enable us to relate $\rho$ and $\theta$ to the time variable and so study motion along curves, we need to know how to express velocity and acceleration in terms of the polar parametric representation. The formulas that we intend to develop for velocity and acceleration will serve two purposes. Given the polar parametric representation of a curve, we shall be able to calculate the velocity and acceleration. Conversely, given the acceleration or velocity formulas, which will usually be determined by the physical forces causing the motion, we shall be able to derive the equations representing the motion and so learn more about the motion.

In the case of rectangular parametric coordinates, we found that the components of velocity and acceleration along the $x$- and $y$-axes were useful, as were the components tangential and normal to the curve. In the case of polar parametric coordinates, the directions of the components that prove most useful are the direction of $\rho$ itself (Fig. 19-4), and the direction *perpendicular* to $\rho$, and in the sense of increasing $\theta$. It is somewhat apparent that these directions should be the useful ones. Because polar coordinates are used when we are interested in motion relative to a fixed point, the pole, the direction toward or away from the pole should be useful. Motion around the pole should also be significant, and the direction of this motion is the direction that results from $\theta$ increasing or decreasing.

We introduce the unit vectors $\mathbf{u}_\rho$ in the direction of increasing $\rho$ and $\mathbf{u}_\theta$ in the direction of increasing $\theta$. We shall express other vectors in terms of

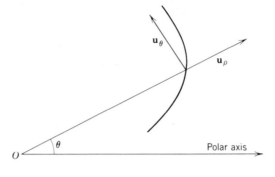

**Figure 19-4**

these unit vectors. The component of a vector in the $\mathbf{u}_\rho$ direction is called the radial component and the component in the $\mathbf{u}_\theta$ direction is called the transverse component. These components may be positive or negative. We should note that $\mathbf{u}_\theta$ is usually *not* tangential to the actual curve along which an object may move.

We shall now derive the vector velocity and acceleration in terms of the radial and transverse components. It is apparent from Fig. 19-5 that

**(1)** $$\mathbf{u}_\rho = \mathbf{i} \cos \theta + \mathbf{j} \sin \theta$$

**(2)** $$\mathbf{u}_\theta = -\mathbf{i} \sin \theta + \mathbf{j} \cos \theta.$$

Before considering the velocity and acceleration vectors themselves let us note that

**(3)** $$\frac{d\mathbf{u}_\rho}{d\theta} = -\mathbf{i} \sin \theta + \mathbf{j} \cos \theta$$

**(4)** $$\frac{d\mathbf{u}_\theta}{d\theta} = -\mathbf{i} \cos \theta - \mathbf{j} \sin \theta.$$

**Figure 19-5**

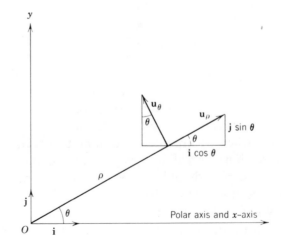

From (3) and (2) we see that

**(5)**
$$\frac{d\mathbf{u}_\rho}{d\theta} = \mathbf{u}_\theta$$

and from (4) and (1) we see that

**(6)**
$$\frac{d\mathbf{u}_\theta}{d\theta} = -\mathbf{u}_\rho.$$

Thus the result of differentiating $\mathbf{u}_\rho$ and $\mathbf{u}_\theta$ with respect to $\theta$ has the effect of rotating these unit vectors 90° in a counterclockwise direction.

Now suppose a particle moves along a curve whose polar coordinate equation is $\rho = f(\theta)$ or whose parametric equations are $\rho = \rho(t)$, $\theta = \theta(t)$. The position vector of the particle with respect to the pole $O$ is

**(7)**
$$\boldsymbol{\rho}(t) = \rho(t)\mathbf{u}_\rho.*$$

As in the case of rectangular parametric equations (Chap. 18, Sect. 7; compare Fig. 19-6), the velocity vector is $d\boldsymbol{\rho}/dt$. From (7) we have that

$$\frac{d\boldsymbol{\rho}}{dt} = \frac{d\rho}{dt}\mathbf{u}_\rho + \rho\frac{d\mathbf{u}_\rho}{dt}$$

$$= \frac{d\rho}{dt}\mathbf{u}_\rho + \rho\frac{d\mathbf{u}_\rho}{d\theta}\frac{d\theta}{dt}.$$

Hence from (5)

**(8)**
$$\frac{d\boldsymbol{\rho}}{dt} = \frac{d\rho}{dt}\mathbf{u}_\rho + \rho\frac{d\theta}{dt}\mathbf{u}_\theta.$$

Thus we have expressed the velocity vector in terms of its components along $\mathbf{u}_\rho$ and $\mathbf{u}_\theta$. If we write the velocity vector as

**(9)**
$$\mathbf{v} = v_\rho\mathbf{u}_\rho + v_\theta\mathbf{u}_\theta$$

**Figure 19-6**

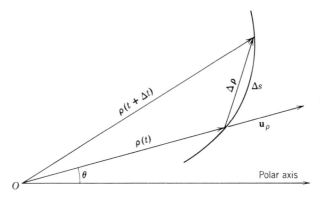

*If we work with the parametric equations $\rho = \rho(t)$ and $\theta = \theta(t)$, then choosing any value of $t$ to discuss $\rho(t)$ also fixes $\theta(t)$ so that the position vector $\boldsymbol{\rho}(t)$ is fully determined.

then

$$(10) \qquad v_\rho = \frac{d\rho}{dt} = \dot\rho, \qquad v_\theta = \rho\frac{d\theta}{dt} = \rho\dot\theta.$$

To obtain the acceleration vector we must now differentiate the velocity vector $\mathbf{v} = d\rho/dt$. Hence by differentiating (8)

$$(11) \;\; \mathbf{a} = \frac{d\mathbf{v}}{dt} = \frac{d^2\rho}{dt^2}\mathbf{u}_\rho + \frac{d\rho}{dt}\frac{d\mathbf{u}_\rho}{dt} + \frac{d\rho}{dt}\frac{d\theta}{dt}\mathbf{u}_\theta + \rho\frac{d^2\theta}{dt^2}\mathbf{u}_\theta + \rho\frac{d\theta}{dt}\frac{d\mathbf{u}_\theta}{dt}.$$

If we note that

$$\frac{d\mathbf{u}_\rho}{dt} = \frac{d\mathbf{u}_\rho}{d\theta}\frac{d\theta}{dt} \qquad \text{and} \qquad \frac{d\mathbf{u}_\theta}{dt} = \frac{d\mathbf{u}_\theta}{d\theta}\frac{d\theta}{dt}$$

and use (5) and (6) we may express each term in (11) as some factor times $\mathbf{u}_\rho$ or $\mathbf{u}_\theta$. We then rearrange terms and obtain

$$(12) \qquad \mathbf{a} = \left[\frac{d^2\rho}{dt^2} - \rho\left(\frac{d\theta}{dt}\right)^2\right]\mathbf{u}_\rho + \left[\rho\frac{d^2\theta}{dt^2} + 2\frac{d\rho}{dt}\frac{d\theta}{dt}\right]\mathbf{u}_\theta.$$

For brevity we shall often write

$$\mathbf{a} = a_\rho\mathbf{u}_\rho + a_\theta\mathbf{u}_\theta$$

so that

$$(13) \qquad a_\rho = \frac{d^2\rho}{dt^2} - \rho\left(\frac{d\theta}{dt}\right)^2 = \ddot\rho - \rho\dot\theta^2$$

$$(14) \qquad a_\theta = \rho\frac{d^2\theta}{dt^2} + 2\frac{d\rho}{dt}\frac{d\theta}{dt} = \rho\ddot\theta + 2\dot\rho\dot\theta = \frac{1}{\rho}\frac{d}{dt}(\rho^2\dot\theta).$$

**Example.** Suppose a particle moves along the curve whose polar parametric equations are $\rho = 2\cos 3t$ and $\theta = 4t$, where $t$ represents time. Find the velocity and acceleration vectors.

**Solution.** By (8) $d\rho/dt = (d\rho/dt)\mathbf{u}_\rho + \rho(d\theta/dt)\mathbf{u}_\theta$. In our example, $\dot\rho = d\rho/dt = -6\sin 3t$ and $\dot\theta = d\theta/dt = 4$. Hence

$$\mathbf{v} = \frac{d\rho}{dt} = -6\sin 3t\,\mathbf{u}_\rho + 8\cos 3t\,\mathbf{u}_\theta.$$

The acceleration vector, by (12), is

$$\mathbf{a} = (\ddot\rho - \rho\dot\theta^2)\mathbf{u}_\rho + (\rho\ddot\theta + 2\dot\rho\dot\theta)\mathbf{u}_\theta.$$

We have $\dot\rho$ and $\dot\theta$. Also $\ddot\rho = -18\cos 3t$ and $\ddot\theta = 0$. Hence

$$\mathbf{a} = (-18\cos 3t - 32\cos 3t)\mathbf{u}_\rho + (0 - 48\sin 3t)\mathbf{u}_\theta.$$

## EXERCISES

**1.** A particle moves along a straight line $\theta = \pi/6$ with a variable velocity $v$. What are the radial and transverse components of the velocity and the acceleration?

$$Ans. \ v_\rho = v; \ v_\theta = 0; \ a_\rho = \frac{dv}{dt}; \ a_\theta = 0.$$

**2.** A particle moves along a circle of radius $R$ with a constant angular velocity $\omega$; that is, $\omega = d\theta/dt = $ constant.
   (a) Find the radial and transverse components of the velocity and the acceleration. $\qquad$ $Ans. \ v_\rho = 0; \ v_\theta = R\omega; \ a_\rho = -R\omega^2; \ a_\theta = 0.$
   (b) Compare the results of Exercise 1 in Section 8 of Chapter 18 for tangential and normal accelerations. Should the results agree and, if so, why?

**3.** Suppose that a particle moves along a circle of radius $R$ with a variable angular velocity $\omega$; that is, $\omega = d\theta/dt$ is a function of $t$. Find the radial and transverse components of the velocity and the acceleration.

$$Ans. \ v_\rho = 0; \ v_\theta = R\omega; \ a_\rho = -R\omega^2; \ a_\theta = R\frac{d\omega}{dt}.$$

**4.** Show that the magnitude of the velocity vector (8) is indeed $ds/dt$.
   *Suggestion:* We know from (33) of Chapter 17 that $ds/d\theta = \sqrt{\rho^2 + (d\rho/d\theta)^2}$ .

**5.** A particle moves along the line whose polar parametric equations are $\rho = p/\cos\phi$ and $\theta = \alpha + \phi$ (see Section 1). Suppose that $\phi$ changes with time so that $\phi = ct$ where $c$ is a constant. Find the radial and transverse components of the velocity and the accelerations.

**6.** Suppose that a particle $P$ moves along a ray $OA$ with constant speed $v$ while $OA$ rotates in a horizontal plane with constant angular velocity $\omega$. What are the radial and transverse accelerations of $P$? $\qquad$ $Ans. \ a_\rho = -\rho\omega^2; \ a_\theta = 2v\omega.$

**7.** Suppose that the polar parametric equations of a curve are $\rho = \rho_0 e^{-kt}$, $\theta = \omega t + \alpha$, where $k$, $\omega$, and $\alpha$ are constants and $t$ represents time. Find the radial and transverse components of the velocity and the acceleration of a point whose coordinates are $\rho$ and $\theta$. Then find the magnitudes of the resultant velocity and acceleration.

**8.** A boat leaves $B$ on the bank of a river (Fig. 19-7) and is rowed with a constant velocity $v$ in the direction of point $A$ directly opposite $B$ with $AB = a$. However, the river has a current of velocity $v$ which also acts on the boat. Show that the radial and transverse components of the resultant velocity are $-v + v \sin\theta$ and $v \cos\theta$, respectively.

**Figure 19-7**

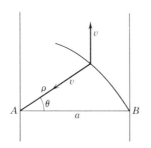

9. Using the result of Exercise 8 find the equation of the path of the boat and describe the path of the boat.

    *Suggestion:* From Exercise 8 obtain an expression for $\dfrac{1}{\rho}\dfrac{d\rho}{d\theta}$.

    $$Ans. \ \rho = \frac{a}{1 - \cos\left(\theta + \dfrac{\pi}{2}\right)}.$$

10. A particle $P$ moves with constant velocity $v$ (Fig. 19-8) along the line $AB$ which is at a distance $a$ from the pole $O$. Find the angular velocity and angular acceleration of the line $OP$ in terms of $v$, $a$, and $\theta$.

    *Suggestion:* $v_\theta = v \cos \theta$.

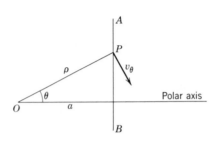

**Figure 19-8**

11. A particle $P$ falls down the line $AB$ (Fig. 19-9), which is at a distance $a$ from the pole $O$, and travels the distance $\frac{1}{2}gt^2$ from $A$ after $t$ seconds. Find the angular velocity and angular acceleration of the line $OP$.

    *Suggestion:* The downward velocity of the particle is $gt$. The transverse velocity $v_\theta = gt \cos \theta$.

    $$Ans. \ \dot\theta = 4agt/(4a^2 + g^2t^4), \ \ddot\theta = 4ag(4a^2 - 3g^2t^4)/(4a^2 + g^2t^4)^2.$$

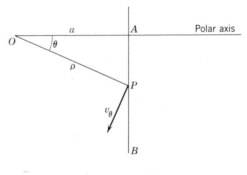

**Figure 19-9**

12. A particle describes a circle of radius $a$ (Fig. 19-10) with uniform speed $v$. Take a diameter as polar axis and one end of this diameter as a pole and find the radial and transverse acceleration of the particle.

    *Suggestion:* $\rho = 2a \cos \theta$, $\theta = vt/2a$.

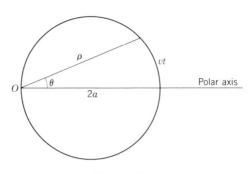

**Figure 19-10**

13. A point transverses a curve under the condition that the radius vector rotates at a constant angular velocity $\omega$. Show that the radial and transverse accelerations are $\omega^2(d^2\rho/d\theta^2 - \rho)$ and $2\omega^2\,d\rho/d\theta$, respectively.

14. (a) A particle $P$ of unit mass free to slide on a straight wire is attracted to a fixed point $O$ of the wire with a force that is $k$ times the distance $OP$. If the wire revolves about $O$ with a constant angular velocity $\omega$ in a horizontal plane, show that the motion of the particle along the wire is simple harmonic with a period $2\pi/\sqrt{k - \omega^2}$ provided that $\omega^2 < k$.

    *Suggestion:* Consider the radial acceleration of $P$.

    (b) Show that when $\omega^2 = k/2$, the path of $P$ in the plane is a circle.

15. A particle moves with a constant angular speed of $\omega$ rad/sec on the curve $\rho = a(1 - \cos\theta)$. Find the radial and transverse components of the velocity and acceleration.   *Ans.* $v_\rho = a\omega\sin\theta,\ v_\theta = a\omega(1 - \cos\theta),$
$$a_\rho = a\omega^2(2\cos\theta - 1),\ a_\theta = 2a\omega^2\sin\theta.$$

16. A particle moves along an ellipse whose latus rectum and eccentricity are $p$ and $e$, respectively, with uniform angular speed $\omega$, the angle being measured at one focus. Find the components of velocity and acceleration along and perpendicular to the radius vector.   *Ans.* $v_\rho = (-\omega/p)\rho^2\sin\omega t,\ v_\theta = \rho\omega;$
$$a_\rho = (\omega^2/p)\rho^2\cos\omega t - (2\omega^2/p^2)\rho^3\sin^2\omega t - \omega^2\rho,\ a_\theta = (-2\omega^2/p)\rho^2\sin\omega t.$$

17. A particle moves in a plane so that the line from a fixed point $O$ in the plane to the position $P$ of the particle sweeps out equal areas in equal times. Show that the acceleration of the particle is along the line $OP$.

    *Suggestion:* Use the polar coordinate formula for area. Also, what does sweeping out equal areas in equal times mean as far as $dA/dt$ is concerned?

18. Three ants each equally distant from its neighbor are situated on the circumference of a circle of radius 1. At each instant starting at $t = 0$ each ant moves counter-clockwise in the direction of the ant nearest him and with a uniform velocity of 1. Where will they meet and how long will it take them to do so?

    *Suggestion:* The motion of each ant is the same. Picture their positions and directions of motion at an arbitrary time $t$ and find the radial velocity of any one. Let $\rho = 0$ in $\rho = -t\sin(\pi/3) + 1$ to find the time.

**3. *Kepler's Laws.*** The greatest inspiration for the calculus came from the efforts to understand the motions of the planets on the basis of the heliocentric hypothesis. The theory introduced by Copernicus in his classic *On the Revolutions of the Heavenly Spheres* published in 1543 still utilized what is called the scheme of deferent and epicycle which had been created by the Greeks, but Copernicus made the all-important change that the sun rather than the earth was to be regarded as the central body around which the planets moved. Johannes Kepler, in his efforts to simplify Copernicus' description of the motion of the planets, introduced three famous laws. These laws, which Kepler accepted solely on the basis of the fact that they fitted his data, are as follows:

1. Each planet moves in an elliptical orbit with the sun at one focus of each ellipse.
2. The line joining the sun and any given planet sweeps out equal areas in equal times.
3. The square of the period of revolution of any planet is proportional to the cube of the semimajor axis of the planet's elliptical path about the sun.

Kepler stated the first two of these laws in a book *On the Motion of the Planet Mars*, published in 1609, and he announced the third in his *The Harmony of the World* which appeared in 1619.

Actually, these laws are correct only if one regards the sun and any one planet as moving independently of the effects exerted by any other planet or comet and if one assumes that the sun is stationary. However, they are an excellent foundation for any refinements one may introduce in order to take into account the mutual interactions of several bodies.

Kepler's laws were an extraordinary achievement. The use of the ellipse to describe planetary motions was a daring and radical innovation. Moreover, coordinate geometry had not yet been created and the calculus was in its infancy, so that Kepler had few mathematical tools at his disposal. Nevertheless, from the standpoint of the scientific program formulated by Galileo and pursued later by Newton, Kepler's laws were foster children because they were not derived from basic laws of motion. The function of science is to provide an explanation of the various classes of physical phenomena. However, science is an organized body of knowledge and it seeks to derive the laws of any one branch from basic principles or laws just as mathematics deduces conclusions from basic axioms about the various types of numbers and geometrical forms. It was therefore an enormous accomplishment when Newton showed that all of Kepler's laws as well as many other celestial phenomena can be deduced from the laws of motion and the law of gravitation, which had already served as the foundation for the deduction of the laws of terrestrial motions. Newton's derivations of Kepler's laws gave a solid basis to the planetary theory of Kepler and established Newtonian mechanics as the firm foundation of physics. We shall reproduce Newton's derivations and, of course, see as a consequence the role played by the calculus in this most momentous scientific achievement.

Let us recall, first, that the law of gravitation states that any two particles of mass $M$ and $m$ attract each other in accordance with the quantitative law

**(15)**
$$F = G \frac{Mm}{r^2}$$

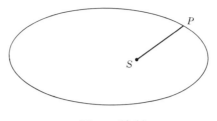

Figure 19-11

where $G$ is a constant and $r$ is the distance between the two particles. The force of attraction is really a vector because it not only has the magnitude given by the right side of (15) but also a direction. Specifically, if one is interested in the attraction that the mass $M$ exerts on $m$, the direction of $F$ is from $m$ to $M$.

We shall utilize also Newton's second law of motion, namely, a force $F$ acting on a mass $m$ gives that mass an acceleration $a$ and

**(16)**                                    $$F = ma.$$

This second law of motion is also a vector law because acceleration, as we know, has a definite direction and the force is a vector having the direction of the acceleration.

Let us consider now the sun $S$ of mass $M$ (Fig. 19-11) attracting a planet $P$ of mass $m$ in accordance with the law of gravitation. We regard the sun as stationary and the planet as moving about the sun along some path whose equation we should like to determine. Also, we can regard the sun and planet as particles because their size is small compared to the distance $SP$.* If the planet $P$ were stationary or had a velocity only along the line of $SP$ when the gravitational force began to act, the effect of this force would be to pull $P$ directly into $S$. Hence the planet must have an initial velocity in a direction other than along $SP$ and then the gravitational attraction of $S$ on $P$ acts to pull $P$ somewhat toward $S$ so that the planet does not wander off along a straight line as it would otherwise do in accordance with Newton's first law of motion. If we suppose that the original or initial velocity is in the plane of the paper, the motion of the planet under the gravitational force will remain in the plane of the paper, because the gravitational force acts in the direction from $P$ to $S$ and this is also in the plane of the paper. Hence the resultant velocity will be in that plane.

To study the motion of one object about another, polar coordinates are convenient. Hence let us introduce this coordinate system with the pole at $S$, so that $SP$ is the $\rho$-value of $P$. The position of the polar axis need not be fixed at the moment, although of course we suppose that the $\theta$-value of $P$ is measured from this axis. What we know from (15) and (16) are some

*Actually, if the sun and earth are assumed to be spherical in shape, we can use previously proven theorems (Chapter 16) to assert that for purposes of gravitational attraction the mass of each sphere can be regarded as concentrated at its center.

facts about the force acting on the planet $P$. In fact, when $F$ in (16) is the gravitational force, we know that

$$\frac{GMm}{\rho^2} = ma,$$

wherein we have written $\rho$ for $r$ because $\rho$ is the distance between the sun and the planet. Then, as far as magnitude is concerned,

$$a = \frac{GM}{\rho^2} .$$

This acceleration acts in the direction $PS$; hence it is a radial acceleration. Moreover, the acceleration acts in the direction of decreasing $\rho$. Hence

$$a_\rho = -\frac{GM}{\rho^2} .$$

The radial acceleration is given by (13), so that

**(17)**
$$\ddot{\rho} - \rho\dot{\theta}^2 = -\frac{GM}{\rho^2} .$$

We also know that because the gravitational force is entirely radial and because this is the only known force producing acceleration, the transverse acceleration must be 0. Then from (14) it follows that

**(18)**
$$\frac{1}{\rho} \frac{d}{dt} (\rho^2 \dot{\theta}) = 0.$$

Equations (17) and (18) contain the basic physical information about the motion, and we should now like to derive from them the equation of the path of $P$. Unfortunately, both equations contain the derivatives of $\rho$ and $\theta$, so that there is no straightforward procedure for solving each one separately. However, let us see what we can deduce.

We can multiply both sides of (18) by $\rho$ and then integrate with respect to $t$. These steps yield

**(19)**
$$\rho^2 \dot{\theta} = h$$

where $h$ is a constant. This result is in itself significant. We learned in connection with polar coordinates [see (29) of Chapter 17] that the area between a curve and the radii vectors $\theta = \alpha$ and $\theta = \beta$ is given by

$$A = \int_\alpha^\beta \tfrac{1}{2}\rho^2 \, d\theta.$$

By the fundamental theorem of the calculus this means that

**(20)**
$$\frac{dA}{d\theta} = \frac{1}{2}\rho^2$$

and by the chain rule that

**(21)** $$\frac{dA}{dt} = \frac{dA}{d\theta}\,\frac{d\theta}{dt} = \frac{1}{2}\,\rho^2\dot\theta.$$

Then (19) tells us that if $A$ is the area swept out by the radius vector $SP$,

**(22)** $$\frac{dA}{dt} = \frac{h}{2}$$

or that $dA/dt$ is a constant. Then the area swept out by the radius vector from $S$ to $P$ is

**(23)** $$A = \frac{ht}{2} + C.$$

This equation implies that the area swept out in equal time intervals is the same; that is, the area swept out from $t = t_1$ to $t = t_2$ is the same as the area swept out from $t = t_3$ to $t = t_4$ if $t_2 - t_1 = t_4 - t_3$. This assertion is precisely what Kepler's second law of motion asserts. Thus we have already derived Kepler's second law from the law of gravitation and the second law of motion.

We have not as yet utilized (17) to see what more we can learn about the path of the planet. We can use (19) to substitute for $\dot\theta$ in (17); then (17) becomes

**(24)** $$\ddot\rho - \frac{h^2}{\rho^3} = -\frac{GM}{\rho^2}\,.$$

We now have a differential equation involving only $\rho$ and $t$, and so we may be more hopeful of doing something with it.

There are several ways of proceeding with (24), no one of which is straightforward. By using an old trick of multiplying both sides of (24) by $2\dot\rho$, we can integrate and thus find an expression for $\dot\rho$. Since $\dot\rho$ is $d\rho/dt$, we can use the theorem on inverse functions to state what $dt/d\rho$ is and then integrate once more to find $t$ as a function of $\rho$. However, this function cannot be solved for $\rho$ as a function of $t$, at least not in a simple usable form. Hence instead of seeking $\rho$ as a function of $t$ and then $\theta$ as a function of $t$, that is, instead of seeking the polar parametric equations, we shall see if we can find the direct equation relating $\rho$ and $\theta$.

Let us try to derive from (24) an expression for $d^2\rho/d\theta^2$. This involves finding an expression for $\ddot\rho$ or $d^2\rho/dt^2$ in terms of $d^2\rho/d\theta^2$. We know that

$$\frac{d\rho}{dt} = \frac{d\rho}{d\theta}\,\frac{d\theta}{dt} = \frac{d\rho}{d\theta}\,\dot\theta.$$

Because we do not wish to become entangled with $\dot\theta$, we shall use (19) to write

**(25)** $$\frac{d\rho}{dt} = \frac{d\rho}{d\theta}\,\frac{h}{\rho^2}\,.$$

Now we can argue that

$$\frac{d^2\rho}{dt^2} = \frac{d}{d\theta}\left(\frac{d\rho}{dt}\right)\frac{d\theta}{dt} = \frac{d}{d\theta}\left(\frac{d\rho}{d\theta}\frac{h}{\rho^2}\right)\dot{\theta} = \frac{d^2\rho}{d\theta^2}\frac{h}{\rho^2}\dot{\theta} - \frac{2h}{\rho^3}\frac{d\rho}{d\theta}\frac{d\rho}{d\theta}\dot{\theta}.$$

In view of (19)

$$\frac{d^2\rho}{dt^2} = \frac{d^2\rho}{d\theta^2}\frac{h^2}{\rho^4} - \frac{2h^2}{\rho^5}\left(\frac{d\rho}{d\theta}\right)^2.$$

If we were to substitute this value of $\ddot{\rho}$ in (24), we would have a rather complicated differential equation and would, in fact, be worse off than we are with (24) itself.

Let us try another approach. We shall still seek the direct equation between $\rho$ and $\theta$. However, this time, noting the presence of powers of $1/\rho$ in (24), let us try to replace $\rho$ by a new variable, namely,

**(26)**
$$u = \frac{1}{\rho}$$

and see what happens to (24).

By the chain rule applied to (26)

$$\frac{du}{d\theta} = -\frac{1}{\rho^2}\frac{d\rho}{d\theta},$$

and by substituting the value of $d\rho/d\theta$ given by this equation in (25)

$$\frac{d\rho}{dt} = -h\frac{du}{d\theta}.$$

If we differentiate this last equation with respect to $t$ by using the chain rule, we obtain

$$\frac{d^2\rho}{dt^2} = \frac{d}{d\theta}\left(-h\frac{du}{d\theta}\right)\frac{d\theta}{dt} = -h\frac{d^2u}{d\theta^2}\frac{d\theta}{dt},$$

and by (19) and (26) we obtain

**(27)**
$$\frac{d^2\rho}{dt^2} = -h\frac{d^2u}{d\theta^2}\frac{h}{\rho^2} = -h^2u^2\frac{d^2u}{d\theta^2}.$$

We substitute this value of $d^2\rho/dt^2$ in (24) and replace $1/\rho$ by $u$. Then

$$-h^2u^2\frac{d^2u}{d\theta^2} - h^2u^3 = -GMu^2$$

or

**(28)**
$$\frac{d^2u}{d\theta^2} + u = \frac{GM}{h^2}.$$

Thus we have a differential equation for $u$ in terms of $\theta$ which is simpler than (24), and we have made some progress.

To integrate (28) we note that, except for the constant term on the right side, it is the differential equation of simple harmonic motion. To eliminate the constant term, we let

**(29)** $$y = u - \frac{GM}{h^2} .$$

Then

$$\frac{d^2y}{d\theta^2} = \frac{d^2u}{d\theta^2},$$

and from (28)

$$\frac{d^2y}{d\theta^2} + y = 0.$$

We know the solution of this differential equation. It is

$$y = A \cos\theta + B \sin\theta,$$

which we can also write [Chapter 10, formula (55)] as

$$y = C \cos(\theta + \alpha)$$

where $C$ and $\alpha$ are constants of integration. (We use cosine here in place of sine, but this merely means using another value of $\alpha$.) Then by (29)

**(30)** $$u = C \cos(\theta + \alpha) + \frac{GM}{h^2} ,$$

which we can also write as

**(31)** $$u = \frac{GM}{h^2} (1 + e \cos(\theta + \alpha))$$

with

**(32)** $$e = \frac{h^2C}{GM} .$$

Finally, since $u = 1/\rho$,

**(33)** $$\rho = \frac{\dfrac{h^2}{GM}}{1 + e \cos(\theta + \alpha)} .$$

Thus we have the direct relationship between $\rho$ and $\theta$. In this equation $G$ and $M$ are known quantities, whereas $h$, $e$, and $\alpha$ are constants of integration whose values depend on the initial conditions of the motion.

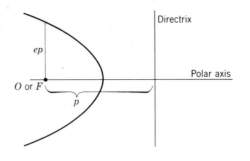

**Figure 19-12**

What kind of a curve does (33) represent? It reminds us of the polar coordinate equation of a conic section. We learned in Chapter 17, Section 3, that the equation of a conic in polar coordinates when the pole, polar axis, focus, and directrix are as shown in Fig. 19-12 is

**(34)**
$$\rho = \frac{ep}{1 + e \cos \theta}$$

where $e$ is the eccentricity of the conic and $p$ is the distance from the focus to the directrix. Equations (33) and (34) are not quite of the same form. However, suppose that we choose as our polar axis not the line from focus to directrix as in Fig. 19-12 but a line making an angle $\alpha$ with the line from focus to directrix (Fig. 19-13). Then the equation of a conic with the line from focus to directrix as polar axis is, of course,

$$\rho = \frac{ep}{1 + e \cos \theta'}$$

where $\theta'$ is as shown in Fig. 19-13. However,

$$\theta' = \theta + \alpha$$

**Figure 19-13**

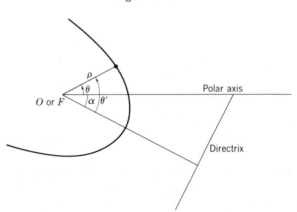

and therefore

**(35)**
$$\rho = \frac{ep}{1 + e \cos(\theta + \alpha)} \, .$$

In other words, (35) is the equation of a conic when $\theta$ is measured, as usual, from the polar axis but the polar axis makes an angle $\alpha$ with the line from the focus to the directrix.

   If we compare (33) and (35), we see that (33) is also the equation of a conic section. Thus the path of a planet moving under the gravitational attraction of the sun is a conic section with one focus at the pole. This focus is also the location of the sun because we started by taking the sun as the pole.

   It is, of course, desirable to know which conic section serves as the path of a planet. We know, however, that the nature of the conic section depends on the value of $e$ in (33) and the value of $e$ in turn depends, in view of (32), on the constants of integration $h$ and $C$. These two constants and the constant $\alpha$ are determined by the initial conditions. If we determine $h$, $e$, and $\alpha$, we can fix (33) completely.

## EXERCISES

1. If $h$ in (19) were 0 then $\dot{\theta}$ would be 0. What is the physical significance of this fact?

2. Show that Kepler's second law holds in a central force field, that is, when the force attracting the moving object is always directed to a fixed center.

3. Show that if Kepler's second law holds, then the force applicable to the moving mass is directed to a fixed center.

4. If a planet moves in an ellipse whose polar coordinate equation is $\rho = ep/(1 + e \cos \theta)$ and if the acceleration is directed toward the origin or pole, that is, if Kepler's first two laws hold, show that the magnitude of the acceleration is proportional to $1/\rho^2$.

   *Suggestion:* The transverse acceleration is 0 by Exercise 2. Compute the radial acceleration. Thus Kepler's first two laws imply an inverse square law of attraction for any one planet. (With the aid of the third law we could show that the proportionality constant in the inverse square law is the same for all the planets.)

5. What change must we make in formula (33) if the equation is to describe the path of a satellite moving around the earth? We assume that the earth is a sphere and its mass can be regarded as concentrated at the center of the earth; that is, the earth can be treated as a particle just as the sun was in the case of planetary motion.

   Let us return to the problem of determining the constants $h$, $e$, and $\alpha$ in (33). Their values depend on the initial conditions. We do not know, of course, how the planets were set into motion but we can learn a lot if we hypothesize some initial conditions. The most instructive case is that in which a planet is given an initial velocity $v_0$ perpendicular to the polar axis

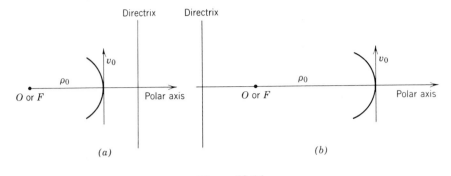

**Figure 19-14**

and the planet is at that instant a distance $\rho_0$ along the polar axis from the focus. Since the velocity is tangential to the path these conditions imply that either of the following two situations obtain. In Fig. 19-14a the line from focus to directrix is in the direction of the polar axis, whereas in Fig. 19-14b the line from focus to directrix is opposite in direction to that of the polar axis. In view of (35) the first figure corresponds to $\alpha = 0$ and the second to $\alpha = \pi$. The angle $\theta$ is, of course, measured from the polar axis as always.

What these initial conditions tell us is first that

**(36)** $$\text{when } \theta = 0, \rho = \rho_0.$$

Secondly, since $v_0$ is in the transverse direction and the transverse component of the velocity is, by (10), $\rho\dot{\theta}$ then

**(37)** $$\rho_0\dot{\theta}_0 = v_0.$$

We use the subscript zero to denote that these conditions hold at $\theta = 0$. We should also note that though $\theta_0$ is 0, $\dot{\theta}_0$ will not be because there is an initial transverse velocity.

We can now determine $h$ at once. By (19), $h = \rho^2\dot{\theta}$. Because $h$ is a constant we can determine it at $\theta = 0$. Then $h = \rho_0^2\dot{\theta}_0$ and by (37)

**(38)** $$h = \rho_0 v_0.$$

Let us first consider (33) with $\alpha = 0$. Then

$$\rho = \frac{h^2}{GM(1 + e \cos \theta)}.$$

But at $\theta = 0$, $\rho = \rho_0$, so that

$$\rho_0 = \frac{h^2}{GM(1 + e)}$$

or

$$e = \frac{h^2}{GM\rho_0} - 1.$$

But $h^2 = \rho_0^2 v_0^2$ and so

$$e = \frac{\rho_0 v_0^2}{GM} - 1$$

and

(39)
$$\rho = \frac{\dfrac{\rho_0^2 v_0^2}{GM}}{1 + \left(\dfrac{\rho_0 v_0^2}{GM} - 1\right)\cos\theta}.$$

Now the eccentricity $e$ must be positive or zero. Hence in any case $(\rho_0 v_0^2/GM) - 1$ must be 0 or greater than 0 or $v_0 \geq \sqrt{GM/\rho_0}$. If $e$ is between 0 and 1, that is, if the path is an ellipse, $\rho_0 v_0^2/GM$ must be less than 2 or $v_0 < \sqrt{2GM/\rho_0}$. Thus for an elliptical path

(40$a$)
$$\sqrt{\frac{GM}{\rho_0}} \leq v_0 < \sqrt{\frac{2GM}{\rho_0}}.$$

If $e$ is 1, that is, if the path is a parabola, then

(40$b$)
$$v_0 = \sqrt{\frac{2GM}{\rho_0}}$$

If $e$ is greater than 1, that is, if the path is a hyperbola, then $\rho_0 v_0^2/GM$ must be greater than 2 or

(40$c$)
$$v_0 > \sqrt{\frac{2GM}{\rho_0}}.$$

These various cases are summed up in Fig. 19-15.

**Figure 19-15**

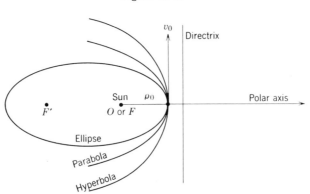

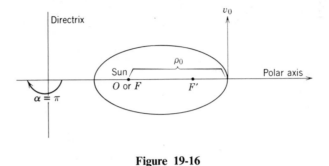

**Figure 19-16**

Now let us consider the situation of Fig. 19-14*b* or Fig. 19-16, that is, when $\alpha = \pi$. In view of (33) the equation of the conic is

$$\rho = \frac{h^2}{GM(1 - e \cos \theta)} .$$

But at $\theta = 0$, $\rho = \rho_0$ and $h^2$ is still $\rho_0^2 v_0^2$. Hence by steps paralleling those above we obtain

$$e = 1 - \frac{\rho_0 v_0^2}{GM}$$

and

**(41)**
$$\rho = \frac{\dfrac{\rho_0^2 v_0^2}{GM}}{1 - \left(1 - \dfrac{\rho_0 v_0^2}{GM}\right)\cos \theta} .$$

Now $e$ must be positive or zero so that

$$\frac{\rho_0 v_0^2}{GM} \leq 1$$

or

**(42)**
$$v_0 \leq \sqrt{\frac{GM}{\rho_0}} .$$

That is, if $\rho_0$ is fixed, then $v_0$ must satisfy (42) and since $e$ must be positive or zero, it will be less than 1 and the path will always be an ellipse. In this case $\rho_0$ is the maximum or aphelion distance from the focus $F$ (or the sun). Because the path is an ellipse, there is another focus $F'$ which lies to the right of $F$. Compare Fig. 17-10.

The case $e = 0$ or

**(43)**
$$\frac{\rho_0 v_0^2}{GM} = 1 \quad \text{or} \quad v_0 = \sqrt{\frac{GM}{\rho_0}}$$

is of special interest. The equation of the conic then is, by (41),

$$\rho = \rho_0$$

which is the equation of a circle. In this case $F$ and $F'$ coincide.

All of the cases discussed can be unified in the following way. Suppose that we keep $\rho_0$ fixed and vary $v_0$. For small $v_0$, the inequality (42) will hold and the path will be an ellipse. As $v_0$ increases but (42) continues to hold, the ellipse broadens (see Chap. 17, Sect. 3, Exercise 13). When $v_0$ increases to the point at which (43) holds, the path is a circle. As $v_0$ increases some more but remains less than $\sqrt{2GM/\rho_0}$ , then by (40a) the path is still an ellipse. When $v_0 = \sqrt{2GM/\rho_0}$ , then (40b) tells us that the path is a parabola. If $v_0 > \sqrt{2GM/\rho_0}$ , the path is a hyperbola. As $v_0$ increases still more, the hyperbola becomes wider. We should note that the circle and parabola each result from one particular value of $v_0$, whereas the ellipse and hyperbola can occur for a range of velocities. All of these facts are represented in Fig. 19-17.

We shall complete the story of Newton's derivation of the Keplerian laws with the proof of the third law. According to (23), if we start to measure the area swept out at the time $t = 0$, then $C = 0$ and

$$A = \tfrac{1}{2}ht.$$

If we restrict ourselves to the elliptical motion of the planets and if we denote by $T$ the time it takes a planet to make one complete revolution, then the area swept out in one revolution is

$$A = \tfrac{1}{2}hT.$$

**Figure 19-17**

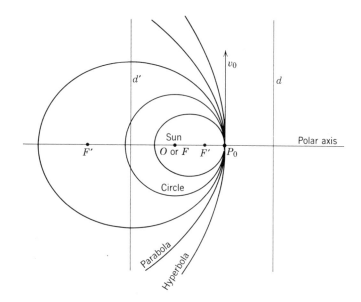

Now, the area of an ellipse is $\pi ab$, where $a$ is the semimajor axis and $b$ the semiminor axis. Then

**(44)**
$$\pi ab = \tfrac{1}{2}hT.$$

We now use two subsidiary facts. The first, obtained by comparing (33) and (35), is that

$$ep = \frac{h^2}{GM}.$$

The second is that $ep$ is the semi-latus rectum of the ellipse.* In terms of $a$ and $b$, the semi-latus rectum is $b^2/a$ (see Chapter 7, Section 5, Exercise 7). Hence

$$\frac{h^2}{GM} = \frac{b^2}{a}$$

or

**(45)**
$$h^2 = GM\frac{b^2}{a}.$$

From (44) we have

$$T^2 = \frac{4\pi^2 a^2 b^2}{h^2},$$

and therefore from (45)

$$T^2 = 4\pi^2 a^2 b^2 \cdot \frac{a}{GMb^2}$$

or

**(46)**
$$T^2 = \frac{4\pi^2}{GM}a^3.$$

Because the quantity $4\pi^2/GM$ is the same no matter which planet is involved, the result (46) states that the square of the period of revolution of a planet is a constant times (or is proportional to) the cube of the semimajor axis of the planet's path about the sun.[†]

---

*This result was obtained in Exercise 9 of Section 3, Chapter 17. However, we can obtain it at once here. When the conic is in either form

$$\rho = \frac{ep}{1 \pm e \cos\theta},$$

the semi-latus rectum is the value of $\rho$ when $\theta = \pi/2$. See Figs. 17-10 and 17-11.

[†]Sometimes Kepler's third law is stated in the form: The square of the period of revolution is proportional to the cube of the *mean distance* from the sun. Actually, the semimajor axis is merely the mean of the aphelion and perihelion distances, but is not the mean of all the distances in the entire orbit. The mean length of the radius vector of an ellipse with respect to time could be shown to be $a[1 + (e^2/2)]$ and the mean length with respect to angle $\theta$ as the independent variable could be shown to be $b$, the semiminor axis.

A fuller investigation of the motion of the planets so as to obtain, for example, the velocity of a planet at any point of its path (see Exercises 7 and 12) or the time required to traverse a given arc of its path, would take us too far from the elements of the calculus and indeed into the branch of science known as celestial mechanics. Our objective has been only to show how a fundamental and classic piece of work of modern science utilizes the calculus.

We would like to point out that the work we have presented is just the beginning of what Newton actually did and is only a first approximation to the accurate story of planetary motion. We have assumed that only the sun and *one* planet are present. Strictly all the planets are present simultaneously and each exerts a gravitational force on the planet under consideration. Secondly, according to the law of gravitation any one planet attracts the sun with the same force that the sun exerts on the planet. Hence the sun too is in motion. However, the acceleration that the planet gives to the sun is $Gm/r^2$ where $m$ is the mass of the planet and $r$ the distance from the planet to the sun. This acceleration is to be contrasted with the acceleration which the sun imparts to a planet, namely, $GM/r^2$, where $M$ is the mass of the sun. Now, the mass of the planet is so much less than the mass of the sun that the acceleration given to the sun is very small. Hence we regard the sun as stationary and treat only the motion of the planet under the gravitational attraction of a fixed sun. Actually, the relative motion of the sun and one planet can be treated, and it turns out that each describes an ellipse with the center of mass of the two bodies as a focus. Advanced work in celestial mechanics does take into account the mutual gravitational interaction of several bodies, the oblate shapes of the earth and moon, the drag due to resisting media, and other factors. Of course, when these factors are taken into account, the path of a planet is no longer an ellipse.

## EXERCISES

1. A body of mass 2 pounds is on the polar axis 12 feet from the pole. It is given a velocity of 6 ft/sec in a direction perpendicular to the axis and thereafter is subject to a gravitational force of $120/\rho^2$ poundals directed toward the pole. Find the equation of the path of the body.     *Ans.* $\rho = \dfrac{432/5}{1 + (31/5)\cos\theta}$.

2. A body of mass 2 pounds is on the polar axis 12 feet from the pole. It is attracted to the pole by a gravitational force of $120/\rho^2$ poundals. What initial velocity perpendicular to the axis should be given to the body so that it moves in the following orbits:
   (a) An elliptic orbit of eccentricity $\frac{1}{2}$.     *Ans.* $\sqrt{45/6}$.
   (b) A circular orbit.     *Ans.* $\sqrt{5}$.
   (c) A parabolic orbit.     *Ans.* $\sqrt{10}$.
   (d) A hyperbolic orbit of eccentricity 2.     *Ans.* $\sqrt{15}$.

3. The eccentricity of the earth's path about the sun is close to 0; that is, the path is almost a circle. Suppose that it is a circle and use this fact to obtain some information about the initial conditions for the earth's motion.
   *Ans.* $\rho_0 v_0^2 / GM = 1$.

4. Using the information gathered in Exercise 3, show that if the sun's mass had been one half its present value, the path of the earth would have become parabolic.

5. Integrate (24) once by multiplying both sides by $2\dot{\rho}$ and show that if a particle is projected with velocity $v_0$ from a point distant $\rho_0$ from the pole and perpendicular to the polar axis, then

$$\dot{\rho}^2 = v_0^2 - (2GM/\rho_0) + (2GM/\rho) - (\rho_0^2 v_0^2/\rho^2).$$

6. Show that if the orbit of (39) is an ellipse, the semimajor axis is $a = GM\rho_0/(2GM - v_0^2\rho_0)$. Does the same result apply to (41)?

7. Suppose that a particle moves subject to the inverse square law of attraction to a fixed point. Then we know that (33) must hold. Show that if $v$ is the magnitude of the velocity of the particle, then

$$v^2 = (G^2 M^2/h^2)(2 + 2e\cos(\theta + \alpha) + e^2 - 1)$$

$$= GM[(2/\rho) + (GM/h^2)(e^2 - 1)].$$

   *Suggestion:* Use (8) and (19).

8. Using the result of Exercise 7, find the points on the conic at which the velocity is a maximum and a minimum. Where are these points in the case of ellipses?

9. Suppose that a particle moves so that it is repelled from a fixed point by a force directed radially away from the point and of magnitude $GM/\rho^2$.
   (a) Show that the orbit is a branch of a hyperbola. (It is that branch which does not contain the fixed point.)

   *Suggestion:* Start with (24) but change the sign of the force.

   (b) Show that if the initial velocity is $\sqrt{GM/\rho_0}$, where $\rho_0$ is the distance from the fixed point to the initial position of the particle, and if the velocity is perpendicular to the initial radius vector, then the orbit is a branch of a hyperbola whose eccentricity is 2.

10. In Chapter 17, Section 7, Exercise 4, we found that $ds/d\theta = \rho^2/d$ where $d$ is the perpendicular distance from the pole to the tangent at the point $(\rho, \theta)$. Using this result, show that the magnitude of the velocity at any point $P$ of the path of a body moving in accordance with the inverse square law is inversely proportional to the perpendicular distance from the origin to the tangent at $P$; in symbols, prove that $ds/dt = h/d$.

11. If a particle is attracted to one fixed point by a force $k\rho$ where $\rho$ is the distance to the fixed point and $k$ is a constant, show that the polar coordinate equation of the orbit of the particle is $\rho^2 = 1/[A + B\cos(2\theta + \alpha)]$, where $A$, $B$, and $\alpha$ are constants.

   *Suggestion:* Use the method of deriving (33).

12. Use the results of Exercises 6 and 7 to show that if $v$ is the speed of a planet at any point in its elliptical path, then $v^2 = GM[2/\rho - 1/a]$ where $a$ is the semimajor axis. This equation, which holds also at time $t = 0$, shows how the initial velocity and initial distance determine the semimajor axis of an elliptical orbit.

13. Find the equation of motion of a planet if its distance at the perihelion or point closest to the sun is $\rho_0$ and the speed there is $v_0$.

   *Suggestion:* $d\rho/d\theta = 0$. Use (39).

   *Ans.* $\rho = \rho_0^2 v_0^2/[GM + (\rho_0 v_0^2 - GM)\cos\theta]$.

**4. Satellites and Projectiles.** In Section 3 we considered theory that describes possible planetary motions about the sun. One of the great values of mathematics is that the very same theory often can be applied to a quite different situation by merely reinterpreting the physical meaning of the variables and constants. We can apply the theory of the preceding section to the motion of artificial or man-made satellites about the earth.

Let $M$ in the foregoing theory now stand for the mass of the earth ($G$ is, of course, always the same value) and let us consider the problem of launching a satellite from a point $P_0$ on the earth's surface so that the satellite will clear the earth and follow a closed path. Of course, the earth acts as though its mass were concentrated at its center. We could show that if the satellite is launched at the surface of the earth and if it is to clear the earth and pursue a closed path it must be fired parallel to the earth's surface. Since the distance from the center of the earth to the launching point must be the minimum or perihelion distance then the situation in Fig. 19-14a or Fig. 19-15 must hold, or in view of (40a),

$$\text{(47)} \qquad \sqrt{\frac{GM}{R}} \leq v_0 < \sqrt{\frac{2GM}{R}} \, .$$

If the satellite is projected in a nonparallel direction, and if $v_0 < \sqrt{2GM/R}$, the satellite will indeed take an elliptical path but it will return to earth. Of course, such paths are also useful as the paths of "peaceful" missiles.

Let us examine more closely the meaning of the inequality (47). Suppose that a shot is fired in a horizontal direction from the surface of the earth. The value of $\sqrt{GM/R}$ is about 5 mi/sec and that of $\sqrt{2GM/R}$ about 7 mi/sec. If the initial velocity of the shot is between 5 and 7 mi/sec, the shot will take an elliptical path with the earth's center as the focus nearer to the launching point (Fig. 19-18) and the path will clear the earth. At 5 mi/sec the path, in view of (43), will be a circle. If the initial velocity is 7 mi/sec, the path will be parabolic and the shot will escape; if the initial velocity is more than 7 mi/sec, the path will be hyperbolic and again the shot will never return to earth. (At velocities of 7 mi/sec or more the parabolic and hyperbolic paths will result even if the angle of fire is not perpendicular to the polar axis.)

**Figure 19-18**

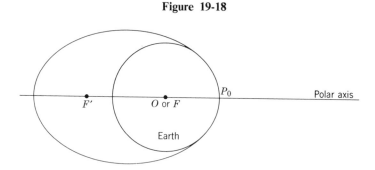

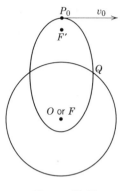

**Figure 19-19**

A significant comparison of paths is more easily made in the cases of velocities less than 5 mi/sec by considering what happens when the shot is fired horizontally from a point $P_0$ somewhat above the earth's surface. The paths will still be elliptical but will cut the earth (Fig. 19-19) so that only the part $P_0Q$ of the ellipse is realized. The center of the earth, $O$ or $F$, is now farther from $P_0$ than the other focus $F'$. As the initial velocity decreases, the ellipse becomes narrower. At points of the actual path $P_0Q$ the directions to the earth's center become more nearly parallel and, if taken to be parallel, will yield a parabolic path, as we found in Chapter 18, Section 4. However, the actual path is always an arc of an ellipse.

In practice satellites are actually raised to a height of one hundred or so miles and then launched horizontally. At such heights there is more room to maneuver. The initial distance is now not $R$ but some larger quantity which, as in Section 3, we denote by $\rho_0$. There are several advantages to launching from this height. First, the air resistance is negligible. Secondly, even if the direction of launching is not precisely parallel to the earth's surface, the satellite can still take an elliptical path well clear of the earth's surface. (We have not discussed all the possible motions in this case.) Thirdly, even for $v_0$ slightly less than $\sqrt{GM/\rho_0}$, there are elliptical paths inside the circular path that will clear the earth, for example, path 3 of Fig. 19-20.

We owe chiefly to Newton the great ideas that we have been pursuing in this chapter. Newton knew all about the parabolic motion of projectiles from the work of Galileo. He also knew that the planets follow elliptical paths from the work of Kepler. His great thought was to incorporate all of these motions under one universal scheme. It occurred to him that if projectiles were launched horizontally from a mountain top with large velocities and if one took into account the sphericity of the earth and the fact that the gravitational pull is toward the center of the earth, these projectiles would follow elliptical paths and, if possessed of enough initial velocity, would clear the earth and become satellites. At this point Newton says in his *Mathematical Principles of Natural Philosophy*:

"And after the same manner that a projectile, by the force of gravity, may be made to revolve in an orbit, and go round the whole earth, the moon also, either by the force of gravity, if it is endowed with gravity, or by

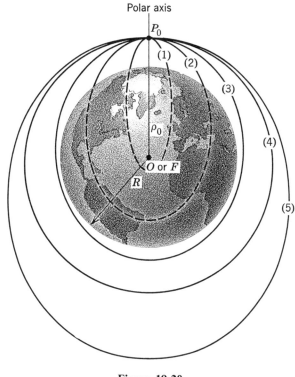

**Figure 19-20**

any other force, that impels it toward the earth, may be continually drawn aside toward the earth, out of the rectilinear way by which its innate force [inertia] it would pursue, and would be made to revolve in the orbit it now describes . . . ."

As the moon revolves in its orbit under the gravitational attraction of the earth, so "the planets do in their orbits" about the sun. Thus Newton conceived that the force of gravitation controls all terrestrial and heavenly motions and worked out the mathematical consequences of the law of gravitation and the laws of motion. When we take into account that Newton also created much of the calculus by which he deduced the motions of projectiles, the moon, and the planets, we cannot but be amazed by such extraordinary achievements.

# EXERCISES

1. A satellite is projected at a distance $\rho_0$ from the center of the earth in a direction parallel to the surface and maintains a circular orbit. Show that $\dot{\rho} = 0$ and that the angular velocity $\dot{\theta}$ is a constant.

2. Under the conditions of Exercise 1 and using the fact that the eccentricity is 0, show that the period $T$ of the satellite's motion is $2\pi\rho_0^{3/2}/\sqrt{GM}$ where $M$ is the mass of the earth.

    *Suggestion:* Use (46).

3. Suppose that a satellite is launched with a velocity that makes it take a circular path and it is desired to have it rotate around the earth's center once in 24

hours so that it rotates in the same period as the earth. At what distance from the earth's center should it be launched?

*Suggestion:* Use (46).                                    *Ans.* About 27,000 miles.

4. If the orbit of a satellite is known to be circular and if the radius of the orbit is known, can one find the mass of the earth?

5. Suppose that $\rho_0$ in Exercise 1 is 4300 miles. Use the result in Exercise 2 to show that $T = 5700$ seconds. In place of $GM$, when $M$ is the mass of the earth, you may use $32R^2$ where $R$ is the radius.

6. A satellite is projected from a distance $\rho_0$ from the center of the earth in a direction parallel to the surface and with a linear velocity $v_0$. Show that if $\rho_0 v_0^2 / GM < 1$, the point at which the satellite is fired is the point of the orbit where the satellite is farthest from the center of the earth (this point is the apogee).

*Suggestion:* See (41).

7. Under the conditions of Exercise 6 calculate the distance from the center of the earth to the satellite when the satellite is closest to the center of the earth, that is, calculate the perigee.                  *Ans.* $\rho_0^2 v_0^2 / (2GM - \rho_0 v_0^2)$.

8. Show that for a given $\rho_0$ the velocity $v_0$ that enables the satellite to clear the earth must satisfy the inequality $v_0^2 > 2GMR/(\rho_0^2 + \rho_0 R)$, where $R$ is the radius of the earth.

*Suggestion:* Use the result of Exercise 7.

9. A rocket of mass 500 pounds is raised to a height of 1000 miles and then shot out horizontally with a velocity of 2000 ft/sec. What is the equation of its path around the earth?

*Suggestion:* Take the earth's center as the pole of the coordinate system and the line from the center to the point at which the rocket is shot out horizontally as the polar axis. Also, when $M$ is the mass of the earth, $GM = 32R^2$ where $R$ is the radius of the earth.

$$Ans. \quad \rho = \frac{195{,}313}{1 - (16{,}771/16{,}896)\cos\theta}.$$

10. Suppose that a satellite is fired from a point distant $\rho_0$ from the center of the earth with a speed $v_0$ directed parallel to the earth's surface. If $(GM/\rho_0) < v_0^2 < 2GM/\rho_0$, show that the point on the elliptical path farthest from the center of the earth is $\rho_0^2 v_0^2 / (2GM - \rho_0 v_0^2)$.

*Suggestion:* See (39).

11. Suppose that a projectile is fired horizontally from the earth's surface with the initial speed of $v_0 = \sqrt{GM/R}$ , where $R$ is the earth's radius. We know from (43) that the path is a circle just along the earth's surface. Moreover, we know that the earth's gravitational force acts toward the center so that there is no tangential acceleration. Then the velocity along the circular path is constant. Using the value of 4.9 mi/sec for $v_0$ [formula (61) of Chapter 6 will give this result when $R = 4000$ miles] and knowing the circumference of the earth, we find that the time to complete one revolution is a little more than 85 minutes. But this is the time it takes an object which is free to move along a tunnel through the earth [Chapter 10, formula (77)] to make one round trip. The equality of these two periods suggests that one motion is related to the other. Suppose that the tunnel goes from the North pole to the South pole and the satellite's path around the earth goes through the poles. Show that the component of the projectile's centripetal acceleration along the vertical direction of the tunnel is precisely the acceleration acting on the object in the tunnel.

# CHAPTER TWENTY
# TAYLOR'S THEOREM AND INFINITE SERIES

**1. The Need to Approximate Functions.** The calculus works with functions and, in particular, with the differentiation and integration of functions. Differentiation is a relatively simple process but integration, as we have seen, is far more complicated. In fact, there are rather simple functions for which we cannot find antiderivatives in terms of the functions that we already know. Some examples are

$$\frac{\sin x}{x}, \quad e^{-x^2}, \quad \text{and} \quad \sqrt{1 - k^2 \sin^2 x}$$

where $k$ is some constant less than 1. The third function, we may recall, comes up in trying to find the length of arc of an ellipse. Despite the inability to integrate such functions in terms of the elementary functions, that is, the ones we studied in the preceding chapters, scientists must work with them.

A second problem that arises in work with functions generally, but especially in problems of the calculus, is that of calculating the values of functions. It is a rather simple matter to calculate the values of, say, the polynomial $3x^2 + 7x + 1$ for various values of $x$. But how do we calculate the values of $\sin x$? We know that $\sin x$ is a ratio of two sides of a right triangle, but this is not of much help in calculating $\sin x$. To use the geometric definition for calculation, we would have to construct a right triangle containing the desired angle $x$ and then presumably measure the opposite side and hypotenuse. This process would not be very accurate if $x$ should, for example, be $35°\ 50'\ 47''$. Aside from the question of accuracy, mathematics does not establish its results by measurement. It proceeds by reasoning which may then lead to arithmetic calculations. Moreover, a proper mathematical process should enable us to calculate any quantity to as great an accuracy as anyone can request.

The answer to the problems that we have cited is to approximate unmanageable functions by manageable ones. However, the notion of approximation must be understood in the proper sense. Mathematicians do not replace one function by any other function that seems to behave similarly. When they approximate one function by another, they not only have good reason for choosing a particular approximating function, but they also insist on determining precisely what the error incurred is. If this error is too large to be tolerated in a given application, they make a better approximation and make certain that the lesser error incurred is not significant for the application in hand. Thus, if the value of $\sin x$ for a particular value of $x$ is needed to five decimal places, the mathematician will make certain that the error is indeed no greater than the quantity 0.000,005.

The subject to which we turn our attention in this chapter is the approximation of functions and the error involved in making approximations.

**2. The Approximation of Functions by Polynomials.** If we are to approximate a given function $f(x)$ by another, $g(x)$ say, then the second function certainly should be a relatively simple one so that we can integrate this second function or calculate its values, because these processes are the ones that cause trouble in the case of the complicated function. Now, the simplest functions to work with are the polynomials, and therefore we shall look into the question of the approximation of functions by polynomials.

Generally, one is interested in the values of a function over some domain of $x$-values. This domain might be the interval over which one is integrating the function or it might be the domain over which one wishes to calculate the values of the function. Hence the problem we face is that of approximating a function over some domain of $x$-values. If we approximate a function very closely at and near some one value of $x$ in that domain, we have some reason to expect that the approximation will still be good at the values in the entire domain, at least if the domain is not large. Let us therefore look into the simpler problem of approximating a function around one value of $x$ and then see what follows.

Suppose that we have a function $f(x)$ and consider approximating it around or in the neighborhood of $x = 0$. Since, as already noted, polynomials are desirable approximating functions, let us consider the approximation

$$(1) \qquad g(x) = c_0 + c_1 x + c_2 x^2 + \cdots + c_n x^n$$

where the coefficients $c_0, c_1, \ldots, c_n$ are to be determined so as to best approximate $f(x)$ around $x = 0$.

We can make $g(x)$ agree with $f(x)$ at $x = 0$; because, by (1), $g(0) = c_0$, we can take $c_0$ to be $f(0)$. What criterion should we now use to determine $c_1, c_2, \ldots$? The suggestion comes from noting Figure 20-1; the tangent to a curve approximates the curve rather closely in the neighborhood of the point of tangency. The tangent approximates the curve closely not only because it has a point in common with the curve but because it has the same slope as the curve. Hence we should seek to make the slope of (1) agree with the slope of $f(x)$ at $x = 0$. By differentiating (1) we have

$$(2) \qquad g'(x) = c_1 + 2c_2 x + 3c_3 x^2 + \cdots nc_n x^{n-1}.$$

**Figure 20-1**

At $x = 0$, $g'(0) = c_1$. If $g'(0)$ is to agree with $f'(0)$, then $c_1$ must equal $f'(0)$. Thus we have the desired value of $c_1$.

Now let us carry the preceding idea further; that is, let us make the second derivative of $g(x)$ agree with $f''(x)$ at $x = 0$. From (2) we have that

**(3)** $$g''(x) = 2c_2 + 2 \cdot 3c_3 x + \cdots + n(n-1)c_n x^{n-2}.$$

Then $g''(0) = 2c_2$, and if $g''(0)$ is to be the same as $f''(0)$, we must have $2c_2 = f''(0)$ or

$$c_2 = \frac{f''(0)}{2}.$$

To have $g''(0)$ agree with $f''(0)$ makes sense geometrically. The curvature of a curve depends on the second and first derivatives of its equation, and by making the first and second derivatives of $f(x)$ and $g(x)$ agree at $x = 0$, we are requiring that the curvature of $g(x)$ agree with that of $f(x)$ at $x = 0$.

We now have a method for determining the coefficients $c_0$, $c_1$, and $c_2$. To determine $c_3$ we could make the third derivatives of $f(x)$ and $g(x)$ agree at $x = 0$. From (3) we have

**(4)** $$g'''(x) = 2 \cdot 3c_3 + \cdots + n(n-1)(n-2)c_n x^{n-3}.$$

Then $g'''(0) = 2 \cdot 3c_3$ and, because this is to equal $f'''(0)$, the result is

$$c_3 = \frac{f'''(0)}{2 \cdot 3}.$$

The process that we have used to determine $c_0$, $c_1$, $c_2$, and $c_3$ can be continued. In fact, we can see from (1) that the $n$th derivative of $g(x)$, which we denote by $g^{(n)}(x)$, is $n(n-1)(n-2) \cdots 2 \cdot 1 c_n$ and, if $g^{(n)}(0)$ is to equal $f^{(n)}(0)$, then

$$c_n = \frac{f^{(n)}(0)}{n(n-1) \cdots 2 \cdot 1}$$

or, to use the factorial notation, namely, $n! = 1 \cdot 2 \cdot 3 \cdots (n-1)n$,

$$c_n = \frac{f^{(n)}(0)}{n!}.$$

To summarize what we have accomplished thus far, if the function $g(x)$ given by (1) is to approximate $f(x)$ at $x = 0$ and if we use the condition that at $x = 0$ the two functions are to agree and each pair of the successive derivatives up to the $n$th derivatives are to agree, then $g(x)$ takes the form

**(5)** $$g(x) = f(0) + f'(0)x + \frac{f''(0)}{2!} x^2 + \cdots + \frac{f^{(n)}(0)}{n!} x^n.$$

Of course, although we have some geometrical evidence to suggest that $g(x)$ should approximate $f(x)$ rather well for values of $x$ near $x = 0$, we really do not know as yet how close numerically this approximation is. Before we consider this point, let us note that instead of approximating $f(x)$ by $g(x)$ at and near $x = 0$, we could equally well make the approximation at and near some other value of $x$, say $x = a$. If we proceeded to do this by using the form (1) for $g(x)$ and the above method of determining the coefficients $c_0, c_1, \ldots,$ we would not suceed. We can see that we would be blocked in the very first step because for $x = a$

$$g(a) = c_0 + c_1 a + c_2 a^2 + \cdots + c_n a^n,$$

and we would like to have this expression equal $f(a)$. However, this time we do not obtain the value of $c_0$ at once as we did in the preceding case of $x = 0$. There might still be some way of proceeding with the form (1) of $g(x)$, but a wiser procedure is to recognize that the proper form of $g(x)$, which generalizes on the form (1), is

**(6)** $$g(x) = c_0 + c_1(x - a) + c_2(x - a)^2 + \cdots + c_n(x - a)^n.$$

That is, we recognize that the $g(x)$ in (1) is really of the form

$$g(x) = c_0 + c_1(x - 0) + c_2(x - 0)^2 + \cdots + c_n(x - 0)^n$$

and that (6) is the proper generalization. With the form (6) for $g(x)$ we can use the procedure above to determine the coefficients so that at $x = a$, $f(x)$ equals $g(x)$ and each of the successive derivatives of $f(x)$ up to the $n$th derivative agrees with the corresponding derivative of $g(x)$. In fact, we can see at once that $g(a) = c_0$ and because this must equal $f(a)$,

$$c_0 = f(a).$$

Likewise, by differentiating (6) we obtain

$$g'(x) = c_1 + 2c_2(x - a) + 3c_2(x - a)^2 + \cdots + nc_n(x - a)^{n-1}.$$

Then $g'(a) = c_1$ and, if this is to equal $f'(a)$, we must have

$$c_1 = f'(a).$$

The procedure can certainly be continued and the result is that if $g(x)$ is to approximate $f(x)$ in the sense that at $x = a$ the two functions are to be equal and each of the successive derivatives up to and including the $n$th derivative of $f(x)$ is to equal the corresponding derivative of $g(x)$, then

$$g(x) = f(a) + f'(a)(x - a) + \frac{f''(a)}{2!}(x - a)^2 + \cdots + \frac{f^{(n)}(a)}{n!}(x - a)^n.$$

**(7)**

Thus (7) is our final formula for approximating any function $f(x)$ by a polynomial $g(x)$ [see (6)] in $x - a$. We can, of course, stop with $n = 2, 3, 4$ or some larger positive integer.

## EXERCISES

**1.** Approximate $\sin x$ by the first degree polynomial $c_0 + c_1 x$ by making $\sin x$ and the polynomial agree at $x = 0$ and their respective first derivatives agree at $x = 0$. What does the result say about the values of $\sin x$ for $x$ near 0?

**2.** Approximate $\sin x$ by a fourth degree polynomial at $x = \pi/4$.

*Ans.* $\frac{1}{\sqrt{2}}\left\{1 + \left(x - \frac{\pi}{4}\right) - \frac{1}{2}\left(x - \frac{\pi}{4}\right)^2 - \frac{1}{6}\left(x - \frac{\pi}{4}\right)^3 + \frac{1}{24}\left(x - \frac{\pi}{4}\right)^4\right\}.$

**3.** Find the $n$th degree polynomial of the form $c_0 + c_1 x + \cdots + c_n x^n$ which approximates $e^x$ in the sense that at $x = 0$ the function and the polynomial agree and each of the successive derivatives of $f(x)$ agrees with the corresponding derivative of $g(x)$. *Ans.* $c_i = 1/i!, i = 0, 1, \ldots, n.$

**4.** Repeat Exercise 3, except that $e^x$ is to be replaced by $\sin x$.

*Ans.* $c_{2i} = 0, c_{2i+1} = (-1)^i/(2i + 1)!, i = 0, 1, \ldots, n.$

**3. *Taylor's Formula.*** We have learned thus far that we can approximate a function $f(x)$ by an $n$th degree polynomial to the extent that at $x = a$ we can make the function agree with the polynomial and make each of the successive derivatives up to and including the $n$th derivative of the function agree with the corresponding derivative of the polynomial. The approximating polynomial then has the form (7). However, we do not know how good the approximation is numerically. Certainly, at $x = a$, $g(a) = f(a)$ and the approximation is exact. However, suppose that we take a value of $x$ different from $a$, say $a + h$, where $h$ can be positive or negative. Now, $f(a + h)$ will generally not equal $g(a + h)$. The difference $f(a + h) - g(a + h)$ is the error in approximating $f(a + h)$ by $g(a + h)$. Let us denote this error by the constant $R$ so that

**(8)**                          $R = f(a + h) - g(a + h)$

and let us seek to compute $R$.

Actually, we are interested in more than the value of $R$. We spoke earlier of approximating a function $f(x)$ in some domain of $x$-values. Hence we might certainly consider the domain from $a$ to $a + h$ and try to see what the error is for any $x$ in that domain. That is, we should evaluate $f(x) - g(x)$ for $x$ in the domain $a$ to $a + h$. This error will depend on $x$, and there is the chance since $g(x)$ has the form (7) that the error might involve

$(x - a)^{n+1}$ because if we were to carry the approximation (6) to one more term we would have to add the term $f^{(n+1)}(a)(x - a)^{n+1}/(n + 1)!$ to (7). However, we have already fixed $R$ so that at $x = a + h$ the error is $R$. This suggests that we try $R(x - a)^{n+1}/h^{n+1}$ for $f(x) - g(x)$ because then at $x = a + h$ the error will be $R$. Thus we are led to the conjecture that

$$(9) \qquad f(x) = g(x) + R \frac{(x - a)^{n+1}}{h^{n+1}}.$$

Now (9) is still not correct for all values of $x$ in the interval $a$ to $a + h$, because $R$ is a constant fixed so as to satisfy (8) and $g(x)$ is a polynomial whereas $f(x)$ is any function. We can introduce the function

$$(10) \qquad F(x) = f(x) - g(x) - R \frac{(x - a)^{n+1}}{h^{n+1}}$$

where, to repeat, $x$ is any value in $a \le x \le a + h$ and $R = f(a + h) - g(a + h)$. This function represents the error in approximating $f(x)$ by the right side of (9). Let us study this function to see what we can learn about the error and the value of $R$.

Because $f(a) = g(a)$, $F(a)$ is certainly 0. Moreover, $F(a + h)$ is also 0 because $f(a + h) - g(a + h)$ equals $R$ in view of (8). Thus $F(x)$ vanishes at $x = a$ and $x = a + h$. By Rolle's theorem $F'(x)$ vanishes at some value $x_1$ between $a$ and $a + h$; that is, $F'(x_1) = 0$. We consider next

$$(11) \qquad F'(x) = f'(x) - g'(x) - R(n + 1) \frac{(x - a)^n}{h^{n+1}}.$$

Because by (7) $f'(a) = g'(a)$, we see from (11) that $F'(a) = 0$. Moreover, we just proved that $F'(x_1) = 0$. Then by Rolle's theorem $F'(x)$ vanishes for some value $x_2$ of $x$ which lies between $a$ and $x_1$. We turn then to $F''(x)$, which from (11) is

$$(12) \qquad F''(x) = f''(x) - g''(x) - R \frac{(n + 1)n(x - a)^{n-1}}{h^{n+1}}.$$

Again, by the very construction of $g(x)$, $g''(a) = f''(a)$ and so from (12), $F''(a) = 0$. We also know that $F''(x_2) = 0$. Another application of Rolle's theorem to $F''(x)$ tells us that there is a value $x_3$ of $x$ such that $F'''(x_3) = 0$. We can continue this process until we reach

$$(13) \qquad F^{(n)}(x) = f^{(n)}(x) - g^{(n)}(x) - R \frac{(n + 1)n(n - 1) \cdots 2(x - a)}{h^{n+1}}.$$

Now, $f^{(n)}(a)$ and $g^{(n)}(a)$ are equal by the very construction of $g^{(n)}(x)$. Hence $F^{(n)}(a) = 0$. The step dealing with $F^{(n-1)}(x)$, which is understood in the process, tells us that $F^{(n)}(x)$ vanishes for some value $x_n$ of $x$ which lies between $x_{n-1}$ and $a$; that is, $F^{(n)}(x_n) = 0$. Hence by a final application of

Rolle's theorem we know that $F^{(n+1)}(x)$ vanishes at some value $x_{n+1}$ of $x$ which lies between $x_n$ and $a$. However, by (13) and since the $(n+1)$st derivative of $g(x)$ vanishes because $g(x)$ is a polynomial of the $n$th degree,

$$(14) \qquad F^{(n+1)}(x) = f^{(n+1)}(x) - \frac{R(n+1)!}{h^{n+1}}.$$

Then

$$(15) \qquad F^{(n+1)}(x_{n+1}) = f^{(n+1)}(x_{n+1}) - R\frac{(n+1)!}{h^{n+1}} = 0.$$

From (15) we see that

$$R = f^{(n+1)}(x_{n+1})\frac{h^{n+1}}{(n+1)!}.$$

Let us note that although we do not know the precise value of $x_{n+1}$, we do know that it lies between $a$ and $a+h$. We denote it by $\mu$. Then

$$(16) \qquad R = f^{(n+1)}(\mu)\frac{h^{n+1}}{(n+1)!}.$$

Let us now put together what we have established. We see from (8) that

$$(17) \qquad f(a+h) = g(a+h) + R.$$

We know from (7) that at $x = a + h$

$$(18) \qquad g(a+h) = f(a) + f'(a)h + f''(a)\frac{h^2}{2!} + \cdots + f^{(n)}(a)\frac{h^n}{n!}.$$

Then if we substitute (18) into (17) and use the value of $R$ in (16), we find that

$$f(a+h) = f(a) + f'(a)h + f''(a)\frac{h^2}{2!} + \cdots + f^{(n)}(a)\frac{h^n}{n!}$$
$$(19) \qquad + f^{(n+1)}(\mu)\frac{h^{n+1}}{(n+1)!},$$

the last term on the right side being, of course, the value of $R$. This quantity is called the remainder after $n + 1$ terms.

Formula (19) is a fundamental result known as Taylor's theorem because the essence of it was first given in 1715 by Brook Taylor (1685–1731), one of the immediate successors to Newton and Leibniz. The particular form of $R$ given in (16) was derived in 1797 by Joseph-Louis Lagrange (1736–1813), one of the great French mathematicians of the eighteenth century.

Taylor's formula can be written in many ways, which differ trivially from one another. For example, $a + h$ is just a value of $x$ different from $a$. Hence we can as well write $x$ in place of $a + h$. But then we must replace $h$ by $x - a$. With these changes formula (19) becomes

**Taylor's Theorem:** For any function $f(x)$ which has $(n + 1)$ derivatives in the interval from $a$ to $x$,

$$f(x) = f(a) + f'(a)(x - a) + f''(a)\frac{(x - a)^2}{2!} + \cdots + f^n(a)\frac{(x - a)^n}{n!}$$

(20) $$+ f^{(n+1)}(\mu)\frac{(x - a)^{n+1}}{(n + 1)!}$$

where $\mu$ lies between $a$ and $x$.

Formula (20) is called Taylor's expansion of $f(x)$ around $x = a$ or, we could say, an expansion in powers of $(x - a)$.

Before utilizing Taylor's formula let us note one or two facts about it. First of all, the value of $n$ in (19) or (20) is at our disposal. We could, for example, choose $n = 0$. For this value of $n$, (20) becomes

(21) $$f(x) = f(a) + f'(\mu)(x - a).$$

This statement, however, is just the law of the mean or the mean value theorem of the differential calculus. Thus Taylor's formula is a generalization of the law of the mean and for this reason is sometimes called the extended law of the mean.

The second point worthy of note is that when $a = 0$ in (20), Taylor's formula becomes

$$f(x) = f(0) + f'(0)x + f''(0)\frac{x^2}{2!} + \cdots$$

(22) $$+ f^{(n)}(0)\frac{x^n}{n!} + f^{(n+1)}(\mu)\frac{x^{n+1}}{(n + 1)!}$$

where $\mu$ now lies between 0 and $x$. In this special case Taylor's theorem is known as Maclaurin's theorem because Colin Maclaurin (1698–1746) stated it in 1742 although, as he himself pointed out, it had already been stated by Taylor. Maclaurin's theorem gives an expansion of $f(x)$ around $x = 0$ or in powers of $x$.

To expand a given function in accordance with (20) is a rather mechanical procedure. Let us expand $\log (1 + x)$ around $x = 1$; that is, $a$ in (20) is 1. Then, since $f(x) = \log(1 + x)$,

$$f(1) = \log 2 .$$

Because $f'(x) = 1/(1 + (x))$,

$$f'(1) = \frac{1}{1 + 1} = \frac{1}{2}.$$

Again, since $f''(x) = -1/(1 + x)^2$,

$$f''(1) = -\frac{1}{(1 + 1)^2} = -\frac{1}{4}.$$

We can, of course, calculate the higher derivatives, but if we decide to carry three on the right side plus the remainder term, we need only the next or third derivative. This is

$$f'''(x) = +\frac{2}{(1 + x)^3}.$$

Now we can substitute in (20) to obtain

$$\log(1 + x) = \log 2 + \tfrac{1}{2}(x - 1) - \tfrac{1}{4}\frac{(x - 1)^2}{2!} + \frac{2}{(1 + \mu)^3}\frac{(x - 1)^3}{3!}.$$

**(23)**

The quantity $\mu$ in the remainder term is not known exactly; we know only that $\mu$ lies between 1 and $x$.

We could have chosen to expand $\log(1 + x)$ around $x = 0$. This means that $a = 0$ and that we are really using the special case (22) of (20). Then, if we use the derivatives already calculated, we have that

$$f(0) = \log 1 = 0, \qquad f'(0) = 1, \qquad f''(0) = -1.$$

By substitution in (22) we obtain

**(24)**
$$\log(1 + x) = 0 + x - \frac{x^2}{2!} + \frac{2}{(1 + \mu)^3}\frac{x^3}{3!}$$

where $\mu$ now lies between 0 and $x$.

## EXERCISES

**1.** Expand the following functions around the value of $x$ indicated. Carry each expansion to three terms plus a remainder term.
(a)  $\cos x$ around $x = \pi/4$.

*Ans.*  $\cos x = \dfrac{1}{\sqrt{2}} - \dfrac{1}{\sqrt{2}}\left(x - \dfrac{\pi}{4}\right) - \dfrac{1}{\sqrt{2}}\dfrac{\left(x - \dfrac{\pi}{4}\right)^2}{2!} + \sin\mu\,\dfrac{\left(x - \dfrac{\pi}{4}\right)^3}{3!}.$

(b)   $\cos x$ around $x = 0$.

(c)   $\sin x$ around $x = \dfrac{\pi}{4}$ .

$$Ans. \quad \sin x = \frac{1}{\sqrt{2}} + \frac{1}{\sqrt{2}}\left(x - \frac{\pi}{4}\right) - \frac{1}{\sqrt{2}}\frac{\left(x - \frac{\pi}{4}\right)^2}{2!} - \cos\mu\frac{\left(x - \frac{\pi}{4}\right)^3}{3!} .$$

(d)   $\sin x$ around $x = 0$.

(e)   $\tan x$ around $x = \dfrac{\pi}{4}$ .

$$Ans. \quad \tan x = 1 + 2\left(x - \frac{\pi}{4}\right) + 4\frac{\left(x - \frac{\pi}{4}\right)^2}{2!}$$
$$+ (4\tan^2\mu \sec^2\mu + 2\sec^4\mu)\frac{\left(x - \frac{\pi}{4}\right)^3}{3!} .$$

(f)   $e^x$ around $x = 1$.

2. Apply formula (20) to the function $y = x^4$ when $a = 0$ and $x = 1$ to obtain $f(1)$ when $n$ is 0; then when $n = 1, 2,$ and 3. Note the values of $\mu$ obtained for these various values of $n$. What can you say about their behavior?

### 4. Some Applications of Taylor's Theorem.

One of the problems which led us to investigate the approximation of functions by polynomials was that of calculating functions such as $\sin x$. Let us now see how Taylor's theorem or Taylor's formula helps us. Suppose that we wish to calculate values of $\sin x$ near $x = 0$. We can apply formula (22) to obtain an expansion of $\sin x$ around $x = 0$. After calculating the derivatives required by (22), we obtain to four terms

$$(25) \qquad\qquad \sin x = x - \frac{x^3}{3!} + \frac{x^5}{5!} - \cos\mu\,\frac{x^7}{7!}$$

where $\mu$ lies between 0 and $x$.

Let us suppose now that we wish to calculate $\sin x$ for $x = 0.1$. This value is, of course, 0.1 radians because our calculus formulas for differentiation and integration of the trigonometric functions presuppose the measure of angles in radians. We can now substitute 0.1 for $x$ in the first three terms on the right side of (25) and calculate their sum. The result will be too large because the exact value of $\sin x$ calls for subtracting the fourth term. We do not know the exact value of the fourth term—if we did, we could calculate the exact value of $\sin x$—but we can argue as follows. The value of $\mu$ lies between 0 and $x$. Now, $x$ is 0.1 and the value of $\cos\mu$ is at most 1. Then for $x = 0.1$,

$$\cos\mu\,\frac{x^7}{7!} < 1 \cdot \frac{(0.1)^7}{7!} .$$

We could, of course, calculate exactly the value of the right-hand side of this inequality, but it is sufficient for our present purposes to note that it is less than 0.000 000 1. This means, then, that the error incurred in using the first three terms on the right side of (25) and neglecting the fourth one is less than 0.000 000 1. We see thus that by using only three terms in the Maclaurin expansion of sin $x$, we can calculate that function to a high degree of accuracy. It is also apparent that if we had calculated more terms in the expansion of sin $x$ than the four given in (25), we would have obtained a still better result, for the remainder term would be of the form

**(26)**
$$\cos \mu \, \frac{x^{2m+1}}{(2m+1)!} \, ,$$

and when $m$ increases beyond 3, which is the value in (25), the numerator in (26) becomes smaller and the denominator increases. Hence the remainder term decreases as $m$ increases.

We see from this example that when we use Taylor's formula to calculate the value of a function, we do not calculate the exact value but can at least in significant cases estimate the maximum error incurred in neglecting the remainder. Then we know that our approximate value of the function is correct to some decimal place, and this suffices for the use of these function values in science or engineering.

It is helpful to see geometrically just how we improve our approximation to sin $x$ by taking more and more terms of the Taylor expansion. Figure 20-2 shows that if we take merely $y = x$ as the first approximation to $y = \sin x$, we obtain the tangent line to $y = \sin x$ at $(0, 0)$. The approximation $y = x - x^3/3!$ gives a cubic curve that approximates $y = \sin x$ rather well up to the value $x = 1$ but then departs more and more from $y = \sin x$. The third approximation, $y = x - x^3/3! + x^5/5!$ approximates $y = \sin x$ rather closely up to the value $x = 1.5$ and then departs more and more from $y = \sin x$.

**Figure 20-2**

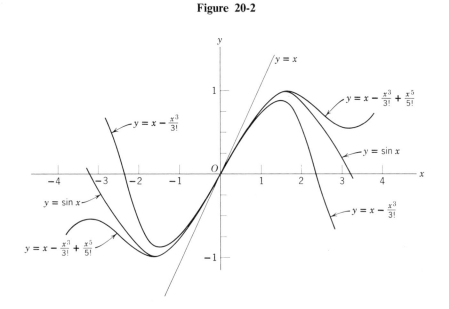

## EXERCISES

1. Calculate the value of $\cos x$ for $x = 0.1$ by using three terms in the Taylor expansion around $x = 0$ and estimate the error involved in neglecting the remainder after three terms.      *Ans.* $\cos .1 = 0.995\ 004\ 17, |R| < 1.4 \cdot 10^{-9}$.

2. Suppose that one used formula (25) to calculate $\sin 0.2$. What estimate can you give of the error involved in neglecting the remainder term?

3. Expand $e^x$ around $x = 0$ to four terms plus a remainder. Then calculate $e^{1/2}$ from the four terms and estimate as best as you can the error in neglecting the remainder.                    *Ans.* $e^{1/2} = 1.65, 0 < R < 0.008$.

4. Carry out the procedures called for in Exercise 3 but for the function $\log(1 + x)$ and for the value $x = \frac{1}{2}$.

5. Calculate the value of $\cos x$ for $x = 0.1$ by using five terms in the Taylor expansion around $x = 0$ and estimate the error in neglecting the remainder. Is the error less in this case than in Exercise 1?
   *Ans.* $\cos .1 = 0.995\ 004\ 165\ 278\ 0258, 0 < R < 0.3 \cdot 10^{-16}$.

**5. The Taylor Series.** Taylor's theorem applied to a function gives an expansion that consists of a finite number of terms plus a remainder. When we wish to use this expansion, we naturally seek to determine how accurately the few terms employed approximate the function; to determine this, we evaluate the remainder; that is, we usually find the maximum value that the remainder can take on, which tells us the maximum error incurred in neglecting the remainder. If we should wish to obtain better and better approximations to the function, we might use more terms in the expansion provided we knew that the remainder became smaller and smaller. To be specific, suppose that we use $n$ terms so that

$$f(x) = f(a) + f'(x - a) + f''(a)\frac{(x - a)^2}{2!} + \cdots$$

$$+ f^{(n-1)}(a)\frac{(x - a)^{n-1}}{(n - 1)!} + R_n$$

where $R_n$ denotes the remainder after $n$ terms. To be certain that by increasing the number of terms we come closer and closer to $f(x)$, we must know that $R_n$ approaches 0 as $n$ becomes infinite.

To speak of $R_n$ approaching 0 as $n$ becomes infinite implies that $R_n$ is a function of $n$. It is in the sense that for each *positive integral* value of $n$ there is a definite quantity $R_n$. Hence the remainders

**(27)**                          $R_1, R_2, R_3, \ldots, R_n, \cdots$ .

form what we called a sequence in Chapter 9, and the statement that $R_n$ approaches 0 as $n$ becomes infinite means that the limit of the sequence (27), that is, the number approached by the $R_n$ as $n$ becomes larger and larger, is 0.

If it is true that $R_n$ approaches 0 as $n$ becomes infinite, then $f(x)$ is approximated better and better as we take more terms in the Taylor expansion of $f(x)$. We indicate this by writing

**(28)**      $$f(x) = f(a) + f'(a)(x - a) + f''(a)\frac{(x - a)^2}{2!} \cdots,$$

where the dots mean that we keep on adding more and more terms of the Taylor expansion without end. This expansion is an infinite series and in the present case is called *Taylor's series*. In the special case in which $a = 0$, the infinite series is

**(29)**      $$f(x) = f(0) + f'(0)x + f''(0)\frac{x^2}{2!} \cdots.$$

This infinite series is called *Maclaurin's series*.

There is some question as to what we mean by representing a function as in (28) and (29) by an infinite series. In a loose way we mean that if we start with the first term, add the second to it, then add the third to that sum, then the fourth to this sum, and so on, we shall come closer and closer to the value of $f(x)$. Of course, to speak of continuing without end to add a term to the sum already obtained is vague because there is no final sum. What we need here is a more precise definition of the quantity that is obtained by summing an infinite series in the manner we have described. We shall turn for a while to the consideration of infinite series as such and then return to the subject of Taylor's and Maclaurin's series.

## EXERCISES

**1.** What is the MacLaurin series for the following:
   (a)  $\sin x$.
   (b)  $\cos x$.
   (c)  $\log(1 + x)$.
   (d)  $e^x$.
   (e)  $e^{-x}$.
   (f)  $\tan x$.

**2.** What is the Taylor series for the following:
   (a)  $\sin x$ around $x = \pi/4$.
   (b)  $e^x$ around $x = 1$.
   (c)  $\log(1 + x)$ around $x = 2$.

**6. *Infinite Series of Constant Terms.*** To begin our study of infinite series, let us start with series of constant terms because that is what (28) and (29) are for a fixed value of $x$. Thus suppose that we consider the series

**(30)**      $$\tfrac{1}{2} + \tfrac{1}{4} + \tfrac{1}{8} + \tfrac{1}{16} + \cdots.$$

Let us ask ourselves what one could possibly mean by the sum of such an infinite set of numbers. The natural inclination would be to add $\tfrac{1}{4}$ to $\tfrac{1}{2}$ and obtain $\tfrac{3}{4}$; then add $\tfrac{1}{8}$ to $\tfrac{3}{4}$ and obtain $\tfrac{7}{8}$; then add $\tfrac{1}{16}$ to $\tfrac{7}{8}$ and obtain $\tfrac{15}{16}$; and to continue adding the next term to the sum already obtained. If we approach the problem of summing the infinite series (30) in this way, we shall never arrive at the sum because no matter how many terms we have already summed there will still be more to be taken into account. However, by a slight modification of our point of view we can obtain the sum.

Let us look at the partial sums that we obtain by taking the first term of (30), then the first two terms, then the first three terms, and so on. These partial sums are

$$\text{(31)} \qquad \frac{1}{2}, \frac{3}{4}, \frac{7}{8}, \frac{15}{16}, \cdots$$

Of course, there is no end to those partial sums and so at the moment we are no better off than before. However, we can look at the *sequence* of partial sums and note what number they may be approaching. This number or limit can be taken to be the sum of the series (29) because the continuing process of adding the next term to the partial sum already obtained does no more than bring us closer and closer to this very limit. If we can determine the limit by examining the sequence, we can short-circuit the unending addition process.

Let us see how the suggestion of taking the number approached by the sequence of partial sums works out for the series (30). This series happens to be a geometric series, that is, each term is obtained from the preceding one by multiplying by a constant factor, which in the present case is $\frac{1}{2}$. Suppose that we consider the sum of the first $n$ terms. The sum of $n$ terms of a geometric series (or progression) is given by the formula

$$S_n = \frac{a - ar^n}{1 - r}$$

where $a$ is the first term and $r$ is the constant factor. In the case of (30), $a$ is $\frac{1}{2}$ and $r$ is $\frac{1}{2}$. Hence the sum of $n$ terms is

$$\text{(32)} \qquad S_n = \frac{\frac{1}{2} - \frac{1}{2}\left(\frac{1}{2}\right)^n}{1 - \frac{1}{2}} = 1 - \left(\frac{1}{2}\right)^n.$$

For $n = 1, 2, 3, \ldots$, $S_n$ is $\frac{1}{2}, \frac{3}{4}, \frac{7}{8}, \ldots$, that is, for $n = 1, 2, 3, \ldots$, $S_n$ represents the sequence of partial sums given in (31). Now let us ask, what is the number approached by $S_n$ as $n$ becomes larger and larger. The quantity $\left(\frac{1}{2}\right)^n$ in (32) approaches 0 as $n$ becomes larger and larger. Then $S_n$ approaches 1. It certainly seems reasonable to take this number to be the sum of the infinite series (30). In fact, all we are doing by taking this number to be the sum is to note to what number the unending process of adding the next term to the partial sum already obtained is leading us and to take the number at once as the sum of the infinite series. Moreover, we do not guess that number, but examine mathematically the precise expression for the $n$th partial sum, that is, $S_n$ in (32), and we calculate what number $S_n$ is approaching.

We can also see geometrically the reasonableness of what we said above. We start (Fig. 20-3) with a line segment of length $\frac{1}{2}$ and add to this a

**Figure 20-3**

line segment of length $\frac{1}{4}$, then a segment of length $\frac{1}{8}$, and so forth. The infinite series (30) is then pictured by the sum of the infinite number of lengths which are obtained in this way. Intuitively, it seems clear that the sum of all these lengths will fill out a length of 1 unit. The partial sums $S_1, S_2, S_3, \ldots$ are the lengths $\frac{1}{2}, \frac{3}{4}, \frac{7}{8}, \ldots$, and these partial sums cover more and more of the unit length. In fact, they differ from the unit length by a smaller and smaller amount as we consider succeeding terms in this sequence $S_1, S_2, S_3 \cdots$.

As a matter of fact, if we have any infinite geometric series

$$a + ar + ar^2 + \cdots + ar^n + \cdots ,$$

and if $r$ lies between $-1$ and $+1$, the end values excluded, then the sequence of partial sums will approach a limit. We know that

**(33)** $$S_n = \frac{a - ar^n}{1 - r} .$$

We shall now show that if $r$ lies between $-1$ and $+1$, then $r^n$ approaches 0 as $n$ becomes larger and larger.

Suppose to start with that $r$ is positive. Since $r$ is less than 1, it can be written in the form $1/(1 + h)$ where $h$ is positive. Thus, if $r = \frac{3}{4}$, it can be written as $1/\frac{4}{3}$ or $1/(1 + \frac{1}{3})$. Then

**(34)** $$r^n = \frac{1}{(1 + h)^n} .$$

By the binomial theorem

$$(1 + h)^n = 1 + nh + \cdots$$

where the values of the remaining terms do not matter, except for the fact that they are positive. Then

$$(1 + h)^n > 1 + nh$$

and by (34)

$$r^n < \frac{1}{1 + nh} .$$

As $n$ becomes larger and larger, the right side of this inequality approaches 0, and so $r^n$ surely approaches 0. If $r$ is negative and greater than $-1$, then $|r|^n$ is positive, and as $n$ becomes larger and larger $|r|^n$ approaches 0.

However, for negative $r$, $r^n$ differs from $|r|^n$ only in that the odd powers are negative. But the numerical value of $r^n$ still approaches 0.

Returning to (33), we see that as long as $r$ lies between $-1$ and $+1$, then as $n$ increases $r^n$ approaches 0 and because $a$ is a fixed number, $ar^n$ approaches 0. As $n$ increases, the value of $S_n$ approaches $a/(1-r)$. Thus the sum $S$ of any infinite geometric series in which $r$, the common ratio, lies between $-1$ and 1 (but not including $-1$ and 1) is

$$S = \frac{a}{1-r}.$$

We can put in more general terms what this example suggests.

**Definition:** Suppose that we have the infinite series

**(35)**               $u_1 + u_2 + u_3 + \cdots + u_n + \cdots.$

where the $u_i$'s are ordinary real numbers. We form the sequence of partial sums

$$S_1 = u_1$$
$$S_2 = u_1 + u_2$$
$$S_3 = u_1 + u_2 + u_3$$
$$\cdots$$

**(36)**               $S_n = u_1 + u_2 + u_3 + \cdots + u_n.$

If as $n$ becomes larger and larger the $S_n$ approach a fixed number $S$, then this number $S$ is, by definition, the sum of the infinite series (35). This number $S$ can also be described as the limit of the sequence $S_1, S_2, S_3, \ldots$ as $n$ becomes infinite and is designated by

**(37)**               $S = \lim_{n \to \infty} S_n.$

We also write

$$S = u_1 + u_2 + u_3 + \cdots + u_n + \cdots.$$

To define the sum of an infinite series as the limit of the sequence of partial sums seems to suggest that this limit will always be available. Let us see if this is the case. Suppose that we consider the series

**(38)**               $1 + 2 + 3 + 4 + \cdots.$

Here the sequence of partial sums is

$$1, 3, 6, 10, \cdots.$$

Does this sequence of partial sums approach some definite number? Clearly it does not. The terms of the sequence become larger and larger and do not come closer to a definite number. One can say that $S_n$ becomes infinite or even write $\lim\limits_{n\to\infty} S_n = \infty$ but one must always keep in mind that $\infty$ is not a symbol for a number; rather it is shorthand for the statement that the variable, $S_n$, takes on larger and larger values, indeed values larger than any number one can name. Then the series (38) does *not* have a sum.

As another example let us consider the series

**(39)** $$1 - 1 + 1 - 1 + 1 \cdots .$$

The sequence of partial sums for this series is

**(40)** $$1, 0, 1, 0, 1, \cdots .$$

This sequence does *not* approach a definite number. It is true that the odd-numbered members are always 1 and so do even better than approach 1, and that the even-numbered members are always 0 and so certainly do better than approach 0. However, when we speak of the members of a sequence approaching a definite number we mean that as $n$ gets larger, *all* the members get closer and closer to one definite number. In the case of the sequence (40), no matter how far out we go, that is, no matter how large $n$ gets, we shall always find 0's and 1's, and so all the members will not get closer and closer to one definite number.

These examples show that we must distinguish among series. For some of them the sequence of partial sums will approach a definite number or will have a limit. In these cases the series have sums and the series are said to be *convergent*. On the other hand, if the sequence of partial sums of a series does not have a limit, the series does not have a sum and is said to be *divergent*.

## EXERCISES

1. Do the following series converge? Use either facts about geometric series or an intuitive argument to support your answer.
   (a) $1 + \frac{1}{3} + \frac{1}{9} + \frac{1}{27} + \cdots .$   *Ans.* Convergent.
   (b) $1 + 2 + 2^2 + 2^3 \cdots .$
   (c) $1 + 0.1 + 0.01 + 0.001 + \cdots .$   *Ans.* Convergent.
   (d) $1 + \frac{1}{4} + \frac{1}{16} + \frac{1}{64} \cdots .$
   (e) $1 + 0.3 + 0.03 + 0.003 + \cdots .$   *Ans.* Convergent.
   (f) $0.01 + 0.02 + 0.03 + 0.04 + \cdots .$   *Ans.* Divergent.

2. Does the geometric series converge in the following cases?
   (a) $r = 1.$
   (b) $r = -1.$

3. Use an argument analogous to that in the text to show that if $r > 1$, $r^n$ becomes infinite as $n$ does. Then show that the geometric series diverges when $r > 1$.

4. What can you say about the convergence or divergence of the geometric series when $r < -1$?

5. Determine whether the following series converge or diverge:
   (a) $\frac{1}{2} - \frac{1}{4} + \frac{1}{8} - \cdots + (-1)^{n+1}\frac{1}{2^n} + \cdots .$   *Ans.* Convergent.

(b)   $1 - \dfrac{1}{3} + \dfrac{1}{9} - \dfrac{1}{27} + \cdots + (-1)^{n+1} \dfrac{1}{3^{n-1}} + \cdots$ .

(c)   $1 - \dfrac{3}{2} + \dfrac{9}{4} - \dfrac{27}{8} + \cdots + (-1)^{n+1} \dfrac{3^{n-1}}{2^{n-1}} + \cdots$ .     *Ans.* Divergent.

**6.** Criticize the following argument. Let

$$S = 1 + 2 + 4 + 8 \cdots .$$

Then

$$2S = 2 + 4 + 8 + 16 + \cdots$$

or

$$2S = S - 1.$$

Then

$$S = -1.$$

**7.** Criticize the following argument. Let

$$S = 1 - 1 + 1 - 1 + 1 - \cdots .$$

Then

$$S = (1 - 1) + (1 - 1) + (1 - 1) + \cdots = 0.$$

**8.** Criticize the following argument. Let

$$S = 1 - 1 + 1 - 1 + 1 - \cdots .$$

Then

$$S = 1 - (1 - 1) - (1 - 1) - \cdots = 1.$$

**9.** Criticize the following argument. Let

$$S = 1 - 1 + 1 - 1 + 1 - \cdots .$$

Then

$$S = 1 - (1 - 1 + 1 - 1 + \cdots )$$
$$= 1 - S.$$

Hence

$$S = \tfrac{1}{2} .$$

**7. Tests for Convergence and Divergence.** Given an infinite series, we would like to know whether it converges, because if the series is to be of use in some application, it should have a (finite) sum.* One of the simplest

---

* Actually, divergent series are used in more advanced mathematics.

tests, although not always helpful, depends on the behavior of $u_n$, the $n$th term of the series, as $n$ increases. Specifically, we have the following theorem:

**Theorem:** If the series $u_1 + u_2 + u_3 + \cdots + u_n + \cdots$ converges, then $u_n$ must approach 0 as $n$ becomes infinite, that is, $\lim_{n \to \infty} u_n = 0$.

Before examining the proof, let us understand the idea. If two numbers differ from 5 by, say, less than $\frac{1}{10}$, what is the most that the two numbers can differ from each other? The answer is $\frac{2}{10}$ because the greatest difference arises when one number is greater than 5 and the other is less than 5. Now suppose that the two numbers differ from 5 by less than $\frac{1}{100}$. What is the most that the two numbers can differ from each other? Clearly it is $\frac{2}{100}$. Moreover, the closer the two numbers come to 5, the closer they must come to each other.

Let us now apply this idea in the proof of the theorem. Because the series in question converges, $S_n$ must come closer and closer to the sum $S$ and $S - S_n$ must approach 0 as $n$ becomes infinite. Then $S_{n+1}$, which is the next term after $S_n$, must also approach $S$ as $n$ becomes infinite, and so $S - S_{n+1}$ must approach 0. Thus as $n$ increases, $S_n$ and $S_{n+1}$ differ from $S$ by smaller and smaller amounts, so that the difference $S_{n+1} - S_n$ must also approach 0. But $S_{n+1} - S_n$ is $u_{n+1}$; therefore, as $n$ becomes infinite, $u_{n+1}$ approaches 0. This proves the theorem because it is immaterial whether we speak of $u_{n+1}$ approaching 0 or $u_n$ approaching 0, for as $n$ increases, $u_n$ and $u_{n+1}$ represent the same set of terms.

This theorem tells us that if the series converges, $u_n$ must approach 0 or, if $u_n$ does not approach 0, the series must diverge. The theorem does not say that if $u_n$ does approach 0, the series converges, and, in fact, this is not true. One says that the approach to 0 of $u_n$ is a necessary condition for convergence but is not sufficient. Thus as a test for convergence or divergence this theorem is useful only in determining divergence.

The test is very easy to apply. Thus, given the series

$$\frac{1}{2} + \frac{2}{3} + \frac{3}{4} + \frac{4}{5} + \cdots + \frac{n}{n+1} + \cdots,$$

we note that $u_n$ approaches 1, and therefore the series must diverge. On the other hand, in the series

$$1 + \frac{1}{2} + \frac{1}{3} + \frac{1}{4} + \cdots \frac{1}{n} + \cdots$$

the $n$th term, $u_n$, does approach 0 but, as we shall see shortly, this series, which is called the harmonic series, does diverge.

The most powerful method of establishing the convergence or divergence of a series is what is called the *comparison test*. Because the very theorems which establish this test explain its nature, let us proceed directly to the theorems.

**Theorem:**  Suppose that

**(41)**                    $u_1 + u_2 + u_3 + \cdots + u_n + \cdots$

is a series of positive terms and

**(42)**                    $a_1 + a_2 + a_3 + \cdots + a_n + \cdots$

is also a series of positive terms which is known to be convergent. If each term of (41) is less than or at most equal to the corresponding term of (42), that is, if for each value of $n$, $0 \leq u_n \leq a_n$, then the series (41) is convergent.

In order to prove that a series is convergent, the only means available to us at the present time is to show that the sequence of partial sums, whose $n$th term is $S_n$, approaches a limit. We do not know anything directly about the behavior of $S_n$ for (41), but we do know that if $T_n$, say, is the sum of the first $n$-terms of the series (42), $T_n$ approaches a definite number $T$ because the series (42) converges. Moreover, because each term of (41) is at most equal to the corresponding term of (42), we know that $S_n \leq T_n$.

Because the terms in both series are positive, we know that as $n$ increases, $S_n$ and $T_n$ increase. Yet $T_n$ approaches closer and closer to $T$. The relation of these quantities may be pictured on a straight line as follows. If the sum $S_n$ is represented as a length from 0 to the point marked $S_n$ in Fig. 20-4, then $T_n$ must be to the right (or identical with $S_n$) since $S_n \leq T_n$. Because as $n$ increases $S_n$ and $T_n$ increase, we show $S_{n+1}$ and $T_{n+1}$ to the right of $S_n$ and $T_n$, respectively, with $T_{n+1}$ to the right of $S_{n+1}$ (although $S_{n+1}$ might coincide with $T_{n+1}$). That is, as $n$ increases, $S_n$ and $T_n$ move to the right and the $T_n$ come closer to $T$. Since the $S_n$ constantly increase but remain no greater than the $T_n$, it is geometrically clear that the $S_n$ cannot increase indefinitely but must come closer and closer to some number which is at most $T$. Although we do not know what number the $S_n$ approach, the important fact is that they do approach some number and hence that the series (41) converges.

Let us apply the theorem. Suppose that we must determine whether the series

**(43)**          $\dfrac{1}{3} + \dfrac{1}{5} + \dfrac{1}{9} + \dfrac{1}{17} + \cdots + \dfrac{1}{(2^n + 1)} + \cdots$

converges. The theorem that we have just proved tells us that if we can find a convergent series whose terms are at least as large as those of the given series, the latter must also converge. We do know that a geometric series converges if the common ratio is less than 1. Inspection of the given series

**Figure  20-4**

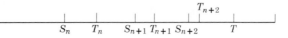

suggests that we compare it with

**(44)**
$$\frac{1}{2} + \frac{1}{4} + \frac{1}{8} + \cdots + \frac{1}{2^n} + \cdots .$$

We see that each term of (43) is less than the corresponding term of (44). But (44) is a geometric series with common ratio $\frac{1}{2}$. Hence (44) converges; by the comparison test the series (43) converges.

We may also use a comparison test to show that a series diverges. Let us consider the following theorem:

**Theorem:** Suppose that

**(45)**
$$u_1 + u_2 + u_3 + \cdots u_n + \cdots$$

is a series of positive terms and

**(46)**
$$a_1 + a_2 + a_3 + \cdots a_n + \cdots$$

is also a series of positive terms which is known to be divergent. If $u_n \geq a_n$ for each $n$, that is, if each term of (45) is at least as large as the corresponding term of (46), then the series (45) diverges.

The proof is simple. Suppose that the series (45) converges. Then by the preceding theorem the series (46) must converge. But we are given that (46) diverges. Hence the series (45) cannot converge and so must diverge.

To illustrate the use of this theorem we shall test a series which is in itself rather important. We shall prove that the series

**(47)**
$$1 + \frac{1}{2} + \frac{1}{3} + \frac{1}{4} + \cdots + \frac{1}{n} + \cdots$$

is divergent. We shall compare the series (47) with another series by writing corresponding terms one beneath the other. Thus

**(48)**   $1 + \frac{1}{2} + \frac{1}{3} + \frac{1}{4} + \frac{1}{5} + \frac{1}{6} + \frac{1}{7} + \frac{1}{8} + \frac{1}{9} + \cdots + \frac{1}{16} + \cdots .$

**(49)**   $\frac{1}{2} + \frac{1}{2} + \frac{1}{4} + \frac{1}{4} + \frac{1}{8} + \frac{1}{8} + \frac{1}{8} + \frac{1}{8} + \frac{1}{16} + \cdots + \frac{1}{16} + \cdots .$

We see that the terms of (48) are equal to or larger than the corresponding terms of the series (49). In the series (49) we observe that the first and second terms are each $\frac{1}{2}$; the sum of the next two terms is $\frac{1}{2}$; from the formation of the series we see that we can continue to get blocks of terms each of which adds up to $\frac{1}{2}$. Moreover, because the number of terms in the series (49) is infinite, we can continue to form blocks of such terms each with sum $\frac{1}{2}$. Then $S_n$, the $n$th term of the sequence of partial sums, can be made as large as we please merely by taking enough blocks of terms; that is, $S_n$ must become infinite, and the series (49) diverges. By the preceding theorem, the series (48) must diverge.

The series (48) is called the *harmonic series* and, because this series is important, we shall record what we have just proved in a theorem:

**Theorem:**  The harmonic series

(50)
$$1 + \frac{1}{2} + \frac{1}{3} + \cdots + \frac{1}{n} + \cdots$$

is divergent.

The geometric series and the harmonic series serve very often as useful series to test a given series for convergence and divergence. Another useful standard series, called the *p*-series or generalized harmonic series, is the following:

(51)
$$1 + \frac{1}{2^p} + \frac{1}{3^p} + \frac{1}{4^p} + \cdots + \frac{1}{n^p} + \cdots .$$

The convergence or divergence of this series depends on the value of $p$. When $p = 1$, this series is identical with the harmonic series, and we know then that it diverges. When $p < 1$, each term of the *p*-series is at least as large as the corresponding term of the harmonic series. By the comparison theorem the *p*-series must diverge. There remains, then, the case $p > 1$. We shall show that for such values of $p$ the *p*-series converges.

Our proof will depend on a comparison with a convergent geometric series. Let us note that

$$\frac{1}{2^p} + \frac{1}{3^p} < \frac{1}{2^p} + \frac{1}{2^p} = \frac{2}{2^p} = \frac{1}{2^{p-1}} .$$

$$\frac{1}{4^p} + \frac{1}{5^p} + \frac{1}{6^p} + \frac{1}{7^p} < \frac{1}{4^p} + \frac{1}{4^p} + \frac{1}{4^p} + \frac{1}{4^p}$$

$$= \frac{4}{4^p} = \frac{2^2}{2^{2p}} = \left( \frac{2}{2^p} \right)^2 = \left( \frac{1}{2^{p-1}} \right)^2 .$$

$$\frac{1}{8^p} + \frac{1}{9^p} + \cdots + \frac{1}{15^p} < \frac{8}{8^p} = \frac{2^3}{2^{3p}} = \left( \frac{2}{2^p} \right)^3 = \left( \frac{1}{2^{p-1}} \right)^3 .$$

We could now take the next 16 terms of the *p*-series and show that their sum is less than $(1/2^{p-1})^4$, and so on. Thus the *p*-series (when the terms are suitably grouped) is less than the series

(52)
$$1 + \frac{1}{2^{p-1}} + \left( \frac{1}{2^{p-1}} \right)^2 + \left( \frac{1}{2^{p-1}} \right)^3 + \cdots .$$

The series (52) is a geometric series with common ratio $1/2^{p-1}$. If $p > 1$, this common ratio is less than 1. Then the series (52) converges.* Because

---

* Strictly speaking, our proof deals with three series: the *p*-series (51), the series $1 + \frac{1}{2p} + \frac{1}{2p} + \frac{1}{4p} + \frac{1}{4p} + \frac{1}{4p} + \frac{1}{4p} + \cdots$, and the series (52). The successive partial sums of the middle series, $S_1, S_2, S_3, S_4, \ldots$ increase steadily. $S_1$ equals the first partial sum $T_1$ of the series (52), $S_5$ is $T_2$; $S_9$ is $T_3$, etc. Since the sequence of $T$-values approaches a limit, the sequence of $S$-values approaches the same limit.

the $p$-series is less term-for-term than the series that gave rise to (52) and because the latter converges, then by the comparison test the $p$-series converges when $p > 1$. We may summarize the results on the $p$-series with the following theorem:

**Theorem:**    The $p$-series

(53)
$$1 + \frac{1}{2^p} + \frac{1}{3^p} + \cdots + \frac{1}{n^p} + \cdots$$

converges for $p > 1$. For all other values of $p$ the series diverges.

We now have several tests for the convergence or divergence of a series. If the $n$th term does not approach 0, the series must diverge. If the series is geometric and if the common ratio is between $-1$ and $+1$, the end values excluded, the series converges; otherwise, the geometric series diverges. The $p$-series converges when $p > 1$; for other values of $p$ it diverges. We also have a comparison test to establish convergence and one to establish divergence. The geometric series and the $p$-series are useful in comparison tests.

## EXERCISES

**1.** Determine whether the following series are convergent or divergent:

(a) $1 + \dfrac{3}{4} + \dfrac{5}{8} + \dfrac{9}{16} + \cdots + \dfrac{2^{n-1} + 1}{2^n} + \cdots$.    *Ans.* Divergent.

(b) $\dfrac{1}{2 + 1} + \dfrac{1}{4 + 1} + \dfrac{1}{8 + 1} + \cdots + \dfrac{1}{2^n + 1} + \cdots$.

(c) $1 + \dfrac{1}{2^2} + \dfrac{1}{3^3} + \cdots + \dfrac{1}{n^n} + \cdots$.    *Ans.* Convergent.

(d) $1 + \dfrac{1}{\sqrt{2^3}} + \dfrac{1}{\sqrt{3^3}} + \cdots + \dfrac{1}{\sqrt{n^3}} \cdots$.

(e) $1 + \dfrac{1}{\sqrt{2}} + \dfrac{1}{\sqrt{3}} + \cdots + \dfrac{1}{\sqrt{n}} \cdots$.    *Ans.* Divergent.

(f) $\dfrac{1}{1 \cdot 2} + \dfrac{1}{2 \cdot 3} + \dfrac{1}{3 \cdot 4} + \cdots + \dfrac{1}{n(n + 1)} + \cdots$.

(g) $\dfrac{2}{2 \cdot 3} + \dfrac{4}{3 \cdot 4} + \dfrac{6}{4 \cdot 5} + \cdots + \dfrac{2n}{(n + 1)(n + 2)} + \cdots$.

    *Ans.* Divergent.

(h) $\dfrac{1}{3} + \dfrac{1}{6} + \dfrac{1}{9} + \cdots + \dfrac{1}{3n} + \cdots$.

    *Suggestion:* Factor out $\frac{1}{3}$ from all of the terms and make an argument based on the harmonic series.

(i) $\dfrac{1}{5} + \dfrac{1}{6} + \dfrac{1}{7} + \cdots + \dfrac{1}{n + 4} + \cdots$.

    *Suggestion:* Note that this is the harmonic series minus the first few terms. Use this fact as a basis for your argument.

(j) $\dfrac{1}{3} + \dfrac{1}{\sqrt{3}} + \dfrac{1}{\sqrt[3]{3}} + \cdots + \dfrac{1}{\sqrt[n]{3}} + \cdots$.    *Ans.* Divergent.

(k) $\dfrac{1}{1 + 1} + \dfrac{1}{4 + 1} + \dfrac{1}{9 + 1} + \cdots + \dfrac{1}{n^2 + 1} + \cdots$.

(l)   $\dfrac{1}{2} + \dfrac{1}{4} + \dfrac{1}{6} + \cdots \dfrac{1}{2n} + \cdots .$                    *Ans.* Divergent.

> *Suggestion:* Factor out $\frac{1}{2}$ from all of the terms and compare with the harmonic series. Base your argument on these facts.

(m)  $1 + \dfrac{1}{3} + \dfrac{1}{5} + \dfrac{1}{7} + \cdots + \dfrac{1}{2(n-1)+1} + \cdots .$

> *Suggestion:* Compare with the series in (l).

(n)   $\dfrac{1}{\log 2} + \dfrac{1}{\log 3} + \dfrac{1}{\log 4} + \cdots .$                    *Ans.* Divergent.

> *Suggestion:* How does $\log n$ compare with $n$?

(o)   $\dfrac{3}{2} + \dfrac{3}{4} + \dfrac{3}{6} + \cdots + \dfrac{3}{2n} + \cdots .$

> *Suggestion:* Compare with the harmonic series.

**2.** Consider the following argument. Each term of the series

$$\tfrac{1}{2} + \tfrac{1}{5} + \tfrac{1}{8} + \tfrac{1}{11} + \cdots +$$

is less than the corresponding term of the series

$$1 + \tfrac{1}{2} + \tfrac{1}{4} + \tfrac{1}{8} + \cdots .$$

The latter series is convergent because it is a geometric series with common ratio $\frac{1}{2}$. Hence the former series converges. On the other hand, the first series is greater term-for-term than the series

$$\tfrac{1}{3} + \tfrac{1}{6} + \tfrac{1}{9} + \tfrac{1}{12} + \cdots ,$$

and the latter diverges (see Exercise 1(h) above). Hence the first series diverges. Explain the contradictory results.

**3.** Criticize the following argument. The series

$$\dfrac{1}{1 \cdot 2} + \dfrac{1}{2 \cdot 3} + \dfrac{1}{3 \cdot 4} + \dfrac{1}{4 \cdot 5} + \cdots$$

converges because each term is less than the corresponding term of the series

$$\tfrac{1}{2} + \tfrac{1}{4} + \tfrac{1}{8} + \tfrac{1}{16} + \cdots .$$

The latter series is geometric with common ratio of $\frac{1}{2}$ and therefore converges. Hence by the comparison test the former series converges.

**4.** Is the following proof of the divergence of the harmonic series correct? Suppose that the series converges and its sum is $S$. Then

$$S = 1 + \tfrac{1}{2} + \tfrac{1}{3} + \tfrac{1}{4} + \cdots .$$

We now replace some of the terms by smaller terms so that

$$S > \tfrac{1}{2} + \tfrac{1}{2} + \tfrac{1}{4} + \tfrac{1}{4} \cdots .$$

By grouping the first two terms, the second two terms, etc., we have

$$S > 1 + \tfrac{1}{2} + \tfrac{1}{3} + \cdots .$$

Then

$$S > S.$$

Since this is impossible, the series diverges.

*Suggestion:* Is grouping valid? Compare Exercise 7 of Section 6. However, the present series consists of positive terms, whereas that in Exercise 7 of Section 6 contains positive and negative terms. Can you give an argument to justify the grouping?

**8. Absolute and Conditional Convergence.** Some of the tests for convergence and divergence which we have already examined cover series in which the terms may be positive and negative. Thus, whether or not the terms vary in sign, if the $n$th term does not approach zero, the series must diverge. Also, in the case of the geometric series, if $r$ lies between 0 and $-1$, the terms will alternate in sign but the series converges. On the other hand, the comparison tests apply only to series with positive terms. Because series with positive and negative terms are quite common, we must look into them a little further to see what we can do about establishing their convergence and divergence.

Let us suppose that we have to establish the convergence or divergence of the series

**(54)**
$$1 - \tfrac{1}{2} + \tfrac{1}{3} - \tfrac{1}{4} + \tfrac{1}{5} - \cdots .$$

In this series the terms alternate in sign. No one of the tests that we have had thus far will help us to settle the question of convergence or divergence. There is, however, an important theorem which does help us in the case of alternating series.

**Theorem:**   If the terms of a series alternate in sign, if their absolute values $|u_n|$ decrease as $n$ increases, that is, $|u_{n+1}| < |u_n|$ for each value of $n$, and if $|u_n|$ approaches 0, then the series converges.

We start with a series

**(55)**
$$u_1 + u_2 + u_3 + \cdots$$

where the terms alternate in sign. Let us suppose that the first term is positive, for if not we can multiply through by a minus sign and the new series will differ from the old only by this factor of $-1$. Moreover, it will be easier to present the proof if we write the series as

$$a_1 - a_2 + a_3 - a_4 + \cdots ,$$

where $a_n = |u_n|$.

Now let us consider the partial sums $S_2, S_4, S_6, \ldots$; that is,

$$S_{2n} = (a_1 - a_2) + (a_3 - a_4) + \cdots + (a_{2n-1} - a_{2n}).$$

Because the terms decrease as $n$ increases, $S_{2n}$ is positive. Furthermore,

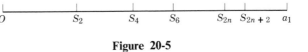

**Figure 20-5**

since we add positive terms to go from $S_2$ to $S_4$ to $S_6$, etc., we have that $S_{2n+2} > S_{2n}$. Thus these partial sums increase as $n$ increases. Finally, since

$$S_{2n} = a_1 - (a_2 - a_3) - (a_4 - a_5) - \cdots - (a_{2n-2} - a_{2n-1}) - a_{2n},$$

we see that for each $n$, $S_{2n} < a_1$. We have then

$$S_2 < S_4 \cdots S_{2n} < a_1.$$

This sequence of partial sums always increases and yet remains less than $a_1$. If we picture (Fig. 20-5) the behavior of these $S_{2n}$, we see that they must come closer to some number which is $a_1$ or less than $a_1$. In either case, the $S_{2n}$ approach a limit which we shall denote by $S$.

We must still show that the odd-numbered partial sums, $S_1$, $S_3$, $S_5, \ldots$ approach the same limit. However, how do $S_{2n+1}$ and $S_{2n}$ differ? We merely add $a_{2n+1}$ to $S_{2n}$ to obtain $S_{2n+1}$. Hence

$$S_{2n+1} - S_{2n} = a_{2n+1}.$$

Now, it is one of the hypotheses that $a_{2n+1}$ approaches 0 as $n$ increases. Then $S_{2n+1}$ must come closer and closer to $S_{2n}$ as $n$ becomes infinite, and since the $S_{2n}$ approach $S$, so must the $S_{2n+1}$. Hence we may say that all the $S_n$, where $n$ is odd or even, approach $S$ and the series (55) converges.

In the case of alternating series such as (55), we can draw another useful conclusion. We showed in the preceding proof that the $S_n$ approach a number $S$ which is at most $a_1$. That is, the sum of an alternating series satisfying the conditions of the preceding theorem is at most the first term $a_1$. Now suppose that we neglect all terms of such an alternating series after the $n$th term. What error have we committed? The terms neglected are themselves an infinite alternating series whose first term is $a_{n+1}$. Hence the sum of these neglected terms cannot exceed $|a_{n+1}|$. Thus we have proved the following corollary:

**Corollary:**   If the absolute values of the terms of an alternating series decrease as $n$ increases and approach 0, then the error in the sum introduced by neglecting all terms after the $n$th one will be no greater than the absolute value of the first of the neglected terms.

We see from the theorem above that there is an additional test for convergence which applies to some alternating series and, in particular, to the series

$$1 - \tfrac{1}{2} + \tfrac{1}{3} - \tfrac{1}{4} + \cdots.$$

This series is significant because, if we consider the corresponding one in which all terms are positive, namely,

$$1 + \tfrac{1}{2} + \tfrac{1}{3} + \tfrac{1}{4} + \cdots,$$

we have the harmonic series and we know that this series diverges. On the other hand, not only does the geometric series

$$1 - \tfrac{1}{2} + \tfrac{1}{4} - \tfrac{1}{8} + \cdots$$

converge, but the corresponding series in which all terms are positive, namely,

$$1 + \tfrac{1}{2} + \tfrac{1}{4} + \tfrac{1}{8} + \cdots$$

also converges. In other words, there are series of positive and negative terms which converge but the corresponding series of all positive terms diverges, and there are series of positive and negative terms which converge and the corresponding positive series also converges. These two types are distinguished by the following definitions.

**Definition:**    The series of positive and negative terms (not necessarily alternating)

**(56)**  $$u_1 + u_2 + u_3 + \cdots + u_n + \cdots,$$

is said to be *conditionally convergent* if the series

**(57)**  $$|u_1| + |u_2| + |u_3| + \cdots + |u_n| + \cdots$$

diverges. On the other hand, the series (56) is said to be *absolutely convergent* if the series (57), which consists of the absolute values of the terms in (56), converges.

The significance of the distinction between conditional and absolute convergence lies in the following. Suppose that we have a series of positive and negative terms and we wish to test it for convergance. It may be easier to test the series of absolute values because they are all positive. Suppose that we do test the latter series and it is convergent; that is, the original series is absolutely convergent. Then one would expect that the original series of positive and negative terms would also converge because the negative terms should make the sum smaller than the sum of the absolute values. In other words, if we can prove that when the series of absolute values converges, the original series must converge, then we shall have a new test for series with varying signs. Let us state and prove the relevant theorem.

**Theorem:**    Given the series

**(58)**  $$u_1 + u_2 + u_3 + \cdots$$

of terms with varying signs, if the series

**(59)**                                $|u_1| + |u_2| + |u_3| + \cdots$

converges, then the original series converges.

Let us denote the positive terms of (58) in the order in which they occur by $p_1, p_2, p_3, \ldots$ and let us denote the negative terms in the order in which they occur by $-q_1, -q_2, -q_3, \ldots$, so that each $q_i$ is positive. If we form the $n$th partial sum $S_n$ of the series (58), then among the $n$-terms that comprise $S_n$ there will be $p$-terms of the $p_i$'s and $q$-terms of the $q_i$'s with $p + q = n$. Moreover,

**(60)**                                $S_n = S_p - S_q$

where $S_p$ denotes the sum of the $p_i$'s and $S_q$ denotes the sum of the $q_i$'s in the $n$-terms of $S_n$.

Now let us use the fact that the series (59) of absolute values converges and converges, say, to the number $T$. Since $S_p$ consists of positive terms, as $p$ increases the value of $S_p$ increases but must always remain less than $T$ because the sum $S_p$ consists of only some of the terms in the absolute value series. Then the $S_p$ must approach some number which is less than $T$. Likewise, $S_q$ consists of positive terms and increases as $q$ increases but because (59) converges must approach some number less than $T$. Hence both $S_p$ and $S_q$ separately approach definite limits.

We should now like to use (60) to state that the limit of $S_n$ as $n$ becomes infinite is the limit of $S_p$ as $p$ becomes infinite minus the limit of $S_q$ as $q$ become infinite. (If $q$, for example, does not become infinite, then there is only a finite number of negative terms. We may then state that $S_n = S_p - Q$ where $-Q$ is the sum of the negative terms and is a fixed number. Since $S_p$ has a limit, so does $S_n$. In fact, $\lim S_n = \lim S_p - Q$.) However, the theorem* we should like to apply is that if

**(61)**                                $S_n = U_n - V_n,$

---

* This theorem on sequences is analogous to the corresponding theorem on functions which reads: if $f(x) = g(x) - h(x)$, then $\lim\limits_{x \to a} f(x) = \lim\limits_{x \to a} g(x) - \lim\limits_{x \to a} h(x)$. We used this theorem in Section 3 of Chapter 6 but did not prove it. We showed merely that it is reasonable. We shall adopt the same position here. Consider the sequence whose $n$th terms is

$$S_n = \frac{3n^2}{n^2 - 1} - \frac{n}{n + 1}.$$

If we simplify this expression, we obtain $(2n^2 + n)/(n^2 - 1)$ and $\lim\limits_{n \to \infty} S_n = 2$. If, on the other hand, we write

$$\lim_{n \to \infty} S_n = \lim_{n \to \infty} \frac{3n^2}{n^2 - 1} - \lim_{n \to \infty} \frac{n}{n + 1},$$

we obtain

$$\lim_{n \to \infty} S_n = 3 - 1.$$

Thus (62), at least as far as one example shows, is correct. We shall consider this theorem in Chapter 25.

then

**(62)** $$\lim_{n\to\infty} S_n = \lim_{n\to\infty} U_n - \lim_{n\to\infty} V_n.$$

Now, (60) is not in the form (61) because the subscripts in (60) are $p$ and $q$, whereas to use (62) they should be $n$. However, by a minor device we can remedy the difficulty.

Let

$$p_j = \frac{u_j + |u_j|}{2}.$$

Then, when $u_j$ is positive, $p_j$ is $u_j$; when $u_j$ is negative, $p_j$ is 0. If we let $j$ run from 1 to $n$, where $n$ is $p + q$, the sum $U_n$ is precisely $S_p$. Likewise, let

$$q_j = \frac{|u_j| - u_j}{2}.$$

When $u_j$ is positive, $q_j$ is 0; when $u_j$ is negative, $q_j$ is $|u_j|$ as it should be. If we let $j$ run from 1 to $n$, the sum $V_n$ is precisely $S_q$. Hence let us replace (60) by

$$S_n = U_n - V_n.$$

We can now apply (62) and assert that the limit approached by $S_n$ must be the limit approached by $S_p$ minus the limit approached by $S_q$.

Our proof actually demonstrates more than the statement of the theorem covers, for the proof shows that the sum of the series (58) is the sum of the series of its positive terms minus the sum of the series of negative terms.

We use the theorem to test for convergence in the following way. To test a series of terms with varying signs we test the series of corresponding absolute values. If the latter converges, so does the former. Thus to test the convergence of

**(63)** $$1 - \frac{1}{2^2} + \frac{1}{3^2} - \frac{1}{4^2} + \cdots$$

we can argue that the series of positive terms

$$1 + \frac{1}{2^2} + \frac{1}{3^2} + \frac{1}{4^2} + \cdots$$

converges because it is the $p$-series for $p = 2$. Then (63) must also converge. In other words, (63) is an absolutely convergent series. On the other hand, the series

$$1 - \frac{1}{\sqrt{2}} + \frac{1}{\sqrt{3}} - \frac{1}{\sqrt{4}} + \cdots$$

is convergent because it satisfies the conditions for the convergence of an alternating series, but it is conditionally convergent because the corresponding series of positive terms is the $p$-series for $p = \frac{1}{2}$, which is divergent.

## EXERCISES

**1.** Determine whether the following series are conditionally convergent, absolutely convergent, or divergent.

(a) $1 - \dfrac{1}{2^3} + \dfrac{1}{3^3} - \cdots + (-1)^{n+1}\dfrac{1}{n^3} + \cdots$ .

*Ans.* Absolutely convergent.

(b) $\dfrac{1}{2} - \dfrac{1}{5} + \dfrac{1}{8} + \cdots + (-1)^{n+1}\dfrac{1}{3n-1} = \cdots$ .

*Ans.* Conditionally convergent.

*Suggestion:* To test the corresponding series of positive terms, use a comparison with the series whose $n$th term is $1/3n$.

(c) $\dfrac{1}{2} - \dfrac{2}{3} + \dfrac{3}{4} - \dfrac{4}{5} + \cdots + (-1)^{n+1}\dfrac{n}{n+1} + \cdots$ . *Ans.* Divergent.

(d) $\dfrac{1}{2\cdot 5} - \dfrac{2}{3\cdot 5} + \dfrac{3}{4\cdot 5} - \cdots + (-1)^{n+1}\dfrac{n}{5(n+1)} + \cdots$ .

(e) $\dfrac{1}{1+9} - \dfrac{1}{4+9} + \dfrac{1}{9+9} - \cdots + (-1)^{n+1}\dfrac{1}{n^2+9} + \cdots$ .

*Ans.* Absolutely convergent.

(f) $\dfrac{2}{1} - \dfrac{4}{4} + \dfrac{6}{9} - \dfrac{8}{16} + \cdots + (-1)^{n+1}\dfrac{2^n}{n^2} + \cdots$ .

**2.** The theorem in the text gives conditions under which an alternating series converges. Would it be possible for an alternating series to converge if:
(a) The $n$th term does not approach 0?
(b) The terms do not decrease monotonically or steadily?

**9. The Ratio Test.** The subject of infinite series is a vast one and there are many tests for convergence and divergence. We shall take time for two more. The first of these is called the ratio test and will be very useful in later work. Let us consider an example of how the test proceeds. Consider the series

**(64)** $$1 + \frac{1}{2!} + \frac{1}{3!} + \cdots + \frac{1}{n!} + \cdots .$$

The notation $n!$ means, of course, $1 \cdot 2 \cdot 3 \cdots n$. The ratio test requires that we first find the ratio of the $(n + 1)$st term to the $n$th term, that is, in general notation, the ratio $u_{n+1}/u_n$. For the series (64)

$$\frac{u_{n+1}}{u_n} = \frac{\dfrac{1}{(n+1)!}}{\dfrac{1}{n!}} = \frac{1}{n+1} .$$

We must next find the limit approached by this ratio as $n$ becomes infinite. In the present example

$$\lim_{n\to\infty}\frac{u_{n+1}}{u_n} = \lim_{n\to\infty}\frac{1}{n+1} = 0.$$

The ratio test says among other things that when

$$\lim_{n\to\infty}\left|\frac{u_{n+1}}{u_n}\right| < 1$$

the series is convergent. Since in the case of (64) this limit is 0, the series is convergent.

The ratio test also gives a criterion for divergence, namely,

$$\lim_{n \to \infty} \left| \frac{u_{n+1}}{u_n} \right| > 1.$$

Unfortunately, the ratio test does not tell us what happens when the limit of the ratio of $u_{n+1}/u_n$ is 1. Let us now note the precise theorem and its proof.

**Theorem:**  Suppose that we have the infinite series

**(65)**          $$u_1 + u_2 + u_3 + \cdots + u_n + \cdots$$

and we find

$$\lim_{n \to \infty} \left| \frac{u_{n+1}}{u_n} \right|.$$

If this limit is less than 1, the series is absolutely convergent. If this limit is greater than 1, the series is divergent. And if this limit equals 1, no conclusion about convergence or divergence can be drawn on the basis of this test.

Now let us prove that the series (65) converges when

**(66)**          $$\lim_{n \to \infty} \left| \frac{u_{n+1}}{u_n} \right| < 1.$$

Since the limit is some number, we denote it by $t$. This number $t$ is less than 1; hence we can find a number $r$ such that $t < r < 1$. The fact that the limit of $\left| \frac{u_{n+1}}{u_n} \right|$ approaches $t$ means that when $n$ is sufficiently large all the ratios will be very close to $t$, indeed as close as we wish to have them. Let us then choose a value $N$ of $n$ such that for $n \geq N$ all the ratios $\left| \frac{u_{n+1}}{u_n} \right|$ are so close to $t$ that they are less than $r$.
    Then

$$\left| \frac{u_{N+1}}{u_N} \right| < r \quad \text{or} \quad |u_{N+1}| < r|u_N|,$$

$$\left| \frac{u_{N+2}}{u_{N+1}} \right| < r \quad \text{or} \quad |u_{N+2}| < r|u_{N+1}| < r^2|u_N|,$$

$$\left| \frac{u_{N+3}}{u_{N+2}} \right| < r \quad \text{or} \quad |u_{N+3}| < r|u_{N+2}| < r^3|u_N|$$

and so on for succeeding terms $u_{N+4}$, $u_{N+5}$, .... Now let us compare

**(67)**          $$|u_{N+1}| + |u_{N+2}| + |u_{N+3}| + \cdots$$

with

**(68)**
$$r|u_N| + r^2|u_N| + r^3|u_N| + \cdots .$$

The inequalities that we have established show that each term of the series (67) is less than the corresponding term of the series (68). But the series (68) is a geometric series with common ratio less than 1. Hence it surely converges. By the comparison test the series (67) converges.

However, the series (67) is not quite the series (65) with which we started. It differs in two respects. First, it deals with the absolute values of terms in (65). However, we found earlier that if the series consisting of the absolute values of the terms of a given series converges, then the original series converges. Hence we can say that

**(69)**
$$u_{N+1} + u_{N+2} + u_{N+3} + \cdots$$

converges and indeed converges absolutely. Secondly, the series (69) does not contain the terms from $n = 1$ to $n = N$ of (65). But since the sum of these first $N$ terms is a finite number, when these terms are added to the series (69) the entire series will still converge. Hence the series (65) converges.

We have proved part of the theorem on the ratio test. We must show that if

$$\lim_{n \to \infty} \left| \frac{u_{n+1}}{u_n} \right| > 1,$$

the series (65) diverges. This part of the proof is relatively easy to carry out. Suppose that

$$\lim_{n \to \infty} \left| \frac{u_{n+1}}{u_n} \right| = t$$

and $t > 1$. As in the first part of the proof, we argue that when $n$ is large enough, all the ratios $\left| \frac{u_{n+1}}{u_n} \right|$ will be as close to $t$ as we wish. Suppose, then, that $N$ is so large that all ratios $\left| \frac{u_{n+1}}{u_n} \right|$ for $n \geq N$ are so close to $t$ that they are larger than 1. Then

$$\left| \frac{u_{n+1}}{u_n} \right| > 1 \quad \text{or} \quad |u_{n+1}| > |u_n| \quad \text{for} \quad n \geq N.$$

We see that the successive terms $u_{N+1}$, $u_{N+2}$, and so on are larger and larger in magnitude than $u_N$; that is, the successive terms increase in magnitude. But we proved earlier (Section 8) that if the $n$th term of a series does not approach 0, the series must diverge. Hence when $\lim_{n \to \infty} \left| \frac{u_{n+1}}{u_n} \right| > 1$, the series (65) diverges.

We said in the statement of the theorem that if

$$\lim_{n \to \infty} \left| \frac{u_{n+1}}{u_n} \right| = 1,$$

no conclusion as to the convergence or divergence of (65) can be drawn. How do we know this? Let us consider some specific series. For the harmonic series

$$1 + \frac{1}{2} + \frac{1}{3} + \cdots + \frac{1}{n} + \cdots$$

we have that

$$\lim_{n \to \infty} \left| \frac{u_{n+1}}{u_n} \right| = \lim_{n \to \infty} \left| \frac{n}{n+1} \right| = \lim_{n \to \infty} \left| \frac{1}{1 + \frac{1}{n}} \right| = 1.$$

The harmonic series, of course, diverges. Now let us consider the series

**(70)** $$1 + \frac{1}{2^2} + \frac{1}{3^2} + \cdots + \frac{1}{n^2} + \cdots.$$

For this series we have

$$\lim_{n \to \infty} \left| \frac{u_{n+1}}{u_n} \right| = \lim_{n \to \infty} \left| \frac{(n+1)^2}{n^2} \right| = \lim_{n \to \infty} \left| 1 + \frac{2}{n} + \frac{1}{n^2} \right| = 1.$$

But the series (70) converges because it is the *p*-series for $p = 2$. We see from these two examples that when

**(71)** $$\lim_{n \to \infty} \left| \frac{u_{n+1}}{u_n} \right| = 1,$$

the series may diverge or converge. Note, also, that in any use of the ratio test it is not the value of $\left| \frac{u_{n+1}}{u_n} \right|$ that counts but $\lim_{n \to \infty} \left| \frac{u_{n+1}}{u_n} \right|$.

## EXERCISES

**1.** Test the following series for convergence or divergence by using the ratio test.

(a) $\dfrac{1}{3} + \dfrac{2}{3^2} + \dfrac{3}{3^3} + \cdots + \dfrac{n}{3^n} + \cdots.$          *Ans.* Convergent.

(b) $\dfrac{2}{1} + \dfrac{2^2}{2} + \dfrac{2^3}{3} + \cdots + \dfrac{2^n}{n} + \cdots.$

(c) $\dfrac{2}{1} + \dfrac{2^2}{2^2} + \dfrac{2^3}{3^2} + \dfrac{2^4}{4^2} + \cdots + \dfrac{2^n}{n^2} + \cdots.$          *Ans.* Divergent.

(d) $1 + \dfrac{2}{10} + \dfrac{3}{10^2} + \cdots + \dfrac{n}{10^{n-1}} + \cdots.$

(e) $\dfrac{2}{3} + 2\left(\dfrac{2}{3}\right)^2 + 3\left(\dfrac{2}{3}\right)^3 + \cdots + n\left(\dfrac{2}{3}\right)^n + \cdots$ .          *Ans.* Convergent.

(f) $\dfrac{1}{10} + \dfrac{2!}{10^2} + \dfrac{3!}{10^3} + \cdots + \dfrac{n!}{10^n} + \cdots$ .

(g) $2 + \dfrac{4}{\sqrt{2}} + \dfrac{8}{\sqrt{3}} + \cdots + \dfrac{2^n}{\sqrt{n}} + \cdots$ .          *Ans.* Divergent.

(h) $\dfrac{1}{3} + \dfrac{1 \cdot 2}{3 \cdot 5} + \dfrac{1 \cdot 2 \cdot 3}{3 \cdot 5 \cdot 7} + \cdots + \dfrac{n!}{3 \cdot 5 \cdot 7 \cdots (2n + 1)} + \cdots$

(i) $1 + \dfrac{1 \cdot 3}{1 \cdot 4} + \dfrac{1 \cdot 3 \cdot 5}{1 \cdot 4 \cdot 7} + \cdots + \dfrac{1 \cdot 3 \cdot 5 \cdots (2n - 1)}{1 \cdot 4 \cdot 7 \cdots (3n - 2)} + \cdots$

*Ans.* Convergent.

(j) $\dfrac{1}{1 \cdot 2} + \dfrac{1}{3 \cdot 4} + \dfrac{1}{5 \cdot 6} + \cdots + \dfrac{1}{(2n - 1)2n} + \cdots$ .          *Ans.* No test.

**10. Power Series.** Although series of constant terms do occur in significant connections both in mathematics proper and in its applications, the main reason for studying them is to help us understand and work with series in which the individual terms are functions of $x$, as is the case in Taylor's series or in Maclaurin's series. In fact, we intend to return to these series. With this goal in mind, let us consider series of the form

**(72)**          $a_0 + a_1x + a_2x^2 + \cdots + a_nx^n + \cdots$

where the $a_i$ are constants. A series of the form (72) is called a *power series*.

To be concrete, let us consider a specific power series, say,

**(73)**          $1 + x + x^2 + x^3 + \cdots + x^{n-1} + \cdots$ .

For any particular value of $x$, say $x = \frac{1}{2}$, the series becomes a series of constant terms and it may converge. For some other value of $x$, say $x = 1\frac{1}{2}$, the resulting series of constant terms may diverge. To use the series (73) for example, in calculating the values of the function that the series represents, the series must converge. Hence we must know for what values of $x$ the series converges. It would seem as though we should test (73) for every possible value of $x$ and so determine the range of $x$-values for which it converges. We can do this testing in one swoop.

The series (73) is a geometric series with common ratio $x$, and we know that when $|x| < 1$, such a series converges. Hence we know at once that the series (73) converges for $-1 < x < 1$. The range of $x$-values for which a power series converges is called the *interval of convergence*.

Of course, power series are not necessarily geometric series. For example, the Maclaurin series for $\sin x$ is

$$\sin x = x - \frac{x^3}{3!} + \frac{x^5}{5!} - \frac{x^7}{7!} + \cdots .$$

Hence we need some method of obtaining the interval of convergence of any power series. The most powerful test is the ratio test, which is in effect the same test as we used for series of constant terms.

We shall state the theorem for the general case of power series of form (72).

**Theorem:** If $\lim\limits_{n \to \infty} \left| \dfrac{a_{n+1}}{a_n} \right| = L$, then the power series (72) converges when $|x| < 1/L$ and diverges when $|x| > 1/L$.

The proof of the theorem is immediate in view of what we learned about the ratio test for series of constant terms. Let us consider the ratio of the $(n + 1)$-st term of (72) to the $n$th term. This ratio is

$$\frac{a_{n+1}x^{n+1}}{a_n x^n} = \frac{a_{n+1}}{a_n} x.$$

For any definite value of $x$ the series (72) is a series of constant terms. The ratio test for a series of constant terms tells us that when

**(74)** $$\lim_{n \to \infty} \left| \frac{a_{n+1}}{a_n} x \right| < 1,$$

the series (72) converges. Now, $x$ does not vary when $n$ increases. Hence we can write (74) as

**(75)** $$|x| \lim_{n \to \infty} \left| \frac{a_{n+1}}{a_n} \right| < 1,$$

or, since we use the notation $L$ for the limit,

$$|x|L < 1$$

or

$$|x| < \frac{1}{L}.$$

Hence when $|x| < 1/L$, that is, when $-1/L < x < 1/L$, the condition (74) will be satisfied and the series (72) will converge.

Likewise, if we start with the condition

$$\lim_{n \to \infty} \left| \frac{a_{n+1}}{a_n} x \right| > 1,$$

we find that when

$$|x| > \frac{1}{L},$$

the series (72) will diverge. That is, when $x < -1/L$ or when $x > 1/L$, the series (72) diverges. Hence both statements of the theorem are proved.

The ratio test does not tell us whether the series (72) converges when $x = 1/L$ or $x = -1/L$. For these two cases we have series of constant terms, and these must be tested by one of the tests for such series.

Let us see how the ratio test works in specific cases. Consider the series

**(76)**
$$\frac{x}{1 \cdot 3} + \frac{x^2}{2 \cdot 3^2} + \frac{x^3}{3 \cdot 3^3} + \cdots + \frac{x^n}{n \cdot 3^n} + \cdots .$$

We form the ratio of $a_{n+1}$ to $a_n$; thus

$$\frac{a_{n+1}}{a_n} = \frac{n \cdot 3^n}{(n+1)3^{n+1}} = \left(\frac{n}{n+1}\right)\frac{1}{3} .$$

Then

$$\lim_{n \to \infty} \left| \frac{a_{n+1}}{a_n} \right| = \frac{1}{3} .$$

We may therefore assert that the series (76) converges for $|x| < 3$ and diverges for $|x| > 3$.

If the values $x = \pm 3$ are of interest, we must test each of them separately. When $x = 3$, the series is the harmonic series which diverges. When $x = -3$, the series is

$$- 1 + \tfrac{1}{2} - \tfrac{1}{3} + \tfrac{1}{4} - \cdots .$$

This is an alternating series, and the numerical values of the terms decrease monotonically or steadily to 0. Hence this series converges.

The full story, then, of the convergence of the series (76) is that it converges for $x = -3$ and for $x$ between $-3$ and 3. It diverges for all other values of $x$. The interval of convergence is denoted by $-3 \le x < 3$.

As another example, let us consider the series that happens to be the Maclaurin series for $\sin x$, namely,

$$x - \frac{x^3}{3!} + \frac{x^5}{5!} - \frac{x^7}{7!} + \cdots + \frac{x^{2n-1}}{(2n-1)!} + \cdots .$$

The ratio test calls for

$$\lim_{n \to \infty} \left| \frac{a_{n+1}}{a_n} \right| = \lim_{n \to \infty} \frac{(2n-1)!}{(2n+1)!} = \lim_{n \to \infty} \frac{1}{(2n+1)(2n)} = 0.$$

The interval of convergence should then be

$$|x| < \frac{1}{0} .$$

Of course, $1/0$ is meaningless, but step (75) of the proof of the ratio test says that the series converges when

$$|x| \lim_{n \to \infty} \left| \frac{a_{n+1}}{a_n} \right| < 1$$

and, since the limit is 0, any value of $x$ satisfies the inequality. In other words, when the limit $L$ proves to be 0, the series converges for all positive and negative values of $x$. One writes this interval of convergence as $-\infty < x < \infty$.

Thus far in our discussion of power series we have treated series of the form (72) which quite often arise as the Maclaurin series of some functions. The Taylor series is of the form

$$\textbf{(77)} \qquad a_0 + a_1(x\text{-}a) + a_2 \frac{(x-a)^2}{2!} + a_3 \frac{(x-a)^3}{3!} + \cdots.$$

Such a series is called a power series in $(x - a)$. Indeed, it really does not differ from series of the form (72), for if we let $t = x - a$, then (77) becomes

$$\textbf{(78)} \qquad a_0 + a_1 t + a_2 \frac{t^2}{2!} + a_3 \frac{t^3}{3!} + \cdots,$$

which is the form (72). To determine the interval of convergence of the series (77), we determine the interval of convergence of (78). Suppose that (78) converges for $|t| \leq c$, that is, for $-c \leq t \leq c$. Then (77) converges for

$$- c \leq x - a \leq c$$

or, since we may add $a$ to these inequalities,

$$\textbf{(79)} \qquad a - c \leq x \leq c + a.$$

Thus no new difficulties arise in treating power series of the form (77).

## EXERCISES

**1.** Determine the interval of convergence (including possible end values) of the following series:

(a) $x - \dfrac{x^2}{2^2} + \dfrac{x^3}{3^2} + \cdots + (-1)^{n+1} \dfrac{x^n}{n^2} + \cdots.$   *Ans.* $-1 \leq x \leq 1.$

(b) $1 + \dfrac{x^2}{2!} + \dfrac{x^4}{4!} + \cdots + \dfrac{x^{2n-2}}{(2n-2)!} + \cdots.$

(c) $x - \dfrac{x^2}{2} + \dfrac{x3}{3} + \cdots + (-1)^{n+1} \dfrac{x^n}{n} + \cdots.$   *Ans.* $-1 < x \leq 1.$

(d) $x + x^4 + x^9 + \cdots + x^{n^2} + \cdots.$

(e) $x + \dfrac{x^2}{\sqrt{2}} + \dfrac{x^3}{\sqrt{3}} + \cdots + \dfrac{x^n}{\sqrt{n}} + \cdots.$   *Ans.* $-1 \leq x < 1.$

(f) $1 + x + \dfrac{x^2}{2!} + \dfrac{x^3}{3!} + \cdots + \dfrac{x^{n-1}}{(n-1)!} + \cdots.$

(g) $1 - \dfrac{x^2}{2!} + \dfrac{x^4}{4!} - \cdots + (-1)^{n+1} \dfrac{x^{2n-2}}{(2n-2)!} + \cdots.$

  *Ans.* All values of $x$.

(h) $1 - 2x + 3x^2 + \cdots + (-1)^{n+1} n x^{n-1} + \cdots.$

(i) $1 + x + \dfrac{x^2}{2^2} + \cdots + \dfrac{x^{n-1}}{(n-1)^2} + \cdots.$   *Ans.* $-1 \leq x \leq 1.$

(j) $1 + 2x + \dfrac{3x^2}{2!} + \cdots + \dfrac{nx^{n-1}}{(n-1)!} + \cdots$ .

(k) $2x + \dfrac{2^2 x^2}{5} + \dfrac{2^3 x^3}{10} + \cdots + \dfrac{2^n x^n}{n^2 + 1} + \cdots$ . $\qquad$ *Ans.* $-\frac{1}{2} \le x \le \frac{1}{2}$ .

(l) $1 + \dfrac{x}{2 \cdot 1} + \dfrac{x^2}{2^2 \cdot 2} + \cdots + \dfrac{x^{n-1}}{2^{n-1} \cdot n} + \cdots$ .

(m) $\dfrac{1}{3} + \dfrac{2x}{2 \cdot 3^2} + \dfrac{3x^2}{2^2 \cdot 3^3} + \cdots + \dfrac{nx^{n-1}}{2^{n-1} \cdot 3^n} + \cdots$ .

$\qquad\qquad\qquad\qquad\qquad\qquad\qquad$ *Ans.* $-6 < x < 6$ .

(n) $\dfrac{x}{1 \cdot 2} + \dfrac{2x^2}{2 \cdot 2 \cdot 3} + \dfrac{3x^3}{2^2 \cdot 3 \cdot 4} + \cdots + \dfrac{nx^n}{2^{n-1} \cdot n(n+1)} + \cdots$ .

2. Determine the interval of convergence (including possible end values) of the following series:

(a) $1 - 2(x - 1) + 3(x - 1)^2 \cdots + (-1)^{n+1} n(x - 1)^{n-1} + \cdots$ .

$\qquad\qquad\qquad\qquad\qquad\qquad\qquad$ *Ans.* $0 < x < 2$ .

(b) $1 + (x - 2) + \dfrac{(x - 2)^2}{2!} + \cdots + \dfrac{(x - 2)^{n-1}}{(n - 1)!} + \cdots$ .

(c) $1 - \dfrac{(x + 4)^2}{2!} + \dfrac{(x + 4)^4}{4!} + \cdots + \dfrac{(x + 4)^{2n-2}}{(2n - 2)!} + \cdots$ .

$\qquad\qquad\qquad\qquad\qquad\qquad\qquad$ *Ans.* All values.

(d) $1 - (x + 3)^2 + (x + 3)^4 + \cdots + (-1)^{n+1}(x + 3)^{2n-2} + \cdots$ .

3. Is a power series absolutely convergent in its interval of convergence?

$\qquad$ *Suggestion:* The interval of convergence is determined by the ratio test. However, this is not true of the end values of the interval of convergence.

## 11. Return to Taylor's Series.

We were led to the subject of infinite series by starting with Taylor's theorem (Section 5) and then considering whether we could improve the approximation to the function represented by Taylor's formula by taking more and more terms. Let us consider Maclaurin's formula since this is the more important case. We know from Maclaurin's formula that

**(80)** $\qquad f(x) = f(0) + f'(0)x + f''(0)\dfrac{x^2}{2!} + \cdots + f^{(n-1)}(0)\dfrac{x^{n-1}}{(n-1)!} + R_n$

where

$$R_n = f^n(\mu)\dfrac{x^n}{n!}$$

and $\mu$ lies between 0 and $x$. We may rewrite (80) as

**(81)** $\qquad\qquad\qquad\qquad f(x) = S_n + R_n$

where $S_n$ stands for the sum of the first $n$-terms in the Maclaurin formula for $f(x)$. Our argument in Section 5 was that if $R_n$ approaches 0 as $n$ becomes larger and larger, then $S_n$ will come closer and closer to $f(x)$ in value and will furnish a better and better approximation to $f(x)$. As $n$ becomes infinite, $S_n$ approaches the sum of the infinite series, and we describe this limiting situation by writing

(82) $$f(x) = f(0) + f'(0)x + f''(0)\frac{x^2}{2!} + f'''(0)\frac{x^3}{3!} \cdots .$$

In other words, since our definition of the sum $S$ of the infinite series in (82) is precisely $\lim_{n\to\infty} S_n$, we see from (81) that if we let $n$ become infinite and if $\lim_{n\to\infty} R_n = 0$, then $S = f(x)$.

Now, $R_n$ is really a function of $x$ as the form of $R_n$ in (80) shows. Hence we can expect the sum of the infinite series on the right side of (82) to equal $f(x)$ for those values of $x$ for which $R_n(x)$ approaches 0 as $n$ becomes infinite. Then, given the Maclaurin series for a function or having obtained such a series by applying Maclaurin's formula and forming the infinite series, we should determine the range of $x$-values for which $R_n$ approaches 0 as $n$ becomes infinite. For such values of $x$ the series represents the function, and the more terms of the series we use to approximate the function the better our approximation will be.

Let us consider a concrete case. By application of Maclaurin's formula we know that

(83) $$e^x = 1 + x + \frac{x^2}{2!} + \frac{x^3}{3!} + \cdots + \frac{x^{n-1}}{(n-1)!} + e^\mu \frac{x^n}{n!}$$

where $\mu$ is some number between 0 and $x$. Here

(84) $$R_n(x) = e^\mu \frac{x^n}{n!} .$$

We would like to know for what range of $x$-values $R_n(x)$ approaches 0 as $n$ becomes infinite.

For some values of $x$ it is easy to show that $R_n$ approaches 0. Consider, for example, any $x$ such that $|x| < 1$. Since $|x| < 1$, $e^\mu < e$. Then for any value of $n$ the numerator in $R_n(x)$ remains less than $e$ and in fact approaches 0 as $n$ becomes infinite, whereas the denominator becomes infinite as $n$ becomes infinite. Hence $R_n$ approaches 0. Then we certainly can assert that the infinite series

(85) $$1 + x + \frac{x^2}{2!} + \frac{x^3}{3!} + \cdots + \frac{x^{n-1}}{(n-1)!} + \cdots$$

equals $e^x$ for all $x$ such that $|x| < 1$.

With a little more work we can prove that (85) represents $e^x$ for all values of $x$. The suspicion that this might be the case comes from considering the form of the remainder (84). For any value of $x$ the value of $e^\mu < e^{|x|}$. It is true that for $|x| > 1$ as $n$ increases $x^n$ also increases as does the denominator $n!$. However, $n!$ increases much faster. To see this let us first select a typical case such as $x = 3$. Then, apart from the fixed quantity $e^\mu$, we have $3^n/n!$ Now, as $n$ increases one unit, it is true that the numerator is multiplied by 3, but for $n > 3$, the denominator increases still more. Thus, when $n$ goes from 100 to 101, the numerator is multiplied by 3 but the denominator is multiplied by 101. We can put this fact into a general proof.

Given a value of $x$, choose a definite $m$ such that $m > 2|x|$. Then for any integer $n$ greater than $m$ we surely have $|x|/n < \frac{1}{2}$. Moreover,

$$\frac{|x^n|}{n!} = \frac{|x^m|}{m!} \cdot \frac{|x|}{m+1} \cdot \frac{|x|}{m+2} \cdots \frac{|x|}{n}.$$

Then for any integer $n$ greater than $m$,

(86)
$$\left| \frac{x^n}{n!} \right| < \frac{|x^m|}{m!} \cdot \frac{1}{2^{n-m}}.$$

Now $m$ is fixed and so $|x^m|/m!$ is fixed, whereas as $n$ increases the second factor on the right side of (86) approaches 0. Hence the left side of (86) must approach 0. $R_n$ also includes the factor $e^\mu$. But, as we have pointed out, $e^\mu < e^{|x|}$ and $x$ is fixed. Hence as $n$ becomes infinite, $R_n$ approaches 0.

This argument holds for any value of $x$, and therefore we have proved that

$$\lim_{n \to \infty} R_n(x) = 0$$

for all values of $x$. Consequently the Maclaurin series (85) represents $e^x$ for all values of $x$.

To prove that the remainder in Taylor's or Maclaurin's formula approaches 0 as $n$ becomes infinite, can be a complicated task. Hence in practice one takes the infinite series that results from the application of Taylor's formula and determines the interval of convergence for this series by one of the tests for convergence, such as the ratio test. There is no guarantee that the series represents the *original function* throughout the interval of convergence although, of course, the series does have a sum for each value of $x$ in the interval of convergence.

Let us see what this latter procedure amounts to in practice. We shall find the Maclaurin series for the function $(1 + x)^\alpha$, where $\alpha$ is any real number positive or negative, rational or irrational. We have

$$f(x) = (1 + x)^\alpha, \qquad f(0) = 1.$$

$$f'(x) = \alpha(1 + x)^{\alpha-1}, \qquad f'(0) = \alpha.$$

$$f''(x) = \alpha(\alpha - 1)(1 + x)^{\alpha-2}, \qquad f''(0) = \alpha(\alpha - 1).$$

$$\cdots$$

$$f^{(n)}(x) = \alpha(\alpha - 1) \cdots (\alpha - n + 1)(1 + x)^{\alpha-n},$$

$$f^{(n)}(0) = \alpha(\alpha - 1) \cdots (\alpha - n + 1).$$

Then the Maclaurin series is

**(87)** $(1 + x)^\alpha = 1 + \alpha x + \dfrac{\alpha(\alpha - 1)}{2!} x^2 + \cdots$

$$+ \dfrac{\alpha(\alpha - 1) \cdots (\alpha - n + 1)}{n!} x^n + \cdots.$$

Here we have ignored the remainder and have written the infinite series at once.

We really do not know for what values of $x$ the infinite series in (87) represents the function $(1 + x)^\alpha$. We could write down the remainder $R_n(x)$ and try to find for what values of $x$ it approaches 0. Instead, we shall apply the ratio test for power series. We have that

$$\lim_{n \to \infty} \left| \frac{a_{n+1}}{a_n} \right| = \lim_{n \to \infty} \frac{\dfrac{|\alpha(\alpha - 1) \cdots (\alpha - n + 1)(\alpha - n)|}{(n + 1)!}}{\dfrac{|\alpha(\alpha - 1) \cdots (\alpha - n + 1)|}{n!}}$$

$$= \lim_{n \to \infty} \frac{|\alpha - n|}{n + 1} = 1.$$

Thus far, then, the ratio test tells us that the series converges for $-1 < x < 1$. For the end values $x = 1$ and $x = -1$, the convergence of the series depends on the value of $\alpha$, and so we shall not bother to investigate these cases.*

## EXERCISES

**1.** Find the Maclaurin series for the following functions and determine the interval of convergence of the series:

(a) $\sin x$.    *Ans.* $x - \dfrac{x^3}{3!} + \dfrac{x^5}{5!} - \cdots + (-1)^n \dfrac{x^{2n+1}}{(2n + 1)!} \cdots$ ; all $x$.

(b) $\cos x$.

(c) $\log(1 + x)$.    *Ans.* $x - \dfrac{x^2}{2} + \dfrac{x^3}{3} - \cdots + (-1)^{n+1} \dfrac{x^n}{n} \cdots$ ;

$$-1 < x \le 1.$$

**2.** Find the ranges of $x$-values for which the remainder $R_n(x)$ of the Maclaurin expansion of the following functions approaches 0:

*Suggestion:* Note the argument of the text for the case of $e^x$.

(a) $\sin x$.    *Ans.* All $x$.

(b) $\cos x$.

---

* We shall mention the results. For $x = +1$, the series converges absolutely when $\alpha > 0$, converges conditionally when $-1 < \alpha < 0$, and diverges when $\alpha \le -1$. For $x = -1$, the series is absolutely convergent when $\alpha > 0$ and divergent when $\alpha < 0$. Of course, if $\alpha$ is a positive integer, the series (87) terminates after a finite number of terms and so converges for all values of $x$.

3. The function $\log(1 + x)$ can be represented by the series $x - \dfrac{x^2}{2} + \dfrac{x^3}{3}$
$+ \cdots$; this series converges for $-1 \le x \le 1$. However, the function has a value for all $x > -1$. On the basis of this example, what general observation would you make about the relation between a function and a series that represents it?

4. The binomial expansion (87) can be used to find approximate values of square roots, cube roots, and higher roots readily. For example,

$$\sqrt[3]{29} = (2 + 27)^{1/3} = 27^{1/3}(1 + \tfrac{2}{27})^{1/3} = 3(1 + \tfrac{2}{27})^{1/3}.$$

We may now apply (87) to expand $(1 + \tfrac{2}{27})^{1/3}$. Calculate $\sqrt[3]{29}$ by using three terms of the binomial expansion (87).                    *Ans.* 3.073.

5. Using the method indicated in Exercise 4 calculate
(a) $\sqrt[3]{30}$ .                    *Ans.* 3.108.
(b) $\sqrt[4]{18}$ .
(c) $\sqrt[5]{34}$ .                    *Ans.* 2.0244.
(d) $\sqrt[4]{8}$ .
   *Suggestion:* $8 = 16 - 8$.
(e) $\sqrt[4]{75}$ .                    *Ans.* 2.943.
(f) $\sqrt[3]{25}$ .

In this chapter we have pursued the idea of applying Taylor's theorem to a function and thereby obtaining an infinite series to represent the function. It is sometimes convenient to obtain this series by another process. Let us suppose that we wished to find the Taylor series for arc sin $x$ expanded around $x = 0$. We know that [Chapter 11, formula (28)]

**(88)**                    $$\text{arc sin } x = \int_0^x \frac{dx}{\sqrt{1 - x^2}} \ .$$

This fact suggests that we expand the integrand on the right side of (88) into a power series and then integrate the series. The advantage of doing so, as opposed to applying Taylor's theorem to arc sin $x$, is that the series representing the integrand is readily obtained by the use of the binomial theorem and the integration of the individual terms is very easy to perform. Let us pursue this procedure to see how it works.

The integrand in (88) is $(1 - x^2)^{-1/2}$. If we now use (87) wherein we let $\alpha = -\tfrac{1}{2}$ and where $x$ is replaced by $-x^2$, we obtain

**(89)**     $(1 - x^2)^{-1/2} = 1 + \tfrac{1}{2}x^2 + \dfrac{1 \cdot 3}{2 \cdot 4} x^4 + \dfrac{1 \cdot 3 \cdot 5}{2 \cdot 4 \cdot 6} x^6 + \cdots .$

Because the binomial series converges for $|x| < 1$, (89) converges for $|x^2| < 1$ or $|x| < 1$. We integrate the left and right sides of (89) and, in view of (88), we have

**(90)**     arc sin $x = x + \dfrac{1}{2} \dfrac{x^3}{3} + \dfrac{1 \cdot 3}{2 \cdot 4} \dfrac{x^5}{5} + \dfrac{1 \cdot 3 \cdot 5}{2 \cdot 4 \cdot 6} \dfrac{x^7}{7} + \cdots .$

Thus we readily obtain the power series for arc sin $x$.

There are two questions about the procedure that we employed to obtain (90). The first arises because we integrated the series on the right side of (89) term-by-term. The question is whether the new series obtained by integrating the old one term-by-term represents the integral of the function on the left side of (89). It may indeed seem reasonable that the answer should be yes, but we must remember that infinite series present special difficulties. For example, although the series in (89) converges for $|x| < 1$, it is conceivable that the series in (90) may not converge at all or that it may converge for some range of $x$-values but not represent the integral of $(1 - x^2)^{-1/2}$. There is, fortunately, a theorem which tells us that, if the interval of $x$-values over which the integral is taken lies within the interval of convergence of the original series, then we may integrate this series term-by-term and the resulting series will represent the integral of the original function. We shall not prove this theorem because the proof involves a concept—uniform convergence of series—which takes us a bit too far into the theory of infinite series. But we shall feel free to integrate power series term-by-term.

The second question which the procedure of obtaining (90) raises is that the final series may not be the Taylor series for arc sin $x$. It is true that the binomial expansion of $(1 - x^2)^{-1/2}$ is the Taylor series for that function. We proved this in (87). However, although integrating the binomial series may produce a power series for arc sin $x$, this power series may not be the one that is obtained by applying Taylor's theorem to arc sin $x$. Let us look into the question of whether a given function can be represented by two different power series for the same range of $x$-values.

Suppose that

**(91)** $$f(x) = a_0 + a_1 x + a_2 x^2 + \cdots$$

and

**(92)** $$f(x) = b_0 + b_1 x + b_2 x^2 + \cdots.$$

Our question is, is it possible for any coefficient in the first series to be different from the corresponding coefficient in the second series? Suppose that we subtract (92) from (91). Then

**(93)** $$0 = (a_0 - b_0) + (a_1 - b_1)x + (a_2 - b_2)x^2 + \cdots.$$

When $x = 0$, we see that $a_0 - b_0 = 0$, so that $a_0 = b_0$. If we differentiate both sides of (93), we obtain

**(94)** $$0 = (a_1 - b_1) + 2(a_2 - b_2)x + \cdots.$$

Again, if we let $x = 0$ in (94), we see that $a_1 - b_1 = 0$, so that $a_1 = b_1$. By differentiating (94) and setting $x = 0$ we obtain $a_2 = b_2$. And so on. Thus it follows that *a function can be represented by a power series in only one way, if at all.*

The considerations of the preceding paragraph do not constitute a proof because we did not prove that if we subtract two series term-by-term, the resulting series represents the difference of the two functions. Nor did we prove that if a series represents a function, we can differentiate the series term-by-term and that the new series represents the derivative of the original function. We could prove these theorems, but we would have to devote more space and time to the theory of series than is desirable at this stage of our work in the calculus.

## EXERCISES

1. Use the fact that $\log(1 + x) = \int_0^x \dfrac{dt}{1 + t}$ to obtain the Taylor series for $\log(1 + x)$.

2. Use the series

$$\sin z = z - \frac{z^3}{3!} + \frac{z^5}{5!} + \cdots$$

to obtain the series for $\sin x^2$ and then obtain the series for $\int_0^x \sin t^2 \, dt$.

*Ans.* $\dfrac{x^3}{3} - \dfrac{x^7}{42} + \dfrac{x^{11}}{7920} - \cdots$.

3. Using integration of series, find the series for the following:

(a) arc tan $x$.     *Ans.* $x - \dfrac{x^3}{3} + \dfrac{x^5}{5} - \cdots$.

(b) $\log(1 - x)$.

(c) $\log \cos x$ given $\tan x = x + \dfrac{x^3}{3} + \dfrac{2}{15} x^5 + \dfrac{17}{315} x^7 + \cdots$.

*Ans.* $-\dfrac{x^2}{2} - \dfrac{x^4}{12} - \dfrac{x^6}{45} - \dfrac{17x^8}{2520} - \cdots$.

4. Use the result of 3(a) to calculate the value of $\pi/4$. This is the value of arc tan $x$ when $x = 1$.

*Ans.* $\dfrac{\pi}{4} = 1 - \tfrac{1}{3} + \tfrac{1}{5} - \tfrac{1}{7} + \cdots$.

## 12. Some Applications of Taylor's Series.*

We saw in Sections 4 and 11 that we could obtain approximate values for functions such as $\sin x$, $\cos x$, and $\log(1 + x)$ by applying Taylor's theorem, obtaining 3 or 4 terms plus a remainder, and then using these 3 or 4 terms while estimating the error incurred in neglecting the remainder. We could, of course, take as many terms as we please and, if the remainder approaches 0, the usual case for ordinary functions, we can improve the accuracy of the values that we compute for the functions. Of course, if we use more and more terms of the Taylor expansion under the condition that the remainder $R_n$ approaches 0 as $n$ becomes infinite, we are really using the Taylor series. In this section we propose to look into additional applications of the Taylor series.

The first of these applications concerns the evaluation of integrals which cannot be expressed in terms of elementary functions. In Chapter 15, formula (40), we found that the length of one quarter of the ellipse is given

---

* This section can be omitted without disrupting the continuity.

by

**(95)**
$$s = a \int_0^{\pi/2} \sqrt{1 - e^2 \sin^2 \theta} \; d\theta$$

where $e$ is the eccentricity of the ellipse and $a$ is the semimajor axis. The integral in (95) is one of the class called elliptic integrals. We are unable to evaluate this definite integral by antidifferentiation because there is no elementary function whose derivative is the integrand in (95). However, we can expand the integrand by the binomial theorem and then integrate term-by-term. Thus, (87),

$$(1 - e^2 \sin^2 \theta)^{1/2} = 1 - \tfrac{1}{2} e^2 \sin^2 \theta - \tfrac{1}{8} e^4 \sin^4 \theta + \cdots .$$

This series converges when $|e^2 \sin^2 \theta| < 1$, which is always the case. Then

$$\int_0^{\pi/2} (1 - e^2 \sin^2 \theta)^{1/2} \, d\theta$$

$$= \int_0^{\pi/2} 1 \, d\theta - \int_0^{\pi/2} \tfrac{1}{2} e^2 \sin^2 \theta \, d\theta - \int_0^{\pi/2} \tfrac{1}{8} e^4 \sin^4 \theta \, d\theta - \cdots .$$

Now

$$\int_0^{\pi/2} 1 \, d\theta = \frac{\pi}{2} .$$

$$\int_0^{\pi/2} \tfrac{1}{2} e^2 \sin^2 \theta \, d\theta = \tfrac{1}{2} e^2 \frac{\pi}{4} .$$

$$\int_0^{\pi/2} \tfrac{1}{8} e^4 \sin^4 \theta \, d\theta = \tfrac{1}{8} e^4 \tfrac{3}{16} \pi.$$

Then, in view of (95),

$$s = a \int_0^{\pi/2} (1 - e^2 \sin^2 \theta)^{1/2} \, d\theta = a \frac{\pi}{2} - \frac{a}{2} \frac{\pi}{4} e^2 - \frac{a}{8} \frac{3\pi}{16} e^4 - \cdots .$$

**(96)**

Given the eccentricity of the particular ellipse, we see that we can calculate the quarter-length $s$ as accurately as we please by taking more and more terms of the convergent series (96).

It is always wise to check one's result by seeing if it applies to some special case in which the result is known. In the present case we can check by noting that an ellipse becomes a circle when the eccentricity $e$ is 0. If $e$ is 0, the result on the right side of (96) is $a\pi/2$, which is the correct value for the length of the quarter-circle of radius $a$. Of course, this check does not show that the terms beyond the first one are correct in all details.

The function $y = e^{-x^2}$ is basic in the theory of probability. The curve of this function (Fig. 20-6) is called the normal probability curve or the

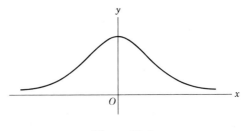

**Figure 20-6**

error curve. The quantity used intensively in that theory is

**(97)**
$$\int_0^x e^{-x^2}\, dx,$$

that is, the area under the curve and between the abscissas 0 and $x$. In this case, too, we cannot evaluate the integral by antidifferentiation, and the most effective method is to use series.

Because

$$e^x = 1 + x + \frac{x^2}{2!} + \frac{x^3}{3!} + \cdots,$$

then

**(98)**
$$e^{-x^2} = 1 - x^2 + \frac{x^4}{2!} - \frac{x^6}{3!} + \cdots.$$

Moreover, since the series for $e^x$ converges for all values of $x$, so does the series for $e^{-x^2}$ because any value of $-x^2$ falls within the interval of convergence of the first series. We now integrate (98) term-by-term so that

**(99)**
$$\int_0^x e^{-x^2}\, dx = x - \frac{x^3}{3} + \frac{x^5}{5 \cdot 2!} - \frac{x^7}{7 \cdot 3!} + \cdots.$$

We see, then, that we can compute the value of the integral as accurately as we wish by using the series in (99).

Let us see next what we can do with the problem of the motion of the pendulum by means of infinite series. When we first discussed the problem [Chapter 10, equation (64)], we found that the differential equation that governed the motion of the pendulum was

**(100)**
$$\ddot{\theta} = -\frac{32}{l} \sin \theta,$$

where $\theta$ is the angle that the string makes with the vertical (Fig. 20-7), $l$ is the length of the string, and $\ddot{\theta}$ is the second derivative with respect to the time. The problem posed by the differential equation (100) is to find $\theta$ as a function of $t$. In our earlier work on this problem we stated that it was not possible to express $\theta$ in terms of elementary functions of $t$, and therefore we

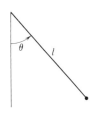

**Figure 20-7**

approximated by replacing $\sin \theta$ by $\theta$ and then solved the equation

**(101)** $$\ddot{\theta} = -\frac{32}{l}\,\theta.$$

The approximation, of course, introduces an error in the resulting solution. Because the pendulum is a very useful scientific device, we would like to know how much error is introduced. We could calculate this error if we could compare the solution of (100) with the solution of (101). Let us see, therefore, how far we can go toward obtaining a solution of (100).

Let us see first if we can obtain the expression for $\dot{\theta}$ from (100). The usual trick for this purpose, and one that we have employed several times previously, is to multiply both sides of (100) by $2\dot{\theta}$. Then

**(102)** $$2\dot{\theta}\,\ddot{\theta} = -\frac{64}{l}\,(\sin \theta)\dot{\theta}.$$

Now, the left side is the derivative with respect to $t$ of $(\dot{\theta})^2$ and the right side is the derivative with respect to $t$ of $(64/l)\cos \theta$. Hence, if we integrate both sides of (102), we have

**(103)** $$(\dot{\theta})^2 = \frac{64}{l}\,\cos \theta + C$$

where $C$ is the constant of integration.

To fix $C$, let us suppose that when the bob is initially pulled aside, the string makes an angle $\theta_0$ with the vertical and the bob is then released. This means that the bob starts out with an initial angular velocity of 0. Thus our initial condition is that $\dot{\theta} = 0$ when $\theta = \theta_0$. From (103) we have

$$C = -\frac{64}{l}\,\cos \theta_0,$$

and equation (103) now becomes

$$(\dot{\theta})^2 = \frac{64}{l}\,(\cos \theta - \cos \theta_0)$$

and

$$\dot{\theta} = \pm\sqrt{\frac{64}{l}\,(\cos \theta - \cos \theta_0)} = \pm\sqrt{\frac{64}{l}}\,\sqrt{\cos \theta - \cos \theta_0}\,.$$

We see that $\dot\theta$, which is of course $d\theta/dt$, is a function of $\theta$. Because the right side is a function of $\theta$, we shall consider

$$\frac{dt}{d\theta} = \frac{\pm\sqrt{\dfrac{l}{64}}}{\sqrt{\cos\theta - \cos\theta_0}}.$$

Then

$$t = \pm\sqrt{\frac{l}{64}}\int \frac{1}{\sqrt{\cos\theta - \cos\theta_0}}\, d\theta.$$

Since we are usually interested in the period $T$ of the pendulum, let us calculate the quarter-period between $\theta = 0$ and $\theta = \theta_0$. Also, as the bob moves from $\theta = 0$ to $\theta = \theta_0$ during any one of its swings, $d\theta/dt$ and so $dt/d\theta$ is positive. Hence

**(104)**
$$\frac{T}{4} = \sqrt{\frac{l}{64}}\int_0^{\theta_0} \frac{1}{\sqrt{\cos\theta - \cos\theta_0}}\, d\theta.$$

The integration called for in (104) presents a problem. Although it is not obvious, it is impossible to express the indefinite integral in terms of elementary functions, and we are going to have to resort to infinite series. However, to replace $\cos\theta$ by an infinite series would not help much, because there is still the square root and the fact that the series is in the denominator. Before employing infinite series let us try to put the integrand in a more useful form.

First, let us use the identities

$$\sin\frac{\theta}{2} = \sqrt{\frac{1 - \cos\theta}{2}} \quad \text{or} \quad \cos\theta = 1 - 2\sin^2\frac{\theta}{2}$$

and

$$\sin\frac{\theta_0}{2} = \sqrt{\frac{1 - \cos\theta_0}{2}} \quad \text{or} \quad \cos\theta_0 = 1 - 2\sin^2\frac{\theta_0}{2}.$$

Then

**(105)**
$$\frac{T}{4} = \sqrt{\frac{l}{64}}\frac{1}{\sqrt{2}}\int_0^{\theta_0} \frac{1}{\sqrt{\sin^2\dfrac{\theta_0}{2} - \sin^2\dfrac{\theta}{2}}}\, d\theta.$$

The advantage of the use of the identities is that we can now make a further transformation which will simplify the radicand appreciably. We let

**(106)**
$$\sin\frac{\theta}{2} = \sin\frac{\theta_0}{2}\sin\phi$$

or

**(107)**
$$\sin \frac{\theta}{2} = k \sin \phi$$

where $k = \sin(\theta_0/2)$; that is, we shall make a change of variable from $\theta$ to $\phi$. We must then also replace $d\theta$ by its equivalent in terms of $\phi$. From (107) we have, by differentiating both sides with respect to $\phi$,

$$\cos \frac{\theta}{2} \frac{1}{2} \frac{d\theta}{d\phi} = k \cos \phi$$

or

$$d\theta = \frac{2k \cos \phi}{\cos \dfrac{\theta}{2}} d\phi$$

or, in view of (107),

**(108)**
$$d\theta = \frac{2k \cos \phi}{\sqrt{1 - k^2 \sin^2 \phi}} d\phi.$$

We now substitute (106) and (108) in (105). Then, after some cancellations, we obtain

**(109)**
$$\frac{T}{4} = \sqrt{\frac{l}{64}} \frac{2}{\sqrt{2}} \int_0^{\pi/2} \frac{d\phi}{\sqrt{1 - k^2 \sin^2 \phi}}.$$

The new end values of the interval of integration are, of course, determined by means of (106). The integral in (109) is, also, one of the class called elliptic integrals.

It is now possible to apply infinite series. We have first by the binomial theorem (87) that

$$(1 - k^2 \sin^2 \phi)^{-1/2} = 1 + \tfrac{1}{2} k^2 \sin^2 \phi + \tfrac{3}{8} k^4 \sin^4 \phi + \tfrac{5}{16} k^6 \sin^6 \phi + \cdots$$

This series converges for $|k^2 \sin^2 \phi| < 1$, which holds here for all values of $\phi$. Then

$$T = 4\sqrt{\frac{l}{32}}$$

$$\times \left\{ \int_0^{\pi/2} 1 \, d\phi + \int_0^{\pi/2} \tfrac{1}{2} k^2 \sin^2 \phi \, d\phi + \int_0^{\pi/2} \tfrac{3}{8} k^4 \sin^4 \phi \, d\phi + \cdots \right\}.$$

Except for the constants, the integrals are the same as those evaluated in connection with (95). Hence

$$T = 4\sqrt{\frac{l}{32}} \left\{ \frac{\pi}{2} + \frac{1}{2} k^2 \frac{\pi}{4} + \frac{3 \cdot 3}{8} \frac{\pi}{16} k^4 + \cdots \right\}$$

or

$$T = 2\pi\sqrt{\frac{l}{32}} \left\{ 1 + \left( \frac{1}{2} \right)^2 k^2 + \left( \frac{1 \cdot 3}{2 \cdot 4} \right)^2 k^4 + \left( \frac{1 \cdot 3 \cdot 5}{2 \cdot 4 \cdot 6} \right)^2 k^6 + \cdots \right\}.$$

(110)

We now have an accurate value for the period of the pendulum, although of course it is in the form of an infinite series. We see that if we neglect the terms involving $k$, we obtain the period $2\pi\sqrt{l/32}$ which we got earlier (Chapter 10 formula (67)) by working with the approximate differential equation (101). Since $k = \sin(\theta_0/2)$ and $\theta_0 < \pi/2$, then $k < 1$. Thus the terms in (110) involving $k$ become smaller and smaller in value. If we do wish to obtain the period to a high degree of approximation, we can, given $\theta_0$, take into account two or more terms of the series in (110). Or, since the coefficients of the various terms are less than 1, we can use the geometric series

(111)                     $$k^2 + k^4 + k^6 + \cdots$$

to estimate the error in neglecting all the terms involving $k$. Let us note that the true period of a pendulum is *not* independent of the amplitude of the swing. The quantity $k$ involves $\theta_0$ and this is the initial displacement or amplitude.

Let us consider one more example of how series aid in scientific investigations. In Chapter 18, Section 4, we studied projectile motion in a vacuum. If the projectile is launched into a medium whose air resistance is proportional to the velocity then the direction equation of the trajectory is

(112)     $$y = \left( V \sin A + \frac{32}{k} \right) \frac{x}{V \cos A} + \frac{32}{k^2} \log\left( 1 - \frac{kx}{V \cos A} \right).$$

Here $V$ is the magnitude of the initial velocity, $A$ is the angle of fire, and $k$ is the proportionality constant determined by the amount of air resistance. Of course, for given numerical values of $V$, $A$, and $k$ we could calculate $y$ for various values of $x$ and we could graph the function (112) as accurately as we please. However, if we wished to compare projectile motion with and without air resistance, it would be difficult to draw any general conclusions about the effect of the resistance. We know that without air resistance the function analogous to (112) is (see formula (10) of Chapter 18)

(113)          $$y = V \sin A \frac{x}{V \cos A} - 16 \frac{x^2}{V^2 \cos^2 A}.$$

One sees some superficial differences between (112) and (113), but this is all that an inspection of the two formulas tells us.

Let us use the series

(114)          $$\log(1 + x) = x - \frac{x^2}{2} + \frac{x^3}{3} - \frac{x^4}{4} + \cdots,$$

which converges for $-1 < x < 1$. In (112) we have $\log\left(1 - \dfrac{kx}{V \cos A}\right)$. Then, if we replace $x$ in (114) by $-kx/V \cos A$, we obtain

$$\log\left(1 - \frac{kx}{V \cos A}\right) = -\frac{kx}{V \cos A} - \frac{k^2 x^2}{2V^2 \cos^2 A} - \frac{k^3 x^3}{3V^3 \cos^3 A} - \cdots .$$

**(115)**

If we use just these three terms of the series, substitute in (112), and simplify, we obtain

$$y = V \sin A \frac{x}{V \cos A} - \frac{1}{2} \frac{32}{V^2 \cos^2 A} x^2 - \frac{1}{3} \frac{32k}{V^3 \cos^3 A} x^3 - \cdots .$$

**(116)**

Because the series (114) is convergent for $|x| < 1$ and we substituted $kx/V \cos A$ for $x$ to obtain (116), the approximation for $y$ in (116) should be good for

**(117)** $$\frac{kx}{V \cos A} < 1.$$

Now $V$ and $A$ are fixed for a given trajectory. Then the quantity on the left side of (117) will be less than 1 when $kx$ is less than $V \cos A$ or, roughly stated, when $k$ is small and $x$ reasonably large or, if $k$ is not small, when $x$ is small. With these limitations on $k$ and $x$ in mind, let us compare (113) and (116). We see that the first two terms are exactly the same. When the projectile first leaves the cannon, $x$ is certainly small. Then the third term on the right side of (116) is small, and so the path of the projectile at the beginning of the flight is practically the same as that in (113), namely, parabolic. As $x$ increases, the third term on the right side of (116) becomes more significant and, since it is negative, we see that the path in the case of air resistance will fall below the parabolic path that obtains when there is no air resistance. Moreover, if we compare two trajectories which result when different air resistances are effective, the trajectory resulting from larger air resistance will be lower because $k$ is larger. Thus we see how the use of series reveals information not apparent from the original function itself.

## EXERCISES

1. The following integrals cannot be evaluated in terms of elementary functions. Use the series for $\sin x$ to evaluate them:

(a) $\displaystyle\int \frac{\sin x}{x}\, dx.$ 

*Ans.* $x - \dfrac{x^3}{3 \cdot 3!} + \dfrac{x^5}{5 \cdot 5!} - \cdots + C.$

(b) $\displaystyle\int \sin x^2\, dx.$

(c) $\displaystyle\int \sqrt{x}\, \sin x\, dx.$

**2. (a)** If a particle is dropped and falls in a medium whose resistance is proportional to the velocity, the velocity at time $t$ is given by $v = (32/k) - (32/k)e^{-kt}$. [See formula (69) of Chapter 12.] By using series, obtain an approximate expression for the velocity.      *Ans.* $v \sim 32t - 16kt^2$.

**(b)** Does the velocity approach the velocity in a vacuum as $k$ approaches 0?

**3. (a)** Under the conditions of Exercise 2 the distance fallen by the particle in time $t$ is given by the formula $y = (32/k)t + (32/k^2)e^{-kt} - (32/k^2)$ [See formula (71) of Chapter 12.] By using series, obtain an approximate expression for the distance.      *Ans.* $y \sim 16t^2 - \frac{16}{3} kt^3$.

**(b)** Does the distance fallen approach that in a vacuum as $k$ approaches 0?

**4. (a)** If an object is projected upward with an initial velocity $v_0$ in a medium whose resistance is proportional to the velocity, the formula for the velocity at time $t$ is

$$v = \left( \frac{32 + kv_0}{k} \right) e^{-kt} - \frac{32}{k} .$$

[Compare formula (75) of Chapter 12.] Using the series for $e^x$, obtain an approximate expression for the velocity.

*Ans.* $v \sim v_0 - 32t - kv_0t + (32 + kv_0)kt^2/2$.

**(b)** Does the velocity approach that in a vacuum as $k$ approaches 0?

**5. (a)** If an object is shot upward with an initial velocity of 1000 ft/sec and if the air resistance is proportional to the velocity, the height above ground obtained in time $t$ is

$$y = - \frac{32}{k} t + \frac{32 + 1000k}{k^2} (1 - e^{-kt}).$$

[See formula (77) of Chapter 12.] Use the series for $e^x$ to obtain an approximate expression for $y$.      *Ans.* $y \sim - 16t^2 + 1000t - 1000kt^2/2$.

**(b)** Does the height above ground approach that in a vacuum as $k$ approaches 0?

**6. (a)** Under the conditions of the preceding problem the time required by the object to reach maximum height is given by the formula $t_1 = (1/k)\log [1 + (1000k/32)]$. (See Exercise 3 in Section 7 of Chapter 12.) Use the first two terms of the series for $\log(1 + x)$ to obtain an approximate value of $t_1$.      *Ans.* $t_1 \sim (1000/32) - (1000)^2k /2(32)^2$.

**(b)** Does the value of $t_1$ approach the value in a vacuum as $k$ approaches 0?

**7. (a)** Under the conditions of Exercise 5 the maximum height $y_1$ attained by the object is given by the formula

$$y_1 = \frac{1000}{k} - \frac{32}{k^2} \log\left( 1 + \frac{1000k}{32} \right).$$

(See Exercise 4 in Section 7 of Chapter 12.) Use the first three terms of the series for $\log(1 + x)$ to obtain an approximate expression for $y_1$.

*Ans.* $y_1 \sim \dfrac{(1000)^2}{64} - \dfrac{(1000)^3k}{3(32)^2} .$

**(b)** Does the expression for $y_1$ approach the value in a vacuum as $k$ approaches 0?

8. If an object is projected upward with a velocity of 1000 ft/sec and if the resistance of the medium is proportional to the square of the velocity, the time $t_1$ required to reach maximum height is given by the formula $t_1 = (1/\sqrt{32k})\tan^{-1}\sqrt{k/32}\,(1000)$. (See Exercise 12 in Section 7 of Chapter 12). Use three terms of the series for arc tan $x$ to obtain an approximate expression for $t_1$.

$$Ans.\ t_1 \sim \frac{1000}{32}\left[1 - \frac{k(1000)^2}{3\cdot 32} + \frac{k^2(1000)^4}{5\cdot(32)^2}\right].$$

9. (a) Under the conditions of the preceding exercise the maximum height $y_1$ reached by the object is given by

$$y_1 = \frac{1}{2k}\log\left[1 + \frac{(1000)^2 k}{32}\right].$$

(See Exercise 13 in Section 7 of Chapter 12.) Use three terms of the series for log $(1 + x)$ to obtain an approximate expression for $y_1$.

$$Ans.\ y_1 \sim \frac{(1000)^2}{64}\left[1 - \frac{(1000)^2 k}{2\cdot 32} + \frac{(1000)^4 k^2}{3(32)^2}\right].$$

(b) Does the expression for $y_1$ approach that in a vacuum as $k$ approaches 0?

10. A cable that supports a load which is the same *for each foot along the cable* takes the shape of a catenary (Chap. 16, Sect. 4). A cable that supports a load which is the same *for each horizontal foot* takes the shape of a parabola (Chap. 4, Sect. 5). For small distances along the catenary starting from the vertex, the distance does not differ much from the horizontal distance (Fig. 20-8). Hence the catenary should be approximated by a parabola near the vertex. Show that the equation of the catenary $y = c(e^{x/c} + e^{-x/c})/2$ is approximated by the equation of a parabola.

*Suggestion:* Use the first three terms of the exponential series.

**Figure 20-8**

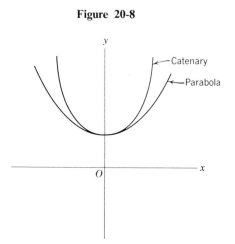

11. In Chapter 16 [see equation (24)] we encountered the problem of determining the value of $c$ in the equation $y = c(e^{x/c} + e^{-x/c})/2$ when $x = l$ and $y = c + d$. Use the first three terms of the series for $e^x$ and determine $c$ approximately.

12. In Chapter 6, Section 8 we calculated the work done by gravity in pulling an object down from a height $r_1$ from the center of the earth to the surface of the earth where the distance from the center is $R$. We found that $W' = GMm/r^2$, where $W' = dW/dr$, $G$ is the gravitational constant, $M$ is the mass of the earth, and $m$ is the mass of the object being pulled down. For brevity, let us write $W' = -k/r^2$ where $k = GMm$. We had no difficulty in integrating $W'$, but in many applications it might be sufficient to approximate the variation of $W'$ with distance from the center of the earth by arguing as follows. Let $r = R + h$, where $h$ is the height above the *surface* of the earth. Then

$$W' = -\frac{k}{r^2} = -\frac{k}{(R+h)^2} = -\frac{k}{R^2\left(1+\dfrac{h}{R}\right)^2}$$

$$= -\frac{k}{R^2}\left(1+\frac{h}{R}\right)^{-2} = -\frac{k}{R^2}\left(1 - 2\frac{h}{R} + \cdots\right).$$

For $h < R$ the series converges, and so we may use as an approximation to $W'$

$$W' = -\frac{k}{R^2}\left(1 - 2\frac{h}{R}\right),$$

where $W'$ here is $dW/dh$. We now have $W'$ expressed as a linear function of $h$. Using this expression for $W'$, calculate the work done by gravity in pulling an object whose mass is 100 pounds from a height of 500 miles to the surface of the earth. As in Chapter 6, formula (60), you may use the fact that $GM = 32(4000 \cdot 5280)^2$. Compare the result with that of Exercise 2 of Chapter 6, Section 8.

13. If a projectile is shot out with initial velocity $V$ from a cannon that is inclined at angle $A$ to the ground and if the air resistance is proportional to the velocity, the time it takes the projectile to reach its maximum height is given by the formula $t_2 = (1/k)\log[1 + (kV\sin A/32)]$. The corresponding value of $t_2$ when the motion takes place in a vacuum is $T_2 = V\sin A/32$. Show by using the series for $\log(1 + x)$ that $t_2 < T_2$.

14. Under the conditions of the preceding exercise the projectile attains the maximum height $y_2$ given by the formula

$$y_2 = \frac{V\sin A}{k} - \frac{32}{k^2}\log\left(1 + \frac{kV\sin A}{32}\right).$$

Under the same conditions but in a vacuum the projectile attains the maximum height $Y_2 = V^2\sin^2 A/64$. Show that $y_2 < Y_2$.

15. The relation between height and time of a projectile moving in a medium whose resistance is proportional to the velocity is given by

$$y = -\frac{32t}{k} + \left(\frac{V\sin A}{k} + \frac{32}{k^2}\right)(1 - e^{-kt}).$$

To obtain the time $t_1$ it takes the projectile to reach the ground, one should set $y = 0$ and solve for $t_1$. A usable value of $t_1$ is not obtained readily in this way. Instead, replace $e^{-kt}$ by the first three terms of its series and then solve for $t_1$. Compare the result with that for projectile motion with no air resistance.

$$t_1 \sim (V\sin A/16)[1 - (kV\sin A/32)].$$

**16.** The horizontal distance reached by a projectile moving in a medium whose resistance is proportional to the velocity is given by $x = (V \cos A / k)(1 - e^{-kt})$. Using the result of the preceding exercise, calculate the (approximate) range $x_1$ of the projectile. Compare the result with that for projectile motion with no air resistance.

$$Ans. \ x_1 \sim \frac{V^2 \sin A \cos A}{16} \left( 1 - \frac{kV \sin A}{32} \right).$$

**13. *Series as Functions.*** Our point of view in introducing series in this chapter was that we have functions which are difficult to work with in various situations and that we represent these functions by series either to replace or approximate the functions. Of course, Taylor's theorem was the chief instrument for obtaining a series from a function. We then went one step further. We encountered indefinite integrals that cannot be expressed in terms of elementary functions, for example,

**(118)**
$$y = \int_0^x e^{-x^2} \, dx.$$

What we did, instead, was to represent this integral by the series given in (99). Thus series serve to represent functions that are neither algebraic, trigonometric, nor any one of the elementary functions. The series gives a useful expression for the function, and practically everything that we wish to do with the function can be done with the series.

We now make still another step. Suppose that we write down any series whatever, such as

**(119)**
$$1 - \left( \frac{x}{2} \right)^2 + \left( \frac{x}{2} \right)^4 - \left( \frac{x}{2} \right)^6 + \cdots .$$

This series, at least for values of $x$ for which the series converges, *is* a function. It is a function because for each value of $x$ within the interval of convergence there is a value for the whole series, that is, a $y$-value. We know, too, that we can integrate and differentiate series. The integral and derivative so obtained are the integral and derivative of the function given by the series (119). In other words, series are functions, and they can be quite different functions from the elementary functions that we already know. Moreover, we need these new functions to represent phenomena that are not representable by elementary functions or even complicated combinations of elementary functions. In mathematics beyond the calculus we use functions that are known to us only as infinite series. The subject of infinite series, then, possesses a significance far broader than as a representation of functions that we already know.

# CHAPTER TWENTY-ONE
# FUNCTIONS OF TWO OR MORE VARIABLES AND THEIR GEOMETRIC REPRESENTATION

*1. Functions of Two or More Variables.* The functions that we have considered thus far—for example, $y = 3x^2$, $y = \sin 2t$, and $y = e^{x^2}$—have one independent variable and one dependent variable. We have found that these functions are useful to represent a variety of physical phenomena, but they do not suffice to represent all of the phenomena that man seeks to study. Hence we shall consider more general functions, the geometrical representation of such functions, and the calculus that applies to them.

Let us see why we need more general functions. In elementary geometry we learn that the formula for the area $A$ of a rectangle is the product of the length $x$ and the width $y$; that is,

$$A = xy.$$

The area $A$, then, depends on two quantities and if either one or both vary, $A$ varies. The variable $A$ is a function of two variables, $x$ and $y$. We should note that $x$ and $y$ can vary independently of each other; that is, no matter what value we assign to $x$, we can assign any other value to $y$. Hence $x$ and $y$ are independent variables and $A$ is the dependent variable. Therefore, to study the behavior of the area as the two dimensions of the rectangle vary we must treat $A$ as a function of both variables.

The formula for the volume of a circular cylinder whose base has the radius $r$ and whose height is $h$ is

$$V = \pi r^2 h.$$

Here again we have a function of two independent variables, and if we wish to study the behavior of the dependent variable $V$ as the dimensions of the cylinder vary, we must regard $V$ as a function of both independent variables $r$ and $h$. The formula for the period of a pendulum, derived in

**Figure 21-1**

Chapter 10, formula (69), is

$$T = 2\pi\sqrt{\frac{l}{g}} \ ,$$

where $T$ is the period, $l$ is the length of the pendulum, and $g$ is the acceleration due to gravity at the location of the pendulum. Because the length of the pendulum can be varied and the acceleration of gravity varies from place to place, $T$ is also a function of two variables.

Consider an elastic string, made of rubber say, which is fixed at the two ends and which occupies the position $AQB$ (Fig. 21-1). If one plucks this string, it will vibrate. We should like to describe the behavior of this string. One might do so by specifying the displacement $z$ of any point $P$ on it from its rest position. However, the value of $z$ will depend on which point $P$ we select and, since the string is vibrating, the instant at which we ask for the position of the string. We can agree to let $x$ represent the distance from $A$ to point $Q$ directly below $P$ and thereby describe the position of any point $P$ on the string in terms of its $x$-value. We can also introduce the time $t$ measured, say, from the instant the string begins to vibrate. Then the displacement $z$ will depend on $x$ and $t$, and $z$ is a function of $x$ and $t$. We do not know the precise function, but we can at least see the need for functions of two independent variables to treat such phenomena.

Functions of three or more independent variables also are needed in geometrical and physical studies. The volume $V$ of a box is $V = xyz$, where $x$, $y$, and $z$ are the dimensions. $V$, then, is a function of three independent variables. To consider a physical problem, suppose that we have a long metal plate so thin that we can idealize it as a rectangle. Let $ABCD$ (Fig. 21-2) be this rectangle. If we apply heat to the edge $AB$, the heat will travel along the plate. Suppose that we wished to study the temperature at any point $P$ of the plate. We could specify the position of $P$ by introducing the

**Figure 21-2**

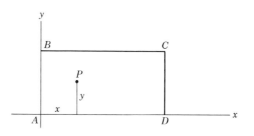

coordinates $x$ and $y$. The temperature $T$ will then depend on $x$ and $y$, but it also varies with the time $t$. Thus $T$ is a function of three independent variables, $x, y$, and $t$.

We intend to work with functions of two and three independent variables. A considerable aid in working with a function is a geometric picture of its behavior. In the case of $y$ as a function of $x$, the picture is a curve. The question which we shall now consider is, what geometric picture can we associate with a function of two independent variables? In speaking of such functions, for example,

$$z = x^2 + y^2,$$

we often use the word equation just as we use the words equation and function interchangeably in the case of a function of one variable. Of course, an equation may sometimes define a function implicitly. Thus the equation

$$x^2 + y^2 + z^2 = 25$$

defines $z$ as a function of $x$ and $y$ implicitly. Actually, this equation defines two functions

$$z = \sqrt{25 - x^2 - y^2} \qquad \text{and} \qquad z = -\sqrt{25 - x^2 - y^2}$$

since by the word function we mean a single-valued function.

## 2. Basic Facts on Three-Dimensional Cartesian Coordinates. To represent functions of two or more independent variables geometrically the basic device, as in the case of functions of one variable, is a coordinate system. Our previous coordinate systems, rectangular and polar, involved two coordinates and located points in a plane. The functions with which we are currently concerned involve at least three variables, and so we shall presumably need three coordinates. What we should investigate first, then, is a three-dimensional coordinate system. This locates points in space.

Instead of starting with two mutually perpendicular axes as we did earlier, let us start with three mutually perpendicular axes (Fig. 21-3) meeting at a common origin $O$. On each of these axes we suppose that numbers are assigned to the points, the zero point of the three axes being the common origin $O$. We suppose that the positive direction on the $x$-axis is directed out of the paper toward the reader, the positive direction on the $y$-axis is to the right, and the positive direction of the $z$-axis is upward. With this choice of directions the three-dimensional coordinate system is called right-handed. If a right-threaded screw (the usual threading) were turned in the direction from the $x$-axis to the $y$-axis through the 90° angle between them, the screw would move in the direction of the positive $z$-axis. (If the $x$- and $y$-axes are interchanged or if the positive direction of the $x$-axis is chosen to be into the paper, the coordinate system is called left-handed.)

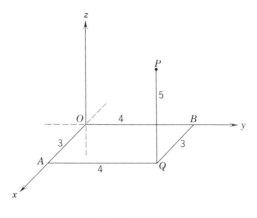

**Figure 21-3**

We can now locate any point in space by means of three numbers or coordinates. Thus consider point $P$ in Fig. 21-3. This point can be reached by going a distance $OA$ along the $x$-axis, then a distance $AQ$ parallel to the $y$-axis, and then the distance $QP$ parallel to the $z$-axis. These three distances are called the coordinates of $P$ and are usually written in the order just described. Thus if $OA$ is 3, $AQ$ is 4, and $QP$ is 5, the coordinates of $P$ are (3, 4, 5). Of course, one or more of the coordinates can be negative.

There is another, often helpful, way of regarding the coordinate system just introduced. The $x$- and $y$-axes determine a plane, called the $xy$-plane. So do the $x$- and $z$-axes and the $y$- and $z$-axes. Thus there are three coordinate planes. We may now think of the coordinates of $P$ as the three distances of $P$ from the coordinate planes (Fig. 21-4). Thus the $x$-coordinate of $P$, which is $QB$, can equally well be taken to the distance $PB'$, which is the (perpendicular) distance from $P$ to the $yz$-plane. Of course, $PB'$ would be negative if $P$ should lie on the other side of the $yz$-plane. Likewise, the $y$-coordinate of $P$, which is $AQ$, can be taken to be the distance $PA'$ or the perpendicular distance from $P$ to the $xz$-plane; again $PA'$ would be negative if $P$ should lie to the left of the $xz$-plane. The $z$-coordinate of $P$, which

**Figure 21-4**

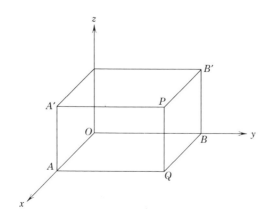

is $PQ$, is also the perpendicular distance from $P$ to the $xy$-plane, with the proper sign.

The coordinate planes divide the space into eight parts, called octants. The first octant is, by definition, the one in which all three coordinates of $P$ are positive. It is, of course, possible to designate what one means by the second, third, and other octants, but it is not worthwhile.

## EXERCISES

1. Indicate as best you can on a set of axes where the following points lie:
   (a) $(2, 3, -5)$.                    (f) $(3, 5, 0)$.
   (b) $(-2, 1, 4)$.                    (g) $(0, 0, 5)$.
   (c) $(2, -3, -4)$.                   (h) $(0, -5, 0)$.
   (d) $(0, 3, 5)$.                     (i) $(-5, 0, 0)$.
   (e) $(3, 0, 5)$.

2. What is the numerical distance of the point $(x, y, z)$ from each of the three axes?

3. When we speak of two points being symmetrically placed with respect to a plane, we mean that the line joining the two points is perpendicular to and bisected by the plane. What points are symmetric to $(3, 4, 5)$ with respect to the following?
   (a) The $yz$-plane.                  (c) The $xy$-plane.
   (b) The $xz$-plane.

4. Where are all the points for which the following hold?
   (a) $x = 0$.        Ans. The $yz$-plane.    (c) $z = 0$.
   (b) $y = 0$.

5. Where are all the points for which the following hold?
   (a) $x = 0$ and $y = 0$.             (c) $y = 0$ and $z = 0$.
                    Ans. The $z$-axis.
   (b) $x = 0$ and $z = 0$.

6. Describe geometrically the following sets of points:
   (a) All points whose perpendicular distance from the $xy$-plane is 7.
   (b) All points whose perpendicular distance from the $xz$-plane is $-5$.

7. Describe geometrically the following sets of points:
   (a) All points whose perpendicular distance to the $z$-axis is 4.
   (b) All points whose perpendicular distances from the $xz$- and $yz$-planes are equal.

In plane or two-dimensional coordinate geometry two auxiliary concepts proved to be very helpful in the main task of arriving at and studying the equations of curves. These were the distance formula and the concept of slope. The corresponding concepts of three-dimensional coordinate geometry are the distance formula and direction cosines.

The distance formula is readily derived. Let $P_1P_2$ in Fig. 21-5 be the distance between the two points $P_1$ with coordinates $(x_1, y_1, z_1)$ and $P_2$ with coordinates $(x_2, y_2, z_2)$. If we introduce point $Q$ which has the same $x$- and $y$-values as $P_2$ but the $z$-value of $P_1$, we see that $P_1P_2$ is the hypotenuse of the right triangle $P_1QP_2$. Hence we can find $P_1P_2$ if we can find the other two sides, $P_1Q$ and $QP_2$. Now $QP_2$ is $z_2 - z_1$. As for $P_1Q$, this is the

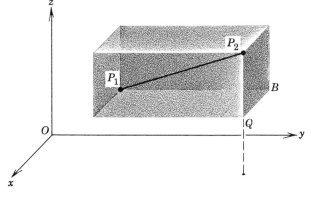

**Figure 21-5**

hypotenuse of the right triangle $P_1BQ$ where $B$ has the $x$- and $z$-values of $P_1$ and the $y$-value of $P_2$. Then $P_1B$ is $y_2 - y_1$; $BQ$ is $x_2 - x_1$; and therefore

$$(P_1Q)^2 = (x_2 - x_1)^2 + (y_2 - y_1)^2.$$

Since

$$(P_1P_2)^2 = (P_1Q)^2 + (QP_2)^2,$$

**(1)**        $$P_1P_2 = \sqrt{(x_2 - x_1)^2 + (y_2 - y_1)^2 + (z_2 - z_1)^2}.$$

Our proof utilized points $P_1$ and $P_2$ that are in the first octant, but we know from plane analytic geometry that a quantity such as $x_2 - x_1$ represents the distance $BQ$, which is parallel to the $x$-axis, no matter what signs $x_1$ and $x_2$ may have. Likewise, $P_1B$ is $y_2 - y_1$, no matter where $P_1$ and $P_2$ lie. The same applies to $QP_2$; that is, it is $z_2 - z_1$, regardless of the positions of $P_1$ and $P_2$ because the assignment of numbers to points on the $z$-axis follows precisely the scheme employed for the $x$- and $y$-axes.

**Example.**    Find the distance between the points $(0, 5, 7)$ and $(3, -2, 5)$.

**Solution.**    We apply (1) with 0, 5, 7 as $x_1, y_1,$ and $z_1$ and 3, $-2$, 5 as $x_2, y_2, z_2$. Then by (1) the distance is

$$\sqrt{(3-0)^2 + (-2-5)^2 + (5-7)^2} = \sqrt{62}.$$

## EXERCISES

1. Find the length of the longest side of the triangle whose vertices are $(0, 0, 0)$, $(3, 0, 0)$, and $(3, 3, 0)$.

2. The triangle whose vertices are $(0, 2, 0)$, $(4, 2, 0)$, and $(0, 2, 3)$ is a right triangle. Find the length of the hypotenuse.

3. Two of the sides of the triangle whose vertices are $(4, -2, 0)$, $(4, 2, 0)$, and $(0, 0, 5)$ are equal. What are their lengths?

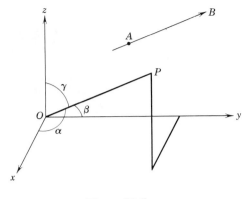

**Figure 21-6**

The notions of angle of inclination and slope in plane coordinate geometry serve to fix the direction of a line. This is what we shall now try to do for lines in space. Suppose that we have (Fig. 21-6) a line $AB$ and that we wish to designate its direction including also the fact that it is directed from $A$ to $B$. If we are concerned only with its direction and not with its actual location, we can as well utilize any line parallel to $AB$. Let us consider, then, the line $OP$ through the origin and parallel to $AB$. Moreover, to represent the direction on $AB$ from $A$ to $B$ we shall take the direction on $OP$ to be from $O$ to $P$. The directed line $OP$ makes an angle, denoted by $\alpha$, with the *positive x*-axis, the angle $\beta$ with the *positive y*-axis, and the angle $\gamma$ with the *positive z*-axis. These angles $\alpha$, $\beta$, and $\gamma$ are called the *direction angles* of $OP$ and of any line having the same direction as $OP$. The values of $\alpha$, $\beta$, and $\gamma$ depend, of course, on the position of $P$; they can vary from $0°$ to $180°$, the end values included. If we were concerned with the very same line $AB$ but directed from $B$ to $A$, we would specify its direction by taking the parallel line $OP'$ directed from $O$ to $P'$ (Fig. 21-7). The direction angles of $OP'$ are, say, $\alpha'$, $\beta'$, $\gamma'$. Since $POP'$ is a straight line which cuts the $x$-axis at $O$, the angles $\alpha$ and $\alpha'$ are supplementary so that $\alpha' = \pi - \alpha$. Likewise, $\beta' = \pi - \beta$ and $\gamma' = \pi - \gamma$, where $\alpha$, $\beta$, and $\gamma$ are the direction angles of $OP$.

**Figure 21-7**

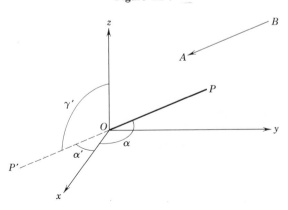

The direction angles of a line do specify its direction. However, just as the slope proves to be more useful than inclination in the case of plane coordinate geometry, mainly because the derivative of $y = f(x)$ equals the slope of the corresponding curve, so in three dimensions the quantities that prove to be more useful are the direction cosines of the direction angles $\alpha$, $\beta$, and $\gamma$. These *direction cosines* are

$$\cos \alpha, \quad \cos \beta, \quad \text{and} \quad \cos \gamma.$$

The presence of three direction angles and three direction cosines may be a little surprising. To fix the direction of a line in a plane we needed only one angle, the angle of inclination, or the slope, that is, the tangent of this angle. Hence intuitively one might expect that two angles or two direction cosines should suffice to fix the direction of a line in space. That is, in fact, the case. We may not choose $\alpha$, $\beta$, and $\gamma$ independently and so we may not choose their cosine values independently. We can see this fact best if we examine Fig. 21-8.

We start with the line $OP$ which we take to be $d$ units long. We now, so to speak, form a box or rectangular parallelepiped of which $OP$ is the diagonal. To form the box we introduce $Q$ which is the foot of the perpendicular from $P$ to the $xy$-plane. Through $PQ$ we consider the plane parallel to the $yz$-plane. This plane cuts the $x$-axis at $A$, and directly above $A$ in this plane and at the height of $P$ we mark off the point $R$. In this plane only the rectangle $AQPR$ is of interest to us; this is one face of the box. Likewise, through $PQ$ we pass a plane parallel to the $xz$-plane. The new plane cuts the $y$-axis at $B$, and directly above $B$ at the height of $P$ we mark off the point $S$. Again, the rectangle $PQBS$ is of interest. This is another face of the box. A third face is $AQBO$. We have now determined the box, the other three faces being easily identified in the figure.

The distances $OA$, $AQ$, and $QP$ are precisely the distances that we used to define the $x$-, $y$- and $z$-values of $P$. Moreover, triangle $OAP$ is a right triangle because the plane of $AQPR$ is perpendicular to the $x$-axis and

**Figure 21-8**

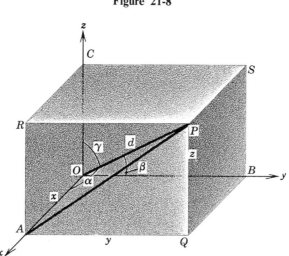

so, by a rather intuitively obvious fact of solid geometry, every line in that plane, and $AP$ in particular, is perpendicular to the $x$-axis. The direction angle $\alpha$ of $OP$ is the angle $AOP$, and so

**(2)**
$$\cos \alpha = \frac{OA}{OP} = \frac{x}{d} .$$

By using triangle $OBP$ and the same line of thought, we obtain

**(3)**
$$\cos \beta = \frac{y}{d} .$$

By using triangle $COP$, we obtain

**(4)**
$$\cos \gamma = \frac{z}{d} .$$

Squaring both sides of (2), (3), and (4) and adding the resulting equalities yields

**(5)**
$$\cos^2 \alpha + \cos^2 \beta + \cos^2 \gamma = \frac{x^2 + y^2 + z^2}{d^2} .$$

However, by formula (1), $x^2 + y^2 + z^2$ is the square of the distance $OP$ because the coordinates of $P$ are $(x, y, z)$ and the coordinates of $O$ are $(0, 0, 0)$. Since this distance is $d$, we have

**(6)**
$$\cos^2 \alpha + \cos^2 \beta + \cos^2 \gamma = 1.$$

This result is very useful. In particular, it tells us that if we choose any two direction cosines, which of course must be numbers between $-1$ and $1$, the third direction cosine is determined, except for sign. This does mean that there are two possible lines with the same $\cos \alpha$ and $\cos \beta$. If $\cos \gamma$ is then calculated by means of (6), the two values of $\cos \gamma$ are

$$\cos \gamma = \pm \sqrt{1 - \cos^2 \alpha - \cos^2 \beta} .$$

The two values of $\gamma$ are supplementary, for we know that for any angle $A$

$$\cos(\pi - A) = -\cos A$$

and our values of $\gamma$ are limited to $0°$ to $180°$. Hence $\gamma$ can be acute or obtuse; one line, $OP$ in Fig. 21-9, will make an acute angle with the positive $z$-axis, and the other, $OP'$ in Fig. 21-9, an obtuse angle with the positive $z$-axis. In a given problem we may know from other facts which of the two lines is wanted.

To define the direction cosines of a directed line $AB$ (see Fig. 21-6) we used the parallel directed line $OP$. However, to calculate the direction cosines of the line we can use information about the line itself. Suppose that $A$ and $B$ in Fig. 21-10 are two points on the directed line $AB$, and that the

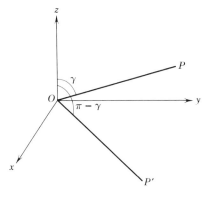

**Figure 21-9**

coordinates of $A$ are $(x_1, y_1, z_1)$ and those of $B$ are $(x_2, y_2, z_2)$. We construct the box with faces parallel to the coordinate planes and with $AB$ as a diagonal. Then the angle that $AB$ makes with $AC$ is $\alpha$ because $AC$ is parallel to the $x$-axis and in the same direction. Since $BC$ is perpendicular to $AC$ (compare triangle $OAP$ in Fig. 21-8), $ABC$ is a right triangle. Hence $\cos \alpha = AC/AB$. But $AC = x_2 - x_1$. Then

$$\cos \alpha = \frac{x_2 - x_1}{AB}.$$

Because the coordinates of $A$ and $B$ are known, formula (1) enables us to compute the distance $AB$. We can make similar arguments for $\cos \beta$ and $\cos \gamma$. Our results are, then, that *the direction cosines of the directed line $AB$ determined by $A$ with coordinates $(x_1, y_1, z_1)$ and $B$ with coordinates $(x_2, y_2, z_2)$ are*

**(7)** $\qquad \cos \alpha = \dfrac{x_2 - x_1}{AB}, \quad \cos \beta = \dfrac{y_2 - y_1}{AB}, \quad \cos \gamma = \dfrac{z_2 - z_1}{AB}$

**Figure 21-10**

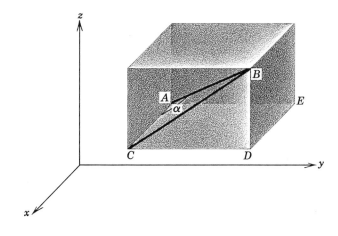

*where AB is the (positive) quantity* $\sqrt{(x_1 - x_2)^2 + (y_1 - y_2)^2 + (z_1 - z_2)^2}$.

A slight modification of the notion of direction cosines is that of direction numbers. The *direction numbers* of a line are any three numbers which are proportional to the direction cosines. That is, if *a*, *b*, and *c* are the direction numbers of a directed line, then by definition

**(8)** $$\frac{a}{\cos \alpha} = \frac{b}{\cos \beta} = \frac{c}{\cos \gamma}.$$

Given the direction numbers of a line, we can find the direction cosines. If we let each of the ratios in (8) be *r*, then

**(9)** $$a = r \cos \alpha, \quad b = r \cos \beta, \quad c = r \cos \gamma.$$

By squaring each equation and adding the results we obtain

$$a^2 + b^2 + c^2 = r^2(\cos^2 \alpha + \cos^2 \beta + \cos^2 \gamma) = r^2.$$

From (9) we have that

**(10)**
$$\cos \alpha = \frac{a}{\sqrt{a^2 + b^2 + c^2}},$$
$$\cos \beta = \frac{b}{\sqrt{a^2 + b^2 + c^2}},$$
$$\cos \gamma = \frac{c}{\sqrt{a^2 + b^2 + c^2}}.$$

Thus we have the direction cosines from the direction numbers. We have chosen the positive square root in (10) because this insures that the direction cosines represent the same *directed* line as do the given direction numbers. For, whatever the signs of the given quantities *a*, *b*, and *c*, formula (10) obliges us to choose α, β, and γ to accord with those signs.

In view of our definition of direction numbers, if *P* is a point on a line *OP* (Fig. 21-8) and *P* has coordinates (*x*, *y*, *z*), then by (2), (3), and (4) or by (7) its direction numbers are

**(11)** $$x = d \cos \alpha, \quad y = d \cos \beta, \quad z = d \cos \gamma,$$

where *d* is the distance *OP*.

**Example 1.** Find the direction cosines of the line determined by the point *A* with coordinates (2, 3, 5) and the point *B* with coordinates (4, 7, 9).

**Solution.**   We use formulas (7). This requires that we first find the distance *AB*. By (1)

$$AB = \sqrt{(4 - 2)^2 + (7 - 3)^2 + (9 - 5)^2} = \sqrt{36} = 6.$$

Then the direction cosines are

$$\cos \alpha = \frac{4 - 2}{6}, \qquad \cos \beta = \frac{7 - 3}{6}, \qquad \cos \gamma = \frac{9 - 5}{6}.$$

Note that if we had been required to find the direction cosines of the line determined by $BA$ we would have to use $(4, 7, 9)$ as $(x_1, y_1, z_1)$ and $(2, 3, 5)$ as $(x_2, y_2, z_2)$. Compare Fig. 21-7.

**Example 2.** Find the direction cosines of the line whose direction numbers are $\sqrt{6}$, $-3$, 7.

**Solution.**  We use formulas (10) in which we let $a = \sqrt{6}$, $b = -3$, and $c = 7$. Then

$$\cos \alpha = \frac{\sqrt{6}}{\sqrt{64}}, \qquad \cos \beta = \frac{-3}{\sqrt{64}}, \qquad \cos \gamma = \frac{7}{\sqrt{64}}.$$

Since $\cos^2 \alpha + \cos^2 \beta + \cos^2 \gamma$ must equal 1, we can check, and we readily find that this is so.

## EXERCISES

1. Draw a rectangular parallelepiped with faces in and parallel to the coordinate planes and having the points $(0, 0, 0)$ and $(3, 4, 5)$ as the end points of one diagonal.

2. Describe the line for which the following hold:
   (a) $\cos \alpha = \cos \beta = 0$.  (b) $\cos \alpha = \cos \gamma = 0$.

3. Where must a line lie to satisfy the following conditions?
   (a) $\cos \gamma = 0$.  (b) $\cos \alpha = 0$.

4. A line makes equal angles with all three axes. Find the angle.    *Ans.* $54° \, 44'$.

5. A line through the origin makes an angle of $45°$ with the $x$-axis and an angle of $60°$ with the $y$-axis. What angles can it make with the $z$-axis? *Ans.* $60°, 120°$.

6. Which of the following sets of numbers can be the direction cosines of a line?
   (a) $\frac{1}{2}, \frac{1}{3}, \frac{1}{4}$.  (c) $0, \sqrt{2}/2, \sqrt{2}/2$.
   (b) $\frac{1}{4}, \frac{1}{5}, \frac{3}{7}$.  (d) $1, 0, \frac{1}{4}$.

7. The direction cosines of a directed line are $\frac{1}{2}, \frac{1}{2}, \sqrt{2}/2$. What are the direction cosines of the oppositely directed line?

8. Find the direction cosines of the directed line joining the following pairs of points:
   (a) $(1, 1, 1)$ to $(2, 2, 2)$.  (c) $(1, -2, 3)$ to $(3, 4, -5)$.
      *Ans.* $1/\sqrt{3}, 1/\sqrt{3}, 1/\sqrt{3}$.   *Ans.* $1/\sqrt{26}, 3/\sqrt{26}, -4/\sqrt{26}$.
   (b) $(0, 0, 0)$ to $(2, 3, 5)$.  (d) $(2, 2, 2)$ to $(1, 1, 1)$.
      (e) $(2, 3, 5)$ to $(0, 0, 0)$.

9. What are the direction angles and direction cosines of the $y$-axis?

10. Find the angle between each axis and the line drawn from the origin to the following points:
   (a) $(4, 3, 12)$.   *Ans.* $\alpha = 72° \, 5', \beta = 76° \, 40', \gamma = 22° \, 37'$.
   (b) $(1, -1, -1)$.   *Ans.* $\alpha = 54° \, 44', \beta = 125° \, 16', \gamma = 125° \, 16'$.
   (c) $(1, 3, -5)$.
   (d) $(-6, 2, 3)$.   *Ans.* $\alpha = 149°, \beta = 73° \, 24', \gamma = 64° \, 37'$.

11. Find the direction cosines and direction angles of a line making an acute angle with the $z$-axis if its direction numbers are the following:

(a)  $-6, 2, 3$.     *Ans.* $\alpha = 149°, \beta = 73° \ 24', \gamma = 64° \ 37'$.

(b)  $1, -1, -1$.     *Ans.* $\alpha = 125° \ 16', \beta = 54° \ 44', \gamma = 54° \ 44'$.

(c)  $4, 1, 0$.

(d)  $-2, -3, 1$.

(e)  $5, -4, 3$.

12. Can any three numbers be the direction numbers of a line?

13. Define for plane analytic geometry the analogue of direction angles and direction cosines.

There is one more basic formula which is highly useful in studying geometrical figures in three-dimensional space—the formula for the angle between any two lines. In the plane two lines either intersect or are parallel. In the first case they certainly form a definite angle, and in the second the angle between them is defined to be $0°$ if the lines have the same direction and $180°$ if they are oppositely directed. In space two lines, say $m$ and $n$ of Fig. 21-11, may not be parallel and yet need not intersect. Nevertheless, it is convenient to introduce an angle formed by these lines. We do this by drawing two lines, $OP$ and $OP'$ through the origin parallel to and in the same direction as each of the given lines, respectively. The angle $\theta$ between these two lines $OP$ and $OP'$ is, by definition, the *angle between the two original lines*.

Let us try to calculate $\theta$. We presume that we know the directions of the two given lines in space, and because $OP$ and $OP'$ are parallel, respectively, to these lines, we know the direction angles of $OP$ and $OP'$. Suppose that $\alpha$, $\beta$, and $\gamma$ are the direction angles of $OP$ and that $\alpha'$, $\beta'$, and $\gamma'$ are the direction angles of $OP'$. We see from Fig. 21-11 that $\theta$ is an angle of triangle $OPP'$. If we knew some facts about this triangle, we could find $\theta$. Insofar as the size of angle $\theta$ is concerned, we can choose $OP$ and $OP'$ each to be of unit length. At the moment we do not know $l$, the length of $PP'$, but let us suppose that we can obtain it and see if this will help.

**Figure 21-11**

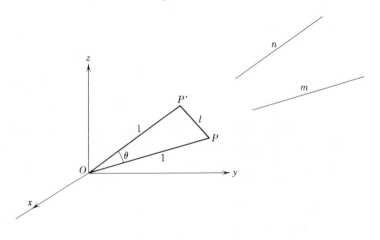

Since we have, or believe that we can obtain, the three sides of triangle $OPP'$, the law of cosines gives us an expression for $\cos \theta$. The law of cosines says that if $a$, $b$, and $c$ are the three sides of a triangle and if $C$ is the angle opposite side $c$, then

$$c^2 = a^2 + b^2 - 2ab \cos C.$$

In our situation, if we think of $c$ as $PP'$ with length $l$, then

**(12)**  $$l^2 = 1 + 1 - 2 \cos \theta.$$

Thus we can find $\cos \theta$ if we can find $l$.

Suppose that the coordinates of $P$ are $(x, y, z)$ and the coordinates of $P'$ are $(x', y', z')$. Then by (1)

**(13)**  $$l^2 = (x - x')^2 + (y - y')^2 + (z - z')^2.$$

We do not know the values of the coordinates, but we do know the direction angles of $OP$ and $OP'$. By (11)

$$x = \cos \alpha, \quad y = \cos \beta, \quad z = \cos \gamma,$$
$$x' = \cos \alpha', \quad y' = \cos \beta', \quad z' = \cos \gamma'.$$

If we substitute these values in (13) and use the fact that the sum of the squares of the direction cosines of a line is 1, we find that

$$l^2 = 2 - (2 \cos \alpha \cos \alpha' + 2 \cos \beta \cos \beta' + 2 \cos \gamma \cos \gamma').$$

In view of (12) we have that

**(14)**  $$\cos \theta = \cos \alpha \cos \alpha' + \cos \beta \cos \beta' + \cos \gamma \cos \gamma'.$$

This result will be used often. Let us summarize what it says.

**Theorem:**  If $\alpha$, $\beta$, and $\gamma$ and $\alpha'$, $\beta'$, and $\gamma'$ are the direction angles, respectively, of two directed lines, the angle $\theta$ between these lines is given by formula (14).

With this result not only can we calculate the angle between two lines but we can also state at once that two lines are perpendicular when and only when

**(15)**  $$\cos \alpha \cos \alpha' + \cos \beta \cos \beta' + \cos \gamma \cos \gamma' = 0.$$

## EXERCISES

**1.** Show that two lines with the direction numbers $a$, $b$, $c$ and $a'$, $b'$, $c'$, respectively, are:

(a)  Parallel when $\dfrac{a}{a'} = \dfrac{b}{b'} = \dfrac{c}{c'}$.

(b)  Perpendicular when $aa' + bb' + cc' = 0$.

2. Show that the line with direction numbers $(12, -3, -4)$ is perpendicular to the line with direction numbers $(4, 12, 3)$.

3. If the direction numbers of two lines are $(2, -3, 4)$ and $(-1, 2, 3)$, find the direction numbers of a line perpendicular to the two given lines.

*Suggestion:* Remember that the direction numbers of a line can be any numbers proportional to the direction cosines. *Ans.* $(17, 10, -1)$.

**3. Equations of Planes.** Our interest in representing or picturing functions of two variables will be furthered if, to start with, we learn to recognize the figures associated with simple functions. In the case of functions of one variable the simplest function is the linear function

$$y = ax + b$$

or, in more general form,

$$Ax + By + C = 0.$$

We know that the graph of this function is always a straight line. The simplest function of two variables is also linear, that is, of the first degree in the two independent variables. It has the form

**(16)** $$z = ax + by$$

or, more generally,

**(17)** $$Ax + By + Cz + D = 0.$$

Hence we should ascertain what figure or graph represents this function. One might guess that the analogue of the line would be the plane and, therefore, that (17) should be the equation of a plane. Let us see if that is correct.

Usually a plane will cut the coordinate axes. Suppose that (Fig. 21-12) it cuts the $x$-, $y$-, and $z$-axes in the points $S$, $T$, and $U$, respectively. Let us drop the perpendicular $OQ$ from the origin onto the plane, and let $P$ with coordinates $(x, y, z)$ be any point in the plane. If a line, $OQ$ in our case, is perpendicular to a plane, it is perpendicular to every line in the plane. This is a fact of solid geometry which we have already noted. Hence the line $PQ$ is perpendicular to $OQ$. If we let the direction cosines of $OQ$ be $\cos \alpha$, $\cos \beta$, and $\cos \gamma$ and if we let the direction cosines of $OP$ be $\cos \alpha'$, $\cos \beta'$, and $\cos \gamma'$, the angle $\theta$ between $OQ$ and $OP$ is given by

**(18)** $$\cos \theta = \cos \alpha \cos \alpha' + \cos \beta \cos \beta' + \cos \gamma \cos \gamma'.$$

However, $OQP$ is a right triangle. Hence

**(19)** $$\cos \theta = \frac{OQ}{OP}.$$

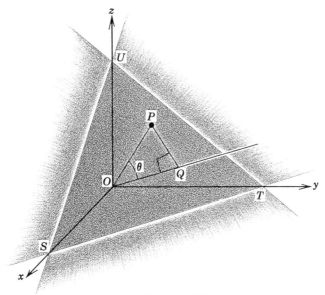

**Figure 21-12**

Moreover, by (11),

**(20)** $$\frac{x}{OP} = \cos \alpha', \quad \frac{y}{OP} = \cos \beta', \quad \frac{z}{OP} = \cos \gamma'.$$

If we substitute (19) and (20) in (18), we obtain

**(21)** $$OQ = x \cos \alpha + y \cos \beta + z \cos \gamma.$$

Now, $OQ$ is a fixed quantity, say $d$. Moreover, for the given plane, the perpendicular $OQ$ has a fixed direction, so that $\cos \alpha$, $\cos \beta$, and $\cos \gamma$ are constant. Then equation (21) is of the form (17). Thus what we have shown is that our plane has a first degree equation in $x$, $y$, and $z$ of the form (17).

We assumed to start with that the plane cut each of the coordinate axes. If it should be parallel to one or two of the axes, the proof would still be the same, although $OQ$ may lie in one of the coordinate planes or along one of the coordinate axes. If the plane should pass through the origin we could still draw a perpendicular $OR$ to the plane from the origin $O$. Let $\cos \alpha$, $\cos \beta$, and $\cos \gamma$ be the direction cosines of this perpendicular. The point $Q$ of the above proof would be $O$ itself and so $OQ$ would be zero. Since $OP$ lies in the plane, the angle $\theta$, which now means the angle between $OR$ and $OP$, is 90° and the proof proceeds as before. Thus we have shown that any plane has a first degree equation in $x$, $y$, and $z$ and of the form (17).

We should also show that any equation of the form (17) represents a plane. We start then with

**(22)** $$Ax + By + C + D = 0.$$

We shall try to convert (22) to the form (21). This is readily done by dividing both sides of (22) by $\sqrt{A^2 + B^2 + C^2}$ to obtain

(23) $\qquad \dfrac{A}{\sqrt{A^2 + B^2 + C^2}} \, x + \dfrac{B}{\sqrt{A^2 + B^2 + C^2}} \, y$

$$+ \dfrac{C}{\sqrt{A^2 + B^2 + C^2}} \, z + \dfrac{D}{\sqrt{A^2 + B^2 + C^2}} = 0.$$

Now we can interpret the coefficients of $x, y$, and $z$ as the direction cosines of a line because the sum of the squares of these three coefficients is 1. Hence consider a plane which is perpendicular to the line with these direction cosines and which meets this line at a distance $D/\sqrt{A^2 + B^2 + C^2}$ (along the line) from the origin. We know from (21) that the equation of this plane is given by (23). [According to (21), the quantity $D/\sqrt{A^2 + B^2 + C^2}$ must be negative and we can attain this by dividing (22) by $-\sqrt{A^2 + B^2 + C^2}$ if necessary. What we have thus far said will still be correct.] Hence we know that (23) represents a plane and so (22), which is the same equation, must also represent, or be the equation of, a plane.

We therefore have proved the following theorem:

**Theorem 1:** The equation $Ax + By + Cz + D = 0$ represents a plane and, conversely, any plane is represented by an equation of this form.

Our proof also shows the following:

**Theorem 2:** The coefficients of $x, y$, and $z$ in the equation of the plane are proportional to the direction cosines, or are the direction numbers, of a line perpendicular to the plane.

**Theorem 3:** The perpendicular distance from the origin to the plane $Ax + By + Cz + D = 0$ is $D/\sqrt{A^2 + B^2 + C^2}$ .*

Theorem 2 is useful in determining what one might call the "direction" of a plane in space. Strictly one cannot speak of the direction of a plane since such a figure extends in many directions, but we can determine how a plane lies by thinking in terms of the direction of a perpendicular to the plane, and the latter direction, according to Theorem 2, is furnished by the coefficients. Thus to learn how the plane

$$3x + 2y - 5z + 7 = 0$$

lies in space we use the fact that the plane is perpendicular to the line with

*Strictly $D/\pm\sqrt{A^2 + B^2 + C^2}$ must be negative, and we can choose the sign of the radical so that it is.

direction numbers 3, 2, $-5$ or direction cosines $3/\sqrt{38}$, $2/\sqrt{38}$, $-5/\sqrt{38}$. Any perpendicular to a plane is called a *normal* to the plane. Theorem 3 tells us the distance from the origin to the plane.

There is a larger point to be noted in connection with Theorem 1. It tells us that the locus or figure corresponding to an equation in three variables, or a function of two independent variables, is a *surface*. This statement is to be compared with the fact that an equation in two variables, or a function of one independent variable, represents a *curve*. However, the situation is a little more complicated.

Let us consider the equation $x + y - 5 = 0$. We can certainly write it as $x + y + 0z - 5 = 0$. In the latter form the equation more evidently represents a plane. Because it is the same as $x + y - 5 = 0$, this equation, too, represents a plane. Moreover, because the coefficient of $z$ is 0, the third direction number of any perpendicular to the plane is 0; then the perpendicular (Fig. 21-13) is parallel to the $xy$-plane, and the plane under discussion is parallel to the $z$-axis. In other words, even an equation in two variables, if it is interpreted geometrically in *three-dimensional* space, represents a surface. The situation that we are discussing has its analogue in two-dimensional coordinate geometry. There an equation such as $x = 5$ represents a straight line.

Now let us go one step further. Consider the equation $x - 5 = 0$. We can write this as $x + 0y + 0z - 5 = 0$ and so, according to Theorem 1, this equation represents a plane. Then the equation $x - 5 = 0$ represents the same plane. Moreover, because the direction numbers of any perpendicular to the plane are 1, 0, 0, this perpendicular has the direction of the $x$-axis and the plane itself is perpendicular to the $x$-axis or is parallel to the $yz$-plane. In other words, even an equation in one variable, when interpreted geometrically in *three-dimensional* space, represents a surface.

**Figure 21-13**

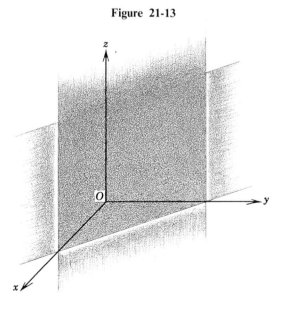

## EXERCISES

1. Find the intercepts of the plane $2x + 2y - z - 6 = 0$; that is, find the coordinates of the points $A$, $B$, and $C$ (Fig. 21-14) in which the plane cuts each of the coordinate axes.

   *Suggestion:* We know that the $y$- and $z$-coordinates of the point $A$ are 0. Hence we substitute these values of $y$ and $z$ in the equation of the plane and obtain $x = 3$. The coordinates of $A$ are $(3, 0, 0)$.

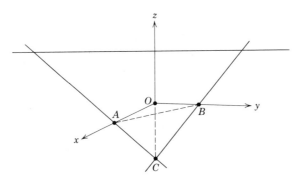

**Figure 21-14**

2. Find the intercepts of the following planes and sketch the planes:
   (a)  $x + y + z - 5 = 0$.                    *Ans.* $(5, 0, 0)$, $(0, 5, 0)$, and $(0, 0, 5)$.
   (b)  $6x - 4y + z - 12 = 0$.
   (c)  $6x - 2y + 3z - 20 = 0$.      *Ans.* $(\frac{10}{3}, 0, 0)$, $(0, -10, 0)$, and $(0, 0, \frac{20}{3})$.
   (d)  $x + y + z = 0$.
   (e)  $x + y - 5 = 0$.

3. What are the direction cosines of the normal to the plane whose equation is the following?
   (a)  $3x - 4y + 5z + 6 = 0$.                *Ans.* $3/\sqrt{50}$, $-4/\sqrt{50}$, $5/\sqrt{50}$.
   (b)  $2x - y - z + 5 = 0$.
   (c)  $2x - y + 5 = 0$.                       *Ans.* $2/\sqrt{5}$, $-1/\sqrt{5}$, $0$.
   (d)  $3x - z + 7 = 0$.
   (e)  $y + z - 5 = 0$.

4. Find the perpendicular distance from the origin to each of the planes in Exercise 3.                                          *Ans.* (a) $6/\sqrt{50}$.

5. Describe the positions of the following planes in terms of parallelism or perpendicularity to the coordinate axes or coordinate planes:
   (a)  $x + y + 7 = 0$.                        *Ans.* Perp. to $xy$-plane.
   (b)  $2y + z - 5 = 0$.
   (c)  $3x + 4z - 5 = 0$.
   (d)  $x + 7 = 0$.                            *Ans.* Parallel to $yz$-plane.
   (e)  $y - 3 = 0$.
   (f)  $z + 5 = 0$.

6. Show that the planes $2x + y - z + 7 = 0$ and $4x + 2y - 2z + 9 = 0$ are parallel.

**7.** Show that the planes $2x + y + z + 7 = 0$ and $-3x - 4y + 10z + 4 = 0$ are perpendicular.

**8.** Write the equation of the plane which is perpendicular to the line from the origin:

(a)  To $(4, 5, 3)$ and passing through the point $(1, 3, 2)$.

*Ans.* $4x + 5y + 3z - 25 = 0$.

(b)  To $(2, -4, 3)$ and passing through the point $(3, -4, -5)$.

**9.** Find the perpendicular distance between the following pairs of parallel planes:

(a)  $x + y + z + 5 = 0$ and $2x + 2y + 2z + 7 = 0$.  *Ans.* $\sqrt{3}/2$.

(b)  $x - y - z + 5 = 0$ and $2x - 2y - 2z + 7 = 0$.

(c)  $6x + 2y - 3z - 15 = 0$ and $6x + 2y - 3z + 25 = 0$.  *Ans.* $40/7$.

**10.** Find the point of intersection of the following planes:

(a)  $x + 2y + z = 0$, $x - 2y - 8 = 0$, $x + y + z - 3 = 0$.

*Ans.* $(2, -3, 4)$.

(b)  $3x - 5y - 4z + 7 = 0$, $6x + 2y + 2z - 7 = 0$, $x + y - 5 = 0$.

**11.** Show that the equation of the plane determined by three points can be obtained by starting with the general form of the equation, namely, $Ax + By + Cz + D = 0$ and by using the known coordinates of the three points to determine $A$, $B$, $C$, and $D$.

**12.** Show that the equation of the plane determined by the three points whose coordinates are $(x_1, y_1, z_1)$, $(x_2, y_2, z_2)$, and $(x_3, y_3, z_3)$ can be represented by the determinant

$$\begin{vmatrix} x & y & z & 1 \\ x_1 & y_1 & z_1 & 1 \\ x_2 & y_2 & z_2 & 1 \\ x_3 & y_3 & z_3 & 1 \end{vmatrix} = 0$$

The theory that we have already developed enables us to answer a question which arises occasionally, namely, what is the angle between two planes? Before answering this question let us understand what is meant by the angle between two planes. If at any point $A$ on the line of intersection (Fig. 21-15) we draw the perpendiculars $AB$ and $AC$ to the line of intersection, the first lying in one plane and the second in the other plane, then the angle $BAC$ is taken to be the angle between the two planes; it is called the dihedral angle. (There is an ambiguity here because we could equally well take the supplementary angle $B'AC$ to be the measure of the dihedral angle, but we shall ignore this point for the moment.) To obtain the size of $\angle BAC$ we can draw the perpendicular to the first plane at $B$ and the perpendicular to the second plane at $C$. Then these two perpendiculars will meet at some point, say $D$, and $ABDC$ is a quadrilateral. Because angles $B$ and $C$ of the quadrilateral are right angles, angle $D$ of the quadrilateral is supplementary to angle $A$. However, angle $D$ is the angle between the two perpendiculars, and we know how to find the angle between two lines if we know the direction cosines of the lines. Because the lines in question are the perpendiculars to the planes, we can find the direction cosines of these lines.

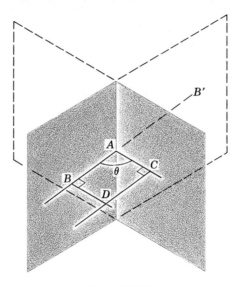

**Figure 21-15**

For example, suppose that we have to find the angle between the planes

$$4x - 3y + 5z = 8 \quad \text{and} \quad 2x + 3y - z = 4.$$

The direction cosines of the perpendicular to the first plane are $4/\sqrt{50}$, $-3/\sqrt{50}$, $5/\sqrt{50}$, and the direction cosines of the perpendicular to the second plane are $2/\sqrt{14}$, $3/\sqrt{14}$, $-1/\sqrt{14}$. Then, according to formula (14) for the angle between two lines, namely,

$$\cos \theta = \cos \alpha \cos \alpha' + \cos \beta \cos \beta' + \cos \gamma \cos \gamma',$$

we have

$$\cos \theta = \frac{4}{\sqrt{50}} \frac{2}{\sqrt{14}} - \frac{3}{\sqrt{50}} \frac{3}{\sqrt{14}} - \frac{5}{\sqrt{50}} \frac{1}{\sqrt{14}}$$

or

$$\cos \theta = -\frac{6}{\sqrt{50}\,\sqrt{14}} = -\frac{6}{5\sqrt{2}\,\sqrt{2}\,\sqrt{7}} = -\frac{3}{5\sqrt{7}}.$$

We could readily express $3/5\sqrt{7}$ as a decimal. Since in the present case $\cos \theta$ is negative, the supplement of $\theta$, that is, $180 - \theta$, can be found in a table.

This work has left open the question of whether we are finding the angle $BAC$ of Fig. 21-15 or the supplementary angle. In fact, we did not assign a direction to the perpendiculars to the planes, and so the direction cosines that we use are ambiguous to the extent of a minus factor. We could be specific and agree that these perpendiculars have the directions of the perpendiculars from the origin to the planes and thus fix the angle between the two planes. However, in any given situation either it will not matter whether we obtain $\angle BAC$ or its supplement or we shall know from facts in the situation which of the two we are obtaining. We have, then, the following theorem:

**Theorem 4:** The angle $\theta$ between two planes $A_1x + B_1y + C_1z + D_1 = 0$ and $A_2x + B_2y + C_2z + D_2 = 0$ is given by

$$(24) \qquad \cos\theta = \frac{A_1A_2 + B_1B_2 + C_1C_2}{\sqrt{A_1^2 + B_1^2 + C_1^2}\ \sqrt{A_2^2 + B_2^2 + C_2^2}}.$$

**Example.** Show that the planes $2x + 4y + 7z = 9$ and $x - 4y + 2z = 10$ are perpendicular to each other.

**Solution.** We know from theorem 2 that 2, 4, and 7 are the direction numbers of the normal to the first plane and that 1, $-4$ and 2 are the direction numbers of the normal to the second plane. The angle between these two normals is given by (14). Though (14) calls for the direction cosines, insofar as establishing perpendicularity is concerned, (15) tells us that we may as well use the direction numbers because the latter are proportional to the direction cosines. In our example, we do find that $2 \cdot 1 + 4 \cdot (-4) + 7 \cdot 2 = 0$.

## EXERCISES

1. Find the angle between the following planes:
   (a) $2x - y + z = 7$, $x + y + 2z = 11$.                     *Ans.* 60° or 120°.
   (b) $4x - 3y + z = 6$, $2x + 3y - 5z = 4$.
   (c) $x + 2y - z = 12$, $x - 2y - 2z = 7$.                    *Ans.* 97° 50′ or 82° 10′.
   (d) $3x - z + 12 = 0$, $x + 3y + 17 = 0$.

**4. Equations of Straight Lines.** We are investigating three-dimensional coordinate geometry primarily to obtain pictorial or geometrical representations of functions of two independent variables. These representations, as we have already had occasion to observe, are surfaces. However, in the applications of mathematics to phenomena taking place in space we shall certainly have occasion to work with curves. For example, the motion of a projectile may well take place along a curve that does not lie entirely in one plane. The question then does arise, how are space-curves represented in three-dimensional coordinate geometry? Because one equation in $x$, $y$, and $z$ represents a surface, surely one equation is not the answer and neither would no equations be. A good guess might be that two equations in $x$, $y$, and $z$ are needed to represent a curve. Let us see if this is correct.

We shall take up the straight line. Although this curve does lie in one plane, we may want to consider lines that do not lie in one of the coordinate planes but are in some general position in space. Then the problem of representing the straight line may well serve as an introduction to the problem of representing curves in space.

We can think of a line as the intersection of any two planes containing that line. Suppose that the equations of the planes are

$$3x + 2y - z - 1 = 0$$
**(25)**
$$2x - y + 2z - 3 = 0.$$

The sets of values of $x$, $y$, and $z$ that satisfy both equations simultaneously must represent points which lie on both planes and which constitute the line of intersection of the two planes. Hence the two equations of the two planes *taken together* or *taken simultaneously* represent the line of intersection. Thus we see that one way of representing the straight line is by means of the equations of the two planes on which the line lies.

It does seem as though we should be able to eliminate one of the two equations in (25) and so be able to represent the straight line by one equation. Suppose that we eliminate $z$ by multiplying the second equation by $\frac{1}{2}$ and adding that result to the first one. This gives

**(26)**
$$4x + \tfrac{3}{2} y - \tfrac{5}{2} = 0.$$

However, (26) is the equation of a plane and so by itself cannot represent the line. What we do know about (26) is that

$$4x + \tfrac{3}{2} y - \tfrac{5}{2} = (3x + 2y - z - 1) + \tfrac{1}{2}(2x - y + 2z - 3).$$

Then any values of $x$, $y$ and $z$ which satisfy both equations (25) will make the right side 0 and so do the same to the left side. In other words, (26) is the equation of a *plane* that also contains the points of the line of intersection of the two original planes. Hence we could represent the line by the two equations

$$4x + \tfrac{3}{2} y - \tfrac{5}{2} = 0$$
**(27)**
$$3x + 2y - z - 1 = 0$$

in place of the two equations in (25). Nevertheless, two equations are still needed.

There is one slight advantage in the use of the pair of equations in (27) as opposed to the pair in (25). The first equation in (27) represents a plane that is more readily visualized. This plane is perpendicular to the $xy$-plane. We can also replace the second equation in (27) by a simpler one. All we need to do is eliminate $y$ or $x$ from the equations in (25) and use the resulting equation together with the first equation in (27). If we eliminate $y$ in (25), we obtain

$$7x + 3z - 7 = 0.$$

Then we can represent the line by the two simpler equations

**(28)**
$$4x + \tfrac{3}{2}y - \tfrac{5}{2} = 0$$

$$7x + 3z - 7 = 0.$$

These planes which contain the line and each of which is perpendicular to one of the coordinate planes are called the *projecting planes* of the line (Fig. 21-16).

Let us note that, although each of the equations in (28) contains only two coordinates, it is still the equation of a plane and not of a line. This point has already been made in Section 3.

Suppose that we have a line which is given by the equations of two planes. What might we like to know about the line and how can we obtain that information? It would be helpful in order to picture the line to know its direction numbers. Let us see if we can obtain them.

Suppose that the line is given by the two equations

**(29)**
$$3x + 2y - z - 1 = 0$$

$$2x - y + 2z - 3 = 0.$$

Let $a$, $b$, and $c$ be the direction numbers of the line. The line lies in each of the planes and therefore is perpendicular to any normal of each of the planes. However, we know that the coefficients of $x$, $y$, and $z$ are the direction numbers of any normal to a plane. To express the perpendicularity of the line and a normal to the first plane in (29) we can use (15) and so state

$$3a + 2b - c = 0.$$

Likewise, from the second equation in (29) we have

$$2a - b + 2c = 0.$$

We have two equations in the three unknowns $a$, $b$, and $c$. These equations

**Figure 21-16**

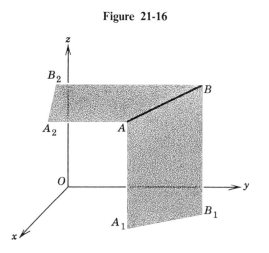

do not determine $a$, $b$, and $c$ uniquely, but we can solve for $a$ and $b$ in terms of $c$. The result is

$$7a = -3c \quad \text{and} \quad 7b = 8c.$$

We can restate this result as

$$\frac{a}{3} = \frac{b}{-8} = \frac{c}{-7}.$$

What we have then is the ratio of $a$ and $b$ to $c$ or the ratio of $a$ to $b$ to $c$. But this is all we need because the direction numbers of a line are not unique. We can if we wish take

$$a = 3, \quad b = -8, \quad c = -7$$

or any set of numbers proportional to these.

What we just did for the two specific planes in (29) we can do more generally for the planes

(30)
$$A_1 x + B_1 y + C_1 z + D_1 = 0$$
$$A_2 x + B_2 y + C_2 z + D_2 = 0.$$

Execution of the algebra gives the following theorem:

**Theorem 1:** If $a$, $b$, and $c$ are the direction numbers of the line represented by the two equations in (30), then

(31)
$$\frac{a}{B_1 C_2 - B_2 C_1} = \frac{b}{C_1 A_2 - C_2 A_1} = \frac{c}{A_1 B_2 - A_2 B_1}.$$

There is another bit of information that one might like to have about a line which is known to us through two given equations of planes, namely, the points in which the line cuts the coordinate planes. These points are called the *traces* of the line in the coordinate planes. Let us consider the line given in (29). To find the coordinates of the point in which the line cuts the $xy$-plane, we can use the fact that for any point in that plane $z = 0$. If, then, we set $z = 0$ in the two equations in (29), we obtain

$$3x + 2y - 1 = 0$$
$$2x - y - 3 = 0.$$

We solve these equations for $x$ and $y$ and obtain $x = 1$, $y = -1$. Then the trace of the line in the $xy$-plane is $(1, -1, 0)$.

## EXERCISES

1. Find the direction numbers and the trace (if it exists) in the $xy$-plane of the line represented by each of the following pairs of planes:
   (a)   $x + 5y + 7z - 3 = 0$, $x - 2y + 3z - 6 = 0$.

   $\textit{Ans.}$   $29, 4, -7; \left( \dfrac{48}{7}, \dfrac{-3}{7}, 0 \right).$

(b)   $6x - 3y + 6z - 7 = 0, 3x + 2y + 3z + 28 = 0$.
(c)   $5x - 7y + 3z - 10 = 0, 3x + 5y - 8z + 4 = 0$.

$$Ans. \ 41, -49, 46; \ \left( \frac{11}{23}, \ \frac{-25}{23}, 0 \right).$$

(d)   $y + z = 4, x + y - 2z = 12$.
(e)   $x + 2y = 8, 2x - 4y = 7$.                    $Ans. \ 0, 0, 1; \ (\frac{23}{4}, \frac{9}{8}, 0).$
(f)   $2x + y - z = 2, x - y + 2z = 4$.
(g)   $4x + 3y - 6z = 0, 4x - 3y = 2$.

**2.** Replace the two given equations in each part of Exercise 1 by two projecting planes defining the same line.

There is one more problem that often arises in dealing with straight lines. Up to now we have supposed that the equations of the line are given to us and we have learned to use the equations to obtain some information about the lines. The converse problem is to start with some information that determines the line and then obtain the equations representing the line. A line is known or determined if it passes through a given point in space and if its direction angles are fixed. The problem is to find the equations representing that line. The answer is readily obtained from equations (7). Suppose that $P_1$ with coordinates $(x_1, y_1, z_1)$ is the given point on the line and $P$ with coordinates $(x, y, z)$ is any other point on the line. Then equations (7) say that

**(32)**                          $x - x_1 = P_1 P \cos \alpha$

**(33)**                          $y - y_1 = P_1 P \cos \beta$

**(34)**                          $z - z_1 = P_1 P \cos \gamma.$

We can now formulate our conclusion in any one of several ways. We supposed that we know $P_1$ and the direction angles. Then from (32), (33), and (34) we may say that

**(35)**                $$\frac{x - x_1}{\cos \alpha} = \frac{y - y_1}{\cos \beta} = \frac{z - z_1}{\cos \gamma}.$$

These are the equations of the line.
We should note that what we really have in (35) are the equations of planes. The equation

$$\frac{x - x_1}{\cos \alpha} = \frac{y - y_1}{\cos \beta}$$

is equivalent to

$$x \cos \beta - y \cos \alpha - x_1 \cos \beta + y_1 \cos \alpha = 0$$

which is the equation of a plane, in fact of the line's projecting plane perpendicular to the $xy$-plane. Likewise, the equation

$$\frac{y - y_1}{\cos \beta} = \frac{z - z_1}{\cos \gamma}$$

is the equation of a plane perpendicular to the $yz$-plane and another of the projecting planes of the line under discussion. By equating the first and third terms in (35), we obtain the equation of the third projecting plane. In other words, the equations of a line as given by (35) are really the equations of three planes, any two of which determine the line.

The result (35) is sufficiently important to be stated as a theorem.

**Theorem 2:** The equations of a line through the point $(x_1, y_1, z_1)$ and with direction angles $\alpha$, $\beta$, and $\gamma$ are

**(36)**
$$\frac{x - x_1}{\cos \alpha} = \frac{y - y_1}{\cos \beta} = \frac{z - z_1}{\cos \gamma}.$$

Equations (32), (33), and (34) yield another form of the equations of a line. Suppose that a line is given by fixing one point $(x_1, y_1, z_1)$ on it and its direction angles $\alpha$, $\beta$, and $\gamma$. The quantity $P_1 P$ in (32), (33), and (34) is the distance from $(x_1, y_1, z_1)$ to any variable point $(x, y, z)$. Let us call this variable distance $d$. Then the three equations become

**(37)**    $x = x_1 + d \cos \alpha, \quad y = y_1 + d \cos \beta, \quad z = z_1 + d \cos \gamma.$

In these equations $x_1$, $y_1$, $z_1$, $\cos \alpha$, $\cos \beta$, and $\cos \gamma$ are fixed and $x$, $y$, $z$, and $d$ are variable. What we really have are the *parametric* equations of the line. The variable $d$ is the parameter and, of course, $x$, $y$, and $z$ are the variable coordinates of any point $P$ on the line. The parametric representation of a line calls for *three* equations. This should not be surprising because we found in the case of curves in the plane that in place of one direct equation involving $x$ and $y$ we had to use two equations when we introduced the parametric form. In contrast to (37) we may call (36), or any two equations of planes determining a line, the *direct* equations of the *line*.

The result (37) is also important and we shall state it as a theorem.

**Theorem 3:** The parametric equations of a line through the point $(x_1, y_1, z_1)$ and with the direction angles $\alpha$, $\beta$, and $\gamma$ are

**(38)**    $x = x_1 + d \cos \alpha, \quad y = y_1 + d \cos \beta, \quad z = z_1 + d \cos \gamma.$

The quantity $d$ represents the distance from $(x_1, y_1, z_1)$ to $(x, y, z)$.

If a line is determined by two points, $P_1$ with coordinates $(x_1, y_1, z_1)$ and $P_2$ with coordinates $(x_2, y_2, z_2)$, we can use the distance formula (1) to calculate $P_1 P_2$ and the formulas (7) to calculate its direction angles.

## EXERCISES

**1.** Use (36) to write the equations of a line through $(x_1, y_1, z_1)$ and with the direction numbers $a$, $b$, and $c$.

**2.** May we use negative values of $d$ in the parametric equations of a line to obtain points on the line?                                                  *Ans.* Yes.

**3.** Would it be correct to write the parametric equations of a line in the form $x = x_1 + at$, $y = y_1 + bt$, $z = z_1 + ct$, where $a$, $b$, and $c$ are the direction numbers of the line?                                              *Ans.* Yes.

**4.** Derive the equations of each of the following lines. The answers may be in terms of the direct equations or the parametric equations.

    (a)   Through $(3, 4, 5)$ with direction angles $60°$, $45°$, $120°$.

$$Ans. \quad \frac{x-3}{\frac{1}{2}} = \frac{y-4}{\sqrt{2}/2} = \frac{z-5}{-\frac{1}{2}}.$$

    (b)   Through $(3, 4, -4)$ with direction angles $30°$, $60°$, $45°$.

    (c)   Through $(3, -2, 1)$ and $(2, 3, 4)$.

    (d)   Through $(3, -2, 1)$ and $(3, -4, 5)$.

$$Ans. \ x = 3, y = -2 - 2t, z = 1 + 4t.$$

    (e)   Through $(3, 2, 1)$ with direction numbers $2, 1, 3$.

    (f)   Through $(3, 2, 1)$ with direction numbers $0, 2, 0$.

$$Ans. \ x = 3, y = 2 + 2t, z = 1.$$

**5.** Find the equations of the line through $(0, -3, 2)$ and parallel to the line joining $(3, 4, -7)$ and $(2, 7, -6)$.    *Ans.* $x = t, y = -3 - 3t, z = 2 - t$.

**6.** Find the equations of the line through $(-2, 4, 0)$ and parallel to the line $x/4 = (y+2)/-3 = (z-4)/-1$.

**7.** Given the parametric equations $x = 1 + d\sqrt{\frac{3}{2}}$, $y = 2 + (d/2)$, $z = 4 - (d/2)$, calculate the coordinates of three other points on the line.

**8.** Sketch the lines whose equations are the following:

    (a)   $x = 2 + \frac{2}{3}t$, $y = 4 + \frac{1}{3}t$, $z = 6 + \frac{2}{3}t$.

    (b)   $x = -3 + \frac{2}{7}t$, $y = 6 - \frac{6}{7}t$, $z = 4 + \frac{3}{7}t$.

**9.** Show that the line

$$\frac{x - x_1}{\frac{1}{2}} = \frac{y - y_1}{\frac{1}{3}} = \frac{z - z_1}{\frac{2}{3}}$$

is parallel to the plane whose equation is $2x + 3y - 3z + 7 = 0$.

**10.** Show that the line $\dfrac{x}{3} = \dfrac{y}{-2} = \dfrac{z}{7}$ is perpendicular to the plane $3x - 2y + 7z = 8$.

**11.** Show that the line $\dfrac{x-2}{3} = \dfrac{y+2}{1} = \dfrac{z-3}{-4}$ lies in the plane $x + y + z - 3 = 0$.

**12.** Find the equations of the following lines:

    (a)   Passing through $(2, -3, 4)$ and perpendicular to the plane $3x - y + 2z = 4$.    *Ans.* $x = 2 + 3t, y = -3 - t, z = 4 + 2t$.

    (b)   Passing through $(-1, 3, 2)$ and perpendicular to the plane $x - 3z = 4$.

    (c)   Passing through $(0, 2, 4)$ and parallel to each of the planes $x - 2z = 1$ and $y - 3z = 2$.

**13.** Find the angle between the line $\dfrac{x-2}{3} = \dfrac{y-4}{2} = \dfrac{z-1}{1}$ and the normal to the plane $3x - y + 2z = 5$.    *Ans.* $50° \ 46'$.

### 5. *Quadric or Second Degree Surfaces.* We have examined the geometrical representation of functions of the form $z = ax + by$, that is, functions

which are of the first degree in $x$ and $y$, and have found that they correspond to planes. Our next question might be, what geometrical figures correspond to second degree functions such as

$$z = xy, \qquad z = x^2 + y^2, \qquad z = x^2 - y^2$$

and to other functions?

Let us start our geometrical study of second degree functions by working backward. When we considered plane curves we found that next to the straight line the circle was about the easiest to tackle algebraically. Let us now ask, what is the equation of the sphere, that is, the surface of the solid figure? Suppose that a sphere (Fig. 21-17) has its center at the point $(h, k, l)$ where $h$, $k$, and $l$ may be positive or negative. By definition the sphere consists of all points that are at a fixed distance, say $r$, from the center. If we let $(x, y, z)$ be the coordinates of any point on the sphere, then by using the distance formula (1) we can say that

$$(39) \qquad (x - h)^2 + (y - k)^2 + (z - l)^2 = r^2.$$

If we carry out the squaring of the terms and rearrange them, we see that the equation is

$$(40) \qquad x^2 + y^2 + z^2 - 2xh - 2yk - 2zl + h^2 + k^2 + l^2 = r^2.$$

We also see that if the center is (0, 0, 0), the equation becomes

$$(41) \qquad x^2 + y^2 + z^2 = r^2.$$

If we think in terms of functions solved for $z$, then (41) yields

$$z = \pm\sqrt{r^2 - x^2 - y^2}\ .$$

Here, as in the case of the circle, we must be careful. The positive radical

**Figure 21-17**

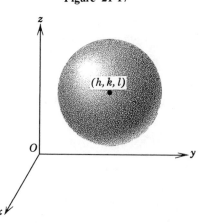

represents points on the upper half of the sphere and the negative radical represents points on the lower half. In other words, if we insist on single-valued functions of $x$ and $y$, two functions are needed to represent the sphere. Let us signalize the result (39).

**Theorem 1:** The equation of a sphere with center $(h, k, l)$ and radius $r$ is

**(42)** $$(x - h)^2 + (y - k)^2 + (z - l)^2 = r^2.$$

We have seen that the sphere is represented by an equation of the form (40) or (42). However, we do not know that every equation of the form (40) represents a sphere. Let us see if we can prove this. Suppose that we consider a concrete case, namely,

**(43)** $$x^2 + y^2 + z^2 - 4x + 5y - 6z + 10 = 20.$$

If we could put this equation into the form (42), we would see that it represents a sphere with center $(h, k, l)$ and radius $r$. Let us group the terms in $x$, in $y$, and in $z$ thus:

**(44)** $$x^2 - 4x + y^2 + 5y + z^2 - 6z = 10.$$

Now we can make a perfect square of the $x$-terms, the $y$-terms, and the $z$-terms separately by using the process called completing the square. Thus in the case of $x^2 - 4x$ we take half the coefficient of $x$, square it, and add it to both sides of the equation. This gives

$$x^2 - 4x + 4 + y^2 + 5y + z^2 - 6z = 10 + 4.$$

If we complete the square for the $y$-terms and the $z$-terms, we obtain

$$x^2 - 4x + 4 + y^2 + 5y + \tfrac{25}{4} + z^2 - 6z + 9 = 10 + 4 + \tfrac{25}{4} + 9$$

or

**(45)** $$(x - 2)^2 + (y + \tfrac{5}{2})^2 + (z - 3)^2 = \tfrac{117}{4}.$$

We know by comparing (45) and (42) that (45) represents a sphere with center $(2, -\tfrac{5}{2}, 3)$ and radius $\sqrt{117}/2$. Because (43) is equivalent to (45) in the sense that the same $x, y,$ and $z$ satisfy both equations, we know that (43) also represents a sphere.

We can, of course, carry out the process that took us from (43) to (45) with the general equation

**(46)** $$x^2 + y^2 + z^2 + Gx + Hy + Iz + K = 0$$

and our result is the following theorem:

**Theorem 2:** The equation $x^2 + y^2 + z^2 + Gx + Hy + Iz + K = 0$ represents a sphere.

We should note that if the constant, which appears where $117/4$ does in (45), should be negative, then no real values of $x$, $y$, and $z$ will satisfy the equation, because each term on the left side is positive for all real $x$, $y$, and $z$. In this case the equation does not represent a real surface. Theorem 2 as stated does not take into account this possibility. We could readily state a condition that would exclude it, but it is not important. We have also not bothered to single out the case of a sphere with radius 0.

## EXERCISES

1. Find the centers and radii of the following spheres:
   (a) $x^2 + y^2 + z^2 - 2x + 3y + 1 = 0$.        *Ans.* $(1, -\frac{3}{2}, 0)$, $\frac{3}{2}$.
   (b) $x^2 + y^2 + z^2 - 4x - 6z = 0$.

   (c) $x^2 + y^2 + z^2 - x + 4y + 10 = 0$.      *Ans.* $(-\frac{1}{2}, -2, 0)$, $\dfrac{\sqrt{23}}{2}$.

   (d) $x^2 + y^2 + z^2 - 12y + 6z - 5 = 0$.
   (e) $x^2 + y^2 + z^2 - 4x + 5y + 8z + 25 = 0$.

2. What geometrical figure corresponds to the equation

$$(x - 3)^2 + (y - 4)^2 + (z - 5)^2 = 0?$$

3. Find the equation of the spheres determined by the following conditions:
   (a) Center (2, 3, 4) and radius 5.
          *Ans.* $x^2 + y^2 + z^2 - 4x - 6y - 8z + 4 = 0$.
   (b) Center (0, 1, 2) and radius $\frac{5}{2}$.
   (c) Center (3, 0, $-$ 2) and radius 1.
   (d) Center ($-$1, 3, 2) and radius $\sqrt{3}$.

4. What geometrical figure is represented by each of the following equations?
   (a) $z = \sqrt{25 - (x - 2)^2 + (y - 3)^2}$.
   (b) $z = 3 + \sqrt{25 - (x - 2)^2 + (y - 3)^2}$.

5. Find the equation of the sphere whose center is (2, $-$ 2, 1) and which is tangent to the $yz$-plane.      *Ans.* $x^2 + y^2 + z^2 - 4x + 4y - 2z + 5 = 0$.

6. Show that the surfaces determined by the conditions given below are spheres:
   (a) The set of all points which are twice as far from (7, 1, $-$ 3) as from $(-\frac{5}{4}, -2, \frac{3}{2})$.
   (b) The set of all points for which the sum of the squares of the distances of any one from (4, $-$ 5, 1) and (0, 2, 4) is 64.

7. Find the equation of the sphere which is concentric with (has the same center as) $x^2 + y^2 + z^2 - 6x + 4z - 36 = 0$ and passes through (2, 5, $-$ 7).
          *Ans.* $x^2 + y^2 + z^2 - 6x + 4z = 38$.

8. Find the equation of the tangent plane (the plane that touches the sphere at one point) to each of the following spheres at the given point:
   (a) $x^2 + y^2 + z^2 - 14 = 0$ at (3, $-$ 2, 1).     *Ans.* $3x - 2y + z - 14 = 0$.
   (b) $x^2 + y^2 + z^2 - 6x + 4z - 36 = 0$ at (1, 6, $-$ 5).
          *Ans.* $2x - 6y + 3z + 49 = 0$.

(c)   $x^2 + y^2 + z^2 - 4x - 2y + 6z = 0$ at $(0, 0, -6)$.

**9.** What condition must we place on $K$ in terms of $G$, $H$, and $I$ in (46) in order that the equation represent a real sphere?

$$Ans. \ \ K < \frac{G^2 + H^2 + I^2}{4}.$$

Let us continue our exploration of second degree equations in $x$, $y$, and $z$ by seeking the geometrical figure that represents

**(47)**                                      $z = x^2 + y^2$.

To determine the geometrical representation of equations we should try to develop some general procedure. One such procedure might be to take sections of the surface by planes and to try to recognize the nature of these sections. Generally, it is useful to take sections cut out by planes parallel to one of the coordinate planes. In the present case let us try planes parallel to the $xy$-plane. Such planes, as we learned in Section 3, have equations of the form $z = $ constant.

To be specific, let us try $z = 5$. Then the coordinates of all of the points on the surface belonging to (47) and for which $z = 5$ must satisfy the equation

**(48)**                                      $5 = x^2 + y^2$.

What collection of points lying in the plane $z = 5$ corresponds to (48)? Our knowledge of plane coordinate geometry suggests a circle with radius $\sqrt{5}$. In the present case this circle, if it is one, must lie in the plane $z = 5$. The center of the circle would most likely be $(0, 0, 5)$. Let us see if the circle is the correct locus. Any point in the plane $z = 5$ has the coordinates $(x, y, 5)$. The set of all such points which are $\sqrt{5}$ units from $(0, 0, 5)$ must, by the distance formula (1), satisfy the equation

$$\sqrt{(x - 0)^2 + (y - 0)^2 + (5 - 5)^2} = \sqrt{5}$$

or

$$x^2 + y^2 = 5.$$

Hence the section cut out of the figure corresponding to $z = x^2 + y^2$ by the plane $z = 5$ is a circle lying in the plane $z = 5$, with center at $(0, 0, 5)$ and radius $\sqrt{5}$.

If in place of $z = 5$ we had used $z = 10$, the curve cut out would have been $x^2 + y^2 = 10$ and so on. That is, the higher we cut the figure, the larger the radius of the circle. At the plane $z = 0$, that is, at the $xy$-plane, the circle is $x^2 + y^2 = 0$; that is, the circle becomes a point.

We now have a picture of the figure corresponding to (47). Figure 21-18 puts together what we have learned by our analysis. This figure is called a paraboloid. Moreover, this particular paraboloid is a figure of revolution, for consider the curve in which the $xz$-plane cuts the figure. The

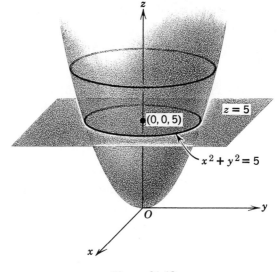

**Figure  21-18**

equation of the $xz$-plane is $y = 0$, and if we set $y = 0$ in the equation $z = x^2 + y^2$, we obtain $z = x^2$ which is the equation of a parabola in the two-dimensional coordinate system of $x$ and $z$. If we rotate this parabola around the $z$-axis, each point will describe a circle. This is exactly what we found to be the cross section of the paraboloid at any $z$-level. Not all paraboloids are figures of revolution, as some of the exercises will point out.

The procedure that we used to determine the figure or locus representing $z = x^2 + y^2$ was to make sections by a collection of planes. Another helpful device is to determine whether the figure is symmetric with respect to any of the coordinate planes. We note in (47) that if we were to replace $x$ by $-x$, the equation would remain the same. This means that if $(a, b, c)$ are the coordinates of any point satisfying the equation, $(-a, b, c)$ would also satisfy the equation. The two points $(a, b, c)$ and $(-a, b, c)$ are symmetrically placed with respect to the $yz$-plane. Then whatever the figure is in front of the $yz$-plane it will also be behind that plane. Likewise, because equation (47) is unaltered when $y$ is replaced by $-y$, the figure is symmetrical with respect to the $xz$-plane. Hence whatever the figure may be to the right of the $xz$-plane it will also be to the left. The consequence of the two symmetries is that if we determine what the figure looks like in the first octant and the octant immediately below it, we shall know what the figure is in all eight octants.

Insofar as the analysis of the figure belonging to $z = x^2 + y^2$ is concerned, since we know what the figure is, the discussion of its symmetries only confirms what we have already found. However, in attempts to determine the figure corresponding to an equation the use of symmetry can be very helpful.

Before terminating the discussion of the surface belonging to $z = x^2 + y^2$, let us note a fact that will be helpful in other connections. The section of the paraboloid by the plane $z = 5$ proved to be a circle. The equations that describe this circle are $x^2 + y^2 = 5$ and $z = 5$. *Both equations are needed.* Clearly, $z = 5$ alone describe a plane and, although we do not know as yet what locus in three-dimensional space corresponds to $x^2 + y^2 = 5$,* we can certainly see that this equation alone does not describe the circle in question. For example, all the points in the $xy$-plane itself which are $\sqrt{5}$ units from the origin also satisfy the equation $x^2 + y^2 = 5$. The point, then, is that a curve in space, like a line is space, must be specified by means of two equations.

## EXERCISES

1. Describe in words the surfaces represented by the following equations:
   (a) $z = 3x^2 + 3y^2$.
   (b) $y = x^2 + z^2$.
   (c) $4x = y^2 + z^2$.
   (d) $z = x^2 + 4y^2$.
   (e) $x = y^2 + 4z^2$.
   (f) $z = x^2 + y^2 + 5$.
   (g) $x + 4 = y^2 + z^2$.
   (h) $z = x^2 + 4y^2 + 7$.
   (i) $cz = \dfrac{x^2}{a^2} + \dfrac{y^2}{b^2}$.

2. What are the equations of the curve in which the paraboloid $z = x^2 + 4y^2$ cuts the following planes?
   (a) The $yz$-plane.
      *Ans.* $z = 4y^2$, $x = 0$.
   (b) The $xz$-plane.
   (c) The plane $z = 5$.
      *Ans.* $x^2 + 4y^2 = 5$, $z = 5$.
   (d) The plane $y = 5$.

3. The focus of a paraboloid of revolution is the focus of the generating parabola.
   (a) Find the coordinates of the focus of the paraboloid $z = (1/4p)(x^2 + y^2)$.
      *Ans.* $(0, 0, p)$.
   (b) Find the diameter of the circular section in the focal plane, that is, at the level of the focus.
      *Ans.* $4p$.

4. Suppose that one wishes to use the finite zone of the paraboloid of revolution $z = (1/4p)(x^2 + y^2)$ cut off by the plane $z = $ constant as a radio or an optical reflector. The circular section cut out by the plane is called the aperture and the finite segment cut off on the axis is called the depth.
   (a) Find the equation of the paraboloid of revolution whose aperture diameter at depth $c$ is $2a$.
      *Ans.* $z = (c/a^2)(x^2 + y^2)$.
   (b) Find the coordinates of the focus of this paraboloid. *Ans.* $(0, 0, a^2/4c)$.

We have been guided by two-dimensional coordinate geometry in an effort to acquire some knowledge of the figures that belong to second degree equations in $x$, $y$, and $z$. Let us pursue this analogy. In two dimensions we know that

**(49)** $$\frac{x^2}{a^2} + \frac{y^2}{b} = 1$$

is the equation of an ellipse with semimajor axis $a$ and semiminor axis $b$. If we introduce one more coordinate or variable, $z$, the analogue of (49)

*We shall discuss this equation later.

becomes

**(50)**
$$\frac{x^2}{a^2} + \frac{y^2}{b^2} + \frac{z^2}{c^2} = 1.$$

Let us determine the figure that represents (50).

We shall try the device already used of cutting the surface by planes parallel to the $xy$-plane. A plane parallel to the $xy$-plane is represented by $z = k$, where $k$ is a constant. If we substitute $k$ for $z$ in (50), we obtain

$$\frac{x^2}{a^2} + \frac{y^2}{b^2} + \frac{k^2}{c^2} = 1.$$

Since $k$ is a constant, let us write the equation as

**(51)**
$$\frac{x^2}{a^2} + \frac{y^2}{b^2} = 1 - \frac{k^2}{c^2} = \frac{c^2 - k^2}{c^2}.$$

This equations suggests the ellipse. To write it in the form (49) let us divide both sides by $(c^2 - k^2)/c^2$. This gives

**(52)**
$$\frac{x^2}{\frac{a^2}{c^2}(c^2 - k^2)} + \frac{y^2}{\frac{b^2}{c^2}(c^2 - k^2)} = 1.$$

The equation is entirely analogous to (49). The kind of argument we used to show that the section $z = 5$ of $z = x^2 + y^2$ is a circle in the plane $z = 5$ tells us here that equation (52) coupled with the equation $z = k$ defines an ellipse lying in the plane $z = k$.

The semimajor axis of the ellipse (52) is

**(53)**
$$\frac{a}{c}\sqrt{c^2 - k^2}$$

and the semiminor axis is

**(54)**
$$\frac{b}{c}\sqrt{c^2 - k^2}.$$

Then the sizes of these axes and consequently the size of the ellipse depends on $k$. When $k = 0$, these axes are $a$ and $b$. But as $k$ increases, the sizes of the axes decrease, and so does the ellipse. When $k = c$, both axes are 0 and the ellipse becomes a point. When $k > c$, there is no curve at all corresponding to (52). As $k$ decreases from 0 and so takes on negative values, the story is the same because formulas (53) and (54) involve $k^2$.

We now have a fairly good picture of what the figure corresponding to (50) is. Starting with the elliptical cross section in the $xy$-plane, the cross sections higher and higher above this one are smaller and smaller ellipses which at $k = c$ shrink to a point. The same is true below. Figure 21-19 shows what the surface looks like. It is called an ellipsoid. It has three axes in place of the two in the ellipse. These axes are $AA'$, $BB'$, and $CC'$. The

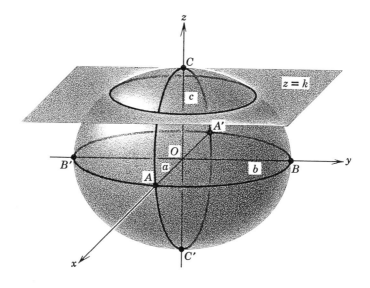

**Figure 21-19**

lengths of the semi-axes are $a$, $b$, and $c$, respectively, as we see from our analysis.

The general ellipsoid, that is, the figure we have just obtained, is not a figure of revolution because one could not generate the surface by rotating a curve around an axis. However, in a special case, $b$ might happen to equal $c$. Then the curve $ABA'$ rotated around the $x$-axis would generate the surface. If $a$ is larger than $b$ and $c$ and if $b = c$, we have the surface of a football. This special case is also called a prolate spheroid. If $a$ is less than $b$ and $c$ and if $b$ still equals $c$, the figure is called an oblate spheroid.

## EXERCISES

1. Describe the surfaces represented by the following equations:
   (a) $\dfrac{x^2}{2} + \dfrac{y^2}{4} + \dfrac{z^2}{6} = 1$.
   (b) $x^2 + 4y^2 + 9z^2 = 36$.
   (c) $x^2 + 4y^2 + 9z^2 = 100$.
   (d) $x^2 + 4y^2 + 4z^2 = 100$.
   (e) $4x^2 + 4y^2 + z^2 = 36$.

2. Describe the curves cut out on the coordinate planes by the following surfaces:
   (a) $x^2 + 4y^2 + 9z^2 = 36$.
   (b) $x^2 + 4y^2 + 4z^2 = 36$.

3. Write the equations of the curve cut out by the plane $z = 1$ on the surface $x^2 + 4y^2 + 9z^2 = 36$.     *Ans.* $x^2 + 4y^2 = 27, z = 1$.

4. In two-dimensional coordinate geometry the equation of the circle is a special case of the equation of the ellipse. Is the corresponding relation true for sphere and ellipsoid?

5. Describe the sections of the surface $x^2 + 4y^2 + 9z^2 = 36$ made by planes $x = k$.

6. Guided by equation (42) for the sphere, guess what figure represents the equation
$$\frac{(x-2)^2}{16} + \frac{(y-3)^2}{25} + \frac{(z-4)^2}{36} = 1.$$

We know from our work in two-dimensional coordinate geometry that the equations

$$\frac{x^2}{a^2} + \frac{y^2}{b^2} = 1 \quad \text{and} \quad \frac{x}{a^2} - \frac{y^2}{b^2} = 1$$

have different loci. We have in (50) an analogous case of the left-hand equation. Now let us investigate a three-dimensional analogy of the right-hand equation. Specifically, let us consider

**(55)**
$$\frac{x^2}{a^2} + \frac{y^2}{b^2} - \frac{z^2}{c^2} = 1.$$

We can determine the surface representing this equation as readily as we handled equation (50). Suppose that we consider sections cut out by planes parallel to the $xy$-plane. Let $z = k$ be one such plane. Then in the plane of $z = k$, $x$ and $y$ satisfy the equation

**(56)**
$$\frac{x^2}{a^2} + \frac{y^2}{b^2} - \frac{k^2}{c^2} = 1.$$

To see what the section in the plane $z = k$ looks like, let us first write this equation as

$$\frac{x^2}{a^2} + \frac{y^2}{b^2} = 1 + \frac{k^2}{c^2} = \frac{c^2 + k^2}{c^2} ;$$

**Figure 21-20**

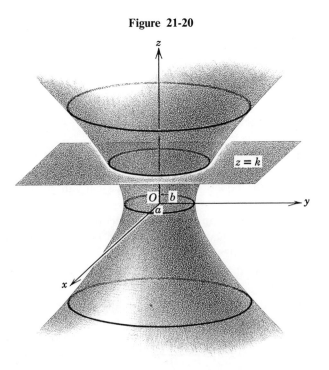

if we divide both sides by $(c^2 + k^2)/c^2$, we obtain

**(57)**
$$\frac{x^2}{\dfrac{a^2}{c^2}(c^2 + k^2)} + \frac{y^2}{\dfrac{b^2}{c^2}(c^2 + k^2)} = 1.$$

We see that each section is an ellipse whose semimajor axis is

$$\frac{a}{c}\sqrt{c^2 + k^2}$$

and whose semiminor axis is

$$\frac{b}{c}\sqrt{c^2 + k^2}\ .$$

If we start with $k = 0$, we see that the section is an ellipse with semimajor axis $a$ and semiminor axis $b$. However, as $k$ increases, both axes increase. Moreover, no matter how large $k$ becomes, there is still an elliptical section. The analogous facts hold for negative $k$. The shape of the surface is now clear and is shown in Fig. 21-20. This surface is called a hyperboloid of one sheet.

## EXERCISES

1. Describe the surface represented by each of the following equations:

   (a) $\dfrac{x^2}{9} + \dfrac{y^2}{12} - \dfrac{z^2}{16} = 1.$

   (b) $x^2 + 4y^2 - 9z^2 = 36.$

   (c) $9x^2 + y^2 - z^2 = 36.$
   (d) $9x^2 - y^2 + z^2 = 36.$
   (e) $9x^2 - 16y^2 + 4z^2 = 64.$

2. Describe the curves cut out on the surface $9x^2 + 4y^2 - z^2 = 36$ by the coordinate planes.

3. Describe the curves cut out on the surface $4x^2 + 9y^2 - z^2 = 36$ by the planes $y = k$.

4. Describe the surface represented by the equation $4x^2 + 4y^2 - 9z^2 = 36.$

5. Write the equations of the curve cut out on $x^2 + 2y^2 - 4z^2 = 5$ by the plane $z = 3$.

In the equation

$$\frac{x^2}{a^2} + \frac{y^2}{b^2} + \frac{z^2}{c^2} = 1,$$

which represents the ellipsoid, all three of the signs of the terms on the left side are positive. In the equation

$$\frac{x^2}{a^2} + \frac{y^2}{b^2} - \frac{z^2}{c^2} = 1,$$

which represents the hyperboloid of one sheet, only two of the variable terms have positive signs. It is possible to have the equation

**(58)**
$$\frac{x^2}{a^2} - \frac{y^2}{b^2} - \frac{z^2}{c^2} = 1,$$

in which only one of the variable terms has a positive sign. Let us determine the shape of the surface that represents (58).

We may as well try the method that has worked well so far. We shall consider sections of the surface cut out by planes $z = k$. Then in the plane $z = k$ the section has the equation

$$\frac{x^2}{a^2} - \frac{y^2}{b^2} - \frac{k^2}{c^2} = 1$$

or

$$\frac{x^2}{a^2} - \frac{y^2}{b^2} = 1 + \frac{k^2}{c^2} = \frac{c^2 + k^2}{c^2}.$$

If we divide by $(c^2 + k^2)/c^2$, the equation of the section becomes

**(59)**
$$\frac{x^2}{\frac{a^2}{c^2}(c^2 + k^2)} - \frac{y^2}{\frac{b^2}{c^2}(c^2 + k^2)} = 1.$$

We note first of all that the section has the equation of a hyperbola. The semimajor axis is

**(60)**
$$\frac{a}{c}\sqrt{c^2 + k^2}$$

and the semiminor axis is

**(61)**
$$\frac{b}{c}\sqrt{c^2 + k^2}.$$

When $k = 0$, these semi-axes are $a$ and $b$. However, as $k$ increases, both semi-axes increase. The fact that the semimajor axes increase means geometrically that the branches of the hyperbolas are farther apart. We learned also in studying the hyperbola that the spread of a hyperbola can be gauged by the two lines called the asymptotes. The slopes of these asymptotes are $b/a$ and $-b/a$ when $a$ is the semimajor axis and $b$, the semiminor axis. In our case, for each value of $k$, the semimajor axis is given by (60) and the semiminor axis by (61). The ratio of (61) to (60) is constant, namely $b/a$. Hence all the hyperbolas cut out by the planes $z = k$ have the same asymptotes. If we were to plot each of these hyperbolas in the *same* $xy$-plane, they would look as in Fig. 21-21. However, as $k$ increases, these hyperbolas lie one above the other or, when $k$ is negative and decreasing, one below the other.

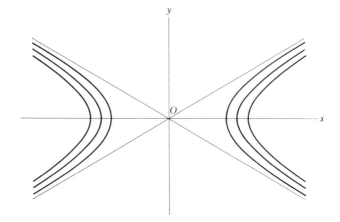

**Figure  21-21**


   This analysis suggests that the surface corresponding to (58) looks as in Fig. 21-22. This surface is called a hyperboloid of two sheets. It is said to lie along the *x*-axis because it opens up in the positive and negative *x*-directions.


## EXERCISES

**1.** To verify that our picture in Fig. 21-22 is correct, let us consider sections of the hyperboloid of two sheets made by planes $x = k$. Determine from (58) what the equations of these sections are; decide from these equations what the geometric character of the sections should be; see if this conclusion is borne out by Fig. 21-22.


**Figure  21-22**

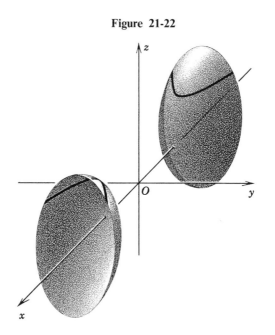

**2.** Describe the surface represented by each of the following equations:

(a) $\dfrac{x^2}{36} - \dfrac{y^2}{9} - \dfrac{z^2}{4} = 1.$           (e) $-\dfrac{x^2}{4} + \dfrac{y^2}{9} - \dfrac{z^2}{36} = 1.$

(b) $x^2 - 4y^2 - 9z^2 = 36.$

(c) $x^2 - 8y^2 - 2z^2 = 16.$           (f) $-\dfrac{x^2}{3} - \dfrac{y^2}{4} + \dfrac{z^2}{12} = 1.$

(d) $x^2 - y^2 - z^2 = 16.$

**3.** Describe the curves cut out on the surface $4x^2 - 3y^2 - 2z^2 = 24$ by the planes $y = k$.

**4.** Write the equations of the curve cut out on the surface $4x^2 - 9y^2 - 36z^2 = 1$ by the plane $z = 4$.

The hyperboloids of one sheet and two sheets are represented, respectively, by the equations

**(62)** $$\frac{x^2}{a^2} + \frac{y^2}{b^2} - \frac{z^2}{c^2} = 1$$

and

**(63)** $$\frac{x^2}{a^2} - \frac{y^2}{b^2} - \frac{z^2}{c^2} = 1.$$

In both equations all of the terms are of the second degree. On the other hand, the paraboloid is represented by the equation

$$z = x^2 + y^2$$

or, more generally, as some of the exercises in the second list of this section show, by

**(64)** $$z = \frac{x^2}{a^2} + \frac{y^2}{b^2}.$$

It would seem likely that an equation of the form

**(65)** $$z = \frac{x^2}{a^2} - \frac{y^2}{b^2}$$

would represent still another type of surface, because it has something of the paraboloidal character of (64) and something of the hyperboloidal character of (62) and (63). Let us determine the nature of the surface represented by (65). We shall use the method applied previously; that is, we shall consider sections of the surface cut out by planes $z = k$. If we let $z = k$ in (65), we obtain

**(66)** $$\frac{x^2}{a^2} - \frac{y^2}{b^2} = k.$$

If $k$ is positive, these sections are certainly hyperbolas. Moreover, if we write (66) in the form

**(67)**
$$\frac{x^2}{a^2 k} - \frac{y^2}{b^2 k} = 1,$$

we can see what the semimajor and semiminor axes are, namely,

$$a\sqrt{k} \qquad \text{and} \qquad b\sqrt{k}.$$

The major axis is parallel to the $x$-axis and the minor axis parallel to the $y$-axis. These axes increase as $k$ increases and, because their ratio, $a/b$, is constant, we have a family of hyperbolas very much like those which we encountered in discussing (58). However, when $k$ is negative, that is, when the section is below the $xy$-plane the form (67) is no longer the standard one for the hyperbola. Suppose that $k$ is $-5$. Then (67) becomes

**(68)**
$$\frac{x^2}{5a^2} - \frac{y^2}{5b^2} = -1.$$

This equation also represents a hyperbola but, as we learned in Chapter 7, Section 5, Exercise 17, this hyperbola opens out along the $y$-axis; that is, its major or transverse axis lies along the $y$-axis and its minor or conjugate axis lies along the $x$-axis. In other words, when $k$ is negative, the hyperbolic sections are turned $90°$ as compared with the sections formed when $k$ is positive.

The transition from the hyperbolic sections that lie above the $xy$-plane, that is, the sections determined by $z = k$ when $k$ is positive, to the hyperbolic sections that lie below the $xy$-plane, that is, the sections determined by $z = k$ when $k$ is negative, occurs at $k = 0$. When $k = 0$, we see from (65) or (66) that the section is

$$\frac{x^2}{a^2} - \frac{y^2}{b^2} = 0$$

and the curve or figure corresponding to this equation consists of two straight lines.

Although we now know the sections of the surface corresponding to (65), it is still not easy to visualize the surface. One can also consider sections made by planes $x = k$ in order to obtain additional aid toward visualization. These sections are parabolas opening downward. Figure 21-23 shows the surface. It is called a hyperbolic paraboloid and around the origin it has the shape of a saddle. For this reason it is also called the saddle-shaped surface.

## EXERCISES

**1.** To verify that Fig. 21-23 is correct, consider the section of the surface corresponding to (65) made by the plane $y = 0$. What is the shape of this section? Does this shape indeed appear in Fig. 21-23?

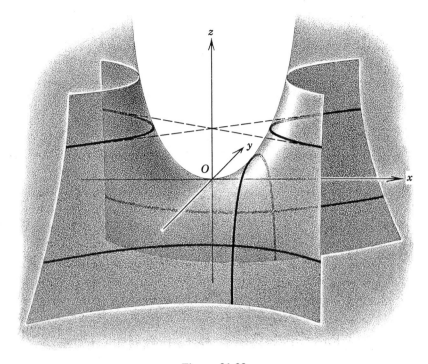

**Figure 21-23**

2. What is the shape of a section of the surface corresponding to (65) made by the following planes:
   (a)  The plane $x = 0$.                    (c)  The plane $x = k$.
   (b)  The plane $y = 5$.                    (d)  The plane $y = k$.

3. Describe the surface represented by each of the following equations:
   (a)  $z = x^2 - y^2$.                       (c)  $4x = y^2 - 2z^2$.
   (b)  $z = y^2 - 4x^2$.
                                              (d)  $2y = \dfrac{x^2}{9} - \dfrac{z^2}{4}$.

4. Describe the surface represented by each of the following equations:

   (a)  $y = \dfrac{x^2}{a^2} - \dfrac{z^2}{c^2}$.                    (b)  $x = \dfrac{y^2}{b^2} - \dfrac{z^2}{c^2}$.

   The equations of the second degree that we have analyzed so far do not include the type

**(69)**                         $x^2 + y^2 - z^2 = 0.$

Here all terms are of the second degree, as in the case of spheres, ellipsoids, and hyperboloids, but the constant term is 0. To obtain a clue to the nature of the surface, consider sections made by the planes $z = k$. The equation of the section in the plane $z = k$ is

$$x^2 + y^2 = k^2.$$

Clearly, these sections are circles, and the radii of these circles increase as $k$ increases through positive values or decreases through negative values. It is

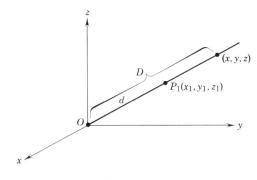

**Figure 21-24**

relatively easy to visualize this surface. At the origin it consists of only a single point and then, above and below, it widens out as though there were two funnels placed tip-to-tip and opening up in opposite directions. However, we can say a little more about it, which is not quite obvious from (69).

Suppose that $P_1$ with coordinates $(x_1, y_1, z_1)$ is a point on the surface (Fig. 21-24). By formulas (2), (3), and (4) the line joining this point to the origin has the direction cosines

$$\frac{x_1}{d}, \ \frac{y_1}{d}, \ \frac{z_1}{d}$$

where $d$ is the distance $OP_1$. Now let us use the fact that the origin is a point on this line for which we have the direction cosines. Then by equations (38), the equations of this line are

$$x = 0 + \frac{x_1}{d} D, \quad y = 0 + \frac{y_1}{d} D, \quad z = 0 + \frac{z_1}{d} D$$

**Figure 21-25**

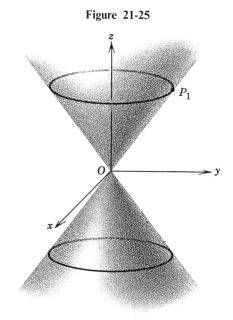

where $D$ is the distance from $(x, y, z)$ to $(0, 0, 0)$. If we substitute these values of $x$, $y$, and $z$ in (69) and remember that $(x_1, y_1, z_1)$ lies on the surface, we have that any $(x, y, z)$ which lies on the line joining the origin to a point $P_1$ on the surface also lies on the surface. Then if $P_1$ (Fig. 21-25) moves along the circular section in the plane $z = k$, the line joining $P_1$ to the origin will always lie on the surface no matter where $P_1$ is on the circle. Such a surface is called a cone.

More generally, a *cone* is the surface formed by the lines which join a fixed point (the origin in our example) to the points of a curve (the circle in the example). Of course, the curve need not be a circle. The lines are called the *elements* of the cone.

## EXERCISES

**1.** Describe the surface represented by each of the following equations:
   (a)  $x^2 + y^2 - 16z^2 = 0$.                  (c)  $4x^2 - y^2 - 16z^2 = 0$.
   (b)  $4x^2 + y^2 - 16z^2 = 0$.                  (d)  $4x^2 - y^2 + 16z^2 = 0$.

**2.** Find the equation of the cone whose vertex is the origin and whose elements cut the circle $x^2 + y^2 = 4$ and $z = 1$.                  *Ans.* $x^2 + y^2 - 4z^2 = 0$.

There is another major type of second degree equation which we have not examined as yet. All of the second degree equations thus far considered contain terms involving $x$, $y$, and $z$. Suppose, however, that we consider the equation

$$(70) \qquad\qquad x^2 + y^2 = 25.$$

What surface does it represent? One's first thought is that this equation does not represent a surface but a curve and, in fact, a circle. However, we had occasion in discussing the equations of planes to consider the equation

$$x + y - 5 = 0,$$

and there we learned that this equation *interpreted in a three-dimensional coordinate system* represents a plane, whereas interpreted in a two-dimensional coordinate system it represents a line. Likewise, (70) interpreted in a three-dimensional coordinate system represents a surface, whereas interpreted in a two-dimensional coordinate system it does, indeed, represent a circle. The question now is, what surface does (70) represent in a three-dimensional system?

It may help our thinking if we write (70) as

$$(71) \qquad\qquad x^2 + y^2 + 0z^2 = 25.$$

Now we try our usual method of analysis. We examine the curves cut out on the surface by planes $z = k$. No matter what the constant $k$, the substitution of its value in (71) gives $x^2 + y^2 = 25$. In the plane $z = k$, this

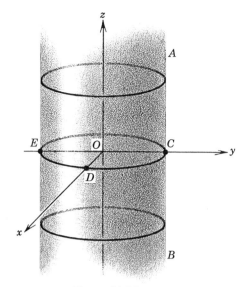

**Figure 21-26**

equation does represent a circle with center at $(0, 0, k)$ and radius 5. This curve is the same no matter what $k$ is. Hence the sections of the surface made by planes $z = k$ are always circles. As $k$ increases from 0, the circles lie one above the other, and as $k$ decreases from 0, the circles lie below one another. The picture that we obtain is shown in Fig. 21-26. The surface is a cylinder.

By definition a *cylinder* is a surface generated by a line called the generator which moves parallel to its original position and intersects a fixed curve called the directrix. In the case of the cylinder in Fig. 21-26, we can think of the surface as generated by the line $AB$ as it moves parallel to its original position while constantly intersecting the fixed circle $CDE$. The equation of a cylinder need not always be of the form (70); that is, one variable need not be absent. When one variable is absent, the generator is parallel to the axis along which that variable is measured.

## EXERCISES

**1.** Describe the surfaces represented by the following equations:
(a) $4x^2 + y^2 = 4$.
(b) $y^2 - 4x = 0$.
(c) $x^2 + z^2 = 25$.
(d) $y^2 + z^2 = 16$.
(e) $z^2 - 4x = 0$.
(f) $x^2 + y^2 + 4x = 0$.
(g) $x^2 - y^2 = 25$.
(h) $xy - 6 = 0$.

**6. *Remarks on Further Work in Solid Analytic Geometry.*** The study of the correspondence between equations in $x$, $y$, and $z$ and the figures they represent is only partially complete. The equations in $x$, $y$, and $z$ that we have analyzed have been of the first degree or of the second degree in these variables. However, we have not analyzed all second degree equations. We could very well ask, what surface does the equation

**(72)** $$x^2 + xy + xz + y^2 - 3z^2 = 25$$

represent? We would have difficulty in determining the shape of this surface. One might guess, on the basis of experience with the conic sections, that every second degree equation in $x, y$, and $z$ should represent one of the types that we have already analyzed, that is, ellipsoid, paraboloid, hyperboloid, cylinder, or cone. This is correct, and we could show this by duplicating what we did for second degree equations in $x$ and $y$; that is, we could introduce rotation and translation of axes for three-dimensional coordinate systems and simplify more complicated equations such as (72) so that they will reduce to the forms that we have already studied.

We could also undertake to study the figures corresponding to third and higher degree algebraic equations and those corresponding to transcendental functions such as $z = \sin(x + y)$ and $z = e^{x^2+y^2}$. Moreover, one can use coordinate systems other than the rectangular Cartesian system, just as one uses polar coordinates in addition to rectangular Cartesian coordinates in two dimensions.

However, we shall not pursue these extensions of our subject at this point but shall proceed to the calculus of functions involving two or more independent variables. Some of the ideas that we have omitted will be taken up as we need them in the next two chapters in connection with the calculus material. This chapter is intended primarily to give the fundamental ideas on the geometric representation of equations involving three variables and some of the methods of analyzing such equations.

At the beginning of this chapter we mentioned that we shall also have occasion to work with functions of three independent variables, for example,

$$w = x^2 + y^2 + z^2.$$

We cannot picture such functions because we need three dimensions merely to plot the various points corresponding to sets of $x$-, $y$-, and $z$-values and, fortunately or unfortunately, physical space is limited to three dimensions. One can and does speak of the four numbers representing one set of values of $x, y, z$ and $w$ as being represented by a point and of the collection of all such points as constituting a hypersurface. This geometrical language is sometimes helpful and suggestive. For example, one might be dealing with two equations in the four variables $x, y, z$, and $w$, and to express the fact that there is no set of values for $x, y, z$, and $w$ which satisfies both equations, one might say that the corresponding hypersurfaces do not intersect. But there is no picture for these hypersurfaces.

# CHAPTER TWENTY-TWO
## **PARTIAL DIFFERENTIATION**

**1. Functions of Two or More Variables.** In the introduction to Chapter 21 we considered a few examples of functions of two and three independent variables. Let us look into this notion a little more carefully.

The formula for the area $A$ of a rectangle whose sides are $x$ and $y$ units, namely,

$$(1) \qquad\qquad A = xy,$$

involves the independent variables $x$ and $y$. When we say that $x$ and $y$ are independent, we mean that the values that $x$ can take on are independent of those that $y$ can take on. In working with functions one is usually interested in particular ranges of values for the independent variables. Thus we might be considering rectangles for which one dimension can range from 1 to 5 and the other, say, from 2 to 6. Then the set of possible $x$-values would be $1 \leq x \leq 5$ and the set of possible $y$-values would be $2 \leq y \leq 6$. The word *domain* is used for the entire set of *pairs* of values—one for $x$ and the other for $y$—which can be assigned to $x$ and $y$. Geometrically, the domain is the interior and boundary of the rectangle shown in Fig. 22-1, because the coordinates of any point in this rectangle are a pair of possible values, the first for $x$ and the second for $y$. Since the values of the variable $A$ in (1) are determined when the values of $x$ and $y$ have been chosen, $A$ is the dependent variable.

If we wish to discuss any function of one independent variable then, as we know, we use the notation $y = f(x)$. To discuss any arbitrary function of two independent variables it is customary to use the notation

$$(2) \qquad\qquad z = f(x, y).$$

Here $x$ and $y$ are the independent variables and $z$, the dependent one. The symbol $f$ or $f(x, y)$ can also stand for a particular function. Thus, if we were

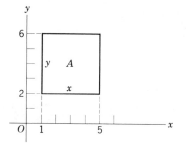

**Figure 22-1**

working with the function

**(3)** $$z = x^2 - y^2 + 2xy + x - y$$

and wished to refer to it without having to repeat all of its terms, we might use $f(x, y)$ to describe the right side.

In using the notation $f(x, y)$ we must note the order of the variables. Thus, if we use the notation $f(3, 5)$ for a function of two variables, we mean the value of the function when 3 is substituted for $x$ and 5 is substituted for $y$. For the function in (3)

$$f(3, 5) = 3^2 - 5^2 + 2 \cdot 3 \cdot 5 + 3 - 5 = 12.$$

If we were careless and substituted 5 for $x$ and 3 for $y$, we would obtain a different value for $z$.

A simple example of a function of three independent variables is the formula for the area of a parallelogram (Fig. 22-2), namely,

**(4)** $$A = xy \sin \theta.$$

Here the three independent variables are $x$, $y$, and $\theta$, whereas $A$ is the dependent variable. The variables might be restricted to certain ranges of values. Thus $x$ might range from 1 to 3, $y$ from 2 to 5, and $\theta$ from 0 to $\pi/2$, the end values included. The domain of the function would then be the set of all possible triplets $(x, y, \theta)$ with $x$, $y$, and $\theta$ having any value in their respective ranges. Geometrically, the domain could be represented by the box shown in Fig. 22-3. The coordinates of any point in the interior or on the boundary of the box are a triplet of numbers in the domain of the function.

**Figure 22-2**

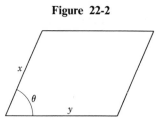

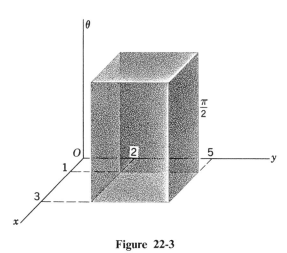

**Figure 22-3**

If one wishes to discuss any function of three independent variables, it is customary to use the notation

**(5)** $$u = f(x, y, z).$$

As in the case of two independent variables, the symbol $f$ or the entire symbol $f(x, y, z)$ can also stand for a specific function which may be lengthy and so can be referred to briefly by this notation. Again, the order in which the variables are written is important. If we deal with the particular function

$$u = x^2 + 2y^2 + 3z^2$$

and use the notation $f(x, y, z)$ to refer to it, then $f(3, -2, 5)$ means the value of the function or of $u$ when 3 is substituted for $x$, $-2$ for $y$, and 5 for $z$. In this case $f(3, -2, 5) = 3^2 + 2(-2)^2 + 3 \cdot 5^2 = 92$.

## EXERCISES

**1.** If $z = x^3 + 3xy - y^2$, what is the value of $z$ when $x$ and $y$ have the following values?

(a) $x = 3, y = 5$.      *Ans.* 63.    (d) $x = 2, y = -2$.

(b) $x = 3, y = 0$.                    (e) $x = -2, y = 2$.    *Ans.* $-24$.

(c) $x = 0, y = 3$.      *Ans.* $-9$.    (f) $x = -3, y = -4$.

**2.** Show that the values of $z$ in the function $z = x^2 - 2xy + y^2$ can never be negative.

**3.** If $z = \sin x \cos y$, what is the value of $z$ when $x$ and $y$ are the following?

(a) $x = \dfrac{\pi}{4}, y = \dfrac{\pi}{2}$.      *Ans.* 0.    (d) $x = \dfrac{3\pi}{2}, y = \pi$.

(b) $x = 0, y = \dfrac{\pi}{4}$.      (e) $x = 2\pi, y = \dfrac{3\pi}{2}$.    *Ans.* 0.

(c) $x = \dfrac{\pi}{4}, y = \dfrac{\pi}{4}$.      *Ans.* $\frac{1}{2}$.

**4.** If $f(x, y) = \dfrac{x^2 y}{x^2 + 3}$ , what is the value of the following?

    (a)  $f(1, 5)$.                        *Ans.* $\frac{5}{4}$.   (c)  $f(5, -3)$.               *Ans.* $-\frac{75}{28}$.

    (b)  $f(0, 5)$.                                        (d)  $f(0, 0)$.

**5.** If $f(x, y, z) = x^2 + 3xyz + z^2$, what is the value of the following?

    (a)  $f(1, -1, 1)$.               *Ans.* $-1$.   (c)  $f(2, -2, -3)$.        *Ans.* 49.

    (b)  $f(0, 0, 1)$.                                (d)  $f(\frac{3}{4}, \frac{1}{2}, \frac{2}{3})$.

**6.** What is the domain of $x$ and $y$ for which the function $z = \sqrt{1 - x^2 - y^2}$ has real values?

**7.** Consider the law of gravitation $F = GMm/r^2$. $G$ is, of course, a constant, but the masses $M$ and $m$ and the distance $r$ between them can take on different values; that is, $M$, $m$, and $r$ are independent variables. To indicate that we wish to consider $F$ as a function of all three variables, we can write $F = f(M, m, r)$. What is the value of the following?

    (a)  $f(2, 3, 4)$.           *Ans.* $3G/8$.  (c)  $f(3, 4, 0)$.       *Ans.* Undefined.

    (b)  $f(2, 3, 5)$.

**8.** If $f(x, y) = \sin(x + y)$, what is $f(0, 0)$, $f(0, \pi)$, $f\left(-\dfrac{\pi}{2}, 0\right)$, $f\left(\dfrac{\pi}{2}, \dfrac{\pi}{4}\right)$?

$$\textit{Ans.}\ \ 0, 0, -1, 1/\sqrt{2}\ .$$

    Let us examine a function that is fundamental in the study of wave motion. Among physical phenomena wave motion is a basic one because light, radio and television messages, and sound usually propagate or move forward in space as waves.

    First, let us consider the plane curve $z = \sin x$ shown in Fig. 22-4 and let $P$ be any point on it with coordinates $(x, z)$. Suppose that the axes are regarded as fixed and the curve is moved to the right (Fig. 22-5) a distance $a$. Then the value of $z$ at a given $x$ is no longer $z = \sin x$ but that which one obtains for the original curve at $x - a$; that is, for a given $x$, the $z$-value is $\sin(x - a)$. The equation of the second curve, then, is $z = \sin(x - a)$.

    Now let us consider the variable $t$ which starts with the value 0 and increases. If we think of the $a$ in $z = \sin(x - a)$ as $t$, then for any positive value of $t$, the function $z = \sin(x - t)$ represents a sine curve which is displaced $t$ units to the right of $z = \sin x$. As $t$ increases, the curve is displaced more and more to the right.

    Suppose now that the curve moves steadily to the right at a constant velocity $c$. The distance it will move to the right in time $t$ is $ct$. If we let the $a$ above be $ct$, the description of the curve at its position at time $t$ is

**Figure 22-4**

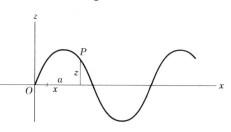

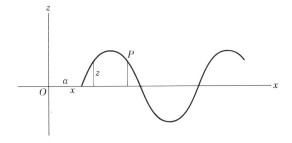

**Figure  22-5**

$z = \sin(x - ct)$. Thus $z = \sin(x - ct)$ represents a shape or curve given initially by $z = \sin x$ and moving to the right with the velocity $c$.

The function $z = \sin(x - ct)$ has just been analyzed in terms of a sinusoidal curve or wave shape that moves to the right, or in terms of a succession of sinusoidal curves, one for each value of $t$. However, the function can also be regarded as a function of two independent variables $x$ and $t$, and the graph should be a surface. Instead of picturing the function as a series of curves successively displaced to the right, let us introduce the $t$-axis and attempt to determine what the surface is like.

We already know that for a fixed $t$ the function $z = \sin(x - ct)$ is the sine curve but displaced a distance $ct$ to the right. To fix $t$ is to cut the surface by a plane $t = $ constant, and we know what that plane section looks like. As $t$ increases, the section remains the same but is displaced farther to the right. Hence the graph of $z = \sin(x - ct)$ is the surface shown in Fig. 22-6.

We see from this method of constructing the surface that fixing $t$ and following the function as $x$ varies amounts to freezing the surface at a particular instant and gliding up and down the waves. On the other hand,

**Figure  22-6**

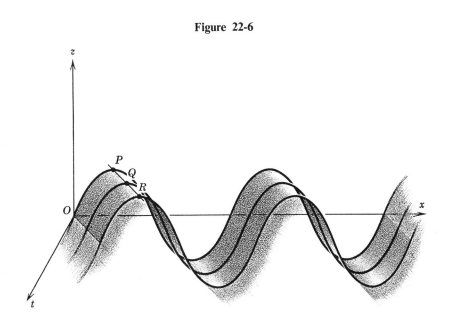

in fixing $x$ and following the function values as $t$ varies, we observe the rising and falling of the surface at a fixed point in space.

The peculiar feature of the function $z = \sin(x - ct)$ is that the two independent variables $x$ and $t$ occur in the fixed combination $x - ct$. When $x$ and $t$ both vary but in such a way as to keep $x - ct$ constant, then $z$ has a constant value. Thus, if $x$ and $t$ are chosen so that $x - ct$ is always $\pi/2$, then $z = 1$. Physically, this choice of $x$- and $t$-values would mean riding the first peak of the wave as it moves out in space and time, that is, staying along the path $PQR$ of Fig. 22-6.

## EXERCISES

1. Describe in graphical terms the difference between $z = \sin(x - 2t)$ and $z = \sin(x - 3t)$.

2. Compare the function $z = 3\sin(x - ct)$ and $z = \sin(x - ct)$.

3. Describe in physical or graphical terms the function $z = \sin(x + ct)$.

4. Describe in graphical terms where the points of the surface of $z = \sin(x - ct)$ are when $x$ and $t$ are chosen so that $x - ct$ always equals $\pi$.

In our work with functions of two and three independent variables we shall be interested in calculus operations, that is, differentiation and integration. As we know from our study of functions of one variable, differentiation and integration involve limit processes and the limits in question must exist. This will be the case if the functions have certain properties.

The first important property is continuity. In the case of functions of one variable we did describe continuity intuitively (Chap. 6, Sect. 2) by stating that the graph of the function, which is a curve, must be constructible with an uninterrupted motion of a pencil. There must be no breaks or gaps. Such an intuitive description of continuity is not adequate for functions of two or more independent variables. We know from our work in Chapter 21 that the graph of a function of two variables is not a curve but a surface. We can describe the continuity of such surfaces in the following intuitive way.

Roughly speaking, continuity means that the surface must be uninterrupted. For example, suppose that one walks in a mountainous region. Then the altitude of each point on the surface is its height above sea level. Continuity would mean that there is no sudden change in altitude at any point. The changes in altitude must be gradual. This description is a bit vague. It will help if we see what the discontinuities might be. If, for example, a surface contains a needle-like projection, the point at which the needle sticks up (it may extend to infinity) is a point of discontinuity because there the altitude changes abruptly. Thus the function $z = 1/(x^2 + y^2)$ has a needle-like projection extending upward to infinity at $(0, 0)$. We can, in fact, visualize this surface. If we take the paraboloid $z = x^2 + y^2$ and replace each $z$-value by its reciprocal, we have the picture. Furthermore, if a surface contains a large rock whose sides rise vertically upward,

the points all around the base are points at which the surface is discontinuous because the altitude changes suddenly there. A cliff, whose wall rises
vertically from a surface, is another example of a discontinuity. The surface
is discontinuous at all points along the base of the cliff because the altitude
changes suddenly there from that of the surface to that at the top of the
cliff. The cliff may be only a very thin ridge rising to a finite or infinite
height. Thus the function $z = 1/(x - y)^2$ is infinite at all points at which
$x = y$, which means at all points along the line $x = y$ in the $xy$-plane.

Sudden drops in the altitude of a surface likewise present discontinuities. These drops may be described as holes. For example, there might be a
hole at one point, and it would not matter whether the hole has a finite
depth or infinite depth. Thus the function $z = -1/(x^2 + y^2)$ has a hole of
infinite depth at $(0, 0)$. The hole may extend over a region, say a crater,
whose walls are vertical. Again, for our purposes it would not matter if the
crater had finite or infinite depth. At the points along the edge of the crater
the altitude changes suddenly, as anyone who walks over the edge can
determine. The kind of hole presented by a chasm is another sort of
discontinuity. Thus the function $z = -1/(x - y)^2$ has a chasm extending
along the line $x = y$ in the $xy$-plane. Each point of the line $x = y$ is a point
of discontinuity.

The function

$$\frac{x^2}{a^2} - \frac{y^2}{b^2} - \frac{z^2}{c^2} = 1$$

presents a double problem. First, we must remember that the calculus deals
with single-valued functions. Hence we must express this implicit function
of $z$ as the two explicit functions

**(6)**     $$z = c\sqrt{\frac{x^2}{a^2} - \frac{y^2}{b^2} - 1} \ , \quad z = -c\sqrt{\frac{x^2}{a^2} - \frac{y^2}{b^2} - 1} \ .$$

Moreover, we know from the picture of this surface (see Fig. 21-22) that
there are no values of $z$ outside the hyperbola $(x^2/a^2) - (y^2/b^2) = 1$.
However within the domains for which $(x^2/a^2) - (y^2/b^2) \geq 1$ each of the
functions is continuous. That is, for an $(x, y)$ within the "shells," the two
functions are continuous.

Let us try to make this idea of continuity a little more precise.
Moreover, because we are going to be interested in differentiation and
because the derivative involves what happens at a particular point, let us
concentrate on the region around one point. We can describe the location
of any point $Q$ on a surface (Fig. 22-7) by the coordinates $(x, y, z)$; the
projection of $Q$ onto the $xy$-plane, which we can think of as sea level, is $Q_0$
with coordinates $(x, y, 0)$; the height or altitude of $Q$ is $z$. Likewise, if $P$ is a
point on the surface with coordinates $(x_0, y_0, z_0)$, the projection of $P$ onto
the $xy$-plane is $P_0$ with coordinates $(x_0, y_0, 0)$. Then, as $Q$ approaches point
$P$ from any direction or along any path on the surface, continuity means
that the $z$-value of $Q$ must approach $z_0$, the $z$-value of $P$. If there should be

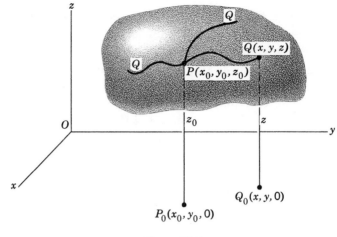

**Figure 22-7**

a sudden drop or sudden rise in the height of the surface at $P_0$, the $z$-values of the variable point $Q$ would not approach the value $z_0$ of $P$, and the surface would be discontinuous at $P$.

Now let us express the notion of continuity in terms of limits. Analytically, the surface is represented by $z = f(x, y)$. The travel of $Q$ to $P$ can be expressed by requiring that the $x$ and $y$ of $Q$'s positions approach the $x_0$ and $y_0$ of $P$'s position. Moreover, because $Q$ can approach $P$ along any path, the $x$ and $y$ can vary in any way as long as $x$ approaches $x_0$ and $y$ approaches $y_0$. Then the statement that $z$ must approach $z_0$ as $x$ and $y$ approach $x_0$ and $y_0$, respectively, can be written

**(7)**
$$\lim_{\substack{x \to x_0 \\ y \to y_0}} z = z_0$$

or

**(8)**
$$\lim_{\substack{x \to x_0 \\ y \to y_0}} f(x, y) = f(x_0, y_0).$$

In the case of functions of more than two independent variables, it is no longer possible to picture the functions because our visual sense is limited to three dimensions whereas we would need four dimensions to picture a function of three variables. The alternative is to resort to analytical definition. We shall not attempt to give the precise analytical definition, but we can give the idea. Let us go back to our statement of what continuity means for a function of two variables. There we said that given any point $P$ on the surface, the $z$-values of a variable point $Q$ on the surface must approach the $z_0$-value of $P$ as $Q$ approaches $P$ or as the $x$-and $y$-values of $Q$ approach the $x_0$ and $y_0$ of $P$. Now, if we have

$$u = f(x, y, z)$$

and if we are considering the continuity of this function at $(x_0, y_0, z_0)$, then when $x$, $y$, and $z$ approach $x_0$, $y_0$, and $z_0$, respectively, by any path whatever, $u = f(x, y, z)$ must approach $u_0 = f(x_0, y_0, z_0)$. In symbols, $f$ is continuous at $(x_0, y_0, z_0)$ if

**(9)** $$\lim_{\substack{x \to x_0 \\ y \to y_0 \\ z \to z_0}} f(x, y, z) = f(x_0, y_0, z_0)$$

for all $(x, y, z)$ which approach $(x_0, y_0, z_0)$.

We propose to consider the differentiation of functions of two or more variables. As in the case of functions of one variable, the differentiability of a function presupposes a little more than continuity. Consider a mountainous surface again. The surface may indeed be continuous or uninterrupted but it may also be very rough or uneven. It may contain crags, which have sharp edges or sharp points. At such edges or points the surface is not differentiable. The essential difficulty at such places is analogous to what we examined in the case of $y = |x|$ (see Chapter 6, Section 2). The sharp corner of this function at $x = 0$ means that there is no derivative there. To be differentiable at a value of $x$ and $y$, the surface of $z = f(x, y)$ must be smooth there or, we can say, there must be a well-defined tangent plane.

The functions that we shall consider will be continuous and differentiable, except perhaps at specific points or along curves that will be easily recognizable. In addition, there is the proviso already made that a function, such as the hyperboloid of two sheets, may be continuous and differentiable in each of its branches but not even exist for the domain between the two sheets.

## EXERCISES

**1.** What value, if any, does the function $z = \dfrac{x^2 + y^2}{x + y}$ have at $(0, 0)$? Is the function continuous there?

*Ans.* No value; no.

**2.** Consider the function $z = 1/(x - y)$. What values, if any, does the function have along the line $x = y$ (in the $xy$-plane)? Is the function continuous along $x = y$? How does the function behave as $x$ and $y$ approach a point $(x_0, y_0)$ on $x = y$ through values of $x$ smaller than $y$ and then through values of $x$ larger than $y$?

**3.** Describe the surface $z = |y|$. Where is it differentiable?

*Ans.* Everywhere except on the $x$-axis.

**4.** (a) Consider the function defined by $z = 1$ for all $x$ and for $y < 2$ and by $z = 3$ for all $x$ and for $y > 2$. Where are the discontinuities of this function?

(b) Answer the same question if $z = 1$ for $x < 2$ and $y < 2$ and $z = 3$ for all other values of $x$ and $y$.

**2. *Partial Differentiation.*** A significant question concerning any function, as we now know from our experiences with functions of one variable, is the rate of change. In the case of functions of two or more variables, there are several different rates of change.

Let us consider the function for the area of a rectangle,

**(10)** $$A = xy.$$

Because $x$ and $y$ are independent variables, we can consider changes in the value of $x$ while $y$ is kept at a fixed value. In this situation $A$ becomes a function of only one variable, $x$, and the familiar notion of instantaneous rate of change, or the derivative, applies to $A$ as a function of $x$ only. To indicate that we are considering the rate of change of $A$ as a function of $x$ only, we use the notations

$$\frac{\partial A}{\partial x} \quad \text{or} \quad A_x$$

and we speak of this derivative as the *partial* derivative of $A$ with respect to $x$. For the function (10), $\partial A / \partial x = y$. Likewise, we can consider the rate of change of $A$ with respect to $y$, while $x$ is kept at any fixed value, and $\partial A / \partial y = x$.

These partial derivatives have familiar geometrical interpretations. Because $A$ is the area of a rectangle of sides $x$ and $y$ (Fig. 22-1), the fact that $\partial A / \partial x = y$ merely means that the rate of change of area with respect to $x$, while $y$ is kept fixed, is the length of the side $y$. A similar interpretation applies to $\partial A / \partial y$.

Since a partial derivative, insofar as the actual differentiation process is concerned, amounts to no more than an ordinary derivative, no new technical knowledge is needed to calculate partial derivatives. We have but to remember that in calculating a partial derivative with respect to $x$, $y$ is to be treated as a constant.

The notion of a partial derivative is readily extended to functions of three or more variables. Thus let us consider the formula for the area of a parallelogram,

$$A = xy \sin \theta.$$

We can consider the rate of change of $A$ with respect to $x$, $y$, or $\theta$. If the rate of change of $A$ with respect to $x$ is desired, $y$ and $\theta$ are held constant. We find, then, that

$$\frac{\partial A}{\partial x} = y \sin \theta, \qquad \frac{\partial A}{\partial y} = x \sin \theta, \qquad \frac{\partial A}{\partial \theta} = xy \cos \theta.$$

Finally, the notion of partial differentiation is extended to higher derivatives. Thus consider the function

$$z = x^3 + 2xy^2.$$

Here

$$z_x = 3x^2 + 2y^2, \qquad z_y = 4xy.$$

We can now ask for the partial derivative of $z_x$ with respect to $x$. This is indicated by $z_{xx}$. Differentiating $z_x$ partially with respect to $x$ yields

$$z_{xx} = 6x.$$

We can also ask for $z_{yy}$ and in the present case

$$z_{yy} = 4x.$$

There are however two other partial derivatives that can be considered. Because $z_x$ is itself a function of $x$ and $y$ we can ask for the partial derivative of $z_x$ with respect to $y$. This partial derivative is indicated by $z_{xy}$ and in the present example it is

$$z_{xy} = 4y.$$

Likewise we can ask for the partial derivative of $z_y$ with respect to $x$ and find from $z_y$ that

$$z_{yx} = 4y.$$

We note that $z_{xy} = z_{yx}$; that is, the order in which we take the partial derivatives does not matter. This result holds under rather general conditions, which we shall not specify precisely, but the importance of the result makes it desirable to note it as a theorem.

**Theorem:**   If the second partial derivatives $z_{xy}$ and $z_{yx}$ of a function $z = f(x, y)$ are continuous, then

**(11)**                                        $$z_{xy} = z_{yx}.$$

As a matter of fact, this theorem can be extended to still higher partial derivatives. For example, if $u = f(x, y, z)$, then

$$u_{xyz} = u_{xzy} = u_{zxy} = \cdots .$$

We have used the notation $\partial z / \partial x$ and $\partial z / \partial y$ as well as $z_x$ and $z_y$ for the first partial derivatives of $z = f(x, y)$. For the second partial derivatives there is the corresponding notation

$$\frac{\partial^2 z}{\partial x^2}, \quad \frac{\partial^2 z}{\partial y \, \partial x}, \quad \frac{\partial^2 z}{\partial x \, \partial y}, \quad \text{and} \quad \frac{\partial^2 z}{\partial y^2}.$$

In the case of $\partial^2 z / \partial y \, \partial x$ the meaning is that $z$ is first differentiated with respect to $x$ and then $\partial z / \partial x$ is differentiated with respect to $y$. In the notation $z_{xy}$ one reads the order of differentiation indicated by the subscripts from left to right.

Although partial differentiation as such involves no new techniques of differentiation, the concept does involve some differences over what holds in the case of ordinary differentiation of functions of one variable. Consider, for example, the equations that enable us to change from rectangular to polar coordinates, namely,

$$x = r \cos \theta, \qquad y = r \sin \theta.$$

We see that $\partial x / \partial r = \cos \theta$. If we were asked to find $\partial r / \partial x$, we might be tempted to use the fact familiar to us from our work with functions of one variable, namely, that $dy/dx = 1/dx/dy$. This fact applied to obtaining $\partial r / \partial x$ would tell us that $\partial r / \partial x = 1/\cos \theta$. However, we know that $r = \sqrt{x^2 + y^2}$ , and from this equation we have

$$\frac{\partial r}{\partial x} = \frac{x}{\sqrt{x^2 + y^2}} = \frac{x}{r} = \cos \theta.$$

We have two different values for $\partial r / \partial x$, and so something is wrong.

Let us go back. When we found $\partial x / \partial r$, we presupposed that $\theta$ is held constant. If we take the same relation $x = r \cos \theta$, write it as $r = x/\cos \theta$, and, keeping $\theta$ constant, find $\partial r / \partial x$, we do indeed obtain $1/\cos \theta$, the reciprocal of $\partial x / \partial r$. However, when we use $r = \sqrt{x^2 + y^2}$ to find $\partial r / \partial x$, we are presupposing that $y$ is constant. If $x$ changes while $y$ is constant, point $P$ (Fig. 22-8) must move so that $\theta$ as well as $r$ varies. Then $\partial r / \partial x$ obtained under the condition that $y$ is held constant is not the same quantity as $\partial r / \partial x$ obtained under the condition that $\theta$ is held constant. In other words, $\partial r / \partial x = 1/\partial x / \partial r$ only if the *same* variable, $\theta$ in the present case, is held constant in obtaining the two derivatives.

Because there are two different quantities $\partial r / \partial x$, it is sometimes necessary to indicate in the notation which one we mean. Thus $(\partial r / \partial x)_\theta$ or $(r_x)_\theta$ would mean the $\partial r / \partial x$ for which $\theta$ is held constant whereas $(\partial r / \partial x)_y$ or $(r_x)_y$ would mean the $\partial r / \partial x$ for which $y$ is held constant.

**Example.**   Find the first and second partial derivatives of the function

$$z = \frac{1}{\sqrt{x^2 + y^2}} .$$

**Figure 22-8**

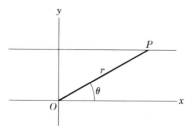

**Solution.**     We can write the function as

$$z = (x^2 + y^2)^{-1/2}.$$

Then, first treating $y$ as a constant we find that

$$z_x = - \frac{x}{(x^2 + y^2)^{3/2}}.$$

Then treating $x$ as a constant yields

$$z_y = - \frac{y}{(x^2 + y^2)^{3/2}}.$$

Now we can ask for the partial derivative of $z_x$ with respect to $x$. Differentiating $z_x$ partially with respect to $x$ by means of the theorem on the quotient of two functions yields

$$z_{xx} = \frac{-(x^2 + y^2)^{3/2} \cdot 1 + x\frac{3}{2}(x^2 + y^2)^{1/2} \cdot 2x}{(x^2 + y^2)^3}$$

$$= \frac{-x^2 - y^2 + 3x^2}{(x^2 + y^2)^{5/2}} = \frac{2x^2 - y^2}{(x^2 + y^2)^{5/2}}.$$

Likewise,

$$z_{yy} = \frac{-(x^2 + y^2)^{3/2} \cdot 1 + y\frac{3}{2}(x^2 + y^2)^{1/2} \cdot 2y}{(x^2 + y^2)^3}$$

$$= \frac{-x^2 - y^2 + 3y^2}{(x^2 + y^2)^{5/2}} = \frac{-x^2 + 2y^2}{(x^2 + y^2)^{5/2}}.$$

Because $z_x$ is itself a function of $x$ and $y$, we can ask for the partial derivatives of $z_x$ with respect to $y$. Using $z_x$ above, we find that

$$z_{xy} = \frac{x \cdot \frac{3}{2}(x^2 + y^2)^{1/2} \cdot 2y}{(x^2 + y^2)^3} = \frac{3xy}{(x^2 + y^2)^{5/2}}.$$

Likewise, $z_y$ is function of $x$ and $y$, and we can ask for the partial derivative of $z_y$ with respect to $x$, that is, for $z_{yx}$. Using $z_y$ above, we find that

$$z_{yx} = \frac{y \cdot \frac{3}{2}(x^2 + y^2)^{1/2} \cdot 2x}{(x^2 + y^2)^3} = \frac{3xy}{(x^2 + y^2)^{5/2}}.$$

## EXERCISES

1. (a)  For the volume formula $V = \pi r^2 h$ find $\partial V / \partial r$ and $\partial V / \partial h$.
Ans. $2\pi rh$; $\pi r^2$.
   (b)  State what each partial derivative means geometrically.
   (c)  Show that $\partial^2 V / \partial r\, \partial h = \partial^2 V / \partial h\, \partial r$.

2. For each of the following functions calculate $z_x$ and $z_y$:
   (a)  $z = \dfrac{a^2 x^2}{x^2 + y^2}$.

   (c)  $z = e^{2x} \sin y$.

   (d)  $z = \sin^{-1} \dfrac{y}{z}$.

   Ans. $z_x = \dfrac{2a^2 x(1 - x^2)}{(x^2 + y^2)^2}$.

   Ans. $z_x = \dfrac{-y}{x\sqrt{x^2 - y^2}}$.

   (b)  $z = \sin xy$.
   Ans. $z_x = y \cos xy$.

3. If $u = \sqrt{x^2 + y^2}$ , find $u_x$, $u_y$, and $u_{xy}$.
   Ans. $u_x = \dfrac{x}{\sqrt{x^2 + y^2}}$ ; $u_{xy} = \dfrac{-xy}{(x^2 + y^2)^{3/2}}$.

4. If $S = \pi r \sqrt{r^2 + h^2}$ , find $\partial S / \partial r$ and $\partial S / \partial h$.

5. If $z = \log \sqrt{x^2 + y^2}$ , show that $\dfrac{\partial^2 z}{\partial x^2} + \dfrac{\partial^2 z}{\partial y^2} = 0$.

6. If $z = \log \dfrac{\sqrt{(x - 1)^2 + y^2}}{\sqrt{(x + 1)^2 + y^2}}$ , show that $\dfrac{\partial^2 z}{\partial x^2} + \dfrac{\partial^2 z}{\partial y^2} = 0$.

7. Show that $\dfrac{\partial^2 z}{\partial t^2} = c^2 \dfrac{\partial^2 z}{\partial x^2}$ for the following functions:
   (a)  $z = (x + ct)^2$.
   (b)  $z = e^{x+ct}$.
   (c)  $z = (x - ct)^2$.
   (d)  $z = \sin(x - ct)$.
   (e)  $z = e^{x-ct} \cos(x - ct)$.

8. If $z = x^2 + 3y^2$, find the instantaneous rate of change of $z$ with respect to $x$ at (2, 5).
Ans. 4.

9. Show that each of the following functions satisfies the equation $z_{xx} + z_{yy} = 0$.
   (a)  $z = \log(x^2 + y^2)$.
   (b)  $z = x^2 - y^2$.
   (c)  $z = 3x^2 - 3y^2$.
   (d)  $z = e^x \cos y$.
   (e)  $z = \tan^{-1} \dfrac{y}{x}$.

10. If $u = 3x^2 + 2y^2 + z^2$, find $u_{xy}$.
Ans. $u_{xy} = 0$.

11. If $u = 3x^2 + 2xy^2 + z^2$, find $u_{yx}$.

12. If $u = e^{ax} \sin y \cos z$, find
Ans. $u_{yz} = -e^{ax} \cos y \sin z$.

13. If $u = \sqrt{x^2 + y^2 + z^2}$ , find $u_x$.

**14.** If $u = \log\sqrt{x^2 + y^2 + z^2}$ , find $u_y$.    *Ans.* $u_y = \dfrac{y}{x^2 + y^2 + z^2}$ .

**15.** If $u = \dfrac{1}{\sqrt{x^2 + y^2 + z^2}}$ , show that $\dfrac{\partial^2 u}{\partial x^2} + \dfrac{\partial^2 u}{\partial y^2} + \dfrac{\partial^2 u}{\partial z^2} = 0$.

**3. The Geometrical Meaning of the Partial Derivatives.** It is always helpful in mathematical work to interpret geometrically the algebraic or analytical ideas. Let us do so for the partial derivatives of a function. Consider the function

**(12)** $$z = x^2 + 2y^2.$$

We know from our work in the preceding chapter that the graphical interpretation of the equation itself is a paraboloidal surface (Fig. 22-9), whose cross section made by a plane $z = $ constant is an ellipse. The definition of $z_x$ presupposes that we first regard $y$ as a constant. Let $y = 2$. Geometrically this means that we limit ourselves to a section of the surface made by the plane $y = 2$. Such a section is the curve $ABCD$ in the figure. The equations of this curve are, in view of (12),

**(13)** $$z = x^2 + 8, \qquad y = 2.$$

The first equation in (13) relates the $z$- and $x$-values of a point on this curve. We could imagine the actual $xz$-plane of Fig. 22-9 moved two units to the right, and in this plane we have a plane curve whose equation is $z = x^2 + 8$. Hence if we compute $\partial z / \partial x$, we obtain precisely what we obtain when working with a plane curve whose equation in a two-dimensional $(x, z)$-coordinate system is $z = x^2 + 8$. Then $\partial z / \partial x$ is the

**Figure 22-9**

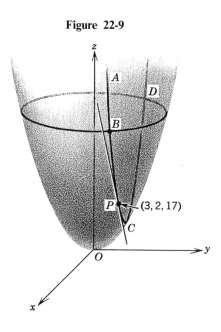

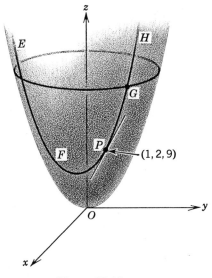

Figure 22-10

slope of this curve at any given $x$. For example, at $x = 3$, since $\partial z / \partial x = 2x$, the slope of the curve is 6. This is the slope of the tangent to the curve $ABCD$ at point $P$ whose coordinates are $(3, 2, 17)$.

Likewise, to interpret $\partial z / \partial y$ geometrically we first think of a plane $x = $ constant, say $x = 1$, cutting the surface (Fig. 22-10). This plane cuts out the curve $EFGH$. Then, by (12),

$$z = 2y^2 + 1, \quad x = 1$$

are the equations of this curve. Again, we may regard

**(14)**                                $z = 2y^2 + 1$

as the equation in the plane $x = 1$, as though the $yz$-plane were moved forward one unit and a $yz$-coordinate system were set up in the plane $x = 1$. Then $\partial z / \partial y = 4y$ represents the slope of the curve $EFGH$ at any value of $y$. Thus at point $P$ whose coordinates are $(1, 2, 9)$ the slope of the curve is 8.

In general, if $z = f(x, y)$, $\partial z / \partial x$ evaluated at $(x, b)$ is the slope of the curve cut out on the surface of $z = f(x, y)$ by a plane $y = b$, and $\partial z / \partial y$ evaluated at $(a, y)$ is the slope of the curve cut out on the surface by the plane $x = a$.

**Example.**   Find the slope of the curve cut out on the paraboloid of elliptical cross section, $z = x^2 + 4y^2$, by the plane $x = 2$ at the point $(2, 1, 8)$.

**Solution.**   What we want is $\partial z / \partial y$ at the point $(2, 1, 8)$. Now $\partial z / \partial y = 8y$ and at $(2, 1, 8)$, $\partial z / \partial y = 8$.

## EXERCISES

**1.** Find the slope of the curve cut out on the paraboloid $z = 2x^2 + 2y^2$ by the plane $y = 4$ at the point whose abscissa is 3. *Ans.* 12.

**2.** Find the slope of the curve cut out at the point $(2, 1, 5)$ on the surface $z = x^2 + y^2$ by the plane $x = 2$.

**3.** Find the slope of the curve cut out on $z = 3x - 4y + 5$ by the plane $y = 2$ at the point $(1, 1, 4)$. Why is the slope independent of $x$?

**4.** (a)   Find the slope of the curve cut out on the ellipsoid $x^2 + 2y^2 + 3z^2 = 12$ by the plane $y = 2$ at the point $(1, 2, 1)$.
(b)   At what point on this curve is the slope 0?

**5.** Show that the slope at any point of the curve cut out on the surface $z^2 = x^2 + y^2$ by the plane $y = 0$ is the same. Account geometrically for the fact that the slope is constant.

There is another geometrical interpretation of the first partial derivatives of a function $z = f(x, y)$. Consider a surface (Fig. 22-11) and a point $P$ on that surface. Through this point one can draw any number of curves lying on the surface. Each of these curves has a tangent at $P$. Now, it is intuitively obvious that these tangent lines all lie in one plane—the plane which just touches the surface at $P$. This plane is called the tangent plane to the surface at $P$. Let us try to find the equation of this plane. Suppose that the coordinates of $P$ are $(x_0, y_0, z_0)$. Then, since any first degree equation in $x, y,$ and $z$ represents a plane, the equation

**(15)** $$A(x - x_0) + B(y - y_0) + C(z - z_0) = 0$$

represents a plane and, since the equation is satisfied by $x = x_0, y = y_0, z = z_0$, this plane goes through $(x_0, y_0, z_0)$. We shall determine $A, B,$ and $C$ so that the plane (15) is indeed the tangent plane at $P$.

We consider the curve cut out on the surface by a plane $y = y_0$, which passes through $P$. The tangent to this curve at $P$ has the slope $\partial z / \partial x$ evaluated at $(x_0, y_0)$, or $(\partial z / \partial x)_0$. This tangent lies in the plane $y = y_0$ and

**Figure 22-11**

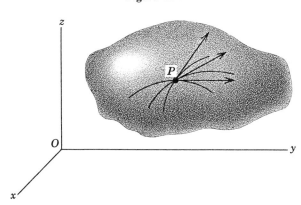

in the plane (15). In the plane $y = y_0$ the equation of the tangent, by (15), is

$$A(x - x_0) + C(z - z_0) = 0.$$

This is the equation of a line in a plane, the plane $y = y_0$, where the coordinates $x$ and $z$ have the same meaning as in the $xz$-plane itself. Then by formula (8) of the appendix to Chapter 3, the slope of the tangent is $-A/C$. Hence

**(16)** $$\left(\frac{\partial z}{\partial x}\right)_0 = -\frac{A}{C}.$$

Likewise, let us consider the curve cut out on the surface by the plane $x = x_0$, which passes through $P$. The tangent to this curve at $P$ has the slope $\partial z/\partial y$ evaluated at $(x_0, y_0)$ or $(\partial z/\partial y)_0$. This tangent lies in the plane $x = x_0$ and the plane (15). In the plane $x = x_0$ the equation of the tangent is

$$B(y - y_0) + C(z - z_0) = 0.$$

This is the equation of a line in a plane, the plane $x = x_0$, and the coordinates $y$ and $z$ have the same meaning as if the line were in the $yz$-plane itself. Then the slope of the tangent is $-B/C$. Hence

**(17)** $$\left(\frac{\partial z}{\partial y}\right)_0 = -\frac{B}{C}.$$

Now, we do not need to determine unique values of $A$, $B$, and $C$. Only the ratios $A/C$ and $B/C$ count, because we can write equation (15) as

**(18)** $$\frac{A}{C}(x - x_0) + \frac{B}{C}(y - y_0) + (z - z_0) = 0.$$

If, therefore, in (18) we replace $A/C$ and $B/C$ by their values in (16) and (17), we obtain

$$\left(\frac{\partial z}{\partial x}\right)_0(x - x_0) + \left(\frac{\partial z}{\partial y}\right)_0(y - y_0) - (z - z_0) = 0$$

as the equation of the plane tangent to the surface $z = f(x, y)$ at $(x_0, y_0, z_0)$. We also see that the direction numbers of the normal to this plane are $\partial z/\partial x$, $\partial z/\partial y$, $-1$, with the partial derivatives evaluated at $(x_0, y_0)$. This result is significant enough to be embodied in a theorem.

**Theorem:**   The equation of the tangent plane to $z = f(x, y)$ at $(x_0, y_0, z_0)$ is

**(19)** $$\frac{\partial z}{\partial x}(x - x_0) + \frac{\partial z}{\partial y}(y - y_0) - (z - z_0) = 0,$$

with the partial derivatives evaluated at $(x_0, y_0)$. Moreover, the direction numbers of the normal to this plane are

$$\left( \frac{\partial z}{\partial x} \right), \left( \frac{\partial z}{\partial y} \right), \ -1.$$

We see, then, another significant geometrical interpretation of the first partial derivatives of $z = f(x, y)$.

## EXERCISES

1. Find the equation of the tangent plane to the following surfaces:
   (a) $z = 2x^2 + 3y^2$ at the point (1, 2, 14).      *Ans.* $4x + 12y - z - 14 = 0$.
   (b) $z = 4x^2 + 6y^2$ at $(1, -1, 10)$.
   (c) $z = 4x^2 - 9y^2$ at $(2, -1, 7)$.      *Ans.* $16x + 18y - z - 7 = 0$.
   (d) $3x^2 + 4y^2 + 8z^2 = 24$ at (2, 1, 1).
   (e) $3x^2 + 4y^2 + 8z^2 = 24$ at $(2, 1, -1)$.      *Ans.* $3x + 2y - 4z - 12 = 0$.
   (f) $z = 3 \sin(x - 2y)$ at $\left( \pi, \frac{\pi}{4}, 3 \right)$.

2. Find the direction numbers of the normal to the sphere $x^2 + y^2 + z^2 = 25$ at the point $(2, 2, \sqrt{17})$ and show that it lies along the radius.      *Ans.* $2, 2, \sqrt{17}$.

3. Show that the normal to the surface $z = \sqrt{xy}$ at any point on the surface is perpendicular to the line joining the point to the origin.

**4. The Directional Derivative.** We mentioned at the beginning of Section 2 that in the case of functions of two or more variables there are several different kinds of rates of change. So far we have studied the partial derivatives. These give the rate of change of the function when only one of the variables changes. Suppose that in the case of a function of two variables both variables change in some definite manner. Is there a corresponding rate of change of the function? Physically, such a rate of change may be quite significant. Suppose that one is traveling down a mountain. The altitude of one's position, as we noted earlier, can be regarded as a function $z$ of the two coordinates $x$ and $y$ which denote the position directly below at sea level. Now, as one descends the mountain, while skiing say, $\partial z / \partial x$ will give the slope of the path of descent if one chooses the path in the plane $y = $ constant through one's position. Likewise, $\partial z / \partial y$ will give the slope of the path of descent if the path lies in the plane $x = $ constant through one's position. However, one may choose to descend along some path for which both $x$ and $y$ change. In fact, one may wish to compare the slopes of the various paths either to select the most gradual one or the steepest one.

To consider the rate of change of the function $z = f(x, y)$ along some path for which both $x$ and $y$ vary, suppose to start with that one is at the position $(x_0, y_0, z_0)$. Let us suppose further that $x$ and $y$ vary so that $(x, y)$ lies along a specific line $PQ$ in the $xy$-plane (Fig. 22-12). Let $s$ denote the positive distance from $P$ at $(x_0, y_0)$ to $Q$ at $(x, y)$. The change in $f$ from its value at $P$ to its value at $Q$ is $f(x, y) - f(x_0, y_0)$. The average rate of change

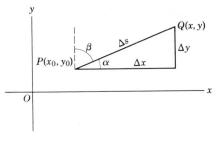

**Figure 22-12**

of $f$ per unit of distance along $PQ$ is

$$\frac{f(x, y) - f(x_0, y_0)}{\Delta s} .$$

The limit of this quotient as $\Delta s$ approaches 0 is the rate of change with respect to horizontal distance of $f$ at $P$, or $(x_0, y_0)$, in the direction of the line segment $PQ$. This rate of change of $f$ is called the directional derivative of $f$ and is denoted by $df/ds$ or $dz/ds$. The word directional is significant because clearly it is the direction of $PQ$ that determines how $f(x, y)$ changes and so determines the derivative. We have, then, by definition,

**(20)** $$\frac{dz}{ds} = \lim_{\Delta s \to 0} \frac{f(x, y) - f(x_0, y_0)}{\Delta s}$$

where $\Delta s$ is the distance from $(x_0, y_0)$ to $(x, y)$ along a specific direction $PQ$.

We must now consider how to calculate $df/ds$. Let us denote $f(x, y) - f(x_0, y_0)$ by $\Delta z$. Then

**(21)** $$\frac{\Delta z}{\Delta s} = \frac{f(x, y) - f(x_0, y_0)}{\Delta s} .$$

We do not know how to find the limit of the right-hand side because both variables $x$ and $y$ are involved. But we do know how to calculate such a limit when only one variable changes. Hence what we shall try to do is to break up the change from $f(x_0, y_0)$ to $f(x, y)$ into two changes, each involving only one of the variables.

We can write

**(22)** $$\frac{f(x, y) - f(x_0, y_0)}{\Delta s} = \frac{f(x, y) - f(x_0, y) + f(x_0, y) - f(x_0, y_0)}{\Delta s} ,$$

because all we have done in the right-hand numerator is to add and subtract the same term. In the first two terms of the right-hand numerator $y$ is the same whereas $x_0$ changes to $x$. The difference suggests using the law of the mean (Chapter 13, Section 2), although it is not clear that this law will help us. If we do apply it, we obtain

**(23)** $$f(x, y) - f(x_0, y) = f_x(x_1, y)\Delta x$$

where $f_x(x_1, y)$ means $\partial f/\partial x$ evaluated at $x_1$ and $y$; $x_1$ is, according to the law of the mean, some value of $x$ between $x$ and $x_0$, and $\Delta x$ is merely $x - x_0$. Because the second pair of terms in the right-hand numerator involves only a change in the $y$-variable, we can apply the law of the mean there too. This application tells us that

**(24)**                        $$f(x_0, y) - f(x_0, y_0) = f_y(x_0, y_1)\Delta y$$

where $f_y(x_0, y_1)$ means $\partial f/\partial y$ evaluated at $(x_0, y_1)$; $y_1$ is some value of $y$ between $y$ and $y_0$, and $\Delta y = y - y_0$. If we use (23) and (24) in (22), we obtain

**(25)**            $$\frac{f(x, y) - f(x_0, y_0)}{\Delta s} = f_x(x_1, y)\frac{\Delta x}{\Delta s} + f_y(x_0, y_1)\frac{\Delta y}{\Delta s}.$$

The directional derivative is the limit of the left side or the right side of (25) as $\Delta s$ approaches 0. As we can see from Fig. 22-12, when $\Delta s$ approaches 0, both $\Delta x$ and $\Delta y$ approach 0. We see also that $\Delta x/\Delta s = \cos\alpha$ where $\alpha$ is the angle that $PQ$ makes with the $x$-axis and $\Delta y/\Delta s = \cos\beta$ where $\beta$ is the angle that $PQ$ makes with the $y$-axis. Because $PQ$ is a line segment, $\alpha$ and $\beta$ remain constant as $\Delta s$ approaches 0. As $\Delta x$ and $\Delta y$ approach 0, $x$ must approach $x_0$, $y$ must approach $y_0$; then $x_1$ approaches $x_0$, and $y_1$ approaches $y_0$. We have, then, from (25) that

**(26)**                $$\frac{dz}{ds} = f_x(x_0, y_0)\cos\alpha + f_y(x_0, y_0)\cos\beta.$$

With (26) we can calculate the directional derivative of a function $z = f(x, y)$ if we specify the direction $PQ$ in which the derivative is to be calculated. To specify $PQ$ is to specify the angle $\alpha$ that $PQ$ makes with the positive $x$-axis and the angle $\beta$ that $PQ$ makes with the positive $y$-axis.

We must be careful in determining the proper $\alpha$ and $\beta$ for a given $PQ$. Figure 22-12 shows a direction of $PQ$ for which $\alpha$ and $\beta$ are (positive) acute angles. Figure 22-13 shows three other *directed* segments $PQ$ and the angles that these segments make with the positively directed $x$- and $y$-axes. We see that $\alpha$ and $\beta$, which are always taken to be positive angles, can lie between $0°$ and $180°$ in value. Let us note that the directed segment in (*b*) here has

**Figure 22-13**

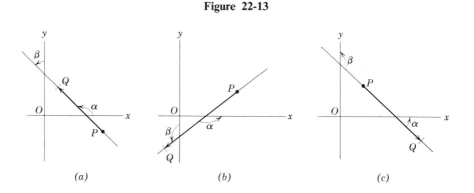

(*a*)                                     (*b*)                                     (*c*)

the opposite direction of *PQ* in Fig. 22-12. Correspondingly, the direction angles $\alpha$ and $\beta$ here are the supplements of those in Fig. 22-12.

The directional derivative is a generalization of the first partial derivatives $f_x$ and $f_y$ of $z = f(x, y)$. The directional derivative in the direction of the *positive* x-axis is $f_x$ because then $\alpha = 0$ and $\beta = \pi/2$. Likewise, the directional derivative in the direction of the *positive* y-axis is $f_y$ because then $\alpha = \pi/2$ and $\beta = 0$. The directional derivative in the direction of the negative x-axis is obtained for $\alpha = 180°$ and $\beta = 90°$ and then $df/ds$ is $-f_x$.

We see, then, that the directional derivative of $z = f(x, y)$ at a point $P$ reduces to $f_x$ and $f_y$ for special angles $\alpha$ and $\beta$. But $f_x$ is the slope of the curve through $P$ cut out on the surface by a plane parallel to the *xz*-plane and $f_y$ is the slope of the curve through $P$ cut out on the surface by a plane parallel to the *yz*-plane. The directional derivative in the direction $\alpha$, $\beta$ should be the slope of the curve cut out on the surface by a plane through $P$ and making an angle $\alpha$ with the x-axis and $\beta$ with the y-axis. This fact is really a consequence of the very definition, but the analytical work that we have done may have obscured it. Figure 22-14 shows a curve *PRQ* cut out on the surface of $z = f(x, y)$ by a vertical plane making an angle $\alpha$ with the x-axis and $\beta$ with the y-axis. Now

$$\frac{df}{ds} = \lim_{\Delta s \to 0} \frac{\Delta z}{\Delta s} \; .$$

Geometrically, $\Delta z$ is $R_1 R$ and $\Delta s$ is $P_0 R_0$ or its equal $PR_1$. Then $\Delta z/\Delta s$ is

**Figure 22-14**

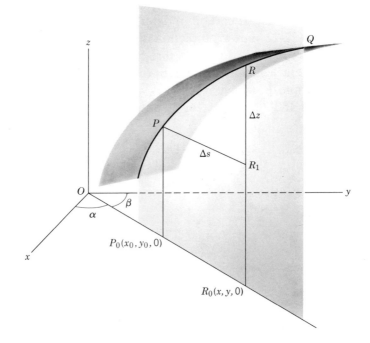

the slope of the secant line $PR$ of the curve, and the limit as $\Delta s$ approaches 0 is the slope of the tangent to the curve $PRQ$ at $P$.

The notion of a directional derivative is not limited to the case in which $x$ and $y$ vary along a straight-line path. The $x$ and $y$ may vary along some curve in the $xy$-plane. The directional derivative of $z = f(x, y)$ along the curve at any point on the curve is the derivative in the direction of the tangent to the curve at that point; hence, again, we are back to the directional derivative along a straight line, the tangent to the curve at the point.

Now let us consider the concept of directional derivative as it may apply to functions of three independent variables, say $u = f(x, y, z)$. In this case the direction is along some line $PQ$ in space (Fig. 22-15). The argument analogous to that used to derive (26) leads to the conclusion that if $P_0$ is $(x_0, y_0, z_0)$ then

**(27)** $\quad \dfrac{du}{ds} = f_x(x_0, y_0, z_0)\cos \alpha + f_y(x_0, y_0, z_0)\cos \beta + f_z(x_0, y_0, z_0)\cos \gamma,$

where $\alpha$, $\beta$, and $\gamma$ are the direction angles that the directed line $PQ$ makes with the positive $x$-, $y$-, and $z$-axes, is the directional derivative of $u$ at $P$ and in the direction determined by $\alpha$, $\beta$, and $\gamma$.

There is one useful fact about the directional derivative which is immediately deducible from its very expression. Suppose that we are at some fixed point $(x, y, z)$ in space. We can write (27) in the form

**(28)**
$$\frac{du}{ds} = \sqrt{f_x^2 + f_y^2 + f_z^2}\left[ \frac{f_x \cos \alpha}{\sqrt{f_x^2 + f_y^2 + f_z^2}} \right.$$
$$\left. + \frac{f_y \cos \beta}{\sqrt{f_x^2 + f_y^2 + f_z^2}} + \frac{f_z \cos \gamma}{\sqrt{f_x^2 + f_y^2 + f_z^2}} \right]$$

where the partial derivatives are all evaluated at the fixed point. Now, $f_x/\sqrt{f_x^2 + f_y^2 + f_z^2}$ and the two companion expressions involving $f_y$ and $f_z$

**Figure 22-15**

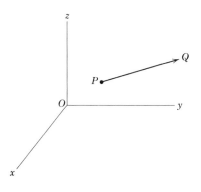

are the direction cosines of some direction in space. Hence by formula (14) of Chapter 21 the quantity in parentheses is the cosine of the angle between this direction in space and the direction, $\cos \alpha$, $\cos \beta$, $\cos \gamma$, in which the directional derivative is taken. The maximum value of this cosine is 1, and this value will obtain when the directional derivative is taken in the direction determined by $f_x$, $f_y$, and $f_z$. Also, the maximum possible value of $du/ds$ is $\sqrt{f_x^2 + f_y^2 + f_z^2}$ because the quantity in parentheses has the maximum value of 1.

**Example.** Find the directional derivative of $u = xy + 2xz - y^2 + z^2$ at the point (1, 2, 1) and in the direction from (1, 2, 1) to (3, 5, 7).

**Solution.** We wish to use formula (27) but to do so we must first find the direction cosines of the direction in which the derivative is to be calculated. These can be calculated by means of (7) of Chapter 21. The distance from (1, 2, 1) to (3, 5, 7) is $\sqrt{(3 - 1)^2 + (5 - 2)^2 + (7 - 1)^2} = 7$. Then by (7) of Chapter 21

$$\cos \alpha = \frac{3 - 1}{7}, \qquad \cos \beta = \frac{5 - 2}{7}, \qquad \cos \gamma = \frac{7 - 1}{7}.$$

Now from the function $u$ itself we have that

$$f_x = y + 2z, \quad f_y = x - 2y, \quad f_z = 2x + 2z.$$

At (1, 2, 1), $f_x = 4$, $f_y = -3$, $f_z = 4$. Then by (27)

$$\frac{du}{ds} = 4\left(\frac{2}{7}\right) + (-3)\left(\frac{3}{7}\right) + 4\left(\frac{6}{7}\right) = \frac{23}{7}.$$

## EXERCISES

1. Given the function $z = x^2 + y^2$, calculate the directional derivative at the point (3, 4) in the direction making an angle of 30° with the x-axis.
   
   *Ans.* $3\sqrt{3} + 4$.

2. Given the function $z = x^2 + y^2$, find the rate of change of the function at the point (3, 4)
   
   (a) In the direction of increasing x and y along the line $x - y = -1$.
   
   *Ans.* $7\sqrt{2}$.
   
   (b) In the direction of decreasing x and y along the same line.

3. Calculate the rate of change of $z = xy$ at the point (1, 2) in the direction of increasing x and y along the line $y = 2x$. *Ans.* $4\sqrt{5}/5$.

4. If $z = y/(x^2 + y^2)$, find the rate of change of z at the point (1, 2) and in the direction making an angle 45° with the (positive) x-axis. *Ans.* $-7\sqrt{2}/50$.

5. (a) Find the direction through the point (2, 1) for which the function $z = 4x^2 + 9y^2$ has the maximum rate of change.
   
   *Suggestion:* Use the result deduced from (28) but for the case of a function of two variables.
   
   *Ans.* $\cos^{-1}(8/\sqrt{145})$ with respect to positive x-axis.

(b)   Show that this direction is normal to the ellipse $4x^2 + 9y^2 = 25$ at the point $(2, 1)$.

(c)   Verify that the maximum rate of change found in (a) is equal to $(z_x^2 + z_y^2)^{1/2}$.

6. (a)   For $z = f(x, y)$ show that the direction at $(x, y)$ for which $dz/ds$ is a maximum is given by $\cos \alpha = f_x/\sqrt{f_x^2 + f_y^2}$, $\cos \beta = f_y/\sqrt{f_x^2 + f_y^2}$.

*Suggestion:* Use the result deduced from (28) but for the two-dimensional case.

(b)   Show that the maximum value of $dz/ds$ is $\sqrt{f_x^2 + f_y^2}$.

7. If $u = xy + yz + zx$, find the directional derivative of $u$ at the point $(-1, 1, 7)$ in the direction of $(7, 7, 7)$.                                              *Ans.* 10.

8. Find the directional derivative of $z = x^2/(x - y)$ at the point $(2, 4)$ in the direction of increasing $x$ on the curve $y = x^2$.

9. Find the direction at the point $(-1, 1, 7)$ for which the directional derivative of $u = xy + yz + zx$ is a maximum and find the maximum value of the directional derivative.

10. Find the directional derivative of $u = \log\sqrt{x^2 + y^2 + z^2}$ at the point $(3, 4, 8)$ in the direction of the point $(5, 7, 10)$.                    *Ans.* $34/(89\sqrt{17})$.

11. Find the directional derivative of $u = x^2 + 2y^2 + z^2$ at the point $(1, -1, -1)$ in the direction of the point $(3, -2, 5)$.

**5. The Chain Rule.** In investigating the calculus of functions of one variable we encountered and found great use for the chain rule which tells us that if $y = f(u)$ and $u = g(x)$, then

(29)
$$\frac{dy}{dx} = \frac{dy}{du}\frac{du}{dx} = f'(u)\,g'(x).$$

There is an analogous theorem for functions of two or more independent variables.

Suppose that $u = x^2 + y^2 + z^2$, while $x$, $y$, and $z$ themselves are the following functions of $s$ and $t$,

$$x = st, \quad y = s + 2t, \quad z = 2s + t.$$

The problem one often faces is that of finding $\partial u/\partial s$ and $\partial u/\partial t$. In this case, where we know the explicit functions, it is certainly possible to replace $x$, $y$, and $z$ by their values in terms of $s$ and $t$ and thus obtain $u$ as a function of $s$ and $t$. Then the problem of finding $\partial u/\partial s$ and $\partial u/\partial t$ presents no new difficulties. However, an extension of the chain rule permits us to obtain $\partial u/\partial s$ and $\partial u/\partial t$ more readily. Moreover, in arguments in which we do not know one or more of the functions explicitly, the chain rule for functions of several variables is indispensable.

Let us first see what the chain rule amounts to and, for simplicity, let us consider

(30)
$$u = f(x, y),$$

while

$$x = g(s, t), \quad y = h(s, t).$$

If $s$ changes to some value $s + \Delta s$, while $t$ remains fixed, then $x$ changes to $x + \Delta x$ and $y$ to $y + \Delta y$. The $u$ changes to $f(x + \Delta x, y + \Delta y)$. Consequently,

$$\frac{\Delta u}{\Delta s} = \frac{f(x + \Delta x, y + \Delta y) - f(x, y)}{\Delta s}.$$

By adding and subtracting equal terms, we may write

$$\frac{\Delta u}{\Delta s} = \frac{f(x + \Delta x, y + \Delta y) - f(x, y + \Delta y) + f(x, y + \Delta y) - f(x, y)}{\Delta s}.$$

In the first two terms of the right-hand numerator only the first variable changes. Hence we may apply the mean value theorem for functions of one variable to these two terms [compare the derivation of (25)]. The analogous statement applies to the second two terms. Then

$$\frac{\Delta u}{\Delta s} = f_x(x_1, y + \Delta y) \frac{\Delta x}{\Delta s} + f_y(x, y_1) \frac{\Delta y}{\Delta s}$$

where $x_1$ lies between $x$ and $x + \Delta x$ and $y_1$, between $y$ and $y + \Delta y$. As $\Delta s$ approaches 0, $\Delta x$ and $\Delta y$ approach 0. Moreover, if $f_x$ is continuous, and we do suppose that it is, $f_x(x_1, y + \Delta y)$ approaches $f_x(x, y)$. The analogous statement applies to $f_y$. Hence

$$(31) \qquad \frac{\partial u}{\partial s} = \lim_{\Delta s \to 0} \frac{\Delta u}{\Delta s} = f_x(x, y) \frac{\partial x}{\partial s} + f_y(x, y) \frac{\partial y}{\partial s}.$$

We write $\partial u / \partial s$ rather than $du / ds$ because $u$ is a function of $s$ and $t$ and we are considering the rate of change of $u$ with respect to $s$ only. Similarly,

$$(32) \qquad \frac{\partial u}{\partial t} = f_x(x, y) \frac{\partial x}{\partial t} + f_y(x, y) \frac{\partial y}{\partial t}.$$

Formulas (31) and (32) are the chain rule for functions of two variables. The same type of argument leads to a number of variations of the chain rule which fit different situations. For example, if

$$u = f(x, y, z)$$

and

$$x = g(s, t), \quad y = h(s, t), \quad z = k(s, t),$$

then

$$(33) \qquad \frac{\partial u}{\partial s} = f_x \frac{\partial x}{\partial s} + f_y \frac{\partial y}{\partial s} + f_z \frac{\partial z}{\partial s},$$

$$(34) \qquad \frac{\partial u}{\partial t} = f_x \frac{\partial x}{\partial t} + f_y \frac{\partial y}{\partial t} + f_z \frac{\partial z}{\partial t}.$$

Next, let us suppose that

$$z = f(x)$$

and

$$x = g(s, t),$$

and that we wish to find $\partial z / \partial s$. We obtain this quantity by considering a special case of (31) in which $f_y$ and $\partial y / \partial s$ are 0. Moreover, because the $f$ here is a function of $x$ only, the $f_x$ of (31) can also be written as $df / dx$. The result is

**(35)** 
$$\frac{\partial z}{\partial s} = \frac{df}{dx} \frac{\partial x}{\partial s} .$$

Actually, the present situation could be treated as well by the chain rule (29) for functions of one variable because $t$ plays the role of a constant.

Let us consider still another situation. Suppose that

$$u = f(x, y, z)$$

and

**(36)** 
$$y = g(x), \quad z = h(x).$$

Here $u$ may be considered a function of $x$ only, and it is meaningful to ask for $du / dx$. There is no harm in writing

$$x = t$$

and in rewriting (36) as

$$x = t, \quad y = g(t), \quad z = h(t).$$

We now see that our problem of finding $du / dx$, which is the same as $du / dt$, is just a special case of (33), the special nature being that $x, y,$ and $z$ are functions of $t$ only. Then (33) yields

$$\frac{du}{dt} = f_x \frac{dx}{dt} + f_y \frac{dy}{dt} + f_z \frac{dz}{dt} .$$

Now let us return to using $x$ in place of $t$. Thus

**(37)** 
$$\frac{du}{dx} = f_x + f_y \frac{dy}{dx} + f_z \frac{dz}{dx} .$$

The examples that follow will illustrate other forms of the chain rule.

Let us take as our first example, the functional relations given at the beginning of this section:

**(38)** 
$$u = x^2 + y^2 + z^2.$$

**(39)** 
$$x = st, \quad y = s + 2t, \quad z = 2s + t.$$

Then by (33)

$$\frac{\partial u}{\partial s} = 2x \cdot t + 2y \cdot 1 + 2z \cdot 2 = 2xt + 2y + 4z.$$

If the expression desired for $\partial u / \partial s$ is one involving only $s$ and $t$, we can replace the $x$, $y$, and $z$ in $\partial u / \partial s$ by their values in terms of $s$ and $t$. The result is

**(40)**                                  $\dfrac{\partial u}{\partial s} = 2st^2 + 10s + 8t.$

As a second example let us consider $u = x^2 e^y \sin z$ where

$$x = \cos t, \qquad y = \sin t, \qquad z = 3t.$$

Here $x, y$, and $z$ are functions of one variable only, and so indirectly $u$ is a function of $t$ only. It is, therefore, proper to ask for $du/dt$ instead of $\partial u / \partial t$. The chain rule that is applicable is just a special case of (33)—the special case which merely takes into account that $x, y$, and $z$ are functions of $t$ only. The rule then reads

**(41)**                  $\dfrac{du}{dt} = f_x \dfrac{dx}{dt} + f_y \dfrac{dy}{dt} + f_z \dfrac{dz}{dt}.$

For our example this rule gives

$$\frac{du}{dt} = 2xe^y \sin z(-\sin t) + x^2 e^y \sin z \cos t + x^2 e^y (\cos z)3.$$

A very important use of the chain rule is to convert expressions involving derivatives with respect to one set of coordinates to expressions involving derivatives with respect to another set of coordinates. Thus suppose that for some function $z = f(x, y)$ we have the expression

**(42)**                             $\dfrac{\partial^2 z}{\partial x^2} + \dfrac{\partial^2 z}{\partial y^2}.$

We might wish to transform $f(x, y)$ to polar coordinates and to know what expression is equal algebraically to (42) when $z$ or $f(x, y)$ is expressed in polar coordinates. We should note first that the functional form of the transformed $f$ will not be the same. That is, if $f(x, y) = x^3 + y^2$, the transformed function will not be $\rho^3 + \theta^2$ or $\theta^3 + \rho^2$. In fact, because

**(43)**                       $x = \rho \cos \theta, \qquad y = \rho \sin \theta,$

the transformed function will be $\rho^3 \cos^3 \theta + \rho^2 \sin^2 \theta$. Hence the transformed function of $f(x, y)$ will be some new functional form $z = F(\rho, \theta)$. Now one might guess that the expression equal to (42) would be $\partial^2 z / \partial \rho^2 + \partial^2 z / \partial \theta^2$ where $z$ is now given by $F(\rho, \theta)$, but this is very unlikely because the functional form has changed radically. We must determine the correct form by using the chain rule.

Our first task is to find out what $\partial^2 z/\partial x^2$, where $z = f(x, y)$, amounts to in terms of derivatives of $z = F(\rho, \theta)$. We know that [Chapter 17, formula (14)]

**(44)** $\qquad \rho = \sqrt{x^2 + y^2}\,, \qquad \cos\theta = \dfrac{x}{\sqrt{x^2 + y^2}}\,, \qquad \sin\theta = \dfrac{y}{\sqrt{x^2 + y^2}}\,.$

Then $F(\rho, \theta)$ is indirectly a function of $x$ and $y$ and, by (31),

**(45)** $\qquad\qquad\qquad\qquad \dfrac{\partial z}{\partial x} = \dfrac{\partial F}{\partial x} = F_\rho\,\dfrac{\partial \rho}{\partial x} + F_\theta\,\dfrac{\partial \theta}{\partial x}\,.$

So far so good. Next

$$\dfrac{\partial^2 z}{\partial x^2} = \dfrac{\partial}{\partial x}\left(F_\rho\,\dfrac{\partial \rho}{\partial x} + F_\theta\,\dfrac{\partial \theta}{\partial x}\right).$$

Each term in the parentheses is directly or indirectly a function of $x$, and therefore we can apply the usual theorems on the differentiation of the sum and product of functions. Thus

**(46)** $\qquad \dfrac{\partial^2 z}{\partial x^2} = \dfrac{\partial (F_\rho)}{\partial x}\,\dfrac{\partial \rho}{\partial x} + F_\rho\,\dfrac{\partial^2 \rho}{\partial x^2} + \dfrac{\partial (F_\theta)}{\partial x}\,\dfrac{\partial \theta}{\partial x} + F_\theta\,\dfrac{\partial^2 \theta}{\partial x^2}\,.$

The only difficulty arises at this point. How should we calculate $\partial (F_\rho)/\partial x$ and $\partial (F_\theta)/\partial x$? Now $F_\rho$ is itself a function of $\rho$ and $\theta$, and $\rho$ and $\theta$ are through (44) functions of $x$ and $y$. Hence we apply the chain rule (45) to $F_\rho$ in place of $F$. This rule applied to $F_\rho$ gives

**(47)** $\qquad\qquad\qquad\qquad \dfrac{\partial (F_\rho)}{\partial x} = F_{\rho\rho}\,\dfrac{\partial \rho}{\partial x} + F_{\rho\theta}\,\dfrac{\partial \theta}{\partial x}\,.$

Likewise, to calculate $\partial (F_\theta)/\partial x$, we apply the chain rule (45) to $F_\theta$ in place of $F$. Then

**(48)** $\qquad\qquad\qquad\qquad \dfrac{\partial (F_\theta)}{\partial x} = F_{\theta\rho}\,\dfrac{\partial \rho}{\partial x} + F_{\theta\theta}\,\dfrac{\partial \theta}{\partial x}\,.$

If we substitute (47) and (48) in (46), we have

**(49)** $\qquad \dfrac{\partial^2 z}{\partial x^2} = F_{\rho\rho}\left(\dfrac{\partial \rho}{\partial x}\right)^2 + F_{\rho\theta}\,\dfrac{\partial \theta}{\partial x}\,\dfrac{\partial \rho}{\partial x} + F_\rho\,\dfrac{\partial^2 \rho}{\partial x^2}$

$$+ F_{\theta\rho}\,\dfrac{\partial \rho}{\partial x}\,\dfrac{\partial \theta}{\partial x} + F_{\theta\theta}\left(\dfrac{\partial \theta}{\partial x}\right)^2 + F_\theta\,\dfrac{\partial^2 \theta}{\partial x^2}\,.$$

To compute the right side, we need the various partial derivatives of $\rho$

and $\theta$. These can be computed from (44). We shall merely note the results.

$$\frac{\partial \rho}{\partial x} = \frac{x}{\sqrt{x^2 + y^2}} = \cos \theta, \qquad\qquad \frac{\partial \theta}{\partial x} = -\frac{y}{x^2 + y^2} = -\frac{1}{\rho} \sin \theta$$

$$\frac{\partial^2 \rho}{\partial x^2} = \frac{y^2}{(x^2 + y^2)^{3/2}} = \frac{1}{\rho} \sin^2 \theta, \qquad \frac{\partial^2 \theta}{\partial x^2} = \frac{2xy}{(x^2 + y^2)^2} = \frac{2 \sin \theta \cos \theta}{\rho^2}.$$

If we substitute these values in (49), we obtain

**(50)**      $$\frac{\partial^2 z}{\partial x^2} = F_{\rho\rho} \cos^2 \theta - 2F_{\rho\theta} \frac{\cos \theta \sin \theta}{\rho^2}$$

$$+ F_{\theta\theta} \frac{\sin^2 \theta}{\rho^2} + F_{\rho} \frac{\sin^2 \theta}{\rho} + F_{\theta} \frac{2 \sin \theta \cos \theta}{\rho^2}.$$

We must now compute $\partial^2 z / \partial y^2$. The method is the same, and we leave the work for an exercise. The result is

**(51)**      $$\frac{\partial^2 z}{\partial y^2} = F_{\rho\rho} \sin^2 \theta + 2F_{\rho\theta} \frac{\cos \theta \sin \theta}{\rho^2}$$

$$+ F_{\theta\theta} \frac{\cos^2 \theta}{\rho^2} + F_{\rho} \frac{\cos^2 \theta}{\rho} - F_{\theta} \frac{2 \sin \theta \cos \theta}{\rho^2}.$$

We now see that if we add the left and right sides of (50) and (51),

**(52)**      $$\frac{\partial^2 z}{\partial x^2} + \frac{\partial^2 z}{\partial y^2} = F_{\rho\rho} + \frac{1}{\rho^2} F_{\theta\theta} + \frac{1}{\rho} F_{\rho}.$$

Let us note that we can write

$$\frac{\partial^2 z}{\partial x^2} + \frac{\partial^2 z}{\partial y^2} = \frac{\partial^2 z}{\partial \rho^2} + \frac{1}{\rho^2} \frac{\partial^2 z}{\partial \theta^2} + \frac{1}{\rho} \frac{\partial z}{\partial \rho},$$

but the $z$ on the right side refers to $z = F(\rho, \theta)$ and the $z$ on the left to $z = f(x, y)$.

# EXERCISES

**1.** Express $u$ in (38) directly as a function of $s$ and $t$ by using (39) and then find $\partial u / \partial s$. Does your result agree with that in (40)?

**2.** Apply the chain rule (34) to the functions in (38) and (39) to find $\partial u / \partial t$.

                                        *Ans.* $2s^2 t + 12s + 12t$.

**3.** Given that $z = f(x, y)$, find the following:
    (a)   When $x$ and $y$ are functions of $t$, find $dz / dt$.
    (b)   When $x$ is independent of $t$ but $y$ is a function of $t$, find $dz / dt$.

                                       *Ans.* $dz / dt = z_y (dy / dt)$.

(c) When $y$ is a function of $x$, find $dz/dx$.

$\quad$ *Suggestion:* Introduce the variable $t$ such that $x = t$ and regard $y$ as a function of $t$. $\qquad$ *Ans.* $dz/dx = z_x + z_y(dy/dx)$.

**4.** (a) Given that $z = f(x + ct)$, find $\partial z/\partial x$.

$\quad$ *Suggestion:* One is tempted to write $\partial f/\partial x$ or $f_x$ as the value of $\partial z/\partial x$ and, indeed, if we knew what $f$ was explicitly, we could find $f_x$. See Exercise 7 of Section 2. Because we do not know the explicit form of $f$, the best we can do is write $z = f(u)$ where $u = x + ct$ and then apply the appropriate chain rule. $\qquad$ *Ans.* $z_x = (\partial f/\partial u) \cdot 1$.

$\quad$ (b) For the same function, find $z_t$. $\qquad\qquad\qquad$ *Ans.* $(\partial f/\partial u) \cdot c$.

$\quad$ (c) Find $z_{xx}$ and $z_{tt}$ and show that $z_{tt} = c^2 z_{xx}$.

**5.** If $z = f(x - y, y - x)$ show that $(\partial z/\partial x) + (\partial z/\partial y) = 0$.

**6.** If $u = f(r)$ and $r = \sqrt{x^2 + y^2}$, show that $u_{xx} + u_{yy} = \dfrac{d^2u}{dr^2} + \dfrac{1}{r}\dfrac{du}{dr}$.

**7.** If $z = f(x, y)$, $x = \rho \cos \theta$, and $y = \rho \sin \theta$, show that for $z = F(\rho, \theta)$

$$z_\rho^2 + \frac{1}{\rho^2} z_\theta^2 = z_x^2 + z_y^2.$$

**8.** Obtain the result (51) in the text.

**9.** If $z = f(x, y)$, $x = \rho \cos \theta$, and $y = \rho \sin \theta$, find $z_{\theta\theta}$ where $z = F(\rho, \theta)$, in terms of the partial derivatives of $f$.

$\qquad$ *Ans.* $z_{\theta\theta} = f_{xx}\rho^2 \sin^2 \theta - 2f_{xy}\rho^2 \sin \theta \cos \theta + f_{yy}\rho^2 \cos^2 \theta$
$\qquad\qquad\qquad\qquad\qquad - f_x\rho \cos \theta - f_y\rho \sin \theta.$

**10.** With the data of Exercise 9, compute $z_{\rho\rho}$ and show that (50) holds.

**11.** Let $u$ and $v$ be functions of $x$ and $y$, for which $u_x = v_y$ and $u_y = -v_x$ and let $x = \rho \cos \theta$ and $y = \rho \sin \theta$. Show that the following hold:

$\quad$ (a) $u_\rho = \dfrac{1}{\rho} v_\theta$. $\qquad\qquad\qquad$ (b) $v_\rho = -\dfrac{1}{\rho} u_\theta$.

**12.** Suppose that $u = f(x, y, z)$ while $x = g(r, s, t)$, $y = h(r, s, t)$, and $z = k(r, s, t)$. Write the chain rule for $\partial f/\partial r$. $\quad$ *Ans.* $\partial f/\partial r = f_x g_r + f_y h_r + f_z k_r$.

**13.** Suppose that $u = f(x, y, z)$ and $z = g(x, y)$. Find the chain rule for $\partial u/\partial x$.

$\qquad\qquad\qquad\qquad\qquad\qquad\qquad$ *Ans.* $\partial u/\partial x = f_x + f_z g_x$.

**14.** If $z = f(x, y)$, $x = r\dfrac{e^\theta + e^{-\theta}}{2}$, and $y = r\dfrac{e^\theta - e^{-\theta}}{2}$, prove that $z_{xx} - z_{yy}$
$= z_{rr} - \dfrac{1}{r^2} z_{\theta\theta} + \dfrac{1}{r} z_r$, where on the right $z = F(r, \theta)$.

**6. Implicit Functions.** One more bit of technique is needed to operate effectively with partial derivatives. We found in dealing with functions of one variable (Chap. 7, Sect. 4) that the functional relation between $x$ and $y$ is often given implicitly as, for example, in $2x^2 + 3y^2 = 7$. To obtain $dy/dx$, it is not necessary to solve for $y$; one can differentiate the implicit function. The same idea carries over to functions of two or more independent variables and the primary reason for differentiating the implicit function is the same, namely, that it may be difficult or impossible to solve for the explicit function. Thus the equation

**(53)** $\qquad\qquad\qquad\qquad z^3 - 3z^2 + x^2 + 2xy + 7 = 0$

defines $z$ as a function of $x$ and $y$ or, more precisely, it defines three different single-valued functions of $x$ and $y$. However, it is difficult to obtain these functions explicitly because the equation is a cubic in $z$. Moreover, the expressions for the three explicit functions would be complicated.

Let us generalize the problem. Suppose that in some theoretical work we had to consider

**(54)** $$F(x, y, z) = 0.$$

How could we express $z_x$ and $z_y$ in terms of $F$? Like (53), this equation may define several different functions of $x$ and $y$. However, we can suppose that we are dealing with one of them which might be selected, for example, by the fact that we know the value of $z$ for a given $x$ and $y$.

Let us put aside (54) for the moment and consider the function

**(55)** $$u = F(x, y, z),$$

about which we are told that $z$ is a function of $x$ and $y$. Then by the chain rule (33), where we specialize the functions $x = g(s, t)$ and $y = h(s, t)$ to $x = s$ and $y = t$, we obtain

**(56)** $$\frac{\partial u}{\partial s} = F_x + F_z \frac{\partial z}{\partial s}$$

since $\partial y / \partial s = 0$. Because $x = s$,

$$\frac{\partial u}{\partial x} = F_x + F_z \frac{\partial z}{\partial x}.$$

Now, (54) is that special case of (55) for which $u \equiv 0$. Then $\partial u / \partial x \equiv 0$ and

**(57)** $$\frac{\partial z}{\partial x} = -\frac{F_x(x, y, z)}{F_z(x, y, z)}.$$

It is important to remember that $F_x$ and $F_z$ mean the partial derivatives of $F$ obtained *by regarding $x$, $y$, and $z$ as independent variables*, because this is what (56) calls for on the basis of the chain rule. Likewise,

**(58)** $$\frac{\partial z}{\partial y} = -\frac{F_y(x, y, z)}{F_z(x, y, z)}.$$

What these results mean in practice can be seen by reconsidering (53), namely,

$$z^3 - 3z^2 + x^2 + 2xy + 7 = 0.$$

By (57)

$$\frac{\partial z}{\partial x} = -\frac{2x + 2y}{3z^2 - 6z}.$$

An argument entirely analogous to that used to derive (57) and (58) tells us that if

**(59)** $$F(x, y) = 0,$$

then the derivative $dy/dx$ of any function $y = f(x)$ defined by (59) is given by

**(60)** $$\frac{dy}{dx} = -\frac{F_x(x, y)}{F_y(x, y)}.$$

Formula (60) is an alternative way of expressing and obtaining $dy/dx$ for functions of the form (59). We obtained $dy/dx$ for such implicit functions in Chapter 7, Section 4, by an argument which avoided any explicit use of partial derivatives.

We can use (57) and (58) to reformulate an earlier result. We found that the normal to the surface or to the tangent plane of the surface $z = f(x, y)$ at any given $(x, y)$ has the direction numbers [see (19)]

$$f_x, f_y, -1.$$

We now see from (57) and (58) that the direction numbers can be taken to be

$$-\frac{F_x}{F_z}, -\frac{F_y}{F_z}, -1,$$

or, because any set of numbers proportional to these three may be used as the direction numbers, we can multiply this set by $-F_z$ and state that

**(61)** $$F_x, F_y, F_z$$

are the direction numbers of the normal to the surface $z = f(x, y)$ defined by $F(x, y, z) = 0$.

**Example.**   Find the slope at the point $(1, 1, 1)$ of the curve cut out on the surface $x^3 + x^2y + y^2z + z^2 = 0$ by the plane $y = 1$.

**Solution.**   We could solve the equation of the surface for $z$, select that one of the two solutions which contains the point $(1, 1, 1)$ and then find $\partial z/\partial x$ at $(1, 1, 1)$. However, since $y$ is constant in the plane $y = 1$ we really have $z$ defined implicitly as a function of $x$. Then we can use (57). Now $F_x = 3x^2 + 2xy$; $F_z = y^2 + 2z$. Then by (57)

$$\frac{\partial z}{\partial x} = \frac{3x^2 + 2xy}{y^2 + 2z}.$$

At the point $(1, 1, 1)$ we find that $\partial z/\partial x = -5/3$.

## EXERCISES

**1.** From (53) and (58) find $\partial z/\partial y$.                  *Ans.* $2x/(3x^2 - 6z)$.

**2.** For the function of $z$ defined by $xy + yz - z^2 = 0$, find $z_x$ and $z_y$.

*Ans.* $z_x = y/(2z - y)$.

**3.** Use (57) to find $\partial^2 z/\partial x^2$.      *Ans.* $\dfrac{-18z^2(z - 2)^2 - 24(x + y)^2(z - 1)}{(3z^2 - 6z)^3}$.

**4.** For each of the following functions find $z_x$ and $z_y$:

(a)   $x^2 + y^2 + z^2 - 4xz = 0$.                   (c)   $\sin(x + y + z) = 0$.

  *Ans.* $z_x = (x - 2z)/(2x - z)$.                     *Ans.* $z_x = -1$.

(b)   $x^3 + y^3 + z^3 - 4xyz = 10$.                 (d)   $z^3 + 3xz + 4y = 0$.

**5.** If $z^3 + 3xz - 3y = 0$, show that $z_{xx} + xz_{yy} = 0$.

**6.** The equation $F(x, y, z) = 0$ can be regarded as defining $x$ as a function of $y$ and $z$. Express $\partial x/\partial y$ and $\partial x/\partial z$.      *Ans.* $\partial x/\partial y = -(F_y/F_x)$.

**7.** Find the equations of the tangent planes to the following surfaces at any given point $(x_0, y_0, z_0)$ on the surface:

(a)   $x^2 + y^2 + z^2 = 25$.                     *Ans.* $x_0 x + y_0 y + z_0 z = 25$.

(b)   $\dfrac{(x - 3)^2}{25} + \dfrac{(y - 2)^2}{16} + (z - 1)^2 = 49$.

(c)   $3x^2 + 4y^2 - 5z^2 = 10$.                 *Ans.* $3x_0 x + 4y_0 y - 5z_0 z = 10$.

(d)   $xy + yz + 3x = 1$.

(e)   $x^2 + z^2 = 1$.                       *Ans.* $x_0 x + z_0 z = 1$.

**8.** Show that the ellipsoid $3x^2 + 4y^2 + 8z^2 = 24$ and the hyperboloid of one sheet $x^2 + 2y^2 - 4z^2 = 4$ are orthogonal to each other at the common point $\left(\dfrac{4\sqrt{5}}{5}, \sqrt{2}, \dfrac{2\sqrt{5}}{5}\right)$. Orthogonality of the two surfaces means that the tangent planes at the point are perpendicular to each other.

**9.** Show that the two surfaces of Exercise 8 are orthogonal to each other at every common point.

**10.** Show that the ellipsoid $3x^2 + 4y^2 + 8z^2 = 24$ and the hyperboloid of two sheets $4x^2 - 4y^2 - z^2 = 4$ are orthogonal to each other at the common point $\left(\dfrac{4\sqrt{5}}{5}, \sqrt{2}, \dfrac{2\sqrt{5}}{5}\right)$.

**11.** Show that the two surfaces of Exercise 10 are orthogonal to each other at every common point.

**12.** We found in our work on the directional derivative that for $u = f(x, y, z)$, $du/ds$ is a maximum in the direction $(f_x, f_y, f_z)$. Show that this direction is normal to the surface $u = $ constant.

**13.** The equation $F(x, y) = 0$ defines $y$ as one or several functions of $x$. It also defines $x$ as one or several functions of $y$. Suppose that $y = f(x)$ is one of the explicit functions of $x$. Show that $dy/dx = 1/(dx/dy)$, assuming of course that the inverse function is the one inverse to $y = f(x)$.

**7. Differentials.** We learned for functions of one variable that the change $\Delta y$ in $y$ which takes place when $x$ is changed to $x + \Delta x$ can be approximated rather well by the differential $dy$, the latter being, by definition,

$y'\,\Delta x$ or $f'(x)\,\Delta x$. Such a useful approximation is also available for functions of several variables. Let us consider a function of two variables, $z = f(x, y)$. If $x$ changes to $x + \Delta x$ and $y$ to $y + \Delta y$, the actual increment in $z$, $\Delta z$, is given by

$$\Delta z = f(x + \Delta x, y + \Delta y) - f(x, y).$$

By adding and subtracting the same term, we can write

$$\Delta z = f(x + \Delta x, y + \Delta y) - f(x, y + \Delta y) + f(x, y + \Delta y) - f(x, y).$$

In the first two terms on the right side we have a function that changes only in $x$. Hence we can apply the law of the mean for functions of one variable to the two terms. Likewise, in the second two terms only $y$ changes. Hence here, too, we can apply the law of the mean for functions of one variable. Then

$$\Delta z = f_x(x_1, y + \Delta y)\,\Delta x + f_y(x, y_1)\,\Delta y$$

where $x_1$ lies between $x$ and $x + \Delta x$ and $y_1$, between $y$ and $y + \Delta y$. Now, if $\Delta x$ and $\Delta y$ are small, $f_x(x_1, y + \Delta y)$ does not differ much from $f_x(x, y)$, provided that $f_x$ is continuous for the domain of $x$- and $y$-values, because continuity means that as $(x_1, y + \Delta y)$ approaches $(x, y)$, $f_x(x_1, y + \Delta y)$ approaches $f_x(x, y)$. Likewise, when $\Delta y$ is small, $f_y(x, y_1)$ does not differ much from $f_y(x, y)$ if $f_y$ is continuous. Hence for small $\Delta x$ and $\Delta y$ a good approximation to $\Delta z$ seems to be

**(62)**                         $$dz = f_x(x, y)\,\Delta x + f_y(x, y)\,\Delta y.$$

It is customary, as in the case of functions of one variable, to write $dx$ and $dy$ for $\Delta x$ and $\Delta y$, respectively, so that we define the approximation to be

**(63)**                         $$dz = f_x(x, y)\,dx + f_y(x, y)\,dx,$$

and call this the differential of $z$.

Now let us see whether (63) does indeed offer a good approximation to $\Delta z$ for small $dx$ and $dy$. Let us consider first the specific function

$$A = xy.$$

If $x$ changes to $x + \Delta x$ and $y$ to $y + \Delta y$, the area of the rectangle (Fig. 22-16) changes to that of the larger rectangle, and $\Delta A$ is the entire shaded area. According to (63)

$$dA = y\,dx + x\,dy.$$

Then $dA$ consists of the two shaded rectangles $R$ and $S$. The difference between $\Delta A$ and $dA$ is the small rectangle in the upper right-hand corner of the figure. This is small compared to $\Delta A$, and its neglect should still leave $dA$ a useful approximation to $\Delta A$.

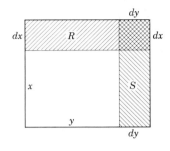

**Figure 22-16**

Let us examine geometrically the general definition (63) of $dz$ and see if this sheds any light on how good an approximation $dz$ is to $\Delta z$. If we evaluate $dz$ at a point $(x_0, y_0)$ and think of $dx$ or $\Delta x$ as $x - x_0$ and $dy$ or $\Delta y$ as $y - y_0$, then (63) states that

**(64)**          $dz = f_x(x_0, y_0)(x - x_0) + f_y(x_0, y_0)(y - y_0).$

We know that $\Delta z = z - z_0$ where $z_0 = f(x_0, y_0)$ and $z = f(x, y)$. If we now think of $dz$ as some change in $z$ from the value of $z_0$, say $Z - z_0$, the question that we face is, what is $Z$? The form

**(65)**          $Z - z_0 = f_x(x_0, y_0)(x - x_0) + f_y(x_0, y_0)(y - y_0)$

reminds us [see (19)] of the equation of the tangent plane (Fig. 22-17) to the surface $z = f(x, y)$ at the point $(x_0, y_0, z_0)$. That is, the $Z$ for which $Z - z_0 = dz$ is the $Z$-value of the point on the tangent plane whose first two coordinates are the $x$ and $y$ of (65). In other words, whereas the $z$ which results from changing $(x_0, y_0)$ to $(x, y)$ or $(x_0, y_0)$ to $(x_0 + \Delta x, y_0 + \Delta y)$ is the $z$-value belonging to the surface itself, the $Z$-value given by (65) is the

·**Figure 22-17**

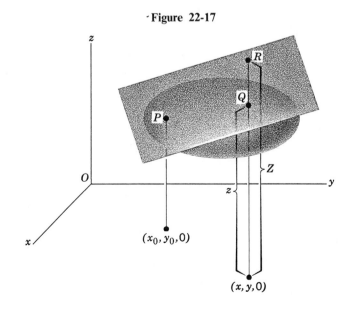

$Z$-value of the tangent plane. Because the tangent plane remains close to the surface when $(x, y)$ is close to $(x_0, y_0)$, we see that $dz$ is a good approximation to $\Delta z$ for small $dx$ and $dy$.

## EXERCISES

1. Suppose that the sides of a rectangle are found to be 10 and 7 feet. The correct values are 10.1 and 7.05 feet, respectively. What is the actual error made in the calculation of the area? Then use the differential of the area to calculate the approximate error. *Ans.* 1.205; 1.2.

2. Calculate $dz$ for each of the following functions:
   (a) $z = x^2 + 2xy - y^2$.  *Ans.* $dz = 2(x + y)dx + 2(x - y)dy$.
   (b) $V = \pi r^2 h$.
   (c) $z = \log(x^2 + y^2)$.  *Ans.* $dz = \dfrac{2}{x^2 + y^2}(x\,dx + y\,dy)$.
   (d) $z = \sin x \sin y$.
   (e) $z = e^{xy}$.  *Ans.* $dz = e^{xy}(y\,dx + x\,dy)$.

3. Suggest a definition of the differential $du$ for a function $u = f(x, y, z)$.

4. The sides of a right-angled triangle are measured and found to be 8.5 and 11.5 feet, respectively, with a possible error of $\frac{1}{5}$ inch in each. Find the approximate error in the hypotenuse. *Ans.* 0.28 in. approx.

5. The area of an ellipse whose semi-axes are $a$ and $b$ is $\pi ab$. Find the approximate error in the area due to possible errors of $\frac{1}{2}$ inch in the measured values of $a$ and $b$ if these are found to be 3 and 2 inches, respectively. *Ans.* 0.65 sq in.

6. The angle $A$ of a triangle is calculated by measuring the three sides and using the law of cosines, namely,

$$\cos A = \frac{b^2 + c^2 - a^2}{2bc}.$$

Find an expression for the approximate error in $A$ due to errors in measurement of $b$, $c$, and $a$.

$$Ans. \quad -\frac{c(b^2 - c^2 + a^2)db + b(c^2 - b^2 + a^2)dc - 2abc\,da}{bc(2a^2b^2 + 2b^2c^2 + 2c^2a^2 - a^4 - b^4 - c^4)^{1/2}}$$

7. The period of oscillation of a simple pendulum is given by $T = 2\pi\sqrt{l/g}$. Show that the error in $T$ caused by a 1% error in $l$ and a 1% error in $g$, if both errors are in the same direction, is approximately 0.

8. The acceleration of gravity can be obtained from the formula $g = 2s/t^2$, if one can measure $s$ and $t$. Find the approximate error in $g$ due to small errors in $s$ and $t$. *Ans.* $2(t\,ds - 2s\,dt)/t^3$.

**8. Maxima and Minima.** One of the applications of the calculus of functions of two or more variables is to find maximum and minimum values of functions. We might, for example, be interested in securing maximum volume in a box-shaped can under the condition that a fixed amount of tin be used. The problem then would be to determine the dimensions that yield maximum volume. The maximum or minimum function values that we generally seek are, as in the case of functions of one variable, relative

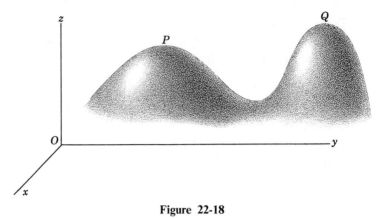

**Figure 22-18**

maxima or minima. Thus the $z$-value of the point $P$ in Fig. 22-18 is larger than the $z$-values of all nearby points, although there may be other points such as $Q$ whose $z$-value is even larger than that of $P$. In analytical terms, function $z = f(x, y)$ has a relative maximum at $z_0 = f(x_0, y_0)$ if

$$f(x_0, y_0) > f(x, y)$$

for all $(x, y)$ near $(x_0, y_0)$. Likewise, $z = f(x, y)$ has a relative minimum at $z_0 = f(x_0, y_0)$ if

$$f(x_0, y_0) < f(x, y)$$

for all $(x, y)$ near $(x_0, y_0)$. Of course, analogous definitions hold for functions of three and more variables.

The method for determining the maximum or minimum value of a function is similar to that for functions of one variable. Let us consider the surface of $z = f(x, y)$ and suppose that $P$ with coordinates $(x_0, y_0, z_0)$ is a maximum point. If we cut this surface by a plane $y = y_0$, which is, of course, parallel to the $xz$-plane and passes through $P$, then a curve is cut out on the surface. If $P$ is a maximum point on the surface, then certainly its $z$-value is larger than other $z$-values on this curve. Then $z_0$ is a maximum value of the function $f(x, y_0)$, which is a function of $x$ alone. By the theory of maxima and minima for functions of one variable, $f_x$ must be 0 at $(x_0, y_0)$. The analogous argument shows that $f_y$ must be 0 at $(x_0, y_0)$.

We might think that we now have the conditions that would enable us to determine the maximum or minimum values of $f(x, y)$, because $f_x$ and $f_y$ are both functions of $x$ and $y$ and by solving the two equations

$$f_x(x, y) = 0 \qquad \text{and} \qquad f_y(x, y) = 0$$

simultaneously we could find the $x_0$ and $y_0$ of the maxima and minima. However, our experience with functions of one variable should forewarn us that the matter is not that simple. In the case of functions of one variable we found that at a maximum or minimum $f'(x) = 0$, but the fact that $f'(x) = 0$ at some value $x_0$ of $x$ is not sufficient to guarantee a maximum or a minimum. The analogous fact holds for functions of two variables. We have but to consider the saddle-shaped surface representing $z = x^2 - y^2$ to see that the vanishing of $f_x$ and $f_y$ is not sufficient to guarantee a maximum or a minimum. As Fig. 21-20 shows, the origin is a maximum with respect to some nearby points on the surface but a minimum with respect to other nearby points. Hence the origin is neither a maximum nor a minimum in the sense demanded of a function of two variables.

In the case of functions of one variable, we had to examine $f''(x)$ and found that if $f''(x) < 0$ at a value of $x$ where $f'(x) = 0$, then $f(x)$ has a maximum at that value of $x$. There is a corresponding condition for functions of two variables.

**Theorem:**  If at $(x_0, y_0)$

(a) $f_x$ and $f_y$ are 0,      (b) $f_{xy}^2 - f_{xx}f_{yy} < 0$,      (c) $f_{xx} < 0$,

then $z = f(x, y)$ has a (relative) maximum at $(x_0, y_0)$. If conditions (a) and (b) hold but (c) becomes

(c') $f_{xx} > 0$,

then $z = f(x, y)$ has a (relative) minimum at $(x_0, y_0)$. If $f_{xy}^2 - f_{xx}f_{yy} > 0$, then $f(x, y)$ has neither a maximum nor a minimum at $(x_0, y_0)$. If $f_{xy}^2 - f_{xx}f_{yy} = 0$, no conclusion can be drawn.

We shall not prove this theorem only because the proof would take us a little farther into the theory than time permits.

The application of this theorem is rather straightforward. Let us examine the function

$$z = x^2 + y^3 - 6y$$

for its relative maxima and minima. We find that $f_x = 2x$ and $f_y = 3y^2 - 6$. We set

$$2x = 0,$$
$$3y^2 - 6 = 0,$$

and we see that $x = 0$, $y = \sqrt{2}$ and $x = 0$, $y = -\sqrt{2}$ are possible points at which a relative maximum or minimum may obtain.

We now apply condition (b). First,

$$f_{xx} = 2, \qquad f_{xy} = 0, \qquad f_{yy} = 6y.$$

Then

$$f_{xy}^2 - f_{xx}f_{yy} = -12y.$$

At $(0, \sqrt{2})$ this expression is negative and $f_{xx} > 0$. Hence the function has a relative minimum at $(0, \sqrt{2})$ and the value of this minimum is $-4\sqrt{2}$.

At $(0, -\sqrt{2}\,)$, $f_{xy}^2 - f_{xx}f_{yy} = 12\sqrt{2}$, and so the function has neither a maximum nor a minimum at $(0, -\sqrt{2}\,)$.

As a second example let us consider the problem mentioned at the beginning of this section. Specifically, a box is to be constructed with 24 sq in. of metal. What dimensions should be chosen to yield maximum volume? If the dimensions of the box are $x$, $y$, and $z$, the volume $V$ is

**(66)**                               $$V = xyz.$$

We see that $V$ is a function of three variables. However, these three variables are not independent because there is the condition that the surface area of the box be 24 sq in. That is

**(67)**                               $$2(xy + yz + zx) = 24.$$

It is possible to solve (67) for $z$ in terms of $x$ and $y$ and substitute this value of $z$ in (66). However, there are problems of the same type in which the elimination of the third variable is not readily done. For the sake of learning a method, therefore, let us adopt a different procedure.

We shall regard $z$ in (66) as a function of $x$ and $y$ and apply the usual method of maxima and minima; that is, we shall seek $V_x$ and $V_y$. To differentiate (66), in which $z$ is to be regarded as a function of $x$ and $y$, we apply the chain rules (33) and (34) to the special situation in which $x = s$ and $y = t$. The chain rule (33) then reads, since $\partial y / \partial s = 0$,

$$\frac{\partial u}{\partial s} = f_x \frac{\partial x}{\partial s} + f_z \frac{\partial z}{\partial s}$$

or, since $x = s$,

**(68)**                               $$\frac{\partial u}{\partial x} = f_x + f_z \frac{\partial z}{\partial x}.$$

The chain rule (34) in this special case where $x = s$ and $y = t$ yields, since $\partial x / \partial t = 0$,

**(69)**                               $$\frac{\partial u}{\partial y} = f_y + f_z \frac{\partial z}{\partial y}.$$

Hence let us apply these rules (68) and (69) to $V$. They yield

**(70)**                     $$V_x = yz + xyz_x; \qquad V_y = xz + xyz_y.$$

To obtain $z_x$ and $z_y$, we can use (67) and differentiate it as an implicit function by means of (57) and (58). Thus

**(71)**                     $$z_x = -\frac{y + z}{y + x}, \qquad z_y = -\frac{x + z}{y + x}.$$

We substitute these values of $z_x$ and $z_y$ in (70) and obtain

**(72)**
$$(y + x)yz + xy(-y - z) = 0$$

$$(y + x)xz + xy(-x - z) = 0.$$

If we divide the first equation by $y$ and the second by $x$ and then subtract, we obtain

$$x^2 - xy = 0.$$

Now $x = 0$ is a possible value but not a practical one. Another possible solution is

$$x = y.$$

If we use this result in either of the equations (72), we obtain

$$x = z.$$

Hence we obtain as the possible values at which a maximum may occur

$$x = y = z.$$

From (67) we find that $x = 2$.

We should now apply conditions (b) and (c) of the theorem to be certain that $x = y = 2$ does indeed furnish a relative maximum, but it is physically evident that this is the case. If we used all 24 sq. in. of tin for the top and bottom of the box, there would be no tin for the sides and the volume would be zero. As we decrease the area of top and bottom and allow more tin for the sides, the volume increases. On the other hand, if we used dimensions such as 1 and 1 for $x$ and $y$, (67) tells us that $z$ would be $5\frac{1}{2}$ and the volume would be less than the maximum of 8. Of course, such numerical evidence does not constitute a proof.

## EXERCISES

1. Show that the tangent plane to the surface of $z = f(x, y)$ at a relative maximum must be parallel to the $xy$-plane.
2. Test each of the following functions for maxima and minima:
    (a) $z = 9x^2 - 18x - 16y^2 - 64y$.     (c) $z = x^4 + y^4 + 32x - 4y + 52$.
           *Ans.* No max. or min.                    *Ans.* Min. value of 1 at $(-2, 1)$.
    (b) $z = x^3 + y^3 - 9xy + 35$.
3. Find the point of the plane $3x + 4y - z = 26$ which is closest to the origin.
           *Ans.* $(3, 4, -1)$.
4. Solve the box problem of the text by substituting the value of $z$ given by (67) into (66).
5. Solve the box problem of the text under the condition that the box has no top.
           *Ans.* $x = y = 2\sqrt{2}$, $z = \sqrt{2}$, $V = 8\sqrt{2}$.
6. If the product of the sines of the angles of a triangle is a maximum, show that the triangle is equilateral.
7. Find the dimensions of a box (top included) which contains a given volume $V$ and uses minimum material (i.e., has minimum surface area).     *Ans.* A cube.

**8.** The volume of an ellipsoid with semi-axes $a$, $b$, and $c$ is $4\pi abc/3$. Show that if $a + b + c$ is fixed, the ellipsoid of maximum volume is a sphere.

**9.** Show that the surface $z = xy$ has neither a maximum nor a minimum point.

**10.** Find the maximum value of the product of any three numbers whose sum is 12.
*Ans.* 64.

**11. (a)** Find the minimum distance from the origin to the surface $x^2 - z^2 = 1$.
    *Caution:* Note that the allowable values of $x$, $y$, and $z$ must lie on the surface. *Ans.* 1.

**(b)** Show that the line from the origin to the point on $x^2 - z^2 = 1$ for which the distance is minimal is normal to the surface.

**12.** Show that the line joining the fixed point $(a, b, c)$ to the point on the surface $\phi(x, y, z) = 0$ for which the distance is least is normal to $\phi = 0$.

***9. Envelopes.*** Another application of our theory on partial differentiation is the calculation of special curves called envelopes. Consider (Fig. 22-19) the paths of projectiles shot from a cannon with fixed velocity $V$ and with angle of fire $A \geq 45°$. We happen to know from our work in Chapter 18, Section 4, that each of these paths is a parabola. The entire collection of curves is called a *family* of parabolas. Surrounding this family of parabolas is a curve $ABCD$ that seems to be tangent to each parabola of the family. This curve, which itself happens to be a parabola, is of interest because all points inside it can be reached by the gun whereas no point outside it can be reached. It is called the parabola of surety; one is sure not to be hit by shells from the cannon if one stays outside the curve. The parabola of surety is an example of an envelope.

Generally, if there is a family of curves and if there is another curve to which each member of the family is tangent, the latter curve is called an *envelope* of the family. This definition is subject to some limitations. For example, the family of projectile paths involved above consists of only those whose angle of fire is 45° or larger and directed both to the left and to the right of the $y$-axis. The envelope consists of the arc of the parabola of surety which lies above the $x$-axis. However, these limitations amount to no

**Figure 22-19**

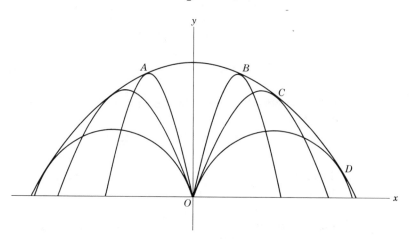

more than what is often understood in other situations. When we speak of the function $y = \sqrt{1 - x^2}$ , we mean to consider it only in the domain $-1 \le x \le 1$. Likewise, the family of curves in the situation above is limited to a domain of $A$-values and the envelope is limited to a domain of $x$-values.

To become familiar with the notion of an envelope, let us note one or two other examples. Let us consider the equation

**(73)** $$(x - a)^2 + y^2 = 1.$$

For fixed $a$, the equation represents a circle (Fig. 22-20) with center at $(a, 0)$ and radius of 1. As $a$ varies, the equation represents different circles, and thus the equation represents a family of circles. It is obvious geometrically that the lines $y = +1$ and $y = -1$ are tangent to the family of circles. Hence the two lines are the envelope of the family. As another example of an envelope we may consider the family of tangents to a curve. The curve itself is the envelope of the family of tangents.

What we should like is some method of obtaining the envelope of a family of curves. Let us suppose that the family is given by an equation of the form

**(74)** $$F(x, y, \alpha) = 0.$$

In this equation $\alpha$ is the quantity which determines the member of the family; that is, when $\alpha$ is fixed, the equation determines one curve of the family. The letter $a$ in (73) is an example of an $\alpha$. Thus $\alpha$ is also a variable, but its role is different from that of the variables $x$ and $y$. The $\alpha$ is called the parameter of the family. This use of the word is somewhat different from the usage in the phrase "the parametric representation of a curve," although in both cases the word indicates a subsidiary variable.

To obtain the envelope of the family (74), we observe first that for any one value of $\alpha$, a particular member of the family is selected. Moreover, for that value of $\alpha$ there is a point $(x, y)$ (or points) on that member at which the envelope touches the member. Hence to each $\alpha$ an $(x, y)$ is determined which lies on the envelope. This fact suggests, since the $x$ and $y$ are

**Figure 22-20**

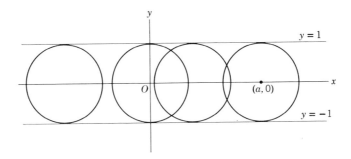

determined by $\alpha$, that we regard the $x$ and $y$ which belong to the envelope as functions of $\alpha$ and that we regard the envelope as defined by the two parametric equations

(75)                         $x = g(\alpha), \qquad y = h(\alpha).$

To find the envelope we must determine $g(\alpha)$ and $h(\alpha)$.

The $x$ and $y$ corresponding to a particular value $\alpha_0$ of $\alpha$ lie on a curve of the family (74), in fact on the very curve determined by the $\alpha_0$ which fixes $x$ and $y$. Hence

$$F\big[\, g(\alpha_0), h(\alpha_0), \alpha_0 \big] = 0.$$

Moreover, the last equation holds for every $\alpha_0$; hence

$$F\big[\, g(\alpha), h(\alpha), \alpha \big] \equiv 0.$$

We can regard this equation as being of the form

$$u = F(x, y, z)$$

where $x = g(\alpha)$, $y = h(\alpha)$, and $z = \alpha$, and $u \equiv 0$ for all $\alpha$. Then by the chain rule (41)

(76)     $F_x\big[\, g(\alpha), h(\alpha), \alpha \big] g'(\alpha) + F_y\big[\, g(\alpha), h(\alpha), \alpha \big] h'(\alpha) + F_\alpha = 0.$

In this equation $F_x$ indicates that one differentiates $F$ as though $x$ were present in place of $g(\alpha)$, but $x$ is then replaced by $g(\alpha)$. The same applies to $F_y$. $F_\alpha$ is the derivative of $F(x, y, \alpha)$ with respect to $\alpha$. The equation does give us some new information about $g(\alpha)$ and $h(\alpha)$ but does not determine these functions.

However, we have not yet used the fact that the envelope and the members of the original family are tangent. The slope of any member of the original family (74) is, by our theorem (60) on implicit functions,

$$\frac{dy}{dx} = -\frac{F_x(x, y, \alpha)}{F_y(x, y, \alpha)}.$$

According to formula (18) of Chapter 18, the slope of the envelope defined by (75) is

$$\frac{dy}{dx} = \frac{h'(\alpha)}{g'(\alpha)}.$$

At the point at which the envelope and a member of the family touch, that is, at $x = g(\alpha)$, $y = h(\alpha)$, the two slopes are the same, or

$$\frac{h'(\alpha)}{g'(\alpha)} = -\frac{F_x\big[\, g(\alpha), h(\alpha), \alpha \big]}{F_y\big[\, g(\alpha), h(\alpha), \alpha \big]}$$

or

**(77)** $\qquad F_x\big[\,g(\alpha),\,h(\alpha),\,\alpha\,\big]\,g'(\alpha) + F_y\big[\,g(\alpha),\,h(\alpha),\,\alpha\,\big]h'(\alpha) = 0.$

Equation (77) tells us that the sum of the first two terms in (76) is 0. Then the remaining term in (76) is 0, that is,

**(78)** $\qquad\qquad\qquad F_\alpha(\,g(\alpha),\,h(\alpha),\,\alpha) = 0,$

where $F_\alpha$ is the partial derivative of $F(x, y, \alpha)$ with respect to the third variable $\alpha$ only.

Equation (78) does give us some new information about $g(\alpha)$ and $h(\alpha)$. What it says is that if we take $F(x, y, \alpha)$ and differentiate only with respect to $\alpha$, then the $x$ and $y$ of points on the envelope will satisfy (78). But points on the envelope also satisfy $F(x, y, \alpha) = 0$. Hence we may take

**(79)** $\qquad\qquad F(x, y, \alpha) = 0, \qquad F_\alpha(x, y, \alpha) = 0$

as two equations describing the envelope. These two equations are sufficient to determine the envelope, for we may eliminate $\alpha$ between them and so obtain one equation in $x$ and $y$ or we may use them to express $x$ and $y$ as functions of $\alpha$, the functions that we described in (75).

The theory of envelopes contains a number of fine points or special facts which we shall not consider here but which are taken up in more advanced courses.

To illustrate how the method of envelopes works, let us find the envelope of the family of normals to the parabola $y^2 = 4x$. If $(x_0, y_0)$ is any point on the parabola, the slope at this point is $2/y_0$. Hence the slope of the normal is $-y_0/2$ and the equation of the normal is

$$y - y_0 = -\frac{y_0}{2}(x - x_0).$$

This equation of the family of normals contains two parameters, $x_0$ and $y_0$, but we have that $y_0^2 = 4x_0$. Therefore, we can write

**(80)** $\qquad\qquad y - y_0 = -\frac{y_0}{2}\left(x - \frac{y_0^2}{4}\right),$

and now $y_0$ is the parameter, the $\alpha$ of our theory. To find what we have denoted by $F_\alpha(x, y, \alpha) = 0$ in our theory, we find the partial derivative of (80) with respect to $y_0$. This is

$$-1 = -\frac{x}{2} + \frac{3y_0^2}{8}$$

or

**(81)** $\qquad\qquad\qquad x = 2 + \frac{3y_0^2}{4}.$

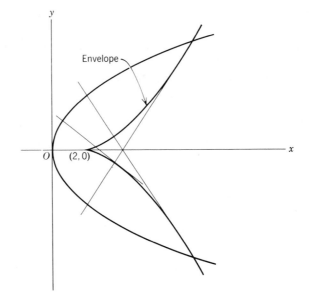

**Figure 22-21**

We can now describe the envelope in two ways. By using the value of $x$ in (81) to eliminate $x$ in (80), we can state that

$$x = 2 + \frac{3y_0^2}{4}, \qquad y = -\tfrac{1}{4} y_0^3$$

are the parametric equations of the envelope. Secondly, by eliminating $y_0$ between these two equations or between (80) and (81), we obtain

$$4(x - 2)^3 = 27y^2,$$

and this is the direct equation of the envelope (Fig. 22-21). Incidentally, the envelope of the family of normals of a plane curve is called the *evolute* of the curve.

## EXERCISES

1. Find the envelope of the family of curves $y = (x - \alpha)^3$ and sketch the curves and their envelope.                                                        *Ans.* $y = 0$.
2. Show that the envelope of the family of circles $(x - a)^2 + y^2 = 1$ is the pair of lines $y = \pm 1$.
3. Find the envelope of the following families of straight lines:
    (a)  $2\alpha y = 2x + \alpha^2$.
                    *Ans.* $y^2 = 2x$.     (c)  $y = \dfrac{m}{a} x + ax$.
    (b)  $x \cos \alpha + y \sin \alpha = 2$.                                  *Ans.* $y^2 = 4mx$.
4. The legs of a right triangle lie along two fixed lines, and the hypotenuse varies so that the area of the triangle is constant. Find the envelope of the family of hypotenuses.

**5.** Consider the family of chords of the parabola $y^2 = x$ which are perpendicular to the axis of the parabola. On each chord a circle is drawn with the chord as diameter. Show analytically that the envelope of the family of circles is a parabola of equal width.

**6.** Find the envelope of the family of circles which have their centers on $y = x^2$ and are tangent to the $x$-axis. *Ans.* $y = 0$ and $x^2 + y^2 = y/2$.

**7.** A straight line moves in such a way that the sum of its intercepts on the two axes is constant. Find the envelope. *Ans.* $\sqrt{x} + \sqrt{y} = l$.

**8.** Find the envelope of the family of circles which pass through the origin and have their centers on the hyperbola $xy = 1$.
*Ans.* The lemniscate $(x^2 + y^2)^2 = 16xy$.

**9.** The family of trajectories of a shell shot out from a cannon with fixed velocity $V$ and varying angle of inclination $A$ is given by (see Chapter 18, Section 4)

$$y = x \tan A - \frac{16(1 + \tan^2 A)}{V^2} x^2.$$

(a)   Show that the envelope of the family, all the members of which lie in one vertical plane, is a parabola—the parabola of surety.

(b)   Find the focus of the parabola of surety.

**10.** The streams of water in a fountain flow upward and outward in all directions from a nozzle which emits them with the same velocity $V$. Show that the surface of the water is a paraboloid of revolution.

   *Suggestion:* See Exercise 9.

**11.** Find the equation of the evolute, the envelope of the normals, of the following:

(a)   The ellipse $x = a \cos \phi$, $y = b \sin \phi$.

   *Suggestion:* The equation of any normal is $y - b \sin \phi = (a/b)$
(x - a \cos \phi)\tan \phi$.      *Ans.* $ax = (a^2 - b^2)\cos^3 \phi$, $by = (b^2 - a^2)\sin^3 \phi$.

(b)   The hyperbola $x = a \sec \phi$, $y = b \tan \phi$.

(c)   The cycloid $x = a(\theta - \sin \theta)$, $y = a(1 - \cos \theta)$.
*Ans.* $x = a\theta + a \sin \theta, y = -a + a \cos \theta$.

**12.** Leibniz first solved the problem of finding the envelope of the family of circles $(x - b)^2 + y^2 = ab$ in which $b$ is the parameter. Find the envelope.

**Figure 22-22**

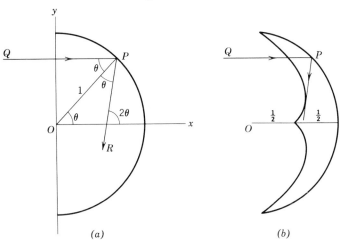

(a)                                         (b)

**13.** Suppose that rays of light come in parallel to the axis of a semicircular concave mirror with center $O$ and radius 1 (Fig. 22-22a) and are reflected in accordance with the law that the angle of reflection equals the angle of incidence ($\angle QPO$ = $\angle OPR$). Find the envelope of the family of reflected rays. This envelope is called a caustic (Fig. 22-22b) and can often be seen when light falls on the concave side of a water glass or a napkin ring and the reflected rays strike the tablecloth.

  *Suggestion:* Choose the axes as shown in Fig. 22-22a and represent the circle by the parametric equations $x = \cos\theta, y = \sin\theta$.

$$Ans. \quad x = \cos\theta - \tfrac{1}{2}\cos 2\theta \cos\theta = \tfrac{3}{4}\cos\theta - \tfrac{1}{4}\cos 3\theta,$$
$$y = \tfrac{3}{4}\sin\theta - \tfrac{1}{4}\sin 3\theta.$$

# CHAPTER
# TWENTY-THREE
# **MULTIPLE**
# **INTEGRALS**

***1. Introduction.*** When we dealt with functions of one variable, we found it advantageous to introduce the concept of the definite integral, that is, the quantity which is the limit of sequences of sums. Our introduction to this concept was motivated by the problem of finding the area under a curve, but we soon discovered that this integral was equally useful in representing volumes of revolution, arc lengths, gravitational attraction, and other quantities. The definite integral can be defined for functions of two or more variables, and, as we shall see, also has many uses. We shall start with the definite integral for functions of two variables and shall see first how it arises in certain problems of volume.

***2. Volume Under a Surface.*** Let us start with the surface

**(1)** $$z = 25 - x^2 - y^2.$$

This is a paraboloid which opens downward and which has its vertex at $(0, 0, 25)$. The surface cuts the $xy$-plane in a circle; this is evident from the fact that when $z = 0$, the points on the surface satisfy the equation $x^2 + y^2 = 25$, which is the equation of a circle in the $z = 0$ plane. There is, then, a volume bounded by the surface and the $xy$-plane. Because the surface is symmetric with respect to the $xz$-plane and the $yz$-plane, the portion of the volume in the first octant is one fourth of the entire volume in question. Let us find the volume of this quarter (Fig. 23-1). We note that it is bounded by the surface, the $xz$-plane, the $yz$-plane, and the $xy$-plane.

To obtain this volume we shall follow the procedure used to obtain the area under a curve. In the latter case we approximated the area by a sum of rectangles and then let the widths of these rectangles approach 0 while increasing their number to fill out the area as much as possible. In the present case the rectangles will be replaced by columns with rectangular cross sections. Specifically, we break up the $x$-interval from 0 to 5 into $j$

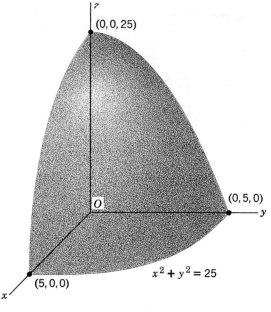

**Figure 23-1**

equal parts $\Delta x$ and the $y$-interval from 0 to 5 into $j$ equal parts $\Delta y$ (Fig. 23-2). At each point of subdivision on one axis we draw lines parallel to the other axis, thus covering the quarter-circle in the $xy$-plane by squares. Not all of the area in the quarter-circle is covered by squares lying entirely within the quarter-circle. We shall consider only those squares which do and assign a number to each of them from 1 to $k$, so that each square has a unique number. In each square we pick any one point. Thus in the typical or $i$th square we pick a point $(x_i, y_i, 0)$.

We consider next the value of our function (1) at $(x_i, y_i, 0)$ and denote it by $z_i$. The quantity $\Delta x \, \Delta y$ is the area of any one square and the quantity $z_i \, \Delta x \, \Delta y$ is the volume of a column (Fig. 23-3) with base $\Delta x \, \Delta y$ and height $z_i$. This column is an approximation to the volume underneath that part of the surface (1) whose projection on the $xy$-plane is $\Delta x \, \Delta y$, or that part of the surface (1) which lies directly above the $i$th square. That the column is

**Figure 23-2**

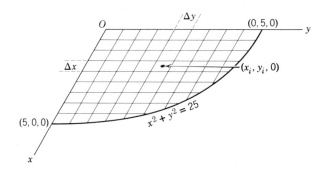

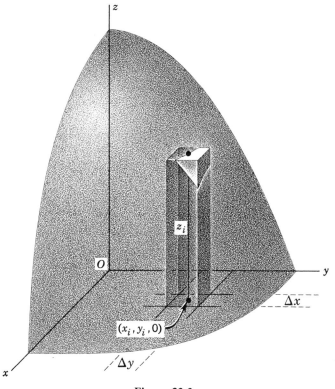

**Figure 23-3**

only an approximation results from the fact that the top surface of the column lies in part above the surface of (1) and in part below.

We now form the sum

**(2)**     $$S_1 = z_1 \, \Delta x \, \Delta y + z_2 \, \Delta x \, \Delta y + \cdots + z_k \, \Delta x \, \Delta y.$$

This sum is an approximation to the volume that we are seeking.

Our next step is to decrease the size of $\Delta x$ while continuing to fill out the $x$-interval from 0 to 5 and to do the same with $\Delta y$. Consequently, there will be some larger number of squares $\Delta x \, \Delta y$ which lie entirely within the quarter-circle of Fig. 23-2 and, in fact, these will fill out more of the quarter-circle than the previous set. We again number the squares from 1 to $l$, say, where $l$ is the number of squares now present, and choose any point $(x_i, y_i, 0)$ in each square. Let $z_i$ be the value of $z$ at each $(x_i, y_i, 0)$. We form the sum

**(3)**     $$S_2 = z_1 \, \Delta x \, \Delta y + z_2 \, \Delta x \, \Delta y + \cdots + z_l \, \Delta x \, \Delta y.$$

The sum $S_2$ is a better approximation to the volume that we are seeking than $S_1$ because the smaller squares $\Delta x \, \Delta y$ fill out more of the quarter-circle and because any column with base $\Delta x \, \Delta y$ and height $z_i$ approximates more closely the volume under that part of the surface which lies over $\Delta x \, \Delta y$.

We can continue the process of making $\Delta x$ and $\Delta y$ smaller while the $\Delta x$'s fill out the interval from 0 to 5 and the $\Delta y$'s do likewise. At the $n$th stage of this process we shall have, say, $m$ squares and the sum

**(4)**                 $$S_n = z_1 \, \Delta x \, \Delta y + z_2 \, \Delta x \, \Delta y + \cdots + z_m \, \Delta x \, \Delta y.$$

We now do precisely what we did in the case of functions of one variable. We let the number of squares become larger and larger, each time securing a new $S_n$ and a better approximation to the volume being sought. We thus obtain a sequence of sums,

$$S_1, S_2, \ldots, S_n, \ldots.$$

Because the approximations furnished by the successive terms of the sequence seem to come closer and closer to the volume under the surface, the limit of this sequence should be the volume that we seek. This limit, that is, $\lim\limits_{n \to \infty} S_n$, is indicated by

**(5)**                 $$\iint_A z \, dx \, dy \quad \text{or} \quad \iint_A (25 - x^2 - y^2) \, dx \, dy.$$

The notation employs two integral signs to show that we are dealing with a function of two variables. The letter $A$ below the two integral signs denotes the region or domain of $x$- and $y$-values to be considered and in the present problem refers to the region in the quarter-circle of the $xy$-plane.

The designation of the limit of the sequence of approximating volumes by the double integral in (5) does not, of course, determine what the volume is. The double integral is merely a symbol and the problem of calculating the volume still remains. We faced precisely the same difficulty when we approached the problem of obtaining the area under a curve as a limit of a sequence of sums of rectangles. We indicated the limit by (cf. Chap. 9, Sect. 3)

$$A = \int_a^b y \, dx$$

(where $A$ denoted area), but the problem of calculating $A$ remained to be handled. The essential technique in this earlier situation proved to be antidifferentiation or the calculation of the indefinite integral. Antidifferentiation will help us here too.

Suppose that in summing the elements of volume, $z_i \, \Delta x \, \Delta y$, each representing one column, we try to involve one variable at a time. Specifically, suppose that we consider a set of squares which are determined by one point $y_i$ of the subdivision of the $y$-axis. These squares lie in a row parallel to the $x$-axis (Fig. 23-4). In each square let us pick one point. Because the choice of this point does not matter in determining the volume, let us choose any $x$-value in any square but let the $y$-value be $y_i$. Thus the $x_i$ all lie on the line $y = y_i$. These choices fix an $x_i$ and $y_i$ in each square. Let $z_i = 25 - x_i^2 - y_i^2$.

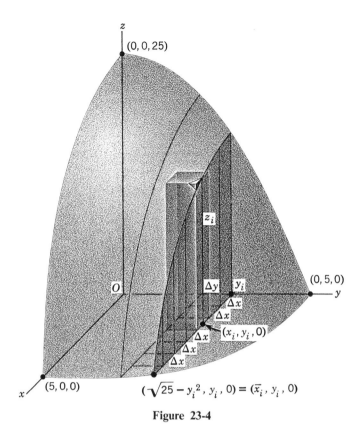

$(\sqrt{25 - y_i^2}, y_i, 0) = (\bar{x}_i, y_i, 0)$

**Figure 23-4**

The volume contributed by the columns over these squares is

**(6)**    $$S_j = z_1 \, \Delta x \, \Delta y + z_2 \, \Delta x \, \Delta y + \cdots + z_j \, \Delta x \, \Delta y,$$

where $j$ is the number of squares in the row. We now let the $\Delta x$ become smaller while we increase the number to fill out the interval from $x = 0$ to $x = \bar{x}$, $\bar{x}$ being the $x$-value on the boundary $x^2 + y^2 = 25$ which corresponds to $y_i$. However, *we keep $\Delta y$ fixed*. Because the $z_i$ vary only with the $x_i$, the sequence of sums furnished by (6) is of exactly the same kind that we set up in Chapter 9 where we were dealing with functions of one variable. This sequence has a limit that we can denote by

**(7)**    $$\lim_{j \to \infty} S_j = \int_0^{\bar{x}} (25 - x^2 - y_i^2) \, dx \, \Delta y.$$

Here the interval of integration is the interval from 0 to $\bar{x}$ where $\bar{x}$ is the value of $x$ on the boundary circle (Fig. 23-4). Of course, $\bar{x}$ depends on the value of the $y_i$ which we choose to keep constant.

We recognize two important facts about (7). First, apart from the factor $\Delta y$, (7) represents the area under the curve determined by cutting the paraboloidal surface by the plane $y = y_i$, the dark area in Fig. 23-4. Secondly, we can calculate (7) because, since $y_i$ is fixed and $\Delta y$ is merely a constant factor, the integrand is a function of one variable, namely $x$.

Before we calculate it, let us note that $\bar{x} = \sqrt{25 - y_i^2}$ . Thus let us calculate

**(8)**
$$\int_0^{\sqrt{25-y_i^2}} (25 - x^2 - y_i^2)\, dx.$$

This integral is

$$\left(25x - \frac{x^3}{3} - y_i^2 x\right)\Bigg|_0^{\sqrt{25-y_i^2}}$$

or, after substituting the end values of the interval of integration,

$$25\sqrt{25 - y_i^2} - \frac{(25 - y_i^2)^{3/2}}{3} - y_i^2\sqrt{25 - y_i^2} = \tfrac{2}{3}(25 - y_i^2)^{3/2}.$$

If we now take the factor $\Delta y$ into account, we have

**(9)**
$$\tfrac{2}{3}(25 - y_i^2)^{3/2}\, \Delta y.$$

This quantity (9) is an approximation to the volume between the two vertical planes $y = y_i$ and $y = y_i - \Delta y$. If we now think of the $y$-interval from 0 to 5 as divided into $n$ subintervals $\Delta y$ and of $y_i$ as a value of $y$ in each $\Delta y$, then the sum of elements such as (9) gives a good approximation to the volume under the paraboloid. In fact, this sum can be taken as the $n$th term of a sequence of sums that approximate the volume under the paraboloid better and better as $\Delta y$ becomes smaller, while of course the set of $\Delta y$'s in each sum fills out the $y$-interval from 0 to 5. Because the element of volume is (9), the volume $V$ is

**(10)**
$$V = \int_0^5 \tfrac{2}{3}(25 - y^2)^{3/2}\, dy.$$

This integral is readily evaluated. By means of the standard form 31 in the Table of Integrals, we have that

$$V = \frac{2}{3}\left[ \frac{y}{8}(125 - 2y^2)\sqrt{25 - y^2} + \frac{1875}{8} \sin^{-1} \frac{y}{5} \right]_0^5.$$

Then

$$V = \frac{625}{8}\, \pi.$$

Let us note what we have accomplished. We set out to find a volume and we saw that it could be expressed as the limit of a sequence of sums of columns, each of volume $z\, \Delta x\, \Delta y$. This limit is expressed as the double integral

**(11)**
$$\int \int_A z\, dx\, dy.$$

In forming any one sum we merely numbered the elements $\Delta x\, \Delta y$ of area in the quarter-circle in some arbitrary order. However, to *evaluate* the double integral we first considered all squares which were determined by a fixed $y$-value, $y_i$, and summed the columns over these squares. By letting $\Delta x$ approach 0, we obtained the volume element (9), namely,

**(12)**
$$\int_0^{\sqrt{25-y_i^2}} z\, dx\, \Delta y,$$

which we could evaluate by keeping $y$ fixed in the function $z = 25 - x^2 - y^2$. The integral is a function of $y_i$. We then summed elements of the form (12) by choosing one $y_i$ in each subdivision of the $y$-interval $(0, 5)$. By repeatedly decreasing $\Delta y$ and summing, we obtained a second sequence of sums. Since (12) is a function of $y$ only, the limit of this second sequence of sums is

**(13)**
$$\int_0^5 \left( \int_0^{\sqrt{25-y^2}} z\, dx \right) dy.$$

In other words, we evaluated the double integral by first integrating the function $z$ with respect to $x$, keeping $y$ fixed, and using as the end values of the integral the values of $x$ corresponding to any *typical* $y$-value. We then integrated with respect to $y$ the result of the first integration, using as end values the end values of the $y$-domain. Thus the double integral (11) was evaluated by two successive ordinary integrations, or by repeated integration.

Of course, it would have been just as sensible to first integrate with respect to $y$, using as end values of the integral the values of $y$ corresponding to a typical value $x_i$ of $x$ (Fig. 23-5). We could then integrate the resulting function of $x$ with respect to $x$, using the end values 0 and 5 for this second integral. That is, we could have evaluated

**(14)**
$$\int_0^5 \left( \int_0^{\sqrt{25-x^2}} z\, dy \right) dx.$$

**Figure 23-5**

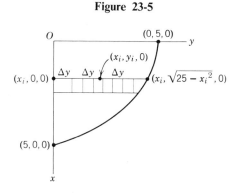

When one writes a repeated integral such as (13) or (14), the inner differential symbol, $dx$ in the case of (13) and $dy$ in the case of (14), goes with the inner integral and its end values; of course then the outer symbol, $dy$ in the case of (13) and $dx$ in the case of (14), goes with the outer integral. It is not necessary to write the parentheses in (13) or (14).

To illustrate further the notion of an integral of a function of two variables and its evaluation by repeated integration, let us find the volume under the surface $z = xy$ and lying over the area in the first quadrant between the two parabolas $y = x^2$ and $y = 18 - x^2$. The surface is a hyperbolic paraboloid turned 45° counterclockwise from that pictured in Fig. 21-23. However, we do not need to picture it. What is essential is that $z$ is positive for $x$ and $y$ positive, so that the surface lies above the $xy$-plane. The domain of integration is the region in the first quadrant illustrated in Fig. 23-6. The integral that we wish to evaluate is

**(15)**
$$V = \int \int_A z \, dx \, dy$$

where $A$ is the domain just described.

To fix $A$ precisely, we must know where the two curves meet. This we determine by solving simultaneously the equations

$$y = x^2 \quad \text{and} \quad y = 18 - x^2.$$

We find that $x = 3, y = 9$ and $x = -3, y = 9$ are the points of intersection of the two parabolas.

Let us integrate (15) by repeated integration. We shall first keep $y$ fixed and try to integrate with respect to $x$. Here a difficulty presents itself. We must determine the interval of integration for $x$ and to do so we take any typical $y$-value and find the range of $x$ for this value of $y$. However, we note that the range of $x$-values is different along $AB$ in Fig. 23-6 from that along $CD$. That is, $B$ lies on the curve of $y = x^2$ whereas $D$ lies on the curve of $y = 18 - x^2$. We might be able to overcome this difficulty, but it may be easier to circumvent it by integrating first with respect to $y$ and then

**Figure 23-6**

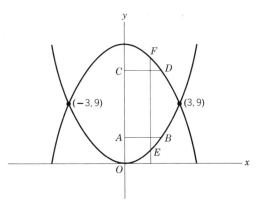

with respect to $x$. Let us, then, keep $x$ fixed and find the typical interval of $y$-values. This is exemplified by $EF$ in Fig. 23-6; we see that $y$ ranges from $y = x^2$ to $y = 18 - x^2$. The range of $x$-values is from 0 to 3. Hence the double integral in (15) becomes

**(16)** $$V = \int_0^3 \int_{x^2}^{18-x^2} xy \, dy \, dx.$$

We integrate with respect to $y$, keeping $x$ fixed. Then

$$V = \int_0^3 \left\{ x \left. \frac{y^2}{2} \right|_{x^2}^{18-x^2} \right\} dx.$$

$$V = \int_0^3 \left\{ x \frac{(18 - x^2)^2}{2} - x \frac{x^4}{2} \right\} dx.$$

$$V = \int_0^3 (162x - 18x^3) \, dx = \frac{729}{2}.$$

We see from this example that even though it is possible in principle to evaluate the double integral by repeated integration in either order, it may be easier to do so in one order rather than the other.

There is another point to be gleaned from this example. Suppose that the original problem had been to find the volume under the surface $z = xy$ and lying over the entire area between $y = x^2$ and $y = 18 - x^2$. The consequent change from what we did above would be to make the $x$-interval of integration run from $-3$ to 3. Evaluation of (16) with this change would yield 0. This result is surprising because, as we found earlier, the volume above half of the area is certainly not 0. The explanation stems from the nature of our double integral. We introduced it by means of the concept of volume, and the element of volume was $z \, \Delta x \, \Delta y$. Now, the area $\Delta x \, \Delta y$ is always chosen to be positive just as $\Delta x$ in the definition of the single integral is always chosen positive. Then $z \, \Delta x \, \Delta y$ represents volume when $z$ is positive, if by volume we mean the pure geometric concept. However, we see that the function $z = xy$ is negative when $x$ and $y$ are in the second quadrant, and therefore the double integral gives the negative of volume when $z$ is negative. In our example the volume given by the integral when $z$ is positive is offset by the "negative volume" when $z$ is negative. (Compare Chap. 9, Sect. 5.)

The double integral serves many other purposes in addition to the calculation of volumes. In the present case, although we shall deal with volumes, the ultimate goal is to evaluate $\int_{-\infty}^{\infty} e^{-x^2} dx$.* We have already encountered the function $z = e^{-x^2}$ in Chapter 20, Section 12, where we

---

* The symbol $\infty$ in the upper and lower bounds of the interval of integration means strictly $\lim_{N \to \infty} \int_{-N}^{N} e^{-x^2} dx$. We shall discuss this matter in Chapter 25, Section 9.

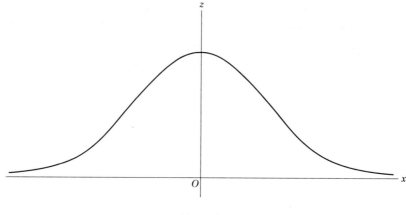

**Figure 23-7**

observed the use of series to calculate $\int_0^x e^{-x^2}\, dx$. However, to calculate the area under the entire curve (Fig. 23-7), that is, from $x = -\infty$ to $x = \infty$, the series method will not do because the end values are infinite. The evaluation of $\int_{-\infty}^{\infty} e^{-x^2}\, dx$ is done by a trick that is rarely useful but, because the result is important and the method does oblige us to think about volumes, we shall look into it.

The trick is to complicate the problem by introducing the surface obtained by rotating the curve $z = e^{-x^2}$ about the $z$-axis (Fig. 23-8). The equation of this surface is

$$z = e^{-x^2 - y^2},$$

**Figure 23-8**

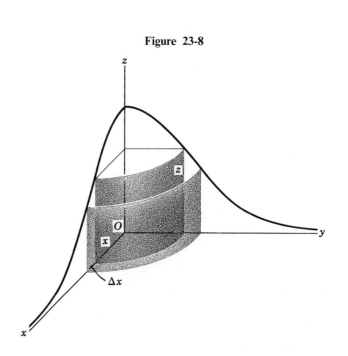

because if we fix $z$, say at $z = \frac{1}{2}$, the locus of all the points in the plane for which $\frac{1}{2} = e^{-x^2-y^2}$ is the circle $x^2 + y^2 = \log 2$.

We now calculate the volume under the entire surface. Since the volume is a volume of revolution we can use the shell method which we first studied in Chapter 15, Section 3. As Fig. 23-8 shows, the volume is the limit of a sequence of sums of cylindrical shells. The thickness of any one shell is $\Delta x$ and the lateral surface of the shell is $2\pi xz$. Hence the volume is

$$V = \int_0^\infty 2\pi xz \; dx.$$

Since $z = e^{-x^2}$,

$$V = \int_0^\infty 2\pi e^{-x^2} x \; dx.$$

$$V = -\pi e^{-x^2}\big|_0^\infty = \pi.^*$$

Now let us express the volume under $z = e^{-x^2-y^2}$ by the method we have been learning in this section. The volume is given by the double integral

$$V = \int\int_A z \; dx \; dy$$

where the domain of integration $A$ is the entire $xy$-plane. Then

$$V = \int_{-\infty}^\infty \int_{-\infty}^\infty e^{-x^2-y^2} \; dx \; dy.$$

But $e^{-x^2-y^2} = e^{-x^2} e^{-y^2}$, so that

$$V = \int_{-\infty}^\infty \int_{-\infty}^\infty e^{-x^2} e^{-y^2} \; dx \; dy.$$

Let us evaluate by repeated integration. If we keep $y$ fixed and integrate first with respect to $x$, we may as well take $e^{-y^2}$ outside the inner integral because this factor is a constant. Then

$$V = \int_{-\infty}^\infty e^{-y^2} \left\{ \int_{-\infty}^\infty e^{-x^2} \; dx \right\} dy.$$

We see that if we evaluate the inner integral, the result does not involve $y$, and so we can regard this integral as a constant insofar as the integration with respect to $y$ is concerned. Thus

$$V = \int_{-\infty}^\infty e^{-x^2} \; dx \cdot \int_{-\infty}^\infty e^{-y^2} \; dy.$$

---

* Strictly speaking, we do not substitute $\infty$ for $x$. We evaluate $-\pi e^{-x^2}\big|_0^N$ which gives $\pi - \pi e^{-N^2}$ and then let $N$ become infinite, thus obtaining $\pi$.

The two integrals have the same value, so that

$$V = \left( \int_{-\infty}^{\infty} e^{-x^2} dx \right)^2 .$$

We know from our evaluation of $V$ by the shell method that $V = \pi$. Then

(17)                            $$\int_{-\infty}^{\infty} e^{-x^2} dx = \sqrt{\pi} .$$

## EXERCISES

1. Evaluate the following repeated integrals:

   (a) $\int_0^2 \int_0^1 (x + y) \, dy \, dx.$     *Ans.* 3.    (d) $\int_0^b \int_t^{10t} \sqrt{st - t^2} \, ds \, dt.$

   (b) $\int_{1/2}^1 \int_0^y y \, dx \, dy.$                      (e) $\int_0^1 \int_{\sqrt{2}}^{2-y} y^2 \, dx \, dy.$     *Ans.* $\frac{11}{84}$.

   (c) $\int_0^{\sqrt{2}} \int_{x^3-x}^{3x-x^3} 1 \, dy \, dx$     *Ans.* 2.

2. Evaluate (14). The result should, of course, be the same as that obtained by the reverse order of integration.

3. Find the volume bounded by the elliptic paraboloid $z = 1 - (x^2/a^2) - (y^2/b^2)$ and the $xy$-plane.                                    *Ans.* $\pi ab/2$.

4. Evaluate the integral (15) by first integrating with respect to $x$ and then with respect to $y$.

   *Suggestion:* Break up the domain of integration into two parts by introducing the line $y = 9$.

5. Evaluate $\iint_A (2xy - x^2) dx \, dy$ where $A$ is the rectangle bounded by $x = -1$, $x = 2, y = 0,$ and $y = 4$.                                    *Ans.* 12.

6. Evaluate $\iint_A (y - 2x) dx \, dy$ where $A$ is the triangle bounded by $x = 0, y = 0$, and $y = 3x + 6$.                                    *Ans.* 20.

7. Find the volume under the plane $x + y + z = 9$ and above the triangle in the $xy$-plane bounded by $y = 0, x = 3,$ and $y = 2x/3$.                *Ans.* 19.

8. Find the volume under the plane $z = 2y$ and above the first quadrant area bounded by $x = 3, y = 0,$ and $x^2 + y^2 = 36$.

9. Find the volume under the cylinder $y = z^2$ and above the area in the $xy$-plane bounded by $y = 0$ and $x^2 + 9y = 9$.                        *Ans.* $3\pi/4$.

10. Find the volume under the surface $z = xy$ and above the area in the first quadrant bounded by $y = 0, y = x,$ and $x^2 + y^2 = 1$.

11. Find the volume under the plane $z = x + y$ and above the area in the first quadrant bounded by the ellipse $4x^2 + 9y^2 = 36$.                  *Ans.* 10.

12. Find the volume bounded by the paraboloid $x^2 + 4z^2 + 8y = 16$ and by the $xz$-plane.

    *Suggestion:* Treat $y$ as the dependent variable.                    *Ans.* $8\pi$.

**13.** Find the volume cut out in the first octant by the plane $2x + 3y + 6z = 6$.

**14.** Find the volume in the first octant bounded by the cylinder $z = 4 - x^2$, the coordinate planes, and the plane $4x + 3y = 12$. *Ans.* 16.

**15.** Describe the volume represented by the following:

(a) $\displaystyle\int_0^a \int_0^x \sqrt{a^2 - x^2}\; dy\; dx.$ (b) $\displaystyle\int_0^a \int_0^{\sqrt{a^2-y^2}} (2a - x - y)dx\; dy.$

**16.** Rewrite the following integrals so that the integrations can be performed in reverse order.

(a) $\displaystyle\int_0^{a/2} \int_{x^2/a}^{x-(x^2/a)} f(x,y)dy\; dx$ *Ans.* $\displaystyle\int_0^{a/4} \int_{(a/2)-\sqrt{(a^2/4)-ay}}^{\sqrt{ay}} f(x,y)dx\; dy.$

(b) $\displaystyle\int_c^a \int_{(b/a)\sqrt{a^2-x^2}}^{b} f(x,y)dy\; dx.$

*Ans.* $\displaystyle\int_{(b/a)\sqrt{a^2-c^2}}^{b} \int_c^a f(x,y)dx\; dy + \int_0^{(b/a)\sqrt{a^2-c^2}} \int_{a\sqrt{b^2-y^2}/b}^{a} f(x,y)dx\; dy.$

(c) $\displaystyle\int_0^a \int_{\sqrt{a^2-x^2}/2}^{\sqrt{a^2-x^2}} f(x,y)dy\; dx.$

*Ans.* $\displaystyle\int_0^{a/2} \int_{\sqrt{a^2-4y^2}}^{\sqrt{a^2-y^2}} f(x,y)dx\; dy + \int_{a/2}^a \int_0^{\sqrt{a^2-y^2}} f(x,y)dx\; dy.$

**17.** Let $V$ be the volume (Fig. 23-9) enclosed by the coordinate planes, the surface $PNTS$, and the planes $PQMN$ and $PQRS$. In terms of this figure, decide on intuitive grounds the geometric meaning of the following

(a) $\dfrac{\partial V}{\partial y}$. *Ans. Area PQRS.* (c) $\dfrac{\partial V}{\partial x}$. *Ans. Area PQMN.*

(b) $\dfrac{\partial}{\partial x}\left(\dfrac{\partial V}{\partial y}\right)$. *Ans. PQ.* (d) $\dfrac{\partial}{\partial y}\left(\dfrac{\partial V}{\partial x}\right)$.

**Figure 23-9**

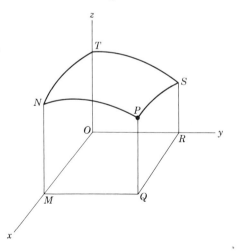

**18.** Find the volume of one of the wedges cut out from the cylinder $x^2 + y^2 = r^2$ by the planes $z = 0$ and $z = mx$. *Ans.* $2m\,r^3/3$.

19. Find the volume cut out from a sphere of radius $a$ by a right circular cylinder of radius $b$, $b < a$, whose axis passes through the center of the sphere.

   *Suggestion:* Break up the desired volume into the volume of a cylinder plus the volume of a spherical cap and choose the proper order of integration in obtaining the latter volume.        *Ans.*  $(4\pi/3)[a^3 - (a^2 - b^2)^{3/2}]$.

20. Find the volume in the first octant bounded by the cylinder $x^2 + y^2 = 9$ and the planes $y = 0$, $z = 0$, and $z = x$.

21. Find the volume in the first octant bounded by the surfaces $y^2 = x$, $x + z = 1$, $y = 0$, and $z = 0$.        *Ans.*  $\frac{4}{15}$.

22. Find the volume in the first octant bounded by the surfaces $y^2 = x$, $x + y + z = 2$, $y = 0$, and $z = 0$.

23. Find the volume common to the two cylinders $x^2 + y^2 = r^2$ and $x^2 + z^2 = r^2$.        *Ans.*  $16r^3/3$.

24. Find the volume of the column standing in the area common to the two parabolas $x = y^2$ and $y = x^2$ as base and cut off by the surface $z = 12 + y - x^2$.

25. Rewrite the integral $\int_0^a \int_0^x f(x, y) dy\, dx$ so that the integrations can be performed in reverse order. The equality of the two integrals is known as Dirichlet's formula.        *Ans.*  $\int_0^a \int_y^a f(x, y) dx\, dy$.

26. Show that $\int_0^x \int_0^u f(u) dt\, du = \int_0^x f(u)(x - u) du$.

   *Suggestion:* Apply integration by parts to the right side.

### 3. Some Physical Applications of the Double Integral.

Let us note, first, that the double integral, which we have introduced to represent a volume, can also represent an area. Suppose that the function $z$ of $x$ and $y$ happens to be the function $z = 1$ and the domain $A$ is the region (Fig. 23-10) between the parabola $y = x^2$ and the straight line $y = x$. Then the double integral

$$\iint_A dx\, dy$$

represents the volume over the domain $A$ and bounded above by the plane $z = 1$. However, it is equally correct to interpret the double integral as representing the *area* $A$ itself,* because the volume is really a cylinder with base $A$ and height 1. Then the area of the base is numerically the same as the volume. Hence we can use the double integral to evaluate the area $A$, and our method of evaluation is the same as that for any double integral. The specific double integral that represents $A$ is

$$A = \int_0^1 \int_{x^2}^x dy\, dx,$$

* We use the letter $A$ for the domain or region whose area we seek and for the area itself, which is a number.

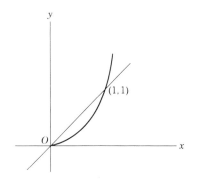

**Figure 23-10**

and the value of this double integral, obtained of course by repeated integration, is $\frac{1}{6}$.

The use of the double integral to find areas does not achieve more than what can be achieved with single integrals (see Chapter 9). A more significant application is that of finding the mass of solids. Because materials must be used in the construction of all objects and material costs money, it is important to know how much mass is involved. With the double integral we can find the mass of bodies that are essentially two-dimensional, such as thin disks. For the moment let us consider disks for which the distribution of mass is uniform throughout. If the disk has total mass $M$, area $A$, and thickness $t$, the mass per unit volume is $M/At$ and the mass per unit area is $M/A$. (Because the disk is thin, one can ignore the thickness and consider the mass distributed only over the area, as though there were no thickness. This idealized disk is often referred to as a lamina. However, it is important to keep in mind that physically every disk has some thickness and that $M$ is the mass of a volume.)

The mass of a disk can be specified in another way, which is important especially when the mass is not uniformly distributed. One can specify the mass $M$ *per unit volume*. If the disk has thickness $t$, the mass of a volume formed by a thin cylinder, whose base is one square unit and thickness $t$, is $M \cdot 1 \cdot t$ and so the mass per unit area of the disk is $Mt$.* The mass of an element of area $\Delta A$ is then $Mt \, \Delta A$.

The mass of a solid can vary from point to point. The concept of density is used to represent this variation of mass from point to point. To give meaning to density at a point, we think of a little volume $\Delta V$ surrounding that point and of mass $\Delta M$ and consider the limit of the ratio $\Delta M / \Delta V$ as $\Delta V$ shrinks to 0 about the point. We thus obtain a function $D(x, y, z)$, the density, which can vary from point to point. Thus density means mass per unit volume at a point. In terms of this density function, the mass of an element of a thin disk of area $\Delta A$ and thickness $t$ is approximately $D(x, y, z)t \, \Delta A$ where $(x, y, z)$ is some point in the volume. Because the disk is thin, one can neglect any variation in density over the thickness and consider only the variation over the surface. Then the

* See also Chapter 16, Section 5.

variation of the density over the surface is a function of $x$ and $y$ only. This density quantitatively is $D(x, y, z)t$ but, because $D$ does not vary with $z$ in the situation under discussion, we agree to speak of density per unit area and write just $D(x, y)$ in place of $D(x, y, z)t$.

Now let us consider how to find the mass of a thin disk with variable density. If we break up the entire area into little squares $\Delta x \, \Delta y$ and choose any point $(x_i, y_i)$ in each square, we have as an approximation to the mass of the disk

$$D(x_1, y_1) \, \Delta x \, \Delta y + D(x_2, y_2) \, \Delta x \, \Delta y + \cdots + D(x_n, y_n) \, \Delta x \, \Delta y.$$

If we now decrease $\Delta x$ and $\Delta y$ but take all squares which lie inside the area of the disk, we obtain a better approximation to the mass. The limit of the sequence of sums as $\Delta x$ and $\Delta y$ approach 0 is the mass of the disk; this limit is denoted by the double integral

**(18)**
$$\int \int_A D(x, y) \, dy \, dx,$$

where $A$ is the area of the disk. Thus the mass is representable as a double integral if the density at each point is known.

Just to see how (18) is used, let us consider the problem of finding the mass of a thin circular disk of radius $a$ if the density at each point varies as the square of the distance of that point from a fixed diameter (Fig. 23-11). We regard the circular disk as placed on a coordinate system with the center of the disk at the origin and the fixed diameter lying along the $x$-axis. Then the density $D(x, y)$ at any point $(x, y)$ is $ky^2$ where $k$ is a constant. The mass of the entire disk then is given by (18); that is,

$$M = \int \int_A ky^2 \, dy \, dx$$

where $A$ is the area of the circular disk and $M$ is the mass of the entire disk.

**Figure 23-11**

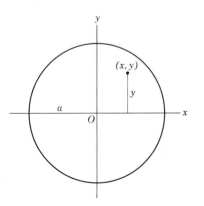

This double integral is evaluated by means of the repeated integral

$$M = \int_{-a}^{a} \int_{-\sqrt{a^2 - x^2}}^{\sqrt{a^2 - x^2}} ky^2 \, dy \, dx$$

or, since the mass is the same in each quadrant, by

**(19)**          $$\frac{M}{4} = \int_{0}^{a} \int_{0}^{\sqrt{a^2 - x^2}} ky^2 \, dy \, dx.$$

## EXERCISES

1. Calculate by double integrals the area bounded by each of the following pairs of curves:
   (a) $y^2 = x^3$ and $y = x$.
   Ans. $\frac{1}{10}$.
   (b) $x^2 + y^2 = 10$ and $y^2 = 9x$.
   (c) $y^2 = x + 1$ and $x + y = 1$.
   Ans. $4\frac{1}{2}$
   (d) $y = 9 - x^2$ and $y = x + 7$.

   (e) $xy = 4$ and $x + y = 5$.
   Ans. $7\frac{1}{2} - 4 \log 4$.
   (f) $y^2 = 5 - x$ and $y^2 = 4x$.
   (g) $y = 2x - x^2$ and $y = 3x^2 - 6x$.
   Ans. $5\frac{1}{3}$.
   (h) $4y = x^3$ and $y = x^3 - 3x$.

2. Evaluate the integral (19) of the text.          Ans. $k\pi a^4 / 16$.

3. The density of a circular disk of radius $a$ varies as the distance of any point from a fixed diameter. Find the mass of the disk.

4. In the isosceles right triangle the density at any point varies as the square of the distance of that point from the vertex of the right angle. Find the mass of the triangle.          Ans. $ka^4 / 6$.

5. The density at any point of a square lamina of side $a$ varies as the square of the distance of that point from one corner. Find the mass of the lamina.
   Ans. $2ka^4 / 3$.

6. The density at any point of an isosceles right triangle is proportional to the distance from one of the equal sides. Find the mass of the triangle.

7. Find the mass of a lamina bounded by $x = 0$, $x = 1$, $y = 0$, and $y = e^x$ if the density at any point varies as the distance of that point from the $x$-axis.
   Ans. $k(e^2 - 1)/4$.

8. Find the mass of the lamina bounded by the parabola $x^2 = 16y$ and the line $y = 4$ if the density at any point is proportional to the distance of that point from the straight side.

9. Find the mass of the lamina in the first quadrant of the circle $x^2 + y^2 = 25$ if the density at any point is proportional to the sum of the distances of that point from the two straight edges.

To see more of the role that double integrals play in physical problems, let us consider rotary motion.* Many objects, including bad arguments, go in circles. In automobiles the wheels, gears, crankshaft, the armature of the generator, and many cams rotate. In airplanes similar

---

\* This application can be omitted.

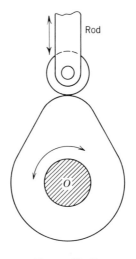

**Figure  23-12**

components as well as turbines and propellers rotate. All machinery has rotating elements.

Consider a cam (Fig. 23-12) rotating around an axis through the point $O$ and perpendicular to the plane of the paper. As the cam rotates, each element of mass $\Delta m$ of the cam must have a centripetal acceleration toward the center of its circular motion; the magnitude of this acceleration is $\dot\theta^2 r$, where $\dot\theta$ is the angular velocity of the element and $r$ is the constant radius of the circular path. [See Chap. 19, formula (13).] According to Newton's second law of motion, a force must be exerted to provide this acceleration, and the force is the mass times the acceleration. Then the radial force, whose magnitude we denote by $f_r$, is

**(20)** $$f_r = \Delta m r \dot\theta^2 = D\,\Delta x\,\Delta y\, r\dot\theta^2,$$

where $D$ is the density of the element of mass $\Delta m$. This centripetal force must be exerted physically by an axle which lies along the mathematical axis of rotation. Because the axle must exert a force to keep each element $\Delta m$ of the cam rotating in its circular path, the axle may be called upon to exert considerable force, particularly if the angular velocity is large. Moreover, if the distribution of mass in the cam is not favorable, the axle will be called upon to exert different forces in different directions. Since no body is perfectly rigid, the axle will flex or bend and may even snap. It would be desirable, therefore, to have the axle exert as little force as possible.

The position of the axle in the cam may be at our disposal, so let us see if we can choose it advantageously. We shall suppose that a coordinate system is set up and that the center of rotation is to be at some point $(a, b)$ which will be determined so as to minimize the total force the axle must exert (Fig. 23-13).

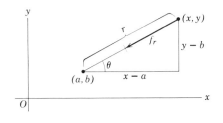

**Figure 23-13**

We cannot sum readily all the centripetal forces that the axle must exert, because they are not in the same direction. However, we can resolve each force into a horizontal and a vertical component and then add the horizontal and vertical components separately. Thus, since $f_r$ is the magnitude of the radial force required to keep the element $\Delta m$ located at $(x, y)$ in its path, and since the force is directed toward $(a, b)$, the horizontal component is $-f_r \cos \theta$. Now

$$\cos \theta = \frac{x - a}{r}.$$

Then the horizontal component $f_h$ of the radial force is

$$f_h = \frac{a - x}{r} f_r$$

$$= \frac{a - x}{r} D \, \Delta x \, \Delta y \, r\dot\theta^2$$

$$= (a - x)D\dot\theta^2 \, \Delta x \, \Delta y.$$

If we sum all the horizontal components for all the elements $\Delta m$ of the cam and let $\Delta x$ and $\Delta y$ approach 0, we obtain the double integral

$$F_h = \int \int (a - x)D\dot\theta^2 \, dx \, dy.$$

Because the angular velocity $\dot\theta$ is the same for all elements of the cam,

$$F_h = \dot\theta^2 \int \int (a - x)D \, dx \, dy.$$

We can make this force 0 by solving for the proper value of $a$. Since the integral can be expressed as a sum of two integrals, we have

$$\dot\theta^2 a \int \int D \, dx \, dy - \dot\theta^2 \int \int xD \, dx \, dy = 0$$

and

**(21)**
$$a = \frac{\int \int Dx \, dx \, dy}{\int \int D \, dx \, dy}$$

If we now do the same for the vertical component of $f_r$, we obtain

**(22)**
$$b = \frac{\iint Dy \ dx \ dy}{\iint D \ dx \ dy} .$$

Thus we can place the axle at a point $(a, b)$ so that the axle does not have to exert radial forces while the cam is moving. The point whose coordinates $(a, b)$ are determined by (21) and (22) is called the center of gravity of the body.*

We should point out that what is done in practice to eliminate the radial force exerted by the axle is not to move the location of the axis. The position of the axis in the cam is dictated by the work that the cam must perform as it rotates. However, we can see from formulas (21) and (22) that we can distribute the density of the material of the cam so that the desired geometrical location of the center of rotation can also satisfy (21) and (22). For example, one can increase the thickness of the cam along one part of the circumference and not affect the cam's functioning. This same trick is used to balance automobile wheels. If the wheel is out of balance, it will exert a force on the axle of the car which might ultimately bend it and, in addition, there will be uneven wear on the tire. Balance is achieved by placing small weights on the rim.

### 4. The Double Integral.

We introduced the double integral in Section 2 to represent volume under a surface and then evaluated the double integral by repeated integration. The concept of the double integral is really an analytical one; that is, it applies to functions of two variables regardless of the physical or geometrical interpretation. Moreover, the distinction between the double integral and the repeated integrals used to evaluate them is a little sharper and more significant than we have thus far made clear. Let us start afresh with the concept of the double integral.

Suppose that we have a two-dimensional domain $A$ (Fig. 23-14). Analytically, this can be described as a collection of pairs of values $(x, y)$. One can think of this domain as a region in the $xy$-plane, as we did in Section 2, but the geometrical interpretation is not essential. We are also given some function $z = f(x, y)$ which is defined for each $(x, y)$ in the domain $A$. We subdivide the domain $A$ into subdomains $\Delta A$ of arbitrary shape. (In Section 2 they were squares.) These subdomains can also be described analytically by specifying the pairs of $x$- and $y$-values in each. Let $\Delta A$ also denote the area of a typical subdomain. The area is a number. We now take into account those subdomains $\Delta A$ which lie entirely within $A$ and number them $\Delta A_1, \Delta A_2, \cdots \Delta A_k$. In each subdomain we choose any pair $(x_i, y_i)$. Let $z_i = f(x_i, y_i)$. We then introduce the sum

**(23)**        $S_1 = z_1 \Delta A_1 + z_2 \Delta A_2 + \cdots + z_k \Delta A_k,$

where $\Delta A_i$ is used to denote the area of the subdomain $\Delta A_i$.

---

* The center of gravity plays a large role in mechanics. The notion is often introduced in other ways.

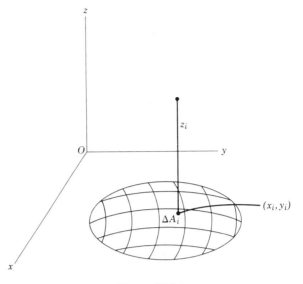

**Figure 23-14**

The two-dimensional domain $A$ is now divided into smaller pieces of area $\Delta A$, and again we take into account those pieces or subdomains $\Delta A$ which lie entirely in $A$. These $\Delta A$ are numbered in some manner; let us suppose that there are $l$ of them. In each $\Delta A$ we choose one $(x_i, y_i)$ and again form the sum

**(24)** $$S_2 = z_1 \Delta A_1 + z_2 \Delta A_2 + \cdots + z_l \Delta A_l$$

where $z_i = f(x_i, y_i)$.

We continue this process of subdividing $A$ into smaller and smaller pieces $\Delta A$ and each time form a sum analogous to (23) and (24). The only restriction on the form of the $\Delta A$ as they are chosen smaller and smaller is that the diameter (the largest possible distance from one point to another in $\Delta A$) approach 0. We thus obtain a sequence of sums

**(25)** $$S_1, S_2, \ldots, S_n, \cdots$$

and if this sequence has a limit, then this limit is what we mean by the double integral of the function $f(x, y)$ over the domain $A$. The $\lim_{n \to \infty} S_n$ is denoted by

**(26)** $$\iint_A f(x, y) dA \quad \text{or} \quad \int_A \int z \, dA.$$

Strictly speaking, there is an additional condition in the definition of the double integral. It is possible to make many different choices of the $\Delta A_i$ not only in the first subdivision of $A$ but also in the succeeding subdivisions. Moreover, it is possible to make many different choices of $(x_i, y_i)$ in each $\Delta A_i$. These possible variations also make possible many different sequences of the type given in (25). For the double integral to exist or to have meaning, each of these possible sequences must have the same limit. There are theorems that tell us when all possible sequences do yield a unique limit, but we shall not investigate them. We shall rely on the intuitive argument that all these sequences approach the volume lying above $A$ and under the surface $z = f(x, y)$.

The definition of the double integral does offer in principle a method of calculating it. Given any domain $A$ and a function $f(x, y)$, one could calculate the individual members of the sequence (25) and then attempt to find the limit of this sequence. We did evaluate some single integrals by this method in Section 2 of Chapter 9. However, this method is impractical even for single integrals, let alone double integrals. The effective method is repeated or iterated integration. In the case of rectangular coordinates and where the $\Delta A_i$ are squares with sides parallel to the $x$- and $y$-axes, this amounted to holding one variable, say $y$, fixed and summing those $z_i \Delta A_i$ which are determined by the fixed $y$-value. This sum, as the $\Delta x$ approach 0, gives rise to a sequence of sums which in turn leads to a single integral as in (7) above. Then a second summation involving the result of the first integration and $\Delta y$, [compare (9)], leads, as $\Delta y$ approaches 0, to a second sequence and a second single integral as in (10). Consequently, the method of repeated or iterated integration involves two separate sequences of sums and their limits, whereas the double integral involves taking the limit of a single sequence of sums. Thus the two notions, the double integral and the iterated integral, are different.

There is, then, some question as to when a double integral may be evaluated by two repeated integrations. In the case of rectangular coordinates we used a geometrical argument to show that repeated integration gives the same volume as the double integral. We shall rely on this geometrical argument to justify evaluating subsequent double integrals by repeated integration.

In defining the double integral (26), we utilized $x, y$, and $z$, and in Fig. 23-14 we pictured a Cartesian coordinate system. However, the definition is really independent of the geometric meaning of $x, y$, and $z$, as our review of it in this section should show. Hence we should be able to apply the notion to a totally different geometrical or physical situation. We shall see in the next section how the definition applies without change to a new geometrical situation.

### 5. The Double Integral in Cylindrical Coordinates.

In working with functions of one variable we found that many problems could be formulated and solved in terms of polar coordinates rather than rectangular coordinates. It is true also for problems involving functions of two or more variables that coordinate systems other than the rectangular system are helpful. One of these is the cylindrical coordinate system.

This system is actually no more than the usual polar coordinate system in one plane—the horizontal plane of Fig. 23-15—to which a third dimension, the $z$-dimension, is added. The $z$-axis is perpendicular to the $\rho\theta$-plane and passes through the pole $O$ of the polar coordinate system. Thus any point in space is represented in the cylindrical coordinate system by three coordinates—a $\rho$-value, a $\theta$-value, and a $z$-value—and these are written in

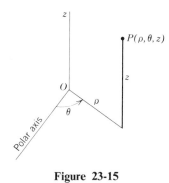

**Figure 23-15**

the order $(\rho, \theta, z)$. The conventions already adopted for polar coordinates apply here unchanged and the $z$-values, as in the rectangular coordinate system, can be positive or negative—positive if the point lies above the $\rho\theta$-plane and negative if below.

It is, of course, possible to write equations for planes, curved surfaces, lines, and curves in the cylindrical coordinate system as well as in the rectangular system. We shall not undertake any systematic study of the equations in cylindrical coordinates and their corresponding figures. Rather, we shall rely on becoming familiar with these correspondences as we encounter the need for them. However, a couple of points may bear mention at this time. We can often identify the figure belonging to an equation in cylindrical coordinates if we keep in mind that the $\rho$- and $\theta$-values of points represented in the cylindrical coordinate system are readily translated into the $x$- and $y$-values of the same points represented in a rectangular coordinate system whose origin is at the pole, whose $xy$-plane is the $\rho\theta$-plane, and whose positive $x$-axis is the polar axis. We need only recall that

$$\rho = \sqrt{x^2 + y^2}, \qquad \sin \theta = \frac{y}{\sqrt{x^2 + y^2}}, \qquad \cos \theta = \frac{x}{\sqrt{x^2 + y^2}}.$$

Secondly, we pointed out in Section 3 of Chapter 21 that an equation such as $x + y = 5$ can be interpreted in two ways. Interpreted as an equation of a figure in the plane, it is the equation of a line. However, interpreted as an equation of a figure in three-dimensional space, it is the equation of a plane. The same applies to cylindrical coordinates. The equation $\rho = 5$, interpreted as an equation in the $\rho\theta$-plane, is the equation of a circle with center at the pole and radius 5. However, interpreted as an equation in three dimensions, it is the equation of a circular cylinder whose axis is the $z$-axis, because all points for which $\rho = 5$, no matter what their $z$-values, satisfy the equation.

## EXERCISES

**1.** Describe the figures represented by the following equations in cylindrical coordinates regarded as equations in three-dimensional space:
   (a)  $\rho = 1$.             *Ans.* Cylinder.    (b)  $\tan \theta = 1$.

(c) $\rho^2 + z^2 = 4$.      *Ans.* Sphere.      (g) $\rho = 4 \cos \theta$.

(d) $z^2 = 3\rho^2$.                          (h) $\rho = 2 \sin \theta$      *Ans.* Cylinder.

(e) $\rho \cos \theta = 4$.      *Ans.* Plane.      (i) $z = 5$.

(f) $\rho \sin \theta = 3$.

A function whose geometrical interpretation is to be in terms of cylindrical coordinates will generally take the form

$$z = f(\rho, \theta).$$

Let us investigate the concept of the double integral as it applies to such functions.

If we review the definition of the double integral

**(27)** $$\iint_A f(x, y) \, dA$$

given in the preceding section we see that it applies verbatim to $z = f(\rho, \theta)$. We must now understand $A$ to be some region in the $(\rho, \theta)$-plane and the $\Delta A$ to be subdomains of $A$. Merely to indicate that we intend to think geometrically in terms of cylindrical coordinates, we can write the double integral as

**(28)** $$\iint_A f(\rho, \theta) \, dA.$$

However, if we are going to use cylindrical coordinates, we must express the $\Delta A$ in this system.

Let us consider, then, a region $A$ in the $(\rho, \theta)$-plane (Fig. 23-16) and let us divide it into elements $\Delta A$ that we can express in terms of the $\rho$- and $\theta$-coordinates. Suppose that insofar as the $\theta$-values are concerned the region

**Figure 23-16**

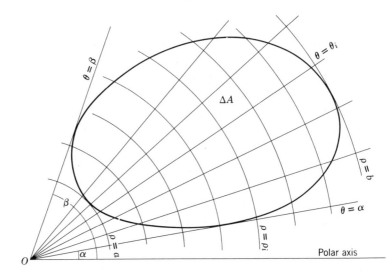

$A$ lies between $\theta = \alpha$ and $\theta = \beta$. We divide the $\theta$-interval from $\alpha$ to $\beta$ into subintervals by choosing values of $\theta$ between $\alpha$ and $\beta$, namely,

$$\alpha, \theta_2, \theta_3, \ldots, \theta_{m-1}, \beta.$$

Likewise, suppose that insofar as $\rho$-values are concerned the region $A$ lies between $\rho = a$ and $\rho = b$. We divide the $\rho$-interval from $\rho = a$ to $\rho = b$ into subintervals by choosing values of $\rho$ between $a$ and $b$, namely,

$$a, \rho_2, \rho_3, \ldots, \rho_{n-1}, b.$$

We draw the lines $\theta = \alpha, \theta = \theta_2, \ldots, \theta = \beta$, all of which pass through the pole $O$, and we draw the circles $\rho = a, \rho = \rho_2, \rho = \rho_3, \ldots, \rho = b$, all of which have their centers at the pole $O$. This set of lines and circles divides the region $A$ into subregions $\Delta A_i$, a typical one of which is shown in Fig. 23-17. We consider only those $\Delta A_i$ which lie entirely within $A$.

To obtain an expression for $\Delta A_i$, we note that it is the difference between two circular sectors. The larger sector has the area

$$\tfrac{1}{2}(\rho_i + \Delta\rho_i)^2 \, \Delta\theta_i$$

where $\Delta\rho_i = \rho_{i+1} - \rho_i$, and the smaller has the area

$$\tfrac{1}{2}\rho_i^2 \, \Delta\theta_i.$$

The area $\Delta A_i$ is then the difference of these two quantities, that is,

$$\Delta A_i = \rho_i \, \Delta\rho_i \, \Delta\theta_i + \tfrac{1}{2}(\Delta\rho_i)^2 \, \Delta\theta_i.$$

Of these two terms, only the first is significant. We must recall here a point made in connection with single integrals (Chapter 15, Section 7). We saw there that if in the sum $S_n$ a factor which is a coefficient of $\Delta x$ approaches 0 as $\Delta x$ approaches 0, the term will not contribute to the integral. The same is true for double integrals and the argument is the same. In the present case the second term is

$$\tfrac{1}{2}\Delta\rho_i \, \Delta\rho_i \, \Delta\theta_i.$$

We are going to let $\Delta\rho_i \, \Delta\theta_i$ approach 0, and the coefficient $\Delta\rho_i/2$ will

**Figure 23-17**                    **Figure 23-18**

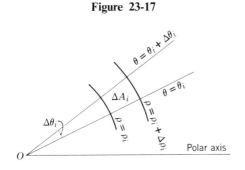

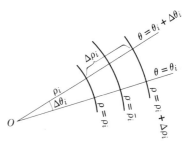

approach 0 when $\Delta\rho_i \, \Delta\theta_i$ does. Hence this entire term will not contribute to the integral.

Alternatively, we can see by another argument that we can take $\Delta A_i$ to be $\rho_i \, \Delta\rho_i \, \Delta\theta_i$. Suppose that we choose the circle $\rho = \bar{\rho}_i$, which cuts the interval from $\rho = \rho_i$ to $\rho = \rho_i + \Delta\rho_i$, halfway between the two circles (Fig. 23-18). Then the area $\Delta A_i$ is again the difference between the areas of two circular sectors, one with radius $\bar{\rho}_i + \Delta\rho_i/2$ and the other with radius $\bar{\rho}_i - \Delta\rho_i/2$. Then

$$\Delta A_i = \tfrac{1}{2}\left(\bar{\rho}_i + \frac{\Delta\rho_i}{2}\right)^2 \Delta\theta_i - \tfrac{1}{2}\left(\bar{\rho}_i - \frac{\Delta\rho_i}{2}\right)\Delta\theta,$$

and this is

**(29)**                                $\bar{\rho}_i \, \Delta\rho_i \, \Delta\theta_i.$

Here we are restricted to the value $\bar{\rho}_i$ in the expression for $\Delta A_i$ but, as we shall see in a moment, this is really no restriction.

In forming the sum $S_n$ that leads to the integral (27), we may take any point $(x_i, y_i)$ in each $\Delta A_i$. In our present coordinate system we can take any point $(\rho, \theta)$ and we may as well take $(\bar{\rho}_i, \bar{\theta}_i)$ where $\bar{\theta}_i$ also lies in the $i$th subregion $\Delta A_i$. Just as we use the notation $dx\, dy$ to indicate that our elements of area are $\Delta x \, \Delta y$, so we now use the notation $\rho \, d\rho \, d\theta$ to indicate that our elements of area are $\bar{\rho}_i \, \Delta\rho_i \, \Delta\theta_i$. We then write (28) as

**(30)**                             $\displaystyle \int\int_A f(\rho, \theta)\rho \, d\rho \, d\theta.$

We should note that the factor $\rho$ in the integrand comes from the element of area.

The expression (30) is a double integral. The question of how to evaluate it now arises. We could present a geometrical argument analogous to that presented in Section 2 to show that the double integral can be evaluated by repeated integration. The essence of the argument would be to interpret (30) as a volume under the surface $z = f(\rho, \theta)$ and to show that the same volume is obtained first by summing all columns belonging to the same $\rho = \rho_i$, which would lead to a single integral with respect to $\theta$, and then summing elements that result from this integration but now taking into account the variation in $\rho$. However, we do not need this argument. We did prove, although by an intuitive geometrical argument, that the double integral

**(31)**                             $\displaystyle \int\int_A f(x, y) \, dy \, dx$

can be evaluated by repeated integration. This argument, if we overlook its reliance on intuition, shows that any *analytical expression* such as (31) can be evaluated by repeated integration. Now

**(32)**                             $\displaystyle \int\int_A f(\rho, \theta)\rho \, d\rho \, d\theta$

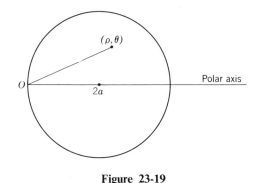

**Figure 23-19**

is an analytical expression like (31). In fact, (32) is of precisely the same type as (31) with $f(\rho, \theta)\rho$ playing the role of $f(x, y)$ and $d\rho\, d\theta$ playing the role of $dy\, dx$. Hence, if (31) can be evaluated by repeated integration, so can (32).

Of course, to evaluate (32), if we first integrate with respect to $\rho$, we must find the end values for $\rho$ corresponding to a typical $\theta$ and then find the end values for $\theta$. If the end values for $\rho$ are $\rho_1$ and $\rho_2$, which will be functions of $\theta$, and if the end values for $\theta$ are $\alpha$ and $\beta$, then the value of (32) will be given by the repeated integral

**(33)**
$$\int_\alpha^\beta \int_{\rho_1(\theta)}^{\rho_2(\theta)} f(\rho, \theta)\rho\, d\rho\, d\theta.$$

Alternatively, if we integrate first with respect to $\theta$ and then with respect to $\rho$, we shall have to evaluate

**(34)**
$$\int_a^b \int_{\theta_1(\rho)}^{\theta_2(\rho)} f(\rho, \theta)\rho\, d\theta\, d\rho.$$

where $\theta_1$ and $\theta_2$ are the end values for $\theta$ and both are functions of $\rho$.

Let us consider an example. The density of a thin circular disk of radius $a$ varies as the distance from a point $O$ on its circumference.* Find the mass of the disk.

We introduce a polar coordinate system with the point $O$ of the disk as the pole and a diameter of the disk as the polar axis (Fig. 23-19). The equation of the bounding circle then is [Chap. 17, formula (4)]

$$\rho = 2a \cos \theta.$$

Because the density at any point $(\rho, \theta)$ of the disk varies as the distance of the point from $O$, the density at $(\rho, \theta)$ is

$$D = k\rho.$$

The mass of the disk is the limit of the sum of the elements of mass $k\rho\, \Delta A$

---

* It may be helpful to review the discussion of density in Section 3.

as $\Delta A$ approaches 0. In other words,

$$M = \int \int_A k\rho \, dA$$

where $A$ is the area of the circle. Since we are using polar coordinates,

$$M = \int \int_A k\rho\rho \, d\rho \, d\theta.$$

Let us note that this integral is of the form (32) where $f(\rho, \theta)$ is $k\rho$. If we keep $\theta$ constant, then for any typical $\theta$, $\rho$ varies from 0 to $2a \cos \theta$. The angle $\theta$ itself varies from $-\pi/2$ to $\pi/2$. Then the integral is

$$M = k \int_{-\pi/2}^{\pi/2} \int_0^{2a \cos \theta} \rho^2 \, d\rho \, d\theta.$$

Integration with respect to $\rho$ gives

$$M = k \int_{-\pi/2}^{\pi/2} \left\{ \frac{\rho^3}{3} \bigg|_0^{2a \cos \theta} \right\} d\theta,$$

or

$$M = \frac{8a^3 k}{3} \int_{-\pi/2}^{\pi/2} \cos^3 \theta \, d\theta = \tfrac{32}{9} ka^3.$$

## EXERCISES

1. Evaluate the following repeated integrals:

   (a) $\displaystyle\int_0^\pi \int_0^{a \cos \theta} \sin \theta \, \rho \, d\rho \, d\theta.$     Ans. $\dfrac{a^2}{3}$.

   (b) $\displaystyle\int_0^\pi \int_0^{a(1 + \cos \theta)} \rho^2 \sin \theta \, d\rho \, d\theta.$

   (c) $\displaystyle\int_0^{\pi/2} \int_{a \cos \theta}^{a} \rho^4 \, d\rho \, d\theta.$     Ans. $(\pi - \tfrac{16}{15}) \dfrac{a^5}{10}$.

2. Find the area inside the circle $\rho = 2a \cos \theta$ and outside the circle $\rho = a$.

   Ans. $a^2 \left( \dfrac{\pi}{3} + \dfrac{\sqrt{3}}{2} \right)$.

3. Find the area inside the circle $\rho = 1$ and to the right of the line $4\rho \cos \theta = 3$.

4. Find the area which is inside the circle $\rho = 3 \cos \theta$ and outside the circle $\rho = \cos \theta$.     Ans. $2\pi$.

5. Find the area inside the cardioid $\rho = 1 + \cos \theta$ and to the right of the line $4\rho \cos \theta = 3$.

6. Find the area which is inside the circle $\rho = 1$ and outside the parabola $\rho(1 + \cos \theta) = 1$.     Ans. $(\pi/2) - (2/3)$.

7. Find the area which is inside the lemniscate $\rho^2 = 2a^2 \cos 2\theta$ and outside the circle $\rho = a$.

**8.** Suppose that the density at any point of a circular disk of radius $a$ varies as the cube of its distance from a fixed point on the circumference. Write an expression for the mass of the disk using polar coordinates.

$$Ans. \ 2\int_0^{\pi/2}\int_0^{2a\cos\theta} k\rho^4 \, d\rho \, d\theta.$$

**9.** In cylindrical coordinates the equation of a sphere of radius $a$, if the center of the sphere is at the pole (Fig. 23-20), is $\rho^2 + z^2 = a^2$. Calculate the volume in the first octant. $Ans. \ \pi a^3/6.$

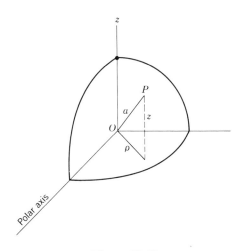

**Figure 23-20**

**10.** A washer in the form of a circular ring with inner radius $a$ and outer radius $b$ has a density at any point which is inversely proportional to the distance of that point from the center. Find the mass of the washer.

**11.** Find the volume in the first octant under the ellipsoidal surface $9\rho^2 + 4z^2 = 36$.

**12.** Consider the region inside the circle $\rho = 2a\cos\theta$ and outside the circle $\rho = a$. If the density at any point $(\rho, \theta)$ is $\sin\theta$, find the mass of the lamina.

$$Ans. \ 2a^2/3.$$

**13.** Find the volume cut from the sphere $x^2 + y^2 + z^2 = 4a^2$ by the cylinder $(x - a)^2 + y^2 = a^2$.

*Suggestion:* See Exercise 9.

**14.** Find the mass of a homogeneous lamina bounded by the cardioid $\rho = a(1 + \sin\theta)$.

$$Ans. \ \frac{3\pi ka^2}{2}.$$

**15.** (a) Find the gravitational attraction exerted by a thin circular disk (Fig. 23-21) of radius $a$ and of mass $M$ per unit volume on a unit mass located at a point $Q$, $l$ units above the center.

*Suggestion:* Suppose that the disk has thickness $t$. Then the mass of a cylinder of unit area and thickness $t$ is $Mt$. By virtue of the symmetry of the disk about the $z$-axis, the gravitational attraction it exerts in any horizontal direction is 0. Hence we need compute only the component in the vertical direction. Consider any element of mass at $P$. This element

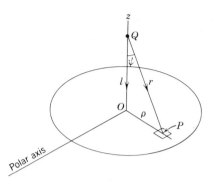

**Figure 23-21**

is $Mt\rho \, d\rho \, d\theta$; the pull of this mass on the unit mass at $Q$ has the magnitude $GMt\rho \, d\rho \, d\theta / r^2$. The vertical component of this pull is $GMt\rho \, d\rho \, d\theta \cos \psi / r^2$.

$$Ans. \quad 2\pi GMt \left( 1 - \frac{l}{\sqrt{a^2 + l^2}} \right).$$

(b)  Compare the method and result with that in Chapter 16, Section 6.

16. A student proposes to find the attraction that a segment of the paraboloid (Fig. 23-22) of revolution $x^2 + y^2 = 4z$ bounded by the plane $z = 1$ and of mass $M$ per unit volume exerts on a unit mass at the origin by using the result for the attraction that a thin disk exerts on a unit mass on the axis of the disk. (See the preceding exercise.) His argument is that the paraboloidal segment is a sum of such disks, each with its own radius $y$ and with the unit mass $z$ units from its center. Hence the student sets up the double integral

$$2\pi GM \int_0^2 \int_{y^2/4}^1 \left( 1 - \frac{z}{\sqrt{y^2 + z^2}} \right) dz \, dy.$$

This integral is not the correct expression for the attraction exerted by the segment. What is wrong?

*Suggestion:* Concentrate on the independence of the variables $y$ and $z$.

**Figure 23-22**

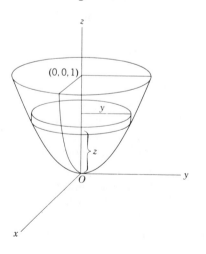

**17.** We found earlier that $\int_{-\infty}^{\infty} \int_{-\infty}^{\infty} e^{-x^2-y^2} \, dx \, dy = \pi$. Express the same integral in polar coordinates and evaluate it.

**18.** When a circular region of the eye's retina is illuminated uniformly the total effective excitation of the retina results from the contribution of all the small areas of that circular region but the contribution of any small area is inversely proportional to $\rho^m$, where $\rho$ is its distance from the center and $m < 2$. Express the total effective excitation of the circular region as a double integral and evaluate it.                                    *Ans.* $2\pi k \rho^{2-m}/(2-m)$.

**6. Triple Integrals in Rectangular Coordinates.** The ideas that we have been discussing concerning integration of functions of two variables can, of course, be extended to functions of three and more variables. Let us confine ourselves to functions of three variables. The motivation for working with integrals of functions of three variables is not to find volumes (although this is a special case, just as area is for double integrals); rather, there is a wealth of applications which stems from the fact that all physical objects are three-dimensional. Thus the gravitational attraction and the mass of a body are properties of bodies, and the calculation of these properties calls for integrals of functions of three variables.

Let us find the weight of a solid object whose mass per unit volume, that is, density, varies from point to point. To keep our opening example simple, let us suppose that we have a hemisphere (the solid) whose mass varies linearly from the base to the top. To be specific, suppose that the surface of the hemisphere (Fig. 23-23) is given by the equation $z = \sqrt{25 - x^2 - y^2}$ and the mass per cubic foot at each point is given by

**Figure 23-23**

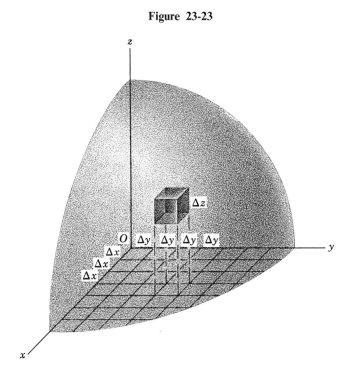

the $z$-value of that point. The problem is to find the mass of the entire hemisphere.

Because the hemisphere and the mass at each point are symmetric with respect to the $xz$- and $yz$-planes, we need find only the mass that lies in the first octant. Let us denote the region in the first octant by $V$. Since the hemisphere runs from $x = 0$ to $x = 5$, we divide the interval $(0, 5)$ into $a$ equal parts and introduce the planes $x = \Delta x, x = 2 \Delta x, \ldots, x = a \Delta x$. Likewise, we divide the $y$-interval $(0, 5)$ into $a$ equal parts and introduce the planes $y = \Delta y, y = 2 \Delta y, \ldots, y = a \Delta y$. The same is done for the $z$-interval $(0, 5)$. The introduction of these planes divides the region $V$ into little cubes, each of volume $\Delta x \, \Delta y \, \Delta z$. Those cubes which lie entirely in $V$ can be numbered, say, from 1 to $k$. The mass of any cube is given approximately by $z_i \, \Delta x \, \Delta y \, \Delta z$ where $z_i$ is the $z$-value of any point in the $i$th cube. Then the quantity

$$(35) \qquad S_1 = z_1 \, \Delta x \, \Delta y \, \Delta z + z_2 \, \Delta x \, \Delta y \, \Delta z + \cdots + z_k \, \Delta x \, \Delta y \, \Delta z$$

is a good approximation to the mass of the region $V$.

By decreasing the sizes of $\Delta x$, $\Delta y$, and $\Delta z$ but increasing the number of each of them to cover the respective $x$-, $y$-, and $z$-intervals, we obtain a better approximation to the mass in two ways. First, when the cubes are smaller, those which lie inside $V$ fill out more of this volume. Secondly, because each cube is smaller, the choice of any $z$ in it to represent the density of the cube is more accurate. Let us suppose that there are $l$ of these smaller cubes. Then the sum

$$S_2 = z_1 \, \Delta x \, \Delta y \, \Delta z + z_2 \, \Delta x \, \Delta y \, \Delta z + \cdots + z_l \, \Delta x \, \Delta y \, \Delta z$$

is a better approximation to the mass in the first octant.

As in the case of double integrals, we obtain a sequence of sums

$$S_1, S_2, \cdots, S_n, \cdots .$$

We take the limit of this sequence to be the mass of the hemisphere and denote the limit by the triple integral

$$(36) \qquad \int \int \int_V z \, dx \, dy \, dz.$$

To evaluate this integral we use repeated integration. Although we can no longer interpret the triple integral as a volume, we can give the same kind of intuitive justification for the use of repeated integration that we gave in Section 2 for double integrals. Consider any one subdivision of the region $V$ into cubes. We choose a definite $\Delta x$ whose end values may be $x_i$ and $x_{i-1}$ and a definite $\Delta y$ with end values $y_i$ and $y_{i-1}$ and consider those cubes which lie in one column above the square $\Delta x \, \Delta y$ (see Fig. 23-24). In each cube of this column take the point $(x_i, y_i, z_i)$ where $z_i$ changes from cube to cube. Now consider the sum

$$(z_1 \, \Delta z + z_2 \, \Delta z + \cdots + z_n \, \Delta z) \, \Delta x \, \Delta y.$$

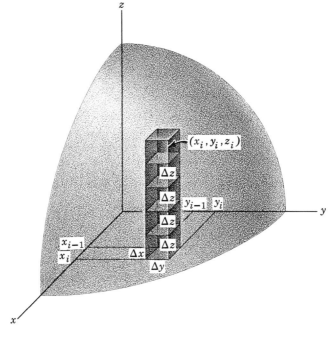

**Figure 23-24**

If we keep $\Delta x$ and $\Delta y$ fixed and let $\Delta z$ approach 0, while the number of the $\Delta z$ continue to fill out the $z$-interval from the $xy$-plane to the surface of the hemisphere, the limit of the sequence of sums so determined is

**(37)**
$$\Delta x \, \Delta y \int z \, dz.$$

The end values of this integral are the extreme $z$-values at the fixed $x_i$- and $y_i$-values. For a typical pair of fixed $x$- and $y$-values the range of $z$-values is 0 to $\sqrt{25 - x^2 - y^2}$ . Hence (37) becomes

**(38)**
$$\Delta x \, \Delta y \int_0^{\sqrt{25 - x^2 - y^2}} z \, dz.$$

We must now sum all such quantities over the domain of $x$- and $y$-values. This domain is the quarter-circle in the $xy$-plane. To take into account the sum of elements such as (38) over the quarter-circle we have but to recognize that (38) is of the form

$$F(x, y) \, \Delta x \, \Delta y$$

where

$$F(x, y) = \int_0^{\sqrt{25 - x^2 - y^2}} z \, dz.$$

Hence the limit to which we are led by the sum of the elements (38) as $\Delta x$

and $\Delta y$ approach 0 is the double integral

**(39)** 
$$\int \int_A F(x, y) \, dx \, dy,$$

where $A$ is the quarter-circle. In view of our method of evaluating double integrals and since the equation of the quarter-circle is given by $x^2 + y^2 = 25$, (39) becomes

**(40)** 
$$\int_0^5 \int_0^{\sqrt{25-y^2}} \int_0^{\sqrt{25-x^2-y^2}} z \, dz \, dx \, dy.$$

    Our method of evaluating the triple integral (36) utilized first integration with respect to $z$, then with respect to $x$, and finally with respect to $y$. We can rephrase the argument and show that any order of the variables could be chosen. Of course, then the appropriate intervals of integration for $x$, $y$, and $z$ must be used.

    The discussion of the concept of the triple integral and its evaluation by repeated or iterated integration dealt with the particular triple integral

$$\int \int \int_V z \, dz \, dx \, dy.$$

The general situation is one in which we start with some function

$$u = f(x, y, z)$$

and are led to the general triple integral

**(41)** 
$$\int \int \int_V f(x, y, z) \, dz \, dx \, dy$$

where $V$ is some three-dimensional domain. Suppose that the triple integral is to be evaluated by integrating first with respect to $z$. The boundary of $V$ consists of one or more surfaces. One seeks those surfaces which determine the boundary insofar as $z$-values are concerned. These surfaces must be expressed in the form $z = f(x, y)$. In our example these bounding surfaces were $z = \sqrt{25 - x^2 - y^2}$ and $z = 0$. One must next determine the $xy$-domain. This must include all $x$- and $y$-values that give rise to a $z$-value. Alternatively described, the $xy$-domain consists of the feet of the perpendiculars from all points $(x, y, z)$ in $V$ to the $xy$-plane. In our example the $xy$-domain was the quarter-circle. The evaluation of the remaining double integral over the $xy$-domain proceeds precisely as in the evaluation of double integrals.

    In the special case when the function $f$ in (41) is 1, the triple integral becomes

**(42)** 
$$\int \int \int_V dz \, dx \, dy,$$

and this integral is just the volume of $V$ itself. This is rather apparent from (35) if each $z_i$ is replaced by 1, because the summation is over the cubes lying in $V$, and as $\Delta x$, $\Delta y$, and $\Delta z$ approach 0, the sum approaches more and more closely the volume.

**Example.** Find the mass of the portion of the cylinder $y^2 + z^2 = 4$ which lies in the first quadrant, is bounded by $x = 0$, $y = 0$, $z = 0$ and the plane $x + 2y = 6$, and has the density $z$ at any point in the volume just described. (Fig. 23-25).

**Solution.** Since mass is density times volume, the mass of any element of volume $\Delta V$ is $z \, \Delta V$ or $z \, \Delta x \, \Delta y \, \Delta z$. The entire mass is given by the triple integral

$$\int \int \int_V z \; dx \; dy \; dz$$

where $V$ is the portion of the cylinder described in the statement of the problem. Let us try to integrate by repeated integration, first with respect to $z$, then with respect to $x$ and finally with respect to $y$. We indicate this intended order by writing

$$\int \int \int_V z \; dz \; dx \; dy.$$

Our next task is to determine the end values of the domain of integration. If we take a typical point $(x, y, z)$ in the domain and keep $x$ and $y$ fixed, the $z$-values will range from 0 to $\sqrt{4 - y^2}$, the value of $z$ on the surface of the cylinder. If we now think of $y$ as fixed, the $x$-values will range from 0 to $6 - 2y$, and, finally, for any $x$ and $z$ the $y$-values will range from

**Figure 23-25**

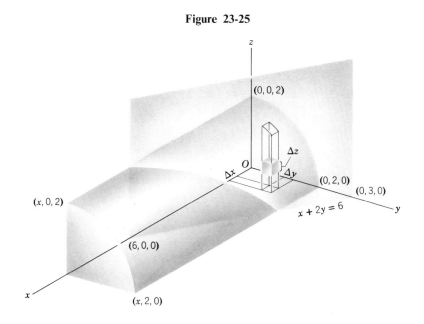

0 to 2 because the volume in question is bounded on the right by the cylinder. Thus we are led to the repeated integral

$$\int_0^2 \int_0^{6-2y} \int_0^{\sqrt{4-y^2}} z \, dz \, dx \, dy.$$

Integration with respect to $z$ yields

$$\int_0^2 \int_0^{6-2y} \frac{z^2}{2} \Big|_0^{\sqrt{4-y^2}} dx \, dy,$$

or

$$\tfrac{1}{2} \int_0^2 \int_0^{6-2y} (4 - y^2) \, dx \, dy.$$

Integration with respect to $x$ gives

$$\tfrac{1}{2} \int_0^2 (4 - y^2) x \big|_0^{6-2y} dy.$$

Substitution of the end values leads to

$$\tfrac{1}{2} \int_0^2 (4 - y^2)(6 - 2y) \, dy.$$

We have now merely to integrate with respect to $y$ and evaluate as in the case of usual single integrals.

## EXERCISES

**1.** Evaluate the following repeated integrals:

(a) $\displaystyle\int_1^2 \int_0^1 \int_2^4 x^2 y^2 z \, dz \, dy \, dx.$                         *Ans.* $\frac{14}{3}$.

(b) $\displaystyle\int_0^1 \int_0^{\sqrt{2x-x^2}} \int_0^{2-x} dz \, dy \, dx.$

(c) $\displaystyle\int_0^1 \int_{y^2}^1 \int_0^{1-x} x \, dz \, dx \, dy.$                          *Ans.* $\frac{4}{35}$.

(d) $\displaystyle\int_0^1 \int_0^{1-x} \int_0^{1-y^2} z \, dz \, dy \, dx.$

(e) $\displaystyle\int_0^a \int_0^b \int_0^c (x^2 + y^2 + z^2) \, dz \, dy \, dx.$      *Ans.* $\dfrac{abc}{3}(a^2 + b^2 + c^2).$

(f) $\displaystyle\int_1^2 \int_0^z \int_0^{x/3} \frac{x}{x^2 + y^2} \, dy \, dx \, dz.$

(g) $\displaystyle\int_0^1 \int_0^{1-x} \int_0^{2-x} xyz \, dz \, dy \, dx.$                  *Ans.* $\frac{13}{240}$.

**2.** Complete the evaluation of (40).

**3.** Evaluate the triple integral (36) by repeated integration first with respect to $y$, then with respect to $z$, and finally with respect to $x$.

4. Express as a triple integral and evaluate the following:
   (a) The volume in the first octant bounded by the coordinate planes and the plane $(x/a) + (y/b) + (z/c) = 1$. *Ans. $abc/6$.*
   (b) The volume bounded by the paraboloid $y^2 + z^2 = x + 1$ and the plane $x = 0$.
   (c) The volume in the first octant bounded by the surfaces $x^2 + z = 1$, $y^2 + z = 1$, $x = 0$, $y = 0$, and $z = 0$. *Ans. $\frac{1}{2}$.*
   (d) The volume of one of the wedges cut out from the cylinder $x^2 + y^2 = r^2$ by the planes $z = 0$ and $z = mx$.
   (e) The volume bounded by the cylinder $x^2 + y^2 = 4$ and the planes $y + z = 4$ and $z = 0$. *Ans. $16\pi$.*
   (f) The volume bounded by the paraboloid $y^2 + z^2 = 4ax$, the parabolic cylinder $y^2 = ax$, and the plane $x = 3a$.
   (g) The volume over the area common to the two parabolas $x = y^2$ and $y = x^2$ and under the surface $z = 12 + y - x^2$. *Ans. $\frac{569}{140}$.*
   (h) The volume bounded by the two paraboloids $z = 8 - x^2 - y^2$ and $z = x^2 + 3y^2$.
   (i) The volume bounded by the paraboloid $z = 2x^2 + y^2$ and the cylinder $z = 4 - y^2$. *Ans. $4\pi$.*

5. Find the weight of half of a spherical shell bounded by $x^2 + y^2 + z^2 = 25$ and $x^2 + y^2 + z^2 = 9$ if the density at any point (mass per unit volume) is the $z$-value of that point.

6. The planes $x = 0$, $y = 0$, $z = 1$, and $x + y - z = 0$ enclose a tetrahedron. Suppose that the density at any point $(x, y, z)$ varies as the distance of this point from the face $z = 1$. Find the mass of the tetrahedron. *Ans. $k/24$.*

7. Consider the solid consisting of that portion of the cylinder $x^2 + y^2 = a^2$ which is bounded by $z = 0$ and $z = h$, $h > 0$ and lying to the right of the $xz$-plane. Suppose that the density at any point is $\rho = kyz$. Find the mass of the solid.

8. Consider the unit cube bounded by the coordinate planes, $x = 1$, $y = 1$, and $z = 1$. Suppose that the density at any point $(x, y, z)$ is $\rho = kyz$. Find the $x$-component of the gravitational attraction that the cube exerts on a mass $m$ at the origin. *Ans. $Gkm(2\sqrt{2} - 1 - \sqrt{3})$.*

9. Describe the volume represented by the iterated integral

$$\int_0^1 \int_0^{1 + \sqrt{1 - x^2}} \int_0^{\sqrt{x^2 + y^2}} dz\, dy\, dx.$$

10. Find the mass of the volume in Exercise 9 if the density at any point varies inversely as the distance from the origin. *Ans. $k[(\pi/4) + 1)] \log(\sqrt{2} + 1)$.*

11. Find the volume bounded by the surfaces $z = 0$, $az = xy$, and $x + y + z = a$.

12. Find the volume in the first octant bounded by the ellipsoid $\dfrac{x^2}{a^2} + \dfrac{y^2}{b^2} + \dfrac{z^2}{c^2} = 1$. *Ans. $\pi abc/6$.*

13. Find the volume of the solid bounded by the elliptic paraboloids $z = 4 - x^2 - \frac{1}{4}y^2$, and $z = 3x^2 + \frac{1}{4}y^2$.

14. Compute the triple integral of $f(x, y, z) = z$ over the volume in the first octant bounded by $y = 0$, $z = 0$, $x + 2y = 6$, $x + y = 2$, and the cylinder $y^2 + z^2 = 4$. *Ans. $\frac{26}{3}$.*

**15.** Describe the volume represented by the integral

$$\int_0^4 \int_0^{\sqrt{16-x^2}} \int_{(x^2+y^2)/4}^4 dz\ dy\ dx.$$

### 7. Triple Integrals in Cylindrical Coordinates. We have introduced the notion of the triple integral by finding the weight of a particular object and by working in the rectangular coordinate system. However, the notion of the triple integral is an analytical concept which is not tied to one geometric interpretation.

Phrased analytically, the concept is defined as follows. Suppose that we have a function $u = f(x, y, z)$ and a three-dimensional domain $V$ that can be specified by stating which triples $(x, y, z)$ compose it. We can now break up this domain $V$ into subdomains $\Delta V$ of arbitrary shape and consider those which lie entirely within $V$. Suppose that there are $m$ of them. Let $\Delta V_1, \Delta V_2, \ldots, \Delta V_m$ denote the volumes of these subdomains. Each volume is, of course, a number. In each $\Delta V_i$ we choose a triple $(x_i, y_i, z_i)$. Let $u_i = f(x_i, y_i, z_i)$. We then form the sum

**(43)** $$S_1 = u_1\,\Delta V_1 + u_2\,\Delta V_2 + \cdots + u_m\,\Delta V_m.$$

We now decrease the size of the subdomains $\Delta V_i$ and increase the number of them so as to fill out as far as possible the domain $V$. We then form a new sum of the type (43). By continuing this process we obtain a sequence of sums

**(44)** $$S_1, S_2, \cdots, S_n, \cdots.$$

As we form new sums we require that the diameter of each $\Delta V_i$ (the largest possible distance between any two triples of $\Delta V_i$) approach 0. The limit of the sequence (44) is, by definition, the triple integral of $f$ over the domain $V$; this limit is denoted by

**(45)** $$\iiint_V f(x, y, z)\,dV$$

or

**(46)** $$\iiint_V u\,dV.$$

There are a number of theoretical matters that enter into a full presentation of the concept of the triple integral. Some of these were mentioned in the analogous case of the double integral. However, we shall not take them up in this introduction to the concept.

We know from our work in Section 6 that one interpretation of the triple integral is that in which $x, y$, and $z$ are interpreted as rectangular Cartesian coordinates and the $\Delta V_i$ are cubes. Let us consider another interpretation. We have already utilized a second three-dimensional coordinate system, namely the cylindrical system, to treat some double integrals. We shall consider a triple integral in cylindrical coordinates.

Before we undertake to do a problem involving cylindrical coordinates, we must dispose of one detail. In order to use (45) when $x$, $y$, and $z$ are the cylindrical coordinates $\rho$, $\theta$, and $z$ we must know what the element of volume $\Delta V$ is. Figure 23-26 shows such a typical element with base $ABCD$ and top $EFGH$. Let us note how this element is determined.

When we used rectangular coordinates, we divided the $x$-interval occupied by the domain of integration $V$ by planes parallel to the $yz$-plane. We did the same with the $y$-interval and the $z$-interval and, as a consequence, the volume $V$ was divided into little cubes. In the case of cylindrical coordinates we do the analogous thing. We consider the interval of $\rho$-values over which the volume $V$ is spread and divide this into subintervals $\Delta\rho$. Thus, if the $\rho$-values run, say, from $a$ to $b$, we introduce the surfaces $\rho = a$, $\rho = a + \Delta\rho$, $\rho = a + 2\Delta\rho$, ..., $\rho = b$. These surfaces are cylinders whose common axis is the $z$-axis. The faces $ADHE$ and $BCGF$ lie on such cylinders. We now consider the $\theta$-interval over which the volume $V$ is spread. If these $\theta$-values run from $\theta = \alpha$ to $\theta = \beta$, we divide the interval into subintervals $\Delta\theta$ and introduce the surfaces $\theta = \alpha$, $\theta = \alpha + \Delta\theta$, $\theta = \alpha + 2\Delta\theta$, ..., $\theta = \beta$. These surfaces are vertical half planes extending out from the $z$-axis. In Fig. 23-26 the faces $ABFE$ and $DCGH$ of the element $\Delta V$ lie on two such half planes. Finally, if the $z$-interval over which the domain of integration $V$ is spread runs from $z = c$ to $z = d$, we divide this interval into subintervals $\Delta z$ and introduce the surfaces $z = c$, $z = c + \Delta z$, $z = c + 2\Delta z$, ..., $z = d$. These surfaces are planes perpendicular to the $z$-axis. The faces $ABCD$ and $EFGH$ (of Fig. 23-26) lie on two such planes.

**Figure 23-26**

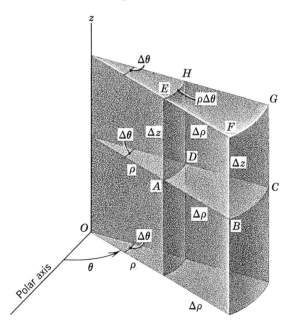

The three families of surfaces, called coordinate surfaces, which we use to divide the volume $V$ into elements $\Delta V$, are the analogues in the cylindrical coordinate system of the three families of planes used in the rectangular coordinate system. The reason for choosing the particular surfaces described in the preceding paragraph is that we shall thereby be able to carry out the evaluation of our triple integral in cylindrical coordinates.

We know now the geometrical shape of our elements of volume $\Delta V$, but we do not have as yet an expression for the volume. We found when we discussed the double integral in cylindrical coordinates that an element of area such as $ABCD$ is given by $\rho \Delta \rho \, \Delta \theta$ [see (29)], where $\rho$ is the value of some point in the area. Consequently the volume of the little piece of cylindrical shell from $ABCD$ to $EFGH$ is

**(47)**                          $$\Delta V = \rho \, \Delta \rho \, \Delta \theta \, \Delta z.$$

Then the triple integral (45) expressed in cylindrical coordinates is

**(48)**                          $$\int \int \int_V f(\rho, \theta, z) \rho \, d\rho \, d\theta \, dz.$$

How are we going to evaluate such a triple integral? The answer is, of course, repeated integration. As in the case of rectangular coordinates, we can give a rough argument to show that repeated integration accomplishes the kind of summation that the triple integral calls for. By considering all elements $\Delta V$ which are determined by fixing $\rho$ and $\theta$ but by letting $u$ of (46) vary with $z$ only, we can form a sum

$$f(\rho, \theta, z) \, \Delta z + f(\rho, \theta, z_2) \, \Delta z + \cdots + f(z, \theta, z_n) \, \Delta z,$$

where the $\Delta z$ fill out the $z$-interval corresponding to a choice of a fixed but typical $\rho$ and $\theta$. Next, the $\Delta z$ are made smaller but more are chosen to fill out the $z$-interval and a new sum is formed. The limit of this sequence of sums as $\Delta z$ approaches 0 is a single integral of the form

$$\int_{z_1}^{z_2} f(\rho, \theta, z) \, dz$$

where $z_1$ and $z_2$ are functions of $\rho$ and $\theta$. This step reduces the triple integral (47) to a double integral in the variables $\rho$ and $\theta$, which can be evaluated by repeated integration first with respect to $\theta$, say, and then with respect to $\rho$. The result of all three integrations would take into account all elements of the form

$$f(\rho_i, \theta_i, z_i) \rho_i \, d\rho \, d\theta \, dz$$

which enter into the triple integral (48). This is the kind of argument that we used in Section 6 to show that the triple integral in rectangular coordinates can be evaluated by repeated integration.

Let us consider an example of the use of (48). We shall find the gravitational attraction that a homogeneous, circular, cylindrical shell of height $h$ and thickness $b - a$ exerts on a unit mass located at the center of the base of the shell. Suppose, then, that the cylindrical shell has an inner surface given by $\rho = a$ and an outer surface given by $\rho = b$. Figure 23-27 shows one quarter of the shell. The unit particle is at $O$. We consider an element of mass $\Delta M$. The force with which the element attracts the unit mass can be regarded as the vector sum of a horizontal force and a vertical force. However, to each such element there will be another on the the the same level and diametrically opposite whose horizontal pull on the unit mass offsets the horizontal pull that $\Delta M$ exerts. Hence we need only consider the vertical component of the force that each element $\Delta M$ exerts. This component is

$$\frac{G \, \Delta M}{r^2} \cos \psi,$$

where $\psi$ is the angle shown in the figure and $r$ is the distance $OP$, which in cylindrical coordinates is $\sqrt{\rho^2 + z^2}$. Now, $\cos \psi = z/r$. Hence the vertical component is

$$\frac{G \, \Delta M z}{r^3}.$$

Because the cylinder is homogeneous, then in view of (47), $\Delta M = D \, \Delta V = D\rho \, \Delta\rho \, \Delta\theta \, \Delta z$, where $D$ is the constant density. Then the total vertical force

**Figure 23-27**

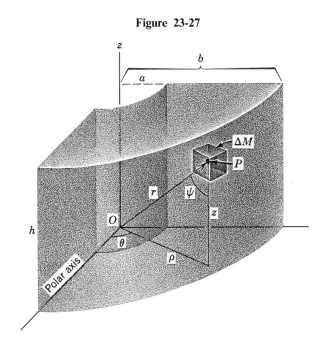

is [see (48)],

**(49)**
$$\iiint_V \frac{GDz\rho \, d\rho \, d\theta \, dz}{(\rho^2 + z^2)^{3/2}} \, .$$

To evaluate this by repeated integration, let us choose the order $d\theta \, dz \, d\rho$. When $z$ and $\rho$ are held constant, $\theta$ varies from 0 to $2\pi$. Then as $\rho$ is held constant, $z$ varies from 0 to $h$. Finally, $\rho$ varies from $a$ to $b$. Thus (49) becomes

**(50)**
$$\int_a^b \int_0^h \int_0^{2\pi} \frac{GDz\rho \, d\theta \, dz \, d\rho}{(\rho^2 + z^2)^{3/2}} \, .$$

Successive integration with respect to $\theta$, $z$, and $\rho$ gives

$$2\pi GD \, (b - a - \sqrt{b^2 + h^2} + \sqrt{a^2 + h^2} \, ).$$

## EXERCISES

1. Evaluate the following integrals:

   (a) $\displaystyle\int_0^{\pi/4} \int_1^{\cos\theta} \int_1^\rho \frac{1}{\rho^2 z^2} \, dz \, d\rho \, d\theta.$       *Ans.* $\dfrac{\pi + 4}{8} - \log(\sqrt{2} + 1).$

   (b) $\displaystyle\int_0^2 \int_0^1 \int_0^2 z\rho^2 \sin\theta \, dz \, d\rho \, d\theta.$

   (c) $\displaystyle\int_0^{\pi/2} \int_0^4 \int_0^{\sqrt{16-z^2}} (16 - \rho^2)^{1/2}\rho z \, d\rho \, dz \, d\theta.$       *Ans.* $256\pi/5.$

2. Calculate the attraction that the cylindrical shell of the text exerts on a unit mass exterior to and on the axis of the shell $c$ units from one base.

$$\textit{Ans. } 2\pi GD\Big(-\sqrt{b^2 + (c + h)^2} + \sqrt{b^2 + c^2}$$
$$+ \sqrt{a^2 + (c + h)^2} - \sqrt{a^2 + c^2} \, \Big).$$

3. Calculate the volume of a right circular cone of radius 2 and altitude 3.

   *Suggestion:* The equation of the cone in cylindrical coordinates is $\rho/z = \frac{2}{3}$. See Fig. 23-28.

4. Calculate the volume of the part of the paraboloid of revolution $x^2 + y^2 = 2z$ cut off by the plane $z = 2$.       *Ans.* $4\pi.$

5. Consider the solid bounded by the planes $y = 0$, $z = 0$, $z = h$, $h > 0$, and the cylinder $x^2 + y^2 = a^2$. Suppose that the density at any point $(\rho, \theta, z)$ is $Dz\rho \sin\theta$. Find the mass of the solid.

6. Find the gravitational attraction that a solid, homogeneous, right circular cone (Fig. 23-28) with base of radius $a$, height $h$, and density $D$ exerts on a unit mass located at the vertex.

   *Suggestion:* The equation of the cone in cylindrical coordinates is $\rho/z = a/h.$

$$\textit{Ans. } 2\pi GDh\Big(1 - \frac{h}{\sqrt{a^2 + h^2}}\Big).$$

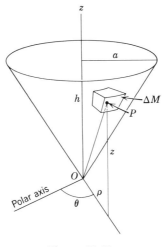

**Figure 23-28**

7. Consider the homogeneous mass below the spherical surface $\rho^2 + z^2 = 2$ and above the paraboloid $z = \rho^2$. Find the gravitational force with which this mass attracts a unit mass at the pole.

8. Consider the homogeneous solid cut off from the cylinder $\rho = 2a \cos \theta$ by the cone $z = c\rho$ and the plane $z = 0$. The quantities $a$ and $c$ are positive. Find the $x$-component of the gravitational force that this solid exerts on a unit mass located at the pole.                                    *Ans.* $\pi GDca / \sqrt{1 + c^2}$ .

9. Find the volume bounded by the planes $z = 0$, $z = 4a + \rho \cos \theta$, and the cylinder $\rho = a \cos 2\theta$.

10. A finite solid of uniform density and of mass $M$ per unit volume is bounded by the paraboloid $x^2 + y^2 = 4az$ or $\rho^2 = 4az$ in cylindrical coordinates, and the plane $z = a$. Prove that the attraction it exerts on unit mass at the pole is $2\pi GMa[1 - \sqrt{5} + 4 \log \frac{1}{2}(1 + \sqrt{5})]$.

11. A uniform solid of mass $M$ per unit volume is in the form of the finite portion of the paraboloid of revolution $\rho^2 = 4az$ (in cylindrical coordinates) cut off by the plane $z = 2a$. Show that the attraction exerted on a unit mass located at the center of the circular top is $4\pi GMa[\sqrt{2} - \log(1 + \sqrt{2})]$.

12. Calculate the triple integral of $f(\rho, \theta, z) = \rho^2$ over the volume bounded by the paraboloid $\rho^2 = 9 - z$ and the plane $z = 0$.                    *Ans.* $243\pi / 2$.

13. Calculate the volume within the cylinder $\rho = 4 \cos \theta$ and bounded by the sphere $\rho^2 + z^2 = 16$ and the plane $z = 0$.                    *Ans.* $\frac{64}{9}(3\pi - 4)$.

***8. Triple Integrals in Spherical Coordinates.*** Although in principle we could formulate all of our triple integration problems in rectangular coordinates, we can see from the preceding section that some problems are more readily formulated and solved in cylindrical coordinates. Moreover, the integration may be simpler in this system than in the rectangular system. Similar advantages are offered by still another three-dimensional coordinate system—the spherical coordinate system.

This system of describing position in space is a modification of the system of latitude and longitude. The location (Fig. 23-29) of any point $P$ is

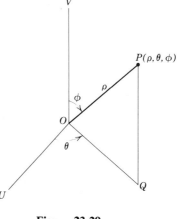

**Figure 23-29**

described by the distance $\rho$ of $P$ from a fixed point $O$,* by the angle $\theta$ that the projection $OQ$ of $OP$ makes with a fixed line $OU$ in a horizontal plane, and by the angle $\phi$ that $OP$ makes with a fixed vertical line $OV$. The angle $\theta$ is often called the longitude of $P$, and $\phi$ is called the colatitude because it is the complement of the latitude angle in the system of latitude and longitude. To describe all points of space, we must let $\rho$ vary from 0 to $\infty$; $\theta$ must vary from 0 to $2\pi$ and $\phi$ from 0 to $\pi$. The coordinates of a point are written in the order $(\rho, \theta, \phi)$.

Of course, the equations of curves and surfaces can be written in spherical coordinates. We shall encounter some of them in our later work. To identify the figures represented by equations in spherical coordinates and conversely to write the equation of a given figure, it is helpful to know the relation between rectangular coordinates and spherical coordinates. If the rectangular system has its origin at $O$ (Fig. 23-30), if the positive $x$-axis lies along $OU$, and if the positive $z$-axis lies along $OV$, it is easy to relate the rectangular and spherical coordinates of any point $P$. We can see from Fig.

**Figure 23-30**

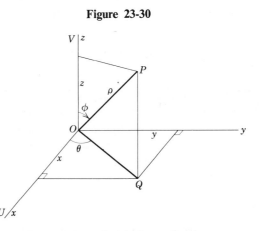

*This $\rho$ is not the same as the $\rho$ of the cylindrical coordinate system.

23-30 that $OQ = \rho \sin \phi$ and, therefore, that

$$x = \rho \sin \phi \cos \theta, \, y = \rho \sin \phi \sin \theta, \, z = \rho \cos \phi.$$

Conversely, if we square each of the first two equations and add them and then add the square of the last one, we obtain

$$\rho = \sqrt{x^2 + y^2 + z^2} \, .$$

From the third equation we obtain directly that

$$\phi = \cos^{-1} \frac{z}{\sqrt{x^2 + y^2 + z^2}}$$

and from the figure we have that

$$\theta = \tan^{-1} \frac{y}{x} \, .$$

In working with spherical coordinates we should also keep in mind that even an equation in one or two variables may represent a surface if the equation is interpreted as representing a figure in three dimensions. Thus the equation $\rho = 5$ represents the sphere with center at the origin and radius 5.

## EXERCISES

**1.** Describe the figures represented by each of the following equations interpreted in three dimensions:

(a) $\rho = 4$.          *Ans.* Sphere.     (e) $\theta = 30°$.          *Ans.* Half plane.
(b) $\phi = 30°$.                            (f) $\theta = 210°$.
(c) $\phi = 120°$.        *Ans.* Cone.      (g) $\rho \sin \phi = 2$.    *Ans.* Cylinder.
(d) $\rho \cos \phi = 1$.                    (h) $\rho = a \cos \phi$.

To work with triple integrals when the geometrical interpretation of the integrand and the volume $V$ are in terms of spherical coordinates, we should break $V$ into volume elements $\Delta V$ which are most simply expressed in that coordinate system. As in the case of cylindrical coordinates, these elements are determined by the coordinate surfaces, that is, the surfaces $\rho = $ const., $\theta = $ const., and $\phi = $ const. The surfaces $\rho = $ const. are spheres with center at $O$ (Fig. 23-30). The surfaces $\theta = $ const. are half planes beginning along the entire vertical line $OV$. The surfaces $\phi = $ const. are single nappes of cones; the vertex of each cone is at $O$. If $\phi < 90°$, the vertex angle of the cone is $\phi$ itself, and the axis is $OV$. If $\phi > 90°$, the cone opens downward, the axis is the lower half of $OV$, and the vertex angle is $(180 - \phi)°$. When $\phi = 90°$, the cone becomes the horizontal plane.

To see what the shape of the volume element $\Delta V$ is and to obtain an expression for it, let us introduce (Fig. 23-31) a single sphere $\rho = $ const. Then the two half planes $\theta = $ const. and $\theta + \Delta\theta = $ const. are introduced.

These cut the sphere in the arcs $KADL$ and $KBCM$. The cone $\phi = $ const. cuts the sphere in a circle of which $AB$ is an arc and the cone $\phi + \Delta\phi = $ const. cuts the sphere in a circle of which $DC$ is an arc. Thus the area cut out on the sphere by the two half planes and the two cones is the curvilinear area $ABCD$. For this area we can obtain an approximate expression which becomes better and better as the quantities $\Delta\theta$ and $\Delta\phi$ become smaller. The arc $AD$ is given exactly by $\rho \, \Delta\phi$. The arc $AB$ is part of a circle with *radius EA*. This is more readily seen if one recalls that $AB$ lies on the cone $\phi = $ const. and on the sphere $\rho = $ const. Now $EA$ is $\rho \sin \phi$ and the angle at $E$ subtended by arc $AB$ is $\Delta\theta$ because $AE$ and $BE$ form the same angle at $E$ that $LO$ and $MO$ do at $O$. Hence arc $AB = \rho(\sin \phi) \, \Delta\theta$. (The arc $DC$ is a little longer than $AB$ and the difference is $\rho \sin(\phi + \Delta\phi) \, \Delta\theta - \rho(\sin \phi) \, \Delta\theta$. It is rather evident that for small $\Delta\phi$ this difference is less significant than $\rho(\sin \phi) \, \Delta\theta$ but let us hold this point for the present and let us treat $DC$ as equal to $AB$.) We regard $ABCD$ as a rectangle with sides $AD$ and $AB$ because when $\Delta\theta$ and $\Delta\phi$ are small, the arcs do not differ much from line segments. Moreover, the edges are perpendicular to each other. Hence the area of $ABCD$ is

$$(\rho \, \Delta\phi)(\rho \sin \phi)\Delta\theta.$$

We now introduce (Fig. 23-32) the sphere $\rho + \Delta\rho = $ const. The planes $\theta = $ const. and $\theta + \Delta\theta = $ const. and the cones $\phi = $ const. and $\phi + \Delta\phi = $ const. cut out on this sphere a region $A'B'C'D'$ which is similar to $ABCD$ on $\rho = $ const. To obtain the area of $A'B'C'D'$, the argument used to obtain the area of $ABCD$ applies intact except that $\rho + \Delta\rho$ replaces $\rho$. Hence the

**Figure 23-31**

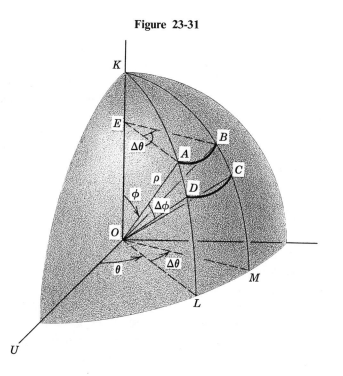

area of $A'B'C'D'$ is

$$(\rho + \Delta\rho)\,\Delta\phi\,(\rho + \Delta\rho)(\sin\phi)\,\Delta\theta.$$

This area differs from the area of $ABCD$ by

$$2\rho(\sin\phi)\,\Delta\rho\,\Delta\theta\,\Delta\phi + (\sin\phi)(\Delta\rho)^2\,\Delta\theta\,\Delta\phi.$$

Let us ignore this difference, too, for the moment and take the area $A'B'C'D'$ to be the same as the area of $ABCD$.

We treat the figure formed by $ABCD$, $A'B'C'D'$, and the length $\Delta\rho$ as a cylinder (or box) with base $ABCD$ and height $\Delta\rho$. Because the length $\Delta\rho$ is perpendicular to $ABCD$ the volume of the cylinder is the area of $ABCD$ times $\Delta\rho$ or

**(51)**                               $\rho^2(\sin\phi)\Delta\rho\,\Delta\theta\,\Delta\phi.$

This is the element of volume determined by the coordinate surfaces.

In deriving (51) we made several approximations. We ignored the differences between $CD$ and $AB$ in Fig. 23-31, we treated $ABCD$ as a rectangle, and we ignored the difference between $ABCD$ and $A'B'C'D'$ in Fig. 23-32. Were we to take into account the difference between (51) and the exact expression for the volume of the region between $ABCD$ and

**Figure 23-32**

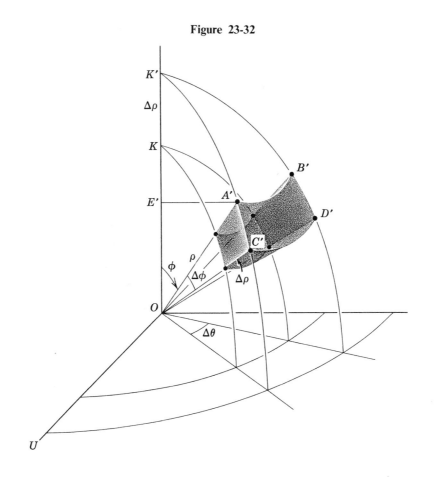

$A'B'C'D'$, we would find that this difference contains the product $\Delta\rho\,\Delta\theta\,\Delta\phi$ and that apart from this product the difference approaches 0 as $\Delta\rho\,\Delta\theta\,\Delta\phi$ approaches 0. Hence this difference will not contribute to the final triple integral. The point involved here is the analogue for triple integrals of the one that we made in Section 7 of Chapter 15 for single integrals.

Thus any triple integral

$$\iiint_V f(x, y, z)\, dV,$$

when the variables have the geometric meaning of spherical coordinates, becomes

**(52)** $$\iiint_V f(\rho, \theta, \phi)\rho^2 \sin\phi\, d\rho\, d\theta\, d\phi.$$

These triple integrals are evaluated by repeated integration. We could give a justification of the kind already given in the cases of rectangular and cylindrical coordinates, but there is not much to be gained by repeating the story.

To acquire some expertise in the use of triple integrals expressed in spherical coordinates, let us consider an example. We shall show that the gravitational attraction that a spherical shell of uniform mass exerts on a unit mass interior to the inner sphere of the shell is 0.

Suppose that the shell is bounded by two spheres (Fig. 23-33) of radii $R_1$ and $R_2$ with $R_2 > R_1$. Let $M$ be the mass per unit volume of the shell. The fact that we are going to work with a spherical shell suggests that

**Figure 23-33**

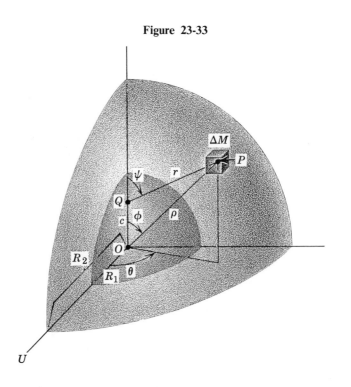

spherical coordinates may prove to be the best to use. We choose the vertical axis from which the $\phi$-coordinate is measured so that it goes through the unit mass which is located at $Q$ in the figure. The spherical coordinates of $Q$ are then $(c, 0, 0)$ with $c < R_1$. The attractive force that an element of the shell, at say $P$, exerts may be regarded as the vector sum of a horizontal and a vertical force. Because the shell is symmetrical about the vertical axis, the gravitational pull that the element exerts in a horizontal direction is offset by a symmetrically placed element. Hence the element and therefore the entire shell can exert only a vertical force on the unit mass at $Q$. We must, therefore, show that this vertical component of the gravitational attraction exerted by the shell is 0.

We should like to set up a triple integral of the form (52) to represent the total vertical attraction of the shell. The attraction exerted by any element of volume $\Delta V$ in the shell, say the typical element located at $P$, is $GM\,\Delta V/r^2$ where $r$ is the distance $QP$. This attraction is directed from $Q$ to $P$. The vertical component of the attractive force is

$$\textbf{(53)} \qquad \frac{GM\,\Delta V}{r^2}\cos\psi$$

where $\psi$ is the angle at $Q$ between $QP$ and the vertical axis. If the coordinates of $P$ are $(\rho, \theta, \phi)$, then (Fig. 23-34)

$$\textbf{(54)} \qquad \cos\psi = \frac{\rho\cos\phi - c}{r}.$$

Then the vertical component of the force exerted by the element $\Delta V$ is

$$\textbf{(55)} \qquad \frac{GM\,\Delta V(\rho\cos\phi - c)}{r^3}.$$

We must also express $r$ in spherical coordinates. To do this we note that $r^2 = RQ^2 + PR^2$ or

$$r^2 = (\rho\cos\phi - c)^2 + (\rho\sin\phi)^2$$

or

$$\textbf{(56)} \qquad r^2 = \rho^2 + c^2 - 2\rho c\cos\phi,$$

**Figure 23-34**

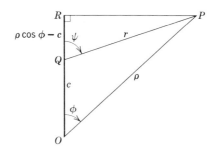

a result that we can obtain also by applying the law of cosines to triangle $OPQ$.

We now use (55), the expression (56) for $r$, and the expression (51) for $\Delta V$ to state that the vertical component of the attraction that the element of volume centered at $P$ (Fig. 23-33) exerts on the unit mass at $Q$ is

(57) $$\frac{GM(\rho \cos \phi - c)}{(\rho^2 + c^2 - 2\rho c \cos \phi)^{3/2}} \rho^2 \sin \phi \, \Delta\phi \, \Delta\theta \, \Delta\rho.$$

These elements must be summed over the volume of the spherical shell. This volume is described as $\theta$ varies from 0 to $2\pi$, $\phi$ varies from 0 to $\pi$, and $\rho$ varies from $R_1$ to $R_2$. Hence the integral that we want is

(58) $$\int_{R_1}^{R_2} \int_0^\pi \int_0^{2\pi} \frac{GM(\rho \cos \phi - c)\rho^2 \sin \phi}{(\rho^2 + c^2 - 2\rho c \cos \phi)^{3/2}} \, d\theta \, d\phi \, d\rho.$$

We can evaluate such integrals by repeated integration using any order we choose of the variables $\rho$, $\theta$, and $\phi$. In the case of (58) we shall integrate first with respect to $\phi$ because this is the crucial variable. To carry out this work, let us ignore for the present the factor $GM\rho^2$ and the integration with respect to $\rho$ and $\theta$. We have then to evaluate

(59) $$\int_0^\pi \frac{(\rho \cos \phi - c) \sin \phi}{(\rho^2 + c^2 - 2\rho c \cos \phi)^{3/2}} \, d\phi.$$

This integral can be expressed as a difference of two integrals. One of these is

(60) $$\int_0^\pi \frac{c \sin \phi}{(\rho^2 + c^2 - 2\rho c \cos \phi)^{3/2}} \, d\phi.$$

If we think of the entire quantity in the parentheses as a function of $\phi$, then, except for a constant factor, the numerator contains the derivative of that function of $\phi$. Hence, using the power formula, we have

(61) $$-\frac{1}{\rho(\rho^2 + c^2 - 2\rho c \cos \phi)^{1/2}} \Bigg|_0^\pi.$$

The radical, in view of (56), is the value of $r$, and this quantity is positive. When we substitute $\pi$ for $\phi$, the radical becomes $\sqrt{\rho^2 + c^2 + 2\rho c}$ , which is $\rho + c$. However, when we substitute 0 for $\phi$, the radical becomes $\sqrt{\rho^2 + c^2 - 2\rho c}$ . This quantity is either $\rho - c$ or $c - \rho$. We see from Fig. 23-33 that the $\rho$-values of points in the shell, which are the $\rho$-values with which we are concerned, are larger than $c$. To keep $r$ positive, we must take the value $\rho - c$. Then (61) yields

**(62)** $$-\frac{1}{\rho(\rho + c)} + \frac{1}{\rho(\rho - c)} = \frac{2c}{\rho(\rho^2 - c^2)}.$$

We evaluate next the other integral in (59), namely,

**(63)** $$\int_0^\pi \frac{\rho \cos \phi \sin \phi}{(\rho^2 + c^2 - 2\rho c \cos \phi)^{3/2}} \, d\phi.$$

This integral is best evaluated by a trick. We know that if the numerator did not contain the $\cos \phi$ factor, we could evaluate it as we did (60). We shall get around this by first multiplying numerator and denominator by $-2c$. This gives

$$\int_0^\pi \frac{-2\rho c \cos \phi \sin \phi}{-2c(\rho^2 + c^2 - 2\rho c \cos \phi)^{3/2}} \, d\phi.$$

We now add and subtract $(\rho^2 + c^2) \sin \phi$ in the numerator and obtain

$$\int_0^\pi \frac{(\rho^2 + c^2) \sin \phi - 2\rho c \cos \phi \sin \phi}{-2c(\rho^2 + c^2 - 2\rho c \cos \phi)^{3/2}} \, d\phi$$

$$+ \int_0^\pi \frac{(\rho^2 + c^2) \sin \phi}{2c(\rho^2 + c^2 - 2\rho c \cos \phi)^{3/2}} \, d\phi.$$

By factoring $\sin \phi$ out of the numerator in the first integral and dividing numerator and denominator by the other factor, we have

$$\int_0^\pi \frac{\sin \phi}{-2c(\rho^2 + c^2 - 2\rho c \cos \phi)^{1/2}} \, d\phi$$

$$+ \int_0^\pi \frac{(\rho^2 + c^2) \sin \phi}{2c(\rho^2 + c^2 - 2\rho c \cos \phi)^{3/2}} \, d\phi.$$

We can now integrate each integral by the method that was used for (60). The result is

$$-\frac{1}{2\rho c^2} (\rho^2 + c^2 - 2\rho c \cos \phi)^{1/2} \Big|_0^\pi - \frac{\rho^2 + c^2}{2\rho c^2} \frac{1}{(\rho^2 + c^2 - 2\rho c \cos \phi)^{1/2}} \Big|_0^\pi,$$

**(64)**

or again, since $\rho > c$ and the value of the radical is positive,

$$-\frac{1}{2\rho c^2} (\rho + c) + \frac{1}{2\rho c^2} (\rho - c) - \frac{\rho^2 + c^2}{2\rho c} \frac{1}{\rho + c} + \frac{\rho^2 + c^2}{2\rho c^2} \frac{1}{\rho - c}.$$

Adding these fractions gives

**(65)**
$$\frac{2c}{\rho(\rho^2 - c^2)}.$$

The integral (59) is the integral (63) minus the integral (60). In view of (62) and (65), we see that the integral (59) is 0.

There is no need to carry out the integrations in (58) with respect to $\rho$ and $\theta$ for, since the integrand is 0, the result will be 0.

This result is of interest on several accounts. The most obvious one is that the attraction of the entire shell on the unit mass interior to the inner sphere of the shell is 0. Now, $R_1$ and $R_2$ in (58) are arbitrary. Hence no matter how thin or thick the shell the attraction is still 0. Secondly, we should compare the method used in Chapter 16, Section 7 with that used here. In the earlier work we were obliged to make several auxiliary steps such as the use of zones, thin shells, and finally a shell of finite thickness to solve the problem by means of an integral of a function of one variable. In the present method we obtained the result with one direct process.

**Example.**   The calculation of the attraction exerted by a spherical shell involves difficulties in integration that may obscure the process of evaluating triple integrals in spherical coordinates. Let us consider, therefore, a simpler example. Let us find the volume bounded by the spheres $\rho = a$, $\rho = b$ and the cone $\phi = \alpha$, $0 < \alpha < (\pi/2)$.

**Solution.**   One quarter of the volume is shown in Fig. 23-35. This quarter volume is represented by the integral (52) in which the function $f$ is now 1. Thus we wish to evaluate

$$\int_0^{\frac{\pi}{4}} \int_0^\alpha \int_a^b \rho^2 \sin\phi \, d\rho \, d\phi \, d\theta.$$

**Figure 23-35**

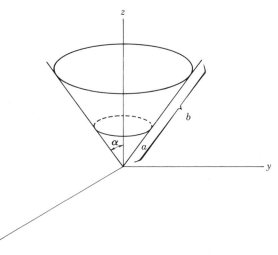

Integration with respect to $\rho$ and substitution of the end values give

$$\int_0^{\frac{\pi}{4}} \int_0^\alpha \frac{b^3 - a^3}{3} \sin \phi \, d\phi \, d\theta.$$

Integration with respect to $\phi$ yields

$$\frac{b^3 - a^3}{3} \int_0^{\frac{\pi}{4}} - (\cos \alpha - 1) \, d\theta.$$

And, finally, integration with respect to $\theta$ results in

$$\frac{b^3 - a^3}{3} (1 - \cos \alpha) \frac{\pi}{4} .$$

Of course the entire volume is four times this quantity.


## EXERCISES

1. Evaluate the following integrals:

   (a) $\displaystyle\int_0^\pi \int_0^{\pi/4} \int_0^{\sec \phi} \sin 2\phi \, d\rho \, d\phi \, d\theta.$            *Ans.* $(2 - \sqrt{2})\pi.$

   (b) $\displaystyle\int_0^{\pi/2} \int_{\pi/4}^{\arctan 2} \int_0^{\sqrt{6}} \rho \sin \phi \, d\rho \, d\phi \, d\theta.$

   (c) $\displaystyle\int_0^{2\pi} \int_0^\pi \int_0^5 \rho^4 \sin \phi \, d\rho \, d\phi \, d\theta.$            *Ans.* $2500\pi.$

2. Use spherical coordinates to find the volume cut from a right circular cone with a 30° semivertical angle (i.e., $\phi = 30°$) by a sphere of radius 6. The vertex of the cone is at the center of the sphere.

3. Find the volume cut out from the cone $\phi = \pi/4$ by the sphere $\rho = 2a \cos \phi.$         *Ans.* $\pi a^3.$

4. Find the mass of a sphere of radius $R$ if the density $D$ varies inversely as the square of the distance from the center.

5. A solid, right circular cone of height $h$ and semivertical angle $\alpha$ is of uniform mass. Find the attraction that it exerts on a unit particle located at its vertex by using spherical coordinates.         *Ans.* $2\pi Gkh(1 - \cos \alpha).$

6. Use the method of the example in the text to show that a spherical shell with uniformly distributed mass attracts a unit mass *external* to the shell as though the mass of the shell were concentrated at its center.

   *Suggestion:* Note that in this problem $c > \rho.$

7. The integral (59) in the text can be evaluated by another method. Make the substitution $u^2 = \rho^2 + c^2 - 2\rho c \cos \phi$ and carry out the integration.

8. (a) Given the homogeneous solid hemisphere bounded by $\rho = a$, $\theta = 0$, and $\theta = \pi$, show that it attracts a unit mass at the origin with a force $F = Gka\pi.$

   (b) Show that the force of part (a) is equivalent to concentrating the mass of the hemisphere at $\rho = \sqrt{\frac{2}{3}}\, a, \theta = \pi/2, \phi = \pi/2.$

9. Find the volume bounded by the surface $\rho = 2a \sin \phi$. (This surface is the same as the one obtained by revolving the circle $(x - a)^2 + z^2 = a^2$ about the $z$-axis.)                                                                    *Ans.* $2\pi^2 a^3$.

10. The surface $\rho = 4 \cos \phi$ is a sphere of radius 2 and center at $\rho = 2$, $\phi = 0$. Find the volume common to this sphere and the sphere $\rho = 3$.

11. Find the gravitational force that a homogeneous mass occupying the volume of Exercise 10 exerts on unit mass at the origin.                    *Ans.* $39\pi Gk/16$.

12. Consider the smaller segment cut from the sphere $\rho = 2$ by the plane $\rho \cos \phi = 1$. If the density at any point is inversely proportional to the distance of that point from the vertical axis, find the mass.

13. Let $M$ be the mass of the larger of the two solids cut out from a homogeneous spherical shell of radii $b$ and $c$, with $b < c$, by one nappe of a right circular cone of semivertical angle $60°$ with vertex at the center of the shell. Show that the gravitational attraction that $M$ exerts on a unit mass at the center of the shell is $3GM/[4(b^2 + bc + c^2)]$.

14. Let $M$ be the mass of the smaller of the two solids cut out from a sphere of radius 2 by one nappe of a right circular cone of semivertical angle $45°$ with vertex at the center of the sphere. If the density at any point is $k$ times its distance from the vertex of the cone, find the gravitational force that $M$ exerts on a unit mass located at the vertex of the cone.          *Ans.* $GM(2 + \sqrt{2})/8$.

15. Evaluate the triple integral of the function $f(\rho, \phi, \theta) = 1/\rho$ over the volume bounded by the cones $\phi = \pi/4$, $\phi = \arctan 2$, and the sphere $\rho = \sqrt{6}$.

## 9. The Moment of Inertia of a Body.* To get some indication of the vast importance of double and triple integration we shall undertake a little excursion into mechanics. A body in motion has a capacity to do work. For example, a pile driver coming down on a pile drives that pile into the ground. The question that one might raise is, how can we obtain a quantitative expression for the work which the body can do if we know its mass and velocity?

Let us take a simple situation. Suppose that a body of mass $m$ is at a height $y$ above the ground. If the body falls to the ground under the action of gravity, the force applied is $32m$ and the force acts through the distance $y$. Hence, since work is the product of force and distance, one measure of the work done by gravity on the body is $32my$. When the body reaches the ground, it has acquired a velocity, and we also know [Chap. 3, formulas (11) and (14)] that the velocity is related to the distance fallen by $v^2 = 64y$. If we substitute this value of $y$ in $32my$, we obtain $mv^2/2$. This quantity $mv^2/2$ is then another expression for the work done by gravity on the body in making it fall $y$ feet. The body, in turn, can deliver this work to another body if it should hit it.

The quantity $mv^2/2$, which represents the work a body of mass $m$ can do by virtue of the fact that it is in motion with velocity $v$, is called the *kinetic energy* of the body. We have derived the expression by considering a fall straight down, but the expression is a measure of the work that a body can do however it acquires the velocity $v$.

Now let us consider a rigid body (Fig. 23-36) which is rotating about

---

* This section can be omitted without interrupting the continuity.

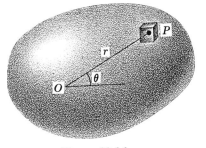

**Figure 23-36**

an axis through $O$ and perpendicular to the plane of the paper. Suppose that the body is rotating with a constant angular velocity $d\theta/dt$ or $\omega$. We should like to know what kinetic energy the body possesses by virtue of the fact that it is rotating. Toward this end consider a bit of mass $\Delta m$ centered about the point $P$ and $r$ units from the axis. Because the angular velocity of the mass is $\omega$, the linear velocity along the circle on which it moves is $r\omega$ and the kinetic energy of this mass then is $\frac{1}{2}\Delta mr^2\omega^2$.

To compute the kinetic energy of the entire body, we should sum the kinetic energies of all the little masses of which the body is composed. We know now that this means taking the limit of a sequence of sums of all the energies of the masses $\Delta m$ as $\Delta m$ approaches 0, that is,

$$\text{kinetic energy} = \int\int\int \tfrac{1}{2}r^2\omega^2\,dm$$

where the integral is taken over the entire body. Now, if $D$ is the density of the mass (we shall again use $D$ to avoid confusion with the coordinate $\rho$), then in rectangular coordinates

**(66)** $$\Delta m = D\,\Delta x\,\Delta y\,\Delta z,$$

so that

$$\text{kinetic energy} = \int\int\int \tfrac{1}{2}r^2\omega^2 D\,dx\,dy\,dz.$$

Of course, $r$ varies with $x, y$, and $z$ because $r$ is the distance from any element of mass to the axis of rotation, but the quantity $\omega$ is constant. Hence we can write

**(67)** $$\text{kinetic energy} = \tfrac{1}{2}\omega^2\int\int\int Dr^2\,dx\,dy\,dz.$$

In this expression the quantity which depends only on the distribution of mass in the body and on the location of the center of rotation, namely,

**(68)** $$I = \int\int\int Dr^2\,dx\,dy\,dz,$$

is called the *moment of inertia* of the body. Thus for a given angular velocity $\omega$, the moment of inertia of a body is a measure of the energy of rotation of the body. The word inertia here has a significance which we shall discuss shortly.

Of course, the calculus is required to calculate moments of inertia. Usually a triple integral must be evaluated, and this has the form (68), that is,

$$\int \int \int_V D r^2 \, dV$$

where $V$ is the volume of the body and $r$ is the variable distance from any point in the body to the fixed axis of rotation. The evaluation can be carried out in any coordinate system that is amenable.

If the body is essentially two-dimensional, for example, a thin disk, then the element of mass can be taken to be

**(69)**                                 $\Delta m = Dt \, \Delta A$

when $t$ is the thickness. There is then no need to integrate over the third dimension of the body because any point in the volume element $t \, \Delta A$ will be about the same distance from the axis as some point in the element of area $\Delta A$. Then the moment of inertia of the body is given by

**(70)**                              $I = t \int \int_A D r^2 \, dA$

where the integration is over the area of the body. The smaller $t$ is, the more accurate will the expression (70) be for the moment of inertia of the body. In practice, one may know the mass $M$ of the entire body. If the mass is homogeneously distributed and if $A$ is the area of the disk, then $M/A$ is the mass per unit area (and thickness $t$). This is the quantity $Dt$ in (69).

Similarly, if a body is essentially one-dimensional, for example, a thin rod, then the element of mass can be taken to be

**(71)**                                 $\Delta m = Da \, \Delta x$

where $a$ is the cross-sectional area. In this case, one need integrate only over the length because any point in the volume element $a \, \Delta x$ will be about the same distance from the axis as some point in the length $\Delta x$. Then the moment of inertia of the one-dimensional body is given by

**(72)**                              $I = a \int D r^2 \, dx,$

where the integral is evaluated over the length of the body. The smaller $a$ is, the more accurately does formula (72) give the moment of inertia of the body. If $M$ is the mass of the entire body of length $l$ and if the mass is uniformly distributed, then $M/l$ is the mass per unit length. This is the quantity $Da$ in (71).

Let us consider an example of the calculation of the moment of inertia of a body. Let us calculate the moment of inertia of a (solid) homogeneous, or uniform, right circular cone (Fig. 23-37) of radius $a$ and height $h$ about its axis and let us use cylindrical coordinates. This coordinate system seems best because the top of the cone as well as the lateral surface is most simply expressed in that system.

We see from Fig. 23-37 that if $Q$ with coordinates $(\rho, \theta, z)$ is a point on the surface of the cone, then $\rho/z = a/h$, so that the equation of the cone in cylindrical coordinates is $z = h\rho/a$. The distance of any element $\Delta m$ of mass, centered at any point $P$ in the cone, from the axis of rotation is the $\rho$-value of $P$. Then the integral to be evaluated is

$$\int\int\int_V \rho^2 \, dm$$

where $V$ is the volume of the cone. If we denote the density by $D$ the integral becomes in cylindrical coordinates

**(73)** $$D\int\int\int_V \rho^2\rho \, dz \, d\rho \, d\theta.$$

We must now evaluate by repeated integration and, therefore, must determine the intervals of integration. We see from the figure that if we fix $\rho$ and $\theta$, $z$ varies from $h\rho/a$ to $h$. The $\rho$-coordinate varies from 0 to $a$ and the $\theta$-coordinate from 0 to $2\pi$. Thus the triple integral becomes

$$D\int_0^{2\pi}\int_0^a\int_{h\rho/a}^h \rho^3 \, dz \, d\rho \, d\theta.$$

**Figure 23-37**

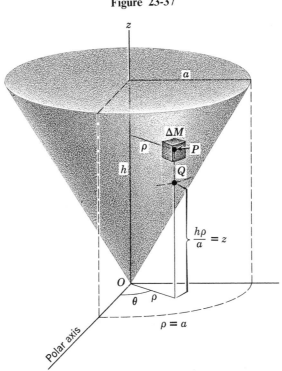

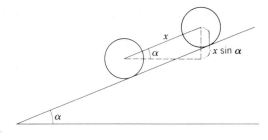

**Figure 23-38**

The value of this integral is $D\pi ha^4/10$. Because the volume of the cone is $\pi a^2 h/3$, its mass is $D\pi a^2 h/3$. Then the moment of inertia is $3Ma^2/10$.

To illustrate the usefulness of the concept of moment of inertia, let us consider a problem. Suppose to start with that a sphere of total mass $M$ and of radius $R$ (Fig. 23-38) *rolls* down an inclined plane without slipping. The plane is inclined at an angle $\alpha$ to the horizontal. What acceleration does the entire sphere acquire insofar as its motion down the plane is concerned; that is, what is the linear acceleration of the center of the sphere?

To answer this question, let us suppose that the sphere has moved down the plane a distance $x$; as Fig. 23-38 shows, this quantity is the distance between the centers of the sphere in the initial and final positions. Because the component of the force of gravity along the plane is $32M \sin\alpha$, the work done by gravity in pulling the sphere down this distance is $32Mx \sin\alpha$. In rolling down the plane the sphere goes through two motions. It rotates about its center and at the same time moves down the plane. It thus acquires two velocities—an angular velocity $\omega$ of rotation and a linear velocity $v$, the velocity of its center, down the plane. The sphere is now capable of doing work which results from both velocities. The rotational velocity can do work just as a wheel in a machine, once it is rotating, is capable of turning other wheels, and the linear velocity can be used to hit and move another object. The work that the sphere is capable of doing by virtue of its motion, that is, the kinetic energy of the sphere, seems intuitively to be the sum of the kinetic energy of translation and the kinetic energy of rotation because each motion should be translatable into work independently of the other.* Let us rely on this intuitive basis. Earlier in this section we found the kinetic energy of translation to be $Mv^2/2$. The kinetic energy of rotation is given by (67). Then the total

$$\text{kinetic energy} = \tfrac{1}{2}Mv^2 + \tfrac{1}{2}I\omega^2.$$

However, for the sphere $I = (\tfrac{2}{5})MR^2$ (see Exercise 5 below). Hence

$$\text{kinetic energy} = \tfrac{1}{2}Mv^2 + \tfrac{1}{2}\cdot\tfrac{2}{5}MR^2\omega^2.$$

The linear velocity $v$ is related to the angular velocity $\omega$ by $v = R\omega$

---

* Watch a young boy send a spinning marble into a stationary marble. The latter is put into translational and rotational motion.

because, as the sphere rotates through an angle $\theta$, it moves down the plane a distance $x = R\theta$ and, by differentiating with respect to time, we obtain $v = R\omega$. Then

$$\text{kinetic energy} = \tfrac{1}{2} Mv^2 + \tfrac{1}{5} Mv^2$$

$$= \tfrac{7}{10} Mv^2.$$

The kinetic energy is acquired because gravity does work on the sphere, and we already have an expression for this work, namely, $32 Mx \sin \alpha$. Then

$$\tfrac{7}{10} Mv^2 = 32\, Mx \sin \alpha$$

or

**(74)** $$\tfrac{7}{10} v^2 = 32\, x \sin \alpha.$$

    Equation (74) is in itself a useful result. It tells us that the sphere, while rotating down the plane and moving a linear distance $x$ (Fig. 23-38), acquires the linear velocity $v$ given by (74). This result differs from the velocity of a smooth body which merely slides down the plane a distance $x$; in the latter case (see Chapter 3, Section 4, Exercise 5$b$) the velocity is $8\sqrt{x \sin \alpha}$. Let us note that the linear velocity acquired by the rotating sphere is *less* than that acquired by a sliding object.

    From (74) we can derive another useful fact. Because this equation holds at any instant $t$, we may differentiate with respect to $t$ and obtain

$$\tfrac{7}{10} \cdot 2v \frac{dv}{dt} = 32v \sin \alpha.$$

Then the linear acceleration (down the plane) is

**(75)** $$\frac{dv}{dt} = \tfrac{5}{7} \cdot 32 \sin \alpha.$$

If an object merely slides down a plane which is inclined at an angle $\alpha$ to the horizontal, its acceleration is $32 \sin \alpha$. We see that a sphere which rolls down an inclined plane acquires less linear acceleration than if it merely slides down. The physical explanation is that the work done by gravity in causing the sphere to roll down the plane is used in part to give the sphere a rotational acceleration.

## EXERCISES

In working out the following exercises choose the appropriate coordinate system.

**1.** Calculate the moment of inertia of a uniform (or homogeneous) thin rod of length $2a$ and of total mass $M$:

    (a)  When the axis of rotation is perpendicular to the rod and through the center.               *Ans.* $\tfrac{1}{3} Ma^2$.

(b)  When the axis of rotation is perpendicular to the rod and through one end.

2.  (a)  Calculate the moment of inertia of a uniform, thin, circular disk of radius $a$ and total mass $M$ when the axis of rotation is perpendicular to the plane of the disk and through its center.                          *Ans.* $\frac{1}{2} Ma^2$.

(b)  Calculate the moment of inertia of a uniform solid circular cylinder of total mass $M$, radius $a$, and length $l$ about its axis.

    *Suggestion:* The cylinder can be regarded as the sum of a large number of thin disks.

3.  Calculate the moment of inertia of a uniform thin ring of radius $a$ and total mass $M$ when the axis of rotation is perpendicular to the plane of the ring and through its center.                          *Ans.* $Ma^2$.

4.  Calculate the moment of inertia of a uniform thin rectangular disk with sides of length $2a$ and $2b$ and of total mass $M$ when the axis of rotation is perpendicular to the plane of the disk and through its center.

5.  Calculate the moment of inertia of a uniform sphere of radius $a$ and total mass $M$ when the axis of rotation is through its center.                          *Ans.* $\frac{2}{5} Ma^2$.

6.  Calculate the moment of inertia of a uniform thin, rectangular disk with sides of length $2a$ and $2b$ and of total mass $M$ when the axis of rotation is a line in the plane of the disk, passing through the center of the disk, and parallel to the side with length $2b$.

7.  (a)  Show that the sum of the moments of inertia of any uniform plane laminar body (thin disk of arbitrary bounding shape) about any two perpendicular axes in the plane of the body is equal to the moment of inertia about an axis through the point of intersection of the two axes and perpendicular to the plane of the lamina.

(b)  Apply the result of part (a) to find the moment of inertia of a uniform circular disk about a diameter.

8.  Evaluate the integral (73) of the text by integrating with respect to $\rho$, then $z$, and then $\theta$.

9.  A homogeneous hemispherical shell of density $D$ has radii $a$ and $b$ with $a > b$. Show that its moment of inertia with respect to any diameter of the base is $4\pi D(a^5 - b^5)/15$.

10.  A ring is cut out from a homogeneous spherical shell of density $D$ and of radii 4 and 5 feet by two parallel planes distant 1 foot and 3 feet from the center and on the same side of the center. Find the moment of inertia of this ring about its axis.                          *Ans.* $291\pi D$.

11.  Consider a homogeneous thin disk of total mass $M$ and occupying the first quadrant outside the circle $\rho = 2a$ and inside the circle $\rho = 4a \cos \theta$. Find the moment of inertia of the disk about an axis through the pole and perpendicular to the plane of the disk.

    *Ans.* $\dfrac{20\pi + 21\sqrt{3}}{2\pi + 3\sqrt{3}} a^2 M$.

12.  The radii of a homogeneous spherical shell of density $d$ are $a$ and $b$ with $b < a$. Through this shell a circular hole of radius $c < b$ is bored, the axis of the hole coinciding with a diameter of the shell. Find the moment of inertia of the remaining solid about the axis of the hole.

    *Suggestion:* Use cylindrical coordinates.

    *Ans.* $\frac{4}{15}\pi d[(2a^2 + 3c^2)(a^2 - c^2)^{3/2} - (2b^2 + 3c^2)(b^2 - c^2)^{3/2}]$.

13.  Find the moment of inertia of a thin, homogeneous, circular disk of total mass

$M$ and bounded by $\rho = 2(\sin \theta + \cos \theta)$ about an axis through the pole and perpendicular to the plane of the disk.

14. Find the moment of inertia of a homogeneous, right circular cone of total mass $M$, radius $a$, and height $h$ about its axis by integrating with respect to $\rho$, $z$, and then $\theta$. *Ans.* $3a^3M/10$.

15. Find the moment of inertia of the cone in Exercise 14 about any line through the vertex and perpendicular to the axis.

16. Consider the homogeneous solid of total mass $M$ cut out from one nappe of a right circular cone of semivertical angle $30°$ by a sphere of radius 2 whose center is at the vertex of the cone. Find the moment of inertia of this mass about the $z$-axis. *Ans.* $(5 - 2\sqrt{3})M/5$.

    *Suggestion:* Use spherical coordinates.

17. Consider the homogeneous solid of total mass $M$ which is bounded by the paraboloid of revolution $z = (x^2 + y^2)/4$ and the plane $z = 4$. Find its moment of inertia about the $z$-axis.

    *Suggestion:* Use cylindrical coordinates.

18. Find the moment of inertia of the solid of Exercise 17 about the $y$-axis.
    *Ans.* $32M/3$.

19. Find the moment of inertia about the $z$-axis of the homogeneous solid of mass $M$ bounded by $z = \rho^2$ (in cylindrical coordinates) and by the plane $z = 2$.

20. Find the moment of inertia of the thin homogeneous disk of total mass $M$:
    (a)  Bounded by $x^2 + y^2 = R^2$ and to the right of the $y$-axis about the $x$-axis.
    *Ans.* $R^2M/4$.

    (b)  The same disk as in (a) but about the $y$-axis.

    (c)  Bounded by the ellipse $\dfrac{x^2}{a^2} + \dfrac{y^2}{b^2} = 1$ about the $x$-axis.

    (d)  Bounded by the ellipse $\dfrac{x^2}{a^2} + \dfrac{y^2}{b^2} = 1$ about the $y$-axis. *Ans.* $a^2M/4$.

    (e)  Bounded by $y^2 = 4x$, $x = 4$, and $y = 0$ about the $x$-axis.
    (f)  Bounded by $y^2 = 4x$, $x = 4$, and $y = 0$ about the $y$-axis.
    *Ans.* $48M/7$.

21. Consider a homogeneous solid cylinder of mass $M$ and radius $R$ rolling down an inclined plane of inclination $\alpha$ without slipping. Find the speed and acceleration of the center when it reaches the bottom. The moment of inertia of the solid cylinder is $MR^2/2$. *Ans.* $v = \sqrt{\frac{4}{3}32h}$ ; $a = \frac{2}{3}32 \sin \alpha$.

22. The yo-yo, a child's toy, is a homogeneous solid wooden cylinder of mass $M$, radius $R$, and length $h$. A string is wound around the middle of the cylinder. The free end is held fixed, and the yo-yo travels straight down as it rotates. Find the linear acceleration of its center. The moment of inertia of the solid cylinder is $MR^2/2$.

23. A string has been wound around a thin-walled hollow cylinder of mass $M$ and radius $R$. The free end of the string is held fixed, and the cylinder travels down as it rotates. Show that the linear acceleration of the axis of the cylinder in its downward motion is one half of the normal acceleration of falling objects, that is, 16 ft/sec². The moment of inertia of the cylinder is $MR^2$.

The concept of moment of inertia enters into problems of rotation in still another way. Anyone who has played on a seesaw knows that the heavier the weight of the person, the greater the effect of the person in causing downward rotation, and the farther the person is from the fulcrum, the greater his effect. In other words, what one might call the force causing rotation depends not only on the force itself (the weight on the seesaw) but on the distance of the point of application of the force from the center of rotation. The "force of rotation" is then the product $Fr$. What one learns from the seesaw is, in fact, generally correct. Implicit there is also the fact that the force, to be most effective, must be perpendicular to the length $r$, which is the case when the seesaw is horizontal.

The force of rotation $Fr$ is called technically the *torque* or *moment of force*. It plays the role in rotation which a force itself plays in pushing an object along some path. If an object does rotate through an angle $\theta$ in time $t$, the actual distance it rotates is $s = r\theta$, where $r$ is the distance from the object to the axis; the linear velocity then is $\dot{s} = r\dot{\theta}$ and the linear acceleration is $\ddot{s} = r\ddot{\theta}$. According to Newton's second law of motion, $F = ma$. Then $F = mr\ddot{\theta}$ and, since the torque $T$ is $rF$,

$$T = mr^2\ddot{\theta}.$$

The interpretation of this equation, then, is that the torque or rotational force is the quantity $mr^2$ times the *angular* acceleration. The quantity $mr^2$ is what we have already met [cf. (68)] as the moment of inertia of an object which can be regarded as localized at one point $r$ units from the center of rotation. Thus the moment of inertia of an object plays the same role in rotational motion as mass does in translational motion, that is, motion along some path.

We have discussed the role of moment of inertia in the rotational motion of a particle, for example, the person at the end of the seesaw. Suppose that one wishes to set a rigid body into rotation (Fig. 23-39). The axis of rotation is to be a line perpendicular to the plane of the paper and through the point $O$. Consider, first, the small element $\Delta m_1$ of the body with distance $r_1$ from $O$. To set it rotating, one can apply a force $F_1$ tangential to the circular path on which $\Delta m_1$ moves. We know that the tangential acceleration is $a_1 = r_1\ddot{\theta}$ and so, by Newton's second law, the force that must be applied tangentially is $F_1 = \Delta m_1 r_1 \ddot{\theta}$. Likewise, to set the small element $\Delta m_2$ rotating, one must apply a tangential force $F_2 = \Delta m_2 r_2 \ddot{\theta}$, $F_2$ being perpendicular to $r_2$ and $\ddot{\theta}$ being the same because the whole rigid

**Figure 23-39**

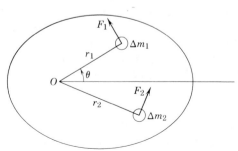

body will rotate with the same angular acceleration. Likewise, there will be the force $F_n = \Delta m_n r_n \ddot{\theta}$ on the $n$th element of mass.

The torque applied to the $i$th element of mass is $\Delta m_i r_i^2 \ddot{\theta}$. Since all these torques produce the same angular acceleration, we may add them; the total $T$ of these torques is

**(76)**
$$T = \ddot{\theta} \left[ r^2 \, \Delta m_1 + r_2^2 \, \Delta m_2 + \cdots + r_n^2 \, \Delta m_n \right].$$

Since, if $D(x, y, z)$ is the density of the rigid body, $\Delta m_i = D_i \, \Delta x \, \Delta y \, \Delta z$,

$$T = \ddot{\theta} \left[ D_1 r_1^2 + D_2 r_2^2 + \cdots + D_n r_n^2 \right] \Delta x \, \Delta y \, \Delta z.$$

We now let each element $\Delta x \, \Delta y \, \Delta z$ approach 0 and continue to sum over all the elements comprising the body. Then the limiting value of $T$, which we shall also denote by $T$, is

**(77)**
$$T = \ddot{\theta} \int \int \int Dr^2 \, dx \, dy \, dz$$

where $r$ is the distance of any element of mass from the axis of rotation.

The integral is what we previously denoted by $I$—the moment of inertia of the body—and what we learn from this equation is that the torque on the extended rigid body is the moment of inertia of the entire body with respect to the axis of rotation times the angular acceleration or

**(78)**
$$T = I\ddot{\theta}.$$

The torque formula (78) teaches us something else about the significance of moment of inertia. If we wish to have a wheel accelerate or decelerate quickly and yet apply small torques, we must make $I$ small. How can we do this? The moment of inertia of a body is always calculated with reference to a specific axis of rotation. Perhaps we can position the axis wisely. Intuitively, we can see that if the $\Delta m_i$ are close to the axis, then the $r_i$ would be small; that is, we should place the axis so that as much mass as possible is close to the axis. Let us see if we can pin this idea down in mathematical terms.

Let us consider a thin disk or wheel of variable density $D$ and let us try to determine the point $(a, b)$ through which the axis should pass to make the moment of inertia as small as possible (Fig. 23-40). By (70) the moment of inertia for our two-dimensional body is

**(79)**
$$I = \int \int D \left[ (x - a)^2 + (y - b)^2 \right] dx \, dy,$$

where the factor $t$ or thickness is omitted because it will play no role. Now, $I$ is a function of the location $(a, b)$ of the axis, and we wish to minimize $I$ by the best choice of $(a, b)$. We know that if we were to carry out the integration, the integral would contain $a$ and $b$. Hence we can use our method for minimizing a function of two variables, that is, find $\partial I / \partial a$ and

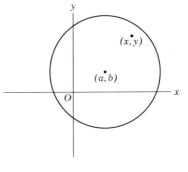

**Figure 23-40**

$\partial I/\partial b$ and set each equal to 0. We shall go a bit beyond our theory to assert that we can differentiate the integral by differentiating the *integrand*. This is possible because the variables of integration are $x$ and $y$ and not $a$ and $b$.* Then

$$\frac{\partial I}{\partial a} = \int \int \frac{\partial}{\partial a} \left\{ D \left[ (x-a)^2 + (y-b)^2 \right] \right\} dx\ dy.$$

Because $D$ is a function of $x$ and $y$ [we can regard this $D$ as the $Dt$ of (69) or just recognize that $D$ varies only with $x$ and $y$ over a thin disk], we can regard it as a constant insofar as differentiation with respect to $a$ is concerned. Thus

$$\frac{\partial I}{\partial a} = -2 \int \int D (x-a)\ dx\ dy.$$

Likewise,

$$\frac{\partial I}{\partial b} = -2 \int \int D (y-b)\ dx\ dy.$$

If we set these partial derivatives equal to 0 and solve for $a$ and $b$, we obtain

**(80)** $$a = \frac{\int \int Dx\ dx\ dy}{\int \int D\ dx\ dy}, \qquad b = \frac{\int \int Dy\ dx\ dy}{\int \int D\ dx\ dy}.$$

This result tells us that to make the moment of inertia least, the axis should pass through the point $(a, b)$ where $a$ and $b$ are given by (80). If we compare

---

*Intuitively, the justification of the differentiation can be put thus. The double integral is, before taking the limit, a sum of a finite number of terms of the form $F(x, y, a, b)\ \Delta x\ \Delta y$. We can differentiate the sum with respect to $a$ or $b$ and then take the limit as $\Delta x$ and $\Delta y$ approach 0.

(21) and (22) with (80), we see that the point $(a, b)$ is what we have called the center of gravity of the disk.

In Section 3 we found that placing the axis at the center of gravity eliminates unbalanced centripetal forces on the axis. The two conditions—no radial force on the axis and minimum torque—can be met by putting the axis through the center of gravity. However, minimum torque is not always a desirable property. For example, the function of a flywheel is to resist any tendency to change its angular velocity. This means, in view of (78), that for a given torque we should make the moment of inertia as large as possible. Since putting the axis through the center of gravity minimizes the torque, it is necessary to put the axis off-center. This, however, would drastically shorten the life of the axle and bearings. Furthermore, the flexing of the shaft would introduce variations in angular velocity, which is exactly what we want to avoid. Flywheels are designed by compromises.

# CHAPTER TWENTY-FOUR
# AN INTRODUCTION TO DIFFERENTIAL EQUATIONS

*1. Introduction.* Strictly speaking, there is no sharp line between the calculus and differential equations. Loosely, a differential equation is an equation involving derivatives and the problem of solving a differential equation is to find the function or functions which satisfy the differential equation. Since in the calculus we solve problems such as

$$\frac{dy}{dx} = 2x,$$

we are technically solving a differential equation and the solution in this case is $y = x^2 + C$. In fact any equation of the type

$$\frac{dy}{dx} = f(x)$$

is a differential equation and the solution is of the form

**(1)** $$y = \int f(x)dx + C.$$

Whether or not one can express the integral in terms of elementary functions one says that (1) is the solution. That is, as long as finding the solution is reduced to an integration or a quadrature, the equation is said to have been solved.

In the course of our work in the calculus we have solved many other types of differential equations. In our work on growth and decay problems (Chap. 12, Sect. 5) we encountered differential equations of the form

$$\frac{dy}{dx} = ky$$

and in our work on straight-line motion in a resisting medium (Chap. 12,

Sect. 6) we solved

$$\frac{dv}{dt} = kv$$

and

$$\frac{dv}{dt} = 32 - kv.$$

All these and many others are of the form

**(2)** $$\frac{dy}{dx} = f(y).$$

We know now that we can solve these equations by using the fact that

$$\frac{dy}{dx} = \frac{1}{\dfrac{dx}{dy}}$$

so that

$$\frac{dx}{dy} = \frac{1}{f(y)}.$$

The solution of this type is

$$x = \int \frac{1}{f(y)} \, dy$$

and whether or not we can express the integral in terms of elementary functions we have at least reduced the problem to a quadrature.

In the study of gravitational attraction (Chap. 7, Sect. 8) and simple harmonic motion (Chap. 10, Sect. 6) we encountered the differential equations

**(3)** $$\frac{d^2r}{dt^2} = - \frac{GM}{r^2}$$

and

**(4)** $$\frac{d^2y}{dx^2} = - ky.$$

In these cases we used special devices to solve the equations. Thus in the case of (3) we used the device of replacing $d^2r/dt^2$ by $v \, dv/dr$ so that (3) became

**(5)** $$v \frac{dv}{dr} = - \frac{GM}{r^2}.$$

We then integrated both sides with respect to $r$ and obtained

$$\frac{v^2}{2} = \frac{GM}{r} + C.$$

Since $v = dr/dt$ this equation reduces to the type (2) and so we can integrate once more. In the case of (4) we multiplied both sides by $2\, dy/dx$ [a device we could have used for (3) also] and thus obtained

$$2\frac{dy}{dx}\frac{d^2y}{dx^2} = -2ky\frac{dy}{dx}$$

which yields, on integration,

$$\left(\frac{dy}{dx}\right)^2 = -ky^2 + C.$$

To integrate this equation we again face an equation of type (2) and so we can integrate once more.

In the study of planetary motion (Chap. 19, Sect. 3) we encountered

**(6)** $$\frac{d^2u}{d\theta^2} + u = \frac{GM}{h^2}.$$

Here a simple transformation

$$y = u - \frac{GM}{h^2}$$

reduced (6) to

**(7)** $$\frac{d^2y}{d\theta^2} + y = 0$$

and so we were back to the type (4).

Obviously the physical problems we have considered are just a few of the hundreds that scientists encounter and we might reasonably expect that the differential equations that can arise are quite different from the ones we have encountered. How do we solve these many types that arise in real problems? One answer, though not a very satisfying one, is to try to use tricks which reduce the differential equations one encounters to the types described above. Thus the original differential equation that arose in the study of planetary motion was not (4) above but was reduced to (4) by a special transformation. Though ingenuity is always in order and in fact is to be welcomed, it will not always serve.

The alternative is to study differential equations systematically and to attempt to find general methods for the solution of the various types that can possibly occur. Toward this end, differential equations are generally classified into two major types, ordinary and partial. Ordinary differential equations involve a function or functions of one independent variable. Thus all of the above examples are ordinary differential equations. Partial differential equations involve functions of two or more independent variables. Thus with the understanding that $u = f(x, y)$,

$$\frac{\partial^2 u}{\partial x^2} + \frac{\partial^2 u}{\partial y^2} = 0$$

is a partial differential equation. Both types, ordinary and partial, include a variety of cases, and techniques have been developed to solve them. In this introduction to differential equations we shall consider the simpler type, namely, ordinary differential equations, and only the commonest cases that occur in practice.

For the sake of learning some terminology let us consider the differential equation

**(8)** $$\frac{d^2 y}{dx^2} + a(x)\left(\frac{dy}{dx}\right)^2 + b(x)y = g(x).$$

It is an ordinary differential equation because it involves $y$ as a function of the one independent variable $x$. It is called a second-order differential equation because the highest-order derivative appearing in it is of the second order. It is also said to be of the first degree because the *highest-order derivative* appears only to the first degree. If the term involving $d^2 y / dx^2$ had been $(d^2 y / dx^2)^3$ we would say that the equation is of the third degree.

**2. First-Order Ordinary Differential Equations.** It is most reasonable to start a systematic study with first-order equations because these are most likely to be easier to solve. Of course a differential equation in $dy / dx$ may be of higher degree but we shall assume it can be solved for $dy / dx$. Thus

$$xy\left(\frac{dy}{dx}\right)^2 - \sin x = 0$$

can be solved for $dy / dx$ so that

$$\frac{dy}{dx} = \pm\sqrt{\frac{\sin x}{xy}} \, .$$

More generally solvability for $dy / dx$ would lead to an equation of the form

$$\frac{dy}{dx} = f(x, y).$$

Unfortunately there are no methods of solving this general equation. We must restrict ourselves to special cases.

We know already that we can solve (or at least reduce to quadrature)

$$\frac{dy}{dx} = f(x)$$

and

$$\frac{dy}{dx} = f(y).$$

However, we can also handle readily the first-order equation of the form

**(9)** $$\frac{dy}{dx} = f(x)\,g(y).$$

We have only to rewrite the equation as

$$\frac{1}{g(y)}\frac{dy}{dx} = f(x)$$

and to integrate both sides with respect to $x$. This equation is often written in differential form

$$\frac{1}{g(y)}\,dy = f(x)\,dx.$$

We may, therefore, write

**(10)** $$\int \frac{1}{g(y)}\,dy = \int f(x)\,dx + C.$$

Clearly we have reduced the solution of the differential equation to quadratures. Let us note that equation (5) is of the form (10). The method we have just described is called separation of variables.

## EXERCISES

Solve the following differential equations by the method of separation of variables:

1. $\dfrac{dy}{dx} = x^2 y^3.$      *Ans.* $-\dfrac{1}{2y^2} = \dfrac{x^3}{3} + C.$

2. $\dfrac{dy}{dx} = \dfrac{x^2}{y^3}.$

3. $\dfrac{dy}{dx} = e^{x-y}.$

4. $\sqrt{1 + y^2}\ dy = \sqrt{1 - x^2}\ dx.$

5. $y\dfrac{dy}{dx} = \dfrac{\log x}{x}.$      *Ans.* $y^2 = (\log x)^2 + C.$

6. $\dfrac{dy}{dx} = \dfrac{3x + xy^2}{y + x^2 y}.$

7. $\sin^2 y\ dx + \cos^2 x\ dy = 0$ subject to the condition $y = \pi/4$ when $x = \pi/4.$

8. $x\sqrt{1 + y^2}\ dx - y\sqrt{1 + x^2}\ dy = 0.$

9. $y' = 8xy + 3y.$

10. Solve $y' = (x + y)^2$ by letting $v = x + y.$

We shall take up one more very common type of first-order ordinary differential equation. First let us reconsider an old problem. A man falls straight down in a medium whose resistance varies directly with the velocity. Find the velocity with which he falls.

As usual we consider the forces at work. Let us take the downward direction as positive. Gravity pulls the man down and the force of gravity is $32m$ (if the fall takes place near the surface of the earth). The resistance of the air is of the form $Kv$ and, because $v$ is positive downward whereas the resistance is upward, the resistance is $-Kv$. Then by Newton's second law

$$m\frac{dv}{dt} = -Kv + 32m$$

or

**(11)**
$$\frac{dv}{dt} = -kv + 32$$

where $k = K/m$. We can and did solve this problem by a simple method (Chap. 12, Sect. 6). However, what is pertinent here is that it is a special case of what is called a linear first-order equation whose general form is

**(12)**
$$\frac{dy}{dx} + P(x)y = Q(x).$$

Equation (12) is called linear because if we think of $y$ and $dy/dx$ as variables, the equation is of the first degree in these variables.

The general case (12) cannot be solved by the method used for (11) because the functions $P(x)$ and $Q(x)$ are present. However, there is a general method of solving (12). We multiply the entire equation by $e^{\int P(x)dx}$ and obtain

**(13)**
$$e^{\int P(x)dx}\frac{dy}{dx} + e^{\int P(x)dx}P(x)y = Q(x)e^{\int P(x)dx}.$$

Now the merit of this step, that is, multiplying by $e^{\int P(x)dx}$, which is called an integrating factor, is that the first two terms are

$$\frac{d}{dx}\left(ye^{\int P(x)dx}\right).$$

Hence (13) can be written as

$$\frac{d}{dx}\left(ye^{\int P(x)dx}\right) = Q(x)e^{\int P(x)dx}.$$

We may now integrate both sides with respect to $x$. Then

$$ye^{\int P(x)dx} = \int Q(x)e^{\int P(x)dx} + C.$$

Hence

**(14)** $$y = e^{-\int P(x)dx} \int Q(x)e^{\int P(x)dx} + Ce^{-\int P(x)dx}.$$

Let us consider an example.

**Example.**  Solve

$$\frac{dy}{dx} + 2xy = x.$$

**Solution.**  We multiply both sides by $e^{\int 2x\,dx} = e^{x^2}$. Then

$$e^{x^2}\frac{dy}{dx} + e^{x^2}2xy = e^{x^2}x.$$

Hence

$$\frac{d}{dx}\left(e^{x^2}y\right) = e^{x^2}x.$$

Integration yields

$$e^{x^2}y = \tfrac{1}{2}e^{x^2} + C.$$

Hence

$$y = e^{-x^2}\left(\tfrac{1}{2}e^{x^2}\right) + Ce^{-x^2}$$

or

$$y = \tfrac{1}{2} + Ce^{-x^2}.$$

One could use (14) directly instead of repeating the method by which (14) is obtained.

## EXERCISES

**1.** Solve each of the following first-order linear equations:

(a) $\dfrac{dy}{dx} + \dfrac{y}{x} = 1.$                    *Ans.* $x^2 - 2xy = C.$

(b) $y' + \dfrac{3}{x}y = x.$

(c) $\dfrac{dr}{dt} + 2r = 10e^{-2t}$; $r = 0$ when $t = 0$.            *Ans.* $r = 10te^{-2t}.$

(d) $\dfrac{dy}{dx} + \dfrac{10}{2x+5}y = 10.$

(e) $x\,dy + y\,dx = \sin x\,dx.$

**2.** If the slope of a curve at any point $(x, y)$ is $2x + 3y$, find the equation of the curve.

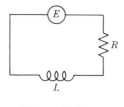

**Figure 24-1**

The commonest physical applications of the first-order linear equation occur in electric circuit theory. Although the concepts of this theory are not as intuitively apparent as those of mechanics, nevertheless let us try to get some indication of why first-order linear equations are important in circuit theory.

The symbol $E$ in Fig. 24-1 denotes a voltage or electromotive force such as is supplied by a flashlight battery or the voltage we tap in an electrical socket in our homes, and which is furnished by an electric company. This voltage causes electric current to flow in the circuit. The zigzag lines marked $R$ in the figure denote what is called a resistor. Physically it is actually the resistance which wires present to the passage of electric current running through them. The more mysteriously behaving element in electric circuits is a coil of wire, called an inductance, and denoted by $L$ in the figure. To understand its action let us note that each element in the circuit consumes voltage. If $i$ is used to denote the current then the resistor consumes a voltage $iR$. This fact is known as Ohm's law. The inductance $L$ consumes voltage and the amount, given essentially by Lenz's law, is $L\, di/dt$ where $t$ is time. (There is a physical explanation of why a coil causes such a loss of voltage.) Now $E$ supplies the voltage consumed by $R$ and $L$. Another basic law, Kirchhoff's, tells us that

**(15)** $$L \frac{di}{dt} + iR = E(t).$$

The current $i$ that flows in the circuit depends then on what elements in it consume the voltage.

In a realistic situation, $E$ itself may be an alternating current such as the type used in modern homes to light our lamps, heat toasters, and run vacuum cleaners and other appliances. The unit in which $E$ is measured is volts; the current $i$ is measured in amperes; the resistance $R$ is a number of ohms; and $L$ is measured in henrys. Then $iR$ and $L\, di/dt$ are each volts, and equation (15) equates voltages. The circuit in Fig. 24-1 is called a series circuit.

## EXERCISES

**1.** Solve (11) by the method used for linear equations. Compare Chapter 12, Section 6.

**2.** Solve equation (15) when $R = 10$ ohms, $L$ is 2 henrys and $E$ is $20 \cos 5t$ volts.

3. An electromotive force of 20 volts is applied to a circuit consisting of an inductance of 2 henrys and a resistance of 40 ohms. Find the current at any time $t$ if it is 0 when $t = 0$.

4. Find the current in a series circuit containing a resistance of 10 ohms, an inductance of 0.1 henry, and a voltage $E(t)$ such that $E(t) = 10$ for $0 \leq t \leq 5$ and $E(t) = 0$ for $t > 5$.

**3. Second-Order Linear Homogeneous Differential Equations.** As in the case of first-order ordinary differential equations it is possible to write down an infinite variety of second-order equations. There are no general methods of solutions for all second-order equations and so mathematicians concentrate on those types that arise in real problems. Of these the most important type is the linear equation with constant coefficients. Such an equation would be of the form

**(16)**
$$3 \frac{d^2y}{dx^2} + 5 \frac{dy}{dx} - 8y = x^2.$$

Even in this type a distinction is made between the case in which the right side is 0 or a function of $x$. In the former case the equation is called homogeneous and in the latter, non-homogeneous. We shall consider both cases.

Let us see first what physical problem gives rise to a second-order linear equation with constant coefficients. We have considered the motion of a weight on a spring (Chap. 10, Sect. 6) but ignored any losses due to friction. As a consequence we obtained a differential equation of the form

**(17)**
$$\frac{d^2y}{dx^2} + ky = 0$$

and, because this is a very special case of (16), we were able to solve it by a special technique. When we derived (17) we argued that the force acting on the mass $m$ is $-32m$ (because the upward direction was chosen positive) and the spring force was $-k(d - y)$ because, for example, where $y$ is negative the stretch of the spring is $d - y$ and the force is upward (see Fig.

**Figure 24-2**

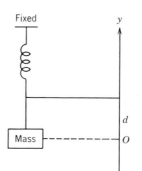

24-2). Then we were led to the differential equation

$$\frac{d^2y}{dt^2} = -ky$$

because the weight $32m$ offsets the quantity $kd$. (Review the reasoning in Chap. 10, Sect. 6.)

Let us now suppose that air resistance is taken into account. The air resistance opposes the motion. Hence when the mass is moving upward and $y$ is increasing so that $dy/dt$ is positive, the air resistance will be downward and is $-l\,dy/dt$ where $l$ is a positive proportionality constant. Correspondingly when the mass moves downward $y$ decreases, $dy/dt$ is negative, and so the air resistance is $-l\,dy/dt$ because it is upward and should be positive. Hence in place of (17) we now have

$$\frac{d^2y}{dt^2} = -l\frac{dy}{dt} - ky$$

and this is clearly of the form (16) in which the right-hand side is 0.

We see therefore that there is reason to consider second-order linear differential equations with constant coefficients. Let us look into the general type. We consider

**(18)** $$\frac{d^2y}{dx^2} + \alpha\frac{dy}{dx} + \beta y = 0$$

where $\alpha$ and $\beta$ are constants. When one thinks about functions whose derivatives are likely to offset each other and the function itself, the possibility of using $e^{mx}$ suggests itself because $d(e^x)/dx = e^x$. Hence we try $e^{mx}$. If we substitute $y = e^{mx}$ in (18) we obtain

**(19)** $$m^2 + \alpha m + \beta = 0.$$

If $m$ satisfies this equation then $e^{mx}$ is a solution of (18). Now (19) is a quadratic equation in $m$, called the auxiliary or characteristic equation, and we must consider the various possible types of roots.

The simplest case is when the roots are real and distinct. Let us suppose that the roots are $m_1$ and $m_2$. Then the solution of (18) is

**(20)** $$y = Ae^{m_1x} + Be^{m_2x}$$

where $A$ and $B$ are arbitrary constants which can be determined only if we have some initial conditions such as the initial displacement and initial velocity of, say, a mass on a spring.

The roots of equation (19) may be equal, that is, $m_1 = m_2$. Then we have only one solution whereas we know from experience with second-order equations (and, in fact, there is a general theorem) that such equations should have two different or independent solutions. There is a minor argument, which we shall not present (see Exercise 2), which leads to the suggestion that if $e^{m_1 x}$ is one solution then

**(21)** $$y = e^{m_1 x}(A + Bx)$$

is the general solution. One can of course substitute (21) into the differential equation and show that it is the general solution when $m_1 = m_2$.

The last possibility is that the quadratic equation (19) has complex roots. Let us suppose that these are $a \pm bi$. Then formally at least the solution of (18) is

**(22)** $$y = Ae^{(a+bi)x} + Be^{(a-bi)x}.$$

Such solutions present us with a new kind of problem, namely, the use of complex numbers, which we have up to now avoided in the calculus. Let us operate intuitively and formally and see if we can recast (22) in a form more useful for our purposes and which also avoids complex numbers.

Let us go back to the special case of (18), namely,

**(23)** $$\frac{d^2 y}{dx^2} + y = 0$$

and suppose we apply to it the method we are exploring for (18) itself. We substitute $e^{mx}$ for $y$ in (23) and obtain

$$m^2 e^{mx} + e^{mx} = 0$$

or

$$m^2 + 1 = 0.$$

Then

$$m = \pm i$$

and the solutions of (23) are then

**(24)** $$y = Ae^{ix} + Be^{ix}.$$

However, we know from our earlier work (Chap. 10, Sect. 6) that the solution is

**(25)** $$y = C \cos x + D \sin x.$$

Now (24) and (25) are both general solutions of the same differential equation and, moreover, both are equally general because both contain two arbitrary constants, which is what should and does result from two integrations. Hence

**(26)** $$Ae^{ix} + Be^{-ix} \equiv C \cos x + D \sin x.$$

Let $x = 0$ and let us use the fact that $e^0 = 1$. Then

**(27)** $$A + B = C.$$

If we differentiate (26) according to the usual rules of the calculus we obtain

**(28)** $$Aie^{ix} - Bie^{-ix} = -C \sin x + D \cos x.$$

Now if $x = 0$, we obtain

**(29)** $$Ai - Bi = D.$$

If we use the values of $C$ and $D$ given by (27) and (28) in (26) we obtain

$$Ae^{ix} + Be^{-ix} = (A + B)\cos x + i(A - B)\sin x$$

**(30)** $$= A(\cos x + i \sin x) + B(\cos x - i \sin x).$$

Now $A$ and $B$ are arbitrary constants. Hence (29) holds for all values of $A$ and $B$. Let $B = 0$ and $A = 1$. Then

**(31)** $$e^{ix} = \cos x + i \sin x.$$

Likewise if in (30) we let $A = 0$ and $B = 1$ we get

**(32)** $$e^{-ix} = \cos x - i \sin x.$$

Incidentally, (31) and (32) are called Euler's formulas. Now $e^{(a+bi)x}$ is a solution of (18) and so is $e^{(a-bi)x}$  But by (31) and (32), since $e^{u+v} = e^u e^v$,

**(33)** $$e^{(a+bi)x} = e^{ax}(\cos bx + i \sin bx).$$

**(34)** $$e^{(a-bi)x} = e^{ax}(\cos bx - i \sin bx).$$

The sum or difference of two solutions of a linear equations such as (18) is a solution. Then by adding and subtracting (33) and (34) we obtain

$$2e^{ax} \cos bx.$$

$$2ie^{ax} \sin bx.$$

Moreover, any constant times a solution of (18) is also a solution. Hence we can write the general solution of (18) for the case of complex roots $a \pm bi$ of the characteristic equation as

**(35)** $$y = Ae^{ax} \cos bx + Be^{ax} \sin bx,$$

wherein $A$ and $B$ are arbitrary constants.

We have performed many formal operations with complex numbers as though they had all the properties of real numbers. Hence there is some question as to whether (35) is the general solution of (18). We can substitute

(35) in (18) and see that it is so. Moreover, since (35) contains two arbitrary constants it is the general solution.

**Example.** Solve

$$\frac{d^2y}{dx^2} + 4\frac{dy}{dx} + 13y = 0.$$

**Solution.** The characteristic equation [see (19)] is

$$m^2 + 4m + 13 = 0.$$

The roots of this quadratic equation are

$$m_i = \frac{-4 + \sqrt{16 - 52}}{2}, \qquad m_2 = \frac{-4 - \sqrt{16 - 52}}{2}$$

or

$$m_1 = -2 + 3i, \qquad m_2 = -2 - 3i.$$

Hence since we have denoted the roots by $a \pm bi$,

$$a = -2 \qquad \text{and} \qquad b = 3.$$

By (35) the general solution is

$$y = Ae^{-2x}\cos 3x + Be^{-2x}\sin 3x.$$

## EXERCISES

**1.** Solve

(a) $\dfrac{d^2y}{dx^2} - y = 0.$  *Ans.* $y = Ae^x + Be^{-x}$.

(b) $\dfrac{d^2y}{dx^2} - 3\dfrac{dy}{dx} - 10y = 0.$  *Ans.* $y = Ae^{5x} + Be^{-2x}$.

(c) $\dfrac{d^2y}{dx^2} + \dfrac{dy}{dx} - y = 0.$

(d) $\dfrac{d^2y}{dx^2} + \dfrac{dy}{dx} + y = 0.$  *Ans.* $y = e^{-x/2}\left(A\cos\dfrac{\sqrt{3}}{2}x + B\sin\dfrac{\sqrt{3}}{2}x\right).$

(e) $\dfrac{d^2y}{dx^2} + 4\dfrac{dy}{dx} + 4y = 0.$

(f) $\dfrac{d^2y}{dx^2} + 6\dfrac{dy}{dx} + 9y = 0.$

**2.** Show that, when the roots of the characteristic equation of $y'' + 2\alpha y' + \beta y = 0$ are equal, and if $m$ is the double root, then $(A + Bx)e^{mx}$ is the general solution.

   *Suggestion:* Assume that the general solution is of the form $y = u(x)e^{mx}$ and determine $u(x)$.

**3.** (a)  A bead is free to slide along a smooth straight horizontal wire. One end of the wire is kept at a fixed point which one can take as the pole or origin and the wire is rotated around the origin in a horizontal plane at a constant angular velocity $\omega$. Find the equation of the path of the bead.

        *Suggestion:* Ignore gravity and use the fact that no radial force acts to keep the bead in one position on the wire.

   (b)  Suppose the bead is at the origin when $t = 0$ and the wire starts rotating at $\theta = 0$. Describe the motion of the bead.

The various types of solutions of the second-order linear differential equation just discussed have important physical significance. Let us consider the physical problem mentioned at the beginning of this section, a mass suspended from a spring and set into motion, with the resistance of the air taken into account. Previously we wrote

$$\frac{d^2y}{dt^2} = -l\frac{dy}{dt} - ky$$

where $l$ and $k$ are proportionality constants. Merely to simplify the subsequent algebra and to use somewhat standard notation let us write this equation as

$$\frac{d^2y}{dt^2} + 2l\frac{dy}{dt} + \omega^2 y = 0.$$

Then the characteristic equation is

$$m^2 + 2lm + \omega^2 = 0$$

and the roots are

**(36)** $$m = -l \pm \sqrt{l^2 - \omega^2}\ .$$

Now let us consider what may happen physically remembering that $l$ is the coefficient of the term which represents the air resistance and $\omega^2$ is the spring constant, which measures the stiffness or elasticity of the spring. (Strictly we have divided through by the mass on the spring.)

    We can see that if $l = \omega$, then the two values of $m$ are equal and the solution is of the form

**(37)** $$y = (A + Bt)e^{-lt}.$$

Because $l$ is positive and $e^{-lt}$ decreases very much faster than $Bt$ increases, the mass on the spring if initially displaced from its equilibrium position will return steadily to the equilibrium position. A typical graph of $y$ versus $t$ is shown in Fig. 24-3.

    Suppose next that $l > \omega$. Then the roots $m$ are real and unequal and, as we can see from (36), both are negative. Hence if we look at the solutions in the form (20) we see that $y$ must decrease steadily with time $t$. A typical

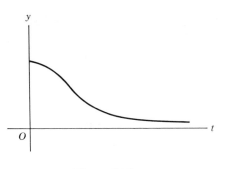

**Figure 24-3**

graph of the motion, which depends on the initial conditions, would be very much like the one above.

The most interesting case and most important practically is that in which $l$ is less than $\omega$ and in fact small compared to $\omega$. The roots $m$ of (36) are now complex and the solution, according to (35), would be

**(38)**    $$y = Ae^{-lt}\cos\sqrt{\omega^2 - l^2}\ t + Be^{-lt}\sin\sqrt{\omega^2 - l^2}\ t.$$

We can, of course, write this solution in the form [cf. Chap. 10, formula (55)]

**(39)**    $$y = Ce^{-lt}\sin\left(\sqrt{\omega^2 - l^2}\ t + \phi\right)$$

where now $C$ and $\phi$ are the arbitrary constants. We see that the factor $e^{-lt}$ will still damp the oscillations so that the mass will ultimately come to rest. We note also that the period of oscillations will be $2\pi/\sqrt{\omega^2 - l^2}$, whereas if there were no air resistance, that is, if $l$ were 0, the period would be smaller. A typical graph of displacement versus time would be of the form (Fig. 24-4).

Though we have illustrated the discussion of the homogeneous linear second-order equation by using the motion of a mass on a spring, the same equation appears in hundreds of physical problems, especially those of electrical circuits.

**Figure 24-4**

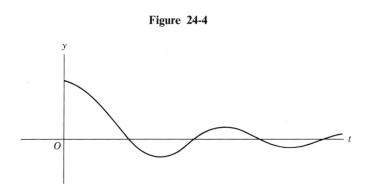

**4. Second-Order Linear Non-homogeneous Differential Equations.** A weight on a spring whose motion soon damps out or an electrical circuit in which the current soon decreases to 0 are occasionally useful. When an automobile strikes a bump in a road the absorption of the shock by the springs and the gradual damping out of the vibrations in the springs are certainly helpful. But in most practical applications the continuing oscillations of the mass on the spring or the continuing flow of current in an electrical circuit are essential. Hence some continually applied force or source of power must be supplied to keep such physical systems in operation. Mathematically the action of an external force (as opposed to, say, the normal restoring force of a spring) is represented by an extra term in the differential equation. Thus in place of (18), that is, in place of

$$\frac{d^2y}{dx^2} + \alpha\,\frac{dy}{dx} + \beta y = 0$$

one considers

**(40)**
$$\frac{d^2y}{dx^2} + \alpha\,\frac{dy}{dx} + \beta y = F(x),$$

where $F(x)$ represents the external force. Physically, if the situation involves a mass on a spring, the application of an external force, which we represent by $F(t)$ in Fig. 24-5 because the force is usually a function of the time, can be achieved by a mechanism which is attached to the mass $M$ and which causes the mass to move in accordance with whatever $F(t)$ calls for.

Equation (40) is called a non-homogeneous linear equation because the term $F(x)$ is present. Our mathematical problem is now how to solve equations of the type (40). If the $F(x)$ term were not present in (40) we would have a homogeneous equation. The solution of this homogeneous equation is now called the complementary solution of (40) and, as we know, this will be of the form

$$y_c = Ae^{m_1 x} + Be^{m_2 x}.$$

The substitution of $y_c$ in the left side of (40) will produce 0. Hence we must find some additional term which when substituted in (40) will produce

**Figure 24-5**

Fixed

$M$

$F(t)$

$F(x)$. The additional term is called the particular integral which we shall denote by $y_p$. Thus the full solution of (40) is of the form

**(41)** $$y = y_c + y_p.$$

There are rather general methods of finding the particular solutions of non-homogeneous equations such as (40) but mathematicians naturally concentrate on those cases which arise in real problems. Perhaps the commonest external force that is applied in mechanical and electrical devices is a sinusoidal or cosinusoidal one. Let us therefore seek to solve an equation of the type (40) with such an external force.

**Example.**   Consider the differential equation

**(42)** $$\frac{d^2y}{dx^2} + 4\frac{dy}{dx} + 9y = 6 \sin 3x.$$

We first find the complementary solution. Since the characteristic equation is

$$m^2 + 4m + 9 = 0$$

and the roots are $-2 \pm \sqrt{-5}$, then in view of (35) the complementary function is

**(43)** $$y_c = e^{-2x}(A \cos\sqrt{5}\, x + B \sin\sqrt{5}\, x).$$

We must now find the particular integral. We note that the right side (42) is a sine function. Hence we ask, what function or functions when substituted in the left side of (42) would, after the differentiations and additions, yield $6 \sin 3x$? We cannot answer this question at once but we do know that the derivatives of sines and cosines are cosines and sines. Let us, therefore, try

**(44)** $$y_p = a \sin 3x + b \cos 3x.$$

If we substitute $y_p$ in (42) and, after differentiating, rearrange terms we find that

$$12a \cos 3x - 12b \sin 3x = 6 \sin 3x.$$

Clearly if we let $a = 0$ and take $b$ to be $-\frac{1}{2}$ then the $y_p$ in (44) will satisfy the non-homogeneous differential equation. Hence the proper $y_p$ is $-(\frac{1}{2}) \cos 3x$ and the full solution of (44) is

**(45)** $$y = y_c + y_p = e^{-2x}(A \cos\sqrt{5}\, x + B \sin\sqrt{5}\, x) - \frac{1}{2} \cos 3x.$$

Let us observe the physical significance of the solution. Because of the factor $e^{-2x}$ in the complementary solution this function will decrease more and more in value as $x$ increases (cf. Fig. 24-4). However, the particular integral, namely $-(\frac{1}{2})\cos 3x$, behaves as a cosine function indefinitely. For this reason the complementary function is called a transient. Its physical significance becomes less and less as $x$ increases, whereas the external force dominates. The particular integral is called the steady-state solution. If (42) represented the motion of a mass on a spring subject to the external force $6 \sin 3x$ and if $x$ were time, then (45) tells us that the mass will, after some time, oscillate with the frequency of $3/2\pi$ cycles per second and the amplitude of its motion will be $\frac{1}{2}$.

The method we have described to solve (42) will not cover all types of non-homogeneous linear equations with constant coefficients but is effective in many realistic problems.

## EXERCISES

Solve the following differential equations:

1. $y'' + 9y = 4e^{2x}$.

> *Suggestion:* Try $ae^{2x}$ to obtain the particular integral.
>
> *Ans.* $y = A \cos 3x + B \sin 3x + \frac{4}{13} e^{2x}$.

2. $\dfrac{d^2y}{dx^2} + 4\dfrac{dy}{dx} + 4y = 6 \sin 3x$.

3. $\dfrac{d^2y}{dx^2} + 4\dfrac{dy}{dx} + 9y = x^2 + 5x$.

> *Suggestion:* To obtain the particular integral, assume that $y_p = ax^2 + bx + c$.

4. $\dfrac{d^2y}{dx^2} + 2\dfrac{dy}{dx} + y = 4 \sin 2x$.

5. $\dfrac{d^2y}{dx^2} + 3\dfrac{dy}{dx} + 2y = 3e^{-2x}$. *Caution:* The assumption that $y_p = ae^{-2x}$ does not lead to a particular integral. Why not? Try $y_p = axe^{-2x}$.

6. (a) $y'' + 9y = \sin 3x$.

> *Suggestion:* To find the particular integral try $y_p = x(a \sin 3x + b \cos 3x)$.

   (b) Discuss the relative importance of the complementary function and the particular integral, that is, of the transient and the steady state, for large $x$.

# CHAPTER
## TWENTY-FIVE
# A RECONSIDERATION
# OF THE FOUNDATIONS

*1. Introduction.* In our work on the calculus we have employed such basic notions as the concept of a function, the limit of a function, the limit of a sequence, the continuity of a function, the derivative, and the integral. In our efforts to understand the basic notions we have often relied on specific examples of functions, on physical interpretations, and on geometrical pictures. For example, we characterized a continuous function (Chap. 6) as one whose graph can be drawn with an uninterrupted motion of a pencil. This is, of course, a physical description. Furthermore, many of the arguments used to establish theorems were based on what happens to particular functions. Thus we "proved" (Chap. 6) that the limit of the sum of two functions of $x$ as $x$ approaches $a$ is the sum of the limits by noting that this is so for two particular functions.

Although these geometrical, physical, and concrete illustrations of general mathematical concepts and proofs are not satisfactory from the standpoint of mathematical rigor, they are an advisable first step. Nevertheless, it is necessary sooner or later to attempt precise formulations of the concepts and to give rigorous proofs. There are several reasons for undertaking this work. Arguments based on geometrical pictures or physical evidence are vulnerable. A geometrical picture of a particular function may not be typical of all functions, and therefore the conclusion drawn from it may not apply to all functions. We are also courting trouble when we conclude that the limit of a sum of two functions is the sum of the limits just because we find that this fact holds for two particular functions.

To make his ideas precise, the mathematician formulates them in terms of purely mathematical concepts; that is, he defines them in terms of number or geometrical forms because these are clear and sharp ideas. In the case of the calculus mathematicians have found that the more efficacious foundation is number. It is also theoretically possible to employ geometry to formulate precise definitions of such concepts as the continuity of a function, a tangent to a curve, and the volume bounded by a surface

**866**

but, as we shall see, it is easier to do so in terms of number. Moreover, for scientific and engineering uses of mathematics quantitative results are essential, and these are obtained most readily from concepts and processes that are based on number. We are, therefore, going to give arithmetical definitions of the concepts and base our arguments on these arithmetical definitions.

As for proofs of the theorems, in accordance with the standard laid down by the Greeks and maintained ever since, these must be deductive. That is, we must use the kind of argument in which each assertion or each step of a proof is justified in terms of definitions, axioms, and previously established theorems. A fuller appreciation of the distinction between the program we now propose to initiate and the one we have followed thus far will be gained as we proceed with the work of this chapter. Our goal will not be to give a full rigorous presentation but rather to give some idea of what it involves.

**2. The Concept of a Function.** We have said that a function is a relation between two variables such that when the values of one variable—the independent variable—change, the values of the other or dependent variable also change. This is the important idea. Yet, this formulation is vague. Exactly what do we mean by a relation between variables? Also, the notion of change is really a physical notion and, if mathematical concepts are to be formulated in terms of number, we must replace such physical notions by their mathematical equivalents. Finally, the loose statement above says nothing about the extent to which either variable may change.

Before we try to form a precise definition of the concept of a function, we should look at some examples. The mathematical concept ought to embrace at least those functions which do occur in physical phenomena because mathematics is devoted to the representation and study of physical phenomena. Insofar as the extent to which $x$ or $y$ can vary is concerned, there is no difficulty. In the case of $y = x^2$, $x$ can vary from $-\infty$ to $\infty$. This language does not imply that $x$ can have $\infty$ or $-\infty$ as a value. It means that the values of $x$ can be all numbers from arbitrarily small negative numbers, for example, $-10^9$, $-10^6$, and so forth, to arbitrarily large positive numbers. However, for the function $y = 1/x$ we must exclude the value $x = 0$ because there is no number $1/0$. One says in this case that the function *does not exist* for $x = 0$ or that the function is *defined* for the interval $-\infty < x < 0$ and for the interval $0 < x < \infty$. For the function $y = \sqrt{25 - x^2}$, $y$ has no real values for values of $x$ greater than 5 or less than $-5$. Hence in this case the function exists or is defined for $-5 \leq x \leq 5$. Thus to have a function, there must be some set of values for $x$ corresponding to which there are values for $y$.

Some terminology here is convenient. If the values of $x$ for which the function is defined include all numbers *between* two given numbers, say all numbers between $-5$ and 5, or all numbers between a given number and $\infty$ (that is, all numbers larger than a given one), or all numbers between a given number and $-\infty$, we say that the values of $x$ constitute an *open interval*. If the end points are finite and are included, we say that we have a *closed interval.* The full set of values of $x$ may include more than one interval. Thus the full set of values for which $y = 1/x$ is defined consists of all values of $x$ in the open interval $0 < x < \infty$ and all values of $x$ in the open interval $-\infty < x < 0$. The full set of values of $x$ for which the function is defined is called the *domain* of the function.

To what extent are the values of the dependent variable $y$ limited in order that we may have a function? The only limitation is that there must be just one value of $y$ for each value of $x$ in the domain of $x$. Thus in the case of $y^2 = x$ we must distinguish the functions $y = \sqrt{x}$ and $y = -\sqrt{x}$. Each of them is a function, whereas strictly $y^2 = x$ is not because to each value of $x$ in the interval $0 \leq x < \infty$ there correspond two values of $y$. One also says that $y^2 = x$ is a multiple-valued function of $x$, whereas $y = \sqrt{x}$ and $y = -\sqrt{x}$ each are single-valued functions of $x$. Beyond this limitation to single-valuedness, the set of values that $y$ may take on can be quite arbitrary. It is customary to include the statement $y = 5$ among functions. Here $y$ is always 5 no matter what value of $x$ is considered. The set of $y$-values corresponding to the values in the domain of $x$ is called the *range* of the function.

To appreciate fully what kinds of relationships we should include under the concept of function, we shall examine some other functions. Let us consider the relation between the postage that one must put on first-class mail and its weight. At one time the United States Post Office required that the amount of postage be 10 cents for each ounce or fraction of an ounce of weight. This means that the postage is 10 cents for any weight (greater than 0) up to and including 1 ounce, 20 cents for any weight greater than 1 ounce but up to and including 2 ounces, and so on. The graph of the function is shown in Fig. 25-1. Here the domain of $x$, which represents weight, is $0 < x < \infty$, because to each value of $x$ in this interval there is a unique value of the postage $y$. The range of $y$-values, however, is only the set of numbers 10, 20, 30 $\cdots$.

To work with this function, one may want the formula which represents it. There is such a formula. It is

**(1)**
$$y = \begin{cases} 10 & \text{for} \quad 0 < x \leq 1 \\ 20 & \text{for} \quad 1 < x \leq 2 \\ 30 & \text{for} \quad 2 < x \leq 3 \\ & \text{etc}. \end{cases}$$

The peculiarity of this formula is that one must use different expressions for the $y$-values in different $x$-intervals. One might be tempted so say that this relation between amount of postage and weight is not a function or at least not one function, because one must use different formulas or analytical expressions for the different $x$-intervals. However, there is just one relation between postage and weight and there is just one value of $y$ for each value of $x$ in the domain of $x$. Hence it would seem desirable to speak of the entire relationship as only one function, and we do so. According to the intuitive notion of continuity, which was introduced in Chapter 6, where we

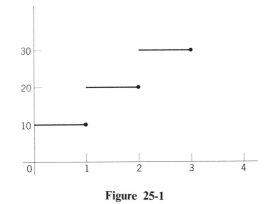

**Figure 25-1**

require that a continuous function be drawn with one uninterrupted motion of a pencil, the function (1) is discontinuous at $x = 1, 2, 3 \cdots$.

Lest one acquire the impression that a function such as the preceding one is too artificial to be worthy of attention, we shall consider a natural phenomenon that behaves similarly.

Water is a basic and common substance. Its behavior is uncommon. Most substances increase in volume as their temperature increases. Figure 25-2 shows how water behaves. Consider 1 gram of water. As the temperature increases from $-4°C$ to $0°$, during which interval water exists (at normal pressure) as ice, the volume of 1 gram of water does indeed increase from about 1.0901 cu cm to a little more than 1.0905 cu cm. At $0°$, when the ice changes to water, the volume drops suddenly to a value of a little more than 1.0001 cu cm. Then as the temperature increases the volume *decreases* until the temperature of $4°C$ is reached, at which stage the volume is 1 cu cm. After that the volume increases with the temperature. Thus the volume is discontinuous at $0°$.

**Figure 25-2**

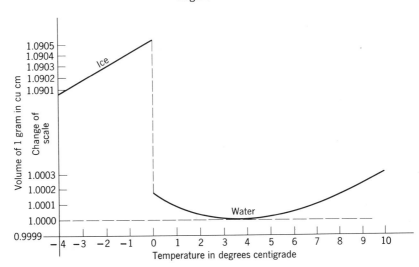

Let us consider still another function in our attempt to appreciate what the concept of a function should embrace. We shall consider the force that the earth of mass $M$ exerts on a small object of mass $m$. When the object is *inside* the earth, the force is given by the formula [see (59) of Chap. 16]

$$(2) \qquad F = \frac{GMm}{R^3}\, r$$

where $R$ is the radius of the earth, $r$ is the distance from the center of the earth to the mass $m$ (which we suppose small enough to be regarded as a point mass), and $G$ is the gravitational constant. However, when the mass $m$ is *outside* the earth, the force is given by

$$(3) \qquad F = \frac{GMm}{r^2}.$$

Hence the function is given in its entirety by the formula

$$(4) \qquad F = \begin{cases} \dfrac{GMm}{R^3}\, r & \text{for} \quad 0 \le r \le R \\[2mm] \dfrac{GMm}{r^2} & \text{for} \quad R \le r < \infty. \end{cases}$$

We note that when $r = R$, that is, when the mass $m$ is just at the surface of the earth, the value of $F$ given by either expression in (4) is the same. Then $F$ changes continuously as $r$ changes from values less than $R$ to values greater than $R$ (Fig. 25-3). However, the derivative of $F$ behaves peculiarly at $r = R$. As is evident from the slope of the graph, the derivative is positive when $r < R$ and negative when $r > R$. Moreover, it changes abruptly from some positive value to some negative value at $r = R$.

There is one more important point in connection with the concept of a function. Let us suppose that we are working with the function $d = 16t^2$ which represents the distance a dropped object falls (in a vacuum) in time $t$. We may be interested in this function only for those values of $t$ during which the object is in motion. If the object hits the ground at $t = 5$, the domain of $t$-values which is of interest is $0 \le t \le 5$. This function happens to be well-behaved for all values of $t$. But even if there were some

**Figure 25-3**

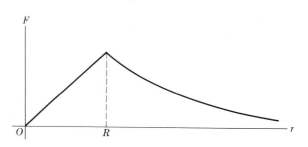

peculiarity in its behavior at, say, $t = 7$ we would not be concerned, because all we would care about is the domain $0 \le t \le 5$.

These examples suggest that the concept of a function should include a far greater variety of relationships than one might have expected at the beginning of his study of functions. Although in our examples we have exhibited the relation of $y$ to $x$ by one or more formulas, strictly speaking the definition of a function does not require that the $y$-values be given by formulas. What does seem to characterize all these functions is that *there is a domain of x-values such that to each value of x in that domain there is a unique value of y.* In our mathematical definition of a function the notion of change is not explicit. Of course, the $y$-values that correspond to the various $x$-values in the domain may change as the $x$-values change, although they may in special cases be constant over the entire domain of $x$-values or over some intervals of the domain, as in the case of the postage function. But the notion of change is only implicit in the mathematical definition.

Since functions can be so different in their behavior, the question arises: to what extent can we apply differentiation and integration to these functions? For example, can we differentiate the irregularly behaving functions at all values of $x$ or just at some values? We shall answer these questions by undertaking a careful study of the properties of functions.

## EXERCISES

1. State in your own words what one means by the statement that $y$ is a function of $x$.

2. What is the domain of a function? The range of a function?

3. What are the domain and range of the following functions?
   (a) The postage-stamp function.
   (b) The force-of-gravitation-versus-distance function as illustrated in Fig. 25-3.

4. Graph the following functions:

   (a) $y = \begin{cases} x^2 & \text{for} \quad 0 \le x \le 1. \\ x & \text{for} \quad 1 \le x \le 5. \end{cases}$

   (c) $y = \begin{cases} x + 2 & \text{for} \quad 0 \le x \le 1. \\ 3x & \text{for} \quad 1 \le x \le 6. \end{cases}$

   (b) $y = \sqrt{x}$ .

5. Sketch the function that represents the slope for the force of gravitation function in Fig. 25-3.

6. Suppose that a rocket is shot up into the air with an initial velocity of 400 ft/sec and loses velocity at the rate of 32 ft/sec each second. After 6 seconds an explosive charge carried by the rocket goes off and adds 100 ft/sec to the speed of the rocket, and thereafter it again loses speed at the rate of 32 ft/sec each second. Write the formula for the speed of the rocket for the interval $0 \le t \le 15$ and graph the function.

   *Ans.* $v = \begin{cases} -32t + 400, & 0 \le t \le 6. \\ -32t + 500, & 6 \le t \le 15. \end{cases}$

7. Draw a graph showing the domain and range of the function $y = \sqrt{x^3 - x}$ for positive and negative values of $x$.

8. Graph the following functions:

   (a)   $y = x + \sqrt{(1 - x)(2 - x)}$ .      (b)   $y = x + \sqrt{(x - 2)(x + 1)}$ .

9. A rocket is at rest. Then a force applied instantaneously at $t = 0$ gives the rocket an upward velocity of 100 ft/sec. Graph the velocity as a function of time from $t = -\infty$ to $t = \infty$. Assume that the acceleration of gravity is 32 ft/sec$^2$.

10. The attraction of a spherical *shell* (idealized as a spherical surface of radius $R$) of mass $M$ per unit *area* on a unit particle inside is 0. The attraction of the shell on a unit particle outside is the same as if the mass were concentrated at the center. If the unit particle outside is $r$ units from the center, the force of attraction is $4\pi R^2 M / r^2$. If the unit particle is just on the shell, the attractive force of the shell on the particle can be shown to be $2\pi M$. Graph the force as a function of the distance $r$ of the unit particle from the center of the shell for $r \geq 0$.

11. Let $[x]$ denote the integer (including 0) which is closest to $x$ and let $f(x) = \|[x] - x\|$. Graph the function for $x$ in the domain (0, 10).

12. Sketch the graph of $y = f(x)$ where $f(x) = x$ for $-1 \leq x \leq 1$ and $f(x)$ is periodic and of period 2.

13. Sketch the graph of $y = 1/(x^2 - 1)$.

### 3. The Concept of the Limit of a Function.

To gain a better understanding of the concept of differentiation and to formulate this concept more precisely than we did at the outset of our work, let us begin by reviewing the process of differentiation.

To obtain the derivative of, say, $s = t^2$ at $t = t_0$, we first calculate $s_0$, the value of $s$ at $t = t_0$. We have that

(5)
$$s_0 = t_0^2.$$

We then let $t$ have the value $t_0 + \Delta t$ and calculate the corresponding value of $s$. This value, denoted by $s_0 + \Delta s$, is

(6)
$$s_0 + \Delta s = (t_0 + \Delta t)^2 = t_0^2 + 2t_0 \Delta t + (\Delta t)^2.$$

By subtracting (5) from (6) we find that

(7)
$$\Delta s = 2t_0 \Delta t + (\Delta t)^2.$$

We obtain, next, the average rate of change of $s$ with respect to $t$ in the interval $\Delta t$ by dividing both sides of (7) by $\Delta t$. Thus

(8)
$$\frac{\Delta s}{\Delta t} = \frac{2t_0 \Delta t + (\Delta t)^2}{\Delta t} .$$

The derivative is the instantaneous rate of change of $s$ with respect to $t$ at $t = t_0$. We know that we cannot obtain this instantaneous rate of change by letting $\Delta t$ be 0 in (8) because the substitution of 0 for $\Delta t$ yields 0/0 and this expression is meaningless. We agreed, therefore, in our early work on the derivative that we would consider the number or limit approached by $\Delta s / \Delta t$ as $\Delta t$ approaches 0, the value of $\Delta s / \Delta t$ for $\Delta t = 0$ being irrelevant.

The important and novel idea, then, in the concept of differentiation is the limit of some expression in $\Delta t$ as $\Delta t$ approaches 0. We may state this idea in other words. The expression (8) for $\Delta s / \Delta t$ is a *function of* $\Delta t$. The independent variable of this function is $\Delta t$, the dependent variable is $\Delta s / \Delta t$, and we are concerned with finding the limit or number approached by this function as $\Delta t$ approaches 0.

We note, parenthetically, that we were able to find the limit in question, by dividing numerator and denominator by $\Delta t$, thus obtaining

$$\textbf{(9)} \qquad \frac{\Delta s}{\Delta t} = 2t_0 + \Delta t.$$

Our argument then was that (8) and (9) are identical except when $\Delta t = 0$ because the division is valid for $\Delta t \neq 0$. Since we do not care about the value of (8) when $\Delta t = 0$, we may use (9) to find the limit. And we saw from (9) that as $\Delta t$ approaches 0, $\Delta s / \Delta t$ approaches $2t_0$. Thus in the case of (9) we were able to find the desired limit rather easily. We were not so fortunate when finding the derivative of $y = \sin x$, $y = e^x$ and $y = \log x$, although we did succeed in these cases too. But the important point is that finding the derivative calls for finding the limit of a function as the independent variable, $\Delta t$ in (8), approaches 0.

It is helpful to formulate the problem of finding the derivative in a slightly different way. Suppose, again, that we wish to find the derivative of $s = t^2$ at $t = t_0$. We can, as before, write

$$\textbf{(10)} \qquad s_0 = t_0^2.$$

Now instead of writing the new value of $t$ as $t_0 + \Delta t$, let us just write $t$, meaning by $t$ some arbitrary value other than $t_0$. Then for this new value of $t$

$$\textbf{(11)} \qquad s = t^2.$$

The quantity $\Delta s$ is the change in $s$ as $t$ changes from $t_0$ to $t$. This change in $s$ is just as well represented by $s - s_0$, and we see from (10) and (11) that

$$\textbf{(12)} \qquad s - s_0 = t^2 - t_0^2.$$

Where we formerly wrote $\Delta t$ for the change in $t$, we now write $t - t_0$. Then the average rate of change of $s$ with respect to $t$ in the interval $t - t_0$ is obtained by dividing both sides of (12) by $t - t_0$. Thus

$$\textbf{(13)} \qquad \frac{s - s_0}{t - t_0} = \frac{t^2 - t_0^2}{t - t_0}.$$

To obtain the instantaneous rate of change of $s$ with respect to $t$ at $t_0$, we see that we cannot replace $t$ by $t_0$ in (13) because this substitution yields

$0/0$. That is, we encounter the same difficulty as in letting $\Delta t$ be 0 in (8). Instead, we seek the limit in (13) as $t$ approaches $t_0$, for as $t$ approaches $t_0$, the quantity $t - t_0$ approaches 0. Thus we see in another way that finding the derivative of a function calls for finding the limit of a function as the independent variable, $t$ in the case of (13), approaches a fixed value.

Thus the entire body of the differential calculus and, therefore, of the work with the antiderivative or the indefinite integral rests on the notion of the limit of a function. The concept of the limit of a function that we have used thus far, namely, the number approached by the function as the independent variable approaches a given value, is intuitively rather clear, and yet this concept is far more subtle than appears on the surface. Let us consider the simple function $y = x^2$. We say that the limit of $y$ as $x$ approaches 2 is 4, or in symbols

$$\lim_{x \to 2} y = \lim_{x \to 2} x^2 = 4.$$

because the closer the values of $x$ come to 2, the closer do the values of $x^2$ come to or approach 4. But words such as close or approach are rather vague. Suppose that we choose some values of $x$ greater than 2 but closer and closer to 2 and calculate the corresponding $y$-values. We obtain the following table:

| $x$ | 3 | 2.5 | 2.4 | 2.3 | 2.2 | 2.1 | 2.05 | 2.04 | 2.03 | 2.02 |
|---|---|---|---|---|---|---|---|---|---|---|
| $y$ | 9 | 6.25 | 5.76 | 5.29 | 4.84 | 4.41 | 4.2025 | 4.1616 | 4.1209 | 4.0804 |

We see from this table that for values of $x$ closer and closer to 2, the corresponding $y$-values do indeed come closer and closer to 4. But they also come closer and closer to 3. Why then do we say that 4 is the limit rather than 3? The answer, of course, is that the $y$-values do not come close enough to 3; they are always at least one unit greater than 3. Thus the words *"come close to"* to define what we mean by a limit apparently mean that the $y$-values must come close in the sense that the difference between the limit and the $y$-values becomes really small.

Suppose, then, that we consider 3.9 as the limit of $x^2$ as $x$ approaches 2. Surely, the $y$-values get very close to 3.9 as $x$ approaches 2, and the difference between 3.9 and the $y$-values is small. Perhaps. The difference is always at least 0.1, and if one had to jump across a chasm whose width were 0.1 miles, one would not call the distance small. What we really want is that the $y$-values should come arbitrarily close to 4, by which we mean that the difference between 4 and the $y$-values should become less than 0.1, less than 0.01, less than 0.001, and in fact less than any number one can name. Since in our example these $y$-values do not come arbitrarily close to 3.9 as $x$ gets closer and closer to 2 because the values of $y$ always lie above 4, then 3.9 cannot be the limit. Thus one requirement on the number that serves as the limit of a function is that the function values come as close as one can specify to this number if the $x$-values are chosen sufficiently close to the value of $x$ at which the limit is being considered.

There is another consideration in our notion of limit. We would not care to say that $y$ approaches 4 if some of the $y$-values did indeed approach 4 as $x$ approaches 2, but other $y$-values corresponding to $x$-values closer and closer to 2 approached, say, 3. Could this happen? It could. Consider the function $y = x^2$ but now modified in the following way. Suppose that $y = x^2$ for all values of $x$ except $x = 2\frac{1}{2}, 2\frac{1}{4}, 2\frac{1}{8}, 2\frac{1}{16}, \cdots$, and suppose that for these $x$-values $y$ is always 3. Is this a legitimate function? It is because to each value of $x$ in some domain, which here is $(-\infty, \infty)$, there is a unique $y$-value. For this function most of the $y$-values approach 4 as $x$ approaches 2, but not all do. No matter how close $x$ gets to 2, there is always at least one $x$-value for which $y$ gets close to (in fact is) 3 and not to 4. In this case we would not say that $y$ approaches 4 as $x$ approaches 2. The point, then, is that we should require that $y$ approach 4 for *all* values of $x$ that approach 2.

Thus we seem to mean by the statement

**(14)** $$\lim_{x \to 2} x^2 = 4$$

that all the $y$-values come arbitrarily close to 4 as $x$ approaches 2. Of course, if we specify a particular degree of closeness, say 0.01, we cannot expect that all the $y$-values will be that close to 4, but we do expect all the $y$-values which belong to all $x$-values sufficiently close to 2 to be that close to 4.

We have narrowed down what we mean by a limit, but our specification is verbose and still uses words, such as arbitrarily close and sufficiently close, which are somewhat vague. We shall try to improve the wording. Suppose that we let $\epsilon$ represent any positive number including as small a number as anyone may care to choose. Thus $\epsilon$ stands for 1, 0.01, 0.001, $10^{-6}$, and for any other positive number one may choose. Then we require that $y - 4$ be less than $\epsilon$ for all values of $x$ sufficiently close to 2. How close is sufficiently close? We really do not care. As long as it is true that for *all* values of $x$ in some interval ending at 2, $y - 4$ is less than $\epsilon$, we have what we want. Let us say then, given any $\epsilon$, if there exists a $\delta$ such that for all $x$ for which $x - 2$ is less than $\delta$, $y - 4$ is less than $\epsilon$, then 4 is the limit of $x^2$ as $x$ approaches 2.

We should note that given the $\epsilon$, we must be able to find a $\delta$ which meets the condition just stated. If $\epsilon$ is chosen smaller, then usually $\delta$ will have to be smaller, because if $\epsilon$ is chosen smaller, which means that $y$ must be closer to 4, then the $x$-values may have to be closer to 2 in order to keep the corresponding $y$-values closer to 4.

We have thus far ignored an essential point in this reconsideration of the concept of limit. When we assert that

**(15)** $$\lim_{x \to 2} x^2 = 4,$$

we should also take into account what happens when $x$ approaches 2 through values of $x$ which are smaller than 2. The reason for this stems from our very first thoughts about the derivative. When we talk about the limit of $\Delta s/\Delta t$ as $\Delta t$ approaches 0, we wish to include negative as well as positive $\Delta t$ because we believe on physical grounds that velocity at an instant is the limit of average velocities taken over time intervals $\Delta t$ before the instant in question as well as after the instant in question (see Exercise 1 of the first list in Chap. 2, Sect. 3). Likewise, the slope of a curve at a point $P$ (Fig. 25-4) should be the limit of the slopes of secants such as $RP$ where $R$ has an abscissa smaller than that of $P$, as well as the limit of slopes of secants such as $PQ$ where $Q$ has an abscissa larger than that of $P$.

In the case of (15) it is readily seen that when $x$ approaches 2 through values such as 1.5, 1.6, 1.7, etc., the $y$-values will approach 4 and get as close to 4 as one can require when $x$ is taken sufficiently close to 2. However, there are functions that approach different values when $x$ approaches the value at which the limit is being taken through larger values than when $x$ approaches this value through smaller values. Geometrically this is readily seen. Consider the postage-stamp function which is graphed in Fig. 25-1. As $x$ approaches 2 through values less than 2, $y$ is constantly 20 and so approaches 20. As $x$ approaches 2 through values larger than 2, $y$ is constantly 30 and so approaches 30. Another example is furnished by the function graphed in Fig. 25-2. As the temperature approaches 0 through values less than 0, the $y$-values approach 1.0905, but as $x$ approaches 0 through values larger than 0, $y$ approaches 1.0001. We must conclude that the two functions just discussed—the postage-stamp function and the volume–temperature function—do not have a limit at the respective values of $x$.

To render precise the statement that as $x$ approaches 2 through values less than 2, $y$ approaches 4, we use the same language and notation that we used to represent the corresponding fact when $x$ approaches 2 through values larger than 2. That is, the function $y = x^2$ has the limit 4 as $x$ approaches 2 through values less than 2 if, given any $\epsilon$, there exists a $\delta$ such that when $2 - x < \delta$, then $4 - y < \epsilon$.

Now, the meaning of

$$\lim_{x \to 2} x^2 = 4$$

**Figure 25-4**

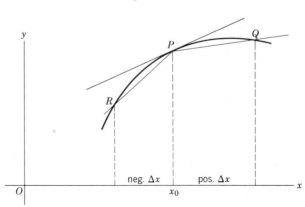

requires that two statements hold—the one made a few paragraphs earlier which deals with what must happen when $x$ approaches 2 through values larger than 2 and the one in the immediately preceding paragraph which states what must be the case when $x$ approaches 2 through values less than 2. We can combine these two statements into one. Instead of saying that $y - 4 < \epsilon$ and $4 - y < \epsilon$ in the two respective situations, we can say $|y - 4| < \epsilon$, where by $|y - 4|$ we mean the numerical value of $y - 4$, that is, the positive value. Likewise, instead of writing $x - 2 < \delta$ and $2 - x < \delta$ in the respective cases, we can write $|x - 2| < \delta$. Then the composite statement becomes: the function $y = x^2$ has the limit 4 as $x$ approaches 2 if, given any positive number $\epsilon$, there exists a $\delta$ such that if $x$ satisfies the inequality $|x - 2| < \delta$, then $|y - 4| < \epsilon$.

There is one final point to be observed about the concept of a limit. One of the major reasons for our concern with the concept is that the derivative is a limit, and it is precisely in connection with the derivative that we encounter the peculiarity that we now wish to discuss. Let us recall (8) which reads

**(16)**
$$\frac{\Delta s}{\Delta t} = \frac{2t_0 \, \Delta t + (\Delta t)^2}{\Delta t} .$$

The difficulty which the difference quotient $\Delta s / \Delta t$ presents as a function of $\Delta t$ is that the difference quotient has no value at $\Delta t = 0$; yet the function does have a limit as $\Delta t$ approaches 0. We see, then, that the value of $\Delta s / \Delta t$ at $\Delta t = 0$ must be ignored in speaking about the values of the function. Hence in formulating the notion of a limit to apply to $\Delta s / \Delta t$, we should not include any condition on what happens at $\Delta t = 0$.

Similarly, in formulating the notion of a limit to apply to, say, $y = x^2$ as $x$ approaches 2, we should ignore the value of the function at $x = 2$. This is readily done by modifying slightly our definition of a limit. Instead of requiring that $|y - 4| < \epsilon$ for $|x - 2| < \delta$, we require that $|y - 4| < \epsilon$ for $0 < |x - 2| < \delta$. In other words, we exclude the value $x = 2$ as a value for which $|y - 4|$ must be less than $\epsilon$. It does happen in this case that the value of $y$ when $x = 2$ satisfies the condition $|y - 4| < \epsilon$, but this fact is purely gratuitous. In the case of the difference quotient (16), the value of $\Delta s / \Delta t$ at $\Delta t = 0$ will not satisfy the condition $|\Delta s / \Delta t - 2t_0| < \epsilon$ because the difference quotient has no value at $\Delta t = 0$.

We have been using specific functions to pin down just what we mean by the limit of a function of $x$ as $x$ approaches a particular number. Let us now formulate the notion in more general terms. Let us suppose that we are dealing with a function given by $y = f(x)$ and that we wish to define what we mean by the statement that $y$ has the limit $b$ as $x$ approaches $a$.

Because the $y$-values can approach $b$ through smaller or larger $y$-values and all we care about is that these $y$-values come close to $b$, we use the absolute value $|y - b|$ to denote the difference between $y$ and $b$. The statement that $y$ must take on values arbitrarily close to $b$ is then expressed by the symbols

$$|y - b| < \epsilon.$$

Of course, we do not wish to require that all the values of $y$ be within any chosen $\epsilon$ of $b$. We wish only that, when $x$ is sufficiently close to $a$, $|y - b|$ be less than $\epsilon$. Hence we require merely that, having chosen a particular value of $\epsilon$, there should exist some quantity $\delta$ such that when

$$0 < |x - a| < \delta \quad \text{then} \quad |y - b| < \epsilon.$$

Thus our definition of the limit of a function now reads:

**Definition:** The function $y = f(x)$ has the limit $b$ as $x$ approaches $a$ (or one also says at $x = a$) if for each positive quantity $\epsilon$ there exists a quantity $\delta$ such that when

$$0 < |x - a| < \delta$$

then

$$|y - b| < \epsilon.$$

Although we do not wish to rely on pictures in our present investigation of the notion of limit of a function, it is nevertheless helpful to have an illustration of what the precise definition of limit means. Figure 25-5 shows a function $y = f(x)$ which takes on values near $x = a$ and $y = b$. To specify that $|y - b| < \epsilon$ means geometrically that the $y$-values must lie between the two horizontal lines $y = b + \epsilon$ and $y = b - \epsilon$. To specify that $|x - a| < \delta$ means geometrically that the $x$-values lie between the two vertical lines $x = a - \delta$ and $x = a + \delta$. Because our rigorous definition of limit does not involve the value $x = a$, we have left a gap in the $y$-value at $x = a$. In geometrical terms the definition of limit states that if for any value of $\epsilon$ we choose the two horizontal lines $y = b + \epsilon$ and $y = b - \epsilon$, there must exist the two vertical lines $x = a - \delta$ and $x = a + \delta$ such that for all $x$-values other than $a$ between the two vertical lines the $y$-values of $y = f(x)$ must lie between the two horizontal lines.

**Figure  25-5**

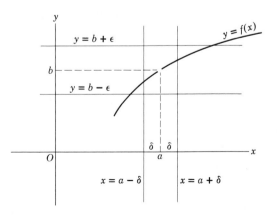

Now that we have a precise definition of the limit of a function, how do we use it? A fuller answer will be given in the next section. Here we shall merely illustrate its meaning with examples. Suppose that we wish to prove that

$$\lim_{x \to 2} 3x = 6.$$

We consider any specific $\epsilon$, say $\frac{1}{2}$. We must now show that there exists a value of $\delta$ such that when

$$0 < |x - 2| < \delta$$

then

$$|3x - 6| < \tfrac{1}{2}.$$

To keep $|3x - 6| < \frac{1}{2}$ means to keep $3|x - 2| < \frac{1}{2}$ or $|x - 2| < \frac{1}{6}$. Hence if we choose $\delta$ to be $\frac{1}{6}$, then certainly when

$$|x - 2| < \tfrac{1}{6},$$

we have

$$|3x - 6| < \tfrac{1}{2}.$$

So far we have shown that the definition of the limit of a function is satisfied when $\epsilon = \frac{1}{2}$. However, we are required by the definition to show that for *any* value of $\epsilon$ there exists the proper $\delta$. We cannot do this by trying particular values of $\epsilon$ for there is an endless number of them. Let us, therefore, consider $\epsilon$ itself. For what values of $x$ near 2 will $|3x - 6|$ be less than $\epsilon$? Since $|3x - 6| = 3|x - 2|$,

$$3|x - 2| < \epsilon$$

when

$$|x - 2| < \epsilon/3.$$

Hence, if we choose $\delta = \epsilon/3$, then, no matter what $\epsilon$ is, when

$$0 < |x - 2| < \delta,$$

we have

$$|3x - 6| < \epsilon.$$

We have shown that a $\delta$ exists for each value of $\epsilon$ and so have satisfied the definition.

There is one extension that we must make of the definition of the limit of a function to take care of the following case. We say quite rightly that as $x$ becomes larger and larger beyond any bound or becomes infinite, the function $y = 1/x$ approaches 0. Just what does this mean in precise

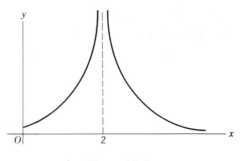

**Figure 25-6**

language? We do mean, first of all, that the domain of $x$-values includes all numbers larger than some fixed number. Thus the domain of $x$ might include all numbers larger than one million or one billion. To describe precisely the fact that the limit of $1/x$ is 0 as $x$ becomes infinite, we can no longer require the existence of a $\delta$ corresponding to any given $\epsilon$, because we are not concerned here with the values of $x$ in the neighborhood of or near some definite number $a$ but with what happens as the values of $x$ become arbitrarily large. What we do mean is that the values of $1/x$ come as close to 0 as one cares to require for values of $x$ which are sufficiently large. We can say this more precisely as follows. Given any positive quantity $\epsilon$, there must exist a number $N$ such that for all $x > N$

$$|1/x - 0| < \epsilon.$$

More generally, $f(x)$ has the limit $b$ as $x$ becomes infinite if, given any positive quantity $\epsilon$, there exists a number $N$ such that for all $x > N$,

$$|f(x) - b| < \epsilon.$$

If, on the other hand, $f(x)$ becomes infinite as $x$ approaches some finite number, as in the case (Fig. 25-6) of $y = 1/(x - 2)^2$ when $x$ approaches 2, $f(x)$ does not have a limit because it is not approaching a definite number. One does mean by the statement that $f(x)$ becomes infinite as $x$ approaches $a$ that, given any positive number $M$, there exists a $\delta$ such that for all $x$ for which

$$0 < |x - a| < \delta,$$

it is true that

$$|f(x)| > M.$$

## EXERCISES

**1.** Sketch the following functions and describe on the basis of the sketch their limiting behavior at the indicated values of $x$:

    (a)   $y = \sin x$ at $x = 0$.                                           *Ans.* 0.

(b) $y = x \sin x$ at $x = 0$.

(c) $y = \sin 1/x$ at $x = 0$.         *Ans.* No limit.

(d) $y = x \sin 1/x$ at $x = 0$.

(e) $y = \dfrac{\sin 2x}{x}$ at $x = 0$.         *Ans.* 2.

(f) $y = \dfrac{\sin (x/2)}{x}$ at $x = 0$.

(g) $y = \begin{cases} x^2 & \text{for } 0 \le x \le 1 \\ 2 - x^2 & \text{for } 1 \le x \le 2 \end{cases}$ at $x = 1$.         *Ans.* 1.

(h) $y = e^{1/x}$ at $x = 0$.

(i) $y = 2^{-1/x^2}$ at $x = 0$.         *Ans.* 0.

(j) $y = 2^{-1/x}$ at $x = 0$.

(k) $y = |x|$ at $x = 0$.         *Ans.* 0.

(l) $y = \dfrac{|x|}{x}$ at $x = 0$.

(m) $y = \dfrac{1}{x^2 - 1}$ at $x = 1$.         *Ans.* $\infty$.

(n) $y = \dfrac{1}{1 + 2^{1/x}}$ at $x = 0$.

        *Ans.* For $x > 0$, $y$ approaches 0; for $x < 0$, $y$ approaches 1.

(o) $y = \arctan 1/x$ at $x = 0$.

(p) $y = \dfrac{e^{1/x} - e^{-1/x}}{e^{1/x} + e^{-1/x}} = \tanh \dfrac{1}{x}$ at $x = 0$.

        *Ans.* For $x > 0$, $y$ approaches 1; for $x < 0$, $y$ approaches $-1$.

(q) $y = x \dfrac{e^{1/x} - e^{-1/x}}{e^{1/x} + e^{-1/x}}$ at $x = 0$.

2. Prove by applying the $\epsilon$-$\delta$ definition of a limit of a function that the following hold:

(a) $\lim\limits_{x \to 2} 4x = 8$.

(b) $\lim\limits_{x \to 3} 3x = 9$.

(c) $\lim\limits_{x \to 2} 4x + 7 = 15$.

(d) $\lim\limits_{x \to 2} 4 = 4$.

(e) $\lim\limits_{x \to 2} x = 2$.

3. Suppose that for a given $\epsilon$ we know there exists a $\delta$ such that when $0 < |x - a| < \delta$, then $|y - b| < \epsilon$. Is it true that when $0 < |x - a| < \delta/2$, then $|y - b| < \epsilon$?

4. Given a function $y = f(x)$, suppose we know that for a given $\epsilon$ there exists a $\delta$ such that when $0 < |x - a| < \delta$ then $|y - b| < \epsilon$. Would $|y - b|$ be less than $\epsilon$ if we replaced $\delta$ by any positive number less than $\delta$?

5. Prove that if $f(x)$ has the limit $b$ as $x$ approaches $a$, then $b$ is unique; that is, there cannot be another limit, say $c$, in addition to $b$.

6. Determine whether the following limits exist and if they do state what they are. No rigorous proof need be given.

(a) $\lim\limits_{x \to 0} \dfrac{\sqrt{1 - x}}{x}$.         *Ans.* No limit (or $\infty$).

(b) $\lim\limits_{x \to 1} \dfrac{\sqrt{2 - x}}{x}$.

(c) $\lim\limits_{x \to 0} \dfrac{\sqrt{1 + x}}{x}$.         *Ans.* No limit (or $\infty$).

(d) $\lim\limits_{x \to 0} \dfrac{x^2 - x}{x}$.

(e) $\lim\limits_{x \to -1} \dfrac{x^3 + 1}{x + 1}$.  *Ans.* 1.

(f) $\lim\limits_{x \to 2} \dfrac{x - 2}{x^2 - x - 2}$.

(g) $\lim\limits_{x \to 0} \dfrac{\sqrt{1 + x} - \sqrt{1 - x}}{x}$.

Suggestion: Multiply numerator and denominator by $\sqrt{1 + x} + \sqrt{1 - x}$.

*Ans.* 1.

(h) $\lim\limits_{x \to 0} \dfrac{x}{|x| + x^2}$.

7. Show that 5 is not the limit of $y = 4x^2$ as $x$ approaches 1.

Suggestion: One method would be to use the result of Exercise 5.

**4. Some Theorems on Limits of Functions.** It is easy to apply the $\epsilon$-$\delta$ definition to show that a function such as $y = 3x$ approaches 6 as $x$ approaches 2. However, to show, for example, that

**(17)** $$y = \frac{x^2 + 4}{x^2 - 5x + 7}$$

approaches 8 as $x$ approaches 2 by applying this definition would not be at all easy. The difficulty would lie in showing that the proper $\delta$ exists for any $\epsilon$. It would seem, then, that the definition is not very helpful because we cannot apply it to functions where there may really be some doubt about what the limit is.

The resolution of the difficulty lies in some theorems about limits which enable us to break down complicated functions into simpler ones. There are four basic theorems on limits of functions:

**Theorem 1:** The limit of the sum of two functions of $x$ at $x = a$ is the sum of the limits of the functions if these separate limits exist. In symbols, if

$$\lim_{x \to a} f(x) = A \quad \text{and} \quad \lim_{x \to a} g(x) = B$$

then

$$\lim_{x \to a} \{f(x) + g(x)\} = A + B.$$

**Theorem 2:** The limit of the difference of two functions of $x$ at $x = a$ is the difference of the limits of the functions if these separate limits exist. In symbols, if

$$\lim_{x \to a} f(x) = A \quad \text{and} \quad \lim_{x \to a} g(x) = B$$

then

$$\lim_{x \to a} \{f(x) - g(x)\} = A - B.$$

**Theorem 3:** The limit of the product of two functions of $x$ at $x = a$ is the product of the limits of the functions if the separate limits exist. In symbols, if

$$\lim_{x \to a} f(x) = A \quad \text{and} \quad \lim_{x \to a} g(x) = B$$

then

$$\lim_{x \to a} f(x) g(x) = AB.$$

**Theorem 4:** The limit of the quotient of two functions of $x$ at $x = a$ is the quotient of the limits of the functions if the separate limits exist and if the limit of the denominator is not 0. In symbols, if

$$\lim_{x \to a} f(x) = A \quad \text{and} \quad \lim_{x \to a} g(x) = B \quad \text{with} \quad B \neq 0$$

then

$$\lim_{x \to a} \frac{f(x)}{g(x)} = \frac{A}{B} .$$

In using these theorems during our work on the calculus we relied on intuitive evidence for their validity. We should now see that these theorems can be proved by applying the precise $\epsilon$-$\delta$ definition of a limit. Let us prove the first theorem.

**Proof of**
**Theorem 1.** We are given that

$$\lim_{x \to a} f(x) = A \quad \text{and} \quad \lim_{x \to a} g(x) = B.$$

We wish to prove that

$$\lim_{x \to a} \{ f(x) + g(x) \} = A + B.$$

In $\epsilon$-$\delta$ language this means that, given any positive quantity $\epsilon$, we must be able to find a $\delta$ such that when

**(18)** $$0 < |x - a| < \delta$$

then

**(19)** $$|f(x) + g(x) - (A + B)| < \epsilon.$$

Now,

**(20)** $$|f(x) + g(x) - (A + B)| = |f(x) - A + g(x) - B|.$$

Moreover,

**(21)** $$|f(x) - A + g(x) - B| \leq |f(x) - A| + |g(x) - B|,$$

because it is a basic fact about numbers that if $c$ and $d$ are any two numbers positive or negative, then

$$|c + d| \leq |c| + |d|.*$$

If we can show that there is a $\delta$ such that when $0 < |x - a| < \delta$,

**(22)** $$|f(x) - A| + |g(x) - B| < \epsilon,$$

then by the steps (21) and (20) we shall have shown that (19) is correct.

Now (22) suggests that we consider

$$\lim_{x \to a} f(x) = A \quad \text{and} \quad \lim_{x \to a} g(x) = B.$$

Given any $\epsilon$, suppose that we select the positive quantity $\epsilon/2$. Since $f(x)$ has the limit $A$ and $\epsilon/2$ is a positive quantity, there must exist a quantity $\delta_1$ such that when

$$0 < |x - a| < \delta_1$$

then

**(23)** $$|f(x) - A| < \epsilon/2.$$

Moreover, since $g(x)$ has the limit $B$ and $\epsilon/2$ is a positive quantity, there must exist a quantity $\delta_2$ such that when

$$0 < |x - a| < \delta_2$$

then

**(24)** $$|g(x) - B| < \epsilon/2.$$

We have used $\delta_1$ and $\delta_2$ in place of the customary $\delta$ because these $\delta$-values may differ. Suppose that $\delta_1$ is the smaller of $\delta_1$ and $\delta_2$. Then, surely, for $0 < |x - a| < \delta_1$ we may assert (23) and (24). Then for this value of $\delta_1$ we have that (22) is correct. Thus given $\epsilon$ we have shown that there exists a $\delta$, namely $\delta_1$, such that when $0 < |x - a| < \delta_1$, then (22) holds and, as noted above, if (22) holds, so does (19).

We shall not prove the other three theorems because the main idea worth acquiring in this first contact with the precise notion of the limit of a function is already illustrated in the proof of Theorem 1. The idea, of course, is that once we have a precise definition of the limit of a function, it can be used to prove rigorously theorems on limits which are essential to the development of the calculus. We shall, however, show how the theorems on limits are used to determine limits of somewhat complicated functions.

*If $c$ and $d$ are both positive numbers or both negative numbers, then $|c + d| = |c| + |d|$. If one is positive and the other negative, then $|c + d| < |c| + |d|$. If one or both are 0, then the equality holds.

Let us reconsider the function given in (17) above, namely,

**(25)**
$$y = \frac{x^2 + 4}{x^2 - 5x + 7} .$$

We can see by rough calculation that as $x$ approaches 2, $y$ approaches 8. But suppose that we wished to prove this fact by an application of the $\epsilon$-$\delta$ definition. This would involve showing that there exists a $\delta$ corresponding to any $\epsilon$ and satisfying the conditions of the definition. To produce the proper $\delta$ for any given $\epsilon$ is not easy. However, by applying the theorems on limits the proof that $y$ approaches 8 as $x$ approaches 2 is readily made.

We note that $y$ is a quotient of two functions. By applying Theorem 4 we need only determine the limit of the numerator separately and the limit of the denominator separately and divide one limit by the other. Now, the numerator is the sum of two functions, namely, $x^2$ and 4. The limit of this sum is, by Theorem 1, the sum of the limits. The limit of 4 as $x$ approaches 2 is 4, since for any given $\epsilon$, any $\delta$ suffices to satisfy the limit definition (see Exercise 2d of Section 3). The term $x^2$ is $x \cdot x$; it is, in other words, a product of two functions and, by Theorem 3, the limit of a product of two functions is the product of the limits. Since the limit of $x$ as $x$ approaches 2 is 2 (see Exercise 2e of Section 3), the limit of $x^2$ as $x$ approaches 2 is 4. We know now that the limit of the numerator of (25) is $4 + 4$ or 8. As for the denominator, let us regard it, first of all, as the sum

$$(x^2 - 5x) + 7.$$

The limit of this sum, by Theorem 1, is the sum of the limits of $x^2 - 5x$ and of 7. The limit of 7 as $x$ approaches 2 is 7. The limit of $x^2 - 5x$ is, by Theorem 2, the difference of the limits. We have already shown that the limit of $x^2$ as $x$ approaches 2 is 4; and, as in Exercise 2a of Section 3, we can show rigorously that the limit of $5x$ is 10. Hence the limit of $x^2 - 5x$ is $-6$ and the limit of the entire denominator is 1. Then the limit of the entire function (25) is 8.

We see, then, how the application of the limit theorems enables us to break down complicated functions into simple ones whose limits are readily established by the $\epsilon$-$\delta$ definition. There is a major point of mathematical method involved in this procedure. By considering functions generally, we established broad theorems about limits and thereby we were able to dispose of a rather complicated special function. Had we tried to apply the $\epsilon$-$\delta$ definition directly, we would have become lost in details. To abstract the general features of a particular problem, consider the abstractions, and then return to the particular problem is often far more successful than tackling the particular problem directly.

## EXERCISES

**1.** Find the limits called for in the following problems by applying the theorems on limits:

   (a)   $\displaystyle\lim_{x \to 2} \frac{x + 4}{x}$ .          *Ans.* 3.     (b)   $\displaystyle\lim_{x \to 2} 5x$.

(c) $\lim\limits_{x \to 3} x^2$.    *Ans.* 9.    (e) $\lim\limits_{\Delta x \to 0} 3x_0^2 + 3x_0\Delta x + (\Delta x)^2$.

$\qquad\qquad\qquad\qquad\qquad\qquad\qquad\qquad\qquad$ *Ans.* $3x_0^2$.

(d) $\lim\limits_{x \to 2} \dfrac{x^2 - 5x}{x^2 + 4x + 6}$ .

2. Consider the function $y = \sin \dfrac{1}{x}$ . By relying upon graphical evidence, determine whether the three limits $\lim\limits_{x \to 0} x$, $\lim\limits_{x \to 0} \sin \dfrac{1}{x}$, and $\lim\limits_{x \to 0} x \sin \dfrac{1}{x}$ exist. Are your results consistent with Theorem 3 of the text?

3. Consider the quadratic equation $ax^2 + bx + c = 0$. The roots are given by the formula

$$x = \frac{-b \pm \sqrt{b^2 - 4ac}}{2a}$$

If $a$ is 0, the equation becomes $bx + c = 0$ and there is just the one root, $x = -c/b$. Show that as $a$ approaches 0, one root of the quadratic equation approaches the root of the linear equation and the other root of the quadratic equation becomes infinite.

$\qquad$ *Suggestion:* Multiply the numerator and denominator of the expressions for $x$ by the numerator.

4. Since $\lim\limits_{x \to 0} \dfrac{\sin mx}{x} = m$ and $\lim\limits_{x \to 0} \dfrac{x}{\sin nx} = \dfrac{1}{n}$ , what is $\lim\limits_{x \to 0} \dfrac{\sin mx}{\sin nx}$ ?

$\qquad\qquad\qquad\qquad\qquad\qquad\qquad\qquad\qquad\qquad\qquad\qquad$ *Ans.* $m/n$.

5. If $f(x) = \begin{cases} x^2 + 1 & \text{for} \quad x > 0 \\ -(x^2 + 1) & \text{for} \quad x < 0 \end{cases}$ , does $\lim\limits_{x \to 0} f(x)$ exist?

6. Given that $g(x) = \begin{cases} 1 & \text{for} \quad x = 0, 1, 2, \cdots \\ \dfrac{1}{x} & \text{for all other values of } x \end{cases}$ , what are the following?

$\quad$ (a) $\lim\limits_{x \to 1} g(x)$.    *Ans.* 1.    (c) $\lim\limits_{x \to 1} \dfrac{g(x)}{x}$ .    *Ans.* 1.

$\quad$ (b) $\lim\limits_{x \to 2} g(x)$.    $\qquad\qquad$ (d) $\lim\limits_{x \to 2} \dfrac{g(x)}{x}$ .

## 5. Continuity and Differentiability.

In order to discuss the derivative of any function at some value $x_0$ of $x$, we had to know that $\Delta y$ approaches 0 as $\Delta x$ approaches 0; otherwise, $\lim\limits_{\Delta x \to 0} (\Delta y / \Delta x)$ could not exist. We "showed" in Chapter 6 Section 2 that the fact that $\Delta y$ does approach 0 when $\Delta x$ does followed from the continuity of the function at $x_0$. However, to understand continuity we described it by the statement that a function is continuous if its graph can be drawn with one uninterrupted motion of a pencil. This definition is poor because it relies on terms that have no precise meaning even in geometry. What do we mean by an uninterrupted motion? Intuitively we believe we know what these words mean but the terms are loose. Moreover, the concept of motion is physical, and mathematics does not rely on physical concepts for its definitions. Hence the problem of defining what we mean by a continuous function is thus far open.

$\qquad$ What do we really require of a function in order that it be continuous? Suppose that we reconsider the function $y = x^2$, which satisfies our intuitive concept of continuity. Because we are interested in continuity in behalf of the derivative and the derivative is defined at a value $x_0$ of $x$, we are really concerned about how the function behaves near and possibly at $x_0$.

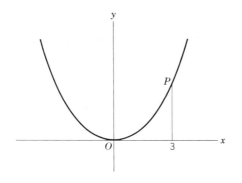

**Figure 25-7**

Let us, then, fix on a definite value of $x$, say $x = 3$. Suppose that one is drawing the curve of $y = x^2$ (Fig. 25-7) and is getting close to the point $P$ whose abscissa is 3 and ordinate is 9. In order to continue to draw the curve through point $P$ in an uninterrupted motion of the pencil, the $y$-values belonging to values of $x$ closer and closer to 3 must approach the $y$-value of $y = x^2$ at $x = 3$. In other words, the function values or $y$-values of points closer and closer to $P$ must approach more and more closely the $y$-value at $P$. This is why the pencil need not be lifted from the paper in order to draw the point belonging to the curve at $x = 3$.

Let us see what happens in the case of a curve that cannot be drawn in one continuous motion of the pencil. Consider the postage-stamp function which we originally studied in Section 2 and the graph of which is reproduced in Fig. 25-8. We can draw the portion of the graph which corresponds to weights from 0 to 1. Since the postage is 10 for weight 1, we have no trouble up to and including the point $P$ whose abscissa is 1. To continue the graph, we must jump just as soon as we go beyond the weight 1 to the value 20. Hence the motion of the pencil is interrupted. In other words, we cannot continue past the point whose abscissa is 1 because the function values to the right are not arbitrarily close to 10; they do not change gradually from the value at 1 but jump. Or we may think of proceeding to point $P$ from the right. As we come closer to the point whose abscissa is 1, the function values do not approach the value at 1. At the

**Figure 25-8**

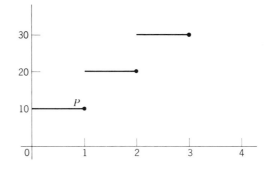

weight 1 the function value suddenly jumps from 20 to 10. It seems, then, that for continuity to hold at a point $P$ whose abscissa is $a$, say, the function values arbitrarily close to this point must approach the function value at $P$, and this must be true of the function values to the left as well as to the right of $P$.

Our analysis of what continuity involves leads to two requirements. First, if the function $y = f(x)$ is to be continuous at some value of $x$, say $x = a$, there must be an $f(a)$, that is, the function must be defined at $x = a$. Otherwise, to put the matter geometrically, there can be no point at $x = a$ through which the curve can go. Secondly, the function values near $x = a$, that is, $f(x)$ for $x$ near $a$, must approach the function value at $a$ or, in the language of limits,

$$\lim_{x \to a} f(x) = f(a).$$

We may frame this last statement in $\epsilon$-$\delta$ language.

**Definition:** A function $y = f(x)$ is continuous at $x = a$ if given any positive quantity $\epsilon$ there exists a quantity $\delta$ such that when

$$|x - a| < \delta$$

then

$$|f(x) - f(a)| < \epsilon.$$

The essential difference between this definition of continuity and the definition of the limit of a function is that the limit of $f(x)$ is now specified to be $f(a)$ rather than some number $b$ which may not be related to $f(a)$. For this reason, too, we no longer state, as we did in the definition of a limit, that $0 < |x - a|$.

We have defined what we mean by a function being continuous at a value $a$ of $x$. However, our intuitive notion of a continuous function has covered what happens over a whole interval of $x$-values, namely, that we can draw an unbroken curve. We can make this notion precise, too, by requiring that at each value of $x$ in this interval we expect the function to do what it does at any one value where it is continuous; that is, as $x$ approaches any number in the interval, say the number $x = c$, we expect the function to approach its value $f(c)$. We state, therefore, the following:

**Definition:** A function is continuous over an interval of $x$-values if it is continuous at each value of $x$ in the interval.

Thus $y = x^2$ is continuous for all values of $x$, and $y = 1/x$ is continuous for $-\infty < x < 0$ and for $0 < x < \infty$.

This definition of continuity in an interval is subject to a qualification. Consider the relation between temperature and volume shown in Fig. 25-2. The domain of the function is the set of temperature values from $-4$ to 10. In this domain the function is discontinuous at $0°$. However, in each of the *open intervals* from $-4°$ to $0°$ and $0°$ to 10, the function is continuous (we are using the graph as a basis for this assertion). Hence we must be careful, in asserting that a function is continuous, to specify what set of $x$-values or of the independent variable we have in mind.

Moreover, if we should wish to confine ourselves, for some purpose, to the *closed* interval $0°$ to $10°$ and assert that the function is continuous in that interval (and it is), we shall have to make an exception of what we require at the end values of that interval. For example, we require that the dependent variable have the value at $0°$ which it approaches only for values of the independent variable *larger* than $0°$. This value is 1.0001 in the present case. Likewise, at the right-hand end value, we require that the dependent variable have the value at $10°$ which it approaches as the independent variable approaches $10°$ only through *smaller* values. This value is 1.0003 in the present example. In general terms, $f(x)$ is continuous in the interval $a \leq x \leq b$ if it is continuous in the usual sense at a value of $x$ between $a$ and $b$; if at $x = a$

$$f(a) = \lim_{x \to a} f(x)$$

for values of $x$ greater than $a$; and if at $x = b$

$$f(b) = \lim_{x \to b} f(b)$$

for values of $x$ less than $b$.

It may be nice to know what mathematics means by a function being continuous at a point or over an interval, but how do we know when a given function is continuous at any value of $x$? The method is practically the same as that used to determine the limits of functions. In fact, there are the theorems which state that if two functions $f(x)$ and $g(x)$ are each continuous at a value of $x$, then the sum, difference, product, and quotient of the two functions are also continuous at that value of $x$, provided that, in the case of the quotient, the denominator is not 0. These theorems on continuous functions are really corollaries of the respective theorems on limits. To see this, let us consider, for example, the assertion concerning the sum of two continuous functions. If the functions are $f(x)$ and $g(x)$, our hypothesis is that

$$\lim_{x \to a} f(x) = f(a) \quad \text{and} \quad \lim_{x \to a} g(x) = g(a).$$

We wish to prove that

$$\lim_{x \to a} \{f(x) + g(x)\} = f(a) + g(a).$$

If we examine the hypothesis and conclusion of the corresponding theorem on limits, we see that $f(a)$ and $g(a)$ here replace the $A$ and $B$ there. In all other respects the proof is exactly the same.

With these theorems on continuous functions one can readily establish that a great variety of functions are continuous. The argument is the same as that used in connection with finding the limit of the function in (25), namely, the function

$$y = \frac{x^2 + 4}{x^2 - 5x + 7} .$$

This function is built up by applying the operations of sum, difference, product and quotient to $x$ itself and to constants. Hence the question of the continuity of this function at, say, $x = 2$ boils down to the question of the continuity of the very simple functions $y = x$ and $y = $ const. Is the function $y = x$ continuous at $x = 2$? Yes, because the very proof that $y = x$ approaches the limit 2 as $x$ approaches 2 (see Exercise 2e of Section 3) proves that $y = x$ is continuous since the limit is the value of the function at $x = 2$. Is every function of the form $y = $ const. continuous? Here, clearly, the limit approached by the function as $x$ approaches any value is the value of the function. Thus we can settle the question of the continuity of many functions by regarding these functions as built up from simpler functions and by applying the theorems on continuous functions.

These theorems will not, however, help us to prove that such functions as $\sin x$, $\log x$, and $e^x$ are continuous. For these functions special arguments are needed which we shall not take up. However, if we do prove that $\sin x$ is continuous at, say, $x = \pi/4$, then we do know that $x \sin x$ is continuous at $x = \pi/4$ because $x \sin x$ is the product of two continuous functions. Actually more theorems on limits and continuity are needed to handle all of the proofs of the calculus, but we shall not examine them here.

## EXERCISES

1. Suppose that $y = f(x)$ is continuous at $x = a$. Does $f(x)$ necessarily approach a limit as $x$ approaches $a$?                                                  *Ans.* Yes.

2. We know that $\lim\limits_{x \to 2} x^2 = 4$ and we know that when $x = 2$, $x^2 = 4$. Do these facts imply that $x^2$ is continuous at $x = 2$?

3. We are given that $\sin x$ and $e^x$ are continuous at each value of $x$. Is $e^x \sin x$ continuous at each value of $x$?                                           *Ans.* Yes.

4. Is $(\sin x)/x$ continuous at $x = 0$?

5. Is $e^{1/x}$ continuous at $x = 0$?

6. Suppose that we were testing the continuity of some function $f(x)$ at $x = a$ and we found that for $\epsilon = \frac{1}{2}$ there did not exist a $\delta$ such that when $|x - a| < \delta$, $|f(x) - f(a)| < \epsilon$.
   (a)  Would it be possible by increasing $\epsilon$ to 1, say, that we could find a suitable $\delta$ to meet the $\epsilon$-$\delta$ condition for this new value of $\epsilon$?     *Ans.* Yes.
   (b)  Would it be possible by decreasing $\epsilon$ to $\frac{1}{4}$, say, that we could find a suitable $\delta$ to meet the $\epsilon$-$\delta$ condition?

7. Suppose that we were testing the continuity of some function $f(x)$ at $x = a$ and we found that for each $\epsilon$ down to 0.001 we could find a $\delta$ to meet the $\epsilon$-$\delta$ condition. Is the function necessarily continuous at $x = a$?     *Ans.* No.

8. Suppose that we were testing the continuity of some function $f(x)$ at $x = a$ and we found that for each $\epsilon$ in the infinite sequence $\frac{1}{2}, \frac{1}{4}, \frac{1}{8}, \cdots$ we could find a $\delta$ to meet the $\epsilon$-$\delta$ condition. Is the function necessarily continuous at $x = a$?

**9.** Show by application of the $\epsilon$-$\delta$ definition that the following functions are continuous at the value of $x$ indicated:

(a)  $y = 2x$ at $x = 3$.

(b)  $y = 4x + 6$ at $x = 2$.

(c)  $y = 3x - 7$ at $x = 1$.

(d)  $y = 5x + 7$ at $x = 2$.

**10.** If $f(x) = \begin{cases} x^2 & \text{for } x \geq 0, \\ -x^2 & \text{for } x < 0, \end{cases}$ is $f(x)$ continuous at $x = 0$?    *Ans.* Yes.

**11.** (a)  What is the value of $f(x) = x \sin(1/x)$ at $x = 0$ insofar as the analytic expression indicates?

(b)  Can we define $f(x)$ at $x = 0$ so as to make the function continuous at $x = 0$?

**12.** Given that $g(x) = \begin{cases} 1 & \text{for } x = 0, 1, 2, \dots \\ \dfrac{1}{x} & \text{for all other values of } x, \end{cases}$ do the following hold?

(a)  Is $g(x)$ continuous at $x = 1$?

*Ans.* Yes.

(b)  Is $g(x)$ continuous at $x = 2$?

(c)  Is $g(x)/x$ continuous at $x = 1$?

*Ans.* Yes.

(d)  Is $g(x)/x$ continuous at $x = 2$?

In the differential calculus we usually wish to know more about a function than that it is continuous. We would also like to know that it has a derivative at some values of $x$. Does the continuity of a function at a value of $x$ guarantee that the function will also have a derivative at that value of $x$? The answer is no. We have but to look at the function which represents the force of gravitation and which is graphed in Fig. 25-3. This function is continuous at $r = R$, but does not have a derivative there, because there is no tangent at that value of $r$. There are, in fact, functions which are continuous throughout an interval but do not have a derivative at any value of $x$ in that interval. However, if a function has a derivative at a value of $x_0$ of $x$, the function must be continuous at that value of $x$.

Intuitively, we can readily see this because we know that if $f(x)$ has a derivative at $x = x_0$, then, if we write the derivative as [cf. (13)]

$$\lim_{x \to x_0} \frac{f(x) - f(x_0)}{x - x_0} = A$$

where $A$ is the derivative at $x_0$, $f(x) - f(x_0)$ must approach 0 as $x - x_0$ approaches 0 or $f(x)$ must approach $f(x_0)$ as $x$ approaches $x_0$. We could prove the assertion by using the rigorous definition of continuity but we have gotten some indication of what rigorous proof involves and so we shall not do so.

The distinction between the limit of a function as $x$ approaches $a$ and the continuity of a function at $x = a$ enables us to understand a little more thoroughly the concept of the derivative. Let us review what we did almost at the outset of our work. To calculate the derivative of, say, $y = x^2$ by the method of increments, we first found that

**(26)**
$$\frac{\Delta y}{\Delta x} = \frac{2x_0 \, \Delta x + (\Delta x)^2}{\Delta x}.$$

Now $\Delta y / \Delta x$ is a function of $\Delta x$. At $\Delta x = 0$ this function has no value and so we are obliged, in order to define the derivative, to consider the limit of $\Delta y / \Delta x$ as $\Delta x$ approaches 0. In the case of (26) it is fortunate that we can divide numerator and denominator by $\Delta x$ and so obtain

**(27)**
$$\frac{\Delta y}{\Delta x} = 2x_0 + \Delta x.$$

The functions of $\Delta x$ which appear in (26) and (27) are *not* the same. They agree in value for each value of $\Delta x$ except $\Delta x = 0$. The function in (26) has no value for $\Delta x = 0$; the function in (27) does. To find the limit of (26) at $\Delta x = 0$ we may use (27) because the limit does *not* depend on the value of the function at $\Delta x = 0$. However, the right-hand side of (27) is a continuous function of $\Delta x$ at $\Delta x = 0$. Hence to find the limit in (27) one may substitute $\Delta x = 0$ in the function, because the limit is the value of the function at $\Delta x = 0$.

Thus for the polynomials, which one studies at the beginning of the calculus, it is possible to calculate the limit of $\Delta y / \Delta x$ as $\Delta x$ approaches 0 by actually substituting the value of $\Delta x$ in a function, for example (27), which is almost the same as the original $\Delta y / \Delta x$, for example (26). It is advisable to start the study of the calculus with polynomial functions because they are simple; but it is also unfortunate because the student gets the impression that the whole fuss about limits being necessary to define the derivative is a sham. He can find it by substituting $\Delta x = 0$ in an almost equivalent function such as (27). Of course, when one gets to the transcendental functions, this alternative of substituting $\Delta x = 0$ in an equivalent function is no longer possible and one is actually obliged to find the limit of $\Delta y / \Delta x$ as $\Delta x$ approaches 0. One should, however, never lose sight of the fact that the derivative is a limit, even though in the case of polynomials it is possible to evaluate that limit by substituting $\Delta x = 0$ in some related function.

The founding of the calculus on an arithmetical basis calls for one more step involving the derivative. In Section 1 of Chapter 4 we "proved" that the derivative of $y = f(x)$ at $x = a$, say, equals the slope of the curve representing $y = f(x)$ at the point $P$ whose abscissa is $a$. A review of the argument given there will show that we observed that $\Delta y / \Delta x$ gives the slope of the secant through $P$ and, since the secants approached the tangent at $P$ as $\Delta x$ approached 0, we concluded that $dy/dx$ must be the slope of the tangent. This argument presumes that we know what we mean by the tangent at $P$ and that we know what we mean by saying that the secants through $P$ approach the tangent at $P$ as $\Delta x$ approaches 0. In other words, the argument rests on geometrical knowledge about secants and tangents. It would be possible to formulate this geometrical knowledge precisely, but because in other connections, such as the theory of limits, it has been found desirable and even necessary to base the calculus on arithmetic concepts, it is desirable to do this throughout the calculus. To avoid having to make our geometrical ideas on secants and tangents precise and for the sake of a consistent arithmetical approach to the calculus, we revise our treatment of the derivative as the slope of a tangent.

The revision takes the following form. We see intuitively or geometrically that there is such a thing as a tangent line to a (smooth) curve at a point and that the secants through that point approach the tangent. Logically we *define* the tangent to be that line through the point whose slope is the derivative of the function at that point. Since the derivative is an arithmetical concept, the definition of the tangent and its slope is now based on the arithmetic concept. The logical basis of the geometry becomes the arithmetical, or one says analytical, theory of the calculus.

Such a definition may seem arbitrary, but it is no more so than defining the instantaneous velocity of a moving object to be the derivative. If our mathematical definitions incorporate what geometrical intuition or physical experience suggest, they can be used to study geometrical and physical phenomena. Whether mathematicians have done wisely to trust the seemingly greater clarity and sharpness of arithmetic concepts as opposed to geometrical ones, is a deep philosophical question that must be passed over at this stage of our study of mathematics.

## EXERCISES

1. Sketch the following functions and determine from the sketch whether the function is continuous and whether it has a derivative at the value of $x$ indicated:

   (a)  $y = x^{1/3}$ at $x = 0$.                                       *Ans.* Yes; no.

   (b)  $y = x^{2/3}$ at $x = 0$.

   (c)  $y = \begin{cases} x^2 & \text{for } 0 \le x \le 1 \\ 2 - x^2 & \text{for } 1 \le x \le 2 \end{cases}$ at $x = 1$.      *Ans.* Yes; no.

   (d)  $y = |x|$ at $x = 0$.

   (e)  $y = \dfrac{|x|}{x}$ at $x = 0$.                                 *Ans.* No; no.

   (f)  $y = \dfrac{1}{1 + 2^{1/x}}$ at $x = 0$.

   (g)  $y = \arctan \dfrac{1}{x}$ at $x = 0$.                          *Ans.* No; no.

   (h)  $y = \begin{cases} x & \text{for } 0 \le x \le 1 \\ x - 1 & \text{for } 1 < x \le 2 \\ x - 2 & \text{for } 2 < x \le 3 \end{cases}$ at $x = 1$.

   (i)  $y = \begin{cases} x & \text{for } x < 0 \\ \frac{1}{2} & \text{for } x = 0 \\ 1 + x & \text{for } x > 0 \end{cases}$ at $x = 0$.

2. Is it permissible to replace the problem of finding

$$\lim_{x \to 0} \frac{x^2 - x}{x}$$

   by the problem of finding

$$\lim_{x \to 0} x - 1?$$

   If so, why?

**3.** Criticize the following reasoning:

$$\lim_{x \to 3} \frac{x^2 - 9}{x - 3} = \lim_{x \to 3} x + 3$$

$$\lim_{x \to 3} x + 3 = 6$$

because $x + 3 = 6$ when $x = 3$.

**6. The Limit of a Sequence.** There are two limit notions in the calculus. The first of these is the limit of a function; this was reviewed in Section 3 as the foundation of the concepts of continuity and differentiation. The second limit concept is the limit of a sequence and this is utilized for the definitions of the definite integral and the sum of an infinite series.

The explanation given in Chapter 9 of the limit of a sequence as the number that the members of the sequence approach more and more closely and indeed arbitrarily closely is loose. The looseness lies in the use of such words as close and arbitrarily close. The objection to these words is entirely analogous to that already pointed out in our reconsideration of the definition of the limit of a function.

Before we attempt to introduce precise language, let us consider the notion of a sequence. What is an infinite sequence? It is an infinite set of numbers taken in a definite order; that is, there is a first member, a second member, a third member, etc. Thus the set of numbers

**(28)**                        $1, \frac{1}{2}, \frac{1}{3}, \frac{1}{4}, \cdots ,$

taken in the order in which they are written and with the three dots implying that the set continues indefinitely, is a sequence. It seems clear from the first few members of the sequence what the succeeding terms should be, but to avoid any possible ambiguity it is usually desirable to write down what is called the $n$th term. In the case of the sequence (28) the $n$th term is $1/n$.

**(29)**                        $s_1, s_2, s_3, \cdots , s_n, \cdots .$

Then $s_1$ is the first term; $s_2$ the second term; $s_n$, the $n$th term; and so on.

To get at the concept of the limit of a sequence let us, for concreteness, consider the sequence

**(30)**                $\frac{1}{2}, \frac{3}{4}, \frac{7}{8}, \frac{15}{16}, \cdots , \frac{(2^n - 1)}{2^n} , \cdots .$

It seems clear from the first few members of the sequence as well as from the $n$th term that they are approaching 1 as a limit. As $n$ increases, the quantity 1 in the numerator becomes less and less significant in comparison with $2^n$ and therefore as $n$ increases, the numerator and denominator become more nearly equal and the fraction approaches 1. Our concept of limit, then, is the number which the members of the sequence approach more and more closely. Of course, the members are also approaching 2 more and more closely, but what we mean really is that the members of the sequences come arbitrarily close to the true limit, which seems to be the case for the number 1 but not for the number 2. How close is arbitrarily close? The precise way of stating this is to use the $\epsilon$-language that we used in connection with the notion of limit of a function. That is, let $\epsilon$ be *any* positive quantity. Then no matter what $\epsilon$ may be, we would like to have the difference between the limit and the members of the sequence become less than $\epsilon$. Let us see what this means in the case of (30). If 1 is the limit, the difference between the limit and the $n$th term is

**(31)** $$1 - \frac{2^n - 1}{2^n} = \frac{2^n - 2^n + 1}{2^n} = \frac{1}{2^n} .$$

Does this difference become less than any positive quantity $\epsilon$? If $\epsilon$ is 0.001, then for $n = 10$, $1/2^n$ is less than 0.001. If $\epsilon$ is 0.000,01, then for $n = 17$, $1/2^n$ is less than 0.000,01. In fact, by making $n$ large enough we can make $1/2^n$ less than any positive quantity.

We have still not stated all that the intuitive meaning of limit requires. Let us consider the sequence

**(32)** $$\frac{1}{2}, \frac{1}{2}, \frac{3}{4}, \frac{1}{2}, \frac{7}{8}, \frac{1}{2}, \frac{15}{16}, \frac{1}{2}, \cdots .$$

Some members of this sequence—the odd-numbered members—do approach 1; in fact, the odd-numbered members are precisely the members of the sequence (30) and we have just seen that for $n$ large enough we can make the difference between the number 1 and the $n$th term of that sequence less than any given $\epsilon$. Yet we would not want to say that 1 is the limit of the sequence (32), and the reason is that some members of the sequence—the even-numbered members—do not approach 1. In other words, our intuitive concept of a limit would require that, having specified an $\epsilon$, we would want *all* the members, at least after a certain one, to come within $\epsilon$ of the limit. If $\epsilon = \frac{1}{4}$, this condition is not satisfied by the sequence (32), because, no matter how far out in the sequence we may go, we will continue to find terms that differ from 1 by more than this $\epsilon$. On the other hand, this condition is satisfied by sequence (30).

Thus so far our intuitive notion of limit requires that, given any positive quantity $\epsilon$, *all* the members after a certain one—which one it is depends on the choice of $\epsilon$—must come within $\epsilon$ of the limit.

Before we try to put the definition of a limit in final form, let us study the sequence

**(33)** $$\frac{1}{2}, 1\frac{1}{2}, \frac{3}{4}, 1\frac{1}{4}, \frac{7}{8}, 1\frac{1}{8}, \frac{15}{16}, 1\frac{1}{16}, \cdots .$$

Do the members of this sequence approach 1 as a limit? They do indeed come closer and closer to 1 and indeed come arbitrarily close. However, the members are alternately less and greater than 1. The question, then, is whether we really wish to include such sequences among those that have a limit. We do.

This is readily done if we introduce the concept of absolute value. We require merely that given any $\epsilon$ the absolute value of the difference between the limit and all members of the sequence from a certain one on be less than $\epsilon$. Thus in the case of the sequence (33) if we choose $\epsilon = \frac{1}{10}$, it is true for all members $s_n$ from the seventh one on that

$$|1 - s_n| < \epsilon.$$

Now let us try to formulate in general language what these examples suggest. Suppose that we have a sequence

$$s_1, s_2, s_3, \cdots s_n, \cdots .$$

We say that the number $S$ is the limit of this sequence if for each positive quantity $\epsilon$, there exists some term, say $s_N$, such that for all succeeding ones, that is, for all $s_n$ where $n > N$,

$$|S - s_n| < \epsilon.$$

This definition is usually stated in the somewhat more elliptical form:

**Definition:** The number $S$ is the limit of the sequence $s_1, s_2, s_3, \ldots, s_n, \ldots$ if given any positive quantity $\epsilon$, there exists an $N$ such that for all $n > N$

**(34)**                         $$|S - s_n| < \epsilon.$$

The definition (34) is often referred to for brevity as the $\epsilon$-$N$ definition of a limit of a sequence.

Just to see how the general definition can be utilized, let us prove that the sequence

**(35)**                     $$0, \frac{1}{2}, \frac{2}{3}, \frac{4}{5}, \cdots, \frac{n-1}{n}, \cdots$$

has the limit 1. We could, of course, choose $\epsilon = \frac{1}{10}$ and find that for all $n$ greater than some one $N$, all the members $s_n$ differ from 1 by less than $\frac{1}{10}$. Then we could try $\epsilon = \frac{1}{100}$ and so on, but we could never exhaust all the possible $\epsilon$ in this way. Let us do it in one swoop. Consider any positive quantity $\epsilon$. For what values of $n$ is

**(36)**                         $$\left| 1 - \frac{n-1}{n} \right| < \epsilon$$

or

**(37)**                         $$\left| \frac{1}{n} \right| < \epsilon?$$

The inequality (37) will be correct if

**(38)**                         $$\frac{n}{1} > \frac{1}{\epsilon}.$$

(We can ignore the absolute value sign in (37) because $1/n$ is positive.) In other words, given any $\epsilon$, then for $n > 1/\epsilon$, (37) holds and so (36) holds. Hence given $\epsilon$, we choose $N$ to be the first integer greater than $1/\epsilon$ and then for all $n > N$, (37) and hence (36) will surely hold.

## EXERCISES

1. What are the first five terms in the sequence whose $n$th term is the following:

(a) $n^2$.

(b) $\dfrac{2n + 1}{n + 2}$.    *Ans.* 1, $\frac{5}{4}$, $\frac{7}{5}$, $\frac{3}{2}$, $\frac{11}{7}$.

(c) $(-1)^n \dfrac{1}{n}$.

(d) $\dfrac{n^2 - 1}{2n^2 + 3n + 1}$.

2. Suppose that for a given sequence which has the limit $S$, one finds that for $\epsilon = \frac{1}{10}$, $s_5$ and all succeeding terms satisfy the condition $|S - s_n| < \epsilon$. Is it necessarily true that for $n > 3$, $|S - s_n| < \epsilon$? Suppose that we now choose $\epsilon = \frac{1}{20}$. Is it necessarily true that for $n > 5$, $|S - s_n| < \epsilon$?

3. For the following sequences and for the given values of $S$ and $\epsilon$ find an $N$ such that for $n > N$, $|S - s_n| < \epsilon$:

(a) 1, $\frac{1}{2}$, $\frac{1}{3}$, $\frac{1}{4}$, $\frac{1}{5}$, $\cdots$ ; $S = 0$ and $\epsilon = \frac{1}{10}$.    *Ans.* 10.

(b) 1, $\frac{1}{2}$, $\frac{1}{4}$, $\frac{1}{8}$, $\frac{1}{16}$, $\cdots$ ; $S = 0$ and $\epsilon = \frac{1}{10}$.

(c) 1, $-\frac{1}{2}$, $\frac{1}{4}$, $-\frac{1}{8}$, $\frac{1}{16}$, $-\frac{1}{32}$, $\cdots$ ; $S = 0$ and $\epsilon = \frac{1}{10}$.    *Ans.* 4.

4. Show that the values of the first 100 terms of any sequence are immaterial in determining the limit of a sequence.

5. Use the precise definition of the limit of a sequence to prove that the following sequences have the limit indicated:

(a) 0, 1, $\frac{4}{3}$, $\frac{6}{4}$, $\frac{8}{5}$, $\cdots$ , $(2n - 2)/n$ $\cdots$ has the limit 2.

(b) $1\frac{1}{2}$, $1\frac{3}{4}$, $1\frac{7}{8}$, $\cdots$ , $(2^{n+1} - 1)/2^n$, $\cdots$ has the limit 2.

(c) $\frac{1}{2}$, $\frac{1}{4}$, $\frac{1}{8}$, $\cdots$ , $1/2^n$, $\cdots$ has the limit 0.

6. Show by application of the precise definition that the sequence (30) of the text cannot have $1\frac{1}{2}$ as a limit.

7. Prove by application of the precise definition that the limit of the sequence for which $s_{2m} = 1/m$ and $s_{2m-1} = 1/2m$ is 0.

8. Prove rigorously that 1 is not the limit of the sequence for which $s_n = 1/n$.

**7. *Some Theorems on Limits of Sequences.*** The definition of the limit of a sequence does not tell us in the case of any given sequence just what the limit is. For simple sequences, inspection of the $n$th term often permits us to "guess" what the limit is and we may then prove that this guess does indeed satisfy the definition of the limit. For example, in the case of the sequence (35), in which the $n$th term is $(n - 1)/n$, it seems clear, that the limit of the sequence is 1 and, as we saw in the preceding section, we can indeed prove that this is the case.

For more complicated sequences, the guess about the correct limit is not so readily made and, even when made, it may be difficult to apply the definition of a limit to show that the guess is indeed correct. Suppose, for example, that the $n$th term of a sequence is

**(39)** $$s_n = \frac{n^2 + 1}{2n^2 + 3n + 1}.$$

To guess the limit one might argue that the $n^2$-terms in the numerator and the denominator are the dominant terms. Hence a rough argument would be that $s_n$ should behave more and more like $n^2/2n^2$ as $n$ becomes infinite, and so the limit should be $\frac{1}{2}$. This rough argument can be made a little more convincing if we first divide the numerator and denominator of $s_n$ by $n^2$ so that

$$
(40) \qquad\qquad s_n = \frac{1 + \dfrac{1}{n^2}}{2 + \dfrac{3}{n} + \dfrac{1}{n^2}}.
$$

Now, as $n$ becomes infinite, the terms $1/n^2$ and $3/n$ approach 0, and so it seems clear that the numerator approaches 1, the denominator approaches 2, and the entire quantity $s_n$ approaches $\frac{1}{2}$.

To prove that $\frac{1}{2}$ is the limit of the sequence, we should show that it satisfies the definition of the limit of a sequence, that is, we should show that, given any positive quantity $\epsilon$, there is an $N$ such that for all $n > N$

$$
(41) \qquad\qquad \left| \frac{n^2 + 1}{2n^2 + 3n + 1} - \frac{1}{2} \right| < \epsilon.
$$

A little effort will show that it is not easy to find an $N$ such that (41) holds for all $n > N$.

We could avoid the difficult demonstration that (41) is satisfied for $n > N$ if we *could* argue as follows. Let us consider $s_n$ in the form (40). The limit of $s_n$ as $n$ becomes infinite is the limit of the numerator divided by the limit of the denominator. Let us see what each separate limit is. The limit of the numerator is the sum of the limits of the separate terms. These limits are 1 and 0. Hence the limit of the numerator is 1. The limit of the denominator is the sum of the limits of the separate terms. These limits are 2, 0, and 0. Hence the limit of the denominator is 2. Then the limit of $s_n$ is $\frac{1}{2}$.

The idea of this at present hypothetical argument is to break up the complicated sequence whose $n$th term is given by (40) into the sum and quotient of simpler sequences. For these separate simpler sequences we can determine the limits readily. Then by arguing that the limit of the quotient of two sequences is the quotient of the limits we reduce the problem to finding the limit of the numerator and the limit of the denominator separately. Then we handle the numerator and the denominator by the argument that the limit of a sum of sequences is the sum of the limits.

To make the kind of argument that we have just indicated we need theorems about the limit of sums and quotients of sequences. These theorems do hold, and we shall indicate what they state.

Suppose that one has two sequences

$$
(42) \qquad\qquad a_1, a_2, a_3, \cdots, a_n, \cdots
$$

and

$$
(43) \qquad\qquad b_1, b_2, b_3, \cdots, b_n, \cdots.
$$

One can define a new sequence by forming the sum of the respective terms of the two sequences. Thus the new sequence would be

$$a_1 + b_1, a_2 + b_2, a_3 + b_3, \cdots, a_n + b_n, \cdots,$$

and this sequence is called the sum of the two sequences (42) and (43). Likewise, the sequence

$$a_1 - b_1, a_2 - b_2, a_3 - b_3, \cdots, a_n - b_n, \cdots$$

is called the difference of the two sequences (42) and (43). The sequence

$$a_1 b_1, a_2 b_2, a_3 b_3, \cdots, a_n b_n, \cdots$$

is called the product of the sequences (42) and (43), and the sequence

$$\frac{a_1}{b_1}, \frac{a_2}{b_2}, \frac{a_3}{b_3}, \cdots, \frac{a_n}{b_n}, \cdots$$

is called the quotient of the sequences (42) and (43).

The following theorems about sequences do hold.

**Theorem 1:** The limit of the sum of two sequences is the sum of the limits of the separate sequences, if these latter limits exist.

**Theorem 2:** The limit of the difference of two sequences is the difference of the limits of the separate sequences, if these latter limits exist.

**Theorem 3:** The limit of the product of two sequences is the product of the limits of the separate sequences, if these latter limits exist.

**Theorem 4:** The limit of the quotient of two sequences is the quotient of the limits of the separate sequences, if these latter limits exist and if the limit of the sequence of denominators is not zero.

These theorems can be proved on the basis of the definitions of sum, difference, and so forth given above and on the basis of the rigorous definition of the limit of a sequence. They are entirely analogous to the theorems on the limits of the sum, difference, product, and quotient of two functions. We shall not present the proofs but merely wish to call attention to the fact that such theorems do exist and can be utilized to determine the limits of sequences. Moreover, as we shall see in the next section, these same theorems and the precise definition of the limit of a sequence enable us to give a proper foundation to the theory of the definite integral.

## EXERCISES

**1.** Determine the limits of the following sequences by using the theorems on limits of sequences cited in the text:

(a) $s_n = \dfrac{n}{n^2 + 2}$.    *Ans.* 0.    (b) $s_n = \dfrac{n + 1}{n + 2}$.

(c) $s_n = \dfrac{n^2 - 3n + 1}{2n^2 - 4n + 1}$. *Ans.* $\frac{1}{2}$. (d) $s_n = \dfrac{2n + 1}{3n + 1}$.

2. Using the proof of the theorem on the limit of the sum of two functions as a guide, see if you can prove that the limit of the sum of two sequences is the sum of the limits of the separate sequences.

3. If $s_1, s_2, s_3, \cdots$ is a sequence of positive numbers whose limit is 0 and if $t_1, t_2, t_3, \cdots$ is another sequence of positive numbers such that $t_n \leq s_n$ for each $n$, prove that the limit of the second sequence is 0.

4. If the sequence $s_1, s_2, s_3, \cdots$ has the limit $s$ and if $c$ is a constant, prove that $cs_1, cs_2, cs_3, \cdots$ has the limit $cs$.

5. If the sequence $s_1, s_2, s_3, \cdots$ has the limit $s$ and $a$ is a constant, prove that the sequence $a + s_1, a + s_2, a + s_3, \cdots$ has the limit $a + s$.

6. Show that if a sequence has a limit, the sequence consisting of just the even-numbered terms has the same limit.

7. Suppose that $\lim\limits_{x \to a} f(x) = b$. Show that $\lim\limits_{n \to \infty} f(x_n) = b$ when $\{x_n\}$ is a sequence of numbers whose limit is $a$.

8. Prove that the limit of a sequence is unique, that is, if there is a limit, there is only one limit.

**8. The Definite Integral.** The first major use that we made of the notion of limit of a sequence was to define the definite integral or the integral as the limit of a sequence of sums. The second use was to define the sum of an infinite series. We shall not do more with the latter application because the basic notion of the sum is rather clear-cut once the notion of limit of a sequence is made precise. The definite integral, however, is a rather complicated notion and requires further study.

In defining the definite integral in Chapter 9 we started with a function $y = f(x)$ defined over some interval $a \leq x \leq b$.*

There we found that if we divided the interval $a \leq x \leq b$ into $n$ parts, $\Delta x_1, \Delta x_2, \cdots, \Delta x_n$, and that if we chose any value of $x$, say $x_i$ and then formed the sequence of sums

(44) $$S_n = f(x_1) \Delta x_1 + f(x_2) \Delta x_2 + \cdots + f(x_n) \Delta x_n$$

for $n = 1, 2, 3, \cdots$, we obtained better and better approximations to the area under the curve $y = f(x)$ between $x = a$ and $x = b$ (Fig. 25-9). The choice of the $x_i$ in each $\Delta x_i$ is arbitrary as are the sizes of the $\Delta x_i$ provided only that the sum of the $\Delta x_i$'s fills out the interval $a \leq x \leq b$. The only condition on the $\Delta x_i$'s is that the maximum $\Delta x$ must get smaller as we pass from one subdivision to the next and, in fact, as the number $n$ of the sum $S_n$ becomes infinite, the maximum $\Delta x$ must approach 0. The reason for this condition is that if the maximum $\Delta x$ of any subdivision approaches 0 as $n$ becomes infinite, so must each subinterval. Then each element $f(x_i) \Delta x_i$ must be a better approximation to the area (Fig. 25-10) under the curve and over the subinterval $\Delta x_i$ because the $f(x_i)$ chosen cannot differ as much from that $f(x)$ which furnishes the proper height of the rectangle. Or we

*It would be helpful if the reader would review the presentation in Chapter 9.

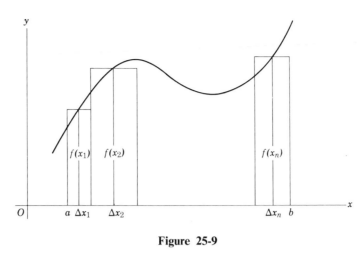

**Figure 25-9**

could say that the smaller $\Delta x_i$ is, the less does $f(x_i)$ differ from the other $y$-values in that $\Delta x_i$.

Each new subdivision of $a \le x \le b$ and each new sum is of the form (44). We thus have a sequence of sums which we asserted has a limit because the sequence approaches the area under the curve. This limit is the definite integral and is denoted by

**(45)**
$$\lim_{n \to \infty} S_n = \int_a^b f(x)\, dx.$$

It is important to recall (Chapter 9) that one can form an infinite number of sequences because in forming any one we can make different choices of the $\Delta x_i$'s and of the $x_i$ in each $\Delta x_i$. Yet all these sequences have the same limit, the area under the curve, and all therefore are denoted by $\int_a^b f(x)\, dx$.

**Figure 25-10**

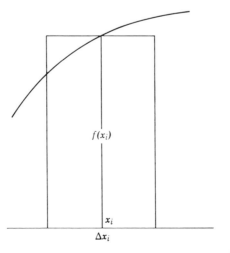

However, in the rigorous approach to the definite integral we cannot rely on the fact that the sequences have a limit and indeed the same limit, just because each approaches the area under the curve. How do we know then that all of them have a limit and indeed the same limit? The answer is supplied by a theorem which is often worded thus:

**Theorem:** If $f(x)$ is continuous in the interval then the definite integral $\int_a^b f(x)\, dx$ exists.

To say that the definite integral exists means that all choices of sequences of the kind that we described above lead to the same limit. The theorem asserts that this will be the case if $f(x)$ is continuous. It is not precluded that this integral will exist even for more irregularly behaving functions, but at least the continuity of $f(x)$ is sufficient to guarantee the existence of the integral. The proof of the theorem, which we shall not give, is purely analytical; that is, it does not depend on the integral representing an area.

The fact that the definite integral can be defined entirely analytically, so that there is no dependence on the geometry, leads to a turn of events which is rather unexpected but important in the development of mathematics. Intuitively we know that the area under a curve and, more generally, areas bounded entirely by curves, can be represented by definite integrals. However, the geometrical area has no precise definition, whereas the definite integral does have a very satisfactory definition. Hence we *define* the geometrical area to be what the definite integral yields. Thus in the logical development we actually reverse the process that we went through in the earlier, intuitive development of the calculus. We do the same thing with volumes, arc lengths, and areas of surfaces of revolution.

On the basis of the analytical definition of the definite integral we can prove, without referring to areas, all of the theorems we "proved" earlier. For example, we can prove that *if c is a value of x in a $\leq$ x $\leq$ b and if f(x) is continuous on that interval, then*

$$(46) \qquad \int_a^b f(x)\, dx = \int_a^c f(x)\, dx + \int_c^b f(x)\, dx.$$

## EXERCISES

**1.** What does the statement that $\int_0^2 3x^2\, dx$ exists mean?

**2.** Show by application of the definition of the definite integral and the theorems on sequences that the following hold:

(a) $\int_a^b [f(x) + g(x)]\, dx = \int_a^b f(x)\, dx + \int_a^b g(x)\, dx.$

(b) $\int_a^b cf(x)\, dx = c \int_a^b f(x)\, dx.$

We assume that all the integrals involved exist.

**3.** Show by any (proper) method that

$$\int_a^b f(x)\, g(x)\, dx \neq \left( \int_a^b f(x)\, dx \right) \left( \int_a^b g(x)\, dx \right).$$

**9. *Improper Integrals.*** The definite integral has been defined for functions that are continuous over the domain of integration. Yet there are occasions when the concept of the integral is useful in representing some geometrical or physical quantity and the integrand, that is, $f(x)$, is not continuous over the entire domain of integration. To make the mathematics fit the geometrical and physical situations, the definition of the integral is extended to include a wider class of integrands. Such a procedure makes sense if, first, it leads to a mathematically definite quantity, a number in the case of the definite integral, and if the extended definition serves a useful purpose. The integrals that we shall define when $f(x)$ is not continuous over the domain of integration or when the domain is infinite are called *improper* integrals.

Thus consider the function $y = f(x)$ which is defined by

**(47)**
$$f(x) = \begin{cases} x/2 & \text{for} \quad 0 \le x \le 1 \\ 2x & \text{for} \quad 1 \le x \le 2 \end{cases}$$

and which is shown graphically in Fig. 25-11. This function is not continuous at $x = 1$ because it approaches the value of $\frac{1}{2}$ as $x$ approaches 1 through values less than 1 and then it jumps at $x = 1$ from $\frac{1}{2}$ to 2. Such functions do occur even in physical problems, as we pointed out in Section 2, and one might want to evaluate

**(48)**
$$\int_0^2 f(x)\, dx.$$

Under the limitation that $f(x)$ be continuous in the domain $(0, 2)$ this integral would have no meaning. However, $f(x)$ is continuous in the interval $(0, 1)$. Here we should recall the remark made in Section 5 that $f(x)$ is continuous in an interval as opposed to its entire domain of definition if

**Figure 25-11**

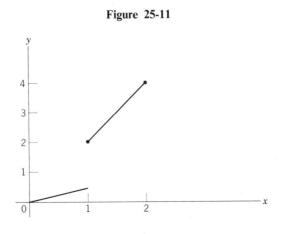

the values of $f(x)$ for values of $x$ *interior* to the interval approach the values of $f(x)$ at the respective end values of the interval and, of course, if $f(x)$ is continuous at each interior point of the interval. The values of $x/2$ for $x < 1$ do approach the value $\frac{1}{2}$, which we can take to be $f(1)$ *as far as the interval* (0, 1) *is concerned.* The same applies at $x = 0$. Hence $f(x)$ is continuous in $0 \leq x \leq 1$. Likewise, it is continuous in the interval $1 \leq x \leq 2$. Hence we can define the integral (48) to mean

**(49)**
$$\int_0^1 f(x)\, dx + \int_1^2 f(x)\, dx.$$

The quantity (49) is a definite number. In fact, in the present case it is

$$\int_0^1 \frac{x}{2}\, dx + \int_1^2 2x\, dx = 3\tfrac{1}{4}.$$

If this number fits the physical situation, the definition of the integral is applicable to such situations. For example, if an object moved with the velocity $t/2$ from $t = 0$ to $t = 1$ and then under a sudden acceleration increased its velocity to $2t$ from $t = 1$ to $t = 2$, the quantity $3\tfrac{1}{4}$ would represent the distance traveled.

Thus the first extension of the concept of the definite integral is to functions with jump or finite discontinuities. In general terms,

**Definition:** If $f(x)$ is continuous over $a \leq x \leq b$ and continuous over $b \leq x \leq c$ but possesses a jump discontinuity at $x = b$, then, by definition,

**(50)**
$$\int_a^c f(x)\, dx = \int_a^b f(x)\, dx + \int_b^c f(x)\, dx.$$

The second extension of the concept of the definite integral is to integrands that become infinite at one end point of the interval of integration. For example, suppose that we had to find the length of arc of the circle $x^2 + y^2 = 25$. We might proceed to find this length by finding the length of the quarter-circle in the first quadrant (Fig. 25-12). Since the arc

**Figure 25-12**

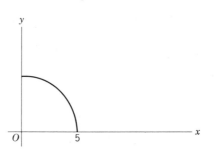

length is given by

$$L = \int_a^b \sqrt{1 + (dy/dx)^2} \; dx,$$

in the present case we are led to the integral

**(51)**
$$L = \int_0^5 \frac{5}{\sqrt{25 - x^2}} \; dx.$$

Now we note that at $x = 5$ the integrand is infinite and so is not continuous in the entire interval $0 \leq x \leq 5$. We are therefore strictly not justified in regarding (51) as a definite integral. It is an improper integral. To define integrals such as (51) we introduce the following device. Let $\epsilon$ be any small positive quantity. Then the integral

**(52)**
$$\int_0^{5-\epsilon} \frac{5}{\sqrt{25 - x^2}} \; dx$$

certainly exists, because over the interval $0 \leq x \leq 5 - \epsilon$, the integrand is a continuous function ($25 - x^2$ is continuous and the square root of a continuous, positive function is continuous). We can then proceed to evaluate (52). The fundamental theorem permits us to apply antidifferentiation and we obtain

$$5 \sin^{-1} \frac{x}{5} \Big|_0^{5-\epsilon}$$

or

**(53)**
$$5 \sin^{-1} \left( \frac{5 - \epsilon}{5} \right).$$

The definition of the improper integral (51) now requires that we seek the limit of (53) as $\epsilon$ approaches 0. As $\epsilon$ approaches 0, $(5 - \epsilon)/5$ approaches 1 and so $\sin^{-1} (5 - \epsilon)/5$ approaches $\pi/2$. Then (53) approaches $5\pi/2$. The definition of the improper integral (51) states that we should take this limit to be the value of (51).

What this example illustrates is the following.

**Definition:** If in the integral

**(54)**
$$\int_a^b f(x) \; dx$$

$f(x)$ is continuous except at $x = b$ where $f(x)$ becomes infinite, then we define

**(55)**
$$\lim_{\epsilon \to 0+} \int_a^{b-\epsilon} f(x) \; dx$$

to be the value of (54) if this limit exists. (We write $\epsilon \to 0 +$ to indicate that $\epsilon$ approaches 0 through positive values.) If the limit (55) does not exist then (54) has no value. Likewise, if in the integral

$$\textbf{(56)} \qquad \int_a^b f(x)\, dx$$

$f(x)$ is continuous except at $x = a$ where $f(x)$ becomes infinite, then we define

$$\textbf{(57)} \qquad \lim_{\epsilon \to 0+} \int_{a+\epsilon}^b f(x)\, dx$$

to be the value of (56) if this limit exists.

The integral

$$\textbf{(58)} \qquad \int_{-5}^{5} \frac{1}{x}\, dx$$

presents a new type of difficulty. Here the integrand becomes infinite not at either end point of the interval but at a value *interior* to the interval of integration. We can, of course, regard (58) as the sum of two integrals

$$\textbf{(59)} \qquad \int_{-5}^{0} \frac{1}{x}\, dx + \int_0^5 \frac{1}{x}\, dx;$$

then the infinity of the integrand occurs at an end value of each interval of integration. If we now treat each interval in accordance with the definitions given in (55) and (57), we are led to

$$\textbf{(60)} \qquad \lim_{\epsilon \to 0} \int_{-5}^{0-\epsilon} \frac{1}{x}\, dx + \lim_{\epsilon \to 0} \int_{0+\epsilon}^5 \frac{1}{x}\, dx.$$

After antidifferentiation we obtain, since the sum of the limits is the limit of the sum,

$$\lim_{\epsilon \to 0} \left\{ \log |x| \,\Big|_{-5}^{0-\epsilon} + \log x \,\Big|_{0+\epsilon}^5 \right\}$$

or

$$\textbf{(61)} \qquad \lim_{\epsilon \to 0} \left\{ \log|-\epsilon| - \log|-5| + \log 5 - \log \epsilon \right\}.$$

Since $\log|-\epsilon| = \log|\epsilon|$ and $\log|-5| = \log 5$, the value of the quantity in the braces in (61) is 0 and so the limit is 0. Thus by splitting (58) into the two integrals in (59) and by applying the definitions (57) and (55) we obtain the value 0 for (58).

This result makes sense. As we can see from Fig. 25-13, the quantity (60) is 0 because the negative area just offsets the positive area for any

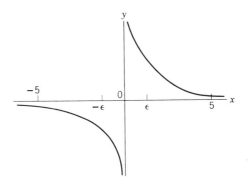

**Figure 25-13**

positive $\epsilon$, and so the net area is 0 and the limit as $\epsilon$ approaches 0 is 0. However, the interpretation of (58) as the sum of the improper integrals in (60) masks the fact that each separate integral becomes infinite, and this fact may be physically important. Hence the definition accepted for an integral of the form (58) is usually the following:

**(62)**
$$\int_{-5}^{5} \frac{1}{x}\, dx = \lim_{\epsilon_1 \to 0} \int_{-5}^{0-\epsilon_1} \frac{1}{x}\, dx + \lim_{\epsilon_2 \to 0} \int_{0+\epsilon_2}^{5} \frac{1}{x}\, dx$$

where $\epsilon_1$ and $\epsilon_2$ are positive quantities. The significance of the $\epsilon_1$ and $\epsilon_2$ instead of a single $\epsilon$ in both integrals is that $\epsilon_1$ and $\epsilon_2$ are to be treated as *independent* quantities; or each of the integrals on the right side must exist. However, integration of the first integral yields

$$\log | - \epsilon_1| - \log | - 5|.$$

Now as $\epsilon_1$ approaches 0, $\log | - \epsilon_1|$ becomes infinite and so the first integral does not have any value. The same is true of the second one. Thus each of the integrals on the right side of (62) is infinite and their sum is meaningless. Then the integral on the left side has no value.

  The general point illustrated by (62) is the following third extension of the concept of the definite integral.

**Definition:**  If in

**(63)**
$$\int_{a}^{b} f(x)\, dx$$

$f(x)$ becomes infinite at the value $x = c$ where $a < c < b$, then the definition of this integral is

**(64)**
$$\lim_{\epsilon_1 \to 0+} \int_{a}^{c-\epsilon_1} f(x)\, dx + \lim_{\epsilon_2 \to 0+} \int_{c+\epsilon_2}^{b} f(x)\, dx.$$

If the two *separate* limits exist, the value of (63) is the sum of the two limits.

That is, each of the two integrals in (64) must have a finite value for the entire improper integral (63) to have a finite value.

Still another type of improper integral occurs in mathematics and its applications. Suppose that we were interested in the area (Fig. 25-14) under the curve $y = 1/x^2$ from $x = 1$ to arbitrarily large values of $x$. How should we represent this area? In mathematical language a reasonable expression would be

**(65)**
$$\int_1^\infty \frac{1}{x^2}\, dx.$$

Indeed, we used this notation in Chapter 23, where we evaluated

$$\int_{-\infty}^\infty e^{-x^2}\, dx.$$

However, what does it mean to have an infinite upper end value? Infinity is not a number and so should not serve as one end value of an interval of integration. The meaning of (65) is suggested by the very problem that gives rise to it, namely,

**(66)**
$$\lim_{b\to\infty} \int_1^b \frac{1}{x^2}\, dx.$$

By $b$ approaching $\infty$ we do not mean that $b$ approaches a fixed quantity $\infty$, but that $b$ takes on larger and larger values, in fact, values larger than any number one cares to name.

The value of (66) is obtained thus. By using the fundamental theorem, (66) becomes

$$\lim_{b\to\infty} \left\{ -\frac{1}{x} \Big|_1^b \right\}$$

or

**(67)**
$$\lim_{b\to\infty} \left\{ -\frac{1}{b} + 1 \right\}.$$

**Figure 25-14**

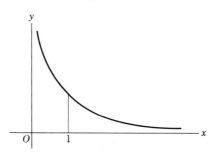

As $b$ becomes infinite, $\lim -1/b = 0$. Hence the value of the limit in (67) is 1.

Thus we make the following

**Definition:** The value of

$$(68) \qquad \int_a^\infty f(x)\, dx$$

is defined to be

$$(69) \qquad \lim_{b \to \infty} \int_a^b f(x)\, dx.$$

Likewise, the general definition of the improper integral

$$(70) \qquad \int_{-\infty}^b f(x)\, dx$$

is

$$(71) \qquad \lim_{a \to -\infty} \int_a^b f(x)\, dx.$$

We would like to emphasize that there is a degree of arbitrariness in all of the above definitions of the improper integrals. In the case of an integral such as (58) we saw that two definitions are possible, one involving a single $\epsilon$ as in (60) and the other involving $\epsilon_1$ and $\epsilon_2$ as in (62). Which one we use depends on what we seek to represent.* The general point involved here is a deep one and comes up in all applications of mathematics. Many concepts of mathematics are suggested directly by physical phenomena or physical problems, and in these cases there is little question about how the mathematical concept is to be framed. Thus the derivative as a representation of instantaneous rate of change and the definite integral as the representation of area under a continuous function are scarcely open to question. However, especially when infinity is involved either in the integrand or as an end value of an interval of integration, there may be some question as to what mathematical formulation fits the geometrical or physical situation. Infinite time intervals and the infinite extent of objects do not occur in our experience. When some quantity extends so far out in time or space that its values become enormously large, we might consider infinity as the best mathematical idealization. But this idealization may be questionable. Let us consider an example.

*In this book we have decided that the definition suggested by (62) is the one that we shall adopt. There are, however, occasions in mathematics when the definition involving only a single $\epsilon$ in place of $\epsilon_1$ and $\epsilon_2$ is adopted. That is, the value of the improper integral (63) is (64), except that $\epsilon$ replaces $\epsilon_1$ and $\epsilon_2$, and we ask for the limit of the entire expression in (64) as $\epsilon$ approaches 0. This limit is called the Cauchy principal value of (63).

Consider the area (Fig. 25-15) under the curve $y = 1/x$ from $x = 1$ to $x = b$. This area, as we know, is given by

**(72)**

$$A = \int_1^b \frac{1}{x} \, dx$$

$$= \log x \Big|_1^b$$

$$= \log b.$$

Now let us consider the volume of revolution generated by this area. The formula for the volume being

$$V = \int_a^b \pi y^2 \, dx,$$

our volume is

**(73)**
$$V = \int_1^b \frac{\pi}{x^2} \, dx = \pi \left( -\frac{1}{x} \right) \Big|_1^b = \pi \left[ 1 - \left( \frac{1}{b} \right) \right].$$

Suppose that we now let $b$ become infinite. Then in place of the integral in (72) we have

$$A = \int_1^\infty \frac{1}{x} \, dx.$$

By our definition of the improper integral

**(74)**
$$A = \lim_{b \to \infty} \int_1^b \frac{1}{x} \, dx = \lim_{b \to \infty} \log b = \infty.$$

On the other hand, when $b$ is infinite the volume integral (73) becomes

$$V = \int_1^\infty \frac{\pi}{x^2} \, dx,$$

**Figure 25-15**

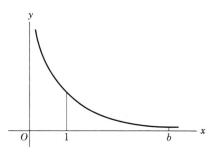

and by our definition of the improper integral

**(75)**
$$V = \lim_{b \to \infty} \int_1^b \frac{\pi}{x^2}\, dx = \lim_{b \to \infty} \left\{ \pi\left(1 - \frac{1}{b}\right)\right\} = \pi.$$

If we compare (74) and (75), we see that an infinite area generates a finite volume of revolution. In other words, our use of the improper integrals to represent area and volume extending indefinitely far out leads to a conclusion which is intuitively objectionable but which we accept nevertheless as long as we do not run into a difficulty in an actual application.

The situation is complicated still more if we consider the area of the surface generated by revolving about the $x$-axis the arc from $x = 1$ to $x = \infty$ of $y = 1/x$. The formula for the area $S$ of a surface of revolution is

$$S = 2\pi \int_a^b y\sqrt{1 + y'^2}\, dx.$$

In the present case

**(76)**
$$S = 2\pi \int_1^\infty \frac{\sqrt{1 + 1/x^4}}{x}\, dx = 2\pi \int_1^\infty \frac{\sqrt{x^4 + 1}}{x^3}\, dx.$$

To integrate this expression, we make the change of variable

$$x = \sqrt{u}\ .$$

Then

$$S = 2\pi \int_1^\infty \frac{\sqrt{u^2 + 1}}{u^{3/2}} \cdot \frac{1}{2\sqrt{u}}\, du = \pi \int_1^\infty \frac{\sqrt{u^2 + 1}}{u^2}\, du.$$

Now, by the meaning of the improper integral,

$$S = \pi \lim_{b \to \infty} \int_1^b \frac{\sqrt{u^2 + 1}}{u^2}\, du.$$

Use of the integral formula 51 in the Table of Integrals gives

**(77)**
$$S = \pi \lim_{b \to \infty} \left\{ -\frac{\sqrt{b^2 + 1}}{b} + \log\left(b + \sqrt{b^2 + 1}\ \right)\right\}$$

$$- \pi\left\{ -\sqrt{2} + \log\left(1 + \sqrt{2}\ \right)\right\}.$$

We must now evaluate the quantity in the first pair of braces as $b$ becomes infinite. As for $-\sqrt{b^2 + 1}\ /b$, this approaches $-1$. The logarithm term becomes infinite. Since the only other quantity involved in (77) is finite, the area of the surface of revolution is infinite.

This result, in the light of the preceding ones, is disturbing. The infinite surface area encloses a finite volume. To put the matter in physical terms, we could fill the volume with a finite amount of paint but cannot paint the surface. As a matter of fact, if we filled the volume with paint, the inside surface, which has the same area as the outside, *would be* painted, but the mathematics says that it is not so.

## EXERCISES

**1.** Evaluate $\int_0^2 f(x)\, dx$ where $f(x) = \begin{cases} x^2 \text{ for } 0 \leq x < 1 \\ 3x^2 \text{ for } 1 \leq x \leq 2. \end{cases}$

**2.** Evaluate the following:

(a) $\int_0^a \dfrac{dx}{\sqrt{a^2 - x^2}}$    *Ans.* $\dfrac{\pi}{2}$.

(b) $\int_0^1 \dfrac{dx}{x^2}$.    *Ans.* No value.

(c) $\int_0^a \dfrac{x\, dx}{\sqrt{a^2 - x^2}}$.    *Ans. a.*

(d) $\int_0^2 \dfrac{dx}{x}$.

(e) $\int_0^1 \dfrac{dx}{x^a}$ for $0 < a < 1$.    *Ans.* $\dfrac{1}{1-a}$.

(f) $\int_0^1 \dfrac{dx}{x^a}$ for $a > 1$.

(g) $\int_0^1 \dfrac{dx}{(x-1)^{2/3}}$.    *Ans.* 3.

(h) $\int_1^2 \dfrac{dx}{(x-1)^{2/3}}$.

(i) $\int_0^1 \dfrac{dx}{(1-x)^2}$.    *Ans.* No value.

(j) $\int_0^1 \cot x\, dx$.

(k) $\int_0^{\pi/2} \sec x\, dx$.    *Ans.* No value.

(l) $\int_{-1}^0 \dfrac{dx}{x^2 - x}$.

**3.** Evaluate the following:

(a) $\int_{-1}^1 \dfrac{dx}{x^2}$.    *Ans.* No value.

(b) $\int_0^2 \dfrac{dx}{(x-1)^2}$.    *Ans.* No value.

(c) $\int_{-1}^1 \dfrac{dx}{x^{2/3}}$.    *Ans.* 6.

(d) $\int_0^{3a} \dfrac{2x\, dx}{(x^2 - a^2)^{2/3}}$    *Ans.* $3a^{2/3}$.

(e) $\int_1^4 \dfrac{dx}{x - 3}$.

(f) $\int_1^4 \dfrac{dx}{(x-3)^2}$.

**4.** Evaluate the following:

(a) $\int_0^\infty e^{-x}\, dx$.    *Ans.* 1.

(b) $\int_0^\infty e^{-ax}\, dx$.    *Ans.* $1/a$.

(c) $\int_1^\infty \dfrac{dx}{x}$.

(d) $\int_1^\infty \dfrac{dx}{x^2}$.    *Ans.* 1.

(e) $\int_1^\infty \dfrac{dx}{x^a}$ for $a > 1$.

(f) $\int_0^\infty \dfrac{x\, dx}{1 + x^2}$.    *Ans.* No value.

(g) $\int_0^\infty \cos x\, dx$.

(h) $\int_2^\infty \dfrac{dx}{(x-1)^2}$.    *Ans.* 1.

(i) $\int_1^\infty \log x\, dx$.

(j) $\int_0^\infty x e^{-x}\, dx$.    *Ans.* 1.

(k) $\int_{-\infty}^\infty \dfrac{dx}{1 + x^2}$.

(l) $\int_0^\infty x e^{-x^2}\, dx$.

(m) $\displaystyle\int_2^\infty \frac{dx}{x^2 - x}$.  *Ans.* log 2.  (n) $\displaystyle\int_0^\infty e^{-x} \cos x \, dx$.

5. If an object is projected along smooth ground with an initial velocity of 100 ft/sec, but is subject to air resistance that is proportional to the velocity, the velocity of the object at any time $t$ is given by $v = 100e^{-kt}$ where $k$ is a constant which depends on the amount of air resistance. The distance covered by the object in infinite time is given by $\displaystyle\int_0^\infty 100e^{-kt} \, dt$. Find this distance.

*Ans.* $100/k$.

6. If an object is projected along smooth ground with an initial velocity of 100 ft/sec, but is subject to air resistance that is proportional to the square of the velocity, the velocity of the object at any time $t$ is given by $v = 100/(1 + 100kt)$ where $k$ is a constant which depends on the amount of air resistance. The distance covered by the object in infinite time is given by $\displaystyle\int_0^\infty 100 \, dt/(1 + 100kt)$. Find this distance.

7. If an object is dropped in a gas for which the resistance is proportional to the velocity and if gravity acts, the velocity at any time $t$ is given by $v = (32/k)(1 - e^{-kt})$ where $k$ is a constant that depends on the amount of resistance. The distance fallen by the object in infinite time is given by $\displaystyle\int_0^\infty \frac{32}{k}(1 - e^{-kt}) \, dt$. Find the distance.

*Ans.* $\infty$.

8. (a)  Calculate the gravitational force that an infinitely extended, thin plane of mass $M$ per unit volume exerts on a mass $m$ situated $h$ units above it.

   *Suggestion:* Use the result in formula (36) of Chapter 16 to formulate the improper integral.  *Ans.* $2\pi GMmt$.

   (b)  The result in part (a) is independent of $h$. Can you explain in physical terms why this is reasonable?

9. Show that the length of arc of the logarithmic or equiangular spiral $\rho = ae^{b\theta}$, $a$ and $b$ positive, from $\theta = 0$ to $\theta = -\infty$ is equal to the length $PQ$ of the tangent (Fig. 25-16) to the curve at $\theta = 0$.

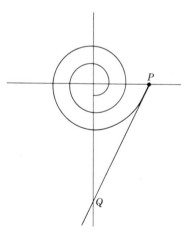

**Figure 25-16**

## 10. The Fundamental Theorem of the Calculus. We know from our earlier work that although the concept of the definite integral as a limit of a

sequence of sums is extremely useful in representing geometrical and physical quantities, the evaluation of the definite integral is carried out by using the fundamental theorem of the calculus; that is, we find the antiderivative of the integrand and then substitute the upper and lower end values of the interval of integration. Hence the fundamental theorem is indispensable. Our proof of the fundamental theorem (Chapter 9, Section 4) rested on the facts that the area under the curve can be expressed as a definite integral and that the same area can be obtained by antidifferentiation. If the concept of the definite integral is freed, as it now is, from any dependence on area, then it would also seem desirable to free the proof of the fundamental theorem from any dependence on geometrical considerations. We shall sketch the purely analytical proof of the fundamental theorem.

Let us first establish just what it is we want to prove. We have

$$\int_a^b f(x)\, dx$$

and we wish to show that we can evaluate this definite integral by finding an antiderivative of $f(x)$, which will be some function $F(x)$, and then calculate $F(b) - F(a)$.

The connection between $F(x)$ and the definite integral $\int_a^b f(x)\, dx$ seems to be elusive because the definite integral is a number which is defined without any reference to differentiation. However, suppose that instead of considering $\int_a^b f(x)\, dx$ we consider

(78) $$\int_a^u f(x)\, dx$$

where $u$ is any value of $x$ between $a$ and $b$. This definite integral now depends on the value of $u$ and so is a function of $u$. Let us introduce the functional symbol $F(u)$ to denote this new function, that is,

(79) $$F(u) = \int_a^u f(x)\, dx.$$

Now let us find out what the derived function of $F(u)$ is. To do this we apply the method of increments. First,

$$F(u + \Delta u) = \int_a^{u+\Delta u} f(x)\, dx.$$

Then

$$F(u + \Delta u) - F(u) = \int_a^{u+\Delta u} f(x)\, dx - \int_a^u f(x)\, dx.$$

Now by a theorem on definite integrals [see (46)],

$$F(u + \Delta u) - F(u) = \int_u^{u + \Delta u} f(x)\, dx$$

and

(80) $$\frac{F(u + \Delta u) - F(u)}{\Delta u} = \frac{\int_u^{u + \Delta u} f(x)\, dx}{\Delta u}.$$

We would like now to find the limit of the right side as $\Delta u$ approaches 0. If we take the limit of the numerator and the limit of the denominator separately and then divide, we shall surely run into trouble. For the limit of the denominator is 0 and the limit of the numerator is also 0. The way out of the difficulty is to use the law of the mean for integrals.* Hence, we may write in place of (80)

$$\frac{F(u + \Delta u) - F(u)}{\Delta u} = \frac{f(c)\, \Delta u}{\Delta u}$$

where $c$ is some value of $x$ in the interval $u \leq x \leq u + \Delta u$. Now we can cancel $\Delta u$ and

$$\frac{F(u + \Delta u) - F(u)}{\Delta u} = f(c).$$

If we let $\Delta u$ approach 0, then $c$, which is always in the interval $(u, u + \Delta u)$, must approach $u$. Hence

(81) $$\lim_{\Delta u \to 0} \frac{F(u + \Delta u) - F(u)}{\Delta u} = f(u)$$

or

$$F'(u) = f(u).$$

(If $\Delta u$ is negative, the argument still holds except for small changes in notation.) It does not matter what letter we use to represent the independent variable, and so we can as well write

$$F'(x) = f(x).$$

---

*The law of the mean for integrals, which we shall not prove, states that if $f(x)$ is continuous, there is a value $c$ such that $\int_a^b f(x)\, dx = f(c)(b - a)$ where $a \leq c \leq b$.

What we have shown so far is that the function $F(u)$ defined by

$$F(u) = \int_a^u f(x)\, dx$$

is an antiderivative of $f(u)$. We say an antiderivative because there is an infinite number of antiderivatives, any two of which differ from each other by a constant (Chapter 13, Section 2). Hence if we take any antiderivative of $f(x)$, say $G(x)$, we can write

$$G(u) = \int_a^u f(x)\, dx + C.$$

When $u = a$,

$$G(a) = 0 + C$$

or

$$C = G(a).$$

Then

$$G(u) = \int_a^u f(x)\, dx + G(a).$$

When $u = b$,

$$G(b) = \int_a^b f(x)\, dx + G(a)$$

or

**(82)** $$G(b) - G(a) = \int_a^b f(x)\, dx.$$

We now have the result that we sought. Equation (82) says that if $G(x)$ is any antiderivative of $f(x)$, then $G(b) - G(a)$ is the value of the definite integral $\int_a^b f(x)\, dx$. In other words, we may evaluate the definite integral by antidifferentiation.

## EXERCISES

1. Without evaluating the following definite integrals give bounds within which they lie, that is, give two numbers, one less than and one more than the value of the integral.

   (a) $\int_0^{\pi/2} \sin^5 x\, dx.$      *Ans.* $0, \dfrac{\pi}{2}.$      (b) $\int_0^{\pi} \sin^5 x\, dx.$

(c) $\int_0^1 (x^{10} + 9x^9)\, dx.$     *Ans.* 0, 10.  (e) $\int_0^1 e^{-x^2}\, dx.$     *Ans.* $e^{-1}$, 1.

(d) $\int_0^1 e^{x^2}\, dx.$

**2.** Given that $F(u) = \int_0^u x\, dx$, calculate $F(3)$.     *Ans.* $\frac{9}{2}$.

**3.** Given that

$$F(u) = \int_1^u (x \sin x + e^x \sin x)^2\, dx,$$

show by any sound argument, geometrical or analytical, that $F(u)$ is an increasing function of $u$.

*Suggestion:* The integrand is positive.

**4.** Given that

$$F(u) = \int_1^u x^{3/2} \sin x\, dx,$$

find $F'(x)$.     *Ans.* $x^{3/2} \sin x$.

**5.** Evaluate the following expressions:

(a) $\displaystyle\lim_{h \to 0} \int_\pi^{\pi + h} \sin x\, dx.$     *Ans.* 0.

(b) $\displaystyle\lim_{h \to 0} \int_{\pi/2}^{(\pi/2)+h} \sqrt{\sin x}\, dx.$

(c) $\displaystyle\frac{d}{dt} \int_0^{t^2} \sin x\, dx.$

        *Suggestion:* Let $t^2 = u$ and use the chain rule.

(d) $\displaystyle\frac{d}{dt} \int_0^{t^2} \sqrt{\sin x}\, dx.$     *Ans.* $2t\sqrt{\sin t^2}$ (if $\sin t^2 > 0$).

(e) $\displaystyle\lim_{h \to 0} \frac{1}{h} \int_a^{a+h} f(t)\, dt.$

(f) $\displaystyle\lim_{x \to 0} \frac{1}{x} \int_0^x \sqrt{t^3 + 4}\, dt.$     *Ans.* 2.

(g) $\displaystyle\lim_{x \to 1} \frac{1}{x - 1} \int_1^x \tan^{-1} t\, dt.$     *Ans.* $\pi/4$.

**6.** The function $F(x) = \displaystyle\int_0^x \frac{dt}{\sqrt{t^3 + 1}}$ cannot be evaluated in terms of elementary functions. Nevertheless, answer the following questions:

(a) What is $F(0)$?     *Ans.* 0.
(b) Is $F(-\frac{1}{2}) > 0$ or $< 0$?
(c) Does $F(-3)$ exist?     *Ans.* No.
(d) What is $F'(x)$?

(e) What is $F''(x)$?     *Ans.* $-\dfrac{3}{2}\, \dfrac{x^2}{\sqrt{(x^3 + 1)^3}}$.

(f) In view of (a), (d), and (e), give an approximate expression for $F(x)$ around $x = 0$ by using Taylor's theorem.
$$\text{\textit{Ans.} } x + F'''(\mu)\frac{x^3}{3!},\ 0 < \mu < x.$$

(g) Is $F(x)$ an increasing function for all $x > -1$?

7. Suppose that $F(x) = \int_0^x (t + 1) \tan^{-1} \dfrac{1}{1 + t^2} \, dt$. Without evaluating the integral find the following:

(a) $F'(x)$.

*Ans.* $(x + 1) \tan^{-1} \dfrac{1}{1 + x^2}$.

(b) $F'(0)$.

8. If $F(x) = \int_0^x e^{-t^2} \, dt$, what is $F'(1)$?

9. Find the formula $\rho(r)$ for the variation of density inside a spherical mass of radius $a$ if the attraction that it exerts at any internal point is constant and equal to its value at the surface and if the mean density $\bar{\rho}$ is known.

*Suggestion:* In Exercise 2 of Chapter 16, Section 7, second list, we found that a sphere with density $\rho(r)$ attracts at an internal point $h$ units from the center with a force of $(G/h^2) \int_0^h 4\pi\rho(r)r^2 \, dr$. According to that exercise, at the surface the entire mass acts as though the mass were concentrated at the center. Set up an equality and differentiate. *Ans.* $\rho(r) = 2\bar{\rho}a/3r$.

**11. The Directions of Future Work.** The few sketchy indications we have given in this chapter of a rigorous approach to the calculus evidently suggest that a full presentation of this approach calls for extensive study. Moreover, such an approach must include the rigorous theory of functions of two and three variables.

In Chapter 24 we began the study of ordinary differential equations. However, this subject is a vast one and vital in the investigations of all the sciences. The types of differential equations that arise in the applications are numerous and a fuller study of the subject calls for learning methods of solution of these types and the properties of new functions, usually called special functions or higher transcendental functions, which solve these types. Hence another direction in which one can proceed is to learn more about ordinary differential equations. The subject of differential equations extends to the vast area of partial differential equations in which partial derivatives occur and which must be solved by techniques peculiar to these equations.

Beyond differential equations the calculus is applied to such subjects as Fourier series, differential geometry, and the calculus of variations. The calculus we have studied and the extensions just mentioned deal with functions in which the values of the independent and dependent variables are real numbers. This suggests that there might be a calculus in which the values of the variables are complex numbers. There is such a calculus and it is known as the theory of functions of a complex variable. This study is another direction which one who has learned the elements of calculus can pursue.

All of the above-mentioned extensions of the calculus and many others are immensely important for the mathematician, the physicist, the chemist, and the engineer and are becoming important for the biological and social scientist. The calculus, then, is the heart of enormously significant and diverse mathematical developments, all of which are generally subsumed under the name of analysis.

# TABLES

Table I
**FORMULAS OF GEOMETRY AND TRIGONOMETRY**

Curved surface of a right circular cylinder with height $h$ and base of radius $r$:
$$2\pi rh.$$
Volume of right circular cylinder of height $h$ and base of radius $r$:
$$\pi r^2 h.$$
Surface of a sphere of radius $r$:
$$4\pi r^2.$$
Volume of a sphere of radius $r$:
$$\tfrac{4}{3}\pi r^3.$$
Curved surface of a right circular cone with altitude $h$ and base of radius $r$:
$$\pi r \sqrt{r^2 + h^2}\,.$$
Volume of a right circular cone with altitude $h$ and base of radius $r$:
$$\tfrac{1}{3}\pi r^2 h.$$
Curved surface of a frustrum of a right circular cone with base of radius $r_1$, top of radius $r_2$, and altitude $h$:
$$\pi(r_1 + r_2)\sqrt{h^2 + (r_2 - r_1)^2}\,.$$

**TRIGONOMETRIC IDENTITIES**

$$\sin x \equiv \sin(180 - x) \equiv -\sin(180 + x) \equiv -\sin(360 - x).$$
$$\sin x \equiv \cos(90 - x) \equiv -\cos(90 + x).$$
$$\cos x \equiv -\cos(180 - x) \equiv -\cos(180 + x) \equiv \cos(360 - x).$$
$$\cos x \equiv \sin(90 - x) \equiv \sin(90 + x).$$
$$\tan x \equiv -\tan(180 - x) \equiv \tan(180 + x) \equiv -\tan(360 - x).$$
$$\sin^2 x + \cos^2 x \equiv 1.$$
$$1 + \tan^2 x \equiv \sec^2 x.$$
$$1 + \cot^2 x \equiv \csc^2 x.$$
$$\sin(x \pm y) \equiv \sin x \cos y \pm \cos x \sin y.$$
$$\cos(x \pm y) \equiv \cos x \cos y \mp \sin x \sin y.$$
$$\tan(x \pm y) \equiv \frac{\tan x \pm \tan y}{1 \pm \tan x \tan y}.$$
$$\sin 2x \equiv 2 \sin x \cos x.$$
$$\cos 2x \equiv \cos^2 x - \sin^2 x.$$
$$\tan 2x \equiv \frac{2 \tan x}{1 - \tan^2 x}.$$
$$\sin \frac{x}{2} \equiv \pm\sqrt{\frac{1 - \cos x}{2}}.$$
$$\cos \frac{x}{2} \equiv \pm\sqrt{\frac{1 + \cos x}{2}}.$$
$$\tan \frac{x}{2} \equiv \pm\sqrt{\frac{1 - \cos x}{1 + \cos x}} = \frac{\sin x}{1 + \cos x}.$$
$$\sin x \pm \sin y \equiv 2 \sin \tfrac{1}{2}(x \pm y) \cos \tfrac{1}{2}(x \mp y).$$
$$\cos x + \cos y \equiv 2 \cos \tfrac{1}{2}(x + y) \cos \tfrac{1}{2}(x - y).$$
$$\cos x - \cos y \equiv -2 \sin \tfrac{1}{2}(x + y) \sin \tfrac{1}{2}(x - y).$$

**RELATIONS AMONG THE SIDES AND ANGLES OF ANY TRIANGLE**

Law of sines: $\hspace{80pt} \dfrac{a}{\sin A} = \dfrac{b}{\sin B} = \dfrac{c}{\sin C}.$

Law of cosines: $\hspace{70pt} c^2 = a^2 + b^2 - 2ab \cos C.$

Table II
**DEGREES TO RADIANS**

| ° | Radians | ′ | Radians | ″ | Radians |
|---|---------|---|---------|---|---------|
| 1 | 0.01745 33 | 1 | 0.00029 09 | 1 | 0.00000 48 |
| 2 | 0.03490 66 | 2 | 0.00058 18 | 2 | 0.00000 97 |
| 3 | 0.05235 99 | 3 | 0.00087 27 | 3 | 0.00001 45 |
| 4 | 0.06981 32 | 4 | 0.00116 36 | 4 | 0.00001 94 |
| 5 | 0.08726 65 | 5 | 0.00145 44 | 5 | 0.00002 42 |
| 6 | 0.10471 98 | 6 | 0.00174 53 | 6 | 0.00002 91 |
| 7 | 0.12217 30 | 7 | 0.00203 62 | 7 | 0.00003 39 |
| 8 | 0.13962 63 | 8 | 0.00232 71 | 8 | 0.00003 88 |
| 9 | 0.15707 96 | 9 | 0.00261 80 | 9 | 0.00004 36 |
| 10 | 0.17453 29 | 10 | 0.00290 89 | 10 | 0.00004 85 |
| 20 | 0.34906 59 | 20 | 0.00581 78 | 20 | 0.00009 70 |
| 30 | 0.52359 88 | 30 | 0.00872 66 | 30 | 0.00014 54 |
| 40 | 0.69813 17 | 40 | 0.01163 55 | 40 | 0.00019 39 |
| 50 | 0.87266 46 | 50 | 0.01454 44 | 50 | 0.00024 24 |
| 60 | 1.04719 76 | 60 | 0.01745 33 | 60 | 0.00029 09 |
| 70 | 1.22173 05 | | | | |
| 80 | 1.39626 34 | | | | |
| 90 | 1.57079 63 | | | | |

Table III
**RADIANS TO DEGREES**

| Radians | 1.0 | 0.1 | 0.01 | 0.001 | 0.0001 |
|---------|-----|-----|------|-------|--------|
| 1 | 57°17′44″.8 | 5°43′46″.5 | 0°34′22″.6 | 0° 3′26″.3 | 0°0′20″.6 |
| 2 | 114°35′29″.6 | 11°27′33″.0 | 1° 8′45″.3 | 0° 6′52″.5 | 0°0′41″.3 |
| 3 | 171°53′14″.4 | 17°11′19″.4 | 1°43′07″.9 | 0°10′18″.8 | 0°1′01″.9 |
| 4 | 229°10′59″.2 | 22°55′05″.9 | 2°17′30″.6 | 0°13′45″.1 | 0°1′22″.5 |
| 5 | 286°28′44″.0 | 28°38′52″.4 | 2°51′53″.2 | 0°17′11″.3 | 0°1′43″.1 |
| 6 | 343°46′28″.8 | 34°22′38″.9 | 3°26′15″.9 | 0°20′37″.6 | 0°2′03″.8 |
| 7 | 401° 4′13″.6 | 40° 6′25″.4 | 4° 0′38″.5 | 0°24′03″.9 | 0°2′24″.4 |
| 8 | 458°21′58″.4 | 45°50′11″.8 | 4°35′01″.2 | 0°27′30″.1 | 0°2′45″.0 |
| 9 | 515°39′43″.3 | 51°33′58″.3 | 5° 9′23″.8 | 0°30′56″.4 | 0°3′05″.6 |

Table IV
## NATURAL TRIGONOMETRIC FUNCTIONS

| Degrees | Radians | Sin | Cos | Tan | Cot | Sec | Csc | | |
|---|---|---|---|---|---|---|---|---|---|
| 0°00′ | .0000 | .0000 | 1.0000 | .0000 | — | 1.000 | — | 1.5708 | 90°00′ |
| 10 | .0029 | .0029 | 1.0000 | .0029 | 343.8 | 1.000 | 343.8 | 1.5679 | 50 |
| 20 | .0058 | .0058 | 1.0000 | .0058 | 171.9 | 1.000 | 171.9 | 1.5650 | 40 |
| 30 | .0087 | .0087 | 1.0000 | .0087 | 114.6 | 1.000 | 114.6 | 1.5621 | 30 |
| 40 | .0116 | .0116 | .9999 | .0116 | 85.94 | 1.000 | 85.95 | 1.5592 | 20 |
| 50 | .0145 | .0145 | .9999 | .0145 | 68.75 | 1.000 | 68.76 | 1.5563 | 10 |
| 1°00′ | .0175 | .0175 | .9998 | .0175 | 57.29 | 1.000 | 57.30 | 1.5533 | 89°00′ |
| 10 | .0204 | .0204 | .9998 | .0204 | 49.10 | 1.000 | 49.11 | 1.5504 | 50 |
| 20 | .0233 | .0233 | .9997 | .0233 | 42.96 | 1.000 | 42.98 | 1.5475 | 40 |
| 30 | .0262 | .0262 | .9997 | .0262 | 38.19 | 1.000 | 38.20 | 1.5446 | 30 |
| 40 | .0291 | .0291 | .9996 | .0291 | 34.37 | 1.000 | 34.38 | 1.5417 | 20 |
| 50 | .0320 | .0320 | .9995 | .0320 | 31.24 | 1.001 | 31.26 | 1.5388 | 10 |
| 2°00′ | .0349 | .0349 | .9994 | .0349 | 28.64 | 1.001 | 28.65 | 1.5359 | 88°00′ |
| 10 | .0378 | .0378 | .9993 | .0378 | 26.43 | 1.001 | 26.45 | 1.5330 | 50 |
| 20 | .0407 | .0407 | .9992 | .0407 | 24.54 | 1.001 | 24.56 | 1.5301 | 40 |
| 30 | .0436 | .0436 | .9990 | .0437 | 22.90 | 1.001 | 22.93 | 1.5272 | 30 |
| 40 | .0465 | .0465 | .9989 | .0466 | 21.47 | 1.001 | 21.49 | 1.5243 | 20 |
| 50 | .0495 | .0494 | .9988 | .0495 | 20.21 | 1.001 | 20.23 | 1.5213 | 10 |
| 3°00′ | .0524 | .0523 | .9986 | .0524 | 19.08 | 1.001 | 19.11 | 1.5184 | 87°00′ |
| 10 | .0553 | .0552 | .9985 | .0553 | 18.07 | 1.002 | 18.10 | 1.5155 | 50 |
| 20 | .0582 | .0581 | .9983 | .0582 | 17.17 | 1.002 | 17.20 | 1.5126 | 40 |
| 30 | .0611 | .0610 | .9981 | .0612 | 16.35 | 1.002 | 16.38 | 1.5097 | 30 |
| 40 | .0640 | .0640 | .9980 | .0641 | 15.60 | 1.002 | 15.64 | 1.5068 | 20 |
| 50 | .0669 | .0669 | .9978 | .0670 | 14.92 | 1.002 | 14.96 | 1.5039 | 10 |
| 4°00′ | .0698 | .0698 | .9976 | .0699 | 14.30 | 1.002 | 14.34 | 1.5010 | 86°00′ |
| 10 | .0727 | .0727 | .9974 | .0729 | 13.73 | 1.003 | 13.76 | 1.4981 | 50 |
| 20 | .0756 | .0756 | .9971 | .0758 | 13.20 | 1.003 | 13.23 | 1.4952 | 40 |
| 30 | .0785 | .0785 | .9969 | .0787 | 12.71 | 1.003 | 12.75 | 1.4923 | 30 |
| 40 | .0814 | .0814 | .9967 | .0816 | 12.25 | 1.003 | 12.29 | 1.4893 | 20 |
| 50 | .0844 | .0843 | .9964 | .0846 | 11.83 | 1.004 | 11.87 | 1.4864 | 10 |
| 5°00′ | .0873 | .0872 | .9962 | .0875 | 11.43 | 1.004 | 11.47 | 1.4835 | 85°00′ |
| 10 | .0902 | .0901 | .9959 | .0904 | 11.06 | 1.004 | 11.10 | 1.4806 | 50 |
| 20 | .0931 | .0929 | .9957 | .0934 | 10.71 | 1.004 | 10.76 | 1.4777 | 40 |
| 30 | .0960 | .0958 | .9954 | .0963 | 10.39 | 1.005 | 10.43 | 1.4748 | 30 |
| 40 | .0989 | .0987 | .9951 | .0992 | 10.08 | 1.005 | 10.13 | 1.4719 | 20 |
| 50 | .1018 | .1016 | .9948 | .1022 | 9.788 | 1.005 | 9.839 | 1.4690 | 10 |
| 6°00′ | .1047 | .1045 | .9945 | .1051 | 9.514 | 1.006 | 9.567 | 1.4661 | 84°00′ |
| 10 | .1076 | .1074 | .9942 | .1080 | 9.255 | 1.006 | 9.309 | 1.4632 | 50 |
| 20 | .1105 | .1103 | .9939 | .1110 | 9.010 | 1.006 | 9.065 | 1.4603 | 40 |
| 30 | .1134 | .1132 | .9936 | .1139 | 8.777 | 1.006 | 8.834 | 1.4573 | 30 |
| 40 | .1164 | .1161 | .9932 | .1169 | 8.556 | 1.007 | 8.614 | 1.4544 | 20 |
| 50 | .1193 | .1190 | .9929 | .1198 | 8.345 | 1.007 | 8.405 | 1.4515 | 10 |
| 7°00′ | .1222 | .1219 | .9925 | .1228 | 8.144 | 1.008 | 8.206 | 1.4486 | 83°00′ |
| 10 | .1251 | .1248 | .9922 | .1257 | 7.953 | 1.008 | 8.016 | 1.4457 | 50 |
| 20 | .1280 | .1276 | .9918 | .1287 | 7.770 | 1.008 | 7.834 | 1.4428 | 40 |
| 30 | .1309 | .1305 | .9914 | .1317 | 7.596 | 1.009 | 7.661 | 1.4399 | 30 |
| 40 | .1338 | .1334 | .9911 | .1346 | 7.429 | 1.009 | 7.496 | 1.4370 | 20 |
| 50 | .1367 | .1363 | .9907 | .1376 | 7.269 | 1.009 | 7.337 | 1.4341 | 10 |
| 8°00′ | .1396 | .1392 | .9903 | .1405 | 7.115 | 1.010 | 7.185 | 1.4312 | 82°00′ |
| 10 | .1425 | .1421 | .9899 | .1435 | 6.968 | 1.010 | 7.040 | 1.4283 | 50 |
| | | Cos | Sin | Cot | Tan | Csc | Sec | Radians | Degrees |

Table IV
(continued)

| Degrees | Radians | Sin | Cos | Tan | Cot | Sec | Csc | | |
|---|---|---|---|---|---|---|---|---|---|
| 20 | .1454 | .1449 | .9894 | .1465 | 6.827 | 1.011 | 6.900 | 1.4254 | 40 |
| 30 | .1484 | .1478 | .9890 | .1495 | 6.691 | 1.011 | 6.765 | 1:4224 | 30 |
| 40 | .1513 | .1507 | .9886 | .1524 | 6.561 | 1.012 | 6.636 | 1.4195 | 20 |
| 50 | .1542 | .1536 | .9881 | .1554 | 6.435 | 1.012 | 6.512 | 1.4166 | 10 |
| 9°00′ | .1571 | .1564 | .9877 | .1584 | 6.314 | 1.012 | 6.392 | 1.4137 | 81°00′ |
| 10 | .1600 | .1593 | .9872 | .1614 | 6.197 | 1.013 | 6.277 | 1.4108 | 50 |
| 20 | .1629 | .1622 | .9868 | .1644 | 6.084 | 1.013 | 6.166 | 1.4079 | 40 |
| 30 | .1658 | .1650 | .9863 | .1673 | 5.976 | 1.014 | 6.059 | 1.4050 | 30 |
| 40 | .1687 | .1679 | .9858 | .1703 | 5.871 | 1.014 | 5.955 | 1.4021 | 20 |
| 50 | .1716 | .1708 | .9853 | .1733 | 5.769 | 1.015 | 5.855 | 1.3992 | 10 |
| 10°00′ | .1745 | .1736 | .9848 | .1763 | 5.671 | 1.015 | 5.759 | 1.3963 | 80°00′ |
| 10 | .1774 | .1765 | .9843 | .1793 | 5.576 | 1.016 | 5.665 | 1.3934 | 50 |
| 20 | .1804 | .1794 | .9838 | .1823 | 5.485 | 1.016 | 5.575 | 1.3904 | 40 |
| 30 | .1833 | .1822 | .9833 | .1853 | 5.396 | 1.017 | 5.487 | 1.3875 | 30 |
| 40 | .1862 | .1851 | .9827 | .1883 | 5.309 | 1.018 | 5.403 | 1.3846 | 20 |
| 50 | .1891 | .1880 | .9822 | .1914 | 5.226 | 1.018 | 5.320 | 1.3817 | 10 |
| 11°00′ | .1920 | .1908 | .9816 | .1944 | 5.145 | 1.019 | 5.241 | 1.3788 | 79°00′ |
| 10 | .1949 | .1937 | .9811 | .1974 | 5.066 | 1.019 | 5.164 | 1.3759 | 50 |
| 20 | .1978 | .1965 | .9805 | .2004 | 4.989 | 1.020 | 5.089 | 1.3730 | 40 |
| 30 | ˙.2007 | .1994 | .9799 | .2035 | 4.915 | 1.020 | 5.016 | 1.3701 | 30 |
| 40 | .2036 | .2022 | .9793 | .2065 | 4.843 | 1.021 | 4.945 | 1.3672 | 20 |
| 50 | .2065 | .2051 | .9787 | .2095 | 4.773 | 1.022 | 4.876 | 1.3643 | 10 |
| 12°00′ | .2094 | .2079 | .9781 | .2126 | 4.705 | 1.022 | 4.810 | 1.3614 | 78°00′ |
| 10 | .2123 | .2108 | .9775 | .2156 | 4.638 | 1.023 | 4.745 | 1.3584 | 50 |
| 20 | .2153 | .2136 | .9769 | .2186 | 4.574 | 1.024 | 4.682 | 1.3555 | 40 |
| 30 | .2182 | .2164 | .9763 | .2217 | 4.511 | 1.024 | 4.620 | 1.3526 | 30 |
| 40 | .2211 | .2193 | .9757 | .2247 | 4.449 | 1.025 | 4.560 | 1.3497 | 20 |
| 50 | .2240 | .2221 | .9750 | .2278 | 4.390 | 1.026 | 4.502 | 1.3468 | 10 |
| 13°00′ | .2269 | .2250 | .9744 | .2309 | 4.331 | 1.026 | 4.445 | 1.3439 | 77°00′ |
| 10 | .2298 | .2278 | .9737 | .2339 | 4.275 | 1.027 | 4.390 | 1.3410 | 50 |
| 20 | .2327 | .2306 | .9730 | .2370 | 4.219 | 1.028 | 4.336 | 1.3381 | 40 |
| 30 | .2356 | .2334 | .9724 | .2401 | 4.165 | 1.028 | 4.284 | 1.3352 | 30 |
| 40 | .2385 | .2363 | .9717 | .2432 | 4.113 | 1.029 | 4.232 | 1.3323 | 20 |
| 50 | .2414 | .2391 | .9710 | .2462 | 4.061 | 1.030 | 4.182 | 1.3294 | 10 |
| 14°00′ | .2443 | .2419 | .9703 | .2493 | 4.011 | 1.031 | 4.134 | 1.3265 | 76°00′ |
| 10 | .2473 | .2447 | .9696 | .2524 | 3.962 | 1.031 | 4.086 | 1.3235 | 50 |
| 20 | .2502 | .2476 | .9689 | .2555 | 3.914 | 1.032 | 4.039 | 1.3206 | 40 |
| 30 | .2531 | .2504 | .9681 | .2586 | 3.867 | 1.033 | 3.994 | 1,.3177 | 30 |
| 40 | .2560 | .2532 | .9674 | .2617 | 3.821 | 1.034 | 3.950 | 1.3148 | 20 |
| 50 | .2589 | .2560 | .9667 | .2648 | 3.776 | 1.034 | 3.906 | 1.3119 | 10 |
| 15°00′ | .2618 | .2588 | .9659 | .2679 | 3.732 | 1.035 | 3.864 | 1.3090 | 75°00′ |
| 10 | .2647 | .2616 | .9652 | .2711 | 3.689 | 1.036 | 3.822 | 1.3061 | 50 |
| 20 | .2676 | .2644 | .9644 | .2742 | 3.647 | 1.037 | 3.782 | 1.3032 | 40 |
| 30 | .2705 | .2672 | .9636 | .2773 | 3.606 | 1.038 | 3.742 | 1.3003 | 30 |
| 40 | .2734 | .2700 | .9628 | .2805 | 3.566 | 1.039 | 3.703 | 1.2974 | 20 |
| 50 | .2763 | .2728 | .9621 | .2836 | 3.526 | 1.039 | 3.665 | 1.2945 | 10 |
| 16°00′ | .2793 | .2756 | .9613 | .2867 | 3.487 | 1.040 | 3.628 | 1.2915 | 74°00′ |
| 10 | .2822 | .2784 | .9605 | .2899 | 3.450 | 1.041 | 3.592 | 1.2886 | 50 |
| 20 | .2851 | .2812 | .9596 | .2931 | 3.412 | 1.042 | 3.556 | 1.2857 | 40 |
| 30 | .2880 | .2840 | .9588 | .2962 | 3.376 | 1.043 | 3.521 | 1.2828 | 30 |
| | | Cos | Sin | Cot | Tan | Csc | Sec | Radians | Degrees |

Table IV
(continued)

| Degrees | Radians | Sin | Cos | Tan | Cot | Sec | Csc | | |
|---|---|---|---|---|---|---|---|---|---|
| 40 | .2909 | .2868 | .9580 | .2994 | 3.340 | 1.044 | 3.487 | 1.2799 | 20 |
| 50 | .2938 | .2896 | .9572 | .3026 | 3.305 | 1.045 | 3.453 | 1.2770 | 10 |
| 17°00′ | .2967 | .2924 | .9563 | .3057 | 3.271 | 1.046 | 3.420 | 1.2741 | 73°00′ |
| 10 | .2996 | .2952 | .9555 | .3089 | 3.237 | 1.047 | 3.388 | 1.2712 | 50 |
| 20 | .3025 | .2979 | .9546 | .3121 | 3.204 | 1.048 | 3.356 | 1.2683 | 40 |
| 30 | .3054 | .3007 | .9537 | .3153 | 3.172 | 1.049 | 3.326 | 1.2654 | 30 |
| 40 | .3083 | .3035 | .9528 | .3185 | 3.140 | 1.049 | 3.295 | 1.2625 | 20 |
| 50 | .3113 | .3062 | .9520 | .3217 | 3.108 | 1.050 | 3.265 | 1.2595 | 10 |
| 18°00′ | .3142 | .3090 | .9511 | .3249 | 3.078 | 1.051 | 3.236 | 1.2566 | 72°00′ |
| 10 | .3171 | .3118 | .9502 | .3281 | 3.047 | 1.052 | 3.207 | 1.2537 | 50 |
| 20 | .3200 | .3145 | .9492 | .3314 | 3.018 | 1.053 | 3.179 | 1.2508 | 40 |
| 30 | .3229 | .3173 | .9483 | .3346 | 2.989 | 1.054 | 3.152 | 1.2479 | 30 |
| 40 | .3258 | .3201 | .9474 | .3378 | 2.960 | 1.056 | 3.124 | 1.2450 | 20 |
| 50 | .3287 | .3228 | .9465 | .3411 | 2.932 | 1.057 | 3.098 | 1.2421 | 10 |
| 19°00′ | .3316 | .3256 | .9455 | .3443 | 2.904 | 1.058 | 3.072 | 1.2392 | 71°00′ |
| 10 | .3345 | .3283 | .9446 | .3476 | 2.877 | 1.059 | 3.046 | 1.2363 | 50 |
| 20 | .3374 | .3311 | .9436 | .3508 | 2.850 | 1.060 | 3.021 | 1.2334 | 40 |
| 30 | .3403 | .3338 | .9426 | .3541 | 2.824 | 1.061 | 2.996 | 1.2305 | 30 |
| 40 | .3432 | .3365 | .9417 | .3574 | 2.798 | 1.062 | 2.971 | 1.2275 | 20 |
| 50 | .3462 | .3393 | .9407 | .3607 | 2.773 | 1.063 | 2.947 | 1.2246 | 10 |
| 20°00′ | .3491 | .3420 | .9397 | .3640 | 2.747 | 1.064 | 2.924 | 1.2217 | 70°00′ |
| 10 | .3520 | .3448 | .9387 | .3673 | 2.723 | 1.065 | 2.901 | 1.2188 | 50 |
| 20 | .3549 | .3475 | .9377 | .3706 | 2.699 | 1.066 | 2.878 | 1.2159 | 40 |
| 30 | .3578 | .3502 | .9367 | .3739 | 2.675 | 1.068 | 2.855 | 1.2130 | 30 |
| 40 | .3607 | .3529 | .9356 | .3772 | 2.651 | 1.069 | 2.833 | 1.2101 | 20 |
| 50 | .3636 | .3557 | .9346 | .3805 | 2.628 | 1.070 | 2.812 | 1.2072 | 10 |
| 21°00′ | .3665 | .3584 | .9336 | .3839 | 2.605 | 1.071 | 2.790 | 1.2043 | 69°00′ |
| 10 | .3694 | .3611 | .9325 | .3872 | 2.583 | 1.072 | 2.769 | 1.2014 | 50 |
| 20 | .3723 | .3638 | .9315 | .3906 | 2.560 | 1.074 | 2.749 | 1.1985 | 40 |
| 30 | .3752 | .3665 | .9304 | .3939 | 2.539 | 1.075 | 2.729 | 1.1956 | 30 |
| 40 | .3782 | .3692 | .9293 | .3973 | 2.517 | 1.076 | 2.709 | 1.1926 | 20 |
| 50 | .3811 | .3719 | .9283 | .4006 | 2.496 | 1.077 | 2.689 | 1.1897 | 10 |
| 22°00′ | .3840 | .3746 | .9272 | .4040 | 2.475 | 1.079 | 2.669 | 1.1868 | 68°00′ |
| 10 | .3869 | .3773 | .9261 | .4074 | 2.455 | 1.080 | 2.650 | 1.1839 | 50 |
| 20 | .3898 | .3800 | .9250 | .4108 | 2.434 | 1.081 | 2.632 | 1.1810 | 40 |
| 30 | .3927 | .3827 | .9239 | .4142 | 2.414 | 1.082 | 2.613 | 1.1781 | 30 |
| 40 | .3956 | .3854 | .9228 | .4176 | 2.394 | 1.084 | 2.595 | 1.1752 | 20 |
| 50 | .3985 | .3881 | .9216 | .4210 | 2.375 | 1.085 | 2.577 | 1.1723 | 10 |
| 23°00′ | .4014 | .3907 | .9205 | .4245 | 2.356 | 1.086 | 2.559 | 1.1694 | 67°00′ |
| 10 | .4043 | .3934 | .9194 | .4279 | 2.337 | 1.088 | 2.542 | 1.1665 | 50 |
| 20 | .4072 | .3961 | .9182 | .4314 | 2.318 | 1.089 | 2.525 | 1.1636 | 40 |
| 30 | .4102 | .3987 | .9171 | .4348 | 2.300 | 1.090 | 2.508 | 1.1606 | 30 |
| 40 | .4131 | .4014 | .9159 | .4383 | 2.282 | 1.092 | 2.491 | 1.1577 | 20 |
| 50 | .4160 | .4041 | .9147 | .4417 | 2.264 | 1.093 | 2.475 | 1.1548 | 10 |
| 24°00′ | .4189 | .4067 | .9135 | .4452 | 2.246 | 1.095 | 2.459 | 1.1519 | 66°00′ |
| 10 | .4218 | .4094 | .9124 | .4487 | 2.229 | 1.096 | 2.443 | 1.1490 | 50 |
| 20 | .4247 | .4120 | .9112 | .4522 | 2.211 | 1.097 | 2.427 | 1.1461 | 40 |
| 30 | .4276 | .4147 | .9100 | .4557 | 2.194 | 1.099 | 2.411 | 1.1432 | 30 |
| 40 | .4305 | .4173 | .9088 | .4592 | 2.177 | 1.100 | 2.396 | 1.1403 | 20 |
| 50 | .4334 | .4200 | .9075 | .4628 | 2.161 | 1.102 | 2.381 | 1.1374 | 10 |
| | | Cos | Sin | Cot | Tan | Csc | Sec | Radians | Degrees |

Table IV
(continued)

| Degrees | Radians | Sin | Cos | Tan | Cot | Sec | Csc | | |
|---|---|---|---|---|---|---|---|---|---|
| 25°00′ | .4363 | .4226 | .9063 | .4663 | 2.145 | 1.103 | 2.366 | 1.1345 | 65°00′ |
| 10 | .4392 | .4253 | .9051 | .4699 | 2.128 | 1.105 | 2.352 | 1.1316 | 50 |
| 20 | .4422 | .4279 | .9038 | .4734 | 2.112 | 1.106 | 2.337 | 1.1286 | 40 |
| 30 | .4451 | .4305 | .9026 | .4770 | 2.097 | 1.108 | 2.323 | 1.1257 | 30 |
| 40 | .4480 | .4331 | .9013 | .4806 | 2.081 | 1.109 | 2.309 | 1.1228 | 20 |
| 50 | .4509 | .4358 | .9001 | .4841 | 2.066 | 1.111 | 2.295 | 1.1199 | 10 |
| 26°00′ | .4538 | .4384 | .8988 | .4877 | 2.050 | 1.113 | 2.281 | 1.1170 | 64°00′ |
| 10 | .4567 | .4410 | .8975 | .4913 | 2.035 | 1.114 | 2.268 | 1.1141 | 50 |
| 20 | .4596 | .4436 | .8962 | .4950 | 2.020 | 1.116 | 2.254 | 1.1112 | 40 |
| 30 | .4625 | .4462 | .8949 | .4986 | 2.006 | 1.117 | 2.241 | 1.1083 | 30 |
| 40 | .4654 | .4488 | .8936 | .5022 | 1.991 | 1.119 | 2.228 | 1.1054 | 20 |
| 50 | .4683 | .4514 | .8923 | .5059 | 1.977 | 1.121 | 2.215 | 1.1025 | 10 |
| 27°00′ | .4712 | .4540 | .8910 | .5095 | 1.963 | 1.122 | 2.203 | 1.0996 | 63°00′ |
| 10 | .4741 | .4566 | .8897 | .5132 | 1.949 | 1.124 | 2.190 | 1.0966 | 50 |
| 20 | .4771 | .4592 | .8884 | .5169 | 1.935 | 1.126 | 2.178 | 1.0937 | 40 |
| 30 | .4800 | .4617 | .8870 | .5206 | 1.921 | 1.127 | 2.166 | 1.0908 | 30 |
| 40 | .4829 | .4643 | .8857 | .5243 | 1.907 | 1.129 | 2.154 | 1.0879 | 20 |
| 50 | .4858 | .4669 | .8843 | .5280 | 1.894 | 1.131 | 2.142 | 1.0850 | 10 |
| 28°00′ | .4887 | .4695 | .8829 | .5317 | 1.881 | 1.133 | 2.130 | 1.0821 | 62°00′ |
| 10 | .4916 | .4720 | .8816 | .5354 | 1.868 | 1.134 | 2.118 | 1.0792 | 50 |
| 20 | .4945 | .4746 | .8802 | .5392 | 1.855 | 1.136 | 2.107 | 1.0763 | 40 |
| 30 | .4974 | .4772 | .8788 | .5430 | 1.842 | 1.138 | 2.096 | 1.0734 | 30 |
| 40 | .5003 | .4797 | .8774 | .5467 | 1.829 | 1.140 | 2.085 | 1.0705 | 20 |
| 50 | .5032 | .4823 | .8760 | .5505 | 1.816 | 1.142 | 2.074 | 1.0676 | 10 |
| 29°00′ | .5061 | .4848 | .8746 | .5543 | 1.804 | 1.143 | 2.063 | 1.0647 | 61°00′ |
| 10 | .5091 | .4874 | .8732 | .5581 | 1.792 | 1.145 | 2.052 | 1.0617 | 50 |
| 20 | .5120 | .4899 | .8718 | .5619 | 1.780 | 1.147 | 2.041 | 1.0588 | 40 |
| 30 | .5149 | .4924 | .8704 | .5658 | 1.767 | 1.149 | 2.031 | 1.0559 | 30 |
| 40 | .5178 | .4950 | .8689 | .5696 | 1.756 | 1.151 | 2.020 | 1.0530 | 20 |
| 50 | .5207 | .4975 | .8675 | .5735 | 1.744 | 1.153 | 2.010 | 1.0501 | 10 |
| 30°00′ | .5236 | .5000 | .8660 | .5774 | 1.732 | 1.155 | 2.000 | 1.0472 | 60°00′ |
| 10 | .5265 | .5025 | .8646 | .5812 | 1.720 | 1.157 | 1.990 | 1.0443 | 50 |
| 20 | .5294 | .5050 | .8631 | .5851 | 1.709 | 1.159 | 1.980 | 1.0414 | 40 |
| 30 | .5323 | .5075 | .8616 | .5890 | 1.698 | 1.161 | 1.970 | 1.0385 | 30 |
| 40 | .5325 | .5100 | .8601 | .5930 | 1.686 | 1.163 | 1.961 | 1.0356 | 20 |
| 50 | .5381 | .5125 | .8587 | .5969 | 1.675 | 1.165 | 1.951 | 1.0327 | 10 |
| 31°00′ | .5411 | .5150 | .8572 | .6009 | 1.664 | 1.167 | 1.942 | 1.0297 | 59°00′ |
| 10 | .5440 | .5175 | .8557 | .6048 | 1.653 | 1.169 | 1.932 | 1.0268 | 50 |
| 20 | .5469 | .5200 | .8542 | .6088 | 1.643 | 1.171 | 1.923 | 1.0239 | 40 |
| 30 | .5498 | .5225 | .8526 | .6128 | 1.632 | 1.173 | 1.914 | 1.0210 | 30 |
| 40 | .5527 | .5250 | .8511 | .6168 | 1.621 | 1.175 | 1.905 | 1.0181 | 20 |
| 50 | .5556 | .5275 | .8496 | .6208 | 1.611 | 1.177 | 1.896 | 1.0152 | 10 |
| 32°00′ | .5585 | .5299 | .8480 | .6249 | 1.600 | 1.179 | 1.887 | 1.0123 | 58°00′ |
| 10 | .5614 | .5324 | .8465 | .6289 | 1.590 | 1.181 | 1.878 | 1.0094 | 50 |
| 20 | .5643 | .5348 | .8450 | .6330 | 1.580 | 1.184 | 1.870 | 1.0065 | 40 |
| 30 | .5672 | .5373 | .8434 | .6371 | 1.570 | 1.186 | 1.861 | 1.0036 | 30 |
| 40 | .5701 | .5398 | .8418 | .6412 | 1.560 | 1.188 | 1.853 | 1.0007 | 20 |
| 50 | .5730 | .5422 | .8403 | .6453 | 1.550 | 1.190 | 1.844 | .0977 | 10 |
| 33°00′ | .5760 | .5446 | .8387 | .6494 | 1.540 | 1.192 | 1.836 | .9948 | 57°00′ |
| 10 | .5789 | .5471 | .8371 | .6536 | 1.530 | 1.195 | 1.828 | .9919 | 50 |
| | | Cos | Sin | Cot | Tan | Csc | Sec | Radians | Degrees |

Table IV
(continued)

| Degrees | Radians | Sin | Cos | Tan | Cot | Sec | Csc | | |
|---|---|---|---|---|---|---|---|---|---|
| 20 | .5818 | .5495 | .8355 | .6577 | 1.520 | 1.197 | 1.820 | .9890 | 40 |
| 30 | .5847 | .5519 | .8339 | .6619 | 1.511 | 1.199 | 1.812 | .9861 | 30 |
| 40 | .5876 | .5544 | .8323 | .6661 | 1.501 | 1.202 | 1.804 | .9832 | 20 |
| 50 | .5905 | .5568 | .8307 | .6703 | 1.492 | 1.204 | 1.796 | .9803 | 10 |
| 34°00′ | .5934 | .5592 | .8290 | .6745 | 1.483 | 1.206 | 1.788 | .9774 | 56°00′ |
| 10 | .5963 | .5616 | .8274 | .6787 | 1.473 | 1.209 | 1.781 | .9745 | 50 |
| 20 | .5992 | .5640 | .8258 | .6830 | 1.464 | 1.211 | 1.773 | .9716 | 40 |
| 30 | .6021 | .5664 | .8241 | .6873 | 1.455 | 1.213 | 1.766 | .9687 | 30 |
| 40 | .6050 | .5688 | .8225 | .6916 | 1.446 | 1.216 | 1.758 | .9657 | 20 |
| 50 | .6080 | .5712 | .8208 | .6959 | 1.437 | 1.218 | 1.751 | .9628 | 10 |
| 35°00′ | .6109 | .5736 | .8192 | .7002 | 1.428 | 1.221 | 1.743 | .9599 | 55°00′ |
| 10 | .6138 | .5760 | .8175 | .7046 | 1.419 | 1.223 | 1.736 | .9570 | 50 |
| 20 | .6167 | .5783 | .8158 | .7089 | 1.411 | 1.226 | 1.729 | .9541 | 40 |
| 30 | .6196 | .5807 | .8141 | .7133 | 1.402 | 1.228 | 1.722 | .9512 | 30 |
| 40 | .6225 | .5831 | .8124 | .7177 | 1.393 | 1.231 | 1.715 | .9483 | 20 |
| 50 | .6254 | .5854 | .8107 | .7221 | 1.385 | 1.233 | 1.708 | .9454 | 10 |
| 36°00′ | .6283 | .5878 | .8090 | .7265 | 1.376 | 1.236 | 1.701 | .9425 | 54°00′ |
| 10 | .6312 | .5901 | .8073 | .7310 | 1.368 | 1.239 | 1.695 | .9396 | 50 |
| 20 | .6341 | .5925 | .8056 | .7355 | 1.360 | 1.241 | 1.688 | .9367 | 40 |
| 30 | .6370 | .5948 | .8039 | .7400 | 1.351 | 1.244 | 1.681 | .9338 | 30 |
| 40 | .6400 | .5972 | .8021 | .7445 | 1.343 | 1.247 | 1.675 | .9308 | 20 |
| 50 | .6429 | .5995 | .8004 | .7490 | 1.335 | 1.249 | 1.668 | .9279 | 10 |
| 37°00′ | .6458 | .6018 | .7986 | .7536 | 1.327 | 1.252 | 1.662 | .9250 | 53°00′ |
| 10 | .6487 | .6041 | .7969 | .7581 | 1.319 | 1.255 | 1.655 | .9221 | 50 |
| 20 | .6516 | .6065 | .7951 | .7627 | 1.311 | 1.258 | 1.649 | .9192 | 40 |
| 30 | .6545 | .6088 | .7934 | .7673 | 1.303 | 1.260 | 1.643 | .9163 | 30 |
| 40 | .6574 | .6111 | .7916 | .7720 | 1.295 | 1.263 | 1.636 | .9134 | 20 |
| 50 | .6603 | .6134 | .7898 | .7766 | 1.288 | 1.266 | 1.630 | .9105 | 10 |
| 38°00′ | .6632 | .6157 | .7880 | .7813 | 1.280 | 1.269 | 1.624 | .9076 | 52°00′ |
| 10 | .6661 | .6180 | .7862 | .7860 | 1.272 | 1.272 | 1.618 | .9047 | 50 |
| 20 | .6690 | .6202 | .7844 | .7907 | 1.265 | 1.275 | 1.612 | .9018 | 40 |
| 30 | .6720 | .6225 | .7826 | .7954 | 1.257 | 1.278 | 1.606 | .8988 | 30 |
| 40 | .6749 | .6248 | .7808 | .8002 | 1.250 | 1.281 | 1.601 | .8959 | 20 |
| 50 | .6778 | .6271 | .7790 | .8050 | 1.242 | 1.284 | 1.595 | .8930 | 10 |
| 39°00′ | .6807 | .6293 | .7771 | .8098 | 1.235 | 1.287 | 1.589 | .8901 | 51°00′ |
| 10 | .6836 | .6316 | .7753 | .8146 | 1.228 | 1.290 | 1.583 | .8872 | 50 |
| 20 | .6865 | .6338 | .7735 | .8195 | 1.220 | 1.293 | 1.578 | .8843 | 40 |
| 30 | .6894 | .6361 | .7716 | .8243 | 1.213 | 1.296 | 1.572 | .8814 | 30 |
| 40 | .6923 | .6383 | .7698 | .8292 | 1.206 | 1.299 | 1.567 | .8785 | 20 |
| 50 | .6952 | .6406 | .7679 | .8342 | 1.199 | 1.302 | 1.561 | .8756 | 10 |
| 40°00′ | .6981 | .6428 | .7660 | .8391 | 1.192 | 1.305 | 1.556 | .8727 | 50°00′ |
| 10 | .7010 | .6450 | .7642 | .8441 | 1.185 | 1.309 | 1.550 | .8698 | 50 |
| 20 | .7039 | .6472 | .7623 | .8491 | 1.178 | 1.312 | 1.545 | .8668 | 40 |
| 30 | .7069 | .6494 | .7604 | .8541 | 1.171 | 1.315 | 1.540 | .8639 | 30 |
| 40 | .7098 | .6517 | .7585 | .8591 | 1.164 | 1.318 | 1.535 | .8610 | 20 |
| 50 | .7127 | .6539 | .7566 | .8642 | 1.157 | 1.322 | 1.529 | .8581 | 10 |
| 41°00′ | .7156 | .6561 | .7547 | .8693 | 1.150 | 1.325 | 1.524 | .8552 | 49°00′ |
| 10 | .7185 | .6583 | .7528 | .8744 | 1.144 | 1.328 | 1.519 | .8523 | 50 |
| 20 | .7214 | .6604 | .7509 | .8796 | 1.137 | 1.332 | 1.514 | .8494 | 40 |
| 30 | .7243 | .6626 | .7490 | .8847 | 1.130 | 1.335 | 1.509 | .8465 | 30 |
| | | Cos | Sin | Cot | Tan | Csc | Sec | Radians | Degrees |

Table IV
(continued)

| Degrees | Radians | Sin | Cos | Tan | Cot | Sec | Csc | | |
|---|---|---|---|---|---|---|---|---|---|
| 40 | .7272 | .6648 | .7470 | .8899 | 1.124 | 1.339 | 1.504 | .8436 | 20 |
| 50 | .7301 | .6670 | .7451 | .8952 | 1.117 | 1.342 | 1.499 | .8407 | 10 |
| 42°00′ | .7330 | .6691 | .7431 | .9004 | 1.111 | 1.346 | 1.494 | .8378 | 48°00′ |
| 10 | .7359 | .6713 | .7412 | .9057 | 1.104 | 1.349 | 1.490 | .8348 | 50 |
| 20 | .7389 | .6734 | .7392 | .9110 | 1.098 | 1.353 | 1.485 | .8319 | 40 |
| 30 | .7418 | .6756 | .7373 | .9163 | 1.091 | 1.356 | 1.480 | .8290 | 30 |
| 40 | .7447 | .6777 | .7353 | .9217 | 1.085 | 1.360 | 1.476 | .8261 | 20 |
| 50 | .7476 | .6799 | .7333 | .9271 | 1.079 | 1.364 | 1.471 | .8232 | 10 |
| 43°00′ | .7505 | .6820 | .7314 | .9325 | 1.072 | 1.367 | 1.466 | .8203 | 47°00′ |
| 10 | .7534 | .6841 | .7294 | .9380 | 1.066 | 1.371 | 1.462 | .8174 | 50 |
| 20 | .7563 | .6862 | .7274 | .9435 | 1.060 | 1.375 | 1.457 | .8145 | 40 |
| 30 | .7592 | .6884 | .7254 | .9490 | 1.054 | 1.379 | 1.453 | .8116 | 30 |
| 40 | .7621 | .6905 | .7234 | .9545 | 1.048 | 1.382 | 1.448 | .8087 | 20 |
| 50 | .7650 | .6926 | .7214 | .9601 | 1.042 | 1.386 | 1.444 | .8058 | 10 |
| 44°00′ | .7679 | .6947 | .7193 | .9657 | 1.036 | 1.390 | 1.440 | .8029 | 46°00′ |
| 10 | .7709 | .6967 | .7173 | .9713 | 1.030 | 1.394 | 1.435 | .7999 | 50 |
| 20 | .7738 | .6988 | .7153 | .9770 | 1.024 | 1.398 | 1.431 | .7970 | 40 |
| 30 | .7767 | .7009 | .7133 | .9827 | 1.018 | 1.402 | 1.427 | .7941 | 30 |
| 40 | .7796 | .7030 | .7112 | .9884 | 1.012 | 1.406 | 1.423 | .7912 | 20 |
| 50 | .7825 | .7050 | .7092 | .9942 | 1.006 | 1.410 | 1.418 | .7883 | 10 |
| 45°00′ | .7854 | .7071 | .7071 | 1.000 | 1.000 | 1.414 | 1.414 | .7854 | 45°00′ |
| | | Cos | Sin | Cot | Tan | Csc | Sec | Radians | Degrees |

Table V†

## NATURAL LOGARITHMS OF NUMBERS—0.00 TO 99

(Base $e = 2.718 \cdots$ )

| N | 0 | 1 | 2 | 3 | 4 | 5 | 6 | 7 | 8 | 9 |
|---|---|---|---|---|---|---|---|---|---|---|
| 0.0 | | 5.395 | 6.088 | 6.493 | 6.781 | 7.004 | 7.187 | 7.341 | 7.474 | 7.592 |
| 0.1 | 7.697 | 7.793 | 7.880 | 7.960 | 8.034 | 8.103 | 8.167 | 8.228 | 8.285 | 8.339 |
| 0.2 | 8.391 | 8.439 | 8.486 | 8.530 | 8.573 | 8.614 | 8.653 | 8.691 | 8.727 | 8.762 |
| 0.3 | 8.796 | 8.829 | 8.861 | 8.891 | 8.921 | 8.950 | 8.978 | 9.006 | 9.032 | 9.058 |
| 0.4 | 9.084 | 9.108 | 9.132 | 9.156 | 9.179 | 9.201 | 9.223 | 9.245 | 9.266 | 9.287 |
| 0.5 | 9.307 | 9.327 | 9.346 | 9.365 | 9.384 | 9.402 | 9.420 | 9.438 | 9.455 | 9.472 |
| 0.6 | 9.489 | 9.506 | 9.522 | 9.538 | 9.554 | 9.569 | 9.584 | 9.600 | 9.614 | 9.629 |
| 0.7 | 9.643 | 9.658 | 9.671 | 9.685 | 9.699 | 9.712 | 9.726 | 9.739 | 9.752 | 9.764 |
| 0.8 | 9.777 | 9.789 | 9.802 | 9.814 | 9.826 | 9.837 | 9.849 | 9.861 | 9.872 | 9.883 |
| 0.9 | 9.895 | 9.906 | 9.917 | 9.927 | 9.938 | 9.949 | 9.959 | 9.970 | 9.980 | 9.990 |
| 1.0 | 0.0 0000 | 0995 | 1980 | 2956 | 3922 | 4879 | 5827 | 6766 | 7696 | 8618 |
| 1.1 | 9531 | *0436 | *1333 | *2222 | *3103 | *3976 | *4842 | *5700 | *6551 | *7395 |
| 1.2 | 0.1 8232 | 9062 | 9885 | *0701 | *1511 | *2314 | *3111 | *3902 | *4686 | *5464 |
| 1.3 | 0.2 6236 | 7003 | 7763 | 8518 | 9267 | *0010 | *0748 | *1481 | *2208 | *2930 |
| 1.4 | 0.3 3647 | 4359 | 5066 | 5767 | 6464 | 7156 | 7844 | 8526 | 9204 | 9878 |
| 1.5 | 0.4 0547 | 1211 | 1871 | 2527 | 3178 | 3825 | 4469 | 5108 | 5742 | 6373 |
| 1.6 | 7000 | 7623 | 8243 | 8858 | 9470 | *0078 | *0682 | *1282 | *1879 | *2473 |
| 1.7 | 0.5 3063 | 3649 | 4232 | 4812 | 5389 | 5962 | 6531 | 7098 | 7661 | 8222 |
| 1.8 | 8779 | 9333 | 9884 | *0432 | *0977 | *1519 | *2058 | *2594 | *3127 | *3658 |
| 1.9 | 0.6 4185 | 4710 | 5233 | 5752 | 6269 | 6783 | 7294 | 7803 | 8310 | 8813 |
| 2.0 | 9315 | 9813 | *0310 | *0804 | *1295 | *1784 | *2271 | *2755 | *3237 | *3716 |
| 2.1 | 0.7 4194 | 4669 | 5142 | 5612 | 6081 | 6547 | 7011 | 7473 | 7932 | 8390 |
| 2.2 | 8846 | 9299 | 9751 | *0200 | *0648 | *1093 | *1536 | *1978 | *2418 | *2855 |
| 2.3 | 0.8 3291 | 3725 | 4157 | 4587 | 5015 | 5442 | 5866 | 6289 | 6710 | 7129 |
| 2.4 | 7547 | 7963 | 8377 | 8789 | 9200 | 9609 | *0016 | *0422 | *0826 | *1228 |
| 2.5 | 0.9 1629 | 2028 | 2426 | 2822 | 3216 | 3609 | 4001 | 4391 | 4779 | 5166 |
| 2.6 | 5551 | 5935 | 6317 | 6698 | 7078 | 7456 | 7833 | 8208 | 8582 | 8954 |
| 2.7 | 9325 | 9695 | *0063 | *0430 | *0796 | *1160 | *1523 | *1885 | *2245 | *2604 |
| 2.8 | 1.0 2962 | 3318 | 3674 | 4028 | 4380 | 4732 | 5082 | 5431 | 5779 | 6126 |
| 2.9 | 6471 | 6815 | 7158 | 7500 | 7841 | 8181 | 8519 | 8856 | 9192 | 9527 |
| 3.0 | 9861 | *0194 | *0526 | *0856 | *1186 | *1514 | *1841 | *2168 | *2493 | *2817 |
| 3.1 | 1.1 3140 | 3462 | 3783 | 4103 | 4422 | 4740 | 5057 | 5373 | 5688 | 6002 |
| 3.2 | 6315 | 6627 | 6938 | 7248 | 7557 | 7865 | 8173 | 8479 | 8784 | 9089 |
| 3.3 | 9392 | 9695 | 9996 | *0297 | *0597 | *0896 | *1194 | *1491 | *1788 | *2083 |
| 3.4 | 1.2 2378 | 2671 | 2964 | 3256 | 3547 | 3837 | 4127 | 4415 | 4703 | 4990 |
| 3.5 | 5276 | 5562 | 5846 | 6130 | 6413 | 6695 | 6976 | 7257 | 7536 | 7815 |
| 3.6 | 8093 | 8371 | 8647 | 8923 | 9198 | 9473 | 9746 | *0019 | *0291 | *0563 |
| 3.7 | 1.3 0833 | 1103 | 1372 | 1641 | 1909 | 2176 | 2442 | 2708 | 2972 | 3237 |
| 3.8 | 3500 | 3763 | 4025 | 4286 | 4547 | 4807 | 5067 | 5325 | 5584 | 5841 |
| 3.9 | 6098 | 6354 | 6609 | 6864 | 7118 | 7372 | 7624 | 7877 | 8128 | 8379 |
| 4.0 | 8629 | 8879 | 9128 | 9377 | 9624 | 9872 | *0118 | *0364 | *0610 | *0854 |
| 4.1 | 1.4 1099 | 1342 | 1585 | 1828 | 2070 | 2311 | 2552 | 2792 | 3031 | 3270 |
| 4.2 | 3508 | 3746 | 3984 | 4220 | 4456 | 4692 | 4927 | 5161 | 5395 | 5629 |
| 4.3 | 5862 | 6094 | 6326 | 6557 | 6787 | 7018 | 7247 | 7476 | 7705 | 7933 |
| 4.4 | 8160 | 8387 | 8614 | 8840 | 9065 | 9290 | 9515 | 9739 | 9962 | *0185 |
| 4.5 | 1.5 0408 | 0630 | 0851 | 1072 | 1293 | 1513 | 1732 | 1951 | 2170 | 2388 |
| 4.6 | 2606 | 2823 | 3039 | 3256 | 3471 | 3687 | 3902 | 4116 | 4330 | 4543 |
| 4.7 | 4756 | 4969 | 5181 | 5393 | 5604 | 5814 | 6025 | 6235 | 6444 | 6653 |
| 4.8 | 6862 | 7070 | 7277 | 7485 | 7691 | 7898 | 8104 | 8309 | 8515 | 8719 |
| 4.9 | 8924 | 9127 | 9331 | 9534 | 9737 | 9939 | *0141 | *0342 | *0543 | *0744 |
| 5.0 | 1.6 0944 | 1144 | 1343 | 1542 | 1741 | 1939 | 2137 | 2334 | 2531 | 2728 |
| 5.1 | 2924 | 3120 | 3315 | 3511 | 3705 | 3900 | 4094 | 4287 | 4481 | 4673 |
| 5.2 | 4866 | 5058 | 5250 | 5441 | 5632 | 5823 | 6013 | 6203 | 6393 | 6582 |
| 5.3 | 6771 | 6959 | 7147 | 7335 | 7523 | 7710 | 7896 | 8083 | 8269 | 8455 |
| 5.4 | 8640 | 8825 | 9010 | 9194 | 9378 | 9562 | 9745 | 9928 | *0111 | *0293 |
| 5.5 | 1.7 0475 | 0656 | 0838 | 1019 | 1199 | 1380 | 1560 | 1740 | 1919 | 2098 |
| 5.6 | 2277 | 2455 | 2633 | 2811 | 2988 | 3166 | 3342 | 3519 | 3695 | 3871 |
| 5.7 | 4047 | 4222 | 4397 | 4572 | 4746 | 4920 | 5094 | 5267 | 5440 | 5613 |
| 5.8 | 5786 | 5958 | 6130 | 6302 | 6473 | 6644 | 6815 | 6985 | 7156 | 7326 |
| 5.9 | 7495 | 7665 | 7834 | 8002 | 8171 | 8339 | 8507 | 8675 | 8842 | 9009 |
| N | 0 | 1 | 2 | 3 | 4 | 5 | 6 | 7 | 8 | 9 |

(For rows 0.0 through 0.9, take tabular value −10.)

$\log_e 0.10$     7.69741 49070 −10

†From Richard Stevens Burington, *Handbook of Mathematical Tables and Formulas*, Third Edition. Handbook Publishers, Inc., Sandusky, Ohio, 1954.

*A star in front of any entry in the table means that the first two digits are to be taken from the next line in the table.

Table V
(continued)

| N | 0 | 1 | 2 | 3 | 4 | 5 | 6 | 7 | 8 | 9 |
|---|---|---|---|---|---|---|---|---|---|---|
| 6.0 | 1.7 9176 | 9342 | 9509 | 9675 | 9840 | *0006 | *0171 | *0336 | *0500 | *0665 |
| 6.1 | 1.8 0829 | 0993 | 1156 | 1319 | 1482 | 1645 | 1808 | 1970 | 2132 | 2294 |
| 6.2 | 2455 | 2616 | 2777 | 2938 | 3098 | 3258 | 3418 | 3578 | 3737 | 3896 |
| 6.3 | 4055 | 4214 | 4372 | 4530 | 4688 | 4845 | 5003 | 5160 | 5317 | 5473 |
| 6.4 | 5630 | 5786 | 5942 | 6097 | 6253 | 6408 | 6563 | 6718 | 6872 | 7026 |
| 6.5 | 7180 | 7334 | 7487 | 7641 | 7794 | 7947 | 8099 | 8251 | 8403 | 8555 |
| 6.6 | 8707 | 8858 | 9010 | 9160 | 9311 | 9462 | 9612 | 9762 | 9912 | *0061 |
| 6.7 | 1.9 0211 | 0360 | 0509 | 0658 | 0806 | 0954 | 1102 | 1250 | 1398 | 1545 |
| 6.8 | 1692 | 1839 | 1986 | 2132 | 2279 | 2425 | 2571 | 2716 | 2862 | 3007 |
| 6.9 | 3152 | 3297 | 3442 | 3586 | 3730 | 3874 | 4018 | 4162 | 4305 | 4448 |
| 7.0 | 4591 | 4734 | 4876 | 5019 | 5161 | 5303 | 5445 | 5586 | 5727 | 5869 |
| 7.1 | 6009 | 6150 | 6291 | 6431 | 6571 | 6711 | 6851 | 6991 | 7130 | 7269 |
| 7.2 | 7408 | 7547 | 7685 | 7824 | 7962 | 8100 | 8238 | 8376 | 8513 | 8650 |
| 7.3 | 8787 | 8924 | 9061 | 9198 | 9334 | 9470 | 9606 | 9742 | 9877 | *0013 |
| 7.4 | 2.0 0148 | 0283 | 0418 | 0553 | 0687 | 0821 | 0956 | 1089 | 1223 | 1357 |
| 7.5 | 1490 | 1624 | 1757 | 1890 | 2022 | 2155 | 2287 | 2419 | 2551 | 2683 |
| 7.6 | 2815 | 2946 | 3078 | 3209 | 3340 | 3471 | 3601 | 3732 | 3862 | 3992 |
| 7.7 | 4122 | 4252 | 4381 | 4511 | 4640 | 4769 | 4898 | 5027 | 5156 | 5284 |
| 7.8 | 5412 | 5540 | 5668 | 5796 | 5924 | 6051 | 6179 | 6306 | 6433 | 6560 |
| 7.9 | 6686 | 6813 | 6939 | 7065 | 7191 | 7317 | 7443 | 7568 | 7694 | 7819 |
| 8.0 | 7944 | 8069 | 8194 | 8318 | 8443 | 8567 | 8691 | 8815 | 8939 | 9063 |
| 8.1 | 9186 | 9310 | 9433 | 9556 | 9679 | 9802 | 9924 | *0047 | *0169 | *0291 |
| 8.2 | 2.1 0413 | 0535 | 0657 | 0779 | 0900 | 1021 | 1142 | 1263 | 1384 | 1505 |
| 8.3 | 1626 | 1746 | 1866 | 1986 | 2106 | 2226 | 2346 | 2465 | 2585 | 2704 |
| 8.4 | 2823 | 2942 | 3061 | 3180 | 3298 | 3417 | 3535 | 3653 | 3771 | 3889 |
| 8.5 | 4007 | 4124 | 4242 | 4359 | 4476 | 4593 | 4710 | 4827 | 4943 | 5060 |
| 8.6 | 5176 | 5292 | 5409 | 5524 | 5640 | 5756 | 5871 | 5987 | 6102 | 6217 |
| 8.7 | 6332 | 6447 | 6562 | 6677 | 6791 | 6905 | 7020 | 7134 | 7248 | 7361 |
| 8.8 | 7475 | 7589 | 7702 | 7816 | 7929 | 8042 | 8155 | 8267 | 8380 | 8493 |
| 8.9 | 8605 | 8717 | 8830 | 8942 | 9054 | 9165 | 9277 | 9389 | 9500 | 9611 |
| 9.0 | 9722 | 9834 | 9944 | *0055 | *0166 | *0276 | *0387 | *0497 | *0607 | *0717 |
| 9.1 | 2.2 0827 | 0937 | 1047 | 1157 | 1266 | 1375 | 1485 | 1594 | 1703 | 1812 |
| 9.2 | 1920 | 2029 | 2138 | 2246 | 2354 | 2462 | 2570 | 2678 | 2786 | 2894 |
| 9.3 | 3001 | 3109 | 3216 | 3324 | 3431 | 3538 | 3645 | 3751 | 3858 | 3965 |
| 9.4 | 4071 | 4177 | 4284 | 4390 | 4496 | 4601 | 4707 | 4813 | 4918 | 5024 |
| 9.5 | 5129 | 5234 | 5339 | 5444 | 5549 | 5654 | 5759 | 5863 | 5968 | 6072 |
| 9.6 | 6176 | 6280 | 6384 | 6488 | 6592 | 6696 | 6799 | 6903 | 7006 | 7109 |
| 9.7 | 7213 | 7316 | 7419 | 7521 | 7624 | 7727 | 7829 | 7932 | 8034 | 8136 |
| 9.8 | 8238 | 8340 | 8442 | 8544 | 8646 | 8747 | 8849 | 8950 | 9051 | 9152 |
| 9.9 | 9253 | 9354 | 9455 | 9556 | 9657 | 9757 | 9858 | 9958 | *0058 | *0158 |
| 10.0 | 2.3 0259 | 0358 | 0458 | 0558 | 0658 | 0757 | 0857 | 0956 | 1055 | 1154 |
| N | 0 | 1 | 2 | 3 | 4 | 5 | 6 | 7 | 8 | 9 |

| N | 0 | 1 | 2 | 3 | 4 | 5 | 6 | 7 | 8 | 9 |
|---|---|---|---|---|---|---|---|---|---|---|
| 1 | 2.30259 | 39790 | 48491 | 56495 | 63906 | 70805 | 77259 | 83321 | 89037 | 94444 |
| 2 | 99573 | *04452 | *09104 | *13549 | *17805 | *21888 | *25810 | *29584 | *33220 | *36730 |
| 3 | 3.40120 | 43399 | 46574 | 49651 | 52636 | 55535 | 58352 | 61092 | 63759 | 66356 |
| 4 | 68888 | 71357 | 73767 | 76120 | 78419 | 80666 | 82864 | 85015 | 87120 | 89182 |
| 5 | 91202 | 93183 | 95124 | 97029 | 98898 | *00733 | *02535 | *04305 | *06044 | *07754 |
| 6 | 4.09434 | 11087 | 12713 | 14313 | 15888 | 17439 | 18965 | 20489 | 21951 | 23411 |
| 7 | 24850 | 26268 | 27667 | 29046 | 30407 | 31749 | 33073 | 34381 | 35671 | 36945 |
| 8 | 38203 | 39445 | 40672 | 41884 | 43082 | 44265 | 45435 | 46591 | 47734 | 48864 |
| 9 | 49981 | 51086 | 52179 | 53260 | 54329 | 55388 | 56435 | 57471 | 58497 | 59512 |

$$\log_e 10 = 2.30258\ 50930$$

Table VI
**VALUES OF $e^x$ AND $e^{-x}$**

| $x$ | $e^x$ | $e^{-x}$ | $x$ | $e^x$ | $e^{-x}$ | $x$ | $e^x$ | $e^{-x}$ |
|------|-------|----------|-----|-------|----------|-----|--------|----------|
| 0.00 | 1.000 | 1.000 | 0.1 | 1.105 | 0.905 | 1 | 2.72 | 0.368 |
| .01 | 1.010 | .990 | .2 | 1.221 | .819 | 2 | 7.39 | .135 |
| .02 | 1.020 | .980 | .3 | 1.350 | .741 | 3 | 20.09 | .0498 |
| .03 | 1.030 | .970 | .4 | 1.492 | .670 | 4 | 54.60 | .0183 |
| .04 | 1.041 | .961 | .5 | 1.649 | .607 | 5 | 148.4 | .00674 |
| .05 | 1.051 | .951 | .6 | 1.822 | .549 | 6 | 403.4 | .00248 |
| .06 | 1.062 | .942 | .7 | 2.014 | .497 | 7 | 1097. | .000912 |
| .07 | 1.073 | .932 | .8 | 2.226 | .449 | 8 | 2981. | .000335 |
| .08 | 1.083 | .923 | .9 | 2.460 | .407 | 9 | 8103. | .000123 |
| .09 | 1.094 | .914 | 1.0 | 2.718 | .368 | 10 | 22026. | .000045 |

*Note.* $e^{x+y} = e^x \cdot e^y$.

*Example.* $e^{2.81} = e^2 \cdot e^{0.8} \cdot e^{0.01} = (7.39)(2.226)(1.01) = 16.6$.

Table VII
**TABLE OF INTEGRALS**

In the following table $u$ stands for any differentiable function of $x$ and can, of course, be $x$ itself. The constant of integration is to be added in each case. The reduction formulas are in many cases valid for values of the constants other than those indicated, but this table does not give the variety of special cases.

1. $\displaystyle \int u^n \, du = \frac{u^{n+1}}{n+1}$

2. $\displaystyle \int \frac{du}{u} = \log|u|$

3. $\displaystyle \int a^u \, du = \frac{a^u}{\log a}, \qquad a > 0, a \neq 1$

4. $\displaystyle \int e^u \, du = e^u$

5. $\displaystyle \int \sin u \, du = -\cos u$

6. $\displaystyle \int \cos u \, du = \sin u$

7. $\displaystyle \int \tan u \, du = \log|\sec u|$

8. $\displaystyle \int \cot u \, du = \log|\sin u|$

9. $\displaystyle \int \sec u \, du = \log|\sec u + \tan u| = \log\left|\tan\left(\frac{u}{2} + \frac{\pi}{4}\right)\right| = \cosh^{-1}(\sec u)$

10. $\displaystyle \int \csc u \, du = \log|\csc u - \cot u| = \log\left|\tan \frac{u}{2}\right| = -\sinh^{-1}(\cot u)$

11. $\displaystyle \int \frac{du}{u^2 + a^2} = \frac{1}{a} \tan^{-1} \frac{u}{a}, \qquad a \neq 0$

12. $\displaystyle \int \frac{du}{a^2 - u^2} = \frac{1}{2a} \log\left|\frac{u + a}{u - a}\right| = \begin{cases} \dfrac{1}{2a} \log \dfrac{a + u}{u - a} = \dfrac{1}{a} \coth^{-1} \dfrac{u}{a}, & u^2 > a^2 \\[2mm] \dfrac{1}{2a} \log \dfrac{a + u}{a - u} = \dfrac{1}{a} \tanh^{-1} \dfrac{u}{a}, & u^2 < a^2 \end{cases}$

13. $\int \dfrac{du}{\sqrt{a^2 - u^2}} = \sin^{-1} \dfrac{u}{|a|}, \qquad u^2 < a^2$

14. $\int \dfrac{du}{u(a + bu)} = \dfrac{1}{a} \log\left| \dfrac{u}{a + bu} \right|, \qquad a \neq 0, b \neq 0$

15. $\int \dfrac{du}{u^2(a + bu)} = -\dfrac{1}{au} + \dfrac{b}{a^2} \log\left| \dfrac{a + bu}{u} \right|, \qquad a \neq 0, b \neq 0$

16. $\int \dfrac{du}{u(a + bu)^2} = \dfrac{1}{a(a + bu)} - \dfrac{1}{a^2} \log\left| \dfrac{a + bu}{u} \right|, \qquad a \neq 0, b \neq 0$

**Forms Involving $\sqrt{a + bu}$, $u > -\dfrac{a}{b}$**

17. $\int u\sqrt{a + bu}\ du = \dfrac{2(3bu - 2a)\sqrt{(a + bu)^3}}{15b^2}, \qquad a \neq 0, b \neq 0$

18. $\int \dfrac{u\ du}{\sqrt{a + bu}} = \dfrac{2(bu - 2a)\sqrt{a + bu}}{3b^2}, \qquad a \neq 0, b \neq 0$

19. $\int u^2\sqrt{a + bu}\ du = \dfrac{2(15b^2u^2 - 12abu + 8a^2)\sqrt{(a + bu)^3}}{105b^3}, \qquad a \neq 0, b \neq 0$

20. $\int \dfrac{u^2\ du}{\sqrt{a + bu}} = \dfrac{2(3b^2u^2 - 4abu + 8a^2)\sqrt{a + bu}}{15b^3}, \qquad a \neq 0, b \neq 0$

21. $\int \dfrac{du}{u\sqrt{a + bu}} = \begin{cases} \dfrac{1}{\sqrt{a}} \log\left| \dfrac{\sqrt{a + bu} - \sqrt{a}}{\sqrt{a + bu} + \sqrt{a}} \right|, & a > 0, b \neq 0 \\[3mm] \dfrac{2}{\sqrt{-a}} \tan^{-1}\sqrt{\dfrac{a + bu}{-a}}, & a < 0, b \neq 0 \end{cases}$

22. $\int \dfrac{\sqrt{a + bu}}{u}\ du = 2\sqrt{a + bu} + a\int \dfrac{du}{u\sqrt{a + bu}}, \qquad a \neq 0, b \neq 0$

23. $\int \dfrac{du}{u^2\sqrt{a + bu}} = -\dfrac{\sqrt{a + bu}}{au} - \dfrac{b}{2a}\int \dfrac{du}{u\sqrt{a + bu}}, \qquad a \neq 0, b \neq 0$

24. $\int \sqrt{\dfrac{a + u}{b + u}}\ du = \sqrt{(a + u)(b + u)} + (a - b)\log(\sqrt{a + u} + \sqrt{b + u})$

25. $\int \sqrt{\dfrac{a - u}{b + u}}\ du = \sqrt{(a - u)(b + u)} + (a + b)\sin^{-1}\sqrt{\dfrac{b + u}{a + b}}$

**Forms Involving $\sqrt{a^2 - u^2}$, $u^2 < a^2$**

We use $\dfrac{u}{|u|} = \begin{cases} 1 \text{ for } u > 0 \\ 0 \text{ for } u = 0 \\ -1 \text{ for } u < 0 \end{cases}$

26. $\int \sqrt{a^2 - u^2}\ du = \dfrac{1}{2}\left( u\sqrt{a^2 - u^2} + a^2 \sin^{-1}\dfrac{u}{|a|} \right)$

27. $\int u\sqrt{a^2 - u^2}\ du = -\dfrac{1}{3}(a^2 - u^2)^{3/2}$

28. $\int u^2\sqrt{a^2 - u^2}\ du = \dfrac{u}{8}(2u^2 - a^2)\sqrt{a^2 - u^2} + \dfrac{a^4}{8}\sin^{-1}\dfrac{u}{|a|}$

29. $\int \dfrac{u\ du}{\sqrt{a^2 - u^2}} = -\sqrt{a^2 - u^2}$

30. $\displaystyle \int \frac{u^2 \, du}{\sqrt{a^2 - u^2}} = -\frac{u}{2} \sqrt{a^2 - u^2} + \frac{a^2}{2} \sin^{-1} \frac{u}{|a|}$

31. $\displaystyle \int (a^2 - u^2)^{3/2} \, du = \frac{u}{8} (5a^2 - 2u^2) \sqrt{a^2 - u^2} + \frac{3a^4}{8} \sin^{-1} \frac{u}{|a|}$

32. $\displaystyle \int \frac{du}{(a^2 - u^2)^{3/2}} = \frac{u}{a^2 \sqrt{a^2 - u^2}}$

33. $\displaystyle \int \frac{u^2 \, du}{(a^2 - u^2)^{3/2}} = \frac{u}{\sqrt{a^2 - u^2}} - \sin^{-1} \frac{u}{|a|}$

34. $\displaystyle \int \frac{du}{u \sqrt{a^2 - u^2}} = \frac{1}{|a|} \log \left| \frac{|a| - \sqrt{a^2 - u^2}}{u} \right| = -\frac{1}{|a|} \frac{u}{|u|} \operatorname{sech}^{-1} \left| \frac{u}{a} \right|$

35. $\displaystyle \int \frac{du}{u^2 \sqrt{a^2 - u^2}} = -\frac{\sqrt{a^2 - u^2}}{a^2 u}$

36. $\displaystyle \int \frac{\sqrt{a^2 - u^2}}{u} \, du = \sqrt{a^2 - u^2} + |a| \log \left| \frac{|a| - \sqrt{a^2 - u^2}}{u} \right|$

37. $\displaystyle \int \frac{\sqrt{a^2 - u^2}}{u^2} \, du = -\frac{\sqrt{a^2 - u^2}}{u} - \sin^{-1} \frac{u}{|a|}$

**Forms Involving $\sqrt{u^2 \pm a^2}$**

It is understood that $u^2 > a^2$ in the case of $\sqrt{u^2 - a^2}$.

Moreover, $\quad \dfrac{u}{|u|} = \begin{cases} 1 \text{ for } u > 0 \\ 0 \text{ for } u = 0 \\ -1 \text{ for } u < 0 \end{cases}$

38. $\displaystyle \int \frac{du}{\sqrt{u^2 + a^2}} = \log|u + \sqrt{u^2 + a^2}\,| = \sinh^{-1} \frac{u}{a}$

39. $\displaystyle \int \frac{du}{\sqrt{u^2 - a^2}} = \log|u + \sqrt{u^2 - a^2}\,| = \cosh^{-1} \left| \frac{u}{a} \right|$

40. $\displaystyle \int \sqrt{u^2 \pm a^2} \, du = \frac{u}{2} \sqrt{u^2 \pm a^2} \pm \frac{a^2}{2} \log|u + \sqrt{u^2 \pm a^2}\,|$

41. $\displaystyle \int u \sqrt{u^2 \pm a^2} \, du = \tfrac{1}{3} (u^2 \pm a^2)^{3/2}$

42. $\displaystyle \int u^2 \sqrt{u^2 \pm a^2} \, du = \frac{u}{8} (2u^2 \pm a^2) \sqrt{u^2 \pm a^2} - \frac{a^4}{8} \log|u + \sqrt{u^2 \pm a^2}\,|$

43. $\displaystyle \int \frac{u^2 \, du}{\sqrt{u^2 \pm a^2}} = \frac{u}{2} \sqrt{u^2 \pm a^2} \mp \frac{a^2}{2} \log|u + \sqrt{u^2 \pm a^2}\,|$

44. $\displaystyle \int (u^2 \pm a^2)^{3/2} \, du = \frac{u}{8} (2u^2 \pm 5a^2) \sqrt{u^2 \pm a^2} + \frac{3a^4}{8} \log|u + \sqrt{u^2 \pm a^2}\,|$

45. $\displaystyle \int \frac{du}{(u^2 \pm a^2)^{3/2}} = \frac{\pm u}{a^2 \sqrt{u^2 \pm a^2}}$

46. $\displaystyle \int \frac{u \, du}{\sqrt{u^2 \pm a^2}} = \sqrt{u^2 \pm a^2}$

47. $\displaystyle \int \frac{u^2 \, du}{(u^2 \pm a^2)^{3/2}} = -\frac{u}{\sqrt{u^2 \pm a^2}} + \log|u + \sqrt{u^2 \pm a^2}\,|$

48. $\displaystyle \int \frac{du}{u^2 \sqrt{u^2 \pm a^2}} = \mp \frac{\sqrt{u^2 \pm a^2}}{a^2 u}$

49. $\displaystyle \int \frac{du}{u^3 \sqrt{u^2 - a^2}} = \frac{\sqrt{u^2 - a^2}}{2a^2 u^2} + \frac{1}{|a|^3} \frac{u}{|u|} \sec^{-1} \frac{u}{|a|}$

50. $\displaystyle\int \frac{\sqrt{u^2 - a^2}}{u}\, du = \sqrt{u^2 - a^2} - |a|\, \frac{u}{|u|} \sec^{-1} \frac{u}{|a|}$

51. $\displaystyle\int \frac{\sqrt{u^2 \pm a^2}}{u^2}\, du = - \frac{\sqrt{u^2 \pm a^2}}{u} + \log|u + \sqrt{u^2 \pm a^2}\,|$

52. $\displaystyle\int \frac{du}{u\sqrt{u^2 + a^2}} = \frac{1}{|a|} \log\left| \frac{\sqrt{u^2 + a^2} - |a|}{u} \right| = - \frac{1}{|a|} \frac{u}{|u|} \operatorname{csch}^{-1}\left| \frac{u}{a} \right|$

53. $\displaystyle\int \frac{du}{u\sqrt{u^2 - a^2}} = \frac{1}{|a|} \frac{u}{|u|} \sec^{-1} \frac{u}{|a|}$

54. $\displaystyle\int \frac{du}{u^3\sqrt{u^2 + a^2}} = - \frac{\sqrt{u^2 + a^2}}{2a^2u^2} - \frac{1}{2|a|^3} \log\left| \frac{|a| - \sqrt{u^2 + a^2}}{u} \right|$

55. $\displaystyle\int \frac{\sqrt{u^2 + a^2}}{u}\, du = \sqrt{u^2 + a^2} + |a|\log\left| \frac{|a| - \sqrt{u^2 + a^2}}{u} \right|$

**Forms Involving $\sqrt{2au \mp u^2}$**

It is understood that $2a > u$ when the minus sign holds and $2a < -u$ when the plus sign holds.

56. $\displaystyle\int \sqrt{2au - u^2}\, du = \frac{u - a}{2} \sqrt{2au - u^2} + \frac{a^2}{2} \sin^{-1} \frac{u - a}{|a|}$

57. $\displaystyle\int \frac{du}{\sqrt{2au - u^2}} = \sin^{-1} \frac{u - a}{|a|}$

58. $\displaystyle\int \frac{u^n\, du}{\sqrt{2au - u^2}} = \frac{-u^{n-1}\sqrt{2au - u^2}}{n} + \frac{a(2n - 1)}{n} \int \frac{u^{n-1}}{\sqrt{2au - u^2}},$

$\qquad\qquad\qquad\qquad\qquad n$ integral and $\geq 1$

59. $\displaystyle\int \frac{du}{u^n\sqrt{2au - u^2}} = \frac{\sqrt{2au - u^2}}{a(1 - 2n)u^n} + \frac{n - 1}{(2n - 1)a} \int \frac{du}{u^{n-1}\sqrt{2au - u^2}},$

$\qquad\qquad\qquad\qquad\qquad n$ integral and $\geq 1$

60. $\displaystyle\int u^n\sqrt{2au - u^2}\, du = \frac{-u^{n-1}(2au - u^2)^{3/2}}{n + 2} + \frac{(2n + 1)a}{n + 2}$

$\qquad\qquad\qquad\qquad \times \displaystyle\int u^{n-1}\sqrt{2au - u^2}\, du, \qquad n$ integral and $\geq 1$

61. $\displaystyle\int \frac{\sqrt{2au - u^2}}{u^n}\, du = \frac{(2au - u^2)^{3/2}}{(3 - 2n)au^n} + \frac{n - 3}{(2n - 3)a} \int \frac{\sqrt{2au - u^2}}{u^{n-1}}\, du,$

$\qquad\qquad\qquad\qquad\qquad n$ integral and $\geq 1$

62. $\displaystyle\int \frac{du}{(2au - u^2)^{3/2}} = \frac{u - a}{a^2\sqrt{2au - u^2}}$

63. $\displaystyle\int \frac{du}{\sqrt{2au + u^2}} = \log|u + a + \sqrt{2au + u^2}\,|$

**Forms Involving $a + bx \pm cx^2$**

The condition below on the discriminant $4ac - b^2$ can be relaxed if $x$ is limited to values for which the radicand is positive.

64. $\displaystyle\int \frac{du}{a + bu + cu^2} = \frac{2}{\sqrt{4ac - b^2}} \tan^{-1} \frac{2cu + b}{\sqrt{4ac - b^2}},$

$\qquad\qquad\qquad\qquad\qquad\qquad 4ac - b^2 > 0,\, c > 0$

65. $\displaystyle\int \frac{du}{a + bu - cu^2} = \frac{1}{\sqrt{b^2 + 4ac}} \log\left| \frac{\sqrt{b^2 + 4ac} - b + 2cx}{\sqrt{b^2 + 4ac} + b - 2cx} \right|,$

$$4ac + b^2 > 0, \, c > 0$$

66. $\displaystyle\int \frac{du}{\sqrt{a + bu - cu^2}} = \frac{1}{\sqrt{c}} \sin^{-1} \frac{2cu - b}{\sqrt{b^2 + 4ac}}, \qquad 4ac + b^2 > 0, \, c > 0$

67. $\displaystyle\int \frac{du}{\sqrt{a + bu + cu^2}} = \frac{1}{\sqrt{c}} \log\left|2cu + b + 2\sqrt{c}\,\sqrt{a + bu + cu^2}\,\right|,$

$$4ac - b^2 > 0, \, c > 0$$

68. $\displaystyle\int \sqrt{a + bu + cu^2}\; du = \frac{2cu + b}{4c} \sqrt{a + bu + cu^2} - \frac{b^2 - 4ac}{8c^{3/2}}$

$$\times \log\left|2cu + b + 2\sqrt{c}\,\sqrt{a + bu + cu^2}\,\right|, \quad 4ac - b^2 > 0, \, c > 0$$

69. $\displaystyle\int \sqrt{a + bu - cu^2}\; du = \frac{2cu - b}{4c} \sqrt{a + bu - cu^2} + \frac{b^2 + 4ac}{8c^{3/2}}$

$$\times \sin^{-1} \frac{2cu - b}{\sqrt{b^2 + 4ac}}, \qquad 4ac + b^2 > 0, \, c > 0$$

70. $\displaystyle\int \frac{u\, du}{\sqrt{a + bu - cu^2}} = -\frac{\sqrt{a + bu - cu^2}}{c} + \frac{b}{2c^{3/2}} \sin^{-1} \frac{2cu - b}{\sqrt{b^2 + 4ac}},$

$$4ac + b^2 > 0, \, c > 0$$

71. $\displaystyle\int \frac{u\, du}{\sqrt{a + bu + cu^2}} = \frac{\sqrt{a + bu + cu^2}}{c} - \frac{b}{2c^{3/2}}$

$$\times \log\left|2cu + b + 2\sqrt{c}\,\sqrt{a + bu + cu^2}\,\right|, \qquad 4ac - b^2 > 0, \, c > 0$$

**Trigonometric Forms**

72. $\displaystyle\int \sin^n u\; du = -\frac{\sin^{n-1} u \cos u}{n} + \frac{n-1}{n} \int \sin^{n-2} u\; du,$

$$n \text{ integral and } \geq 2$$

73. $\displaystyle\int \cos^n u\; du = \frac{\cos^{n-1} u \sin u}{n} + \frac{n-1}{n} \int \cos^{n-2} u\; du,$

$$n \text{ integral and } \geq 2$$

74. $\displaystyle\int \tan^n u\; du = \frac{\tan^{n-1} u}{n-1} - \int \tan^{n-2} u\; du, \qquad n \text{ integral and } \geq 2$

75. $\displaystyle\int \cot^n u\; du = -\frac{\cot^{n-1} u}{n-1} - \int \cot^{n-2} u\; du, \qquad n \text{ integral and } \geq 2$

76. $\displaystyle\int \sec^n u\; du = \frac{\tan u \sec^{n-2} u}{n-1} + \frac{n-2}{n-1} \int \sec^{n-2} u\; du, \qquad n \text{ integral and } \geq 2$

77. $\displaystyle\int \csc^n u\; du = -\frac{\cot u \csc^{n-2} u}{n-1} + \frac{n-2}{n-1} \int \csc^{n-2} u\; du, \qquad n \text{ integral and } \geq 2$

78. $\displaystyle\int \cos^m u \sin^n u \, du = \frac{\cos^{m-1} u \sin^{n+1} u}{m+n} + \frac{m-1}{m+n} \int \cos^{m-2} u \sin^n u \, du,$

$m$ and $n$ integral, $m \geq 2, n \geq 0$

$\displaystyle = -\frac{\sin^{n-1} u \cos^{m+1} u}{m+n} + \frac{n-1}{m+n} \int \cos^m u \sin^{n-2} u \, du,$

$m$ and $n$ integral, $m \geq 0, n \geq 2$

$\displaystyle = -\frac{\sin^{n+1} u \cos^{m+1} u}{m+1} + \frac{m+n+2}{m+1} \int \cos^{m+2} u \sin^n u \, du,$

$m$ and $n$ integral, $m \geq 0, n \geq 0$

$\displaystyle = \frac{\sin^{n+1} u \cos^{m+1} u}{n+1} + \frac{m+n+2}{n+1} \int \cos^m u \sin^{n+2} u \, du,$

$m$ and $n$ integral, $m \geq 0, n \geq 0$

79. $\displaystyle\int \sin au \sin bu \, du = \frac{\sin(a-b)u}{2(a-b)} - \frac{\sin(a+b)u}{2(a+b)}, \qquad |a| \neq |b|$

80. $\displaystyle\int \cos au \cos bu \, du = \frac{\sin(a-b)u}{2(a-b)} + \frac{\sin(a+b)u}{2(a+b)}, \qquad |a| \neq |b|$

81. $\displaystyle\int \sin au \cos bu \, du = -\frac{\cos(a-b)u}{2(a-b)} - \frac{\cos(a+b)u}{2(a+b)}, \qquad |a| \neq |b|$

82. $\displaystyle\int u^n \sin u \, du = -u^n \cos u + n \int u^{n-1} \cos u \, du, \qquad n$ integral and $\geq 1$

83. $\displaystyle\int u^n \cos u \, du = u^n \sin u - n \int u^{n-1} \sin u \, du, \qquad n$ integral and $\geq 1$

84. $\displaystyle\int \frac{du}{a + b \cos u} = \begin{cases} \dfrac{2}{\sqrt{a^2 - b^2}} \tan^{-1} \dfrac{\sqrt{a^2 - b^2} \tan \frac{u}{2}}{a+b}, & a^2 - b^2 > 0 \\[4ex] \dfrac{1}{\sqrt{b^2 - a^2}} \log \left| \dfrac{a + b + \sqrt{b^2 - a^2} \tan \frac{u}{2}}{a + b - \sqrt{b^2 - a^2} \tan \frac{u}{2}} \right|, & b^2 - a^2 > 0 \end{cases}$

85. $\displaystyle\int \frac{du}{a + b \sin u} = \begin{cases} \dfrac{2}{\sqrt{a^2 - b^2}} \tan^{-1} \dfrac{a \tan \frac{u}{2} + b}{\sqrt{a^2 - b^2}}, & a^2 - b^2 > 0 \\[4ex] \dfrac{1}{\sqrt{b^2 - a^2}} \log \left| \dfrac{a \tan \frac{u}{2} + b - \sqrt{b^2 - a^2}}{a \tan \frac{u}{2} + b + \sqrt{b^2 - a^2}} \right|, & b^2 - a^2 > 0 \end{cases}$

86. $\displaystyle\int \frac{du}{a^2 \cos^2 u + b^2 \sin^2 u} = \frac{1}{ab} \tan^{-1} \frac{b \tan u}{a}, \qquad ab \neq 0$

### Inverse Trigonometric Forms, Principal Values Understood

87. $\displaystyle\int \sin^{-1} u \, du = u \sin^{-1} u + \sqrt{1 - u^2}, \qquad u^2 < 1$

88. $\displaystyle\int \cos^{-1} u \, du = u \cos^{-1} u - \sqrt{1 - u^2}, \qquad u^2 < 1$

89. $\int \tan^{-1} u \, du = u \tan^{-1} u - \frac{1}{2} \log(1 + u^2)$

90. $\int \cot^{-1} u \, du = u \cot^{-1} u + \frac{1}{2} \log(1 + u^2)$

91. $\int \sec^{-1} u \, du = u \sec^{-1} u - \log|u + \sqrt{u^2 - 1}|, \qquad u^2 > 1$

92. $\int \csc^{-1} u \, du = u \csc^{-1} u + \log|u + \sqrt{u^2 - 1}|, \qquad u^2 > 1$

93. $\int u \sin^{-1} u \, du = \frac{1}{4}\left[(2u^2 - 1)\sin^{-1} u + u\sqrt{1 - u^2}\right], \qquad u^2 < 1$

94. $\int u \tan^{-1} u \, du = \frac{1}{2}\left[(u^2 + 1)\tan^{-1} u - u\right]$

### Forms Involving Exponential and Logarithmic Functions

95. $\int u^n e^{au} \, du = \dfrac{u^n e^{au}}{a} - \dfrac{n}{a} \int u^{n-1} e^{au} \, du, \qquad\qquad n$ integral and $\geq 1, a \neq 0$

96. $\int u^n \log u \, du = u^{n+1}\left[\dfrac{\log u}{n + 1} - \dfrac{1}{(n + 1)^2}\right], \qquad\qquad n$ integral and $\geq 1$

97. $\int u^n \log^m u \, du = \dfrac{u^{n+1} \log^m u}{n + 1} - \dfrac{m}{n + 1} \int u^n \log^{m-1} u \, du,$

$m$ and $n$ integral and $\geq 1$

98. $\int e^{au} \sin nu \, du = \dfrac{e^{au}(a \sin nu - n \cos nu)}{a^2 + n^2}, \qquad a^2 + n^2 \neq 0$

99. $\int e^{au} \cos nu \, du = \dfrac{e^{au}(n \sin nu + a \cos nu)}{a^2 + n^2}, \qquad a^2 + n^2 \neq 0$

100. $\int \dfrac{du}{a + be^{nu}} = \dfrac{1}{an}[nu - \log|a + be^{nu}|], \qquad an \neq 0, a + be^{nu} \neq 0$

101. $\int \dfrac{du}{ae^{nu} + be^{-nu}} = \begin{cases} \dfrac{1}{n\sqrt{ab}} \tan^{-1}\left(e^{nu}\sqrt{\dfrac{a}{b}}\right), & ab > 0 \\[3mm] \dfrac{1}{2n\sqrt{-ab}} \log\left|\dfrac{ae^{nu} - \sqrt{-ab}}{ae^{nu} + \sqrt{-ab}}\right|, & ab < 0 \end{cases}$

102. $\int \dfrac{ue^u \, du}{(1 + u)^2} = \dfrac{e^u}{1 + u}$

103. $\int \sin(\log u) \, du = \dfrac{u}{2}[\sin(\log u) - \cos(\log u)]$

104. $\int \cos(\log u) \, du = \dfrac{u}{2}[\sin(\log u) + \cos(\log u)]$

### Forms Involving Hyperbolic Functions

105. $\int \sinh u \, du = \cosh u$

106. $\int \cosh u \, du = \sinh u$

107. $\int \tanh u \, du = \log \cosh u$

108.  $\displaystyle\int \operatorname{sech} u \; du = 2 \tan^{-1} e^{u}$

109.  $\displaystyle\int \sinh^2 u \; du = -\tfrac{1}{2}u + \tfrac{1}{4}\sinh 2u$

110.  $\displaystyle\int \cosh^2 u \; du = \tfrac{1}{2}u + \tfrac{1}{4}\sinh 2u$

111.  $\displaystyle\int \operatorname{sech}^2 u \; du = \tanh u$

112.  $\displaystyle\int \operatorname{csch}^2 u \; du = -\coth u$

113.  $\displaystyle\int \operatorname{sech} u \tanh u \; du = -\operatorname{sech} u$

114.  $\displaystyle\int \operatorname{csch} u \coth u \; du = -\operatorname{csch} u$

**Miscellaneous Integrals**

115.  $\displaystyle\int u^m (a + bu^n)^p \; du =$
$$
\begin{cases}
\dfrac{u^{m-n+1}(a+bu^n)^{p+1}}{b(np+m+1)} - \dfrac{(m-n+1)a}{b(np+m+1)} \\[2mm]
\qquad\qquad \times \displaystyle\int u^{m-n}(a+bu^n)^p \; du \\[4mm]
\dfrac{u^{m+1}(a+bu^n)^p}{np+m+1} + \dfrac{npa}{np+m+1} \\[2mm]
\qquad\qquad \times \displaystyle\int u^m (a+bu^n)^{p-1} \; du \\[4mm]
\dfrac{u^{m+1}(a+bu^n)^{p+1}}{a(m+1)} - \dfrac{b(np+n+m+1)}{a(m+1)} \\[2mm]
\qquad\qquad \times \displaystyle\int u^{m+n}(a+bu^n)^p \; du \\[4mm]
\dfrac{-u^{m+1}(a+bu^n)^{p+1}}{na(p+1)} + \dfrac{np+n+m+1}{na(p+1)} \\[2mm]
\qquad\qquad \times \displaystyle\int u^m (a+bu^n)^{p+1} \; du,
\end{cases}
$$

$m, n, p$ integral and $> 0$ in all four forms

116.  $\displaystyle\int_0^{\pi} \sin^2 nu \; du = \int_0^{\pi} \cos^2 nu \; du = \dfrac{\pi}{2}$

117.  $\displaystyle\int_0^{\pi/2} \sin^n u \; du = \int_0^{\pi/2} \cos^n u \; du$

$$
= \begin{cases}
\dfrac{(n-1)(n-3)(n-5)\cdots 4\cdot 2}{n(n-2)(n-4)\cdots 5\cdot 3} \\[2mm]
\qquad\qquad \text{for } n \text{ an odd integer and } > 1 \\[4mm]
\dfrac{(n-1)(n-3)(n-5)\cdots 3\cdot 1}{n(n-2)(n-4)\cdots 4\cdot 2} \cdot \dfrac{\pi}{2} \\[2mm]
\qquad\qquad \text{for } n \text{ an even integer and } > 0
\end{cases}
$$

118. $\displaystyle\int_0^{\pi/2}\sin^m u\,\cos^n u\,du =$
$$\begin{cases}
\dfrac{(n-1)(n-3)(n-5)\cdots 4\cdot 2}{(m+n)(m+n-2)\cdots(m+5)(m+3)(m+1)} \\
\qquad\qquad\text{for } n \text{ an odd integer} > 1 \\[4pt]
\dfrac{(m-1)(m-3)(m-5)\cdots 4\cdot 2}{(n+m)(n+m-2)\cdots(n+5)(n+3)(n+1)} \\
\qquad\qquad\text{for } m \text{ an odd integer} > 1 \\[4pt]
\dfrac{(m-1)(m-3)\cdots 1\cdot(n-1)(n-3)\cdots 1}{(m+n)(m+n-2)\cdots 4\cdot 2}\cdot\dfrac{\pi}{2} \\
\qquad\qquad\text{for } m \text{ and } n \text{ both even integers and} > 0
\end{cases}$$

# INDEX

**939**